D0211060

Cassell's Concise Spanish-English English-Spanish Dictionary

Compiled by

Brian Dutton
M.A., Ph.D., Professor of Spanish,
University of Illinois

L. P. Harvey
M.A., D.Phil., Cervantes Professor of
Spanish, King's College, University of
London

Roger M. Walker
B.A., Ph.D., Reader in Spanish,
Birkbeck College, University of London

MACMILLAN • USA

Macmillan General Reference
A Simon & Schuster Macmillan Company
1633 Broadway
New York, NY 10019-6785

CASSELL'S COMPACT
SPANISH-ENGLISH ENGLISH-SPANISH DICTIONARY
(1977, title changed to CASSELL'S CONCISE
SPANISH-ENGLISH ENGLISH-SPANISH DICTIONARY)

Library of Congress Cataloging in Publication Data
Dutton, Brian.
    Cassell's concise Spanish-English English-Spanish Dictionary,
Reprint of the ed. published by Funk & Wagnalls, New York,
under title: Cassell's new compact Spanish-English,
        English-Spanish Dictionaries—English.
1. Spanish language—Dictionaries—English.
2. English Language—Dictionaries—Spanish.
I. Harvey, Leonard Patrick, joint author.
II. Walker, Roger M., joint author.
III. Title.
    PC4640.D85   1977   463'.21   77-7615
ISBN 0-02-522660-6

20

Printed in the United States of America

Contents

This concise Dictionary aims to provide the user with a modern reference book that will serve for most general purposes. The listings have been carefully selected with regard to both frequency and importance in normal speech and writing, as well as technical vocabulary that is more and more frequent in the twentieth century.

The base-language is the Spanish of Spain, though we have given close attention to the current variations in Spanish America. The definitions have been selected on the basis of similarity of register, e.g. **barriga** is defined *belly*, not *stomach*, since *belly*/**barriga** have a very similar tone and level.

The dictionary also bears in mind school and college users who read classical literature, and so lists literary and poetical items with appropriate equivalents. On the other hand, racy expressions common in normal day-to-day speech are also listed abundantly, sometimes uniquely.

In order to contain so much in a compact dictionary, certain word-groups of the type **geólogo, geología, geológico; biólogo, biología, biológico** are often represented only by the - **ía** form. Similarly, adverbs in -**mente** have been omitted where they simply correspond to the adjective + *ly* in English.

The listing of irregularities in verbs has been carried out in a very clear tabular form, with references in the text of the dictionary.

In general, this dictionary should be sufficient for the student of Spanish from the very beginning to college-level studies, and also for the traveller and tourist.

B.D.

Advice to the User

Arrangement of Entries

Entries are given in strict alphabetical order, in both English and Spanish. The sequence of definitions is based on frequency. Similar meanings are separated by a comma, distinct meanings by a semicolon. Idiomatic phrases are entered after the definitions of the individual word. Usually idioms occur under the first noun, verb, adjective or adverb which is present in the idiom.

Words that are spelt alike but semantically quite distinct are given separate numbered entries.

Grammar

Parts of speech are indicated by abbreviations in italics (*a.*, *v.t.* etc.), all of which are included in the List of Abbreviations.

Genders are indicated in both halves of the dictionary by *m.* or *f.* following the word. In the English-Spanish half, a group of two or more nouns followed by one of these two letters will be nouns of the same gender, although no genders have been indicated for masculine words in **–o** or feminine words in **–a**.

Verbs. Irregular verbs in both Spanish and English have been listed in tables. In the Spanish-English section verbs having orthographic changes are indicated with a letter that refers to the explanatory table. A verb indicated by a number is irregular in form as well as spelling and will be listed in the corresponding table. Where a verb has both a spelling and a form difference, such as **rogar** (**ruego, rogué**) it will bear both a letter and a number.

The suffix **-se** has been omitted from Spanish reflexive verbs when they occur as keywords.

Variants

Usually variant forms are listed as separate entries with a reference in small capitals to the commonest form.

Accents

The latest rulings of the Real Academia de la Lengua have been observed.

Phonetics

The symbols of the International Phonetic Association have been used as far as possible, with some slight simplifications. Phonetic transcriptions are given only for English words, given the ease with which Spanish pronunciation can be determined by the spelling. A key to the I.P.A. symbols and to Spanish pronunciation is given. In the phonetic transcriptions, the mark ′ precedes the stressed syllable.

Disposición de los artículos

En ambas partes, española e inglesa, los artículos figuran en riguroso orden alfabético. La secuencia de las definiciones se basa en un criterio de frecuencia. Una coma separa las acepciones semejantes, un punto y coma las acepciones diferentes. Las frases idiomáticas aparecen después de las definiciones de palabras individuales. Normalmente los modismos aparecen bajo el primer sustantivo, verbo, adjetivo o adverbio, al cual hace referencia el artículo.

Las palabras de la misma grafía pero de valor semántico distinto figuran por separado en artículos numerados.

Gramática

Partes de la oración van indicadas en abreviaturas en bastardilla (*a.*, *v.t.* etc.), todas las cuales figuran en la Lista de Abreviaturas.

Géneros van indicados en ambas partes del diccionario por *m.* o *f.* después de cada palabra. En la mitad Inglés–Español, un grupo de dos o más sustantivos seguidos de una de estas dos letras serán sustantivos del mismo género, si bien no se han indicado los géneros de las palabras masculinas en **–o** ni de las palabras femeninas en **–a**.

Verbos. Tanto los verbos irregulares ingleses como españoles han sido agrupados en tablas. En la parte Español–Inglés, los verbos de cambio ortográfico van indicados con una letra que remite a la tabla explicativa. Un verbo indicado por un número es irregular en forma y en ortografía y figurará en la tabla correspondiente. Cuando un verbo tenga una irregularidad de forma y ortografía, como **rogar** (**ruego, rogué**), llevará un número y una letra.

Se ha omitido el sufijo **–se** de los verbos reflexivos españoles cuando éstos figuren como vocablos principales.

Variantes

Normalmente las variantes figuran como artículos separados con referencia a la forma más común en letra versalita.

Acentos

Se han observado las normas más recientes de la Real Academia de la Lengua.

Fonética

En la medida de lo posible se han empleado los símbolos de la Asociación Fonética Internacional con ligeras simplificaciones. Sólo se dan transcripciones fonéticas para las palabras inglesas, dada la relativa semejanza de la pronunciación española con su ortografía. Incluimos una clave de símbolos de la A.F.I. y de la pronunciación española. En las transcripciones fonéticas, el signo ′ precede a la sílaba acentuada.

Advice to the User

Regional variations

American variants in both Spanish and English have been given as far as possible, within the limits of a dictionary of this size. Often words that are purely British or peninsular Spanish have been indicated as such.

Register

Where a word in one language is used only at one level of speech (poetic, literary, familiar, vulgar etc.) the equivalent in the other language has been selected to match as far as possible the tone of the original.

Spelling

Standard Spanish Academy spelling has been adopted. Changes of spelling in the plural of nouns and adjectives, other than the simple addition of **-s,** have been indicated in the entries.

Variantes regionales

Dentro de los límites de un diccionario de este tamaño, hemos intentado dar variantes americanas tanto del inglés como del español. Las palabras que son exclusivamente británicas o españolas peninsulares han sido indicadas a veces como tales.

Registro

Cuando una palabra en un idioma se usa solamente en un nivel específico (poético, literario, familiar, vulgar etc.) hemos seleccionado el equivalente en el otro idioma para coincidir lo más posible con el tono del original.

Ortografía

Se han adoptado las normas ortográficas usuales de la Real Academia Española. Se han indicado en los artículos los cambios ortográficos de sustantivos y adjetivos, a excepción de la simple adición de -s para formar el plural.

Key to Pronunciation

Phonetic symbol	English example		Rough Spanish equivalent

VOWELS

i:	[si:t]	seat	como la *i* de f*i*n
i	[fiʃ]	fish	*i* muy corta
e	[nek]	neck	*e* de p*e*rro
æ	[mæn]	man	*a* muy corta, casi *e* corta
ɑ:	[pɑ:t]	part	*a* muy larga
ɔ	[blɔk]	block	*o* muy corta
ɔ:	[ʃɔ:l]	shawl	*o* de t*o*rre
u	[gud]	good	*u* muy corta
u:	[mu:n]	moon	*u* de l*u*na
ʌ	[kʌt]	cut	*u* muy corta, casi *a*
ə:	[sə:tʃ]	search	vocal larga relajada
ə	['nevə]	never	vocal corta relajada

DIPHTHONGS

ei	[reit]	rate	*ey* de l*ey*
ou	[stou]	stow	*ou* portuguesa
ai	[hai]	high	h*ay*
au	[kraud]	crowd	*au* de c*au*to
ɔi	[bɔi]	boy	*oy* de v*oy*
iə	[stiə]	steer	*ía* de p*ía*, pero con un *a* muy relajada
ɛə	[hɛə]	hair	*e* de s*ie*rra más *a* muy relajada
uə	[muə]	moor	*u* de l*u*na más *a* muy relajada

CONSONANTS

p	[peil]	pail	*p* de *p*aso
b	[beil]	bail	*b* de *b*ajo
t	[teil]	tail	*t* de al*t*o
d	[deil]	dale	*d* de bal*d*e
k	[keil]	kale	*k* de *k*ilo
g	[geil]	gale	*g* de *g*anas
m	[meil]	male	*m* de *m*ás
n	[neil]	nail	*n* de *n*o
ŋ	[siŋ]	sing	*n* de ta*n*go
f	[feil]	fail	*f* de *f*ino
v	[veil]	veil	*v* valenciana, *f* sonora
θ	[θin]	thin	*c* de *c*inco
ð	[ðain]	thine	*d* de na*d*a
s	[seil]	sail	*s* de esto
z	[leiz]	laze	*s* de des*d*e
ʃ	[ʃeil]	shale	*s* portuguesa, *sch*
ʒ	['viʒən]	vision	*ll* argentina de ca*ll*e
r	[reil]	rail	*r* de pasa*r*
h	[heil]	hail	*j* suave andaluza
x	[lɔx]	loch (Scots)	*j* castellana

SEMI-CONSONANTS

j	[jeil]	Yale	*y* de va*y*a
w	[weil]	wail	*hu* de *hue*vo

PHONETIC VALUES OF SPANISH (CASTILIAN)

	Phonetic symbol	Spanish example		Rough English equivalent

VOWELS

i	i	fin	[fin]	*ee* in s*ee*n
e	e	leche	['letʃe]	*a* in l*a*te
a	a	saca	['saka]	*a* in f*a*ther
o	ọ	solo	['solo]	*o* in s*o*ldier
u	u	luna	['luna]	*oo* in b*oo*t

DIPHTHONGS

ie	je	tiene	['tjene]	*ya* in *Ya*le
ei	ej	peine	['pejne]	*ay* in p*ay*ing
eu	εu	deuda	['dεuða]	ε as *ai* in *ai*r; *u* as in J*u*ly
ai, ay	aj	baile	['bajle]	*y* in sk*y*
au	aw	cauto	['kawto]	*ow* in c*ow*
oi, oy	oj	doy	[doj]	*oy* in b*oy*
ue	we	bueno	['bweno]	*way*

CONSONANTS

b, v (initial)	b	beso	['beso]	*b* in *b*est
		vaso	['baso]	
b, v (intervocalic)	β	cabo, cavo	['kaβo]	like *b* without lips touching
ca, co, cu	k	coca	['koka]	*k* in *k*ind
		cuna	['kuna]	
que, qui, k	k	que	[ke]	
		quiso	['kiso]	
		kilo	['kilo]	
ce, ci	θ	cero	['θero]	*th* in *th*ink
		cinco	['θiŋko]	
z	θ	caza	['kaθa]	
		zona	['θona]	
d (initial)	d	dice	['diθe]	*d* in *d*ear
d (intervocalic)	ð	nada	['naða]	*th* in *th*ere
f	f	fino	['fino]	*f* in *f*ind
g	ɡ	gana	['gana]	*g* in *g*ain
h	zero	hace	['aθe]	*h* in *h*onour
ch	tʃ	chico	['tʃiko]	*ch* in *ch*oose, ri*ch*
j, ge, gi	x	gigante	[xi'gante]	*ch* in lo*ch* (Scots)
		caja	['kaxa]	
l	l	bala	['bala]	*l* in *l*ong
ll	λ	calla	['kaλa]	*lli* in mi*lli*on
m	m	mozo	['moθo]	*m* in *m*ice
n	n	gana	['gana]	*n* in ba*nn*er
ñ	ɲ	caña	['kaɲa]	*ni* in o*ni*on
p	p	capa	['kapa]	*p* in co*p*per
r	r	caro	['karo]	*r* in Scots la*r*ge
rr	r̃	carro	['kar̃o]	*r* in Scots *r*ound
s	s	casa	['kasa]	*s* in goo*s*e
t	t	tanto	['tanto]	*t* in *t*ank
w	treated like *v*, *b*, occurs only in foreign words			
x	ɡz	examen	[eg'zamen]	*gs* in e*gg*s
	s	extremo	[es'tremo]	*s* in be*s*t
y	j	vaya	['baja]	*y* in la*y*er

Key to Pronunciation

American Spanish

The following are the major features which distinguish the pronunciation of American from that of Castilian Spanish; they also occur in Southern Spain:

ci, ce and *z* are all pronounced as *s.*

Castilian		*American*
casa	['kasa]	['kasa]
caza	['kaθa]	['kasa]
has	[as]	[as]
haz	[aθ]	[as]
ase	['ase]	['ase]
hace	['aθe]	['ase]

ll is pronounced in many regions as **y** [j], both in Spain and Spanish America. It is also pronounced [ʒ] (=the *s* in pleasure) in Argentina and Uruguay.

Castilian		*Regional pronunciations*
haya	['aja]	['aʒa]
halla	['aʎa]	['aja, 'aʒa]
cayó	[ka'jo]	[ka'ʒo]
calló	[ka'ʎo]	[ka'jo] [ka'ʒo]

s at the end of a word or before a consonant is pronounced as a weak *h* in parts of Southern Spain and America:

Castilian		*Regional*
esto	['esto]	['ehto]
los mismos	[los 'mizmos]	[loh 'mihmoh]

List of Abbreviations

a.	adjective	*lit.*	literary
abbrev.	abbreviation	*m.*	masculine
adv.	adverb	*math.*	mathematics
aer.	aeronautics	*mech.*	mechanics
agr.	agriculture	*med.*	medicine
anat.	anatomy	*metal.*	metallurgy
arch.	architecture	*mil.*	military
art.	arts	*min.*	mining
astr.	astronomy	*mus.*	music
aut.	automobiles	*myth.*	mythology
aux.	auxiliary	*n.*	noun
Bibl.	Biblical	*naut.*	nautical
biol.	biology	*nav.*	naval
bot.	botany	*neg.*	negative
Brit.	British	*neol.*	neologism
C.A.	Central America	*obs.*	obsolete
carp.	carpentry	*orn.*	ornithology
chem.	chemistry	*p.p.*	past participle
cin.	cinema	*paint.*	painting
com.	commerce	*pej.*	pejorative
compar.	comparative	*pers.*	personal
cond.	conditional	*phot.*	photography
conj.	conjunction	*phr.*	phrase
cul.	culinary	*phys.*	physics
dial.	dialect	*pl.*	plural
dem.	demonstrative	*poet.*	poetic
eccl.	ecclesiastical	*pol.*	politics
educ.	education	*poss.*	possessive
elec.	electricity	*prep.*	preposition
eng.	engineering	*pret.*	preterite
ent.	entomology	*print.*	printing
esp.	especially	*pron.*	pronoun
f.	feminine	*prov.*	provincial
fam.	familiar	*r.*	reflexive
fig.	figurative	*rad.*	radio
fut.	future	*rail.*	railways
gem.	gemmology	*rel.*	relative
geog.	geography	*S.A.*	South America
geol.	geology	*s.o.*	someone
gram.	grammar	*s.th.*	something
her.	heraldry	*sg.*	singular
hist.	history	*Sp.*	Spain
hunt.	hunting	*sup.*	superlative
i.	intransitive	*t.*	transitive
ichth.	ichthyology	*T.V.*	television
impers.	impersonal	*taur.*	tauromachy
indef.	indefinite	*tech.*	technical
inf.	infinitive	*tel.*	telephone
interj.	interjection	*theat.*	theatre
interrog.	interrogative	*theol.*	theology
inv.	invariable	*U.S.*	United States
iron.	ironic	*v.*	verb
irr.	irregular	*var.*	variant
joc.	jocular	*vet.*	veterinary
jur.	jurisprudence	*vulg.*	vulgar; popular
Lat.	Latin	*zool.*	zoology

A, a, *n.f.* first letter of the Spanish alphabet.
a, *prep.* to; on; by; at.
abad, *n.m.* abbot.
abadesa, *n.f.* abbess.
abadía, *n.f.* abbey; dignity of abbot.
abajo, *adv.* under(neath), below.—*interj.*
¡abajo . . .! down with . . .!
abalanzar [C], *v.t.* balance; throw.—*v.r.*
rush.
abalorio, *n.m.* glass bead.
abanderado, *n.m.* colour-sergeant.
abanderamiento, *n.m.* (*naut.*) registration.
abandonado, -da, *a.* forsaken; forlorn;
profligate.
abandonar, *v.t.* forsake; leave; give up.—*v.r.*
give oneself up.
abandono, *n.m.* forlornness; slovenliness;
debauchery.
abanicar, *v.t.* fan.
abanico, *n.m.* fan.
abano, *n.m.* hanging fan, punkah.
abarca, *n.f.* rawhide *or* rubber sandal.
abarcar [A], *v.t.* clasp; cover, take up;
include.
abarloar, *v.t.* (*naut.*) dock, bring alongside.
abarquillar, *v.t., v.r.* curl up, warp.
abarrancadero, *n.m.* precipice; steep slope.
abarrancar [A], *v.t.* erode.—*v.i.* (*naut.*) run
aground.—*v.r.* fall into a hole.
abarrote, *n.m.* (*naut.*) packing; stop-gap.—
pl. (*S.A.*) groceries.
abastar, *v.t.* supply, provision.
abastecedor, -ra, *a.* providing.—*n.m.f.*
victualler, caterer.
abastecer [9], *v.t.* supply, provision.—*v.r.*
obtain supplies; provision oneself (*de,* with).
abastecimiento, abasto, *n.m.* provisioning;
provision(s), supplies.
abatimiento, *n.m.* depression; (*naut.*) leeway;
(*aer.*) drift.
abatir, *v.t.* throw down; demolish.—*v.r.* be
downcast; (*naut.*) have leeway.
abdicación, *n.f.* abdication.
abdicar [A], *v.t.* abdicate; renounce.
abdomen, *n.m.* abdomen.
abdominal, *a.* abdominal.
abecé, *n.m.* A.B.C., alphabet.
abedul, *n.m.* (*bot.*) birch.
abeja, *n.f.* (*ent.*) bee.
abejarrón, *n.m.* (*ent.*) bumble-bee, humble-
bee.
abejón, *n.m.* (*ent.*) hornet.
aberración, *n.f.* aberration; deviation.
abertura, *n.f.* opening; gap.
abierto, -ta, *a.* open; frank, sincere.—*p.p.*
[ABRIR].
abigarrado, -da, *a.* motley, particoloured;
variegated.
Abisinia, *n.f.* Abyssinia.
abisinio, -nia, *a., n.m.f.* Abyssinian.
abismal, *a.* abysmal.
abismo, *n.m.* abyss, depths.
abjurar, *v.t.* abjure, forswear.
ablandador de agua, *n.m.* water softener.

ablandante, *a.* soothing, mollifying.
ablandar, ablandecer [9], *v.t.* soften,
mollify, assuage.—*v.i.* soften, mellow.
ablativo, -va, *a.* (*gram.*) ablative.
ablución, *n.f.* ablution, washing.
abnegación, *n.f.* self-denial, abnegation.
abnegar [1B], *v.t.* renounce.—*v.r.* deny
oneself.
abobar, *v.t.* stupefy.—*v.r.* grow stupid.
abocar [A], *v.t.* decant; bring near.—*v.r.*
meet by agreement.
abocardar, *v.t.* (*eng.*) ream; countersink.
abocetar, *v.t.* (*art.*) sketch roughly.
abochornar, *v.t., v.r.* wilt, shrivel (*plants*);
(*fig.*) (make) blush.
abofetear, *v.t.* slap.
abogacía, *n.f.* advocacy, pleading; bar,
profession of law.
abogado, *n.m.* barrister, lawyer, advocate.
abogar [B], *v.i.* plead; — **por,** advocate.
abolengo, *n.m.* ancestry; (*jur.*) inheritance.
abolición, *n.f.* abolition.
abolicionista, *a., n.m.f.* abolitionist.
abolir [Q], *v.t.* revoke, abolish.
abollar, *v.t.* dent; bruise; emboss.
abombar, *v.t.* make bulge; (*fam.*) stun.
abominable, *a.* abominable.
abominación, *n.f.* abomination.
abominar, *v.t.* abominate, detest.
abonado, -da, *a., n.m.f.* subscriber (*to
magazine*); season ticket holder (*person*).
abonar, *v.t.* certify, vouch for; fertilize,
manure.—*v.r.* take out a subscription.
abonaré, *n.m.* (*com.*) (promissory) note;
debenture.
abono, *n.m.* guarantee; subscription; (*com.*)
credit entry; fertilizer, manure.
abordaje, *n.m.* (*naut.*) collision.
abordar, *v.t.* (*naut.*) run foul of; board;
approach.
aborigen, *a.* (*pl.* **aborígenes**) aboriginal.—
n.m. aborigine.
aborrascar [A], *v.r.* get stormy.
aborrecer [9], *v.t.* hate, detest.
aborrecible, *a.* abhorrent, detestable.
aborrecimiento, *n.m.* abhorrence, hate.
abortar, *v.t.* make abortive.—*v.i.* miscarry;
have a miscarriage; abort.
abortivo, -va, *a.* abortive.
aborto, *n.m.* abortion; miscarriage; aborted
foetus.
abotonar, *v.t.* button.—*v.i.* bud; crack in
boiling (*egg*).
abovedar, *v.t.* arch, vault, groin.
abozalar, *v.t.* muzzle.
abra, *n.f.* bay, cove; (*S.A.*) clearing; crack.
abrasar, *v.t.* set fire to; nip (*frost*).—*v.i.*
burn.
abrasión, *n.f.* abrasion.
abrasivo, -va, *a.* abrasive, abradent.
abrazadera, *n.f.* clamp, clasp; (*print.*)
bracket.
abrazar [C], *v.t.* embrace; (*fig.*) accept.—
v.r. embrace.

abrazo, *n.m.* embrace.
ábrego, *n.m.* south-west wind.
abrelatas, *n.m. inv.* tin-opener, (*esp. U.S.*) can opener.
abrevadero, *n.m.* water-hole; trough.
abrevar, *v.t.* water.
abreviación, *n.f.* abbreviation; abridgement.
abreviar, *v.t.* shorten; abridge.
abrigar [B], *v.t.* shelter, protect; (*fig.*) cherish.—*v.r.* take shelter; wrap up warmly.
abrigo, *n.m.* shelter; overcoat; (*naut.*) haven; **al — de,** under protection of.
abril, *n.m.* April.
abrillantar, *v.t.* polish; cut (*diamonds*).
abrir [*p.p.* **abierto**], *v.t., v.i.* open.—*v.r.* open; unbosom oneself; gape.
abrochar, *v.t.* button; buckle.
abrogación, *n.f.* abrogation, repeal.
abrogar [B], *v.t.* abrogate, annul.
abrojo, *n.m.* (*bot.*) thistle; (*fig. esp. pl.*) difficulty.
abrumar, *v.t.* crush, overwhelm; weary.—*v.r.* become foggy; worry.
abrupto, -ta, *a.* abrupt; craggy, rugged.
abrutado, -da, *a.* brutish, bestial.
absceso, *n.m.* (*med.*) abscess.
absentismo, *n.m.* absenteeism.
ábside, *n.m.f.* (*arch.*) apse.
absintio, *n.m.* wormwood, absinthe.
absolución, *n.f.* absolution.
absoluta, *n.f.* dogma, dictum; (*mil.*) discharge *or* exemption.
absolutismo, *n.m.* despotism, autocracy.
absolutista, *a., n.m.f.* absolutist.
absoluto, -ta, *a.* absolute; despotic; **en —,** absolutely (*negative*).
absolvente, *a.* absolving.
absolver [5, *p.p.* **absuelto**], *v.t.* absolve; acquit.
absorbencia, *n.f.* absorbence, absorption.
absorbente, *a.* absorbent; (*fig.*) engrossing.
absorber, *v.t.* absorb; (*fig.*) engross.
absorción, *n.f.* absorption.
absorto, -ta, *a.* absorbed, wrapped in thought.
abstemio, -mia, *a.* abstemious.
abstención, *n.f.* abstention.
abstener [33], *v.r.* abstain, forbear (**de,** from).
abstinencia, *n.f.* abstinence, self-denial, fasting.
abstinente, *a.* abstemious.
abstracto, -ta, *a., n.m.* abstract.
abstraer [34], *v.t.* abstract.
abstruso, -sa, *a.* abstruse, difficult.
absuelto, -ta, *p.p.* [ABSOLVER].
absurdidad, *n.f.* absurdity.
absurdo, -da, *a.* absurd, nonsensical.—*n.m.* absurdity.
abubilla, *n.f.* (*orn.*) hoopoe.
abuela, *n.f.* grandmother; **tía —,** great-aunt.
abuelo, *n.m.* grandfather; **tío —,** great-uncle.—*n.m.pl.* grandparents; forefathers.
abundamiento, *n.m.* abundance; **a mayor —,** furthermore.
abundancia, *n.f.* abundance; fertility.
abundar, *v.i.* abound.
abundoso, -sa, *a.* abundant.
aburilar, *v.t.* engrave.
aburrar, *v.r.* become brutish.
aburrido, -da, *a.* bored; boring.
aburrimiento, *n.m.* boredom, tedium.

aburrir, *v.t.* annoy, vex, bore, weary.—*v.r.* be bored.
abusar, *v.t.* abuse, misuse; profit unduly from; impose upon.
abusivo, -va, *a.* abusive.
abuso, *n.m.* abuse, misuse.
abyección, *n.f.* abjectness.
abyecto, -ta, *a.* abject; servile.
acá, *adv.* here; this way; **desde entonces —,** from that time on.
acabado, -da, *a.* perfect, consummate; (*fam.*) shabby.—*n.m.* (*tech.*) finish.
acabamiento, *n.m.* end, completion; (*fig.*) death.
acabar, *v.t., v.i.* finish, end, conclude; **— de** (+ *inf.*), have just (*done something*); **— con,** put an end to, finish off.—*v.r.* end; run out.
acacia, *n.f.* (*bot.*) acacia.
academia, *n.f.* academy.
académico, -ca, *a.* academic.—*n.m.f.* academician.
acaecer [9], *v.i.* happen.
acaecimiento, *n.m.* event, incident.
acalenturar, *v.r.* become feverish.
acalorar, *v.t.* warm; urge on, encourage.—*v.r.* (*fig.*) grow excited.
acallar, *v.t.* quiet, hush.
acampamento, *n.m.* (*mil.*) encampment, camp.
acampar, *v.t., v.i., v.r.* encamp, camp.
acanalar, *v.t.* make a channel in; (*arch.*) flute; (*carp.*) groove.
acantilado, -da, *a.* steep, sheer.—*n.m.* cliff.
acanto, *n.m.* (*bot., arch.*) acanthus.
acantonar, *v.t.* (*mil.*) quarter (*troops*).
acaparar, *v.t.* monopolize.
acápite, *n.m.* (*S.A.*) paragraph.
acar(e)ar, *v.t.* confront.
acariciar, *v.t.* caress; fondle; cherish.
acarrear, *v.t.* carry, transport; cause.
acarreo, *n.m.* carrying, freight.—*pl.* supplies.
acaso (1), *n.m.* chance.
acaso (2), *adv.* perhaps, maybe; **por si —,** just in case.
acatamiento, *n.m.* esteem; view.
acatar, *v.t.* respect, esteem.
acatarrar, *v.r.* catch cold.
acaudalado, -da, *a.* wealthy, opulent.
acaudalar, *v.t.* hoard.
acaudillar, *v.t.* lead, command.
acceder, *v.i.* accede, agree, consent.
accesibilidad, *n.f.* accessibility.
accesible, *a.* accessible.
accesión, *n.f.* accession; (*med.*) access.
acceso, *n.m.* access; (*jur.*) accession (*to property*); (*med.*) attack.
accesorio, -ria, *a. n.m.* accessory.—*n.f.* outbuilding.
accidentado, -da, *a.* broken (*ground*); eventful.
accidental, *a.* accidental, fortuitous.
accidente, *n.m.* accident, chance.
acción, *n.f.* action; (*com.*) share.
accionar, *v.t.* (*mech.*) operate.—*v.i.* gesticulate.
accionista, *n.m.f.* (*com.*) shareholder.
acebo, *n.m.* (*bot.*) holly.
acebuche, *n.m.* (*bot.*) wild olive tree.
acecinar, *v.t.* salt and smoke *or* dry (*meat*).
acechanza, *n.f.* [ACECHO].
acechar, *v.t.* waylay, lie in ambush for; (*fig.*) watch closely for.

acecho, *n.m.* waylaying, ambush.
acedar, *v.t., v.r.* sour.
acedera, *n.f.* (*bot.*) sorrel.
acedía, *n.f.* acidity; heartburn.
acedo, -da, *a.* acid, sour; (*fig.*) harsh, cutting.
acéfalo, -la, *a.* acephalous, headless.
aceitar, *v.t.* oil, lubricate.
aceite, *n.m.* oil.
aceitero, -ra, *a.* relative to oil.—*n.f.* oil cruet; oil-can.
aceitoso, -sa, *a.* oily, greasy.
aceituna, *n.f.* olive.
aceituno, *n.m.* (*bot.*) olive tree.
aceleración, *n.f.* acceleration.
acelerador, *n.m.* accelerator.
acelerar, *v.t.* accelerate, hasten, expedite.
acelga, *n.f.* (*bot.*) salt-wort; (*cul.*) spinach-beet, Swiss chard.
acémila, *n.f.* mule.
acendrar, *v.t.* refine; (*fig.*) purify.
acento, *n.m.* accent, stress.
acentuación, *n.f.* accentuation.
acentuar, *v.t.* accentuate, stress.
aceña, *n.f.* water-mill (*for corn etc.*).
acepción, *n.f.* acceptation; (*gram.*) acceptation, sense, meaning; — **de personas,** favouritism.
acepillar, *v.t.* (*carp.*) plane; brush (*clothes*).
aceptable, *a.* acceptable.
aceptación, *n.f.* acceptance; approbation.
aceptar, *v.t.* accept.
acequia, *n.f.* channel (*for irrigation*).
acera, *n.f.* pavement, (*U.S.*) sidewalk.
acerbo, -ba, *a.* tart; (*fig.*) cruel, severe.
acerca de, *prep.* about, concerning.
acercar [A], *v.t.* bring near, draw up.—*v.r.* approach (*a*).
acero, *n.m.* steel.
acerolo, *n.m.* (*bot.*) hawthorn, may.
acérrimo, -ma, *sup. a.* very harsh; very strong (*taste, smell*); (*fig.*) very staunch.
acertar [1], *v.t.* hit the mark; hit by chance; guess correctly.—*v.i.* succeed.
acertijo, *n.m.* riddle.
acetato, *n.m.* acetate.
acetileno, *n.m.* acetylene.
acetona, *n.f.* acetone.
aciago, -ga, *a.* unfortunate, sad.
acíbar, *n.m.* aloe(s).
acicalar, *v.t.* burnish.
acicate, *n.m.* long spur; (*fig.*) spur.
acidez, *n.f.* acidity.
acidificar, *v.t.* acidify.
ácido, -da, *a.* acid, sour.—*n.m.* acid.
acierto, *n.m.* good shot; dexterity; success; right answer.
aclamación, *n.f.* acclamation.
aclamar, *v.t.* acclaim.
aclarar, *v.t.* make clear, clarify; explain; rinse.—*v.i., v.r.* clear up (*weather*).
aclaratorio, -ria, *a.* explanatory.
aclimatación, *n.f.* acclimatization; absorption (*of immigrants*).
aclimatar, *v.t.* acclimatize.
acne, *n.m.* (*med.*) acne.
acobardar, *v.t.* intimidate.—*v.r.* become daunted.
acoger [E], *v.t.* receive; welcome, shelter.—*v.r.* take shelter; (*fig.*) resort to (*a pretext*).
acogida, *n.f.* reception; place of meeting;

dar — a una letra, (*com.*) honour a draft; **buena —,** welcome.
acólito, *n.m.* acolyte.
acometedor, -ra, *a.* aggressive.—*n.m.f.* aggressor.
acometer, *v.t.* attack; undertake; overcome, overtake.
acometida, *n.f.* attack; fit of illness.
acomodación, *n.f.* accommodation; integration, absorption (*of immigrants*).
acomodado, -ada, *a.* well-to-do; fond of comfort; convenient; reasonable.
acomodador, -ra, *a.* conciliating.—*n.m.* (*theat.*) usher.—*n.f.* usherette.
acomodar, *v.t.* accommodate, put up; compromise.—*v.i.* suit.—*v.r.* comply; put up (*a*, with).
acompañamiento, *n.m.* retinue; (*mus.*) accompaniment.
acompañar, *v.t.* accompany; (*com.*) enclose.
acompasado, -da, *a.* measured, rhythmic; (*fam.*) slow, monotonous.
acompasar, *v.t.* measure with dividers; (*mus.*) divide into bars (*score*).
acondicionar, *v.t.* prepare, arrange; condition.—*v.r.* qualify (*for a position*).
aconsejable, *a.* advisable.
aconsejar, *v.t.* advise, counsel.—*v.r.* consult (*con*, with).
aconsonantar, *v.t., v.i.* rhyme.
acontecedero, -ra, *a.* possible.
acontecer [9] (*used only in inf. and 3rd person*) *v.i.* happen.
acontecimiento, *n.m.* event, occurrence.
acopiar, *v.t.* collect, garner; corner (*goods*).
acopio, *n.m.* gathering; cornering.
acoplar, *v.t.* couple.—*v.t., v.r.* (*zool.*) mate.
acoquinar, *v.t.* (*fam.*) scare.
acorazado, *n.m.* battleship.
acorazar [C], *v.t.* armour-plate.
acorchar, *v.r.* shrivel; (*fig.*) go to sleep (*limbs*).
acordada, *n.f.* (*jur.*) order, decision.
acordar [4], *v.t.* remind; tune; make flush or level.—*v.i.* agree.—*v.r.* remember (*de*).
acorde, *a.* in tune; in accord.—*n.m.* (*mus.*) chord; harmony.
acordeón, *n.m.* (*mus.*) accordion.
acorralar, *v.t.* round up, pen, (*U.S.*) corral; intimidate.
acorrer, *v.t.* avail.
acortar, *v.t.* shorten, lessen; obstruct.—*v.r.* shrivel; shrink; be bashful; (*mil.*) fall back.
acosar, *v.t.* harass.
acostar [4], *v.t.* lay down; put to bed.—*v.i.* (*naut.*) tilt.—*v.r.* lie down; go to bed.
acostumbrado, -da, *a.* usual, customary.
acostumbrar, *v.t.* accustom.—*v.i.* be accustomed to, be used to.—*v.r.* become accustomed (*a*, to).
acotación, *n.f.* bounds, limit; annotation; (*theat.*) directions.
acotar, *v.t.* limit; banish; annotate; accept for a certain price; vouch for.
acotillo, *n.m.* sledge hammer.
acre, *a.* acrid.
acrecentar [1], **acrecer** [9], *v.t., v.r.* increase; advance.
acreditar, *v.t.* assure; verify; (*com.*) guarantee; authorize; prove.—*v.r.* gain a reputation (*de*, as).
acribar, *v.t.* sift; (*fig.*) riddle.

acriminar, *v.t.* accuse.
acrimonia, *n.f.* acrimony.
acrisolar, *v.t.* (*metal.*) refine; (*fig.*) purify; (*fig.*) clear up.
acróbata, *n.m.f.* acrobat.
acrobático, -ca, *a.* acrobatic.
acta, *n.f.* record of proceedings, minutes; certificate.
actitud, *n.f.* attitude.
activar, *v.t.* make active, activate; expedite.
actividad, *n.f.* activity; nimbleness.
activo, -va, *a.* active; quick.—*n.m.* (*com.*) assets.
acto, *n.m.* act; event; public function; (*theat.*) act.
actor, *n.m.* actor; (*jur.*) plaintiff.
actriz, *n.f.* actress.
actuación, *n.f.* actuation, action; performance; (*jur.*) proceedings.
actual, *a.* present, current.
actualidad, *n.f.* present time.—*pl.* current events.
actualmente, *adv.* at present.
actuar [M], *v.t.* actuate, set in action.—*v.i.* act (*de,* as); perform; perform judicial acts.
actuario, *n.m.* clerk of the court; actuary.
acuarela, *n.f.* (*art.*) water-colour.
Acuario, *n.m.* (*astr.*) Aquarius; **acuario,** *n.m.* aquarium.
acuartelar, *v.t.* (*mil., her.*) quarter.
acuático, -ca, *a.* aquatic.
acuatizar [C], *v.i.* (*aer.*) alight on the water.
acucia, *n.f.* zeal, diligence; longing.
acuciar, *v.t.* stimulate, hasten; covet.
acuclillar, *v.r.* crouch, squat.
acuchillado, -da, *a.* (*fig.*) toughened by experience.
acuchillar, *v.t.* stab, cut, slash.
acudir, *v.i.* resort; assist; attend.
acueducto, *n.m.* aqueduct.
acuerdo, *n.m.* resolution; remembrance; agreement, pact; harmony; **de —,** in agreement; agreed.
acuitar, *v.t.* afflict.
acullá, *adv.* yonder.
acumulación, *n.f.* accumulation.
acumular, *v.t.* accumulate, hoard; impute to.
acumulativo, -va, *a.* joint; cumulative.
acuñar (1), *v.t.* mint, coin.
acuñar (2), *v.t.* wedge.
acuoso, -sa, *a.* watery, aqueous.
acurrucar, *v.r.* huddle.
acusación, *n.f.* accusation.
acusado, -da, *a., n.m.f.* accused; marked.
acusar, *v.t.* accuse; prosecute; show; (*com.*) acknowledge (*receipt*).
acusativo, -va, *a., n.m.* (*gram.*) accusative.
acuse, *n.m.* (*com.*) acknowledgement.
acusón, -sona, *a., n.m.f.* tell-tale.
acústico, -ca, *a.* acoustic.—*n.f.* acoustics.
achacar [A], *v.t.* impute, blame.
achacoso, -sa, *a.* ailing.
achaparrado, -da, *a.* thick-set; stunted.
achaque, *n.m.* ailment; failing; excuse.
achicar [A], *v.t.* reduce, diminish.
achicoria, *n.f.* (*bot.*) chicory.
achochar, *v.r.* (*fam.*) become senile.
adagio (1), *n.m.* adage.
adagio (2), *n.m.* (*mus.*) adagio.
adalid, *n.m.* (*obs.*) chief, champion.
adaptable, *a.* adaptable.
adaptación, *n.f.* adaptation.

adaptar, *v.t.* adapt, fit.
adarga, *n.f.* (oval) shield.
adarme, *n.m.* small amount.
adecuado, -da, *a.* adequate; suitable.
adecuar, *v.t.* fit, accommodate.
adefesio, *n.m.* (*fam.*) extravagance, folly; ridiculous person.
adelantado, -da, *a.* advanced; forward; fast (*clock*); early (*fruit*); **por —,** in advance.— *n.m.* governor of a province.
adelantamiento, *n.m.* progress; betterment; anticipation.
adelantar, *v.t.* advance; promote; pay in advance.—*v.i.* be fast, gain (*clock*).—*v.r.* take the lead; overtake (*a*).
adelante, *adv.* ahead; forward.—*interj.* come in!
adelanto, *n.m.* advance; (*com.*) advance payment.
adelfa, *n.f.* (*bot.*) oleander.
adelgazar [C], *v.t.* make thin; taper; attenuate.—*v.i., v.r.* slim; taper off.
ademán, *n.m.* gesture; manner; **en — de,** about to, prepared to.—*pl.* manners.
además, *adv.* moreover; besides.— **— de,** besides.
adentro, *adv.* within, inside; **mar —,** out to sea.—*n.m.pl.* innermost thoughts; **para sus adentros,** to oneself.
adepto, -ta, *a.* adept, initiated.
aderezar [C], *v.t.* adorn; (*cul.*) cook; (*cul.*) dress (*salad*).
aderezo, *n.m.* dressing; finery.
adestrar [1], *v.t.* lead; train.—*v.r.* practise.
adeudar, *v.t.* owe; (*com.*) debit.—*v.r.* run into debt.
adeudo, *n.m.* indebtedness; (*com.*) debit.
adherencia, *n.f.* adhesion, adherence; bond.
adherente, *a.* adhesive.—*n.m.* adherent, follower; accessory, equipment.
adherir [6], *v.t., v.r.* adhere, stick.
adhesión, *n.f.* adhesion, adherence.
adhesivo, -va, *a.* adhesive.—*n.m.* adhesive, glue.
adición, *n.f.* addition.
adicional, *a.* additional.
adicto, -ta, *a.* addicted; attached.
adiestramiento, *n.m.* training.
adiestrar, *v.t., v.r.* practise.
adinerado, -da, *a.* well-to-do, wealthy.
adiposo, -sa, *a.* adipose, fat.
¡adiós! *interj.* good-bye! good day!
aditamento, *n.m.* addition; attachment.
aditivo, -va, *a., n.m.* additive.
adivinaja, *n.f.* conundrum.
adivinar, *v.t.* foretell; guess right.
adivino, -na, *n.m.f.* soothsayer, fortune-teller; guesser.
adjetival, *a.* adjectival.
adjetivo, -va, *a., n.m.* adjective.
adjudicar, *v.t.* adjudge, adjudicate; sell (*at auction*).—*v.r.* appropriate.
adjunta, *n.f.* (*com.*) enclosure (*in letter*).
adjunto, -ta, *a.* enclosed; associate.
administración, *n.f.* administration; (*com. etc.*) management.
administrador, *n.m.* administrator; manager; (*com.*) director; trustee.
administrar, *v.t.* administer; govern.
administrativo, -va, *a.* administrative; managerial.
admirable, *a.* admirable; marvellous.

4

admiración, *n.f.* admiration; wonder; (*gram.*) exclamation mark.
admirar, *v.t.* admire; marvel at; cause to wonder.—*v.r.* wonder, be astonished (*de, at*).
admisible, *a.* admissible.
admisión, *n.f.* admission, acceptance; input.
admitir, *v.t.* receive, admit; permit.
adobar, *v.t.* prepare (*food*); pickle (*meat*); tan (*hide*).
adobe, *n.m.* mud brick, adobe.
adobo, *n.m.* repairing; pickle sauce; dressing.
adolecente, *a.* suffering.
adolecer [9], *v.i.* suffer (*de,* from).—*v.r.* condole.
adolescencia, *n.f.* adolescence.
adolescente, *a., n.m.f.* adolescent.
adonde, *adv.* where, whither. (*As interrog.* ¿adónde?).
adopción, *n.f.* adoption.
adoptar, *v.t.* adopt.
adoptivo, -va, *a.* adoptive; foster.
adoquier, adoquiera, *adv.* anywhere.
adoquín, *n.m.* paving stone; (*fig.*) rogue.
adorable, *a.* adorable.
adoración, *n.f.* adoration.
adorar, *v.t.* adore, worship.
adormecer [9], *v.t.* lull.—*v.r.* fall asleep.
adormilar, adormitar, *v.r.* doze, drowse.
adornamiento, *n.m.* adornment.
adornar, *v.t.* adorn, embellish, ornament.
adorno, *n.m.* ornament; accomplishment; furniture.
adquirir [6], *v.t.* acquire, obtain.
adquisición, *n.f.* acquisition.
adrede, *adv.* on purpose, deliberately.
adriático, -ca, *a.* Adriatic.
aduana, *n.f.* customs.
aduanero, -ra, *a.* customs.—*n.m.* customs officer.
aducir [15], *v.t.* adduce.
adueñar, *v.r.* take possession.
adulación, *n.f.* adulation, flattery.
adular, *v.t.* adulate, flatter.
adulteración, *n.f.* adulteration.
adulterar, *v.t.* adulterate.—*v.i.* commit adultery.
adulterino, -na, *a.* adulterine.
adulterio, *n.m.* adultery.
adúltero, -ra, *a.* adulterous.—*n.m.* adulterer.—*n.f.* adulteress.
adulto, -ta, *a., n.m.f.* adult, grown-up.
adusto, -ta, *a.* parched; austere; sullen, dour.
advenedizo, -za, *a., n.m.f.* immigrant; outsider, newcomer; parvenu, upstart.
advenimiento, *n.m.* arrival; accession (*of ruler*).
adventicio, -cia, *a.* adventitious.
adverbial, *a.* adverbial.
adverbio, *n.m.* adverb.
adversario, -ria, *n.m.f.* opponent, foe, adversary.
adversidad, *n.f.* adversity, misfortune.
adverso, -sa, *a.* adverse; calamitous; unfavourable.
advertencia, *n.f.* admonition; remark; foreword.
advertido, -da, *a.* intelligent; sagacious.
advertir [6], *v.t.* observe; give warning of; advise (*person*).
Adviento, *n.m.* (*eccl.*) Advent.
adyacente, *a.* adjacent.

aeración, *n.f.* aeration.
aéreo, -rea, *a.* aerial, by air; (*fig.*) airy.
aerodeslizador, *n.m.* hovercraft.
aerodinámica, *n.f.* aerodynamics.
aerodinámico, -ca, *a.* aerodynamic.
aeródromo, *n.m.* aerodrome, airfield, airport.
aerograma, *n.m.* air letter.
aerolito, *n.m.* aerolite, meteorite.
aeronáutico, -ca, *a.* aeronautical.—*n.f.* aeronautics.
aeronave, *n.f.* (*aer.*) aircraft, air liner; airship.
aeroplano, *n.m.* (*aer.*) aeroplane, airplane, aircraft.
aeropuerto, *n.m.* airport.
aerosol, *n.m.* aerosol.
aerostato, *n.m.* aerostat.
afabilidad, *n.f.* affability, approachableness.
afable, *a.* affable, approachable.
afamar, *v.t.* make famous.
afán, *n.m.* anxiety; eagerness; toil.
afanadamente, *adv.* laboriously; anxiously.
afanar, *v.t.* press, urge.—*v.i., v.r.* toil.
afanoso, -sa, *a.* anxious; painstaking.
afear, *v.t.* deform; (*fig.*) decry.
afección, *n.f.* affection, fondness; (*med.*) affection.
afectación, *n.f.* affectation; (*com.*) earmarking (*funds*).
afectado, -da, *a.* affected, foppish.
afectar, *v.t.* affect; (*mil.*) attach.—*v.r.* be moved.
afecto, -ta, *a.* affectionate; fond (*a,* of).—*n.m.* affection; (*med.*) affect.
afectuoso, -sa, *a.* affectionate.
afeitar, *v.t., v.r.* make up; shave; **máquina de —,** (electric) shaver; **maquinilla de —,** safety razor.
afeite, *n.m.* cosmetic, make-up; shave.
afeminar, *v.t.* make effeminate.
aferrado, -da, *a.* headstrong, obstinate.
aferrar, *v.t.* grasp.—*v.r.* (*fig.*) persist obstinately (*a,* in).
el Afganistán, *n.m.* Afghanistan.
afgano, -na, *a., n.m.f.* Afghan.
afianzar [C], *v.t.* guarantee, go bail for; prop.
afición, *n.f.* affection (*a,* for); enthusiasm.
aficionado, -da, *a.* fond (*a,* of).—*n.m.* amateur; (*fam.*) fan.
aficionar, *v.t.* cause a liking (*a,* for).—*v.r.* take a fancy (*a,* to).
afilar, *v.t.* sharpen; taper.
afiliar, *v.t.* adopt; affiliate.
afilón, *n.m.* whetstone; smoothing steel.
afín, *a.* contiguous, close by.—*n.m.f.* relation by affinity; (*fam.*) in-law.
afinación, *n.f.* (*mus., T.V.*) tuning; (*metal.*) refining.
afinar, *v.t.* complete; (*mus., T.V.*) tune; (*metal.*) refine.
afincar [A], *v.i., v.r.* acquire real estate.
afinidad, *n.f.* relationship.
afirmar, *v.t.* make fast; affirm.
afirmativo, -va, *a.* affirmative.
aflicción, *n.f.* affliction.
aflictivo, -va, *a.* distressing; **pena aflictiva,** corporal punishment.
afligir [E], *v.t.* afflict.—*v.r.* grieve.
aflojar, *v.t.* loosen, slacken.—*v.i., v.r.* grow weak; slack.
aflorar, *v.t.* sift (*flour*).

afluencia, *n.f.* abundance; crowd, jam; fluency.
afluente, *a.* abundant; affluent.—*n.m.* (*geog.*) tributary.
afluir [O], *v.i.* congregate; flow (into).
aflujo, *n.m.* inrush; (*med.*) afflux.
afondar, *v.t., v.i., v.r.* sink.
aforar, *v.t.* gauge; appraise.
aforismo, *n.m.* aphorism, maxim.
aforro, *n.m.* lining.
afortunado, -da, *a.* fortunate, lucky.
afrancesar, *v.t.* Gallicise, Frenchify.
afrenta, *n.f.* insult; affront.
africano, -na, *a., n.m.f.* African.
afrodisíaco, -ca, *a.* aphrodisiac.
afrontar, *v.t.* confront.—*v.i.* face.
afuera, *adv.* outside.—*n.f.pl.* **outskirts;** surrounding country.
agachadiza, *n.f.* (*orn.*) snipe.
agachar, *v.t.* bow down.—*v.r.* crouch.
agalla, *n.f.* oak-apple.
agalludo, -da, *a.* (*S.A.*) stingy; (*S.A.*) foxy.
agareno, -na, *a.* Mohammedan; Arab.
agarrado, -da, *a.* tight-fisted.
agarrar, *v.t.* grasp, seize.—*v.r.* hold on (*de*, to).
agarre, *n.m.* grip, gripping.
agarrotar, *v.t.* garrotte; compress (*bales*).
agasajar, *v.t.* receive kindly, fête; fondle.
agasajo, *n.m.* friendly treatment; reception, party; kindness; gift.
ágata, *n.f.* (*gem.*) agate.
agencia, *n.f.* agency, bureau.
agenda, *n.f.* note-book; diary.
agente, *n.m.* agent.
agigantado, -da, *a.* gigantic.
ágil, *a.* agile, nimble.
agilidad, *n.f.* agility.
agitación, *n.f.* agitation; stirring; (*naut.*) choppiness.
agitador, -ra, *n.m.f.* agitator.
agitar, *v.t.* agitate; stir.
aglomeración, *n.f.* agglomeration.
aglomerado, *n.m.* briquette.
aglomerar, *v.t.* agglomerate.
aglutinación, *n.f.* agglutination.
aglutinante, *n.m.* cement.
aglutinar, *v.t.* agglutinate.
agnóstico, -ca, *a., n.m.f.* agnostic.
agobiar, *v.t.* bow down; (*fig.*) oppress, overwhelm.
agolpar, *v.t.* pile up.—*v.r.* crowd.
agonía, *n.f.* agony; pangs of death.
agonioso, -sa, *a.* importunate, persistent.
agonizante, *a.* dying.—*n.m.f.* person on the point of death.
agonizar [C], *v.i.* be dying.
agorar [10], *v.t.* divine, foretell.
agostar, *v.t.* parch; consume.
agosto, *n.m.* August; harvest; **hacer su —,** get rich quick(ly); make hay while the sun shines.
agotado, -da, *a.* out of print; sold out.
agotar, *v.t.* exhaust; use up.—*v.r.* go out of print; become exhausted.
agraciar, *v.t.* embellish; favour.
agradable, *a.* agreeable, pleasant.
agradar, *v.t.* please.
agradecer [9], *v.t.* thank for; be grateful for.
agradecido, -da, *a.* grateful.
agradecimiento, *n.m.* gratitude.

agrado, *n.m.* agreeableness; pleasure; gratitude; liking.
agramilar, *v.t.* point (*brickwork*).
agrandamiento, *n.m.* enlargement; aggrandisement.
agrario, -ria, *a.* agrarian.
agravación, *n.f.* aggravation.
agravar, *v.t.* exaggerate; oppress.—*v.r.* become grave.
agraviador, -ra, *n.m.f.* injurer; offender.
agraviante, *a.* wronging; aggravating.
agraviar, *v.t.* wrong, harm.—*v.r.* take offence.
agravio, *n.m.* offence; harm; grievance.
agravioso, -sa, *a.* offensive; injurious.
agraz, *n.m.* (*pl.* **-aces**) unripe grape; (*fam., fig.*) displeasure; **en —,** prematurely.
agredir, *v.t.* attack, assault.
agregado, *n.m.* aggregate; attaché.
agregar, *v.t.* aggregate; add.
agresión, *n.f.* aggression.
agresividad, *n.f.* aggressiveness.
agresivo, -va, *a.* aggressive.
agresor, -ra, *n.m.f.* aggressor.
agreste, *a.* rustic; wild (*plant*); (*fam.*) uncouth.
agriar [L *or regular*], *v.t.* make sour.
agrícola, *a.* agricultural.
agricultor, *n.m.* farmer, agriculturist.
agricultura, *n.f.* agriculture.
agridulce, *a.* bitter-sweet.
agrietar, *v.t., v.r.* crack, split.
agrimensor, *n.m.* land surveyor.
agrio, -ria, *a.* sour, sharp; (*bot.*) citrous.
agro, -ra, *a.* [AGRIO].—*n.m.* citron.
agronomía, *n.f.* agronomy, agriculture.
agrónomo, -ma, *n.m.f.* agronomist, agricultural expert.
agrupar, *v.t.* group.—*v.r.* cluster.
agua, *n.f.* water; **aguas mayores, excrement; aguas menores,** urine.
aguacate, *n.m.* avocado pear.
aguacero, *n.m.* downpour.
aguaducho, *n.m.* refreshment stall.
aguafiestas, *n.m.f.* (*fam.*) kill-joy, wet blanket.
aguafuerte, *n.f.* etching.
aguaje, *n.m.* tidal wave; sea current; wake.
aguamanil, *n.m.* water jug; washstand.
aguamarina, *n.f.* aquamarine.
aguamiel, *n.f.* honey and water; mead.
aguanieve, *n.f.* sleet.
aguantar, *v.t.* suffer, endure; put up with.—*v.r.* forbear.
aguar [H], *v.t.* dilute with water, water; (*fig.*) mar.
aguardar, *v.t.* wait for, await.—*v.i.* wait.
aguardiente, *n.m.* spirits; brandy.
aguarrás, *n.m.* turpentine.
aguaturma, *n.f.* (*bot.*) Jerusalem artichoke.
agudeza, *n.f.* sharpness; acuteness; wit.
agudo, -da, *a.* sharp; acute; clever; (*mus.*) high-pitched.
agüero, *n.m.* augury.
aguijada, *n.f.* spur, goad.
aguijar, *v.t.* spur, goad.—*v.i.* **hasten.**
aguijón, *n.m.* sting; spur, goad.
águila, *n.f.* eagle.
aguileño, -ña, *a.* aquiline.—*n.f.* (*bot.*) columbine.
aguilón, *n.m.* boom (*of crane*).
aguilucho, *n.m.* eaglet.
aguinaldo, *n.m.* New Year's present; Christmas gift.

aguja, *n.f.* needle; (*rail.*) switch; hand (*of watch*); (*arch.*) spire.
agujazo, *n.m.* prick.
agujerear, *v.t.* pierce, prick.
agujero, *n.m.* hole.
agujeta, *n.f.* lace (*for shoes etc.*).—*pl.* pins and needles, cramp, twinges.
agujón, *n.m.* hatpin.
¡agur! *interj.* (*fam.*) good-bye!
agusanar, *v.r.* become worm-eaten.
Agustín, *n.m.* Augustine.
agustiniano, -na, agustino, -na, *a., n.m.f.* (*eccl.*) Augustinian, (*obs.*) Austin.
aguzanieves, *n.m. inv.* (*orn.*) wagtail.
aguzar [C], *v.t.* sharpen, whet.
ahechar, *v.t.* winnow.
ahí, *adv.* there; yonder; *por* —, that way; somewhere over there.
ahijada, *n.f.* god-daughter.
ahijado, *n.m.* god-son.
ahilar, *v.r.* become faint; turn sour.
ahilo, *n.m.* faintness.
ahinco, *n.m.* earnestness; ardour.
ahitar, *v.t., v.r.* surfeit, gorge.
ahito, -ta, *a.* satiated, gorged; bored.—*n.m.* surfeit; indigestion.
ahogadizo, -za, *a.* heavier than water, sinkable.
ahogador, *n.m.* hangman.
ahogamiento, *n.m.* drowning; suffocation.
ahogar [B], *v.t., v.r.* stifle; choke; drown.
ahogo, *n.m.* anguish; suffocation; penury.
ahondar, *v.t.* go deep into.—*v.i.* go deep; investigate.
ahonde, *n.m.* excavation, sinking.
ahora, *adv.* now; *de* — *en adelante,* from now on, henceforward.
ahorcar [A], *v.t.* hang.
ahorita, *adv.* (*fam.*) right away.
ahormar, *v.t.* fit, shape.
ahorrado, -da, *a.* unencumbered, exempt.
ahorramiento, *n.m.* saving.
ahorrar, *v.t.* save; spare.
ahorrativo, -va, *a.* thrifty; sparing.
ahorro, *n.m.* economy.—*pl.* savings; *caja de ahorros,* savings bank.
ahuecar [A], *v.t.* excavate; hollow.—*v.r.* become hollow; put on airs.
ahumado, -da, *a.* smoky; smoked, smoke-cured.—*n.m.* smoking, curing.
ahumar, *v.t.* smoke; fumigate.—*v.i.* smoke, emit smoke.—*v.r.* get smoky.
ahusar, *v.t.* taper.
ahuyentar, *v.t.* frighten away; put to flight.—*v.r.* flee.
airado, -da, *a.* angry, wrathful.
airar, *v.t.* anger, irritate.—*v.r.* grow angry.
aire, *n.m.* air; (*mus.*) air; choke (*in cars*); *al libre,* in the open air; *hacer* —, be windy.
airear, *v.t.* ventilate.—*v.r.* take the air.
airoso, -sa, *a.* airy, windy; graceful; successful.
aislamiento, *n.m.* isolation; (*phys.*) insulation.
aislar, *v.t.* isolate; (*phys.*) insulate.
¡ajá! *interj.* aha! good!
ajado, -da (1), *a.* garlicky.—*n.f.* garlic sauce.
ajado, -da (2), *a.* withered.
ajar, *v.t.* spoil, mar; tarnish.
ajedrecista, *n.m.f.* chess-player.
ajedrez, *n.m.* chess.
ajenjo, *n.m.* (*bot.*) wormwood; absinthe; (*fig.*) bitterness.

ajeno, -na, *a.* belonging to another; foreign; strange.
ajetreo, *n.m.* fatigue; agitation.
ají, *n.m.* (*bot.*) chili, capsicum.
ajimez, *n.m.* arched (Moorish) window divided by a central pillar.
ajo, *n.m.* garlic; (*fam.*) oath.
ajobo, *n.m.* burden.
ajuar, *n.m.* trousseau; household furniture.
ajustador, *n.m.* brassière; jacket.
ajustar, *v.t.* adjust; regulate; make (*an agreement*); reconcile; settle (*accounts*).
ajuste, *n.m.* adjustment; settlement; coupling.
ajusticiar, *v.t.* execute, put to death.
al [A EL].
ala, *n.f.* wing; brim (*hat*).
Alá, *n.m.* Allah.
alabanza, *n.f.* praise.
alabar, *v.t.* praise, extol.—*v.r.* boast; show oneself pleased (*de,* at).
alabarda, *n.f.* halberd.
alabardero, *n.m.* halberdier; (*theat.*) member of the claque.
álabe, *n.m.* blade, vane (*of turbine*).
alabear, *v.t., v.r.* warp.
alacena, *n.f.* cupboard; closet; (*naut.*) locker.
Alacrán, *n.m.* (*astr.*) Scorpio; **alacrán, n.m.** scorpion.
alacridad, *n.f.* alacrity.
alambicar [A], *v.t.* distil; refine excessively (*style*).
alambique, *n.m.* still.
alambrada, *n.f.* barbed-wire entanglement.
alambrado, *n.m.* wiring.
alambrar, *v.t.* wire; fasten with wire.
alambre, *n.m.* wire; — *de púas* or *espinas,* barbed-wire.
alambrera, *n.f.* wire netting; wire cover (*for food etc.*).
alameda, *n.f.* poplar grove; public avenue.
álamo, *n.m.* poplar; — *temblón,* aspen.
alano, *n.m.* mastiff.
alar, *n.m.* overhanging roof.
alarbe, *a., n.m.f.* (*obs.*) Arab; Arabian.
alarde, *n.m.* parade, (*mil.*) review; ostentation.
alardear, *v.i.* boast, brag.
alargar [B], *v.t.* lengthen, extend; hand out; increase; protract.—*v.r.* become longer; move off.
alarido, *n.m.* outcry; scream.
alarma, *n.f.* alarm.
alarmante, *a.* alarming.
alavés, -vesa, *a., n.m.f.* rel. to Alava.
alazán, -zana, *a.* sorrel-coloured.
alba, *n.f.* dawn; (*eccl.*) alb.
albacea, *n.m.* executor.—*n.f.* executrix.
albada, *n.f.* aubade, dawn song.
albahaca, *n.f.* (*bot.*) sweet basil.
albalá, *n.m.f.* (*obs.*) royal letters patent.
albanega, *n.f.* hair net.
albanés, -nesa, *a., n.m.f.* Albanian.
albañal, *n.m.* sewer.
albañil, *n.m.* mason; bricklayer.
albañilería, *n.f.* masonry.
albarán, *n.m.* 'to let' sign.
albarda, *n.f.* packsaddle.
albardilla, *n.f.* small packsaddle; (*cul.*) batter; coping stone.
albaricoque, *n.m.* apricot.
albaricoquero, *n.m.* apricot tree.

albatros

albatros, *n.m. inv.* (*orn.*) albatros.
albayalde, *n.m.* white lead.
albear, *v.i.* glow white, turn white.
albedrío, *n.m.* free will.
albéitar, *n.m.* horse doctor.
alberca, *n.f.* pond; tank; vat.
albérchigo, *n.m.*, **albérchiga,** *n.f.* peach; apricot.
albergar [B], *v.t., v.i., v.r.* lodge, shelter.
albergue, *n.m.* lodging, shelter, hostel; den.
alberguería, *n.f.* inn; poorhouse.
albino, -na, *a.* albino.
albo, -ba, *a.* (*poet.*) white.
albogue, *n.m.* pastoral flute.
albollón, *n.m.* sewer; drain.
albóndiga, *n.f.* rissole; meat *or* fish ball.
albor, *n.m.* dawn; whiteness; (*fig.*) beginning.
alborada, *n.f.* dawn; dawn serenade.
albornoz, *n.m.* burnoose; dressing gown.
alborotado, -da, *a.* turbulent, restive.
alborotar, *v.t.* disturb, excite.—*v.i., v.r.* get excited; riot.
alboroto, *n.m.* disturbance; riot, outcry.
alborozar [C], *v.t.* exhilarate.
alborozo, *n.m.* merriment, gaiety.
albricias, *n.f.pl.* reward for bringing good news; expression of joy.
álbum, *n.m.* album.
albúmina, *n.f.* (*chem.*) albumin.
albuminoso, -sa, *a.* albuminous.
albura, *n.f.* whiteness; white of egg.
alca, *n.f.* (*orn.*) razorbill.
alcabala, *n.f.* excise.
alcachofa, *n.f.* (*bot.*) artichoke.
alcahueta, *n.f.* bawd, procuress.
alcahuete, *n.m.* pimp, procurer.
alcahuetear, *v.t., v.i.* pander, procure (*women*).
alcaide, *n.m.* (*obs.*) governor, warden.
alcalde, *n.m.* mayor; justice of the peace.
alcaldía, *n.f.* office of ALCALDE.
álcali, *n.m.* (*chem.*) alkali.
alcalino, -na, *a.* (*chem.*) alkaline.
alcalizar [C], *v.t.* (*chem.*) alkalize.
alcaloide, *n.m.* alkaloid.
alcance, *n.m.* reach, scope, range; (*print.*) stop-press, late news; (*com.*) deficit.
alcancía, *n.f.* money box, (child's) piggy-bank.
alcanfor, *n.m.* camphor.
alcantarilla, *n.f.* culvert; sewer.
alcanzado, -da, *a.* necessitous; indebted.
alcanzar [C], *v.t.* follow; catch up with; overtake; get to; reach.
alcaparra, *n.f.*, **alcaparro,** *n.m.* (*bot.*) caper bush; caper.
alcaraván, *n.m.* (*orn.*) stone curlew.
alcaravea, *n.f.* (*bot.*) caraway seed.
alcatraz (1), *n.m.* (*orn.*) pelican, gannet.
alcatraz (2), *n.m.* (*bot.*) arum.
alcazaba, *n.f.* (*mil.*) keep, donjon.
alcázar, *n.m.* castle, fortress; (*naut.*) quarter-deck.
alce (1), *n.m.* moose, elk.
alce (2), *n.m.* cut (*at cards*); (*print.*) gathering.
alcista, *n.m.* (*com.*) bull (*Stock Exchange*).
alcoba, *n.f.* bedroom; alcove.
alcohol, *n.m.* alcohol; kohl, eye shadow.
alcohólico, -ca, *a.* alcoholic.
alcor, *n.m.* hill.
alcornoque, *n.m.* cork tree.
alcorza, *n.f.* (*cul.*) icing.

alcotana, *n.f.* pickaxe.
alcuña, alcurnia, *n.f.* ancestry, lineage.
alcuza, *n.f.* oil bottle; oilcan.
alcuzcuz, *n.m.* (*cul.*) couscous.
aldaba, *n.f.* door knocker; (*eng.*) iron flap.
aldabonazo, *n.m.* knock on the door.
aldea, *n.f.* village, hamlet.
aldeano, -na, rel. to a village; rustic.—*n.m.f.* villager; peasant.
aleación, *n.f.* (*metal.*) alloy; alloying.
alear (1), *v.t.* alloy.
alear (2), *v.i.* flutter.
aledaño, -ña, *a.* bordering.—*n.m.* boundary, border.
alegación, *n.f.* allegation; argument.
alegar [B], *v.t.* allege, affirm; quote.
alegato, *n.m.* (*jur.*) allegation, summing-up.
alegoría, *n.f.* allegory.
alegórico, -ca, *a.* allegorical.
alegorizar [C], *v.t.* allegorize.
alegrar, *v.t.* gladden; enliven.—*v.r.* be glad, rejoice (*de*, at).
alegre, *a.* merry, gay; funny; tipsy.
alegría, *n.f.* mirth; joy; pleasure.
alegro, *n.m.* (*mus.*) allegro.
Alejandría, *n.f.* Alexandria.
alejandrino, -na, *a., n.m.* alexandrine.
Alejandro, *n.m.* Alexander.
alejar, *v.t.* remove to a distance; separate.—*v.r.* recede.
aleluya, *n.f.* hallelujah, alleluia; joy; doggerel.
alemán, -mana, *a., n.m.f.* German.
Alemania, *n.f.* Germany.
alentador, -ra, *a.* encouraging, cheering.
alentar [1], *v.t.* inspire; encourage.—*v.i.* breathe.
alerce, *n.m.* (*bot.*) larch.
alero, *n.m.* eaves, gable end.
alerón, *n.m.* (*aer.*) aileron.
alerta, *n.m.* (*mil.*) alert.—*interj.* watch out!
alertar, *v.t.* put on guard.—*v.r.* be on one's guard.
alerto, -ta, *a.* alert, vigilant.
aleta, *n.f.* (*ichth.*) fin; (*Brit.*) mudguard; (*U.S.*) fender; (*aer.*) flap, fin.
aletear, *v.i.* flutter, flap.
aleve, *a.* perfidious.
alevosía, *n.f.* perfidy.
alevoso, -sa, *a.* perfidious.
alfabético, -ca, *a.* alphabetical.
alfabeto, *n.m.* alphabet.
alfalfa, *n.f.* alfalfa, lucerne.
alfanje, *n.m.* scimitar; cutlass.
alfaquí, *n.m.* alfaki, priest of Islam.
alfarería, *n.f.* pottery, earthenware.
alfarero, -ra, *n.m.f.* potter.
alféizar, *n.m.* (*arch.*) embrasure.
alfeñicado, -da, *a.* weakly; finicky.
alfeñique, *n.m.* sugar paste; (*fam.*) delicate person.
alférez, *n.m.* (*mil.*) ensign; second lieutenant.
alfil, *n.m.* bishop (*chess*).
alfiler, *n.m.* pin; brooch.—*pl.* pin-money.
alfolí, *n.m.* granary; salt warehouse.
alfombra, *n.f.* carpet; rug, mat.
alfonsí, *a.* Alfonsine.
alforja, *n.f.* saddle-bag; pannier.
alforza, *n.f.* plait; tuck.
alga, *n.f.* (*bot.*) alga, seaweed.
algalia, *n.f.* civet (*perfume*).—*n.m.* civet cat.
algara, *n.f.* raiding party.
algarabía, *n.f.* Arabic; jargon; clamour.

8

algarroba, *n.f.* carob bean.
álgebra, *n.f.* algebra.
algebraico, -ca, *a.* algebraic.
algo, *pron.* something.—*adv.* somewhat, rather.
algodón, *n.m.* cotton; — hidrófilo, cotton wool; — *pólvora*, gun-cotton.
algodonoso, -sa, *a.* cottony; insipid (*of fruit*).
alguacil, *n.m.* constable.
alguien, *pron.* somebody.
algún, *a. m. contracted form of* ALGUNO *before n.m.sg.*
alguno, -na, *a.* some, any; — *que otro*, a few.
—*pron.* somebody, someone.
alhaja, *n.f.* jewel; highly prized thing; showy furniture.
al(h)elí, *n.m.* (*bot.*) wallflower; stock.
alheña, *n.f.* (*bot.*) privet; henna (*dye*); (*agr.*) rust.
alhóndiga, *n.f.* public granary.
alhucema, *n.f.* lavender.
aliado, -da, *a.* allied.—*n.m.f.* ally.
alianza, *n.f.* alliance, league; wedding ring; (*Bibl.*) covenant.
aliar [L], *v.r.* form an alliance.
alias, *adv.* (*Lat.*) alias.—*n.m.* alias.
alicaído, -da, *a.* with drooping wings; (*fig.*) discouraged.
alicantino, -na, *a., n.m.f.* (one) from Alicante.
alicates, *n.m.pl.* pliers, pincers, nippers.
aliciente, *n.m.* attraction, inducement.
alienable, *a.* alienable.
alienación, *n.f.* (*med., jur.*) alienation.
alienar, *v.t.* alienate.
aliento, *n.m.* breath; inspiration; bravery.
aligerar, *v.t.* lighten; ease.
alijar, *v.t.* (*naut.*) lighten (*cargo*); gin (*cotton*); smuggle; (*carp.*) sandpaper.
alijo, *n.m.* (*naut.*) lightening (*cargo*); ginning (*cotton*); smuggling.
alimaña, *n.f.* (*pej.*) animal.
alimentación, *n.f.* nutrition; feeding.
alimentar, *v.t.* feed; nourish.
alimenticio, -cia, *a.* nutritious.
alimento, *n.m.* food, nutriment.—*pl.* (*jur.*) alimony.
alineación, *n.f.* alignment.
aliñar, *v.t.* adorn; (*cul.*) dress.
aliño, *n.m.* ornament; preparation.
alisadura, *n.f.* smoothing; planing.—*pl.* shavings.
alisios, *n.m.pl.* trade winds.
aliso, *n.m.* (*bot.*) alder; — *blanco*, (*bot.*) birch.
alistar, *v.t., v.r.* enlist, enrol; get ready.
aliteración, *n.f.* alliteration.
aliviar, *v.t.* lighten, relieve.
alivio, *n.m.* relief; comfort.
aljama, *n.f.* mosque; synagogue; assembly (*of Moors or Jews*).
aljamía, *n.f.* Moorish name for Spanish; Spanish written with Arabic characters.
aljibe, *n.m.* cistern; well.
aljófar, *n.m.* asymmetrical pearl; (*poet.*) dewdrop.
alma (1), *n.f.* soul, spirit.
alma (2), *n.f.* (*arch.*) scaffold pole, newel.
almacén, *n.m.* warehouse, store, shop; naval arsenal.
almádena, *n.f.* sledge hammer.
almadía, *n.f.* raft.

almadreña, *n.f.* clog.
almagra, *n.f.* almagre, *n.m.* red ochre.
almanaque, *n.m.* almanac.
almeja, *n.f.* (*zool.*) cockle; clam.
almendra, *n.f.* almond.
almendrado, *n.m.* macaroon.
almendrilla, *n.f.* gravel; buckwheat coal; file.
almendro, *n.m.* almond-tree.
almiar, *n.m.* haystack.
almíbar, *n.m.* syrup.
almibarar, *v.t.* (*cul.*) preserve in syrup *or* sugar; (*fig.*) conciliate.
almidón, *n.m.* starch.
almidonar, *v.t.* starch.
alminar, *n.m.* minaret.
almirantazgo, *n.m.* admiralty.
almirante, *n.m.* admiral.
almirez, *n.m.* (*pl.* -eces) mortar.
almizcle, *n.m.* (*bot.*) musk.
almocafre, *n.m.* (*agr.*) dibble; hoe.
almofrej, almofrez (*S.A.*), *n.m.* (*pl.* -eces) bedding roll.
almohada, *n.f.* pillow; cushion.
almohadilla, *n.f.* cushion; pad.
almojarife, *n.m.* king's tax-gatherer.
almoneda, *n.f.* auction.
almorzar [4C], *v.i.* lunch.
almud, *n.m.* a dry measure; half an acre.
almuédano, *n.m.* muezzin.
almuerzo, *n.m.* lunch, luncheon.
alnada, *n.f.* step-daughter.
alnado, *n.m.* step-son.
alocución, *n.f.* allocution, address.
áloe, *n.m.* aloes.
aloja, *n.f.* mead.
alojamiento, *n.m.* lodging.
alojar, *v.t., v.i.* lodge; (*mil.*) (be) billet(ed).
alondra, *n.f.* (*orn.*) lark.
alongar [4B], *v.t.* enlarge; extend; separate.
alotropia, *n.f.* (*chem.*) allotropy.
alpaca, *n.f.* (*zool., textile*) alpaca.
alpargata, *n.f.* rope-soled sandal.
alpinismo, *n.m.* mountaineering.
alquería, *n.f.* (isolated) farmhouse.
alquilar, *v.t.* let, hire, rent.
alquiler, *n.m.* hire, rent.
alquilona, *n.f.* charwoman.
alquimia, *n.f.* alchemy.
alquitrán, *n.m.* tar, pitch.
alquitranado, *n.m.* tarpaulin.
alrededor, *adv.* around.—— *de*, around, about. —*n.m.pl.* outskirts, environs.
altanería, *n.f.* haughtiness.
altanero, -ra, *a.* haughty, insolent; proud.
altar, *n.m.* altar.
altavoz, *n.m.* (*rad.*) loudspeaker.
alteración, *n.f.* alteration; change; taint.
alterar, *v.t.* alter, change (*for the worse*); debase; weather.
altercación, *n.f.* altercation, wrangle.
alternación, *n.f.* alternation.
alternadamente, *adv.* alternately.
alternar, *v.t.* alternate.—*v.i.* alternate; have friendly relations with, (*fam.*) hob-nob with.
alternativa, *n.f.* alternative, turn; (*taur.*) ceremony of becoming a matador.
alternativamente, *adv.* alternatively.
alternativo, -va, alterno, -na, *a.* alternate, by turns; (*elec.*) alternating.
Alteza, *n.f.* Highness (*title*); alteza, *n.f.* height.

altibajo(s), *n.m.(pl.)* ups and downs.
altímetro, *n.m.* (*aer.*) altimeter.
altisonante, *a.* high-sounding, grandiloquent, (*fam.*) high-falutin.
altitud, *n.f.* altitude; height.
altivez, *n.f.* haughtiness, pride.
altivo, -va, *a.* haughty.
alto (1) **-ta,** *a.* high, lofty, tall; (*mus.*) alto; — **horno,** blast furnace; *dar de alta,* pronounce fit; *en voz alta,* out loud, in a loud voice.
¡alto! (2), *interj.* halt!
altramuz, *n.f.* (*bot.*) lupin.
altura, *n.f.* height; altitude; (*naut.*) latitude; *estar a la — de,* be equal to, be up to.
alubia, *n.f.* bean.
alucinación, *n.f.,* **alucinamiento,** *n.m.* hallucination; spell.
alucinar, *v.t.* hallucinate; delude; fascinate.
alucón, *n.m.* tawny owl.
alud, *n.m.* avalanche.
aludir, *v.i.* allude, refer.
alumbrado, -da, *a.* (*fam.*) tipsy; enlightened. —*n.m.* lighting.
alumbramiento, *n.m.* illumination; childbirth.
alumbrar, *v.t.* illuminate, light.
alumbre, *n.m.* alum.
alumino, *n.m.* (*Brit.*) aluminium, (*U.S.*) aluminum.
alumno, -na, *n.m.f.* foster-child; pupil; student.
alusión, *n.f.* allusion.
aluvión, *n.m.* (*geol.*) alluvium.
alveolar, *a.* alveolar.
alza, *n.f.* (*com.*) rise (*in price*); (*mil.*) **sight** (*guns*).
alzado, *n.m.* fraudulent bankrupt; (*arch.*) elevation.
alzamiento, *n.m.* raising; raising a bid; rising, insurrection.
alzaprima, *n.f.* crowbar, lever; (*mech.*) fulcrum.
alzar [C], *v.t.* raise; cut (*cards*); (*naut.*) heave. —*v.r.* rise (*in revolt*); rise; (*com.*) embezzle.
allá, *adv.* there, in that place; *por —,* thereabouts.
allanar, *v.t.* level, flatten.—*v.r.* acquiesce (*a,* in).
allegar [B], *v.t.* reap; collect; procure.—*v.r.* approach.
allende, *adv.* on the far side.
allí, *adv.* there, in that place.
ama, *n.f.* mistress of the house; owner; *— de llaves,* housekeeper; *— de cría,* wet-nurse.
amabilidad, *n.f.* amiability; kindness.
amable, *a.* amiable; kind.
amado, -da, *a.* beloved.—*n.m.f.* **beloved,** sweetheart.
amador, *n.m.* lover.
amaestrado, -da, *a.* experienced; schooled.
amaestrar, *v.t.* instruct, teach.
amagar [B], *v.t.* threaten; show signs of; feign. —*v.i.* threaten; be impending.
amago, *n.m.* threat; sign, hint; empty promise.
amainar, *v.t.* relax.—*v.i.* subside; lessen.
amalgama, *n.f.* (*metal.*) amalgam.
amalgamar, *v.t.* amalgamate.
amamantar, *v.t.* suckle.
amancebamiento, *n.m.* concubinage.
amancebar, *v.r.* live in concubinage.
amancillar, *v.t.* stain, pollute.

amanecer [9], *v.i.* dawn; be (at a place) at dawn.—*n.m.* dawn.
amanerar, *v.r.* become affected.
amansar, *v.t.* tame, domesticate, break in (*horses*).
amante, *a.* loving.—*n.m.f.* lover; sweetheart.
amanuense, *n.m.f.* amanuensis, clerk.
amañar, *v.t.* do cleverly, doctor (*accounts etc.*).—*v.r.* be handy.
amapola, *n.f.* poppy.
amar, *v.t.* love.
amargar [B], *v.t.* make bitter; embitter.—*v.i.* be bitter.—*v.r.* become embittered.
amargo, -ga, *a.* bitter.
amargón, *n.m.* (*bot.*) dandelion.
amargor, *n.m.,* **amargura,** *n.f.* bitterness.
amaricado, -da, *a.* (*fam., pej.*) effeminate, sissy.
amarillez, *n.f.* yellowness.
amarillo, -lla, *a.* yellow.—*n.m.* jaundice.
amarra, *n.f.* (*naut.*) cable, hawser.
amarre, *n.m.* (*naut.*) mooring, tying-up.
amartelar, *v.t.* court; love devotedly.—*v.r.* fall in love.
amartillar, *v.t.* hammer.
amasadera, *n.f.* kneading-trough.
amasadora, *n.f.* mixer (*dough etc.*).
amasar, *v.t.* knead, mould; (*med.*) massage.
amasijo, *n.m.* dough; kneading; mortar.
amatista, *n.f.* (*gem.*) amethyst.
amayorazgar [B], *v.t.* (*jur.*) entail.
amazona, *n.f.* riding habit; horsewoman; (*myth.*) Amazon.
Amazonas, *n.m.sg.* Amazon (*river*).
amazónico, -ca, *a.* Amazonian.
ambages, *n.m.pl.* circumlocutions.
ámbar, *n.m.* amber.
ambición, *n.f.* ambition.
ambicionar, *v.t.* aspire to.
ambicioso, -sa, *a.* ambitious; covetous.
ambidextro, -tra, *a.* ambidextrous.
ambiente, *n.m.* environment; atmosphere.
ambigüedad, *n.f.* ambiguity.
ambiguo, -gua, *a.* ambiguous, doubtful.
ámbito, *n.m.* circuit; compass; scope.
ambos, -bas, *a., pron. pl.* both.
ambulancia, *n.f.* ambulance.
ambulante, *a.* ambulant; *vendedor —,* pedlar, itinerant salesman.
ameba [AMIBA].
amedrantar, *v.t.* frighten.
amén, *n.m.* amen.— *de,* besides, in addition to.
amenaza, *n.f.* threat.
amenazante, *a.* menacing.
amenazar [C], *v.t.* threaten, menace (*con,* with, to).
amenidad, *n.f.* amenity; urbanity.
ameno, -na, *a.* pleasant; elegant; urbane.
americana, *n.f.* jacket.
americanismo, *n.m.* (*gram.*) Americanism.
americano, -na, *a., n.m.f.* American (*esp. applied to S.A.*).
amerindio, -dia, *a., n.m.f.* Amerindian.
ametrallador, *n.m.* machine gunner.
ametralladora, *n.f.* machine-gun.
ametrallar, *v.t.* machine-gun, strafe.
amiba, *n.f.* amoeba.
amiga (1), *n.f.* friend; mistress, concubine.
amiga (2), *n.f.* (*prov., obs.*) girls' school.
amigablemente, *adv.* amicably.
amígdalas, *n.f.pl.* (*med.*) tonsils.

amigdalitis, n.f. (med.) tonsillitis.
amigo, n.m. friend; lover.
amistad, n.f. friendship; concubinage.
amistoso, -sa, a. friendly, amicable.
amistar, v.t. bring together.—v.r. make friends.
amnesia, n.f. (med.) amnesia.
amnistia, n.f. amnesty.
amnistiar [L], v.t. amnesty.
amo, n.m. master; employer; (fam.) boss.
amodorrar, v.r. drowse.
amodorrido, -da, a. drowsy.
amojamado, -da, a. dried-up.
amoladora, n.f. (eng.) grinder, grinding machine.
amolar [4], v.t. whet, grind; (fam.) bore.
amoldar, v.t. mould; adjust.—v.r. adapt oneself.
amonestación, n.f. advice; warning.—pl. banns.
amonestar, v.t. advise, counsel.
amoníaco, n.m. (chem.) ammonia.
amontillado, n.m. variety of pale dry sherry, amontillado.
amontonar, v.t. heap; pile; accumulate.—v.r. (fam.) fly into a rage; (fam.) live in sin.
amor, n.m. love.
amoral, a. amoral.
amordazar [C], v.t. gag, muzzle.
amorfo, -fa, a. amorphous.
amorío, n.m. love affair, amour.
amoroso, -sa, a. amorous; loving.
amortajar, v.t. shroud.
amortiguar [H], v.t. deaden; absorb; temper.
amortizable, a. (com.) redeemable.
amortizar [C], v.t. amortize, write off.
amotinar, v.t. incite to rebellion.—v.r. rebel.
amparar, v.t. shelter; protect; support.—v.r. claim protection; seek shelter.
amparo, n.m. protection; aid.
amperaje, n.m. (elec.) amperage.
amperio, n.m. (elec.) ampere.
ampliación, n.f. extension; (phot. etc.) enlargement.
ampliar [L] v.t. amplify, enlarge.
amplificación, n.f. enlargement.
amplificador, -ra, a. enlarging, amplifying.—n.m. (photo., rad.) amplifier.
amplio, -lia, a. ample; large, roomy.
amplitud, n.f. extent; largeness; (phys. etc.) amplitude.
ampolla, n.f. blister; bulb (lamp); bubble.
amputación, n.f. amputation.
amueblar, v.t. furnish.
amurallar, v.t. wall up; surround with walls.
anacoreta, n.m. (eccl.) anchorite, hermit.
anacronismo, n.m. anachronism.
anadón, n.m. duckling.
anagrama, n.m. anagram.
anal, a. anal.
anales, n.m.pl. annals.
analfabetismo, n.m. illiteracy.
analfabeto, -ta, a. illiterate.
análisis, n.m. or f. inv. analysis.
analizar [C], v.t. analyse.
analogía, n.f. analogy.
analógico, -ca, a. analogical.
análogo, -ga, a. analogous.
ananás, n.f. (bot.) pineapple.
anaquel, n.m. shelf.
anarquía, n.f. anarchy.

anárquico, -ca, a. anarchic(al).
anarquismo, n.m. anarchism.
anatema, n.m. or f. anathema.
anatematizar [C], v.t. anathematize, excommunicate.
anatomía, n.f. (med.) anatomy; dissection.
anatómico, -ca, a. anatomical.—n.m.f. anatomist.
anca, n.f. croup; haunch.
anciano, -na, n.m.f. elderly person, elder.
ancla, n.f. anchor.
ancladero, n.m. anchorage.
anclar, v.i. cast anchor, anchor.
ancón, n.m. small cove, inlet.
áncora, n.f. anchor.
ancho, -cha, a. broad, wide, large.—n.m. width, breadth; (rail.) gauge; **a sus anchas,** at one's ease.
anchoa, n.f. anchovy.
andada, n.f. track, trail; **volver a las andadas,** backslide.
andaluz, -za, a., n.m.f. (pl. -uces, -uzas) Andalusian.
andaluzada, n.f. (fam.) long yarn, tall story.
andamiaje, n.m. scaffolding.
andamio, n.m. scaffold, platform.
andante, a. walking; errant (knight).—n.m. (mus.) andante.
andanza, n.f. occurrence.
andar (11), v.i. go, come; walk; ¡anda! come on! gracious!
andariego, -ga, a. restless, roving.
andarrío, n.m. (orn.) wagtail.
andas, n.f.pl. litter.
andén, n.m. (rail.) platform, footpath.
andino, -na, a. Andean.
andrajo, n.m. rag.
andrajoso, -sa, a. ragged.
andurriales, n.m.pl. by-roads.
anea, n.f. (bot.) rush; basket-work.
anécdota, n.f. anecdote.
anecdótico, -ca, a. anecdotal.
anegable, a. submersible; floodable.
anegar [B], v.t. inundate; submerge; drown.—v.r. become flooded or submerged or soaked.
anejo, -ja, a. annexed, joined.—n.m. annex.
aneldo, n.m. (bot.) common dill.
anemia, n.f. (med.) anaemia.
anémona, anémone, n.f. (bot.) anemone.
anestesiar, v.t. anaesthetize.
anexo, -xa, a. [ANEJO].
anfibio, -bia, a. amphibious.
anfiteatro, n.m. amphitheatre; lecture-theatre.
angarillón, n.m. large basket.
ángel, n.m. angel; **tener —,** have a way with one.
angélica, n.f. (bot., med.) angelica.
angina, n.f. (med.) angina.—pl. sore throat.
anglicano, -na, a., n.m.f. Anglican.
anglicismo, n.m. (gram.) Anglicism.
anglo, -gla, a. Anglian.—n.m.f. Angle.
angloamericano, -na, a. Anglo-American.
anglófilo, -la, a., n.m.f. Anglophile.
anglófobo, -ba, a., n.m.f. Anglophobe.
anglomanía, n.f. Anglomania.
anglosajón, -jona, a., n.m.f. Anglo-Saxon; British and American.
angosto, -ta, a. narrow; insufficient.
angostura, n.f. narrowness; narrows.
anguila, n.f. (ichth.) eel.

angular, *a.* angular; *piedra* —, cornerstone.
ángulo, *n.m.* angle, corner.
angustia, *n.f.* anguish, affliction.
angustiar, *v.t.* anguish, afflict.
anhelar, *v.t.* long for, covet.—*v.i.* fight for breath.
anhelo, *n.m.* anxiousness; vehement desire.
anheloso, -sa, *a.* breathless; anxious (*de*, to, for).
anidar, *v.i.* nest.
anilina, *n.f.* (*chem.*) aniline.
anillo, *n.m.* ring; (*pol.*) *de* —, honorary.
ánima, *n.f.* soul; (*mil.*) bore (*of fire-arms*).
animación, *n.f.* animation, bustle, liveliness.
animado, -da, *a.* lively.
animadversión, *n.f.* animadversion, remark.
animal, *a., n.m.* animal, brute.
animar, *v.t.* animate; enliven; inspire, encourage.—*v.r.* cheer up; grow energetic; take courage.
ánimo, *n.m.* soul, spirit; valour, bravery.— *interj.* come on!
animosidad, *n.f.* valour; animosity.
animoso, -sa, *a.* bold.
aniquilación, *n.f.* annihilation.
aniquilar, *v.t.* annihilate.
anís, *n.m.* (*bot.*) anise; aniseed; anisette.
anisar, *v.t.* flavour with aniseed.
anisete, *n.m.* anisette.
aniversario, -ria, *a., n.m.* anniverary.
ano, *n.m.* (*med.*) anus.
anoche, *adv.* last night.
anochecer [9], *v.i.* grow dark; be (at a place) at nightfall.—*v.r.* grow dark.—*n.m.* dark, dusk.
anochecida, *n.f.* nightfall.
anodino, -na, *a.* (*med.*) anodyne; (*fig.*) inoffensive.
ánodo, *n.m.* (*phys.*) anode.
anónimo, -ma, *a.* anonymous.—*n.m.* anonymity.
anormal, *a.* abnormal.
anormalidad, *n.f.* abnormality.
anotación, *n.f.* annotation, note.
anotar, *v.t.* annotate.
ánsar, *n.m.* goose; — *macho*, gander.
ansarino, -na, *a.* goosy.—*n.m.* gosling.
ansarón, *n.m.* big goose.
ansia, *n.f.* anxiety; anguish; longing.
ansiar, *v.t.* desire, hanker for or after.
ansioso, -sa, *a.* anxious; eager.
anta (1), *n.f.* (*zool.*) elk.
anta (2), *n.f.* obelisk; pillar.
antagonismo, *n.m.* antagonism.
antaño, *adv.* yesteryear.
antártico, -ca, *a.* Antarctic.
ante (1), *prep.* before; in the presence of; — *todo*, above all.
ante (2), *n.m.* (*zool.*) elk; doeskin; suede; buff (*colour*).
anteanoche, *adv.* the night before last.
anteayer, *adv.* the day before yesterday.
antebrazo, *n.m.* fore-arm.
antecámara, *n.f.* antechamber, lobby.
antecedencia, *n.f.* antecedence; lineage.
antecesor, -ra, *a.* antecedent.—*n.m.f.* predecessor.—*n.m.pl.* ancestors.
antedicho, -cha, *a.* aforesaid.
con antelación, de antemano, *adv. phr.* beforehand.
antena, *n.f.* (*rad.*) aerial; (*ent.*) antenna; (*naut.*) lateen yard.

antenatal, *a.* pre-natal, ante-natal.
anteojera, *n.f.* spectacle case.—*pl.* blinkers, eyeflaps.
anteojo, *n.m.* telescope; (*obs.*) spy-glass. —*pl.* spectacles; *anteojos de camino,* goggles.
antepasado, -da, *a.* passed, elapsed.— *n.m.pl.* ancestors, forebears.
anteponer [25], *v.t.* prefer; place before.— *v.r.* push oneself forward.
antepuesto, -ta, *a.* preferred.—*p.p.* [ANTEPONER].
anterior, *a.* anterior, former, previous.
anterioridad, *n.f.* priority; precedence; *con* —, previously.
antes, *adv.* before(hand); first; rather; *cuanto* —, as quickly as possible.— *de,* — *de que,* before (*of time*).
antesala, *n.f.* anteroom, antechamber.
anticiclón, *n.m.* anticyclone.
anticipación, *n.f.* anticipation; foretaste; *con* —, in advance.
anticipado, -da, *a.* in advance.
anticipar, *v.t.* anticipate; forestall; advance.
anticipo, *n.m.* anticipation; advance, advance payment or loan.
anticombustible, *a.* non-inflammable.
anticoncepcionismo, *n.m.* contraception.
anticoncepcionista, *a.* contraceptive.
anticongelante, *n.m.* anti-freeze.
anticuado, -da, *a.* antiquated.
anticuario, -ria, *a., n.m.f.* antiquarian.
antídoto, *n.m.* antidote.
antiestético, -ca, *a.* unaesthetic.
antifaz, *n.m.* mask.
antífona, *n.f.* antiphon.
antigualla, *n.f.* monument of antiquity; antique; out-of-date custom or object.
antiguamente, *adv.* in ancient times; formerly.
antigüedad, *n.f.* antiquity; seniority.
antiguo, -gua, *a.* antique, old, ancient; former.—*n.m.* veteran, senior.
antihigiénico, -ca, *a.* unhygienic.
antílope, *n.m.* (*zool.*) antelope.
antillano, -na, *a., n.m.f.* West Indian.
Antillas, *n.f.pl.* West Indies, Antilles.
antiministerial, *a.* opposition.—*n.m.f.* member of the opposition.
antioxidante, *a.* rust-preventive.
antipara, *n.f.* screen.
antipartícula, *n.f.* (*phys.*) antiparticle.
antipatía, *n.f.* antipathy; dislike.
antipático, -ca, *a.* disagreeable, unpleasant.
antípoda, *a.* antipodal.—*n.f.pl.* Antipodes.
antiquísimo, -ma, *sup. a.* very ancient; (*fam.*) out of the Ark.
antirrino, *n.m.* (*bot.*) antirrhinum.
antisemita, *a.* anti-Semitic.—*n.m.f.* anti-Semite.
antiséptico, -ca, *a., n.m.* (*med.*) antiseptic.
antítesis, *n.f.* antithesis.
antitético, -ca, *a.* antithetic(al).
antitoxina, *n.f.* (*med.*) antitoxin.
antojadizo, -za, *a.* capricious, whimsical; fickle.
antojar, *v.r.* long for, fancy; surmise.
antojo, *n.m.* whim, caprice; longing; surmise.
antología, *n.f.* anthology.
antonomasia, *n.f.* antonomasia; ... *por* —, the outstanding example of ...
antorcha, *n.f.* torch, cresset.

antracita, *n.f.* (*min.*) anthracite.
ántrax, *n.m.* (*med.*) anthrax.
antro, *n.m.* (*poet.*) cavern, grotto; (*fam.*) night-club.
antropófago, -ga, *a., n.m.f.* cannibal.
antropoide, *a.* anthropoid.
antropología, *n.f.* anthropology.
antuvión, *n.m.* (*fam.*) sudden attack; **de —,** unexpectedly.
anual, *a.* annual, yearly.
anualidad, *n.f.* annuity; annual instalment.
anuario, *n.m.* year-book; directory.
anublar, *v.t.* cloud, overcast.—*v.r.* become cloudy.
anublo, *n.m.* mildew.
anudar, *v.t.* knot; unite.—*v.r.* become knotted.
anular (1), *v.t.* annul, make void, rescind.—*v.r.* (*math.*) vanish.
anular (2), *a.* annular, ring-shaped; **dedo —,** ring finger.
Anunciación, *n.f.* (*eccl.*) Annunciation; **anunciación,** *n.f.* announcement.
anunciar, *v.t.* announce; notify; advertise.
anuncio, *n.m.* announcement; prediction; advertisement.
anzuelo, *n.m.* fish-hook; (*fig.*) allurement, attraction.
añadidura, *n.f.*, **añadimiento,** *n.m.* addition; increase.
añadir, *v.t.* add; increase.
añafea, *n.f.* **papel de —,** brown paper.
añafil, *n.m.* Moorish trumpet.
añagaza, *n.f.* lure, decoy.
añejo, -ja, *a.* old; mature (*wine etc.*); stale (*news*).
añicos, *n.m.pl.* smithereens.
añil, *n.m.* indigo.
año, *n.m.* year.
añoranza, *n.f.* homesickness, nostalgia.
añorar, *v.t., v.i.* long (for); regret.
aojar, *v.t.* bewitch, cast the evil eye upon.
aojo, *n.m.* fascination; evil eye.
aovado, -da, *a.* egg-shaped.
aovillar, *v.t.* wind (*into balls*).—*v.r.* roll oneself into a ball; shrink.
apabilar, *v.t.* trim (*wick*).—*v.r.* lose courage.
apacentar [1], *v.t.* graze (*cattle*); feed on.
apacible, *a.* peaceable; placid.
apaciguar [H], *v.t.* pacify.—*v.r.* calm down.
apadrinar, *v.t.* act as godfather to; act as second to; patronize.
apagadizo, -za, *a.* which burns badly.
apagado, -da, *a.* dull (*colour*); submissive; humble.
apagafuegos, *n.m. inv.* fire extinguisher.
apagaincendios, *n.m. inv.* fire engine; fire-extinguisher.
apagar [B], *v.t.* extinguish; put out; soften (*colours*); quench (*thirst*).
apalear, *v.t.* drub, beat.
apanalado, -da, *a.* honey-combed.
apantanar, *v.t.* flood.
apañado, -da, *a.* skilful; (*fam.*) suitable.
apañador, -ra, *a.* pilfering.—*n.m.f.* pilferer.
apañar, *v.t.* seize; pilfer; dress; fit close.—*v.r.* be skilful; manage, contrive.
apaño, *n.m.* seizing; knack; patch.
aparador, *n.m.* sideboard, dresser; workshop; display window.
aparato, *n.m.* apparatus; device, appliance; pomp; system; party machine.

aparatoso, -sa, *a.* showy, pompous.
aparcamiento, *n.m.* parking (*cars*); car-park.
aparcar [A], *v.t., v.i.* park (*car*).
aparcero, *n.m.* (*agr.*) partner; share cropper.
aparear, *v.t.* match, mate, couple.
aparecer [9], *v.i., v.r.* appear, turn up.
aparecido, *n.m.* ghost.
aparejador, *n.m.* master builder; general foreman; (*aer.*) rigger.
aparejar, *v.t.* prepare, get ready; saddle.
aparejo, *n.m.* preparation; harness, gear; tackle.—*pl.* tools.
aparente, *a.* apparent; manifest.
aparición, *n.f.* apparition; coming into sight.
apariencia, *n.f.* appearance, aspect; likeness; probability.
apartadero, *n.m.* (*rail.*) siding, (*U.S.*) side track; lay-by.
apartadizo, -za, *a.* unsociable.—*n.m.f.* recluse.—*n.m.* small (partitioned) room.
apartado, -da, *a.* remote; separate.—*n.m.* separate room; Post Office box; (*taur.*) shutting up bulls before a fight.
apartamiento, *n.m.* separation; apartment, flat; (*com.*) waiver.
apartar, *v.t.* separate; (*rail.*) shunt; sort.—*v.r.* withdraw; retire.
aparte, *n.m.* paragraph; section; (*theat.*) aside; **punto y —,** new paragraph.—*adv.* aside; apart.
apasionar, *v.t.* impassion; afflict.—*v.r.* become passionately fond (*de, por,* of).
apatía, *n.f.* apathy.
apátrida, *a., n.m.f.* stateless (person).
apeadero, *n.m.* horseblock; (*rail.*) flag stop; pied-à-terre.
apeador, *n.m.* land surveyor.
apear, *v.t.* set down; survey; hobble.—*v.r.* alight, dismount.
apedrear, *v.t.* stone, lapidate.—*v.i.* hail.—*v.r.* be injured by hail.
apegar [B], *v.r.* become attached (*a,* to).
apego, *n.m.* attachment.
apelación, *n.f.* (*jur.*) appeal.
apelado, -da, *n.m.f.* (*jur.*) successful appellant.
apelante, *n.m.f.* (*jur.*) appellant.
apelar, *v.i.* (*jur.*) appeal; have recourse (*a,* to).
apelmazar [C], *v.t.* compress, make hard and lumpy.
apelotonar, *v.t.* wind into a ball.
apellidar, *v.t.* name; call by name.
apellido, *n.m.* surname, family name.
apenar, *v.t.* cause pain.—*v.r.* grieve.
apenas, *adv.* hardly, scarcely.
apéndice, *n.m.* appendix.
apendicitis, *n.f.* appendicitis.
apercibimiento, *n.m.* foresight; preparation; advice; (*jur.*) summons.
apercibir, *v.t.* provide; get ready; warn; (*jur.*) summon.
aperitivo, -va, *a.* aperitive, appetizing.—*n.m.* cocktail snack, canapé.
apero, *n.m.* tool(s), equipment; sheep fold.
apertura, *n.f.* (solemn) opening.
apesadumbrar, *v.t.* sadden.—*v.r.* grieve.
apesgar [B], *v.t.* overburden.—*v.r.* become aggrieved.
apestar, *v.t.* infect with the plague; (*fig.*) pester.—*v.i.* stink.
apetecer [9], *v.t.* long for, crave.—*v.i.* appeal to.

apetecible, *a.* desirable.
apetencia, *n.f.* appetite; hunger; desire.
apetito, *n.m.* appetite.
apiadar, *v.t.* inspire pity.—*v.r.* take pity (*de,* on).
apicarar, *v.r.* become depraved.
ápice, *n.m.* apex; iota.
apicultor, -ra, *n.m.f.* apiarist, bee keeper.
apilar, *v.t., v.r.* pile up.
apimpollar, *v.r.* sprout.
apiñadura, *n.f.*, **apiñamiento,***n.m.* crowding, congestion.
apiñar, *v.t., v.r.* crowd.
apisonadora, *n.f.* (steam-)roller road-roller.
aplacar [A], *v.t.* appease; calm.
aplacible, *a.* pleasant.
aplanar, *v.t.* level.
aplastar, *v.t.* flatten; crush.—*v.r.* collapse.
aplaudir, *v.t.* applaud.
aplauso, *n.m.* applause; praise.
aplazar [C], *v.t.* convene; postpone.
aplazo, *n.m.* postponement.
aplicación, *n.f.* application; assiduity; appliqué work.
aplicado, -da, *a.* industrious.
aplicar [A], *v.t.* apply; destine.—*v.r.* apply oneself.
aplomo, *n.m.* tact, prudence; aplomb; (*tech.*) plumb.
apocamiento, *n.m.* bashfulness, diffidence.
apocar [A], *v.t.* lessen.—*v.r.* belittle oneself.
apócope, *n.f.* (*gram.*) apocope; apocopation.
apócrifo, -fa, *a.* apocryphal.—*n.m.pl.* (*Bib.*) Apocrypha.
apodar, *v.t.* give nick-names to; ridicule.
apoderar, *v.t.* empower.—*v.r.* take possession (*de,* of).
apodo, *n.m.* nick-name.
apogeo, *n.m.* apogee; peak.
apolilladura, *n.f.* moth hole.
apolillar, *v.t.* (*of moths*) eat holes in.—*v.r.* become moth-eaten.
apologia, *n.f.* apologia, defence.
apólogo, *n.m.* apologue, fable.
apoltronar, *v.r.* grow lazy *or* cowardly.
apoplejía, *n.f.* apoplexy.
aporrar, *v.i.* (*fam.*) stand tongue-tied.—*v.r.* (*fam.*) become importunate.
aporrear, *v.t.* beat, cudgel.—*v.r.* cudgel one's brains, study hard.
aportación, *n.f.* contribution.
aportar, *v.t.* bring, contribute.—*v.i.* (*naut.*) make port.
aposentar, *v.t., v.r.* lodge.
aposento, *n.m.* room; inn.
apostar [4], *v.t.* bet, wager; post (*troops*); **apostarlas** *or* **apostárselas a** *or* **con alguien,** compete with s.o.—*v.i.* contend.
apostasia, *n.f.* apostasy.
apóstata, *n.m.f.* apostate.
apostema, *n.f.* (*med.*) abscess.
apostilla, *n.f.* marginal note, gloss.
apóstol, *n.m.* apostle.
apostolado, *n.m.* apostleship, apostolate; the twelve apostles.
apostrofar, *v.t.* apostrophize.
apóstrofe, *n.f.* (*rhetoric*) apostrophe.
apóstrofo, *n.m.* (*gram.*) apostrophe.
apostura, *n.f.* gentleness, pleasant disposition.
apoteosis, *n.f.* apotheosis.
apoyabrazos, *n.m.* arm rest.
apoyadero, *n.m.* prop, support.

apoyar, *v.t.* rest, lean (*en,* on); support; bear out.—*v.i.* rest.—*v.r.* depend (*en,* upon), rely (*en,* upon); lean (*en,* on, against).
apoyo, *n.m.* prop, support; help; backing.
apreciable, *a.* valuable; respectable; *Apreciable Señor,* Dear Sir (*showing respect*).
apreciación, *n.f.* valuation.
apreciar, *v.t.* estimate; esteem, appreciate.
apreciativo, -va, *a.* appreciative.
aprecio, *n.m.* valuation; appreciation.
apremiante, *a.* urgent, pressing.
apremiar, *v.t.* press, urge; oblige.
apremio, *n.m.* constraint.
aprender, *v.t.* learn.
aprendiz, -za, *n.m.f.* apprentice, trainee.
aprendizaje, *n.m.* apprenticeship.
aprensivo, -va, *a.* apprehensive.
apresador, *n.m.* (*naut.*) privateer.
apresar, *v.t.* seize, capture; take captive.
aprestar, *v.t.* prepare.
apresurar, *v.t.* hasten.—*v.r.* make haste.
apretador, *n.m.* tightener; waistcoat; hairnet.
apretar [1], *v.t.* tighten; compress; clench; squeeze.—*v.i.* pinch (*of shoes*); begin (*a,* to).
apretón, *n.m.* pressure; squeeze; handshake.
apretura, *n.f.* confined space; (*fig.*) straits.
aprieto, *n.m.* crowd; stringency; danger; (*fam.*) tight spot.
aprisa, *adv.* swiftly.
aprisco, *n.m.* sheep-fold.
aprisionar, *v.t.* imprison.
aprobable, *a.* approvable.
aprobar [4], *v.t.* approve; pass (*an examinee*).—*v.i.* pass (*an examination*).
apropiar, *v.t.* give possession of; adapt, fit.—*v.r.* appropriate, take possession of.
apropincuar, *v.r.* (*joc.*) approach.
aprovechable, *a.* available; useful, utilizable.
aprovechar, *v.t.* make good use of.—*v.i.* be useful *or* profitable; make progress; *que* (*le*) *aproveche,* I hope you enjoy your meal.—*v.r.* avail oneself (*de,* of).
aprovisionar, *v.t.* victual, supply.
aproximar, *v.t.* approximate; move near.—*v.r.* move near (*a,* to).
aptitud, *n.f.* aptitude, ability.
apto, -ta, *a.* fit, apt.
apuesta, *n.f.* bet, wager.
apuesto, -ta, *a.* elegant; spruce, well-dressed.
apuntación, *n.f.* note; (*mus.*) notation.
apuntador, *n.m.* (*theat.*) prompter; (*mil.*) gun layer.
apuntalar, *v.t.* prop, shore up.
apuntar, *v.t.* point at; note; stitch; (*theat.*) prompt.—*v.i.* begin to appear.—*v.r.* begin to go sour.
apunte, *n.m.* note; (*theat.*) promptbook.
apuñalar, *v.t.* stab.
apuñear, apuñetear, *v.t.* punch.
apuradamente, *adv.* (*fam.*) in the nick of time, exactly; precisely.
apurado, -da, *a.* destitute, hard-up; dangerous.
apurar, *v.t.* purify; verify; finish; annoy.—*v.r.* worry; (*S.A.*) hasten; strive (*por hacer,* to do).
apuro, *n.m.* want, need; sorrow; (*S.A.*) urgency; (*fam.*) difficult situation, tight spot.

aquel, aquella, *dem. a.* (*pl.* **aquellos, aquellas**) that.—*pl.* those.
aquél, aquélla, *dem. pron.* (*pl.* **aquéllos, aquéllas**) that one; the former.—*pl.* those. —*n.m.* (*fam.*) appeal, it.
aquelarre, *n.m.* witches' Sabbath.
aquello, *dem. pron. neuter.* that, that thing *or* matter.
aquende, *adv.* (*obs.. lit.*) on this side.
aquerenciar, *v.r.* become fond (*de*, of).
aquí, *adv.* here; hither.
aquilatar, *v.t.* assay; (*fig.*) weigh the merits of.
aquilea, *m.f.* (*bot.*) arrow.
Aquiles, *n.m.* (*myth.*) Achilles.
aquilón, *n.m.* (*poet.*) north wind.
Aquisgrán, *n.m.* Aachen, Aix-la-Chapelle.
aquistar, *v.t.* acquire.
ara, *n.f.* altar.
árabe, *a.* Arabic.—*n.m.f.* Arab.—*n.m.* Arabic.
arabesco, -ca, *a.* (*art.*) arabesque; [ÁRABE].— *n.m.* (*art.*) arabesque.
la Arabia Saudita, *n.f.* Saudi Arabia.
arábigo, -ga, *a.* Arabic; Arabian.—*n.m.* Arabic.
arabio, -bia, *a.* [ÁRABE]; Arabian.
arabismo, *n.m.* Arabism.
arabizar [C], *v.t.* Arabize.—*v.i., v.r.* go Arab.
arable, *a.* (*agr.*) arable.
arada, *n.f.* (*agr.*) ploughed land; ploughing.
arado, *n.m.* (*agr.*) plough; ploughshare.
aragonés, -nesa, *a.* Aragonese.
arambel, *n.m.* tatter.
aramio, *n.m.* fallow land.
arancel, *n.m.* tariff, rate (*customs etc.*).
arándano, *n.m.* (*bot.*) cranberry; (*S.A.*) bilberry, whortleberry.
arandela, *n.f.* (*mech.*) washer, ring; candlestick.
araña, *n.f.* (*zool.*) spider; (*bot.*) love-in-a-mist; chandelier; (*fam.*) thrifty person; whore.
arañada, *n.f.* scratch.
arañar, *v.t.* scratch; score; scrape.
arañazo, *n.m.* scratch.
arar, *v.t.* plough.
araucano, -na, *a., n.m.f.* Araucanian.
arbitrador, -ra, *a.* arbitrating.—*n.m.* arbitrator, umpire, referee.—*n.f.* arbitress.
arbitrar, *v.t.* arbitrate; referee, umpire (*sports*).—*v.r.* manage well.
arbitrariedad, *n.f.* arbitrariness.
arbitrario, -ria, *a.* arbitrary; (*jur.*) arbitral.
arbitrio, *n.m.* free will; arbitration; arbitrariness; ways, means.—*pl.* excise taxes.
arbitrista, *n.m.f.* schemer.
árbitro, -tra, *a.* autonomous.—*n.m.f.* referee, umpire; arbiter.—*n.f.* arbitress.
árbol, *n.m.* tree; (*mech.*) shaft, spindle; (*naut.*) mast.
arbolado, -da, *a.* wooded.—*n.m.* woodland.
arboladura, *n.f.* (*naut.*) masts and spars.
arbolar, *v.t.* hoist.
arboleda, *n.f.* grove.
arbollón, *n.m.* outlet; gutter.
arbusto, *n.m.* shrub.
arca, *n.f.* chest, coffer; safe; reservoir; — *de Noé,* Noah's ark; (*fam.*) treasure-house.
arcabuz, *n.m.* (*pl.* **-uces**) arquebus.
arcada, *n.f.* retch; (*arch.*) arcade.
arcaduz, *n.m.* (*pl.* **-uces**) conduit; pipe.
arcaico, -ca, *a.* archaic.

arcaismo, *n.m.* archaism.
arcángel, *n.m.* archangel.
arce, *n.m.* (*bot.*) maple.
arcediano, *n.m.* (*eccl.*) archdeacon.
arcilla, *n.f.* clay.
arcipreste, *n.m.* (*eccl.*) archpriest.
arco, *n.m.* bow; (*math., elec.*) arc; (*arch.*) arch; — *iris,* rainbow.
arcón, *n.m.* bin, large chest, linen-chest.
archidiácono, *n.m.* (*eccl.*) archdeacon.
archiduque, *n.m.* archduke.
archimillonario, -ria, *a., n.m.f.* multi-millionaire.
archipiélago, *n.m.* (*geog.*) archipelago.
archivar, *v.t.* deposit in an archive; (*com. etc.*) file.
archivo, *n.m.* archive, archives; file, filing cabinet; (*S.A.*) office.
arder, *v.t., v.i.* burn.
ardid, *n.m.* stratagem, ruse, trick.
ardido, -da, *a.* bold, brave.
ardiente, *a.* burning, fervent; ardent, passionate; (*poet.*) glowing red.
ardilla, *n.f.* (*zool.*) squirrel.
ardite, *n.m.* farthing.
ardor, *n.m.* ardour; vehemence; intrepidity.
arduo, -dua, *a.* arduous, hard.
área, *n.f.* area; are (*unit of measure*).
arena, *n.f.* sand; arena; (*med.*) gravel.
arenal, *n.m.* sandy ground; quicksand; sand pit.
arengar, *v.t.* harangue.
arenisca, *n.f.* (*min.*) sandstone.
arenque, *n.m.* (*ichth.*) herring.
arete, *n.m.* ear-ring.
argamasa, *n.m.* mortar, cement.
argamasar, *v.t.* cement; plaster.—*v.i.* mix cement *or* mortar.
árgana, *n.f.,* **árgano,** *n.m.* (*industry*) crane; pannier.
argayo, *n.m.* landslide.
Argel, *n.m.* Algiers.
Argelia, *n.f.* Algeria.
argelino, -na, *a., n.m.f.* Algerian.
argentar, *v.t.* plate; (*fig.*) silver.
la Argentina, *n.f.* Argentina, the Argentine.
argentino (1), **-na,** *a.* silvery.
argentino (2), **-na,** *a. n.m.f.* Argentine, Argentinian.
argolla, *n.f.* large ring, staple.
argucia, *n.f.* subtlety, sophistry.
argüir [I], *v.t.* imply.—*v.i.* argue.
argumentación, *n.f.* argumentation.
argumento, *n.m.* argument; plot (*of a story*).
aria, *n.f.* (*mus.*) aria; tune.
aridez, *n.f.* aridity, drought.
árido, -da, *a.* arid, barren.—*n.m.pl.* dry goods.
ariete, *n.m.* battering-ram; (*tech.*) ram.
ario, -ria, *a., n.m.f.* Aryan.
arisco, -ca, *a.* churlish; surly; dour.
arista, *n.f.* (*arch.*) arris; edge.
aristocracia, *n.f.* aristocracy.
aristócrata, *n.m.f.* aristocrat.
aristocrático, -ca, *a.* aristocratic.
Aristóteles, *n.m.* Aristotle.
aristotélico, -ca, *a., n.m.f.* Aristotelian.
aritmético, -ca, *a.* arithmetical.—*n.m.f.* arithmetician.—*n.f.* arithmetic.
arlequín, *n.m.* harlequin; Neapolitan ice cream.

arma, *n.f.* arm, weapon; — *blanca*, sword etc., cold steel; — *de fuego*, firearm.
armada, *n.f.* (*naut.*) fleet, navy, Armada.
armadía, *n.f.* raft.
armadijo, *n.m.* trap, snare.
armadura, *n.f.* armour; (*elec.*) armature; (*arch.*) framework.
armamento, *n.m.* armament; (*naut.*) fitting-out.
armar, *v.t.* arm; assemble; equip, fit out; reinforce (*concrete*); load (*weapon*); (*fam.*) cause, stir up; *armarla*, start a row.—*v.r.* arm; arm oneself (*de*, with).
armario, *n.m.* closet; wardrobe; cupboard.
armazón, *n.f.* framework.
armiño, *n.m.* (*zool.*, *her.*) ermine.
armisticio, *n.m.* armistice.
armonía, *n.f.* harmony.
armónico, **-ca**, *a.* harmonious; harmonic.—*n.m.* harmonic.—*n.f.* harmonica.
armonio, *n.m.* (*mus.*) harmonium.
armonioso, **-sa**, *a.* harmonious.
arnés, *n.m.* harness; armour.
aro, *n.m.* hoop; rim; staple; — *de émbolo*, piston ring.
aroma, *n.m.* aroma, perfume.
aromático, **-ca**, *a.* aromatic.
arpa, *n.f.* (*mus.*) harp.
arpar, *v.t.* rend, claw.
arpista, *n.m.f.* (*mus.*) harpist.
arpón, *n.m.* harpoon.
arpon(e)ar, *v.t.* harpoon.
arquear, *v.t.* arch; (*naut.*) gauge.—*v.i.* retch.
arqueo, *n.m.* arching; (*naut.*) tonnage; (*com.*) audit.
arquelogía, *n.f.* archeology.
arqueólogo, **-ga**, *n.m.f.* archeologist.
arquero, *n.m.* treasurer; archer.
arquetipo, *n.m.* archetype.
arquiepiscopal, *a.* archiepiscopal.
arquitecto, *n.m.* architect.
arquitectónico, **-ca**, *a.* architectural, architectonic.
arquitectura, *n.f.* architecture.
arrabal, *n.m.* suburb, quarter.
arrabalero, **-ra**, *a.* suburban; ill-bred.
arraigado, **-da**, *a.* rooted, secure; inveterate.
arraigar [B], *v.i.*, *v.r.* take root.
arrancar [A], *v.t.* root up; extirpate; pull out.—*v.i.* start off; originate (*de*, in).
arranque, *n.m.* extirpation; sudden impulse; starting-up; starter.
arras, *n.f.pl.* deposit; pledge; dowry.
arrasar, *v.t.* raze; smooth; fill to the brim.—*v.i.*, *v.r.* clear up.
arrastrar, *v.t.* drag (along); drag down.—*v.r.* creep, crawl; follow (*suit at cards*).
arrastre, *n.m.* dragging, haulage, towage; (*taur.*) towing out the dead bull.
arrayán, *n.m.* (*bot.*) myrtle.
¡arre! *interj.* gee up!
arrear, *v.t.* drive, urge on (*mules etc.*).
arrebatadamente, *adv.* headlong; recklessly.
arrebatado, **-da**, *a.* sudden; violent; impetuous.
arrebatar, *v.t.* carry off (*a*, from); captivate.—*v.r.* get carried away; (*cul.*) get burnt.
arrebato, *n.m.* surprise; sudden attack; paroxysm; rapture.
arrebol, *n.m.* red glow (*in the sky*); rosiness (*of cheeks*); rouge.

arrebolar, *v.t.* redden; rouge.—*v.r.* redden.
arrebujar, *v.t.* jumble together; huddle.—*v.r.* cover oneself up well.
arreciar, *v.i.*, *v.r.* grow stronger *or* more severe.
arrecife, *n.m.* (*naut.*) reef.
arrecir [Q], *v.r.* become numb.
arrechucho, *n.m.* (*fam.*) fit, impulse; (*fam.*) slight indisposition.
arredrar, *v.t.* drive back; frighten.—*v.r.* draw back; be frightened.
arregazar [C], *v.t.* tuck up.
arreglar, *v.t.* adjust, regulate; settle; arrange; repair.—*v.r.* get ready; come to terms (*con*, with); *arreglárselas*, to manage as best one can.
arreglo, *n.m.* adjustment; arrangement; agreement; *con* — *a*, in accordance with.
arrejaco, **arrejaque**, *n.m.* (*orn.*) swift; (*S.A.*) blackmartin.
arremangar [B], *v.r.* roll *or* tuck up one's sleeves.
arremeter, *v.t.*, *v.i.* attack.
arrendajo, *n.m.* (*orn.*) jay; (*S.A.*, *U.S.*) mocking-bird.
arrendar [1], *v.t.* rent, lease; tie (*a horse*); mimic.
arrendatario, **-ria**, *n.m.f.* lessee, leaseholder, renter.
arreo, *n.m.* dress; ornament.—*pl.* harness, trappings.
arrepentimiento, *n.m.* repentance.
arrepentir [6], *v.r.* repent, be sorry (*de*, for).
arrequives, *n.m.pl.* finery; attendant circumstances.
arrestado, **-da**, *a.* bold, audacious.
arrestar, *v.t.* arrest; stop.
arresto, *n.m.* detention, arrest, imprisonment.
arria, *n.f.* drove (*of beasts*).
arriano, **-na**, *a.*, *n.m.f.* (*eccl.*) Arian.
arriar [L], *v.t.* flood; (*naut.*) dip, strike; (*naut.*) slacken.
arriata, *n.f.*, **arriate**, *n.m.* (herbaceous) border.
arr'az, *n.m.* (*pl. -aces*) quillion, hilt.
arriba, *adv.* above, over, overhead; upstairs; (*naut.*) aloft; *¡* — *el rey!* long live the King!
arribaje, *n.m.* (*naut.*) arrival.
arribar, *v.i.* arrive; (*naut.*) put in; (*fam.*) make a come-back.
arriero, *n.m.* muleteer.
arriesgado, **-da**, *a.* dangerous; daring.
arriesgar [B], *v.t.* risk; jeopardize.—*v.r.* run a risk; *arriesgarse a hacer*, risk doing; *arriesgarse en hacer*, venture on doing.
arrimar, *v.t.* bring close; (*naut.*) stow.—*v.r.* lean (*a*, against); depend (*a*, upon).
arrinconamiento, *n.m.* seclusion.
arroba, *n.f.* arroba (*Spanish measure of weight*, 25 *lb. approx.*).
arrobamiento, *n.m.* ecstasy, rapture.
arrobar, *v.t.* charm, transport.—*v.r.* be enraptured.
arrodillar, *v.t.* make (*s.o.*) kneel.—*v.i.*, *v.r.* kneel (down).
arrogancia, *n.f.* arrogance, haughtiness.
arrogante, *a.* haughty; arrogant.
arrogar [B], *v.t.* adopt.—*v.r.* arrogate (*to oneself*).
arrojallamas, *n.m. inv.* (*mil.*) flame-thrower.
arrojar, *v.t.* fling; dash; shed; (*fam.*) vomit.

arrojo, *n.m.* boldness.
arrollamiento, *n.m.* (*elec.*) winding.
arrollar, *v.t.* roll (up); wind, coil; rout.
arrope, *n.m.* grape syrup, boiled must.
arrostrar, *v.t.*, *v.i.* face.—*v.r.* fight face to face; *arrostrarse con,* to defy.
arroyo, *n.m.* stream, brook.
arroyuelo, *n.m.* rill, rivulet.
arroz, *n.m.* rice.
arruga, *n.f.* wrinkle, pucker, crease.
arrugar [B], *v.t.* wrinkle; corrugate.
arruinar, *v.t.* ruin; demolish; destroy.—*v.r.* fall into ruin; go bankrupt.
arrullar, *v.t.* lull.—*v.i.* coo; bill and coo.
arrullo, *n.m.* cooing; lullaby.
arrumbar, *v.t.* cast aside; (*naut.*) take bearings.—*v.i.* steer a course.—*v.r.* take bearings; get seasick.
arrurruz, *n.m.*(*cul.*) arrowroot.
arsenal, *n.m.* arsenal; dockyard.
arsénico, *n.m.* arsenic.
arte, *n.f.* or *m.* art; cunning; tackle.
artefacto, *n.m.* device, appliance; artefact.
artejo, *n.m.* knuckle.
arteria, *n.f.* (*med.*) artery; (*rail.*) trunk line; (*elec.*) feeder.
artería, *n.f.* artifice; cunning.
artero, -ra, *a.* cunning, artful.
artesa, *n.f.* trough, kneading trough.
artesanía, *n.f.* craftsmanship; artisan class.
artesano, *n.m.* artisan, craftsman.
artesiano, -na, *a.* artesian.
artesonado, -da, *a.* panelled.—*n.m.* panelled roof.
ártico. -ca, *a.* arctic.
articular, *v.t.* articulate.
artículo, *n.m.* article; joint, articulation; (*gram.*) article.
artífice, *n.m.f.* artificer; craftsman.
artificial, *a.* artificial; *fuegos artificiales,* fireworks.
artificiero, *n.m.* (*mil.*) artificer; fireworks manufacturer.
artificio, *n.m.* artifice, craft; device, contrivance.
artificioso, -sa, *a.* ingenious; crafty, artful.
artilugio, *n.m.* (*pej.*) contraption.
artillería, *n.f.* artillery.
artillero, *n.m.* gunner, artilleryman.
artimaña, *n.f.* trap, trick.
artimón, *n.m.* (*naut.*) mizzen.
artista, *n.m.f.* artist.
artístico, -ca, *a.* artistic.
artritis, *n.f.* (*med.*) arthritis.
Arturo, (*obs.* **Artús**), *n.m.* Arthur.
arveja, *n.f.* (*bot.*) vetch; tare; (*bot.*) carob; (*S.A.*) green pea.
arzobispado, *n.m.* (*eccl.*) archbishopric.
arzobispal, *a.* archiepiscopal.
arzobispo, *n.m.* archbishop.
arzón, *n.m.* saddle-tree.
as, *n.m.* ace (*also fig.*).
asa, *n.f.* handle.
asado, *n.m.* roast; — *de vaca,* roast beef.
asador, *n.m.* (*cul.*) spit.
asadura, *n.f.* offal, entrails.
asalariado, -da, *a., n.m.f.* wage earner, employee.
asaltar, *v.t.* assault.
asalto, *n.m.* assault; (*sport*) **round.**
asamblea- *n.f.* assembly.
asar, *v.t.* roast.

asaz, *adv.* (*poet.*, *obs.*, *joc.*) enough.
asbesto, *n.m.* asbestos.
ascalonia, *n.f.* (*bot.*) shallot.
ascendencia, *n.f.* lineage, ancestry.
ascendente, *a.* ascendent.
ascender [2], *v.t.* promote.—*v.i.* ascend, climb; (*com.*) amount (*a,* to).
ascendiente, *a.* ascendent.—*n.m.f.* ancestor, forebear.—*n.m.* ascendency.
Ascensión, *n.f.* Ascension.
ascenso, *n.m.* ascent; rise, (*U.S.*) raise; promotion.
ascensor, *n.m.* lift, (*U.S.*) elevator; hoist.
asceta, *n.m.f.* ascetic.
asceticismo, *n.m.* asceticism.
asco, *n.m.* disgust; disgusting thing; (*fam.*) *dar —,* make sick.
ascua, *n.f.* ember; *en ascuas,* agitated.
asechamiento, *n.m.*, **asechanza,** *n.f.* snare, waylaying.
asechar, *v.t.* waylay, ambush.
asediador, -ra, *a.* besieging.—*n.m.f.* besieger.
asediar, *v.t.* besiege; blockade; (*fig.*) importune.
asedio, *n.m.* siege.
aseguración, *n.f.* insurance (*policy*).
asegurar, *v.t.* make safe; assure; insure.
asemejar, *v.t.* compare.—*v.i.*, *v.r.* be like (*a*).
a asentadillas, *adv. phr.* sidesaddle.
asentamiento, *n.m.* establishment; settlement; judgement.
asentar [1], *v.t.* seat; establish; hone, sharpen; (*jur.*) award; tamp down.—*v.i.* be becoming.—*v.r.* sit down; settle down.
asentimiento, *n.m.* assent.
asentir [6], *v.i.* assent.
aseo, *n.m.* cleanliness; tidiness; toilet; *cuarto de —,* bathroom, cloakroom.
asepsia, *n.f.* (*med.*) asepsis.
asequible, *a.* obtainable, accessible.
aserrador, -ra, *a.* saw, sawing.—*n.m.* sawyer.—*n.f.* circular saw.
aserradura, *n.f.* saw cut.
aserrar [1], *v.t.* saw.
aserruchar, *v.t.* saw (*by hand*).
asesinar, *v.t.* assassinate, murder.
asesinato, *n.m.* assassination, murder.
asesino, -na, *a.* murderous.—*n.m.* murderer, assassin.—*n.f.* murderess.
asestar, *v.t.* aim; shoot; deal (*a blow*).
aseverar, *v.t.* assert.
asfaltar, *v.t.* asphalt.
asfalto, *n.m.* asphalt.
asfixia, *n.f.* asphyxia, asphyxiation.
asfixiante, *a.* asphyxiating.
asfixiar, *v.t.* asphyxiate.
asfódelo, *n.m.* (*bot.*) asphodel.
así, *adv.* thus, so; — *como,* — *que,* as soon as.
asiático, -ca, *a., n.m.f.* Asiatic.
asidero, *n.m.* handle, grip.
asiduidad, *n.f.* assiduity.
asiduo, -dua, *a.* assiduous; persistent.
asiento, *n.m.* seat; bottom; sediment; wisdom; agreement.
asignación, *n.f.* assignation; salary.
asignar, *v.t.* assign.
asignatura, *n.f.* course, subject (*at school etc.*).
asilar, *v.t.* shelter; put in an asylum.
asilo, *n.m.* asylum; home (*for poor etc.*); refuge.
asimétrico, -ca, *a.* asymmetrical.

asimilación, *n.f.* assimilation.
asimilar, *v.t.*, *v.i.*, *v.r.* assimilate.
asimismo, *adv.* likewise.
asir [12], *v.t.* grasp, seize.—*v.i.* take root.—
  v.r. take hold (*de*, of); grapple (*con*, with).
asistencia, *n.f.* attendance; assistance; social
  service.
asistenta, *n.f.* charwoman, daily help.
asistente, *a.* assisting.—*n.m.f.* attendant;
  assistant; (*mil.*) orderly.
asistir, *v.t.* attend; assist, help.—*v.i.* be
  present; follow suit.
asma, *n.f.* (*med.*) asthma.
asmático, **-ca**, *a.*, *n.m.f.* asthmatic.
asna, *n.f.* she-ass.—*pl.* (*carp.*) rafters.
asno, *n.m.* ass, donkey.
asociación, *n.f.* association.
asociado, **-da**, *a.* associate, associated.—
  n.m.f. associate, partner.
asociar, *v.t.* associate.—*v.r.* associate; become
  a partner.
asolar (1), *v.t.* parch.—*v.r.* become parched.
asolar (2) [4], *v.t.* destroy, raze.
asolear, *v.r.* get sunburnt; bask.
asomar, *v.t.* show, stick out (*the head etc.*).—
  v.i. appear, come into view.—*v.r.* appear,
  lean out (*of a window etc.*).
asombrar, *v.t.* shade; darken (*colours*);
  frighten; astonish.—*v.r.* be frightened; be
  amazed.
asombro, *n.m.* fear; astonishment.
asombroso, **-sa**, *a.* amazing.
asomo, *n.m.* appearance; indication.
asonancia, *n.f.* (*lit.*) assonance.
asonante, *a.* assonant.
asosegar [1B], *v.t.* calm.—*v.i.*, *v.r.* calm
  down.
aspa, *n.f.* cross; sail of a windmill.
aspar, *v.t.* reel; crucify.—*v.r.* take great pains.
aspaviento, *n.m.* fuss, excitement.
aspecto, *n.m.* aspect.
aspereza, *n.f.* roughness; bitterness; coarseness; ruggedness (*of ground*); asperity.
áspero, **-ra**, *a.* rough; harsh; sour; rugged,
  craggy.
aspérrimo, **-ma**, *a. sup. of* ÁSPERO.
áspid, **áspide**, *n.m.* (*zool.*) asp.
aspidistra, *n.f.* (*bot.*) aspidistra.
aspillera, *n.f.* (*mil.*) embrasure, loophole.
aspiración, *n.f.* aspiration; inhalation;
  suction.
aspirador, **-ra**, *a.* relative to suction.—*n.m.*
  or *f.* vacuum cleaner.
aspirante, *a.* aspiring; aspirating.—*n.m.f.*
  applicant, candidate; (*mil.*) cadet.
aspirar, *v.t.* suck in; inhale; aspirate.—*v.i.*
  aspire.
aspirina, *n.f.* (*med.*) aspirin.
asquerosidad, *n.f.* loathsomeness.
asqueroso, **-sa**, *a.* loathsome, disgusting;
  squeamish.
asta, *n.f.* shaft; spear; mast; flagpole; handle;
  horn (*of an animal*).
astado, **-da**, *a.* horned.—*n.m.* (*taur.*) bull.
asterisco, *n.m.* asterisk.
asteroide, *a.*, *n.m.* asteroid.
astil, *n.m.* handle (*of an axe*); shaft (*of an
  arrow*); beam (*of a balance*).
astilla, *n.f.* splinter.
astillero, *n.m.* shipyard; rack for spears.
astringente, *a.*, *n.m.* astringent.

astro, *n.m.* (*poet.*) star; heavenly body
  luminary.
astrolabio, *n.m.* (*astr.*) astrolabe.
astrología, *n.f.* astrology.
astrólogo, *n.m.* astrologer.
astronauta, *n.m.* astronaut.
astronomía, *n.f.* astronomy.
astronómico, **-ca**, *a.* astronomic(al).
astrónomo, *n.m.* astronomer.
astroso, **-sa**, *a.* unfortunate; contemptible.
astucia, *n.f.* cunning; astuteness.
astur, **-ra**, **asturiano**, **-na**, *a.*, *n.m.f.* Asturian.
asturión, *n.m.* (*ichth.*) sturgeon; pony.
astuto, **-ta**, *a.* astute; cunning.
asueto, *n.m.* (*esp. educ.*) short holiday; half
  holiday.
asumir, *v.t.* assume.
asunción, *n.f.* assumption.
asunto, *n.m.* subject, matter; business, affair.
asustar, *v.t.* scare, frighten.—*v.r.* to be
  frightened (*de*, *con*, at).
atabal, *n.m.* kettledrum.
atacante, *a.* attacking.—*n.m.f.* attacker.
atacar [A], *v.t.* attack; pack, ram (down); fit.
atado, **-da**, *a.* timid; irresolute; hammered.—
  n.m. bundle.
atadura, *n.f.* tying, fastening, bond.
ataguía, *n.f.* coffer-dam.
atajar, *v.t.* cut short; partition; interrupt.—
  v.i. take a short cut.—*v.r.* be abashed.
atajo, *n.m.* short cut; cross cut.
atalaya, *n.f.* watch-tower, gazebo.—*n.m.*
  guard.
atanor, *n.m.* pipe.
atañer [K], *v.t.* concern.
ataque, *n.m.* attack.
atar, *v.t.* tie, fasten.
ataracea, *n.f.* (*carp.*) marquetry.
atarantar, *v.t.* stun.
atarazana, *n.f.* arsenal; (*slang*) fence.
atardecer, *n.m.* late afternoon, evening.
atarear, *v.t.* allot a task to.—*v.r.* toil;
  atarearse a hacer, be busy doing.
atarjea, *n.f.* culvert; drainpipe; sewer.
atascadero, *n.m.* mudhole, bog; obstruction.
atascar [A], *v.t.* clog.—*v.r.* clog; get bogged
  down; stuff oneself; jam.
atasco, *n.m.* clogging; jamming; — *de
  circulación*, traffic jam.
ataúd, *n.m.* coffin.
ataviar [L], *v.t.* adorn.
atavío, *n.m.* dress, adornment.
ateísmo, *n.m.* atheism.
atención, *n.f.* attention.—*interj.* watch out!
atender [2], *v.t.* attend to.—*v.i.* pay attention.
atener [33], *v.r.* abide (*a*, by); depend.
atentadamente, *adv.* illegally; cautiously.
atentado, **-da**, *a.* prudent, cautious.—*n.m.*
  transgression, offence.
atentar, *v.t.* attempt to commit (*a crime*).—
  v.i. attempt a crime.
atento, **-ta**, *a.* attentive, kind; polite.—*n.f.*
  (*com.*) favour (*i.e. letter*).
atenuación, *n.f.* attenuation; extenuation.
atenuar [M], *v.t.* attenuate; extenuate.
ateo, **atea**, *a.*, *n.m.f.* atheist.
aterecer [9], **aterir** [Q], *v.r.* become numb
  (*with cold*).
aterrador, **-ra**, *a.* dreadful, terrifying.
aterrajar, *v.t.* (*tech.*) thread, tap.
aterraje, *n.m.* (*aer.*) landing.
aterrar (1), *v.t.* terrify.

aterrar (2) [1], *v.t.* demolish; earth up.—*v.i.* (*aer.*) land.—*v.r.* (*naut.*) stand inshore.
aterrizaje, *n.m.* (*aer.*) landing.
aterrizar [C], *v.i.* (*aer.*) land.
aterrorizar [C], *v.t.* terrorize.
atesar [1], [ATIESAR].
atesorar, *v.t.* treasure up; hoard up.
atestación, *n.f.* attestation, deposition.
atestadura, *n.f.*, **atestamiento**, *n.m.* cramming, stuffing.
atestar (1), *v.t.* (*jur.*) attest.
atestar (2) [1], *v.t.* cram, stuff, fill.
atestiguación, *n.f.*, **atestiguamiento**, *n.m.* attestation, deposition.
atestiguar [H], *v.t.* testify, depose.—*v.i.* attest (to).
atiborrar, *v.t.* stuff.
at(i)esar, *v.t.* stiffen.
atildado, -da, *a.* neat, stylish.
atildar, *v.t.* put a tilde over; adorn; find fault with.
atinado, -da, *a.* keen; pertinent.
atinar, *v.t.* come upon, find.—*v.i.* guess (right).
atisbar, *v.t.* spy on, watch.
atisbo, *n.m.* prying; slight likeness.
atizador, -ra, *a.* stirring; inciting.—*n.m.* poker.
atizar [C], *v.t.* stir; rouse.
Atlante, *n.m.* (*myth.*) Atlas.
atlántico, -ca, *a.*, *n.m.* Atlantic.
atlas, *n.m. inv.* atlas.
atleta, *n.m.f.* athlete.
atlético, -ca, *a.* athletic.
atletismo, *n.m.* athletics.
atmósfera, *n.f.* atmosphere.
atmosférico, -ca, *a.* atmospheric.
atocha, *n.f.* esparto.
atolón, *n.m.* (*geog.*) atoll.
atolondrado, -da, *a.* scatterbrained.
atolondrar, *v.t.* amaze; bewilder.
atollar, *v.i.*, *v.r.* get stuck in the mud.
atómico, -ca, *a.* atomic.
atomizar [C], *v.t.* atomize.
átomo, *n.m.* atom.
atónito, -ta, *a.* astonished; aghast.
átono, -na, *a.* atonic, unstressed.
atontar, *v.t.* stun; bewilder.
atormentar, *v.t.* torment.
atosigar [B], *v.t.* poison; harass.—*v.r.* be hurried.
atóxico, -ca, *a.* non-poisonous.
atrabancar [A], *v.t.* hurry through (*work*).
atracar [A], *v.t.* (*naut.*) bring alongside; hold-up, assault.—*v.i.* (*naut.*) come alongside; (*S.A.*) quarrel.
atracción, *n.f.* attraction.
atraco, *n.m.* hold-up, attack.
atractivo, -va, *a.* attractive.—*n.m.* attractiveness, attraction.
atraer [34], *v.t.* attract.
atrafagar [B], *v.i.* toil.
atrampar, *v.r.* be trapped, get stuck, get blocked.
atramuz, *n.m.* (*pl. -uces*) (*bot.*) lupin.
atrancar [A], *v.t.* obstruct.—*v.i.* take large strides.
atranco, atranque, *n.m.* difficulty.
atrapar, *v.t.* (*fam.*) catch.
atrás, *adv.* back(ward)(s); behind; previously.
atrasado, -da, *a.* backward; slow (*clock*); late; in arrears.

atrasar, *v.t.* slow; put back (*clock*); leave behind; delay; postdate.—*v.i.* go slow; be late; fall behind.
atraso, *n.m.* delay; lateness; backwardness.
atravesar [1], *v.t.* put *or* lay across; cross; go through.—*v.r.* get in the way (**en**, of); have an encounter *or* a fight with.
atreguar [H], *v.t.* grant a truce *or* an extension to.
atrever, *v.r.* dare; *atreverse a*, venture to.
atrevido, -da, *a.* bold; impudent.
atrevimiento, *n.m.* boldness; effrontery.
atribuir [O], *v.t.* attribute.
atril, *n.m.* lectern.
atrincherar, *v.t.* entrench.
atrocidad, *n.f.* atrocity; (*fam.*) enormous amount.
atronar [4], *v.t.* deafen; stun.
atropellado, -da, *a.* hasty; violent; tumultuous.
atropellar, *v.t.* trample down; run over; violate.
atropello, *n.m.* trampling; running over; outrage.
atroz, *a.* (*pl.-oces*) atrocious; (*fam.*) enormous.
atuendo, *n.m.* pomp; dress, adornment.
atún, *n.m.* (*ichth.*) tuna, tunny.
aturdido, -da, *a.* reckless; scatter-brained.
aturdimiento, *n.m.* amazement; stunning.
aturdir, *v.t.* stun; amaze.
audacia, *n.f.* audacity.
audaz, *a.* (*pl. -aces*) audacious.
audición, *n.f.* audition, hearing.
audiencia, *n.f.* audience, hearing; (*jur.*) superior court.
audífono, *n.m.* audiphone, hearing aid.
auditivo, -va, *a.* auditory.—*n.m.* (*tel.*) earpiece.
auditor, *n.m.* (*jur.*) judge; (*com.*) auditor.
auditorio, *n.m.* (*theat. etc.*) audience; auditorium.
auge, *n.m.* (*astr.*) apogee; boom, vogue.
augurio, *n.m.* augury.
augusto, -ta, *a.* august.
aula, *n.f.* (lecture) hall; (*poet.*) palace.
aulaga, *n.f.* (*bot.*) furze, gorse.
aullar [P], *v.i.* howl.
aullido, *n.m.* howl.
aumentar, *v.t.*, *v.i.*, *v.r.* augment, increase.
aumento, *n.m.* increase; augmentation.
aun, *adv.* still, even.
aún, *adv.* still, yet.
aunque, *conj.* although, even though.
¡aúpa! *interj.* up! *de* —, (*fam.*) swanky.
aupar [P], *v.t.* (*fam.*) give a hoist up, hitch up.
aura, *n.f.* gentle breeze; acclamation.
áureo, -rea, *a.* aureate, golden.
aureola, *n.f.* aureole; halo.
auricular, *a.* auricular; *dedo* —, little finger. —*n.m.* (*tel.*) receiver.
ausencia, *n.f.* absence.
ausentar, *v.t.* send away.—*v.r.* absent oneself.
ausente, *a.* absent.
ausentismo, *n.m.* absenteeism.
auspicio, *n.m.* auspice (*usually pl.*).
austeridad, *n.f.* austerity.
austero, -ra, *a.* austere.
Australia, *n.f.* Australia.
australiano, -na, *a.*, *n.m.f.* Australian.
Austria, *n.f.* Austria.

austríaco, -ca, *a., n.m.f.* Austrian.
austro, *n.m.* south wind.
autarcía, autarquía, *n.f.* (*pol.*) autarchy, (*U.S.*) autarky; home-rule.
auténtico, -ca, *a.* authentic, genuine, real.—*n.f.* certificate.
auto (1), *n.m.* (*jur.*) decree; writ; (*theat.*) auto.—*pl.* proceedings.
auto (2), *n.f.* (*fam.*) [AUTOMÓVIL].
autobiografía, *n.f.* autobiography.
autobote, *n.m.* power boat.
autobús, *n.m.* omnibus, bus.
autocar, *n.m.* motor coach, (*U.S.*) interurban bus.
autocracia, *n.f.* (*pol.*) autocracy.
autocrático, -ca, *a.* autocratic.
autocrítica, *n.f.* self-criticism.
autóctono, -na, *a.* autochthonous, native.
autodeterminación, *n.f.* (*pol.*) self-determination.
autodidacto, -ta, *a.* self-taught, self-educated.
autodirigido, -da, *a.* homing (*missile*).
autógrafo, -fa, *a., n.m.* autograph.
automacia, *n.f.* automation.
autómata, *n.m.* automaton.
automaticidad, *n.f.* automatic nature; automation.
automático, -ca, *a.* automatic.
automotor, -ra, *a.* self-propelled.—*n.m.* railway motor coach.
automóvil, *a.* self-propelled.—*n.m.* (motor) car, (*U.S.*) automobile.
automovilista, *a.* rel. to motoring.—*n.m.f.* driver, motorist.
autonomía, *n.f.* (*pol.*) autonomy, home rule; (*aer.*) operational range.
autónomo, -ma, *a.* autonomous.
autopista, *n.f.* motorway, (*U.S.*) turnpike.
autopropulsado, -da, *a.* self-propelled.
autopsia, *n.f.* autopsy.
autor, -ra, *n.m.f.* author; (*obs. theat.*) manager.
autoridad, *n.f.* authority.
autorizar [C], *v.t.* authorize (*a,* to).
autorretrato, *n.m.* (*art.*) self-portrait.
auxiliante, *a.* helping.
auxiliar (1), *a.* auxiliary.—*n.m.* (*educ.*) assistant.
auxiliar (2) [L *or regular*], *v.t.* help; attend (*dying person*).
auxilio, *n.m.* help; relief; — **social,** social service.
avalar, *v.t.* (*com.*) stand security for.
avaluar [M], *v.t.* estimate.
avance, *n.m.* advance; (*tech.*) feed.
avanzar [C], *v.t.* advance.—*v.i.* (*com.*) have a credit balance.
avaricia, *n.f.* avarice.
avaricioso, -sa, *a.* avaricious.
avariento, -ta, avaro, -ra, *a.* avaricious. —*n.m.f.* miser.
avasallar, *v.t.* subject, enslave.
ave, *n.f.* bird; — **de rapiña,** bird of prey.
avecindar, *v.t.* domicile.—*v.r.* set up residence.
avefría, *n.f.* (*orn.*) lapwing.
avellana, *n.f.* hazel-nut, filbert, cob.
avellano, *n.m.* hazel (*bush*).
avena, *n.f.* oats; **harina de —,** oatmeal.
avenencia, *n.f.* bargain; agreement.
avenida, *n.f.* avenue; flood, inflow.

avenir [36], *v.t.* reconcile.—*v.r.* agree (*a,* to); **avenirse con,** get along with.
aventajado, -da, *a.* superior, outstanding.
aventajar, *v.t.* advance, raise, give an advantage to, prefer.—*v.r.* excel.
aventar [1], *v.t.* fan; winnow.—*v.r.* swell up; (*fam.*) run away.
aventura, *n.f.* adventure; risk.
aventurado, -da, *a.* venturesome; hazardous.
aventurar, *v.t.* adventure, hazard.
aventurero, -ra, *a.* adventurous.—*n.m.* adventurer.—*n.f.* adventuress.
avergonzar [10C], *v.t.* shame.—*v.r.* be ashamed (*de,* to).
avería (1), *n.f.* breakdown, failure, defect; (*naut.*) average.
avería (2), *n.f.* aviary.
averiar [L], *v.t.* damage.—*v.r.* break down.
averiguable, *a.* ascertainable.
averiguación, *n.f.* ascertainment; investigation.
averiguar [H], *v.t.* ascertain, verify.
aversión, *n.f.* aversion.
avestruz, *n.m.* (*pl.* -uces) (*orn.*) ostrich.
avetoro, *n.m.* (*orn.*) bittern.
avezar [C], *v.t.* accustom.—*v.r.* become accustomed (*a,* to).
aviación, *n.f.* aviation; (*mil.*) air force.
aviador, -ra, *a.* rel. to flying; equipping.— *n.m.f.* aviator.
aviar [L], *v.t., v.r.* get ready, prepare.
avidez, *n.f.* eagerness, avidity; covetousness.
ávido, -da, *a.* eager, anxious (*de,* for); covetous (*de,* of).
avieso, -sa, *a.* distorted; perverse.
avilés, -lesa, *a.* rel. to Avila.—*n.m.f.* inhabitant of Avila.
avinagrar, *v.t.* make sour.
avío, *n.m.* preparation; money advanced.— *pl.* equipment.
avión, *n.m.* (*aer.*) aeroplane, airplane; (*orn.*) martin.
avisado, -da, *a.* prudent, wise; **mal —,** rash.
avisador, -ra, *a.* warning.—*n.m.f.* informer; adviser.—*n.m.* electric bell; alarm.
avisar, *v.t.* advise; inform; warn.
aviso, *n.m.* advice; notice; warning.
avispa, *n.f.* (*ent.*) wasp.
avispero, *n.m.* wasps' nest; (*fam.*) mess.
avispón, *n.m.* (*ent.*) hornet.
avistar, *v.t.* descry.—*v.r.* have a meeting (*con,* with).
avivar, *v.t.* revive; enliven.
avutarda, *n.f.* (*orn.*) bustard; (*S.A.*) wild turkey.
axioma, *n.m.* axiom.
axiomático, -ca, *a.* axiomatic.
¡ay! *interj.* oh! ouch! alas!*¡* — **de mí!** woe is me!
aya, *n.f.* governess, nurse.
ayer, *adv.* yesterday.
ayo, *n.m.* tutor.
ayuda, *n.f.* aid, help.—*n.m.* page, aide.
ayudanta, *n.f.* female assistant; relief teacher; maid.
ayudante, *n.m.* assistant; (*mil.*) aide-de-camp; adjutant.
ayudar, *v.t.* help, aid, assist.
ayunar, *v.i.* fast.
ayuno, -na, *a.* fasting.—*n.m.* fast; fasting; **en ayunas,** on an empty stomach.

ayuntamiento, *n.m.* town council, municipal government.
azabache, *n.m.* (*min.*) jet.
azada, *n.f.* hoe; spade.
azadón, *n.m.* hoe; — **de peto,** pick-axe.
azafata, *n.f.* (*aer.*) air hostess; (*obs.*) lady of the wardrobe.
azafate, *n.m.* tray.
azafrán, *n.m.* (*bot.*) saffron.
azafranar, *v.t.* flavour *or* colour with saffron.
azahar, *n.m.* orange blossom.
azar, *n.m.* chance; fate; hazard; **al** —, at random.
azaroso, -sa, *a.* hazardous.
ázimo, -ma, *a.* azymous, unleavened.
azimut, *n.m.* (*pl.* **-s**) (*astr.*) azimuth.
azogar [B], *v.t.* coat with quicksilver, silver.—*v.r.* have mercurialism; (*fam.*) shake.
azogue, *n.m.* quicksilver, mercury.
azor, *n.m.* (*orn.*) goshawk.
azorar, *v.t.* abash; excite.
azotaina, *n.f.* (*fam.*) spanking.
azotar, *v.t.* whip, lash.
azote, *n.m.* whip, lash; (*fig.*) scourge.
azotea, *n.f.* flat roof, terrace.
azteca, *a.*, *n.m.f.* Aztec.
azúcar, *n.m.* sugar.
azucarar, *v.t.* sugar; ice.
azucarero, -ra, *a.* rel. to sugar *or* the sugar industry.—*n.m.* sugar producer *or* dealer; sugar bowl.
azucena, *n.f.* (*bot.*) Madonna lily.
azud, *n.m.*, **azuda,** *n.f.* weir; water wheel.
azuela, *n.f.* adze.
azufre, *n.m.* (*chem.*) sulphur, (*U.S.*) sulfur; brimstone.
azul, *a.*, *n.m.* blue; — **celeste,** sky-blue; — **marino,** navy-blue.
azulado, -da, *a.* blue, bluish.
azulejo, *n.m.* glazed (coloured) tile; (*orn.*) bee-eater.
azumbre, *n.m.* azumbre (*a liquid measure, about 4 pints*).
azuzar [C], *v.t.* set on (*a dog*); (*fig.*) incite.

B

B, b, *n.f.* second letter of the Spanish alphabet.
baba, *n.f.* slobber; slime.
babador, *n.m.* bib.
babear, *v.i.* slobber, drool.
Babel, *n.m. or f.* Babel; (*fig.*) babel.
babero, -ra, *n.m.f.* bib.
Babia, *n.f.* area of León; **estar en** —, be in the clouds, be absent-minded.
babieca, *a.*, *n.m.f.* (*fam.*) fool.
babilónico, -ca, *a.* Babylonian; (*fig.*) sumptuous.
babilonio, -nia, *a.*, *n.m.f.* Babylonian.
bable, *n.m.* Asturian dialect.
babor, *n.m.* (*naut.*) port (side).
babosa, *n.f.* (*zool.*) slug.
babosear, *v.t.* drool over; (*C.A.*) hoodwink.
baboso, -sa, *a.* slobbery; callow.—*n.m.* (*S.A.*) fool; (*C.A.*) rotter.

babucha, *n.f.* Moorish slipper.
babuino, *n.m.* baboon.
baca, *n.f.* top (*of vehicle*).
bacalada, *n.f.* cured cod.
bacalao, *n.m.* cod; dried salt cod.
bacanal, *a.* bacchanal.—*n.f.* orgy.
bacante, *n.f.* bacchante; (*fig.*) drunken hussy.
bacía, *n.f.* basin; shaving dish.
bacilo, *n.m.* bacillus.
bacín, *n.m.* urinal; poor box; wastrel.
Baco, *n.m.* Bacchus.
bacteria, *n.f.* microbe, bacterium.
bactericida, *a.* bactericidal.—*n.m.* bactericide.
bacteriología, *n.f.* bacteriology.
bacteriológico, -ca, *a.* bacteriological.
báculo, *n.m.* staff; crook; crozier; (*fig.*) aid, comfort.
bache, *n.m.* pothole, rut; air pocket.
bachiller, -ra. *n.m.f.* bachelor (*degree*); (*fam.*) wiseacre.
bachillerato, *n.m.* baccalaureate, bachelor's degree; school-leaving examination.
badajo, *n.m.* bell clapper; chatterbox.
badana, *n.f.* sheep leather; (*fam.*) hide, skin.
badea, *n.f.* tasteless melon; (*fam.*) dimwit; (*fam.*) bauble, nothing.
badén, *n.f.* ford; open drain.
badulaque, *n.m.* (*fam.*) nincompoop; (*S.A.*) scoundrel.
bagaje, *n.m.* (*mil.*) baggage; baggage mule.
bagatela, *n.f.* trifle, bagatelle.
bagre, *a.* (*S.A.*) showy, vulgar; loose, immoral.—*n.m.* catfish.
bahía, *n.f.* bay, bight.
bahorrina, *n.f.* bilge; (*fam.*) riff-raff.
bailable, *n.m.* (*fam.*) dance-tune.
bailadero, *n.m.* dance hall.
bailador, -ra, *a.* dancing.—*n.m.f.* dancer.
bailar, *v.t.*, *v.i.* dance.
bailarín, -rina, *a.* dancing.—*n.m.f.* dancer.— *n.f.* ballerina.
baile, *n.m.* dance, dancing; dance, ball.
bailotear, *v.i.* dance badly, jig about.
baja, *n.f.* fall (*in price*); (*mil.*) casualty, loss; (*fig.*) withdrawal, resignation; **dar** —, **ir en** —, lose value, wane; **estar de** —, be on the decline.
bajada, *n.f.* descent; way down; drop.
bajamar, *n.f.* low tide.
bajar, *v.t.* lower; bring *or* take down.—*v.i.* descend, go *or* come down; alight, get off; drop.—*v.r.* dismount; stoop.
bajel, *n.m.* vessel, ship.
bajeza, *n.f.* lowness, meanness; lowliness.
bajío, *n.m.* (*naut.*) sandbank, shallow; (*S.A.*) lowland, plain.
bajista, *n.m.* (*com.*) bear (*in shares*).
bajo, -ja, *a.* low, lower; short; base, vulgar; ground (*floor*).—*n.m.* (*naut.*) shallow, shoal; (*mus.*) bass.—*adv.* below, down; in a low voice.—*prep.* under(neath).
bajón (1), *n.m.* decline, drop; relapse.
bajón (2), *n.m.* bassoon.
bajorelieve, *n.m.* bas-relief.
bajura, *n.f.* lowness; shortness; lowlands.
bala, *n.f.* bullet, shell; bale.
balada, *n.f.* ballad; ballade.
baladí, *a.* (*pl.* **-íes**) paltry, worthless.
baladrar, *v.i.* screech, whoop.
baladrón, -ona, *a.* boastful.—*n.m.f.* braggart.

balance, *n.m.* swaying, vacillation; *(com.)* balance sheet.
balancear, *v.t.* balance.—*v.i., v.r.* rock, swing; waver; sway.
balancín, *n.m.* balance beam; balancing pole; see-saw; *(mech.)* crank.
balanza, *n.f.* scales, balance; judgement.
balar, *v.i.* bleat.
balaustrada, *n.f.* balustrade.
balaustre, *n.m.* baluster, banister.
balazo, *n.m.* shot; bullet wound.
balbucear, *v.i.* stammer, stutter; mumble.
balbucencia, *n.f.,* **balbuceo,** *n.m.* stammer, stutter, mumbling.
balbucir [Q] [BALBUCEAR].
Balcanes, *n.m.pl.* the Balkans.
balcánico, -ca, *a.* Balkan.
balcón, *n.m.* balcony.
baldaquín, baldaquino, *n.m.* canopy, baldaquin.
baldar, *v.t.* cripple, maim; trump.
balde (1), *n.m.* baling bucket.
balde (2), *adv. de* —, gratis, free; *en* —, in vain; *estar de* —, stand idle.
baldío, -día, *a.* idle *(land)*; useless, pointless.
baldón, *n.m.* insult.
baldonar, *v.t.* affront, insult.
baldosa, *n.f.* floor tile; *(S.A.)* gravestone.
balear (1), *a.* Balearic.—*n.m.f.* native of the Balearic Islands.
balear (2), *v.t.* *(S.A.)* shoot at, shoot.
Baleares, *n.f./pl.* Balearic Islands.
baleárico, -ca, *a.* Balearic.
balido, *n.m.* bleat.
balístico, -ca, *a.* ballistic.—*n.f.* ballistics.
baliza, *n.f.* buoy.
balneario, -ria, *a.* rel. to a spa.—*n.m.* spa, hydro, watering-place.
balompié, *n.m.* football *(game)*.
balón, *n.m.* (foot)ball; balloon; bale.
baloncesto, *n.m.* basketball.
balonvolea, *n.m.* volley-ball.
balotaje, *n.m.* balloting.
balotar, *v.i.* ballot.
balsa, *n.f.* pond, pool; raft; *(bot.)* balsa.
balsámico, -ca, *a.* balsamic, soothing.
bálsamo, *n.m.* balsam, balm.
báltico, -ca, *a.* Baltic.
baluarte, *n.m.* bulwark, rampart.
balumba, *n.f.* bulk, mass; *(S.A.)* uproar.
ballena, *n.f.* whale; whalebone.
ballenero, -ra, *a.* whaling.—*n.m.* whaler.
ballesta, *n.f.* cross-bow; bird snare; *(mech.)* vehicle spring.
ballestero, *n.m.* cross-bowman.
ballet, *n.m.* *(pl.* -s) ballet.
bambalina, *n.f.* *(theat.)* fly drop, back-cloth.
bambolear, *v.i., v.i.* swing, sway, totter.
bamboleo, *n.m.* swaying, swinging, wobbling, tottering.
bambú, *n.m.* *(pl.* -úes) bamboo.
banana, *n.f.* banana tree; *(S.A.)* banana.
banano, *n.m.* banana tree.
banasta, *n.f.* large basket.
banasto, *n.m.* large round basket; *(low)* jug, jail.
banca, *n.f.* bench, form; market stall; *(com.)* banking.
bancal, *n.m.* vegetable plot.
bancario, -ria, *a.* banking.
bancarrota, *n.f.* bankruptcy; *hacer* —, go bankrupt.

bance, *n.m.* rail, bar.
banco, *n.m.* bank; bench; shoal; sandbank; — *de hielo,* iceberg.
banda, *n.f.* sash; band, gang; riverbank; *(mus.)* military band; *(naut.)* gunwale.
bandada, *n.f.* covey, flock; *a bandadas,* *(fam.)* in droves.
bandeado, -da, *a.* striped.
bandeja, *n.f.* tray; *(S.A.)* serving dish.
bandera, *n.f.* flag, banner.
banderilla, *n.f.* *(taur.)* barbed decorated dart.
banderillero, *n.m.* *(taur.)* bullfighter who inserts the banderillas.
banderín, *n.m.* small flag; pennant; military colours; leading soldier; recruiting office.
bandidaje, banditismo, *n.m.* banditry.
bandido, *n.m.* bandit, outlaw; *(fam.)* crook, swindler.
bando, *n.m.* edict; faction, band; shoal.
bandolera, *n.f.* bandolier; gangster's moll.
bandolerismo, *n.m.* banditry, brigandage.
bandolero, *n.m.* bandit, brigand.
bandolín, *n.m.* *(mus.)* mandolin.
bandolina, *n.f.* hair grease; *(S.A.)* mandolin.
bandurria, *n.f.* *(mus.)* bandore.
banquero, *n.m.* banker.
banqueta, *n.f.* foot-stool; *(C.A.)* pavement, *(U.S.)* sidewalk.
banquete, *n.m.* banquet; small stool.
banquillo, *n.m.* *(jur.)* dock; small bench.
banzo, *n.m.* jamb.
bañado, *n.m.* chamber-pot; *(S.A.)* floodlands.
bañador, -ra, *n.m.f.* bather.—*n.m.* swimsuit.
bañar, *v.t.* dip; bathe; drench.—*v.r.* have a bath; bathe; *(C.A.)* do well *(in business)*.
bañera, *n.f.* bath, bath-tub.
baño, *n.m.* bath; bathe; spa; Turkish prison.
baque, *n.m.* thud, bump.
baquelita, *n.m.* bakelite.
baqueta, *n.f.* *(mil.)* ramrod; horse-switch; drumstick; *carrera de baquetas,* running the gauntlet.
baquía, *n.f.* familiarity with tracks *etc.* of a region; *(S.A.)* dexterity, skill.
baquiano, -na, *a.* skilled, experienced.—*n.m.* scout, path-finder, guide.
báquico, -ca, *a.* Bacchic; bacchanal.
bar, *n.m.* bar, café.
barahunda, *n.f.* hurly-burly, din, rumpus.
baraja, *n.f.* pack *(of cards)*; row, quarrel.
barajar, *v.t.* shuffle; *(S.A.)* understand.—*v.i.* squabble.—*v.r.* get mixed up.
baranda, *n.f.* railing, edge.
barandilla, *n.f.* railing, guard-rail.
barata, *n.f.* barter; cheapness; *a la* —, confusedly.
baratear, *v.t.* cheapen, sell under value.
baratija, *n.f.* knick-knack, trinket.
baratillo, *n.m.* second-hand shop; bargain counter.
barato, -ta, *a.* cheap.—*n.m.* bargain sale.—*adv.* cheap, cheaply; *de* —, gratis, interest free; *echar* or *meter a* —, heckle; *dar de* —, grant, admit.
báratro, *n.m.* *(poet.)* hell.
baratura, *n.f.* cheapness.
baraúnda [BARAHUNDA].
baraustar [P], *v.t.* aim; ward off.
barba, *n.f.* beard; chin; burr, frayed edge; *hacer la* —, shave; annoy; cajole.
barbacoa, barbacúa, *n.f.* *(S.A.)* barbecue; various lattice structures.

la **Barbada**, *n.f.* Barbados.
barbaridad, *n.f.* barbarism, barbarity; rashness, rudeness; (*fam.*) vast amount; *¡qué —!* what a nerve! how shocking!
barbarie, *n.f.* barbarism, cruelty, savagery.
barbarismo, *n.m.* barbarism.
barbarizar [C], *v.t.* barbarize.—*v.i.* say outrageous things.
bárbaro, **-ra**, *a.* barbaric, barbarous; (*fam.*) terrific, fantastic.—*n.m.f.* barbarian.
barbear, *v.t.* reach with the chin; (*S.A.*) shave; (*S.A.*) flatter; — *con*, be as high as.
barbecho, *n.m.* fallow, fallow land.
barbería, *n.f.* barbershop.
barbero, *n.m.* barber; (*S.A.*) flatterer.
barbiblanco, **-ca**, *a.* white-bearded.
barbilampiño, **-ña**, *a.* smooth-faced, beardless.
barbilla, *n.f.* tip of the chin; barbel.
barbiponiente, *a.* beginning to grow a beard.—*n.m.f.* beginner, novice.
barbiturato, *n.m.* barbiturate.
barbo, *n.m.* (*ichth.*) barbel.
barbón, *n.m.* bearded man; billy goat; (*fam.*) old fuddy-duddy.
barbot(e)ar, *v.t., v.i.* mumble.
barbudo, **-da**, *a.* heavy-bearded.
barbulla, *n.f.* (*fam.*) hullabaloo.
barbullar, *v.i.* gabble, jabber.
barca, *n.f.* rowing boat.
barcaza, *n.f.* (*naut.*) lighter.
barcelonés, **-nesa**, *a.* rel. to Barcelona.—*n.m.f.* person from Barcelona.
barco, *n.m.* boat, ship.
barda, *n.f.* horse armour; wall-thatch; (*naut.*) low dark cloud.
bardaguera, *n.f.* osier.
bardo, *n.m.* bard.
bario, *n.m.* barium.
barítono, *n.m.* baritone.
barjuleta, *n.f.* knapsack, tool-bag.
barloar, *v.t.* (*naut.*) bring alongside.
barloventear, *v.i.* (*naut.*) ply windward; (*fig.*) rove about.
barlovento, *n.m.* windward.
barman, *n.m.* barman.
barniz, *n.m.* varnish; pottery glaze; (*fig.*) smattering.
barnizar [C], *v.t.* varnish; glaze.
barómetro, *n.m.* barometer.
barón, *n.m.* baron.
baronesa, *n.f.* baroness.
baronía, *n.f.* barony, baronage.
barquero, *n.m.* boatman.
barquía, *n.f.* rowing boat.
barquilla, *n.f.* (*cul.*) cake mould; airship car; balloon basket; (*naut.*) log.
barquillo, *n.m.* tiny boat; ice-cream cone; wafer biscuit; waffle.
barra, *n.f.* bar, rod; ingot; (*mech.*) lever; (*naut.*) sand-bar; (*law, mus.*) bar; — *de labios*, lipstick.
barraca, *n.f.* rustic cottage; (*S.A.*) storage shed.
barranca, *n.f.*, **barranco**, *n.m.* gully, ravine; great difficulty, snag.
barrar, *v.t.* bar; mire.
barreda, *n.f.* barrier, fence.
barredero, **-ra**, *a.* sweeping; (*fig.*) sweeping all before.
barrena, *n.f.* drill-bit; (*aer.*) spin; — *de mano*, (*carp.*) gimlet.

barrenar, *v.t.* drill, bore; scuttle; break (*the law*).
barrendero, *n.m.* sweeper.
barreno, *n.m.* large bit, auger; drilled hole; (*S.A.*) mania, whim.
barreño, *n.m.* earthenware bowl.
barrer, *v.t.* sweep (away); brush against.
barrera, *n.f.* barrier; barricade; front seats in bullring; clay-pit; crockery cupboard; — *del sonido*, sound barrier.
barrero, *n.m.* potter; clay-pit; (*S.A.*) saltpetre marsh.
barriada, *n.f.* quarter, ward, precinct.
barrial, *n.m.* (*S.A.*) quagmire.
barrica, *n.f.* medium barrel.
barricada, *n.f.* barricade.
barriga, *n.f.* (*fam.*) belly; (*fig.*) bulge.
barril, *n.m.* cask, barrel; water jug.
barrio, *n.m.* quarter, district, suburb.
barrisco, *only in a —*, *adv. phr.* pell-mell, indiscriminately.
barrizal, *n.m.* quagmire.
barro, *n.m.* mud, clay; earthenware; red pimple; (*S.A.*) unintended *or* thoughtless harm; — *cocido*, terra cotta.
barroco, **-ca**, *a., n.m.* baroque.
barroquismo, *n.m.* baroque style; extravagance, bad taste.
barroso, **-sa**, *a.* muddy; pimply.
barruntar, *v.t.* foresee, conjecture.
barrunte, *n.m.* presentiment; indication.
barrunto, *n.m.* guess, conjecture, presentiment.
bartola, *n.f. only in a la —*, *adv.phr.* (*fam.*) in a lazy old way.
bártulos, *n.m.pl.* gear, paraphernalia, belongings.
baruca, *n.f.* (*fam.*) wangle, trick; (*fam.*) snag.
barullero, **-ra**, *a.* clumsy, bungling.—*n.m.f.* bungler; rowdy.
barullo, *n.m.* (*fam.*) rumpus; mess.
barullón, **-llona** [BARULLERO].
basa, *n.f.* (*arch.*) base, pedestal.
basalto, *n.m.* (*geol.*) basalt.
basar, *v.t.* base (*en*, on).
basca, *n.f.* queasiness; (*fam.*) tantrum.
bascoso, **-sa**, *a.* queasy; (*S.A.*) foul.
báscula, *n.f.* platform scale.
base, *n.f.* base, basis; (*mil.*) base; *a — de*, on the basis of, with, using.
básico, **-ca**, *a.* basic.
basílica, *n.f.* basilica.
basilisco, *n.m.* basilisk; (*fig.*) furious person.
basquear, *v.i.* feel queasy.
basquiña, *n.f.* overskirt, basquine.
bastante, *a.* enough, sufficient.—*adv.* enough; rather, fairly.
bastar, *v.i.* be enough, suffice.—*v.r.* be self-sufficient.
bastardilla, letra bastardilla, *n.f.* italics.
bastardo, **-da**, *a.* illegitimate, bastard; degenerate; spurious, mongrel.
bastedad, basteza, *n.f.* coarseness, roughness.
bastidor, *n.m.* frame; (*mech.*) chassis; (*art.*) easel; (*theat.*) flat; *entre bastidores*, behind the scenes, off stage.
bastilla, *n.f.* hem.
bastimento, *n.m.* provisions, victuals; (*obs.*) ship.
bastión, *n.m.* bastion.
basto, **-ta**, *a.* coarse, crude, rough.—*n.m.* club (*in cards*).

23

bastón

bastón, *n.m.* cane, walking stick; *(mil.)* baton.
bastonada, *n.f.*, **bastonazo,** *n.m.* blow with stick, bastinado.
bastonera, *n.f.* umbrella stand.
basura, *n.f.* rubbish, refuse, trash; manure, ordure.
basurero, *n.m.* dustman, *(U.S.)* trash collector; rubbish dump.
bata, *n.f.* dressing gown; smock; *(S.A.)* bat.
batacazo, *n.m.* thud, bump; *(fam.)* let-down, failure.
batalla, *n.f.* battle; fight; joust.
batallar, *v.i.* battle, fight; waver, struggle with oneself.
batallón, -llona, *a.* moot, debatable; causing discord.—*n.m.* battalion.
batán, *n.m.* fulling mill; *(S.A.)* flourmill.
batata, *n.f.* sweet potato, yam; *(S.A.)* jitters, fear.
batayola, *n.f. (naut.)* rail.
bate, *n.m. (S.A.)* baseball bat.
batea, *n.f.* wooden tray, wooden vessel; flat-bottomed boat; *(rail.)* flatcar.
batería, *n.f. (mil., elec.)* battery; drums, drummer; *(S.A.)* nuisance; *(theat.)* footlights.
batido, -da, *a.* shot *(silk etc.)*; well-beaten *(road).*—*n.m.* batter; milk-shake.
batidor, *n.m. (mil.)* scout, outrider; *(cul.)* whisk, beater; *(hunt.)* beater; comb.
batiente, *n.m.* door-jamb; piano damper.
batihoja, *n.m.* gold-beater; sheet-metal worker.
batín, *n.m.* smoking jacket.
batintín, *n.m.* gong.
batir, *v.t.* beat; clap; overcome, ruin; strike *(coins)*; patrol.—*v.r.* fight.
bato, *n.m.* ninny.
batueco, -ca, *a.* simple, yokelish; addled.
baturro, -rra, *a.* yokelish, simple.—*n.m.f.* Aragonese peasant; ninny.
batuta, *n.f. (mus.)* baton; *llevar la —, (fam.)* be in charge.
baúl, *n.m.* trunk, chest; *(fam.)* belly.
bauprés, *n.m. (naut.)* bowsprit.
bausán, *n.m. (mil.)* strawman, dummy; *(fam.)* fool, dummy.
bautismal, *a.* baptismal.
bautismo, *n.m.* baptismo.
bautista, *n.m.* baptizer; baptist.
bautizar [C], *v.t.* baptize, christen; *(fam.)* dilute *(wine).*
bautizo, *n.m.* christening.
bávaro, -ra, *a., n.m.f.* Bavarian.
Baviera, *n.f.* Bavaria.
baya (1), *n.f.* berry.
bayeta, *n.f.* baize; floor mop.
bayo, -ya (2) *a., n.m.f.* bay *(horse).*
bayoneta, *n.f.* bayonet.
baza (1), *n.f.* trick *(cards)*; *hacer —,* prosper; *meter —, (fam.)* stick an oar in.
bazar, *n.m.* bazaar; department store.
bazo, -za (2), *a.* yellow-brown.—*n.m.* spleen.
bazofia, *n.f.* pig-swill; garbage.
bazucar [A], **bazuquear,** *v.t.* shake *(liquid in container)*; meddle with, tamper with.
be (1), *n.m.* bleat.
be (2), *n.f.* name of letter B; *— por —,* in detail.
beatería, *n.f.* bigotry.
beatificar [A], *v.t.* beatify.
beatitud, *n.f.* beatitude.

beato, -ta, *a.* blessed; happy; devout; bigoted.—*n.m.f.* bigot; prude.
beatón, -tona, *a.* bigoted, sanctimonious.—*n.m.f.* prude; bigot.
bebé, *n.m.* baby; doll.
bebedero, -ra, *a.* drinking, drinkable.—*n.m.* watertrough; spout.
bebedizo, -za, *a.* drinkable.—*n.m.* potion, philtre; poison.
beber, *n.m.* drink.—*v.t.* drink; absorb.—*v.i.* drink, tipple.—*v.r.* drink, swallow.
bebida, *n.f.* drink, beverage.
bebido, -da, *a.* drunk, tipsy, merry.
bebistrajo, *n.m. (fam.)* rot-gut, nasty drink.
beca, *n.f.* scholarship, studentship; academic sash.
becario, -ria, *n.m.* scholarship holder.
becerrada, *n.f.* yearling bullfight.
becerro, *n.m.* yearling calf; calfskin; cartulary.
becuadro, *n.m. (mus.)* natural sign.
bedel, *n.m.* university porter.
beduíno, -na, *a., n.m.f.* Bedouin.
befa, *n.f.* taunt.
befar, *v.t.* jeer at.
befo, -fa, *a.* blubber-lipped; knock-kneed.—*n.m.* blubber lip.
behetría, *n.f. (hist.)* free city; *(fam.)* pandemonium.
bejín, *n.m. (bot.)* puff-ball; *(fam.)* touchy person.
bejuco, *n.m.* rattan, liana.
beldad, *n.f.* beauty.
beldar [I], *v.t.* winnow *(with a fork).*
Belén, *n.m.* Bethlehem; **belén,** *n.m.* crib; *(fam.)* bedlam; *(fam.)* risky business.
beleño, *n.m. (bot.)* henbane; poison.
belfo, -fa, *a.* blubber-lipped.—*n.m.* lip *(of animal).*
belga, *a., n.m.f.* Belgian.
Bélgica, *n.f.* Belgium.
bélgico, -ca, *a.* Belgian.
bélico, -ca, *a.* warlike; rel. to war.
belicoso, -sa, *a.* bellicose, aggressive.
beligerante, *a., n.m.* belligerent.
belitre, *a. (fam.)* mean, vile.—*n.m.* wretch, cur.
bellaco, -ca, *a.* knavish, villainous, cunning.—*n.m.f.* scoundrel.
belladona, *n.f.* belladonna.
bellaquería, *n.f.* villainy, roguery.
belleza, *n.f.* beauty.
bello, -lla, *a.* beautiful, fine; *el — sexo,* the fair sex; *bellas artes,* fine arts.
bellota, *n.f.* acorn; *(fam.)* Adam's apple.
bembo, -ba, *a. (S.A.)* thick-lipped.
bemol, *a., n.m. (mus.)* flat.
bencina, *n.f.* benzine.
bendecir [77, *but p.p.* **bendecido** *(obs.* **bendito),** *fut.* **bendeciré,** *cond.* **bendeciría],** *v.t.* bless.
bendición, *n.f.* blessing.
bendito, -ta, *a.* blessed, happy; *(fam.)* confounded; *(fam.)* simple, silly.—*n.m.* simpleton.
benedictino, -na, *a., n.m.f.* Benedictine.
beneficencia, *n.f.* charity, welfare.
beneficentísimo, -ma, *sup. of* BENÉFICO.
beneficiación, *n.f.* benefit; cultivation, tilling; *(min.)* exploitation; *(industry)* processing; *(com.)* concession, discount.
beneficiar, *v.t.* benefit; cultivate, till; exploit *(mines)*; process *(raw materials)*; *(com.)*

24

allow a discount to; (*S.A.*) slaughter (*stock*). —*v.r.* avail oneself (*de*, of); (*S.A.*) kill, account for.
beneficiario, -ria, *n.m.f.* beneficiary.
beneficio, *n.m.* benefaction; benefit; benefice; (*theat.*, *sport*) benefit; (*agr.*) cultivation; (*min.*) yield; (*com.*) profit; (*S.A.*) slaughtering; (*S.A.*) processing plant; (*S.A.*) fertilizer.
beneficioso, -sa, *a.* profitable, advantageous.
benéfico, -ca, *a.* beneficent, charitable; beneficial.
la Benemérita, *n.f.* (*Sp.*) Civil Guard.
benemérito, -ta, *a., n.m.f.* worthy; — *de la patria,* national hero.
beneplácito, *n.m.* approval, consent.
benevolencia, *n.f.* benevolence.
benévolo, *a.* benevolent [*sup.* **benevolentísimo, -ma**].
benignidad, *n.f.* kindness.
benigno, -na, *a.* benignant, kind; mild.
Benito, *n.m.* Benedict; **benito, -ta,** *n.m.f.* Benedictine.
beodez, *n.f.* drunkenness.
beodo, -da, *a.* drunk.—*n.m.f.* drunkard.
berberecho, *n.m.* (*zool.*) cockle.
Berbería, *n.f.* Barbary.
berberisco, -ca, *a.* Berber.
berbiquí, *n.m.* (*carp.*) brace and bit.
bereber, *a., n.m.f.* Berber.
berenjena, *n.f.* eggplant, aubergine.
berenjenal, *n.m.* eggplant plot; (*fig.*) predicament.
bergante, *n.m.* scoundrel.
bergantín, *n.m.* (*naut.*) brig; (*S.A.*) black eye.
berilo, *n.m.* (*gem.*) beryl.
berlina, *n.f.* berlin; *en* —, in the cart, in a silly position.
berlinés, -nesa, *a., n.m.f.* Berliner.
bermejear, *v.i.* look *or* become bright red.
bermejo, -ja, *a.* vermilion.
bermellón, *n.m.* vermilion.
Bermudas, *n.f.pl.* Bermuda.
bernardina, *n.f.* tall story, cock-and-bull story.
berrear, *v.i.* low, bellow.
berrenchín, *n.m.* (*fam.*) tantrum; bad breath.
berrido, *n.m.* lowing, bellow.
berrín, *n.m.* (*fam.*) touchy person *or* child.
berrinche, *n.m.* (*fam.*) tantrum, rage; (*S.A.*) squabble.
berro, *n.m.* watercress.
berza, *n.f.* cabbage.
besana, *n.f.* furrow; arable land.
besar, *v.t.* kiss; (*fam.*) brush against.—*v.r.* (*fam.*) collide; — *la mano* or *los pies a,* pay one's respects to.
beso, *n.m.* kiss; (*fam.*) bump.
bestia, *n.f.* beast.—*n.m.f.* brute, boor, lout.
bestiaje, *n.m.* beasts of burden.
bestial, *a.* bestial, beastly; (*fam.*) terrific.
bestialidad, *n.f.* beastliness.
besucar [A], *v.t., v.i.* kiss repeatedly.
besucón, -cona, *a., n.m.f.* (person) much given to kissing.—*n.m.* (*fam.*) big kiss.
besugo, *n.m.* sea-bream.
besuquear [BESUCAR].
besuqueo, *n.m.* kissing, billing and cooing.
betarraba (*S.A.*), **betarraga** (*Sp.*), *n.f.* beetroot.
bético, -ca, *a.* Andalusian.

betún, *n.m.* bitumen; shoe polish; pitch; asphalt.
bezo, *n.m.* thick lip.
biberón, *n.m.* baby's feeding bottle.
Biblia, *n.f.* Bible.
bíblico, -ca, *a.* biblical.
bibliófilo, *n.m.* bibliophile.
bibliografía, *n.f.* bibliography.
bibliógrafo, *n.m.* bibliographer.
biblioteca, *n.f.* library; large bookcase.
bibliotecario, -ria, *n.m.f.* librarian.
bicarbonato, *n.m.* bicarbonate (*esp. of soda*).
bicentenario, -ria, *a., n.m.* bicentenary.
bíceps, *n.m. inv.* biceps.
bicerra, *n.f.* wild goat.
bicicleta, *n.f.* bicycle.
bicoca, *n.f.* (*fam.*) trifle, small thing.
bicolor, *a.* bicoloured.
bicornio, *n.m.* two-pointed hat.
bicha, *n.f.* (*dial.*) snake; (*obs.*) caryatid.
bichar, *v.t.* spy on.—*v.i.* pry.
bichero, *n.m.* boathook.
bicho, *n.m.* bug; (*fam.*) anything living; *mal* —, (*fam.*) ugly customer; savage bull; (*S.A.*) spite.
bidé, *n.m.* bidet.
biela, *n.f.* (*mech.*) connecting rod.
bielda, *n.f.,* **bieldo, bielgo,** *n.m.* winnowing fork.
bien, *n.m.* good, welfare.—*pl.* property, goods. —*adv.* well; properly; very; really; — *a* —, willingly; — *que,* although; *en* — *de,* for the good of; *hombre de* —, honest man; *no* —, as soon as; *o* —, or else, otherwise; *¡qué* —*!* splendid! *si* —, although.
bienal, *a.* biennial.
bienandante, *a.* prosperous, happy.
bienandanza, *n.f.* prosperity, success.
bienaventurado, -da, *a.* blissful, blessed.
bienaventuranza, *n.f.* bliss.—*pl.* (*eccl.*) Beatitudes.
bienestar, *n.m.* well-being.
bienhechor, -ra, *a.* charitable, kind.—*n.m.* benefactor.—*n.f.* benefactress.
bienhechuría, *n.f.* (*S.A.*) improvements (*to property*).
bienintencionado, -da, *a.* well-meaning.
bienllegada, *n.f.* welcome.
bienmandado, -da, *a.* compliant, obedient.
bienoliente, *a.* fragrant.
bienquerencia, *n.f.* goodwill, affection.
bienquerer [26], *v.t.* be fond of, be well disposed towards.—*n.m.* goodwill, affection.
bienquisto, -ta, *a.* well-loved widely esteemed.
bienvenido, -da, *a., n.f.* welcome; *dar la bienvenida a,* welcome.
bife, *n.m.* (*S.A.*) beefsteak; (*S.A., fam.*) slap.
bifocal, *a.* bifocal.
biftec, *n.m.* beefsteak.
bifurcación, *n.f.* bifurcation; (*rail.*) branch; fork (*in road*).
bigamia, *n.f.* bigamy; (*jur.*) second marriage.
bígamo, -ma, *a.* bigamous.—*n.m.f.* bigamist; remarried person.
bigardía, *n.f.* hoodwinking; lechery.
bigardo, -da, *a.* wanton.
bigornia, *n.f.* anvil.
bigote, *n.m.* moustache; (*print.*) ornate dash.— *pl.* moustache.
bigotudo, -da, *a.* moustachioed.

bilbaíno, -na, *a., n.m.f.* (*person*) native of Bilbao.
bilingüe, *a.* bilingual.
bilioso, -sa, *a.* (*med.*) bilious; (*fig.*) tetchy.
bilis, *n.f.* bile; **descargar la —,** vent one's spleen.
billar, *n.m.* billiards; billiard table; billiard room.
billete, *n.m.* ticket; note; banknote; **— de ida y vuelta,** return ticket; **— de abonado,** season ticket; **— kilométrico,** mileage ticket.
billón, *n.m.* (*Brit.*) billion, (*U.S.*) trillion (10^{12}).
billonario, -ria, *a., n.m.f.* billionaire.
bimba, *n.f.* (*fam.*) top hat.
bimembre, *a.* two-part.
bimensual, *a.* twice-monthly.
bimestre, bimestral, *a.* bi-monthly.—*n.m.* two months.
bimotor, -ra, *a., n.m.f.* twin-engine(d).
binóculo, *n.m.* binoculars; lorgnette.
biografía, *n.f.* biography.
biógrafo, -fa, *n.m.f.* biographer.
biología, *n.f.* biology.
biológico, -ca, *a.* biological.
biólogo, *n.m.* biologist.
biombo, *n.m.* folding screen.
bioquímica, *n.f.* biochemistry.
bióxido, *n.m.* dioxide.
bípede, bípedo, -da, *a., n.m.* biped.
biplano, *n.m.* (*aer.*) biplane.
birlar, *v.t.* (*fam.*) bring down with one blow or shot; (*fam.*) pinch, filch.
birlocha, *n.f.* kite (*toy*).
a la birlonga, *adv. phr.* (*fam.*) sloppily.
Birmania, *n.f.* Burma.
birmano, -na, *a., n.m.f.* Burmese.
birreta, *n.f.* cardinal's hat.
birrete, *n.m.* academic or judge's cap.
bis, *interj.* (*theat.*, *mus.*) encore! (*mus.*) bis.
bisabuelo, -la, *n.m.f.* great-grandfather, great-grandmother.
bisagra, *n.f.* door hinge.
bisar, *v.t.* (*mus.*) repeat.—*v.i.* give an encore.
bisbisar, *v.t.* (*fam.*) mutter.
bisbita, *n.f.* (*orn.*) pipit.
bisecar [A], *v.t.* bisect.
bisector, -triz, *a.* bisecting.—*n.f.* bisector.
bisel, *n.m.* bevel.
bisemanal, *a.* twice-weekly.
bisiesto, *a.* **año —,** leap year.
bismuto, *n.m.* bismuth.
bisnieto,-ta, *n.m.f.* great-grandson, great-granddaughter.
bisojo, -ja, *a.* squinting, cross-eyed.
bisonte, *n.m.* bison.
bisoño, -ña, *a.* (*mil.*) raw.—*n.m.f.* novice, greenhorn; raw recruit.
bistec, *n.m.* beefsteak.
bisturí, *n.m.* (*pl.* **-íes**) scalpel.
bisulfato, *n.m.* bisulphate.
bisulfuro, *n.m.* bisulphide.
bisunto, -ta, *a.* greasy, dirty.
bisutería, *n.f.* imitation jewellery, paste.
bituminoso, -sa, *a.* bituminous.
bizantino, -na, *a., n.m.f.* Byzantine.
bizarría, *n.f.* valour; magnanimity; splendour.
bizarro, -rra, *a.* valiant; magnanimous; splendid.
bizcar [A], *v.t.* wink (*one's eye*).—*v.i.* squint.
bizco, -ca, *a.* cross-eyed, squinting; (*fam.*) dumbfounded.

bizcocho, *n.m.* cake (*esp. sponge-cake*); biscuit.
bizma, *n.f.* poultice.
blanco, -ca, *a.* white; blank; (*fam.*) yellow, cowardly. **quedarse en —,** not understand. —*n.m.* white; blank; target; (*fam.*) coward; **dar en el —,** hit the mark. —*n.f.* **estar sin blanca,** be penniless.
blancor, *n.m.,* **blancura,** *n.f.* whiteness.
blandear, *v.t.* mollify, persuade; brandish.—*v.i., v.r.* soften, give in.
blandir [Q], *v.t.* brandish.—*v.i., v.r.* wave about, shake.
blando, -da, *a.* soft; smooth; mild; weak; timid; (*mus.*) flat.—*adv.* gently, softly.
blandura, *n.f.* softness, gentleness; flattery, blandishment; flabbiness; weakness.
blanquear, *v.t.* whiten, bleach; whitewash; blanch; (*S.A.*) hit or kill with the first shot. —*v.i., v.r.* turn white, blanch.
blanquecino, -na, *a.* whitish.
blanqueo, *n.m.* whitening, bleaching; whitewashing; blanching.
blasfemar, *v.i.* blaspheme.
blasfemia, *n.f.* blasphemy.
blasfemo, -ma, *a.* blasphemous.—*n.m.f.* blasphemer.
blasón, *n.m.* heraldry; coat of arms; (*fig.*) glory.
blasonar, *v.t.* emblazon.—*v.i.* boast (**de,** of being).
blasonería, *n.f.* bragging.
bledo, *n.m.* (*bot.*) goosefoot; (*fam.*) tinker's damn.
blenda, *n.f.* (*geol.*) blende.
blindaje, *n.m.* armour plating.
blindar, *v.t.* (*mil.*) armour-plate.
blofear, *v.t.* (*S.A.*) bluff.
blondo, -da, *a.* flaxen, blond; (*S.A.*) curly.
bloque, *n.m.* block; note pad; lot; (*S.A.*) block (of houses).
bloquear, *v.t.* blockade; brake; (*com.*) block, freeze.
bloqueo, *n.m.* blockade.
blusa, *n.f.* blouse; smock.
boa, *n.f.* boa constrictor.
boato, *n.m.* pomp.
bobada, *n.f.* stupidity.
bobalicón, -cona, *a., n.m.f.* fool.
bobear, *v.i.* act the fool; dawdle.
bobería, *n.f.* stupidity; trifle, trinket, knick-knack.
bobina, *n.f.* bobbin; (*elec.*) coil.
bobo, -ba, *a.* stupid; **estar — con,** be mad about.—*n.m.f.* simpleton, dolt; clown.
boca, *n.f.* mouth; (*fig.*) flavour; **a pedir de —,** to one's heart's desire; **se me viene a la —,** it tastes horrid to me.
bocacalle, *n.f.* end of a street.
bocadillo, *n.m.* roll, sandwich; morsel; snack.
bocado, *n.m.* mouthful, morsel; bit, bridle.
bocallave, *n.f.* keyhole.
bocamanga, *n.f.* cuff.
bocanada, *n.f.* mouthful; puff; rush; gust; (*fam.*) boast.
bocel, *n.m.* (*arch.*) moulding; (*carp.*) moulding plane.
bocera, *n.f.* smear (*on lips*).
boceto, *n.m.* sketch, outline.
bocina, *n.f.* trumpet, horn; car horn, hooter; (*S.A.*) blowgun.
bocio, *n.m.* goitre.
bock, *n.m.* (*pl.* **-cks**) small beer glass.

bocudo, -da, *a.* big-mouthed.
bocha, *n.f.* bowl (*ball*).
bochar, *v.t.* hit the jack (*in bowls*); (*S.A.*) snub; fail (*an examinee*).
boche, *n.m.* marble hole; Boche; (*S.A.*) squabble, row; *dar — a,* (*S.A.*) snub.
bochinche, *n.m.* din, uproar, to-do; (*S.A.*) pub.
bochinchero, -ra, *a.* rowdy, trouble-making. —*n.m.f.* rowdy, hooligan.
bochorno, *n.m.* sultry weather; flush, embarrassment.
bochornoso, -sa, *a.* sultry, sweltering; embarrassing.
boda(s), *n.f. pl.* wedding; (*fig.*)feast; rowdy party; *bodas de plata,* silver wedding *or* jubilee.
bodega, *n.f.* wine vault, wine cellar; pantry; (*naut.*) hold; (*S.A.*) grocer's shop.
bodegón, *n.m.* cheap restaurant, inn; (*art.*) still life.
bodeguero, -ra, *n.m.f.* wine dealer; (*S.A.*) grocer.
bodigo, *n.m.* votive bread.
bodijo, *n.m.* (*fam.*) ill-matched couple; quiet wedding.
bodoque, *n.m.* (*fam.*) dimwit; (*C.A.*) botched job.
bodrio, *n.m.* hodge-podge; bad meal; pig pudding.
bofe, *n.m.*, **bofena,** *n.f.* light, animal lung.
bofetada, *n.f.* slap.
bofetón, *n.m.* hard slap.
boga, *n.f.* vogue; rowing; kind of fish.
bogar [B], *v.i.* row, sail.
bogavante, *n.m.* leading oarsman; lobster.
bogotano, -na, *a., n.m.f.* Bogotan.
bohemiano, -na, *a., n.m.f.* (*geog.*) Bohemian.
bohemio, -mia, *a., n.m.f.* Bohemian; bohemian.
boicotear, *v.t.* boycott.
boicoteo, *n.m.* boycott.
boina, *n.f.* beret.
boj, *n.m.* (*bot.*) box.
bojiganga, *n.f.* strolling players; weird dress; sham.
bol, *n.m.* punch-bowl; net; red earth.
bola, *n.f.* ball; shoeshine; slam (*at cards*); (*fam.*) swindle, lie; (*C.A.*) shindig; *hacer bolas,* play truant.
bolada, *n.f.* ball-throw; (*S.A.*) cinch; bargain.
bolchevique, *a., n.m.f.* Bolshevik.
bolcheviquista, bolchevista, *n.m.f.* Bolshevist.
bolear, *v.t.* (*fam.*) chuck, throw.—*v.i.* play (*a game for fun only*); (*fam.*) fib.—*v.r.* (*S.A.*) stumble.
bolero, -ra, *a.* (*fam.*) lying.—*n.m.f.* truant; fibber.—*n.m.* bolero (*dance and garment*).
boleta, *n.f.* ticket, pass; (*mil.*) billet; warrant; (*S.A.*) certificate; voting slip.
boleto, *n.m.* (*bot.*) boletus; (*S.A.*) ticket, form.
bolichada, *n.f.* (*fam.*) windfall.
boliche, *n.m.* bowl, jack; (*S.A.*) cheap shop *or* bar; dragnet.
bólido, *n.m.* shooting star; hot rod (*car*).
bolígrafo, *n.m.* ball-point pen.
bolina, *n.f.* (*naut.*) bowline; flogging; (*fam.*) shindy.
boliviano, -na, *a., n.m.f.* Bolivian.
bolo, *n.m.* skittle, ninepin; ignoramus; company of strolling players.

bolsa, *n.f.* purse, pouch, bag; stock exchange; (*S.A.*) pocket; sack; *— de trabajo,* labour exchange.
bolsillo, *n.m.* pocket.
bolsista, *n.m.* stock-broker; (*S.A.*) pickpocket.
bolso, *n.m.* bag; handbag.
bolsón, *n.m.* large bag; (*S.A.*) satchel, briefcase.
bollo, *n.m.* bun; bump, dent; row, shindy.
bollón, *n.m.* stud (*nail*).
bomba, *n.f.* bomb; pump; fire-engine; (*S.A.*) fire-cracker; (*S.A.*) lie; rumour; (*C.A.*) drunkenness; *— atómica,* atom bomb; *— de hidrógeno,* hydrogen bomb.
bombar, *v.t.* pump.
bombardear, *v.t.* bomb, bombard.
bombardeo, *n.m.* bombing, bombardment.
bombardero, *n.m.* bomber.
bombástico, -ca, *a.* bombastic.
bombazo, *n.m.* bomb explosion *or* hit.
bombear, *v.t.* bomb; make bulge; (*S.A.*) spy out.
bombilla, *n.f.* (*elec.*) bulb; (*naut.*) lantern.
bombillo, *n.m.* hand-pump; (*S.A., elec.*) bulb.
bombita, *n.f.* firework; (*S.A.*) shame.
bombo, -ba, *a.* (*fam.*) flabbergasted.—*n.m.* big bass drum; fulsome praise, ballyhoo; (*naut.*) sea-barge.
bombón, *n.m.* sweet, candy.
Bona, *n.f.* Bonn.
bonachón, -chona, *a.* good-natured, credulous.
bonaerense, *a., n.m.f.* rel. to, *or* native of, Buenos Aires.
bonanza, *n.f.* (*naut.*) fair weather; (*fig.*) prosperity, bonanza.
bonazo, -za, *a.* (*fam.*) good-natured.
bondad, *n.f.* goodness, kindness; *tener la — de,* be kind enough to.
bondadoso, -sa, *a.* kind, good-natured.
bonete, *n.m.* bonnet, hat; academic cap; *a tente —,* (*fam.*) eagerly; *gran —,* (*fam.*) big-wig.
boniato, *n.m.* sweet potato.
bonico, -ca, *a.* pretty; cute.
bonísimo, -ma, *sup. of* BUENO.
bonítalo, *n.m.* (*ichth.*) bonito.
bonito, -ta, *a.* pretty, nice; (*fig.*) crafty.— *n.m.* (*ichth.*) bonito.
bono, *n.m.* voucher; bond.
boqueada, *n.f.* last gasp, dying breath.
boquear, *v.t.* utter.—*v.i.* breathe one's last; (*fam.*) tail off.
boquerón, *n.m.* anchovy; large opening.
boquiabierto, -ta, *a.* open-mouthed, gaping.
boquilla, *n.f.* mouthpiece; cigarette holder; lamp burner; opening; cigarette tip.
boquimuelle, *a.* (*fam.*) easily imposed on.
boquirroto, -ta, *a.* (*fam.*) wordy.—*n.m.f.* chatterbox.
boquiverde, *a.* (*fam.*) smutty.—*n.m.f.* dirtpeddler.
bórax, *n.m.* borax.
borbollar, borbollear, *v.i.* bubble.
borbollón, *n.m.* bubble, bubbling.
Borbón, *n.m.* Bourbon.
borbotar, *v.i.* bubble.
borbotón, *n.m.* bubble.
borceguí, *n.m.* laced boot.
bordado, *n.m.* embroidery.

bordar, *v.t.* embroider.
borde, *n.m.* edge, side, fringe; bastard.
bordear, *v.t.* skirt.—*v.i.* be *or* go along the edge; (*naut.*) sail windward.
bordillo, *n.m.* curb.
bordo, *n.m.* (*naut.*) board; *a* —, on board; *al* —, alongside; *de alto* —, large (*vessel*); (*fam.*) high-ranking.
bordón, *n.m.* pilgrim's staff; refrain, burden.
bordonear, *v.i.* rove, roam; (*S.A.*) buzz.
Borgoña, *n.f.* Burgundy; **borgoña,** *n.m.* burgundy.
borgoñés, -ñesa, borgoñón, -ñona, *a., n.m.f.* Burgundian.
borinqueño, -ña, *a., n.m.f.* Puerto Rican.
borla, *n.f.* tassel; powder puff, (*fig.*) doctorate.
borne, *n.m.* (*elec.*) terminal.
bornear, *v.t.* twist, warp; set; size up.—*v.i.* (*naut.*) lie at anchor.—*v.r.* warp.
borní, *n.m.* (*orn.*) lanner; harrier.
boro, *n.m.* boron.
borra, *n.f.* young ewe; flock, raw wool; fluff; borax.
borrachera, borrachería, borrachez, *n.f.* drunkenness; carousal; folly.
borracho, -cha, *a.* drunk; violet coloured.— *n.m.f.* drunkard.
borrador, *n.m.* rough draft; note book; (*S.A.*) eraser.
borradura, *n.f.* erasure.
borraj, *n.m.* borax.
borrajear, *v.t.* doodle, scribble.
borrajo, *n.m.* embers.
borrar, *v.t.* erase; efface; blot, smear.
borrasca, *n.f.* tempest, storm; (*fam.*) spree.
borrascoso, -sa, *a.* stormy.
borrego, -ga, *n.m.f.* young sheep; (*fam.*) nitwit.—*n.m.pl.* fleecy clouds.
borrico, -ca, *n.m.f.* ass, donkey.—*n.m.* (*carp.*) trestle.
borricón, borricote, *n.m.* plodder, drudge.
borrón, *n.m.* blot; draft.
borronear, *v.i.* doodle.
borroso, -sa, *a.* blurred; fluffy.
boscaje, *n.m.* grove, coppice.
boscoso, -sa, *a.* (*S.A.*) well-wooded.
bosque, *n.m.* wood, woods.
bosquejar, *v.t.* sketch, outline.
bosquejo, *n.m.* sketch.
bosquete, *n.m.* spinney, coppice.
bostezar [C], *v.i.* yawn.
bostezo, *n.m.* yawn.
bota (1), *n.f.* boot.
bota (2), *n.f.* leather wine bottle; butt (*measure*).
botadura, *n.f.* launching.
botamen, *n.m.* phials and jars; (*naut.*) water store.
botana, *n.f.* bung, plug; patch, scar; (*S.A.*) [TAPA].
botánico, -ca, *a.* botanical.—*n.m.f.* botanist. —*n.f.* botany.
botar, *v.t.* hurl, throw away; launch; (*S.A.*) squander, get rid of.—*v.i.* bounce; buck.
botarate, *n.m.* (*fam.*) blusterer, show-off. (*S.A.*) spendthrift.
bote, *n.m.* thrust; bounce; prancing; can; pot; rowboat; (*fam.*) clink, jail; *de* — *en* —, (*fam.*) packed tight; *en el* —, (*fam.*) in the bag.
botella *n.f.* bottle.

botero, *n.m.* maker *or* repairer of BOTAS (**2**); boatman.
botica, *n.f.* pharmacy; (*fam.*) shop.
boticario, *n.m.* apothecary.
botija, *n.f.* earthen water-jug.
botijo, *n.m.* unglazed BOTIJA; (*fam.*) tubby (*person*).
botillo, *n.m.* wineskin.
botín, *n.m.* booty; gaiter, spat; (*S.A.*) sock.
botina, *n.f.* boot.
botiquín, *n.m.* first aid box, medicine chest; (*S.A.*) wine shop.
boto, -ta, *a.* blunt, dull.
botón, *n.m.* button; knob; bud; (*S.A., fam.*) cop, policeman; — *de oro,* buttercup.
botonero, *n.m.* buttonmaker; (*elec.*) control buttons.
botones, *n.m. inv. pl.* pageboy, (*U.S.*) bellhop.
bóveda, *n.f.* vault; crypt, cavern.
bovino, -na, *a.* bovine.
boxear, *v.t.* box.
boxeo, *n.m.* boxing.
boya, *n.f.* buoy.
boyada, *n.f.* drove of oxen.
boyante, *a.* buoyant; lucky, successful.
boyar, *v.i.* float.
boyera, boyeriza, *n.f.* ox stall.
boyerizo, boyero, *n.m.* ox drover.
boyuno, -na, *a.* bovine.
bozal, *a.* pure-blooded (*Negro*); callow, green; stupid; wild; (*S.A.*) speaking broken Spanish.—*n.m.* muzzle.
bozo, *n.m.* down on face; headstall.
braceaje, *n.m.* coining; furnace tapping; brewing; (*naut.*) fathoming.
bracear, *v.t.* tap (*furnace*); brew; fathom, sound.—*v.i.* swing the arms; wrestle.
braceo, *n.m.* arm swing; crawl (*swimming*).
bracero, -ra, *a.* manual, thrown.—*n.m.* escort; dav labourer; brewer; *de* — or *de bracete,* arm in arm.
braga, *n.f.* hoisting rope; baby's diaper.—*pl.* knickers, panties.
bragazas, *n.m. inv.* (*fam.*) hen-pecked husband; weak-willed man.
bragueta, *n.f.* fly (*of trousers*).
bramar, *v.i.* roar, bellow, howl.
bramido, *n.m.* bellow, howl, roar.
bramón, -mona, *n.m.f.* (*fam.*) squealer, stool pigeon.
brasa, *n.f.* live coal.
brasero, *n.m.* brazier; place for burning heretics.
Brasil, *n.m.* Brazil.
brasileño, -ña, *a., n.m.f.* Brazilian.
bravata, *n.f.* bravado; *echar bravatas,* talk big, make boastful threats.
bravear, *v.i.* boast, bully.
braveza, *n.f.* ferocity; courage; fury.
bravío, -vía, *a.* wild.—*n.m.* fierceness.
bravo, -va, *a.* manful, brave; wild; (*fam.*) bullying; (*fam.*) cussed; (*fam.*) classy; angry; *fiesta brava,* bull-fighting.—*n.m., interj.* bravo!
bravucón, -cona, *a.* swaggering, bragging.— *n.m.f.* braggart.
bravura, *n.f.* fierceness; courage; bravado.
braza, *n.f.* (*naut.*) fathom; breaststroke.
brazada, *n.f.* armstroke; armful; stroke (*swimming*).
brazado, *n.m.* armful.

brazal, *n.m.* armband; branch channel; headrail.

brazalete, *n.m.* bracelet.

brazo, *n.m.* arm; foreleg; *a — partido*, hand to hand (*fighting*); *de —*, (*S.A.*) arm in arm. —*pl.* hands, workers; sponsors, backers.

brea, *n.f.* pitch, tar; resin.

brebaje, *n.m.* nasty potion; (*naut.*) grog.

brécol(es), *n.m.* (*pl.*) broccoli.

brecha, *n.f.* breach; impact, impression.

brega, *n.f.* struggle, fight; trick.

bregar [B], *v.t.* knead.—*v.i.* toil; struggle.

breña, *n.f.* rough scrubland.

breñoso, **-sa**, *a.* rough (*ground*); craggy, rocky.

Bretaña, *n.f.* Brittany; (*la*) *Gran —*, Great Britain; **bretaña**, *n.f.* (*bot.*) hyacinth.

brete, *n.m.* fetter; (*fig.*) tight spot.

bretón, **-tona**, *a.*, *n.m.f.* Breton.

bretones, *n.m.pl.* sprouts, kale.

breva, *n.f.* cinch; bargain; early fig; flat cigar.

breve, *a.* short, brief; *en —*, shortly; in short. —*n.m.* papal brief.—*n.f.* (*mus.*) breve.

brevedad, *n.f.* brevity.

brevete, *n.m.* memorandum.

breviario, *n.m.* breviary; short treatise.

brezal, *n.m.* heath, moor.

brezo, *n.m.* (*bot.*) heather, heath.

bribón, **-bona**, *n.m.f.* scoundrel, loafer.

bribonería, *n.f.* roguery.

brida, *n.f.* bridle; (*fig.*) curb.

brigada, *n.f.* brigade.—*n.m.* sergeant major.

Briján, *n.m. saber más que —*, (*idiom*) know what's what, be as wise as an owl.

brillante, *a.* brilliant, shining; outstanding; gaudy.—*n.m.* brilliant, diamond.

brillantez, *n.f.* brilliance, splendour.

brillantina, *n.f.* hair grease; metal polish.

brillar, *v.i.* shine, beam.

brillo, *n.m.* shine, splendour, brilliance.

brincar [A], *v.t.* bounce; (*fam.*) skip, pass over.—*v.i.* skip, gambol; (*fam.*) be touchy.

brinco, *n.m.* leap, bound, hop.

brindar, *v.t.* offer.—*v.i.* drink the health (*a*, of).—*v.r.* offer to.

brindis, *n.m. inv.* toast; offer, invitation.

brinquillo, **brinquiño**, *n.m.* trinket; sweetmeat; *hecho un brinquiño*, (*fam.*) all dolled up.

brinza, *n.f.* (*bot.*) sprig, blade.

brío, *n.m.* mettle, vigour, spirit.

brioso, **-sa**, *a.* mettlesome, spirited, lively.

briqueta, *n.f.* briquette.

brisa, *n.f.* breeze.

británico, **-ca**, *a.* British.

britano, **-na**, *a.* British.—*n.m.f.* Briton.

briza, *n.f.* haze.

brizna, *n.f.* chip, splinter; string, filament; blade.

briznoso, **-sa**, *a.* splintery; stringy.

brizo, *n.m.* cradle.

broa (1), *n.f.* biscuit.

broa (2), *n.f.* (*naut.*) small bay, cove.

broca, *n.f.* shuttle bobbin; drill bit; nail.

brocal, *n.m.* edge, rim, mouth; scabbard.

brocino, *n.m.* lump, bump.

bróculi, *n.m.* broccoli.

brocha, *n.f.* brush; *de — gorda*, (*fam.*) slapdash.

brochada, *n.f.* brush stroke.

broche, *n.m.* clasp; brooch; (*S.A.*) paperclip.

brocheta, *n.f.* skewer.

broma, *n.f.* joke, fun; (*zool.*) woodworm; (*S.A.*) disappointment; *de —*, in fun; *dar — a*, tease; *en —*, jokingly.

bromato, *n.m.* bromate.

bromear, *v.i.*, *v.r.* joke; have a good time.

bromista, *n.m.f.* joker, practical joker, merry person.

bromo, *n.m.* bromine.

bromuro, *n.m.* bromide.

bronca, *n.f.* (*fam.*) row, quarrel; *soltar una — a*, rant and rave at.

bronce, *n.m.* bronze, brass.

broncear, *v.t.*, *v.r.* bronze; sun-tan.

bronco, **-ca**, *a.* rough, harsh; abrupt, crusty; brittle.

bronquedad, *n.f.* roughness; gruffness; brittleness.

bronquial, *a.* bronchial.

bronquitis, *n.f.* bronchitis.

brontosauro, *n.m.* brontosaurus.

broquel, *n.m.* (*poet.*) shield, buckler.

broquelillo, *n.m.* ear-ring.

broqueta, *n.f.* skewer.

brota, *n.f.* shoot, bud.

brotadura, *n.f.* budding, sprouting; (*med.*) rash.

brotar, *v.t.* sprout, send out.—*v.i.* sprout, bud; break out (*in a rash*).

brote, *n.m.* shoot, sprout; (*med.*) rash.

broza, *n.f.* brushwood; garden rubbish; printer's brush.

bruces, **de**, *adv. phr.* face down.

bruja, *n.f.* witch; (*fam.*) old hag; (*orn.*) barn owl; (*S.A.*) spook.—*a. inv.* (*S.A.*) broke, penniless.

Brujas, *n.f.* Bruges.

brujería, *n.f.* witchcraft.

brujir [GRUJIR].

brujo, **-ja**, *a.* magic.—*n.m.* sorcerer, wizard.

brújula, *n.f.* compass, magnetic needle; gunsight; peephole; *perder la —*, lose the knack.

brujulear, *v.t.* scrutinise, examine; (*fam.*) suspect; (*S.A.*) plot; (*S.A.*) have a spree.

brulote, *n.m.* fireship; (*S.A.*) swear word.

bruma, *n.f.* mist, fog.

brumazón, *n.m.* thick fog.

brumoso, **-sa**, *a.* foggy, misty.

bruno, **-na**, *a.* dark brown.

bruñido, *n.m.*, **bruñidura**, *n.f.*, **bruñimiento**, *n.m.* burnishing, polishing.

bruñir [K], *v.t.* burnish.

brusco, **-ca**, *a.* gruff, abrupt, brusque.

bruselas, *n.f.pl.* tweezers.

Bruselas, *n.f.* Brussels.

brusquedad, *n.f.* abruptness, brusqueness.

brutal, *a.* brutal; sudden; (*fam.*) stunning, terrific.—*n.m.* brute.

brutalidad, *n.f.* brutality; (*fam.*) terrific amount.

brutalizar [C], *v.t.* brutalize.

brutesco, **-ca**, *a.* grotesque.

bruteza, *n.f.* brutishness; roughness.

bruto, **-ta**, *a.* brutish; crude, rough.—*n.m.* brute, beast.

bruza, *n.f.* brush, bristle brush.

bu, *n.m.* (*fam.*) bogeyman.

búa, **buba**, *n.f.* (*med.*) pustule; (*med.*) bubo.

bubón, *n.m.* tumour.

bubónico, **-ca**, *a.* bubonic.

bucanero, *n.m.* buccaneer.

bucear, *v.i.* dive; (*fig.*) delve (**en,** into).
bucle, *n.m.* curl, ringlet, loop.
buco, *n.m.* gap, opening; (*zool.*) buck; (*S.A.*) yarn.
bucólico, -ca, *a.* bucolic.—*n.m.* pastoral poet. —*n.f.* pastoral poetry; (*fam.*) grub, food.
buchada, *n.f.* (*fam.*) mouthful.
buche, *n.m.* craw, crop (*of birds*); belly; **sacar el — a uno,** (*fam.*) make s.o. spill the beans.
buchón, -chona, *a.* (*fam.*) baggy, bulging. —*n.f.* pouter pigeon.
budín, *n.m.* (*S.A.*) pudding.
budismo, *n.m.* Buddhism.
budista, *a.,* *n.m.f.* Buddhist.
buen, *a.m.* *contracted form of* BUENO *before n.m.sg.*
buenamente, *adv.* willingly; easily.
buenaventura, *n.f.* good luck, good fortune.
buenazo, -za, [BONAZO].
bueno, -na, *a.* good; kind; fit; **de buenas a primeras,** suddenly; **estar de buenas,** be in a good mood.
buenparecer, *n.m.* good appearance; good opinion.
buey, *n.m.* ox, bullock; **a paso de —,** at a snail's pace.
¡buf! *interj.* ugh!
bufa, *n.f.* jest.
búfalo, *n.m.* buffalo.
bufanda, *n.f.* scarf.
bufar, *v.i.* snort, puff.
bufete, *n.m.* desk; lawyer's office; (*S.A.*) buffet, snack.
bufido, *n.m.* snort.
bufo, -fa, *a.* farcical.—*n.m.* buffoon, clown.
bufonada, *n.f.* buffoonery.
bugle, *n.m.* bugle.
buharda, *n.f.* garret; dormer window.
buhardilla, *n.f.* [BUHARDA]; (*S.A.*) skylight.
buharro, *n.m.* (*orn.*) eagle-owl.
buhedera, *n.f.* loophole.
buho, *n.m.* eagle-owl; tawny owl; (*fam.*) miser, misery; (*fam.*) squealer.
buhón, buhonero, *n.m.* pedlar.
buhonería, *n.f.* peddling.
buitre, *n.m.* vulture.
buitrero, -ra, *a.* vulturine.
buje, *n.m.* axle box.
bujería, *n.f.* bauble, trinket.
bujeta, *n.f.* box made of boxwood.
bujía, *n.f.* candle; spark plug.
bula, *n.f.* (*eccl.*) bull.
bulbo, *n.m.* (*bot.,* *med.*) bulb.
bulboso, -sa, *a.* bulbous.
bulevar, *n.m.* boulevard.
búlgaro, -ra, *a.,* *n.m.f.* Bulgarian.
bulto, *n.m.* bulk, mass; bundle; (*S.A.*) briefcase; **a —,** broadly, by and large; **de —,** evident; (*S.A.*) important.
bulla, *n.f.* din, uproar.
bullanga, *n.f.* tumult, riot.
bullanguero, -ra, *a.* riotous.—*n.m.f.* rioter.
bullarengue, *n.m.* (*fam.*) bustle (*of dress*); (*S.A.*) dud, anything false.
bullicio, *n.m.* bustle, noise, excitement.
bullicioso, -sa, *a.* restless, noisy, turbulent.
bullir [J], *v.t.* move, stir.—*v.i.* boil; teem, swarm; bustle; budge.—*v.r.* budge. stir.
bullón, *n.m.* ornamental stud; boiling dye.

buñuelo, *n.m.* bun, doughnut; (*fam.*) botched job.
buque, *n.m.* ship, vessel; hull; **— cisterna,** tanker; **— de desembarco,** landing craft; **— de guerra,** warship; **— lanzaminas,** minelayer; **— mercante,** merchant ship.
buqué, *n.m.* wine bouquet.
burato, *n.m.* crêpe; transparent veil.
burbuja, *n.f.* bubble.
burbujear, *v.i.* bubble, burble.
burbujeo, *n.m.* bubbling.
burdel, *n.m.* brothel.
Burdeos, *n.f.* Bordeaux.
burdeos, *n.m.* *inv.* claret.
burdo, -da, *a.* coarse, common.
bureta, *n.f.* burette.
burgalés, -lesa, *a.,* *n.m.f.* rel. to, *or* native of, Burgos.
burgo, *n.m.* (*obs.*) township, borough.
burgomaestre, *n.m.* burgomaster.
burgués, -guesa, *a.,* *n.m.f.* bourgeois.—*n.m.f.* burgess.
burguesía, *n.f.* bourgeoisie, middle class.
buriel, *a.* dark red.—*n.m.* coarse woollen cloth.
buril, *n.m.* burin, engraver; dentist's probe.
burilar, *v.t.* engrave.
burjaca, *n.f.* beggar's pouch.
burla, *n.f.* mocking; joke, jest; trick, hoax; gibe; **— burlando,** gently, on the quiet; **de burlas,** jokingly.
burlador, -ra, *a.* joking, mocking.—*n.m.f.* wag, practical joker.—*n.m.* seducer.
burlar, *v.t.* gibe at; hoax; outwit; evade (*the law*).—*v.r.* make fun (*de,* of).
burlería, *n.f.* drollery; hoaxing; yarn.
burlesco, -ca, *a.* (*fam.*) funny, comic, ludicrous.
burlón, -lona, *a.* mocking, joking.—*n.m.f.* banterer.
buró, *n.m.* bureau.
burocracia, *n.f.* bureaucracy.
burócrata, *n.m.f.* bureaucrat.
burocrático, -ca, *a.* bureaucratic.
burra, *n.f.* she-ass; drudge (*woman*).
burro, -rra, *a.* stupid.—*n.m.f.* donkey, ass; sawhorse; windlass; (*S.A.*) stepladder.
bursátil, *a.* rel. to stock exchange *or* to shares.
busca, *n.f.* search; pursuit.—*pl.* (*S.A.* *coll.*) perquisites.
buscada, *n.f.* search.
buscapié, *n.m.* hint, clue.
buscapiés, *n.m.* *inv.* jumping jack, firework.
buscapleitos, *n.m.* *inv.* (*S.A.*) shyster; trouble-maker; touting lawyer.
buscar [C], *v.t.* look for, seek; (*fam.*) pinch, filch; **se la busca,** (*fam.*) he's asking for it!
buscavidas, *n.m.f.* *inv.* busybody, snooper.
buscón, -cona, *a.* seeking.—*n.m.f.* cheat, petty pilferer.
busilis, *n.m.* (*fam.*) trouble, tricky problem; (*fam.*) cash.
búsqueda, *n.f.* search.
busto, *n.m.* bust.
butaca, *n.f.* easy chair; (*theat.*) orchestra seat.
butano, *n.m.* butane.
buzo, *n.m.* diver.
buzón, *n.m.* mail box, post box; conduit; lid; sluice.

C

C, c, *n.f.* third letter of the Spanish alphabet.
ca, *conj.* (*obs.*) for, since.—*interj.* no! never!
cabal, *a.* exact; complete; **no estar en sus cabales,** not to be in one's right mind.— *adv.* exactly.—*interj.* right! fine!
cábala, *n.f.* cabal; intrigue; superstition.
cabalgada, *n.f.* cavalry sortie.
cabalgadura, *n.f.* mount; beast of burden.
cabalgar [B], *v.i.* ride (**en, sobre,** on).
cabalgata, *n.f.* cavalcade.
cabalista, *n.m.f.* cabalist; intriguer.
caballar, *a.* equine.
caballerear, *v.i.* simulate gentility.
caballeresco, -ca, *a.* courteous; gentlemanly; chivalric.
caballería, *n.f.* (*mil.*) cavalry; chivalry; mount.
caballeriza, *n.f.* stable.
caballerizo, *n.m.* groom.
caballero, *n.m.* gentleman; knight; horseman; **— de industria,** sharper, confidence man; **armar a uno —,** knight.
caballerosidad, *n.f.* gentlemanliness, chivalry.
caballeroso, -sa, *a.* gentlemanly, chivalrous.
caballete, *n.m.* ridge (*roof, furrow*); bridge (*nose*); trestle; easel; torture horse.
caballista, *n.m.* horseman, horse-breaker.— *n.f.* horsewoman.
caballito, *n.m.* small horse; hobbyhorse; **— del diablo,** dragonfly; **— de mar,** sea horse.
caballo, *n.m.* horse; knight (*chess*); (*S.A.*) blockhead; **— de vapor** or **de fuerza,** horsepower; **a mata —,** full tilt; **— blanco,** sponsor, backer.
caballuno, -na, *a.* horselike; equine.
cabaña, *n.f.* hut; herd; track.
cabaret, *n.m.* cabaret, night-club.
cabecear, *v.t.* head (*wine*); thicken (*letters*). —*v.i.* shake one's head; nod (*in sleep*); (*naut.*) lurch.
cabeceo, *n.m.* shake, nod; lurch; (*naut.*) pitching.
cabecera, *n.f.* head (*bed, table etc.*); regional capital; headline; bolster; **— de puente,** (*mil.*) bridge-head.
cabecilla, *n.m.* ringleader.
cabellera, *n.f.* locks, hair.
cabello, *n.m.* hair; **traerlo por los cabellos,** drag it in, mention it somehow.
cabelludo, -da, *a.* hairy.
caber [13], *v.i.* fit, have room; befall; **no cabe duda,** there's no room for doubt; **no cabe en sí,** he is beside himself; **no cabe más,** that's the end; **todo cabe,** everything goes.
cabestrante, *n.m.* capstan.
cabestrillo, *n.m.* sling (*for arm*); small halter.
cabestro, *n.m.* halter; lead ox.
cabeza, *n.f.* head; chief; top; **dar de —,** (*fam.*) come a cropper; **irse de la —,** (*fam.*) go off one's head.
cabezada, *n.f.* butt; nod.
cabezalero, *n.m.* executor.
cabezo, *n.m.* hillock; reef, rock.
cabezón, -zona, *a.* large-headed; (*fam.*) stubborn.

cabezota, *a.* stubborn.—*n.m.f.* mulish person.
cabezudo, -da, *a.* large-headed; (*fam.*) stubborn.—*n.m.* man wearing huge mask (*in festive processions*).
cabida, *n.f.* space, room; **tener gran con,** (*fam.*) have great influence with.
cabildear, *v.i.* lobby.
cabildero, *n.m.* lobbyist.
cabildo, *n.m.* (*eccl.*) chapter; council.
cabina, *n.f.* (*aer.*) cabin; telephone booth.
cabizbajo, -ja, *a.* crestfallen.
cable, *n.m.* cable; lifeline.
cablegrafiar [L], *v.t., v.i.* cable.
cablegrama, *n.m.* cable, cablegram.
cabo, *n.m.* end, tip; (*geog.*) cape; handle; (*naut.*) rope; foreman; (*mil.*) corporal; **al fin y al —,** after all; **dar — a,** complete; **llevar a —,** carry out.—*pl.* odds and ends; **atar cabos,** (*fam.*) put two and two together.
cabra, *n.f.* goat; loaded dice; (*med.*) leg blister.
cabrahigo, *n.m.* wild fig.
cabrero, -ra, *n.m., n.m.f.* goatherd, goatherdess.
cabrestante, *n.m.* capstan.
cabria, *n.f.* three-legged hoist.
cabrilla, *n.f.* (*carp.*) sawing horse; (*med.*) leg blister; whitecap (*wave*).
cabrio, *n.m.* (*carp.*) roof spar, beam, joist.
cabrío, -ría, *a.* rel. to goats.—*n.m.* herd of goats.
cabriola, *n.f.* gambol, somersault, caper.
cabriolar, *v.i.* gambol, caper.
cabrito, *n.m.* kid (*goat*).
cabrón, *n.m.* male goat [*Avoid: use* **macho cabrio** *instead*]; cuckold.
cabruno, -na, *a.* rel. to goats.
cacahuete, *n.m.* peanut, groundnut.
cacao, *n.m.* cacao; (*S.A.*) chocolate.
cacaraña, *n.f.* pock, pit.
cacarear, *v.t.* (*fam.*) crow about.—*v.i.* cackle, crow.
cacareo, *n.m.* crowing, cackling; (*fam.*) bragging.
cacatúa, *n.f.* cockatoo.
cacería, *n.f.* hunt; hunting party; game caught, bag.
cacerola, *n.f.* (*cul.*) pot, casserole.
cacique, *n.m.* Indian chief; (*fam.*) bossy fellow; (*fam.*) string-puller; (*U.S.*) political boss.
caciquismo, *n.m.* (*fam.*) string-pulling; (*U.S.*) bossism.
cacofonía, *n.f.* cacophony.
cacto, *n.m.* cactus.
cacumen, *n.m.* (*fam.*) nous, acumen.
cachano, *n.m.* (*fam.*) Old Nick; **llamar a —,** (*fam.*) waste one's breath.
cachar, *v.t.* shatter; harrow; (*S.A.*) mock; cheat; (*S.A.*) catch (*Anglicism: all meanings*).
cacharro, *n.m.* crock, pot; crockery; (*fam.*) bone-shaker, rickety machine; (*C.A.*) (*coll.*) jug, jail.
cachaza, *n.f.* (*fam.*) slowness, phlegm.
cachazudo, -da, *a.* (*fam.*) slow, phlegmatic. —*n.m.f.* slowcoach, sluggard.
cachear, *v.t.* frisk (*a suspect*).
cachete, *n.m.* (*taur.*) dagger; slap (*on face*); cheek.
cachetina, *n.f.* scuffle, brawl.
cachicán, *n.m.* overseer; (*fam.*) sharper.
cachidiablo, *n.m.* hobgoblin; (*fam.*) imp, rogue.

cachifollar, *v.t.* (*fam.*) snub; cheat.
cachillada, *n.f.* litter (*of young*).
cachimba, *n.f.* pipe (*smoking*).
cachiporra, *n.f.* club, cudgel.
cachivache, *n.m.* (*fam.*) thingummy, contraption; (*fam.*) wretch, fool; (*fam.*) pot, pan, *etc.*
cacho, -cha, *a.* bent.—*n.m.* bit; slice; (*ichth.*) chub; (*S.A.*) (*zool.*) horn; (*S.A.*) yarn, fib.
cachón, *n.m.* (*naut.*) breaker.
cachondeo, *n.m.* (*low*) larking, messing about.
cachorro, -rra, *n.m.f.* puppy; cub.
cachucha, *n.f.* small boat; cap; Andalusian dance.
cachupín, -pina, *n.m.f.* (*C.A. pej.*) Spanish settler.
cada, *a. inv.* each, every; — *cual,* each one, one and all; — *quisque,* (*fam.*) every man jack.
cadalso, *n.m.* scaffold; platform.
cadáver, *n.m.* corpse.
cadavérico, -ca, *a.* cadaverous.
cadena, *n.f.* chain; chain gang; — *perpetua,* life imprisonment.
cadencia, *n.f.* cadence; (*mus.*) cadenza.
cadencioso, -sa, *a.* rhythmical, cadenced.
cadente, *a.* moribund; rhythmic.
cadera, *n.f.* hip.
cadetada, *n.f.* prank.
cadete, *n.m.* cadet.
caducar [A], *v.i.* expire, lapse; dodder; wear out.
caducidad, *n.f.* expiry, caducity; decrepitude.
caduco, -ca, *a.* expired; decrepit.
caduquez, *n.f.* dotage; decrepitude.
caedizo,-za, *a.* ready to fall.—*n.m.* (*S.A.*) lean-to.
caer [14], *v.i.* fall, drop; decline; suit, fit; lie, be located; — *del burro,* see one's mistake; — *en la cuenta,* see the point; *¡ya caigo!* I get it! Oh, I see!—*v.r.* fall down; lie.
café, *n.m.* coffee; café; — *solo,* black coffee; — *con leche,* white coffee.
cafeína, *n.f.* caffeine.
cafetero, -ra, *a.* coffee.—*n.m.f.* coffee worker. —*n.f.* coffee pot.
cafeto, *n.m.* coffee bush.
cáfila, *n.f.* (*fam.*) bunch, troop.
cafre, *a., n.m.f.* Kaffir; (*fig.*) savage.
cagafierro, *n.m.* slag.
cagalaolla, *n.m.* (*fam.*) clown.
cagatintas, *n.m. inv.* (*fam., pej.*) pen-pusher.
caída, *n.f.* fall; collapse; flop; setting (*of sun*).
caído, -da, *a.* fallen; drooping; dejected.— *n.m.pl.* the fallen; income due; (*min.*) rubble. [CAER]
caigo [CAER].
caimán, *n.m.* alligator; (*fam.*) shark, crook.
caimiento, *n.m.* fall; droop; dejection.
Caín, *n.m.* (*Bib.*) Cain; *pasar las de —,* go through hell.
el Cairo, *n.m.* Cairo.
caja, *n.f.* box, chest; cash desk, cashier's office; casing; drum; body (*of vehicle*); well (*stairs, lift*); fund; (*carp.*) mortise; — *de ahorros,* savings bank; — *fuerte,* safe; — *de registro,* manhole; — *registradora,* till, cash register; *despedir con cajas destempladas,* send packing.
cajero, -ra, *n.m.f.* cashier.

cajetilla, *n.f.* packet; matchbox.
cajista, *n.m.* (*print.*) compositor.
cajón, *n.m.* case, crate; drawer; stall, stand; caisson; (*C.A.*) shop; (*S.A.*) gorge; — *de sastre,* muddle; *de —,* ordinary.
cajonería, *n.f.* chest of drawers.
cal, *n.f.* lime; *de — y canto,* (*fam.*) hefty.
cala, *n.f.* inlet; (*min.*) test boring; (*naut.*) hold; probe.
calabacear, *v.t.* (*fam.*) flunk (*examinee*); (*fam.*) give the brush off to.
calabaza, *n.f.* pumpkin; marrow.—*n.m.f.* (*fam.*) bonehead; *dar calabazas a,* give the brush off to; *salir —,* (*fam.*) be a wash-out.
calabobos, *n.m.sg.* (*fam.*) drizzle.
calabozo, *n.m.* dungeon, cell.
calabrote, *n.m.* hawser.
calada, *n.f.* soaking; plunge, swoop.
calado, *n.m.* fretwork; drawn thread work; stencil; depth; (*naut.*) draught.
calafate, *n.m.* shipwright; caulker.
calafatear, *v.t.* caulk; point (*walls*); plug up.
calamar, *n.m.* (*zool.*) squid.
calambre, *n.m.* (*med.*) cramp.
calamidad, *n.f.* calamity.
calamita, *n.f.* loadstone; magnetic needle.
calamitoso, -sa, *a.* calamitous.
cálamo, *n.m.* reed; (*poet.*) pen, flute.
calamoco, *n.m.* icicle.
calandrajo, *n.m.* tatter; (*fam.*) scruff.
calandria, *n.f.* (*orn.*) calandria lark; calender (*press*); treadmill.—*n.m.f.* malingerer, lead-swinger.
calaña, *n.f.* pattern; calibre, character.
calar (1), *a.* limy.—*n.m.* limestone quarry.— *v.t.* lime.
calar (2), *v.t.* pierce, penetrate; soak; do CALADO work; test-bore; fix (*bayonet*); lower (*nets etc.*); (*naut.*) draw; (*fam.*) size up (*someone*); (*fam.*) see through (*someone*); (*fam.*) pick (*pockets*); (*S.A.*) stare at.—*v.r.* get soaked *or* drenched; squeeze in; swoop down; (*fam.*) stick on (*hat etc.*).
calavera, *n.f.* skull.—*n.m.* rake (*person*).
calaverada, *n.f.* escapade, tomfoolery.
calcañar, calcaño, *n.m.* heel.
calcar [A], *v.t.* trace, copy; model (*en,* on); trample on.
calce, *n.m.* iron tip, edge *or* rim.
calceta, *n.f.* hose, stocking; knitting.
calcetero, -ra, *n.m.f.* hosier.
calcetín, *n.m.* sock (*men's*).
calcio, *n.m.* calcium.
calco, *n.m.* tracing, copy.
calcografía, *n.f.* calchography, engraving.
calcomanía, *n.f.* transfer (*picture*).
calcular, *v.t.* calculate.
calculista, *a.* scheming; (*S.A.*) prudent.— *n.m.f.* schemer.
cálculo, *n.m.* calculation; calculus; gallstone.
calda, *n.f.* heating; (*fig.*) encouragement.
caldear, *v.t.* heat; weld.—*v.r.* get hot.
caldeo, *n.m.* heating; welding.
caldera, *n.f.* cauldron; pot; (*S.A.*) kettle; tea- *or* coffee-pot; (*eng.*) boiler.
calderero, *n.m.* boilermaker; tinker.
caldereta, *n.f.* cooking pot; stew.
calderilla, *n.f.* small change, coppers.
caldero, *n.m.* large cauldron.
calderoniano, -na, *a.* Calderonian.
caldillo, *n.m.* gravy.

caldo, *n.m.* broth; stock; salad dressing.
caldoso, -sa, *a.* thin, brothy.
cale, *n.m.* (*fam.*) tap, slap.
calefacción, *n.f.* heating; — **central,** central heating.
calendario, *n.m.* calendar.
calentador, -ra, *a.* heating, warming.—*n.m.* heater.
calentar [1], *v.t.* heat, warm; urge on; (*fam.*) thrash, beat.—*v.r.* get warm; (*fig.*) get heated; **calentarse los sesos** or **la cabeza,** rack one's brains.
calentura, *n.f.* fever.
calenturiento, -ta, *a.* feverish.
calera, *n.f.* limestone quarry; lime kiln.
caleta, *n.f.* small cove; (*S.A.*) dockers' union; (*S.A.*) minor port.
caletre, *n.m.* (*fam.*) nous, acumen.
calibrador, *n.m.* callipers.
calibrar, *v.t.* calibrate, gauge.
calibre, *n.m.* calibre; gauge.
calicanto, *n.m.* roughcast.
calicata, *n.f.* (*min.*) prospecting.
calicó, *n.m.* (*pl.* **-cós**) calico.
caliche, *n.m.* flake (*of plaster etc.*).
calidad, *n.f.* quality, worth; condition; capacity; **en — de,** in the capacity of.
cálido, -da, *a.* warm.
calidoscopio, *n.m.* kaleidoscope.
caliente, *a.* warm, hot; (*fig.*) heated.
califa, *n.m.* caliph.
califato, *n.m.* caliphate.
calificación, *n.f.* assessment; mark (*in exam.*); qualification.
calificado, -da, *a.* qualified; competent; sound; important.
calificar [A], *v.t.* assess; justify; qualify; describe; ennoble.
calificativo, -va, *a.* qualifying.
calígine, *n.f.* (*poet.*) murk; (*fam.*) sultry weather.
caligrafía, *n.f.* calligraphy.
calígrafo, *n.m.* calligrapher.
calina, *n.f.* light mist.
cáliz, *n.m.* chalice; calyx.
calizo, -za, *a.* limy.—*n.f.* chalk.
calmante, *a.* calming.—*n.m.* sedative.
calmar, *v.t.* calm.—*v.i.* calm down, abate.
calmo, -ma, *a.* treeless; calm.—*n.f.* calm; lull; **calma chicha,** dead calm.
calmoso, -sa, *a.* calm; (*fam.*) slow.
caló, *n.m.* Spanish gipsy dialect.
calofriar [L], *v.r.* shiver.
calofrío, *n.m.* shiver, chill.
calor, *n.m.* heat, warmth; **hace —,** it is hot (*weather*); **tengo —,** I am hot.
caloría, *n.f.* calorie.
calorífero, -ra, *a.* giving heat.—*n.m.* heater.
calorífico, -ca, *a.* calorific.
calorífugo, -ga, *a.* heat insulating; fire-proof.
caloroso, -sa, *a.* hot, warm.
calumnia, *n.f.* slander, calumny.
calumniar, *v.t.* slander, calumniate.
calumnioso, -sa, *a.* slanderous, calumnious.
caluroso, -sa, *a.* hot, warm; heated.
calvario, *n.m.* Calvary; (*fam.*) Baldy; (*fam.*) troubles.
calvatrueno, *n.m.* bald head.
calvero, *n.m.* clearing (*in woods*).
calvicie, *n.f.* baldness.
calvinismo, *n.m.* Calvinism.
calvinista, *a., n.m.f.* Calvinist.

Calvino, *n.m.* Calvin.
calvo, -va, *a.* bald; barren; threadbare.—*n.f.* bald spot; clearing.
calza, *n.f.* hose.—*pl.* tights.
calzado, -da, *a.* shod.—*n.m.* footwear.—*n.f.* causeway; Roman road.
calzador, *n.m.* shoehorn.
calzar [C], *v.t.* wear (*shoes*); put on (*shoes*); wedge; fit.—*v.r.* put on (*shoes etc.*); (*fig.*) make one's fortune.
calzo, *n.m.* (*mech.*) wedge, chock; shoe.
calzón, *n.m.*, **calzones,** *n.m.pl.* breeches.
calzonarias, *n.f.pl.* (*S.A.*) braces, (*U.S.*) suspenders.
calzonazos, *n.m.* *inv.* weak-willed husband *or* man.
calzoncillos, *n.m.pl.* underpants.
callada, *n.f.* silence; lull; **de —** or **a las calladas,** stealthily, on the quiet.
callado, -da, *a.* silent; secret; vague.
callandico, callandito, *adv.* stealthily, on the quiet.
callar, *v.t.* silence; keep quiet; not mention.— *v.i., v.r.* be silent; become silent.
calle, *n.f.* street; (*fam.*) way out (*of predicament*); — **mayor,** main street; **hacer —** or **abrir —,** clear the way.
calleja, *n.f.* narrow street; (*fam.*) bolt-hole, way out.
callejear, *v.i.* loiter about.
callejeo, *n.m.* loitering, loafing.
callejero, -ra, *a.* of the street, low.—*n.m.f.* gadabout, loiterer.
callejón, *n.m.* alley; — **sin salida,** blind alley.
callejuela, *n.f.* alley, side-street; (*fam.*) way-out, dodge.
callicida, *n.m.* corn-remover.
callo, *n.m.* corn, callosity.—*pl.* cooked tripe.
calloso, -sa, *a.* calloused, horny.
cama, *n.f.* bed; bedding; **caer en (la) —,** fall ill; **guardar (la) —,** be ill in bed.
camada, *n.f.* litter, brood; layer.
camafeo, *n.m.* cameo.
camaleón, *n.m.* chameleon.
camándula, *n.f.* rosary; (*fam.*) trickery.
camandulero, -ra, *a.* (*fam.*) slippery, sly.— *n.m.f.* (*fam.*) sly one, slippery customer.
cámara, *n.f.* chamber, hall; (*aer.*) cockpit; (*jur.*) camera; berth; — **de aire,** inner tube; — **de comercio,** chamber of commerce.
camarada, *n.m.f.* comrade, friend.
camaradería, *n.f.* comradeship.
camaranchón, *n.m.* attic.
camarera, *n.f.* waitress; chamber maid; lady-in-waiting.
camarero, *n.m.* waiter; steward; valet.
camarilla, *n.f.* pressure group, clique.
camarín, *n.m.* small room; niche; (*theat.*) dressing room.
camarlengo, *n.m.* chamberlain.
cámaro, camarón, *n.m.* shrimp.
camarote, *n.m.* (*naut.*) cabin.
camasquince, *n.m.* *inv.* (*fam.*) busybody.
camastro, *n.m.* bunk, rickety bed.
camastrón, -rona, *n.m.f.* (*fam.*) sly person, double-dealer.
cambalachear, *v.t.* (*fam.*) swap, swop.
cámbaro, *n.m.* crayfish.
cambiadiscos, *n.m.* *inv.* record changer.
cambial, *a.* (*com.*) rel. to exchange.
cambiamiento, *n.m.* change, alteration.

cambiante, *a.* changing.—*n.m.f.* money-changer.
cambiar, *v.t.* change; exchange (*por,* for); convert (*en,* into).—*v.i.* alter, change.—*v.r.* change, be changed; — *de propósito,* change plans.
cambio, *n.m.* change; exchange; (*com.*) share quotation; exchange rate; (*rail.*) switch; (*mech.*) — *de marchas,* gear change; *en* —, on the other hand; *libre* —, free trade.
cambista, *n.m.* money-changer; banker.
Camboya, *n.f.* Cambodia.
camboyano, -na, *a., n.m.f.* Cambodian.
camelar, *v.t.* (*fam.*) flirt with; seduce.
camelia, *n.f.* camelia.
camelo, *n.m.* (*fam.*) flirtation; (*fam.*) let-down.
camello, *n.m.* camel.
Camerón, *n.m.* Cameroons.
camilla, *n.f.* stretcher; couch.
camillero, *n.m.* stretcher-bearer.
caminante, *a.* walking.—*n.m.f.* walker, traveller.
caminar, *v.t., v.i.* travel, walk.
caminata, *n.f.* (*fam.*) stroll, trip.
caminero, -ra, *a.* rel. to roads.
camino, *n.m.* road; *a medio* —, half-way; *en* —, on the way.
camión, *n.m.* lorry, (*U.S.*) truck; (*S.A.*) bus.
camioneta, *n.f.* van, small truck.
camisa, *n.f.* shirt; chemise; (*bot.*) skin; lining; mantle; — *de fuerza,* strait jacket.
camisería, *n.f.* draper's; haberdashery.
camiseta, *n.f.* vest, (*U.S.*) undershirt.
camisola, *n.f.* blouse, shirt (*ruffled*).
camisón, *n.m.* nightdress.
camomila, *n.f.* camomile.
camorra, *n.f.* (*fam.*) row, quarrel.
campal, *a.* pitched (*battle*).
campamento, *n.m.* camp, encampment.
campana, *n.f.* bell.
campanada, *n.f.* stroke of bell; (*fig.*) scandal.
campanario, *n.m.* belfry, steeple.
campanear, *v.t., v.i.* peal, chime.
campaneo, *n.m.* peal, pealing.
campanilla, *n.f.* hand bell; door-bell; bubble; tassel.
campanillear, *v.i.* tinkle, ring.
campante, *a.* outstanding; (*fam.*) glad, self-satisfied.
campanudo, -da, *a.* bell-shaped; (*fam.*) high-flown.
campaña, *n.f.* open countryside; campaign; (*naut.*) cruise.
campar, *v.i.* stand out; (*mil.*) camp; — *por su respeto,* act independently.
campeador, *n.m.* valiant warrior (*said of* **El Cid**).
campear, *v.t.* (*S.A.*) survey, look for.—*v.i.* campaign; graze.
campechanía, campechanería, *n.f.* (*fam.*) heartiness.
campechano, -na, *a.* (*fam.*) hearty, lively.
campeón, *n.m.* champion.
campeonato, *n.m.* championship.
campesino, -na, *a.* rural, rustic.—*n.m.f.* peasant.
campestre, *a.* rural.
campiña, *n.f.* farmlands.
campo, *n.m.* country, countryside; field;

background; *a — traviesa* or *travieso,* across country; *dar — a,* give free range to.
camposanto, *n.m.* cemetery, grave-yard.
camueso, -sa, *n.m.* pippin tree.—*n.f.* pippin apple.
camuflaje, *n.m.* camouflage.
camuflar, *v.t.* camouflage.
can, *n.m.* dog, hound; khan.
cana, *n.f.* grey hair; *echar una — al aire,* have a good time; *peinar canas,* be getting on (*old*).
Canadá, *n.m.* Canada.
canadiense, *a., n.m.f.* Canadian.
canal, *n.m.* canal; channel.—*n.f.* gutter; trough; conduit, pipe; carcass; *el Canal de la Mancha,* the English Channel.
canalización, *n.f.* canalization; conduits, piping; (*elec.*) wiring.
canalizar [C], *v.t.* channel, canalize.
canalón, *n.m.* water spout.
canalla, *n.f.* rabble, canaille.—*n.m.* (*fig.*) swine, rotter.
canallada, *n.f.* filthy trick.
canallesco, -ca, *a.* low, swinish.
canapé, *n.m.* sofa, settee.
Canarias, *n.f.* Canaries, Canary Islands.
canariense, *a., n.m.f.* Canarian.
canario, -ria, *a., n.m.f.* Canarian; canary (*bird*).
canasta, *n.f.* large basket; canasta; layette; bottom drawer.
canastillo, -lla, *n.m.f.* small basket, wicker tray.
canasto, *n.m.* tall round basket.
cancamurria, *n.f.* (*fam.*) the blues.
cancamusa, *n.f.* (*fam.*) stunt, trick.
cancán, *n.m.* cancan.
cáncano, *n.m.* (*fam.*) louse, bug.
cancel, *n.m.* porch; (*C.A.*) screen.
cancela, *n.f.* lattice gate.
cancelación, canceladura, *n.f.* cancellation.
cancelar, *v.t.* cancel.
cancelario, *n.m.* chancellor.
Cáncer, *n.m.* (*astr.*) Cancer; **cáncer,** *n.m.* cancer.
cancerar, *v.t.* canker.—*v.r.* become cancerous.
canceroso, -sa, *a.* cancerous.
cancilla, *n.f.* half-door.
canciller, *n.m.* chancellor.
cancilleresco, -ca, *a.* rel. to chancellery.
cancillería, *n.f.* chancellery; Foreign Ministry.
canción, *n.f.* song; (*lit.*) canzone.
cancionero, *n.m.* song-book.
cancionista, *n.m.f.* song-writer; singer.
cancro, *n.m.* canker.
cancha, *n.f.* arena; (*S.A.*) open space.
cancho, *n.m.* boulder.
candado, *n.m.* padlock.
cande, *a.* candied.
candela, *n.f.* candle; (*fam.*) light.
candelabro, *n.m.* candelabra.
Candelaria, *n.f.* Candlemas.
candelero, *n.m.* candlestick; (*fig.*) high office.
candelilla, *n.f.* small candle; (*med.*) catheter; (*S.A.*) glow-worm, firefly, weevil.
candelizo, *n.m.* icicle.
candencia, *n.f.* white heat.
candente, *a.* white hot; *cuestión* —, burning question.
candi, *a.* candied; *azúcar* —, sugar candy.
candidato, -ta, *n.m.f.* applicant; candidate.
candidatura, *n.f.* candidature.

candidez, *n.f.* whiteness; candour; naïveté.
cándido, -da, *a.* candid, naïve; white.
candil, *n.m.* oil lamp.
candileja, *n.f.* tiny lamp.—*pl.* (*theat.*) footlights.
candor, *n.m.* candour; whiteness.
candoroso, -sa, *a.* frank, sincere.
canelo, -la, *a.* cinnamon coloured.—*n.f.* cinnamon; (*fam.*) peach, fine thing.
canelón, *n.m.* spout; icicle; piping (*sewing*).
canevá, *n.m.* canvas.
cangrejo, *n.m.* crab; crayfish.
canguro, *n.m.* kangaroo.
caníbal, *a.,* *n.m.f.* cannibal.
canibalino, -na, *a.* cannibalistic.
canibalismo, *n.m.* cannibalism.
canica, *n.f.* marble (*toy*).
canicie, *n.f.* whiteness (*of hair*).
canícula, *n.f.* (*astr.*) dog star; dog days.
canijo, -ja, *a.* ailing, infirm.—*n.m.f.* weakling, invalid.
canilla, *n.f.* arm *or* shin bone; tap, cock; bobbin.
canino, -na, *a.* canine.
canje, *n.m.* exchange.
canjear, *v.t.* exchange.
cano, -na, *a.* grey, hoary.
canoa, *n.f.* canoe.
canon, *n.m.* (*pl.* **cánones**) (*eccl.*) canon precept.—*pl.* canon law.
canónico, -ca, *a.* canonical.
canónigo, *n.m.* (*eccl.*) canon (*person*).
canonizar [C], *v.t.* (*eccl.*) canonize.
canonjía, *n.f.* canonry; (*fam.*) soft job.
canoro, -ra, *a.* melodious.
canoso, -sa, *a.* grey- *or* white-haired.
cansado, -da, *a.* tired, weary; wearisome.
cansancio, *n.m.* tiredness, weariness.
cansar, *v.t.* tire, weary.—*v.r.* get tired.
cansera, *n.f.* (*fam.*) wearisome pest.
cantábrico, -ca, *a.* Cantabrian.
cantada, *n.f.* (*mus.*) cantata; (*C.A.*) folk song.
cantal, *n.m.* stone block; stony ground.
cantaleta, *n.f.* tin-pan serenade, mockery.
cantante, *a.* singing.—*n.m.f.* professional singer.
cantar, *n.m.* song; singing.—*v.t., v.i.* sing; (*fam.*) peach, squeal.
cantarín, *a.* singing.—*n.m.f.* singer.
cántaro, *n.m.* pitcher; **llover a cántaros,** rain cats and dogs.
cantata, *n.f.* (*mus.*) cantata.
cantatriz, *n.f.* (*pl.* **-ices**) singer.
cante, *n.m.* singing; — **hondo,** — **flamenco,** Andalusian style of gypsy singing.
cantera, *n.f.* quarry; (*fig.*) gift, talent.
cantero, *n.m.* stonemason.
cántico, *n.m.* canticle; song.
cantidad, *n.f.* quantity.
cantiga, *n.f.* lay, song.
cantilena, *n.f.* song, ballad; **la misma —,** (*fam.*) the same old song.
cantillo, *n.m.* pebble; corner.
cantimplora, *n.f.* water bottle, canteen.
cantina, *n.f.* canteen, buffet; wine cellar.
cantizal, *n.m.* stony ground.
canto (1), *n.m.* song; canto; singing.
canto (2), *n.m.* edge, corner; stone; pebble.
cantonada, *n.f.* corner; **dar — a,** (*fam.*) shake off, dodge.
cantonear, *v.i.* lounge on street corners.
cantonera, *n.f.* corner piece *or* guard.

cantor, -ra, *a.* sweet-singing.—*n.m.* songster, choirmaster; bard.—*n.f.* songstress.
Cantórbery, *n.m.* Canterbury.
cantoso, -sa, *a.* rocky, stony.
cantueso, *n.m.* lavender.
canturrear, canturriar, *v.i.* (*fam.*) hum, sing.
canturreo, *n.m.,* **canturria,** *n.f.* humming, singing.
caña, *n.f.* cane; reed, stalk; pipe, tube; beer glass; — **del timón,** helm.
cañada, *n.f.* track; dale.
cañamazo, *n.m.* canvas, hempcloth.
cáñamo, *n.m.* hemp.
cañavera, *n.f.* reed-grass.
cañería, *n.f.* pipe(s); — **maestra,** main.
cañero, *n.m.* pipe-maker; plumber.
cañizal, *n.m.* reed bed.
caño, *n.m.* pipe; (*naut.*) channel.
cañón, *n.m.* gun-barrel; cannon; shaft; quill; gorge, canyon.
cañonazo, *n.m.* artillery shot; (*fam.*) big surprise.
cañonería, *n.f.* cannon, artillery.
caoba, *n.f.* mahogany.
caolín, *n.m.* kaolin.
caos, *n.m. sg.* chaos.
caótico, -ca, *a.* chaotic.
capa, *n.f.* cloak, coat; layer; **de — caída,** in a bad way, in decline.
capacidad, *n.f.* capacity.
capacitar, *v.t.* enable; empower.
capacho, *n.m.* tool basket.
capar, *v.t.* geld.
caparazón, *n.m.* caparison; shell (*of insects etc.*); chicken carcass.
capataz, *n.m.* foreman.
capaz, *a.* (*pl.* **-aces**) capable; capacious; holding.
capcioso, -sa, *a.* captious.
capear, *v.t.* (*taur.*) wave the cape **at;** (*fam.*) fool.
capellán, *n.m.* chaplain, priest.
Caperucita Roja, *n.f.* Red Riding Hood.
caperuza, *n.f.* hood.
capilla, *n.f.* chapel; — **ardiente,** funeral chapel; **en (la) —,** (*fam.*) on tenterhooks.
capillo, *n.m.* baby's hood; toe-cap.
capirote, *n.m.* conical hood; hood, (*U.S.*) top (*of car*); fillip.
capital, *a.* capital, main; basic, important.—*n.m.* capital (*money*).—*n.f.* capital (*city*).
capitalismo, *n.m.* capitalism.
capitalista, *a.,* *n.m.f.* capitalist.
capitalizar [C], *v.t.* capitalize.
capitán, *n.m.* (*mil.*) captain; (*aer.*) squadron leader; — **de corbeta,** (*naut.*) lieutenant-commander; — **de fragata,** (*naut.*) commander; — **de navío,** (*naut.*) captain.
capitana, *n.f.* (*naut.*) flagship; (*fam.*) captain's wife.
capitanear, *v.t.* lead, captain.
capitanía, *n.f.* captaincy.
capitel, *n.m.* (*arch.*) capital.
Capitolio, *n.m.* Capitol.
capitulación, *n.f.* capitulation.—*pl.* marriage contract.
capitular, *a.* capitular.—*v.t.* accuse; settle.—*v.i.* capitulate.
capítulo, *n.m.* chapter.
capón, *n.m.* capon; rap; faggot.
caporal, *n.m.* overseer.

capotaje, *n.m.* overturning.
capotar, *v.i.* overturn.
capote, *n.m.* cloak; greatcoat; cover.
capotear, *v.t.* dodge; wave (*cloak*); (*theat.*) cut.
Capricornio, *n.m.* Capricorn.
capricho, *n.m.* caprice, whim.
caprichoso, -sa, *a.* whimsical, capricious.
caprino, -na, *a.* caprine, goatish.
cápsula, *n.f.* capsule.
captación, *n.f.* attraction; catchment; (*rad.*) tuning.
captar, *v.t.* catch; attract, win over; (*rad.*) tune in to.—*v.r.* win, attract.
captura, *n.f.* capture.
capturar, *v.t.* capture.
capucha, *n.f.* cowl; circumflex (^).
capuchino, *n.m.* (*eccl., zool.*) capuchin.
capucho, *n.m.* hood; cowl.
capullo, *n.m.* bud, bloom; cocoon.
caqui, *a., n.m.* khaki.
cara, *n.f.* face; — **de hereje,** (*fam.*) ugly mug; — **de pascua,** cheerful face; **a — o cruz,** heads **or** tails.
carabela, *n.f.* caravel.
carabina, *n.f.* carbine; (*joc.*) chaperon.
carabinero, *n.m.* customs guard.
caracol, *n.m.* snail; curl; spiral.
carácter, *n.m.* (*pl.* **caracteres**) character; nature.
característico, -ca, *a., n.f.* characteristic.
caracterizar [C], *v.t.* characterize.
carado, -da, *a.* faced.
¡caramba! *interj.* dear me! well, well!
carámbano, *n.m.* icicle.
carambola, *n.f.* cannon (*billiards*); (*fam.*) ruse.
caramelo, *n.m.* caramel.
caramillo, *n.m.* thin flute; jumble; false rumour.
carantamaula, *n.f.* (*fam.*) ugly mug.
carantoña, *n.f.* (*fam.*) ugly mug; (*fam.*) dolled-up old hag.—*pl.* wheedling.
carapacho, *n.m.* shell, carapace.
carátula, *n.f.* mask; (*fig.*) the boards, theatre.
caravana, *n.f.* caravan.
caray, *n.m.* tortoise.—*interj.* gosh!
carbohidrato, *n.m.* carbohydrate.
carbólico, -ca, *a.* carbolic.
carbón, *n.m.* charcoal; coal.
carbonato, *n.m.* carbonate.
carbonera, *n.f.* charcoal kiln; coal shed.
carbonero, -ra, *a.* rel. to coal.—*n.m.* coalman; (*orn.*) great *or* coal tit.
carbónico, -ca, *a.* carbonic.
carbonilla, *n.f.* coal dust; coking, carbonizing (*car*).
carbonizar [C], *v.t., v.r.* carbonize, char.
carbono, *n.m.* (*chem.*) carbon.
carborundo, *n.m.* carborundum.
carbunclo, *n.m.* carbuncle.
carburador, *n.m.* carburettor.
carburo, *n.m.* carbide.
carcaj, *n.m.* quiver, holder.
carcajada, *n.f.* guffaw.
carcamán, *n.m.* (*naut.*) old tub.
cárcava, *n.f.* gully, ditch; grave.
cárcel, *n.f.* prison; clamp.
carcelario, -ria, *a.* rel. to prison.
carcelería, *n.f.* imprisonment.
carcelero, *n.m.* jailer.

carcoma, *n.f.* woodworm; (*fig.*) **gnawing worry.**
carcomer, *v.t.* gnaw away.—*v.r.* become worm-eaten.
cardenal, *n.m.* cardinal; bruise.
cardenillo, *n.m.* verdigris.
cárdeno, -na, *a.* violet, rich purple.
cardíaco, -ca, *a.* cardiac.
cardinal, *a.* cardinal.
cardiografía, *n.f.* cardiography.
cardo, *n.m.* thistle.
carear, *v.t.* bring face to face.—*v.r.* face (*con,* up to).
carecer [9], *v.i.* lack (*de*), be lacking (*de,* in).
carencia, *n.f.* need; shortage.
carente, *a.* lacking (*de,* in), devoid (*de,* of).
careo, *n.m.* confronting.
carestía, *n.f.* shortage, scarcity; rising prices.
careta, *n.f.* mask.
carey, *n.m.* turtle.
carga, *n.f.* load; charge.
cargadero, *n.m.* loading bay.
cargamento, *n.m.* load, cargo.
cargante, *a.* (*fam.*) crushing, boring.
cargar [B], *v.t.* load, overload; charge; (*fam.*) bore.—*v.r.* (*fam.*) get rid (*de,* of).
cargazón, *n.f.* cargo; heaviness (*health, weather*).
cargo, *n.m.* load; charge; office, duty; **hacerse — de,** undertake (to).
cargoso, -sa, *a.* onerous, bothersome.
cari, *n.m.* (*cul.*) curry.
cariacontecido, -da, *a.* woebegone.
el Caribe, *n.m.* the Caribbean.
caribe, *a., n.m.* Carib; (*fig.*) savage.
caricatura, *n.f.* caricature, cartoon.
caricia, *n.f.* caress.
caridad, *n.f.* charity.
caridoliente, *a.* glum.
carilucio, -cia, *a.* shiny-faced.
carillón, *n.m.* carillon, chime.
carinegro, -gra, *a.* swarthy.
cariño, *n.m.* love, affection; darling.
cariñoso, -sa, *a.* loving, affectionate.
caritativo, -va, *a.* charitable.
cariz, *n.m.* aspect, look.
carlinga, *n.f.* (*aer.*) cockpit; saloon.
carlismo, *n.m.* Carlism.
carlista, *a., n.m.f.* Carlist.
Carlomagno, *n.m.* Charlemagne.
Carlos, *n.m.* Charles.
carmelita, *a., n.m.f.* Carmelite.
Carmen, *n.f.* Carmen; Carmelite Order; **carmen,** *n.m.* song, poem, carmen; villa.
carmesí, *a., n.m.* (*pl.* **-íes**) crimson.
carmín, *n.m.* carmine, cochineal; wild rose; lip-stick.
carnadura, *n.f.* (*low*) beefiness, muscularity.
carnal, *a.* carnal; related by blood.—*n.m.* non-Lenten period.
carnaval, *n.m.* carnival; **martes de Carnaval,** Shrove Tuesday.
carnavalesco, -ca, *a.* rel. to carnival.
carne, *n.f.* flesh, meat; **echar carnes,** to put on weight; **— de gallina,** goose pimples; **ser uña y —,** be very intimate.
carnestolendas, *n.f.pl.* Shrovetide.
carnet, *n.m.* identity card; licence; note book.
carnicería, *n.f.* butcher's shop; butchery.
carnicero, -ra, *a.* carnivorous.—*n.m.* butcher.
carniseco, -ca, *a.* lean, scraggy.

carnívoro, -ra, *a.* carnivorous.—*n.m.* carnivore.
carnoso, -sa, *a.* fleshy, meaty.
caro, -ra, *a.* dear.—*adv.* dear, dearly.
carolingio, -gia, *a.* Carolingian.
Carón, Caronte, *n.m.* Charon.
carpa, *n.f.* (*ichth.*) carp; (*S.A.*) tent.
carpeta, *n.f.* folder, portfolio.
carpetazo, *n.m.* *dar — a,* shelve, file away.
carpintería, *n.f.* carpentry, joinery; carpenter's shop.
carpintero, *n.m.* carpenter, joiner; (*orn.*) woodpecker.
carpir, *v.t.* (*S.A.*) weed.
carraca, *n.f.* (*naut.*) carrack, old tub; rattle.
carrada, *n.f.* cartload.
carrasca, *n.f.* holm oak.
carraspear, *v.i.* croak, be hoarse.
carraspeño, -ña, *a.* gruff, hoarse.
carrera, *n.f.* race, course; career; row, line; way; girder, beam; ladder (*in stocking*); *— armamentista,* arms race.
carrerista, *n.m.f.* punter, race-goer; racer.
carrero, *n.m.* carter.
carreta, *n.f.* ox-cart.
carrete, *n.m.* bobbin; fishing reel; (*elec.*) coil; (*phot.*) spool.
carretear, *v.t.* haul, cart; (*aer.*) (also *v.i.*) taxi.
carretera, *n.f.* road, highway.
carretero, *n.m.* carter, cartwright.
carretilla, *n.f.* truck, wheelbarrow; *saber de —,* know parrot-fashion.
carretón, *n.m.* pushcart; *— de remolque,* trailer.
carril, *n.m.* rail; lane; rut.
carrilera, *n.f.* rut.
carrizo, *n.m.* reed-grass.
el Carro, *n.m.* (*astr.*) the Plough.
carro, *n.m.* cart; (*mech.*) carriage; truck; (*S.A.*) car.
carrocería, *n.f.* body shop; body-work.
carrocero, *n.m.* coachbuilder.
carroña, *n.f.* carrion.
carroñ(os)o, -ñ(os)a, *a.* rotten, putrid.
carroza, *n.f.* coach, carriage.
carruaje, *n.m.* vehicle.
carruco, *n.m.* primitive cart.
carrucha, *n.f.* pulley.
carta, *n.f.* letter; card; chart; charter; *a — cabal,* thoroughly, completely; *— blanca,* carte blanche.
cartaginense, cartaginés, -nesa, *a.* Carthaginian.
Cartago, *n.f.* Carthage.
cartapacio, *n.m.* writing-case; dossier; notebook; satchel.
cartear, *v.r.* correspond (with), write letters to (*con*).
cartel, *n.m.* poster, placard; cartel.
cartelera, *n.f.* bill-board.
carteo, *n.m.* correspondence.
cárter, *n.m.* (*mech.*) casing, case.
cartera, *n.f.* wallet; brief-case; (*pol.*) portfolio.
carterista, *n.m.* pickpocket.
cartero, *n.m.* postman.
cartesiano, -na, *n.m.f.* Cartesian.
cartílago, *n.m.* cartilage, gristle.
cartilla, *n.f.* note; primer (*book*); dossier.
cartografía, *n.f.* cartography, map-making.
cartón, *n.m.* cardboard; carton; cartoon; papier-mâché.
cartoné, *n.m.* boards (*bookbinding*).

cartucho, *n.m.* cartridge; paper cornet.
Cartuja, *n.f.* Carthusian order.
cartujo, -ja, *a., n.m.f.* Carthusian.
cartulario, *n.m.* cartulary.
cartulina, *n.f.* fine cardboard.
carura, *n.f.* (*S.A.*) [CARESTIA].
casa, *n.f.* house; home; *— de correos,* post office; *a —,* home (*to one's home*); *en —,* at home; *poner —,* set up house.
casaca, *n.f.* dress coat.
casación, *n.f.* cassation.
casadero, -ra, *a.* marriageable.
casal, *n.m.* country house; (*S.A.*) couple, pair.
casalicio, *n.m.* dwelling, house.
casamentero, -ra, *a.* match-making.—*n.m.f.* match-maker.
casamiento, *n.m.* wedding, marriage.
casar (1), *n.m.* hamlet.
casar (2), *v.t.* marry, marry off; (*jur.*) annul.—*v.i.* marry; to match (*con*).—*v.r. casarse con,* marry, get married to.
casarón, *n.m.* big rambling house.
casatienda, *n.f.* dwelling shop.
casca, *n.f.* grape-skin; tanning bark.
cascabel, *n.m.* tinkle bell.
cascabelear, *v.t.* (*fam.*) bamboozle.—*v.i.* (*fam.*) be feather-brained; (*S.A.*) tinkle, jingle.
cascabelero, -ra, *a.* (*fam.*) feather-brained. —*n.m.f.* (*fam.*) feather-brain.—*n.m.* baby's rattle.
cascada, *n.f.* cascade.
cascajo, *n.m.* gravel; nuts; (*fam.*) junk, old wreck.
cascanueces, *n.m. inv.* nut-crackers.
cascar [A], *v.t.* split, crack; (*fam.*) bust.—*v.i.* chatter.—*v.r.* break (*voice*); (*fam.*) fail (*health*).
cáscara, *n.f.* shell, rind, bark; cascara.
cascarón, *n.m.* eggshell.
cascarria, *n.f.* mud-splash.
casco, *n.m.* helmet; skull; potsherd; (*naut.*) hull, hulk; *— urbano,* built-up area.—*pl.* (*fam.*) brains, head.
cascote, *n.m.* rubble, debris.
casería, *n.f.* manor, farm; (*S.A.*) clientele.
caserío, *n.m.* hamlet.
casero, -ra, *a.* home-made, homely.—*n.m.f.* tenant; caretaker.—*n.m.* landlord.—*n.f.* landlady.
caserón, *n.m.* big rambling house.
caseta, *n.f.* bathing hut.
casi, *adv.* almost, nearly.
casilla, *n.f.* hut, kiosk; pigeon-hole; square (*chess*).
casillero, *n.m.* pigeon-holes.
casino, *n.m.* club, casino.
caso, *n.m.* event; (*jur., med., gram.*) case; matter; *al —,* to the point; *hacer — de,* take notice of.
casorio, *n.m.* (*fam.*) hasty marriage.
caspa, *n.f.* scurf, dandruff.
¡cáspita! *interj.* by Jove!
casquete, *n.m.* helmet; skull-cap.
casquijo, *n.m.* gravel.
casquillo, *n.m.* ferrule, tip.
casquivano, -na, *a.* feather-brained.
casta, *n.f.* caste, lineage.
castañeta, *n.f.* snap, click; castanet.
castañetazo, *n.m.* click, snap, crack.
castañetear, *v.t.* snap (*fingers*).—*v.i.* play castanets; chatter (*teeth*); crack (*joints*).

castaño

castaño, -ña, a. chestnut.—n.m. chestnut tree; — de Indias, horse chestnut.—n.f. chestnut; bun (of hair).
castañuela, n.f. castanet.
castellanismo, n.m. Castilianism.
castellanizar [C], v.t. Castilianize, Hispanicize.
castellano, -na, a., n.m.f. Castilian; (S.A.) Spanish.
casticidad, n.m. purity, correctness.
casticismo, n.m. purism.
castidad, n.f. chastity.
castigar [B], v.t. punish.
castigo, n.m. punishment.
Castilla, n.f. Castile; — la Nueva (la Vieja), New (Old) Castile.
castillejo, n.m. scaffolding.
castillo, n.m. castle.
castizo, -za, a. pure (language, blood).
casto, -ta, a. chaste.
castor, n.m. beaver.
castrar, v.t. castrate; prune.
castrense, a. military, army.
casual, a. accidental, casual; (gram.) rel. to case.
casualidad, n.f. accident, chance.
casuca, casucha, n.f. shanty, slum house.
casuista, a., n.m.f. casuist.
casuístico, -ca, a. casuistic(al).—n.f. casuistry.
casulla, n.f. chasuble.
cata, n.f. taste, sample; sampling.
catacaldos, n.m.f. inv. (fam.) rolling stone; meddler.
cataclismo, n.m. cataclysm.
catacumba, n.f. catacomb.
catadura, n.f. sampling; (obs.) mien.
catafalco, n.m. catafalque.
catalán, -lana, a., n.m.f. Catalan, Catalonian.
catalanismo, n.m. Catalanism; Catalan nationalism.
catalanista, n.m.f. Catalan nationalist; Catalan scholar.
catalejo, n.m. spyglass.
Catalina, n.f. Catherine.
catálisis, n.f. catalysis.
catalizador, n.m. catalyst.
catalogación, n.f. cataloguing.
catalogar [B], v.t. catalogue.
catálogo, n.m. catalogue.
Cataluña, n.f. Catalonia.
catamarán, n.m. catamaran.
cataplasma, n.f. poultice.
¡cataplum! interj. bump!
catapulta, n.f. catapult.
catar, v.t. taste, sample; (obs.) look at.
catarata, n.f. cataract.
catarro, n.m. heavy cold; catarrh.
catarroso, -sa, a. prone to catarrh.
catarsis, n.f. catharsis.
catástrofe, n.f. catastrophe.
catastrófico, -ca, a. catastrophic.
catavinos, n.m. inv. wine-taster; (fam.) pub-crawler.
catear, v.t. seek; sample; (S.A.) search.
catecismo, n.m. catechism.
catecúmeno, -na, a., n.m.f. catechumen.
cátedra, n.f. cathedra, chair, professorship.
catedral, n.f. cathedral.
catedrático, -ca, n.m.f. professor.
categoría, n.f. category.
categórico, -ca, a. categorical.

catequesis, n.f., catequismo, n.m. religious instruction.
catequista, n.m.f. catechist.
catequizar [C], v.t. catechize.
caterva, n.f. throng, mob.
cateto, -ta, n.m.f. (pej.) bumpkin.
catilinaria, n.f. violent diatribe.
cátodo, n.m. cathode.
catolicidad, n.f. catholicity; Catholicity.
catolicismo, n.m. Catholicism.
católico, -ca, a., n.m.f. catholic; Catholic; (fam.) no estar muy —, to feel ill.
Catón, n.m. Cato; catón, n.m. reading primer.
catorce, a., n.m. fourteen.
catorceno, -na, a. fourteenth.
catre, n.m. cot; — de tijera, camp bed.
caucásico, -ca, a. Caucasian.
Cáucaso, n.m. Caucasus.
cauce, n.m. river bed; ditch; course.
caución, n.f. caution; pledge.
caucionar, v.t. caution; guard against.
cauchal, n.m. rubber plantation.
cauchero, -ra, a. rubber.—n.m.f. rubber worker.
caucho, n.m. rubber; — esponjoso, sponge rubber.
caudal, a. large.—n.m. wealth; volume (of water).
caudaloso, -sa, a. of heavy flow (rivers).
caudatorio, n.m. bishop's attendant; (fam.) yes-man.
caudillaje, n.m. leadership; (S.A.) political bossism.
caudillo, n.m. leader; (S.A.) political boss.
causa, n.f. cause; lawsuit; a — de, on account of.
causal, a. causal.
causalidad, n.f. causality.
causante, a. causing; (fam.) responsible.—n.m.f. litigant.
causar, v.t. cause; (jur.) sue.
causativo, -va, a. causative.
causticidad, n.f. causticness.
cáustico, -ca, a. caustic.
cautela, n.f. caution, heed; artfulness.
cautelar, v.t., v.r. guard (de, against).
cauteloso, -sa, a. wary; cunning.
cauterizar [C], v.t. cauterize.
cautivar, v.t. capture; captivate.
cautiverio, n.m., cautividad, n.f. captivity.
cautivo, -va, a., n.m.f. captive.
cauto, -ta, a. cautious.
cavadura, n.f. digging.
cavar, v.t. dig.
cavazón, n.f. digging.
caverna, n.f. cavern.
cavernícola, n.m.f. cave-dweller.
cavernoso, -sa, a. cavernous.
cavial, caviar, n.m. caviar.
cavidad, n.f. cavity.
cavilación, n.f. cavilling.
cavilar, v.t. cavil at.
caviloso, -sa, a. captious, cavilling.
cayada, n.f., cayado, n.m. shepherd's crook; crozier.
Cayena, n.f. Cayenne.
cayente, a. falling.
caza, n.f. hunt, chase; game, quarry; a — de, hunting for; — de grillos, wild-goose chase; — mayor, big game.—n.m. (aer.) fighter.

cazabe, *n.m.* cassava.
cazabombadero, *n.m.* (*aer.*) fighter-bomber.
cazador, -ra, *a.* hunting.—*n.m.* hunter; (*mil.*) chasseur; — **furtivo,** poacher.—*n.f.* huntress.
cazar [C], *v.t.* hunt, chase; (*fam.*) catch, take in; (*fam.*) wangle.
cazatorpedero, *n.m.* (*naut.*) destroyer.
cazcalear, *v.i.* (*fam.*) bumble about.
cazcorvo, -va, *a.* bowlegged.
cazo, *n.m.* ladle; saucepan.
cazolero, a.m. old-womanish.—*n.m.* fuss-pot, "old woman".
cazoleta, *n.f.* pipe-bowl; sword guard; pan.
cazuela, *n.f.* casserole, pan, dish; (*theat.*) upper gallery, (*obs.*) women's gallery.
cazumbre, *n.m.* oakum.
cazurro, -rra, *a.* (*obs.*) vulgar; (*fam.*) grumpy.—*n.m.* (*obs.*) low minstrel.
ce, *n.f.* name of letter C; — **por be,** in detail. —*interj.* hey!
cebada, *n.f.* barley.
cebadura, *n.f.* fattening; priming.
cebar, *v.t.* fatten (*cattle etc.*); stoke; bait; prime; start (*a motor*); nourish (*passions*).— *v.i.* bite (*nail, screw*).—*v.r.* rage (*disease*); **cebarse en,** gloat over; devote oneself to.
cebellina, *n.f.* sable (fur).
cebo, *n.m.* animal feed; bait; priming.
cebolla, *n.f.* onion; bulb; nozzle.
cebón, -bona, *a.* fattened.—*n.m.* fattened animal.
cebra, *n.f.* zebra.
cebrado, -da, *a.* zebra-striped.
ceca, *only in* **de — en Meca,** *adv. phr.* hither and thither.
cecear, *v.i.* lisp; pronounce *s* as *z* [θ] in Spanish.
ceceo, *n.m.* lisp, lisping.
ceceoso, -sa, *a.* lisping.
cecial, *n.m.* dried fish.
cecina, *n.f.* dried meat.
cecografía, *n.f.* braille.
ceda (1), *n.f.* bristle.
ceda (2), *n.f.* name of letter Z.
cedazo, *n.m.* riddle, sieve.
ceder, *v.t.* give up, cede.—*v.i.* yield, give in.
cedilla, *n.f.* cedilla.
cedro, *n.m.* cedar.
cédula, *n.f.* slip, form; charter; patent.
céfiro, *n.m.* zephyr.
cegajoso, -sa, *a.* bleary, watery (*eyes*).
cegar [1B], *v.t.* blind; block up.—*v.i.* go blind.
cegarra, *a. inv.,* **cegato, -ta,** *a.* (*fam.*) short-sighted.
ceguedad, ceguera, *n.f.* blindness.
Ceilán, *n.m.* Ceylon.
ceilanés, -nesa, *a., n.m.f.* Ceylonese.
ceja, *n.f.* eyebrow; brow.
cejar, *v.i.* back; slacken off.
cejijunto, -ta, *a.* (*fam.*) heavy browed, scowling.
cejo, *n.m.* morning mist; esparto cord.
cejudo, -da, *a.* bushy-browed.
celada, *n.f.* ambush, trap; (*obs.*) helmet.
celaje, *n.m.* scattered cloud; skylight; foretaste.
celar, *v.t.* show zeal in; keep an eye on; hide; engrave.—*v.i.* watch (*sobre, por,* over).
celda, *n.f.* cell.
celebérrimo, -ma, *a. sup.* very celebrated.

celebración, *n.f.* celebration.
celebrante, *a.* celebrating.—*n.m.f.* celebrator. —*n.m.* celebrant.
celebrar, *v.t.* celebrate; be glad about, hold (*meetings etc.*).—*v.i.* be glad to.—*v.r.* take place.
célebre, *a.* celebrated; (*fam.*) cute.
celebridad, *n.f.* celebrity; celebration.
celemín, *n.m.* Spanish dry measure (= 1 *gallon approx.*).
celeridad, *n.f.* celerity.
celeste, *a.* celestial (*rel. to sky*); sky blue. —*n.m.* sky blue.
celestial, *a.* heavenly, celestial; (*fam.*) silly.
celestina, *n.f.* bawd, procuress.
celibato, *n.m.* celibacy; (*fam.*) bachelor.
célibe, *a., n.m.f.* celibate.
celidonia, *n.f.* celandine.
celo, *n.m.* zeal; rut; heat; **en —,** on heat.—*pl.* jealousy; **dar celos a,** make jealous; **tener celos,** be jealous.
celofán, -fana, celófana, *n.m.* or *f.* cellophane.
celosía, *n.f.* lattice (*over window*), grill, grating.
celoso, -sa, *a.* jealous; zealous; (*S.A.*) tricky, unsafe.
celsitud, *n.f.* grandeur; highness.
celta, *a., n.m.* Celtic.—*n.m.f.* Celt.
celtibérico, -ca, celtíbero, -ra, *a., n.m.f.* Celtiberian.
céltico, -ca, *a.* Celtic.
célula, *n.f.* (*biol., elec., pol.*) cell.
celular, *a.* cellular.
celuloide, *n.f.* celluloid.
celulosa, *n.f.* cellulose.
cementar, *v.t.* cement (*metals*); precipitate.
cementerio, *n.m.* cemetery.
cemento, cimento, *n.m.* cement; — **armado,** reinforced concrete.
cena, *n.f.* supper.
cenaaoscuras, *n.m.f. inv.* (*fam.*) recluse; skinflint.
cenáculo, *n.m.* cenacle; Cenacle.
cenacho, *n.m.* market basket.
cenador, -ra, *n.m.f.* diner.—*n.m.* summerhouse, arbour.
cenagal, *n.m.* quagmire.
cenagoso, -sa, *a.* marshy, muddy.
cenar, *v.t.* eat for supper.—*v.i.* have supper.
cenceño, -ña, *a.* thin, lean; unleavened.
cencerrear, *v.i.* clatter, clang.
cencerro, *n.m.* cow-bell.
cendal, *n.m.* gauze, tulle.
cendolilla, *n.f.* flighty girl.
cendra, cendrada, *n.f.* cupel paste.
cenicero, *n.m.* ash-tray, ash-box.
ceniciento, -ta, *a.* ashen, ashy; **la Cenicienta,** Cinderella.
cenit, *n.m.* zenith.
ceniza, *n.f.* ash, ashes.
cenizo, -za, *a.* ashy, ashen.—*n.m.f.* (*fam.*) wet-blanket, Jonah, jinx.
cenobio, *n.m.* monastery, cenoby.
cenobita, *n.m.f.* cenobite.
cenotafio, *n.m.* cenotaph.
censar, *v.t.* (*S.A.*) take a census of.
censo (1), *n.m.* census.
censo (2), *n.m.* tax; lien, mortgage; (*fam.*) burden, drain.
censor, *n.m.* censor, proctor; accountant.
censura, *n.f.* censure; censorship; auditing.
censurar, *v.t.* censure; censor.

censurista, *a.* censorious.—*n.m.f.* fault-finder.

centauro, *n.m.* centaur.

centavo, -va, *a.* hundredth.—*n.m.* hundredth; cent.

centella, *n.f.* lightning flash; (*fig.*) spark.

centellar, centellear, *v.i.* flash, sparkle.

centelleo, *n.m.* flash, sparkle.

centena, *n.f.* a hundred (*approx.*).

centenada, *n.f.,* **centenar,** *n.m.* about a hundred.

centenario, -ria, *a.* age-old, centenarian, centenary.—*n.m.f.* centenarian.—*n.m.* centenary.

centeno *n.m.* rye.

centesimal, *a.* centesimal.

centésimo, -ma, *a.* hundredth.—*n.m.* cent.

centígrado, *n.m.* centigrade.

centilitro, *n.m.* centilitre.

centímetro, *n.m.* centimetre.

céntimo, -ma, *a.* hundredth.—*n.m.* cent.

centinela, *n.f.* sentinel, guard, sentry.

centípedo, *n.m.* centipede.

centiplicado, -da, *a.* hundredfold.

centón, *n.m.* patchwork quilt; cento.

central, *a.* central.—*n.f.* head office; power station; (*tel.*) exchange.

centralismo, *n.m.* centralism.

centralista, *a., n.m.f.* centralist.

centralizar [C], *v.t., v.r.* centralize.

centrar, *v.t.* centre; square up.

céntrico, -ca, *a.* central.

centrífugo, -ga, *a.* centrifugal.—*n.f.* centrifuge.

centrípeto, -ta, *a.* centripetal.

centro, *n.m.* centre; aim, object.

Centro América, *n.f.* Central America.

centroamericano, -na, *a., n.m.f.* Central American.

centroeuropeo, -pea, *a., n.m.f.* Central European.

centuplicar [A]. *v.t.* centuple, centuplicate.

centuria, *n.f.* century.

centurión, *n.m.* centurion.

cénzalo, *n.m.* mosquito.

ceñido, -da, *a.* thrifty; close-fitting.

ceñidor, *n.m.* belt, girdle, sash.

ceñidura, *n.f.* girding; limiting.

ceñir [8K], *v.t.* gird, girdle; encircle; limit, shorten.—*v.r.* tighten one's belt; **ceñirse a,** limit oneself to.

ceño, *n.m.* frown; hoop, band.

ceñoso, -sa, ceñudo, -da, *a.* frowning, stern.

cepa, *n.f.* stump, bole, stock.

cepillar, *v.t.* brush; (*carp.*) plane.

cepillo, *n.m.* brush; (*carp.*) smoothing plane.

cepo, *n.m.* bough; stump; trap; pillory; poor-box.

cera, *n.f.* wax; wax polish.

cerámico, -ca, *a.* ceramic.—*n.f.* ceramics.

cerbatana, *n.f.* peashooter; blowgun; ear trumpet.

cerca (1), *n.f.* fence, wall; — **viva,** hedge.

cerca (2), *adv.* near, nearby; almost, about.—*prep.* near (*de*), close (*de*, to); nearly (*de*) *de* —, near, at close range.

cercado, *n.m.* enclosure; fence.

cercanía, *n.f.* nearness.—*pl.* outskirts.

cercano, -na, *a.* near, nearby, adjoining.

cercar [A], *v.t.* fence in, enclose; surround, besiege.

a cercén, *adv. phr.* completely, to the root.

cercenar, *v.t.* clip, trim, curtail.

cerciorar, *v.t.* inform, assure.—*v.r.* find out, assure oneself (*de*, about), ascertain (*de*).

cerco, *n.m.* siege; ring, rim; frame; circle; (*S.A.*) fence.

cerda, *n.f.* bristle; sow; snare.

Cerdeña, *n.f.* Sardinia.

cerdo, *n.m.* hog, pig, boar; — **marino,** porpoise.

cerdoso, -sa, *a.* bristly.

cereal, *a., n.m.* cereal.

cerebración, *n.f.* cerebration.

cerebral, *a.* cerebral.

cerebro, *n.m.* brain.

ceremonia, *n.f.* ceremony.

ceremonial, *a., n.m.* ceremonial.

ceremoniático, -ca, *a.* extremely formal.

ceremoniero, -ra, (*fam.*) **ceremonioso, -sa**) ceremonious, formal.

céreo, -rea, *a.* waxen.

cerero, *n.m.* wax dealer; chandler.

cerevisina, *n.f.* brewer's yeast.

cereza, *n.f.* cherry.

cerezal, *n.m.* cherry orchard.

cerezo, *n.m.* cherry tree.

cerilla, *n.f.* match; earwax; taper.

cerillo, *n.m.* taper; (*C.A.*) match.

cerner [2], *v.t.* sift; scan.—*v.i.* bud; drizzle.—*v.r.* hover; waddle.

cernícalo, *n.m.* (*orn.*) kestrel; (*fam.*) lout.

cernidillo, *n.m.* drizzle; waddle.

cernir [3], *v.t.* sift.

cero, *n.m.* zero.

ceroso, -sa, *a.* waxy.

cerote, *n.m.* cobbler's wax; (*fam.*) fright.

cerquillo, *n.m.* tonsure, hair ring.

cerquita, *adv.* quite near.

cerradero, -ra, *a.* locking.—*n.m.* lock, bolt; purse string.

cerrado, -da, *a.* close; overcast; heavy (*accent*).

cerradura, *n.f.* lock; closing.

cerraja, *n.f.* lock; thistle.

cerrajero, *n.m.* locksmith.

cerrajón, *n.m.* steep hill, cliff.

cerramiento, *n.m.* closing; enclosure; partition.

cerrar [1], *v.t.* shut; close, lock.—*v.r.* close.

cerrazón, *n.f.* darkness, overcast sky.

cerrejón, *n.m.* hillock.

cerrero, -ra, cerril, *a.* wild; brusque.

cerro, *n.m.* hill; backbone; **en —,** bareback; **por los cerros de Úbeda,** up hill and down dale.

cerrojillo, *n.m.* (*orn.*) coaltit.

cerrojo, *n.m.* bolt, latch.

certamen, *n.m.* contest.

certero, -ra, *a.* accurate.

certeza, certidumbre, *n.f.* certainty.

certificado, *n.m.* certificate; registered letter.

certificar [A], *v.t.* register (*mail*); certify.

certitud, *n.f.* certainty.

cerúleo, -lea, *a.* cerulean.

cerval, *a.* deerlike, rel. to deer.

cervantino, -na, *a.* Cervantine.

cervantista, *n.m.f.* Cervantist.

cervato, *n.m.* fawn.

cervecería, *n.f.* brewery; beer house.

cervecero, -ra, *a.* brewing.—*n.m.f.* brewer.

cerveza, *n.f.* beer; — **negra,** stout.

cerviz, *n.f.* (*pl.* -**ices**) neck, nape.

cesación, n.f., cesamiento, *n.m.* cessation.

cesante, *a.* forced to retire on half pay.—*n.m.f.* civil servant so retired.
cesantía, *n.f.* condition of a CESANTE.
César, *n.m.* Caesar.
cesar, *v.i.* cease, stop; — *de,* stop (+*gerund*).
cesáreo, -rea, *a.* Caesarean; caesarean.
cese, *n.m.* dismissal.
cesionario, -ria, *n.m.f.* assignee.
césped, *n.m.* turf, lawn.
cesta, *n.f.* basket.
cestería, *n.f.* basketry.
cesto, *n.m.* large basket; cestus.
cesura, *n.f.* caesura.
cetina, *n.f.* whale oil.
cetrería, *n.f.* falconry.
cetrino, -na, *a.* citrine, lemon; gloomy.
cetro, *n.m.* sceptre; roost.
ceutí, *a.* (*pl.* **-íes**) rel. to Ceuta.—*n.m.f.* native of Ceuta.
cianhídrico, -ca, *a.* hydrocyanic.
cianotipo, *n.m.* blueprint, cyanotype.
cianuro, *n.m.* cyanide.
ciática, *n.f.* sciatica.
cicatero, -ra, *a.* niggardly.—*n.m.f.* skinflint.
cicatriz, *n.f.* scar.
cicatrizar [C], *v.r.* heal (*of wound*).
cícero, *n.m.* pica type.
Cicerón, *n.m.* Cicero.
cicerone, *n.m.* cicerone.
ciceroniano, -na, *a.* Ciceronian.
cíclico, -ca, *a.* cyclic(al).
ciclismo, *n.m.* cycling; cycle racing.
ciclista, *n.m.f.* cyclist.
ciclo, *n.m.* cycle (*not bicycle*).
ciclón, *n.m.* cyclone.
Cíclope, *n.m.* Cyclops.
ciclostil(o), *n.m.* cyclostyle, mimeograph.
cicuta, *n.f.* hemlock.
cidra, *n.f.* citrus, citron.
cidrada, *n.f.* candied peel.
cidro, *n.m.* citrus *or* citron tree.
ciego, -ga, *a.* blind; blocked.—*n.m.* blindman. —*n.f.* blind woman; *a ciegas,* blindly.
cielo, *n.m.* sky; heaven; paradise; roof, canopy; *a — raso,* in the open air.
ciempiés, *n.m.* *inv.* centipede; (*fam.*) (written) drivel.
cien, *a.* a hundred.—*n.m.* (*fam.*) a hundred, [CIENTO].
ciénaga, *n.f.* bog, quagmire.
ciencia, *n.f.* science, learning.
cieno, *n.m.* mud, silt.
científico, -ca, *a.* scientific.—*n.m.f.* scientist.
ciento, *a., n.m.* a hundred, one hundred; *por —,* per cent. [*As a. before nouns* CIEN].
cierne, *n.m.* blooming, burgeoning.
cierre, *n.m.* closure; lock, latch; — *metálico,* metal roller-blind; — *cremallera or relámpago,* zip, zipper.
cierto, -ta, *a.* certain, sure; right; a certain; *por —,* certainly.
ciervo, -va, *n.m.f.* deer.—*n.m.* stag.—*n.f.* hind, doe.
cierzo, *n.m.* north wind.
cifra, *n.f.* number; code, cypher; monogram.
cifrar, *v.t.* code, cypher; summarize; — *la esperanza en,* put one's hopes in.
cigala, *n.f.* crayfish, squilla.
cigarra, *n.f.* (*ent.*) cicada.
cigarrero, -ra, *n.m.f.* cigar maker *or* seller.— *n.f.* cigar box.
cigarrillo, *n.m.* cigarette.

cigarro, *n.m.* cigar, cigarette; — *puro,* cigar.
cigoñal, *n.m.* crankshaft; winch.
cigüeña, *n.f.* (*orn.*) stork; (*mech.*) winch.
cilicio, *n.m.* hairshirt, sackcloth.
cilindrada, *n.f.* cylinder capacity.
cilindrar, *v.t.* roll.
cilíndrico, -ca, *a.* cylindrical.
cilindro, *n.m.* cylinder; roller.
cillero, *n.m.* store; tithe man.
cima, *n.f.* summit, top; *dar — a,* round off.
cimarrón, -rrona, *a.* (*S.A.*) wild; fugitive, gone wild.
címbalo, *n.m.* cymbal.
cimborio, cimborrio, *n.m.* (*arch.*) dome.
cimbr(e)ar, *v.t., v.r.* sway; bend.
cimbreño, -ña, *a.* supple, willowy.
cimentación, *n.f.* foundation.
cimentar, *v.t.* lay the foundation for.
cimento [CEMENTO].
cimera, *n.f.* plume, crest.
cimero, -ra, *a.* uppermost, crowning.
cimiento, *n.m.* foundation, groundwork.
cimitarra, *n.f.* scimitar.
cinabrio, *n.m.* cinnabar.
cinc, *n.m.* zinc.
cincel, *n.m.* graver, chisel.
cincelar, *v.t.* chisel, carve, engrave.
cinco, *a., n.m.* five.
cincuenta, *a., n.m.* fifty.
cincuentavo, -va, *a.* fiftieth.
cincuentenario, -ria, *a., n.m.* semicentenary.
cincuentena, *n.f.* fifty (*approx.*).
cincuentón, -tona, *a., n.m.f.* (*fam.*) fifty-year-old.
cincha, *n.f.* girth, cinch.
cinchar, *v.t.* cinch, band, hoop.
cincho, *n.m.* girdle, sash; girth; hoop.
cine, *n.m.* cinema; — *hablado,* talkie; — *mudo,* silent film.
cineasta, *n.m.f.* film producer; film actor *or* actress.
cinedrama, *n.m.* film drama, photoplay.
cinemático, -ca, *a.* kinematic.
cinematografía, *n.f.* cinematography.
cinematografiar [L], *v.t.* film.
cinematográfico, -ca, *a.* cinematographic.
cinematógrafo, *n.m.* cinematograph; filming; cinema.
cinéreo, -rea, *a.* ash-grey, cinerous.
cinético, -ca, *a.* kinetic.—*n.f.* kinetics.
cíngaro, -ra, *a., n.m.f.* zíngaro, gipsy.
cinglar (1), *v.t.* forge (*iron*).
cinglar (2), *v.t., v.i.* scull (*boat*).
cíngulo, *n.m.* cingulum.
cínico, -ca, *a.* cynical; (*fig.*) brazen, immoral. —*n.m.f.* cynic, Cynic.
cinismo, *n.m.* cynicism, Cynicism; (*fig.*) brazen immorality.
cinta, *n.f.* ribbon, tape; strip; film; curb.
cintarazo, *n.m.* blow with flat of sword.
cintero, -ra, *n.m.f.* ribbon seller.—*n.m.* belt, sash; rope.
cintillo, *n.m.* hat-band.
cinto, *n.m.* girdle, belt.
cintra, *n.f.* (*arch.*) curvature, arching.
cintura, *n.f.* waist; girdle.
cinturón, *n.m.* belt.
ciño, etc. [CEÑIR].
ciprés, *n.m.* cypress.
ciprino, -na, ciprio, -ria, *a., n.m.f.* Cypriot.
circo, *n.m.* circus, amphitheatre; coomb.
circuir [O], *v.t.* encircle.

circuito, *n.m.* circuit; *corto —,* (*elec.*) short circuit.
circulación, *n.f.* circulation; traffic.
circular, *a., n.f.* circular.—*v.t., v.i.* circulate, circularize.
circularidad, *n.f.* circularity.
circulatorio, -ria, *a.* circulatory.
círculo, *n.m.* circle; club; *— polar ártico,* Arctic Circle.
circuncidar, *v.t.* circumcise.
circuncisión, *n.f.* circumcision.
circundar, *v.t.* surround.
circunferencia, *n.f.* circumference.
circunflejo, -ja, *a., n.m.* circumflex.
circunlocución, *n.f.,* **circunloquio,** *n.m.* circumlocution.
circunnavegar [B], *v.t.* circumnavigate.
circunscribir, *v.t.* (*p.p.* **circunscrito**) circumscribe.
circunscripción, *n.f.* circumscription; territorial division.
circunspección, *n.f.* circumspection.
circunspecto, -ta, *a.* circumspect.
circunstancia, *n.f.* circumstance.
circunstanciado, -da, *a.* detailed.
circunstancial, *a.* circumstantial.
circunstante, *a.* surrounding; present.—*n.m.f.* onlooker, bystander.
circunvalar, *v.t.* circumvallate, surround.
circunvención, *n.f.* circumvention.
circunvenir [36], *v.t.* circumvent.
circunvolar [4], *v.t.* fly round.
circunvolución, *n.f.* circumvolution.
cirigallo, -lla, *n.m.f.* layabout, gadabout.
cirio, *n.m.* (*eccl.*) large candle.
cirolero, *n.m.* plum tree.
ciruela, *n.f.* plum; *— pasa,* prune.
ciruelo, *n.m.* plum tree; (*fam.*) numskull.
cirugía, *n.f.* surgery.
cirujano, *n.m.* surgeon.
cisco, *n.m.* slack, fine charcoal; (*fam.*) row, din; *meter —,* stir up trouble.
ciscón, *n.m.* cinders.
cisión, *n.f.* incision, cut.
cisma, *n.f.* schism.
cismático, -ca, *a., n.m.f.* schismatic.
cisne, *n.m.* swan.
Cister, *n.m.* Cistercian Order.
cisterciense, *a., n.m.f.* Cistercian.
cisterna, *n.f.* tank, cistern.
cisura, *n.f.* fissure; incision.
cita, *n.f.* appointment, date; quotation.
citación, *n.f.* summons; quotation.
citano, -na, *n.m.f.* (*fam.*) so-and-so.
citar, *v.t.* make an appointment with; quote, cite; summon; (*taur.*) provoke.
cítara, *n.f.* zither; cithern.
cítrico, -ca, *a.* citric.
citrón, *n.m.* lemon.
ciudad, *n.f.* city.
ciudadanía, *n.f.* citizenship.
ciudadano, -na, *a.* civic; town-bred.—*n.m.f.* citizen; townsman, townswoman.
ciudadela, *n.f.* citadel.
civeta, *n.f.* civet.
cívico, -ca, *a.* civic.—*n.m.* (*fam.*) copper, policeman.
civil, *a.* civil; civilian.—*n.m.f.* civilian; policeman.
civilidad, *n.f.* civility.
civilización, *n.f.* civilization.
civilizar [C], *v.t.* civilize.

civismo, *n.m.* civicism; patriotism.
cizaña, *n.f.* darnel, tare; (*fig.*) discord.
cinzañero, -ra, *n.m.f.* (*fam.*) troublemaker.
clamor, *n.m.* clamour, outcry; knell.
clamoreada, *n.f.* outcry; shrieking.
clamorear, *v.t.* clamour for.—*v.i.* toll; clamour (*por,* for).
clandestino, -na, *a.* clandestine.
clangor, *n.m.* (*poet.*) blare, clarion.
claque, *n.m.* claque.
claraboya, *n.f.* skylight.
clarear, *v.t.* brighten; dawn.—*v.r.* be transparent.
clarecer [9], *v.i.* dawn.
clareo, *n.m.* clearing (*in woods*).
clarete, *n.m.* claret.
clareza (*lit.*), **claridad,** *n.f.* clarity, clearness; brightness; daylight.—*pl.* plain truths.
clarificación, *n.f.* clarification.
clarificar [A], *v.t.* clarify; brighten.
clarín, *n.m.* clarion; trumpeter.
clarinada, *n.f.* clarion call; (*fam.*) uncalled-for remark.
clarinero, *n.m.* bugler.
clarinete, *n.m.* clarinet.
clarioncillo, *n.m.* crayon.
clarividencia, *n.f.* clairvoyance; perspicacity.
clarividente, *a.* clairvoyant; perspicacious.
claro, -ra, *a.* clear, bright; light; obvious; famous.—*n.m.* blank, gap; clearing; skylight.—*n.f.* egg white; thin patch; break, bright patch.—*adv.* clearly.—*interj.* of course! naturally! *poner en —,* make clear; *a las claras,* clearly.
claror, *n.m.* brightness, splendour, light.
claroscuro, *n.m.* (*art.*) chiaroscuro.
clarucho, -cha, *a.* (*fam.*) watery thin.
clase, *n.f.* class.
clasicismo, *n.m.* classicism.
clasicista, *n.m.f.* classicist.
clásico, -ca, *a.* classic(al).—*n.m.* classic; classicist.
clasificador, -ra, *a.* classifying.—*n.m.* filing cabinet.
clasificar [A], *v.t.* classify.—*v.r.* qualify.
claudicación, *n.f.* limping; bungling.
claudicar [A], *v.i.* limp; bungle.
claustral, *a.* cloistral.
claustro, *n.m.* cloister; university council.
claustrofobia, *n.f.* claustrophobia.
cláusula, *n.f.* clause.
clausura, *n.f.* cloistered life; close, closure.
clausurar, *v.t.* adjourn; close.
clavado, -da, *a.* studded; sharp, punctual; stopped (*watch*); (*fam.*) to the life, exact.
clavar, *v.t.* nail; drive in (*nail, dagger etc.*); fix; (*fam.*) cheat.
clavazón, *n.f.* nails.
clave, *n.f.* key (*to code*); (*mus.*) clef.—*n.m.* harpsichord.
clavel, *n.m.* carnation, pink.
clavellina, *n.f.* (*bot.*) pink.
clavero (1), **-ra,** *n.m.f.* keeper of the keys.
clavero (2), *n.m.* clove tree.
claveta, *n.f.* peg.
clavete, *n.m.* tack; plectrum.
clavicordio, *n.m.* clavichord.
clavícula, *n.f.* clavicle, collar-bone.
clavija, *n.f.* peg; (*elec.*) plug.

clavijero, *n.m.* coat rack; peg-box; (*tel.*) switch board.
clavo, *n.m.* nail; (*cul.*) clove; (*fig.*) pain, anguish; (*med.*) corn; **dar en el —,** hit the nail on the head.
clemencia, *n.f.* clemency.
clemente, *a.* clement.
cleptomanía, *n.f.* kleptomania.
cleptómano, -na, *a., n.m.f.* kleptomaniac.
clerecía, *n.f.* clergy.
clerical, *a.* clerical.—*n.m.* clericalist.
clericalismo, *n.m.* clericalism.
clericato, *n.m.,* clericatura, *n.f.* clergy, priesthood.
clerigalla, *n.f.* (*pej.*) priests, dog-collar men.
clérigo, *n.m.* clergyman, cleric.
clerigón, *n.m.* acolyte, server.
clero, *n.m.* clergy.
clerofobia, *n.f.* hatred of priests.
clerófobo, -ba, *a.* priest-hating.—*n.m.f.* priest-hater.
cliché, *n.m.* cliché.
cliente, *n.m.f.* client, customer.
clientela, *n.f.* clientele; customers, custom; patronage.
clima, *n.m.* climate, (*poet.*) clime.
climactérico, -ca, *a.* climacteric.
climático, -ca, *a.* climatic.
clínico, -ca, *a.* clinical.—*n.m.f.* clinical doctor.—*n.f.* clinic; clinical medicine.
clíper, *n.m.* (*naut., aer.*) clipper.
clisar, *v.t.* stereotype.
clisé, *n.m.* (*phot., print.*) plate; stencil.
cloaca, *n.f.* sewer.
clocar [4A], cloquear, *v.i.* cluck.
clorhídrico, -ca, *a.* hydrochloric.
cloro, *n.m.* chlorine.
clorofila, *n.f.* chlorophyll.
cloroformizar [C], *v.t.* chloroform.
cloroformo, *n.m.* chloroform.
cloruro, *n.m.* chloride.
club, *n.m.* (*pl.* -bs *or* -bes) club.
clubista, *n.m.f.* club member.
clueco, -ca, *a.* broody.—*n.f.* broody hen.
cluniacense, *a.,* Cluniac.
coacción, *n.f.* coercion.
coaccionar, *v.t.* force, compel.
coactivo, -va, *a.* coercive.
coagulación, *n.f.* coagulation.
coagular, *v.t., v.r.* coagulate.
coalición, *n.f.* coalition.
coartada, *n.f.* alibi.
coartar, *v.t.* limit, restrict.
coautor, -ra, *n.m.f.* co-author, fellow author.
coba, *n.f.* (*fam.*) leg-pull; cajolery, wheedling.
cobalto, *n.m.* cobalt.
cobarde, *a.* cowardly.—*n.m.f.* coward.
cobardía, *n.f.* cowardice.
cobayo, -ya, *n.m.f.* guinea pig.
cobertera, *n.f.* pot cover; bawd.
cobertizo, *n.m.* lean-to; cover.
cobertor, *n.m.* coverlet.
cobertura, *n.f.* covering, cover; knighting.
cobija, *n.f.* cover.—*pl.* bedclothes.
cobijar, *v.t.* cover, shelter; lodge.
cobijo, *n.m.* shelter, cover.
cobista, *n.m.f.* (*fam.*) cajoler, smooth-tongued character.
cobra, *n.f.* (*hunt.*) retrieving; (*zool.*) cobra.
cobrable, cobrandero, -ra, *a.* collectable, recoverable.

cobrador, *n.m.* bus conductor; collector; retriever.
cobranza, *n.f.* recovery, retrieving; cashing.
cobrar, *v.t.* recover, collect; cash; acquire; (*hunt.*) retrieve.—*v.r.* recover (*de,* from).
cobre, *n.m.* copper.—*pl.* (*mus.*) brass.
cobreño, -ña, *a.* made of copper.
cobrizo, -za, *a.* coppery.
cobro, *n.m.* collection, cashing; **en —,** in a safe place.
coca, *n.f.* (*bot.*) coca; berry; rap; (*fam.*) head.
cocaína, *n.f.* cocaine.
cocción, *n.f.* baking, cooking.
cocear, *v.i.* kick; jib, balk.
cocer [5D], *v.t.* cook, bake, boil; seethe.—*v.r.* suffer agonies.
coces [COZ].
cocido, *n.m.* Spanish stew with chick peas.—*p.p.* [COCER].
cociente, *n.m.* quotient.
cocimiento, *n.m.* cooking, baking; decoction.
cocina, *n.f.* kitchen; cuisine, cookery.
cocinar, *v.t.* cook; (*fam.*) meddle.
cocinero, -ra, *n.m.f.* cook.
cocinilla, *n.f.* kitchenette; camping stove.
coco, *n.m.* coconut; coconut palm; coccus; (*fam.*) bogeyman; **hacer cocos,** (*fam.*) pull faces; make eyes.
cocodrilo, *n.m.* crocodile.
cocoliche, *n.m.* (*S.A.*) broken Spanish.
cócora, *a.* pestering, pesky.—*n.m.f.* pest, bore.
cocotero, *n.m.* coconut palm.
coctel, *n.m.* cocktail.
coctelera, *n.f.* cocktail shaker.
cochambre, *n.m.* (*fam.*) greasy filth.
coche, *n.m.* coach; car; bus; **en el — de San Francisco,** on Shanks's mare.
coche-cama, *n.m.* (*pl.* coches-cama) (*rail.*) sleeper, wagon-lit.
cochera, *n.f.* coach house, garage.
cochero, *n.m.* coachman.
cochinilla, *n.f.* cochineal, cochineal beetle; woodlouse.
cochinillo, *n.m.* sucking-pig; piglet.
cochino, -na, *a.* piggish.—*n.m.f.* pig.—*n.m.* hog.—*n.f.* sow.
cochite-hervite, *adv.* helter-skelter; slap-dash.
cochitril [CUCHITRIL].
cochura, *n.f.* baking; dough.
codal, *a.* rel. to elbow, cubital.—*n.m.* strut, brace.
codazo, *n.m.* nudge, poke.
codear, *v.i.* elbow; (*S.A.*) cadge; **codearse con,** hob-nob with.
codera, *n.f.* elbow-patch.
códice, *n.m.* codex, manuscript.
codicia, *n.f.* greed, lust.
codiciar, *v.t., v.i.* covet.
codicilo, *n.m.* codicil.
codicioso, -sa, *a.* covetous; (*fam.*) hard-working.
codificar [A], *v.t.* codify.
código, *n.m.* (*jur.*) statute book; code.
codo, *n.m.* elbow, cubit; **por los codos,** (*fam.*) nineteen to the dozen, extravagantly.
codoñate, *n.m.* quince preserves.
codorniz, *n.f.* (*pl.* -ices) (*orn.*) quail.
coeducación, *n.f.* co-education.
coeducacional, *a.* co-educational.
coeficiente, *a., n.m.* coefficient.

coercer [D], *v.t.* coerce.
coerción, *n.f.* coercion.
coetáneo, -nea, *a.* contemporary.
coevo, -va, *a.* coeval.
coexistencia, *n.f.* coexistence.
coexistente, *a.* coexistent.
coexistir, *v.i.* coexist.
cofia, *n.f.* coif.
cofrade, *n.m.f.* fellow member; member of COFRADÍA.
cofradía, *n.f.* confraternity, guild.
cofre, *n.m.* coffer, chest; — *fuerte,* safe.
cofto, -ta, *a.* Coptic.—*n.m.f.* Copt.
cogedero, -ra, *a.* ready for picking.—*n.m.* handle.
cogedor, -ra, *n m.f.* picker, gatherer.—*n.m.* shovel; rubbish box.
cogedura, *n.f.* picking, gathering.
coger [E], *v.t.* seize; catch; gather; pick up; hold; cover; (*taur.*) toss.—*v.i.* be situated; (*fam.*) fit. [*This word NEVER used in Argentina*].
cogida, *n.f.* gathering; catch; (*taur.*) toss.
cognado, -da, *a.,* *n.m.f.* cognate.
cognición, *n.f.* cognition.
cogollo, *n.m.* (*bot.*) heart; shoot; tree-top; (*fig.*) pick, best.
cogolludo, -da, *a.* (*fam.*) terrific, great, fine.
cogorza, *n.f.* *coger una* —, (*fam.*) get tipsy.
cogotazo, *n.m.* rabbit punch, blow on nape.
cogote, *n.m.* nape, back of neck.
cogotudo, -da, *a.* thick-necked; (*fam.*) stiff-necked, proud.
cogujada, *n.f.* (*orn.*) crested lark.
cogulla, *n.f.* cowl.
cohabitar, *v.i.* cohabit.
cohechar, *v.t.* bribe; plough.
cohecho, *n.m.* bribe.
coherencia, *n.f.* coherence.
coherente, *a.* coherent.
cohesión, *n.f.* cohesion.
cohete, *n.m.* rocket; jet; rocket motor.
cohetería, *n.f.* rocketry.
cohibir, *v.t.* inhibit.
cohombrillo, *n.m.* gherkin.
cohombro, *n.m.* cucumber.
cohonestar, *v.t.* gloss over.
cohorte, *n.m.* cohort.
coincidencia, *n.f.* coinciding; coincidence.
coincidir, *v.i.* coincide; concur.
coipo, coipú, *n.m.* (*zool.*) coypu, nutria.
cojear, *v.i.* limp, wobble; (*fam.*) slip up.
cojera, *n.f.* limp.
cojijo, *n.m.* (*ent.*) insect, (*fam.*) creepy-crawly; moan, grouse.
cojijoso, -sa, *a.* peevish, grumpy.
cojín, *n.m.* cushion.
cojinete, *n.m.* pad; (*mech.*) bearing.
cojo, -ja, *a.* lame, limping; crippled; wobbly, shaky.—*n.m.f.* cripple, lame person.
cok, [COQUE].
col, *n.f.* cabbage.
cola, *n.f.* tail; train (*of dress*); queue; glue; *hacer (la)* —, queue up, (*U.S.*) form a line.
colaboración, *n.f.* collaboration.
colaborador, -ra, *a.* collaborating.—*n.m.f.* collaborator.
colaborar, *v.i.* collaborate.
colación, *n.f.* collation; conferment; glebe; *sacar a* —, (*fam.*) bring up, mention.
colada, *n.f.* soaking; lye; wash(ing); track; ravine.

coladizo, -za, *a.* runny.
colador, *n.m.* colander; strainer.
coladura, *n.f.* straining; (*fam.*) slip-up.
colanilla, *n.f.* small bolt, catch.
colapso, *n.m.* collapse; — *nervioso,* nervous breakdown.
colar [4], *v.t.* strain; boil (*clothes*); pour; bore. —*v.i.* squeeze through; ooze, leak; (*fam.*) booze.—*v.r.* seep; slip in; — *a fondo,* (*naut.*) sink; *eso no cuela,* (*fam.*) that's impossible.
colateral, *a.,* *n.m.f.* co-lateral.
colcrén, *n.m.* cold cream.
colcha, *n.f.* quilt, bedspread.
colchón, *n.m.* mattress.
colear, *v.t.* throw (*cattle*).—*v.i.* wag one's tail; (*fam.*) remain unsettled.
colección, *n.f.* collection.
coleccionar, *v.t.* collect (*as hobby*).
coleccionista, *n.m.f.* collector.
colecta, *n.f.* (*eccl.*) collect.
colectividad, *n.f.* collectivity; community.
colectivismo, *n.m.* collectivism.
colectivización, *n.f.* collectivization.
colectivizar [C], *v.t.* collectivize.
colectivo, -va, *a.* collective.—*n.m.* (*S.A.*) bus.
colector, *n.m.* collector, gatherer; drain; (*elec.*) commutator.
colega, *n.m.f.* colleague.
colegiata, *n.f.* collegiate church.
colegio, *n.m.* college; high school.
colegir [8E], *v.t.* gather, infer.
cólera, *n.f.* bile, wrath.—*n.m.* cholera.
colérico, -ca, *a.,* *n.m.f.* choleric, angry, wrathful; choleraic.
coleta, *n.f.* (*taur.*) bullfighter's pigtail; queue; postscript.
coletillo, *n.m.* waistcoat.
coleto, *n.m.* doublet; (*fam.*) oneself.
colgadero, *n.m.* hanger.
colgadizo, -za, *a.* hanging.—*n.m.* lean-to.
colgado, -da, *a.* drooping; unsettled; thwarted.
colgadura, *n.f.* drapery, hangings.
colgajo, *n.m.* tatter.
colgante, *a.* hanging; *puente* —, suspension bridge.
colgar [4B], *v.t.* hang; drape; fail (*an examinee*).—*v.i.* hang, dangle.
colibrí, *n.m.* (*pl.* **-íes**) humming bird.
cólico, -ca, *a.,* *n.m.* colic.
coliflor, *n.f.* cauliflower.
coligación, *n.f.* union, alliance.
coligado, -da, *n.m.f.* ally.
coligar [B], *v.r.* join forces.
colijo [COLEGIR].
colilla, *n.f.* end, butt (*cigar etc.*).
colina, *n.f.* hill.
colindante, *a.* adjacent.
coliseo, *n.m.* coliseum.
colisión, *n.f.* collision.
colmar, *v.t.* fill to the brim; fulfil; overwhelm (*de*), with).
colmena, *n.f.* beehive.
colmillo, *n.m.* canine tooth, eye-tooth; tusk; fang.
colmilludo, -da, *a.* tusked, fanged; (*fam.*) canny.
colmo, -ma, *a.* full to the brim.—*n.m.* height, peak; overflowing; (*fam.*) the last straw.
colocación, *n.f.* collocation; job.
colocar [A], *v.t.* place; locate.

colofón, *n.m.* colophon.
colombiano, -na, *a., n.m.f.* Colombian.
colombino, -na, *a.* rel. to Columbus, Columbine.
Colón, *n.m.* Columbus; **colón,** *n.m.* (*anat., gram.*) colon.
colonato, *n.m.* colonization.
Colonia, *n.f.* Cologne; **colonia,** *n.f.* colony; eau-de-Cologne.
colonial, *a.* colonial.—*n.m.pl.* imported foods.
colonización, *n.f.* colonization.
colonizar [C], *v.t.* colonize.
colono, -na, *n.m.f.* settler; colonial; tenant farmer.
coloquio, *n.m.* colloquy, talk.
color, *n.m.* colour; **de —,** coloured; **so — de,** on pretext of.
coloración, *n.f.* coloration.
colorado, -da, *a.* red; coloured; risqué; specious.
colorante, *a., n.m.* colouring.
colorar, *v.t.* colour.
colorativo, -va, *a.* colouring.
colorear, *v.t.* colour; palliate.—*v.i.* turn red, ripen.
colorete, *n.m.* rouge.
colorido, -da, *a.* colourful.—*n.m.* colouring.
colorín, *n.m.* bright colour; (*orn.*) goldfinch.
colorir [Q], [COLOREAR].
colorista, *a.* colourist.
colosal, *a.* colossal.
coloso, *n.m.* colossus.
coludir, *v.i., v.r.* act in collusion.
columbino, -na, *a.* columbine, dovelike.
columbrar, *v.t.* discern, glimpse.
columbrete, *n.m.* reef, islet.
columna, *n.f.* column.
columnata, *n.f.* colonnade.
columpiar, *v.t., v.r.* swing, rock.
columpio, *n.m.* swing.
colusión, *n.f.* collusion.
colusorio, -ria, *a.* collusive.
collado, *n.m.* hill; mountain pass.
collar, *n.m.* necklace; collar (*for dogs, slaves etc.*).
collazo, *n.m.* farmhand; (*obs.*) serf.
coma, *n.f.* (*gram.*) comma.—*n.m.* (*med.*) coma.
comadre, *n.f.* midwife; grandmother; (*fam.*) gossip; (*fam.*) woman friend.
comadrear, *v.i.* (*fam.*) gossip, chin-wag.
comadreja, *n.f.* weasel.
comadrero, -ra, *a.* (*fam.*) gossipy.—*n.m.f.* gossip.
comadrona, *n.f.* midwife.
comandancia, *n.f.* (*mil.*) high command.
comandante, *n.m.* (*mil.*) commander, commandant, major; (*aer.*) wing commander.
comandar, *v.t.* (*mil.*) command.
comandita, *n.f.* silent partnership.
comanditar, *v.t.* invest (*in a business*).
comando, *n.m.* (*mil.*) commando; command, control.
comarca, *n.f.* region, district.
comarcal, *a.* regional, local.
comarcano, -na, *a.* neighbouring, bordering.
comarcar [A], *v.i.* border.
comatoso, -sa, *a.* comatose.
comba (1), *n.f.* bend, curve, camber.
comba (2), *n.f.* skipping; skipping-rope; **saltar a la —,** skip.
combadura, *n.f.* bend, camber; sag.

combar, *v.t.* bend, warp.—*v.r.* sag, bulge, bend.
combate, *n.m.* fight, combat; **fuera de —,** out of action, hors de combat.
combatiente, *a., n.m.* combatant.
combatir, *v.t.* fight, combat; harass.—*v.i., v.r.* struggle, fight.
combatividad, *n.f.* combativeness; fighting spirit.
combinación, *n.f.* combination; (*rail.*) connexion.
combinar, *v.t.* combine; work out.
combo, -ba, *a.* bulging, bent, warped.
combustible, *a.* combustible.—*n.m.* fuel.
combustión, *n.f.* combustion.
comedero, -ra, *a.* eatable.—*n.m.* manger.
comedia, *n.f.* play, drama; comedy; (*fig.*) shamming.
comediante, -ta, *n.m.* actor.—*n.f.* actress; (*fig.*) hypocrite.
comediar, *v.t.* halve.
comedido, -da, *a.* courteous, moderate.
comedimiento, *n.m.* politeness, moderation.
comedio, *n.m.* middle; interval.
comedir [8], *v.r.* be polite *or* moderate.
comedor, -ra, *a.* eating much.—*n.m.* dining room.
comején, *n.m.* termite; fretter moth.
comendador, *n.m.* commander (*of an Order*).
comensal, *n.m.f.* retainer; fellow diner.
comentador, -ra, *n.m.f.* commentator.
comentar, *v.t.* comment (on).—*v.i.* (*fam.*) natter.
comentario, *n.m.* commentary; comment.
comentarista, *n.m.* commentator.
comento, *n.m.* comment; falsehood.
comenzar [1C], *v.t., v.i.* begin, commence (*a,* to, *por,* by).
comer, *n.m.* food; eating.—*v.t.* eat, eat away. —*v.i.* eat; have lunch; itch.
comerciable, *a.* marketable; sociable.
comercial, *a.* commercial.
comercialización, *n.f.* commercialization.
comercializar [C], *v.t.* commercialize.
comerciante, *a.* trading.—*n.m.f.* trader, merchant.
comerciar, *v.t.* trade, deal (*con,* with).
comercio, *n.m.* commerce, business; intercourse.
comestible, *a.* edible.—*n.m.pl.* food.
cometa, *n.m.* comet.—*n.f.* kite (*toy*).
cometer, *v.t.* commit; assign.
cometido, *n.m.* assignment, commitment.
comezón, *n.m.* itch.
comicidad, *n.f.* comicality.
cómico, -ca, *a.* comic, comical; dramatic.— *n.m.* actor; comedian.—*n.f.* actress; comedienne.
comida, *n.f.* lunch; meal; food.
comidilla, *n.f.* (*fam.*) right thing, "cup of tea"; (*fam.*) hobby; (*fam.*) gossip, talk, scandal.
comienzo, *n.m.* beginning; **dar —,** begin.
comilón, -lona, *a.* (*fam.*) guzzling.—*n.m.f.* (*fam.*) guzzler, big eater.—*n.f.* spread, big meal.
comillas, *n.f.pl.* quotation marks.
cominero, *n.m.* "old woman", fuss-pot.
comino, *n.m.* (*bot.*) cumin.
comiquear, *v.i.* put on amateur plays.
comisar, *v.t.* impound.
comisaría, *n.f.* police station.

comisariato, *n.m.* commissariat.
comisario, *n.m.* commissioner, commissar.
comisión, *n.f.* committee; commission.
comisionista, *n.m.f.* commission agent.
comiso, *n.m.* seizure, impounding.
comisquear, *v.t.* nibble.
comistrajo, *n.m.* rotten meal, hodge-podge.
comité, *n.m.* committee.
comitente, *n.m.f.* client, constituent.
comitiva, *n.f.* retinue, party.
como, *adv.* like, as; how; about; as if.—*conj.*
    as; when; how; so that; if; *así* —, as soon
    as; just as; — *que,* seeing that; — *quien*
    dice, so to speak.
cómo, *adv. interrog.* how ? what ?—*interj.* how!
    what! *¿* — *no?* why not ? for sure, yes.
comóda, *n.f.* commode.
comodidad, *n.f.* comfort, ease, convenience.
comodín, *n.m.* joker (*in cards*); gadget; alibi,
    excuse.
comodista, *a.* selfish, comfort-loving.—
    n.m.f. self-seeker, comfort-lover.
cómodo, -da, *a.* convenient; comfortable.
comodón, -dona, *a.* comfort-loving.
comodoro, *n.m.* commodore.
compacidad, *n.f.* compressibility, compact-
    ness.
compactar, *v.t.* make compact.
compacto, -ta, *a.* compact.
compadecer [9], *v.t.* pity, feel sorry for.—*v.r.*
    concur, tally; sympathize (*de,* with).
compadraje, *n.m.* clique, ring.
compadrar, *v.i.* become a godfather; become
    friends.
compadre, *n.m.* godfather; (*fam.*)   pal,
    chum; (*S.A.*) swanker, braggart.
compadrear, *v.i.* (*fam.*) be chummy.
compaginación, *n.f.* pagination; arranging.
compaginar, *v.t.* arrange; page.—*v.r.* fit,
    agree.
compañerismo, *n.m.* companionship; com-
    radeship.
compañero, -ra, *n.m.f.* companion, fellow,
    friend, comrade.
compañía, *n.f.* company.
comparable, *a.* comparable.
comparación, *n.f.* comparison.
comparar, *v.t.* compare.
comparativo, -va, *a., n.m.* comparative.
comparecer [9], *v.i.* (*jur.*) appear.
comparsa, *n.f.* (*theat.*) extras.—*n.m.f.* extra.
compartimiento, *n.m.* division, compart-
    ment.
compartir, *v.t.* share, divide.
compás, *n.m.* compass; compasses; (*mus.*)
    time, beat; (*mus.*) bar.
compasado, -da, *a.* moderate, measured.
compasar, *v.t.* cut to size, adapt.
compasión, *n.f.* compassion.
compasivo, -va, *a.* compassionate.
compatibilidad, *n.f.* compatibility.
compatible, *a.* compatible.
compatriota, *n.m.f.*   compatriot,   fellow
    countryman *or* -woman.
compeler, *v.t.* compel.
compendiar, *v.t.* summarize.
compendio, *n.m.* summary, compendium.
compendioso, -εa, *a.* compendious.
compenetrar, *v.r.* interpenetrate; *com-*
    penetrarse de, absorb, immerse oneself
    in; *compenetrarse con,* understand.
compensación, *n.f.* compensation.

compensar, *v.t.* compensate (for).
competencia, *n.f.* competence; competition.
competente, *a.* competent, adequate.
competer, *v.i.* appertain, concern.
competición, *n.f.* competition.
competidor, -ra, *a.* competing.—*n.m.f.*
    competitor.
competir [8], *v.i.* compete.
compilación, *n.f.* compilation.
compilar, *v.t.* compile.
compinche, *n.m.f.* (*fam.*) crony.
complacencia, *n.f.* pleasure, satisfaction.
complacer [23], *v.t.* please; humour.—*v.r.*
    be pleased (*de, con, en,* with).
complaciente, *a.* complaisant, pleasing.
complejidad, *n.f.* complexity.
complejo, -ja, *a., n.m.* complex.
complementar, *v.t.* complete, complement.
complementario, -ria, *a.* complementary.
complemento, *n.m.* complement; completion.
completar, *v.t.* complete.
completo, -ta, *a.* complete; full (*vehicle*).—
    n.f.pl. (*eccl.*) compline.
complexidad, *n.f.* complexity.
complexión, *n.f.* (*med.*) constitution.
complexo [COMPLEJO].
complicación, *n.f.* complication.
complicar [A], *v.t.* complicate.
cómplice, *n.m.f.* accomplice, accessory.
complicidad, *n.f.* complicity.
complot, *n.m.* plot.
complutense, *a.* rel. to Alcalá.
componedor, -ra, *n.m.f.* compositor; com-
    poser, arbitrator.
componenda, *n.f.* compromise, settlement.
componente, *a., n.m.* (*mech. n.f.*) component.
componer [25], *v.t.* compose, arrange; mend,
    trim; reconcile.—*v.r.* come to terms; be
    composed (*de,* of).
comportamiento, *n.m.* conduct, behaviour.
comportar, *v.t.* bear; (*S.A.*) entail.—*v.r.*
    behave.
comporte, *n.m.* bearing, behaviour.
composición, *n.f.* composition; settlement.
compositor, -ra, *n.m.f.* (*mus.*) composer.
compostelano, -na, *a., n.m.f.* Compostelan
    (*rel. to Santiago de Compostela*).
compostura, *n.f.* structure; settlement;
    composure; repair.
compota, *n.f.* stewed fruit.
compra, *n.f.* shopping, purchase; *ir de*
    compras, go shopping.
comprar, *v.t.* buy, purchase.—*v.i.* shop.
compraventa, *n.f.* transaction; second-hand
    business.
comprender, *v.t.* understand; comprise.
comprensible, *a.* understandable.
comprensión, *n.f.* understanding; compre-
    hension.
comprensivo, -va, *a.* comprehensive; under-
    standing.
compresa, *n.f.* compress; sanitary towel.
compresible, *a.* compressible.
compresión, *n.f.* compression.
compresor, -ra, *a.* compressing.—*n.m.*
    (*med.*) *n.f.* (*mech.*) compressor.
comprimido, *n.m.* tablet.—*p.p.* [COMPRIMIR].
comprimir, *v.t.* compress, condense; repress.
comprobación, *n.f.* proof, verification.
comprobante, *a.* proving.—*n.m.* proof;
    voucher.
comprobar [4], *v.t.* prove, verify, check.

comprometer, *v.t.* oblige; compromise.— *v.r.* undertake (**a,** to).

comprometido, -da, *a.* embarrassing.

comprometimiento, *n.m.* compromise; predicament.

compromisario, -ria, *n.m.f.* arbitrator.

compromiso, *n.m.* compromise; commitment; embarrassment, compromising situation.

compuerta, *n.f.* sluice gate, lock gate; half door.

compuesto, -ta, *a.* compound, composed, composite—*p.p.* [COMPONER].—*n.m.* compound.

compulsa, *n.f.* collation; authenticated copy.

compulsación, *n.f.* collation.

compulsar, *v.t.* collate, check.

compulsión, *n.f.* compulsion.

compulsivo, -va, *a.* compulsive; compulsory.

compunción, *n.f.* compunction.

compungir [E], *v.t.* move to remorse.—*v.r.* feel remorse.

compuse [COMPONER].

computación, *n.f.* computation.

computador, *n.m.* (*S.A.*), **computadora,** *n.f.* (*Sp.*) computer.

computar, *v.t.* compute.

cómputo, *n.m.* computation, calculation.

comulgante, *n.m.f.* (*eccl.*) communicant.

comulgar [A], *v.t.* (*eccl.*) administer communion to.—*v.i.* communicate, receive communion; — **con,** (*fig.*) agree with.

comulgatorio, *n.m.* communion rail.

común, *a.* common.—*n.m.* commonalty; the common run; lavatory, toilet; *por lo —,* commonly, generally.

comuna, *n.f.* commune; (*S.A.*) township.

comunal, *a.* common; communal.—*n.m.* the common people.

comunero, -ra, *a.* popular.—*n.m.* joint owner; (*hist.*) commoner.

comunicable, *a.* communicable.

comunicación, *n.f.* communication.

comunicado, *n.m.* communiqué.

comunicante, *a., n.m.f.* communicant.

comunicar [A], *v.t.* communicate.

comunicativo, -va, *a.* communicative.

comunidad, *n.f.* community; *Comunidad Británica de Naciones,* British Commonwealth.

comunión, *n.f.* communion.

comunismo, *n.m.* Communism.

comunista, *a., n.m.f.* Communist.

comunizante, *n.m.f.* fellow traveller, Communist sympathizer.

comunizar [C], *v.t.* communize.—*v.r.* turn Communist.

cón, *prep.* with; in spite of; by; — *que,* so that; — *tal que,* provided that; — *todo,* nevertheless.

conato, *n.m.* endeavour; attempt.

concadenación, concatenación, *n.f.* concatenation.

concadenar, concatenar, *v.t.* concatenate.

cóncavo, -va, *a.* concave.—*n.m.f.* concavity.

concebible, *a.* conceivable.

concebir [8], *v.t.* conceive.

conceder, *v.t.* concede, grant.

concejal, *n.m.* alderman, councillor.

concejo, *n.m.* council.

concentración, *n.f.* concentration.

concentrado, -da, *a.* concentrated, (*fig.*) retiring.—*n.m.* concentrate.

concentrar, *v.t.* concentrate.—*v.r.* concentrate (**en,** on); be centred (**en,** on, around).

concéntrico, -ca, *a.* concentric.

concepción, *n.f.* conception.

conceptismo, *n.m.* conceptism.

conceptista, *a., n.m.f.* conceptist.

conceptivo, -va, *a.* conceptive.

concepto, *n.m.* concept, opinion; conceit, witticism.

conceptual, *a.* conceptual.

conceptuar [M], *v.t.* deem.

conceptuoso, -sa, *a.* epigrammatic, witty, conceited (*style*).

concerniente, *a.* concerning.

concernir [3Q], *v.t.* concern, apply to.

concertar [1], *v.t.* arrange, harmonize, mend. —*v.i.* agree.—*v.r.* come to terms.

concertina, *n.f.* concertina.

concertista, *n.m.f.* concert performer.

concesible, *a.* allowable.

concesión, *n.f.* concession.

conciencia, *n.f.* conscience; consciousness.

concienzudo, -da, *a.* conscientious.

concierto, *n.m.* agreement, harmony; (*mus.*) concert; concerto.

conciliación, *n.f.* conciliation.

conciliar, *a.* rel. to council.—*n.m.* councillor. —*v.t.* conciliate; gain.—*v.r.* win, earn (*esteem etc.*)

conciliatorio, -ria, *a.* conciliatory.

concilio, *n.m.* council; council decrees.

concisión, *n.f.* concision.

conciso, -sa, *a.* concise.

concitar, *v.t.* incite.

conciudadano, -na, *a.* fellow citizen.

cónclave, conclave, *n.m.* conclave.

concluir [O], *v.t.* conclude; convince.—*v.i.,* *v.r.* conclude, end.

conclusión, *n.f.* conclusion.

conclusivo, -va, *a.* concluding.

concluso, -sa, *a.* concluded.

concluyente, *a.* conclusive.

concomer, *v.r.* fidget; shrug; be impatient.

concomitante, *a.* concomitant.

concordancia, *n.f.* concordance, concord.

concordante, *a.* concordant.

concordar [4], *v.t.* harmonize.—*v.i.* agree (**con,** with).

concordato, *n.m.* concordat.

concorde, *a.* agreeing, in agreement.

concordia, *n.f.* concord.

concretar, *v.t.* limit; make concrete *or* definite, substantiate.—*v.r.* confine oneself (**a,** to).

concreto, -ta, *a.* concrete; definite.—*n.m.* concrete; concretion.

concubina, *n.f.* concubine.

por concuerda, *adv. phr.* accurately (*copied*).

conculcar [A], *v.t.* trample on, violate.

concupiscencia, *n.f.* concupiscence.

concupiscente, *a.* concupiscent.

concurrencia, *n.f.* concurrence; gathering, assembly; competition.

concurrente, *a.* concurrent; competing.— *n.m.f.* competitor.

concurrido, -da, *a.* crowded, much frequented.

concurrir, *v.i.* concur; assemble; compete.

concurso, *n.m.* concourse; contest; show, exhibition.

concusión, *n.f.* concussion; extortion.
concusionario, -ria, *n.m.f.* extortioner.
concha, *n.f.* shell, conch, shellfish; (*theat.*) prompter's box.
conchabanza, *n.f.* comfort; (*fam.*) conniving.
conchabar, *v.t.* blend, join; (*S.A.*) employ, obtain a job.—*v.r.* (*fam.*) connive.
conchabo, *n.m.* (*S.A.*) employment (*esp. as servant*).
conchudo, -da, *a.* crustacean, shell-covered; (*fam.*) crafty, sly.
condado, *n.m.* county; earldom.
conde, *n.m.* count, earl; (*dial.*) foreman.
condecoración, *n.f.* decoration, honour.
condecorar, *v.t.* decorate, honour.
condena, *n.f.* (*jur.*) conviction, sentence.
condenación, *n.f.* condemnation; damnation.
condenado, -da, *a.* condemned, damned.—*n.m.f.* condemned prisoner; (*fam.*) blighter.
condenar, *v.t.* condemn, damn.
condensación, *n.f.* condensation.
condensador, -ra, *a.* condensing.—*n.m.* (*elec.*) condenser.
condensar, *v.t.*, *v.r.* condense.
condesa, *n.f.* countess.
condescendencia, *n.f.* condescendence, condescension.
condescender [2], *v.i.* acquiesce (*a*, to, in).
condescendiente, *a.* acquiescent.
condestable, *n.m.* constable.
condición, *n.f.* condition; *a — (de) que,* on condition that.
condicional, *a.* conditional.
condicionar, *v.t.* condition, adjust.—*v.i.* agree.
condigno, -na, *a.* appropriate (*de*, to).
condimentar, *v.t.* season, condiment.
condimento, *n.m.* seasoning, condiment.
condiscípulo, -la, *n.m.f.* fellow-student.
condolencia, *n.f.* condolence.
condoler [5], *v.r.* condole, sympathize (*de*, with).
condominio, *n.m.* condominium.
condonar, *v.t.* condone, pardon.
cóndor, *n.m.* condor.
conducción, *n.f.* conduction; driving; transport; piping.
conducir [15], *v.t.* guide, lead, conduct; drive; convey.—*v.r.* behave, conduct oneself.
conducta, *n.f.* conduct; guidance, management; conveyance.
conductividad, *n.f.* conductivity.
conductivo, -va, *a.* conductive.
conducto, *n.m.* conduit, duct; agency.
conductor, -ra, *a.* leading, guiding, conducting.—*n.m.f.* conductor, leader, guide; driver; (*S.A.*) bus conductor.
conectar, *v.t.* connect.
conectivo, -va, *a.* connective.
conejero, -ra, *a.* rabbit-hunting.—*n.f.* rabbit-warren *or* hutch; (*fam.*), dive, den.
conejillo de Indias, *n.m.* guinea pig.
conejo, *n.m.* rabbit.
conejuno, -na, *a.* rel. to rabbits.—*n.f.* coney fur.
conexión, *n.f.* connexion.
conexionar, *v.t.* connect.
conexo, -xa, *a.* connected.
confabulación, *n.f.* confabulation.
confabular, *v.i.*, *v.r.* confabulate.

confección, *n.f.* ready-made suit; making; concoction.
confederación, *n.f.* confederation, confederacy.
confederado, -da, *a.*, *n.m.f.* confederate.
confederar, *v.t.*, *v.r.* confederate.
conferencia, *n.f.* lecture; conference; (*tel.*) trunk call, toll call.
conferenciante, *n.m.f.* lecturer.
conferenciar, *v.i.* confer, discuss.
conferir [6], *v.t.* confer, bestow, discuss.
confesado, -da, *n.m.f.* penitent.
confesante, *n.m.f.* penitent, one who confesses (*guilt etc.*).
confesar [1], *v.t.*, *v.r.* confess.
confesión, *n.f.* confession.
confesor, *n.m.* confessor (*priest, believer*).
confeti, *n.m.* confetti.
confiable, *a.* reliable.
confiado, -da, *a.* trusting, confident.
confianza, *n.f.* confidence; informality; *de —,* reliable; intimate.
confianzudo, -da, *a.* (*fam.*) forward, too informal.
confiar [L], *v.t.*, *v.i.* trust, confide (*en, de,* in).—*v.r.* rely (*en, de,* on).
confidencia, *n.f.* confidence, secret.
confidencial, *a.* confidential.
confidente, *a.* faithful; reliable.—*n.m.f.* confidant(e), informer.
configuración, *n.f.* configuration.
configurar, *v.t.* shape, form.
confín, *a.* bordering.—*n.m.* border, confine.
confinar, *v.t.* confine.—*v.i.* border (*con,* on).
confinidad, *n.f.* proximity.
confirmación, *n.f.* confirmation.
confirmador, -ra, confirmante, *a.* confirming, confirmatory.—*n.m.f.* confirmant, confirmer.
confirmar, *v.t.* confirm.
confiscación, *n.f.* confiscation.
confiscar [A], *v.t.* confiscate.
confitar, *v.t.* preserve, candy.
confite, *n.m.* preserves; toffee, candy.
confitería, *n.f.* confectionery.
confitura, *n.f.* jam, preserves.
conflagración, *n.f.* conflagration.
conflagrar, *v.t.* set ablaze.
conflicto, *n.m.* conflict, struggle, fight; anguish.
confluencia, *n.f.* confluence.
confluente, *a.* confluent.—*n.m.* confluence.
confluir [O], *v.i.* flow together, meet.
conformación, *n.f.* conformation.
conformar, *v.t.*, *v.i.*, *v.r.* conform, agree.
conforme, *a.* agreeable, agreeing; fitting.—*adv.* accordingly.—*conj.* as, just as, according to what.
conformidad, *n.f.* conformity, agreement.
conformista, *a.*, *n.m.f.* conformist.
confort, *n.m.* comfort, ease.
confortable, *a.* comforting, comfortable.
confortación, *n.f.*, **confortamiento,** *n.m.* comfort; encouragement.
confortante, *a.* comforting; invigorating.—*n.m.* tonic; mitten.
confortar, *v.t.* comfort; invigorate.
confraternar, confraternizar [C], *v.i.* fraternize.
confrontación, *n.f.* comparison, checking; confrontation.

confrontar, *v.t.* confront, compare.—*v.i., v.r.* border (on); agree (**con,** with).
Confucio, *n.m.* Confucius.
confundir, *v.t.* confuse, confound; mix (up). —*v.r.* get confused, make a mistake.
confusión, *n.f.* confusion.
confuso, -sa, *a.* confused.
confutación, *n.f.* confutation.
confutar, *v.t.* confute.
congelación, *n.f.* freezing, congealing.
congelante, *a.* freezing.
congelar, *v.t., v.r.* freeze, congeal.
congénere, *a.* congeneric.
congenial, *a.* congenial.
congeniar, *v.i.* be congenial; get on well (**con,** with).
congénito, -ta, *a.* congenital.
congerie, *n.f.* mass, congeries.
congestión, *n.f.* congestion.
congestionar, *v.t.* congest.
conglomeración, *n.f.* conglomeration.
conglomerar, *v.t., v.r.* conglomerate.
Congo, *n.m.* the Congo.
congo, -ga, *a., n.m.f.* Congolese.—*n.f.* conga.
congoja, *n.f.* anguish, grief.
congojoso, -sa, *a.* grievous, anguished.
congoleño, -ña, congolés, -lesa, *a., n.m.f.* Congolese.
congraciamiento, *n.m.* ingratiation.
congraciar, *v.t.* win over, ingratiate.
congratulación, *n.f.* congratulation.
congratular, *v.t.* congratulate (**de, por,** on). —*v.r.* rejoice (**de,** at).
congratulatorio, -ria, *a.* congratulatory.
congregación, *n.f.* congregation.
congregar [B], *v.t., v.r.* congregate.
congresal, *n.m.* (*S.A.*) [CONGRESISTA].
congresional, *a.* congressional.
congresista, *n.m.f.* member of a congress.
congreso, *n.m.* congress.
congrio, *n.m.* conger eel; (*fam.*) dope, fool.
congruencia, *n.f.* congruence, congruity.
congruente, *a.* congruent.
congruo, -rua, *a.* congruous.
cónico, -ca, *a.* conical, conic.
conífero, -ra, *a.* coniferous.—*n.f.* conifer.
conjetura, *n.f.* conjecture.
conjetural, *a.* conjectural.
conjeturar, *v.t.* conjecture, surmise.
conjugación, *n.f.* conjugation.
conjugar [B], *v.t.* conjugate.
conjunción, *n.f.* conjunction.
conjunctivo, -va, *a.* conjunctive.
conjunto, -ta, *a.* conjunct, allied.—*n.m.* entirety, whole; **en —,** as a whole.
conjura, conjuración, *n.f.* conspiracy.
conjurado, -da, *n.m.f.* conspirator.
conjurar, *v.t.* entreat, conjure; exorcize.—*v.i. v.r.* conspire.
conjuro, *n.m.* conjuration, entreaty.
conllevar, *v.t.* share (*burden*); bear with, suffer.
conmemoración, *n.f.* commemoration.
conmemorar, *v.t.* commemorate.
conmemorativo, -va, *a.* commemorative.
conmensurable, *a.* commensurable, commensurate.
conmigo, with me.
conminar, *v.t.* threaten.
conmiseración, *n.f.* commiseration.
conmisto, -ta, *a.* mingled, (*obs.*) commixed.
conmoción, *n.f.* commotion.

conmovedor, -ra, a. moving, touching.
conmover [5], *v.t.* move, touch.—*v.r.* be moved.
conmutable, *a.* commutable.
conmutación, *n.f.* commutation.
conmutar, *v.t.* commute.
conmutatriz, *n.f.* (*elec.*) converter (of A.C. or D.C.).
connaturalizar [C], *v.r.* become acclimatized.
connivencia, *n.f.* connivance.
connivente, *a.* conniving.
connotación, *n.f.* connotation.
connotar, *v.t.* connote.
cono, *n.m.* cone.
conocedor, -ra, *a.* knowledgeable, well-informed, expert.—*n.m.f.* connoisseur, expert.
conocencia, *n.f.* (*jur.*) statement, confession.
conocer [9], *v.t.* know, be acquainted with; get to know; (*jur.*) try (*a case*).—*v.i.* know (**en, de,** about).
conocible, *a.* knowable.
conocido, -da, *a.* familiar; well-known.— *n.m.f.* acquaintance.
conocimiento, *n.m.* knowledge; consciousness; (*com.*) bill of lading; acquaintance; (*jur.*) substantiation.
conque, *conj., adv.* so that, so then, then.— *n.m.* (*fam.*) terms, condition; (*S.A.*) wherewithal.
conquista, *n.f.* conquest.
conquistador, *n.m.* conqueror; conquistador; (*fam.*) lady-killer.
conquistar, *v.t.* conquer; capture; win over gain.
consabido, -da, *a.* aforesaid; well-known.
consagración, *n.f.* consecration.
consagrar, *v.t.* consecrate, dedicate.
consanguíneo, -nea, *a.* consanguineous.
consciente, *a.* conscious, aware; conscientious.
conscripción, *n.f.* conscription, (*U.S.*) draft.
conscripto, *n.m.* conscript, (*U.S.*) draftee.
consecución, *n.f.* acquisition.
consecuencia, *n.f.* consequence.
consecuente, *a.* consequent, coherent.
consecutivo, -va, *a.* consecutive.
conseguir [8G], *v.t.* obtain, attain; bring about.—*v.i.* manage, succeed.
conseja, *n.f.* yarn, tale.
consejero, -ra, *a.* advisory.—*n.m.f.* counsellor; councillor.
consejo, *n.m.* advice, counsel; council, board; **— de guerra,** court martial.
consenso, *n.m.* assent; consensus.
consentido, -da, *a.* spoiled (*child*); complaisant (*husband*); (*S.A.*) haughty.
consentimiento, *n.m.* consent.
consentir [6], *v.t.* permit, allow; pamper.—*v.i.* consent (**en,** to); believe.—*v.r.* come apart; (*S.A.*) be haughty.
conserje, *n.m.* concierge.
conserjería, *n.f.* porter's desk or room or position.
conserva (1), *n.f.* preserves; jam; pickles; **conservas alimenticias,** tinned food.
conserva (2), *n.f.* (*naut.*) convoy.
conservación, *n.f.* maintenance; preservation, conservation.
conservador, -ra, *a.* preservative; (*pol.*) conservative.—*n.m.f.* conservative, (*pol.*) Conservative.—*n.m.* curator.
conservaduría, *n.f.* curatorship.

conservar

conservar, *v.t.* conserve, preserve, keep, save. —*v.r.* look after oneself; keep, last well.
conservatismo, *n.m.* conservatism.
conservatorio, -ria, *a., n.m.* conservatory.
conservería, *n.f.* canning, preserving; canning factory.
considerable, *a.* considerable.
consideración, *n.f.* consideration; importance; regard.
considerado, -da, *a.* considerate; considered; esteemed.
considerar, *v.t.* consider.
consigna, *n.f.* (*mil.*) order, charge; (*rail.*) left-luggage office, (*U.S.*) checkroom.
consignación, *n.f.* consignment; apportionment.
consignar, *v.t.* consign; apportion; state; deliver.
consignatorio, -ria, *n.m.f.* (*com.*) consignee.
consigo, with him, her, it, them; with you; with himself, herself *etc.*
consiguiente, *a.* consequent, consequential; *por* —, consequently.
consistencia, *n.f.* consistency.
consistente, *a.* consistent; consisting (*en,* of, in).
consistir, *v.i.* consist (*en,* of, in).
consistorio, *n.m.* consistory, council.
consola, *n.f.* console.
consolación, *n.f.* consolation.
consolador, -ra, *a.* consoling.—*n.m.f.* consoler.
consolar [4], *v.t.* console, comfort.
consolidación, *n.f.* consolidation.
consolidados, *n.m.pl.* consols.
consolidar, *v.t., v.r.* consolidate.
consonancia, *n.f.* consonance, rhyme; harmony.
consonantado, -da, *a.* rhymed.
consonante, *a.* consonant; rhyming.—*n.m.* rhyme word.—*n.f.* consonant.
consonántico, -ca, *a.* consonantal.
consonar [4], *v.t.* rhyme; harmonize.
consorcio, *n.m.* consortium.
consorte, *n.m.f.* consort; partner; accomplice.
conspicuo, -cua, *a.* outstanding; conspicuous.
conspiración, *n.f.* conspiracy.
conspirado, *n.m.,* **conspirador, -ra,** *n.m.f.* conspirator.
conspirar, *v.i.* conspire.
constancia, *n.f.* constancy; proof, evidence.
constante, *a., n.f.* (*math.*) constant.
constar, *v.i.* be clear, certain, right; — *de* consist of.
constatación, *n.f.* proof, proving.
constatar, *v.t.* prove, establish.
constelación, *n.f.* constellation; climate.
constelar, *v.t.* spangle.
consternación, *n.f.* consternation.
consternar, *v.t.* distress, dismay.
constipado, *n.m.* head cold.
constipar, *v.r.* catch cold; *estar constipado,* have a cold.
constitución, *n.f.* constitution.
constitucional, *a.* constitutional.
constituir [O], *v.t.* constitute, establish; force into (*en*).—*v.r.* set oneself up, be established (*en, por,* as).
constituyente, *a., n.m.* (*pol. etc.*) constituent.
constreñimiento, *n.m.* constraint; (*med.*) constipation.

constreñir [8K], *v.t.* constrain; (*med.*) constipate.
constricción, *n.f.* constriction.
construcción, *n.f.* construction, structure.
constructivo, -va, *a.* constructive.
constructor, -ra, *a.* constructing.—*n.m.f.* constructor; builder.
construir [O], *v.t.* construct.
consuelo, *n.m.* consolation, comfort; *sin* —, to excess, inconsolably.
consueta, *n.m.* (*theat.*) prompter.
cónsul, *n.m.* consul.
consulado, *n.m.* consulate; consulship.
consular, *a.* consular.
consulta, consultación, *n.f.* consultation.
consultar, *v.t.* consult; discuss; advise.
consultivo, -va, *a.* consultative.
consultor, -ra, *a.* consulting.—*n.m.f.* consultant.
consultorio, *n.m.* advice bureau; clinic.
consumación, *n.f.* consummation.
consumar, *v.t.* consummate.
consumición, *n.f.* consumption; drink, food.
consumir, *v.t.* consume; take communion; (*fam.*) vex, wear down.—*v.r.* pine, waste away; be consumed.
consumo, *n.m.* consumption; consumers.—*pl.* octroi, excise.
consunción, *n.f.* (*med. etc.*) consumption.
de consuno, *adv. phr.* jointly, in accord.
consuntivo, -va, *a.* consumptive.
contabilidad, *n.f.* accountancy, book-keeping.
contabilista, *n.m.* accountant.
contable, *n.m.f.* book-keeper.
contacto, *n.m.* contact.
contadero, -ra, *a.* countable, to be counted. —*n.m.* turnstile.
contado, -da, *a.* scarce, infrequent; (*obs.*) famous; *al* —, for cash; *por de* —, of course.
contador, *n.m.* counter, meter; auditor; till; — *de Geiger,* Geiger counter.
contaduría, *n.f.* accountancy; accountant's office; (*theat.*) box office; treasury.
contagiar, *v.t.* infect.—*v.r.* become infected (*de,* with).
contagio, *n.m.* contagion.
contagioso, -sa, *a.* contagious.
contaminación, *n.f.* contamination.
contaminar, *v.t.* contaminate; infringe; corrupt.
contante, *a.* ready (*cash*); (*fam.*) *dinero — y sonante,* ready cash.
contar [4], *v.t.* count; tell, narrate; debit; consider; — *con,* count on, rely on.
contemplación, *n.f.* contemplation.
contemplar, *v.t.* contemplate; be lenient towards.
contemplativo, -va, *a.* contemplative; condescending.
contemporáneo, -nea, *a., n.m.f.* contemporary.
contención, *n.f.* contention, strife.
contencioso, -sa, *a.* contentious.
contender [2], *v.i.* contend.
contendiente, *n.m.* contender.
contener [33], *v.t.* contain.
contenido, -da, *a.* restrained.—*n.m.* contents.
contenta, *n.f.* gift, treat; (*com.*) endorsement.
contentadizo, -za, *a.* easy to please; *mal* —, hard to please.
contentamiento, *n.m.* contentment.

contentar, *v.t.* content, please.—*v.r.* be content (*de, con,* with).
contento, -ta, *a.* glad, content.—*n.m.* contentment.
contera, *n.f.* metal tip; refrain; bell; (*fam.*) the end.
conterráneo, -nea, *a.,n.m.f.* person or thing from the same country or region.
contestable, *a.* answerable.
contestación, *n.f.* answer, reply; dispute.
contestar, *v.t.* answer; confirm.—*v.i.* reply (*a,* to); agree.
contexto, *n.m.* context; interweaving.
contienda, *n.f.* dispute, fight.
contigo, with you.
contiguo, -gua, *a.* contiguous.
continental, *a., n.m.f.* continental.
continente, *a.* continent.—*n.m.* container; continent; countenance.
contingencia, *n.f.* contingency.
contingente, *a.* contingent.—*n.m.* contingent; quota; contingency.
contingible, *a.* possible.
continuación, *n.f.* continuation; *a* —, below, as follows.
continuadamente, *adv.* continuously; continually.
continuar [M], *v.t.* continue.—*v.i., v.r.* be adjacent (*con,* to); *continuará,* to be continued.
continuidad, *n.f.* continuity.
continuo, -nua, *a.* continual; continuous; perservering; *de* —, continuously.
contómetro, *n.m.* comptometer.
contonear, *v.r.* strut, swagger, waddle.
contoneo, *n.m.* strut, swagger, waddle.
contorcer [5D], *v.r.* writhe.
contorsión, *n.f.* writhing, contortion.
contorno, *n.m.* outline; contour; *en* —, round about.—*pl.* environs.
contorsión, *n.f.* contortion.
contorsionista, *n.m.f.* contortionist.
contra, *n.m.* contra, con.—*n.f.* (*fam.*) bother, pest; (*S.A.*) antidote; *llevar la* — *a,* (*fam.*) go against.—*prep.* against; facing.—*prefix.* counter-, contra-.
contraalmirante, *n.m.* rear-admiral.
contraatacar [A], *v.t., v.i.* counter-attack.
contraataque, *n.m.* counter-attack.
contrabajo, *n.m.* (*mus.*) double bass.
contrabalancear, *v.t.* counterbalance.
contrabalanza, *n.f.* counterbalance, counterpoise.
contrabandear, *v.i.* smuggle.
contrabandista, *n.m.f.* smuggler.
contrabando, *n.m.* contraband; smuggling.
contrabarrera, *n.f.* (*taur.*) second row seats.
contracción, *n.f.* contraction.
contracifra, *n.f.* cypher-key.
contráctil, *a.* contractile.
contracto, -ta, *a.* contracted.
contractual, *a.* contractual.
contradecir [17], *v.t.* contradict.
contradicción, *n.f.* contradiction.
contradictorio, -ria, *a.* contradictory.
contradicho [CONTRADECIR].
contraer [34], *v.t.* contract; condense.—*v.r.* contract.
contraespionaje, *n.m.* counterespionage.
contrafigura, *n.f.* counterpart.
contrafuerte, *n.m.* girth strap; stiffener; buttress.

contrahacedor, -ra, *a.* counterfeiting.—*n.m.f.* counterfeiter; imitator.
contrahacer [20], *v.t.* counterfeit; imitate; feign.
contrahaz, *n.f.* (*pl.* **-aces**) reverse side.
contrahecho [CONTRAHACER].
contrahechura, *n.f.* counterfeit, forgery.
a contrahilo, *adv. phr.* on the cross, against the grain.
contraigo [CONTRAER].
contralto, *n.m.f.* contralto.
contraluz, *n.f.* view (*facing the light*); *a* —, against the light.
contramaestre, *n.m.* overseer; (*naut.*) petty officer, bosun.
contramandar, *v.t.* countermand.
a contramano, *adv. phr.* in the wrong direction.
contramarcha, *n.f.* countermarch; reverse.
contramarchar, *v.i.* countermarch; reverse.
contranatural, *a.* unnatural, against nature.
a contrapelo, *adv. phr.* against the (*lie of the*) hair; (*fig.*) against the grain.
contrapesar, *v.t.* counterbalance.
contrapeso, *n.m.* counterbalance; *puente de* —, cantilever bridge.
contraponer [25], *v.t.* compare; oppose.
contraposición, *n.f.* contraposition, contrast.
contraproducente, *a.* self-defeating.
contrapuerta, *n.f.* screen door, storm door.
contrapuesto [CONTRAPONER].
contrapunto, *n.m.* counterpoint; sarcasm.
contrapuse [CONTRAPONER].
contrariar [L], *v.t.* oppose, run counter to; disappoint, annoy.
contrariedad, *n.f.* obstacle; contrariness; opposition.
contrario, -ria, *a.* contrary, opposite.—*n.m.f.* opponent, adversary.—*n.m.* impediment; contradiction; *al* — or *por* (*el*) —, on the contrary; *llevar la contraria a,* (*fam.*) go against, oppose.
Contrarreforma, *n.f.* (*hist.*) Counter-Reformation.
contrarrestar, *v.t.* counteract, resist.
contrarrevolución, *n.f.* counterrevolution.
contrasentido, *n.m.* misinterpretation; contradiction.
contraseña, *n.f.* countersign; counterfoil; ticket.
contrastar, *v.t.* resist; assay.—*v.i.* resist; contrast.
contraste, *n.m.* contrast; resistance; assay, assaying; hall-mark.
contrata, *n.f.* contract.
contratante, *a.* contracting.—*n.m.f.* contractor.
contratar, *v.t.* engage, hire; trade.
contratiempo, *n.m.* contretemps.
contratista, *n.m.* contractor.
contrato, *n.m.* contract.
contravención, *n.f.* contravention.
contraveneno, *n.m.* antidote.
contravenir [36], *v.i.* contravene, violate (*a*).
contraventana, *n.f.* shutter.
contraventor, -ra, *a.* contravening.—*n.m.f.* contravener.
contravine [CONTRAVENIR].
contrayente, *a., n.m.f.* contracting party.
contrecho, -cha, *a.* crippled.
contribución, *n.f.* contribution; tax.
contribuir [O], *v.t., v.i.* contribute.

contributivo, -va, *a.* contributive; tax, rel. to taxes.
contribuyente, *n.m.f.* contributor; taxpayer.
contrición, *n.f.* contrition.
contrincante, *n.m.* rival, competitor.
contristar, *v.t.* sadden.
contrito, -ta, *a.* contrite.
control, *n.m.* control; inspection, supervision.
controlar, *v.t.* control; supervise, inspect.
controversia, *n.f.* controversy.
controvertir [6], *v.t.* controvert, call in question.
contumacia, *n.f.* contumacy; (*jur.*) contempt.
contumaz, *a.* (*pl.* **-aces**) contumacious; (*med.*) disease-carrying; (*jur.*) guilty of contempt.
contumelia, *n.f.* contumely.
contundente, *a.* bruising, blunt; forceful.
contundir, *v.t.* bruise, contuse.
conturbación, *n.f.* anxiety, perturbation.
conturbar, *v.t.* perturb, disquiet.
contusión, *n.f.* contusion.
contuso, -sa, *a.* contused, bruised.
contuve [CONTENER].
convalecencia, *n.f.* convalescence.
convalecer [9], *v.i.* convalesce, recover.
convaleciente, *a.,* *n.m.f.* convalescent.
convalidar, *v.t.* ratify, confirm.
convección, *n.f.* convection.
convecino, -na, *a.* neighbouring.—*n.m.f.* next-door neighbour.
convencer [D], *v.t.* convince.
convención, *n.f.* convention.
convencional, *a.* conventional.
conveniencia, *n.f.* conformity; settlement; suitability; convenience, advantage.—*pl.* wealth; proprieties, social conventions.
convenienciero, -ra, *a.* self-centred, selfish.
conveniente, *a.* appropriate; convenient, advantageous.
convenio, *n.m.* pact; settlement.
convenir [36], *v.i.* be appropriate; suit, be advantageous *or* important; agree (**en,** to).—*v.r.* come to an agreement; **conviene a saber,** that is to say, namely.
conventillo, *n.m.* (*S.A.*) tenement house.
convento, *n.m.* convent; monastery.
convergencia, *n.f.* convergence; concurrence.
convergente, *a.* convergent.
converger, convergir [E], *v.i.* converge; concur.
conversable, *a.* sociable.
conversación, *n.f.* conversation.
conversador, -ra, *a.* conversing.—*n.m.f.* conversationalist.
conversar, *v.i.* converse; (*mil.*) wheel about.
conversión, *n.f.* conversion.
converso, -sa, *a.* converted.—*n.m.f.* convert; lay brother.
convertibilidad, *n.f.* convertibility.
convertible, *a.* convertible.
convertir [6], *v.t.* convert.—*v.r.* be converted; turn, change.
convexidad, *n.f.* convexity.
convexo, -xa, *a.* convex.
convicción, *n.f.* conviction.
convicto, -ta, *a.* convicted.—*n.m.f.* convict.
convidado, -da, *n.m.f.* guest.
convidar, *v.t.* invite; treat.—*v.r.* offer one's services.
convincente, *a.* convincing.

convine [CONVENIR].
convite, *n.m.* invitation; treat; banquet.
convivencia, *n.f.* coexistence; life together.
convivir, *v.i.* coexist, live together.
convocación, *n.f.* convocation.
convocar [A], *v.t.* convoke.
convocatorio, -ria, *a.* convoking, summoning.—*n.f.* summons, call.
convolución, *n.f.* convolution.
convoy, *n.m.* convoy; cruet set; (*fam.*) retinue; (*S.A.*) train.
convoyar, *v.t.* convoy.
convulsión, *n.f.* convulsion.
convulsionar, *v.t.* convulse.
convulsivo, -va, *a.* convulsive.
convulso, -sa, *a.* convulsed.
conyugal, *a.* conjugal.
cónyuge, *n.m.f.* spouse.
coñac, *n.m.* cognac, brandy.
cooperación, *n.f.* co-operation.
cooperar, *v.i.* co-operate.
cooperativo, -va, *a., n.f.* co-operative.
coordinación, *n.f.* co-ordination.
coordinar, *v.t.* co-ordinate.
copa, *n.f.* wine- *or* spirit-glass, goblet; tree-top; crown (*of hat*); (*sport, fig.*) cup.
copar, *v.t.* take by surprise; (*fam.*) sweep (*election*).
coparticipación, *n.f.* copartnership.
copartícipe, *n.m.f.* copartner.
copero, *n.m.* cup-bearer; cocktail cabinet.
copeta, *n.f.* small wine glass.
copete, *n.m.* forelock; tuft; crest; top; (*fig.*) haughtiness; **de alto —,** high-ranking, aristocratic.
copetudo, -da, *a.* crested, tufted; (*fig.*) snobbish, haughty.
copia (1), *n.f.* plenty, abundance.
copia (2), *n.f.* copy.
copiante, *n.m.f.* copier, copyist.
copiar, *v.t.* copy.
copioso, -sa, *a.* copious.
copista, *n.m.f.* copyist.
copla, *n.f.* couplet; stanza; popular song; **coplas de ciego,** doggerel.
coplero, -ra, coplista, *n.m.f.* ballad-monger; poetaster.
copo, *n.m.* skein; (snow)flake.
coposo, -sa, *a.* bushy; woolly.
copra, *n.f.* copra.
cóptico, -ca, *a.* Coptic.
copto, -ta, *a.* Coptic.—*n.m.f.* Copt.
cópula, *n.f.* copula.
copulativo, -va, *a., n.f.* copulative.
coque, *n.m.* coke.
coqueluche, *n.f.* whooping cough.
coquera, *n.f.* cavity; coke scuttle.
coqueta, *a.* coquettish.—*n.f.* coquette, flirt; dressing-table.
coquetear, *v.i.* flirt, be coquettish.
coquetería, *n.f.* flirtation; flirtatiousness; coquetry; affectation; (*S.A.*) good taste.
coquetismo, *n.m.* coquetry.
coquetón, -tona, *a.* coquettish.—*n.m.* lady-killer.
coquito, *n.m.* amusing grimace.
coraje, *n.m.* anger; mettle.
corajina, *n.f.* (*fam.*) tantrum, outburst.
corajudo, -da, *a.* (*fam.*) bad-tempered.
coral (1), *a.* choral.—*n.m.* chorale.
coral (2), *n.m.* coral.—*pl.* coral beads.
Corán, *n.m.* Koran.

coránico, -ca, a. Koranic.
coraza, n.f. cuirass; armour.
corazón, n.m. heart; core; (fig.) courage; de —, sincerely; hacer de tripas —, find courage in fear.
corazonada, n.f. impulse; hunch; (fam.) guts.
corbata, n.f. tie, cravat.
corbatín, n.m. bow-tie.
corbeta, n.f. (naut.) corvette; capitán de —, lieutenant commander.
Córcega, n.f. Corsica.
corcel, n.m. charger, steed.
corcova, n.m. hump, hunch.
corcovado, -da, a. hunch-backed.—n.m.f. hunchback.
corcovar, v.t. bend.
corcovear, v.i. buck; (S.A.) grumble; (C.A.) be afraid.
corcovo, n.m. buck, bucking; (fam.) crookedness.
corcusir, v.t. (fam.) mend roughly.
corcha, n.f. raw cork.
corcheta, n.f. eye (of fastening).
corchete, n.m. hook (of fastening); fastener; square bracket [ ]; (obs.) constable.
corcho, n.m. cork; cork, stopper.
corchoso, -sa, a. corky.
cordaje, n.m. strings (of guitar); (naut.) rigging.
cordal, n.m. (mus.) string-bar; wisdom tooth.
cordel, n.m. cord; a —, in a straight line.
cordelazo, n.m. lash or blow with rope.
cordelería, n.f. cordmaking, cordage; (naut.) rigging.
cordería, n.f. cordage.
corderino, -na, a. rel. to lambs.—n.f. lambskin.
cordero, -ra, n.m.f. lamb.
cordial, a., n.m. cordial.
cordialidad, n.f. cordiality.
cordillera, n.f. chain or range of mountains.
cordita, n.f. cordite.
Córdoba, n.f. Cordova.
cordobán, n.m. cordovan (leather).
cordobés, -besa, a., n.m.f. Cordovan.
cordón, n.m. cord; cordon; strand; lace.—pl. aiguillettes.
cordoncillo, n.m. braid; milled edge.
cordura, n.f. wisdom, good sense.
Corea, n.f. Korea.
coreano, -na, a., n.m.f. Korean.
corear, v.t., v.i. chorus; choir.
coreografía, n.f. choreography.
coreógrafo, n.m. choreographer.
corezuelo, n.m. piglet; crackling.
Corinto, n.f. Corinth; pasa de —, currant.
corista, n.m.f. chorister.—n.f. (theat.) chorus girl.
corladura, n.f. gold varnish.
corma, n.f. wooden stocks; (fig.) hindrance.
cormorán, n.m. (orn.) cormorant.
cornada, n.f. horn thrust or wound.
cornadura, cornamenta, n.f. horns, antlers.
cornamusa, n.f. bagpipes; brass horn.
córnea, n.f. cornea.
corneal, a. corneal.
cornear, v.t. butt, gore.
corneja, n.f. crow; scops owl.
córneo, -nea, a. horny.
córner, n.m. corner (in football).
corneta, n.f. (mus.) cornet; bugle; pennant.—n.m. bugler.

cornetilla, n.f. hot pepper.
cornezuelo, n.m. (bot.) ergot.
córnico, -ca, a. Cornish.
cornisa, n.f. cornice.
corno, n.m. dogwood; (mus.) horn.
Cornualles, n.m. Cornwall.
cornucopia, n.f. cornucopia.
cornudo, -da, a. horned.—a.m., n.m. cuckold.
cornúpeta, cornupeto, a.m. butting.—n.m. (fam.) bull.
coro (1), n.m. choir; chorus; hacer — a, echo, second; a coros, alternately.
coro (2), de —, by heart.
corolario, n.m. corollary.
corona, n.f. crown; tonsure; corona; wreath; coronet; ceñir(se) la —, come to the throne.
coronación, n.f. coronation; crowning.
coronamiento, n.m. completion, termination.
coronar, v.t. crown; cap; complete.
coronel, n.m. colonel; (aer.) group captain.
coronela, n.f. colonel's wife.
coronilla, n.f. crown (of the head); estar hasta la — (de), (fam.) be fed up (with).
corotos, n.m.pl. (S.A.) gear, tackle.
coroza, n.f. conical cap (for criminals); peasant cap.
corpa(n)chón, n.m. (fam.) big carcass; fowl's carcass.
corpazo, n.m. (fam.) big body.
corpecico, corpiño, n.m. small body; bodice.
corporación, n.f. corporation.
corporal, a. corporal, bodily.
corporativo, -va, a. corporat(iv)e.
corpóreo, -ea, a. corporeal.
corpulencia, n.f. corpulence.
corpulento, -ta, a. corpulent.
Corpus, n.m. Corpus Christi.
corpúsculo, n.m. corpuscle; particle.
corral, n.m. yard, farm yard; (obs.) open-air theatre; corral; hacer corrales, (fam.) play truant.
correa, n.f. belt, strap; leatheriness; besar la —, eat humble pie; tiene mucha —, (fam.) he can take it! — de seguridad, safety belt.
correcalles, n.m. inv. idler, loafer.
corrección, n.f. correction; correctness.
correccional, a. correctional.—n.m. reformatory.
correctivo, -va, a., n.m. corrective.
correcto, -ta, a. correct.
corrector, -ra, a. correcting.—n.m.f. corrector; proof-reader.
corredera (1), n.f. track, rail; runner; slide valve; (naut.) log line; (S.A.) rapids; de —, sliding (door etc.).
corredera (2), n.f. (ent.) cockroach.
corredizo, -za, a. running (knot), sliding.
corredor, -ra, a. running.—n.m.f. runner.—n.m. corridor; gallery; (com.) broker; (mil. obs.) scout.
corredura, n.f. overflow.
corregidor, -ra, a. correcting.—n.m. (obs.) corregidor, Spanish magistrate.
corregir [8E], v.t. correct.
correlación, n.f. correlation.
correlacionar, v.t. correlate.
correlativo, -va, a., n.m. correlative.
correntío, -tía, a. runny, running; (fig.) easy going.

correo, *n.m.* post, mail; post office; mail train; courier; — **aéreo,** airmail; **echar al —,** post.

correón, *n.m.* large strap.

correoso, -sa, *a.* leathery.

correr, *v.t.* run; travel over; chase; overrun; slide, draw; shame, confuse; *(taur.)* fight; auction; *(fam.)* pinch, steal.—*v.i.* run; flow; pass; be current; be valid; **correrla,** *(fam.)* spend a night on the town; **a todo —,** at full speed; **que corre,** current.—*v.r.* run, drip; *(fam.)* overstep the mark; *(fam.)* become embarrassed; slide, slip; turn.

correría, *n.f.* incursion; excursion.

correspondencia, *n.f.* correspondence; harmony; connexion; intercourse.

corresponder, *v.i.* correspond; communicate; — **a,** return, reciprocate; concern, be the duty of.

correspondiente, *a.* corresponding.—*n.m.f.* correspondent.

corresponsal, *n.m.f.* *(press, com.)* correspondent.

corretear, *v.t.* *(S.A.)* chase, pester.—*v.i.* *(fam.)* gad about, race around.

correve(i)dile, *n.m.f.* *(fam.)* gossip, tell-tale.

corrido, -da, *a.* surplus; cursive; fluent; experienced; continuous; *(fam.)* confused. —*n.m.* lean-to; **de —,** fluently, without pause.—*n.f.* bullfight; run, race; *(S.A.)* binge; **de corrida,** without pausing.

corriente, *a.* running, flowing; current; ordinary, common; normal.—*n.m.* current month; **al — de,** posted on, up to date with. —*n.f.* current; stream; draught.—*interj.* fine! all right!

corrillo, *n.m.* clique, coterie.

corrimiento, *n.m.* running; flow; abashment; landslide.

corrincho, *n.m.* bunch of no-goods, riff-raff.

corro, *n.m.* group, circle; ring, space.

corroboración, *n.f.* corroboration.

corroborar, *v.t.* corroborate; fortify.

corroborativo, -va, *a.* corroborative.

corroer [29], *v.t.* corrode, eat away.

corromper, *v.t.* corrupt; rot; *(fam.)* bother.

corrosión, *n.f.* corrosion.

corrosivo, -va, *a., n.m.* corrosive.

corrugación, *n.f.* contraction; corrugation.

corrumpente, *a.* corrupting; *(fam.)* bothersome.

corrupción, *n.f.* corruption; rotting.

corruptela, *n.f.* corruption; abuse.

corruptible, *a.* corruptible.

corrusco, *n.m.* *(fam.)* chunk of bread, crust.

corsario, -ria, *a.* *(naut.)* privateering.—*n.m.* privateer, pirate.

corsé, *n.m.* corset.

corsear, *v.i.* *(naut.)* privateer.

corso, -sa, *a., n.m.f.* Corsican.—*n.m.* privateering; *(S.A.)* promenade.

corta, *n.f.* felling, cutting.

cortacorriente, *n.m.* *(elec.)* switch.

cortada, *n.f.* *(S.A.)* cut; haircut.

cortado, -da, *a.* proportioned; jerky *(style)*; with a little milk *(coffee)*; *(S.A.)* broke, hard up.—*n.m.* caper, leap; small glass.

cortador, -ra, *a.* cutting.—*n.m.* cutter *(person)*; butcher.—*n.f.* cutter; slicer; mower.

cortadura, *n.f.* cutting; cut, gash.—*pl.* trimmings, cuttings.

cortafuego, *n.m.* fire barrier.

cortalápices, *n.m. inv.* pencil-sharpener.

cortante, *a.* cutting, sharp.—*n.m.* butcher's knife.

cortapicos, *n.m. inv.* *(ent.)* earwig; — **y callares,** *(fam.)* less lip! *(to children)*.

cortaplumas, *n.m. inv.* penknife.

cortar, *v.t.* cut; cut off, out, down, up; *(elec.)* switch off; — **de vestir,** *(fam.)* backbite.— *v.r.* become speechless; chap; curdle.

cortavidrios, *n.m. inv.* glass cutter.

cortaviento, *n.m.* windshield.

la Corte, *n.f.* Madrid.—*pl.* Spanish Parliament.

corte (1), *n.m.* cut; cutting; cutting edge; *(elec.)* break; **darse —,** *(S.A.)* put on airs.

corte (2), *n.f.* court, royal household; *(S.A.)* law court; **hacer la — a,** pay court to, court.

cortedad, *n.f.* shortness; scantiness; timidity.

cortejar, *v.t.* court; escort.

cortejo, *n.m.* courtship; entourage; cortège; *(fam.)* beau, lover.

cortero, *n.m.* *(S.A.)* day labourer.

cortés, *a.* courteous, polite.

cortesanía, *n.f.* courtliness; flattery.

cortesano, -na, *a.* courtly.—*n.m.* courtier.— *n.f.* courtesan.

cortesía, *n.f.* courtesy; bow, curtsy.

corteza, *n.f.* bark; peel, rind; crust; coarseness; *(orn.)* sand grouse.

cortezudo, -da, *a.* barky, crusty; boorish, coarse.

cortical, *a.* cortical.

cortijo, *n.m.* farm, farmhouse.

cortil, *n.m.* farmyard.

cortina, *n.f.* curtain; screen; **correr la —,** open *or* close the curtain.

cortinaje, *n.m.* curtaining.

cortinilla, *n.f.* window netting; curtain.

cortisona, *n.f.,* **cortisono,** *n.m.* cortisone.

corto, -ta, *a.* short; scanty; weak; shy; wanting; — **de oído,** hard of hearing; — **de vista,** short-sighted; **corta edad,** early childhood.

cortocircuito, *n.m.* *(elec.)* short circuit.

la Coruña, *n.f.* Corunna.

coruñés, -sa, *a.* rel. to Corunna.—*n.m.f.* native of Corunna.

coruscar [A], *v.i.* *(poet.)* glow, shine.

corvadura, *n.f.* curvature, bend.

corvejón, *n.m.* hock; spur *(of cock)*.

córvidos, *n.m.pl.* *(orn.)* Corvidae.

corvino, -na, *a.* corvine, raven-like.

corvo, -va, *a.* curved, arched.— *m.* hook.

corzo, -za, *n m f.* roe-deer, fallow-de..r.

cosa, *n.f.* thing; **a — hecha,** as good as done; **como si tal —,** *(fam.)* as if nothing had happened; — **de,** a matter of, about; — **que,** *(S.A.)* so that, in order that.

cosaco, -ca, *a., n.m.f.* Cossack.

coscarse, *v.r.* *(fam.)* shrug.

coscoja, *n.f.* kermes oak.

coscojita, *n.f.* hop-scotch.

coscón, -cona, *a.* *(fam.)* crafty, sly.

coscorrón, *n.m.* bump *(on the head)*, bruise.

cosecante, *n.f.* *(math.)* cosecant.

cosecha, *n.f.* harvest, crop; **de su —,** *(fam.)* out of his own head.

cosechar, *v.t.* harvest, reap.

cosechero, -ra, *n.m.f.* harvester.

coseno, *n.m.* *(math.)* cosine.

coser, *v.t.* sew; join closely.

cosicosa, *n.f.* riddle, puzzle.
cosido, *n.m.* sewing.
cosmético, -ca, *a., n.m.* cosmetic.
cósmico, -ca, *a.* cosmic.
cosmopolita, *a., n.m.f.* cosmopolitan.
cosmos, *n.m. sg.* cosmos.
coso (1), *n.m.* bullring.
coso (2), *n.m.* wood-worm.
cosquillas, *n.f.pl.* ticklishness; (*fig.*) touchiness; (*fig., fam.*) weak spot; **tener —,** be ticklish; **tener malas —,** be touchy.
cosquillear, *v.t.* tickle.
cosquilleo, *n.m.* tickling.
cosquilloso, -sa, *a.* ticklish; touchy.
costa (1), *n.f.* cost.
costa (2), *n.f.* coast; **Costa de Marfil,** Ivory Coast.
costado, *n.m.* side; (*mil.*) flank.
costal, *n.m.* sack.
costanero, -ra, *a.* coastal; sloping.—*n.f.* slope; rafter.
costanilla, *n.f.* narrow steep street.
costar [4], *v.t.* cost.
costarricense, costarriqueño, -ña, *a., n.m.f.* Costa Rican.
coste, *n.m.* cost, price.
costear, *v.t.* pay the cost of; (*naut.*) coast.
costeño, -ña, *a.* coastal.
costero, -ra, *a.* coastal.—*n.m.* side.—*n.f.* side; slope; coast; fishing season.
costilla, *n.f.* rib; (*fam.*) better half, wife.—*pl.* back, shoulders.
costilludo, -da, *a.* (*fam.*) well-built (*person*).
costo, *n.m.* cost; **el — de la vida,** the cost of living.
costoso, -sa, *a.* costly.
costra, *n.f.* scab; crust.
costroso, -sa, *a.* crusty; scaled; scabby.
costumbre, *n.f.* custom; habit; **de —,** usual; usually; **tener la —,** be in the habit of.
costumbrista, *a., n.m.f.* (*lit.*) author who chronicles the customs of his period.
costura, *n.f.* seam; sewing.
costurera, *n.f.* seamstress, dressmaker.
costurón, *n.m.* (*pej.*) thick seam; (*fig.*) heavy scar.
cota, *n.f.* coat (*of mail etc.*); quota; elevation (*in maps*).
cotangente, *n.f.* (*math.*) cotangent.
cotarrera, *n.f.* (*fam.*) chin-wagger; (*pej.*) slut.
cotarro, *n.m.* side of a ravine; flophouse.
cotejar, *v.t.* compare.
cotejo, *n.m.* comparison; comparing.
cotidiano, -na, *a.* daily, everyday.
cotillo, *n.m.* hammer-head *or* -face.
cotillón, *n.m.* cotillion.
cotización, *n.f.* quotation (*of price*); quota.
cotizar [C], *v.t.* quote (*a price*); impose, collect *or* pay dues.—*v.r.* be esteemed *or* valued.
coto (1), *n.m.* estate, preserve; boundary stone; **poner —ʼa,** put a stop to.
coto (2), *n.m.* (*ichth.*) chub.
coto (3), *n.m.* (*S.A.*) goitre.
cotón, *n.m.* printed cotton; (*S.A.*) smock.
cotonada, *n.f.* printed cotton.
cotorra, *n.f.* (*orn.*) parakeet; magpie; (*fam.*) gossiper, chatterer.
cotorrear, *v.i.* chatter, gossip.
cotufa, *n.f.* Jerusalem artichoke; titbit; (*S.A.*) pop-corn.

coturna, *n.m.* buskin.
covacha, *n.f.* small cave; (*S.A.*) box-room, storage room; (*C.A.*) shanty.
covachuelista, *n.m.* (*fam.*) civil servant.
coy, *n.m.* (*naut.*) hammock.
coyote, *n.m.* coyote, prairie wolf.
coyunda, *n.f.* yoking strap; (*fam.*) marriage; (*fig.*) bondage.
coyuntura, *n.f.* joint; juncture.
coz, *n.f.* (*pl.* **coces**) kick; recoil; return blow; (*fam.*) churlishness.
crac, *n.m.* crash, failure.
crampón, *n.m.* crampon.
cran, *n.m.* (*print.*) nick.
cráneo, *n.m.* cranium, skull.
crápula, *n.f.* dissipation.
crapuloso, -sa, *a.* crapulous, dissolute.
crascitar, *v.i.* caw.
crasitud, *n.f.* fatness; (*fam.*) stupidity.
craso, -sa, *a.* thick, greasy; crass; gross.
cráter, *n.m.* crater.
creación, *n.f.* creation.
creador, -ra, *a.* creating, creative.—*n.m.f.* creator.
crear, *v.t.* create.
creativo, -va, *a.* creative.
crecer [9], *v.i.* grow, increase; swell.—*v.r.* acquire more authority.
creces, *n.f.pl.* increase; extra; **con —,** abundantly, with interest.
crecida, *n.f.* swelling (*of rivers*).
crecido, -da, *a.* large, big; swollen.
creciente, *a.* growing; crescent.—*n.m.* crescent.—*n.f.* flood-tide; crescent moon.
crecimiento, *n.m.* growth; increase.
credencial, *a., n.f.* credential.
credibilidad, *n.f.* credibility.
crediticio, -cia, *a.* rel. to credit.
crédito, *n.m.* credit.
credo, *n.m.* creed, credo; (*fam.*) trice, moment; **con el — en la boca,** with his heart in his mouth.
credulidad, *n.f.* credulity.
crédulo, -la, *a.* credulous.
creedero, -ra, *a.* credible, believable.
creedor, -ra, *a.* credulous.
creencia, *n.f.* credence, credit; belief; creed.
creer [N], *v.t.* believe, think; **— en,** to believe in; **¡ya lo creo!** of course!—*v.r.* believe oneself to be.
creíble, *a.* believable, credible.
creído, -da, *a.* (*S.A.*) credulous; vain.
crema (1), *n.f.* cream.
crema (2), *n.f.* diaeresis (¨).
cremación, *n.f.* cremation.
cremallera, *n.f.* (*mech.*) rack; rack rail; zipper.
crematorio, -ria, *a.* crematory.—*n.m.* crematorium.
crémor tártaro, *n.m.* cream of tartar.
crencha, *n.f.* parting (*in hair*).
creosota, *n.f.* creosote.
crep, crepé, *n.m.* crêpe.
crepitación, *n.f.* crepitation, crackling.
crepitar, *v.i.* crepitate, crackle.
crepuscular, crepusculino, -na, *a.* crepuscular, twilight.
crepúsculo, *n.m.* twilight, crepuscule.
cresa, *n.f.* larva, maggot.
Creso, *n.m.* Croesus; **creso,** *n.m.* wealthy man.
crespo, -pa, *a.* curly; crispy; (*fig.*) angry; (*fig.*) over-elegant.

crespón, *n.m.* crêpe; crape.
cresta, *n.f.* crest.
crestado, -da, *a.* crested.
crestomatía, *n.f.* chrestomathy.
crestón, *n.m.* large crest; (*min.*) outcrop.
crestudo, -da, *a.* large-crested; (*fam.*) haughty.
Creta, *n.f.* Crete; **creta,** *n.f.* chalk.
cretáceo, -cea, *a.* cretaceous.
cretense, *a., n.m.f.* Cretan.
cretino, -na, *a.* cretinous.—*n.m.f.* cretin.
cretona, *n.f.* cretonne.
creyente, *a.* believing.—*n.m.f.* believer.
cría, *n.f.* brood; breeding; (*S.A.*) stock, lineage.
criadero, -ra, *a.* prolific.—*n.m.* nursery; hatchery; (*min.*) seam.
criado, -da, *a.* bred.—*n.m.f.* servant.—*n.f.* maid, servant.
criador, -ra, *a.* fruitful; raising.—*n.m.f.* creator; raiser.—*n.m.* God, the Creator.—*n.f.* wet-nurse.
crianza, *n.f.* rearing; nursing; breeding; manners.
criar [L], *v.t.* rear, bring up; nurse; grow, raise; create.
criatura, *n.f.* creature; baby, child.
criba, *n.f.* riddle, screen.
cribar, *v.t.* sieve, screen.
cribo, *n.m.* sieve, riddle.
cric, *n.m.* jack, lifting jack.
crimen, *n.m.* crime.
criminal, *a.* criminal.
criminalidad, *n.f.* criminality.
criminalista, *n.m.* criminologist; criminal lawyer.
criminar, *v.t.* incriminate; censure.
criminología, *n.f.* criminology.
criminoso, -sa, *a., n.m.f.* criminal, delinquent.
crin, *n.f.* mane; horse-hair.
crinolina, *n.f.* crinoline.
crío, *n.m.* (*fam.*) nipper, child; young (*of animals etc.*).
criollo, -lla, *a., n.m.f.* Creole; (*S.A.*) American-born.
cripta, *n.f.* crypt.
criptografía, *n.f* cryptography.
crisálida, *n.f.* chrysalis, pupa.
crisantema, -mo, *n.f.* or *m.* chrysanthemum.
crisis, *n.f. inv.* crisis; judgement; — *de la vivienda,* housing shortage; — *nerviosa,* nervous breakdown.
crisma, *n.m.* or *f.* (*eccl.*) chrism; (*fam.*) noddle, head.
crisol, *n.m.* crucible.
crispar, *v.t.* convulse.—*v.r.* twitch.
cristal, *n.m.* crystal; glass; pane; mirror; — *hilado,* glass wool.
cristalino, -na, *a.* crystalline.
cristalización, *n.f.* crystallization.
cristalizar [C], *v.t., v.r.* crystallize.
cristalografía, *n.f.* crystallography.
cristalógrafo, -fa, *n.m.f.* crystallographer.
cristianar, *v.t.* (*fam.*) christen.
cristiandad, *n.f.* Christendom.
cristianismo, *n.m.* Christianity; (*fam.*) christening.
cristianizar [C], *v.t.* christianize.
cristiano, -na, *a., n.m.f.* Christian.—*n.m.* soul, person; (*fam.*) the Spanish language; *vino —,* (*joc.*) watered-down wine.

Cristo, *n.m.* Christ; crucifix.
Cristóbal, *n.m.* Christopher.
cristus, *n.m.* Christ-cross (*beginner's primer*); (*fig.*) the rudiments.
criterio, *n.m.* criterion; judgement.
criticar [A], *v.t.* criticize.
criticismo, *n.m.* (*philos.*) criticism.
crítico, -ca, *a.* critical.—*n.m.f.* critic; (*fam.*) pedant.—*n.f.* criticism; critique.
criticón, -cona, *a.* fault-finding.—*n.m.f.* (*fam.*) fault-finder.
critiquizar [C], *v.t.* (*fam.*) be over-critical.
croar, *v.i.* croak (*frogs*).
croco, *n.m.* crocus.
croché, *n.m.* crochet.
cromar, *v.t.* chrome, chromium-plate.
cromático, -ca, *a.* chromatic.—*n.f.* chromatics.
cromo, *n.m.* chromium, chrome; chromo-lithograph.
cromosoma, *n.m.* chromosome.
crónica, *n.f.* chronicle; news, report.
cronicidad, *n.f.* chronic nature *or* condition.
crónico, -ca, *a.* chronic.
cronicón, *n.m.* short chronicle.
cronista, *n.m.f.* chronicler; reporter, (*U.S.*) newsman.
cronístico, -ca, *a.* rel. to chronicles, news.
cronología, *n.f.* chronology.
cronológico, -ca, *a.* chronological.
cronometraje, *n.m.* (*sport*) timing.
cronometrar, *v.t.* (*sport*) time.
cronómetro, *n.m.* chronometer.
croqueta, *n.f.* croquette.
croquis, *n.m. inv.* sketch.
crótalo, *n.m.* rattle-snake; castanet.
cruce, *n.m.* crossing, cross; intersection, crossroads.
crucero, *n.m.* crossing; cruise; cross-beam; (*naut.*) cruiser.
cruceta, *n.f.* cross-piece; cross-tree.
crucial, *a.* crucial.
crucificar [A], *v.t.* crucify.
crucifijo, *n.m.* crucifix.
crucifixión, *n.f.* crucifixion.
cruciforme, *a.* cruciform.
crucigrama, *n.m.* crossword puzzle.
crudelísimo, -ma, *a. sup.* most *or* very cruel.
crudeza, *n.f.* rawness; crudity; hardness; harshness.
crudo, -da, *a.* raw; hard; harsh; crude; boastful.
cruel, *a.* cruel.
crueldad, *n.f.* cruelty.
cruento, -ta, *a.* bloody.
crujidero, -ra, *a.* creaking; rustling; crackling.
crujido, *n.m.* creak; rustle; clatter; crackle.
crujir, *v.i.* creak; rustle; clatter; crackle.
crúor, *n.m.* (*poet.*) blood; (*med.*) cruor.
crup, *n.m.* (*med.*) croup.
crustáceo, -cea, *a.* crustaceous.—*n.m.* crustacean.
cruz, *n.f.* (*pl.* **cruces**) cross; tails (*of coin*); plus sign; (*vet.*) withers; *¡ — y raya !* (*fam.*) enough! no more of that!
cruzado, -da, *a.* crossed; cross (*bred*).—*n.m.* crusader.—*n.f.* crusade; intersection.
cruzamiento, *n.m.* crossing.
cruzar [C], *v.t.* cross; decorate, honour.—*v.i.* cruise.—*v.r.* cross paths; cross.

cu, *n.f.* name of letter Q.
cuaderno, *n.m.* exercise book; (*print.*) gathering, quarternion.
cuadra, *n.f.* stable; large room; ward, dormitory; rump, croup; (*S.A.*) block (*of houses*).
cuadradillo, *n.m.* square rule; sugar cube.
cuadrado, -da, *a.* square; complete.—*n.m.* square; ruler.
cuadragenario, -ria, *a., n.m.f.* quadragenarian.
cuadragésimo, -ma, *a.* fortieth.—*n.f.* (*eccl.*) Lent; Quadragesima.
cuadral, *n.m.* truss, angle-brace.
cuadrángulo, -la, *a.* quadrangular.—*n.m.* quadrangle.
cuadrante, *n.m.* fourth; face (*of watch*); quadrant; angle-brace; — **solar,** sun dial.
cuadrar, *v.t.* square; suit perfectly.—*v.i.* fit; suit, please.—*v.r.* square one's shoulders; (*fam.*) become solemn; (*C.A.*) strike it rich.
cuadricular, *a.* checkered, ruled in squares.—*v.t.* graticulate.
cuadrienio, *n.m.* quadrennium.
cuadrilátero, -ra, *a., n.m.* quadrilateral.
cuadrilongo, -ga, *a., n.m.* oblong.
cuadrilla, *n.f.* gang, team, crew; quadrille.
cuadrillero, *n.m.* gang leader, squad leader.
cuadripartido, -da, *a.* quadripartite.
cuadrivio, *n.m.* crossroads; quadrivium.
cuadro, *n.m.* square; picture, painting; frame; cadre; panel; (*theat.*) scene; **en** —, square; (*fam.*) on one's uppers; **a cuadros,** squared.
cuadrúpedo, -da, *a., n.m.* quadruped.
cuajado, -da, *a.* (*fam.*) flabbergasted.—*n.m.* mincemeat.—*n.f.* curds.
cuajaleche, *n.m.* (*bot.*) cheese rennet.
cuajar, *v.t.* curdle; coagulate; cake; set, thicken; over-decorate.—*v.i.* turn out well; (*C.A.*) prattle.—*v.r.* curdle, go sour; set, go thick; sleep well; (*fam.*) get crowded (*de,* with).
cuajarón, *n.m.* clot.
cuáquero, -ra [CUÁQUERO].
cual, *rel. a., rel. pron.* (*pl.* **cuales**) which; who, whom; such as; — ... *tal,* like ... like, just as ... so; **por lo** —, for which reason. (*As interrog.* **cuál, cuáles.**)
cualesquier(a) [CUALQUIER(A)].
cualidad, *n.f.* characteristic, quality.
cualitativo, -va, *a.* qualitative.
cualquier, *indef. a., contracted form of* CUALQUIERA *used before noun or other a.*
cualquier(a), *indef. a.* (*pl.* **cualesquier(a)**) any, some or other.—*rel. a.* whichever.—*indef. pron.* anyone.—*rel. pron.* whoever, whichever.—*n.m.* (*fam.*) a nobody.
cuan, *adv.* (*contracted form of* CUANTO *used before a. or other adv.*).
cuán, *adv.* interrog., interj. how, how much.
cuando, *adv., conj.* when; although; **de** — **en** —, from time to time; — **más** (**menos**), at most (least); — **quiera,** whenever.—*prep.* (*fam.*) at the time of, during. (*As interrog.* **cuándo.**)
cuantía, *n.f.* amount, quantity; importance, rank.
cuantiar [L], *v.t.* appraise.
cuantioso, -sa, *a.* substantial, large.
cuantitativo, -va, *a.* quantitative.
cuanto (1), **-ta,** *a., rel. pron., adv.* as much as,

as many as, whatever; as soon as; whilst; all that; — *antes,* as soon as possible; — *más ... tanto más,* the more ... the more; **en** —, as soon as; **en** — **a,** as regards, as for; **por** —, inasmuch as; **cuantos,** all those who, all those that.
cuanto (2), *n.m.* (*pl.* **cuanta**) (*phys.*) quantum.
cuánto, -ta, *interrog., adv., pron.* how much? how many? how long?—*interj.* how much! how many! how long!
cuáquero, -ra, *a., n.m.f.* Quaker.
cuarenta, *a., n.m.* forty.
cuarentavo, -va, *a.* fortieth.
cuarentena, *n.f.* two score; quarantine; forty days *or* nights *or* years.
cuarentón, -tona, *a., n.m.f.* forty-year-old.
cuaresma, *n.f.* Lent.
cuaresmal, *a.* Lenten.
cuartago, *n.m.* pony.
cuartana, *n.f.* quartan fever.
cuartazos, *n.m.* (*fam., pej.*) fatty.
cuartear, *v.t.* quarter; zig-zag along; (*C.A.*) whip.—*v.i.* dodge.—*v.r.* crack; dodge.
cuartel, *n.m.* barracks; quarter, section; quarter, mercy; — **general,** (*mil.*) headquarters.—*pl.* quarters.
cuartelada, *n.f.* (*S.A.* **cuartelazo,** *n.m.*) military revolt.
cuartelero, -ra, *a.* rel. to barracks *or* camp.— *n.m.* (*mil.*) camp policeman.
cuarterón, -rona, *a., n.m.f.* quadroon.—*n.m.* quarter; door panel; postern.
cuarteta, *n.f.* quatrain.
cuartete, cuarteto, *n.m.* quartet(te); quatrain.
cuartilla, *n.f.* quart; quarto; sheet (*paper*).
cuartillo, *n.m.* quart; pint; (*obs.*) groat.
cuarto, -ta, *a., n.m.* fourth.—*n.m.* quarter; room; quarto; (*fam.*) cent, penny; **de tres al** —, (*fam.*) ten a penny.—*n.f.* quarter; palm-span; (*C.A.*) whip.
cuartucho, *n.m.* hovel.
cuarzo, *n.m.* quartz.
cuasi, *adv.* quasi.
cuatrero, *n.m.* rustler, horse *or* cattle thief.
cuatrillizo, -za, *n.m.f.* quadruplet.
cuatrillón, *n.m.* quadrillion.
cuatrimestre, *a.* four-monthly.—*n.m.* four months.
cuatrinca, *n.f.* foursome.
cuatro, *a., n.m.* four.
cuatrocientos, -tas, *a., n.m.* four hundred.
Cuba, *n.f.* Cuba; **cuba,** *n.f.* barrel, cask, vat.
cubano, -na, *a., n.m.f.* Cuban.
cubeta, *n.f.* keg; pail; cup; dish.
cubicar [A], *v.t.* calculate the volume of; cube.
cúbico, -ca, *a.* cubic.
cubículo, *n.m.* cubicle.
cubierta, *n.f.* cover; covering; envelope; car bonnet, (*U.S.*) hood; dust jacket (*of book*); (*naut.*) deck; casing.
cubierto, -ta, *a.* covered.—*p.p.* [CUBRIR].—*n.m.* cover, shelter; table service, place at table; fixed-price meal; **a** —, under cover.
cubil, *n.m.* lair, den; river bed.
cubillo, -lla, *n.m.f.* Spanish fly.—*n.m.* earthenware jug (*for cooling water*).
cubismo, *n.m.* Cubism.
cubista, *a., n.m.f.* Cubist.
cubo, *n.m.* bucket, pail; cube; hub; socket; (*mech.*) drum.
cubrecadena, *n.m.* or *f.* chain-cover (*of bicycle*).

cubrecama, *n.m.* bedspread.
cubrefuego, *n.m.* curfew.
cubretetera, *n.f.* tea cosy.
cubrir [*p.p.* **cubierto**], *v.t.* cover, cover over or up.
cucamonas, *n.f.pl.* (*fam.*) sweet nothings, wheedling.
cucaña, *n.f.* greasy pole; (*fam.*) walk-over, cinch.
cucar, *v.t.* wink; (*fam.*) tease.
cucaracha, *n.f.* cockroach; cochineal beetle.
cucarda, *n.f.* cockade.
cuclillas, *adv.* **en —,** squatting; *ponerse en —,* squat, crouch.
cuclillo, *n.m.* (*orn.*) cuckoo; (*fam.*) cuckold.
cuco, -ca, *a.* sly; spruce, smart.—*n.m.* cuckoo.—*n.m.f.* caterpillar; (*fam.*) gambler.
cucú, *n.m.* (*pl.* **-úes**) cuckoo (*call*).
cuculla, *n.f.* cowl.
cucurucho, *n.m.* paper cone.
cuchara, *n.f.* spoon; ladle, scoop; (*S.A.*) trowel; *media —,* (*fam.*) wet hen, ungifted person; *meter su —,* (*fam.*) stick one's oar in.
cucharada, *n.f.* spoonful, ladleful.
cucharear, *v.t.* spoon out, ladle out.
cucharilla, cucharita, *n.f.* teaspoon.
cucharón, *n.m.* tablespoon; ladle; (*fam.*) the pickings.
cuchichear, *v.i.* whisper.
cuchicheo, *n.m.* whisperings.
cuchichero, -ra, *n.m.f.* whisperer.
cuchilla, *n.f.* blade; carver, cleaver; (*S.A.*) penknife.
cuchillada, *n.f.* cut, gash, slash.—*pl.* fight, squabble.
cuchillo, *n.m.* knife; (*carp.*) upright; *pasar a —,* put to the sword.
cuchitril, *n.m.* cubby-hole; hovel.
cuchuchear, *v.i.* whisper; (*fam.*) gossip.
cuchufleta, *n.f.* (*fam.*) joke, fun.
cuelga, *n.f.* bunch; (*fam.*) birthday present.
cuello, *n.m.* neck; collar; *levantar el —,* get on one's feet again.
cuenca, *n.f.* river basin; wooden bowl; eye socket.
cuenco, *n.m.* earthenware bowl; cavity.
cuenta, *n.f.* count, calculation; account; bill; bead; *a (buena) —,* on account; *caer en la —,* (*fam.*) see the point, get it; *dar de,* account, for; (*coll.*) use up, finish off; *darse — de,* realize; *de —,* of some account; *por la —,* apparently; *tener en —,* take into account; *— corriente,* current account; *cuentas galanas,* (*fam.*) day-dreams, castles in Spain; *en resumidas cuentas,* in short; *a fin de cuentas,* when all's said and done.
cuentacorrentista, *n.m.f.* person having current account.
cuentagotas, *n.m. inv.* dropper, drop-bottle.
cuentakilómetros, *n.m. inv.* milometer.
cuentero, -ra, *a.* (*fam.*) fibbing.—*n.m.f.* fibber, gossip.
cuentista, *n.m.f.* story writer or teller; (*fam.*) fibber.
cuento, *n.m.* story, tale; yarn; count; (*obs.*) million; prop; (*fam.*) trouble; *a —,* opportune(ly); *sin —,* countless.
cuerda, *n.f.* string, rope, cord; watch spring; fishing line; *dar — a,* wind up (*watch*); give free rein to; *bajo —,* underhandedly.

cuerdo, -da, *a.* wise, sensible.
cuerna, *n.f.* horn; antler.
cuerno, *n.m.* horn; (*ent.*) antenna.
cuero, *n.m.* leather; hide; wineskin; (*S.A.*) whip; *en cueros (vivos),* stark naked.
cuerpo, *n.m.* body; substance; corpus; (*mil.*) corps; *— a —,* hand to hand; *hurtar el — a,* dodge, avoid.
cuervo, *n.m.* raven; *— marino,* cormorant.
cuesta (1), *n.f.* hill, slope; *— abajo,* downhill; *— arriba,* uphill; *a cuestas,* on one's shoulders *or* back.
cuesta (2), **cuestación,** *n.f.* charity appeal.
cuestión, *n.f.* question, matter, affair.
cuestionable, *a.* questionable.
cuestionar, *v.t.* call in question, dispute.
cuestionario, *n.m.* questionnaire.
cuesto, *n.m.* hill.
cuestuario, -ria, cuestuoso, -sa, *a.* lucrative.
cueto, *n.m.* crag; fortified crag.
cueva, *n.f.* cave; cellar.
cuévano, *n.m.* grape basket.
cuico, -ca, *a.* (*S.A.*) half-breed.—*n.m.f.* (*S.A., pej.*) foreigner; (*S.A.*) Indian.
cuidado, *n.m.* care; heed; caution; worry; *tener —,* be careful (*con,* with, of).—*interj.* look out! be careful!
cuidadoso, -sa, *a.* careful; concerned.
cuidar, *v.t.* care for, mind, take care of.—*v.i.* take care (*de,* of).—*v.r.* be careful (*de,* of, to); look after oneself.
cuido, *n.m.* care.
cuita, *n.f.* woe, travail; (*C.A.*) dung.
culantro, *n.m.* coriander.
culata, *n.f.* buttock; butt (*of gun*); cylinder head.
culatada, *n.f.,* **culatazo,** *n.m.* recoil; buttblow.
culebra, *n.f.* snake; (*fam.*) rowdy disturbance; (*fam.*) lark, trick.
culebrazo, *n.m.* lark, trick.
culebrear, *v.i.* wriggle (along).
culebreo, *n.m.* wriggling.
culebrino, -na, *a.* snaky.
culera (1), *n.f.* seat-patch (*in trousers*).
culero (1), **-ra** (2), *a.* lazy.
culero (2), *n.m.* nappy, (*U.S.*) diaper.
culí, *n.m.* (*pl.* **-íes**) coolie.
culinario, -ria, *a.* culinary.
culminación, *n.f.* culmination.
culminante, *a.* predominating, supreme.
culminar, *v.t.* culminate.
culo, *n.m.* (*low*) rump, bottom; *— de vaso,* cheap jewel.
culpa, *n.f.* blame, fault, guilt; *tener la — (de),* be to blame (for).
culpabilidad, *n.f.* culpability.
culpable, culpado, -da, *a.* guilty.—*n.m.f.* culprit.
culpar, *v.t.* blame; accuse (*de,* of).—*v.r.* take the blame (*de,* for).
cultedad, *n.f.* fustian; affectation of culture.
culteranismo, *n.m.* (*lit.*) Spanish euphuism.
culterano, -na, *a.* euphuistic; fustian.—*n.m.* euphuist.
cultismo, *n.m.* euphuism; learned word.
cultivación, *n.f.* cultivation.
cultivador, -ra, *a.* cultivating.—*n.m.f.* farmer, cultivator.
cultivar, *v.t.* cultivate.
cultivo, *n.m.* cultivation.

culto, -ta, *a.* cultured; learned.—*n.m.* worship; cult.

cultor, -ra, *a.* worshipping; cultivating.—*n.m.f.* worshipper; cultivator.

cultura, *n.f.* culture.

cultural, *a.* cultural.

culturar, *v.t.* cultivate.

cumbre, *n.f.* summit; (*fig.*) pinnacle.

cumbrera, *n.f.* ridge coping; lintel; (*S.A.*) summit.

cumpa, *n.m.* (*S.A.*, *low*) mate, pal.

cúmplase, *n.m.* official confirmation.

cumpleaños, *n.m. inv.* birthday.

cumplidero, -ra, *a.* be completed; expiring; requisite, necessary.

cumplido, -da, *a.* full, complete; polite correct.—*n.m.* compliment, courtesy.

cumplimentar, *v.t.* compliment, congratulate; fulfil (*an order*).

cumplimiento, *n.m.* compliment; fulfilment; formality.

cumplir, *v.t.* fulfil; reach (*an age*).—*v.i.* expire; fall due; — **con,** fulfil (*duty etc.*); behave correctly towards; **cumple a Pedro hacerlo,** it behooves Peter to do it.—*v.r.* be fulfilled, come true.

cumquibus, *n.m.* (*fam.*) wherewithal, cash.

cúmulo, *n.m.* heap, pile; cumulus.

cuna, *n.f.* cradle; orphans' home; (*fig.*) family.

cundir, *v.i.* spread; swell; multiply.

cunero, -ra, *n.m.f.* foundling; (*pol.*) outside candidate, carpet-bagger.

cuneta, *n.f.* ditch.

cuña, *n.f.* wedge; cobblestone; (*S.A.*) bigwig.

cuñada, *n.f.* sister-in-law.

cuñado, *n.m.* brother-in-law.

cuñete, *n.m.* keg.

cuño, *n.m.* coin die; (*fig.*) stamp, mark.

cuodlibeto, *n.m.* quodlibet; witticism.

cuota, *n.f.* quota; dues.

cuotidiano, -na, *a.* daily, quotidian.

cupe, *etc.* [CABER].

cupé, *n.m.* coupé.

Cupido, *n.m.* Cupid; **cupido,** *n.m.* gallant, lover; cupid.

cupo, *n.m.* quota, share.—*v.* [CABER].

cupón, *n.m.* coupon; **cupón-respuesta,** reply coupon.

cúprico, -ca, *a.* cupric.

cuproso, -sa, *a.* cuprous.

cúpula, *n.f.* cupola, dome; (*bot.*) cupule; (*naut.*) turret.

cuquería, *n.f.* slyness.

cura, *n.m.* parish priest; **este —,** (*fam.*) yours truly.—*n.f.* cure, curing; — **de almas,** care of souls.

curaca, *n.m.* (*S.A.*) Indian chief.

curación, *n.f.* healing, treatment.

curador, -ra, *n.m.f.* guardian; curator; curer.

curandero, -ra, *n.m.f.* quack, medicaster; witch-doctor.

curar, *v.t.* cure, heal; dry.—*v.i.* recover; pay attention; — **de,** recover from; look after *or* to.—*v.r.* heal up; recover; take a cure; (*S.A.*) get drunk; **curarse de,** recover from.

curare, *n.m.* curare.

curatela, *n.f.* (*jur.*) guardianship.

curativo, -va, *a., n.f.* curative.

curato, *n.m.* curacy; parish.

curazao, *n.m.* curaçao. **Curazao,** *n.f.* Curaçao.

cúrcuma, *n.f.* curcumin, turmeric.

curdo, -da, *a.* Kurdish.—*n.m.f.* Kurd; **coger una curda,** (*fam.*) get stoned, drunk.

cureña, *n.f.* gun carriage.

curia, *n.f.* curia.

curial, *a.* curial.—*n.m.* (*jur.*) clerk.

curialesco, -ca, *a.* (*pej.*) legalistic.

curiosear, *v.i.* (*fam.*) pry, snoop.

curiosidad, *n.f.* curiosity; curio; care.

curioso, -sa, *a.* curious; diligent; tidy.—*n.m.f.* busy-body, snooper; (*S.A.*) quack doctor.

Curro, *n.m.* (*fam.*) form of Francisco; **curro, -rra,** *a.* (*fam.*) flashy, loud.

curruca, *n.f.* (*orn.*) warbler; whitethroat.

currutaco, -ca, *a.* dandyish, fashion-conscious.—*n.m.* dandy, (*U.S.*) dude.

cursado, -da, *a.* versed, skilled.

cursante, *a.* attending, studying.—*n.m.f.* pupil, student.

cursar, *v.t.* frequent; study; expedite.

cursería [CURSILERÍA].

cursi, *a.* (*pl.* **-sis** *or* (*low*) **cúrsiles**) (*fam.*) flashy, shoddy, vulgar.

cursilería, *n.f.* flashiness, vulgarity.

cursillista, *n.f.* student on short course.

cursillo, *n.m.* short course.

cursivo, -va, *a.* cursive.

curso, *n.m.* course; academic year; — **legal,** legal tender.

curtido, *n.m.* tanning.—*pl.* leather.

curtidor, *n.m.* tanner.

curtiente, *a.* tanning.—*n.m.* tanning material.

curtimiento, *n.m.* tanning.

curtir, *v.t.* tan; inure; season.

curuca, curuja, *n.f.* barn owl.

curva, *n.f.* curve, bend.

curvado, -da, *a.* curved.

curvatura, *n.f.* curvature.

curvilíneo, -a, *a.* curvilinear.

curvo, -va, *a.* curved.

cusir, *v.t.* (*fam.*) sew badly.

cúspide, *n.f.* apex; cusp; vertex.

custodia, *n.f.* custody; guard; (*eccl.*) monstrance.

custodiar, *v.t.* guard, take care of.

custodio, *n.m.* custodian, guard.

cúter, *n.m.* (*naut.*) cutter.

cutí, *n.m.* (*pl.* **-íes**) ticking.

cutícula, *n.f.* cuticle.

cutio, *n.m.* labour.

cutir, *v.t.* knock, hit.

cutis, *n.m. inv.* skin; complexion.

cutre, *a.* miserly.—*n.m.f.* skinflint.

cuy, *n.m.* (*S.A.*) guinea-pig.

cuyo, -ya, *rel. a.* whose (*obs. as interrog.*).—*n.m.* (*fam.*) beau, lover.

¡cuz! *interj.* here! (*to dog*).

czar [ZAR].

Ch

Ch, ch, *n.f.* fourth letter of the Spanish alphabet.

cha, *n.m.* (*S.A.*) tea.

chabacanada, chabacanería, *n.f.* vulgarity, grossness.
chabacano, -na, *a.* vulgar, gross, crude.
chacal, *n.m.* jackal.
chacolotear, *v.i.* clatter (*hooves*).
chacota, *n.f.* noisy mirth.
chacra, *n.f.* (*S.A.*) farm, plantation.
chacha, *n.f.* (*fam.*) lass; (*fam.*) nurse.
cháchara, *n.f.* (*fam.*) blather, chatter.
chacho, *n.m.* (*fam.*) lad.
chafaldita, *n.f.* (*fam.*) little joke.
chafallar, *v.t.* (*fam.*) patch up, botch.
chafallo, *n.m.* (*fam.*) botched repair.
chafallón, -llona, *a.* (*fam.*) botching.—*n.m.f.* botcher.
chafandín, *n.m.* (*fam.*) vain clod,fool.
chafarrinada, *n.f.* blotch, daub.
chafarrinar, *v.t.* blotch, stain.
chaflán, *n.m.* chamfer, bevel.
chagrín, *n.m.* shagreen.
chah, *n.m.* shah.
chal, *n.m.* shawl.
chalado, -da, *a.* (*fam.*) daft, silly, infatuated.
chalán, -lana, *a.* horse-dealing.—*n.m.f.* horse-dealer.
chalana, *n.f.* lighter, flatboat.
chalar, *v.t.* (*fam.*) drive daft *or* crazy.—*v.r.* be gone, be daft (*por*, on).
chaleco, *n.m.* waistcoat.
chalet, *n.m.* chalet.
chalina, *n.f.* neckerchief.
chalote, *n.m.* (*bot.*) shallot.
chalupa, *n.f.* sailing boat; lifeboat.
chamar, *v.t.* (*fam.*) barter, swap.
chámara, chamarasca, *n.f.* brushwood.
chamarillero, -ra, *n.m.f.* scrap dealer.
chamarra, *n.f.* sheepskin jacket.
chamba, *n.f.* (*fam.*) fluke.
chambelán, *n.m.* chamberlain.
chambergo, -ga, *a.* Schomberg.—*n.m.* slouch hat.
chambón, -bona, *a.* (*fam.*) clumsy.—*n.m.f.* blunderer.
chamiza, *n.f.* thatching reed; twigs.
chamizo, *n.m.* half-burnt tree *or* log; cottage; hovel.
chamorrar, *v.t.* (*fam.*) crop (*hair*).
Champaña, *n.f.* Champagne; **champán, champaña,** *n.m.* champagne.
champiñón, *n m.* mushroom.
champú, *n.m.* (*pl.* **-úes**) shampoo.
champurrar, *v.t.* (*fam.*) mix (*drinks*).
chamuscar [A], *v.t.* singe, scorch.
chamusco, *n.m.* singe, scorch.
chamusquina, *n.f.* singe; (*fam.*) row, squabble; **oler a —,** (*fam.*) be fishy.
chanada, *n.f.* (*fam.*) swindle.
chancear, *v.i.*, *v.r.* joke.
chancero, -ra, *a.* joking, merry.
chanciller, *n.m.* chancellor.
chancillería, *n.f.* chancery.
chancla, *n.f.* old shoe; slipper.
chanclo, *n.m.* clog; pattern; galosh.
chancho, -cha, *a.* (*S.A.*) filthy.—*n.m.f.* (*S.A.*) pig.
chanchullo, *n.m.* (*fam.*) trick, sharp practice.
chanfaina, *n.f.* offal stew.
chanflón, -flona, *a.* misshapen.
changüí, *n.m.* (*pl.* **-íes**) (*fam.*) trick, hoax.
chantaje, *n.m.* blackmail.
chantajista, *n.m.f.* blackmailer.
chantre, *n.m.* precentor.

chanza, *n.f.* joke, fun.
chanzoneta, *n.f.* chansonnette; (*fam.*) lark, joke.
chapa, *n.f.* metal plate, sheet; veneer; (*fam.*) nous, sense.—*pl.* tossing coins; (*fam.*) blush, redness.
chapado, -da, *a.* plated; veneered; **— a la antigua,** olde-worlde, old-fashioned.
chapalear, *v.i.* lap, splash; patter.
chapaleteo, *n.m.* splashing, lapping; patter.
chapapote, *n.m.* asphalt.
chapar [CHAPEAR].
chaparra, *n.f.* brush oak; scrub.
chaparrada, *n.f.* shower, downpour.
chaparro, *n.m.* oak scrub.
chaparrón, *n.m.* heavy shower.
chapear, *v.t.* plate; veneer; (*C.A.*) weed.—*v.i.* clatter.
chapería, *n.f.* metal-plating.
chapetón, -tona, *a.* (*S.A.*) new, green (*immigrant*); novice.
chapitel, *n.m.* (*arch.*) spire, pinnacle; capital.
chapón, *n.m.* blot.
chapotear, *v.t.* sponge; damp.—*v.i.* splash.
chapucear, *v.t.* bungle, botch; dabble in.
chapucería, *n.f.* botching; botched job; fib, lie.
chapucero, -ra, *a.* botchy.—*n.m.f.* dabbler; bungler; fibber.
chapurrar, *v.t.* jabber, (*fam.*) murder (*a language*); mix (*drinks*).
chapurrear, *v.t.*, *v.i.* jabber.
chapuz, *n.m.* botching; ducking (*in water*); (*naut.*) spar.
chapuza, *n.f.* botched job.
chapuzar, *v.t.* duck (*in water*).
chapuzón, *n.m.* ducking.
chaqué, *n.m.* morning-coat.
chaqueta, *n.f.* jacket.
chaquira, *n.f.* (*S.A.*) bead.
charabán, *n.m.* charabanc.
charada, *n.f.* charade.
charanga, *n.f.* (*mus.*) brass band.
charanguero, -ra, *a.* [CHAPUCERO].
charca, *n.f.* pool.
charco, *n.m.* puddle; (*fam.*) pond, sea.
charla, *n.f.* (*fam.*) chat; (*orn.*) missel thrush.
charlar, *v.i.* chatter; chat.
charlatán, -tana, *a.* prattling.—*n.m.f.* prattler; charlatan.
charlatanería, *n.f.* quackery; prattle.
charnela, *n.f.* hinge; (*mech.*) knuckle.
charol, *n.m.* varnish; patent leather.
charpa, *n.f.* gun-belt; arm-sling.
charqui, *n.m.* (*S.A.*) dried meat.
charrada, *n.f.* peasant dance; loutishness; over-ornamentation.
charrán, *n.m.* scoundrel.
charrasca, *n.f.* (*joc.*) sword; throat-cutter.
charrería, *n.f.* over-ornamentation.
charretera, *n.f.* (*mil.*) epaulet.
charro, -rra, *a.* churlish; (*fam.*) tawdry.—*n.m.f.* Salamantine peasant.
charrúa, *n.f.* (*naut.*) tug.
chascar, *v.t.* click (*tongue*); crush up.—*v.i.* [CHASQUEAR].
chascarrillo, *n.m.* (*fam.*) spicy yarn.
chasco, -ca, *a.* (*S.A.*) curly, thick (*hair*).—*n.m.* disappointment; joke.
chasis, *n.m.* inv. chassis; (*phot.*) plate-frame.
chasponazo, *n.m.* bullet mark.

chasquear, *v.t.* crack (*a whip*); disappoint.—*v.i.* crack.—*v.r.* be disappointed.
chasquido, *n.m.* snap, crack.
chatarra, *n.f.* scrap iron.
chato, -ta, *a.* flat, snub-nosed.—*n.m.* (*fam.*) wine-glass; glass of wine.
chatre, *a.* (*S.A.*) dolled-up.
chauvinismo, *n.m.* chauvinism, jingoism.
chaval, -la, *n.m.* (*fam.*) laddie, lad.—*n.f.* lass, lassie.
chaveta, *n.f.* (*mech.*) cotter pin.
che (1), *n.f.* name of letter CH.
¡che! (2), *interj.* (*dial.*,*S.A.*) say! hey!
checa (1), *n.f.* police terrorist group, cheka.
checo -ca (2), *n.m.f.* Czech.
checoslovaco, -ca, *a.*, *n.m.f.* Czechoslovak.
Checoslovaquia, *n.f.* Czechoslovakia.
chelín, *n.m.* shilling.
cheque, *n.m.* cheque, (*U.S.*) check.
chica, *n.f.* girl.
chicarrón, -rrona, *a.* (*fam.*) forward, over-grown (*child*).
chicle, *n.m.* chicle; chewing gum.
chico, -ca, *a.* small.—*n.m.* boy; youth.—*n.f.* girl.—*n.m.f.* child.
chicolear, *v.i.* (*fam.*) pay compliments.—*v.r.* (*S.A.*) have a good time.
chicoria, *n.f.* chicory.
chicote, -ta, *n.m.f.* (*fam.*) strapping youth.—*n.m.* cigar; cigar butt; (*S.A.*) lash.
chicha, *n.f.* (*fam.*) meat; (*S.A.*) chicha (*drink*).
chícharo, *n.m.* (*bot.*) pea.
chicharra, *n.f.* (*ent.*) cicada.
chicharrón, *n.m.* crackling; burnt food.
chichear, *v.t.*, *v.i.* hiss.
chichisbeo, *n.m.* passionate wooing; cicisbeo.
chichón, *n.m.* lump, bruise.
chifla, *n.f.* whistle; hiss.
chiflado, -da, *a.* (*fam.*) nutty.—*n.m.f.* (*fam.*) crank, nut.
chifladura, *n.f.* (*fam.*) silliness; crazy whim.
chiflar, *v.t.* whistle at; hiss, boo.—*v.r.* (*fam.*) be crazy (**por**, about).
chiflato, chiflete, chiflido, chiflo, *n.m.* whistle.
Chile, *n.m.* Chile; **chile**, *n.m.* chili.
chileno, -na, chileño, -ña, *a.*, *n.m.f.* Chilean.
chiltipiquín, *n.m.* chili.
chillar, *v.i.* scream, shriek, squeal; sizzle.
chillido, *n.m.* shriek, screech, scream.
chillón-llona, *a.* (*fam.*) shrieking; shrill; loud (*colour*).—*n.m.f.* (*S.A.*) squealer, informer.
chimenea, *n.f.* chimney; fire-place; (*naut.*) funnel; (*min.*) shaft.
chimpancé, *n.m.* chimpanzee.
China, *n.f.* China; **china**, *n.f.* china; pebble. [CHINO]
chinchar, *v.t.* (*fam.*) pester, bother.—*v.r.* get fed up.
chinche, *n.m.* or *f.* bug; drawing-pin, (*U.S.*) thumbtack; (*fam.*) pest.
chincheta, *n.f.* drawing-pin, (*U.S.*) thumbtack.
chinchilla, *n.f.* (*zool.*) chinchilla.
chinchín, *n.m.* street-music; (*fam.*) ballyhoo.
chinchoso, -sa, *a.* (*fam.*) bothersome.
chinela, *n.f.* slipper.
chinesco, -ca, *a.* Chinese.
chino, -na, *a.*, *n.m.f.* Chinese; (*S.A.*) half-breed; (*S.A.*) love, dearie (*mode of address*).

de chipé(n), *a. phr.* (*fam.*) first-rate.
Chipre, *n.f.* Cyprus.
chipriota, chipriote, *a.*, *n.m.f.* Cypriot.
chiquillada, *n.f.* child's prank.
chiquillo, -lla, *n.m.f. diminutive of* CHICO.
chiquirritico, -ca; -tillo, -lla; -tín, -tina; chiquitín, -tina, *a.* (*fam.*) tiny, weeny; very young.
chiribitil, *n.m.* attic, cubby-hole.
chirimbolo, *n.m.* (*fam.*) gadget, utensil.
chirimía, *n.f.* (*mus.*) flageolet.
chirimoya, *n.f.* (*bot.*) custard apple.
chiripa, *n.f.* fluke.
chirivía, *n.f.* parsnip.
chirlar, *v.i.* (*fam.*) yell, gabble.
chirle, *a.* (*fam.*) flat, tasteless.—*n.m.* dung.
chirlo, *n.m.* slash, scar (*on face*).
chirlomirlo, *n.m.* (*orn.*) morsel; (*orn.*) blackbird.
chirriadero, -ra, chirriante, *a.* squeaking, shrieking.
chirriar, *v.i.* squeak, shriek; chirp; caterwaul; sizzle.
chirrido, *n.m.* shriek, squeak, creak; sizzling.
chirumen, *n.m.* (*fam.*) gumption; acumen.
¡chis! *interj.* sh! hush! **¡ chis chis !** hey!
chiscón, *n.m.* hovel.
chisgarabís, *n.m.* (*fam.*) busybody.
chisguete, *n.m.* (*fam.*) swig, drink.
chisme, *n.m.* titbit of gossip; (*fam.*) thingummy.
chismear, *v.i.* tale-tattle, gossip.
chismería, *n.f.* tale-tattling, gossip.
chismero, -ra, *a.* gossiping.—*n.m.f.* gossip.
chismorrear, *v.i.* (*fam.*) [CHISMEAR].
chismoso, -sa, *a.* gossipy.—*n.m.f.* gossip, tattler.
chispa, *n.f.* spark, (*fam.*) live wire; flash (*of lightning*); drop (*of liquid*); drunkenness; **echar chispas**, be furious.
chispazo, *n.m.* spark, sparking; tale, gossip.
chispeante, *a.* sparkling.
chispear, *v.i.* sparkle; spark; drizzle.
chispero, *n.m.* blacksmith; (*fam.*) spiv, sharper.
chispo, -pa, *a.* (*fam.*) tipsy.—*n.m.* (*fam.*) swig, drink.
chispoleto, -ta, *a.* lively.
chisporrotear, *v.i.* (*fam.*) throw sparks.
chisposo, -sa, *a.* sparking.
chistar, *v.i.* say a word; **sin — (ni mistar)**, (*fam.*) without saying a word.
chiste, *n.m.* joke, witticism.
chistera, *n.f.* fish basket; cesta; top-hat.
chistoso, -sa, *a.* witty.—*n.m.f.* wit (*person*).
chita, *n.f.* anklebone; quoit; **a la — callando**, (*fam.*) as quiet as a mouse.
¡chitón! *interj.* sh! hush!
chivato, *n.m.* kid, young goat; (*fam.*) telltale, squealer.
chivo, -va, *n.m.f.* goat.—*n.m.* billy-goat.
chocante, *a.* surprising, shocking; (*S.A.*) pesky.
chocar, *v.t.* shock, shake; (*low*) [GUSTAR].—*v.i.* collide; clash.
chocarrero, -ra, *a.* coarse, ribald.
choclo, *n.m.* clog; (*S.A.*) ear of corn.
chocolate, *n.m.* chocolate.
chocha, *n.f.* (*orn.*) woodcock.
chochear, *v.i.* dodder, dote.
chochera, chochez, *n.f.* dotage, doting.
chochita, *n.f.*, **chochín**, *n.m.* (*orn.*) wren.
chocho, -cha, *a.* doddering; doting.
chofe [BOFE].

chófer, chofer, *n.m.* (*pl.* **chóferes, choferes, chofers**) driver; chauffeur.
cholo, -la, *a.*, *n.m.f.* (*S.A.*) Indian; mestizo.— *n.f.* [CHOLLA].
cholla, *n.f.* (*fam.*) noddle, head; nous.
chopo, *n.m.* black poplar; (*fam.*) gun.
choque, *n.m.* shock; collision, impact; clash.
choricero, -ra, *n.m.f.* CHORIZO maker *or* seller; (*fam.*) [EXTREMEÑO].
chorizo, *n.m.* smoked seasoned pork sausage.
chorlito, *n.m.* plover; stone-curlew; (*fam.*) *cabeza de* —, ninny, bird-brain.
chorrear, *v.i.* gush, spurt; drip,
chorrera, *n.f.* spout; gulley; rapids; water stains.
chorrillo, *n.m.* (*fam.*) stream (*of money etc.*); *irse por el* —, follow the herd.
chorro, *n.m.* jet; flow; *propulsión a* —, jet propulsion; *a chorros,* in large amounts.
chotacabras, *n.m.* (*orn.*) nightjar.
choto, -ta, *n.m.f.* kid, sucking kid.
chova, *n.f.* (*orn.*) chough; rook.
choz, *n.f.* novelty, surprise; *hacer* — *a,* surprise.
choza, *n.f.* hut, cabin.
chubasco, *n.m.* rain storm, downpour; squall.
chucruta, *n.f.* sauerkraut.
chuchear, *v.i.* whisper.
chuchería (1), *n.f.* tit-bit; trinket.
chuchería (2), *n.f.* snaring.
chucho, -cha, *n.m.f.* (*fam.*) dog.—*interj.* down! away! (*to dogs*).—*n.f.* spree; laziness.
chueca, *n.f.* hockey; (*fam.*) lark, joke.
chufa, *n.f.* (*bot.*) chufa; scoffing, mockery.
chufar, *v.t.*, *v.i.*, *v.r.* scoff (*at*).
chufleta [CUCHUFLETA].
chulada, *n.f.* vulgarity; (*fam.*) carefree wit.
chulería, *n.f.* (*fam.*) sparkle, wit, flashiness; bunch of CHULOS.
chuleta, *n.f.* chop, cutlet; (*carp.*) chip; (*educ. fam.*) crib.
chulo, -la, *a.* snappy, flashy; vulgar.—*n.m.* or *f.* flashy type from Madrid slums. —*n.m.* bullfighter's assistant.
chumacera, *n.f.* rowlock; (*mech.*) journal bearing.
chumbera, *n.f.* (*bot.*) prickly-pear cactus.
chumbo, higo chumbo, *n.m.* prickly pear.
chunga, *n.f.* larking, joking; *de* —, in a merry mood.
chupada, *n.f.* suck, sucking.
chupado, -da, *a.* (*fam.*) scrawny.
chupador, *n.m.* teething ring, dummy, (*U.S.*) pacifier.
chupar, *v.t.* suck; sip; (*S.A.*) smoke *or* tipple. —*v.r.* waste away; *chuparse los dedos,* (*fig.*) smack one's lips.
chupatintas, *n.m.f. inv.* (*fam.*) pen-pusher.
chupete, *n.m.* baby's dummy, (*U.S.*) pacifier; *de* —, tasty.
chupetón, *n.m.* suck, sucking.
churra, *n.f.* (*orn.*) sand grouse.
churrasco, *n.m.* (*S.A.*) barbecue, roast.
churre, *n.m.* (*fam.*) muck, dirt.
churrero, -ra, *n.m.f.* CHURRO maker *or* seller.
churrete, *n.m.* dirty mark (*on person*).
churriburri, *n.m.* (*fam.*) rotter.
churriento, -ta, *a.* filthy.
churrigueresco, -ca, *a.* (*arch.*) churrigue-resque; tawdry, overdone.

churro, *n.m.* doughnut finger, Spanish sweetmeat.
churrullero, -ra, *a.* chattering.—*n.m.f.* chatterer.
churruscar [A], *v.t.* burn (*food*).
churrusco, *n.m.* burnt crust.
¡chus! *interj.* here! (*to dog*); *sin decir* — *ni mus,* without saying a word.
chusco, -ca, *a.* funny.
chusma, *n.f.* galley slaves; rabble.
chutar, *v.t.*, *v.i.* shoot (*in football*).
chuzo, *n.m.* (*mil.*) pike; (*fam.*) boast; *llover a chuzos,* rain in buckets.
chuzón, -zona, *a.* sharp, waggish.

D

D, d, *n.f.* fifth letter of the Spanish alphabet.
dable, *a.* feasible.
dáctilo, *n.m.* dactyl.
dactilografía, *n.f.* typewriting.
dadaísmo, *n.m.* (*lit.*, *art.*) Dadaism.
dádiva, *n.f.* gift, bounty.
dadivoso, -sa, *a.* bountiful.
dado (1), **-da,** *a.*, *p.p.* given; — *que,* granted that; provided that.
dado (2), *n.m.* die; (*mech.*) block.—*pl.* dice.
dador, -ra, *a.* giving.—*n.m.f.* giver, donor; bearer; (*com.*) drawer.
daga, *n.f.* dagger.
daguerrotipo, *n.m.* daguerreotype.
dalia, *n.f.* (*bot.*) dahlia.
Dalila, Dálila, *n.f.* (*Bib.*) Delilah.
dálmata, *a.*, *n.m.f.* Dalmatian (*also dog*).
dalmático, -ca, *a.* Dalmatian.—*n.f.* dalmatic.
dama, *n.f.* lady; dame; (*chess*) queen.—*pl.* draughts, (*U.S.*) checkers.
damajuana, *n.f.* demijohn.
damasceno, -na, *a.*, *n.m.f.* Damascene.
Damasco, *n.m.* Damascus; **damasco,** *n.m.* damask; damson.
damasquina (1), *n.f.* French marigold.
damasquino, -na (2), *a.* damascene.
damería, *n.f.* prudery.
damisela, *n.f.* maiden.
damnación, *n.f.* damnation.
damnificar [A], *v.t.* hurt, damage.
dandismo, *n.m.* dandyism.
danés, -nesa, *a.* Danish.—*n.m.f.* Dane.— *n.m.* Danish.
dánico, -ca, *a.* Danish.
dantesco, -ca, *a.* Dantesque; (*fam.*) fantastic.
Danubio, *n.m.* Danube.
danza, *n.f.* dance; (*fam.*) merry dance; squabble.
danzante, -a, *a.* dancing.—*n.m.f.* dancer.
danzar [C], *v.t.*, *v.i.* dance; (*fam.*) butt in.
danzarín, -rina, *a.* dancing.—*n.m.f.* good dancer.
dañable, *a.* prejudicial.
dañado, -da, *a.* wicked; spoiled.—*n.m.f.* damned soul.
dañar, *v.t.* damage; harm, hurt.
dañino, -na, *a.* harmful, destructive.

daño, *n.m.* harm, hurt; damage; *en — de,* to the detriment of; *hacer —,* harm, hurt, damage.

dañoso, -sa, *a.* harmful.

dar [16], *v.t.* give, provide.—*v.i.* strike (*the hour*); fall; *— a,* give onto, overlook; *— con,* come across, bump into; *— de sí,* give, stretch; *— en,* hit, hit on, get; give onto; run *or* fall into; *— por,* consider to be; *— sobre,* give onto; *— tras,* chase, pursue.—*v.r.* yield; occur; *darse contra,* run into, come up against; *dárselas de,* put on a show of being; *darse por,* be thought to be; consider oneself to be.

dardo, *n.m.* dart; spear.

dares y tomares, *n.m.pl.* (*fam.*) give and take; (*fam.*) squabbles, rowing.

dársena, *n.f.* dock, harbour.

darviniano, -na, *a.* Darwinian.

darvinismo, *n.m.* Darwinism.

data, *n.f.* date; (*com.*) item.

datar, *v.t., v.i.* date.

dátil, *n.m.* (*bot.*) date.

datilera, *n.f.* date palm.

dativo, -va, *a., n.m.* (*gram.*) dative.

dato, *n.m.* fact, datum.

de (1), *n.f.* name of letter D.

de (2), *prep.* of; from; by; with; *— ser así,* if it should be so.

dé [DAR].

dea, *n.f.* (*poet.*) goddess.

deán, *n.m.* (*eccl.*) dean.

debajo, *adv.* underneath, below.—*prep.* underneath, below (*de*).

debate, *n.m.* debate; struggle.

debatir, *v.t.* debate; fight.—*v.r.* struggle.

debe, *n.m.* (*com.*) debit.

debelación, *n.f.* conquest.

debelar, *v.t.* conquer.

deber, *n.m.* duty; debt; homework.—*v.t.* owe; must; should; *debe haber venido,* he should have come; *debe de haber venido,* he must have come.

debido, -da, *a.* due, proper, fit.

débil, *a.* weak.

debilidad, *n.f.* weakness.

debilitación, *n.f.* debilitation.

debilitar, *v.t.* debilitate.—*v.r.* grow weak.

debitar, *v.t.* (*com.*) debit.

débito, *n.m.* debit; duty.

debut, *n.m.* debut.

debutante, *n.m.* debutant.—*n.f.* debutante.

debutar, *v.i.* make a debut.

década, *n.f.* decade.

decadencia, *n.f.* decadence.

decadente, *a.* decadent.

decadentismo, *n.m.* (*lit.*) decadence.

decaer [14], *v.i.* decline, fade, decay.

decagramo, *n.m.* decagramme.

decaimiento, *n.m.* decline, decay.

decalitro, *n.m.* decalitre.

decálogo, *n.m.* decalogue.

decalvar, *v.t.* crop, shave (*convicts*).

decámetro, *n.m.* decametre.

decampar, *v.i.* decamp.

decano, *n.m.* (*educ.*) dean; doyen.

decantar, *v.t.* decant; exaggerate.

decapitación, *n.f.* decapitation.

decapitar, *v.t.* decapitate.

decárea, *n.f.* decare (1000 *sq. metres*).

decasílabo, -ba, *a.* decasyllabic.—*n.m.* decasyllable.

decena, *n.f.* ten.

decenal, *a.* decennial.

decencia, *n.f.* decency, decorum.

decenio, *n.m.* decade.

decentar [1], *v.t.* start on; begin to lose (*health etc.*).

decente, *a.* decent, proper; reasonable.

decepción, *n.f.* disappointment; deception.

decepcionar, *v.t.* disappoint.

decibel, decibelio, decíbelo, *n.m.* (*phys.*) decibel.

decible, *a.* utterable.

decidero, -ra, *a.* mentionable.

decidir, *v.t.* decide; persuade (*a,* to).—*v.r.* decide (*a,* to, *por,* on).

decidor, -ra, *a.* witty, fluent.—*n.m.f.* witty talker.

deciduo, -dua, *a.* deciduous.

décima, *n.f.* tenth; Spanish verse metre.

decimación, *n.f.* decimation.

decimal, *a., n.m.* decimal.

decímetro, *n.m.* decimetre.

décimo, -ma, *a.* tenth.—*n.m.* tenth; tenth of lottery ticket.

décimoctavo, -va, *a., n.f.* eighteenth.

décimocuarto, -ta, *a., n.f.* fourteenth.

décimonono, -na, décimonoveno, -na, *a., n.m.* nineteenth.

décimoquinto, -ta, *a., n.f.* fifteenth.

décimoséptimo, -ma, *a., n.f.* seventeenth.

décimosexto, -ta, *a., n.f.* sixteenth.

décimotercero, -ra, décimotercio, -cia, *a., n.f.* thirteenth.

decir, *n.m.* saying; gossip.—*v.t.* say; tell; call; fit, suit; *como quien dice,* so to speak; *como quien no dice nada,* now this is important; *— entre* or *para sí,* say to oneself; *— por —,* say for saying's sake; *— que sí,* say yes; *¡diga!* hello! (*on telephone*); *es —,* that is to say; *mejor dicho* or *por mejor —,* rather; *querer —,* mean; *se dice,* people say, it is said.

decisión, *n.f.* decision.

decisivo, -va, *a.* decisive.

declamación, *n.f.* declamation.

declamar, *v.t., v.i.* declaim.

declaración, *n.f.* declaration; statement.

declarar, *v.t.* state; declare; explain.—*v.i.* testify.—*v.r.* arise, break out.

declinable, *a.* declinable.

declinación, *n.f.* declination; (*gram.*) declension.

declinar, *v.t.* decline.

declive, *n.m.* slope; decline.

declividad, *n.f., declivio,** *n.m.* slope, declivity.

decoloración, *n.f.* decoloration.

decoración, *n.f.* decoration; decorating.—*pl.* (*theat.*) scenery.

decorado, *n.m.* decoration; (*theat.*) decor.

decorador, -ra, *n.m.f.* decorator.

decorar, *v.t.* decorate; (*obs.*) memorize.

decorativo, -va, *a.* decorative.

decoro, *n.m.* decorum; respect.

decoroso, -sa, *a.* decorous.

decrecer [9], *v.i.* decrease.

decreciente, *a.* decreasing, diminishing.

decrecimiento, *n.m.* decrease.

decrepitar, *v.i.* crackle.

decrépito, -ta, *a.* decrepit.

decrepitud, *n.f.* decrepitude.

decretal, *a., n.f.* decretal.

decretar, *v.t.* decree.
decreto, *n.m.* decree.
dechado, *n.m.* model, example; pattern; sampler.
dedada, *n.f.* drop, touch.
dedal, *n.m.* thimble; finger-stall.
dedalera, *n.f.* (*bot.*) foxglove.
dedicación, *n.f.* dedication.
dedicante, *a.* dedicating.—*n.m.f.* dedicator.
dedicar [A], *v.t.* dedicate, devote.—*v.r.* devote oneself; be dedicated *or* devoted (*a*, to).
dedicatorio, -ria, *a.* dedicatory.—*n.f.* dedication (*in book etc.*).
dedil, *n.m.* finger-stall.
dedillo, *n.m.* little finger; *al* —, perfectly.
dedo, *n.m.* finger; toe; *a dos dedos de,* within an ace of.
deducción, *n.f.* deduction.
deducir [15], *v.t.* deduce (*de, por,* from); deduct.
deductivo, -va, *a.* deductive.
defección, *n.f.* defection.
defeccionar, *v.i.* desert.
defectible, *a.* faulty, unsure.
defecto, *n.m.* defect, failing; lack.
defectuoso, -sa, *a.* faulty, defective.
defendedero, -ra, *a.* defensible.
defendedor, -ra, *a.* defending.—*n.m.f.* defender.
defender [2], *v.t.* defend; hinder; (*obs.*) forbid.
defendible, *a.* defendable; defensible.
defensa, *n.f.* defence.—*n.m.* (*sport*) back, defence.
defensión, *n.f.* protection, defence, safeguard.
defensivo, -va, *a.* defensive.—*n.m.* defence, safeguard; *a la defensiva,* on the defensive.
defensor, -ra, *n.m.f.* defender; (*jur.*) counsel for the defence.
deferencia, *n.f.* deference.
deferente, *a.* deferential.
deficiencia, *n.f.* deficiency, defect.
deficiente, *a.* deficient, defective.
déficit, *n.m.* *inv.* deficit.
definible, *a.* definable.
definición, *n.f.* definition.
definido, -da, *a.* definite; defined.
definir, *v.t.* define.
definitivo, -va, *a.* definitive; *en definitiva,* definitely.
deflector, *n.m.* deflector.
deflexión, *n.f.* deflection.
deformación, *n.f.* deformation; (*rad.*) distortion.
deformar, *v.t.* deform, distort.
deforme, *a.* deformed.
deformidad, *n.f.* deformity.
defraudación, *n.f.* defrauding, fraud; usurping.
defraudar, *v.t.* defraud; disappoint.
defuera, *adv.* outside.
defunción, *n.f.* demise, decease.
degeneración, *n.f.* degeneration, degeneracy.
degenerado, -da, *a., n.m.f.* degenerate.
degenerar, *v.i.* degenerate.
degollación, *n.f.* beheading.
degolladura, *n.f.* throat-cutting; décolletage.
degollar [10], *v.t.* cut the throat of; cut low (*clothes*); ruin, spoil, murder; (*fam.*) bore to tears.
degollina, *n.f.* (*fam.*) slaughter.

degradación, *n.f.* degradation.
degradante, *a.* degrading.
degradar, *v.t.* degrade; demote.
degüello, *n.m.* throat-cutting.
degustación, *n.f.* tasting, sampling.
degustar, *v.t.* taste, sample.
dehesa, *n.f.* pasture, meadow.
deicida, *a.* deicidal.—*n.m.f.* deicide (*person*).
deicidio, *n.m.* deicide (*act*).
deidad, *n.f.* deity.
deificación, *n.f.* deification.
deificar [A], *v.t.* deify.
deísmo, *n.m.* deism.
deísta, *a.* deistic.—*n.m.f.* deist.
dejación, *n.f.* relinquishment.
dejadez, *n.f.* laziness, slovenliness; low spirits.
dejado, -da, *a.* negligent, slovenly; dejected; *— de la mano de Dios,* Godforsaken.
dejamiento, *n.m.* relinquishment; slovenliness; dejection.
dejar, *v.t.* leave; let, allow; produce; lend; *— caer,* drop. *v.i.* cease, stop; *— de,* leave off, give up; *no — de,* not fail to.—*v.r.* be slipshod; allow oneself.
deje, dejillo, *n.m.* regional accent, lilt; after-taste.
dejo, *n.m.* relinquishment; end; regional accent; after-taste; carelessness; drop (*in voice*).
del [DE EL].
delación, *n.f.* denunciation, betrayal, informing.
delantal, *n.m.* apron, pinafore.
delante, *adv.* before, in front, ahead.—*prep.* in front (*de,* of).
delantero, -ra, *a.* forward, foremost, front. —*n.m.* (*sport*) forward; postillion.—*n.f.* front, front row; lead, advantage.
delatar, *v.t.* denounce, inform on, betray.
delator, -ra, *a.* denouncing, betraying.— *n.m.f.* accuser, informer.
deleble, *a.* erasable.
delectación, *n.f.* delectation.
delegación, *n.f.* delegation.
delegado, -da, *n.m.f.* delegate; (*com.*) agent.
delegar [B], *v.t.* delegate.
deleitar, *v.t.* delight.—*v.r.* delight, take delight (*en,* in).
deleite, *n.m.* delight.
deleitoso, -sa, *a.* delightful.
deletéreo, -rea, *a.* deleterious; poisonous (*gas*).
deletrear, *v.t.* spell; decipher.
deletreo, *n.m.* spelling.
deleznable, *a.* slippery; crumbly; perishable.
délfico, -ca, *a.* Delphic.
delfín, *n.m.* dolphin; dauphin.
Delfos, *n.m.* Delphi.
delgadez, *n.f.* slenderness; lightness; sharpness.
delgado, -da, *a.* thin, slender; sharp, fine.
delgaducho, -cha, *a.* lanky, spindly.
deliberación, *n.f.* deliberation.
deliberar, *v.t., v.i.* deliberate, decide.
deliberativo, -va, *a.* deliberative.
delicadez, *n.f.* delicateness, weakness; touchiness.
delicadeza, *n.f.* delicacy; ingenuity; scrupulosity; good manners.
delicado, -da, *a.* delicate; sharp, clever; touchy; chary.
delicia, *n.f.* delight.

delicioso, -sa, a. delicious, delightful.
delictivo, -va, delictuoso, -sa, a. criminal.
delimitar, v.t. delimit.
delincuencia, n.f. delinquency.
delincuente, a., n.m.f. delinquent.
delineante, n.m. designer, draughtsman.
delinear, v.t. delineate.
delinquimiento, n.m. transgression.
delinquir [F], v.i. transgress, be delinquent.
deliquio, n.m. swoon.
delirante, a. delirous, raving.
delirar, v.i. be delirious, rave.
delirio, n.m. delirium; raving, nonsense.
delito, n.m. crime.
delta, n.f. delta.
deludir, v.t. delude.
delusivo, -va, delusorio, -ria, a. delusive, delusory.
demacrar, v.t. emaciate.—v.r. waste away.
demagogia, n.f. demagogy.
demagógico, -ca, a. demagogic.
demagogo, -ga, a. demagogic.—n.m.f. demagogue.
demanda, n.f. demand; claim; request; en — de, in search of; tener —, be in demand.
demandante, n.m.f. (jur.) plaintiff.
demandar, v.t. demand, request, desire; (jur.) sue.
demarcación, n.f. demarcation.
demarcar [A], v.t. demarcate.
demás, a. rest of the; (los — días, las — personas).—pron. the rest (lo —, las or los —); estar —, be in the way, be useless; por —, in vain; excessively; por lo —, as for the rest, furthermore.
demasía, n.f. excess, surplus; audacity; outrage.
demasiadamente, adv. too much, too.
demasiado, -da, a., pron. too much, too many.—adv. too, too much.
demasiar, v.r. (fam.) overdo it, go too far.
demediar, v.t. halve; reach the middle of.—v.i. be cut in half.
demencia, n.f. dementia, madness.
dementar, v.t. drive mad.
demente, a. demented.—n.m. madman.—n.m.f. lunatic.
demérito, n.m. demerit.
demisión, n.f. submission, humility.
democracia, n.f. democracy.
demócrata, a. democratic.—n.m.f. democrat.
democrático, -ca, a. democratic.
democratizar [C], v.t., v.r. democratize.
demografía, n.f. demography.
demoler [5], v.t. demolish.
demolición, n.f. demolition.
demonche, n.m. (fam.) devil.
demoníaco, -ca, a., n.m.f. demoniac.
demonio, n.m. demon, devil.
demonismo, n.m. demonism
demontre, n.m. (fam.) devil.—interj. the deuce!
demora, n.f. delay; (naut.) bearing.
demorar, v.t., v.i. delay; halt; (naut.) bear.
Demóstenes, n.m. Demosthenes.
demostrable, a. demonstrable.
demostración, n.f. demonstration.
demostrar [4], v.t. demonstrate; show clearly.
demostrativo, -va, a., n.m. (gram.) demonstrative.
demótico, -ca, a. demotic.

demudar, v.t. alter, change; disguise.—v.r. change, alter.
denario, a. denary.—n.m. denarius.
dende, adv. (dial., obs.) thence.
denegación, n.f. denial, refusal.
denegar [1B], v.t. deny, refuse.
denegrecer [9], v.t. blacken, darken.
denegrido, -da, a. blackened.
dengoso, -sa, a. fussy, (fam.) finicky.
dengue, n.m. affectedness, fastidiousness; long cape; (med.) dengue.
denigración, n.f. denigration.
denigrante, a. denigrating.
denigrar, v.t. denigrate, defame.
denodado, -da, a. bold, daring.
denominación, n.f. denomination.
denominador, -ra, a. denominating.—n.m. (math) denominator.
denominar, v.t. denominate.
denostar [4], v.t. revile.
denotar, v.t. denote.
densidad, n.f. density; obscurity.
densificar [A], v.t. densify.
denso, -sa, a. dense; obscure; crowded.
dentado, -da, a. toothed, dentate; perforated.—n.m. perforation (on stamps).
dentadura, n.f. denture.
dental, a., n.f. dental.
dentar [1], v.t. tooth; perforate (stamps).—v.i. teethe; sin —, imperforate (stamps).
dentellada, n.f. bite; gnashing; tooth-mark.
dentellado, -da, a. denticulated, serrated.
dentellar, v.i. gnash the teeth; chatter (teeth).
dentellear, v.t. nibble.
dentera, n.f. tingle (sensation in teeth as reaction to certain tastes, sounds etc.); eagerness; envy; dar — a, set (s.o.'s) teeth on edge; whet the appetite of.
dentezuelo, n.m. small tooth.
dentición, n.f. dentition.
dentífrico, -ca, a. for the teeth.—n.m. dentifrice, tooth-paste.
dentista, n.m.f. dentist.
dentistería, n.f. dentistry.
dentro, adv. inside, within.—prep. inside (space) (de); within (time) (de).
denudar, v.t. lay bare, denude.—v.r. be stripped bare.
denuedo, n.m. daring.
denuesto, n.m. affront, abuse.
denuncia, n.f. announcement, proclamation; denunciation.
denunciación, n.f. denunciation.
denunciar, v.t. denounce; proclaim; foretell.
deparar, v.t. provide; present.
departamental, a. departmental.
departamento, n.m. department; compartment; (S.A.) flat.
depauperar, v.t. impoverish; debilitate.
dependencia, n.f. dependence; dependency; agency; branch; employees.
depender, v.i. depend (de, on).
dependienta, n.f. shop assistant (female).
dependiente, a. dependant.—n.m.f. dependent; shop-assistant; employee, clerk.
deplorable, a. deplorable.
deplorar, v.t. deplore.
deponente, a., n.m.f. (gram., jur.) deponent.
deponer [25], v.t. depose; put aside; take down; testify, affirm.
deportación, n.f. deportation.
deportar, v.t. deport.

deporte, *n.m.* sport.
deportismo, *n.m.* sport, sports.
deportista, *n.m.* sportsman.—*n.f.* sportswoman.
deportivo, -va, *a.* sporting, rel. to sport.
deposición, *n.f.* deposition.
depositar, *v.t.* deposit.—*v.r.* settle (*as sediment*).
depósito, *n.m.* depot; deposit; reserve; tank, reservoir.
depravación, *n.f.* depravity.
depravar, *v.t.* deprave.
deprecar [A], *v.t.* entreat.
depreciación, *n.f.* depreciation.
depreciar, *v.t.*, *v.i.* depreciate.
depredación, *n.f.* depredation.
depredar, *v.t.* depredate; pillage.
depresión, *n.f.* depression, drop, dip.
depresivo, -va, *a.* depressive.
deprimente, *a.* depressing, depressive.
deprimir, *v.t.* depress; dent; lower.
depuesto, *p.p.* [DEPONER].
depurar, *v.t.* purify, cleanse, refine.
depuse [DEPONER].
derecha, *n.f.* right (*side, political*).
derechera, *n.f.* straight road.
derechista, *a.* (*pol.*) rightwing.—*n.m.f.* right-winger.
derecho, -cha, *a.* right-hand, right-handed; upright; straight.—*n.m.* law (*as subject*); right; **no hay —,** nobody has the right to do or say that.—*pl.* dues, taxes.—*n.f.* right side; right wing.—*adv.* rightly; directly.
deriva, *n.f.* drift; **a la —,** adrift.
derivación, *n.f.* derivation; diverting; (*elec.*) shunt.
derivado, -da, *a.*, *n.m.* derivative.—*n.m.* by-product.
derivar, *v.t.* derive; divert; (*elec.*) shunt.—*v.i.*, *v.r.* derive (*de,* from); drift.
derivativo, -va, *a.*, *n.m.* derivative.
dermatitis, *n.f.* dermatitis.
derogación, *n.f.* repeal, annulment; deterioration.
derogar [B], *v.t.* abolish, destroy; reform.
derramadero, *n.m.* dump; overspill.
derramamiento, *n.m.* spilling, shedding, over-flow; scattering; waste.
derramar, *v.t.* pour; spread; spill, shed; waste.—*v.r.* spread; overflow.
derrame, *n.m.* [DERRAMAMIENTO]; chamfer, bevel; (*med.*) discharge.
derredor, *n.m.* circumference; **al** or **en —,** round, round about; **al — de,** around.
derrelicto, -ta, *n.m.* (*naut.*) wreck; jetsam.
derrelinquir [F], *v.t.* abandon, forsake.
derrengar [1B, *modern* B], *v.t.* maim, break the back of; twist.
derretido, -da, *a.* (*fam.*) love-lorn.—*n.m.* concrete.
derretimiento, *n.m.* melting, thaw; (*fam.*) crush, passion.
derretir [8], *v.t.* melt, thaw; squander; (*fam.*) change (*money*).—*v.r.* melt, thaw; (*fam.*) fall in love easily; (*fam.*) be like a cat on hot bricks.
derribar, *v.t.* demolish; knock down; overthrow.—*v.r.* tumble down; collapse.
derribo, *n.m.* demolition; overthrow.—*pl.* debris.
derrocadero, *n.m.* precipice.

derrocar [4A, *modern* A], *v.t.* fling or throw down; knock down, destroy; oust.
derrochar, *v.t.* squander.
derroche, *n.m.* waste, squandering.
derrota, *n.f.* rout, defeat; route; (*naut.*) course.
derrotar, *v.t.* rout; wear down; squander; ruin.—*v.r.* (*naut.*) stray off course.
derrotero, *n.m.* (*naut.*) course.
derrotismo, *n.m.* defeatism.
derrotista, *a.*, *n.m.f.* defeatist.
derruir [O], *v.t.* ruin, destroy.
derrumbamiento, *n.m.* plunge, fall; collapse; landslide.
derrumbar, *v.t.* fling down, throw flat.—*v.r.* fall flat; collapse, cave in.
derrumbe, *n.m.* precipice; landslide.
derviche, *n.m.* dervish.
desabarrancar [A], *v.t.* pull out, extricate.
desabollar, *v.t.* planish, flatten.
desabor, *n.m.* tastelessness.
desaborido, -da, *a.* tasteless, insipid; flimsy; (*fam.*) boring, dull.
desabotonar, *v.t.* unbutton.—*v.i.* bloom.
desabrido, -da, *a.* tasteless; gruff, harsh; bleak.
desabrigar [B], *v.t.* expose, uncover; bare.
desabrigo, *n.m.* nakedness; exposure.
desabrimiento, *n.m.* insipidity; severity; glumness.
desabrochar, *v.t.* unbutton, unfasten; reveal.
desacalorar, *v.r.* cool off.
desacatar, *v.t.* behave disrespectfully towards.
desacato, *n.m.* disrespect.
desacertar [1], *v.i.* be in error, err.
desacierto, *n.m.* error, blunder.
desacomodar, *v.t.* inconvenience; dismiss.—*v.r.* lose one's job.
desacomodo, *n.m.* dismissal.
desaconsejar, *v.t.* dissuade.
desacoplar, *v.t.* uncouple.
desacordar [4], *v.t.* ill-tune.—*v.r.* be out of tune; forget.
desacorde, *a.* out of tune; discordant.
desacostumbrado, -da, *a.* unusual, unaccustomed.
desacostumbrar, *v.t.* break (*s.o.*) of a habit. —*v.r.* lose the habit (*de,* of).
desacreditar, *v.t.* discredit.
desacuerdo, *n.m.* disagreement; forgetting.
desafección, *n.f.* dislike.
desafecto, -ta, *a.* disaffected, opposed.—*n.m.* ill-will.
desafiador, -ra, *a.* challenging, defiant.—*n.m.f.* challenger; duellist.
desafiar [L], *v.t.* challenge; defy; rival.
desafición, *n.f.* dislike.
desaficionar, *v.t.* stop the desire to.—*v.r.* lose one's liking (*de,* for).
desafilar, *v.t.* blunt, dull.
desafinar, *v.i.*, *v.r.* get out of tune; (*fam.*) speak indiscreetly.
desafío, *n.m.* challenge; rivalry.
desaforado, -da, *a.* disorderly, lawless; uncalled-for.
desaforar [4], *v.t.* encroach on the rights of. —*v.r.* overstep the mark.
desafortunado, -da, *a.* unfortunate.
desafuero, *n.m.* excess, outrage; encroachment.
desagradable, *a.* unpleasant.

desagradar, *v.t.* displease.
desagradecer [9], *v.t.* be ungrateful for.
desagradecido, -da, *a.* ungrateful.
desagradecimiento, *n.m.* ingratitude.
desagrado, *n.m.* displeasure.
desagraviar, *v.t.* make amends to.
desagravio, *n.m.* amends.
desagregar [B], *v.t., v.r.* disintegrate.
desaguar [H], *v.t.* drain; squander.
desagüe, *n.m.* drainage; outlet.
desahogado, -da, *a.* brazen; roomy; comfortable; carefree; easy.
desahogar [B], *v.t.* ease, relieve; give vent to. —*v.r.* recover, take it easy; get free of one's difficulties; open one's heart (*de,* about).
desahogo, *n.m.* easement, comfort; relief; vent, free rein; unburdening.
desahuciar, *v.t.* drive to despair; despair of; evict.—*v.r.* despair.
desahucio, *n.m.* eviction.
desairado, -da, *a.* graceless; thwarted.
desairar, *v.t.* slight, snub.
desaire, *n.m.* lack of charm; slight.
desajuste, *n.m.* fault, break-down; disagreement.
desalado, -da, *a.* hasty, eager.
desalar (1), *v.t.* remove the salt from.
desalar (2), *v.t.* clip the wings of.—*v.r.* rush; yearn (*por,* for).
dasalentar [1], *v.t.* make breathless; discourage.—*v.r.* get out of breath; get discouraged.
desaliento, *n.m.* depression, discouragement.
desaliñar, *v.t.* rumple.
desaliño, *n.m.* slovenliness; neglect.
desalmado, -da, *a.* merciless, inhuman.
desalmar, *v.r.* crave (*por,* for).
desalojar, *v.t.* dislodge; evict.—*v.i.* move away.
desalterar, *v.t.* allay, assuage.
desamar, *v.t.* dislike, detest; stop loving.
desamor, *n.m.* coldness; hatred; dislike.
desamortizar [C], *v.t.* disentail.
desamparar, *v.t.* desert; forsake, abandon.
desamparo, *n.m.* abandonment; helplessness.
desamueblado, -da, *a.* unfurnished.
desandar [11], *v.t.* retrace (*lo andado,* one's steps).
desangrar, *v.t., v.i.* bleed heavily.
desanimación, *n.f.* down-heartedness.
desanimar, *v.t.* dcject, dishearten.
desánimo, *n.m.* low spirits.
desanublar, *v.t.* clarify.—*v.r.* clear up (*weather*).
desanudar, *v.t.* untie; disentangle.
desapacible, *a.* disagreeable.
desaparecer [9], *v.t.* make disappear.—*v.i., v.r.* disappear.
desaparición, *n.f.* disappearance.
desaparroquiar, *v.t.* take customers away from.—*v.r.* lose trade.
desapasionado, -da, *a.* dispassionate.
desapego, *n.m.* indifference, coolness, dislike.
desaplacible, *a.* unpleasant.
desaplicación, *n.f.* idleness, laziness.
desaplicar [A], *v.t.* make idle.—*v.r.* be idle.
desapoderado, -da, *a.* impetuous, wild.
desapoderar, desaposesionar, *v.t.* dispossess.
desapreciar, *v.t.* underestimate.
desaprensar, *v.t.* take the shine off; free, ease.

desaprensivo, -va, *a.* unworried; unscrupulous.
desaprobación, *n.f.* disapproval.
desaprobar [4], *v.t.* disapprove of.
desapropiar, *v.t.* divest, deprive (*de,* of).—*v.r.* surrender, give up (*property*).
desaprovechado, -da, *a.* unrewarding, unproductive.
desaprovechar, *v.t.* fail to make use of.
desarbolar, *v.t.* unmast; clear (*woodland*).
desarmar, *v.t.* disarm; dismantle.—*v.r.* disarm.
desarme, *n.m.* disarmament; dismantling.
desarraigar [B], *v.t.* root out; extirpate.
desarrapado, -da, *a.* ragged.
desarrebujar, *v.t.* disentangle, unravel.
desarreglar, *v.t.* disarrange, put out of order, derange.
desarreglo, *n.m.* disorder, confusion.
desarrimar, *v.t.* separate; dissuade.
desarrollar, *v.t., v.i., v.r.* develop, unfold, unroll.
desarrollo, *n.m.* development, unfolding.
desarrugar [B], *v.t., v.r.* smooth out.
desarticular, *v.t.* disarticulate, dislocate.
desaseo, *n.m.* slovenliness, untidiness.
desasir [12], *v.t.* let go, release.—*v.r.* let go of, give up (*de*).
desasociar, *v.t.* dissociate.
desasosegar [1B], *v.t.* disquiet.
desasosiego, *n.m.* uneasiness, anxiety.
desastrado, -da, *a.* unfortunate; ragged.
desastre, *n.m.* disaster; misfortune.
desastroso, -sa, *a.* wretched, unfortunate.
desatar, *v.t.* untie, undo.—*v.r.* run wild; break out.
desatascar [A], *v.t.* extricate.
desate, *n.m.* loosening, untying; looseness; lack of restraint.
desatención, *n.f.* disregard.
desatender [2], *v.t.* disregard.
desatento, -ta, *a.* inattentive, thoughtless.
desatiento, *n.m.* anxiety, worry.
desatinado, -da, *a.* unwise, extravagant, unruly.—*n.m.f.* madcap: blunderer.
desatinar, *v.t.* bewilder, derange.—*v.i.* act or speak wildly; reel.—*v.r.* get confused.
desatino, *n.m.* folly; bewilderment; tactlessness.
desaturdir, *v.t.* bring to, rouse.
desautorizar [C], *v.t.* deprive of authority; discredit.
desavahar, *v.t.* air, cool.—*v.r.* cheer up.
desavenencia, *n.f.* disagreement; misunderstanding.
desavenir [36], *v.t.* cause trouble with.—*v.r.* disagree, quarrel (*de, con,* with).
desaventajado, -da, *a.* disadvantageous.
desaviar [L], *v.t.* mislead; ill-equip; deprive.
desavisado, -da, *a.* uninformed; ill-advised.
desayudar, *v.t.* hinder.
desayunar, *v.i.* have breakfast.—*v.r.* breakfast (*con,* on); hear (*de,* of) for the first time.
desayuno, *n.m.* breakfast.
desazón, *n.f.* tastelessness; displeasure, discomfort; poor heart, poverty (*of land*).
desazonado, -da, *a.* indisposed; peevish; poor (*land*).
desazonar, *v.t.* make tasteless; annoy, embitter.
desbancar [A], *v.t.* oust.

desbandada, *n.f.* disbandment; **a la —,** helter-skelter.
desbandar, *v.r.* flee in disorder; desert.
desbarajustar, *v.t.* throw into confusion.
desbarajuste, *n.m.* disorder, confusion.
desbaratar, *v.t.* destroy; waste; ruin; (*mil.*) rout.—*v.i.,* *v.r.* be unreasonable.
desbarate, desbarato, *n.m.* ruin; waste; rout.
desbarbar, *v.t.* shave; trim.
desbarrar, *v.t.* unbar.—*v.i.* slip away; be foolish.
desbarretar, *v.t.* unbolt.
desbarro, *n.m.* slip, folly; quiet departure.
desbastar, *v.t.* rough-hew; waste; weaken; educate.
desbocado, -da, *a.* wide-mouthed; broken-edged; runaway; foul-mouthed.
desbocar [A], *v.t.* break the spout, mouth *or* edge of.—*v.i.* run into, meet (*rivers, streets*). —*v.r.* run wild, break loose; swear, curse; become licentious.
desbordamiento, *n.m.* overflowing.
desbordar, *v.i.,* *v.r.* overflow; lose self-control.
desborde, *n.m.* overflowing; inundation.
desbragado, -da, *a.* (*fam.*) scruffy, ragged.
desbravar, *v.t.* break in, tame.—*v.i.,* *v.r.* get tame, calm down.
desbravecer [9], *v.i.,* *v.r.* [DESBRAVAR].
desbrazar, *v.r.* wave one's arms violently.
desbridar, *v.t.* unbridle.
desbrujar, *v.t.* wear away.
desbuchar, *v.t.* disgorge (*of birds*); reveal (*secrets*).
descabal, *a.* imperfect.
descabalgar, *v.t.,* *v.i.* dismount.
descabellado, -da, *a.* wild, rash; dishevelled.
descabellar, *v.t.* dishevel, rumple; (*taur.*) kill the bull by piercing the nape of his neck.
descabezado, -da, *a.* rash, headstrong.
descabezamiento, *n.m.* beheading; quandary.
descabezar [C], *v.t.* behead; lop off; (*fam.*) break the back of (*a task*); **— un sueño,** take a nap.—*v.r.* rack one's brains.
descabullir [J], *v.r.* sneak away.
descaecer [9], *v.t.* languish.
descalabrar, *v.t.* brain; harm, ruin.—*v.r.* hurt one's head.
descalabro, *n.m.* misfortune, damage, loss.
descalificar [A], *v.t.* disqualify.
descalzado, -da, *a.* bare-foot, bare-footed.
descalzar [C], *v.r.* take one's shoes off. —*v.t.* undermine.
descalzo, -za, *a.* bare-foot, unshod; (*eccl.*) discalced.
descambiar, *v.t.* exchange again (*esp. goods bought in error*).
descaminar, *v.t.* mislead.—*v.r.* go astray; run off the road.
descamino, *n.m.* leading *or* going astray.
descamisado, -da, *a.* ragged, shirtless.— *n.m.f.* ragamuffin, wretch.
descampado, -da, *a.* open (*terrain*).
descansadero, *n.m.* resting place.
descansado, -da, *a.* rested; unworried, tranquil.
descansar, *v.t.* rest; help out.—*v.i.* rest; stop work; lean.
descanso, *n.m.* rest, peace, quiet; interval, break; support; relief, aid; stair-landing.
descantillar, *v.t.* pare.

descapotable, *a., n.m.* convertible (*car*).
descarado, -da, *a.* brazen, shameless.
descarar, *v.r.* be shameless *or* impudent; have the nerve (**a,** to).
descarburar, *v.t.* decarbonize.
descarga, *n.f.* unloading; discharge; discount; customs clearance.
descargadero, *n.m.* unloading bay; wharf.
descargar [B], *v.t.* unload; discharge; clear; strike (*a blow*).—*v.i.* discharge, open, burst, empty.—*v.r.* get rid (**de,** of); free oneself of.
descargo, *n.m.* unloading; exoneration; discharge.
descargue, *n.m.* unloading.
descariño, *n.m.* lovelessness, indifference, coolness.
descarnado, -da, *a.* thin, lean; (*fig.*) bald, plain.—*n.f.*Death.
descarnar, *v.t.* remove the flesh from; wear down.—*v.r.* lose weight.
descaro, *n.m.* effrontery, sauciness.
descarriar, *v.t.* [DESCAMINAR].—*v.r.* get separated (**de,** from); go wrong.
descarrilamiento, *n.m.* derailment.
descarrilar, *v.t.* derail.—*v.i.,* *v.r.* be derailed.
descarrío, *n.m.* erring; ruin.
descartar, *v.t.* discard, reject.—*v.r.* shirk (**de**).
descarte, *n.m.* rejection; shirking.
descasar, *v.t.* annul the marriage of; disturb the good order of.—*v.r.* have one's marriage annulled; be deranged.
descascar [A], *v.t.* shell, peel.—*v.r.* shatter; blabber.
descastar, *v.t.* exterminate (*pests*).—*v.r.* lose one's natural affections.
descatolizar [C], *v.t.* cause to lapse.—*v.r.* lapse (*said of Catholics*).
descendencia, *n.f.* descent, descendants.
descendente, *a.* descending.
descender [2], *v.t.* descend; lower; bring down; take down.—*v.i.* descend; go *or* come down; descend, derive (**de,** from); stoop (**a,** to).
descendiente, *n.m.f.* descendant.
descensión, *n.f.* descent, descending.
descenso, *n.m.* descent; drop, decline.
descentralizar [C], *v.t.* decentralize.
desceñir [8K], *v.t.* ungird.
descercar [A], *v.t.* tear down the fences of; break the siege of.
descerebrar, *v.t.* decerebrate.
descerrajado, -da, *a.* (*fig.*) corrupt, evil.
descerrajar, *v.t.* break the lock of; (*fig.*) fire (*shots*).
descifrar, *v.t.* make out, decipher.
descivilizar [C], *v.t.* barbarize, decivilize.
desclasificar [A], *v.t.* disqualify.
descocado, -da, *a.* (*fam.*) cheeky, saucy.
descocer [5D], *v.t.* digest.
descoco, *n.m.* (*fam.*) cheek, nerve.
descolar, *v.t.* dock; (*S.A.*) snub; dismiss (*employees*).
descolgar [4B], *v.t.* unhang.—*v.r.* fall down, drop; (*fam.*) blurt (**con,** out).
descolocado, -da, *a.* misplaced, out of place.
descoloramiento, *n.m.* discoloration.
descolorar, *v.t.* discolour.
descolorido, -da, *a.* discoloured.
descolorimiento, *n.m.* discoloration.
descolorir [DESCOLORAR].
descollar [4], *v.t.* stand out.

desembargar

descomedido, -da, a. excessive; impolite.
descomedimiento, n.m. disrespect.
descomedir [8], v.r. be rude.
descomodidad, n.f. discomfort.
descompás, n.m. excess.
descompasado, -da, a. immoderate.
descomponer [25], v.t. upset; decompose; alienate.—v.r. decompose; change for the worse; alter (of the face); fall out (con, with).
descomposición, n.f. decomposition; disorder, confusion; disagreement; discomposure.
descompostura, n.f. decomposition; disorder; brazenness.
descompresión, n.f. decompression.
descompuesto, -ta, a. impudent; exasperated; out of order.—p.p. [DESCOMPONER].
descomulgado, -da, a. wicked, evil.
descomulgar [B], v.t. excommunicate.
descomunal, a. huge; extraordinary.
desconceptuar [M], v.t. discredit.
desconcertar [1], v.t. disconcert, baffle, disturb; dislocate.—v.r. get upset; be reckless.
desconcierto, n.m. disorder; imprudence; mismanagement; disagreement; dismay.
desconectar, v.t. disconnect.
desconexión, n.f. disconnexion.
desconfiado, -da, a. distrustful.
desconfianza, n.f. distrust.
desconfiar [L], v.i. distrust (de).
desconforme, a. disagreeing; unlike.
desconformidad, n.f. disagreement; disparity; discord.
descongelar, v.t., v.i., v.r. melt, defrost.
descongestionar, v.t. clear.
desconocer [9], v.t. not know (about); ignore, snub; disown.—v.r. be unrecognizable.
desconocido, -da, a. unknown; strange; ungrateful.—n.m.f. stranger.
desconocimiento, n.m. disregard; ingratitude; ignorance.
desconsiderado, -da, a. inconsiderate; ill-considered.
desconsolar [4], v.t., v.i. grieve.
desconsuelo, n.m. distress, grief.
descontagiar, v.t. disinfect.
descontaminación, n.f. decontamination.
descontaminar, v.t. decontaminate.
descontar [4], v.t. discount; take for granted.
descontentadizo, -za, a. hard to please.
descontentamiento, n.m. discontentment; disagreement.
descontentar, v.t. displease, dissatisfy.
descontento, -ta, a. discontent(ed), displeased.—n.m. discontent.
descontinuar [M], v.t. discontinue.
descontinuo, -nua, a. discontinuous.
desconvenible, a. unsuitable, incompatible.
desconveniencia, n.f. inconvenience; discord.
desconveniente, a. inconvenient; discordant.
desconvenir [36], v.i., v.r. disagree; match badly.
descorazonar, v.t. dishearten.
descorchar, v.t. uncork.
descorrer, v.t. draw back.—v.i. flow.
descortés, a. discourteous.
descortesía, n.f. discourtesy.
descortezar [C], v.t. strip; (fam.) polish (manners).
descoser, v.t. rip, unstitch.—v.r. prattle; come unstitched.

descosido, -da, a. indiscreet; disjointed; unstitched; immoderate; disorderly. —n.m. rip, tear. —n.m.f. (fam.) wild person.
descote [ESCOTE].
descoyuntar, v.t. disjoint; (fig.) vex.
descrédito, n.m. discredit.
descreer [N], v.t. disbelieve; deny due credit to.
descreído, -da, a. unbelieving.—n.m.f. unbeliever.
describir [p.p. descrito], v.t. describe.
descripción, n.f. description.
descriptible, a. describable.
descriptor, -ra, a. descriptive.—n.m.f. describer.
descrito, p.p. [DESCRIBIR].
descuajar, v.t. dissolve; uproot; dispirit.
descuartizar [C], v.t. quarter; carve up.
descubierta, n.f. reconnaissance, scanning.
descubierto, -ta, a. manifest; bare-headed, unveiled; exposed.—p.p. [DESCUBRIR].—n.m. exposition of the Eucharist; discovery; al —, openly; en —, (com.) overdrawn.
descubridor, -ra, a. discovering.—n.m.f. discoverer; (mil.) scout.
descubrimiento, n.m. discovery.
descubrir [p.p. descubierto] v.t. discover; disclose; uncover; (mil.) reconnoitre.—v.r. take off one's hat.
descuello, n.m. excellence, prominence; great stature.
descuento, n.m. discount; deduction.
descuidado, -da, a. careless.
descuidar, v.t. neglect, overlook; distract.—v.i., v.r. be careless; not worry (de, about).
descuido, n.m. carelessness; neglect, omission.
desde, prep. from (place); since (time); — entonces, ever since; — luego, at once; admittedly; of course.
desdecir [17], v.i. degenerate; be unworthy (de, of).—v.r. gainsay, retract (de).
desdén, n.m. disdain, contempt.
desdentado, -da, a. toothless.
desdeñable, a. despicable.
desdeñar, v.t. disdain, scorn.—v.r. be disdainful; loathe; not deign (de, to).
desdeñoso, -sa, a. disdainful, scornful.
desdibujar, v.r. become blurred.
desdicha, n.f. misfortune, misery.
desdichado, -da, a. unfortunate, wretched.
desdoblar, v.t., v.r. unfold, spread out.
desdorar, v.t. take the gilt off; tarnish, sully.
deseable, a. desirable.
desear, v.t. want, desire, wish.
desecar [A], v.t., v.r. desiccate.
desechar, v.t. reject; expel; underrate; turn (keys).
desecho, n.m. residue; debris; rejection; (S.A.) short-cut.
desedificar [A], v.t. set a bad example for.
desembalar, v.t. unpack.
desembarazada, -da, a. open, easy, free.
desembarazar [C], v.t. free, disencumber.—v.r. get free; be cleared.
desembarazo, n.m. ease, freedom.
desembarcadero, n.m. quay, pier.
desembarcar [A], v.t., v.i., v.r. disembark.
desembarco, n.m. disembarkation.
desembargar [B], v.t. free, disembargo.

69

desembarque, *n.m.* unloading; disembarkation.
desembarrar, *v.t.* clean of mud.
desembocadero, desemboque, *n.m.*, **desembocadura,** *n.f.* estuary; outlet.
desembocar [A], *v.i.* flow (*en*, into); end at, lead into (*en*).
desembolsar, *v.t.* disburse.
desembolso, *n.m.* outlay, expenditure.
desemborrachar, *v.t.*, *v.r.* sober up.
desemboque, [DESEMBOCADERO].
desembragar [B], *v.t.* (*mech.*) disengage, declutch.
desembrollar, *v.t.* unravel.
desemejante, *a.* different (*de*, from).
desemejanza, *n.f.* dissimilarity, difference.
desemejar, *v.t.* disfigure.—*v.i.* differ.
desempacho, *n.m.* ease, forwardness.
desempatar, *v.t.* decide, replay.
desempate, *n.m.* deciding game, vote *etc.* after a tie; replay, decider.
desempeñar, *v.t.* carry out; play (*a part*); redeem; free.
desempeño, *n.m.* fulfilment, discharge; redemption.
desempleo, *n.m.* unemployment.
desempolvar, *v.t.* dust; (*fig.*) brush up.
desenamorar, *v.t.* disenchant.
desencadenamiento, *n.m.* unchaining; outbreak.
desencadenar, *v.t.* unchain, unleash.—*v.r.* break loose *or* out.
desencajar, *v.t.* disjoint.—*v.r.* look distorted.
desencajonar, *v.t.* unpack; (*taur.*) release bulls from their travelling boxes.
desencallar, *v.t.* refloat.
desencantar, *v.t.* disenchant, disillusion.
desencanto, *n.m.* disillusionment; disenchantment.
desencapotar, *v.r.* take one's cloak off; clear up (*sky*); calm down (*person*).
desencoger [E], *v.t.* unfold.—*v.r.* grow bold.
desencogimiento, *n.m.* ease, assuredness.
desencolerizar [C], *v.t.*, *v.r.* calm down.
desenconar, *v.t.* calm, allay.—*v.r.* calm down, soften.
desencono, *n.m.* calming, allaying.
desenchufar, *v.t.* unplug.
desendiosar, *v.t.* humble, bring down to earth.
desenfadado, -da, *a.* free and easy, carefree; roomy.
desenfadar, *v.t.* appease; cheer.—*v.r.* calm down, cheer up.
desenfado, *n.m.* ease, calm.
desenfrenado, -da, *a.* unbridled, wanton.
desenfrenar, *v.t.* unbridle.—*v.r.* lose all restraint.
desenfreno, *n.m.* wantonness, unruliness.
desenganchar, *v.t.* unhook, undo.
desengañar, *v.t.* disabuse; disillusion.—*v.r.* get disillusioned.
desengaño, *n.m.* disillusion; disappointment; bitter truth.
desengranar, *v.t.* put out of gear.
desenjaezar [C], *v.t.* unharness.
desenjaular [A], *v.t.* uncage, let out.
desenlace, *n.m.* outcome, dénouement.
desenlazar [C], *v.t.* untie; unravel.—*v.r.* unfold (*story, plot etc.*).
desenlodar, *v.t.* remove the mud from.
desenmarañar, *v.t.* disentangle.

desenmascaradamente, *adv.* bare-facedly.
desenmascarar, *v.t.* unmask.
desenojar, *v.t.* calm the anger of.—*v.r.* calm down.
desenojo, *n.m.* appeasement; composure.
desenredar, *v.t.* disentangle, sort out.—*v.r.* extricate oneself.
desenredo, *n.m.* disentanglement; dénouement.
desenrollar, *v.t.* unroll, unfurl, unwind.
desenroscar [A], *v.t.* unscrew.
desensillar, *v.t.* unsaddle.
desentender, *v.r.* take no part (*de*, in).
desentendido, -ida, *a.* unmindful, feigning ignorance.
desenterramiento, *n.m.* disinterment; unearthing.
desenterrar [I], *v.t.* unearth; disinter exhume; dig up.
desentonar, *v.t.* humble.—*v.i.* be out of tune.—*v.r.* overstep the mark.
desentono, *n.m.* false note; disrespect.
desentrañar, *v.t.* disembowel; figure out.—*v.r.* bleed oneself white.
desenvainar, *v.t.* unsheathe, draw.
desenvoltura, *n.f.* free-and-easy ways; wantonness.
desenvolver [5, *p.p.* **desenvuelto**], *v.t.* unfold, unroll; develop; unravel.—*v.r.* develop, evolve; extricate oneself; be too forward.
desenvolvimiento, *n.m.* unfolding; development; sorting out.
desenvuelto, -ta, *a.* wanton, impudent; free-and-easy.
deseo, *n.m.* desire, wish.
deseoso, -sa, *a.* desirous; eager.
desequilibrar, *v.t.* unbalance.
deserción, *n.f.* desertion.
desertar, *v.t.* desert; (*jur.*) forfeit.—*v.i.* desert (*de, a,* from, to).
desertor, *n.m.* deserter.
deservicio, *n.m.* disservice.
deservir [8], *v.t.* do (a) disservice to.
desesperación, *n.f.* despair, desperation.
desesperado, -da, *a.* desperate; hopeless.
desesperante, *a.* despairing; exasperating.
desesperanza, *n.f.* hopelessness.
desesperanzar [C], *v.t.* deprive of hope.—*v.r.* lose hope.
desesperar, *v.t.* drive to despair.—*v.i.*, *v.r.* despair.
desespero, *n.m.* [DESESPERACIÓN].
desestima, desestimación, *n.f.* lack of esteem, low regard.
desfachatado, -da, *a.* (*fam.*) brazen, hardfaced.
desfachatez, *n.f.* (*fam.*) cheek, impudence.
desfalcar [A], *v.t.* lop off; embezzle.
desfalco, *n.m.* lopping off; embezzlement.
desfallecer [9], *v.t.*, *v.i.* weaken.
desfalleciente, *a.* languishing.
desfallecimiento, *n.m.* weakening; languor; fainting.
desfavorable, *a.* unfavourable.
desfavorecer [9], *v.t.* disfavour; despise; injure.
desfiguración, *n.f.* disfigurement; distortion.
desfigurar, *v.t.* disfigure; disguise; cloud; distort.
desfiladero, *n.m.* pass, defile.
desfilar, *v.i.* defile, march past, parade.

desfile, *n.m.* parade, march-past.
desflorar, *v.t.* deflower; skim over.
desflorecer [9], *v.i.*, *v.r.* wither, fade.
desflorecimiento, *n.m.* withering, fading.
desfogar [B], *v.t.* give vent to; slake.—*v.i.* break (*storm clouds*).—*v.r.* vent one's anger.
desfrenar, *v.i.* take off the brakes; [DESENFRENAR].
desgaire, *n.m.* slovenliness; scorn.
desgajar, *v.t.* tear off, break off.—*v.r.* come off, break off; pour with rain.
desgalgadero, *n.m.* cliff, precipice.
desgana, *n.f.* lack of appetite *or* interest; *a* —, unwillingly.
desganar, *v.t.* take away interest *or* appetite.—*v.r.* lose one's appetite *or* interest.
desgañitar, *v.r.* (*fam.*) yell and bawl.
desgarbado, -da, *a.* graceless, uncouth.
desgargantar, *v.r.* (*fam.*) shout oneself blue in the face.
desgaritar, *v.i.* go astray.—*v.r.* lose one's way; give up a job.
desgarrado, -da, *a.* tattered, torn; shameless.
desgarrar, *v.t.* tear; ruin.—*v.r.* retire.
desgarro, *n.m.* tear, tatter; effrontery; boasting; outburst.
desgarrón, *n.m.* tear, rent; shred, tatter.
desgastar, *v.t.*, *v.r.* wear away.
desgaste, *n.m.* wear; attrition.
desgaznatar, *v.r.* (*fam.*) yell and scream.
desgobernado, -da, *a.* uncontrollable.
desgobernar [1], *v.t.* misgovern; dislocate.
desgobierno, *n.m.* misgovernment; mismanagement; dislocation.
desgonzar [C], **desgoznar,** *v.t.* unhinge.
desgracia, *n.f.* misfortune; disfavour; gracelessness; *por* —, unfortunately.
desgraciado, -da, *a.* unfortunate, luckless; graceless; unpleasant; wretched.
desgraciar, *v.t.* displease; spoil.—*v.r.* decline; quarrel; fail.
desgranar, *v.t.* thresh, shell, husk, pick.—*v.r.* drop off.
desgravar, *v.t.* lower the tax on.
desgreñar, *v.t.* dishevel.
deshabitado, -da, *a.* uninhabited.
deshabitar, *v.t.* abandon, leave (*a dwelling*).
deshabituar, *v.t.* break of a habit.—*v.r.* become unaccustomed.
deshacer [20], *v.t.* undo; take apart; use up; spoil; right (*wrongs*).—*v.r.* fall to pieces; melt; get rid of (*de,* of); strive (*por,* to).
deshambrido, -da, *a.* starving.
desharrapado, -da, *a.* ragged.
deshecha, *n.f.* feint, evasion; farewell.
deshechizo, *n.m.* breaking of a spell; disappointment.
deshecho, -cha, *a.* hard, violent; ruined.—*p.p.* [DESHACER].
deshelar [1], *v.t.* thaw; de-ice.
desherbar [1], *v.t.* weed.
desheredado, -da, *a.* disinherited; underprivileged.
desheredar, *v.t.* disinherit.—*v.r.* betray one's heritage.
deshidratar, *v.t.* dehydrate.
deshielo, *n.m.* thaw; defrosting.
deshierba, *n.f.* weeding.
deshilachar, *v.r.* fray.
deshilado, -da, *a.* in single file; *a la deshilada,* single file; secretly.
deshilar, *v.t.* draw (*threads*).

deshilvanado, -da, *a.* disjointed.
deshipotecar [A], *v.t.* end the mortgage on.
deshojar, *v.t.* strip of leaves; tear the pages from.—*v.r.* lose its leaves; fall to bits (*book*).
deshollinador, *n.m.* chimney-sweep.
deshollinar, *v.t.* sweep (*chimneys*); (*fam.*) eye all over.
deshonestidad, *n.f.* indecency.
deshonesto, -ta, *a.* indecent, immodest.
deshonor, *n.m.* dishonour.
deshonorar, *v.t.* dishonour.
deshonra, *n.f.* dishonour, disgrace.
deshonrar, *v.t.* dishonour; defame.
deshonroso, -sa, *a.* dishonourable.
deshora, *n.f.* inopportune moment; *a* —, inopportunely.
desiderátum, *n.m.* (*pl.* -rata) desideratum.
desidioso, -sa, *a.* indolent.
desierto, -ta, *a.* deserted.—*n.m.* desert.
designación, *n.f.* designation.
designar, *v.t.* designate; design.
designio, *n.m.* purpose, design.
desigual, *a.* unequal; unlike; uneven; difficult.
desigualar, *v.t.* make unequal.—*v.r.* excel.
desigualdad, *n.f.* unevenness; inequality.
desilusión, *n.f.* disillusionment.
desilusionar, *v.t.* disillusion.—*v.r.* be disillusioned.
desimanar, *v.t.* demagnetize.
desimpresionar, *v.t.* undeceive.
desinencia, *n.f.* (*gram.*) ending, inflexion.
desinfección, *n.f.* disinfection.
desinfectante, *a.*, *n.m.* disinfectant.
desinfectar, desinficionar, *v.t.* disinfect.
desinflamar, *v.t.* reduce the inflammation in.
desintegración, *n.f.* disintegration.
desintegrar, *v.t.*, *v.r.* disintegrate.
desinterés, *n.m.* disinterest.
desinteresado, -da, *a.* disinterested, impartial.
desistir, *v.i.* desist (*de,* from); (*jur.*) waive a right.
desjarretar, *v.t.* hamstring.
desjuiciado, -da, *a.* senseless, brainless.
desjuntar, *v.t.* sever.
deslabonar, *v.t.* unlink; break up.
deslavado, -da, *a.* barefaced.
desleal, *a.* disloyal.
deslealtad, *n.f.* disloyalty.
deslenguado, -da, *a.* foul-mouthed.
deslenguar, *v.t.* cut the tongue out of.—*v.r.* (*fam.*) blab.
desliar [L.], *v.t.* untie; unroll; unravel.
desligar [B], *v.t.* untie; unravel; exempt.
deslindador, *n.m.* surveyor.
deslindamiento, *n.m.* demarcation.
deslindar, *v.t.* mark the boundaries of; (*fig.*) define.
desliz, *n.m.* (*pl.* -ices) slip (*also fig.*).
deslizadizo, -za, *a.* slippery.
deslizamiento, *n.m.* slip, slide.
deslizar [C], *v.t.* (make) slide; let slip.—*v.i.* slip, slide.—*v.r.* slip, slide, glide; slip out; get away.
deslucido, -da, *a.* dull, uninteresting.
deslucir [9], *v.t.* dull, tarnish.
deslumbramiento, *n.m.* glare; bafflement.
deslumbrante, *a.* dazzling; bewildering.
deslumbrar, *v.t.* dazzle; baffle.
deslustrar, *v.t.* tarnish; frost (*glass*).
deslustre, *n.m.* tarnish, dullness; discredit.

deslustroso, -sa, *a.* unbecoming, ugly.
desmadejar, *v.t.* enervate.
desmadrado, -da, *a.* motherless, abandoned.
desmagnetizar [C], *v.t.* demagnetize.
desmán, *n.m.* mishap; excess, misbehaviour.
desmanchar, *v.t.* (*S.A.*) clean (*clothes*).
desmandado, -ada, *a.* lawless, out of hand.
desmandar, *v.t.* countermand, revoke.—*v.r.* be unruly.
desmantelamiento, *n.m.* dismantling; dilapidation.
desmantelar, *v.t.* dismantle; dilapidate; (*naut.*) demast.—*v.r.* fall into disrepair.
desmaña, *n.f.* clumsiness.
desmañado, -da, *a.* clumsy, fumbling, awkward.
desmayado, -da, *a.* languid; dull (*colour*).
desmayar, *v.t.,* *v.i.* dismay.—*v.r.* faint.
desmayo, *n.m.* swoon; dismay; faltering.
desmazalado, -da, *a.* dispirited, dejected.
desmedido, -da, *a.* excessive.
desmedir [8], *v.r.* forget oneself.
desmedrar, *v.t.* impair.—*v.r.* deteriorate.
desmedro, *n.m.* detriment, decay.
desmejorar, *v.t.* spoil, make worse.—*v.i., v.r.* get worse; fade.
desmelenar, *v.t.* dishevel.
desmembración, *n.f.* dismembering.
desmembrar, *v.t.* dismember.—*v.r.* break up.
desmemoriado, -da, *a.* forgetful.
desmemoriar, *v.r.* lose one's memory.
desmenguar [H], *v.t.* diminish.
desmentida, *n.f.* denial, giving the lie.
desmentir [6], *v.t.* give the lie to, belie; hide.
desmenuzar [C], *v.t.* crumble; scrutinize.—*v.r.* crumble.
desmerecer [9], *v.t.* be unworthy of.—*v.i.* lose worth; look bad in comparison.
desmerecimiento, *n.m.* unworthiness.
desmesura, *n.f.* immoderation.
desmesurado, -da, *a.* immoderate; uncouth.
desmesurar, *v.t.* discompose, disorder.—*v.r.* be insolent.
desmigajar, desmigar [B], *v.t., v.r.* crumble.
desmilitarización, *n.f.* demilitarization.
desmilitarizar [C], *v.t.* demilitarize.
desmirriado, -da, *a.* (*fam.*) lean; run-down.
desmochar, *v.t.* poll(ard); dehorn; abridge.
desmonetizar [C], *v.t.* demonetize.
desmontable, *a.* detachable; collapsible.
desmontadura, *n.f.,* **desmontaje,** *n.m.* dismantling.
desmontar, *v.t.* dismantle; clear of trees; level off (*ground*); uncock; unhorse.—*v.i., v.r.* dismount.
desmonte, *n.m.* felling; levelling; (*S.A.*) mine rubble.
desmoralización, *n.f.* demoralization.
desmoralizar [C], *v.t.* demoralize.—*v.r.* become demoralized.
desmoronamiento, *n.m.* crumbling, decay.
desmoronar, *v.t.* wear away.—*v.r.* crumble.
desmovilización, *n.f.* demobilization.
desmovilizar [C], *v.t.* demobilize.
desnacionalizar [C], *v.t.* denationalize.
desnatar, *v.t.* skim (*milk*).
desnaturalizar [C], *v.t.* denaturalize; pervert.—*v.r.* become unnatural; lose citizenship.
desnivel, *n.m.* unevenness; drop.

desnivelar, *v.t.* make uneven.
desnucar [A], *v.t.* break the neck off.—*v.r.* break one's neck.
desnudar, *v.t.* undress; strip; reveal.—*v.r.* undress; get rid (*de,* of); shed (*de*).
desnudez, *n.f.* nakedness.
desnudo, -da, *a.* naked, bare, nude; (*fam.*) broke, penniless.
desnutrición, *n.f.* malnutrition.
desnutrido, -da, *a.* undernourished.
desobedecer [9], *v.t.* disobey.
desobediencia, *n.f.* disobedience.
desobediente, *a.* disobedient.
desobligar [B], *v.t.* release from an obligation; disoblige, alienate.
desocupación, *n.f.* leisure; unemployment.
desocupado, -da, *a.* vacant, free; unemployed.—*n.m.f.* unemployed person.
desocupar, *v.t.* empty, vacate.—*v.r.* be doing nothing.
desodorante, *a.,* *n.m.* deodorant.
desoír [22], *v.t.* ignore, not heed.
desolación, *n.f.* desolation.
desolar [4], *v.t.* desolate, lay waste.
desollado, -da, *a.* (*fam.*) brazen, cheeky.
desolladura, *n.f.* flaying, fleecing; graze, hurt.
desollar [4], *v.t.* skin, flay; (*fam.*) fleece; condemn.
desorbitado, -da, *a.* (*S.A.*) wild-eyed.
desorden, *n.m.* disorder.
desordenado, -da, *a.* unruly, disorderly.
desordenar, *v.t.* disorder.—*v.r.* get out of order.
desorganizar [C], *v.t.* disorganize.
desorientar, *v.t.* confuse.—*v.r.* lose one's bearings, get lost.
desovillar, *v.t.* unravel, disentangle.
despabilado, -da, *a.* wide-awake, smart.
despabilar, *v.t.* snuff (*candles*); (*fam.*) eat up; kill off; fritter away; liven up.—*v.r.* wake up; (*S.A.*) go away.
despacio, *adv.* slowly; gently.—*interj.* steady! —*n.m.* (*S.A.*) delay.
despacioso, -sa, *a.* slow, sluggish.
despacito, *adv.* (*fam.*) very slowly.
despachaderas, *n.f.pl.* (*fam.*) wit, resourcefulness.
despachante, *n.m.* (*S.A.*) shop assistant.
despachar, *v.t.* dispatch; attend to; send, ship; sell.—*v.i., v.r.* hurry; get things settled; give birth.
despacho, *n.m.* dispatch; office, study; shop; sending, shipping; message.
despachurrar, *v.t.* (*fam.*) squash, mangle.
despampanante, *a.* (*fam.*) shaking, stunning.
despampanar, *v.t.* prune (*vines*); (*fam.*) shake, dumbfound.—*v.i.* (*fam.*) tell all.—*v.r.* (*fam.*) come a cropper.
desparejo, -ja, *a.* uneven; unsteady.
desparpajar, *v.t.* tear to bits; (*S.A.*) spill.—*v.i.* (*fam.*) gabble.
desparpajo, *n.m.* (*fam.*) cheek, nerve; (*C.A.*) chaos.
desparramado, -da, *a.* wide, open.
desparramamiento, *n.m.* scattering, spilling; prodigality.
desparramar, *v.t.* scatter; spill; squander.—*v.r.* scatter; be spilled; revel, carouse.
despartir, *v.t.* separate, part.
despear, *v.t.* damage the feet of.—*v.r.* get sore feet.

despectivo, -va, *a.* pejorative, disparaging.
despechar, *v.t.* spite, enrage.—*v.r.* fret; give up hope.
despecho, *n.m.* spite; despair; **a — de,** despite.
despedazar [C], *v.t.*, *v.r.* break into pieces.
despedida, *n.f.* farewell, parting; dismissal.
despedimiento, *n.m.* parting, farewell.
despedir [8], *v.t.* hurl; give off; dismiss; see off.—*v.r.* take one's leave (**de,** of).
despegado, -da, *a.* (*fam.*) gruff, surly.
despegar [B], *v.t.* unstick, open, detach.— *v.i.* (*aer.*) take off.—*v.r.* come loose; become distant.
despego, *n.m.* coldness; surliness.
despegue, *n.m.* (*aer.*) take-off.
despeinar, *v.t.* ruffle, muss, let down (*hair*).
despejado, -da, *a.* cloudless; bright, smart.
despejar, *v.t.* clear, clear up.—*v.r.* be bright; clear up (*weather*); get better.
despejo, *n.m.* clearing; ability; brightness.
despeluzar [C], *v.t.* ruffle the hair of; make the hair stand on end.
despeluznante, *a.* hair-raising.
despeluznar [DESPELUZAR].
despellejar, *v.t.* skin, flay; (*fam.*) back-bite.
despenar, *v.t.* console; (*fam.*) kill.
despensa, *n.f.* pantry, larder; provisions.
despensero, -ra, *n.m.f.* steward, storekeeper.
despeñadamente, *adv.* rashly.
despeñadero, -ra, *a.* steep.—*n.m.* precipice, cliff; danger.
despeñadizo, -za, *a.* steep, precipitous.
despeñar, *v.t.* throw over a cliff.—*v.r.* fall from rocks; plunge.
despeño, *n.m.* throwing *or* falling from a cliff; failure, ruin, fall.
despepitar, *v.t.* remove seed.—*v.r.* scream with fury; yearn (**por,** for).
desperdiciar, *v.t.* waste; lose, miss.
desperdicio, *n.m.* waste.—*pl.* waste, by-products.
desperdigar [B], *v.t.* scatter.
desperezar [C], *v.r.* stretch (*limbs on waking etc.*).
desperfecto, *n.m.* flaw, blemish.
despernar [1], *v.t.* injure the legs of.
despertador, *n.m.*, **despertadora,** *n.f.* alarm-clock; (*fig.*) warning.
despertamiento, *n.m.* awakening.
despertar [1], *v.t.* wake, rouse.—*v.r.* wake up, awake, stir.
despiadado, -da, *a.* merciless.
despicar [A], *v.t.* satisfy, make amends.—*v.r.* have one's honour satisfied.
despichar, *v.t.* dry out.—*v.i.* (*low*) kick off (*die*).
despierto, -ta, *a.* awake.
despilfarrado, -da, *a.* ragged; wasteful.— *n.m.f.* squanderer.
despilfarrar, *v.t.* squander, waste.—*v.r.* (*fam.*) blue it in (*money*).
despilfarro, *n.m.* squandering, waste; shabbiness.
despintar, *v.t.* strip the paint off; spoil.—*v.r.* fade, wash off.
despique, *n.m.* requital, satisfaction.
despistar, *v.t.* throw off the scent.—*v.r.* lose the track; get muddled.
despiste, *n.m.* losing the way; putting off the scent; muddle, mistake; lack of care.
despizcar [A], *v.t.* crush, grind up.

desplacer, *n.m.* displeasure.—*v.t.* [23] displease.
desplantar, *v.t.* dig up; throw out of the vertical.—*v.r.* lose the upright position.
desplante, *n.m.* bad posture; (*S.A.*) impudence.
desplazar [C], *v.t.* displace; supplant.—*v.r.* move.
desplegar [1B], *v.t.* unfold, unroll; display; deploy.—*v.r.* unfold; deploy.
despliegue, *n.m.* unfolding; display; deployment.
desplomar, *v.t.* put out of plumb.—*v.r.* move out of plumb; collapse; faint; fall; (*aer.*) pancake.
desplome, *n.m.* collapse; fall; downfall.
desplomo, *n.m.* leaning, tilting.
desplumar, *v.t.* pluck; (*fam.*) fleece.—*v.r.* moult.
despoblación, *n.f.* depopulation.
despoblado, *n.m.* deserted place, wilds.
despoblar [4], *v.t.* depopulate; lay waste.— *v.r.* become depopulated.
despojar, *v.t.* plunder, despoil, divest.—*v.r.* undress; divest oneself (**de,** of).
despolvar, *v.t.* dust; (*S.A.*) sprinkle.
despopularizar [C], *v.t.* make unpopular.
desportillar, *v.t.* chip, nick.
desposado, -da, *a.* handcuffed.—*a.*, *n.m.f.* newly-wed.
desposar, *v.t.* betroth, marry.—*v.r.* get engaged *or* married.
desposeer [N], *v.t.* dispossess.
desposorios, *n.m.pl.* betrothal; nuptials.
déspota, *n.m.* despot.
despótico, -ca, *a.* despotic.
despotismo, *n.m.* despotism.
despotizar [C], *v.t.* (*S.A.*) tyrannize.
despotricar [A], *v.i.*, *v.r.* (*fam.*) rant, rave.
despreciable, *a.* contemptible.
despreciar, *v.t.* despise; slight; reject.—*v.r.* not deign (**de,** to).
desprecio, *n.m.* contempt, scorn; slight.
desprender, *v.t.* unfasten, separate; emit.— *v.r.* come loose; be clear (**de,** from); give up (**de**).
desprendido, -da, *a.* unselfish.
desprendimiento, *n.m.* coming loose; release; generosity; landslide.
despreocupación, *n.f.* freedom from bias; unconcernedness.
despreocupado, -da, *a.* unconcerned; unconventional.
despreocupar, *v.r.* forget one's cares.
desprestigiar, *v.t.* bring into disrepute.—*v.r.* lose one's good standing.
desprestigio, *n.m.* loss of standing; unpopularity.
desprevención, *n.f.* unpreparedness.
desprevenido, -da, *a.* unprepared; unawares.
desproporción, *n.f.* disproportion.
desproporcionado, -da, *a.* disproportionate.
despropositado, -da, *a.* absurd, nonsensical.
despropósito, *n.m.* absurdity, nonsense.
desprovisto, -ta, *a.* deprived of, lacking entirely in (**de**).
después, *adv.* after, later, next.—*prep.* after (**de**).—*conj.* after (**de que** that).
despuntar, *v.t.* take the edge *or* point off; nibble.—*v.i.* start sprouting; dawn; stand out.
despunte, *n.m.* blunting.

desquiciar, *v.t.* unhinge; upset; (*fam.*) spoil things for.—*v.r.* come unhinged; collapse.
desquijarar, *v.t.* break the jaw of.—*v.r.* roar (*de risa*, with laughter).
desquilatar, *v.t.* alloy (*gold*); devaluate.
desquitar, *v.t.* recoup; avenge.—*v.r.* recoup; get even (*con*, with).
desquite, *n.m.* recouping, recovery; retaliation, getting even.
desrazonable, *a.* unreasonable.
desreputación, *n.f.* bad name, disrepute.
destacado, -da, *a.* outstanding.
destacamento, *n.m.* (*mil.*) detachment.
destacar [A], *v.t.* highlight; (*mil.*) detail.—*v.r.* stand out, excel.
destajar, *v.t.* let out (*work*) on piece-rate; cut (*cards*).
destajo, *n.m.* job, piece-work; *a —,* on piece-rate, by the job; eagerly.
destapar, *v.t.* uncover; uncork.
destaponar, *v.t.* uncork, open.
destartalado, -da, *a.* shabby, jumbled, ill-furnished.
destejer, *v.t.* unweave, ravel.
destellar, *v.i.* flash, beam, sparkle.
destello, *n.m.* flash.
destemplanza, *n.f.* lack of moderation *or* regularity.
destemplar, *v.t.* put out of tune; disconcert.—*v.r.* become irregular; be indisposed; act immoderately.
destemple, *n.m.* dissonance; lack of moderation; indisposition.
desteñir [8K], *v.t.*, *v.r.* fade.
desternillar, *v.r.* split one's sides.
desterrar [1], *v.t.* exile, banish.
a destiempo, *adv. phr.* inopportunely.
destierro, *n.m.* exile, banishment; wilds.
destilación, *n.f.* distillation, distilling.
destilar, *v.t.* distil; filter.—*v.r.* drip, ooze.
destilería, *n.f.* distillery.
destinación, *n.f.* destination, assignment.
destinar, *v.t.* destine (*a*, to, *para*, for); assign.
destinatario, -ria, *n.m.f.* addressee.
destino, *n.m.* destiny; destination; employment; *con — a,* bound for.
destitución, *n.f.* destitution; dismissal.
destituir [O], *v.t.* deprive; dismiss.
destorcer [5D], *v.t.*, *v.r.* untwist.
destornillado, -da, *a.* reckless, crazy.
destornillador, *n.m.* screwdriver.
destornillar, *v.t.* unscrew.—*v.r.* (*fig.*) be rash.
destral, *n.m.* hatchet.
destrejar, *v.i.* act with dexterity.
destreza, *n.f.* skill, dexterity.
destripar, *v.t.* disembowel; smash; (*fam.*) spoil, ruin.
destripaterrones, *n.m. inv.* (*fam.*) clodhopper.
destrísimo, -ma, *a.* most skilful.
destrizar [C], *v.t.* tear to shreds.—*v.r.* be furious.
destronamiento, *n.m.* dethronement.
destronar, *v.t.* dethrone.
destrozar [C], *v.t.* destroy, shatter, smash; squander.
destrozo, *n.m.* havoc, ruin, destruction.
destrucción, *n.f.* destruction.
destructivo, -va, *a.* destructive.

destructor, -ra, *a.* destroying.—*n.m.* (*mil.*) destroyer.
destruir [O], *v.t.* destroy.
desudar, *v.t.* wipe the sweat off.
desuello, *n.m.* skinning; brazenness; (*fam.*) daylight robbery (*exorbitant price*).
desuetud, *n.f.* desuetude.
desunión, *n.f.* disunion.
desunir, *v.t.*, *v.r.* disunite.
desusado, -da, *a.* obsolete, out of use.
desusar, *v.t.* disuse.—*v.r.* become disused.
desuso, *n.m.* disuse.
desvaído, -da, *a.* spindly; dull (*colour*).
desvalido, -da, *a.* destitute, helpless.
desvalijar, *v.t.* steal (*from baggage*); plunder, rob.
desvalimiento, *n.m.* helplessness.
desvalorar, *v.t.* devalue.
desvalorización, *n.f.* devaluation.
desvalorizar [C], *v.t.* devaluate.
desván, *n.m.* loft, attic.
desvanecer [9], *v.t.* make vanish; dissipate.—*v.r.* disappear, vanish; swoon.
desvanecido, -da, *a.* faint; haughty.
desvanecimiento, *n.m.* disappearance; vanity; faintness, swoon.
desvariado, -da, *a.* nonsensical; luxuriant.
desvariar [L], *v.i.* rave, be delirious.
desvarío, *n.m.* delirium, raving; extravagance, whim.
desvelado, -da, *a.* watchful, wakeful; worried.
desvelar, *v.t.* keep awake; unveil.—*v.r.* stay awake, not sleep; be very worried (*por*, about).
desvelo, *n.m.* wakefulness; sleeplessness; worry.
desvencijado, -da, *a.* rickety.
desvencijar, *v.t.* pull to bits, loosen.—*v.r.* come loose, come to bits.
desvendar, *v.t.* unbandage.
desventaja, *n.f.* disadvantage.
desventajoso, -sa, *a.* disadvantageous.
desventura, *n.f.* misfortune.
desventurado, -da, *a.* unfortunate; mean, miserable; faint-hearted.
desvergonzado, -da, *a.* shameless.
desvergonzar [4C], *v.r.* be shameless, be insolent (*con*, to).
desvergüenza, *n.f.* shamelessness.
desvestir [8], *v.t.*, *v.r.* undress.
desviación, *n.f.* deflection.
desviado, -da, *a.* devious; astray.
desviar [L], *v.t.* divert, deflect, avert; dissuade.—*v.r.* deviate, wander, swerve.
desvío, *n.m.* deviation, diversion, deflection; dislike; detour; (*rail.*) siding.
desvirtuar [M], *v.t.* detract from, spoil.
desvivir, *v.r.* be eager (*por*, to, for).
desvolver [5, *p.p.* **desvuelto**], *v.t.* change the shape of; till (*the soil*); unscrew.
detallar, *v.t.* detail; retail.
detalle (1), *n.m.* detail; (*fam.*) sign of good manners.
detalle (2), *n.m.* (*S.A.*) retail.
detallista (1), *n.m.f.* retailer.
detallista (2), *n.m.f.* person fond of detail.
detective, *n.m.* detective.
detector, *n.m.* (*rad.*) detector.
detención, *n.f.* detention; delay; meticulousness; arrest.

detener [33], *v.t.* detain, delay, check, arrest, retain.—*v.r.* stop; linger, pause.
detenido, -da, *a.* sparing; lengthy; careful; hesitant.
detenimiento, *n.m.* [DETENCIÓN].
detergente, *a.*, *n.m.* detergent.
deteriorar, *v.t.*, *v.r.* deteriorate.
deterioro, *n.m.* deterioration; damage, wear.
determinable, *a.* determinable.
determinación, *n.f.* determination.
determinado, -da, *a.* determined; determinate; (*gram.*) definite.
determinante, *a.*, *n.m.* determinant.
determinar, *v.t.* determine; induce; specify. —*v.r.* decide, determine (*a*, to).
determinismo, *n.m.* determinism.
detestación, *n.f.* detestation; cursing.
detestar, *v.t.* curse; detest.—*v.i.* detest (*de*).
detonación, *n.f.* detonation.
detonador, *n.m.* detonator.
detonante, *a.* detonating.
detonar, *v.i.* detonate.
detorsión, *n.f.* (*med.*) sprain.
detracción, *n.f.* detraction.
detractar, *v.t.* detract, defame.
detractor, -ra, *a.* detracting.—*n.m.f.* detractor.
detraer [34], *v.t.* detract; libel.
detrás, *adv.* behind.—*prep.* behind (*de*).
detrimento, *n.m.* detriment, harm, damage.
detrito, *n.m.* detritus; debris.
deuda, *n.f.* debt; fault.
deudo, -da, *n.m.f.* relative, kinsman *or* kinswoman.—*n.m.* kinship.
deudor, -ra, *n.m.f.* debtor.
Deuteronomio, *n.m.* (*Bib.*) Deuteronomy.
devanar, *v.t.* wind, spool.—*v.r.* (*S.A.*) writhe; *devanarse los sesos,* cudgel one's brains.
devanear, *v.i.* rave; fritter time away.
devaneo, *n.m.* frenzy, raving; time-wasting; flirting.
devastación, *n.f.* devastation.
devastar, *v.t.* devastate.
devengar [B], *v.t.* earn, receive.
devenir [36], *v.i.* happen; (*phil.*) become.
devoción, *n.f.* devotion.
devocionario, *n.m.* prayer-book.
devolución, *n.f.* return, restitution.
devolver [5, *p.p.* **devuelto**], *v.t.* return, give back, pay back; (*fam.*) vomit.—*v.r.* (*S.A.*) come back.
devorante, *a.* devouring.
devorar, *v.t.* devour.
devotería, *n.f.* bigotry; sanctimoniousness.
devoto, -ta, *a.* devout; devoted.—*n.m.f.* devotee.
devuelto, *n.m.* (*fam.*) vomiting.—*p.p.* [DEVOLVER].
día, *n.m.* day; daylight; *al* —, per day; up to date; *buenos días,* good morning; *dar los días a,* a wish many happy returns to; *de* —, in the daytime; *del* —, in fashion; today's; — *de guardar* or *de precepto,* holiday; — *de Reyes,* Epiphany; — *onomástico,* saint's day; — *útil* or *laborable,* working day; *el* — *menos pensado,* (*fam.*) *al menor* —, when you least expect it; *en el* — *de hoy,* these days; *en pleno* —, in broad daylight; *en su* —, in due course, at the proper time;

entrado en días, advanced in years; *vivir al* —, live for the day *or* moment, live from day to day.
diabetes, *n.f.* (*med.*) diabetes.
diabético, -ca, *a.*, *n.m.f.* diabetic.
diablesa, *n.f.* (*fam.*) she-devil.
diablillo, *n.m.* imp; (*fam.*) schemer.
diablo, *n.m.* devil.
diablura, *n.f.* devilment, deviltry; escapade, naughtiness.
diabólico, -ca, *a.* diabolical, devilish.
diácono, *n.m.* deacon.
diadema, *n.f.* diadem, tiara.
diado, -da, *a.* appointed (*day*).
diáfano, -na, *a.* diaphanous.
diafragma, *n.m.* diaphragm.
diagnosis, *n.f. inv.* diagnosis.
diagnosticar [A], *v.t.* diagnose.
diagnóstico, -ca, *a.*, *n.m.* diagnostic.—*n.m.* diagnosis.
diagonal, *a.*, *n.f.* diagonal.
diagrama, *n.m.* diagram.
dialectal, *a.* dialectal.
dialéctico, -ca, *a.* dialectic.—*n.f.* dialectics.
dialecto, *n.m.* dialect.
dialogar [B], *v.i.* maintain a dialogue.
diálogo, *n.m.* dialogue.
diamantado, -da, *a.* diamond-like.
diamante, *n.m.* diamond.
diamantino, -na, *a.* rel. to diamonds; (*poet.*) adamantine.
diamantista, *n.m.* diamond cutter *or* merchant.
diametral, *a.* diametrical.
diámetro, *n.m.* diameter.
diana, *n.f.* (*mil.*) reveille; bull's-eye.
dianche, diantre, *n.m.* (*fam.*) the devil.—*interj.* the deuce!
diapasón, *n.m.* (*mus.*) diapason; tuning fork; pitch pipe.
diapositiva, *n.f.* (*phot.*) diapositive; slide.
diario, -ria, *a.* daily.—*n.m.* daily (*paper*); diary; daily allowance; day book; *a* —, every day.
diarismo, *n.m.* (*S.A.*) journalism.
diarista, *n.m.f.* diarist; (*S.A.*) journalist.
diarrea, *n.f.* (*med.*) diarrhoea.
Diáspora, *n.f.* (*Bib.*) Diaspora.
diatriba, *n.f.* diatribe.
dibujante, *n.f.* drawer, illustrator.—*n.m.* draughtsman.
dibujar, *v.t.* draw, sketch; depict; outline.—*v.r.* take shape, appear.
dibujo, *n.m.* drawing.
dicaz, *a.* (*pl.* **-aces**) sarcastic.
dicción, *n.f.* diction; word.
diccionario, *n.m.* dictionary.
diccionarista, *n.m.f.* lexicographer.
diciembre, *n.m.* December.
diciente, *a.* saying.
dicotomía, *n.f.* dichotomy.
dictado, *n.m.* dictation; title, honour.—*pl.* dictates.
dictador, *n.m.* dictator.
dictadura, *n.f.* dictatorship.
dictáfono, *n.m.* dictaphone.
dictamen, *n.m.* opinion, judgement.
dictaminar, *v.i.* pass judgement, express an opinion.
dictar, *v.t.* dictate; suggest; (*S.A.*) give (*lectures*).
dictatorial, dictatorio, -ria, *a.* dictatorial.

75

dicterio, *n.m.* taunt.
dicha, *n.f.* happiness, luck.
dicharachero, -ra, *a.* (*fam.*) foul-mouthed.
dicharacho, *n.m.* (*fam.*) smuttiness, obscenity.
dicho, -cha, *a.* said.—*p.p.* [DECIR].—*n.m.* saying; promise; witticism; (*fam.*) insult; — *y hecho,* no sooner said than done.
dichoso, -sa, *a.* happy, lucky; (*fam. iron.*) blessed.
didáctico, -ca, *a.* didactic(al).
diecinueve, *a.,* *n.m.* nineteen.
dieciochesco, -ca, *a.* eighteenth-century.
dieciocho, *a.,* *n.m.* eighteen.
dieciséis, *a.,* *n.m.* sixteen.
diecisiete, *a.,* *n.m.* seventeen.
Diego, *n.m.* James.
diente, *n.m.* tooth; fang; tusk; cog; *a regaña dientes,* grudgingly; — *de león,* (*bot.*) dandelion; *dar — con —,* (*fam.*) chatter (*of teeth*); *estar a —,* (*fam.*) be famished.
diéresis, *n.f.* diaeresis.
diesel, *n.m.* diesel engine.
diestro, -tra, *a.* skilful, expert, dexterous; shrewd; propitious; right; (*her.*) dexter.— *n.m.* bullfighter; master fencer.
dieta, *n.f.* diet; *a —,* on a diet.—*pl.* daily fee.
dietar, *v.t.,* *v.r.* diet.
dietario, *n.m.* day book.
dietético, -ca, *a.* dietary, dietetic.—*n.f.* dietetics.
diez, *a.,* *n.m.* ten.
diezmal, *a.* decimal.
diezmar, *v.t.* decimate; tithe.
diezmo, *n.m.* tithe.
difamación, *n.f.* defamation.
difamar, *v.t.* defame.
difamatorio, -ria, *a.* defamatory.
diferencia, *n.f.* difference; (*obs.*) delay; *a — de,* unlike.
diferenciación, *n.f.* differentiation.
diferencial, *a.,* *n.f.* (*math., mech.*) differential.
diferenciar, *v.t.* differentiate.—*v.i.,* *v.r.* differ.
diferente, *a.* different.
diferir [6], *v.t.* defer.—*v.i.,* *v.r.* differ.
difícil, *a.* difficult, hard (*de,* to).
difícilmente, *adv.* with difficulty.
dificultad, *n.f.* difficulty.
dificultar, *v.t.* make difficult, impede; consider difficult.—*v.i.* raise objections.— *v.r.* get difficult.
dificultoso, -sa, *a.* difficult, troublesome.
difidencia, *n.f.* distrust.
difidente, *a.* distrustful.
difracción, *n.f.* diffraction.
difractar, *v.t.* diffract.
difteria, *n.f.* (*med.*) diphtheria.
difundido, -da, *a.* widespread, widely known.
difundir, *v.t.* spread, broadcast.
difunto, -ta, *a.,* *n.m.f.* deceased; *día de los Difuntos,* All Souls' Day.
difusión, *n.f.* diffusion; spreading; broadcasting.
difusivo, -sa, *a.* diffusive.
difuso, -sa, *a.* diffuse.
digerir [6], *v.t.* digest; bear, suffer.
digestión, *n.f.* digestion.
digestivo, -va, *a.,* *n.m.* digestive.
digesto, *n.m.* (*jur.*) digest.
digital, *a.* digital.—*n.f.* (*bot.*) digitalis.
dígito, *n.m.* digit.

dignar, *v.r.* deign to.
dignatario, *n.m.* dignitary.
dignidad, *n.f.* dignity.
dignificar [A], *v.t.* dignify; honour.
digno, -na, *a.* worthy (*de,* of); fitting.
digo [DECIR].
digresión, *n.f.* digression.
digresivo, -va, *a.* digressive.
dije, *n.m.* amulet; (*fam.*) jewel (*good person*); (*fam.*) smart person. —*pl.* bragging [DECIR].
dilación, *n.f.* delay.
dilapidación, *n.f.* dilapidation; wasting.
dilapidar, *v.t.* dilapidate; squander.
dilatación, *n.f.* dilation; prolixity; serenity (*in grief*).
dilatado, -da, *a.* vast; prolix; dilated.
dilatar, *v.t.* dilate; defer; spread.—*v.r.* dilate, expand; be prolix; be deferred.
dilecto, -ta, *a.* beloved, loved.
dilema, *n.m.* dilemma.
diletante, *a.,* *n.m.f.* dilettante.
diletantismo, *n.m.* dilettantism.
diligencia, *n.f.* diligence; stage-coach; speed; errand.
diligenciar, *v.t.* expedite.
diligente, *a.* diligent; prompt.
dilucidar, *v.t.* elucidate.
dilución, *n.f.* dilution.
diluir [O], *v.t.* dilute.
diluviar, *v.i.* pour down rain.
diluvio, *n.m.* deluge; (*Bib.*) the Flood.
dimanar, *v.i.* spring, arise (*de,* from).
dimensión, *n.f.* dimension.
dimensional, *a.* dimensional.
dimes, *n.m. pl. andar en — y diretes,* (*fam.*) squabble, bicker (*con,* with).
diminución, *n.f.* diminution.
diminuir [O], *v.t.,* *v.i.,* *v.r.* diminish.
diminutivo, -va, *a.* diminutive.
diminuto, -ta, *a.* diminutive; imperfect.
dimisión, *n.f.* resignation.
dimisionario, -ria, dimitente, *a.* resigning. —*n.m.f.* person resigning.
dimitir, *v.t.* resign from, renounce.—*v.i.* resign.
Dinamarca, *n.f.* Denmark.
dinamarqués, -quesa [DANÉS].
dinámico, -ca, *a.* dynamic.—*n.f.* dynamics.
dinamita, *n.f.* dynamite.
dinamitar, *v.t.* dynamite.
dinamitero, -ra, *a.* rel. to dynamite.—*n.m.f.* dynamiter.
dínamo, *n.m.* dynamo.
dinastía, *n.f.* dynasty.
dinerada, *n.f.,* **dineral,** *n.m.* large sum of money, (*fam.*) fortune.
dinero, *n.m.* money; currency.
dineroso, -sa, *a.* moneyed.
dingo, *n.m.* (*zool.*) dingo.
dinosaurio, *n.m.* dinosaur.
dintel, *n.m.* (*arch.*) lintel.
diocesano, -na, *a.* diocesan.
diócesi(s), *n.f.* (*pl.* **diócesis**) diocese.
Dionisio, *n.m.* Dionysius; Denis.
Dios, *n.m.* God; *a la buena de —,* (*fam.*) goodnaturedly, without malice; *¡ por — !* for goodness' sake! *¡ válgame — !* bless me! *¡ vaya con — !* God speed!; be off! *¡ vive — !* by heaven! **dios,** *n.m.* god.
diosa, *n.f.* goddess.
diploma, *n.m.* diploma; document.

diplomacia, *n.f.* diplomacy.
diplomado, -da, *a., n.m.f.* graduate.
diplomático, -ca, *a.* diplomatic.—*n.m.f.* diplomat.—*n.f.* diplomatics; diplomacy.
dipsomanía, *n.f.* dipsomania.
dipsomaníaco, -ca, dipsómano, -na, *a., n.m.f.* dipsomaniac.
diptongar [B], *v.t., v.r.* diphthongize.
diptongo, *n.m.* diphthong.
diputación, *n.f.* deputation; (*hist.*) ruling council when the Cortes were not in session.
diputado, -da, *n.m.f.* deputy; member (*of Parliament*).
diputar, *v.t.* depute; deputize.
dique, *n.m.* dyke, dam; dry dock; (*fig.*) check.
diré [DECIR].
dirección, *n.f.* direction; management; steering; trend; address; — **única,** one-way (*streets etc.*).
direccional, *a.* directional.
directo, -ta, *a.* direct; clear; straight.
director, -ra, *a.* directing, guiding.—*n.m.f.* director; manager; principal; editor (*of paper*); (*mus.*) conductor.
directorado, *n.m.* directorship.
directorio, -ria, *a.* directory; directorial.—*n.m.* directory; directorship; board of directors; directive.
directriz, *n.f.* (*pl.* **-ices**) directive.
dirigente, *n.m.f.* head, director, manager; ruler, minister.
dirigible, *a., n.m.* dirigible.
dirigir [E], *v.t.* direct, manage; conduct; address; steer.—*v.r.* address (*a*); apply (*a,* to).
dirimir, *v.t.* annul; pour; settle.
discante, *n.m.* descant; treble.
discerniente, *a.* discerning.
discernimiento, *n.m.* discernment.
discernir [3], *v.t.* discern; (*jur.*) entrust.
disciplina, *n.f.* discipline; education; lash.
disciplinar, *v.t.* discipline; educate; whip.
disciplinario, -ria, *a.* disciplinary.
disciplinazo, *n.m.* lash.
discípulo, -la, *n.m.f.* disciple; pupil, student.
disco, *n.m.* phonograph record; disc, disk, discus; (*rail.*) signal; tap washer; (*tel.*) dial.
díscolo, -la, *a.* unruly, wayward.
disconforme, *a.* disagreeing.
disconformidad, *n.f.* non-, in- *or* disconformity; disagreement.
discontinuar [M], *v.t.* discontinue.
discordante, *a.* discordant.
discordar [4], *v.i.* disagree, be out of tune (*de,* with).
discorde, *a.* discordant, dissonant.
discordia, *n.f.* discord.
discoteca, *n.f.* record cabinet.
discreción, *n.f.* discretion; prudence; wit.
discrecional, *a.* discretional, optional.
discrepancia, *n.f.* discrepancy; disagreement.
discrepante, *a.* discrepant; disagreeing.
discrepar, *v.i.* disagree, differ.
discretear, *v.i.* attempt cleverness.
discreto, -ta, *a.* discreet, prudent; witty; discrete.
discrimen, *n.m.* risk; difference.
discriminación, *n.f.* discrimination.
discriminante, *a.* discriminating.
discriminar, *v.t., v.i.* discriminate, differentiate.

disculpa, *n.f.* apology; excuse.
disculpable, *a.* excusable.
disculpar, *v.t.* excuse, pardon.—*v.r.* apologize (*con,* to, *de,* for).
discurrir, *v.t.* contrive; conjecture.—*v.i.* roam; flow; reason; discourse.
discursear, *v.i.* (*fam.*) speechify.
discursivo, -va, *a.* reflective.
discurso, *n.m.* speech; passage (*of time*).
discusión, *n.f.* discussion.
discutible, *a.* arguable.
discutir, *v.t.* discuss; argue about.—*v.i.* argue (*sobre,* about).
disecación, *n.f.* dissection.
disecar [A], *v.t.* dissect; stuff.
disección, *n.f.* dissection; taxidermy.
disector, *n.m.* dissector.
diseminación, *n.f.* dissemination.
diseminar, *v.t.* disseminate.—*v.r.* spread.
disensión, *n.f.* dissension.
disenso, *n.m.* dissent.
disentería, *n.f.* (*med.*) dysentery.
disentimiento, *n.m.* dissension.
disentir [6], *v.i.* dissent.
diseñar, *v.t.* design, draw.
diseño, *n.m.* design, sketch.
disertación, *n.f.* dissertation.
disertar, *v.i.* discourse.
disfavor, *n.m.* disfavour.
disforme, *a.* deformed; monstrous, ugly.
disfraz, *n.m.* (*pl.* **-aces**) disguise.
disfrazar [C], *v.t.* disguise.
disfrutar, *v.t.* enjoy; have at one's disposal.—*v.i.* take pleasure (*con,* in); — *de,* enjoy, have the benefit of.
disfrute, *n.m.* use, enjoyment, benefit.
disgregar [B], *v.t., v.r.* disintegrate.
disgustado, -da, *a.* annoyed; insipid.
disgustar, *v.t.* displease.—*v.r.* be displeased (*con, de,* with, about).
disgusto, *n.m.* displeasure, annoyance; worry, sorrow; squabble; *a —,* against one's will.
disgustoso, -sa, *a.* unpleasant.
disidencia, *n.f.* dissidence.
disidente, *a.* dissident.—*n.m.f.* dissenter.
disidir, *v.i.* dissent.
disímil, *a.* dissimilar.
disimilación, *n.f.* dissimilation.
disimilitud, *n.f.* dissimilarity.
disimulación, *n.f.* dissembling.
disimulado, -da, *a.* underhand; reserved.
disimular, *v.t.* hide, pretend not to have *or* to be, dissemble; forgive.
disimulo, *n.m.* dissembling; toleration.
disipación, *n.f.* dissipation.
disipar, *v.t.* dissipate.—*v.r.* be dissipated, vanish.
dislate, *n.m.* nonsense, absurdity.
dislocación, dislocadura, *n.f.* dislocation.
dislocar [A], *v.t., v.r.* dislocate.
disminución, *n.f.* diminution.
disminuir [O], *v.t., v.i., v.r.* diminish, decrease.
disociar, *v.t., v.r.* dissociate.
disoluble, *a.* dissoluble.
disolución, *n.f.* dissolution; disoluteness.
disoluto, -ta, *a.* dissolute.—*n.m.f.* debauchee.
disolver [5, *p.p.* **disuelto**], *v.t., v.r.* dissolve.
disonancia, *n.f.* dissonance.
disonante, *a., n.m.* dissonant.
disonar [4], *v.i.* be dissonant; grate, jar.
dísono, -na, *a.* dissonant.

dispar, *a.* unlike, unmatched, disparate.
disparadero, disparador, *n.m.* trigger; catch.
disparar, *v.t.* shoot, fire; hurl.—*v.i.* talk rubbish.—*v.r.* dash off; go off (*gun*); bolt.
disparatado, -da, *a.* absurd, foolish.
disparatar, *v.i.* talk rubbish; blunder.
disparate, *n.m.* piece of foolery, blunder; (*fam.*) scandal, outrage.
disparidad, *n.f.* disparity.
disparo, *n.m.* shot, discharge; nonsense.
dispendio, *n.m.* waste, squandering.
dispensa, dispensación, *n.f.* dispensation.
dispensar, *v.t.* dispense; excuse; pardon (*de,* for).—*v.i.* dispense (*con,* with).
dispensario, *n.m.* dispensary.
dispersar, *v.t.,* *v.r.* disperse.
dispersión, *n.f.* dispersal, dispersion.
disperso, -sa, *a.* scattered, dispersed; worried.
displicencia, *n.f.* lukewarmness; discouragement.
displicente, *a.* disagreeable; peevish.
disponer [25], *v.t.* arrange; direct.—*v.i.* dispose, make use, have the use (*de,* of).—*v.r.* get ready, prepare (*a, para,* to).
disponibilidad, *n.f.* availability.
disponible, *a.* available.
disposición, *n.f.* disposition; arrangement; inclination; lay-out; disposal.
dispositivo, *n.m.* device.
dispuesto, -ta, *a.* disposed; ready, willing; sprightly.—*p.p.* [DISPONER].
disputa, *n.f.* dispute.
disputable, *a.* disputable.
disputar, *v.t.* dispute; fight for.—*v.i.* argue, fight (*de, por, sobre,* over, about).
disquisición, *n.f.* disquisition.
distancia, *n.f.* distance.
distanciar, *v.t.* outdistance; place apart.
distante, *a.* distant.
distar, *v.i.* be distant, be far.
distender [2], *v.t.,* *v.r.* distend.
distensión, *n.f.* distension.
distinción, *n.f.* distinction.
distinguible, *a.* distinguishable.
distinguir [G], *v.t.* distinguish.
distintivo, -va, *a.* distinctive.—*n.m.* mark, badge, insignia.
distinto, -ta, *a.* different; distinct.—*pl.* various.
distorsión, *n.f.* distortion.
distracción, *n.f.* distraction; amusement; embezzlement.
distraer [34], *v.t.* distract, divert; seduce; misappropriate; amuse.
distraído, -da, *a.* absent-minded; dissolute; (*S.A.*) slovenly.
distribución, *n.f.* distribution; supply system; (*mech.*) gear system.
distribuidor, -ra, *a.* distributing.—*n.m.f.* distributor.
distribuir [O], *v.t.* distribute.
distributivo, -va, *a.* distributive.
distrito, *n.m.* district.
disturbar, *v.t.* disturb.
disturbio, *n.m.* disturbance.
disuadir, *v.t.* dissuade (*de,* from).
disuasión, *n.f.* dissuasion.
disuasivo, -va, *a.* dissuasive.
disuelto, *p.p.* [DISOLVER].
disyuntivo, -va, *a.* disjunctive.—*n.f.* dilemma.

dita, *n.f.* surety, bond; (*S.A.*) debt; credit.
diva, *n.f.* (*poet.*) goddess; (*mus.*) diva.
divagación, *n.f.* wandering, divagation.
divagar [B], *v.i.* ramble, digress.
diván, *n.m.* divan.
divergencia, *n.f.* divergence.
divergente, *a.* divergent.
divergir [E], *v.i.* diverge.
diversidad, *n.f.* diversity, variety.
diversificación, *n.f.* diversification.
diversificar [A], *v.t.,* *v.r.* diversify.
diversión, *n.f.* diversion; amusement.
diverso, -sa, *a.* diverse, different.—*pl.* several.
divertido, -da, *a.* funny; (*S.A.*) merry.
divertimiento, *n.m.* amusement; distraction.
divertir [6], *v.t.* amuse, divert.—*v.r.* have fun, enjoy oneself (*en,* by).
dividendo, *n.m.* dividend.
dividir, *v.t.,* *v.r.* divide.
divieso, *n.m.* (*med.*) boil.
divinidad, *n.f.* divinity; adored person.
divino, -na, *a.* divine; *a lo* —, rewritten to convey religious concepts.
divisa, *n.f.* emblem, device; foreign currency; (*taur.*) breeder's colours.
divisar, *v.t.* espy, perceive.
divisible, *a.* divisible.
división, *n.f.* division.
divisor, -ra, *a.* dividing.—*n.m.f.* divider.—*n.m.* (*math., rad.*) divisor.
divisorio, -ria, *a.* dividing.—*n.f.* dividing-line; (*geol.*) divide.
divo, -va, *a.* (*poet.*) godlike.—*n.m.* (*poet.*) god; (*mus.*) opera singer. [DIVA].
divorciar, *v.t.* divorce, end the marriage of.—*v.r.* get a divorce, divorce (*de*).
divorcio, *n.m.* divorce.
divulgación, *n.f.* divulging.
divulgar [B], *v.t.* divulge, reveal, spread.
do (1), *adv.* (*obs., poet.*) [DONDE].
do (2), *n.m.* (*mus.*) (key of) C; — *de pecho,* top C (*also fig.*).
dobladillo, *n.m.* hem.
doblado, -da, *a.* stocky; uneven; deceitful.
dobladura, *n.f.* fold, crease.
doblamiento, *n.m.* folding, doubling.
doblar, *v.t.* fold, crease; turn (*a corner*); dissuade; dub (*films*); double.—*v.i.* double; toll; turn.—*v.r.* fold, bend; stoop; yield.
doble, *a.* double; thickset; deceitful.—*n.m.* double, twice the amount; double, stand-in; fold; toll(ing); deceitfulness.—*adv.* doubly; *al* —, doubly; double.
doblegable, *a.* easily folded, pliant.
doblegar [B], *v.t.* fold, bend; dissuade; overcome; brandish.—*v.r.* yield; fold.
doblete, *a.* medium.—*n.m.* imitation gem; doublet.
doblez, *n.f.* crease, fold, pleat; turn-up.—*n.m.* or *f.* duplicity.
doblón, *n.m.* doubloon.
doce, *a., n.m.* twelve.
docena, *n.f.* dozen.
docente, *a.* teaching.
dócil, *a.* docile; ductile.
docto, -ta, *a.* learned.—*n.m.f.* scholar.
doctor, -ra, *n.m.f.* doctor.—*n.f.* (*fam.*) doctor's wife; (*fam.*) blue-stocking.
doctorado, *n.m.* doctorate.
doctoral, *a.* doctoral.

dramatización

doctorar, *v.t.* award a doctorate to.—*v.r.* obtain one's doctorate (*por* (*la Universidad de*), at).
doctrina, *n.f.* doctrine.
doctrinal, *a.*, *n.m.* doctrinal.
doctrinar, *v.t.* indoctrinate, instruct.
doctrinario, -ria, *a.* doctrinaire.
doctrino, *n.m.* charity child; (*fig.*) timid person.
documentación, *n.f.* documentation; documents.
documental, *a.*, *n.m.* documentary.
documentar, *v.t.* document.
documento, *n.m.* document.
dogal, *n.m.* halter; noose.
dogma, *n.m.* dogma.
dogmático, -ca, *a.* dogmatic.
dogmatismo, *n.m.* dogmatism.
dogmatizar [C], *v.t.*, *v.i.* dogmatize; teach heresies.
dogo, -ga, *n.m.f.* bulldog.
dolamas, *n.f.pl.*, **dolames,** *n.m.pl.* (*vet.*) defects; (*S.A.*) ailment.
dolar [4], *v.t.* hew.
dólar, *n.m.* dollar.
dolencia, *n.f.* ailment, complaint.
doler [5], *v.t.* hurt, pain; distress.—*v.i.* ache. —*v.r.* complain (*de,* about); feel sorry (*de,* for).
doliente, *a.* ailing; sorrowing.—*n.m.f.* patient, sick person; mourner.
dolo, *n.m.* guile.
dolor, *n.m.* pain; sorrow, grief; repentance.
dolorido, -da, *a.* painful; heart-broken.
doloroso, -sa, *a.* painful; dolorous.—*n.f.* Mater Dolorosa.
doloso, -sa, *a.* deceitful.
doma, *n.f.* breaking, taming.
domador, -ra, *a.* taming.—*n.m.* horse-breaker.
domar, *v.t.* tame, break in (*horses*); master.
domeñar, *v.t.* tame; master.
domesticación, *n.f.* domestication.
domesticidad, *n.f.* domesticity.
doméstico, -ca, *a.*, *n.m.f.* domestic.
domestiquez, *n.f.* tameness.
domiciliar, *v.t.* domicile.—*v.r.* settle.
domicilio, *n.m.* dwelling; home address.
dominación, *n.f.* domination, dominance.
dominante, *a.* dominant; domineering, overbearing.
dominar, *v.t.* dominate; know completely *or* perfectly; domineer.—*v.r.* control oneself.
domingo, *n.m.* Sunday.
dominguero, -ra, *a.* (*fam.*) Sunday.
dominical, *a.* rel. to the Sabbath; feudal; *la oración —,* the Lord's Prayer.
dominicano, -na, *a.*, *n.m.f.* (*eccl.*, *geog.*) Dominican.
dominio, *n.m.* dominion; (*jur.*) ownership; domain; knowledge (*of a subject*).
dominó, *n.m.* (*pl.* **-ós**) domino; dominoes.
dómino, *n.m.* dominoes.
Don, *n.m.* Don, Sir; **don,** *n.m.* gift; talent.
donación, *n.f.* donation.
donador, -ra, *n.m.f.* donor.
donaire, *n.m.* elegant clever wit; graceful witticism.
donairoso, -sa, *a.* witty, clever; graceful.
donante, *n.m.f.* donor.
donar, *v.t.* donate, give.
donativo, *n.m.* gift, donation.

doncel, *n.m.* knight's page; virgin (*man*).
doncella, *n.f.* maiden, virgin.
doncellez, *n.f.* maidenhood, virginity.
doncellueca, *n.f.* (*fam.*) old maid, spinster.
donde, *conj.* where; wherever; in which.— *prep.* (*S.A.*) at *or* to the home, office, shop *etc.* of (*like Fr.* chez); *por —,* through which, whereby; *— no,* otherwise.
¿dónde? *interrogative adv.* where?
dondequiera, *adv.* anywhere.
dondiego, *n.m.* dandy; (*bot.*) morning glory.
donjuanesco, -ca, *a.* like Don Juan.
donoso, -sa, *a.* witty, graceful.
donostiarra, *a.*, *n.m.f.* rel. to *or* native of San Sebastian.
donosura, *n.f.* wittiness; elegance.
Doña, *n.f.* Miss, Mrs., Madam (*title used before Christian name of ladies*).
doñear, *v.t.* woo.—*v.i.* (*fam.*) womanize.
doquier(a), *adv.* wherever.
dorado, -da, *a.* golden, gilt.—*n.m.* gilding, gilt; (*ichth.*) dorado.
dorar, *v.t.* gild; (*fig.*) sugar-coat; (*cul.*) brown.
dórico, -ca, *a.* Doric.
dormida, *n.f.* sleeping; night's sleep; lair, den; (*S.A.*) bedroom; night's lodgings.
dormidero, -ra, *a.* soporific.—*n.f.* (*bot.*) opium poppy.—*pl.* sleepiness.
dormido, -da, *a.* asleep; sleepy.
dormilón, -lona, *a.* (*fam.*) sleepy.—*n.m.f.* (*fam.*) sleepyhead; pyjama-case.—*n.f.* earring (*for small child*).
dormir [7], *v.t.* sleep; sleep off; (*S.A.*) deceive.—*v.i.* sleep.—*v.r.* go to sleep, fall asleep.
dormitar, *v.i.* snooze, doze.
dormitorio, *n.m.* bedroom; dormitory.
Dorotea, *n.f.* Dorothy.
dorsal, *a.* dorsal.
dorso, *n.m.* back, dorsum.
dos, *a.*, *n.m.* two; *en un — por tres,* (*fam.*) in a flash.
doscientos, -tas, *a.*, *n.m.* two hundred.
dosel, *n.m.* canopy.
dosificación, *n.f.* dosage, dosing.
dosificar [A], *v.t.* dose; measure out.
dosis, *n.f. inv.* dose.
dotación, *n.f.* endowment; dowry; (*naut.*, *aer.*) complement, crew; equipment.
dotar, *v.t.* give a dowry to; endow; equip; man; staff.
dote, *n.m. or f.* dowry.—*n.f.* gift, talent.
doy [DAR].
dozavado, -da, *a.* twelve-sided.
dozavo, -va, *a.*, *n.m.* twelfth; *en —,* 12°.
dracma, *n.f.* drachma; dram, drachm.
draga, *n.f.* dredging; (*naut.*) dredger.
dragaminas, *n.m. inv.* (*naut.*) mine-sweeper.
dragar [B], *v.t.* dredge.
dragomán, *n.m.* dragoman.
dragón, *n.m.* dragon; (*mil.*) dragoon.
dragona, *n.f.* (*mil.*) shoulder tassel; (*C.A.*) cape.
dragoncillo, *n.m.* (*bot.*) tarragon.
dragonear, *v.i.* (*S.A.*) boast (*de, of being*); flirt.
drama, *n.m.* drama.
dramático, -ca, *a.* dramatic; theatrical.— *n.m.* dramatist; actor.—*n.f.* drama, the dramatic art.
dramatismo, *n.m.* dramatic quality, drama.
dramatización, *n.f.* dramatization.

79

dramatizar [C], *v.t.* dramatize.
dramaturgo, *n.m.* dramatist.
drástico, -ca, *a.* drastic.
dren, *n.m.* drain.
drenaje, *n.m.* draining.
drenar, *v.t.* drain.
dril, *n.m.* drill (*cloth*).
driza, *n.f.* (*naut.*) halyard.
droga, *n.f.* drug; swindle; pest; (*S.A.*) bad debt; (*fam.*) white elephant (*useless object*).
drogmán, *n.m.* dragoman.
droguería, *n.f.* pharmacy.
droguero, -ra, *n.m.f.* druggist, pharmacist; (*S.A.*) bad debtor; cheat.
droguista, *n.m.f.* cheat; (*S.A.*) druggist.
dromedario, *n.m.* dromedary.
druida, *n.m.* druid.
dual, *n.m.* dual.
dualidad, *n.f.* duality.
dualismo, *n.m.* dualism.
dualista, *a.* dualistic.—*n.m.f.* dualist.
dubitación, *n.f.* dubitation, doubt.
dubitativo, -va, *a.* dubitative.
ducado, *n.m.* duchy, dukedom; ducat.
ducal, *a.* ducal.
dúctil, *a.* ductile.
ductivo, -va, *a.* conducive.
ducha, *n.f.* shower-bath; douche, shower.
duchar, *v.t.* douche; give a shower to.—*v.r.* take a shower.
duda, *n.f.* doubt.
dudable, *a.* doubtful.
dudar, *v.t., v.i.* doubt; — *en,* hesitate to.
dudoso, -sa, *a.* doubtful, dubious.
duelista, *n.m.* duellist.
duelo (1), *n.m.* duel.
duelo (2), *n.m.* sorrow, grief; bereavement.—*pl.* travails.
duende, *n.m.* elf, goblin; spirit.
duendo, -da, *a.* tame, domestic.
dueño, -ña, *n.m.f.* owner.—*n.m.* landlord; master; — *de sí mismo,* self-controlled; **ser** — *de,* be quite at liberty to.—*n.f.* landlady; mistress; matron; duenna, chaperone.
duermevela, *n.f.* (*fam.*) doze, snooze.
dulce, *a.* sweet; mild; soft; fresh (*water*).—*n.m.* sweet, toffee; — *de membrillo,* quince jelly.
dulcería, *n.f.* sweet-shop.
dulcero, -ra, *a.* (*fam.*) sweet-toothed.—*n.m.f.* confectioner.
dulcificar [C], *v.t.* sweeten; dulcify.
dulcinea, *n.f.* (*fam.*) lady-love; (*fig.*) dream.
dulzaino, -na, *a.* (*fam.*) over-sweet, sickly.—*n.f.* (*mus.*) flageolet; (*fam.*) sweet sticky mess.
dulz(arr)ón, -ona, *a.* (*fam.*) too sweet, sickly.
dulzor, *n.m.* sweetness; pleasantness.
dulzura, *n.f.* sweetness, mildness.
duna, *n.f.* dune.
Dunquerque, *n.m.* Dunkirk.
dúo, *n.m.* (*mus.*) duet.
duodecimal, *a.* duodecimal.
duodécimo, -ma, *a.* twelfth.
duplicación, *n.f.* duplication.
duplicado, *n.m.* duplicate; *por* —, in duplicate.
duplicar [A], *v.t.* duplicate; (*jur.*) reply to.
dúplice, *a.* double.
duplicidad, *n.f.* duplicity.

duplo, -la, *a., n.m.* double.
duque, *n.m.* duke.
duquesa, *n.f.* duchess.
dura (*fam.*), **durabilidad,** *n.f.* durability.
durable, *a.* durable.
duración, *n.f.* duration; durability.
duradero, -ra, *a.* durable, lasting.
durante, *prep.* during.
durar, *v.i.* last; last well, wear well.
durazno, *n.m.* peach.
dureza, *n.f.* hardness.
durmiente, *a.* sleeping.—*n.m.f.* sleeper.—*n.m.* cross-beam, tie; (*S.A., rail.*) tie.
duro, -ra, *a.* hard; tough; rough; cruel; harsh.—*n.m.* duro, five pesetas.—*adv.* hard.

E

E, e, *n.f.* sixth letter of the Spanish alphabet.
e, *conj.* and (*used instead of* y *before* i *or* hi, *but not before* hie *or at the beginning of a sentence*).
¡ea! *interj.* hey!
ebanista, *n.m.* cabinet-maker.
ébano, *n.m.* ebony.
ebriedad, *n.f.* drunkenness.
ebrio, -ria, *a., n.m.f.* drunk.
ebrioso, -sa, *a.* drunken.
ebulición, ebullición, *n.f.* ebullition, boiling.
ebúrneo, -nea, *a.* ivory.
eclecticismo, *n.m.* electicism.
ecléctico, -ca, *a.* eclectic.
eclesiástico, -ca, *a.* ecclesiastical.—*n.m.* ecclesiastic.
eclipsar, *v.t.* eclipse.—*v.r.* be eclipsed.
eclipse, *n.m.* eclipse.
eclíptico, -ca, *a., n.f.* ecliptic.
eco, *n.m.* echo.
ecología, *n.f.* ecology.
ecómetro, *n.m.* echo-meter.
economato, *n.m.* co-operative store.
economía, *n.f.* economy; frugality.—*pl.* savings.
económico, -ca, *a.* economic; economical, thrifty.
economista, *n.m.f.* economist.
economizar [C], *v.t., v.i.* economize.
ecónomo, *n.m.* trustee.
ecuación, *n.f.* equation.
Ecuador, *n.m.* Ecuador; **ecuador,** *n.m.* equator.
ecuánime, *a.* calm, equanimous.
ecuanimidad, *n.f.* equanimity; impartiality.
ecuatorial, *a.* equatorial.
ecuatoriano, -na, *a., n.m.f.* Ecuadorian.
ecuestre, *a.* equestrian.
ecuménico, -ca, *a.* ecumenical.
eczema, *n.m.f.* (*med.*) eczema.
echadizo, -za, *a.* waste; discarded; spying.—*n.m.f.* foundling; spy.
echado, -da, *a.* lying down; (*S.A.*) lazy.

echar, *v.t.* throw, fling; dismiss; pour; emit; turn (*a key*); put on (*a play*); begin to grow (*shoots etc.*); cut (*teeth*); deal (*cards*); cast (*a glance*); shed (*blood*); post, mail (*letters*); *echarla de,* (*fam.*) claim to be; — *a perder,* spoil; — *por,* turn towards; — *a pique,* sink; *echarse a hacer,* begin to do; *echarse sobre,* rush upon.

echazón, *n.m.* (*naut.*) jettison.

edad, *n.f.* age; epoch; — *media,* Middle Ages.

edecán, *n.m.* (*mil.*) aide-de-camp.

edición, *n.f.* edition; impression; publication.

edicto, *n.m.* edict.

edificación, *n.f.* construction; edification.

edificante, *a.* edifying.

edificar [A], *v.t.* construct; edify.

edificio, *n.m.* building; edifice.

Edimburgo, *n.m.* Edinburgh.

Edipo, *n.m.* (*myth.*) Oedipus.

editar, *v.t.* publish, edit (*a text*).

editor, -ra, *a.* publishing.—*n.m.f.* publisher.

editorial, *a.* publishing; editorial.—*n.m.* editorial (*article*).—*n.f.* publishing house.

editorialista, *n.m.f.* (*S.A.*) editorial writer.

edredón, *n.m.* eiderdown.

educable, *a.* educable, teachable.

educación, *n.f.* education; good manners, politeness.

educador, -ra, *a.* educating.—*n.m.f.* education(al)ist.

educando, -da, *n.m.f.* student (*in a college*).

educar [A], *v.t.* educate, train; bring up.

educativo, -va, *a.* educational.

educir [15], *v.t.* educe, bring out.

efe, *n.f.* name of letter F.

efectivamente, *adv.* effectively; really; actually; quite so.

efectivo, -va, *a.* real, actual; effective, effectual; permanent (*employment*).—*n.m.* cash.—*pl.* (*mil.*) effectives, troops.

efecto, *n.m.* effect; end; impression; *en* —, in effect; indeed.—*pl.* effects, assets; *efectos de consumo,* consumer goods.

efectuar [M], *v.t.* effect, carry out.

efeméride, *n.f.* anniversary.—*pl.* diary.

efervescencia, *n.f.* effervescence.

eficacia, *n.f.* efficacy, effectiveness.

eficaz, *a.* (*pl.* -aces) effective, effectual.

eficiencia, *n.f.* efficiency.

eficiente, *a.* efficient.

efigie, *n.f.* effigy.

efímero, -ra, *a.* ephemeral.—*n.f.* may-fly.

eflorescencia, *n.f.* (*chem., bot.*) efflorescence; (*med.*) eruption.

efluente, *a., n.m.* effluent.

efluvio, *n.m.* effluvium, emanation.

efusión, *n.f.* effusion; — *de sangre,* bloodshed.

efusivo, -va, *a.* effusive.

egida, égida, *n.f.* aegis.

egipcio, -cia, *a., n.m.f.* Egyptian.

egiptología, *n.f.* Egyptology.

égloga, *n.f.* eclogue.

egoísmo, *n.m.* selfishness, egoism.

egoísta, *a.* selfish, egoistic(al).—*n.m.f.* egoist.

egotismo, *n.m.* egotism.

egotista, *a.* egotistic(al), self-centred.

egregio, -gia, *a.* distinguished, eminent.

egresar, *v.t.* (*S.A.*) withdraw (*money*).—*v.i.* (*S.A.*) leave; (*S.A.*) graduate.

egreso, *n.m.* debit; expense; (*S.A.*) graduation; (*S.A.*) departure.

¡eh! *interj.* ah! here!

eje, *n.m.* axle; spindle; axis.

ejecución, *n.f.* execution; implementation.

ejecutante, *a.* executing.—*n.m.f.* performer.

ejecutar, *v.t.* execute; implement.

ejecutivo, -va, *a.* executive; insistent.

ejecutor, -ra, *a.* executive.—*n.m.f.* executive; executor, executrix.

ejecutoria, *n.f.* title of nobility.

ejecutoriar, *v.t.* confirm (*a judicial sentence*).

ejecutorio, -ria, *a.* (*jur.*) executory.

ejemplar, *a.* exemplary.—*n.m.* copy (*of a book*), sample, model; example.

ejemplaridad, *n.f.* exemplary nature.

ejemplificar [A], *v.t.* exemplify.

ejemplo, *n.m.* example, instance.

ejercer [D], *v.t.* practise, exercise.

ejercicio, *n.m.* exercise; drill; exertion; fiscal year.

ejercitar, *v.t.* exercise (*a profession etc.*); train.

ejército, *n.m.* army; — *del aire,* air force.

ejido, *n.m.* common land.

el, *definite article, m.* (*pl.* **los**) the.

él, *pers. pron. m.* (*pl.* **ellos**) he; him; it.—*pl.* they; them.

elaboración, *n.f.* elaboration; processing, manufacture.

elaborar, *v.t.* elaborate; process, manufacture.

elación, *n.f.* haughtiness; magnanimity; pomposity.

elasticidad, *n.f.* elasticity.

elástico, -ca, *a.* elastic.—*n.m.* elastic.—*n.f.* undershirt.—*n.f.pl.* (*S.A.*) braces, (*U.S.*) suspenders.

ele, *n.f.* name of letter L.

elección, *n.f.* election; choice.

electivo, -va, *a.* elective.

electo, -ta, *a.* chosen, elect.

elector, -ra, *a.* electing.—*n.m.f.* elector.

electorado, *n.m.* electorate.

electoral, *a.* electoral.

electricidad, *n.f.* electricity.

electricista, *n.m.* electrician.

eléctrico, -ca, *a.* electric(al).

electrificación, *n.f.* electrification.

electrificar [A], *v.t.* electrify.

electrizar [C], *v.t.* electrify.—*v.r.* become charged with electricity.

electro, *n.m.* amber; electrum.

electrocución, *n.f.* electrocution.

electrocutar, *v.t.* electrocute.

electrodeposición, *n.f.* electric plating.

electrodo, eléctrodo, *n.m.* electrode.

electroimán, *n.m.* electromagnet.

electrólisis, *n.f.* electrolysis.

electrolizar [C], *v.t.* electrolyze.

electromotora, *n.f.* electric motor.

electrón, *n.m.* electron.

electrónico, -ca, *a.* electronic.—*n.f.* electronics.

electrotecnia, *n.f.* electrical engineering.

electrotipia, *n.f.* (*print.*) electrotyping.

electuario, *n.m.* electuary.

elefante, -ta, *n.m.f.* elephant.

elefantino, -na, *a.* elephantine.

elegancia, *n.f.* elegance.

elegante, *a.* elegant, stylish.

elegía, *n.f.* elegy.

elegíaco, -ca, *a.* elegiac.
elegibilidad, *n.f.* eligibility.
eligible, *a.* eligible.
elegir [8E], *v.t.* elect; select.
elemental, *a.* elementary; elemental, fundamental.
elemento, *n.m.* element; member; (*elec.*) cell.
elenco, *n.m.* index, list; selection.
elevación, *n.f.* elevation.
elevador, *n.m.* hoist; lift, (*U.S.*) elevator.
elevar, *v.t.* elevate.—*v.r.* rise, ascend.
Elías, *n.m.* (*Bib.*) Elijah, Elias.
elidir, *v.t.* (*gram.*) elide.
eliminación, *n.f.* elimination.
eliminador, -ra, *a.* eliminating.—*n.m.f.* eliminator.—*n.m.* (*rad.*, *T.V.*) suppressor.
eliminar, *v.t.* eliminate.
elipse, *n.f.* ellipse.
elipsis, *n.f. inv.* (*gram.*) ellipsis.
elíptico, -ca, *a.* elliptic(al).
Eliseo (1), *n.m.* Elisha.
Elíseo (2), *n.m.* (*myth.*) Elysium.
elíseo, -sea, elisio, -sia, *a.* Elysian.
elisión, *n.f.* elision.
elíxir, elixir, *n.m.* elixir.
elocución, *n.f.* elocution.
elocuencia, *n.f.* eloquence.
elocuente, *a.* eloquent.
elogiar, *v.t.* praise, eulogize.
elogio, *n.m.* eulogy, praise.
elogioso, -sa, *a.* eulogistic.
elucidar, *v.t.* elucidate.
eludible, *a.* avoidable.
eludir, *v.t.* elude, avoid.
ella, *pers. pron. f.* (*pl.* **ellas**) she; her; it.—*pl.* they; them.
elle, *n.f.* name of letter LL.
ello, *pers. pron. neuter,* it.
ellos, ellas, *pers. pron. pl.* they; them.
emanación, *n.f.* emanation.
emanar, *v.i.* emanate, proceed from.
emancipación, *n.f.* emancipation.
emancipar, *v.t.* emancipate.
emascular, *v.t.* emasculate.
embadurnar, *v.t.* daub, smear, coat.
embajada, *n.f.* embassy.
embajador, *n.m.* ambassador.
embajadora, *n.f.* ambassadress; ambassador's wife.
embajatorio, -ria, *a.* ambassadorial.
embalador, -ra, *n.m.f.* packer.
embalaje, embalamiento, *n.m.* packing; package; rush, hurry.
embalar, *v.t.* pack, bale.—*v.r.* rush.
embaldosado, *n.m.* tile paving.
embalsadero, *n.m.* swamp.
embalsamar, *v.t.* embalm.
embalsar, *v.t.* dam; put on a raft.
embalse, *n.m.* dam; damming.
embarazada, *a.f.* pregnant.—*n.f.* pregnant woman.
embarazadamente, *adv.* with difficulty.
embarazar [C], *v.t.* hinder; make pregnant. —*v.r.* be obstructed; become pregnant.
embarazo, *n.m.* embarrassment, obstacle; pregnancy.
embarazoso, -sa, *a.* embarrassing; complicated.
embarcación, *n.f.* vessel, ship; embarcation; — *de alijo,* lighter.
embarcadero, *n.m.* pier; loading dock.
embarcar [A], *v.t.* embark.

embarco, *n.m.* embarcation.
embargar [B], *v.t.* embargo; impede; stupefy.
embargo, *n.m.* embargo; (*jur.*) seizure; *sin* —, however, nevertheless.
embarque, *n.m.* shipment, embarcation (*of goods*).
embarrar, *v.t.* splash with mud; smear.
embarullar, *v.t.* (*fam.*) muddle.
embastecer [9], *v.i.* get fat *or* flabby.—*v.r.* become coarse.
embate, *n.m.* sudden attack; dashing (*of the waves*).
embaucar [A], *v.t.* deceive, trick.
embeber, *v.t.* absorb, soak up; shrink (*of cloth*); soak.—*v.i.* shrink, contract.—*v.r.* be enchanted; become well versed (*de,* in).
embeleco, *n.m.* fraud, imposture.
embelesar, *v.t.* charm, enrapture.
embeleso, *n.m.* entrancement; fascination.
embellecer [9], *v.t.* embellish.
emberrenchinar, emberrinchinar, *v.r.* (*fam.*) fly into a rage.
embestida, *n.f.* attack, assault.
embestir [8], *v.t.* assail, attack; charge.
embetunar, *v.t.* cover with pitch.
emblanquecer [9], *v.t.* bleach; whiten.—*v.r.* turn white.
emblema, *n.m.* emblem.
emblemático, -ca, *a.* emblematic.
embobar, *v.t.* fascinate; amuse.—*v.r.* stand gaping.
embobecer [9], *v.t.* make foolish.
embocadero, *n.m.* outlet, mouth.
embocadura, *n.f.* nozzle; mouthpiece; outlet, mouth; taste (*of wine*); (*arch.*) proscenium arch; tip (*of a cigarette*).
embocar [A], *v.t.* put into the mouth; put through a narrow passage.
embolada, *n.f.* stroke (*of a piston*).
embolia, *n.f.* (*med.*) embolism, blood-clot.
embolismo, *n.m.* intercalation (*in the calendar*).
émbolo, *n.m.* piston; (*med.*) blood-clot.
embolsar, *v.t.* pocket.
embolso, *n.m.* pocketing.
emboquillar, *v.t.* tip (*cigarettes*).
emborrachar, *v.t.* intoxicate.—*v.r.* get drunk.
emborrar, *v.t.* pad.
emborrascar [A], *v.t.* provoke.—*v.r.* become stormy; fail (*of a business, a mine*).
emborronar, *v.t.* cover with blots; scribble.
emboscada, *n.f.* ambush.
emboscar [A], *v.t.* ambush.—*v.r.* lie in ambush; go deep into the woods.
embotar, *v.t.* blunt; dull.
embotellamiento, *n.m.* bottling; traffic jam.
embotellar, *v.t.* bottle.
embotijar, *v.t.* put into jars.—*v.r.* be in a rage.
embovedar, *v.t.* arch, vault.
embozalar, *v.t.* muzzle.
embozar [C], *v.t.* muffle; disguise.
embozo, *n.m.* muffler; turn-over of a sheet; *sin* —, frankly.
embragar [B], *v.t.* throw in the clutch; couple.
embrague, *n.m.* clutch; engaging the clutch.
embrazadura, *n.f.* clasp.
embrazar [C], *v.t.* clasp; buckle.—*v.i.* engage (*of gears*).

embriagar [B], *v.t.* intoxicate.
embriaguez, *n.f.* intoxication; rapture.
embrión, *n.m.* embryo.
embrionario, -ria, *a.* embryonic.
embroca, embrocación, *n.f.* embrocation.
embrocar [A], *v.t.* place upside down; tack (*soles*); (*taur.*) toss between the horns.
embrollar, *v.t.* embroil.
embrollo, *n.m.* imbroglio.
embromar, *v.t.* tease; cheat.
embrujar, *v.t.* bewitch.
embrutecer [9], *v.t.* brutalize.
embuchado, *n.m.* sort of sausage.
embuchar, *v.t.* stuff; cram down (*food*).
embudo, *n.m.* funnel; trick.
embullo, *n.m.* (*C.A.*) excitement.
embuste, *n.m.* trick, fraud.
embustero, -ra, *a.* lying, deceitful.—*n.m.f.* cheat, fraud.
embutido, *n.m.* sausage; marquetry.
embutir, *v.t.* stuff; inlay; set flush.
eme, *n.f.* name of letter M.
emergencia, *n.f.* emergence; emergency.
emergente, *a.* emergent.
emerger [E], *v.i.* emerge.
emético, -ca, *a.* emetic.
emigración, *n.f.* emigration.
emigrado, -da, *n.m.f.* emigrant, émigré.
emigrar, *v.i.* emigrate.
emigratorio, -ria, *a.* rel. to emigration.
eminencia, *n.f.* eminence.
emisario, -ria, *n.m.f.* emissary.
emisión, *n.f.* emission; issue (*of money*); (*rad.*) broadcast, programme; (*phys.*) radiation.
emisor, -ra, *a.* emitting.—*n.m.* (*rad.*) transmitter.—*n.f.* (*rad.*) station.
emitir, *v.t.* emit; (*rad.*) broadcast; issue.
emoción, *n.f.* emotion.
emocional, *a.* emotional.
emocionante, *a.* touching; stirring, exciting.
emocionar, *v.t.* touch; stir.—*v.r.* be moved or stirred; get excited.
emoliente, *a., n.m.* emollient.
emolumento, *n.m.* emolument.
emotivo, -va, *a.* emotive.
empacar [A], *v.t.* pack, bale; (*S.A.*) anger.—*v.r.* get angry.
empachar, *v.t.* hinder; surfeit.—*v.r.* feel ashamed or bashful.
empacho, *n.m.* bashfulness; obstacle; surfeit.
empachoso, -sa, *a.* shameful; embarrassing.
empadronamiento, *n.m.* census.
empadronar, *v.t., v.r.* register.
empalagar [B], *v.t.* surfeit; weary.
empalago, empalagamiento, *n.m.* surfeit.
empalagoso, -sa, *a.* cloying, sickening.
empalar, *v.t.* impale.
empaliada, *n.f.* bunting.
empalizada, *n.f.* pallisade, stockade.
empalizar [C], *v.t.* fence in, stockade.
empalmadura, *n.f.* [EMPALME].
empalmar, *v.t.* join, connect.—*v.i.* connect.
empalme, *n.m.* joint; splice; (*rail.*) connexion; (*rail.*) junction.
empanada, -da, *a.* windowless.—*n.f.* pasty, meat or vegetable pie; fraud.
empantanar, *v.t.* flood, swamp.
empañadura, *n.f.* swaddling clothes.
empañar, *v.t.* swaddle; blur; tarnish.
empapar, *v.t., v.r.* soak.

empapelado, *n.m.* wall-paper; paper-hanging; paper-lining.
empapelador, -ra, *n.m.f.* paper-hanger.
empaque, *n.m.* packing; appearance; stiffness; (*S.A.*) brazenness.
empaquetar, *v.t.* pack; stuff.
emparedado, *n.m.* sandwich.
emparedar, *v.t.* wall in; immure.
emparejar, *v.t.* pair; match; level off.—*v.i.* be even (*con*, with).
emparentar [1], *v.i.* become related (*by marriage*).
emparrado, *n.m.* bower.
empastar, *v.t.* cover or fill with paste; fill (*a tooth*).
empaste, *n.m.* filling (*of a tooth*).
empastelar, *v.t.* botch; compromise.
empatar, *v.t.i., v.i., v.r.* tie, draw (*in sport etc.*).
empate, *n.m.* draw, tie; hindrance.
empavesar, *v.t.* bedeck with flags, (*naut.*) dress.
empecinado, -da, *a.* (*S.A.*) stubborn.
empedernir [Q], *v.t.* harden.—*v.r.* get hard, harden.
empedrado, -da, *a.* flecked, dappled.—*n.m.* stone pavement.
empedrar [1], *v.t.* pave; bespatter.
empega, *n.f.* pitch, tar.
empegado, *n.m.* tarpaulin.
empegar [B], *v.r.* coat or mark with pitch.
empeine, *n.m.* groin; instep.
empelotar, *v.r.* (*fam.*) get tangled up; (*C.A.*) strip.
empellón, *n.m.* push, shove.
empenta, *n.f.* prop, stay.
empeñado, -da, *a.* persistent; heated (*argument*).
empeñar, *v.t.* pawn; pledge.—*v.r.* persist (*en*, in).
empeño, *n.m.* pledge; persistence, perseverance.
empeoramiento, *n.m.* deterioration.
empeorar, *v.t.* make worse.—*v.r.* get worse.
emperador, *n.m.* emperor.
emperatriz, *n.f.* (*pl. -ices*) empress.
emperezar [C], *v.t.* make lazy.—*v.r.* be or become lazy.
empero, *conj.* (*obs.*) however, yet.
empezar [1C], *v.t., v.i.* begin (*a*, to, *por*, by).
empicotar, *v.t.* pillory.
empilar, *v.t.* pile up.
empinado, -da, *a.* high; steep; conceited.
empinar, *v.t.* raise; — *el codo,* (*fam.*) drink heavily.
empíreo, -rea, *a., n.m.* empyrean.
empírico, -ca, *a.* empirical.
empirismo, *n.m.* empiricism.
empizarrar, *v.t.* slate.
emplastadura, *n.f.,* **emplastamiento,** *n.m.* plastering.
emplastar, *v.t.* plaster; smear; (*fam.*) obstruct.
emplastecer [9], *v.t.* stop (*cracks before painting*).
emplasto, *n.m.* plaster, poultice; tyre patch.
emplazar [C], *v.t.* summon; site, locate.
empleado, -da, *n.m.f.* employee; clerk.
emplear, *v.t.* employ.—*v.r.* be employed; (*fam.*) **le esté bien empleado,** it serves him right.
empleo, *n.m.* employment, occupation, job; public office.

83

emplomar, *v.t.* lead; seal with lead.
emplumar, *v.t.* put feathers *or* plumes on; tar and feather; **emplumarlas,** (*S.A. fam.*) beat it, go away.
emplumecer [9], *v.i.* fledge.
empobrecer [9], *v.t.* impoverish.
empodrecer [9], *v.i., v.r.* rot.
empolvar, *v.t.* cover with dust.
empollador, *n.m.* incubator.
empolladura, *n.f.* (*fam.*) swotting, grinding (*for examinations*).
empollar, *v.t.* hatch, brood; (*fam.*) swot.
empollón, -llona, *n.m.f.* (*pej.*) swot, (*U.S.*) grind.
emponzoñar, *v.t.* poison.
emporio, *n.m.* emporium.
empotrar, *v.t.* (*arch.*) embed, fix in a wall, build-in.
emprender, *v.t.* undertake.
empreñar, *v.t.* impregnate.
empresa, *n.f.* enterprise, undertaking; design; firm.
empresario, -ria, *n.m.f.* contractor; impresario.
empréstito, *n.m.* loan.
emprimar, *v.t.* prime (*with paint*); (*fam.*) hoodwink.
empujadora, *n.f.* bulldozer.
empujar, *v.t.* push.
empuje, *n.m.* push; (*phys.*) thrust; energy.
empujón, *n.m.* push, shove.
empulgueras, *n.f.pl.* thumbscrews.
empuñadura, *n.f.* hilt; beginning of a story.
empuñar, *v.t.* clutch, grasp.
emulación, *n.f.* emulation.
emular, *v.t.* emulate.
emulsión, *n.f.* emulsion.
en, *prep.* in; at; on; for.
enagua, *n.f.* (*esp. pl.*) underskirt(s), petticoat.
enajenación, *n.f.*, **enajenamiento,** *n.m.* alienation; distraction; madness; rapture.
enajenar, *v.t.* alienate, transfer; enrapture.
enamoradizo, -za, *a.* susceptible (*to passion*).
enamorado, -da, *a.* in love.—*n.m.f.* lover, sweetheart.
enamorar, *v.t.* enamour; make love to.—*v.r.* fall in love (*de*, with).
enano, -na, *a., n.m.f.* dwarf.
enarbolar, *v.t.* hoist (*flags etc.*).
enardecer [9], *v.t.* inflame.—*v.r.* be inflamed.
encabalgamiento, *n.m.* gun-carriage; (*poet.*) enjambement.
encabezamiento, *n.m.* census; headline, title, heading.
encabezar [C], *v.t.* draw up (*a list*); put a heading to; fortify (*wine*); be at the head (of).
encadenar, *v.t.* chain; enchain; brace.
encajar, *v.t.* insert, fit; tell (*a story etc.*) inopportunely.
encaje, *n.m.* insertion; recess; lace.
encajonar, *v.t.* box, crate.—*v.r.* become narrow (*of a river*).
encalar, *v.t.* whitewash; (*agr.*) lime.
encalmado, -da, *a.* (*naut.*) becalmed; (*com.*) quiet (*market*).
encallar, *v.i.* run aground.
encallecer [9], *v.i.* get corns *or* calluses.
encaminadura, *n.f.*, **encaminamiento,** *n.m.* directing, forwarding.
encaminar, *v.t.* direct, put on the right track; forward.—*v.r.* set out, be on the way (*a*, to).

encanalar, encanalizar [C], *v.t.* channel.
encanallar, *v.t.* corrupt.—*v.r.* become corrupt *or* depraved.
encanecer [9], *v.i.* turn grey.
encantado, -da, *a.* delighted, enchanted; absent-minded.
encantador, -ra, *a.* enchanting.—*n.m.* charmer, enchanter.—*n.f.* enchantress.
encantamiento, *n.m.* enchantment.
encantar, *v.t.* bewitch; charm, delight.
encante, *n.m.* auction.
encanto, *n.m.* charm.
encañada, *n.f.* gorge.
encañado, *n.m.* conduit.
encapotar, *v.t.* cloud; veil.—*v.r.* get cloudy; (*fig.*) glower.
encaprichar, *v.r.* persist in one's fancy.
encaramar, *v.t.* raise; extol.—*v.r.* get on top.
encarar, *v.t.* face; aim.—*v.r.* face, confront (*con*).
encarcelar, *v.t.* imprison; (*carp.*) clamp.
encarecer [9], *v.t.* raise the price of; extol; recommend.
encarecimiento, *n.m.* overrating; enhancement; augmentation; **con —,** earnestly.
encargado, -da, *n.m.f.* person in charge; manager; **— de negocios,** chargé d'affaires.
encargar [B], *v.t.* entrust; urge, warn; order (*goods*); request.—*v.r.* take charge (*de*, of).
encargo, *n.m.* charge; assignment; (*com.*) order.
encariñar, *v.t.* inspire affection.—*v.r.* become fond (*de*, of).
encarnación, *n.f.* incarnation.
encarnadino, -na, *a.* incarnadine, reddish-pink.
encarnado, -da, *a.* incarnate; flesh-coloured.
encarnar, *v.t.* incarnate.—*v.i.* become incarnate.
encarnecer [9], *v.i.* grow fat.
encarnizado, -da, *a.* bloody; fierce.
encarnizar [C], *v.t.* flesh (*a hound*); infuriate.—*v.r.* be infuriated.
encaro, *n.m.* stare; aim.
encartar, *v.t.* outlaw; enrol; lead (*at cards*).—*v.r.* be unable to discard (*at cards*).
encartonar, *v.t.* cover *or* protect with cardboard; bind (*books*).
encasar, *v.t.* set (*bones*).
encasillar, *v.t.* pigeonhole, classify.
encasquetar, *v.t.* clap on (*a hat*); put (*an idea*) in someone's mind.—*v.r.* clap on (*one's hat*); get (*an idea*) fixed in one's mind.
encastillado, -da, *a.* castellated; proud.
encastillador, *n.m.* scaffolder.
encastillar, *v.t.* fortify; scaffold.—*v.r.* withdraw; be stubborn.
encastrar, *v.t.* engage (*gears*).
encauchar, *v.t.* coat with rubber.
encáustico, -ca, *a.* encaustic.
encauzamiento, *n.m.* channelling.
encauzar [C], *v.t.* channel; guide.
encebollado, *n.m.* stewed beef and onions.
encenagar [B], *v.r.* get into the mire, wallow.
encendedor, -ra, *a.* lightning.—*n.m.* lighter, igniter.
encender [2], *v.t.* light, kindle; (*fig.*) inflame.—*v.r.* catch fire.
encendido, -da, *a.* inflamed, flushed.—*n.m.* (*auto.*) ignition.
encendimiento, *n.m.* lighting; incandescence; ardour.

encepar, *v.t.* put in the stocks; stock.—*v.i.*, *v.r.* take root.

encerado, -da, *a.* waxy; hard-boiled (*eggs*).—*n.m.* oilcloth; tarpaulin; blackboard; waxing (*furniture etc.*).

encerar, *v.t.* wax.

encerradura, *n.f.*, **encerramiento**, *n.m.* locking up; imprisonment.

encerrar [I], *v.t.* shut in, lock up; contain, include.

encerrona, *n.f.* (*fam.*) voluntary confinement; trap.

encía, *n.f.* (*anat.*) gum.

enciclopedia, *n.f.* encyclopedia.

enciclopédico, -ca, *a.* encyclopedic.

encierro, *n.m.* locking up; enclosure; (*taur.*) driving bulls into the pen (*before the fight*); retreat.

encima, *adv.* above, over; besides.—*prep.* on, upon, above (*de*).

encina, *n.f.* (*bot.*) holm oak, ilex.

encinal, encinar, *n.m.* wood *or* grove of holm oaks.

encinta, *a.f.* pregnant.

encintado, *n.m.* kerb, (*U.S.*) curb.

encintar, *v.t.* beribbon; curb (*a street*).

enclaustrar, *v.t.* cloister; hide.

enclavar, *v.t.* nail; pierce.

enclave, *n.m.* (*geog.*) enclave.

enclavijar, *v.t.* peg (together), dowel.

enclenque, *a.* weak, sickly, puny.

enclítico, -ca, *a.* (*gram.*) enclitic.

enclocar [4A], *v.i., v.r.* go broody, brood.

encobar, *v.i., v.r.* brood.

encofrar, *v.t.* (*min.*) timber; (*arch.*) shutter, build a form for (*concrete*).

encoger [E], *v.t.* shrink; intimidate.—*v.i.* shrink.—*v.r.* shrink; cringe; be bashful.

encogimiento, *n.m.* shrinking; timidity; crouching.

encojar, *v.t.* cripple.—*v.r.* go lame; (*fam.*) malinger.

encolar, *v.t.* glue, size; clarify (*wine*).

encolerizar [C], *v.t.* anger.—*v.r.* become angry.

encomendar [I], *v.t.* entrust; give an ENCOMIENDA.—*v.i.* hold an ENCOMIENDA.—*v.r.* commend oneself; send one's compliments.

encomiador, -ra, *a.* eulogistic, panegyric.—*n.m.f.* panegyrist.

encomiar, *v.t.* eulogize.

encomienda, *n.f.* (*hist.*) encomienda, grant of crown land; commandership (*in a military order*); badge of a knight commander; charge, commission; commendation; (*S.A.*) parcel-post; *en* —, (*eccl.*) in commendam.

encomio, *n.m.* eulogy.

enconamiento, *n.m.* (*med.*) inflammation; (*fig.*) rancour.

enconar, *v.t.* irritate, inflame.—*v.r.* be irritated; fester.

encono, *n.m.* rancour; sore spot.

enconoso, -sa, *a.* sore; malevolent.

encontradizo, -za, *a.* likely to be met with.

encontrado, -da, *a.* opposite; opposing; at odds (*con*, with).

encontrar [4], *v.t.* meet, encounter.—*v.r.* be situated; *encontrarse con*, meet; run across.

encontrón, *n.m.* collision.

encopetar, *v.t.* arrange (*the hair*) high.—*v.r.* become conceited.

encorar [4], *v.t.* cover with leather.—*v.i., v.r.* heal over, grow new skin.

encorchetar, *v.t.* fasten with hooks and eyes; sew hooks and eyes on.

encordelar, encordonar, *v.t.* tie (*with string*).

encoriación, *n.f.* healing (*of a wound*).

encornadura, *n.f.* (*esp. taur.*) horns, shape of the horns.

encornudar, *v.t.* cuckold.—*v.i.* grow horns.

encorrear, *v.t.* strap.

encorvada, *n.f.* bending; *hacer la* —, (*fam.*) malinger.

encorvar, *v.t.* bend.—*v.r.* stoop; be biased.

encostrar, *v.t.* encrust, crust.

encovar [4], *v.t.* put in the cellar.

encrasar, *v.t.* thicken; (*agr.*) fertilize.

encrespador, *n.m.* curling iron.

encrespamiento, *n.m.* curling; roughness (*of the sea*).

encrespar, *v.t.* curl; ruffle (*feathers etc.*).—*v.r.* curl; become rough (*of waves etc.*); get angry.

encrucijada, *n.f.* crossroads, (*U.S.*) intersection; ambush.

encuadernación, *n.f.* (book-)binding.

encuadernar, *v.t.* bind (*books*); *sin* —, unbound.

encuadrar, *v.t.* frame; insert.

encuadre, *n.m.* film version (*of a book etc.*).

encubierto, -ta, *p.p.* [ENCUBRIR].—*n.f.* fraud.

encubridor, -ra, *n.m.f.* concealer; (*jur.*) accessory.

encubrir [*p.p.* **encubierto**], *v.t.* hide.

encuentro, *n.m.* meeting, encounter.

encuesta, *n.f.* enquiry; poll.

encumbrar, *v.t.* raise.—*v.r.* rise; be proud.

encurtir, *v.t.* pickle.

enchapado, *n.m.* veneer; plywood; overlay, plating.

enchapar, *v.t.* veneer; overlay, plate.

encharcada, *n.f.* puddle.

encharcar [A], *v.t.* turn into a puddle.—*v.r.* be inundated; stagnate.

enchufar, *v.t.* connect (*two pipes etc.*); (*elec.*) plug in; *estar bien enchufado*, be able to pull strings.

enchufe, *n.m.* socket, coupling; (*elec.*) plug; contact; (*fam.*) contact; (*fam.*) fat job.

por ende, *adv. phr.* (*obs.*) therefore.

endeble, *a.* feeble.

endeblez, *n.f.* feebleness.

endecágono, *n.m.* hendecagon.

endecasílabo, -ba, *a.* hendecasyllabic.—*n.m.* hendecasyllable.

endecha, *n.f.* dirge.

endechadera, *n.f.* hired mourner.

endechar, *v.t.* bewail.—*v.r.* grieve.

endémico, -ca, *a.* endemic.

endentar [I], *v.t., v.r.* mesh, engage (*gears*).

endentecer [9], *v.i.* teethe.

enderezadamente, *adv.* rightly, honestly.

enderezar [C], *v.t.* straighten; regulate; direct.—*v.i.* go straight.—*v.r.* straighten up.

endeudar, *v.r.* run into debt.

endiablar, *v.t.* corrupt.

endibia, *n.f.* (*bot.*) endive; chicory.

endilgar [B], *v.t.* (*fam.*) direct; (*fam.*) help; (*fam.*) spring (*a surprise*) on.

endomingar, *v.r.* put on one's Sunday best.

endorsar, endosar, *v.t.* (*com.*) endorse.

endosante, *n.m.f.* (*com.*) endorser.
endosatorio, -ria, *n.m.f.* (*com.*) endorsee.
endriago, *n.m.* dragon, fabulous monster.
endrino, -na, *a.* sloe-coloured.—*n.m.* (*bot.*) sloe (*tree*).—*n.f.* sloe (*fruit*).
endulzar [C] *v.t.* sweeten.
endurador, -ra, *a.* parsimonious.—*n.m.f.* miser.
endurancia, *n.f.* (*sport*) endurance.
endurar, *v.t.* harden; endure.
endurecer [9], *v.t.* harden.
ene, *n.f.* name of letter N.
enea, *n.f.* (*bot.*) rush.
eneágono, *n.m.* nonagon.
eneasílabo, -ba, *a.* of nine syllables.—*n.m.* nine-syllable line.
enebro, *n.m.* (*bot.*) juniper.
eneldo, *n.m.* (*bot.*) common dill.
enemigo, -ga, *a.* hostile, enemy.—*n.m.f.* enemy.
enemistad, *n.f.* enmity.
enemistar, *v.t.* make an enemy of.—*v.r.* become enemies; become an enemy (**con,** of).
energía, *n.f.* energy.
enérgico, -ca, *a.* energetic.
enero, *n.m.* January.
enervación, *n.f.* enervation.
enervar, *v.t.* enervate.—*v.r.* become enervated *or* effeminate.
enésimo, -ma, *a.* (*math.*) nth.
enfadar, *v.t.* offend.—*v.r.* become annoyed.
enfado, *n.m.* anger; trouble.
enfadoso, -sa, *a.* bothersome.
enfangar [B] *v.t.* soil with mud.—*v.r.* sink in the mud.
enfardelador, -ra, *n.m.f.* packer.—*n.f.* baler, baling press.
enfardelar, *v.t.* bale.
énfasis, *n.m.* or *f. inv.* emphasis.
enfático, -ca, *a.* emphatic.
enfermar, *v.t.* make sick.—*v.i.* fall ill (**de,** with).
enfermedad, *n.f.* sickness, illness, disease.
enfermería, *n.f.* infirmary; sanatorium; (*naut., mil.*) sick bay.
enfermero, -ra, *n.m.f.* nurse.
enfermizo, -za, *a.* sickly.
enfermo, -ma, *a.* sick, ill.—*n.m.f.* patient.
enfeudar, *v.t.* (*jur.*) enfeoff.
enfilar, *v.t.* line up; (*mil.*) enfilade; string (*beads*).
enflaquecer [9], *v.t.* make thin.—*v.i.* get thin; lose heart.—*v.r.* get thin.
enfocar [A], *v.t.* focus; (*fig.*) visualise (*from a certain viewpoint*).
enfoque, *n.m.* focus, focusing; (*fig.*) viewpoint, approach.
enfoscar [A], *v.t.* fill in (*with mortar*).—*v.r.* become grumpy.
enfrascar [A], *v.t.* bottle.—*v.r.* become involved.
enfrenar, *v.t.* bridle, check, curb.
enfrentar, *v.t.* confront.—*v.r.* meet face to face; stand up (**con,** to).
enfrente, *adv.* opposite.—*prep.* opposite (**de**); against (**de**).
enfriar [L], *v.t.* refrigerate, cool, chill.
enfurecer [9], *v.t.* infuriate.—*v.r.* rage.
engalanar, *v.t.* deck, adorn.
enganchar, *v.t.* hook; couple, connect; (*fam.*)

inveigle (*esp. into the army*).—*v.r.* (*fam.*) enlist (*in the army etc.*).
enganche, *n.m.* hooking; coupling; (*fam.*) enlistment.
engañadizo, -za, *a.* easily deceived.
engañador, -ra, *a.* deceptive.—*n.m.f.* cheat.
engañapastores, *n.m. inv.* (*orn.*) nightjar.
engañar, *v.t.* mislead, deceive.—*v.r.* make a mistake.
engaño, *n.m.* fraud, deceit.
engañoso, -sa, *a.* deceitful, fraudulent.
engarce, *n.m.* mounting; (*gem*) setting; linking.
engarzar [C], *v.t.* link; set (*gems*).
engastar, *v.t.* set (*gems*).
engaste, *n.m.* setting (*of gems*).
engatusar, *v.t.* (*fam.*) inveigle.
engendrar, *v.t.* engender, beget.
engendro, *n.m.* foetus; misbegotten creature.
englobar, *v.t.* enclose, lump together.
engolosinar, *v.t.* allure.—*v.r.* take a liking (**con,** to).
engordar, *v.t.* fatten.
engorroso, -sa, *a.* troublesome.
engoznar, *v.t.* put hinges on, hang (*a door*).
engranaje, *n.m.* (*tech.*) gearing.
engranar, *v.t., v.i.* gear, mesh.
engrandecer [9], *v.t.* enlarge, magnify.—*v.i.* grow big(ger).
engrandecimiento, *n.m.* enlargement, amplification.
engrasar, *v.t.* lubricate, grease.
engrase, *n.m.* lubrication; fouling (*spark plugs*).
engreimiento, *n.m.* vanity.
engreír [28], *v.t.* make vain.—*v.r.* become vain.
engrosar [4], *v.t.* broaden; enlarge.—*v.i.* get fat.—*v.r.* broaden; become enlarged.
engrudar, *v.t.* paste, glue.
engrudo, *n.m.* paste, glue.
engruesar, *v.i.* get fat.
enguirnaldar, *v.t.* garland, bedeck.
engullir [J], *v.t.* gulp down, swallow.
enhebrar, *v.t.* string, thread (*a needle*).
enherbolar, *v.t.* poison (*with herbs*).
enhestar [1], *v.t.* erect; hoist.—*v.r.* stand upright; tower.
enhiesto, -ta, *a.* erect, upright.
enhilar, *v.t.* thread.
enhorabuena, *adv.* well and good, all right.—*n.f.* congratulations.
enhoramala, *adv.* unluckily, in an evil hour.
enigma, *n.m.* puzzle.
enigmático, -ca, *a.* enigmatic(al).
enjabonar, *v.t.* soap; (*fam.*) soft-soap; (*fam.*) give a good dressing down (to).
enjaezar [C], *v.t.* harness, adorn.
enjaguar [H], [ENJUAGAR].
enjalbegado, *n.m.* whitewashing.
enjalbegar [B], *v.t.* whitewash.
enjalma, *n.f.* light packsaddle.
enjambrar, *v.t.* empty (*a hive*).—*v.i.* swarm.
enjambre, *n.m.* swarm.
enjarciar, *v.t.* rig (*a ship*).
enjebe, *n.m.* alum; lye.
enjergar [B], *v.t.* (*fam.*) start up (*a business etc.*).
enjertación, *n.f.* grafting.
enjertar, *v.t.* engraft.
enjerto, *n.m.* graft, grafted plant.
enjoyar, *v.t.* bejewel.

enjuagadientes, *n.m. inv.* mouthwash.
enjuagar [B], *v.t.* rinse.
enjuagatorio, *n.m.* rinsing; finger bowl.
enjuague, *n.m.* rinsing; finger bowl; plot, scheme.
enjugador, *n.m.* drier; clothes-horse; squeegee.
enjugar [B], *v.t.* dry.
enjuiciar, *v.t.* (*jur.*) sue, indict; (*jur.*) sentence.
enjundia, *n.f.* kidney-fat; grease; (*fig.*) force, substance.
enjundioso, -sa, *a.* fatty; substantial.
enjunque, *n.m.* (*naut.*) heavy ballast, kentledge.
enjuto, -ta, *a.* lean; dried.—*n.m.pl.* tinder, brushwood; salty tit-bits.
enlabiar, *v.t.* wheedle; bamboozle.
enlace, *n.m.* connexion; link; (*chem.*) linkage; (*rail.*) connexion; marriage.
enladrillado, *n.m.* brick pavement; brickwork.
enladrillar, *v.t.* brick; pave with bricks *or* red tiles.
enlatar, *v.t.* tin, (*esp. U.S.*) can; (*S.A.*) roof with tin.
enlazar [C], *v.t.* tie; link; lasso; (*rail.*) connect.—*v.r.* be joined (*in wedlock*).
enlistonar, *v.t.* lath.
enlodar, *v.t.* soil with mud, bemire.
enloquecer [9], *v.t.* madden, drive to distraction.—*v.i.* go mad.
enlosar, *v.t.* pave with flagstones.
enlucir [10], *v.t.* plaster; polish (*metal*).
enlutar, *v.t.* put into mourning.—*v.r.* wear mourning.
enmaderar, *v.t.* board, plank.
enmagrecer [9], *v.t.* make thin.—*v.i., v.r.* grow thin.
enmarañamiento, *n.m.* entanglement.
enmarañar, *v.t.* entangle.
enmascarar, *v.t.* mask.—*v.r.* masquerade.
enmasillar, *v.t.* putty.
enmendación, *n.f.* emendation.
enmendar [1], *v.t.* correct; amend.
enmienda, *n.f.* correction, amendment; amends.
enmohecer [9], *v.t.* mildew, mould (*U.S.* mold), rust.—*v.r.* go mouldy, rust.
enmudecer [9], *v.t.* hush.—*v.i.* fall silent.
ennegrecer [9], *v.t.* blacken; denigrate.—*v.r.* turn *or* be black.
ennoblecer [9], *v.t.* ennoble.—*v.r.* become ennobled.
ennoblecimiento, *n.m.* ennoblement.
enodio, *n.m.* fawn.
enojar, *v.t.* anger; offend; annoy.—*v.r.* be angry; be offended.
enojo, *n.m.* anger, passion; annoyance.
enojoso, -sa, *a.* annoying; troublesome.
enorgullecer [9], *v.r.* make proud.—*v.r.* be proud (*de,* of); pride oneself (*de,* on).
enorme, *a.* enormous; huge.
enormidad, *n.f.* enormity.
enquiciar, *v.t.* put on hinges, hang (*a door*).
enquillotrar, *v.t.* (*fam.*) fall in love.
enrabiar, *v.t.* enrage.—*v.i.* have rabies.—*v.r.* become enraged.
enraizar [C & P], *v.i.* take root.
enredadera, *n.f.* (*bot.*) bindweed, climbing plant.

enredar, *v.t.* entangle; ensnare.—*v.i.* romp.—*v.r.* become entangled.
enredo, *n.m.* tangle; mischief; intricacy; plot (*of a play etc.*).
enredoso, -sa, *a.* intricate.
enrejado, *n.m.* trellis, lattice; — **de alambre,** wire netting.
enrejar, *v.t.* surround with a trellis *or* a grating.
enriar [L], *v.t.* ret.
enrielar, *v.t.* cast into ingots; (*S.A.*) lay rails on (*a road*); (*S.A. fig.*) put on the right track.
Enrique, *n.m.* Henry.
enriquecer [9], *v.t.* enrich.
enriscado, -da, *a.* craggy, mountainous.
enriscar [A], *v.t.* raise.—*v.r.* take refuge in the rocks.
enristrar, *v.t.* couch (*the lance*); string (*onions*); straighten out (*a difficulty*).
enrocar [A], *v.t., v.i.* castle (*in chess*).
enrojar, enrojecer [9], *v.t., v.r.* redden; flush.
enrollar, *v.t.* roll, wind.
enromar, *v.t.* blunt.
enronquecer [9], *v.t.* make hoarse.—*v.r.* become hoarse.
enroque, *n.m.* castling (*in chess*).
enroscar [A], *v.t.* twist.—*v.r.* curl, coil.
enrubiar, *v.t.* bleach (*the hair*).
enrubio, *n.m.* bleaching, dyeing blond; blond dye.
ensaimada, *n.f.* kind of bun.
ensalada, *n.f.* salad; hodge-podge.
ensaladera, *n.f.* salad bowl.
ensalmador, -ra, *n.m.f.* bone-setter; quack.
ensalmar, *v.t.* set (*bones*).
ensalmista, *n.m.f.* quack, charlatan.
ensalmo, *n.m.* spell, charm.
ensalzar [C], *v.t.* extol.—*v.r.* boast.
ensamblador, *n.m.* (*carp.*) joiner.
ensambladura, *n.f.,* **ensamble,** *n.m.* joinery; joint.
ensamblar, *v.t.* join; assemble; (*carp.*) joint.
ensanchador, -ra, *a.* expanding, stretching.—*n.m.* stretcher, expander.
ensanchar, *v.t.* widen; stretch; let out (*clothes*).—*v.r.* widen; be high and mighty.
ensanche, *n.m.* widening; extension.
ensandecer [9], *v.i.* grow crazy or stupid.
ensangrentar [1], *v.t.* stain with blood.—*v.r.* cover oneself with gore; (*fig.*) have murderous thoughts (*con uno,* about s.o.).
ensañamiento, *n.m.* cruelty; (*jur.*) aggravating circumstance.
ensañar, *v.t.* irritate; enrage.—*v.r.* be ruthless.
ensartar, *v.t.* string (*beads*); thread (*a needle*).
ensayador, -ra, *n.m.f.* assayer; rehearser.
ensayista, *n.m.f.* essayist.
ensayo, *n.m.* trial; assay; essay; rehearsal; (*com.*) sample.
ensebar, *v.t.* grease, tallow.
ensenada, *n.f.* inlet, cove.
enseña, *n.f.* ensign, standard.
enseñable, *a.* teachable.
enseñamiento, *n.m.,* **enseñanza,** *n.f.* teaching, education.
enseñar, *v.t.* teach, instruct; point out, show the way.—*v.r.* school oneself; become inured.

enseñorear, *v.t.* domineer.—*v.r.* take possession (*de,* of).

enseres, *n.m.pl.* chattels, implements; fixtures.

ensilar, *v.t.* (*agr.*) put into a silo, ensile.

ensillar, *v.t.* saddle.

ensimismar, *v.r.* become absent-minded *or* lost in thought.

ensoberbecer [9], *v.t.* make proud.—*v.r.* become proud.

ensombrecer [9], *v.t.* darken.

ensordecer [9], *v.t.* deafen.—*v.i.* grow deaf; become silent.

ensordecimiento, *n.m.* deafness.

ensortijar, *v.t.* curl, form ringlets in.

ensuciar, *v.t.* pollute, defile, soil.

ensueño, *n.m.* illusion, daydream, dream.

entablación, *n.f.* (*carp.*) flooring; boarding.

entabladura, *n.f.* flooring; boarding.

entablamento, *n.m.* (*arch.*) entablature.

entablar, *v.t.* floor; board; start, initiate.

entable, *n.m.* position (*of chessmen*); (*S.A.*) circumstances.

entalegar [B], *v.t.* bag; hoard.

entallador, *n.m.* engraver; carver.

entalladura, *n.f.,* **entallamiento,** *n.m.* carving; engraving; slot.

entallar, *v.t.* carve; engrave; slot.

entapizar [C], *v.t.* drape, hang with tapestry; upholster.

entarimar, *v.t.* floor; put a parquet *or* inlaid floor on.

ente, *n.m.* being; entity; (*fam.*) queer fish.

entena, *n.f.* (*naut.*) lateen yard.

entenado, -da, *n.m.f.* stepchild.

entendedor, -ra, *n.m.f.* understander, one who understands.

entender [2], *v.t., v.i.* understand, comprehend; — *de,* be familiar with; be experienced as; — *en,* be in charge of.—*v.r.* be meant; *entenderse con,* get along with.

entendidamente, *adv.* knowingly.

entendido, -da, *a.* expert, trained; prudent; *darse por —,* take a hint.

entendimiento, *n.m.* understanding.

enterar, *v.t.* acquaint, inform.

entereza, *n.f.* integrity; entirety; — *virginal,* virginity.

entérico, -ca, *a.* enteric.

enterizo, -za, *a.* in one piece.

enternecer [9], *v.t.* soften, move.—*v.r.* be moved (*to pity etc.*).

enternecimiento, *n.m.* pity, compassion.

entero, -ra, *a.* entire, whole; honest; (*math.*) integral, whole; strong (*cloth*).—*n.m.* (*math.*) integer.

enterrador, *n.m.* grave-digger.

enterramiento, *n.m.* burial, interment.

enterrar [1], *v.t.* inter, bury.

entesar [1], *v.t.* stretch, make taut.

entibar, *v.t.* prop (*esp. min.*).—*v.i.* rest, lean.

entibiar, *v.t.* make lukewarm, moderate.—*v.r.* cool off.

entibo, *n.m.* (*min.*) pit-prop; foundation.

entidad, *n.f.* entity.

entierro, *n.m.* burial, interment.

entoldar, *v.t.* cover with an awning; adorn with hangings.

entomología, *n.f.* entomology.

entonación, *n.f.* intonation, intoning; blowing the bellows.

entonar, *v.t.* intone; sing (*something*) in tune; harmonize; blow (*an organ*) with bellows.—*v.r.* sing in tune; assume grand airs.

entonces, *adv.* then; *en aquel —,* at that time.

entono, *n.m.* intonation; arrogance.

entontecer [9], *v.t.* make foolish.—*v.i., v.r.* grow foolish.

entontecimiento, *n.m.* foolishness.

entorchado, *n.m.* gold braid; (*fig.*) promotion.

entornado, -da, *a.* ajar, half-closed.

entornillar, *v.t.* thread (*a screw*); screw (up).

entorpecer [9], *v.t.* benumb; obstruct; clog (*machines*).—*v.r.* stick, jam.

entortar [4], *v.t.* bend.

entosigar [B], *v.t.* poison.

entrado, -da, *a.* — *en años,* advanced in years.—*n.f.* entrance; admission; admission ticket; (*cul.*) entrée; (*min.*) shift; (*com.*) entry.

entrambos, -bas, *a., pron.* (*obs.*) both.

entrante, *a.* entering, incoming; *el mes —,* (*com.*) prox.—*n.m.f.* entrant.

entraña, *n.f.* entrail, bowel; (*fig.*) heart, affection.

entrañable, *a.* intimate; deep (*affection*).

entrañar, *v.t.* contain; bury deep.

entrar, *v.t.* bring *or* show in; invade.—*v.i.* enter (*en*); begin (*a,* to).

entre, *prep.* between; among; — *mí,* to myself, myself; — *tanto,* meanwhile.

entreabierto, -ta, *a.* ajar, half-open.

entreabrir [*p.p.* **entreabierto**], *v.t.* half open.

entreacto, *n.m.* (*theat.*) interval, intermission; entr'acte.

entrecano, -na, *a.* greying (*hair*).

entrecejo, *n.m.* space between the eyebrows; frown.

entrecoger [E], *v.t.* catch; compel (*by arguments*).

entrecoro, *n.m.* (*arch.*) chancel.

entrecortado, -da, *a.* intermittent, faltering.

entrecruzar [C], *v.t., v.r.* interweave.

entrecuesto, *n.m.* (*cul.*) loin, sirloin; backbone.

entrechoque, *n.m.* collision.

entredicho, *n.m.* prohibition, interdict.

entrega, *n.f.* delivery; batch, instalment, issue.

entregar [B], *v.t.* deliver; surrender, hand over.—*v.r.* surrender; take charge (*de,* of).

entrelazar [C], *v.t.* interweave, interlace.

entrelucir [10], *v.t.* show through.

entremedias, *adv.* in the meantime; half-way.

entremés, *n.m.* (*cul.*) hors d'oeuvre; (*theat.*) interlude.

entremeter, *v.t.* insert.—*v.r.* meddle; butt in.

entremetido, -da, *a.* meddlesome, officious.

entremezclar, *v.t., v.r.* intermingle.

entrenamiento, *n.m.* (*sport*) training.

entrenar, *v.t., v.r.* (*sport*) train.

entrepaño, *n.m.* (*arch.*) bay; panel.

entreparecer [9], *v.r.* show through.

entrepierna, *n.f.* (*esp. pl.*) crotch, fork.

entreponer [25], *v.t.* interpose.

entresacar [A], *v.t.* select; thin out (*plants*).

entresuelo, *n.m.* mezzanine, entresol.

entretalla, entretalladura, *n.f.* bas-relief.

entretallar, *v.t.* carve in bas-relief.—*v.r.* fit together.

entretanto, *adv.* meanwhile.

entretejer, *v.t.* interweave.

entretela, *n.f.* interlining.—*pl.* (*fam.*, *fig.*) heart.
entretención, *n.f.* (*S.A.*) amusement, pastime.
entretenedor, -ra, *a.* entertaining.—*n.m.f.* entertainer.
entretener [33], *v.t.* entertain, amuse; delay; (*neol.*) maintain.—*v.r.* amuse oneself.
entretenido, -da, *a.* entertaining.
entretenimiento, *n.m.* entertainment; delay; (*neol.*) maintenance.
entretiempo, *n.m.* spring *or* autumn.
entrever [37], *v.t.* glimpse; guess.
entreverado, -da, *a.* streaky (*bacon etc.*).
entreverar, *v.t.* mingle.
entrevista, *n.f.* interview, meeting.
entrevistar, *v.r.* have a meeting *or* an interview.
entripado, -da, *a.* intestinal; not gutted (*dead animal*).—*n.m.* veiled anger *or* displeasure.
entristecer [9], *v.t.* sadden.—*v.r.* grieve.
entronar, *v.t.* enthrone.
entroncar [A], *v.i.*, *v.r.* be descended from the same stock, be related (**con,** to); (*C.A. rail.*) connect.
entronizar [C], *v.t.* enthrone, exalt.
entuerto, *n.m.* injustice, wrong.
entumecer [9], *v.t.* benumb.—*v.r.* become numb, (*fam.*) go to sleep; surge.
entupir, *v.t.* compress; block.
enturbiar, *v.t.* stir up, muddy; obscure.
entusiasmar, *v.t.* enrapture.—*v.r.* be enthusiastic.
entusiasmo, *n.m.* enthusiasm.
entusiasta, *a.* enthusiastic.—*n.m.f.* enthusiast.
entusiástico, -ca, *a.* enthusiastic.
enumeración, *n.f.* enumeration.
enumerar, *v.t.* enumerate.
enunciar, *v.t.* enunciate.
envainar, *v.t.* sheathe.
envalentonar, *v.t.* embolden.—*v.r.* pluck up courage; brag.
envarar, *v.t.* benumb.
envasador, -ra, *n.m.f.* filler; packer.—*n.m.* funnel.
envasar, *v.t.* pack; bottle.—*v.i.* (*fam.*) booze.
envase, *n.m.* packing; bottling; canning; bottle, jar, can.
envejecer [9], *v.t.* age.—*v.i.* age, grow old.
envenenar, *v.t.* poison, envenom.
enverdecer [9], *v.i.*, *v.r.* turn green.
envergadura, *n.f.* span (*of wings etc.*), spread, compass; (*fig.*) scope, importance.
envergue, *n.m.* sail-rope, rope-band.
envero, *n.m.* golden red, ripeness.
envés, *n.m.* wrong side, back; **al —,** inside out.
envestidura, *n.f.* investiture.
enviada, *n.f.* consignment.
enviado, *n.m.* envoy.
enviar [L], *v.t.* send, remit.
enviciar, *v.t.* corrupt, vitiate.—*v.r.* become addicted (**con,** to).
envidador, -ra, *n.m.f.* bidder (*at cards*).
envidar, *v.t.* bid against.
envidia, *n.f.* envy; desire.
envidiable, *a.* enviable.
envidiar, *v.t.* envy; covet.
envidioso, -sa, *a.* envious.
envilecer [9], *v.t.* degrade; vilify.

envío, *n.m.* shipment, consignment; remittance.
envite, *n.m.* stake (*at cards*); invitation; push; **al primer —,** at once.
envoltorio, *n.m.* bundle; knot (*in cloth*).
envoltura, *n.f.* wrapping.—*n.f.pl.* swaddling clothes.
envolver [5, *p.p.* **envuelto**], *v.t.* wrap; wind; swaddle; (*mil.*) surround.—*v.r.* become involved.
envuelto, -ta, *p.p.* [ENVOLVER].
enyesado, *n.m.*, **enyesadura,** *n.f.* plasterwork.
enyesar, *v.t.* plaster.
enyugar [B], *v.t.* yoke.
enzainar, *v.r.* look askance; (*fam.*) become crooked.
enzima, *n.f.* (*chem.*) enzyme.
enzímico, -ca, *a.* (*chem.*) enzymatic.
eñe, *n.f.* name of letter Ñ.
eón, *n.m.* aeon.
epactilla, *n.f.* liturgical calendar.
epéntesis, *n.f. inv.* epenthesis.
eperlano, *n.m.* (*ichth.*) smelt.
épico, -ca, *a.* epic.—*n.f.* epic poetry.
epicúreo, -rea, *a.* epicurean.
epidemia, *n.f.* epidemic.
epidemial, epidémico, -ca, *a.* epidemic.
epidermis, *n.f. inv.* epidermis.
Epifanía, *n.f.* Epiphany.
epiglotis, *n.f. inv.* epiglottis.
epígrafe, *n.m.* inscription; epigraph.
epigrafía, *n.f.* epigraphy.
epigrama, *n.m.* or *f.* epigram.
epigramático, -ca, *a.* epigrammatic.
epilepsia, *n.f.* (*med.*) epilepsy.
epiléptico, -ca, *a.*, *n.m.f.* epileptic.
epílogo, *n.m.* epilogue.
episcopado, *n.m.* bishopric; episcopacy.
episcopal, *a.* episcopal.
episodio, *n.m.* episode; digression; subplot.
epístola, *n.f.* epistle.
epistolar, *a.* epistolary.
epitafio, *n.m.* epitaph.
epiteto, *n.m.* (*gram.*) epithet.
epitomar, *v.t.* epitomize.
época, *n.f.* epoch, era, age.
epónimo, -ma, *a.* eponymous.
epopeya, *n.f.* epic poem.
epsomita, *n.f.* Epsom salts.
equidad, *n.f.* equity.
equidistante, *a.* equidistant.
equilibrar, *v.t.*, *v.r.* balance; counterbalance.
equilibrio, *n.m.* equilibrium; balance.
equilibrista, *n.m.f.* rope-dancer, tight-rope-walker.
equinoccial, *a.* equinoctial.
equinoccio, *n.m.* equinox.
equipaje, *n.m.* luggage; (*naut.*) crew; (*mil.*) baggage-train.
equipar, *v.t.* equip, fit out.
equiparable, *a.* comparable.
equiparar, *v.t.* compare.
equipo, *n.m.* fitting out, equipment; (*sport*) team.
equis, *n.f.* name of letter X.
equitación, *n.f.* equitation.
equitativo, -va, *a.* equitable, fair.
equivalencia, *n.f.* equivalence; compensation.
equivalente, *a.* equivalent, tantamount; compensatory.

equivaler [35], *v.i.* be of equal value; be equivalent.
equivocación, *n.f.* blunder, misconception, mistake.
equivocar [A], *v.t.* mistake.—*v.r.* be mistaken; make a mistake.
equívoco, -ca, *a.* equivocal, ambiguous.— *n.m.* equivocation; pun; mistake.
era (1), *n.f.* era, age, epoch.
era (2), *n.f.* threshing-floor.
era (3), [SER].
erario, *n.m.* exchequer, public treasury.
ere, *n.f.* name of letter R.
erección, *n.f.* erection; elevation; establishment.
erector, -ra, *a.* erecting.—*n.m.f.* erector, founder.
eres [SER].
ergio, *n.m.* (*phys.*) erg.
ergotizar [C], *v.i.* argue, split hairs.
erguir [8 *or* 3, *in which case initial* i *is changed to* y: *yergo etc.*], *v.t.* erect, raise up.
erial, *a.* unploughed, barren.—*n.m.* waste land.
erica, *n.f.* (*bot.*) heath, heather.
erigir [E], *v.t.* erect, build; set up.
erío, ería, *a.* unploughed, barren.
erizar [C], *v.t.* set on end.—*v.r.* bristle, stand on end.
erizo, *n.m.* (*zool.*) hedgehog; prickly husk; (*ichth.*) sea-urchin.
ermita, *n.f.* hermitage.
ermitaño, -ña, *n.m.f.* hermit.—*n.m.* hermit-crab.
erosión, *n.f.* erosion.
erótico, -ca, *a.* erotic.
erotismo, *n.m.* eroticism.
errabundo, -da, *a.* wandering, errant.
e(r)radicación, *n.f.* eradication.
e(r)radicar [A], *v.t.* eradicate.
erraj, *n.m.* fuel made from olive stones.
errante, *a.* errant, wandering, itinerant.
errar [1; *initial* i *is changed to* y: *yerro etc.*], *v.t.* miss.—*v.i.*, *v.r.* wander; be mistaken; err; sin.
errata, *n.f.* erratum; **fe de erratas,** (*print.*) errata.
errático, -ca, *a.* erratic, vagabond.
erre, *n.f.* name of letter RR.
erróneo, -nea, *a.* erroneous, mistaken.
error, *n.m.* error, mistake.
eructar, *v.i.* belch.
eructo, *n.m.* eructation, belch(ing).
erudición, *n.f.* erudition, scholarship.
erudito, -ta, *a.* erudite, learned, scholarly.
erumpir, *v.i.* erupt (*of a volcano*).
erupción, *n.f.* eruption.
ervilla [ARVEJA].
es [SER].
esbeltez, esbelteza, *n.f.* slenderness, litheness; gracefulness.
esbelto, -ta, *a.* slender, svelte; graceful.
esbirro, *n.m.* bailiff; hired thug.
esbozar [C], *v.t.* sketch.
esbozo, *n.m.* sketch.
escabechar, *v.t.* pickle, souse; (*fam., pej.*) paint (*the face*), dye (*the hair*); plough, (*U.S.*) flunk (*an examinee*).
escabeche, *n.m.* pickle.
escabel, *n.m.* stool; (*fig.*) stepping-stone.
escabioso, -sa, *a.* scabious, mangy.—*n.f.* (*bot.*) scabious.

escabro, *n.m.* sheep-scab.
escabrosidad, *n.f.* scabrousness.
escabroso, -sa, *a.* scabrous; harsh, rough.
escabullir [J], *v.r.* escape, slip off.
escafandra, *n.f.,* **escafandro,** *n.m.* diving suit; — **spacial,** space suit.
escala, *n.f.* ladder, step-ladder; (*math., mus.*) scale; (*naut.*) port of call.
escalada, *n.f.* climbing, escalade.
escalador, -ra, *a.* burglarious.—*n.m.f.* housebreaker, cat burglar.
escalafón, *n.m.* register, graded list of established staff.
escalamera, *n.f.* rowlock.
escalamiento, *n.m.* scaling; burglary.
escalar, *v.t.* climb, scale; burgle.
Escalda, *n.m.* (*geog.*) Scheldt.
escaldar, *v.t.* scald; make red-hot.
escalera, *n.f.* stairs, staircase, stairway; ladder; — **de caracol,** spiral staircase; — **doble,** pair of steps, step-ladder; — **extensible,** extension ladder; — **mecánica,** moving staircase, escalator.
escalfar, *v.t.* (*cul.*) poach (*eggs*).
escalmo, *n.m.* rowlock.
escalofrío, *n.m.* shiver; shudder.
escalón, *n.m.* step, stair; rung; grade; (*mil.*) échelon; (*rad.*) stage.
escaloña, *n.f.* (*bot.*) shallot.
escalpelo, *n.m.* scalpel.
escama, *n.f.* (*ichth.*) scale; (*fig.*) grudge.
escamar, *v.t.* scale (*fish*); (*fam.*) arouse the suspicions of.
escamocho, *n.m.* left-overs, dregs.
escamondar, *v.t.* prune.
escamoso, -sa, *a.* scaly, squamous.
escamotear, *v.t.* palm away, whisk away; (*fam.*) swipe, pinch.
escamoteo, *n.m.* sleight of hand; (*fam.*) swiping.
escampada, *n.f.* clear spell, bright interval (*weather*).
escampar, *v.t.* clear out (*a place*).—*v.i.* clear up (*of the weather*), stop raining.
escampo, *n.m.* clearing out (*a place*); clearing up (*of the weather*).
escanciar, *v.t.* pour out (*wine*).
escandalizar [C], *v.t.* scandalize.—*v.r.* be scandalized; be angered.
escándalo, *n.m.* scandal; commotion.
escandaloso, -sa, *a.* scandalous; turbulent.
Escandinavia, *n.f.* Scandinavia.
escandinavo, -va, *a.,* *n.m.f.* Scandinavian.
escandio, *n.m.* (*chem.*) scandium.
escandir, *v.t.* scan (*verse*).
escansión, *n.f.* scansion.
escaño, *n.m.* settle, bench; (*S.A.*) park bench.
escañuelo, *n.m.* foot-stool.
escapada, *n.f.* escape; **en una —,** at full speed.
escapar, *v.t.* free, deliver; drive hard (*a horse*).—*v.i.* escape.—*v.r.* escape; run away (*a,* from); **se me escapó el tren,** I just missed the train.
escaparate, *n.m.* show cabinet, window display, shop window.
escapatoria, *n.f.* escape; (*fig.*) subterfuge.
escape, *n.m.* flight, escape; escapement (*of a watch*); exhaust; **a —,** on the run.
escapulario, *n.m.* scapulary.
escaque, *n.m.* square (*of a chessboard*).
escaqueado, -da, *a.* chequered.

escarabajo, *n.m.* (*ent.*) black-beetle; (*fig. esp. pl.*) scrawl.
escaramujo, *n.m.* (*bot.*) dog-rose.
escaramuza, *n.f.* skirmish.
escaramuzar [C], *v.i.* skirmish.
escarbar, *v.t.* scrape, scratch; poke (*the fire*).
escarbo, *n.m.* scraping, scratching.
escarcha, *n.f.* hoar frost, rime.
escarchar, *v.t.* ice (*cakes*).—*v.i.* freeze.
escardador, -ra, *a.* weeding.—*n.m.f.* weeder. —*n.m.* hoe.
escardar, escardillar, *v.t.* weed.
escarlata, *n.f.* scarlet; scarlet cloth.
escarlatina, *n.f.* scarlet fever.
escarmentar, *v.t.* inflict an exemplary punishment on.—*v.i.* take warning.
escarmiento, *n.m.* warning; chastisement.
escarnecer [9], *v.t.* mock at, ridicule.
escarnio, *n.m.* jeer; ridicule.
escarola, *n.f.* (*bot.*) endive.
escarpa, *n.f.* bluff, slope; (*esp. mil.*) escarpment, scarp.
escarpia, *n.f.* tenterhook.
escarpín, *n.m.* dancing pump (*shoe*).
escasear, *v.t.* give sparingly; spare.—*v.i.* be scarce; grow less.
escasez, *n.f.* scarcity; meanness; lack.
escaso, -sa, *a.* scarce, scanty; little; lacking in.
escatimar, *v.t.* curtail; scrimp.
escatimoso, -sa, *a.* malicious, cunning.
escatología (1), *n.f.* eschatology.
escatología (2), *n.f.* scatology.
escayola, *n.f.* plaster (*of Paris*).
escayolar, *v.t.* put in plaster.
escena, *n.f.* stage; scene.
escenario, *n.m.* stage; (*cine.*) scenario.
escénico, -ca, *a.* scenic, rel. to the stage *or* stage effects.
escenografía, *n.f.* (*theat.*) stage-setting, set designing.
escepticismo, *n.m.* scepticism.
escéptico, -ca, *a., n.m.f.* sceptic.
Escila, *n.f.* (*myth.*) Scylla; **escila,** *n.f.* (*bot.*) squill.
escinco, *n.m.* (*zool.*) skink.
escisión, *n.f.* division.
escita, *a., n.m.f.* Scythian.
esclarecer [9], *v.t.* illuminate; elucidate; enlighten.—*v.i.* dawn.
esclavitud, *n.f.* slavery, servitude.
esclavizar [C], *v.t.* enslave.
esclavo, -va, *a.* enslaved.—*n.m.f.* slave.
esclavón, -vona [ESLAVO].
esclusa, *n.f.* sluice.
escoba, *n.f.* broom; (*bot.*) broom.
escobajo, *n.m.* old broom; stalk of a bunch of grapes.
escobar, *v.t.* sweep.
escobilla, *n.f.* brush.
escocer [5D], *v.t.* irritate.—*v.i.* smart.
escocés, -cesa, *a.* Scottish, Scots.—*n.m.* Scot.
Escocia, *n.f.* Scotland.
escofina, *n.f.* rasp.
escoger [E], *v.t.* select, choose.
escolar, *a.* scholastic.—*n.m.* school-boy, scholar.
escolástico, -ca, *a.* scholastic.—*n.m.* (*hist.*) schoolman.
escolio, *n.m.* gloss.
escolopendra, *n.f.* (*zool.*) centipede.

escolta, *n.f.* (*mil.*) escort.
escollera, *n.f.* breakwater.
escollo, *n.m.* reef; (*fig.*) difficulty.
escombro (1), *n.m.* rubbish; debris.
escombro (2), *n.m.* (*ichth.*) mackerel.
esconder, *v.t.* hide; disguise.
a escondidas, *adv. phr.* on the sly.
escondite, *n.m.* hiding place.
escopeta, *n.f.* shotgun.
escopetero, *n.m.* musketeer.
escoplo, *n.m.* (*carp.*) chisel.
escorbuto, *n.m.* (*med.*) scurvy.
escorchar, *v.t.* flay (*hides*).
escoria, *n.f.* slag, dross.
escorial, *n.m.* slag-heap.
Escorpión, *n.m.* (*astr.*) Scorpio; **escorpión,** *n.m.* (*zool.*) scorpion.
escorzar [C], *v.t.* (*art.*) foreshorten.
escorzón, *n.m.* (*zool.*) toad.
escotado, *n.m.,* **escotadura,** *n.f.* low neck (*in dress*).
escotar, *v.t.* cut to fit; cut low at the neck.—*v.i.* club together, go Dutch.
escote, *n.m.* low neck (*in dress*); quota, share.
escotilla, *n.f.* hatch.
escotillón, *n.m.* hatchway; (*theat.*) trapdoor.
escozor, *n.m.* smarting; affliction.
escribanía, *n.f.* court clerkship; escritoire.
escribano, *n.m.* court clerk; clerk; (*naut.*) purser.
escribir [*p.p.* **escrito**], *v.t., v.i.* write; **—a máquina,** type; **máquina de —,** typewriter.—*v.r.* enroll.
escrito, -ta, *p.p.* [ESCRIBIR].—*n.m.* writing; document; (*jur.*) writ.
escritor, -ra, *n.m.f.* writer, author.
escritorio, *n.m.* desk; study, office.
escritura, *n.f.* handwriting; writing; scripture; deed.
escrófula, *n.f.* (*med.*) scrofula, king's evil.
escroto, *n.m.* scrotum.
escrúpulo, *n.m.* scruple; scruple (20 *grains*).
escrupulosidad, *n.f.* scrupulosity, scrupulousness.
escrupuloso, -sa, *a.* scrupulous.
escrutación, *n.f.* scrutiny.
escrutar, *v.t.* scrutinize; invigilate; count votes.
escrutinio, *n.m.* scrutiny; counting of votes.
escuadra, *n.f.* set-square; angle-iron; squad; (*naut.*) squadron.
escuadrilla, *n.f.* (*aer.*) squadron.
escuadro, *n.m.* (*ichth.*) skate.
escuadrón, *n.m.* (*mil.*) squadron (*of cavalry*); swarm.
escualidez, *n.f.* squalor.
escuálido, -da, *a.* squalid; weak.
escualo, *n.m.* (*ichth.*) spotted dogfish.
escuchar, *v.t.* listen to; heed.
escudero, *n.m.* page, squire, shield-bearer, esquire.
escudilla, *n.f.* bowl.
escudo, *n.m.* shield, escutcheon.
escudriñar, *v.t.* scrutinize, pry into.
escuela, *n.f.* school.
escuerzo, *n.m.* (*zool.*) toad.
escueto, -ta, *a.* disengaged; plain, unadorned.
esculpir, *v.t.* sculpt, carve.
escultor, -ra, *n.m.f.* sculptor, sculptress.
escultura, *n.f.* sculpture.
escultural, *a.* sculptural.
escupidura, *n.f.* spittle.

escupir, *v.t.*, *v.i.* spit.
escurreplatos, *n.m. inv.* plate-rack.
escurridizo, -za, *a.* slippery.
escurridor, *n.m.* colander; plate-rack.
escurriduras, escurrimbres, *n.f.pl.* rinsings, dregs.
escurrir, *v.t.* drain; wring out.—*v.i.* drip, trickle, ooze; slip out.
esdrújulo, -la, *a.* proparoxytonic, proparoxytonal.—*n.m.* proparoxytone.
ese (1), *n.f.* name of letter S.
ese (2), **esa,** *a. dem. m. f.* (*pl.* **esos, esas**) that.—*pl.* those.
ése, ésa, *pron. dem. m.f.* (*pl.* **ésos, ésas**) that, that one.—*pl.* those, those ones.
esencia, *n.f.* essence.
esencial, *a.* essential.
esfera, *n.f.* sphere; dial (*of a clock*).
esferal, esférico, -ca, *a.* spherical, globular.
esfinge, *n.f.* sphinx.
esforzado, -da, *a.* valiant; vigorous, enterprising.
esforzar [4C], *v.t.* strengthen; encourage.—*v.r.* exert oneself.
esfuerzo, *n.m.* effort; vigour.
esfumar, *v.t.* blur, (*art.*) stump; (*art.*) tone down, soften.
esgrima, *n.f.* (*sport*) fencing.
esgrimidor, -ra, *n.m.f.* fencer.
esgrimir, *v.t.* wield; brandish.—*v.i.* fence.
esguince, *n.m.* dodge, twist; sprain.
eslabón, *n.m.* link; steel (*for striking fire or for sharpening*).
eslavo, -va, *a., n.m.f.* Slav.
eslovaco, -ca, *a., n.m.f.* Slovak.
esloveno, -na, *a., n.m.f.* Slovene.
esmaltar, *v.t.* enamel; (*fig.*) adorn.
esmalte, *n.m.* enamel, enamelling; **— de uñas,** nail-polish.
esmerado, -da, *a.* painstaking; highly finished.
esmeralda, *n.f.* (*gem*) emerald.
esmerar, *v.t.* polish.—*v.r.* take great pains; do one's best.
esmeril, *n.m.* emery.
esmero, *n.m.* careful attention; correctness.
eso, *pron. dem. neuter* (*pl.* **esos**) that; **— es,** that's it; **a — de las cinco,** at about five o'clock.—*pl.* those, those ones.
esotérico, -ca, *a.* esoteric.
espabilar, *v.t.* to snuff (*a candle*).—*v.r.* (*fam.*) look lively.
espaciar, *v.t.* space.—*v.r.* expatiate; relax; walk to and fro.
espacio, *n.m.* space; period, interval; delay.
espaciosidad, *n.f.* spaciousness.
espacioso, -sa, *a.* spacious.
espada, *n.f.* sword; spade (*at cards*); (*ichth.*) swordfish.—*n.m.* (*taur.*) bullfighter.
espadachín, *n.m.* swordsman; bully.
espadaña, *n.f.* (*bot.*) bulrush, reed-mace; belfry.
espadilla, *n.f.* scull; jury rudder; ace of spades; hair bodkin; (*bot.*) gladiolus.
espadín, *n.m.* rapier.
espadón, *n.m.* broadsword; (*mil. fam.*) brass hat.
espadrapo [ESPARADRAPO].
espalda, *n.f.* back; shoulder; **de espaldas,** with the back turned (*a,* towards).
espaldar (1), *n.m.* back (*of a seat etc.*).
espaldar (2), *n.m.* (*bot.*) espalier.
espaldera, *n.f.* (*bot.*) espalier.

espaldilla, *n.f.* shoulder-blade.
espaldudo, -da, *a.* broad-shouldered.
espantable, *a.* frightful.
espantadizo, -za, *a.* shy, easily frightened.
espantajo, *n.m.* scarecrow.
espantar, *v.t.* scare, frighten; drive away.—*v.r.* be surprised *or* astonished.
espanto, *n.m.* fright; threat; (*S.A.*) ghost.
espantoso, -sa, *a.* frightful, dreadful; wonderful.
España, *n.f.* Spain.
español, -la, *a.* Spanish.—*n.m.f.* Spaniard.—*n.m.* Spanish (*language*).
esparadrapo, *n.m.* plaster, sticking-plaster.
esparaván, *n.m.* (*vet.*) spavin; (*orn.*) sparrow-hawk.
esparcimiento, *n.m.* scattering; amusement, recreation.
esparcir [D], *v.t.* scatter.—*v.r.* amuse oneself.
espárrago, *n.m.* (*bot.*) asparagus.
espártano, -na, *a.* Spartan.
esparto, *n.m.* (*bot.*) esparto-grass.
espasmo, *n.m.* spasm.
espasmódico, -ca, *a.* spasmodic.
espato, *n.m.* (*min.*) spar.
espátula, *n.f.* spatula, putty knife; (*orn.*) spoonbill.
espaviento, *n.m.* consternation, fuss.
espavorido, -da, *a.* terrified.
especia, *n.f.* spice.
especial, *a.* special, especial.
especialidad, *n.f.* speciality, (*U.S.*) specialty.
especialista, *a., n.m.f.* specialist.
especialización, *n.f.* specialization.
especializar [C], *v.t., v.i., v.r.* specialize.
especiar, *v.t.* spice.
especie, *n.f.* kind, sort; matter, affair; (*zool. etc.*) species; **en —,** in kind.
especiería, *n.f.* spice store.
especificación, *n.f.* specification.
especificar [A], *v.t.* specify.
especificativo, -va, *a.* specificatory; (*gram.*) restrictive.
específico, -ca, *a.* specific.—*n.m.* patent medicine.
espécimen, *n.m.* (*pl.* **especímenes**) specimen.
especiosidad, *n.f.* beauty; speciosity.
especioso, -sa, *a.* beautiful; specious.
espectacular, *a.* spectacular.
espectáculo, *n.m.* spectacle, show.
espectador, -ra, *a.* observing.—*n.m.f.* spectator, onlooker.
espectro, *n.m.* spectre, phantom; spectrum.
especulación, *n.f.* speculation, contemplation; (*com.*) speculation.
especulador, -ra, *a.* speculating.—*n.m.f.* speculator.
especular, *v.t.* inspect; speculate on.—*v.i.* speculate (*esp. com.*).
especulativo, -va, *a.* speculative.
espejeo, espejismo, *n.m.* mirage.
espejo, *n.m.* mirror, looking-glass.
espelunca, *n.f.* cavern.
espeluznante, *a.* hair-raising.
espeluznar, *v.t.* set the hair of (*s.o.*) on end; ruffle (*U.S.* muss) the hair of (*s.o.*).
espera, *n.f.* expectation; waiting; (*mus.*) pause, rest.
esperanza, *n.f.* hope; expectancy.
esperar, *v.t.* expect; hope.—*v.r.* stay, wait.
esperezar, *v.r.* stretch (*one's arms and legs*).
esperma, *n.f.* sperm.

espermático, -ca, *a.* spermatic, seminal.
esperpento, *n.m.* (*fam.*) absurdity; absurd person; fright.
espesar, *v.t.* thicken, inspissate; coagulate.
espeso, -sa, *a.* thick, dense; bulky, heavy; slovenly.
espesor, *n.m.* thickness, gauge (*of plates etc.*); density.
espesura, *n.f.* density, closeness; thicket; slovenliness.
espetar, *v.t.* skewer.
espetera, *n.f.* dresser, kitchen-rack.
espetón, *n.m.* spit; poker.
espía, *n.m.f.* spy.
espiar [L], *v.t.* spy on.—*v.i.* spy.
espicanardi, *n.f.,* **espicanardo,** *n.m.* (*bot.*) spikenard.
espichar, *v.t.* prick.—*v.i.* (*fam.*) peg out, die.
espiche, *n.m.* spigot.
espiga, *n.f.* spike; ear (*of grain*); (*carp.*) tenon; shank; fuse (*of a bomb*); (*naut.*) masthead.
espigar [B], *v.t.* glean; tenon, pin.—*v.i.* form ears.—*v.r.* grow tall.
espigón, *n.m.* sting (*of a bee*); point; break-water.
espín, *n.m.* **puerco —,** porcupine.
espina, *n.f.* thorn; spine; fishbone; splinter; (*fig.*) doubt, uncertainty; **— de pescado,** herringbone (*cloth*).
espinaca, *n.f.* (*bot.*) spinach.
espinal, *a.* spinal.
espinazo, *n.m.* backbone.
espinel, *n.m.* trawl.
espinera, *n.f.* (*bot.*) hawthorn.
espingarda, *n.f.* long Moorish musket; (*obs.*) sort of cannon.
espinilla, *n.f.* shin-bone; blackhead.
espino, *n.m.* (*bot.*) hawthorn.
espinoso, -sa, *a.* thorny; bony (*fish*).—*n.m.* (*ichth.*) stickleback.
espiocha, *n.f.* pickaxe.
espión, *n.m.* spy.
espionaje, *n.m.* espionage, spying.
espira, *n.f.* coil, turn.
espiral, *a.* spiral.— *n.f.* hairspring.—*n.f.* (*geom.*) spiral.
espirar, *v.t., v.i.* breathe, exhale.
espiritar, *v.t.* possess with the devil; agitate. —*v.r.* get agitated.
espiritismo, *n.m.* spiritualism, spiritism.
espiritoso, -sa, *a.* spirited; spirituous.
espíritu, *n.m.* spirit; (*gram.*) breathing; **— de cuerpo,** esprit de corps; **Espíritu Santo,** Holy Spirit, Holy Ghost.
espiritual, *a.* spiritual.—*n.f.* spiritual (*song*).
espiritualidad, *n.f.* spirituality.
espiritualismo, *n.m.* (*Phil.*) spiritualism.
espirituoso, -sa [ESPIRITOSO].
espiroqueta, *n.f.* (*med.*) spirochete.
espita, *n.f.* cock, tap, spigot.
espitar, *v.t.* tap (*a barrel*).
esplendidez, *n.f.* splendour, magnificence.
espléndido, -da, *a.* splendid, magnificent; resplendent.
esplendor, *n.m.* splendour.
esplendoroso, -sa, *a.* resplendent; magnificent.
esplenético, -ca, esplénico, -ca, *a.* splenetic.
espliego, *n.m.* (*bot.*) lavender.
espolada, *n.f.* spurring, prick with the spur.
espolear, *v.t.* spur; (*fig.*) spur on.
espoleta, *n.f.* fuse (*of a bomb*); wishbone.

espolón, *n.m.* spur (*of a cock*); (*geog.*) spur; (*naut.*) beak, ram; mole, jetty; (*arch.*) buttress; (*mil.*) trail spade (*of a gun*); chilblain.
espondaico, -ca, *a.* (*poet.*) spondaic.
espondeo, *n.m.* (*poet.*) spondee.
esponja, *n.f.* sponge; (*fig.*) sponger.
esponjar, *v.t.* sponge, soak.—*v.r.* become puffed up (*with conceit*); glow with health.
esponjosidad, *n.f.* sponginess.
esponjoso, -sa, *a.* spongy.
esponsales, *n.m.pl.* betrothal, engagement.
espontanear, *v.r.* own up, come forward.
espontaneidad, *n.f.* spontaneity, spontane-ousness.
espontáneo, -nea, *a.* spontaneous.—*n.m.* spectator who jumps into the bull-ring.
espora, *n.f.* (*bot. etc.*) spore.
esporádico, -ca, *a.* sporadic.
esportilla, *n.f.* small basket.
esportillero, *n.m.* errand boy, carrier.
esportillo, *n.m.* basket, frail.
esposo, -sa, *n.m.f.* spouse.—*n.m.* husband.— *n.f.* wife.—*n.f.pl.* handcuffs.
espuela, *n.f.* spur.
espuerta, *n.f.* basket (*esp. as used by labourers*); **a espuertas,** in abundance.
espulgar [B], *v.t.* delouse; clean of fleas.
espuma, *n.f.* foam; spume; scum; **goma —** or **de caucho,** foam rubber.
espumajoso, -sa, *a.* frothy, foamy.
espumante, *a.* frothy, foaming; sparkling (*wine*).
espumar, *v.t.* scum, skim.—*v.i.* froth.
espumosidad, *n.f.* frothiness; foaminess.
espurio, -ria, *a.* spurious; illegitimate.
esputo, *n.m.* sputum, spittle.
esquela, *n.f.* note; announcement.
esquelético, -ca, *a.* skeletal, very thin.
esqueleto, *n.m.* skeleton; (*C.A.*) (application etc.) form.
esquema, *n.m.* scheme; schema.
esquemático, -ca, *a.* schematic.
esquematismo, *n.m.* schematism.
esquena, *n.f.* spine.
esquí, *n.m.* ski.
esquiar [L], *v.i.* ski.
esquiciar, *v.t.* sketch.
esquicio, *n.m.* sketch.
esquife, *n.m.* skiff, small boat.
esquila, *n.f.* small bell; prawn; water spider; (*bot.*) squill.
esquilar, *v.t.* shear; (*fig.*) fleece.
esquilmar, *v.t.* harvest; impoverish.
esquilón, *n.m.* small bell.
esquimal, *a., n.m.f.* Eskimo.
esquina, *n.f.* corner.
esquinco, *n.m.* (*zool.*) skink.
esquirla, *n.f.* splinter (*of bone, glass etc.*).
esquirol, *n.f.* strike-breaker, blackleg.
esquisto, *n.m.* (*geol.*) schist.
esquivar, *v.t.* avoid, elude.—*v.r.* withdraw.
esquivez, *n.f.* coyness; disdain; scorn.
esquivo, -va, *a.* shy; elusive; reserved.
estabilidad, *n.f.* stability; constancy.
estabilizar [C], *v.t.* stabilize.
estable, *a.* stable, permanent.
establecer [9], *v.t.* establish, found; decree.— *v.r.* settle (*in a place*).
establecimiento, *n.m.* establishment, settle-ment; store; institution; decree.
establo, *n.m.* stable.

estaca, *n.f.* picket, stake; cudgel.
estacada, *n.f.* stockade, palisade.
estacar [A], *v.t.* stake; enclose.
estación, *n.f.* condition, situation; season; (*rail.*) station.
estacional, *a.* seasonal.
estacionar, *v.r.* remain stationary; (*auto.*) park.
estacionario, -ria, *a.* stationary, fixed.
estadio, *n.m.* stadium.
estadista, *n.m.f.* statesman; statistician.
estadístico, -ca, *a.* statistical.
estado, *n.m.* state; condition; estate (*of the realm*); — **mayor,** (*mil.*) staff; *Estados Unidos,* United States.
estafa, *n.f.* swindle, trick.
estafador, -ra, *n.m.f.* swindler.
estafar, *v.t.* swindle.
estafeta, *n.f.* courier.
estafilococo, *n.m.* (*med.*) staphylococcus.
estalactita, *n.f.* (*geol.*) stalactite.
estalagmita, *n.f.* (*geol.*) stalagmite.
estallar, *v.i.* explode; (*fig.*) break out.
estallido, *n.m.* crack, report.
estambre, *n.m.* yarn, worsted; (*bot.*) stamen.
estameña, *n.f.* serge.
estampa, *n.f.* print; engraving; printing press.
estampar, *v.t.* print, imprint; impress, stamp.
estampida, *n.f.* (*S.A.*) stampede.
estampido, *n.m.* crack, report; crash.
estampilla, *n.f.* small print; (*S.A.*) postage-stamp.
estancar [A], *v.t.* staunch; check; (*com.*) monopolize; embargo.—*v.r.* be stagnant.
estancia, *n.f.* stay, sojourn; dwelling; living-room; (*poet.*) stanza; (*S.A.*) farm, estate.
estanciero, *n.m.* owner of an estate; farm-overseer.
estanco, -ca, *a.* watertight; seaworthy.—*n.m.* monopoly; shop for monopoly goods (*esp. tobacco and postage stamps*); repository.
estándar(d), *n.m.* (*neol.*) standard.
estandar(d)izar, *v.t.* standardize.
estandarte, *n.m.* standard, banner.
estanque, *n.m.* pond; reservoir.
estanquero, -ra, *n.m.f.* retailer of monopoly goods, esp. tobacco; keeper of reservoirs.
estante, *a.* being; permanent.—*n.m.* shelf.
estantería, *n.f.* shelving; bookcase.
estantigua, *n.f.* procession of phantoms and hobgoblins; (*fam.*) fright, scarecrow.
estañar, *v.t.* tin; solder.
estaño, *n.m.* tin.
estar [18], *v.i.* be (*temporarily, or in a state or condition*); *estamos a lunes,* it is Monday; — **con,** have (*a disease*); — **de viaje,** be on a journey; — **de** (*capitán*), be acting as (captain); *estoy en lo que Vd. me dice,* I follow what you are telling me; — **para,** be about to; *estoy por romperle la cabeza,* I have a good mind to break his head; *está por hacer,* it remains to be done; — *sobre un negocio,* conduct a business well.—*v.r.* stay, remain.
estático, -ca, *a.* static.—*n.f.* statics.
estatua, *n.f.* statue.
estatuario, -ria, *a.* statuary.—*n.m.* sculptor.
estatuir [O], *v.t.* ordain, establish.
este (1), *n.m.* east.
este (2), **esta,** *a.* *dem.* (*pl.* **estos, estas**) this; latter.—*pl.* these.

éste, ésta, *pron. dem.* (*pl.* **éstos, éstas**) this; the latter.—*pl.* these.
estela, *n.f.* (*naut.*) wake; (*aer.*) trail.
estelar, *a.* stellar, sidereal.
estenografía, *n.f.* stenography, shorthand.
estenográfico, -ca, *a.* shorthand.
estenógrafo, -fa, *n.m.f.* stenographer, shorthand-writer.
estepa (1), *n.f.* (*bot.*) rock-rose.
estepa (2), *n.f.* (*geog.*) steppe.
estera, *n.f.* mat, matting.
estercolar, *n.m.* manure heap, dunghill.—*v.t.* [4] dung, manure.
estereotipar, *v.t.* stereotype (*also fig.*).
estereotipia, *n.f.* stereotype.
estéril, *a.* sterile; fruitless.
esterilidad, *n.f.* sterility.
esterilizador, -ra, *a.* sterilizing.—*n.m.* sterilizer (*apparatus*).
esterilizar, *v.t.* sterilize.
esterilla, *n.f.* small mat; hopsack (*textile weave*); (*S.A.*) canvas.
esterlina, *n.f.* sterling.
esternón, *n.m.* (*anat.*) sternum, breastbone.
estero, *n.m.* matting; tidal marsh; (*S.A.*) swamp; (*S.A.*) stream.
estertor, *n.m.* noisy breathing; death rattle.
esteta, *n.m.f.* aesthete.
estético, -ca, *a.* aesthetic.—*n.f.* aesthetics.
esteva, *n.f.* plough-handle.
estiaje, *n.m.* low-water mark.
estibador, *n.m.* stevedore, docker, (*U.S.*) longshoreman.
estibar, *v.t.* pack, (*naut.*) stow.
estibio, *n.m.* (*chem.*) stibium.
estiércol, *n.m.* dung, manure.
estigio, -gia, estigioso, -sa, *a.* Stygian.
estigma, *n.m.* stigma.
estigmatismo, *n.m.* (*med.*) stigmatism.
estigmatizar [C], *v.t.* stigmatize.
estilete, *n.m.* stiletto; style, stylus (*of recording instrument*); (*med.*) stylet.
estilista, *n.m.f.* (*lit.*) stylist.
estilístico, -ca, *a.* (*lit.*) stylistic.—*n.f.* stylistics.
estilización, *n.f.* stylization.
estilo, *n.m.* style; stylus; *por el —,* of that kind.
estilográfico, -ca, *a.* stylographic.—*n.f.* fountain pen.
estima, *n.f.* esteem.
estimable, *a.* estimable, worthy.
estimación, *n.f.* estimation; esteem.
estimar, *v.t.* esteem, respect; judge; (*fam.*) be fond of.
estimulación, *n.f.* stimulation.
estimulante, *a.* stimulating.—*n.m.* stimulant.
estimular, *v.t.* stimulate; irritate; goad.
estímulo, *n.m.* stimulus, sting.
estío, *n.m.* summer.
estipendio, *n.m.* stipend, salary.
estipulación, *n.f.* stipulation.
estipular, *v.t.* stipulate.
estirable, *a.* stretchable.
estirar, *v.t.* draw, stretch; — *la pata,* (*fam.*) die.—*v.r.* stretch; put on airs.
estirón, *n.m.* stretch; strong pull.
estirpe, *n.f.* stock, race.
estival, estivo, -va, *a.* summer.
esto, *pron. dem. neuter* this.
estocada, *n.f.* thrust, stab.
Estocolmo, *n.m.* Stockholm.

estofa, *n.f.* (*rare*) quilted material; (*fig.*) stuff, quality.
estofado, *n.m.* meat stew.
estofar, *v.t.* quilt; stew.
estoicismo, *n.m.* Stoicism.
estoico, -ca, *a.* stoic(al).—*n.m.f.* stoic.
estomagar [B], *v.t.* upset (*the stomach*); pall; (*fam.*) annoy.
estómago, *n.m.* stomach.
estonio, -nia, *a.*, *n.m.f.* Estonian.
estopa, *n.f.* tow, oakum.
estopilla, *n.f.* fine flax; cambric.
estoque, *n.m.* rapier; (*bot.*) gladiolus.
estorbar, *v.t.* hinder, impede, hamper.
estorbo, *n.m.* impediment, hindrance.
estorboso, -sa, *a.* hindering, in the way.
estornino, *n.m.* (*orn.*) starling.
estornudar, *v.i.* sneeze.
estornudo, *n.m.* sneeze.
estrabismo, *n.m.* (*med.*) strabismus, squint.
estrada, *n.f.* causeway; highway.
estrado, *n.m.* dais; drawing-room; lecturing platform.—*pl.* court of justice.
estrafalario, -ria, *a.* (*fam.*) slovenly; (*fam.*) outlandish.
estragamiento, *n.m.* corruption.
estragar [B], *v.t.* corrupt, deprave, spoil.
estrago, *n.m.* damage, havoc, devastation; depravity.
estragón, *n.m.* (*bot.*) tarragon.
estrambote, *n.m.* (*poet.*) burden (*of a song*).
estrambótico, -ca, *a.* (*fam.*) odd, freakish.
estrangulación, *n.f.* strangulation; choke (*in machinery*).
estrangulador, *n.m.* throttle, choke (*in machinery*).
estrangular, *v.t.* throttle, strangle, choke.
estraperlista, *a.* rel. to the black market.—*n.m.f.* black marketeer.
estraperlo, *n.m.* black market.
estratagema, *n.f.* stratagem.
estrategia, *n.f.* strategy.
estratégico, -ca, *a.* strategic(al).
estratificar [A], *v.t.*, *v.r.* stratify.
estrato, *n.m.* layer, stratum.
estratosfera, *n.f.* stratosphere.
estraza, *n.f.* rag.
estrechar, *v.t.* tighten; constrict; narrow; press; — *la mano,* shake hands (*a,* with). —*v.r.* become narrow; reduce expenses; come closer together.
estrechez, *n.f.* narrowness; tightness; penury.
estrecho, -cha, *a.* narrow; tight; intimate; stingy.—*n.m.* (*geog.*) strait; (*fig.*) danger, predicament.
estrechón, *n.m.* (*fam.*) handshake.
estrechura, *n.f.* narrowness; closeness, familiarity; predicament; penury.
estregadera, *n.f.* scrubbing brush.
estregar [1B], *v.t.* scrub, scour; rub.
estrella, *n.f.* star; *estrellas y listas,* Stars and Stripes.
estrelladera, *n.f.* (*cul.*) slice, turnover (*implement*).
estrellar, *v.t.* (*fam.*) break; (*cul.*) scramble (*eggs*); crash.—*v.r.* crash (**contra,** into).
estrellón, *n.m.* large star; (*S.A.*) collision.
estremecer [9], *v.t.* shake.—*v.r.* shake, shiver.
estremecimiento, *n.m.* shaking, shivering.
estrena, *n.f.* gift (*of appreciation*); (*obs.*) first use.

estrenar, *v.t.* use *or* wear *or* stage (*etc.*) for the first time.—*v.r.* make one's debut, appear (*etc.*) for the first time.
estreno, *n.m.* beginning; debut; first performance.
estrenuo, -nua, *a.* strenuous.
estreñimiento, *n.m.* constipation.
estreñir [8K], *v.t.* bind, tighten; constipate. —*v.r.* be constipated.
estrépito, *n.m.* noise, racket; fuss.
estrepitoso, -sa, *a.* noisy; notorious.
estriadura, *n.f.* fluting; striation.
estriar [L], *v.t.* flute; striate.
estríbar, *v.i.* rest (**en,** on).
estribillo, *n.m.* (*poet.*) burden, refrain.
estribo, *n.m.* stirrup; (*geog.*) spur.
estribor, *n.m.* (*naut.*) starboard.
estricto, -ta, *a.* strict.
estridente, *a.* strident.
estridor, *n.m.* stridence, loud noise.
estrige, *n.f.* (*orn.*) barn owl.
estro (1), *n.m.* (*poet.*) inspiration.
estro (2), *n.m.* (*ent.*) botfly.
estrofa, *n.f.* strophe.
estrófico, -ca, *a.* strophic.
estroncio, *n.m.* (*chem.*) strontium.
estropajo, *n.m.* (*bot.*) loofah; dishcloth, dishmop.
estropear, *v.t.* abuse; spoil; cripple.—*v.r.* spoil; fail.
estropeo, *n.m.* mistreatment; damage.
estructura, *n.f.* structure.
estruendo, *n.m.* clamour; turmoil, uproar.
estrujar, *v.t.* squeeze, press, crush.
estuario, *n.m.* estuary.
estuco, *n.m.* stucco.
estuche, *n.m.* case, box, casket.
estudiante, *n.m.f.* student.
estudiantina, *n.f.* group of students; students' band.
estudiar, *v.t.*, *v.i.* study.
estudio, *n.m.* study; studio.
estudioso, -sa, *a.* studious.
estufa, *n.f.* stove; hothouse; sweating room.
estufador, *n.m.* stew-pan.
estufilla, *s.f.* foot-warmer.
estulto, -ta, *a.* silly.
estupefaciente, *a.*, *n.m.* narcotic.
estupefacto, -ta, *a.* dumbfounded; petrified.
estupendo, -da, *a.* stupendous, wonderful; (*fam.*) marvellous.
estupidez, *n.f.* stupidity.
estúpido, -da, *a.* stupid.
estupor, *n.m.* stupor.
estuprar, *v.t.* rape, violate.
estupro, *n.m.* rape.
esturión, *n.m.* (*ichth.*) sturgeon.
estuve, estuvo, *etc.* preterite of ESTAR.
etapa, *n.f.* stage (*of a journey*; *rad.*).
etcétera, et cetera.—*n.f.* (*print.*) ampersand.
éter, *n.m.* (*chem.*) ether.
etéreo, -ea, *a.* ethereal.
eternal, *a.* eternal.
eternidad, *n.f.* eternity.
eternizar [C], *v.t.* make eternal.—*v.r.* go on for ever.
eterno, -na, *a.* eternal.
ético, -ca (1), *a.* ethical, moral.
ético, -ca (2), *a.* (*med.*) consumptive.
etilo, *n.m.* ethyl.
etimología, *n.f.* etymology.
etimológico, -ca, *a.* etymological.

95

etíope, etiopio, -pia, *a., n.m.f.* Ethiopian.
Etiopía, *n.f.* Ethiopia.
etiqueta, *n.f.* etiquette; label, price tag; *de* —, formal.
étnico, -ca, *a.* ethnic.
etnografía, *n.f.* ethnography.
etnología, *n.f.* ethnology.
eucalipto, *n.m. (bot.)* eucalyptus.
eucaristía, *n.f. (eccl.)* eucharist, communion.
euclidiano, -na, *a.* Euclidean.
eufemismo, *n.m.* euphemism.
eufonía, *n.f.* euphony.
eufónico, -ca, *a.* euphonic, euphonious.
euforia, *n.f.* euphoria, sense of well-being.
eunuco, *n.m.* eunuch.
eupéptico, -ca, *a.* eupeptic, digestive.
eurasiano, -na, *a., n.m.f.* Eurasian.
euro, *n.m. (poet.)* east wind.
Europa, *n.f. (geog., myth.)* Europe.
europeizar [C], *v.t.* Europeanize.
europeo, -pea, *a., n.m.f.* European.
europio, *n.m. (chem.)* europium.
éuscaro, -ra, eusquero, -ra, *a., n.m.f.* Basque.—*n.m.* Basque *(language)*.
eutanasia, *n.f.* euthanasia.
evacuación, *n.f.* evacuation.
evacuar, *v.t., v.i.* evacuate.
evacuatorio, -ria, *a.* evacuant.—*n.m.* public convenience.
evadir, *v.t.* avoid, evade.—*v.r.* flee, escape.
evaluación, *n.f.* evaluation.
evaluar [M], *v.t.* evaluate.
evanescente, *a.* evanescent.
evangélico, -ca, *a.* evangelic; evangelical.
Evangelio, *n.m.* Gospel; *(fam.)* gospel truth.
evangelista, *n.m.* evangelist; gospeller.
evangelizar [C], *v.t., v.i.* evangelize.
evaporable, *a.* evaporable.
evaporación, *n.f.* evaporation.
evaporar, *v.t., v.r.* evaporate.
evaporizar [C], *v.t.* vaporize.
evasión, *n.f.* evasion; escape.
evasivo, -va, *a.* evasive, elusive.
evento, *n.m.* contingency, chance event; *a todo* —, (prepared *etc.*) for any eventuality.
eventual, *a.* eventual, fortuitous.
eventualidad, *n.f.* eventuality.
evicción, *n.f. (jur.)* eviction, dispossession.
evidencia, *n.f.* evidence.
evidenciar, *v.t.* make evident.—*v.r.* be evident.
evidente, *a.* evident.
evitable, *a.* avoidable.
evitar, *v.t.* avoid, shun.
evocación, *n.f.* evocation.
evocar [A], *v.t.* evoke.
evolución, *n.f.* evolution; change *(in ideas)*.
evolucionar, *v.i.* evolve; *(mil.)* manoeuvre.
evolucionismo, *n.m.* evolutionism, Darwinism.
evolutivo, -va, *a.* evolutionary.
ex, *prefix.* ex-; *ex mujer*, ex-wife.
ex abrupto, *n.m.* outburst; sudden violent remark.
exacerbar, *v.t.* exacerbate.—*v.r.* become exacerbated.
exactitud, *n.f.* exactitude.
exacto, -ta, *a.* exact, accurate; punctual.
exageración, *n.f.* exaggeration.
exagerar, *v.t.* exaggerate.
exaltación, *n.f.* exaltation.

exaltado, -da, *a.* hot-headed; ultra-radical; extremist.
exaltar, *v.t.* exalt.—*v.r.* become excited.
examen, *n.m.* examination.
examinador, -ra, *a.* examining.—*n.m.f.* examiner.
examinando, -da, *n.m.f.* examinee.
examinar, *v.t.* examine, inspect.—*v.t.* take an examination *(de,* in).
exangüe, *a.* bloodless; anaemic.
exánime, *a.* lifeless; fainting.
exasperación, *n.f.* exasperation.
exasperar, *v.t.* exasperate.
excarcelar, *v.t.* release *(from prison)*.
excavación, *n.f.* excavation.
excavador, -ra, *a.* excavating.—*n.m.f.* excavator.—*n.f.* steam shovel.
excavar, *v.t.* excavate.
excedente, *a.* excess; redundant.—*n.m.* excess.
exceder, *v.t., v.i.* exceed.—*v.r.* go too far; *excederse a sí mismo*, outdo oneself.
Excelencia, *n.m.f.* Excellency *(title)*; excelencia, *n.f.* excellence; *por* —, par excellence.
excelsitud, *n.f.* sublimity.
el Excelso, *n.m.* the Most High; excelso, -sa, *a.* lofty, sublime.
excentricidad, *n.f.* eccentricity.
excéntrico, -ca, *a.* eccentric.
excepción, *n.f.* exception; *a* — *de*, except, with the exception of.
excepcional, *a.* exceptional.
excepto, *prep.* except(ing), but.
exceptuar [M], *v.t.* except; exempt.
excesivo, -va, *a.* excessive, immoderate.
exceso, *n.m.* excess; — *de peso*, excess weight.
excitable, *a.* excitable.
excitación, *n.f.* excitation, excitement.
excitante, *a.* exciting.
excitar, *v.t.* excite.
exclamación, *n.f.* exclamation.
exclamar, *v.i.* exclaim.
exclamativo, -va, exclamatorio, -ria, *a.* exclamatory.
exclaustrar, *v.t.* secularize *(a monk)*.
excluir [O], *v.t.* exclude.
exclusión, *n.f.* exclusion; *con* — *de*, with the exclusion of, excluding.
exclusive, *adv.* exclusively.
exclusivo, -va, *a.* exclusive.—*n.f.* refusal; exclusive rights.
excomulgar [B], *v.t.* excommunicate; *(fam.)* send to Coventry.
excomunión, *n.f.* excommunication.
excoriar, *v.t.* excoriate.—*v.r.* skin.
excrecencia, *n.f.* excrescence.
excremental, *a.* excremental.
excrementar, *v.i.* move the bowels.
excrementicio, -cia, *a.* excremental.
excremento, *n.m.* excrement.
excretar, *v.t., v.i.* excrete.
exculpación, *n.f.* exculpation.
exculpar, *v.t.* exculpate.
excursión, *n.f.* excursion, trip.
excursionista, *a.* rel. to an excursion.—*n.m.f.* excursionist.
excusa, *n.f.* excuse.
excusable, *a.* excusable, pardonable.
excusadamente, *adv.* unnecessarily.
excusado, -da, *a.* exempt; unnecessary; reserved, private.—*n.m.* lavatory.

excusar, *v.t.* excuse; avoid; hinder; exempt; *excusas venir,* you do not have to come.—*v.r.* make one's apologies; decline (*de hacer,* to do).
execrable, *a.* execrable.
execración, *n.f.* execration.
exención, *n.f.* exemption.
exencionar, *v.t.* exempt.
exentar, *v.t.* exempt.
exento, -ta, *a.* exempt.
exequible, *a.* attainable, feasible.
exhalación, *n.f.* exhalation; shooting star; fume; *como una* —, (*fam.*) like a shot.
exhalar, *v.t.* exhale, emit (*vapours*).—*v.r.* exhale; breathe hard.
exhaustivo, -va, *a.* exhaustive.
exhausto, -ta, *a.* exhausted.
exheredar, *v.t.* disinherit.
exhibición, *n.f.* exhibition.
exhibir, *v.t.* exhibit.
exhilarante, *a.* exhilarating; laughing (*gas*).
exhortar, *v.t.* exhort.
exhumar, *v.t.* exhume.
exigencia, *n.f.* exigency.
exigente, *a.* exacting, demanding, exigent.
exigible, exigidero, -ra, *a.* exigible.
exigir [E], *v.t.* exact, demand.
exiguo, -gua, *a.* exiguous.
exil(i)ar, *v.t.* exile.
exilio, *n.m.* exile.
eximio, -mia, *a.* select, choice.
eximir, *v.t.* exempt.
existencia, *n.f.* existence.—*pl.* stock(s).
existencial, *a.* existential.
existencialista, *a.*, *n.m.f.* existentialist.
existente, *a.* existent; extant; (*com.*) to hand.
existir, *v.i.* exist.
éxito, *n.m.* outcome, result; success.
éxodo, *n.m.* exodus.
exogamia, *n.f.* exogamy.
exonerar, *v.t.* exonerate, acquit.—*v.r.* relieve oneself, defecate.
exorbitante, *a.* exorbitant.
exorcismo, *n.m.* exorcism.
exorcizar [C], *v.t.* exorcize.
exordio, *n.m.* exordium.
exornar, *v.t.* adorn.
exoticidad, *n.f.* exoticism.
exótico, -ca, *a.* exotic; foreign-grown (*timber etc.*).
exotismo, *n.m.* exoticism.
expansible, *a.* expansible, dilatable.
expansión, *n.f.* expansion; expansiveness; recreation.
expansivo, -va, *a.* expansive.
expatriado, -da, *a.* expatriate.—*n.m.f.* expatriate; displaced person.
expatriar, *v.t.* expatriate.—*v.r.* go *or* settle abroad.
expectación, *n.f.* expectation, expectance.
expectante, *a.* expectant.
expectativa, *n.f.* expectation.
expectorar, *v.t.* expectorate.
expedición, *n.f.* expedition; shipment; despatch.
expedicionario, -ria, *a.* expeditionary.
expedidor, -ra, *a.* (*com.*) forwarding, shipping.—*n.m.f.* (*com.*) shipper, merchant.
expediente, *n.m.* expedient; (*jur.*) proceedings, dossier; motive.
expedir [8], *v.t.* send, ship, remit; expedite.

expeditivo, -va, expedito, -ta, *a.* expeditious.
expeler, *v.t.* expel.
expendedor, -ra, *a.* spending.—*n.m.f.* dealer, agent; utterer (*of coins*).
expendeduría, *n.f.* retail shop (*for monopoly goods*).
expender, *v.t.* spend, expend; sell (*retail*); (*jur.*) pass (*counterfeit coins*).
expendio, *n.m.* expense; (*S.A.*) retail store; (*S.A.*) retailing.
expensas, *n.f.pl.* expenses.
experiencia, *n.f.* experience; experiment.
experimentado, -da, *a.* experienced, expert.
experimentar, *v.t.* experience; test; undergo.—*v.i.* experiment.
experimento, *n.m.* experiment, test.
experto, -ta, *a.*, *n.m.f.* expert.
expiable, *a.* expiable.
expiar, *v.t.* expiate.
expiración, *n.f.* expiration.
expirante, *a.* expiring.
expirar, *v.i.* expire.
explanada, *n.f.* esplanade.
explanar, *v.t.* level; explain.
explayar, *v.t.* extend.—*v.r.* dwell upon a subject; unbosom oneself.
expletivo, -va, *a.* expletive.
explicable, *a.* explainable, explicable.
explicación, *n.f.* explanation.
explicar [A], *v.t.* explain.—*v.r.* give an explanation; understand.
explicativo, -va, *a.* explanatory.
explícito, -ta, *a.* explicit.
exploración, *n.f.* exploration.
explorador, -ra, *a.* exploring; scouting.—*n.m.f.* explorer; boy-scout; (*mil.*) scout.—*n.m.* (*T.V.*) scanner.
explorar, *v.t.* explore; investigate; (*mil.*) scout; (*T.V.*) scan.
exploratorio, -ria, *a.* exploratory.
explosión, *n.f.* explosion, burst.
explosivo, -va, *a.* explosive.
explotable, *a.* exploitable.
explotación, *n.f.* exploitation; (*min.*) working; operation.
explotar, *v.t.* exploit; operate (*an airline etc.*); (*neol.*) explode (*also v.i.*).
exponente, *a.* exponent.—*n.m.f.* exponent; (*com.*) exhibitor.
exponer [25], *v.t.* expose; expound; disclose; exhibit.—*v.r.* run a risk.
exportación, *n.f.* export, exportation.
exportador, -ra, *a.* exporting.—*n.m.f.* exporter.
exportar, *v.t.* export.
exposición, *n.f.* display, exhibition; (*phot.*) exposure; explanation; (*eccl.*) benediction.
expositivo, -va, *a.* explanatory.
expósito, -ta, *a.*, *n.m.f.* foundling.
expositor, -ra, *a.* explaining; exhibiting.—*n.m.f.* expounder; exhibitor.
expresado, -da, *a.* aforesaid.
expresar, *v.t.* express; utter.
expresión, *n.f.* expression; gift; pressing out.
expresivo, -va, *a.* expressive.
expreso, -sa, *a.* expressed; express.—*adv.* on purpose.—*n.m.* express train.
exprimidera, *n.f.* squeezer.
exprimir, *v.t.* squeeze (out).
expropiación, *n.f.* expropriation.
expropiar, *v.t.* expropriate.

expuesto, -ta, *a.* exposed; liable, in danger.— *p.p.* [EXPONER].
expugnar, *v.t.* (*mil.*) take by storm.
expulsar, *v.t.* eject, drive out.
expulsión, *n.f.* expulsion.
expulso, -sa, *a.* expelled; ejected, outcast.
expurgar [B], *v.t.* expurgate.
exquisito, -ta, *a.* exquisite.
extasiar [L], *v.r.* be delighted; go into ecstasies.
éxtasis, *n.f. inv.* ecstasy.
extático, -ca, *a.* ecstatic.
extemporaneamente, *adv.* untimely; extempore.
extemporáneo, -a, *a.* ill-timed.
extender [2], *v.t., v.r.* extend, stretch; widen.
extensión, *n.f.* extension; stretch.
extensivo, -va, *a.* extensive.
extenso, -sa, *a.* extensive; extended; *por —,* in full.
extenuar [M], *v.t.* attenuate, diminish.—*v.r.* languish.
exterior, *a.* exterior; external; foreign; overlooking the street (*room*).—*n.m.* exterior, outside; abroad.
exteriorizar [C], *v.t.* make manifest.—*v.r.* unbosom oneself.
exterminar, *v.t.* exterminate.
exterminio, *n.m.* extermination.
externado, *n.m.* day-school.
externo, -na, *a.* external; outward; exterior. —*n.m.f.* day-pupil.
extinción, *n.f.* extinction.
extinguible, *a.* extinguishable.
extinguir [G], *v.t.* extinguish, quench; extirpate.
extinto, -ta, *a.* extinguished; extinct; (*S.A.*) deceased.
extintor, *n.m.* fire-extinguisher.
extirpación, *n.f.* extirpation.
extirpar, *v.t.* extirpate.
extorsión, *n.f.* extortion.
extra, *prefix.* extra-; *— de,* in addition to.— *n.m.f.* (*theat.*) extra.—*n.m.* tip.
extracción, *n.f.* extraction.
extracto, *n.m.* extract; abstract; summary.
extradición, *n.f.* extradition.
extraer [34], *v.t.* extract.
extranjero, -ra, *a.* foreign.—*n.m.f.* foreigner. —*n.m.* en or *a —,* abroad.
extrañamiento, *n.m.* alienation; deportation.
extrañar, *v.t.* alienate; expatriate; find strange; be surprised at.—*v.i.* be strange.—*v.r.* be surprised; wonder; refuse.
extrañez, extrañeza, *n.f.* strangeness.
extraño, -ña, *a.* strange; foreign; extraneous. —*n.m.f.* stranger; foreigner.
extraordinario, -ria, *a.* extraordinary, out of the ordinary; extra; *horas extraordinarias,* overtime.
extrarradio, *n.m.* outskirts.
extravagancia, *n.f.* extravagance; oddness.
extravagante, *a.* extravagant; eccentric.
extraviar [L], *v.t.* mislead; misplace; embezzle.—*v.r.* go astray; err.
extravío, *n.m.* deviation, aberration.
extremado, -da, *a.* extreme, consummate.
extremeño, -ña, *a.* (*geog.*) rel. to Extremadura.—*n.m.f.* native of Extremadura.
extremidad, *n.f.* extremity.
extremista, *a., n.m.f.* extremist.

extremo, -ma, *a.* extreme, last.—*n.m.* extreme.
exuberancia, *n.f.* exuberance.
exudar, *v.t., v.i.* exude.
exultación, *n.f.* exultation.
exvoto, *n.m.* (*relig.*) votive offering.
eyacular, *v.t.* (*med.*) ejaculate.
eyección, *n.f.* ejection.
eyector, *n.m.* ejector (*of a gun*).
Ezequías, *n.m.* (*Bib.*) Hezekiah.
Ezequial, *n.m.* (*Bib.*) Ezekiel.

F

F, f, *n.f.* seventh letter of the Spanish alphabet.
fa, *n.m.* (*mus.*) (key of) F.
fabada, *n.f.* pork and beans.
fábrica, *n.f.* factory, mill; building, structure, (*esp. eccl.*) fabric.
fabricación, *n.f.* manufacture.
fabricante, *a.* manufacturing.—*n.m.f.* manufacturer.
fabricar [A], *v.t.* manufacture, make; devise.
fábula, *n.f.* fable.
fabuloso, -sa, *a.* fabulous.
faca, *n.f.* sheath-knife.
facción, *n.f.* faction; (*esp. pl.*) feature (*face*); (*mil.*) duty.
faccioso, -sa, *a.* factious.—*n.m.f.* agitator.
faceta, *n.f.* facet.
facial, *a.* facial; *valor —,* face value.
facies, *n.f.* (*med.*) facies, appearance.
fácil, *a.* easy; facile; compliant; probable.
facilidad, *n.f.* facility, ease.
facilitar, *v.t.* facilitate; provide.
facineroso, -sa, *a.* villainous.—*n.m.f.* rascal; criminal.
facistol, *n.m.* lectern.
facsímil, facsímile, *n.m.* facsimile.
factible, *a.* feasible.
facticio, -cia, *a.* factitious.
factor, *n.m.* factor; freight agent; victualler.
factoría, *n.f.* factory, trading post; factorage.
factura, *n.f.* execution, workmanship; invoice, bill.
facturar, *v.t.* invoice; (*rail.*) register, (*U.S.*) check.
facultad, *n.f.* faculty; permission, licence.
facultar, *v.t.* authorize, empower.
facultativo, -va, *a.* optional, facultative. —*n.m.* physician; surgeon.
facundia, *n.f.* eloquence.
facundo, -da, *a.* eloquent; loquacious.
facha, *n.f.* (*fam.*) face, appearance.
fachada, *n.f.* façade; frontispiece (*of a book*).
fachado, -da, *a. bien* (or *mal*) *—,* good- (*or* unpleasant-) looking.
fada, *n.f.* fairy; witch; (sort of) apple.
faena, *n.f.* task, chore, job; (*mil.*) fatigue; each part of a bull-fight.
faenero, *n.m.* (*S.A.*) farm labourer.
fagocita, *n.m.* (*med.*) phagocyte.
fagot, *n.m.* (*mus.*) bassoon; bassoonist.
fagotista, *n.m.f.* (*mus.*) bassoonist.

faisán, *n.m.* pheasant.
faja, *n.f.* sash, girdle, belt, cummerbund; wrapper (*book*); zone; (*rad.*) channel; (*aer.*) strip; (*aer.*) apron (*airport*); (*arch.*) fascia; swaddling clothes.
fajar, *v.t.* swaddle, swathe; girdle; (*S.A.*) thrash; — **con,** (*S.A.*) set upon.
fajardo, *n.m.* (*cul.*) meat pie; vol-au-vent.
fajina, *n.f.* faggot; (*mil.*) lights out, retreat; (*agr.*) shock, stook.
fajo, *n.m.* bundle, sheaf.
falacia, *n.f.* fraud, deceit.
Falange, *n.f.* (*pol.*) Falange; **falange, n.f.** phalanx.
falangero, *n.m.* (*zool.*) phalanger.
falangia, n.f., falangio, n.m. (*zool.*) daddy-long-legs.
falangista, a., n.m.f. (*pol.*) Falangist.
falaz, a. (*pl.* **-aces**) deceitful; treacherous.
falca, n.f. weatherboard; (*naut.*) gunwale.
falce, n.f. sickle.
falda, n.f. skirt; lower slope (*of a hill*); loin (*of meat*); (*esp. pl., fam.*) women.
faldero, -ra, a. rel. to the lap; **perro —,** lap-dog.
faldeta, n.f. small skirt; (*theat.*) drop-curtain.
faldillas, n.f.pl. skirts; coat-tails.
faldistorio, n.m. (*eccl.*) faldstool.
faldón, n.m. coat-tail; shirt-tail; flap; hip (*roof*).
faldriquera, n.f. pocket.
falencia, n.f. fallacy; mistake; (*S.A.*) bankruptcy.
falible, a. fallible.
fálico, -ca, a. phallic.
falo, n.m. phallus.
de falondres, *adv. phr.* (*naut., S.A.*) suddenly, briskly.
falsario, -ria, a. falsifying.—*n.m.f.* forger.
falsear, v.t. falsify, forge, counterfeit; pierce.—*v.i.* sag; be out of tune (*string*).
falsedad, n.f. falsehood; deceit; perfidy.
falseo, n.m. bevelling.
falsete, n.m. spigot; (*U.S.*) tap; small door; falsetto.
falsificación, n.f. falsification.
falsificar [A], *v.t.* falsify; forge, counterfeit.
falso, -sa, a. untrue; false; sham, mock.—*n.m.* facing (*clothes*).—*n.f.* (*mus.*) dissonance.
falta, n.f. lack; want; fault; flaw; (*med.*) missed period; **a — de,** for want of; **hacer —,** be necessary; **me hacían —,** I needed them, I missed them; **— de pago,** non-payment; **sin —,** without fail.
faltante, a. wanting, missing.
faltar, v.t. offend.—*v.i.* be wanting; be missing *or* deficient; lack; fall short; **— a su palabra,** be untrue to one's word; **¡ no faltaba más !** but of course!
falto, -ta, a. wanting, lacking; mean; short (*weight*).
faltoso, -sa, a. (*fam.*) non compos mentis.
faltriquera, n.f. pocket; pouch.
falúa, n.f. (*naut.*) gig, tender.
falucho, n.m. (*naut.*) felucca, lateen-rigged vessel.
falla, n.f. (*S.A.*) defect, fault; (*geol.*) fault, break; (*dial.*) float.
fallar, v.t. trump, ruff (*at cards*).—*v.i.* fail, be deficient; break, give way.
falleba, n.f. latch, bolt, fastener.
fallecer [9], *v.i.* die, pass away; expire.

fallecimiento, n.m. decease.
fallido, -da, a. frustrated; bankrupt.
fallo, -lla, a. (*S.A.*) simple, silly; (*cards*) — **a,** lacking in; **estoy — a bastos,** I have no clubs.—*n.m.* judgement, decision.
fama, n.f. fame; reputation; rumour.
famélico, -ca, a. hungry, ravenous.
familia, n.f. family; household.
familiar, a. domestic; familiar.—*n.m.* household servant; familiar spirit; (*eccl.*) familiar.
familiaridad, n.f. familiarity.
familiarizar [C], *v.t.* familiarize; popularize.—*v.r.* accustom oneself (**con,** to).
famoso, -sa, a. celebrated; famous; notorious.
fámulo, -la, n.m.f. (*fam.*) servant.
fanal, n.m. lighthouse.
fanático, -ca, a. fanatic.
fanatismo, n.m. fanaticism.
fandango, n.m. fandango; disorder.
fanega, n.f. a grain measure (*c.* 1.5 *bushels*); a surface measure (*c.* 1.5 *acres*).
fanfarria, n.f. (*fam.*) arrogance, swagger.
fanfarrón, -rrona, a. swaggering, boasting; bullying.
fanfarronear, v.i. bluster.
fangal, fangar, n.m. swamp, bog.
fango, n.m. mud; ooze; sludge.
fangoso, -sa, a. muddy.
fantasear, v.t. dream of.—*v.i.* daydream.
fantasía, n.f. imagination; fancy; fantasy, caprice; (*mus.*) fantasia; **de —,** fancy.
fantasma, n.m. phantom; apparition, ghost.
fantasmagoría, n.f. phantasmagoria.
fantasmagórico, -ca, a. phantasmagoric.
fantástico, -ca, a. imaginary; fantastic; conceited.
fantoche, n.m. puppet; (*fam.*) nincompoop.
farad, faradio, n.m. (*elec.*) farad.
farallón, n.m. headland, cliff; outcrop.
faramalla, n.f. (*fam.*) cajoling; claptrap.
farándula, n.f. (*obs.*) strolling troupe; (*S.A.*) bunch, crowd; din.
faraón, n.m. pharaoh; faro (*cards*).
faraute, n.m. herald, messenger; prologue (*actor*).
fardel, n.m. bag, bundle.
fardela, n.f. (*orn.*) shearwater.
fardo, n.m. bale, bundle.
fárfara, n.m. (*bot.*) coltsfoot; membrane (*of an egg*); **en —,** immature, (*fam.*) half-baked.
farfolla, n.f. husk (*maize*); (*fam.*) sham, fake.
farfullar, v.t. gabble; stumble through (*a lesson*).
fargallón, -llona, a. (*fam.*) slapdash.—*n.m.f.* botcher; bungler.
farináceo, -cea, a. farinaceous.
fariseo, n.m. Pharisee.
farmacéutico, -ca, a. pharmaceutical.—*n.m.f.* pharmacist, dispensing chemist.—*n.f.* pharmaceutics.
farmacia, n.f. pharmacy, (*Brit.*) chemist's shop, (*U.S.*) drugstore.
farmacología, n.f. pharmacology.
farmacológico, -ca, a. pharmacological.
farmacólogo, -ga, n.m.f. pharmacologist.
farmacopea, n.f. pharmacopoeia.
faro, n.m. lighthouse; (*auto.*) headlight; beacon.
farol, n.m. lantern; street lamp; (*fam.*) conceited fellow.
farola, n.f. large street lamp; beacon.

farra, *n.f.* (*ichth.*) sea trout; (*S.A.*) spree.
fárrago, *n.m.* farrago; hodgepodge.
farro, *n.m.* peeled barley; spelt wheat.
farsa, *n.f.* farce.
farsante, *a.*, *n.m.f.* humbug.
fascículo, *n.m.* fascicle *or* fascicule.
fascinación, *n.f.* fascination, bewitchment.
fascinador, *a.* fascinating.—*n.m.f.* charmer.
fascinante, *a.* fascinating.
fascinar, *v.t.* fascinate, bewitch; allure.
fascismo, *n.m.* fascism.
fascista, *a.*, *n.m.f.* fascist.
fase, *n.f.* phase, stage.
fásol, *n.m.* (*esp. pl.*) French bean; string bean.
fastidiar, *v.t.* sicken; annoy; disappoint.
fastidio, *n.m.* squeamishness; loathing; boredom; fatigue.
fastidioso, -sa, *a.* sickening; annoying; boring; vexed.
fastigio, *n.m.* pinnacle.
fasto, -ta, *a.* auspicious (*event*).—*n.m.* pomp, pageantry.—*pl.* annals.
fastoso, -sa, *a.* pompous, ostentatious.
fatal, *a.* fatal; mortal, deadly; (*fam.*) inevitable.
fatalidad, *n.f.* destiny; ill-fortune; necessity.
fatalismo, *n.m.* fatalism.
fatídico, -ca, *a.* fatidic; fateful.
fatiga, *n.f.* weariness; fatigue; stress.
fatigante, fatigador, -ra, *a.* [FATIGOSO].
fatigar [B], *v.t.* tire; annoy; strain.—*v.r.* get tired.
fatigoso, -sa, *a.* troublesome; wearisome, tiring; tedious.
fatuidad, *n.f.* fatuity; stupidity.
fatuo, -tua, *a.* fatuous; conceited; *fuego —,* will-o'-the-wisp.
fauno, *n.m.* faun.
fausto, -ta, *a.* fortunate; prosperous.—*n.m.* splendour; pomp.
faustoso, -sa, *a.* pompous, luxurious.
fautor, -ra, *n.m.f.* abettor, one who countenances.
favor, *n.m.* favour; *por —,* please.
favorable, *a.* favourable.
favorecer [9], *v.t.* favour.—*v.r.* avail oneself (*de,* of).
favorito, -ta, *a.*, *n.m.f.* favourite.
fayanca, *n.f.* unsteady posture; *de —,* carelessly.
faz, *n.m.* (*pl.* faces) face; (*fig.*) — *a —,* face to face.
fe, *n.f.* faith; religion; certificate; testimony; *dar — de,* attest to; — *de erratas,* errata slip.
fealdad, *n.f.* ugliness; turpitude.
feble, *a.* feeble, weak; light-weight (*coin*).—*n.m.* foible.
Febo, *n.m.* (*myth.*) Phoebus.
febrero, *n.m.* February.
febril, *a.* febrile.
fecal, *a.* faecal.
fécula, *n.f.* starch.
feculento, -ta, *a.* feculent; starchy.
fecundante, *a.* fertilizing, fecundating.
fecundar, *v.t.* fertilize, fecundate.
fecundidad, *n.f.* fecundity. fruitfulness.
fecundo, -da, *a.* fecund.
fecha, *n.f.* date, time.
fechador, *n.m.* (*S.A.*) cancelling stamp.
fechar, *v.t.* date (*a letter*).
fechoría, *n.f.* misdeed.

federación, *n.f.* federation.
federal, *a.* federal.
federalismo, *n.m.* federalism.
federar, *v.t.* federate.
Federico, *n.m.* Frederick.
fehaciente, *a.* (*jur.*) authentic.
feldespato, *n.m.* (*min.*) feldspar.
felicidad, *n.f.* felicity.
felicitación, *n.f.* congratulation, felicitation.
felicitar, *v.t.* congratulate, felicitate.
félido, -da, *a.* feline.—*n.m.* (*zool.*) felid.
feligrés, -gresa, *n.m.f.* parishioner.
feligresía, *n.f.* parish.
felino, -na, *a.*, *n.m.* feline, (*zool.*) felid.
Felipe, *n.m.* Philip.
feliz, *a.* (*pl.* -ices) happy; lucky.
felón, -lona, *a.* treacherous; felonious, criminal.
felonía, *n.f.* treachery.
felpa, *n.f.* plush; (*fam.*) good dressing-down.
felpado, -da, *a.* plushy, velvety.
felpilla, *n.f.* chenille.
felposo, -sa, *a.* plushy, velvety; downy.—*n.m.* mat.
felpudo, *n.m.* mat.
femenil, *a.* feminine, womanish.
femenino, -na, *a.* feminine; (*bot.*) female.
feminidad, *n.f.* feminity.
feminismo, *n.m.* feminism.
fenda, *n.f.* crack, split.
fenecer [9], *v.t.* finish, terminate.—*v.i.* end, die.
fenecimiento, *n.m.* end, termination; death.
fenicio, -cia, *a.*, *n.m.f.* Phoenician.
fénico, -ca, *a.* carbolic.
fénix, *n.m.* (*myth.*) phoenix.
fenol, *n.m.* phenol, carbolic acid.
fenomenal, *a.* phenomenal.
fenómeno, *n.m.* phenomenon.
feo, fea, *a.* ugly; alarming.
feraz, *a.* (*pl.* -aces) fertile.
féretro, *n.m.* bier.
feria, *n.f.* fair, market; weekday; holiday; (*S.A.*) tip.
feriado, -da, *a.* *día —,* holiday.
feriar, *v.t.* buy; sell.—*v.i.* take a holiday.
ferino, -na, *a.* wild; savage; *tos ferina,* whooping cough.
fermentable, *a.* fermentable.
fermentación, *n.f.* fermentation.
fermentar, *v.t.*, *v.i.* ferment.
fermento, *n.m.* ferment. leaven.
Fernando, *n.m.* Ferdinand.
ferocidad, *n.f.* ferocity.
feroz, *a.* (*pl.* -oces) ferocious, savage.
ferrar [1], *v.t.* cover with iron.
ferrato, *n.m.* (*chem.*) ferrate.
férreo, -rrea, *a.* iron, ferreous; *vía férrea,* railway.
ferrería, *n.f.* ironworks, foundry.
ferrete, *n.m.* sulphate of copper; iron punch.
ferretería, *n.f.* ironmongery, hardware store.
férrico, -ca, *a.* ferric.
ferrocarril, *n.m.* railway, (*U.S.*) railroad.
ferrocarrilero, -ra, *a.*, *n.m.f.* (*S.A.*) railway employee.
ferroconcreto, ferrohormigón, *n.m.* ferroconcrete.
ferroso, -sa, *a.* ferrous.
ferrovía, *n.f.* railway, (*U.S.*) railroad.
ferrovial, *a.* rel. to the railway.

ferroviario, -ria, *a.* rel. to the railway.—
n.m.f. railway employee.
ferruginoso, -sa, *a.* ferruginous, iron.
fértil, *a.* fertile.
fertilidad, *n.f.* fertility.
fertilización, *n.f.* fertilization.
fertilizante, *a.* fertilizing.—*n.m.* fertilizer
(*manure*).
fertilizar [C], *v.t.* fertilize.
férula, *n.f.* ferule, cane; (*fig.*) yoke; (*med.*)
splint.
férvido, -da, *a.* fervid.
ferviente, *a.* fervent.
fervor, *n.m.* fervour.
fervoroso, -sa, *a.* fervent.
festejar, *v.t.* fête, entertain; court; (*S.A.*)
thrash.
festejo, *n.m.* feast, entertainment; courtship.
festín, *n.m.* banquet.
festival, *n.m.* festival.
festividad, *n.f.* festivity; witticism.
festivo, -va, *a.* gay; festive; witty; *día* —,
holiday.
fetal, *a.* foetal.
fetiche, *n.m.* fetish.
fetichismo, *n.m.* fetishism.
fetidez, *n.f.* fetidity; stink.
fétido, -da, *a.* fetid, stinking.
feto, *n.m.* foetus.
feudal, *a.* feudal.
feudalidad, *n.f.,* **feudalismo,** *n.m.* feudalism.
feudo, *n.m.* fief; feudal due.
fiable, *a.* trustworthy.
fiado, -da, *a.* trusting; *al* —, on credit; *en* —,
on bail.
fiador, -ra, *n.m.f.* bondsman, guarantor, bail,
surety.—*n.m.* pawl; trigger; safety-catch;
tumbler (*of lock*).
fiambre, *a.* served cold (*of food*).—*n.m.* cold
meat; cold lunch; (*fig.*) stale joke, chestnut.
fiambrera, *n.f.* lunch basket; dinner pail,
lunch pail.
fianza, *n.f.* guarantee, surety.
fiar [L], *v.t.* guarantee, go surety for; entrust;
sell on trust.—*v.r.* trust (*a, de,* in).
fiasco, *n.m.* fiasco.
fibra, *n.f.* fibre; grain (*of wood*); (*fig.*) vigour.
fibravidrio, *n.m.* fibreglass.
fibroideo, -dea, *a.* fibroid.
fibroso, -sa, *a.* fibrous.
ficción, *n.f.* fiction.
ficcionario, -ria, *a.* fictional.
fice, *n.m.* (*ichth.*) whiting; hake.
ficticio, -cia, *a.* fictitious.
ficha, *n.f.* counter, chip; index-card; (*police*)
dossier; — *perforada,* punched card.
fichador, -ra, *a.* filing.—*n.m.f.* filing clerk.
fichar, *v.t.* file (*cards, papers etc.*); play (*a
piece at dominoes*); (*fam.*) black-list.
fichero, *n.m.* filing cabinet; file.
fidedigno, -na, *a.* reliable, trustworthy.
fideicomisario, *n.m.* trustee; fideicommis-
sary.
fidelidad, *n.f.* fidelity; punctiliousness.
fidelísimo, -ma, *a. sup. of* FIEL.
fideos, *n.m.pl.* vermicelli.
fiduciario, -ria, *a.* fiduciary.
fiebre, *n.f.* fever.
fiel, *a.* faithful, honest; punctilious.—*n.m.*
inspector of weights and measures; pointer
(*of scales*).
fieltro, *n.m.* felt.

fiereza, *n.f.* ferocity, cruelty; ugliness.
fiero, -ra, *a.* fierce; terrible; cruel; ugly;
proud, haughty; wild.—*n.m.pl.* beasts.—*n.f.*
wild animal; (*taur.*) bull.
fiesta, *n.f.* feast, holy day; holiday; festivity;
— *brava,* bullfighting.
figura, *n.f.* figure; countenance; face-card;
(*theat.*) character.
figuración, *n.f.* figuration; (*theat.*) extras;
(*S.A.*) rôle in society.
figuranta, *n.f.* figurante, ballet-dancer.
figurante, *n.m.* figurant, ballet-dancer.
figurar, *v.t.* figure; depict; feign.—*v.i.*
figure, participate.—*v.r.* imagine.
figurativo, -va, *a.* figurative.
figurilla, figurita, *n.f.* figurine; (*fam.*) runt.
figurín, *n.m.* dummy, lay figure; (*fig.*) dandy.
figurón, *n.m.* (*fam.*) pretentious nobody;
(*naut.*) — *de proa,* figurehead.
fijación, *n.f.* fixation; fastening.
fijador, -ra, *a.* fixing.—*n.m.f.* fixer.—*n.m.*
(*phot.*) fixing solution; — *de pelo,* hair
cream.
fijar, *v.t.* fix, fasten; glue; settle, establish;
(*phot.*) fix.—*v.r.* settle; *fijarse en,* notice,
look closely at.
fijeza, *n.f.* firmness; fixity.
fijo, -ja, *a.* fixed, permanent; firm; secure;
de —, (*S.A.*) *a la fija,* surely; without
doubt.
fila, *n.f.* row, file, rank; *en filas,* (*mil.*) on
active service.
filamento, *n.m.* filament.
filantropía, *n.f.* philanthropy.
filantrópico, -ca, *a.* philanthropic(al).
filatelia, *n.f.* philately.
filatura, *n.f.* spinning; spinning-mill.
filete, *n.m.* fillet (*of meat*); welt; thread (*of a
screw*).
filfa, *n.f.* (*fam.*) fib, fake, hoax.
filiación, *n.f.* filiation; relationship.
filial, *a.* filial.—*n.f.* (*com.*) affiliate, subsidiary.
filibustero, *n.m.* freebooter.
filigrana, *n.f.* filigree; watermark.
las Filipinas, *n.f.pl.* the Philippines.
filipino, -na, *a.* Filipino *or* Philippine.—
n.m.f. Filipino.
filisteo, -tea, *a., n.m.f.* Philistine.
film, *n.m.* (*cine.*) film.
filmar, *v.t.* (*cine.*) film.
filo, *n.m.* edge, cutting edge; dividing-line;
arris; *dar* — *a,* sharpen; *por* —, exactly.
filología, *n.f.* philology.
filológico, -ca, *a.* philological.
filón, *n.m.* (*min.*) vein; lode; (*fig.*) gold mine.
filoseda, *n.f.* silk and wool *or* cotton.
filosofal, *a. piedra* —, philosopher's stone.
filosofar, *v.i.* philosophize.
filosofía, *n.f.* philosophy.
filosófico, -ca, *a.* philosophic(al).
filtración, *n.f.* filtration.
filtrador, *n.m.* filter.
filtrar, *v.t.* filter.—*v.i., v.r.* filter through,
seep through.
filtro, *n.m.* filter; philtre.
filván, *n.m.* wire-edge (*on a tool*).
fimo, *n.m.* mire.
fin, *n.m. or f.* end, conclusion.—*n.m.* end,
object, purpose; *al* —, at last; *en* —, *por* —,
finally; *a fines de,* towards the end of;
un sin — *de,* an infinity of.
finado, -da, *a.* dead, deceased, late.

final

final, *a.* final.—*n.m.* end, conclusion.
finalidad, *n.f.* end, purpose.
finalizar [C], *v.t., v.i.* conclude.
finamiento, *n.m.* decease.
financiero, -ra, *a.* financial.—*n.m.f.* financier.
finar, *v.i.* die.—*v.r.* long for, (*fam.*) be dying for (*por,* for).
finca, *n.f.* property, (real) estate; farm.
fincar [A], *v.i.* buy real estate.—*v.r.* (*esp. S.A.*) reside.
finés, -nesa, *a.* Finnish.—*n.m.f.* Finn.—*n.m.* Finnish (*language*).
fineza, *n.f.* fineness; favour.
fingir [E], *v.t., v.i.* feign, pretend.—*v.r.* pretend to be.
finiquito, *n.m.* (*com.*) final settlement.
finito, -ta, *a.* finite.
finlandés, -desa, *a.* Finnish.—*n.m.f.* Finn.—*n.m.* Finnish (*language*).
Finlandia, *n.f.* Finland.
fino, -na, *a.* fine; sheer; courteous, refined, polite; cunning, shrewd.
finura, *n.f.* fineness; courtesy.
firma, *n.f.* signature; (*com.*) firm.
firmamento, *n.m.* firmament.
firmante, *a., n.m.f.* signatory.
firmar, *v.t., v.i.* sign.
firme, *a.* firm, steady; *de* —, steadily, constantly; *¡ firmes !* (*mil.*) attention!
firmeza, *n.f.* firmness; resolution.
fiscal, *a.* fiscal.—*n.m.* attorney-general; district attorney.
fiscalizar [C], *v.t.* prosecute; criticize; pry into; inspect; (*rad.*) monitor.
fisco, *n.m.* exchequer, treasury.
fisga, *n.f.* harpoon; banter, chaff.
fisgar [B], *v.t.* harpoon; pry into.—*v.i.* pry; mock.—*v.r.* mock.
fisgón, -na, *n.m.f.* jester, joker; busybody.
físico, -ca, *a.* physical.—*n.m.f.* physicist.—*n.m.* physique; (*obs.*) physician.—*n.f.* physics.
físil, *a.* fissile.
fisiología, *n.f.* physiology.
fisiológico, -ca, *a.* physiological.
fisión, *n.f.* (*phys.*) fission.
fisionomía, *n.f.* physiognomy.
fisioterapia, *n.f.* physiotherapy.
fisonomía, *n.f.* physiognomy.
fistol, *n.m.* crafty person; (*S.A.*) scarf pin.
fístula, *n.f.* (*med.*) fistula; (*mus.*) reed; conduit.
fisura, *n.f.* fissure.
fláccido, -da, *a.* flaccid, soft, lax.
flaco, -ca, *a.* weak; frail; lank, lean.—*n.m.* foible.
flacura, *n.f.* thinness; weakness.
flagelante, *a., n.m.f.* flagellant.
flagelar, *v.t.* flagellate, scourge, flay.
flagelo, *n.m.* whip, scourge.
flagrancia, *n.f.* flagrancy; ardour.
flagrante, *a.* (*poet.*) ardent; rampant; *en* —, in the act, red-handed.
flagrar, *v.i.* (*poet.*) blaze.
flamante, *a.* bright; brand-new; spick and span.
flamear, *v.i.* flame; (*naut., aer.*) flutter.
flamenco, -ca, *a.* Flemish; buxom; Andalusian gypsy, flamenco.—*n.m.f.* Fleming.—*n.m.* Flemish (*language*); (*orn.*) flamingo.
flamenquilla, *n.f.* (*bot.*) marigold.
flameo, *n.m.* (*aer.*) flutter.
flámula, *n.f.* streamer.

flan, *n.m.* (*cul.*) crème caramel; custard.
flanco, *n.m.* flank, face; side wall (*of tyre*).
Flandes, *n.m.* (*geog.*) Flanders.
flanquear, *v.t.* flank.
flanqueo, *n.m.* flanking, out-flanking.
flaquear, *v.i.* weaken, flag.
flaqueza, *n.f.* weakness; faintness.
flato, *n.m.* flatus, wind; (*S.A.*) gloominess.
flatulencia, *n.f.* flatulence, wind.
flatulento, -ta, *a.* flatulent.
flauta, *n.f.* (*mus.*) flute.
flautín, *n.m.* (*mus.*) piccolo.
flautista, *n.m.f.* flautist, flute-player.
fleco, *n.m.* fringe.
flecha, *n.f.* arrow.
flechador, *n.m.* archer.
flechar, *v.t.* draw (*the bow*); wound (*with an arrow*); (*fam.*) infatuate.
flechazo, *n.m.* shot with an arrow; love at first sight.
fleje, *n.m.* hoop; strip steel.
flema, *n.f.* phlegm; low wines (*alcohol*).
flemático, -ca, *a.* phlegmatic.
flequillo, *n.m.* fringe (*of hair*).
Flesinga, *n.f.* (*geog.*) Flushing.
fletador, *n.m.* (*naut., aer.*) charterer.
fletamento, *n.m.* chartering; charter party.
fletante, *n.m.* ship-owner.
fletar, *v.t.* (*naut., aer.*) charter; load; (*S.A.*) hire (*animal*).—*v.r.* (*S.A.*) vamoose.
flete, *n.m.* (*naut.*) cargo; (*naut.*) freightage; (*S.A.*) freight; (*S.A.*) horse.
flexibilidad, *n.f.* flexibility.
flexible, *a.* flexible, soft.—*n.m.* (*elec.*) cord; soft hat.
flexión, *n.f.* flexion; inflexion.
flexional, *a.* flexional; inflexional.
flirtear, *v.i.* flirt.
flojear, *v.i.* slacken.
flojedad, *n.f.* looseness, slackness, laxity.
flojel, *n.m.* nap (*of cloth*); down; *pato del* —, (*orn.*) eider.
flojo, -ja, *a.* loose, slack, sagging.
flor, *n.f.* flower; (*fig.*) compliment; — *de harina,* fine flour; *a* — *de,* flush with, along the surface of; *dar en la* —, get the knack.
floral, *a.* floral.
florar, *v.i.* flower, bloom.
florear, *v.t.* adorn with flowers; bolt (*flour*).—*v.i.* flourish a sword; pay compliments.
florecer [9], *v.i.* flower, bloom; flourish.—*v.r.* go mouldy.
floreciente, *a.* flourishing; blooming.
Florencia, *n.f.* (*geog.*) Florence.
florentino, -na, *a., n.m.f.* Florentine.
floreo, *n.m.* flourish (*in fencing or music*); idle talk.
florero, -ra, *a.* flattering; jesting.—*n.m.f.* flatterer; jester; florist.—*n.m.* flowerpot.
floresta, *n.f.* forest, grove; rural pleasance; anthology.
florete, *a.* (*com.*) top-grade.—*n.m.* foil (*in fencing*).
floretear, *v.t.* decorate with flowers.—*v.i.* fence.
Florida, *n.f.* Florida.
florido, -da, *a.* flowery, full of flowers; florid; choice; *Pascua florida,* Easter.
floridano, -na, *a. n.m.f.* Floridan or Floridian.
florilegio, *n.m.* anthology.

florista, *n.m.f.* florist; maker of artificial flowers.
flota, *n.f.* fleet (*ships, cars etc.*).
flotable, *a.* floatable.
flotación, *n.f.* flotation.
flotante, *a.* floating; flowing (*beard*).
flotar, *v.i.* float.
flote, *n.m.* floating; *a* —, afloat.
flotilla, *n.f.* flotilla.
flox, *n.m.* (*bot.*) phlox.
fluctuación, *n.f.* fluctuation.
fluctante, *a.* fluctuating.
fluctuar [M], *v.i.* fluctuate.
fluencia, *n.f.* flowing; creep (*metals*).
fluidez, *n.f.* fluidity; fluency (*of style*).
flúido, -da, *a.* fluid; fluent (*language*).—*n.m.* fluid; — *eléctrico,* electric current.
fluir [O], *v.i.* flow.
flujo [O], *n.m.* flow; discharge; flux; rising tide.
flúor, *n.m.* (*chem.*) fluorine.
fluorescente, *a.* fluorescent.
fluorhídrico, -ca, *a.* (*chem.*) hydrofluoric.
fluórico, -ca, *a.* fluoric.
fluorina, fluorita, *n.f.* (*chem.*) fluor spar, fluorite.
fluorización, *n.f.* fluoridation.
fluoruro, *n.m.* (*chem.*) fluoride.
fluvial, *a.* fluvial.
flux, *n.m.* flush (*at cards*); **hacer** —, (*fam.*) go bust.
fluxión, *n.f.* fluxion; catarrh, cold in the head.
foca, *n.f.* (*zool.*) seal.
focal, *a.* focal.
foco, *n.m.* focus; centre; core; (*theat.*) spot(light); (*S.A.*) electric light.
focha, *n.f.* (*orn.*) coot.
fofo, -fa, *a.* spongy, soft.—*n.m.* bulk (*papers*).
fogata, *n.f.* blaze; bonfire; fougasse.
fogón, *n.m.* hearth; (cooking) stove; galley; flash-hole.
fogosidad, *n.f.* vehemence; dash, spirit.
fogoso, -sa, *a.* ardent; impetuous.
foja, *n.f.* (*obs., jur.*) leaf, sheet.
foliación, *n.f.* foliation; (*geol.*) rock cleavage.
folio, *n.m.* folio, leaf; *al primer* —, straight off; *de a* —, (*fam.*) enormous.
folklórico, -ca, *a.* rel. to folklore.
folla, *n.f.* medley, hodge-podge.
follada, *n.f.* (*cul.*) puff-pastry patty.
follaje, *n.m.* foliage; (*fig.*) fustian.
follar (1), *v.t.* foliate, shape like a leaf.
follar (2) [4], *v.t.* blow (*bellows*).
folletín, *n.m.* feuilleton; serial, story.
folletinesco, -ca, *a.* rel. to serial stories; cheap.
folleto, *n.m.* pamphlet, tract, brochure.
follón, -llona, *a.* lazy, indolent; cowardly; laggard.—*n.m.* knave, good-for-nothing.
fomentación, *n.f.* (*med.*) fomentation.
fomentar, *v.t.* foment; promote; encourage, foster.
fomento, *n.m.* development; encouragement; (*med.*) fomentation.
fon, *n.m.* (*phys.*) phone.
fonda, *n.f.* inn; restaurant.
fondillos, *n.m.pl.* seat (*of trousers*).
fondista, *n.m.* innkeeper.
fondo, *n.m.* bottom; back; background; (*fig.*) fund, reserve; *a* —, thoroughly; *artículo de* —, leading article.—*pl.* funds.
fondón, -dona, *a.* flabby, old.
fonema, *n.m.* phoneme.

fonémico, -ca, *a.* phonemic.—*n.f.* phonemics.
fonético, -ca, *a.* phonetic.—*n.f.* phonetics.
fonetista, *n.m.f.* phonetician.
fonógrafo, *n.m.* gramophone, (*U.S.*) phonograph.
fonología, *n.f.* phonology.
fontanal, fontanar, *n.m.* spring.
fontanería, *n.f.* plumbing; pipelaying; water-supply system.
fontanero, *n.m.* plumber; pipelayer.
foquito, *n.m.* (*S.A.*) flashlight bulb.
forajido, -da, *a., n.m.f.* outlaw.
foral, *a.* (*jur.*) statutory.
forastero, -ra, *a.* outside, strange.—*n.m.f.* outsider, stranger.
forcej(e)ar, *v.i.* struggle.
forcej(e)o, *n.m.* struggling; contention.
forcejudo, -da, *a.* robust, (*U.S. coll.*) husky.
forense, *a.* forensic.
forero, -ra, *a.* statutory.—*n.m.f.* leaseholder.
forestal, *a.* rel. to a forest.
forja, *n.f.* forge, foundry.
forjar, *v.t.* forge (*metal*); forge, falsify.
forma, *n.f.* form; way; format; *de — que,* so that.
formación, *n.f.* formation; training.
formal, *a.* formal; serious; proper, reliable, definite.
formalidad, *n.f.* formality; seriousness; reliability.
formalismo, *n.m.* formalism; red-tape.
formalizar [C], *v.t.* formalize; formulate.—*v.r.* grow serious; take offence.
formar, *v.t.* form; educate.
formativo, -va, *a.* formative.
formidable, *a.* formidable.
formón, *n.m.* (*carp.*) chisel.
fórmula, *n.f.* formula.
formulación, *n.f.* formulation.
formular, *v.t.* formulate.
fornicación, *n.f.* fornication.
fornicar [A], *v.i.* fornicate.
fornido, -da, *a.* robust, (*U.S. coll.*) husky.
foro, *n.m.* (*hist.*) forum; (*jur.*) bar; rear (*of stage*).
forraje, *n.m.* fodder, forage.
forrajear, *v.t., v.i.* forage.
forrar, *v.t.* line (*clothes*); cover (*books*).
forro, *n.m.* lining; (*naut.*) planking.
fortalecer [9], *v.t.* strengthen; fortify.
fortalecimiento, *n.m.* fortification; tonic.
fortaleza, *n.f.* fortitude; courage; fortress.
fortificación, *n.f.* fortification.
fortificante, *a.* fortifying.
fortificar [A], *v.t.* fortify; corroborate.
fortuito, -ta, *a.* fortuitous.
fortuna, *n.f.* fortune, chance; tempest; *por* —, luckily.
forúnculo, *n.m.* (*med.*) boil.
forzado, -da, *a.* forced.—*n.m.* convict, galley-slave.
forzador, *n.m.* ravisher.
forzal, *n.m.* back (*of a comb*).
forzar [4C], *v.t.* force; constrain.
forzoso, -sa, *a.* unavoidable, obligatory; strong.
forzudo, -da, *a.* robust, (*U.S. coll.*) husky.
fosa, *n.f.* grave; pit; — *séptica,* septic tank.
fosca, *n.f.* haze.
fosco, -ca, *a.* sullen, dour.
fosfático, -ca, *a.* (*chem.*) phosphatic.
fosfato, *n.m.* (*chem.*) phosphate.

fosforecer

fosforecer [9], *v.i.* phosphoresce.
fosforero, -ra, *n.m.f.* match-seller.—*n.f.* matchbox.
fosforescencia, *n.f.* phosphorescence.
fosforescente, *a.* phosphorescent.
fosfórico, -ca, *a.* (*chem.*) phosphoric.
fósforo, *n.m.* (*chem.*) phosphorus; match; (*poet.*) morning star.
fosforoso, -sa, *a.* phosphorous.
fosfuro, *n.m.* (*chem.*) phosphide.
fósil, *a.* fossile.—*n.m.* fossil (*also fig.*).
fosilización, *n.f.* fossilization.
fosilizar [C], *v.r.* become fossilized.
foso, *n.m.* pit, hole; moat.
fotingo, *n.m.* (*S.A. coll.*) jalopy.
fotocelda, fotocélula, *n.f.* photocell.
fotograbado, *n.m.* photogravure.
fotografía, *n.f.* photography; photograph.
fotografiar [L], *v.t., v.i.* photograph.
fotográfico, -ca, *a.* photographic.
fotógrafo, -fa, *n.m.f.* photographer.
fototipia, *n.f.* phototypy.
foz [HOZ].
frac, *n.m.* swallow-tailed coat, tails.
fracasar, *v.i.* fail.
fracaso, *n.m.* failure, collapse.
fracción, *n.f.* fraction.
fraccionar, *v.t.* divide into fractions, break up; crack (*oil*).
fraccionario, -ria, *a.* fractional.
fractura, *n.f.* fracture.
fracturar, *v.i., v.r.* fracture.
fragancia, *n.f.* fragrance.
fragante, *a.* fragrant; *en —,* [EN FLAGRANTE].
fragata, *n.f.* (*naut.*) frigate; *capitán de —,* commander.
frágil, *a.* fragile, frail; weak (*morally*); (*S.A.*) needy.
fragilidad, *n.f.* fragility; moral lapse.
fragmentación, *n.f.* fragmentation.
fragmentar, *v.t.* fragment.
fragmentario, -ria, *a.* fragmentary.
fragmento, *n.m.* fragment.
fragor, *n.m.* din, uproar.
fragosidad, *n.f.* roughness (*of terrain*).
fragoso, -sa, *a.* rough (*terrain*); noisy.
fragua, *n.f.* forge, smithy; (*fig.*) hotbed.
fraguar [H], *v.t.* forge (*iron, lies, plots*).—*v.i.* set (*concrete*).
fraile, *n.m.* friar; *— rezador,* (*ent.*) praying mantis.
frailecillo, *n.m.* (*orn.*) lapwing; puffin.
frailengo, -ga, fraileño, -ña, frailuno, -na, *a.* monkish, friar-like.
frambesia, *n.f.* (*med.*) yaws.
frambuesa, *n.f.* raspberry (*fruit*).
frambueso, *n.m.* raspberry(bush).
francachela, *n.f.* (*fam.*) feast, spread.
francés, -cesa, *a.* French.—*n.m.* Frenchman; French (*language*).—*n.f.* Frenchwoman; *irse a la francesa,* take French leave.
Francia, *n.f.* France.
franciscano, -na, *a., n.m.f.* Franciscan.
francmasón, *n.m.* Freemason, Mason.
francmasonería, *n.f.* Freemasonry.
franco, -ca, *a.* frank; liberal; free; Frankish; *— a bordo,* free on board; *— de porte,* postpaid; *puerto —,* free port.—*n.m.f.* Frank.—*n.m.* franc.
francoalemán, -mana, *a.* Franco-German.
francobordo, *n.m.* (*naut.*) freeboard.

franchote, -ta, franchute, -ta, *n.m.f.* (*pej.*) Frenchy, Froggy.
franela, *n.f.* flannel (*also fig.*).
frangible, *a.* brittle.
franja, *n.f.* fringe, strip.
franquear, *v.t.* exempt; enfranchise; manumit; frank (*a letter*).—*v.r.* yield; unbosom oneself.
franqueo, *n.m.* manumission; postage.
franqueza, *n.f.* liberty; sincerity.
franquicia, *n.f.* franchise; exemption, privilege.
franquista, *a., n.m.f.* rel. to supporters of Gen. Franco.
frasco, *n.m.* flask.
frase, *n.f.* phrase; sentence; epigram.
fraternal, *a.* fraternal.
fraternidad, *n.f.* fraternity.
fraternizar [C], *v.i.* fraternize.
fraterno, -na, *a.* fraternal.—*n.f.* reprimand.
fratría, *n.f.* phratry, siblings.
fratricida, *a.* fratricidal.—*n.m.f.* fratricide (*person*).
fratricidio, *n.m.* fratricide (*crime*).
fraude, *n.m.* fraud.
fraudulento, -ta, *a.* fraudulent.
fray, *n.m.* Brother (*title used in certain orders*), Fra.
frazada, *n.f.* blanket.
frecuencia, *n.f.* frequency.
frecuentación, *n.f.* frequentation.
frecuentar, *v.t.* frequent, haunt; repeat.
frecuente, *a.* frequent.
fregadero, *n.m.* sink.
fregador, -ra, *n.m.f.* dish-washer.—*n.m.* dish-cloth, dish-mop.
fregadura, *n.f.,* **fregamiento,** *n.m.* dish-washing, (*Brit.*) washing-up.
fregar [1B], *v.t.* rub; scrub; mop; scour; (*Brit.*) wash up, (*U.S.*) wash (*the dishes*); (*S.A.*) annoy.
fregona, *n.f.* kitchen maid.
freidura, *n.f.* frying.
freile, *n.m.* knight *or* priest of a military order.
freír [28, *p.p.* **frito**], *v.t.* fry.
fréjol [FRIJOL].
frenar, *v.t.* brake, check; lock (*nuts*).
frenero, *n.m.* bridle-maker; (*rail.*) brakeman.
frenesí, *n.m.* (*pl.* **-íes**) frenzy, madness.
frenético, -ca, *a.* mad, frantic.
freno, *n.m.* bit; bridle; brake; restraint.
frenología, *n.f.* phrenology.
frental, *a.* frontal, rel. to the forehead.
frente, *n.f.* forehead, brow; countenance.—*n.m. or f.* front, fore part; obverse.—*n.m.* (*mil., pol.*) front.—*prep. — a,* opposite; vis-à-vis; *en — de,* opposite.—*adv. a —,* straight ahead; *al —,* (*com.*) carried forward; *del —,* (*com.*) brought forward; *de —,* forward, abreast.
fresa, *n.f.* strawberry; milling tool, cutter.
fresadora, *n.f.* milling machine, miller.
fresal, *n.m.* strawberry bed.
fresar, *v.t.* mill.
frescachón, -chona, *a.* bouncing, buxom.
frescal, *a.* slightly salted.
fresco, -ca, *a.* fresh, cool; recent; (*fam.*) fresh, cheeky; fresh (*breeze*); ruddy; *quedarse tan —,* not turn a hair. —*n.m.* fresh air; (*S.A.*) cool drink; (*art.*) fresco.—*n.f.* fresh air, cool.

104

frescor, *n.m.* freshness; (*art.*) flesh tint.
frescura, *n.f.* coolness; cheek, insolence.
fresneda, *n.f.* ash-grove.
fresno, *n.m.* ash-tree.
fresquera, *n.f.* ice-box, meat-safe.
frey, *n.m.* Brother (*title used in certain military orders*).
frez, *n.f.* dung.
freza, *n.f.* dung; spawning season; spawn.
frezar [C], *v.i.* dung; spawn; root (*of pigs*).
friabilidad, *n.f.* friability, brittleness.
friable, *a.* friable; brittle.
frialdad, *n.f.* coldness; frigidity.
fricasé, *n.m.* (*cul.*) fricassee.
fricción, *n.f.* friction; embrocation.
friega, *n.f.* rubbing, massage; (*S.A.*) drubbing; (*S.A.*) nuisance.
friera, *n.f.* chilblain.
frigidez, *n.f.* frigidity, coldness.
frigorífico, -ca, *a.* refrigerating.—*n.m.* refrigerator; (*S.A.*) meat-packing plant; cold-storage plant.
frijol, frijol, *n.m.* kidney-bean; *frijol de media luna,* butter-bean, (*U.S.*) Lima bean.
frijolar, *n.m.* bean-patch.
frío, fría, *a.* cold; *hacer —,* be cold (*weather*); *tener —,* be cold (*person*); *tomar —,* catch cold.—*n.m.* cold(ness).
friolento, -ta, *a.* chilly.
friolera, *n.f.* trifle, bauble.
frisa, *n.f.* frieze; gasket.
frisar, *v.t.* frieze, frizz (*cloth*); (*naut.*) pack.—*v.i.* resemble; — *con,* border on, approach.
frisón, -sona, *a., n.m.f.* Friesian.
frito, -ta, *p.p.* [FREÍR].—*n.m.* fry.
frivolidad, *n.f.* frivolity.
frívolo, -la, *a.* frivolous.
frondosidad, *n.f.* foliage, luxuriant growth.
frondoso, -sa, *a.* leafy.
frontal, *a.* frontal, rel. to the forehead.—*n.m.* frontal.
frontera, *n.f.* frontier, border, boundary; frontage.
frontero, -ra, *a.* opposite.
frontispicio, *n.m.* frontispiece.
frontón, *n.m.* (*arch.*) pediment; front wall (*in pelota*); (fives-)court (*for pelota*).
frotador, -ra, *a.* rubbing.—*n.m.* (*elec.*) shoe, brush.
frotante, *a.* rubbing.
frotar, *v.t.* rub.
fructificar [A], *v.i.* bear fruit.
fructuoso, -sa, *a.* fruitful, profitable.
fruente, *a.* enjoying.
frugal, *a.* frugal.
frugalidad, *n.f.* frugality.
frugívoro, -ra, *a.* frugivorous, fruit-eating.
fruición, *n.f.* fruition; enjoyment.
fruir [O], *v.i.* be gratified, enjoy oneself.
frunce, *n.m.* gather, shirr (*sewing*).
fruncir [D], *v.t.* pucker; shirr (*sewing*).—*v.r.* affect modesty.
fruslería, *n.f.* bauble.
fruslero, -ra, *a.* trifling, futile.—*n.f.* bauble.
frustración, *n.f.* frustration.
frustrar, *v.t.* frustrate, disappoint, baulk.—*v.r.* miscarry, fall through.
fruta, *n.f.* fruit (*esp. as food*); result; — *de sartén,* pancake.
frutal, *a.* fruit (*tree*).—*n.m.* fruit-tree.
frutería, *n.f.* fruit-shop, fruiterers.

frutero, -ra, *a.* rel. to fruit.—*n.m.f.* fruiterer. —*n.m.* fruit dish.
fruto, *n.m.* fruit (*as containing seed*); (*esp. fig.*) fruit(s), result; *dar —,* yield fruit; *sin —,* fruitlessly.
¡**fu!** *interj.* fie! faugh! phooey!
fucilar, *v.i.* flash.
fucilazo, *n.m.* (heat-)lightning.
fucsia, *n.f.* (*bot.*) fuchsia.
fue [SER & IR].
fuego, *n.m.* fire; light (*for a cigarette etc.*); hearth; (*mil.*) fire; *fuegos artificiales,* fireworks.
fuelle, *n.m.* bellows; blower.
fuente, *n.f.* fountain, spring; source; font; platter, dish; — *de gasolina,* gas pump.
fuer, *adv.* **a** —, in the manner of.
fuera, *adv.* without, outside; — *de,* out of besides; — *de sí,* beside oneself; *estar —,* not be at home.
fuero, *n.m.* law, statute; privilege, charter; — *interior* or *interno,* conscience.
fuerte, *a.* strong; heavy-weight; hard.—*adv.* hard; loud; heavily.—*n.m.* fort.
fuerza, *n.f.* strength; power; (*phys.*) force.—*n.f.pl.* forces, troops.
fuete, *n.m.* (*S.A.*) whip.
fuga, *n.f.* escape, leak; flight; ardour; (*mus.*) fugue.
fugar [B], *v.r.* flee, run away.
fugaz, *a.* (*pl.* -aces) fleeting, fugitive, brief.
fugitivo, -va, *a.* fugitive, brief.
fuina, *n.f.* (*zool.*) marten.
fulano, -na, *n.m.f.* such a one, so-and-so; —, *zutano y mengano,* Tom, Dick and Harry.
fulcro, *n.m.* fulcrum.
fulgente, *a.* refulgent.
fulgor, *n.m.* resplendence.
fulgurante, *a.* resplendent.
fulgurar, *v.i.* flash.
fuliginoso, -sa, *a.* fuliginous, obscure.
fulminante, *a.* fulminating.—*n.m.* percussion cap.
fulminar, *v.t., v.i.* fulminate.
fullero, -ra, *a.* cheating.—*n.m.f.* cheat, crook.
fumable, *a.* smokable.
fumadero, *n.m.* smoking-room.
fumador, -ra, *n.m.f.* smoker.
fumante, *a.* smoking; fuming.
fumar, *v.t., v.i.* smoke.—*v.r.* waste; *fumarse la clase,* to play truant.
fumigar [B], *v.t.* fumigate.
fumigatorio, -ria, *a.* fumigatory.
fumista, *n.m.* stove maker; stove repairer.
funambulesco, -ca, *a.* funambulatory; extravagant.
funámbulo, -la, *n.m.f.* tight-rope walker.
función, *n.f.* function.
funcional, *a.* functional.
funcionar, *v.i.* work, function; be in working order.
funcionario, -ria, *n.m.f.* functionary, civil servant.
funda, *n.f.* case; sheath; cover; holdall; — *de almohada,* pillow-slip.
fundación, *n.f.* foundation.
fundadamente, *adv.* with good reason.
fundador, -ra, *a.* founding.—*n.m.f.* founder.
fundamental, *a.* fundamental.
fundamentar, *v.t.* found; lay the basis for.

fundamento, *n.m.* foundation; grounds; trustworthiness; weft, woof.
fundar, *v.t.* found, base.
fundente, *a.* fusing, melting.—*n.m.* (*chem.*) flux, fluxing agent.
fundería, *n.f.* foundry.
fundible, *a.* fusible.
fundición, *n.f.* fusion; fuse blow-out; melting; (*print.*) fount.
fundillo, *n.m.* (*S.A.*) behind.—*pl.* seat (*of trousers*).
fundir, *v.t.* fuse; smelt; cast; merge.—*v.r.* melt; fuse; merge.
fundo, *n.m.* rural property.
fúnebre, *a.* funereal; funeral.
funeral, *a.* funereal; funeral.—*n.m. esp. pl.* funeral.
funerario, -ria, *a.* funeral, funerary.—*n.m.* undertaker, (*U.S.*) mortician.—*n.f.* undertaking establishment.
funesto, -ta, *a.* fatal, ill-fated; doleful.
fungir [E], *v.i.* (*S.A.*) function, be employed.
fungoso, -sa, *a.* fungous.
funicular, *a.,* *n.m.* funicular.
furgón, *n.m.* van.
furgoneta, *n.f.* light truck, delivery truck *or* van.
furia, *n.f.* fury; rage.
furibundo, -da, *a.* furious.
furioso, -sa, *a.* furious, infuriated.
furor, *n.m.* fury; rage.
furriel, furrier, *n.m.* quartermaster.
furtivo, -va, *a.* furtive.
furúnculo, *n.m.* (*med.*) boil.
fusa, *n.f.* (*mus.*) demi-semiquaver.
fusco, -ca, *a.* brown, dark.
fuselaje, *n.m.* (*aer.*) fuselage.
fusibilidad, *n.f.* fusibility.
fusible, *a.* fusible.—*n.m.* fuse.
fusil, *n.m.* rifle, gun.
fusilar, *v.t.* shoot, kill by shooting.
fusión, *n.f.* fusion, melting; — **de empresas,** (*com.*) merger.
fusta (1), *n.f.* brushwood.
fusta (2), *n.f.* (*naut.*) small lateen-rigged vessel.
fustán, *n.m.* fustian.
fuste, *n.m.* wood; shaft; shank; substance, importance.
fustigar [B], *v.t.* lash; censure severely.
fútbol, *n.m.* football.
futbolista, *n.m.* football player.
futesa, *n.f.* trifle.
fútil, *a.* futile; worthless.
futilidad, *n.f.* futility.
futre, *n.m.* (*S.A.*) fop, (*U.S.*) dude.
futuro, -ra, *a.* future, forthcoming.—*n.m.f.* (*fam.*) fiancé(e).—*n.m.* (*gram.*) future; future.

G

G, g, *n.f.* eighth letter of the Spanish alphabet.
gabacho, -cha, *a.,* *n.m.f.* (*fam. pej.*) Froggie, Frenchie.

gabán, *n.m.* overcoat.
gabardina, *n.f.* gabardine; raincoat.
gabarra, *n.f.* lighter, barge.
gabarro, *n.m.* flaw; error; bother.
gabela, *n.f.* tax, duty.
gabinete, *n.m.* study; cabinet; boudoir; lavatory.
gacel, -la, *n.m.f.* (*zool.*) gazelle.
gaceta, *n.f.* gazette; (*S.A.*) newspaper.
gacetero, *n.m.* gazetteer; newspaper vendor.
gacetilla, *n.f.* gossip column.
gacetillero, *n.m.* gossip writer.
gacha, *n.f.* mush.—*pl.* pap, sops.
gacho, -cha, *a.* drooping; **a gachas,** (*fam.*) on all fours.
gachón, -chona, *a.* (*fam.*) nice, sweet.
gachumbo, *n.m.* (*S.A.*) gourd, pot.
gachupín, -pina, *n.m.f.* (*C.A. pej.*) Spanish settler.
gaditano, -na, *a.,* *n.m.f.* rel. to *or* native of Cadiz.
gafa, *n.f.* hook.—*pl.* glasses, spectacles.
gafar, *v.t.* hook, claw.
gafe, *n.m.* (*fam.*) jinx, Jonah.
gafete, *n.m.* hook and eye.
gafo, -fa, *a.* claw-handed, leprous.—*n.m.* (*fam.*) jinx.
gago, -ga, *a.* (*S.A., dial.*) stammering.
gaita, *n.f.* bagpipe; (*fam.*) neck; (*fam.*) bother.
gaje, *n.m.* wage; **gajes del oficio,** (*joc.*) snags that go with the job, occupational hazards.
gajo, *n.m.* broken branch; cluster; pip: quarter (*of lemon etc.*); prong; spur; foothills.
gala, *n.f.* gala, elegance, finery; **de —,** in full dress; **hacer — de,** show off, glory in.—*pl.* regalia; talents; delights.
galafate, *n.m.* sneak-thief.
galaico, -ca, *a.* Galician.
galán, *a.* [GALANO].—*n.m.* gallant, beau; (*theat.*) male lead.
galano, -na, *a.* smart, spruce, elegant.
galante, *a.* elegant, courtly; attentive to women; coquettish.
galantear, *v.t.* woo, flirt with.
galanteo, *n.m.* wooing, flirting.
galantería, *n.f.* courtesy, elegance; gallantry; generosity.
galanura, *n.f.* finery, elegance; charm.
galápago, *n.m.* tortoise, turtle; ingot; (*fam.*) sharper.
galardón, *n.m.* reward, guerdon.
galaxia, *n.f.* (*astr.*) galaxy; Milky Way.
galbana, *n.f.* (*fam.*) idleness, laziness.
galbanoso, -sa, *a.* (*fam.*) shiftless, idle.
galeón, *n.m.* (*naut.*) galleon.
galeote, *n.m.* galley slave; (*obs.*) convict.
galera, *n.f.* (*naut., print.*) galley; large cart; hospital ward; women's prison; (*carp.*) jack plane.—*pl.* galleys (*as penal sentence*).
galería, *n.f.* gallery.
galerín, *n.m.* (*print.*) galley.
Gales, *n.f.* **el país de —,** Wales.
galés, -lesa, *a.,* *n.m.* Welsh.—*n.m.f.* Welshman, Welshwoman.
galfarro, *n.m.* loafer.
galgo, -ga, *n.m.f.* greyhound.
Galia, *n.f.* Gaul.
gálibo, *n.m.* template.
galicano, -na, *a.* (*eccl.*) Gallican.
Galicia, *n.f.* Galicia.
galicismo, *n.m.* Gallicism.

galicista, *a.*Gallicizing.—*n.m.f.*Gallicizer.
galimatías, *n.m.* rigmarole, gibberish.
galiparla, *n.f.* Frenchified Spanish.
galo, -la, *a.* Gallic.—*n.m.f.* Gaul.
galocha, *n.f.* wooden shoe.
galófobo, -ba, *a., n.m.f.* Gallophobe.
galomanía, *n.f.* Gallomania.
galón, *n.m.* galloon, braid; gallon.
galonear, *v.t.* braid.
galopada, *n.f.* gallop, galloping.
galopar, *v.i.* gallop.
galope, *n.m.* gallop.
galopear, *v.i.* gallop.
galopillo, *n.m.* scullion.
galopo, *n.m.* rogue.
galvanismo, *n.m.* galvanism.
galvanizar [C], *v.t.* galvanize.
gallardear, *v.i., v.r.* be elegant, gallant.
gallardete, *n.m.* pennant, riband.
gallardía, *n.f.* elegance, nobility, gallantry.
gallardo, -da, *a.* elegant, gallant, brave; strong.
gallego, -ga, *a., n.m.f.* Galician; (*S.A.*) Spaniard.
gallera, *n.f.* cockpit.
galleta, *n.f.* biscuit; anthracite; (*fam.*) slap.
gallina, *n.f.* hen.—*n.m.f.* (*fam.*) coward, chicken.
gallinazo, -za, *n.m.f.* (*S.A.*) buzzard.—*n.f.* hen dung.
gallinero, -ra, *n.m.f.* chicken merchant.— *n.m.* hencoop; (*theat.*) gods, gallery; bedlam.
gallipuente, *n.m.* foot-bridge.
gallito, *n.m.* beau, coxcomb.
gallo, *n.m.* cock; false note; (*fam.*) boss;(*fam.*) cockiness; — **en la garganta,** frog in the throat.
gallofero, -ra, gallofo, -fa, *a.* begging, scrounging.—*n.m.f.* beggar, scrounger.
gallón, *n.m.* clod, sod.
gama, *n.f.* gamut; [GAMO].
gamba, *n.f.* shrimp, prawn.
gamberrismo, *n.m.* hooliganism.
gamberro, -rra, *a., n.m.f.* rowdy, hooligan.
gambeta, *n.f.* prance, caper.
gambito, *n.m.* gambit.
gamo, -ma, *n.m.f.* (*zool.*) fallow-deer.
gamuza, *n.f.* chamois.
gana, *n.f.* desire; **de buena —,** willingly; **de mala —,** unwillingly; **me da la — de,** I feel like (*doing etc.*); **tener ganas de,** feel like, have a mind to.
ganadería, *n.f.* ranch; ranching; livestock.
ganadero, -ra, *a.* ranching, rel. to cattle breeding.—*n.m.f.* stock breeder, cattle raiser.
ganado, *n.m.* cattle; livestock; (*fam.*) swarm, mob; — **caballar,** horses; — **lanar,** sheep; — **mayor,** cattle, horses, mules; — **menor,** sheep, goats, pigs.
ganador, -ra, *a.* earning.—*n.m.f.* winner; earner.
ganancia, *n.f.* profit, gain.
ganancioso, -sa, *a.* profitable; gaining.
ganapán, *n.m.* odd-job man; lout.
ganar, *v.t.* win, gain; earn; beat, defeat; reach.—*v.i.* win, gain.—*v.r.* earn; win over; (*S.A.*) run off.
ganchillo, *n.m.* crocheting hook; crochet.
gancho, *n.m.* hook; (*fam.*) sponger.
ganchoso, -sa, ganchudo, -da, *a.* hooked.

gándara, *n.f.* wasteland.
gandaya, *n.f.* loafing, scrounging.
gandul, -la, *a.* (*fam.*) bone-idle.—*n.m.f.* idler.
gandulear, *v.i.* laze, loaf.
gandulería, *n.f.* (*fam.*) idleness, laziness.
ganga, *n.f.* (*orn.*) sand grouse; (*fig.*) bargain.
gangoso, -sa, *a.* snuffling, with a cold in the nose.
gangrena, *n.f.* gangrene.
gángster, *n.m.* gangster.
gangsterismo, *n.m.* gangsterism.
ganguear, *v.i.* snuffle.
ganguero, -ra, ganguista, *n.m.f.* self-seeker; bargain-hunter; (*fam.*) lucky fellow.
ganoso, -sa, *a.* desirous.
gansarón, *n.m.* gander.
ganso, -sa, *n.m.f.* ninny; bumpkin; slob; (*orn.*) goose, gander.
Gante, *n.f.* Ghent.
ganzúa, *n.f.* lock-picker; (*fig.*) wheedler.
gañán, *n.m.* farm labourer.
gañido, *n.m.* yelp, yell, howl.
gañir, *v.i.* yelp, howl; croak.
gañón, gañote, *n.m.* (*fam.*) gizzard, throat.
garabatear, *v.t.* scribble.—*v.i.* hook; mess about.
garabato, *n.m.* hook; pothook, scrawl.
garabatoso, -sa, *a.* scribbly; attractive.
garabito, *n.m.* market stall.
garage, garaje, *n.m.* garage.
garambaina, *n.f.* ugly trinket.—*pl.* (*fam.*) simpering; (*fam.*) scrawl.
garante, *n.m.* guarantor.
garantía, *n.f.* guarantee.
garantir [Q], **garantizar** [C], *v.t.* guarantee.
garañón, *n.m.* stud donkey; (*S.A.*) stallion.
garapiña, *n.f.* (*cul.*) icing; braid.
garapiñar, *v.t.* ice, sugar-coat.
garatusa, *n.f.* (*fam.*) wheedling.
garbanzo, *n.m.* chick-pea.
garbear, *v.i.* put on airs.
garbillo, *n.m.* sieve.
garbo, *n.m.* jauntiness, elegance; nobility.
garboso, -sa, *a.* jaunty, elegant.
garbullo, *n.m.* rumpus, ructions.
garceta, *n.f.* egret.
garduño, -ña, *n.m.f.* sneak-thief.—*n.f.* (*zool.*) marten.
garfa, *n.f.* claw.
garfio, *n.m.* gaff, hook; climbing iron.
gargajear, *v.i.* clear one's throat.
gargajeo, *n.m.* clearing of one's throat, spitting.
gargajo, *n.m.* phlegm.
garganta, *n.f.* throat, neck; gorge.
gargantear, *v.i.* warble.
gárgara, *n.f.* gargle, gargling.
gargarismo, *n.m.* gargle (*liquid*).
gargarizar [C], *v.i.* gargle.
garita, *n.f.* box, cabin.
garlocha, *n.f.* goad.
garra, *n.f.* claw, talon; (*fig.*) clutch.
garrafa, *n.f.* carafe.
garrafiñar, *v.t.* (*fam.*) grab, snatch.
garramar, *v.t.* (*fam.*) pinch, steal.
garrapata, *n.f.* (*zool.*) tick.
garrapatear, *v.i.* scribble.
garrapato, *n.m.* pothook, scrawl.
garrido, -da, *a.* comely.
garrocha, *n.f.* goad; vaulting pole.
garrón, *n.m.* talon, spur.

garrote, *n.m.* cudgel; garrotte; (*C.A.*) brake.
garrotero, *n.m.* (*S.A.*) thug; (*C.A.*) brakeman.
garrotillo, *n.m.* (*med.*) croup.
garrucha, *n.f.* pulley.
gárrulo, -la, *a.* garrulous.
garulla, *n.f.* (single) grape; (*fam.*) bunch, mob.
garza, *n.f.* (*orn.*) heron; crane.
garzo, -za, *a.* blue.
garzón, *n.m.* lad, stripling.
garzota, *n.f.* (*orn.*) night heron; plume.
gas, *n.m.* gas; — *de guerra* or *tóxico,* poison gas; — (*ex*)*hilarante,* laughing gas.
gasa, *n.f.* muslin; mourning crêpe.
gascón, -cona, *a., n.m.f.* Gascon.
gasconada, *n.f.* gasconade, bravado.
gaseoso, -sa, *a.* gaseous.—*n.f.* mineral water, (*fam.*) pop.
gasificar [A], *v.t.* gasify.
gasista, *n.m.* gas fitter.
gasolina, *n.f.* petrol; (*U.S.*) gasoline, gas.
gasómetro, *n.m.* gasometer; gas tank.
gastado, -da, *a.* spent, worn-out.
gastamiento, *n.m.* consumption, wear.
gastar, *v.t.* spend; use up; waste; use very often; play (*jokes*); wear out.
gasto, *n.m.* outlay, expense; wear, use; waste.
gastoso, -sa, *a.* costly; wasteful.
gástrico, -ca, *a.* gastric.
gastronomía, *n.f.* gastronomy.
gastronómico, -ca, *a.* gastronomic.
gastrónomo, -ma, *n.m.f.* gastronome, gourmet.
gata, *n.f.* she-cat; (*fam.*) Madrid woman; *a gatas,* on all fours.
gatallón, *n.m.* (*fam.*) cheat, rogue.
gatatumba, *n.f.* (*fam.*) pretence, shamming, show.
gatear, *v.t.* (*fam.*) scratch; (*fam.*) pinch, steal.—*v.i.* clamber; crawl; (*S.A.*) philander.
gatería, *n.f.* bunch of cats; (*fam.*) gang; (*fam.*) guile.
gatillo, *n.m.* trigger, hammer (*of gun*).
gato, *n.m.* cat, tom-cat; money-bag; (*mech.*) jack; clamp; (*fam.*) pickpocket; (*fam.*) Madrid man; hook; — *encerrado,* fly in the ointment; *vender — por liebre,* (*fam.*) pull a fast one.
gatuno, -na, *a.* catlike.
gauchesco, -ca, *a.* Gaucho.
gaucho, -cha, *a., n.m.f.* Gaucho; (*fig.*) rustic.
gaveta, *n.f.* drawer (*in desk*); till.
gavia, *n.f.* ditch; (*orn.*) gull; padded cell; (*naut.*) top-sail.
gavieta, *n.f.* (*naut.*) crow's nest.
gavilán, *n.m.* (*orn.*) sparrow-hawk; hair: stroke (*in penmanship*); quillon (*of sword*); metal tip.
gavilla, *n.f.* sheaf; (*fam.*) gang.
gaviota, *n.f.* (*orn.*) sea-gull.
gavota, *n.f.* gavotte.
gaya, *n.f.* stripe; magpie.
gayo, -ya, *a.* merry, gay; *gaya ciencia,* poesy.—*n.m.* jay.
gayola, *n.f.* cage; (*fam.*) clink; vineyard watchtower.
gazapa, *n.f.* (*fam.*) fib, lie.
gazapatón, *n.m.* (*fam.*) howler, blooper.
gazapina, *n.f.* gang; brawl.

gazapo, *n.m.* young rabbit; (*fam.*) **sharper;** (*fam.*) howler.
gazmoñero, -ra, gazmoño, -ña, *a.* prudish, priggish.
gaznápiro, *n.m.* boob, churl.
gaznate, *n.m.* gullet; fritter.
gazpacho, *n.m.* gazpacho, cold soup.
gazuza, *n.f.* (*fam.*) hunger.
ge, *n.f.* name of letter G.
gea, *n.f.* mineral geography.
géiser, *n.m.* geyser.
gelatina, *n.f.* gelatine.
gélido, -da, *a.* (*poet.*) gelid, frigid.
gema, *n.f.* gem; (*bot.*) bud.
gemelo, -la, *a., n.m.f.* twin.—*n.m.pl.* pair of theatre glasses *or* cuff links; (*astr.*) Gemini.
gemido, *n.m.* groan, moan.
Géminis, *n.m.* (*astr.*) Gemini.
gemir [8], *v.i.* groan; whine; roar.
gen, *n.m.* gene.
genealogía, *n.f.* genealogy.
genealógico, -ca, *a.* genealogical.
genealogista, *n.m.f.* genealogist.
generación, *n.f.* generation.
generador, -ra, *a.* generating.—*n.m.* generator.
general, *a., n.m.* general; (*aer.*) air marshal; — *de brigada,* brigadier.
generala, *n.f.* general's wife; call to arms.
generalidad, *n.f.* generality; Catalonian Parliament.
generalísimo, *n.m.* generalissimo.
generalización, *n.f.* generalization.
generalizar [C], *v.t.* generalize.—*v.r.* become general.
generar, *v.t.* generate.
genérico, -ca, *a.* generic; common (*noun*).
género, *n.m.* kind, type; genus, class; genre; gender; — *humano,* human race, mankind. —*pl.* goods, wares.
generosidad, *n.f.* generosity; nobility.
generoso, -sa, *a.* generous; noble; brave; superb.
Génesis, *n.m.* (*Bib.*) Genesis; **génesis,** *n.f.* genesis.
genet(ic)ista, *n.m.f.* geneticist.
genético, -ca, *a.* genetic.—*n.f.* genetics.
genetista, *n.m.f.* geneticist.
geniado, *a. bien —,* good-tempered; *mal* —, bad-tempered.
genial, *a.* brilliant, of genius; temperamental; pleasant.
genialidad, *n.f.* natural disposition; genius.
genio, *n.m.* temperament, disposition; character, spirit; genius; genie, jinn; *mal —,* bad temper.
genital, *a.* genital.
genitivo, -va, *a., n.m.* (*gram.*) genitive.
genocidio, *n.m.* genocide.
Génova, *n.f.* Genoa.
genovés, -vesa, *a., n.m.f.* Genoese.
gente, *n.f.* people; troops; nation; (*fam.*) family; (*S.A.*) somebody; — *de bien,* decent people; — *principal,* gentry.
gentecilla, *n.f.* the rabble.
gentil, *a.* genteel; Gentile.—*n.m.f.* Gentile.
gentileza, *n.f.* gentility, elegance; courtesy.
gentilhombre, *n.m.* gentleman; good man.
gentilicio, -cia, *a.* national, family.
gentílico, -ca, *a.* heathen.
gentilidad, *n.f.,* **gentilismo,** *n.m.* heathendom.

gentío, *n.m.* throng, crowd.
gentualla, gentuza, *n.f.* rabble, mob.
genuflexión, *n.f.* genuflexion.
genuino, -na, *a.* genuine.
geofísica, *n.f.* geophysics.
geografía, *n.f.* geography.
geográfico, -ca, *a.* geographic(al).
geógrafo, *n.m.* geographer.
geología, *n.f.* geology.
geológico, -ca, *a.* geological.
geólogo, *n.m.* geologist.
geometría, *n.f.* geometry.
geométrico, -ca, *a.* geometric(al).
geopolítico, -ca, *a.* geopolitical.—*n.f.* geo-
politics.
geórgica, *n.f.* georgic.
geranio, *n.m.* (*bot.*) geranium.
gerencia, *n.f.* management.
gerente, *n.m.* manager; director.
gerifalte, *n.m.* (*orn.*) gerfalcon.
germanesco, -ca, *a.* rel. to underworld
slang.
germanía, *n.f.* underworld slang· criminals'
fraternity.
germánico, -ca, *a.* Germanic.
germano, -na, *a.* Germanic, Teutonic.—
—*n.m.f.* German, Teuton; (*obs.*) member of
thieves' fraternity.
germen, *n.m.* germ.
germicida, *a.* germicidal.—*n.m.* germicide.
germinación, *n.f.* germination.
germinar, *v.i.* germinate.
gerundio, *n.m.* (*gram.*) gerund; (*fam.*) wind-
bag.
gerundivo, *n.m.* (*gram.*) gerundive.
gesta, *n.f.* (*obs.*) gest; feat.
gestación, *n.f.* gestation.
gestear, *v.i.* make faces.
gesticulación, *n.f.* facial expression; gesture.
gesticular, *v.i.* make faces; gesture.
gestión, *n.f.* management; measure, action,
step.
gestionar, *v.t.* negotiate; take steps to obtain.
gesto, *n.m.* facial expression; gesture; (*fig.*)
mood.
gestor, *n.m.* agent, manager.
Getsemaní, *n.m.* (*Bib.*) Gethsemane.
giba, *n.f.* hump; (*fam.*) bugbear.
gibón, *n.m.* (*zool.*) gibbon.
giboso, -sa, *a.* humped, gibbous.
Gibraltar, *n.m.* Gibraltar.
gibraltareño, -ña, *a.*, *n.m.f.* Gibraltarian.
giga, *n.f.* (*mus.*) jig [JIGA].
giganta, *n.f.* giantess.
gigante, *a.*, *n.m.* giant.
gigantesco, -ca, *a.* gigantic.
gigantez, *n.f.* gigantic size.
gigantón, -tona, *n.m.f.* giant figure in festival
processions.
gigote, *n.m.* potted meat.
Gil, *n.m.* Giles.
gilí, *a.* (*pl.* -íes) (*fam.*) daft, silly.
gimnasia, *n.f.* gymnastics.
gimnasio, *n.f.* gymnasium.
gimnasta, *n.m.f.* gymnast.
gimnástico, -ca, *a.* gymnastic.—*n.f.* gymnastics.
gimotear, *v.i.* (*fam.*) whimper, whine.
Ginebra, *n.f.* Geneva.
ginebra (1), *n.f.* gin.
ginebra (2), *n.f.* bedlam.
ginecología, *n.f.* gynaecology.

ginecólogo, *n.m.* gynaecologist.
gira, *n.f.* outing, trip [JIRA].
giralda, *n.f.* weathervane.
girante, *a.* rotating.
girar, *v.t.* (*com.*) draw.—*v.i.* revolve, turn.
girasol, *n.m.* sunflower.
giratorio, -ria, *a.* revolving.—*n.f.* revolving
stand.
giro, *n.m.* turn, rotation; trend; turn of
phrase; bragging; money order; gash.
girocompás, *n.m.* gyrocompass.
giroscopio, giróscopo, *n.m.* gyroscope.
gitanear, *v.i.* live like a gipsy; fawn.
gitanería, *n.f.* gipsies; fawning.
gitanesco, -ca, *a.* gipsy, romany.
gitanismo, *n.m.* gipsyism, gipsy lore.
gitano, -na, *a.* gipsy; artful; flattering.—
n.m.f. gipsy.
glacial, *a.* glacial; icy.
glaciar, *n.m.* glacier.
glaciario, -ria, *a.* glacial.
gladiador, *n.m.* gladiator.
glándula, *n.f.* gland.
glandular, *a.* glandular.
glauco, -ca, *a.* glaucous.
gleba, *n.f.* plough-land.
glera, *n.f.* sandy place.
glicerina, *n.f.* glycerine.
global, *a.* total; global.
globo, *n.m.* globe; balloon; **en —,** in general;
in bulk.
globoso, -sa, *a.* globose, spherical.
globular, *a.* globular.
glóbulo, *n.m.* globule; (*anat.*) corpuscle.
glogló [GLUGLÚ].
gloria, *n.f.* glory.—*n.m.* (*eccl.*) Gloria;
(*theat.*) curtain call; **oler** *or* **saber a —,**
smell *or* taste heavenly; **en sus glorias,**
in one's glory.
gloriar [L], *v.r.* glory (*de, en,* in).
glorieta, *n.f.* summer-house; traffic circle,
square.
glorificación, *n.f.* glorification.
glorificar [C], *v.t.* glorify.—*v.r.* win glory.
la Gloriosa, *n.f.* Our Lady.
glorioso, -sa, *a.* glorious; vainglorious.
glosa, *n.f.* gloss.
glosar, *v.t.* gloss.
glosario, *n.m.* glossary.
glosopeda, *n.f.* (*vet.*) foot-and-mouth disease.
glotis, *n.f.* inv. (*anat.*) glottis.
glotón, -tona, *a.* gluttonous.—*n.m.f.* glutton.
glotonear, *v.i.* gormandise.
glotonería, *n.f.* gluttony.
glucosa, *n.f.* glucose.
gluglú, *n.m.* glug, gurgle; turkey's gobble.
gluglutear, *v.i.* gobble (*of turkeys*).
glutinoso, -sa, *a.* glutinous.
gnomo, *n.m.* gnome.
gnóstico, -ca, *a.*, *n.m.f.* gnostic.
gobelino, *n.m.* goblin.
gobernable, *a.* governable, controllable.
gobernación, *n.f.* home affairs; **Ministerio
de la Gobernación,** Home Office.
gobernador, -ra, *a.* governing.—*n.m.* governor.—*n.f.* governor's wife.
gobernalle, *n.m.* helm, rudder.
gobernante, *a.* ruling.—*n.m.f.* ruler.
gobernar [I], *v.t.* govern; steer; control.
gobernoso, -sa, *a.* (*fam.*) orderly.
gobiernista, *a.* (*S.A.*) governmental.

gobierno, *n.m.* government; control; steering; guidance; — *doméstico,* housekeeping.
goce, *n.m.* pleasure, enjoyment.
gocho, -cha, *n.m.f.* (*fam.*) pig, porker.
godesco, -ca, *a.* cheery, merry.
godo, -da, *a.* Gothic.—*n.m.f.* Goth; blue-blooded person; (*S.A., pej.*) Spaniard.
gofo, -fa, *a.* crude, boorish.
gol, *n.m.* (*sport*) goal.
gola, *n.f.* gullet; (*mil.*) gorget.
goleta, *n.f.* schooner.
golfín, *n.m.* dolphin.
golfista, *n.m.f.* golfer.
golfo, -fa, *n.m.f.* street urchin.—*n.m.* gulf, bay; main, open sea; mass; mess.
Gólgota, *n.f.* Golgotha.
Goliat, *n.m.* Goliath.
golilla, *n.f.* ruff, gorget; (*S.A.*) tie.
golondrina, *n.f.* (*orn.*) swallow.
golondrino, *n.m.* (*mil.*) deserter.
golondro, *n.m.* (*fam.*) desire, whim.
golosina, *n.f.* tit-bit; eagerness.
goloso, -sa, *a.* greedy; sweet-toothed.—*n.m.f.* gourmand.
golpazo, *n.m.* thump.
golpe, *n.m.* blow, knock; shock, clash; mass, abundance; surprise; wittiness; *dar* —, be a hit; *de* —, suddenly; — *de estado,* coup d'état; — *de gracia,* coup de grâce; — *de mano,* surprise attack; — *de teatro,* dramatic turn of events; — *de vista* or *de ojo,* glance, look.
golpear, *v.t.* beat, knock, bump.
golpeo, *n.m.* beating, knocking, bumping.
golpetear, *v.t.* hammer, pound.
gollería, *n.f.* morsel; (*fam.*) pernicketiness.
golletazo, *n.m.* breaking (*of bottle-neck*); abrupt finishing; (*taur.*) thrust through bull's lungs.
gollete, *n.m.* neck.
goma, *n.f.* rubber, gum; (rubber) eraser; rubber band; tyre; (*S.A.*) hangover; — *de mascar,* chewing gum; — *espumosa,* foam rubber.
gomoso, -sa, *a.* gummy; rubbery.—*n.m.* fop, coxcomb.
gonce [GOZNE].
góndola, *n.f.* gondola.
gondolero, *n.m.* gondolier.
gongo, *n.m.* gong.
gongorino, -na, *a., n.m.f.* Gongorist.
gongorismo, *n.m.* Gongorism (*Spanish euphuism*).
gordiano, -na, *a.* Gordian.
gordi(n)flón, -flona, *a.* (*fam.*)tubby, pudgy.
gordo, -da, *a.* fat, plump; greasy; large, big; thick, coarse; *se armó la gorda,* (*fam.*) there was hell to pay.—*n.m.* fat; first prize in lottery.
gordura, *n.f.* fatness; fat.
Gorgona, *n.f.* (*myth.*) Gorgon.
gorgorito, *n.m.* (*fam.*) trill.
gorgorotada, *n.f.* gulp.
gorgotear, *v.i.* gurgle.
gorgoteo, *n.m.* gurgle.
gorguera, *n.f.* ruff; gorget.
gorila, *n.m.* (*zool.*) gorilla.
gorja, *n.f.* throat; *estar de* —, (*fam.*) be full of fun.
gorjear, *v.i.* warble.—*v.r.* gurgle.
gorjeo, *n.m.* warbling; gurgle.
gorra (1), *n.f.* cap.

gorra (2), *n.f.* sponging; *de* —, on the sponge; *colarse de* —, (*fam.*) gate-crash.
gorrero, -ra, *n.m.f.* cap-maker; (*fam.*) sponger.
gorrino, -na, *n.m.f.* piglet; (*fam.*) pig.
gorrión, *n.m.* sparrow.
gorrionera, *n.f.* den of thieves.
gorrista, *a.* sponging.—*n.m.f.* sponger.
gorro, *n.m.* cap; bonnet.
gorrón (1), **-rrona,** *a.* sponging.—*n.m.f.* sponger.
gorrón (2), *n.m.* pebble; (*mech.*) pivot.
gorronear, *v.i.* sponge.
gorullo, *n.m.* ball, lump.
gota, *n.f.* drop; (*med.*) gout.
gotear, *v.i.* drip; splatter.
goteo, *n.m.* dripping.
gotera, *n.f.* dripping; leak.
gótica, *n.f.* (*print.*) gothic type.
gótico, -ca, *a.* Gothic; noble.
gotoso, -sa, *a.* gouty.—*n.m.f.* gout sufferer.
gozar [C], *v.t.* enjoy, possess.—*v.i.* enjoy, rejoice (*de,* in).—*v.r.* enjoy oneself; delight (*en,* in).
gozne, *n.m.* hinge.
gozo, *n.m.* joy, glee; mirth.
gozoso, -sa, *a.* joyful, merry.
gozque(jo), *n.m.* small dog.
grabado, *n.m.* engraving; print.
grabar, *v.t.* engrave; record (*sounds*).—*v.r.* be fixed *or* engraved (*on one's memory*).
gracejar, *v.i.* be a charmer.
gracejo, *n.m.* wit, charm; (*C.A.*) clowner.
gracia, *n.f.* grace; piece of wit; funniness; *de* —, gratis; *en* — *a,* because of; *hacer* —, amuse, be funny; *hacer* — *de,* let (*s.o.*) off; *pedir una* —, ask a favour; *tener* —, be funny, amusing.—*pl.* thanks, thank-you.
grácil, *a.* gracile, slender.
gracioso, -sa, *a.* graceful, gracious; funny, witty; gratuitous.—*n.m.* (*theat.*) comic, comic rôle.
grada, *n.f.* grandstand; step; tier; (*naut.*) slipway, (*agr.*) harrow.—*pl.* steps.
gradación, *n.f.* gradation; (*gram.*) comparison.
gradería, *n.f.* stand, row of seats; steps.
gradiente, *n.m.* (*math.*) gradient; (*S.A.*) slope, gradient.
gradilla, *n.f.* step-ladder.
grado, *n.m.* step, tread (*of stair*); grade; degree; (*mil.*) rank; *de* (*buen*) —, gladly, willingly; *en alto* —, to a high degree.
graduación, *n.f.* graduation; grading; rank.
graduado, -da, *a., n.m.f.* graduate.
gradual, *a.* gradual.
graduar [M], *v.t.* graduate; evaluate, grade; (*mil.*) confer the rank (*de,* of) on.—*v.r.* graduate (*de,* as).
grafía, *n.f.* graphy, graph.
gráfico, -ca, *a.* graphic(al); rel. to printing.—*n.m.* diagram.—*n.f.* graph.
grafito, *n.m.* graphite; graffito.
gragea, *n.f.* tiny candy.
grajo, -ja, *n.m.f.* (*orn.*) rook; jackdaw; chough.
gramática, *n.f.* grammar; — *parda,* (*fam.*) slyness, cunning.
gramatical, *a.* grammatical.
gramático, -ca, *a.* grammatical.—*n.m.f.* grammarian.
gramo, *n.m.* gramme.

gramófono, *n.m.* phonograph.
gramola, *n.f.* record-player and cabinet.
gran, *a.* contracted form of GRANDE, *before sg. nouns.*
grana (1), *n.f.* running to seed.
grana (2), *n.f.* kermes; red cloth.
granada, *n.f.* pomegranate; grenade, shell.
granadero, *n.m.* grenadier.
granadino, -na, *a., n.m.f.* rel. to *or* native of Granada.
granado (1), **-da,** *a.* notable; expert; seedy; large.
granado (2), *n.m.* pomegranate-tree.
granalla, *n.f.* filings, granules.
granar, *v.t.* coarse-grind.—*v.i.* run to seed, fruit.
grande, *a.* big, large; great; *en —*, largely. [GRAN].—*n.m.* grandee.
grandeza, *n.f.* greatness; size; grandeur.
grandilocuente, grandílocuo, -cua, *a.* grandiloquent.
grandillón, -llona, *a.* (*fam.*) over-big.
grandiosidad, *n.f.* grandeur.
grandioso, -sa, *a.* grandiose.
grandor, *n.m.* size.
granear, *v.t.* sow; stipple.
granero, -ra, *a.* rel. to grain.—*n.m.f.* grain-merchant.—*n.m.* granary.
granillo, *n.m.* fine grain; profit.
granilloso, -sa, *a.* granular.
granito, *n.m.* granite.
granizada, *n.f.* hail-storm; (*S.A.*) iced drink.
granizar [C], *v.t., v.i.* hail.
granizo, *n.m.* hail.
granja, *n.f.* dairy farm; dairy grange.
granjear, *v.t.* win, earn.—*v.r.* win over, gain.
granjeo, *n.m.* winning; gain.
granjería, *n.f.* gain; husbandry.
granjero, -ra, *n.m.f.* farmer.
grano, *n.m.* grain; berry, bean, grape; pimple; *ir al —*, get to the point.—*pl.* corn, grain.
granuja, *n.f.* (single) grape; pip.—*n.m.* rogue.
granular, *a.* granular.—*v.t.* granulate.
gránulo, *n.m.* granule.
granza, *n.f.* (*bot.*) madder.—*pl.* chaff; dross.
grao, *n.m.* shore; beach-port.
grapa, *n.f.* clamp; staple.
grasa, *n.f.* fat, grease.—*pl.* slag.
graseza, *n.f.* fattiness.
grasiento, -ta, *a.* greasy.
graso, -sa, *a.* fatty.—*n.m.* fattiness.
grata (1), *n.f.* favour, esteemed (*letter*).
grata (2), *n.f.* wire brush.
gratificación, *n.f.* gratification; reward.
gratificar [A], *v.t.* gratify; reward, tip.
al gratín, *a., adv. phr.* (*cul.*) au gratin.
gratitud, *n.f.* gratitude.
grato, -ta, *a.* pleasing; gratuitous; (*S.A.*) grateful.
gratulación, *n.f.* felicitation.
gratular, *v.t.* congratulate.—*v.r.* rejoice.
grava, *n.f.* gravel.
gravamen, *n.m.* obligation; load, burden.
gravar, *v.t.* burden.
grave, *a.* heavy; grave; serious (*illness*); difficult.
gravedad, *n.f.* gravity.
gravedoso, -sa, *a.* pompous, ponderous.
gravidez, *n.f.* pregnancy.
grávido, -da, *a.* gravid; pregnant.
gravitación, *n.f.* gravitation.

gravitacional, *a.* gravitational.
gravitar, *v.i.* gravitate; rest; be a burden (*sobre*, to).
gravoso, -sa, *a.* onerous.
graznar, *v.i.* caw, croak.
graznido, *n.m.* caw, croak.
Grecia, *n.f.* Grecce.
greco, -ca, *a., n.m.f.* Greek.
grecolatino, -na, *a.* Graeco-Latin.
grecorromano, -na, *a.* Graeco-Roman.
greda, *n.f.* marl, fuller's earth.
gregario, -ria, *a.* gregarious; slavish.
Gregorio, *n.m.* Gregory.
greguería, *n.f.* din, hubbub.
gregüescos, *n.m.pl.* 17th century breeches.
gremial, *a.* rel. to union *or* guild.—*n.m.* guildsman, trade-unionist.
gremio, *n.m.* guild, trade union; lap.
greña, *n.f.* mop, shock, tangled hair; *andar a la —*, (*fam.*) squabble, fight.
gresca, *n.f.* uproar; wrangle.
grey, *n.f.* flock; herd; nation.
Grial, *n.m.* Grail.
griego, -ga, *a., n.m.f.* Greek.
grieta, *n.f.* crack, split.
grietar, *v.t.* crack, split.
grietoso, -sa, *a.* cracked, crannied.
grifo, -fa, *a.* curly.—*n.m.* tap, (*U.S.*) faucet; (*myth.*) griffin.
grifón, *n.m.* spigot, faucet.
grilla, *n.f.* (*rad.*) grid; (*fam.*) fib.
grillete, *n.m.* shackle, fetter.
grillo (1), *n.m.* (*ent.*) cricket.
grillo (2), *n.m.* usually *pl.* fetters, irons; drag, impediment; *andar a grillos*, (*fam.*) fritter time away.
grima, *n.f.* horror; *dar — a,* irritate.
gringo, -ga, *a., n.m.f.* (*pej.*) Gringo (*Anglo-Saxon*).
gripe, *n.f.* influenza.
gris, *a.* grey.—*n.m.* cold weather; grey.
grisáceo, -cea, *a.* greyish.
grisú, *n.m.* (*min.*) fire-damp.
grita, *n.f.* shouting.
gritar, *v.i.* shout; scream; cry out.
gritería, *n.f.*, **griterío,** *n.m.* outcry, clamouring, shouting.
grito, *n.m.* shout, cry; scream; *poner el — en el cielo,* (*fam.*) raise the roof (*contra*, against).
groenlandés, -desa, *a., n.m.f.* Greenlander.
Groenlandia, *n.f.* Greenland.
grosella, *n.f.* currant.
grosería, *n.f.* coarseness; stupidity.
grosero, -ra, *a.* coarse; vulgar; stupid.
grosísimo, -ma, *a.* sup. of GRUESO.
grosor, *n.m.* thickness, bulk.
grosura, *n.f.* fat, suet; meat diet; offal.
grúa, *n.f.* crane, derrick, hoist.
grueso, -sa, *a.* thick, bulky, massive; coarse, rough; dense; (*fig.*) stupid.—*n.m.* bulk; size, thickness.—*n.f.* gross (144).
grulla, *n.f.* (*orn.*) crane.
grumo, *n.m.* clot; lump.
gruñente, *a.* grunting.
gruñido, *n.m.* grunt; growl.
gruñir [K], *v.i.* grunt; growl; creak.
gruñón, -ñona, *a.* (*fam.*) grumpy.
grupa, *n.f.* croup, rump.
grupera, *n.f.* crupper; pillion.
grupo, *n.m.* group; (*mech.*) unit.
gruta, *n.f.* grotto, cave.

guaca, *n.f.* (*S.A.*) Indian tomb; (*fig.*) hidden treasure; nest-egg.
guachapear, *v.t.* kick, splash (*water with feet*); (*fam.*) botch.—*v.i.* rattle.
guácharo, -ra, *a.* ailing, sickly.
guachinango, -ga, *a.* (*C.A.*) crafty, cunning. —*n.m.f.* (*C.A. pej.*) Mex, Mexican.
guacho, -cha, *a.* orphaned.—*n.m.* chick.
guadamací *or* **-cil, guadamecí** *or* **-cil,** *n.m.* embossed leather. (*pl.* **-cíes**)
guadaña, *n.f.* scythe.
guadañar, *v.t.* mow, scythe.
guagua, *n.f.* trifle; (*S.A.*) kid, baby; (*dial., C.A.*) bus.
guaita, *n.f.* night-guard.
guajiro, -ra, *a.* (*Cuba*) rustic.—*n.m.f.* white Cuban peasant.
gualdo, -da, *a.* yellow. —*n.f.* weld.
gualdrapa, *n.f.* trappings; (*fam.*) tatter.
guano, *n.m.* guano.
guantada, *n.f.,* **guantazo,** *n.m.* slap *or* blow with glove.
guante, *n.m.* glove.
guantelete, *n.m.* gauntlet.
guapear, *v.i.* (*fam.*) show off.
guapeza, *n.f.* (*fam.*) good looks; (*fam.*) daring; (*fam.*) showing-off.
guapo, -pa, *a.* (*fam.*) good-looking; showy.— *n.m.* bully; (*fam.*) girl-chaser. —*n.m.f.* (*fam.*) chum, dear (*in vocative*).
guapura, *n.f.* (*fam.*) good looks.
guarapo, *n.m.* sugar-cane juice.
guarda, *n.m.f.* guard, keeper.—*n.m.* guard, ranger, officer.—*n.f.* guard, safekeeping; flyleaf.
guardabarreras, *n.m.* (*rail.*) gate-keeper.
guardabarros, *n.m. inv.* mudguard, (*U.S.*) fender.
guardabosque, *n.m.* gamekeeper.
guardabrisa, *n.f.* windscreen, (*U.S.*) windshield.
guardacadena, *n.m. or f.* chain-guard.
guardacostas, *n.m. inv.* coast-guard cutter.— *pl.* coast-guard service.
guardafrenos, *n.m. inv.* (*rail.*) brakeman.
guardainfante, *n.m.* farthingale.
guardalado, *n.m.* rails, railing.
guardalmacén, *n.m.f.* store-keeper.
guardalodos, *n.m. inv.* (*S.A.*) mudguard.
guardamano, *n.m.* hand-guard of sword.
guardamarina, *n.m.* (*naut.*) midshipman.
guardameta, *n.m.* (*sport*) goalkeeper.
guardapuerta, *n.f.* storm-door.
guardar, *v.t.* guard; keep; look after; observe, obey; save.—*v.r.* be on one's guard; guard (*de,* against); look out (*de,* for).
guardarropa, *n.f.* wardrobe; cloakroom.— *n.m.f.* costumier.
guardarropía, *n.f.* (*theat.*) wardrobe, props.; *de —,* make-believe, sham.
guardasilla, *n.f.* chair-rail.
guardavía, *n.m.* (*rail.*) linesman.
guardería, *n.f.* guard; day-nursery.
guardia, *n.m.* policeman, guard.—*n.f.* guard, watch; protection; duty; *de —,* on guard; on duty; *— civil, m.* country policeman; *f.* country police; *— de corps,* bodyguard (*m. person; f. group*).
guardián, -diana, *n.m.f.* guardian.
guardilla, *n.f.* attic; end-guard (*comb*).
guardoso, -sa, *a.* careful; mean, stingy.

guarecer [9], *v.t.* shelter.—*v.r.* take refuge *or* shelter.
guarida, *n.f.* den, lair; shelter.
guarín, *n.m.* piglet.
guarismo, *n.m.* cypher, number.
guarnecer [9], *v.t.* garnish; edge; provide; plaster; equip; garrison, man.
guarnición, *n.f.* trimmings, edging; setting; sword-guard; garrison; harness; (*mech.*) lining, bush; (*cul.*) garnish.—*pl.* fixtures, fittings.
guarnicionar, *v.t.* garrison.
guarro, -rra, *n.m.f.* pig.
¡guarte! *interj.* look out!
guasa, *n.f.* (*fam.*) dullness; (*fam.*) joking.
guaso, -sa, *a.* (*S.A.*) churlish.—*n.m.f.* peasant.
guasón, -sona, *a.* (*fam.*) churlish; (*fam.*) waggish.—*n.m.f.* (*fam.*) lout; (*fam.*) wag.
guatemalteco, -ca, *a., n.m.f.* Guatemalan.
¡guau! *n.m., interj.* bow-wow!
¡guay! *interj.* (*poet.*) alack!
guaya, *n.f.* lament, plaint.
guayaba, *n.f.* guava; (*S.A., fam.*) fib, yarn.
Guayana, *n.f.* Guyana.
guayanés, -nesa, *a., n.m.f.* Guyanese.
gubernamental, *a.* governmental; pro-government.
gubernativo, -va, *a.* governmental.
gubia, *n.f.* (*carp.*) gouge.
guedeja, *n.f.* mane (*of lion*); long hair.
güero, -ra, *a.* (*C.A.*) blond(e).—*n.m.f.* (*C.A., fam.*) dear.
guerra, *n.f.* war, warfare; *dar —,* (*fam.*) be a nuisance; *— fría,* cold war; *Guerra Mundial,* World War; *— relámpago,* blitzkrieg.
guerrear, *v.i.* war, fight.
guerrero, -ra, *a.* warlike, warring, war.— *n.m.f.* fighter, warrior, soldier.
guerrilla, *n.f.* guerrilla band *or* warfare.
guerrillero, *n.m.* guerrilla.
guía, *n.m.f.* guide; leader.—*n.f.* guide, guidance; marker, post; (*rail.*) timetable; handle-bars; *— sonora,* (*cine.*) sound-track; *— telefónica,* telephone directory.
guiar [L], *v.t.* lead; drive, pilot, steer.—*v.r.* be guided (*de, por,* by).
guija, *n.f.* pebble.—*pl.* (*fam.*) go, energy.
guijarro, *n.m.* cobble, large pebble.
guijo, *n.m.* gravel; (*mech.*) gudgeon.
Guillermo, *n.m.* William.
guillotina, *n.f.* guillotine; *de —,* sash (*window*).
guillotinar, *v.t.* guillotine.
guinchar, *v.t.* goad, prick.
güinche, *n.m.* (*S.A.*) winch.
guincho, *n.m.* goad, pricker.
guinda, *n.f.* mazard, sour cherry.
guindal, *n.m.,* **guindaleza,** *n.f.* (*naut.*) hawser.
guindar, *v.t.* hoist; (*fam.*) snap up.
guindilla, *n.f.* small sour cherry; pepper (*fruit*).—*n.m.* (*fam.*) copper (*policeman*).
guindo, *n.m.* sour-cherry tree.
guindola, *n.f.* bosun's chair; lifebuoy.
Guinea, *n.f.* Guinea.
guineo, -ea, *a., n.m.f.* Guinean.—*n.f.* guinea (*coin*).
guiñada, *n.f.* wink; (*naut.*) lurch.
guiñapo, *n.m.* tatter; ragamuffin.
guiñar, *v.t.* wink.—*v.i.* wink; (*naut.*) lurch.
guiño, *n.m.* wink; grimace.

guión, *n.m.* guide; hyphen, dash; outline, notes; script; scenario.
guionista, *n.m.f.* scriptwriter; (*cine.*) scenarist; dubber.
guirlache, *n.m.* almond brittle.
guirnalda, *n.f.* garland.
guisa, *n.f.* way, wise; *a — de,* as, in the manner of.
guisado, *n.m.* stew.
guisante, *n.m.* pea.
guisar, *v.t.* cook; stew; arrange.
guiso, *n.m.* dish, stew; seasoning.
guita, *n.f.* twine; (*fam.*) cash.
guitarra, *n.f.* guitar.
guitarrear, *v.i.* strum a guitar.
guitarreo, *n.m.* strumming (*of guitar*).
guitarrista, *n.m.f.* guitarist.
guitarro, *n.m.* small four-stringed guitar.
guitarrón, *n.m.* big guitar; (*fam.*) sly scamp.
guitón, -tona, *n.m.f.* tramp, vagrant; (*fam.*) scamp.
guizque, *n.m.* boat-hook.
gula, *n.f.* gluttony.
guloso, -sa, *a.* gluttonous.
gulusmear, *v.i.* hang around the food.
gullería [GOLLERÍA].
gurdo, -da, *a.* silly.
guripa, *n.m.* (*low*) soldier; scoundrel.
gurriato, *n.m.* young sparrow.
gurrufero, *n.m.* broken-down old horse.
gurrumino, -na, *a.* weak, wretched; (*S.A.*) cowardly.—*n.m.* (*fam.*) doting *or* henpecked husband.—*n.f.* luxuriousness.—*n.m.f.* (*C.A.*) kid, child.
gurullo, *n.m.* lump; knot.
gusanear, *v.i.* teem.
gusanera, *n.f.* worm heap; (*fam.*) mania.
gusanillo, *n.m.* small grub *or* worm; silk twist; threaded tip.
gusano, *n.m.* grub, worm, maggot.
gustación, *n.f.* tasting, taste.
gustadura, *n.f.* tasting, sampling.
gustar, *v.t.* please; taste, try.—*v.i.* be nice; please; *— de,* like, enjoy; *me gusta leer,* I like to read, *me gusta el pan,* I like bread; *como Vd. gusta,* as you please, as you will.
gustatorio, -ria, *a.* gustatory.
gustazo, *n.m.* delight; malignant delight.
gustillo, *n.m.* trace, slight taste.
gusto, *n.m.* pleasure; whim; taste, flavour; *a —,* at will; *con mucho —,* only too happy, delighted; *dar —,* be very pleasant, please; *estar a —,* be happy, be in one's element; *tomar — a,* take a liking to.
gustoso, -sa, *a.* glad, delighted; tasty; pleasant.
gutapercha, *n.f.* gutta-percha.
gutural, *a., n.f.* guttural.

H

H, h, *n.f.* ninth letter of the Spanish alphabet.
ha [HABER].
haba, *n.f.* bean; broad bean.

habado, -da, *a.* dappled.
la Habana, *n.f.* (*geog.*) Havana.
habanero, -ra, *a., n.m.f.* Havanese.—*n.f.* habanera (*dance*).
habano, -na, *a.* from Havana (*tobacco*).—*n.m.* Havana cigar.
haber (1) [19], *v.t.* (*obs.*) have.—*v.i.* (*impersonal:* pres. **hay**) there to' be; *tres años ha,* three years ago.—*v.r.* **habérselas con,** have it out with; deal with.—*auxiliary v.* have; *— que hacer,* be necessary to do; *— de: he de salir temprano,* I am to leave early; *he de escribir,* I have to write, I must write.
haber (2), *n.m.* (*com.*) credit (*side*); income; (*esp. pl.*) property, wealth.
habichuela, *n.f.* kidney bean; *habichuelas verdes,* French beans.
hábil, *a.* skilful, able; (*jur.*) fit, qualified; *día —,* working day.
habilidad, *n.f.* ability; skill; cunning.
habilitación, *n.f.* qualification; (*naut.*) fitting out.
habilitar, *v.t.* entitle, qualify; finance; equip, fit out.
habitable, *a.* habitable, inhabitable.
habitación, *n.f.* dwelling; room; habitat.
habitar, *v.t.* inhabit.
hábito, *n.m.* dress, habit; habit, custom.
habituación, *n.f.* habituation.
habitual, *a.* habitual; usual.
habituar [M], *v.t.* accustom, habituate.
habitud, *n.f.* habit, custom; connexion.
habla, *n.f.* speech; language, dialect; *al —,* (*tel.*) speaking.
hablador, -ra, *a.* talkative.—*n.m.f.* gossip.
habladuría, *n.f.* idle talk; gossip.
hablante, *a.* speaking.—*n.m.f.* speaker.
hablar, *v.t., v.i.* speak; talk.
hablilla, *n.f.* rumour; gossip.
hacanea, *n.f.* nag.
hacedero, -ra, *a.* feasible.
Hacedor, *n.m.* Maker.
hacedor, *n.m.* (farm-)manager.
hacendado, -da, *a.* landed, property-owning.—*n.m.f.* property-owner; (*S.A.*) rancher.
hacendar [1], *v.t.* transfer (*property*).—*v.r.* buy property.
hacendero, -ra, *a.* industrious; sedulous.—*n.f.* public work.
hacendista, *n.m.* economist.
hacendoso, -sa, *a.* industrious.
hacer [20], *v.t.* make; do; act; believe (**s.o.** to be): *yo hacía a Juan en París,* I thought John was in Paris.—*v.r.* become; *hacerse a,* become accustomed to; *hace,* ago: *hace un año,* a year ago; *desde hace,* for: *está aquí desde hace un mes,* he has been here (for) a month; *hacer hacer,* have done; *— de,* act as.
hacia, *prep.* toward(s); about; *— adelante,* forward(s).
hacienda, *n.f.* landed property; farm, ranch; (*S.A.*) livestock; (*pol.*) Treasury.—*pl.* chores.
hacina, *n.f.* stack; pile.
hacinamiento, *n.m.* accumulation.
hacinar, *v.t.* stack; pile.
hacha (1), *n.f.* axe.
hacha (2), *n.f.* torch.
hache, *n.f.* aitch, name of letter **H**.
hach(e)ar, *v.t.* hew.

113

hachero, *n.m.* woodcutter; (*mil.*) sapper, pioneer.
hacheta, *n.f.* small axe; small torch.
hachich, *n.m.* hashish.
hacho, *n.m.* firebrand, torch; beacon (*hill*).
hada, *n.f.* fairy.
hadar, *v.t.* foretell; fate.
hado, *n.m.* fate.
hagiografía, *n.f.* hagiography.
hagiógrafo, *n.m.* hagiographer.
hago [HACER].
Haití, *n.m.* Haiti.
haitiano, -na, *a.* Haitian.
¡hala! *interj.* get up! gee up!
halagador, -ra, *a.* flattering.
halagar [B], *v.t.* flatter; cajole; fondle.
halago, *n.m.* (*esp. pl.*) flattery; cajolery; caress.
halagüeño, -ña, *a.* attractive; flattering.
halar, *v.t.* (*naut.*) haul.—*v.i.* (*naut.*) pull ahead.
halcón, *n.m.* falcon.
halconear, *v.i.* (*fam.*) be brazen.
halconero, *n.m.* falconer.
halda, *n.f.* skirt; burlap (*for packing*).
haldudo, -da, *a.* full-skirted.
haleche, *n.m.* (*ichth.*) anchovy.
hálito, *n.m.* breath; (*poet.*) breeze.
halo, *n.m.* halo.
hallar, *v.t.* find.—*v.r.* find oneself; be (situated).
hallazgo, *n.m.* finding, discovery; reward for discovery.
hamaca, *n.f.* hammock; deck-chair.
hámago, *n.m.* beebread; nausea.
hambre, *n.f.* hunger; famine.
hambrear, *v.t., v.i.* starve.
hambriento, -ta, *a.* hungry (*de*, for).
hamo, *n.m.* fish-hook.
hampa, *n.f.* low-life, underworld.
hampesco, -ca, *a.* villainous.
hampón, *n.m.* bully, lout.
hangar, *n.m.* (*aer.*) hangar.
haragán, -gana, *a.* idle, loafing.—*n.m.f.* idler, loafer.
haraganear, *v.i.* idle, loaf.
harapiento, -ta, haraposo, -sa, *a.* ragged.
harapo, *n.m.* tatter, rag.
harén, *n.m.* harem.
harija, *n.f.* mill-dust, flour-dust.
harina, *n.f.* flour; *ser* — *de otro costal,* be quite a different kettle of fish.
harinero, -ra, rel. to flour.—*n.m.* flour-dealer.
harinoso, -sa, *a.* mealy; farinaceous.
harmonía [ARMONÍA].
harnero, *n.m.* sieve, riddle.
harón, -rona, *a.* lazy.—*n.m.* loafer.
harpa, *n.f.* harp.
harpía, *n.f.* harpy.
harpillera, *n.f.* burlap, sack-cloth.
hartar, *v.t.* sate; stuff.—*v.i.* be satiated.—*v.r.* be satiated; be bored, fed up (*de,* with).
hartazgo, *n.m.* fill, glut, (*fam.*) bellyful.
harto, -ta, *a.* full, satiated; fed up (*de,* with). —*adv.* sufficiently; exceedingly.
hartura, *n.f.* satiety; abundance.
hasta, *adv.* even.—*prep.* until, as far as, (*U.S.*) through; — *luego* or *la vista,* good-bye, until we meet again.
hastial, *n.m.* (*arch.*) gable-end; yokel.
hastiar [L], *v.t.* surfeit; cloy; disgust.
hastío, *n.m.* disgust, nausea; surfeit; boredom.

hastioso, -sa, *a.* sickening, disgusting; boring.
hataca, *n.f.* large wooden spoon; rolling-pin.
hatear, *v.t.* (*fam.*) pack up.—*v.i.* pack one's equipment.
hatería, *n.f.* equipment; provision for several days.
hato, *n.m.* herd, flock; (shepherds') lodge *or* hut, bothie; outfit, clothes; gang.
haxix [HACHICH].
hay, *v. impers.* there is *or* are [HABER (1)].
La Haya, *n.f.* The Hague.
haya (1), *n.f.* (*bot.*) beech.
haya (2), [HABER (1)].
hayaca, *n.f.* (*S.A.*) mince pie.
hayal, hayedo, *n.m.* beech grove.
hayo, *n.m.* (*S.A. bot.*) coca.
hayuco, *n.m.* beech mast.
haz (1), *n.m.* (*pl.* **haces**) bundle, sheaf; beam; jet (*cathode ray*).
haz (2), *n.m.* (*pl.* **haces**) troops drawn up in array; (*mil.*) file.
haz (3), *n.f.* (*pl.* **haces**) (*esp. fig.*) face; surface; upper side (*leaf*).
haz (4), [HACER].
haza, *n.f.* field (*arable*).
hazaña, *n.f.* exploit, deed.
hazañería, *n.f.* fuss, dismay.
hazañero, -ra, *a.* easily dismayed *or* fussed.
hazañoso, -sa, *a.* heroic, valiant.
hazmerreír, *n.m.* laughing-stock.
he (1), *adv.* here is *or* are; *heme aquí,* here I am.
he (2), [HABER (1)].
hebdómada, *n.f.* period of seven days *or* years.
hebdomadario, -ria, *a.* hebdomadal, hebdomadary, weekly.
hebilla, *n.f.* buckle, clasp.
hebra, *n.f.* fibre; thread; grain (*of wood*).
hebraico, -ca, *a.* Hebrew, Hebraic.
hebraizar [C & P], *v.t., v.i.* Hebraize; Judaize.
hebreo, -rea, *a.* Hebrew.—*n.m.f.* Hebrew.— *n.m.* Hebrew (*language*); (*pej.*) usurer.
Hébridas, *n.f.pl.* Hebrides.
hebroso, -sa, *a.* stringy, fibrous.
hectárea, *n.f.* hectare.
héctico, -ca, *a.* (*med.*) consumptive.
hectiquez, *n.f.* (*med.*) consumption, phthisis.
hectolitro, *n.m.* hectolitre.
hectómetro, *n.m.* hectometre.
hechicería, *n.f.* sorcery, witchcraft; glamour.
hechicero, -ra, *a.* enchanting; charming.— *n.m.* wizard.—*n.f.* witch.
hechizar [C], *v.t.* bewitch, enchant.
hechizo, -za, *a.* artificial; fake; detachable; (*S.A.*) home-produced.—*n.m.* spell; magic; glamour.
hecho, -cha, *p.p.* [HACER].—*a.* accustomed; perfect; ready-made.—*n.m.* act; event; fact; *de* —, in fact, (*jur.*) de facto.
hechura, *n.f.* making; workmanship; creature; shape; (*S.A.*) treat.
hedentina, *n.f.* stink.
heder [2], *v.t.* annoy.—*v.i.* stink.
hediondez, *n.f.* stink.
hediondo, -da, *a.* stinking, fetid; lewd.— *n.m.* (*bot.*) wild Syrian rue; (*zool.*) skunk.
hedonismo, *n.m.* hedonism.
hedor, *n.m.* stink.
hegemonía, *n.f.* hegemony.
hégira, *n.f.* Hegira, hegira.

heladería, *n.f.* (*esp. S.A.*) ice-cream parlour.
helado, -da, *a.* frozen; frost-bitten; chilly.—
n.m. ice-cream.—*n.f.* frost.
helar [1], *v.t.* freeze; discourage.—*v.i.* freeze.
—*v.r.* freeze; be frost-bitten.
helecho, *n.m.* (*bot.*) fern.
helénico, -ca, *a.* Hellenic.
helenismo, *n.m.* Hellenism.
helenístico, -ca, *a.* Hellenistic.
heleno, -na, *a.* Hellenic.—*n.m.f.* Hellene.
helero, *n.m.* snow-cap; glacier.
helgado, -da, *a.* jag-toothed.
helgadura, *n.f.* gap (*in the teeth*).
hélice, *n.f.* heliz, spiral; screw, propeller.
hélico, -ca, *a.* helical.
helicoide, *n.m.* helicoid.
helicóptero, *n.m.* (*aer.*) helicopter.
helio, *n.m.* helium.
heliotropio *or better* **heliotropo,** *n.m.* (*bot.,*
min.) heliotrope.
helvecio, -cia, *a., n.m.f.* Helvetian.
helvético, -ca, *a.* Helvetic.—*n.m.f.* Helvetian.
hematíe, *n.m.* (*med.*) red (blood) cell.
hembra, *n.f.* female (*of animals and plants*);
(*low*) woman; eye (*of a hook*); female part
(*of plug etc.*), socket; gudgeon.
hembrilla, *n.f.* small socket *or* staple.
hemeroteca, *n.f.* newspaper library.
hemiciclo, *n.m.* semicircle.
hemisferio, *n.m.* hemisphere.
hemistiquio, *n.m.* hemistich.
hemofilia, *n.f.* (*med.*) hemophilia.
hemoglobina, *n.f.* (*med.*) hemoglobin.
hemorragia, *n.f.* hemorrhage.
hemorroida, hemorroide, *n.f.* (*esp. pl.*)
(*med.*) hemorrhoids.
henal, *n.m.* hayloft.
henar, *n.m.* hayfield.
henchimiento, *n.m.* filling-up; abundance;
repletion.
henchir [8], *v.t.* fill; stuff.
hendedura, *n.f.* crack, fissure.
hender [2], *v.t.* split, cleave, crack.
hendible, *a.* cleavable.
hendidura, *n.f.* crack, fissure.
henil, *n.m.* hayloft.
heno, *n.m.* hay.
heñir [8K], *v.t.* knead.
heptagonal, *a.* heptagonal.
heptágono, -na, *a.* heptagonal.—*n.m.* hep-
tagon.
heptámetro, *n.m.* heptameter.
heptasílabo, -ba, *a.* heptasyllabic.—*n.m.*
heptasyllable.
heráldico, -ca, *a.* heraldic.—*n.f.* heraldry.
heraldo, *n.m.* herald, king-at-arms.
herbáceo, -cea, *a.* herbaceous.
herbaje, *n.m.* pasture, herbage.
herbaj(e)ar, *v.t., v.i.* graze.
herbario, -ria, *a.* herbal.—*n.m.* herbarium;
herbalist.
herbero, *n.m.* oesophagus (*of a ruminant*).
herbicida, *a., n.m.* herbicide, weed-killer.
herbívoro, -ra, *a.* herbivorous.
herbolario, *n.m.* herbalist; (*fam.*) scatter-
brain.
herborizar [C], *v.i.* herbalize.
herboso, -sa, *a.* grassy.
herciano, -na, *a.* (*phys.*) Hertzian.
hercúleo, -lea, *a.* Herculean, herculean.
heredable, *a.* inheritable, hereditable.

heredamiento, *n.m.* inheritance; landed
estate, hereditament.
heredar, *v.t.* inherit; institute as heir.
heredero, -ra, *a.* inheritable; inheriting.—
n.m. heir, inheritor; — **presunto,** heir
presumptive.—*n.f.* heiress, inheritor.
hereditario, -ria, *a.* hereditary.
hereje, *n.m.f.* heretic.
herejía, *n.f.* heresy.
herén, *n.m.* vetch.
herencia, *n.f.* inheritance; heritage.
herético, -ca, *a.* heretical.
herido, -da, *a.* wounded; hurt.—*n.m.f.*
injured *or* wounded person, casualty.—*n.f.*
wound.
herir [6], *v.t.* hurt, injure; wound; strike;
pluck (*an instrument*); touch, offend.
hermana, *n.f.* sister [HERMANO].
hermanar, *v.t.* match; join; harmonize.—
v.r. match; love one another as brothers.
hermanastra, *n.f.* step-sister.
hermanastro, *n.m.* step-brother.
hermanazgo, *n.m.* brotherhood.
hermandad, *n.f.* brotherhood; fraternity;
conformity.
hermanear, *v.t.* call brother; treat as a
brother.
hermano, -na, *a.* sister (*language*); matched
(*objects*).—*n.m.* brother; mate, companion; —
carnal, full brother; — **de leche,** foster
brother; **medio—,** half-brother; —**político,**
brother-in-law; **hermanos siameses,**
Siamese twins.
hermético, -ca, *a.* hermetic; air-tight; (*fig.*)
impenetrable.
hermosear, *v.t.* beautify.
hermoso, -sa, *a.* beautiful, handsome,
comely.
hermosura, *n.f.* beauty, handsomeness;
belle.
hernioso, -sa, *a.* herniated, suffering from
hernia.
héroe, *n.m.* hero.
heroico, -ca, *a.* heroic(al).
heroína, *n.f.* heroine.
heroismo, *n.m.* heroism.
herrada, *n.f.* wooden pail.
herradero, *n.m.* place *or* season for branding
cattle.
herrador, *n.m.* smith.
herradura, *n.f.* horse-shoe.
herraj [ERRAJ].
herramental, *n.m.* tool-box; tool-bag.
herramienta, *n.f.* tool, implement; set of
tools; (*fam.*) horns; (*fam.*) teeth.
herrar [1], *v.t.* shoe (*horses*); brand (*cattle*);
hoop, bind with iron.
herrén, *n.m.* mixed fodder.
herrería, *n.f.* smithy.
herrerico, herrerillo, *n.m.* (*orn.*) blue tit;
great tit; marsh tit.
herrero, *n.m.* smith, blacksmith; — **de obra,**
structural steelworker, scaffolder.
herreruelo, *n.m.* (*orn.*) coal tit.
herrete, *n.m.* ferrule, metal tip.
herrín, *n.m.* rust (*iron*).
herrón, *n.m.* quoit; washer.
herrumbre, *n.f.* rust (*iron*).
herrumbroso, -sa, *a.* rusty.
herventar, *v.t.* boil.
hervidor, *n.m.* boiler (*domestic*), kettle.
hervir [6], *v.i.* boil; seethe.

hervor, *n.m.* boiling; vigour; — *de la sangre,* rash.
hervoroso, -sa, *a.* ardent, impetuous.
hesitación, *n.f.* (*rare*) hesitation.
heteróclito, -ta, *a.* (*gram.*) heteroclite.
heterodoxia, *n.f.* heterodoxy.
heterodoxo, -xa, *a.* heterodox.
heterogeneidad, *n.f.* heterogeneity.
heterogéneo, -nea, *a.* heterogeneous.
hético, -ca [HÉCTICO].
hetiquez [HECTIQUEZ].
hexagona, *a.* hexagonal.
hexágono, -na, *a.* hexagonal.—*n.m.* hexagon.
hexámetro, *n.m.* hexameter.
hez, *n.f.* (*pl.* **heces**) sediment; dregs; scum, dross; (*fig.*) dregs, scum.—*pl.* excrement.
hiato, *n.m.* hiatus; gap.
hibernar, *v.i.* hibernate.
hibernés,-nesa,hibernio,-nia, *a.* Hibernian.
híbrido, -da, *a.* hybrid.
hice [HACER].
hidalgo, -ga, *a.* noble.—*n.m.f.* noble.—*n.m.* nobleman.—*n.f.* noblewoman.
hidalguez, hidalguía, *n.f.* nobility.
hidrato, *n.m.* (*chem.*) hydrate.
hidráulico, -ca, *a.* hydraulic(al).—*n.f.* hydraulics.
hidroavión, *n.m.* seaplane; flying-boat.
hidrocarburo, *n.m.* (*chem.*) hydrocarbon.
hidrodeslizador, *n.m.* hydroplane.
hidroeléctrico, -ca, *a.* hydro-electric.
hidrófilo, -la, *a.* (*chem.*) hydrophilic; absorbent (*cotton*).
hidrófugo, -ga, hidrofugante, *a.* water-repellent.
hidrógeno, *n.m.* hydrogen.
hidrógrafo, *n.m.* hydrographer.
hidromel, hidromiel, *n.m.* hydromel, mead.
hidropesía, *n.f.* (*med.*) dropsy.
hidrópico, -ca, *a.* hydropic, dropsical.
hidroplano, *n.m.* hydroplane; seaplane, flying-boat.
hidrosulfuro, *n.m.* (*chem.*) hydrosulphide.
hidrotecnia, *n.f.* hydraulic engineering.
hidruro, *n.m.* (*chem.*) hydride.
hiedra, *n.f.* (*bot.*) ivy.
hiel, *n.f.* gall, bile; bitterness.
hielo, *n.m.* ice; frost; cold; *punto de —,* freezing-point.
hiemal, *a.* hibernal, winter.
hiena, *n.f.* hyena.
hienda, *n.f.* dung.
hierba, *n.f.* grass; herb; *mala —,* weed.—*pl.* pasture; herbal poison; herb soup.
hierbabuena, *n.f.* (*bot.*) mint.
hierro, *n.m.* iron; brand; weapon; — *albo,* white-hot iron; — *colado,* cast iron; — *de fragua,* wrought iron; — *a Vizcaya,* coals to Newcastle.—*pl.* irons (*shackles*).
higa, *n.f.* amulet; mockery.
hígado, *n.m.* liver.—*pl.* (*fam.*) guts; *malos hígados,* ill-will.
higiene, *n.f.* hygiene; sanitation.
higiénico, -ca, *a.* hygienic(al); *papel —,* lavatory paper.
higo, *n.m.* fig; (*vet.*) thrush; (*fig.*) rap, fig; — *chumbo,* prickly pear.
higuera, *n.f.* (*bot.*) fig-tree; — *chumba,* prickly pear; — *del diablo* or *infernal,* castor-oil plant.
hija, *n.f.* daughter [HIJO].

hijastro, -tra, *n.m.f.* stepchild.—*n.m.* stepson.—*n.f.* stepdaughter.
hijo, -ja, *n.m.f.* child; young (*of animals*); issue, product.—*n.m.* son; — *político,* son-in-law.—*n.f.* daughter.
hijodalgo, *n.m.* [HIDALGO].
hijuela, *n.f.* little daughter; gore, gusset; branch drain *or* path *etc.*
hijuelo, *n.m.* little son; (*bot.*) sucker.
hila, *n.f.* row, line; spinning.—*pl.* (*med.*) lint; (*S.A.*) cotton waste.
hilacha, *n.f.,* **hilacho,** *n.m.* loose thread; fraying; (*S.A.*) tatter, rag.
hilado, *n.m.* spinning; thread.
hilandería, *n.f.* spinning-mill.
hilandero, -ra, *n.m.f.* spinner.—*n.m.* spinning mill.
hilar, *v.t., v.i.* spin.
hilarante, *a.* mirthful; laughing (*gas*).
hilaridad, *n.f.* hilarity.
hilatura, *n.f.* spinning.
hilaza, *n.f.* yarn; uneven thread.
hilera, *n.f.* row, line.
hilo, *n.m.* thread; linen; yarn; edge (*of a blade*); filament; wire; — *de perlas,* string of pearls; *a —,* successively; *al —,* with the thread.
hilván, *n.m.* tacking (*in sewing*); (*S.A.*) hem; *de —,* rapidly.
hilvanar, *v.t.* tack (*in sewing*); (*fig.*) throw together in a hurry; (*S.A.*) hem.
La Himalaya, *n.f.* the Himalayas.
himalayo, -ya, *a.* Himalayan.
himnario, *n.m.* hymnal.
himno, *n.m.* hymn; — *nacional,* national anthem.
himnología, *n.f.* hymnology.
hin, *n.m.* neigh.
hincadura, *n.f.* driving; thrusting.
hincapié, *n.m.* **hacer — en algo,** insist on s.th.
hincar [A], *v.t.* fix, drive in (*a nail etc.*); — (*la rodilla*), bend (*the knee*).—*v.r.* kneel (down).
hincón, *n.m.* hitching- *or* mooring-post.
hincha, *n.f.* (*fam.*) grudge.—*n.m.* (*fam.*) fan, supporter.
hinchar, *v.t.* inflate, swell.—*v.r.* swell (up); become puffed up.
hinchazón, *n.m.* swelling; vanity.
hindú, -dúa, *a., n.m.f.* (*pl.* **-úes, -úas**) Hindu; Indian.
hiniesta, *n.f.* (*bot.*) broom.
hinojo (1), *n.m.* (*bot.*) fennel; — *marino,* samphire.
hinojo (2), *n.m.* (*obs.*) knee; *de hinojos,* on one's knees.
hipar, *v.i.* hiccup; pant (*of dogs*); whine; (*fig.*) — *por,* long for.
hipérbola, *n.f.* (*geom.*) hyperbola.
hipérbole, *n.f.* (*lit.*) hyperbole.
hiperbólico, -ca, *a.* (*geom., lit.*) hyperbolical.
hipercrítico, -ca, *a.* hypercritical.—*n.m.f.* severe critic.—*n.f.* severe criticism.
hipertensión, *n.f.* (*med.*) hypertension; high blood-pressure.
hípico, -ca, *a.* equine.—*n.f.* show-jumping; horse-racing.
hípido, *n.m.* whining.
hipismo, *n.m.* horse-training; equestrianism.
hipnosis, *n.f. inv.* hypnosis.

hipnótico, -ca, a., n.m.f. hypnotic.—n.m. hypnotic (drug).
hipnotismo, n.m. hypnotism.
hipnotizar [C], v.t. hypnotize.
hipo, n.m. hiccup; longing; grudge.
hipocampo, n.m. sea-horse.
hipocondría, n.f. hypochondria.
hipocondriaco, hipocondríaco, hipocóndrico, -ca, a., n.m.f. hypochondriac.
hipocrás, n.m. hippocras, grog.
hipocrático, -ca, a. Hippocratic.
hipocresía, n.f. hypocrisy.
hipócrita, a. hypocritical.—n.m.f. hypocrite.
hipodérmico, -ca, a. hypodermic.
hipódromo, n.m. hippodrome.
hipopótamo, n.m. hippopotamus.
hiposo, -sa, a. having hiccups.
hipoteca, n.f. mortgage.
hipotecable, a. mortgageable.
hipotecar [A], v.t. mortgage, hypothecate.
hipotensión, n.f. (med.) low blood-pressure.
hipotenusa, n.f. hypotenuse.
hipótesis, n.f. inv. hypothesis.
hipotético, -ca, a. hypothetical.
hiriente, a. stinging, cutting, hurting.
hirma, n.f. selvedge.
hirsuto, -ta, a. hirsute; (fig.) gruff.
hirviente, a. boiling.
hisca, n.f. bird-lime.
hisop(e)ar, v.t. (eccl.) asperse.
hisopillo, n.m. small aspergill; mouth-swab; (bot.) winter-savory.
hisopo, n.m. (bot.) hyssop; (eccl.) hyssop, aspergill.
hispalense, a., n.m.f. Sevillian.
hispánico, -ca, a. Hispanic.
hispanidad, n.f. Spanish character or spirit; Spanish-speaking community.
hispanismo, n.m. Hispanicism, Spanish idiom or turn of phrase; Spanish studies.
hispanista, n.m.f. Hispanist, Spanish scholar.
hispanizar [C], v.t. Hispanicize.
hispano, -na, a. Spanish, Hispanic.—n.m.f. Spaniard, man or woman of Spanish stock.
Hispanoamérica, n.f. Spanish America, Latin America.
hispanoamericano, -na, a. Spanish American, Latin American.
hispanohablante, a. Spanish-speaking.—n.m.f. speaker of Spanish.
histérico, -ca, a. hysterical.
histerismo, n.m. hysteria.
histología, n.f. histology.
historia, n.f. history; tale, story; — natural, natural history; de —, infamous, notorious.
historiador, -ra, n.m.f. historian.
historial, a. historical.—n.m. record sheet.
historiar, v.t. relate (history, story); (art.) depict, illustrate.
histórico, -ca, a. historic(al).
historieta, n.f. anecdote.
hita, n.f. brad, panel-pin, nail.
hito, -ta, a. (obs.) adjoining (house, street).—n.m. landmark; milestone; target; dar en el —, hit the nail on the head.
hitón, n.m. large headless cut nail.
hocico, n.m. snout; poner —, pout.
hocicón, -cona, hocicudo, -da, a. big-snouted.
hocino, n.m. sickle, bill-hook; gorge.
hogaño, adv. (obs.) this year.

hogar, n.m. hearth, fire-place; fire-chamber, furnace; home; hostel.
hogaza, n.f. large loaf.
hoguera, n.f. bonfire.
hoja, n.f. leaf (of plant, book, door); — de ruta, waybill.
hojalata, n.f. tin, tin-plate.
hojaldre, n.m. or f. puff-pastry.
hojear, v.t. leaf through, skim through.—v.t. flutter (of leaves).
hojuela, n.f. small leaf; pancake; foil.
¡hola! interj. hello!
Holanda, n.f. Holland; holanda, n.f. cambric, (U.S.) chambray.
holandés, -desa, a. Dutch.—n.m. Dutchman; Dutch (language).—n.f. Dutchwoman.
holgadamente, adv. amply; easily.
holganza, n.f. ease; leisure; enjoyment.
holgar [4B], v.i. rest; be idle; be unnecessary; be too loose; be glad (con, at).—v.r. be idle; amuse oneself.
holgazán, -zana, a. idle, indolent.—n.m.f. idler, loafer.
holgazanear, v.i. idle; loiter.
holgorio, n.m. mirth; spree.
holgura, n.f. mirth; spree; ease; looseness, (mech.) play.
holocausto, n.m. holocaust; burnt-offering.
hológrafo, -fa, a. holograph.
hollar [4], v.t. trample, tread upon.
hollejo, n.m. skin, peel, husk.
hollín, n.m. soot, smut.
holliniento, -ta, a. sooty, fuliginous.
hombracho, n.m. well-built man.
hombradía, n.f. manliness.
hombre, n.m. man; mankind; (low) husband; ombre (cards); — de estado, statesman.
hombrear, v.i. shoulder, vie (con, with).—v.r. vie (con, with).
hombrecillo, n.m. little man; (bot.) hop.
hombrera, n.f. epaulette; shoulder-strap.
hombría, n.f. manliness.
hombrillo, n.m. yoke (of a shirt).
hombro, n.m. shoulder.
hombruno, -na, a. mannish (of a woman).
homenaje, n.m. homage.
Homero, n.m. Homer.
homicida, a. homicidal, murderous.—n.m. murderer.—n.f. murderess.
homicidio, n.m. murder, homicide, manslaughter.
homilía, n.f. homily.
homogeneidad, n.f. homogeneity.
homogen(e)izar [C], v.t. homogenize; normalize (steel).
homogéneo, -nea, a. homogeneous.
homologar [B], v.t. validate (a record).
homólogo, -ga, a. homologous.
homonimia, n.f. homonymy.
homónimo, -ma, a. homonymous.—n.m.f. namesake.—n.m. homonym.
honda, n.f. sling.
hondo, -da, a. deep; low.—n.m. depth; bottom.
hondón, n.m. bottom (of cup); eye (of needle); dell; hole.
hondonada, n.f. dell, ravine.
hondura, n.f. depth; profundity.
Honduras, n.f., pl. Honduras.
hondureño, -ña, a., n.m.f. Honduran.
honestidad, n.f. modesty; decency; honourableness.

honesto, -ta, *a.* decent, chaste; honourable.
hongo, *n.m.* mushroom, fungus; bowler hat.
honor, *n.m.* honour; reputation.
honorable, *a.* honourable.
honorario, -ria, *a.* honorary.—*n.m.* honorarium.
honorífico, -ca, *a.* honorific, honourable.
honra, *n.f.* honour; reputation.—*pl.* obsequies.
honradez, *n.f.* integrity.
honrado, -da, *a.* honest, honourable, upright.
honrar, *v.t.* honour.—*v.r.* deem it an honour (*de,* to).
honrilla, *n.f.* keen sense of honour.
honroso, -sa, *a.* honourable (*action*).
hopo, *n.m.* bushy tail, brush.
hora, *n.f.* hour; time; — *de cenar,* supper time; *a la* —, on time; *¿qué — es?* what is the time? *horas extraordinarias,* overtime.
Horacio, *n.m.* Horace.
horadar, *v.t.* perforate, bore.
horario, -ria, *a.* hour.—*n.m.* hour-hand; time-table.
horca, *n.f.* gallows, gibbet; pitch-fork.
a horcajadas, a horcajadillas, *adv.phr.* astride.
horchata, *n.f.* horchata, orgeat.
horda, *n.f.* horde.
hordiate, *n.m.* pearl barley.
horizontal, *a.* horizontal.
horizonte, *n.m.* horizon.
horma, *n.f.* mould, last.
hormiga, *n.f.* ant.
hormigón, *n.m.* concrete; — *armado,* reinforced concrete.
hormigonera, *n.f.* concrete mixer.
hormiguear, *v.i.* itch; swarm (*as with ants*).
hormigueo, *n.m.* crawling sensation; itch.
hormiguero, *n.m.* ant-hill.
hormiguillo, *n.m.* (*vet.*) founders; human chain.
hormón, *n.m.* hormone.
hormonal, *a.* hormonal.
hornero, -ra, *n.m.f.* baker.
hornillo, *n.m.* stove (*for cooking*).
horno, *n.m.* oven, kiln, furnace; *alto* —, blast furnace.
horóscopo, *n.m.* horoscope.
horquilla, *n.f.* fork; fork-socket; (*mil.*) bracket (*in gunnery*); (*naut.*) rowlock.
horrendo, -da, *a.* horrible, awful.
hórreo, *n.m.* granary.
horrible, *a.* horrible.
horridez, *n.f.* dreadfulness.
hórrido, -da, horrífico, -ca, *a.* horrible, horrific.
horripilante, *a.* horrifying.
horro, -rra, *a.* free; freed; barren.
horror, *n.m.* horror.
horrorizar [C], *v.t.* horrify.
horroroso, -sa, *a.* horrible.
hortaliza, *n.f.* (*fresh*) vegetable, garden produce.
hortelano, -na, *a.* rel. to gardens.—*n.m.f.* gardener.
hortensia, *n.f.* (*bot.*) hydrangea.
hortícola, *a.* horticultural.
horticultura, *n.f.* gardening, horticulture.
hosco, -ca, *a.* swarthy; sullen, dour.
hospedaje, *n.m.* lodging.
hospedar, *v.t.* lodge, give lodging, put up.—*v.i., v.r.* lodge, stop at.

hospedería, *n.f.* hostelry, hostel, guest-house.
hospicio, *n.m.* hospice; asylum.
hospital, *n.m.* hospital, infirmary.
hospitalario, -ria, *a.* hospitable.—*n.m.* (*hist.*) Hospitaller.
hospitalidad, *n.f.* hospitality.
hostal, *n.m.* hostelry.
hostia, *n.f.* (*eccl.*) host, wafer.
hostigar [B], *v.t.* lash; chastise; censure severely; trouble.
hostigo, *n.m.* lash.
hostil, *a.* hostile.
hostilidad, *n.f.* hostility.
hostilizar [C], *v.t.* harass, raid.
hotel, *n.m.* hotel; mansion; — *de ventas,* auction rooms.
hotelero, -ra, *a.* rel. to hotels.—*n.m.* hotelier hotel-keeper.
hoy, *adv.* today; — *día* or — *en día,* nowadays; — *por la tarde,* this evening.
hoya, *n.f.* hole, pit; grave.
hoyo, *n.m.* hole, pit; grave.
hoyoso, -sa, *a.* pitted.
hoyuelo, *n.m.* dimple.
hoz, *n.f.* sickle, bill-hook; ravine.
hozar [C], *v.t.* root (*as pigs*).
hua- *see also* [GUA-].
huacal, *n.m.* crate.
hucha, *n.f.* large chest; money-box, (*child's*) piggy-bank.
hueco, -ca, *a.* hollow.—*n.m.* hollow; gap.
huelga, *n.f.* rest; strike (*in industry*).
huelgo, *n.m.* breath (*mech.*) clearance, slack.
huelguista, *n.m.* striker.
huella, *n.f.* footprint; trace.
huello, *n.m.* trodden path; treading.
huérfano, -na, *a., n.m.f.* orphan.
huero, -ra, *a.* addled; empty, vain; (*C.A.*) blond(e) [GÜERO].
huerta, *n.f.* stretch of irrigable land; market-gardening region.
huerto, *n.m.* orchard; fruit and vegetable garden.
huesa, *n.f.* grave.
hueso, *n.m.* bone; stone, core.
huesoso, -sa, *a.* bony, osseous.
huésped, -da, *n.m.f.* guest; host; inn-keeper.
hueste, *n.f.* host, army.
huesudo, -da, *a.* bony.
hueva, *n.f.* spawn, roe.
huevera, *n.f.* egg-woman; ovary (*of fowls*); egg-cup.
huevo, *n.m.* egg.
huida, *n.f.* flight; escape.
huidizo, -za, *a.* fugitive, fleeting.
huir, *v.i., v.r.* flee.
hule, *n.m.* oil-cloth, American cloth; (*S.A.*) rubber.
hulla, *n.f.* (pit-)coal.
hullero, -ra, *a.* rel. to coal.—*n.m.* colliery.
humanidad, *n.f.* humanity.—*pl.* humanities.
humanismo, *n.m.* humanism.
humanista, *n.m.* humanist.
humanitario, -ria, *a.* humanitarian.
humano, -na, *a.* human; humane.—*n.m.* human being.
humarada, humareda, *n.f.* cloud of smoke.
humeante, *a.* smoking, fuming.
humear, *v.i.* smoke, emit smoke.
humedad, *n.f.* humidity.

humedecer [9], *v.t.* moisten.
húmedo, *a.* humid; wet, damp.
húmero, *n.m.* (*anat.*) humerus, funny-bone.
humildad, *n.f.* humility, modesty, lowliness.
humilde, *a.* humble; modest.
humillación, *n.f.* humiliation.
humillante, *a.* humiliating.
humillar, *v.t.* humiliate, humble.—*v.r.* humble oneself.
humo, *n.m.* smoke; fume.
humor, *n.m.* humour; disposition; (*med.*) humour; **buen —,** good nature; **mal —,** ill-temper.
humorismo, *n.m.* (*med.*) theory of the humours; humorous style.
humorístico, -ca, *a.* comic, humorous.
hundible, *a.* sinkable.
hundimiento, *n.m.* subsidence; sinking; downfall.
hundir, *v.t.* sink; immerse; pull down; ruin. —*v.r.* sink; collapse.
húngaro, -ra, *a., n.m.f.* Hungarian.
Hungría, *n.f.* Hungary.
huno, -na, *a.* Hunnish.
hupe, *n.f.* touchwood, tinder.
huracán, *n.m.* hurricane.
huraño, -ña, *a.* shy, wild.
hurgar [B], *v.t.* poke (*fire*); stir up.
hurgón, *n.m.* poker; ash rake.
hurón, -rona, *a.* shy; intractable.—*n.m.f.* ferret.
¡hurra! *interj.* hurrah!
a hurtadillas, *adv. phr.* stealthily.
hurtar, *v.t.* steal.—*v.r.* steal off.
hurto, *n.m.* theft, robbery.
husma, *n.f.* (*fam.*) snooping.
husmear, *v.t.* scent, get wind of; (*fam.*) pry. —*v.i.* smell high.
husmo, *n.m.* high smell; **andarse al —,** be on the scent.
huso, *n.m.* spindle; bobbin; gore (*of parachute*).
huta, *n.f.* hut; (*huntsman's*) hide, blind.
hutía, *n.f.* (*zool.*) hutia, Cuban rat.
¡huy! *interj.* expressing surprise, grief *or* pain.

I

I, i, *n.f.* tenth letter of the Spanish alphabet.
iba [IR].
ibérico, -ca, iberio, -ria, *a.* Iberian.
ibero, -ra, *a., n.m.f.* Iberian.
iberoamericano, -na, *a., n.m.f.* Ibero-American.
íbice, *n.m.* ibex.
ibicenco, -ca, *a., n.m.f.* rel. to *or* native of Iviza.
ibis, *n.f.* ibis.
Ibiza, *n.f.* Iviza.
icón, *n.m.* icon.
iconoclasia, *n.f.* **iconoclasmo,** *n.m.* iconoclasm.
iconoclasta, *a.* iconoclastic.—*n.m.f.* iconoclast.
ictericia, *n.f.* (*med.*) jaundice.
ictiología, *n.f.* ichthyology.

ida, *n.f.* going, departure; impetuosity; trail; sally; **de — y vuelta,** return (*ticket*); **idas y venidas,** comings and goings.
idea, *n.f.* idea.
ideal, *a., n.m.* ideal.
idealismo, *n.m.* idealism.
idealista, *a.* idealist(ic).—*n.m.f.* idealist.
idealización, *n.f.* idealization.
idealizar [C], *v.t.* idealize.
idear, *v.t.* plan, contrive.
ideario, *n.m.* ideology, idearium.
ideático, -ca, *a.* (*S.A.*) whimsical.
idéntico, -ca, *a.* identical.
identidad, *n.f.* identity; identicalness.
identificable, *a.* identifiable.
identificación, *n.f.* identification.
identificar [C], *v.t.* identify.
ideograma, *n.m.* ideogram.
ideología, *n.f.* ideology.
ideológico, -ca, *a.* ideological.
ideólogo, *n.m.* ideologist.
idílico, -ca, *a.* idyllic.
idilio, *n.m.* idyll.
idioma, *n.m.* language; parlance, jargon, idiom.
idiomático, -ca, *a.* idiomatic.
idiosincrasia, *n.f.* idiosyncrasy.
idiosincrático, -ca, *a.* idiosyncratic.
idiota, *a., n.m.f.* idiot.
idiotez, *n.f.* idiocy.
idiótico, -ca, *a.* idiotic.
idiotismo, *n.m.* idiom; crass ignorance.
ido, -da, *a.* (*fam.*) wild, daft; tipsy, drunk.—*p.p.* [IR].
idólatra, *a.* idolatrous.—*n.m.* idolater, idolizer.—*n.f.* idolatress, idolizer.
idolatrar, *v.t.* idolize; idolatrize.
idolatría, *n.f.* idolatry; idolization.
ídolo, *n.m.* idol.
idóneo, -nea, *a.* suitable, proper.
idus, *n.m.pl.* ides.
iglesia, *n.f.* church.
iglú, *n.m.* (*pl.* **-úes**) igloo.
Ignacio, *n.m.* Ignatius.
ignaro, -ra, *a.* ignorant.
ignición, *n.f.* ignition.
ignícola, *n.m.f.* fire-worshipper.
ignifugar [B], *v.t.* flame-proof (*cloth etc.*).
ignoble, *a.* ignoble.
ignominia, *n.f.* ignominy.
ignominioso, -sa, *a.* ignominious.
ignorancia, *n.f.* ignorance; unawareness.
ignorante, *a.* ignorant; unaware.—*n.m.f.* ignoramus.
ignorar, *v.t.* not know.
ignoto, -ta, *a.* unknown.
igual, *a.* equal; level, even; consistent; same, alike.—*adv.* the same, similarly; **al — que,** just as, like; **en — de,** in lieu of; **por —,** equally; **me es —,** it's all the same to me; **sin —,** matchless, unequalled.
iguala, *n.f.* equalization; agreement; stipend.
igualación, *n.f.* equalization; levelling; matching; agreement.
igualar, *v.t.* equalize; level off; match, pair; equate; settle, adjust, iron out.—*v.i., v.r.* be equal.
igualdad, *n.f.* equality; levelness; sameness; evenness.
igualitario, -ria, *a., n.m.f.* egalitarian.
igualmente, *adv.* likewise; (*fam.*) the same to you.

iguana, *n.f.* iguana.
ijada, *n.f.* flank; loin; stitch, pain in side; (*fig.*) weak spot.
ijadear, *v.i.* pant.
ijar, *n.m.* flank, loin.
ilegal, *a.* illegal, unlawful.
ilegalidad, *n.f.* illegality.
ilegibilidad, *n.f.* illegibility.
ilegible, *a.* illegible.
ilegitimidad, *n.f.* illegitimacy.
ilegítimo, -ma, *a.* illegitimate.
ileso, -sa, *a.* unharmed.
Ilíada, *n.f.* Iliad.
ilícito, -ta, *a.* illicit.
ilimitado, -da, *a.* unlimited, limitless.
ilógico, -ca, *a.* illogical.
iludir, *v.t.* mislead, delude.
iluminación, *n.f.* illumination; enlightenment.
iluminado, -da, *a.* illuminated; enlightened. —*n.m.pl.* illuminati.
iluminar, *v.t.* illuminate; enlighten.
ilusión, *n.f.* illusion.
ilusionar, *v.t.* fascinate, give illusions to.—*v.r.* have illusions.
ilusionista, *n.m.f.* illusionist.
ilusivo, -va, *a.* illusive.
iluso, -sa, *a.* deluded; visionary.
ilusorio, -ria, *a.* illusory.
ilustración, *n.f.* illustration; learning, enlightenment; ennobling.
ilustrado, -da, *a.* illustrated; learned; enlightened.
ilustrar, *v.t.* illustrate; ennoble; inspire; educate.
ilustrativo, -va, *a.* illustrative.
ilustre, *a.* illustrious.
imagen, *n.f.* (*pl.* **imágenes**) image.
imaginable, *a.* imaginable.
imaginación, *n.f.* imagination.
imaginar, *v.t., v.i., v.r.* imagine.
imaginario, -ria, *a.* imaginary.—*n.f.* (*mil.*) reserves.
imaginería, *n.f.* imagery; statuary.
imán, *n.m.* magnet, lodestone; magnetism; (*relig.*) imam.
iman(t)ación, *n.f.* magnetizing.
iman(t)ar, *v.t.* magnetize.
imbécil, *a., n.m.f.* imbecile.
imbecilidad, *n.f.* imbecility.
imberbe, *a.* beardless; raw, green.
imborrable, *a.* ineradicable, indelible.
imbuir [O], *v.t.* imbue (**de, en,** with).
imitación, *n.f.* imitation.
imitador, -ra, *a.* imitative.—*n.m.f.* imitator.
imitar, *v.t.* imitate.
impaciencia, *n.f.* impatience.
impacientar, *v.t.* make impatient.—*v.r.* get impatient.
impaciente, *a.* impatient.
impacto, *n.m.* impact.
impago, -ga, *a.* (*S.A.*) unpaid.
impalpabilidad, *n.f.* impalpability.
impalpable, *a.* impalpable.
impar, *a.* odd, uneven.—*n.m.* odd number.
imparcial, *a.* impartial, disinterested.
imparcialidad, *n.f.* impartiality.
imparidad, *n.f.* oddness, imparity.
impartir, *v.t.* impart.
impasible, *a.* impassive.
impavidez, *n.f.* intrepidity.
impávido, -da, *a.* dauntless, intrepid.

impecable, *a.* impeccable.
impedido, -da, *a.* disabled.
impedimenta, *n.f.* impedimenta.
impedimento, *n.m.* impediment.
impedir [8], *v.t.* prevent, impede.
impeler, *v.t.* propel, impel.
impenetrabilidad, *n.f.* impenetrability.
impenetrable, *a.* impenetrable.
impenitente, *a.* impenitent.
impensado, -da, *a.* unforeseen.
imperar, *v.i.* rule, hold sway.
imperativo, -va, *a., n.m.* imperative.
imperceptible, *a.* imperceptible.
imperdible, *n.m.* safety-pin.
imperdonable, *a.* unpardonable.
imperecedero, -ra, *a.* imperishable.
imperfecto, -ta, *a., n.m.* imperfect.
imperforable, *a.* imperforable; puncture-proof.
imperial, *a.* imperial.—*n.f.* top-deck.
imperialismo, *n.m.* imperialism.
imperialista, *a., n.m.f.* imperialist.
impericia, *n.f.* inexpertness, lack of skill.
imperio, *n.m.* empire; dominion, sway.
imperioso, -sa, *a.* imperious.
imperito, -ta, *a.* inexpert.
impermanente, *a.* impermanent.
impermeabilizar [C], *v.t.* waterproof.
impermeable, *a.* impermeable; waterproof.—*n.m.* raincoat.
impersonal, *a.* impersonal.
impersonalidad, *n.f.* impersonality.
impertérrito, -ta, *a.* dauntless.
impertinencia, *n.f.* impertinence.
impertinente, *a.* impertinent.—*n.m.pl.* lorgnettes.
imperturbabilidad, *n.f.* imperturbability.
imperturbable, *a.* imperturbable.
impetrar, *v.t.* entreat; get by entreaty.
ímpetu, *n.m.* impetus; impetuousness.
impetuosidad, *n.f.* impetuosity.
impetuoso, -sa, *a.* impetuous.
impiedad, *n.f.* impiety; pitilessness.
impío, -pía, *a.* impious, godless; cruel.
implacabilidad, *n.f.* implacability.
implacable, *a.* implacable.
implantar, *v.t.* implant, introduce.
implicación, *n.f.* contradiction; implication.
implicar [A], *v.t.* imply; implicate.—*v.i.* oppose, contradict.
implícito, -ta, *a.* implicit.
implorar, *v.t.* implore.
impolítico, -ca, *a.* impolitic; impolite.—*n.f.* discourtesy.
imponderable, *a., n.m.* imponderable.
imponente, *a.* imposing, impressive.
imponer [25], *v.t.* impose; invest; acquaint (**en,** with), instruct (**en,** in); impute falsely.—*v.i.* command respect, be imposing.—*v.r.* dominate; acquaint oneself (**de,** with); **se impone,** it becomes essential (to).
impopular, *a.* unpopular.
importación, *n.f.* importing, imports.
importador, -ra, *a.* importing.—*n.m.f.* importer.
importancia, *n.f.* importance; concern.
importante, *a.* important; considerable.
importar, *v.t.* amount to, be worth; imply; concern; (*com.*) import.—*v.i.* matter, be important.
importe, *n.m.* amount; value.
importunación, *n.f.* importuning.

importunar, *v.t.* importune, pester.
importunidad, *n.f.* importunity.
importuno, -na, *a.* importunate; inopportune.
imposibilidad, *n.f.* impossibility.
imposibilitar, *v.t.* render unable; make impossible; disable.—*v.r.* become unable; be disabled; become impossible.
imposible, *a.* impossible.
imposición, *n.f.* imposition.
impostor, -ra, *a.* cheating.—*n.m.f.* impostor.
impostura, *n.f.* imposture; false accusation.
impotencia, *n.f.* impotence.
impotente, *a.* impotent.
impracticable, *a.* impracticable; impassable.
impráctico, -ca, *a.* impractical.
imprecación, *n.f.* imprecation.
imprecar [A], *v.t.* imprecate, curse.
impreciso, -sa, *a.* imprecise, indefinite.
impregnación, *n.f.* impregnation.
impregnar, *v.t.* impregnate, saturate.
impremeditado, -da, *a.* unpremeditated.
imprenta, *n.f.* printing; press; printed matter; impress(ion).
imprescindible, *a.* indispensable.
impresión, *n.f.* printing; impression; stamp; (*phot.*) print; — digital, finger print.
impresionable, *a.* impressionable.
impresionante, *a.* impressing, impressive.
impresionar, *v.t.* impress; (*phot.*) expose.
impresionismo, *n.m.* impressionism.
impresionista, *a.*, *n.m.f.* impressionist.
impreso, -sa, *a.* printed.—*n.m.* printed book.
—*pl.* printed matter.
impresor, -ra, *n.m.f.* printer.
imprevisible, *a.* unforseeable.
imprevisión, *n.f.* improvidence.
imprevisto, -ta, *a.* unforeseen.
imprimir, [*p.p.* impreso], *v.t.* impress; print; stamp.
improbabilidad, *n.f.* improbability.
improbable, *a.* improbable.
improbar, *v.t.* disapprove, censure.
ímprobo, -ba, *a.* dishonest; laborious.
improcedente, *a.* unlawful; inappropriate.
impronta, *n.f.* stamp, mark.
impronunciable, *a.* unpronounceable.
improperio, *n.m.* insult, affront.
impropiedad, *n.f.* impropriety.
improprio, *a.* improper, unsuited; alien.
impróvido, -da, *a.* improvident.
improvisación, *n.f.* improvisation; impromptu; unmerited success.
improvisar, *v.t.*, *v.i.* improvise.
improviso, -sa, improvisto, -ta, *a.* unforeseen, unexpected; al or de improviso, or a la improvista, unexpectedly.
imprudente, *a.* imprudent.
impudencia, *n.f.* shamelessness, impudence.
impudente, *a.* shameless, impudent.
impúdico, -ca, *a.* immodest, shameless.
impuesto, *a.* imposed; informed (de, about).
—*n.m.* tax, duty.—*p.p.* [IMPONER].
impugnar, *v.t.* contest, impugn.
impulsar, *v.t.* impel; (*mech.*) drive.
impulsión, *n.f.* impulsion; impulse.
impulsivo, -va, *a.* impulsive.
impulso, *n.m.* impulse; impulsion.
impulsor, -ra, *a.* impelling; (*mech.*) driving.
impune, *a.* unpunished.
impunidad, *n.f.* impunity.
impureza, impuridad, *n.f.* impurity.

impuro, -ra, *a.* impure.
impuse, -so [IMPONER].
imputación, *n.f.* imputation.
imputar, *v.t.* impute; (*com.*) credit on account.
inabordable, *a.* unapproachable.
inacabable, *a.* interminable, endless.
inaccesibilidad, *n.f.* inaccessibility.
inaccesible, *a.* inaccessible.
inacción, *n.f.* inaction.
inaceptable, *a.* unacceptable.
inactividad, *n.f.* inactivity.
inactivo, -va, *a.* inactive.
inadecuado, -da, *a.* inadequate; unsuited.
inadmisible, *a.* inadmissible.
inadvertencia, *n.f.* inadvertency; oversight.
inadvertido, -da, *a.* unnoticed; inadvertent.
inagotable, *a.* inexhaustible.
inaguantable, *a.* intolerable.
inajenable, *a.* inalienable.
inalterable, *a.* unalterable.
inalterado, -da, *a.* unchanged.
inane, *a.* inane.
inanidad, *n.f.* inanity.
inanimado, -da, *a.* inanimate.
inapagable, *a.* inextinguishable.
inapelable, *a.* without appeal; unavoidable.
inapetencia, *n.f.* lack of appetite.
inaplicable, *a.* inapplicable.
inaplicación, *n.f.* indolence, inapplication.
inaplicado, -da, *a.* indolent, careless.
inapreciable, *a.* inappreciable; inestimable.
inapto, -ta, *a.* inapt.
inarticulado, -da, *a.* inarticulate.
inasequible, *a.* unattainable, inaccessible.
inatención, *n.f.* inattention.
inatento, -ta, *a.* inattentive.
inaudible, *a.* inaudible.
inauguración, *n.f.* inauguration; opening, opening ceremony.
inaugural, *a.* inaugural.
inaugurar, *v.t.* inaugurate.
inaveriguable, *a.* unverifiable.
inca, *n.m.f.* Inca.
incaico, -ca, *a.* Inca.
incalculable, *a.* incalculable.
incalificable, *a.* unspeakable.
incambiable, *a.* unchangeable.
incandescencia, *n.f.* incandescence.
incandescente, *a.* incandescent.
incansable, *a.* tireless.
incapacidad, *n.f.* incapacity; incapability.
incapacitar, *v.t.* incapacitate; make impossible; declare incapable.
incapaz, *a.* (*pl.* -aces) incapable; incompetent.
incásico, -ca [INCAICO].
incautar, *v.r.* (*jur.*) seize, attach.
incauto, -ta, *a.* incautious, unwary.
incendiar, *v.t.* set fire to.—*v.r.* catch fire.
incendiario, -ria, *a.*, *n.m.f.* incendiary.
incendio, *n.m.* fire, blaze.
incensar [I], *v.t.* incense, cense.
incensario, *n.m.* censer.
incentivo, -va, *a.*, *n.m.* incentive.
incertidumbre, incertitud, *n.f.* uncertainty.
incesable, incesante, *a.* incessant, ceaseless.
incesto, *n.m.* incest.
incestuoso, -sa, *a.* incestuous.
incidencia, *n.f.* incidence; incident.
incidental, *a.* incidental.
incidente, *a.*, *n.m.* incident.

incidir, *v.t.* (*med.*) make an incision.—*v.i.* fall (*en*, into).

incienso, *n.m.* incense.

incierto, -ta, *a.* uncertain; untrue.

incineración, *n.f.* incineration, cremation.

incinerar, *v.t.* incinerate, cremate.

incipiente, *a.* incipient.

incircunciso, -sa, *a.* uncircumcised.

incisión, *n.f.* incision.

incisivo, -va, *a.* incisive.

incitación, *n.f.* inciting, incitement.

incitante, *a.* inciting; tempting.

incitar, *v.t.* incite (*a*, to).

incivil, *a.* uncivil, incivil.

incivilidad, *n.f.* incivility.

incivilizado, -da, *a.* uncivilized.

inclasificable, *a.* unclassifiable.

inclemencia, *n.f.* inclemency; **a la —,** exposed to the elements.

inclemente, *a.* inclement.

inclinación, *n.f.* inclination; bow; gradient.

inclinar, *v.t.* incline.—*v.i.*, *v.r.* incline, be inclined; bow.

ínclito, -ta, *a.* renowned, illustrious.

incluir [O], *v.t.* include; enclose.

inclusión, *n.f.* inclusion; acquaintanceship.

inclusive, *a.* inclusively.

inclusivo, -va, *a.* inclusive.

incluso, -sa, *a.* enclosed.—*adv.* even; included, besides.

incoativo, -va, *a.* inchoative.

incógnito, -ta, *a.* unknown, incognito; **de —,** incognito.—*n.m.* incognito.—*n.f.* (*math.*) unknown quantity.

incoherencia, *n.f.* incoherence.

incoherente, *a.* incoherent.

íncola, *n.m.f.* inhabitant.

incoloro, -ra, *a.* colourless.

incólume, *a.* safe, unharmed.

incombustible, *a.* incombustible.

incomible, *a.* uneatable.

incomodar, *v.t.* inconvenience.—*v.r.* get angry.

incomodidad, *n.f.* inconvenience; uncomfortableness; vexation.

incómodo, -da, *a.* uncomfortable; inconvenient; cumbersome.—*n.m.* discomfort; inconvenience.

incomparable, *a.* incomparable.

incomparado, -da, *a.* matchless.

incompasivo, -va, *a.* pitiless.

incompatibilidad, *n.f.* incompatibility.

incompatible, *a.* incompatible.

incompetencia, *n.f.* incompetence, (*jur.*) incompetency.

incompetente, *a.* incompetent.

incompleto, -ta, *a.* incomplete.

incomprensible, *a.* incomprehensible.

incomprensión, *n.f.* lack of understanding.

incomunicable, *a.* untransferable.

incomunicación, *n.f.* solitary confinement, isolation.

incomunicado, -da, *a.* incommunicado.

inconcebible, *a.* inconceivable.

inconciliable, *a.* irreconcilable.

inconcluso, -sa, *a.* unfinished; inconclusive.

inconcuso, -sa, *a.* unquestionable.

incondicional, *a.* unconditional.

inconexión, *n.f.* incoherence; lack of connexion.

inconexo, -xa, *a.* unconnected, incoherent.

inconfundible, *a.* unmistakable.

incongruencia, *n.f.* incongruence, incongruity.

incongruente, *a.* incongruent.

incongruidad, *n.f.* incongruity.

incongruo, -rua, *a.* incongruous.

inconmensurable, *a.* incommensurable; immense.

inconmovible, *a.* unmovable, unyielding.

inconocible, *a.* unknowable.

inconquistable, *a.* impregnable; incorruptible.

inconsciencia, *n.f.* unconsciousness; unawareness.

inconsciente, *a.* unconscious; unknowing, unaware.

inconsecuencia, *n.f.* inconsequence.

inconsecuente, *a.* inconsequent; inconsistent.

inconsideración, *n.f.* inconsideration.

inconsiderado, -da, *a.* inconsiderate; unconsidered.

inconsiguiente, *a.* inconsistent.

inconsistencia, *n.f.* inconsistency.

inconsistente, *a.* inconsistent.

inconstancia, *n.f.* inconstancy.

inconstante, *a.* inconstant.

inconstitucional, *a.* unconstitutional.

incontable, *a.* uncountable, countless.

incontaminado, -da, *a.* uncontaminated.

incontestable, *a.* unquestionable, indisputable.

incontestado, -da, *a.* undisputed.

incontinencia, *n.f.* incontinence.

incontinente, *a.* incontinent.—*adv.* (*also* **incontinenti**) at once.

incontrastable, *a.* irresistible; unquestionable; unshakable.

incontrovertible, *a.* incontrovertible.

inconvenible, *a.* inconvenient; uncompromising.

inconveniencia, *n.f.* inconvenience; unfitness; impropriety; unlikeliness.

inconveniente, *a.* inconvenient; impolite; unsuitable.—*n.m.* objection, difficulty.

incorporación, *n.f.* incorporation.

incorporar, *v.t.* incorporate; embody.—*v.r.* sit up.

incorpóreo, -rea, *a.* incorporal.

incorrecto, -ta, *a.* incorrect.

incorregible, *a.* incorrigible.

incorruptible, *a.* incorruptible.

incorrupto, -ta, *a.* incorrupt, uncorrupted.

increado, -da, *a.* uncreated.

incredibilidad, *n.f.* incredibility.

incredulidad, *n.f.* incredulousness.

incrédulo, -la, *a.* incredulous.—*n.m.f.* unbeliever.

increíble, *a.* incredible, unbelievable.

incrementar, *v.t.* increase.

incremento, *n.m.* increment.

increpar, *v.t.* chide, rebuke.

incriminación, *n.f.* incrimination.

incriminar, *v.t.* incriminate.

incrustación, *n.f.* incrustation.

incrustar, *v.t.* encrust.

incubación, *n.f.* incubation, hatching.

incubar, *v.t.* incubate, hatch.

íncubo, *n.m.* incubus.

inculcar [A], *v.t.* inculcate.—*v.r.* be stubborn.

inculpable, *a.* blameless.

inculpar, *v.t.* accuse, inculpate.

inculto, -ta, *a.* uncultured, uncivilized; uncultivated.

ineludible

incultura, *n.f.* lack of culture.
incumbencia, *n.f.* incumbency; concern.
incumbente, *a.* incumbent.
incumbir, *v.i.* be incumbent (*a*, on).
incumplido, -da, *a.* unfulfilled.
incunable, *n.m.* incunabulum.
incurable, *a., n.m.f.* incurable.
incurrir, *v.i.* lapse; incur, become liable (*en*, to).
incursión, *n.f.* incursion, inroad.
indagación, *n.f.* investigation.
indagar [B], *v.t.* investigate.
indebido, -da, *a.* undue; improper; uncalled-for.
indecencia, *n.f.* indecency.
indecente, *a.* indecent.
indecible, *a.* unspeakable.
indecisión, *n.f.* indecision.
indeciso, -sa, *a.* indecisive, undecided; vague.
indecoroso, -sa, *a.* indecorous.
indefectible, *a.* unfailing, indefectible.
indefendible, indefensable, indefensible, *a.* indefensible.
indefenso, -sa, *a.* defenceless.
indefinible, *a.* undefinable.
indefinido, -da, *a.* indefinite; undefined.
indeleble, *a.* indelible.
indelicadeza, *n.f.* indelicacy.
indelicado, -da, *a.* indelicate.
indemnidad, *n.f.* indemnity.
indemnizar [C], *v.t.* indemnify.
independencia, *n.f.* independence.
independiente, *a.* independent (*de*, of).
indescifrable, *a.* undecipherable.
indescriptible, *a.* indescribable.
indeseable, *a., n.m.f.* undesirable.
indestructible, *a.* indestructible.
indeterminable, *a.* indeterminable.
indeterminación, *n.f.* indetermination.
indeterminado, -da, *a.* indeterminate.
la India, *n.f.* India.
indiano, -na, *a., n.m.f.* Indian (*West, East*). —*n.m.* nabob, emigrant who returns rich from the Americas.
Indias, *n.f.pl.* the Indies (*esp. West Indies*).
indicación, *n.f.* indication.
indicador, -ra, *a.* indicating.—*n.m.f.* indicator.
indicar [A], *v.t.* indicate.
indicativo, -va, *a., n.m.* indicative.
índice, *n.m.* index; index finger.
indicio, *n.m.* sign, mark, token; *indicios vehementes*, (*jur.*) circumstantial evidence.
índico, -ca, *a.* (*East*) Indian.
indiferencia, *n.f.* indifference.
indiferente, *a.* indifferent; immaterial.
indígena, *a., n.m.f.* native.
indigencia, *n.f.* indigence.
indigente, *a.* indigent.
indigestión, *n.f.* indigestion.
indigesto, -ta, *a.* indigestible; undigested.
indignación, *n.f.* indignation.
indignar, *v.t.* anger.—*v.r.* become indignant.
indignidad, *n.f.* indignity; unworthiness.
indigno, -na, *a.* unworthy.
indigo, *n.m.* indigo.
indio (1), -dia, *a., n.m.f.* Indian.
indio (2), *a.* blue.
indirecto, -ta, *a.* indirect.—*n.f.* innuendo, hint.
indisciplina, *n.f.* indiscipline.

indisciplinado, -da, *a.* undisciplined.
indiscreción, *n.f.* indiscretion.
indiscreto, -ta, *a.* indiscreet.
indisculpable, *a.* inexcusable.
indiscutible, *a.* unquestionable, undeniable.
indisoluble, *a.* indissoluble.
indispensable, *a.* unpardonable; indispensable.
indisponer [25], *v.t.* indispose; prejudice.—*v.r.* become indisposed; quarrel; be cross.
indisposición, *n.f.* disinclination; indisposition.
indispuesto, -ta, *a.* indisposed; at variance. —*p.p.* [INDISPONER].
indisputable, *a.* indisputable.
indistinguible, *a.* indistinguishable.
indistinto, -ta, *a.* indistinct; joint (*account*).
individual, *a.* individual.
individualidad, *n.f.* individuality.
individualismo, *n.m.* individualism.
individualista, *a., n.m.f.* individualist.
individualizar [C], *v.t.* individualize.
individuo, -dua, *a.* individual.—*n.m.f.* member, fellow; individual; (*fam.*) character; self.
indivisible, *a.* indivisible.
indiviso, -sa, *a.* undivided.
indo, -da, *a., n.m.f.* Hindu.
indócil, *a.* indocile, unteachable.
indocto, -ta, *a.* unlearned.
la Indochina, *n.f.* Indo-China.
indochino, -na, *a., n.m.f.* Indo-Chinese.
indoeuropeo, -pea, *a., n.m.f.* Indo-European.
indogermánico, -ca, *a., n.m.* Indo-Germanic.
índole, *n.f.* disposition, temper; class, kind.
indolencia, *n.f.* indolence.
indolente, *a.* indolent.
indoloro, -ra, *a.* painless.
indómito, -ta, *a.* indomitable; unruly.
la Indonesia, *n.f.* Indonesia.
indonésico, -ca, indonesio, -sia, *a., n.m.f.* Indonesian.
inducción, *n.f.* inducing; induction.
inducido, *n.m.* (*elec.*) armature.
inducir [15], *v.t.* induce; lead (*en*, into).
inductivo, -va, *a.* inductive.
indudable, *a.* indubitable, undoubted.
indulgencia, *n.f.* indulgence.
indulgente, *a.* indulgent.
indultar, *v.t.* pardon.
indulto, -ta, *a.* (*jur.*) pardon.
indumentario, -ria, *a.* rel. to clothing.—*n.f.* attire, garb.
indumento, *n.m.* attire, apparel.
industria, *n.f.* industry; industriousness; profession; *de* —, on purpose.
industrial, *a.* industrial.—*n.m.* industrialist.
industrialismo, *n.m.* industrialism.
industrializar [C], *v.t.* industrialize.
industriar, *v.r.* find a way, manage.
industrioso, -sa, *a.* industrious.
induzco [INDUCIR].
inédito, -ta, *a.* unpublished.
inefable, *a.* ineffable.
ineficacia, *n.f.* inefficacy.
ineficaz, *a.* ineffectual.
ineficiencia, *n.f.* inefficiency.
ineficiente, *a.* inefficient.
inelegante, *a.* inelegant.
ineluctable, *a.* inevitable.
ineludible, *a.* unavoidable.

inepcia, ineptitud, *n.f.* ineptitude, inaptitude.
inepto, -ta, *a.* inept, inapt.
inequívoco, -ca, *a.* unequivocal.
inercia, *n.f.* inertia.
inerme, *a.* unarmed.
inerrable, *a.* unerring.
inerte, *a.* inert.
inescrutable, *a.* inscrutable.
inesperado, -da, *a.* unexpected.
inestable, *a.* unstable.
inestimable, *a.* inestimable.
inevitable, *a.* inevitable.
inexactitud, *n.f.* inexactitude.
inexacto, -ta, *a.* inexact; incorrect.
inexcusable, *a.* inexcusable.
inexistente, *a.* non-existent.
inexorable, *a.* inexorable.
inexperiencia, *n.f.* inexperience.
inexperto, -ta, *a.* inexpert; inexperienced.
inexplicable, *a.* inexplicable.
inexplorado, -da, *a.* unexplored.
inexpresivo, -va, *a.* inexpressive.
inexpugnable, *a.* impregnable.
inextinguible, *a.* inextinguishable.
inextricable, *a.* inextricable.
infalibilidad, *n.f.* infallibility.
infalible, *a.* infallible.
infamación, *n.f.* defamation.
infamador, -ra, *a.* defamatory.—*n.m.f.* defamer, slanderer.
infamar, *v.t.* defame, slander.
infame, *a.* infamous; sordid.—*n.m.f.* infamous wretch.
infamia, *n.f.* infamy.
infancia, *n.f.* infancy; infants.
infanta, *n.f.* infanta (*Spanish king's daughter*).
infante, *n.f.* infante (*Spanish king's son*); infantryman.
infantería, *n.f.* infantry.
infanticida, *a.* infanticidal.—*n.m.f.* infanticide (*person*).
infanticidio, *n.m.* infanticide (*crime*).
infantil, *a.* infantile; children's; childish.
infatigable, *a.* indefatigable, tireless.
infatuación, *n.f.* infatuation; vanity.
infatuar, *v.t.* make vain.—*v.r.* become vain.
infausto, -ta, *a.* luckless, unfortunate.
infección, *n.f.* infection.
infeccioso, -sa, *a.* infectious.
infectar, *v.t.* infect.
infecto, -ta, *a.* infected; foul.
infecundidad, *n.f.* infertility.
infecundo, -da, *a.* infertile.
infelicidad, *n.f.* unhappiness.
infeliz, *a.* (*pl.* **-ices**) unhappy.—*n.m.f.* (*fam.*) poor devil.
inferencia, *n.f.* inference.
inferior, *a.* inferior; lower (*a,* than).—*n.m.f.* inferior.
inferioridad, *n.f.* inferiority.
inferir [6], *v.t.* infer; inflict; entail.—*v.r.* follow, be deduced.
infernal, *a.* infernal.
infernar [1], *v.t.* (*fam.*) upset.
infestación, *n.f.* infestation.
infestar, *v.t.* infest.
inficionar, *v.t.* infect.
infidelidad, *n.f.* infidelity; infidels.
infidente, *a.* disloyal, faithless.
infiel, *a.* unfaithful; disloyal.—*a., n.m.f.* infidel.

infiernillo, *n.m.* chafing dish; stove.
infierno, *n.m.* hell.
infiltración, *n.f.* infiltration.
infiltrar, *v.t., v.r.* infiltrate.
ínfimo, -ma, *a.* lowest, worst.
infinidad, *n.f.* infinity.
infinitesimal, *a.* infinitesimal.
infinitivo, -va, *a., n.m.* infinitive.
infinito, -ta, *a., n.m.* infinite.—*adv.* immensely.
infinitud, *n.f.* infinitude.
inflación, *n.f.* inflation; vanity.
inflacionismo, *n.m.* inflationism.
inflacionista, *a.* inflationary, inflationist. —*n.m.f.* inflationist.
inflador, *n.m.* pump (*for tyres, balls etc.*).
inflamable, *a.* inflammable.
inflamación, *n.f.* inflammation; ardour.
inflamar, *v.t.* inflame; set on fire.—*v.r.* become inflamed; catch fire.
inflamatorio, -ria, *a.* inflammatory.
inflar, *v.t.* blow up, inflate.
inflexible, *a.* inflexible.
inflexión, *n.f.* bending; inflexion.
inflexionar, *v.t.* inflect.
infligir [E], *v.t.* inflict (*a,* on).
influencia, *n.f.* influence.
influenciar, *v.t.* influence.
influir [O], *v.i.* have (an) influence (*en, sobre,* on, over).
influjo, *n.m.* influence; (*naut.*) rising tide.
influyente, *a.* influential.
infolio, *n.m.* folio volume.
información, *n.f.* information; inquiry; report; (*jur.*) brief.
informal, *a.* irregular, unreliable, improper; informal.
informalidad, *n.f.* breach of etiquette; informality.
informante, *a.* informing.—*n.m.f.* informer, informant.
informar, *v.t.* inform, apprise; shape.—*v.r.* find out (*de,* about).
informativo, -va, *a.* informative.
informe, *a.* shapeless, formless; misshapen.— *n.m.* report; piece of information.—*pl.* information.
infortunado, -da, *a.* unfortunate, ill-starred.
infortunio, *n.m.* misfortune.
infracción, *n.f.* infringement, breach.
infractor, -ra, *n.m.f.* violator, transgressor.
infrangible, *a.* unbreakable.
infranqueable, *a.* impassable.
infrarrojo, -ja, *a.* infra-red.
infrascri(p)to, -ta, *a., n.m.f.* undersigned, undermentioned.
infrecuente, *a.* infrequent.
infringir [E], *v.t.* infringe.
infructuoso, -sa, *a.* fruitless, unfruitful.
infundado, -da, *a.* unfounded.
infundio, *n.m.* (*fam.*) rumour, fib.
infundir, *v.t.* infuse, imbue.
infusión, *n.f.* infusion.
ingeniar, *v.t.* contrive, think up.—*v.r.* manage (*a, para,* to).
ingeniería, *n.f.* engineering.
ingeniero, *n.m.* engineer.
ingenio, *n.m.* mind, intelligence, wit; talent, skill; engine.
ingenioso, -sa, *a.* talented, ingenious.
ingénito, -ta, *a.* innate; unbegotten.
ingente, *a.* huge, immense.

ingenuidad, *n.f.* ingeniousness.
ingenuo, -ua, *a.* ingenuous, naïve; open, frank.
ingerir [6], *v.t.* consume, swallow. [INJERIR].
Inglaterra, *n.f.* England.
ingle, *n.f.* groin.
inglés,-glesa,a.,n.m. English.—*n.m.* Englishman.—*n.f.* Englishwoman.—*n.m.f.* (*iron.*) creditor.
inglesismo, *n.m.* Anglicism.
ingratitud, *n.f.* ingratitude.
ingrato, -ta, *a.* ungrateful; thankless; unpleasant; fruitless.
ingravidez, *n.f.* weightlessness (*of spacemen*).
ingrávido, -da, *a.* weightless (*spaceman*).
ingrediente, *n.m.* ingredient.
ingresar, *v.t.* deposit; put in.—*v.i.* enter (*en*); accrue.—*v.r.* (*C.A.*) enlist.
ingreso, *n.m.* entrance, entry.—*pl.* receipts, income.
íngrimo, -ma, *a.* (*S.A.*) all alone.
inhábil, *a.* incompetent, incapable.
inhabilidad, *n.f.* inability, incompetency.
inhabilitar, *v.t.* incapacitate; disqualify.
inhabitable, *a.* uninhabitable.
inhabitado, -da, *a.* uninhabited.
inhalar, *v.t.* inhale.
inherente, *a.* inherent.
inhibición, *n.f.* inhibition.
inhibir, *v.t.* inhibit; (*jur.*) stay.—*v.r.* keep out (*de*, of).
inhospitalario, -ria, *a.* inhospitable.
inhumanidad, *n.f.* inhumanity.
inhumano, -na, *a.* inhuman.
inhumar, *v.t.* inter, inhume.
iniciación, *n.f.* initiation.
inicial, *a.*, *n.f.* initial.
iniciar, *v.t.* initiate.
iniciativa, *n.f.* initiative.
inicuo, -cua, *a.* iniquitous; unjust.
inimaginable, *a.* unimaginable.
inimitable, *a.* inimitable.
ininteligente, *a.* unintelligent.
ininteligible, *a.* unintelligible.
iniquidad, *n.f.* iniquity; injustice.
injerir [6], *v.t.* (*agr.*) graft; insert.
injerta, *n.f.* blood orange.
injertar, *v.t.* (*agr.*, *med.*) graft.
injerto, *n.m.* (*agr.*, *med.*) graft.
injuria, *n.f.* offence, insult, wrong, harm.
injuriar, *v.t.* offend, wrong, insult.
injurioso, -sa, *a.* offensive, insulting, harmful.
injusticia, *n.f.* injustice.
injustificable, *a.* unjustifiable.
injustificado, -da, *a.* unjustified.
injusto, -ta, *a.* unjust.
la Inmaculada, *n.f.* Our Lady.
inmaculado, -da, *a.* immaculate, pure.
inmanejable, *a.* unmanageable.
inmanente, *a.* immanent.
inmarcesible, inmarchitable, *a.* unfading; imperishable.
inmaterial, *a.* immaterial.
inmaturo, -ra, *a.* immature.
inmediaciones, *n.f.pl.* environs, neighbourhood.
inmediato, -ta, *a.* immediate; close, next (*a*, to).—*n.f.pl.* crux; sore point.
inmejorable, *a.* unbeatable, peerless.
inmemorial, *a.* immemorial.
inmensidad, *n.f.* immensity.
inmenso, -sa, *a.* immense.

inmensurable, *a.* immeasurable.
inmerecido, -da, *a.* undeserved.
inmergir [E], *v.t.* immerse.—*v.r.* be immersed.
inmersión, *n.f.* immersion.
inmigración, *n.f.* immigration.
inmigrado, -da, inmigrante, *a.*, *n.m.f.* immigrant.
inmigrar, *v.i.* immigrate.
inminencia, *n.f.* imminence.
inminente, *a.* imminent.
inmoble, *a.* immovable; firm.
inmoderación, *n.f.* immoderation.
inmoderado, -da, *a.* immoderate.
inmodestia, *n.f.* immodesty, indecency.
inmodesto, -ta, *a.* immodest, indecent.
inmolación, *n.f.* immolation.
inmolar, *v.t.* immolate, sacrifice.
inmoral, *a.* immoral.
inmoralidad, *n.f.* immorality.
inmortal, *a.* immortal.
inmortalidad, *n.f.* immortality.
inmortalizar [C], *v.t.* immortalize.
inmotivado, -da, *a.* motiveless, unfounded.
inmovible, *a.* immovable.
inmóvil, *a.* motionless; unshaken.
inmovilidad, *a.* immobility.
inmovilizar [C], *v.t.* immobilize.
inmundicia, *n.f.* filth; lewdness.
inmundo, -da, *a.* filthy; lewd.
inmune, *a.* immune (*contra*, to); exempt.
inmunidad, *n.f.* immunity.
inmunización, *n.f.* immunization.
inmunizar [C], *v.t.* immunize.
inmutable, *a.* immutable.
inmutar, *v.t.*, *v.r.* change, alter.
innato, -ta, *a.* innate, inborn.
innatural, *a.* unnatural.
innavegable, *a.* unnavigable.
innecesario, -ria, *a.* unnecessary.
innegable, *a.* undeniable.
innoble, *a.* ignoble.
innocuo, -cua, *a.* innocuous.
innovación, *n.f.* innovation.
innovar, *v.t.* innovate.
innumerable, *a.* innumerable.
innúmero, -ra, *a.* numberless, countless.
inobediente, *a.* disobedient.
inobservado, -da, *a.* unobserved.
inocencia, *n.f.* innocence.
inocentada, *n.f.* (*fam.*) blooper; stunt.
inocente, *a.*, *n.m.f.* innocent; (*fam.*) gullible (*person*); *día de los inocentes,* All Fools' Day (*in Spain*, 28 *December*).
inoculación, *n.f.* inoculation.
inocular, *v.t.* inoculate; (*fig.*) pervert.
inocuo [INNOCUO].
inodoro, -ra, *a.* odourless.—*n.m.* deodorant.
inofensivo, -va, *a.* inoffensive.
inolvidable, *a.* unforgettable.
inoperable, *a.* (*med.*) inoperable.
inopia, *n.f.* penury.
inopinado, -da, *a.* unexpected.
inoportunidad, *n.f.* inopportuneness.
inoportuno, -na, *a.* inopportune, untimely.
inorgánico, -ca, *a.* inorganic.
inoxidable, *a.* inoxidizable, stainless (*steel etc.*).
inquietador, -ra, inquietante, *a.* disquieting, disturbing.
inquietar, *v.t.* disquiet, disturb, worry.—*v.r.* worry (*con, de, por,* about).

inquieto, -ta, *a.* worried, uneasy, anxious; restless.
inquietud, *n.f.* worry, anxiety; restlessness.
inquilinato, *n.m.* tenancy; rent; rates.
inquilino, -na, *n.m.f.* tenant.
inquina, *n.f.* dislike.
inquirir [3, *as if* inquerir], *v.t.* enquire into, investigate.
inquisición, *n.f.* inquisition.
inquisidor, *n.m.* inquisitor.
inquisitivo, -va, inquisitorio, -ria, *a.* investigatory.
inquisitorial, *a.* inquisitorial.
insaciable, *a.* insatiable, greedy.
insalubre, *a.* unhealthy, insalubrious.
insania, insanidad, *n.f.* insanity.
insano, -na, *a.* unhealthy; insane, mad.
insatisfecho, -cha, *a.* unsatisfied.
inscribir [*p.p.* inscrito], *v.t.* inscribe; enrol. —*v.r.* enrol, register.
inscripción, *n.f.* inscription; enrolment.
insecticida, *n.m.* insecticide.
insectívoro, -ra, *a.* insectivorous.—*n.m.* insectivore.
insecto, *n.m.* insect.
inseguridad, *n.f.* insecurity; uncertainty.
inseguro, -ra, *a.* insecure; unsafe; uncertain.
inseminación, *n.f.* insemination.
inseminar, *v.t.* inseminate.
insensatez, *n.f.* senselessness, folly.
insensato, -ta, *a.* senseless, insensate.
insensibilidad, *n.f.* insensibility; insensitivity.
insensibilizar [C], *v.t.* make insensible.
insensible, *a.* insensible; insensitive, unfeeling.
inseparable, *a.* inseparable.
inserción, *n.f.* insertion.
insertar, *v.t.* insert.
inserto, -ta, *a.* inserted.
inservible, *a.* useless, unserviceable.
insidioso, -sa, *a.* insidious.
insigne, *a.* celebrated, renowned, noted.
insignia, *n.f.* badge; banner, standard; medal; pennant.—*pl.* insignia.
insignificancia, *n.f.* insignificance.
insignificante, *a.* insignificant.
insincero, -ra, *a.* insincere.
insinuación, *n.f.* insinuation.
insinuar [M], *v.t.* insinuate, hint.—*v.r.* slip in, work one's way in (*en*).
insipidez, *n.f.* insipidity.
insípido, -da, *a.* insipid.
insipiente, *a.* unwise; ignorant.
insistencia, *n.f.* insistence.
insistente, *a.* insistent.
insistir, *v.i.* insist (*en, sobre*, on).
insociable, insocial, *a.* unsociable.
insolación, *n.f.* insolation; (*med.*) sun-stroke.
insolar, *v.t.* insolate; expose to the sun.—*v.r.* get sun-stroke.
insolencia, *n.f.* insolence.
insolente, *a.* insolent.
insólito, -ta, *a.* unwonted, unaccustomed.
insolubilidad, *n.f.* insolubility.
insoluble, *a.* insoluble.
insolvencia, *n.f.* insolvency.
insolvente, *a.* insolvent.
insomne, *a.* sleepless, insomnious.
insomnio, *n.m.* insomnia, sleeplessness.
insoportable, *a.* intolerable.
insospechado, -da, *a.* unsuspected.

insostenible, *a.* indefensible.
inspección, *n.f.* inspection; control; inspectorate.
inspeccionar, *v.t.* inspect.
inspector, -ra, *a.* inspecting.—*n.m.f.* inspector.
inspiración, *n.f.* inspiration; inhalation.
inspirar, *v.t.* inspire; inhale.—*v.r.* be inspired (*en*, by).
instalación, *n.f.* installation.—*pl.* plant, works, machinery, fittings.
instalar, *v.t.* install.
instancia, *n.f.* instance, entreaty; petition; *de primera —*, (*jur.*) of first instance; in the first place, originally.
instantáneo, -nea, *a.* instantaneous.—*n.f.* (*phot.*) snap, snapshot.
instante, *n.m.* instant, moment; *al —*, at once, this very minute.
instantemente, *adv.* insistently; instantly.
instar, *v.t.* urge, press (*a*, to).—*v.i.* be urgent.
instaurar, *v.t.* restore; establish; install.
instigación, *n.f.* instigation.
instigador, -ra, *a.* instigating.—*n.m.f.* instigator.
instigar [B], *v.t.* instigate.
instilar, *v.t.* instil.
instintivo, -va, *a.* instinctive.
instinto, *n.m.* instinct.
institución, *n.f.* institution.
instituir [O], *v.t.* institute, found.
instituto, *n.m.* institute; high *or* grammar school; rule, constitution.
institutor, -ra, *a.* instituting, founding.— *n.m.f.* founder, institutor; grammar-school teacher.
institutriz, *n.f.* (*pl.* -ices) governess; teacher.
instrucción, *n.f.* instruction; education.
instructivo, -va, *a.* instructive.
instructor, -ra, *a.* instructing.—*n.m.* instructor.—*n.f.* instructress.
instruído, -da, *a.* educated.
instruir [O], *v.t.* instruct.
instrumentación, *n.f.* instrumentation.
instrumental, *a.* instrumental.—*n.m.* instruments.
instrumentista, *n.m.f.* instrumentalist; instrument-maker.
instrumento, *n.m.* instrument.
insubordinación, *n.f.* insubordination.
insubordinado, -da, *a.* insubordinate.
insubordinar, *v.r.* rebel.
insuficiencia, *n.f.* insufficiency.
insuficiente, *a.* insufficient.
insufrible, *a.* insufferable.
insular, *a.* insular.—*n.m.f.* islander.
insulina, *n.f.* (*med.*) insulin.
insulso, -sa, *a.* tasteless, insipid, dreary.
insultante, *a.* insulting.
insultar, *v.t.* insult.
insulto, *n.m.* insult; swoon.
insumergible, *a.* unsinkable.
insumiso, *a.* rebellious, unsubmissive.
insuperable, *a.* insuperable.
insurgente, *a.*, *n.m.f.* insurgent.
insurrección, *n.f.* insurrection.
insurreccionar, *v.t.* incite to rebel.—*v.r.* rise in rebellion.
insurrecto, -ta, *a.*, *n.m.f.* rebel.
intacto, -ta, *a.* intact.
intachable, *a.* irreproachable.
intangible, *a.* intangible.

integración, *n.f.* integration.
integral, *a.* integral.
integrante, *a.* component; integrant.
integrar, *v.t.* integrate; make up; reimburse.
integridad, *n.f.* integrity; maidenhead; whole.
íntegro, -ra, *a.* whole, integral; upright, honest.
intelectivo, -va, *a.* intellective.—*n.f.* understanding.
intelecto, *n.m.* intellect.
intelectual, *a., n.m.f.* intellectual.
inteligencia, *n.f.* intelligence.
inteligente, *a.* intelligent.
inteligible, *a.* intelligible.
intemperancia, *n.f.* intemperance.
intemperante, *a.* intemperate.
intemperie, *n.f.* rough weather, inclemency.
intempestivo, -va, *a.* untimely.
intención, *n.f.* intention; nasty temper (*in animals*); **con** or **de** —, deliberately, knowingly.
intencionado, -da, *a.* **bien** or **mal** —, well-or ill-intentioned.
intencional, *a.* intentional; inner, volitional.
intendencia, *n.f.* administration; intendancy.
intendente, *n.m.* intendant, manager, commander.
intensar, *v.t.* intensify.
intensidad, *n.f.* intensity.
intensificar [A], *v.t.* intensify.
intensivo, -va, *a.* intensive.
intenso, -sa, *a.* intense.
intentar, *v.t.* try out; attempt, try.
intento, *n.m.* purpose, intent; **de** —, on purpose.
intentona, *n.f.* (*pej.*) rash plan or attempt.
interacción, *n.f.* interaction.
intercalar, *v.t.* intersperse, intercalate.
intercambiar, *v.t.* interchange; exchange.
intercambio, *n.m.* interchange; exchange.
interceder, *v.i.* intercede.
interceptación, *n.f.* interception.
interceptar, *v.t.* intercept.
interceptor, *n.m.* (*aero.*) fighter.
intercesión, *n.f.* intercession.
intercomunicación, *n.f.* intercommunication.
intercontinental, *a.* intercontinental.
interdecir [17], *v.t.* interdict.
interdependencia, *n.f.* interdependence.
interdicción, *n.f.* interdiction.
interdicto, *n.m.* interdict.
interés, *n.m.* interest; **intereses creados,** vested interests.
interesado, -da, *a.* interested; self-interested.
interesante, *a.* interesting.
interesar, *v.t.* interest; affect.—*v.r.* be interested (**en, por,** in).
interferencia, *n.f.* interference.
interfoliar, *v.t.* interleave.
ínterin, *n.m.* interim, meantime.—*adv.* meanwhile.—*conj.* (*fam.*) until; till; while.
interino, -na, *a.* interim, temporary.
interior, *a., n.m.* interior.
interioridad, *n.f.* inside, interior.—*pl.* family secrets.
interiormente, *adv.* inwardly.
interjección, *n.f.* interjection.
interlinear, *v.t.* interline.
interlocutor, -ra, *n.m.f.* interlocutor; (*rad.*) interviewer.

intérlope, *a.* (*com., pol.*) interloping.
interludio, *n.m.* interlude.
intermediar, *v.i.* intermediate; stand between.
intermediario, -ria, *a., n.m.f.* intermediary.
intermedio, -dia, *a.* intermediate; intervening.—*n.m.* interlude, intermission.
interminable, *a.* interminable.
intermisión, *n.f.* intermission.
intermitente, *a.* intermittent.
internacional, *a.* international.
internacionalismo, *n.m.* internationalism.
internacionalizar [C], *v.t.* internationalize.
internar, *v.t.* intern; send inland.—*v.i., v.r.* move inland; penetrate (**en,** into).
interno, -na, *a.* internal, inward, inner.—*n.m.f.* (*educ.*) boarder.
interpaginar, *v.t.* interpage.
interpelar, *v.t.* appeal to; demand an explanation of; (*jur.*) summon.
interpenetración, *n.f.* interpenetration.
interplanetario, -ria, *a.* interplanetary.
interpolación, *n.f.* interpolation.
interpolar, *v.t.* interpolate.
interponer [25], *v.t.* interpose.—*v.r.* intervene.
interpretación, *n.f.* interpretation.
interpretar, *v.t.* interpret.
interpretativo, -va, *a.* interpretative.
intérprete, *n.m.f.* interpreter.
interpuesto, *p.p.* [INTERPONER].
interracial, *a.* interracial.
interregno, *n.m.* interregnum.
interrogación, *n.f.* interrogation, questioning.
interrogante, *a.* interrogating.—*n.m.f.* interrogator.—*n.m.* question-mark.
interrogar [B], *v.t.* interrogate, question.
interrogativo, -va, *a., n.m.* interrogative.
interrumpir, *v.t.* interrupt; break, switch off.
interrupción, *n.f.* interruption.
interruptor, -ra, *a.* interrupting.—*n.m.f.* interrupter.—*n.m.* (*elec.*) switch.
intersección, *n.f.* intersection.
intersticio, *n.m.* interstice; interval.
intervalo, *n.m.* interval.
intervención, *n.f.* intervention; inspection; control; (*med.*) operation; auditing.
intervenir [36], *v.t.* audit; supervise; (*med.*) operate; tap (*telephones*).—*v.i.* intervene; occur.
interventor, *n.m.* comptroller, superintendent; auditor.
intervievar, interviewar, *v.t.* [ENTREVISTAR].
interview, interviú, *n.m.* [ENTREVISTA].
intestado, -da, *a.* intestate.
intestinal, *a.* intestinal.
intestino, -na, *a.* inner, interior.—*n.m.* intestine.
intimación, *n.f.* intimation, announcement.
intimar, *v.t.* intimate, indicate.—*v.i., v.r.* become close friends.
intimidación, *n.f.* intimidation.
intimidad, *n.f.* intimacy.
intimidar, *v.t.* intimidate.
íntimo, -ma, *a.* intimate.
intitular, *v.t.* entitle, give a title to.
intocable, *a., n.m.f.* untouchable.
intolerable, *a.* intolerable.
intolerancia, *n.f.* intolerance.
intolerante, *a.* intolerant.
intonso, -sa, *a.* ignorant; uncut.

intoxicación, *n.f.* (*med.*) poisoning.
intoxicar [A], *v.t.* (*med.*) poison.
intraducible, *a.* untranslatable.
intranquilizar [C], *v.t.* disquiet, worry.—*v.r.* worry.
intranquilo, -la, *a.* uneasy, worried.
intransigencia, *n.f.* intransigence.
intransigente, *a.* intransigent.
intransitable, *a.* impassable.
intransitivo, -va, *a., n.m.* intransitive.
intratable, *a.* unsociable, intractable.
intrepidez, *n.f.* intrepidity.
intrépido, -da, *a.* intrepid.
intricado, -da, *a.* intricate.
intriga, *n.f.* intrigue.
intrigante, *a.* intriguing.—*n.m.f.* intriguer.
intrigar [B], *v.t., v.i.* intrigue.
intrincado, -da, *a.* intricate.
intrincar [A], *v.t.* entangle, complicate.
intríngulis, *n.m.* inv. (*fam.*) hidden motive; puzzle.
intrínseco, -ca, *a.* intrinsic(al).
introducción, *n.f.* introduction.
introducir [15], *v.t.* introduce.—*v.r.* get (*en*, into); intervene, interfere.
introductivo, -va, *a.* introductive.
introductor, -ra, *a.* introductory.—*n.m.f.* introducer.
introito, *n.m.* (*eccl.*) introit; prologue.
introspectivo, -va, *a.* introspective.
intrusión, *n.f.* intrusion; quackery.
intruso, -sa, *a.* intruding, intrusive.—*n.m.f.* intruder; quack.
intuición, *n.f.* intuition.
intuir [O], *v.t.* intuit.
intuitivo, -va, *a.* intuitive.
intuito, *n.m.* view, glance.
inundación, *n.f.* inundation, flood.
inundar, *v.t.* inundate, flood.
inurbano, -na, *a.* uncivil.
inútil, *a.* useless.
inutilidad, *n.f.* uselessness.
inutilizado, -da, *a.* unused, unutilized.
inutilizar [C], *v.t.* make useless.—*v.r.* become useless *or* disabled.
invadir, *v.t.* invade.
invalidar, *v.t.* invalidate.
invalidez, *n.f.* invalidity.
inválido, -da, *a., n.m.f.* invalid.
invariable, *a.* invariable.
invasión, *n.f.* invasion.
invasor, -ra, *n.m.f.* invader.
invectiva, *n.f.* invective.
invencible, *a.* invincible.
invención, *n.f.* discovery; invention.
inventar, *v.t.* invent; create.
inventario, *n.m.* inventory.
inventiva, *n.f.* inventiveness.
inventivo, -va, *a.* inventive.
invento, *n.m.* invention.
inventor, -ra, *n.m.f.* inventor.
invernáculo, *n.m.* greenhouse.
invernal, *a.* hibernal.
invernar [1], *v.i.* winter.
invernizo, -za, *a.* wintry.
inverosímil, *a.* unlikely, improbable.
inverosimilitud, *n.f.* unlikelihood, improbability.
inversión, *n.f.* inversion; investment.
inverso, -sa, *a.* inverse, opposite.
invertebrado, -da, *a., n.m.* invertebrate.
invertir [6], *v.t.* invert; invest.

investidura, *n.f.* investiture.
investigación, *n.f.* investigation.
investigador, -ra, *a.* investigating.—*n.m.f.* investigator.
investigar [B], *v.t.* investigate.
investir [8], *v.t.* vest, invest, install.
inveterado, -da, *a.* inveterate.
inveterar, *v.r.* get old; become chronic.
invicto, -ta, *a.* unconquered.
invidente, *a.* sightless.
invierno, *n.m.* winter.
inviolabilidad, *n.f.* inviolability.
inviolable, *a.* inviolable.
inviolado, -da, *a.* inviolate, unviolated.
invisible, *a.* invisible.
invitación, *n.f.* invitation.
invitado, -da, *n.m.f.* guest, invited person.
invitar, *v.t.* invite; treat (*a*, to).
invocación, *n.f.* invocation.
invocar [A], *v.t.* invoke.
involucrar, *v.t.* jumble up with, tangle.
involuntario, -ria, *a.* involuntary.
invulnerabilidad, *n.f.* invulnerability.
invulnerable, *a.* invulnerable.
inyección, *n.f.* injection.
inyectar, *v.t.* inject.
inyector, *n.m.* injector.
iñiguista, *a., n.m.f.* Jesuit.
ion, *n.m.* (*phys.*) ion.
iota, *n.f.* iota.
ir [21], *v.i.* go, walk, move; be getting on (*para*, for); go in (*por*, for); go for (*por*).—*v.r.* go away; pass away; slip; leak; wear out.
ira, *n.f.* wrath, ire.
iracundo, -da, *a.* wrathful.
Irak, *n.m.* Iraq.
Irán, *n.m.* Iran.
iranio, -nia, *a., n.m.f.* Iranian, Persian.
iraqués, -quesa, *a., n.m.f.* Iraqi.
irascible, *a.* irascible.
iridescencia, *n.f.* iridescence.
iridiscente, *a.* iridescent.
iris, *n.m.* (*bot.*) iris; rainbow; (*anat.*) iris.
irisado, -da, *a.* rainbow-hued.
Irlanda, *n.f.* Ireland; Eire; **irlanda,** fine linen *or* cotton.
irlandés, -desa, *a.* Irish.—*n.m.* Irishman; Irish (*language*).—*n.f.* Irishwoman.
ironía, *n.f.* irony.
irónico, -ca, *a.* ironic(al).
ironizar [C], *v.i.* be ironic.
irracional, *a.* irrational.
irradiación, *n.f.* (ir)radiation; (*rad.*) broadcast.
irradiar, *v.t.* (ir)radiate; (*rad.*) broadcast.
irrazonable, *a.* unreasonable.
irrealizable, *a.* impossible, unrealizable.
irrebatible, *a.* irrefutable.
irreconciliable, *a.* irreconcilable.
irredimible, *a.* irredeemable.
irreducible, *a.* irreducible; stubborn.
irreemplazable, *a.* irreplaceable.
irrefrenable, *a.* uncontrollable, unbridled.
irrefutable, *a.* irrefutable.
irregular, *a.* irregular.
irregularidad, *n.f.* irregularity.
irreligión, *n.f.* irreligion.
irreligioso, -sa, *a.* irreligious.
irremediable, *a.* irremediable.
irreparable, *a.* irreparable.
irreprochable, *a.* irreproachable.

irresistible, *a.* irresistible.
irresoluto, -ta, *a.* irresolute.
irresponsabilidad, *n.f.* irresponsibility.
irresponsable, *a.* irresponsible.
irresuelto, -ta, *a.* irresolute; unsolved.
irreverencia, *n.f.* irreverence.
irreverente, *a.* irreverent.
irrevocable, *a.* irrevocable.
irrigación, *n.f.* irrigation.
irrigar [B], *v.t.* (agr., med.) irrigate.
irrisible, *a.* laughable, risible.
irrisión, *n.f.* derision.
irrisorio, -ria, *a.* ridiculous.
irritabilidad, *n.f.* irritability.
irritable, *a.* irritable.
irritación, *n.f.* irritation; (jur.) invalidation.
irritante, *a., n.m.* irritant.
irritar, *v.t.* irritate; (jur.) invalidate.—*v.r.* get *or* become irritated.
irruir [O], *v.t.* invade, to assail.
irrumpir, *v.i.* irrupt, burst (**en**, into); invade.
irrupción, *n.f.* invasion, irruption.
Isabel, *n.f.* Elizabeth, Isabel(la).
isabelino, -na, *a., n.m.f.* Isabeline; Elizabethan.
Isaías, *n.m.* (Bib.) Isaiah.
Isidoro, *n.m.* Isidore.
isidro, -ra, *n.m.f.* bumpkin.
isla, *n.f.* island; block of houses; — **de seguridad**, traffic island.
Islam, *n.m.* Islam.
islámico, -ca, *a.* Islamic.
islandés, -desa, *a.* Icelandic.—*n.m.* Icelandic (language).—*n.m.f.* Icelander.
Islandia, *n.f.* Iceland.
islándico, -ca, *a.* Icelandic.
isleño, -ña, *a.* rel. to an island.—*n.m.f.* islander.
isleta, *n.f.* islet.
islote, *n.m.* barren islet.
isobara, *n.f.* isobar.
isomórfico, -ca, *a.* isomorphic.
isósceles, *a.* isosceles.
isoterma, *n.f.* isotherm.
isótopo, *n.m.* isotope.
Israel, *n.m.* Israel.
israelí, *a., n.m.f.* (pl. -ies) Israeli.
israelita, *a., n.m.f.* Israelite.
Istambul, *n.f.* Istanbul.
istmo, *n.m.* isthmus.
Italia, *n.f.* Italy.
italiano, -na, *a., n.m.f.* Italian.
itálico, -ca, *a., n.f.* italic.
ítem, *adv.* item.—*n.m.* section, paragraph.
iterar, *v.t.* iterate.
itinerario, -ria, *a., n.m.* itinerary.
izar [C], *v.t.* (naut.) hoist, haul up.
izquierda, *n.f.* left, left-hand; (pol.) the Left.
izquierdear, *v.i.* go wrong; (pol.) be Leftish.
izquierdista, *a., n.m.f.* (pol.) Leftist.
izquierdo, -da, *a.* left, left-hand; left-handed; crooked.

J

J, j, *n.f.* eleventh letter of the Spanish alphabet.
¡ja! *interj.* ha!

jabalí, *n.m.* wild boar.
jabalina (1), *n.f.* javelin.
jabalina (2), *n.f.* wild sow.
jabardo, *n.m.* small swarm.
jábega, *n.f.* drag-net; fishing smack.
jabón, *n.f.* soap; (fam.) flattery; telling-off.
jabonar, *v.t.* soap; (fam.) tell off.
jaboncillo, *n.m.* toilet soap, **cake** of soap.
jabonera, *n.f.* soap-dish.
jabonete, -ta, *n.m.* or *f.* cake of soap.
jabonoso, -sa, *a.* soapy.
jaca, *n.f.* cob, nag, pony; (S.A.) fighting cock.
jacal, *n.m.* (zool.) jackal; (C.A.) hovel.
jácara, *n.f.* gay ballad; serenaders; story; pest.
jacarear, *v.i.* sing gay ballads; (fam.) be annoying.
jacarero, -ra, *a.* serenading; (fam.) waggish. —*n.m.f.* serenader; (fam.) wag, wit.
jácaro, -ra, *a.* bragging, bullying.—*n.m.* bully.
jacinto, *n.m.* hyacinth.
jacobino, -na, *a., n.m.f.* Jacobin.
jacobita, *n.m.f.* pilgrim to St. James of Compostela; Jacobite.
Jacobo, *n.m.* James, Jacob.
jactancia, *n.f.* boasting, bragging.
jactancioso, -sa, *a.* boastful.
jactar, *v.r.* boast, brag.
jaculatorio, -ria, *a.* ejaculatory.—*n.f.* ejaculatory *or* short sudden prayer.
jade, *n.m.* jade.
jadeante, *a.* panting, out of breath.
jadear, *v.i.* pant.
jaez, *n.m.* (pl. **jaeces**) harness, trappings; (fig.) kind, type.
jaguar, *n.m.* jaguar.
Jaime, *n.m.* James.
jalar, *v.t.* (low) tug; (C.A.) flirt with.—*v.r.* (S.A.) get tipsy.
jalbegue, *n.m.* whitewash; (fam.) make-up.
jalde, jaldo, -da, *a.* bright yellow.
jalea, *n.f.* jelly.
jalear, *v.t.* cheer on; flirt with.—*v.r.* dance the JALEO; have noisy fun.
jaleo, *n.m.* noisy fun; jaleo, Spanish dance.
jaletina, *n.f.* gelatine.
jalifa, *n.f.* caliph.
jalisco, -ca, *a.* (C.A.) tipsy.
jalma, *n.f.* packsaddle.
jalón, *n.m.* surveyor's pole; stage, point; (S.A.) tug; (C.A.) swig.
jalonar, *v.t.* mark, stake out.
Jamaica, *n.f.* Jamaica; **jamaica**, *n.m.* rum.
jamaicano, -na, *a., n.m.f.* Jamaican.
jamar, *v.t.* (low) gorge, guzzle (eat).
jamás, *adv.* never; **nunca** —, never ever; **por siempre** —, for ever and ever.
jamba, *n.f.* jamb.
jamelgo, *n.m.* (fam.) skinny horse.
jamón, *n.m.* ham.
jándalo, -la, *a., n.m.f.* (fam.) Andalusian.
jangada, *n.f.* (fam.) stupid trick; raft.
Jano, *n.m.* (myth.) Janus.
el Japón, *n.m.* Japan.
japonés, -nesa, *a., n.m.f.* Japanese.
jaque, *n.m.* check (in chess); (fam.) bully; **dar** — **a**, check; **estar muy** —, (fam.) be full of beans; — **mate**, checkmate; **¡—de aquí!** get out of here!
jaquear, *v.t.* check (in chess); harass.—*v.i.* (fam.) bully.

jaqueca

jaqueca, *n.f.* migraine.
jaquel, *n.m.* (*her.*) square.
jaquetón, *n.m.* shark; (*fam.*) bully.
jarabe, *n.m.* syrup; — **de pico,** (*fam.*) flattery, hot air, lip service.
jarana, *n.f.* (*fam.*) spree, larking, merriment.
jarano, *n.m.* Mexican sombrero.
jarcia, *n.f.* rigging; tackle; (*fam.*) jumble.
jardín, *n.m.* garden, flower garden; — **zoológico,** zoological gardens; — **de la infancia,** kindergarten.
jardinería, *n.f.* gardening.
jardinero, -ra, *n.m.f.* gardener.
jardinista, *n.m.f.* gardening expert.
jaro, *n.m.* thicket; (*bot.*) (*also* **jarillo**) arum.
jarocho, -cha, *a.* bluff, blunt.—*n.m.* John Blunt, abrupt, brusque person.
jarope, *n.m.* syrup; potion.
jarra, *n.f.* jar, jug, pitcher; *de* or *en jarras,* arms akimbo.
jarrero, -ra, *n.m.f.* potter.
jarrete, *n.m.* hock, gambrel.
jarretera, *n.f.* garter.
jarro, *n.m.* pitcher, ewer.
jarrón, *n.m.* urn, vase.
jaspe, *n.m.* jasper.
jaspear, *v.t.* marble.
Jauja, *n.f.* Shangri-La, El Dorado (*place of abundant wealth*).
jaula, *n.f.* cage.
jauría, *n.f.* pack (*of dogs*).
jayán, -yana, *n.m.f.* big, strong person.
jazmín, *n.m.* (*bot.*) jasmine.
¡je! *interj.* [JI].
jefa, *n.f.* woman head; (*fam.*) woman boss.
jefatura, *n.f.* chieftainship; headship; headquarters.
jefe, *n.m.* chief, head; boss; (*mil.*) field officer; *en* —, in chief; — *del estado,* head of state.
Jehová, *n.m.* Jehovah.
jengibre, *n.m.* ginger.
jeque, *n.m.* sheik.
jerarquía, *n.f.* hierarchy; *altas jerarquías,* personalities, high-ranking officials.
jerárquico, -ca, *a.* hierarchical.
Jeremías, *n.m.* Jeremiah.
jerez, *n.m.* sherry.
jerga, *n.f.* serge, coarse cloth; jargon; straw bed.
jergal, *a.* rel. to jargon.
Jericó, *n.f.* Jericho.
jerife, *n.m.* shereef.
jerigonza, *n.f.* slang, jargon; gibberish.
jeringa, *n.f.* syringe; hypodermic; grease gun; (*fam.*) pest.
jeringar, *v.t.* syringe, inject; (*fam.*) pester.
jeringazo, *n.m.* shot, injection.
jeringuilla (I), *n.f.* hypodermic syringe.
jeringuilla (2), *n.f.* (*bot.*) syringa.
jeroglífico, -ca, *a., n.m.* hieroglyphic.—*n.m.* hieroglyph.
jerónimo, -ma, *a., n.m.f.* Hieronymite.—*n.m.* Jerome.
jerosolimitano, -na, *a., n.m.f.* rel. to or native of Jerusalem.
jersey, *n.m.* jersey.
Jerusalén, *n.m.* Jerusalem.
Jesucristo, *n.m.* Jesus Christ.
jesuita, *a., n.m.f.* Jesuit.
jesuítico, -ca, *a.* Jesuitical.
jesuitismo, *n.m.* Jesuitism.

Jesús, *n.m.* Jesus; **en un —,** in a moment.—*interj.* heavens!
jeta, *n.f.* pig's snout; blubber lips; (*fam.*) mug, face.
¡ji, ji! *interj.* tee-hee!
jíbaro, -ra, *a., n.m.f.* peasant.
jibia, *n.f.* (*zool.*) cuttlefish, sepia.
jícara, *n.f.* chocolate-cup; (*S.A.*) gourd.
jicarazo, *n.m.* poisoning.
jifa, *n.f.* offal.
jifero, *n.m.* butcher, slaughterman.
jiga, *n.f.* jig, dance, [GIGA].
jilguero, *n.m.* (*orn.*) goldfinch.
jilí, jilando, jilaza, *a.* (*fam.*) silly [GILí].
jineta, *n.f.* mode of riding with bent legs and high stirrups; (*zool.*) genet; *tener los cascos a la —,* (*fam.*) be hare-brained.
jinete, *n.m.* horseman, rider; thoroughbred horse.
jinetear, *v.t.* (*S.A.*) break in (*horses*).—*v.i.* ride about, show one's horsemanship.—*v.r.* (*S.A.*) show off, parade oneself.
jinglar, *v.t.* sway, rock.
jingoísmo, *n.m.* jingoism.
jingoísta, *a., n.m.f.* jingoist.
jira, *n.f.* strip, shred, tatter; picnic [GIRA].
jirafa, *n.f.* giraffe.
jirón, *n.m.* shred, tatter; pennant; piece.
¡jo! *interj.* whoa!
Joaquín, *n.m.* Joachim.
jocoserio, -ria, *a.* seriocomic.
jocosidad, *n.f.* jocosity, jocularity.
jocoso, -sa, *a.* jocular; jocose.
jocundo, -da, *a.* jocund.
jofaina, *n.f.* wash-stand; wash-basin.
jolgorio, *n.m.* merrymaking, jollification.
jolito, *n.m.* calm, leisure; *en —,* in suspense; disappointed.
jollín, *n.m.* (*fam.*) uproar; spree.
Jonás, *n.m.* Jonah.
Jordán, *n.m.* Jordan; (*fig.*) fountain of youth.
jordano, -na, *a., n.m.f.* Jordanian.
Jorge, *n.m.* George.
jornada, *n.f.* day's journey; day's work; journey; (*theat.*) act; lifetime; passing on; (*mil.*) expedition; occasion; *a grandes* or *largas jornadas,* by forced marches.
jornal, *n.m.* day's wage, wages; day's work; diary.
jornalero, *n.m.* day-labourer, labourer.
joroba, *n.m.* hump, hunched back; (*fam.*) pest.
jorobado, -da, *a.* hunchbacked.—*n.m.f.* hunchback.
jorobar, *v.t.* (*fam.*) pester, annoy.
José, *n.m.* Joseph.
Josué, *n.m.* Joshua.
jota, *n.f.* name of letter J; jota, Aragonese dance; iota, tittle.
joven, *a.* (*pl.* **jóvenes**) young.—*n.m.f.* youth, young man, woman; *de —,* as a young man *or* woman.
jovial, *a.* jovial.
jovialidad, *n.f.* joviality.
joya, *n.f.* jewel.
joyel, *n.m.* gem.
joyelero, *n.m.* jewel case.
joyería, *n.m.* jeweller's shop; jewel(le)ry.
joyero, -ra, *n.m.f.* jeweller.—*n.m.* jewel case.
Juan, *n.m.* John; *Buen—,* dupe, easy mark; *— Soldado,* GI Joe.

Juana, *n.f.* Jane, Joan, Jean; — *de Arco,* Joan of Arc.

Juanete, *n.m.* prominent cheek-bone; bunion; (*naut.*) top-gallant.

jubilación, *n.f.* pension; retirement.

jubilado, -da, *a.* retired; (*educ.*) emeritus.

jubilar, *v.t.* retire, pension off; (*fam.*) chuck out.—*v.i.* celebrate; retire.—*v.r.* retire; celebrate, rejoice.

jubileo, *n.m.* jubilee; *por* —, once in a blue moon.

júbilo, *n.m.* jubilation.

jubiloso, -sa, *a.* jubilant.

jubón, *n.m.* doublet, jerkin.

Judá, *n.m.* Judah.

judaico, -ca, *a.* Judaic.

judaísmo, *n.m.* Judaism.

judaizar [PC], *v.i.* Judaize.

Judas, *n.m.* Judas; — *Iscariote,* Judas Iscariot; *estar hecho un* —, look like a rag-bag.

judeo-español, -la, *a., n.m.* Judaeo-Spanish.

judería, *n.f.* Jewry; ghetto.

judía (1), *n.f.* Jewess.

judía (2), *n.f.* bean; — *blanca,* haricot bean; — *pinta,* red kidney bean; — *verde,* kidney bean; French bean.

judicatura, *n.f.* judgeship; judicature.

judicial, *a.* judicial, rel. to judge.

judiciario, -ria, *a.* astrological.—*n.m.f.* astrologer.

judío, -día, *a.* Jewish.—*n.m.f.* Jew, Jewess.

Judit, *n.f.* Judith.

judo, *n.m.* judo.

juego, *n.m.* game; play, playing; gambling, gaming; set; suite; working, movement; *hacer el* — *a,* play into the hands of; *hacer* — *con,* match; — *de ajedrez,* chess set *or* game of chess; — *de bolas,* (*mech.*) ball bearing.

juerga, *n.f.* (*fam.*) spree, binge.

juerguista, *n.m.f.* (*fam.*) reveller.

jueves, *n.m.* Thursday; *cosa del otro* —, a thing seldom seen.

juez, *n.m.* (*pl.* **jueces**) judge; — *de guardia,* coroner; — *de instrucción,* magistrate; (*sport*) umpire, linesman, starter, *etc.*

jugada, *n.f.* play; stroke, move, throw; dirty trick.

jugador, -ra, *n.m.f.* player; gambler.

jugar [4B, *conjugated as if* **jogar**], *v.t.* play; stake, gamble; wield.—*v.i.* match; work, function.—*v.r.* gamble, risk; — *a,* play (*games*); — *con,* match; — *en,* have a hand in.

juglar, *n.m.* (*obs.*) minstrel.

jugo, *n.m.* juice; gravy; (*fig.*) substance.

jugoso, -sa, *a.* juicy, succulent.

juguete, *n.m.* toy, plaything; (*theat.*) skit.

juguetear, *v.i.* frolic, sport, dally.

juguetón, -tona, *a.* playful, frolicsome.

juicio, *n.m.* judgement; (*jur.*) trial; reason, sense; wisdom; astrological forecast, horoscope; — *de Dios,* trial by ordeal; — *de divorcio,* divorce decree.

juicioso, -sa, *a.* judicious, wise.

julepe, *n.m.* julep; (*fam.*) reprimand; (*S.A.*) fright; (*C.A.*) busy time.

Julio, *n.m.* Julius, Julian; **julio,** *n.m.* July.

¡jum! *interj.* hum!

jumento, -ta, *n.m.f.* donkey.

juncia, *n.f.* (*bot.*) sedge; *vender* —, brag.

junco, *n.m.* (*bot.*) rush; rattan cane; (*naut.*) junk.

jungla, *n.f.* jungle.

junio, *n.m.* June.

junípero, *n.m.* juniper.

Juno, *n.f.* (*myth.*) Juno.

junquera, *n.f.* (*bot.*) rush.

junquillo, *n.m.* (*bot.*) jonquil; rattan, reed; (*carp.*) beading.

junta, *n.f.* board, council; session; union; junction, joint; coupling; washer, gasket; — *de comercio,* board of trade; — *de sanidad,* board of health; — *militar,* military junta.

juntamente, *adv.* together.

juntar, *v.t.* join, connect, unite; gather together; leave ajar.—*v.r.* assemble, gather; unite.

junto, -ta, *a.* united, joined.—*pl.* together.—*adv.* together; jointly; near (*a,* to); *por* —, all together, in bulk.

juntura, *n.f.* joint, seam; connexion.

Júpiter, *n.m.* Jupiter.

jura, *n.f.* oath, swearing.

jurado, *n.m.* jury; juror.

juramentar, *v.t.* swear in, put on oath.—*v.r.* take the oath, be sworn in.

juramento, *n.m.* oath; — *de Hipócrates,* Hippocratic oath.

jurar, *v.t.i., v.i.* swear.—*v.r.* swear, curse.

jurídico, -ca, *a.* juridical.

jurisconsulto, *n.m.* jurisconsult, jurist.

jurisdicción, *n.f.* jurisdiction.

jurisperito, *n.m.* legal expert.

jurisprudencia, *n.f.* jurisprudence.

jurista, *n.m.* jurist.

justa, *n.f.* joust, tournament.

justamente, *adv.* justly; exactly, precisely.

justar, *v.i.* joust, tilt.

justicia, *n.f.* justice; (*fam.*) execution, death sentence; *de* —, duly, deservedly.

justiciable, *a.* actionable.

justiciero, -ra, *a.* stern, rigorous.

justificable, *a.* justifiable.

justificación, *n.f.* justification.

justificar [A], *v.t.* justify.

justiprecio, *n.m.* just appraisal.

justo, -ta, *a.* just; exact; right, correct; fair; honest; tight, flush.—*adv.* tightly; duly, rightly.

juvenil, *a.* youthful, juvenile.

juventud, *n.f.* youth.

juzgado, *n.m.* tribunal, court.

juzgar [B], *v.t.* judge.—*v.i.* judge, pass judgement (*de,* on); *a* — *por,* judging by, to judge by.

K

K, k, *n.f.* twelfth letter of the Spanish alphabet.

ka, *n.f.* name of the letter K.

keroseno, kerosene, kerosén, *n.m.* kerosene, coal oil.

kiliárea, *n.f.* kiliare.

kilo, *n.m.* kilo.

kilociclo, *n.m.* kilocycle.
kilométrico, -ca, *a.* kilometric.
kilómetro, *n.m.* kilometre.
kilovatio, *n.m.* kilowatt.
kiosko, *n.m.* kiosk [QUIOSCO].
Kremlín, *n.m.* Kremlin.
Kuwait, Estado del, *n.m.* Kuwait.

L

L, l, *n.f.* thirteenth letter of the Spanish alphabet.
la (1), *f. def. art.* the.—*f. accus. pron.* her; it; you.
la (2), *n.m.* (*mus.*) (key of) A.
laberinto, *n.m.* labyrinth, maze.
labia, *n.f.* (*fam.*) gift of the gab.
labial, *a., n.f.* labial.
labihendido, -da, *a.* hare-lipped.
labio, *n.m.* lip.
labor, *n.f.* work, labour; needle-work; farm work; *campo de* —, tilled field.
laborable, *a.* tillable; working (day).
laboral, *a.* rel. to labour, work.
laborante, *a.* working.—*n.m.* political pressure-man.
laborar, *v.t.* work, till.—*v.i.* intrigue.
laboratorio, *n.m.* laboratory.
laborear, *v.t.* work (*a mine*).
laborioso, -sa, *a.* industrious; laborious.
laborismo, *n.m.* Labour, socialism.
laborista, *a.* Labour.—*n.m.f.* Labour supporter.
labradero, -ra, labradío, -día, *a.* arable, tillable.
labrador, -ra, *a.* working, farming.—*n.m.f.* farmer, peasant.—*n.m.* ploughman.
labrantío, -tía, *a.* arable, tillable.
labranza, *n.f.* farming, tillage; farm-land; working.
labrar, *v.t.* work, fashion; plough, till; construct; bring about.—*v.i.* make a strong impression (*en*, on).
labriego, -ga, *n.m.f.* peasant.
laca, *n.f.* lac; lacquer, japan.
lacayo, *n.m.* lackey.
laceración, *n.f.* laceration.
lacerar, *v.t.* lacerate; damage.
lacería, *n.f.* misery.
lacio, -cia, *a.* withered; languid.
lacónico, -ca, *a.* laconic.
laconismo, *n.m.* laconism.
lacra, *n.f.* mark left by illness; defect; (*S.A.*) wound, sore.
lacrar, *v.t.* strike down; harm.—*v.r.* be stricken.
lacre, *n.m.* sealing wax.
lacrimógeno, -na, *a.* tear-causing.—*n.m.* or *f.* tear-gas.
lacrimoso, -sa, *a.* lachrymose.
lactación, lactancia, *n.f.* lactation.
lactar, *v.t., v.i.* suckle.
lácteo, -tea, *a.* lacteous, milky.
lacticinio, *n.m.* milk food.
láctico, -ca, *a.* lactic.
ladear, *v.t., v.i., v.r.* tilt, turn, level.

ladeo, *n.m.* tilt, turn, leaning.
ladera, *n.f.* hillside.
ladino, -na, *a.* crafty, cunning; Romansch; Sephardic Spanish.—*n.m.f.* Ladin.
lado, *n.m.* side; place; *de* —, sideways; *hacer* —, make room; *hacerse a un* —, step aside.—*pl.* advisers; *por todos lados,* on all sides, everywhere.
ladrar, *v.t., v.i.* bark.
ladrido, *n.m.* bark.
ladrillar, *v.t.* brick.
ladrillo, *n.m.* brick; tile.
ladrón, -drona, *a.* thieving.—*n.m.f.* thief, robber.
ladronear, *v.i.* thieve.
ladronería, *n.f.* thievery; thieves.
lagar, *n.m.* wine-press, press.
lagartija, *n.f.* small lizard.
lagarto, *n.m.* lizard; (*fam.*) sly man.
lago, *n.m.* lake.
lágrima, *n.f.* tear; drop, drip.
lagrimar, *v.i.* weep.
lagrimoso, -sa, *a.* tearful; runny (*eyes*).
laguna, *n.f.* lagoon, pool; lacuna.
lagunoso, -sa, *a.* fenny, marshy.
laical, *a.* lay.
laicizar [C], *v.t.* laicize, secularize.
laico, -ca, *a.* lay.—*n.m.f.* lay person.
laja, *n.f.* slab.
lama, *n.f.* slime, mud; lamé.—*n.m.* lama.
lamasería, *n.f.* lamasery.
lambrija, *n.f.* worm.
lamedura, *n.f.* licking.
lamentable, *a.* lamentable.
lamentación, *n.f.* lamentation.
lamentar, *v.t., v.i., v.r.* lament, weep (*de, por,* for).
lamento, *n.m.* lament.
lamentoso, -sa, *a.* lamentable; mournful.
lamer, *v.t.* lick; lap against.
lámina, *n.f.* plate; sheet, lamina.
laminar, *v.t.* laminate; roll (*metals*).
lamoso, -sa, *a.* slimy.
lámpara, *n.f.* lamp; light bulb; radio tube; grease spot.
lamparilla, *n.f.* small lamp; night-light.
lamparón, *n.m.* grease spot; (*med.*) king's evil, scrofula.
lampazo, *n.m.* (*bot.*) dock; (*naut.*) swab.
lampiño, -ña, *a.* beardless, hairless.
lamprea, *n.f.* lamprey.
lampreazo, *n.m.* lash, stroke.
lana, *n.f.* wool.
lanar, *a.* rel. to wool; wool-bearing.
lance, *n.m.* cast, throw; stroke, move; catch; chance; juncture; affair; quarrel; *de* —, bargain, second hand.
lancero, *n.m.* lancer.
lanceta, *n.f.* lancet.
lancha, *n.f.* slab; (*naut.*) long-boat; lighter.
landa, *n.f.* lande, moor, woodland.
landó, *n.m.* landau.
lanería, *n.f.* woolshop.—*pl.* woollen goods.
lanero, -ra, *a.* rel. to wool, woollen.—*n.m.* wool-store; (*orn.*) lanner.
langosta, *n.f.* (*ent.*) locust; (*zool.*) lobster; (*fam.*) scourge.
langostín, langostino, *n.m.* crayfish.
languidecer [9], *v.i.* languish.
languidez, *n.f.* languor.
lánguido, -da, *a.* languid, languishing, languorous.

lanilla, *n.f.* nap; flannel.
lanolina, *n.f.* lanolin.
lanoso, -sa, lanudo, -da, *a.* woolly, fleecy.
lanza, *n.f.* lance, spear; nozzle; coach pole.
lanzabombas, *n.m. inv.* (*mil.*) mortar; (*aer.*) bomb-doors.
lanzacohetes, *n.m. inv.* (*mil.*) rocket-launcher.
lanzada, *n.f.* lance thrust *or* wound.
lanzadera, *n.f.* shuttle.
lanzallamas, *n.m. inv.* (*mil.*) flame-thrower.
lanzamiento, *n.m.* throw; launching; leap; *plataforma de —,* launching pad (*rockets etc.*).
lanzaminas, *n.m. inv.* (*naut.*) mine-layer.
lanzar [C], *v.t.* hurl, throw; launch; throw out.—*v.r.* rush, dash; leap.
Lanzarote, *n.m.* Lancelot.
laocio, -cia, *a.,n.m.f.* Laotian.
Laos, *n.m.* Laos.
lapicero, *n.m.* pencil-case; drawing pencil.
lápida, *n.f.* stone tablet.
lapidario, -ria, *a., n.m.* lapidary.
lapislázuli, *n.m.* lapis lazuli.
lápiz, *n.m.* (*pl.* **lápices**) graphite, black lead; pencil; *— de labios,* lipstick; *— tinta,* indelible pencil.
lapo, *n.m.* (*fam.*) slap; swig, drink.
lapón, -pona, *a., n.m.f.* Lapp.
Laponia, *n.f.* Lapland.
lapso, *n.m.* lapse.
laquear, *v.t.* lacquer.
lard(e)ar, *v.t.* (*cul.*) baste; grease.
lardero, *a.* applied to Thursday before Lent.
lardo, *n.m.* lard.
largar [B], *v.t.* release, loosen; unfurl; (*fam.*) let slip, say.—*v.r.* set sail; (*fam.*) clear off.
largo, -ga, *a.* long; generous; ready, prompt; abundant.—*n.m.* length; (*mus.*) largo.— *interj.* be off! get out! *a la larga,* in the long run; *a lo — de,* along, throughout; *— de uñas,* light-fingered; *pasar de —,* pass by; pass over.
largueza, *n.f.* length; generosity.
larguirucho, -cha, *a.* (*fam.*) lanky.
largura, *n.f.* length.
laringe, *n.f.* larynx.
larva, *n.f.* (*ent.*) larva.
las, *f.pl. def. art.* the.—*f.pl. accus. pron.* them; those.
lascivia, *n.f.* lasciviousness.
lascivo, -va, *a.* lascivious; sportive.
lasitud, *n.f.* lassitude.
laso, -sa, *a.* weary; lax; unspun.
lastar, *v.t.* pay *or* suffer for another.
lástima, *n.f.* pity; plaint; pitiful object; *¡ qué — !* what a pity!
lastimar, *v.t.* hurt, bruise; pity.—*v.r.* feel sorry (*de,* for), pity; complain (*de,* about).
lastimero, -ra, *a.* pitiful; harmful.
lastimoso, -sa, *a.* pitiful.
lastra, *n.f.* slab.
lastrar, *v.t.* ballast.
lastre, *n.m.* ballast.
lata, *n.f.* tin, can; tin-plate; lath; small dog; (*fam.*) bore, drag; *dar la —,* be a nuisance.
latente, *a.* latent.
lateral, *a.* lateral.
látex, *n.m.* latex.
latido, *n.m.* beat, throb; yap, yelp.
latiente, *a.* heating, throbbing.
latifundio, *n.m.* large rural estate.

latifundista, *n.m.f.* big land-owner.
latigazo, *n.m.* lash, crack.
látigo, *n.m.* whip, lash; cinch-strap; (*fam.*) thin person.
latín, *n.m.* Latin (*language*); (*fam.*) Latinism; *saber (mucho) —,* be canny.
latinajo, *n.m.* (*fam.*) dog Latin; (*fam.*) Latin phrase.
latinidad, *n.f.* Latinity.
latinismo, *n.m.* Latinism.
latinista, *n.m.f.* Latinist.
latinizar, *v.t., v.i.* Latinize.
latino, -na, *a., n.m.f.* Latin.
latinoamericano, -na, *a.* Latin-American.
latir, *v.i.* beat, throb; yap, yelp.
latitud, *n.f.* latitude.
latitudinal, *a.* latitudinal.
lato, -ta, *a.* broad; general.
latón, *n.f.* brass.
latoso, -sa, *a.* (*fam.*) pesky, boring.
latrocinio, *n.m.* thievery, theft.
latvio, -via, *a., n.m.f.* Latvian.
laúd, *n.m.* lute.
laudable, *a.* laudable.
laude, *n.f.* grave-stone.—*pl.* lauds.
laudo, *n.m.* (*jur.*) findings.
laureado, -da, *a., n.m.f.* laureate; prize-winner.
laurear, *v.t.* crown with laurel, honour; award a degree to.
laurel, *n.m.* laurel; laurels.
láureo, -rea, *a.* rel. to laurel.—*n.f.* laurel wreath.
lauréola, *n.f.* laurel crown; halo.
lauro, *n.m.* laurel; laurels.
lauto, -ta, *a.* sumptuous.
lava, *n.f.* lava.
lavable, *a.* washable.
lavabo, *n.m.* wash-basin; lavatory.
lavadedos, *n.m. inv.* finger-bowl.
lavadero, *n.m.* wash-house; washing place; laundry.
lavado, -da, *a.* (*fam.*) brazen.—*n.m.* washing, laundry; *— a seco,* dry cleaning.
lavador, -ra, *a.* washing.—*n.f.* washing machine.
lavajo, *n.m.* pool, pond; morass.
lavamanos, *n.m. inv.* wash-basin, wash-stand.
lavanco, *n.m.* wild duck.
lavanda, *n.f.* lavender.
lavandera, *n.f.* laundress, washerwoman; (*orn.*) wagtail.
lavandería, *n.f.* laundry.
lavandero, *n.m.* launderer, laundryman.
lavaplatos, *n.m.* or *f. inv.* dishwasher.
lavar, *v.t.* wash.—*v.r.* wash, have a wash.
lavativa, *n.f.* enema; (*fam.*) pest.
lavatorio, *n.m.* wash; lavatory; (*med.*) lotion; (*eccl.*) Maundy.
lavazas, *n.f.pl.* dirty suds.
laxación, *n.f.* laxation, easing.
laxamiento, *n.m.* laxation; laxity.
laxante, *a., n.m.* (*med.*) laxative.
laxar, *v.t., v.r.* slacken, loosen.
laxidad, laxitud, *n.f.* laxity, laxness.
laxo, -xa, *a.* lax, slack.
laya, *n.f.* spade; kind, ilk; (*fam.*) shame.
lazar [C], *v.t.* snare, lasso.
lazareto, *n.m.* lazaretto.
lazarillo, *n.m.* blind man's guide.
lazarino, -na, *a., n.m.f.* leper.

Lázaro, *n.m.* Lazarus; **lázaro,** *n.m.* ragged pauper; **hecho un —,** covered with sores.
lazaroso, -sa, *a.* leprous.
lazo, *n.m.* bow, knot; loop; bond; lasso; snare, trap; tie.
le, *dat. pers. pron.* to him, to her, to it, to you. [SE].—*accus.* him, you.
leal, *a.* loyal, faithful, trustworthy.
lealtad, *n.f.* loyalty, faithfulness.
lebrato, lebratón, *n.m.* leveret.
lebrel, -la, *n.m.f.* whippet.
lebrero, -ra, *a.* hare-hunting.
lebrillo, librillo, *n.m.* washing-up bowl.
lebroncillo, *n.m.* leveret.
lebruno, -na, *a.* hare-like, leporine.
lección, *n.f.* lesson; reading, interpretation.
leccionista, *n.m.f.* tutor, coach.
lectivo, -va, *a.* term-time, school (*day, year etc.*).
lector, -ra, *n.m.f.* reader; (*educ.*) native language teacher, lector.
lectura, *n.f.* reading; lecture; reading matter.
lechada, *n.f.* lime-water; paper-pulp.
lechar, *v.t.* (*S.A.*) milk; (*C.A.*) whitewash.
leche, *n.f.* milk.
lechecillas, *n.f.pl.* sweetbreads; offal.
lechería, *n.f.* dairy.
lechero, -ra, *a.* milky, milk.—*n.m.* milkman, dairyman.—*n.f.* milkmaid, dairymaid; milk jug *or* churn.
lechida, *n.f.* litter, brood.
lecho, *n.m.* bed.
lechón, -chona, *n.m.f.* piglet.
lechoso, -sa, *a.* milky.
lechuga, *n.f.* lettuce.
lechugada, *n.f.* (*fam.*) flop, wash-out.
lechuguilla, *n.f.* wild lettuce; ruff, frill.
lechuguino, -na, *a.* stylish, natty.—*n.m.f.* young flirt.
lechuza, *n.f.* barn owl.
lechuzo, -za, *a.* owlish.—*n.m.* bailiff, debt collector.
ledo, -da, *a.* (*poet.*) happy, joyful.
leer [N], *v.t.* read.
lega, *n.f.* lay sister.
legación, *n.f.* legation.
legado, *n.m.* legate; legacy.
legajo, *n.m.* file, bundle; dossier.
legal, *a.* legal; correct, dutiful.
legalidad, *n.f.* legality.
legalizar [C], *v.t.* legalize; authorize.
légamo, *n.m.* ooze, slime, silt.
legaña, *n.f.* bleariness.
legar, *v.t.* bequeath; send as legate.
legendario, -ria, *a.* legendary.
legibilidad, *n.f.* legibility.
legible, *a.* legible.
legión, *n.f.* legion.
legionario, -ria, *a., n.m.f.* legionary.
legislación, *n.f.* legislation.
legislador, -ra, *a.* legislating.—*n.m.f.* legislator.
legislar, *v.i.* legislate.
legislativo, -va, *a.* legislative.
legislatura, *n.f.* legislature.
legisperito, legista, *n.m.* legal expert.
legitimación, *n.f.* legitimation.
legitimar, *v.t.* legitimize.
legítimo, -ma, *a.* legitimate; fair; genuine.
lego, -ga, *a.* lay.—*n.m.* layman; lay brother.
legón, *n.m.* hoe.
legrar, *v.t.* scrape.

legua, *n.f.* league (*about* 3 *miles*).
legulcyo, *n.m.* pettifogger, petty lawyer.
legumbre, *n.f.* vegetable; legume.
leguminoso, -sa, *a.* leguminous.
leible, *a.* readable.
leísta, *n.m.f.* person who uses **le** instead of **lo.**
lejanía, *n.f.* distance, remoteness.
lejano, -na, *a.* far-away, distant.
lejía, *n.f.* lye; (*fam.*) dressing-down.
lejísimo(s), *adv. sup. of* LEJOS.
lejito(s), *adv.* pretty far.
lejos, *adv.* far, distant; **a lo —,** in the distance.
lelo, -la, *a.* silly, stupid.—*n.m.f.* fool, dolt.
lema, *n.m.* motto; theme.
lemosín, -sina, *a.* Limousin, Languedocian. —*n.m.* Langue d'Oc.
lencería, *n.f.* linen goods; linen room.
lendroso, -sa, *a.* full of nits, lousy.
lene, *a.* gentle, soft, mild.
lengua, *n.f.* tongue; language; **mala —,** gossip; **hacerse lenguas de,** (*fam.*) to rave about.
lenguado, *n.m.* (*ichth.*) sole.
lenguaje, *n.m.* language, manner of speaking.
lenguaraz, lenguaz, *a.* (*pl.* **-aces**) loose-tongued; garrulous; foul-mouthed.
lengüeta, *n.f.* needle, pointer; shoe-tongue; tongue; wedge; (*mus.*) reed.
lenidad, *n.f.* lenity, leniency.
lenificar [A], *v.t.* soothe, ease.
Lenín, *n.m.* Lenin.
Leningrado, *n.m.* Leningrad.
lenitivo, -va, *a.* lenitive.
lente, *n.m.* or *f.* lens; magnifying glass.—*pl.* glasses; **lentes de contacto,** contact lenses.
lenteja, *n.f.* lentil; pendulum weight; duck-weed.
lentejuela, *n.f.* sequin.
lentitud, *n.f.* slowness.
lento, -ta, *a.* slow.
leña, *n.f.* firewood; (*fam.*) hiding, beating.
leñador, *n.m.* woodman.
leñame, *n.m.* timber; fire-wood.
leñero, *n.m.* fire-wood dealer; wood-shed.
leño, *n.m.* wood, timber; log; (*poet.*) bark, ship; (*fam.*) dunce.
leñoso, -sa, *a.* woody.
León, *n.m.* Leo; Leon; **león,** *n.m.* lion.
leona, *n.f.* lioness.
leonado, -da, *a.* tawny.
leonera, *n.f.* lion cage; lion's den; (*fam.*) dive, joint; (*fam.*) loft.
leonés, -nesa, *a., n.m.f.* Leonese.
leonino, -na, *a.* leonine.
leopardo, *n.m.* leopard.
lepra, *n.f.* leprosy.
leproso, -sa, *a.* leprous.—*n.m.f.* leper.
lerdo, -da, *a.* slow, heavy; coarse.
les, *pron. m., pl.* dative; to them, to you. [SE]. —*accus.* them, you.
lesión, *n.f.* lesion; harm.
lesionar, *v.t.* hurt, harm, injure.
lesivo, -va, *a.* injurious, harmful.
leso, -sa, *a.* hurt; perverted; **lesa majestad,** lese majesty.
letal, *a.* lethal.
letanía, *n.f.* litany.
letárgico, -ca, *a.* lethargic.
letargo, *n.m.* lethargy.
Lete, *n.m.* (*myth.*) Lethe.
letificar [A], *v.t.* animate, cheer.

letón, -tona, *a., n.m.* Lettish.—*n.m.f.* Lett, Latvian.
letra, *n.f.* letter, character; handwriting; type face; words (*of song*); letter, strict sense; **a la —,** to the letter; **— de cambio,** (*com.*) bill of exchange.—*pl.* letters, literature; **bellas letras,** belles lettres; **primeras letras,** (*educ.*) the three R's.
letrado, -da, *a.* lettered, learned.—*n.m.* lawyer; man of letters.
letrero, *n.m.* sign, poster, label.
letrina, *n.f.* latrine.
letrista, *n.f.* lyricist.
leucemia, *n.f.* leukæmia.
leudar, *v.t.* leaven.
leva, *n.f.* (*naut.*) weighing anchor; (*mil.*) levy; (*naut.*) swell; (*mech.*) tooth, cog.
levadura, *n.f.* leaven, yeast.
levantamiento, *n.m.* raising; rising, insurrection; sublimity; **— del censo,** census taking.
levantar, *v.t.* raise, lift; rouse, agitate; clear (*the table*); build; make (*survey*); levy.—*v.r.* get up, rise; stand up; rebel.
Levante, *n.m.* Levant; east coast of Spain; **levante,** *n.m.* east wind.
levantino, -na, *a., n.m.f.* Levantine.
levantisco, -ca, *a.* turbulent, restless.
leve, *a.* light; slight.
levedad, *n.f.* lightness; levity.
Leví, *n.m.* Levi.
leviatán, *n.m.* leviathan.
levita (1), *n.m.* Levite; deacon.
levita (2), *n.f.* frock-coat.
levitación, *n.f.* levitation.
Levítico, *n.m.* (*Bib.*) Leviticus; **levítico, -ca,** *a.* Levitical.
léxico, -ca, *a.* lexical.—*n.m.* lexicon.
lexicografía, *n.f.* lexicography.
lexicográfico, -ca, *a.* lexicographical.
lexicógrafo, -fa, *n.m.f.* lexicographer.
lexicología, *n.f.* lexicology.
lexicológico, -ca, *a.* lexicological.
lexicólogo, *n.m.* lexicologist.
lexicón, *n.m.* lexicon.
ley, *n.f.* law; norm, standard; loyalty; grade (*of metal*); **a — de caballero,** on the word of a gentleman; **de buena —,** genuine, sterling.
leyenda, *n.f.* legend.
lía, *n.f.* esparto rope.—*pl.* lees.
liar [L], *v.t.* bind; tie *or* wrap up; roll (*cigarettes*); (*fam.*) draw in, embroil.—*v.r.* come together; form a liaison; (*fam.*) get mixed up *or* involved (**a, en,** in); **liarlas,** (*fam.*) escape; (*fam.*) kick off (*die*).
liatón, *n.m.* esparto cord.
libación, *n.f.* libation.
libanés, -nesa, *a., n.m.f.* Lebanese.
Líbano, *n.m.* (the) Lebanon.
libar, *v.t.* suck; taste.—*v.i.* perform a libation.
libelista, *n.m.f.* lampooner, libeller.
libelo, *n.m.* lampoon, libel; (*jur.*) petition.
libélula, *n.f.* dragonfly.
liberación, *n.f.* liberation; settlement, quittance.
liberador, -ra, *a.* liberating.—*n.m.f.* liberator.
liberal, *a., n.m.f.* liberal.
liberalidad, *n.f.* liberality.
liberalismo, *n.m.* liberalism.

liberalizar [C], *v.t.* liberalize.
liberar, *v.t.* free, liberate.
liberiano, -na, *a., n.m.f.* Liberian.
libérrimo, -ma, *a. sup. of* LIBRE.
libertad, *n.f.* liberty, freedom.
libertado, -da, *a.* bold, taking liberties.
libertador, -ra, *a.* liberating.—*n.m.f.* liberator, deliverer.
libertar, *v.t.* free, liberate (**de,** from).
libertario, -ria, *a., n.m.f.* anarchist.
liberticida, *a.* liberticidal.—*n.m.f.* destroyer of freedom.
libertinaje, *n.m.* libertinism.
libertino, -na, *a., n.m.f.* libertine.
liberto, -ta, *n.m.f.* freed slave.
Libia, *n.f.* Libya.
libídine, *n.f.* libido; lewdness.
libidinoso, -sa, *a.* libidinous, lewd.
libio, -bia, *a., n.m.f.* Libyan.
Libra, *n.f.* (*astr.*) Libra; **libra,** *n.f.* pound (*£, lb.*).
librado, -da, *a.* (*fam.*) done-for.—*n.m.f.* (*com.*) drawee.
librador, -ra, *n.m.f.* deliverer; (*com.*) drawer; scoop.
libramiento, *n.m.* delivery; warrant.
libranza, *n.f.* (*com.*) draft, bill of exchange.
librar, *v.t.* free, deliver (**de,** from); exempt; expedite; pass (*sentence*); issue (*a decree*); give (*battle*); (*com.*) draw.—*v.i.* give birth; **a bien** *or* **buen —,** as well as could be expected; **— bien,** succeed; **— mal,** fail.—*v.r.* escape; get rid (**de,** of); **librarse de buena,** (*fam.*) have a close shave.
libre, *a.* free; loose, immoral; rash, brash; unmarried; innocent.
librea, *n.f.* livery.
librecambio, *n.m.* free trade.
librepensador, -ra, *n.m.f.* free-thinker.
librería, *n.f.* book-shop; library; book-case.
libreril, *a.* rel. to books *or* booksellers.
librero, *n.m.* bookseller.
libresco, -ca, *a.* bookish.
libreta, *n.f.* note-book; cheque book; (*Madrid*) loaf.
libreto, *n.m.* libretto.
librillo, *n.m.* packet; booklet. [LEBRILLO].
libro, *n.m.* book; (*fig.*) impost.
licencia, *n.f.* licence; permission, permit; leave, furlough: licentiate, bachelor's degree.
licenciado, -da, *a.* licensed; on leave; free; pedantic.—*n.m.f.* (*educ.*) bachelor, licentiate; discharged soldier; lawyer.
licenciamiento, *n.m.* (*educ.*) graduation; (*mil.*) discharge.
licenciatura, *n.f.* (*educ.*) graduation; licentiate, Spanish bachelor's degree.
licencioso, -sa, *a.* licentious.
liceo, *n.m.* lycée, lyceum.
licitar, *v.t.* bid for; (*S.A.*) buy *or* sell at auction.
lícito, -ta, *a.* licit, lawful; just.
licor, *n.m.* liquor; liqueur.
licoroso, -sa, *a.* spirituous; rich, generous (*wine*).
licuefacer [20], *v.t., v.r.* liquefy.
licuescente, *a.* liquescent.
lid, *n.f.* fight; dispute.
líder, *n.m.* leader.
lidia, *n.f.* fight, battle, contest; bull-fight.
lidiador, -ra, *a.* fighting.—*n.m.f.* fighter.—*n.m.* bull-fighter.

lidiar, *v.t.* fight (*bulls*).—*v.i.* fight, battle.
liebre, *n.f.* hare; coward.
liendre, *n.f.* nit, louse egg.
lienzo, *n.m.* linen; piece of linen; (*paint.*) canvas; (*arch.*) face, facing.
liga, *n.f.* league, union; garter; alloy; bird-lime; mistletoe; rubber band.
ligación, *n.f.* bond; binding; alloying.
ligada, *n.f.* lashing, binding.
ligado, *n.m.* (*print.*, *mus.*) ligature.
ligadura, *n.f.* ligature; lashing, binding.
ligamaza, *n.f.* bird-lime.
ligamento, *n.m.* ligament.
ligar [B], *v.t.* bind, tie, lash; join; alloy; bind, oblige, commit.—*v.r.* form an alliance; bind oneself (*a*, to).
ligazón, *n.f.* bond, union, connexion.
ligereza, *n.f.* lightness; swiftness; levity, fickleness.
ligero, -ra, *a.* light; swift; flippant; fickle; *de —*, without, thinking; *— de cascos*, feather-brained.
ligur, ligurino, -na, *a.*, *n.m.f.* Ligurian.
ligustro, *n.m.* (*bot.*) privet.
lija, *n.f.* sand-paper; (*ichth.*) dog-fish.
lijar, *v.t.* sand-paper, sand.
lila, lilac (*pl.* **lilaques**), *n.f.* (*bot.*) lilac.
lilaila, *n.f.* (*fam.*) wiliness.
lilao, *n.m.* (*fam.*) swank, empty show.
liliputiense, *a.*, *n.m.f.* Lilliputian.
lima, *n.f.* file, rasp; polish.
limadura, *n.f.* filing.
limalla, *n.f.* filings.
limar, *v.t.* file; touch up, polish.
limatón, *n.m.* rasp, rough round file.
limaza, *n.f.* (*zool.*) slug.
limbo, *n.m.* (*eccl.*) limbo; edge; (*astr.*, *bot.*) limb.
limen, *n.m.* threshold.
limeño, -ña, *a.*, *n.m.f.* rel. to *or* native of Lima.
limero, *n.m.* sweet-lime tree.
limitación, *n.f.* limitation.
limitar, *v.t.* limit (*a*, to); bound; constrict, reduce.
límite, *n.m.* limit, confine.
limítrofe, *a.* bordering, limiting, conterminous.
limo, *n.m.* slime, mud; (*S.A.*) [LIMERO].
limón, *n.m.* lemon; lemon-tree; shaft, pole.
limonado, -da, *a.* lemon.—*n.f.* lemonade.
limonar, *n.m.* lemon grove.
limonero, *n.m.* lemon-tree; lemon-seller.
limosina, *n.f.* limousine.
limosna, *n.f.* alms.
limosnear, *v.i.* beg alms.
limosnero, -ra, *a.* charitable.—*n.m.* almoner.—*n.m.f.* (*S.A.*) beggar.
limoso, -sa, *a.* slimy, muddy.
limpia, *n.f.* cleaning.
limpiabotas, *n.m. inv.* boot-black.
limpiachimeneas, *n.m. inv.* chimney-sweep.
limpiadientes, *n.m. inv.* toothpick.
limpiadura, *n.f.* cleaning.
limpiaparabrisas, *n.m. inv.* windshield wiper.
limpiar, *v.t.* clean; (*fam.*) steal; clean out.
límpido, -da, *a.* (*poet.*) limpid.
limpieza, *n.f.* cleanness, cleanliness; cleaning; purity; neatness.
limpio, -pia, *a.* clean, cleanly; neat; pure; free, clear; fair; *en —*, clearly, neatly; net.

linaje, *n.m.* lineage; progeny; extraction; (*fig.*) class.
linajista, *n.m.f.* genealogist.
linajudo, -da, *a.* high-born.
linaza, *n.f.* linseed.
lince, *a.*, *n.m.* lynx.
lincear, *v.t.* (*fam.*) see through, spot.
linchamiento, *n.m.* lynching.
linchar, *v.t.* lynch.
lindante, *a.* adjoining, contiguous.
lindar, *v.i.* border (*con*, on).
lindazo, *n.m.* boundary.
linde, *n.m.* or *f.* boundary, limit.
lindero, -ra, *a.* bordering.—*n.m.f.* edge, border.
lindeza, *n.f.* prettiness.
lindo, -da, *a.* pretty; fine; *de lo —*, wonderfully.—*n.m.* fop, (*fam.*) sissy.
línea, *n.f.* line.
lineal, *a.* linear, lineal.
linear, *v.t.* outline, sketch; demarcate.
linfa, *n.f.* lymph.
linfático, -ca, *a.* lymphatic.
lingote, *n.m.* ingot, pig.
lingual, *a.*, *n.f.* lingual.
linguete, *n.m.* ratchet.
lingüista, *n.m.f.* linguist.
lingüístico, -ca, *a.* linguistic.—*n.f.* linguistics.
linimento, *n.m.* liniment.
lino, *n.m.* linen; flax; (*poet.*) sail.
linóleo, *n.m.* linoleum.
linón, *n.m.* lawn (*cloth*).
linotipia, *n.f.* linotype.
lintel, *n.m.* lintel.
linterna, *n.f.* lantern; torch.
lío, *n.m.* bundle, parcel; (*fam.*) mess, muddle; liaison; *armar un —*, (*fam.*) make trouble.
Liorna, *n.f.* Leghorn; **liorna,** *n.f.* (*fam.*) uproar.
lioso, -sa, *a.* (*fam.*) troublesome; trouble-making.
liquen, *n.m.* lichen.
liquidación, *n.f.* liquidation; settlement.
liquidar, *v.t.* liquidate; liquefy; settle.
liquidez, *n.f.* liquidity.
líquido, -da, *a.*, *n.m.* liquid; (*com.*) net.
lira, *n.f.* lyre; lyrical poetry; inspiration of poet; a verse form.
lírico, -ca, *a.* lyric(al); (*S.A.*) utopian, day-dreaming.—*n.m.* lyrical poet; (*S.A.*) utopian.—*n.f.* lyric poetry.
lirio, *n.m.* (*bot.*) iris, flag; lily.
lir†smo, *n.m.* lyricism.
lirón, *n.m.* dormouse; (*fam.*) sleepy-head.
lis, *n.m.* iris; lily.
Lisboa, *n.f.* Lisbon.
lisbonense, lisbonés, -nesa, *a.*, *n.m.f.* rel. to *or* native of Lisbon.
lisiado, -da, *a.* crippled; wild, eager.—*n.m.f.* cripple.
lisiar, *v.t.* hurt, cripple.—*v.r.* become crippled.
liso, -sa, *a.* smooth; plain, simple; straight-forward.
lisonja, *n.f.* flattery; (*her.*) lozenge.
lisonjear, *v.t.* flatter; delight.
lisonjero, -ra, *a.* flattering; pleasing.—*n.m.f.* flatterer.
lista, *n.f.* list; stripe; strip; muster, roll; *— de correos*, poste restante, general delivery.
listar, *v.t.* list.
list(e)ado, -da, *a.* striped.

listeza, *n.f.* (*fam.*) alertness.
listo, -ta, *a.* ready; alert; prompt; clever.
listón, *n.m.* tape, ribbon; (*carp.*) lath.
lisura, *n.f.* smoothness; simplicity; sincerity; (*S.A.*) nerve, cheek.
litera, *n.f.* litter (*bed*); bunk, berth.
literal, *a.* literal.
literario, -ria, *a.* literary.
literato, -ta, *a.* lettered, literary, learned.—*n.m.f.* lettered *or* literary person.—*pl.* literati.
literatura, *n.f.* literature.
litigación, *n.f.* litigation.
litigante, *a., n.m.f.* litigant.
litigar [B], *v.t., v.i.* litigate.
litigio, *n.m.* lawsuit, litigation; dispute.
litografía, *n.f.* lithograph, lithography.
litografiar, *v.t.* lithograph.
litoral, *a., n.m.f.* littoral, coast.
litro, *n.m.* litre.
Lituania, *n.f.* Lithuania.
lituano, -na, *a., n.m.f.* Lithuanian.
liturgia, *n.f.* liturgy.
litúrgico, -ca, *a.* liturgical.
liviandad, *n.f.* lightness; frivolity; lewdness.
liviano, -na, *a.* light; frivolous; lewd.—*n.m.pl.* lungs, lights.
lividecer [9], *v.t., v.r.* turn livid.
lividez, *n.f.* lividity, lividness.
lívido, -da, *a.* livid.
livor, *n.m.* livid colour; envy, malice.
liza, *n.f.* lists, tournament.
lo, *def. art. neuter,* the.—*accus. pron. m.* it, him; — *bueno,* what is good, the good thing; — *rápido,* the rapidness; how rapidly.
loa, *n.f.* praise; panegyric.
loable, *a.* praiseworthy.
loar, *v.t.* praise.
loba (1), *n.f.* she-wolf.
loba (2), *n.f.* cassock.
lobanillo, *n.m.* wen; gall.
lobato, lobezno, *n.m.* wolf cub.
lobo, *n.m.* wolf; lobe; *coger un* —, (*fam.*) get tight; *desollar un* —, (*fam.*) sleep it off; — *marino,* (*zool.*) seal; (*fam.*) sea-dog.
lóbrego, -ga, *a.* gloomy, murky.
lóbulo, *n.m.* lobule, lobe.
lobuno, -na, *a.* rel. to wolves, wolfish.
locación, *n.f.* (*jur.*) lease.
local, *a.* local.—*n.m.* premises.
localidad, *n.f.* locality; (*theat.*) seat, location.
localismo, *n.m.* localism.
localización, *n.f.* location; localization.
localizar [C], *v.t.* localize; locate.
locatario, -ria, *n.m.f.* tenant.
locería, *n.f.* china-shop; (*S.A.*) pottery.
loción, *n.f.* lotion; lavation.
loco, -ca, *a.* mad; (*fam.*) terrific, wonderful; wild, raging; enthusiastic (*por,* about, *de,* with); *estar* —, be mad, angry *or* enthusiastic; *ser un* —, be insane; — *de atar,* — *rematado*; raving mad; raving lunatic.—*n.m.f.* lunatic; *la loca de la casa,* the imagination.—*n.m.* madman.
locomoción, *n.f.* locomotion.
locomotivo, -va, *a.* locomotive.
locomotor, -ra (*f. also* **locomotriz,** *pl.* **-ices,** *as a.*), *a.* locomotive, locomotor.—*n.f.* (*rail.*) locomotive, engine.
locuacidad, *n.f.* loquacity.
locuaz, *a.* (*pl.* **-aces**) loquacious.

locución, *n.f.* expression; locution.
locuelo, -la, *a.* giddy, wild (*youth*).—*n.m.f.* madcap, giddy youth, giddy girl.—*n.f.* personal manner of speech.
locura, *n.f.* madness.
locutor, -ra, *n.m.f.* (*rad.*) announcer.
locutorio, *n.m.* telephone booth; locutory.
lodazal, lodazar, *n.m.* quagmire, muddy place.
lodo, *n.m.* mud.
lodoso, -sa, *a.* muddy.
logaritmo, *n.m.* logarithm.
logia, *n.f.* (Freemasons') lodge; loggia.
lógico, -ca, *a.* logical.—*n.m.f.* logician.—*n.f.* logic.
logístico, -ca, *a.* logistic(al).—*n.f.* logistics.
logrado, -da, *a.* successful.
lograr, *v.t.* gain, obtain; attain, produce; succeed, manage.—*v.i.* do well; manage (*to*), succeed (*in*).—*v.r.* be successful.
lograr, *v.i.* profiteer.
logrería, *n.f.* usury.
logrero, -ra, *a.* usurious, profiteering.—*n.m.f.* profiteer, usurer.
logro, *n.m.* gain, profit; attainment; usury, interest.
loísta, *a., n.m.f.* said of those who use **lo** instead of **le**.
lombriz, *n.f.* (*pl.* **-ices**) worm, grub.
lomo, *n.m.* back; ridge.—*pl.* ribs.
lona, *n.f.* canvas, sailcloth.
londinense, *a.* London.—*n.m.f.* Londoner.
Londres, *n.m.* London.
longánimo, -ma, *a.* magnanimous.
longaniza, *n.f.* pork sausage.
longevidad, *n.f.* longevity.
longevo, -va, *a.* long-lived, longevous.
longitud, *n.f.* length; longitude.
longitudinal, *a.* longitudinal.
longuísimo, -ma, *a. sup. of* LUENGO.
lonja, *n.f.* slice, strip; slap, step; market, exchange; warehouse; portico; grocer's shop.
lonjista, *n.m.f.* grocer.
lontananza, *n.f.* (*art.*) background; distance.
loor, *n.m.* praise.
lopista, *a.* rel. to Lope de Vega.—*n.m.f.* Lope scholar.
loquear, *v.i.* rave, play the madman.
loquera, *n.f.* madhouse; (*S.A.*) madness.
loquesco, -ca, *a.* half-mad; (*fam.*) screamingly funny.
loranto, *n.m.* Eastern mistletoe.
lord, *n.m.* (*pl.* **lores**) lord, Lord.
Lorena, *n.f.* Lorraine.
Lorenzo, *n.m.* Laurence, Lawrence.
loriga, *n.f.* lorica, cuirass.
loro, -ra, *a.* dark brown.—*n.m.* parrot.
los, *def. article, m.pl.* the.—*pron. acc. pl.* them.—*demonstrative rel.* those.
losa, *n.f.* flagstone, slab.
losange, *n.m.* lozenge.
loseta, *n.f.* small flagstone; trap.
lote, *n.m.* lot, portion.
lotería, *n.f.* lottery.
loto, *n.m.* lotus.
loza, *n.f.* crockery.
lozanear, *v.i., v.r.* be luxuriant; be lusty.
lozanía, *n.f.* luxuriance; elegance; lustiness; pride.
lozano, -na, *a.* luxuriant; lusty; haughty.
lubricación, *n.f.* lubrication.
lubricante, *a., n.m.* lubricant.

lubricar [A], *v.t.* lubricate.
lúbrico, -ca, *a.* lubricious.
Lucano, *n.m.* Lucan.
Lucas, *n.m.* Luke.
lucero, *n.m.* Venus, morning star, evening star; bright star; small window; brilliance. —*pl.* (*poet.*) eyes.
Lucía, *n.f.* Lucy, Lucia.
lucidez, *n.f.* lucidity.
lúcido, -da, *a.* lucid.
lucido, -da, *a.* brilliant; gorgeous.
luciente, *a.* shining.
luciérnaga, *n.f.* (*ent.*) glow-worm.
lucífero, -ra, *a.* (*poet.*) shining, brilliant.
lucimiento, *n.m.* lustre, brilliance; success, applause.
lucio, -cia (1), *a.* bright, lucid.
lucio (2), *n.m.* (*ichth.*) pike.
lución, *n.m.* (*zool.*) slow worm.
lucir [9], *v.t.* illumine; display, sport; aid.— *v.i.* gleam, shine.—*v.r.* dress up; be brilliant (*fig.*).
lucrar, *v.t.* obtain.—*v.r.* make a profit.
lucrativo, -va, *a.* lucrative.
lucro, *n.m.* profit; lucre.
lucroso, -sa, *a.* profitable.
luctuoso, -sa, *a.* gloomy, mournful.
lucubración, *n.f.* lucubration.
lucubrar, *v.t., v.i.* lucubrate.
lucha, *n.f.* fight, struggle; strife; wrestling.
luchador, -ra, *n.m.f.* fighter; wrestler.
luchar, *v.i.* fight, struggle (*por,* for); wrestle; contend.
ludibrio, *n.m.* mockery, derision.
luego, *adv.* presently, later; (*obs.*) immediately; then, next.—*conj.* then; so; **desde —,** naturally; at once; *¡ hasta —!* so long! au revoir! *— que,* after, as soon as.
luengo, -ga, *a.* long.
lugar, *n.m.* place, site; room, space; village; chance, time, occasion; *dar — a,* give rise to; *en — de,* instead of; *— común,* commonplace; lavatory; *no ha —,* (*jur.*) petition not granted; *tener —,* take place; have time or the chance (*de,* to).
lugarcillo, lugarcito, lugarejo, lugarete, lugarillo, *n.m.* hamlet.
lugareño, -ña, *a.* village.—*n.m.f.* villager.
lugarteniente, *n.m.* lieutenant, deputy.
lúgubre, *a.* lugubrious, dismal, gloomy.
Luis, *n.m.* Louis, Lewis; **luis,** *n.m.* louis (*coin*).
lujo, *n.m.* luxury; excess; *de —,* de luxe.
lujoso, -sa, *a.* luxurious.
lujuria, *n.f.* lechery, lust; excess.
lujuriante, *a.* luxuriant.
lujuriar, *v.i.* be lustful.
lujurioso, -sa, *a.* lustful, lecherous.—*n.m.f.* lecher.
Lulio, *n.m.* Lull.
lumbago, *n.m.* lumbago.
lumb(ra)rada, *n.f.* blaze, great fire.
lumbre, *n.f.* fire; light; brilliance; learning; *dar — a,* give a light to; *— del agua,* surface of the water.—*pl.* tinder-box.
lumbrera, *n.f.* light; air- or light-vent; shining light, high example.
luminar, *n.m.* luminary.
luminaria, *n.f.* (*eccl.*) altar light, monstrance lamp.—*pl.* illuminations, lights.
luminescencia, *n.f.* luminescence.
luminescente, *a.* luminescent.
luminosidad, *n.f.* luminosity light.

luminoso, -sa, *a.* luminous.
luna, *n.f.* moon; moonlight; mirror; (*fam.*) whim, mood; *a la — de Valencia,* left out in the cold; *— de miel,* honeymoon.
lunar, *a.* lunar.—*n.m.* mole; spot.
lunático, -ca, *a., n.m.f.* lunatic.
lunes, *n.m.* Monday.
luneta, *n.f.* eyeglass; (*theat.*) orchestra seat.
lunfardo, *n.m.* Argentine gangster; Argentine criminal slang.
lupa, *n.f.* magnifying glass.
lupino, -na, *a.* lupine.—*n.m.* lupine.
lúpulo, *n.m.* (*bot.*) hop, hops.
Lurdes, *n.f.* Lourdes.
lurio, -ria, *a.* (*C.A.*) love-crazed.
lusismo, lusitanismo, *n.m.* Lusitanism.
lusitano, -na, *a., n.m.f.* Lusitanian; Portuguese.
lustrar, *v.t.* polish; lustrate.—*v.i.* roam.
lustre, *n.m.* lustre, gloss, polish.
lustro, *n.m.* lustrum; chandelier.
lustroso, -sa, *a.* glossy, lustrous.
lúteo, -tea, *a.* luteous, miry; vile.
luterano, -na, *a., n.m.f.* Lutheran.
Lutero, *n.m.* Luther.
luto, *n.m.* mourning; bereavement; *de —,* in mourning.—*pl.* mourning clothes.
luz, *n.f.* (*pl.* luces) light; opening, window; *dar a —,* give birth to; publish; *salir a —,* come to light; appear (*book*).—*pl.* culture; *a todas luces,* anyway; everywhere; *entre dos luces,* at dusk or dawn.
luzco [LUCIR].

Ll

Ll, ll, fourteenth letter of the Spanish alphabet.
llaga, *n.f.* ulcer; wound.
llagar [B], *v.t.* wound, hurt.
llama (1), *n.f.* flame, blaze.
llama (2), *n.m.* or *f.* (*zool.*) llama.
llamada, *n.f.* call; ring, knock; signal, sign; peal.
llamado, *n.m.* call.
llamador, -ra, *n.m.f.* caller.—*n.m.* door-knocker; door-bell; messenger.
llamamiento, *n.m.* call; calling, vocation.
llamar, *v.t.* call; call upon, summon; name; attract.—*v.i.* knock, ring; have an appeal.— *v.r.* be named, be called.
llamarada, *n.f.* flare-up, flash; sudden blush.
llamativo, -va, *a.* flashy, showy.
llamear, *v.i.* flame, flash.
llanero, -ra, *n.m.f.* plain-dweller.
llaneza, *n.f.* simplicity, plainness.
llano, -na, *a.* level, smooth, plain, flat; homely, frank; simple, clear.—*n.m.* plain; stair-landing; *de —* or *a la llana,* simply, plainly.
llanta, *n.f.* (metal) tyre; wheel-rim.
llantén, *n.m.* (*bot.*) plantain.
llantera, *n.f.* (*fam.*) blubbering.
llanto, *n.m.* weeping.
llanura, *n.f.* levelness; plain.
llapa, *n.f.* (*S.A.*) extra bit, bonus.

llave, *n.f.* key; spanner, wrench; tap, faucet; (*elec.*) switch; — *inglesa,* monkey wrench.
llavero, -ra, *n.m.f.* turn-key.—*n.m.* key-ring.
llavín, *n.m.* latch key.
llegada, *n.f.* arrival.
llegar [B], *v.t.* move nearer.—*v.i.* arrive (*a,* at), reach; amount (*a,* to).—*v.r.* come or go nearer.
llena, *n.f.* overflow, flood.
llenar, *v.t.* fill; satisfy; cover; fulfil.—*v.r.* fill, get full; get covered (*de,* with).
llenero, -ra, *a.* complete, entire.
lleno, -na, *a.* full.—*n.m.* fill, fullness, plenty; full moon; (*theat.*) full house; **de —,** entirely, fully.
llenura, *n.f.* fullness, plenty.
lleva, llevada, *n.f.* carrying.
llevadero, -ra, *a.* bearable.
llevar, *v.t.* carry, take; lead; carry off, take away; wear, have on; bear, suffer; run, manage.—*v.r.* carry off, take away; get on (*con,* with); get carried away; **lleva un año aquí,** he has been here for a year; **Paco me lleva dos años,** Paco is two years older than I; **nos llevan ocho horas,** they are eight hours ahead of us.
llorar, *v.t.* weep, lament, mourn.—*v.i.* weep, cry; stream.
lloriquear, *v.i.* (*fam.*) whimper.
lloriqueo, *n.m.* (*fam.*) blubbering, whimpering.
lloro, *n.m.* weeping, mourning, crying.
llorón, -rona, *a.* weepy, tearful; weeping (*willow etc.*).—*n.m.f.* weeper, mourner.—*n.m.* plume.
lloroso, -sa, *a.* tearful; mournful.
llovedizo, -za, *a.* leaky; **agua llovediza,** rain-water.
llover [5], *v.t., v.i.* rain; **como llovido,** out of the blue; — **sobre mojado,** never to come alone (*said of misfortunes*); **llueva o no,** rain or shine; **llueve,** it is raining.—*v.r.* leak.
llovido, -da, *n.m.f.* stowaway.
llovizna, *n.f.* drizzle.
lloviznar, *v.i.* drizzle.
llueca, *a., n.f.* broody (*hen*).
lluvia, *n.f.* rain; rain-water; (*fig.*) abundance.
lluvioso, -sa, *a.* rainy, showery, wet.

M

M, m, *n.f.* fifteenth letter of the Spanish alphabet.
maca, *n.f.* blemish.
macabro, -ra, *a.* macabre.
macadam, macadán, *n.m.* macadam.
macarrón, *n.m.* macaroon.—*pl.* macaroni.
macear, *v.t.* hammer.—*v.i.* (*fam.*) be a bore.
maceta, *n.f.* flower-pot; mallet; handle.
macfarlán, macferlán, *n.m.* rain-cape.
macicez, *n.f.* solidity.
macilento, -ta, *a.* lean, wan.
macillo, *n.m.* piano hammer.

macis, *n.f.* (*bot., cul.*) mace.
macizar [C], *v.t.* fill up or in.
macizo, -za, *a.* solid; massive.—*n.m.* massif; mass; bulk; flower-bed.
mácula, *n.f.* blemish; (*fam.*) trick; — **solar,** sun-spot.
machacar [A], *v.t.* crush, pound.—*v.i.* be persistent or a bore.
machado, *n.m.* hatchet.
a machamartillo, *adv. phr.* firmly, solidly.
machar, *v.t.* crush.
machete, *n.m.* machete, chopper.
machihembrar, *v.t.* (*carp.*) tongue and groove; mortise.
machina, *n.f.* derrick; pile-driver.
macho (1), *a. inv.* male; masculine; robust; stupid.—*n.m.* male; buttress; dolt; mule.
macho (2), *n.m.* sledge hammer; anvil.
machucar [A], *v.t.* batter, pound.
machucho, -cha, *a.* mature, wise; elderly.
machuno, -na, *a.* mannish; manly.
madamisela, *n.f.* (*pej.*) young lady.
madeja, *n.f.* hank, skein; — **sin cuenda,** tangle; muddled person.
madera, *n.f.* wood, timber; (*fig.*) stuff, makings.—*n.m.* Madeira (*wine*).
maderable, *a.* timber-yielding.
maderaje, maderamen, *n.m.* timber; wooden framework.
maderero, -ra, *a.* rel. to timber.—*n.m.* timber merchant.
madero, *n.m.* beam, log; dolt; (*poet.*) bark, ship.
madrastra, *n.f.* step-mother.
madre, *n.f.* mother; source, origin; river-bed; lees, mother; main channel; matrix; womb; main-beam; **lengua —,** mother tongue; — **patria,** mother country.
madreperla, *n.f.* pearl oyster; mother-of-pearl.
madreselva, *n.f.* honeysuckle.
madrigal, *n.m.* madrigal.
madriguera, *n.f.* warren; den.
madrileño, -ña, *a., n.m.f.* rel. to or native of Madrid.
madrina, *n.f.* godmother; protectress; — **de boda,** bridesmaid.
madroño, *n.m.* arbutus, strawberry-tree; fruit of same; tassel.
madrugada, *n.f.* the early hours, dawn.
madrugar [B], *v.i.* get up very early; (*fig.*) be well ahead.
madurar, *v.t., v.i., v.r.* ripen, mature, mellow.
madurez, *n.f.* ripeness; maturity.
maduro, -ra, *a.* ripe, mellow; mature.
maestra, *n.f.* mistress; schoolmistress; guide-line.
maestrazgo, *n.m.* (*hist.*) mastership of military order.
maestre, *n.m.* master of military order; (*naut.*) master.
maestrear, *v.t.* take charge of, direct.
maestría, *n.f.* mastery; mastership; stratagem.
maestro, -tra, *a.* master; main, major; trained; **obra maestra,** masterpiece.—*n.m.* master; schoolmaster; maestro.
magia, *n.f.* magic.
mágico, -ca, *a.* magic(al).—*n.m.f.* magician.—*n.f.* magic.
magín, *n.m.* (*fam.*) mind, imagination; ability.

magisterial, *a.* rel. to teaching *or* school-masters.

magisterio, *n.m.* (school-)teaching; school-teachers; teaching profession.

magistrado, *n.m.* magistrate.

magistral, *a.* masterly; magisterial.

magnanimidad, *n.f.* magnanimity.

magnánimo, -ma, *a.* magnanimous.

magnate, *n.m.* magnate.

magnesia, *n.f.* magnesia.

magnesio, *n.m.* magnesium; (*phot.*) flash.

magnético, -ca, *a.* magnetic.

magnetismo, *n.m.* magnetism.

magnetizar [C], *v.t.* magnetize.

magneto, *n.m.* or *f.* magneto.

magnetofónico, -ca, *a.* rel. to tape-recorder; *cinta magnetofónica,* recording tape.

magnetófono, magnetofón (*pl.* **-fones**), *n.m.* tape-recorder.

magnificar [A], *v.t.* magnify.

magníficat, *n.m.* Magníficat.

magnificencia, *n.f.* magnificence.

magnífico, -ca, *a.* magnificent; generous, liberal.

magnitud, *n.f.* magnitude.

magno, -na, *a.* Great; *Alejandro Magno,* Alexander the Great.

mago, -ga, *a., n.m.f.* magian; *los Reyes Magos,* the Three Wise Men. —*n.m.* wizard.

magra, *n.f.* rasher, slice.

magro, -ra, *a.* thin, lean; scant.

maguer, *conj.* (*obs.*) albeit.

magullar, *v.t.* bruise.

Mahoma, *n.m.* Mohammed.

mahometano, -na, *a., n.m.f.* Mohammedan.

mohametismo, *n.m.* Mohammedanism.

maído, *n.m.* mew, miaow.

maitines, *n.m.pl.* (*eccl.*) matins.

maíz, *n.m.* maize, Indian corn.

majada, *n.f.* sheepfold; dung; (*S.A.*) flock.

majadería, *n.f.* pest; silliness.

majadero, -ra, *a.* stupid, boring.—*n.m.f.* fool; bore.—*n.m.* pestle.

majadura, *n.f.* pounding.

majar, *v.t.* pound, crush; (*fam.*) pester.

majestad, *n.f.* majesty.

majestuoso, -sa, *a.* majestic.

majeza, *n.f.* (*fam.*) nattiness, flashiness.

majo, -ja, *a.* bonny, flashy, natty.—*n.m.* beau, young blood.—*n.f.* belle.

majuelo, *n.m.* (*bot.*) white hawthorn; young vine.

mal, *a. contracted form of* MALO, *before n.m.sg.*—*n.m.* evil; harm; wrong; damage; illness; fault; — *de la tierra,* homesickness; — *de mar,* seasickness; — *de ojo,* evil eye.—*adv.* badly, ill, wrongly; wickedly; hardly; *de — en peor,* from bad to worse; *echar a —,* despise; *estar —,* be ill; be on bad terms (*con,* with); *¡ — haya ... !* confound ...! — *que bien,* by hook or by crook.

malabarista, *n.m.f.* juggler.

Malaca, *n.f.* Malaya.

malacate, *n.m.* windlass, hoist.

malacostumbrado, -da, *a.* pampered; having bad habits.

malagueño, -ña, *a., n.m.f.* rel. to *or* native of Malaga.

malamente, *adv.* badly; wrongly.

maladanza, *n.f.* misfortune, ill-chance.

malaria, *n.f.* malaria.

Malasia, *n.f.* Malaysia.

malasiano, -na, *a., n.m.f.* Malaysian.

malaventura, *n.f.* misfortune.

malaventurado, -da, *a.* unfortunate, luck-less.

Malaya, *n.f.* Malaya.

malayo, -ya, *a., n.m.f.* Malayan, Malay.

malbaratar, *v.t.* cut the price of; squander.

malcasado, -da, *a.* ill-matched; unfaithful (*husband, wife*).

malcontento, -ta, *a., n.m.f.* malcontent.

malcriar [L], *v.t.* spoil (*a child*).

maldad, *n.f.* evil, wickedness.

maldecir [17, *fut.* **maldeciré**; *p.p.* **maldito**], *v.t.* curse.—*v.i.* speak ill (*de,* of).

maldiciente, *a.* cursing; slanderous.—*n.m.f.* slanderer.

maldición, *n.f.* malediction, curse.

maldito, -ta, *a.* cursed; wicked; (*fam.*) a single, any (*negative*).

maleante, *a., n.m.f.* miscreant.

malear, *v.t.* corrupt, spoil.

maledicencia, *n.f.* evil talk.

maleficiar, *v.t.* damage, harm; curse.

maleficio, *n.m.* harm; curse, evil spell.

maléfico, -ca, *a.* malicious, evil.

malestar, *n.m.* malaise; uneasiness.

maleta, *n.f.* suitcase.—*n.m.* (*fam.*) bungler.

maletín, *n.m.* satchel; attaché case.

malevolencia, *n.f.* malevolence.

malévolo, -la, *a.* malevolent.

maleza, *n.f.* weeds; scrub; (*S.A.*) pus.

malgastar, *v.t.* squander.

malhablado, -da, *a.* ill-spoken.

malhecho, -cha, *a.* malformed.—*n.m.* misdeed.

malhechor, -ra, *n.m.f.* malefactor.

malhumorado, -da, *a.* ill-humoured.

malicia, *n.f.* evil; malice; slyness.

maliciar, *v.t.* suspect maliciously.—*v.r.* go wrong, err.

malicioso, -sa, *a.* malicious; crafty, sly.

malignar, *v.t.* vitiate, deprave.—*v.r.* spoil; become depraved.

malignidad, *n.f.* malignance, malice.

maligno, -na, *a.* malignant, malign.

malintencionado, -da, *a.* intending evil.

malmandado, -da, *a.* disobedient, wayward.

malmaridada, *n.f.* faithless wife.

malmeter, *v.t.* estrange; waste.

malmirado, -da, *a.* disliked; indiscreet.

malo, -la, *a.* bad; ill; wicked; wrong.—*n.m.* wicked person; the Devil; *por (las) malas o por (las) buenas,* willy-nilly.

malogrado, -da, *a.* lamented, late, ill-fated.

malograr, *v.t.* miss, lose; spoil.—*v.r.* come amiss, fail; come to an untimely end.

malogro, *n.m.* failure; disappointment; untimely end.

maloliente, *a.* foul-smelling.

malparar, *v.t.* hurt, harm, ill-treat.

malparir, *v.i.* miscarry.

malparto, *n.m.* miscarriage.

malquerencia, *n.f.* ill-will, dislike.

malquerer [26], *v.t.* hate, dislike.

malquistar, *v.t.* estrange.

malquisto, -ta, *a.* unpopular, detested.

malsano, -na, *a.* unhealthy.

malsonante, *a.* offensive, sounding objectionable.

malsufrido, -da, *a.* impatient.

malta, *n.f.* malt; coffee substitute.

maltés, -tesa, *a., n.m.f.* Maltese.
maltratar, *v.t.* ill-treat, maltreat.
maltrato, *n.m.* maltreatment.
maltrecho, -cha, *a.* ill-treated, damaged, battered.
maltusiano, -na, *a.* Malthusian.
maluco, -ca, malucho, -cha, *a.* (*fam.*) sickly, poorly.
malva, *n.f.* (*bot.*) mallow; hollyhock; *ser (como) una —,* be kind and gentle.
malvado, -da, *a.* wicked.
malvasía, *n.f.* malmsey (*grape, wine*).
malvavisco, *n.m.* (*bot.*) marsh mallow.
malvender, *v.t.* sell at a loss.
malversación, *n.f.* embezzlement.
malversar, *v.t.* embezzle.
las Malvinas, *n.f.pl.* Falkland Islands.
malla, *n.f.* mesh; chain-mail.
mallete, *n.m.* mallet.
Mallorca, *n.f.* Majorca.
mallorquín, -quina, *a., n.m.f.* Majorcan.
mamá, *n.f.* (*pl.*-**más**) (*fam.*) mummy.
mamar, *v.t.* suck (*mother's milk*); (*fam.*) gulp down; (*fam.*) wangle; (*fam.*) swallow, be fooled by.—*v.r.* (*low*) get sozzled; (*fam.*) wangle; *mamarse el dedo,* be fooled, be taken in.
mamarracho, *n.m.* (*fam.*) daub, mess; wretch.
mameluco, *n.m.* mameluke; (*fam.*) dolt.
mamífero, -ra, *a.* mammalian.—*n.m.* mammal.
mamola, *n.f.* chuck under the chin.
mamotreto, *n.m.* ledger; bundle of papers.
mampara, *n.f.* folding screen.
mamparo, *n.m.* (*naut.*) bulkhead.
mampostería, *n.f.* rubble-work.
mampuesto, *n.m.* rough stone; rubble; parapet; *de —,* spare, set aside.
mamut, *n.m.* (*pl.* -**ts**) (*zool.*) mammoth.
maná, *n.m.* manna.
manada, *n.f.* herd, drove, pack; handful.
manante, *a.* flowing.
manantial, *a.* flowing.—*n.m.* spring, source.
manantío, -tía, *a.* flowing.
manar, *v.t.* run with, pour forth.—*v.i.* pour, flow.
mancar [A], *v.t.* maim.
manceba, *n.f.* concubine.
mancebo, *n.m.* youth; bachelor; lad.
mancilla, *n.f.* stain, blot.
mancillar, *v.t.* blemish, stain.
manco, -ca, *a.* one-handed; one-armed; maimed.
de mancomún, *adv. phr.* by common consent, jointly.
mancomunar, *v.t.* pool, combine.
mancha, *n.f.* stain, blot; patch; *— solar,* sun-spot.
manchar, *v.t.* spot, strain.
manchego, -ga, *a., n.m.f.* rel. to *or* native of La Mancha.
mandadero, -ra, *n.m.f.* messenger.
mandado, *n.m.* order; errand.
mandamiento, *n.m.* (*Bib.*) commandment.
mandar, *v.t.* command; send; bequeath; — *por,* send for.—*v.r.* interconnect (*con,* with); go (*por,* up, through (*stairs, room etc.*)).
mandarín, *n.m.* mandarin.
mandarina, *n.f.* mandarin orange.
mandato, *n.m.* mandate; (*eccl.*) maundy.
mandíbula, *n.f.* mandible, jaw.

mandil, *n.m.* apron.
mando, *n.m.* command, authority; (*mech.*) control.
mandolina, *n.f.* mandolin.
mandria, *a. inv.* cowardly; worthless.
mandril, *n.m.* (*zool.*) mandrill; (*mech.*) chuck.
manducar [A], *v.t., v.i.* (*fam.*) eat, tuck in.
manear, *v.t.* hobble; wield.
manecilla, *n.f.* small hand; watch-hand; clasp; tendril.
manejar, *v.t.* manage; handle; (*S.A.*) drive (*cars*).
manejo, *n.m.* handling; management; stratagem.
manera, *n.f.* manner, way; kind, type; *a — de,* in the way of, like; *de — que,* so that; *sobre —,* exceedingly.
manezuela, *n.f.* small hand; handle.
manga, *n.f.* sleeve; hose, pipe; armed band; whirlwind; *de — ancha,* broad-minded.
manganeso, *n.m.* manganese.
mangle, *n.m.* (*bot.*) mangrove.
mango, *n.m.* handle; (*bot.*) mango (*fruit and tree*).
mangosta, *n.f.* (*zool.*) mongoose.
manguera, *n.f.* (*naut.*) hose; air-vent.
maní, *n.m.* (*pl.* **manises**) (*bot.*) peanut.
manía, *n.f.* mania.
maníaco, -ca [MANIÁTICO].
maniatar, *v.t.* tie the hands of.
maniático, -ca, *a., n.m.f.* maniac.
manicomio, *n.m.* lunatic asylum.
manicorto, -ta, *a.* stingy.
manicuro, -ra, *n.m.f.* manicurist.—*n.f.* manicure.
manido, -da, *a.* tattered; stale.—*n.f.* den, haunt.
manifacero, -ra, *a.* (*fam.*) meddlesome.
manifestación, *n.f.* manifestation; (*jur.*) writ of habeas corpus.
manifestar [1], *v.t.* show, reveal, manifest.
manifiesto, -ta, *a.* clear, obvious, manifest.—*n.m.* manifesto; (*com.*) manifest.
manija, *n.f.* handle, haft; clamp; shackles.
manilargo, -ga, *a.* long-handed; generous.
manilla, *n.f.* small hand; bracelet; manacle.
manillar, *n.m.* handle-bars.
maniobra, *n.f.* operation; (*mil., naut.*) manœuvre; (*rail.*) shunting.
maniobrar, *v.i.* perform; manœuvre; (*rail.*) shunt.
maniota, *n.f.* hobble; manacle.
manipulación, *n.f.* manipulation.
manipular, *v.t.* manipulate.
maniquí, *n.m.* (*pl.* -**íes**) manikin; (*fig.*) puppet.
manirroto, -ta, *a.* lavish, spendthrift.
manivela, *n.f.* (*mech.*) crank; lever.
manjar, *n.m.* morsel, dish.
mano, *n.f.* hand; forefoot, trotter; pestle; coat (*of paint*); elephant's trunk; reproof; *a la —,* to hand; *a —,* at *or* by hand; *dar de manos,* fall flat; *echar — de,* make use of; *echar una —,* lend a hand; *— de gato,* master touch; (*fam.*) face-paint; *— de obra,* labour; *ser —,* lead, be first (*in games*).— *pl.* labour, hands; *entre manos,* on hand; *llegar a las manos,* come to blows.
manojo, *n.m.* bunch.
Manolo, *n.m.* (*fam. form of*) MANUEL; **manolo, -la,** *n.m.f.* flashy young person of Madrid.
manopla, *n.f.* mitten.

manosear, *v.t.* paw, handle.
manotada, *n.f.*, **manotazo,** *n.m.* slap.
manotear, *v.t.* slap, cuff.—*v.i.* gesticulate.
manquear, *v.i.* feign a limp; be maimed.
manquedad, manquera, *n.f.* lack of hand *or* arm; defect.
a mansalva, *adv. phr.* without danger (*de,* of, from).
mansedumbre, *n.f.* meekness, tameness.
mansión, *n.f.* sojourn; abode.
manso, -sa, *a.* gentle; tame.
manta, *n.f.* blanket; cloak.
mantear, *v.t.* toss in a blanket.
manteca, *n.f.* lard; butter.
mantecado, *n.m.* ice-cream; butter biscuit.
mantel, *n.m.* table-cloth; altar cloth.
mantelería, *n.f.* table-linen.
mantellina, *n.f.* mantilla.
mantenencia, *n.f.* maintenance.
mantener [33], *v.t.* maintain.—*v.r.* keep oneself; stay firm.
a manteniente, *adv.phr.* with might and main.
mantenimiento, *n.m.* maintenance, sustenance.
manteo, *n.m.* tossing in a blanket; mantle.
mantequera, *n.f.* butter-dish; churn; butter-girl.
mantequilla, *n.f.* butter.
mantilla, *n.f.* mantilla; horse-blanket.
manto, *n.m.* mantle, cloak.
mantón, *n.m.* shawl; stole.
mantuve [MANTENER].
manual, *a.* manual; handy.—*n.m.* manual.
manubrio, *n.m.* crank; handle.
Manuel, *n.m.* Emmanuel.
manufactura, *n.f.* manufacture; factory.
manufacturar, *v.t.* manufacture.
manufacturero, -ra, *a.* manufacturing.
manumitir, *v.t.* manumit.
manuscrito, -ta, *a., n.m.* manuscript.
manutención, *n.f.* maintenance.
manzana, *n.f.* apple; block of houses; pommel.
manzanar, *n.m.* apple orchard.
manzanilla, *n.f.* camomile; manzanilla sherry; point of chin.
manzano, *n.m.* apple-tree.
maña, *n.f.* skill, knack; wile; trick; bad habit; *darse* —, manage (*para,* to).
mañana, *n.f.* morning.—*n.m.* morrow.—*adv.* tomorrow.
mañear, *v.t., v.i.* wangle.
mañero, -ra, *a.* cunning; easy.
maño, -ña, *a., n.m.f.* (*fam.*) Aragonese.
mañoso, -sa, *a.* clever; cunning.
mapa, *n.m.* map.—*n.f.* (*fam.*) the tops, the cream.
mapamundi, *n.m.* map of the world.
maque, *n.m.* lacquer.
maqueta, *n.f.* (*arch.*) scale model.
maquiavélico, -ca, *a.* Machiavellian.
maquiavelista, *a., n.m.f.* Machiavellian.
Maquiavelo, *n.m.* Machiavelli.
maquillaje, *n.m.* make-up.
maquillar, *v.t., v.r.* make up.
máquina, *n.f.* machine; engine; locomotive; contrivance; invention; vast structure; (*C.A.*) car; **— de escribir,** typewriter; *escrito a* —, typewritten.
maquinación, *n.f.* machination.
máquina-herramienta, *n.f.* machine-tool.
maquinal, *a.* mechanical.

maquinar, *v.t.* machinate.
maquinaria, *n.f.* machinery; mechanics.
maquinista, *n.m.f.* mechanic, machinist; engine-driver.
mar, *n.m.* or *f.* sea; (*fig.*) vast amount; *alta* —, the high seas; *hacerse a la* —, set sail; *hablar de la* —, (*fam.*) rave; *meterse — adentro,* get into deep water; **— alta,** rough sea.
maraña, *n.f.* thicket; tangle; swindle; puzzle.
marañón, *n.m.* (*bot.*) cashew-tree *or* nut.
maravedí, *n.m.* (*pl.* **-ís, -íses** *or* **-íes**) marvedí, old small coin.
maravilla, *n.f.* wonder, marvel; surprise; (*bot.*) marigold; *a* —, wonderfully; *por* —, very seldom; *a las mil maravillas,* superbly.
maravillar, *v.t.* amaze, surprise.—*v.r.* marvel, be astonished (*con, de,* at).
maravilloso, -sa, *a.* wonderful, marvellous; amazing.
marbete, *n.m.* label; edge.
marca, *n.f.* mark; brand; trade mark; (*sport*) record; measure; marker; march, frontier region; standard; size; *de* —, branded; outstanding.
marcar [A], *v.t.* mark; brand; embroider; (*tel.*) dial; designate; score; point out; show; (*naut.*) take bearings.
marcial, *a.* martial.
marcialidad, *n.f.* martialness.
marciano, -na, *a., n.m.f.* Martian.
marco, *n.m.* frame; standard; mark (*coin*).
Marcos, *n.m.* (*Bib.*) Mark.
marcha, *n.f.* march; operation, action; speed; (*mech.*) gear; progress; *en* —, in motion, working.
marchar, *v.i.* march; run, function; progress. —*v.r.* go away.
marchitar, *v.t., v.i.* wither, wilt.
marchitez, *n.f.* witheredness; languor.
marchito, -ta, *a.* wilted, withered; languid.
marea, *n.f.* tide; sea breeze; dew, drizzle.
marear, *v.t.* navigate; (*fam.*) pester.—*v.r.* get sea-sick *or* dizzy; suffer damage at sea; (*fam.*) get a little drunk.
marejada, *n.f.* (*naut.*) swell; (*fig.*) commotion.
maremagno, *n.m.,* **mare mágnum,** *n.m. inv.* (*fam.*) mess, commotion; vast crowd.
mareo, *n.m.* nausea; sea- *or* travel-sickness; dizziness; (*fam.*) bother.
marfil, *n.m.* ivory.
margarina, *n.f.* margarine.
Margarita, *n.f.* Margaret; **margarita,** *n.f.* pearl; (*bot.*) common daisy.
margen, *n.m.* or *f.* (*pl.* **márgenes**) margin; occasion.
marginal, *a.* marginal.
marginar, *v.t.* annotate in the margin; margin.
María, *n.f.* Mary; **maría,** *n.f.* wax taper; *al baño (de)* —, (*cul.*) steamed.
mariano, -na, *a.* Marian.
marica, *n.f.* (*orn.*) magpie; cissy, pansy.
Maricastaña, *n.f.* **en tiempo(s) de** —, in days of yore.
maridaje, *n.m.* conjugal life; (*fig.*) union.
marido, *n.m.* husband.
mariguana, *n.f.* marijuana.
marimacho, *n.m.* (*fam.*) virago, mannish woman.
marimorena, *n.f.* (*fam.*) row, fight.

marina, *n.f.* navy; sea-coast.
marinar, *v.t.* marinate, salt; man (*a ship*).
marinero, -ra, *a.* seaworthy; sea-going, seafaring.—*n.m.* mariner, sailor, seaman.
marinesco, -ca, *a.* nautical, sailorly.
marino, -na, *a.* marine, of the sea.—*n.m.* sailor, seaman.
marioneta, *n.f.* marionette.
mariposa, *n.f.* butterfly, moth; night-light; wing nut.
mariposear, *v.i.* flutter about, be fickle.
mariquita, *n.f.* (*fam.*) sissy; (*ent.*) ladybird.
marisabidilla, *n.f.* blue-stocking.
mariscal, *n.m.* marshal.
marisco, *n.m.* shell-fish.—*pl.* sea-food.
marisma, *n.f.* salt-marsh, fen.
marital, *a.* rel. to a husband; marital.
marítimo, -ma, *a.* maritime.
marjal, *n.m.* fen, boggy moor.
marjoleto, *n.m.* (*bot.*) hawthorn.
marmita, *n.f.* stew-pot.
marmitón, *n.m.* scullion.
mármol, *n.m.* marble.
marmóreo, -rea, *a.* rel. to *or* made of marble.
marmota, *n.f.* (*zool.*) marmot; (*fam.*) sleepy-head.
maroma, *n.f.* esparto rope; (*S.A.*) acrobatics.
marqués, *n.m.* marquis, marquess.
marquesa, *n.f.* marchioness.
marquesina, *n.f.* awning, marquee.
marquetería, *n.f.* marquetry.
marra (1), *n.f.* gap, lacuna.
marra (2), *n.f.* sledge-hammer.
marrajo, -ja, *a.* cunning, sly.—*n.m.* shark.
marrano, -na, *n.m.f.* pig.
marras, *adv.* **de —,** of yore.
marro, *n.m.* quoits; failure; swerve.
marrón, *a.* *inv.,* *n.m.* brown.
marroquí (*pl.* **-íes**), **marroquín, -quina, marrueco, -ca,** *a., n.m.f.* Moroccan.
Marruecos, *n.m.* Morocco.
marrullería, *n.f.* cajolery.
marrullero, -ra, *a.* cajoling.—*n.m.f.* cajoler.
Marsella, *n.f.* Marseilles.
marsopa, *n.f.* (*zool.*) porpoise.
marsupial, *a., n.m.* marsupial.
marta, *n.f.* (*zool.*) marten; **— cebellina,** sable.
martagón, -gona, *n.m.f.* (*fam.*) sly person.
Marte, *n.m.* (*myth., astr.*) Mars.
martes, *n.m.* Tuesday.
martillar, *v.t.* hammer.
marillazo, *n.m.* hammer-blow.
martilleo, *n.m.* hammering.
martillo, *n.m.* hammer; (*fig.*) scourge; auction;.**a macha —,** robustly, roughly.
Martín, *n.m.* Martin; **le viene su San —,** his time (*to pay etc.*) is coming; **martín pescador,** (*orn.*) kingfisher.
martinete, *n.m.* (*orn.*) night-heron; piledriver; piano-hammer.
martingala, *n.f.* martingale.
martinico, *n.m.* (*fam.*) elf, ghost.
mártir, *n.m.* martyr.
martirio, *n.m.* martyrdom.
martirizar [C], *v.t.* martyr.
Maruja, *n.f.* (*fam. form of* MARÍA) Mary.
marullo, *n.m.* (*naut.*) swell.
marxismo, *n.m.* Marxism.
marxista, *a., n.m.f.* Marxist.
marzo, *n.m.* March.
mas, *conj.* but.

más, *adv.* more, most; any more.—*n.m.* (*math.*) plus; more; **a lo —,** at most; **a — de,** besides; **de —,** in addition; in excess; **— bien,** rather; **no . . . —,** no longer; **por — que,** however much; **sin — ni —,** (*fam.*) with no more ado.
masa, *n.f.* dough; mass; mortar; disposition.
masacrar, *v.t.* (*S.A.*) massacre.
masada, *n.f.* farm-house.
masaje, *n.m.* massage.
masajista, *n.m.* masseur.—*n.f.* masseuse.
masar, *v.t.* knead; massage.
mascadura, *n.f.* chewing; fraying.
mascar [A], *v.t.* chew.—*v.r.* fray.
máscara, *n.f.* mask; masquerade.—*n.m.f.* masquerader.
mascarada, *n.f.* masked ball, masquerade.
mascarilla, *n.f.* small mask; death-mask.
mascarón, *n.m.* ugly person; gargoyle; (*naut.*) figurehead.
mascota, *n.f.* mascot.
masculinidad, *n.f.* masculinity.
masculino, -na, *a.* masculine.
mascullar, *v.t.* mutter.
masería, masía, *n.f.* farm-house.
masilla, *n.f.* putty.
masón(1), *n.m.* (free)mason.
masón (2), *n.m.* hen-mash.
masonería, *n.f.* freemasonry.
masónico, -ca, *a.* masonic.
mastelero, *n.m.* top-mast.
masticación, *n.f.* mastication.
masticar [A], *v.t.* masticate, chew.
mástil, *n.m.* mast; stem; upright; quill.
mastín, *n.m.* mastiff.
mastuerzo,.*n.m.* (*bot.*) cress; (*fam.*) mutt, fool.
mata, *n.f.* bush; sprig; coppice; (*bot.*) mastic; tousled hair.
matacandelas, *n.m. inv.* candle-snuffer.
matachín, *n.m.* slaughterman; (*fam.*) bully.
matadero, *n.m.* slaughterhouse; drudgery.
matador, -ra, *a.* killing.—*n.m.* bullfighter; killer.
matafuego, *n.m.* fire extinguisher.
matalascallando, *n.m.f.* sly-boots, cunning person.
matamoros, *n.m. inv.* braggart; bravo, bully.
matamoscas, *n.m. inv.* fly swatter; fly-paper.
matancero, *n.m.* (*S.A.*) slaughterman.
matanza, *n.f.* slaughter; massacre.
mataperros, *n.m. inv.* street-urchin.
matapolvo, *n.m.* drizzle.
matar, *v.t.* kill; put out; slake; gall; **matarse por,** be dying to *or* for.
matasanos, *n.m. inv.* (*fam.*) sawbones, medic.
matasellos, *n.m. inv.* postmark.
matasiete, *n.m. inv.* bravo, bully.
mate, *a.* dull, matt.—*n.m.* (check)mate; (*bot., cul.*) maté; **— ahogado,** stalemate; **dar — (a),** (check)mate.
matemática(s), *n.f.* (*pl.*) mathematics.
matemático, -ca, *a.* mathematical.—*n.m.* mathematician.
Mateo, *n.m.* Matthew.
materia, *n.f.* matter; material; subject-matter; (*med.*) pus; **materias prim(er)as,** raw materials.
material, *a.* material; physical; materialistic. —*n.m.* material; ingredient; (*print.*) copy.
materialidad, *n.f.* materiality; literalness.

materialismo, *n.m.* materialism.
materialista, *a.* materialistic.—*n.m.f.* materialist.
maternal, *a.* maternal, motherly.
maternidad, *n.f.* maternity, motherhood.
materno, -na, *a.* maternal, mother.
matinal, *a.* morning, matutinal.
matiné, *n.m.* matinée.
matiz, *n.m.* (*pl.* **-ices**) shade, hue, nuance.
matizar [C], *v.t.* shade, tint.
matón, *n.m.* (*fam.*) bully, braggart.
matorral, *n.m.* thicket, undergrowth.
matraca, *n.f.* wooden rattle; (*fam.*) banter.
matraquear, *v.i.* make a clatter; jeer.
matrero, -ra, *a.* cunning.—*n.m.* (*S.A.*) tramp, hobo.
matriarca, *n.f.* matriarch.
matriarcado, *n.m.* matriarchy.
matriarcal, *a.* matriarchal.
matricida, *n.m.f.* matricide (*person*).
matricidio, *n.m.* matricide (*act*).
matrícula, *n.f.* register; matriculation; registration; (*auto.*) registration-number.
matricular, *v.t.* register; enroll; matriculate.
matrimonesco, -ca. (*fam.*); **matrimonial,** *a.* matrimonial.
matrimonio, *n.m.* matrimony, marriage; married couple; **cama de —,** double bed.
matritense [MADRILEÑO].
matriz, *n.f.* (*pl.* **-ices**) womb; matrix.
matrona, *n.f.* matron; midwife.
Matusalén, *n.m.* Methuselah.
matute, *n.m.* smuggling.
matutino, -na, matutinal, *a.* morning, matutinal.
maula, *n.f.* junk, rubbish; trickery.—*n.m.f.* (*fam.*) cheat, sharper.
maulero, -ra, *n.m.f.* scrap dealer; trickster.
maullar [P], *v.i.* miaow.
maullido, *n.m.* miaow.
Mauricio, *n.m.* Maurice, Morris.
mausoleo, *n.m.* mausoleum.
máxima, *n.f.* maxim.
máxime, *adv.* principally, especially.
máximo, -ma, *a.* very great, major, chief.—*n.m.* maximum.
maya, *a.,* *n.m.f.* Mayan.—*n.f.* daisy.
mayal, *n.m.* flail.
mayar, *v.i.* miaow.
mayestático, -ca, *a.* majestic, imperial.
mayo, *n.m.* May; maypole.
mayonesa, *n.f.* mayonnaise.
mayor, *a.* greater; larger; elder, older; greatest; largest; eldest, oldest; major, main; senior, adult.—*n.m.* major, chief, head; **por —,** wholesale.—*pl.* elders; ancestors.
mayoral, *n.m.* foreman, overseer; (*obs.*) coachman.
mayorazgo, *n.m.* primogeniture.
mayordomo, *n.m.* majordomo, steward.
mayoría, *n.f.* majority; superiority.
mayoridad, *n.f.* majority (*age*).
mayúscula, *a.f.,* *n.f.* capital (*letter*).
maza, *n.f.* mace, club; pestle; pile-driver.
mazapán, *n.m.* marzipan.
mazmorra, *n.f.* dungeon.
mazo, *n.m.* mallet; bunch; (*fig.*) botherer.
mazorca, *n.f.* ear, cob (*of maize*); spindle.
mazurca, *n.f.* (*mus.*) mazurka.
me, *personal pron.* me, to me.

meandro, *n.m.* meander.
mear, *v.t.,* *v.i.,* *v.r.* (*low*) urinate.
Meca, *n.f.* Mecca; [CECA].
mecánico, -ca, *a.* mechanical; (*fam.*) mean, low.—*n.m.* mechanic; driver.—*n.f.* mechanics; machinery; (*fam.*) chore; (*fam.*) mean ruse.
mecanismo, *n.m.* mechanism.
mecanización, *n.f.* mechanization.
mecanizar [C], *v.t.,* *v.r.* mechanize.
mecanografía, *n.f.* typewriting.
mecanografiar [L], *v.t.,* *v.i.* type.
mecanográfico, -ca, *a.* typewriting.
mecanógrafo, -fa, *n.m.f.* typist.
mecedor, *n.f.* rocking-chair.
Mecenas, *n.m.* Maecenas; **mecenas,** *n.m.* maecenas.
mecer [D], *v.t.* stir; rock.—*v.r.* swing; rock.
mecha, *n.f.* wick; fuse; lock of hair; tinder.
mechera, *n.f.* shoplifter.
mechero, *n.m.* burner; lighter.
medalla, *n.f.* medal, medallion.
medallón, *n.m.* medallion; locket.
media, *n.f.* stocking; (*S.A.*) sock; (*math.*) mean; **a medias,** half.
mediación, *n.f.* mediation.
mediado, -da, *a.* half-full; **a mediados de mayo,** about the middle of May.
mediador, -ra, *a.* mediating.—*n.m.f.* mediator.
medianero, -ra, *a.* dividing, intermediate.—*n.m.* mediator; next-door neighbour.
medianía, *n.f.* middle position, halfway; middlingness, mediocrity; (*fam.*) a nobody.
mediano, -na, *a.* middling; intermediate.
medianoche, *n.f.* midnight.
mediante, *prep.* by means of, through; **Dios —,** God willing.
mediar, *v.t.* half-fill.—*v.i.* be halfway; mediate; intervene; be in the middle; elapse; happen.
mediatizar [C], *v.t.* control, manipulate.
mediato, -ta, *a.* mediate.
medicación, *n.f.* medication.
medicamento, *n.m.* medicament.
medicina, *n.f.* medicine.
medicinal, *a.* medicinal.
medicinar, *v.t.* treat (*a patient*).
médico, -ca, *a.* medical.—*n.m.f.* doctor, physician.—*n.f.* woman doctor; doctor's wife.
medida, *n.f.* measure; moderation; **a — de,** according to; **a — que,** according to, as as.
medieval, *a.* mediaeval.
medievo, *n.m.* Middle Ages.
medio, -dia, *a.* half; middle; average.—*n.m.* half; middle; centre; measure, step; means; medium.—*adv.* half; **de por —,** half; in between; **en — de,** in the midst of; **estar de por —,** mediate; **quitar de en —,** (*fam.*) get rid of.
mediocre, *a.* medium, mediocre.
mediocridad, *n.f.* mediocrity.
mediodía, *n.m.* noon, midday; south.
medioev- [MEDIEV-].
medir [8], *v.t.,* *v.i.* measure.—*v.r.* act with moderation.
meditabundo, -da, *a.* pensive.
meditación, *n.f.* meditation.
meditar, *v.t.,* *v.i.* meditate.
Mediterráneo, *n.m.,* **mediterráneo, -nea,** *a.* Mediterranean.

medrar, *v.i.* thrive, flourish.
medro, *n.m.* thriving.—*pl.* progress.
medroso, -sa, *a.* fearful, afraid.
médula, *n.f.* marrow, medulla, pith.
Mefistófeles, *n.m.* Mephistopheles.
mefistofélico, -ca, *a.* Mephistophelian.
megáfono, *n.m.* megaphone.
megalomanía, *n.f.* megalomania.
megalómano, -na, *a.,* *n.m.f.* megalomaniac.
megatón, *n.m.* megaton.
mego (1), **-ga,** *a.* meek, gentle.
mego (2), *n.m.* (*obs.*) warlock.
mejicano, -na, *a.,* *n.m.f.* Mexican.
Méjico, *n.m.* Mexico.—*n.f.* Mexico City.
mejilla, *n.f.* cheek.
mejillón, *n.m.* (*zool.*) mussel.
mejor, *a.* better; best.—*adv.* better; best; rather; *a lo* —, (*fam.*) perhaps, maybe; with any luck; — *dicho,* rather, better.
mejora, *n.f.* improvement; highest bid.
mejoramiento, *n.m.* amelioration.
mejorar, *v.t.* improve.—*v.i.,* *v.r.* get better, improve.
mejoría, *n.f.* improvement, turn for the better.
melado, -da, *a.* honey-coloured.—*n.m.* honey cake.
melancolía, *n.f.* melancholy, melancholia.
melancólico, -ca, *a.,* *n.m.f.* melancholic; melancholy.
melancolizar [C], *v.t.* make melancholy.—*v.r.* get melancholy.
melaza, *n.f.* molasses.
melena, *n.f.* forelock; long hair; mane (*of lion*).
melenudo, -da, *a.* hairy, with long hair.
melifluo, -flua, *a.* mellifluent, mellifluous.
melindre, *n.m.* (*cul.*) honey fritter, lady-finger.—*pl.* prudery, finickiness, fads.
melindrear, *v.i.* (*fam.*) be finicky.
melindrero, -ra, melindroso, -sa, *a.* finicky, faddy.
melocotón, *n.m.* peach.
melocotonero, *n.m.* peach-tree.
melodía, *n.f.* melody; melodiousness.
melodioso, -sa, *a.* melodious.
melodrama, *n.m.* melodrama.
melodramático, -ca, *a.* melodramatic.
melón, *n.m.* (*bot.*) melon (*plant, fruit*); nitwit, dolt; (*fam.*) pate, bald head.
meloso, -sa, *a.* honeyed, mellow.
mella, *n.f.* notch, gap; *hacer* — *a,* leave a mark on; *hacer* — *en,* harm, damage.
mellar, *v.t.* notch, groove; harm.
mellizo, -za, *a.,* *n.m.f.* twin.
membrana, *n.f.* membrane; (*rad., tel.*) diaphragm.
membrete, *n.m.* memo, note; letter-head.
membrillo, *n.m.* (*bot.*) quince; *carne* or *queso de* —, quince jelly.
membrudo, -da, *a.* hefty, burly.
memo, -ma, *a.* simple.—*n.m.f.* simpleton.
memorable, memorando, -da, *a.* memorable.
memorándum, *n.m.* *inv.* memorandum; letter-head.
memoria, *n.f.* memory; memoir; *de* —, by heart; *hacer* — *de,* bring to mind.
memorial, *n.m.* petition; memorandum book; (*jur.*) brief.
menaje, *n.m.* furnishings; school equipment.
mención, *n.f.* mention.
mencionar, *v.t.* mention.

mendaz, *a.* (*pl.* **-aces**) mendacious.—*n.m.f.* liar.
mendicante, *a.,* *n.m.f.* mendicant.
mendicidad, *n.f.* mendicancy.
mendigar [B], *v.t.* beg.
mendigo, -ga, *n.m.f.* beggar.
mendrugo, *n.m.* crust, scrap of bread.
menear, *v.t.* shake; wag; manage.—*v.r.* shake, wag, waggle; (*fam.*) get a move on; *peor es meneallo,* let sleeping dogs lie.
meneo, *n.m.* shaking, stirring, wagging; (*fam.*) thrashing.
menester, *n.m.* want, need, lack; job, métier; *haber* —, need; *ser* —, be necessary.
menesteroso, -sa, *a.* needy.—*n.m.f.* needy person.
menestra, *n.f.* vegetable stew; dried vegetable.
mengano, -na, *n.m.f.* (*fam.*) so-and-so, who's it (*after FULANO*).
mengua, *n.f.* decline; decrease; want; discredit.
menguado, -da, *a.* cowardly; silly; fatal.
menguante, *a.* declining, waning.—*n.f.* waning; ebb-tide; decline.
menguar, *v.t.,* *v.i.* diminish, decrease; *v.i.* wane; fall.
menina, *n.f.* maid of honour.
menor, *a.* less, lesser; least; smaller; smallest; younger; youngest; minor.—*n.m.f.* minor; *al por* —, retail; *por* —, in detail; retail.
Menorca, *n.f.* Minorca.
menoría, *n.f.* minority (*age*).
menorquín, -quina, *a.,* *n.m.f.* Minorcan.
menos, *adv.* less; least; rather not.—*prep.* less, minus, except, *al* —, or *por lo* —, at least; *a* — *que,* unless; *de* —, less; missing; *echar (de)* —, miss; *no poder* — *de,* not be able to help . . .; *tener a* or *en* —, think badly of; *venir a* —, decay, decline.
menoscabar, *v.t.* lessen; damage; discredit.
menoscabo, *n.m.* detriment; lessening.
menospreciar, *v.t.* underrate; despise.
menosprecio, *n.m.* underrating; scorn.
mensaje, *n.m.* message; errand.
mensajero, -ra, *a.,* *n.m.f.* messenger.
menstruar [M], *v.i.* menstruate.
mensual, *a.* monthly.
mensualidad, *n.f.* monthly payment.
menta, *n.f.* (*bot.*) mint; peppermint.
mental, *a.* mental.
mentalidad, *n.f.* mentality.
mentar [1], *v.t.* mention, name.
mente, *n.f.* mind.
mentecato, -ta, *a.* foolish, silly.—*n.m.f.* fool.
mentido, -da, *a.* lying, false.
mentir [6], *v.t.* lie to, deceive.—*v.i.* lie; clash (*of colours*).
mentira, *n.f.* lie, falsehood; slip of the pen; *parece* —, it's unbelievable.
mentiroso, -sa, *a.* lying; deceitful; full of mistakes.—*n.m.f.* liar.
mentís, *n.m.* insult; lie; *dar el* — *a,* give the lie to.
mentol, *n.m.* menthol.
mentolado, -da, *a.* mentholated.
mentón, *n.m.* chin.
mentor, *n.m.* mentor.
menú, *n.m.* (*pl.* **-ús**) menu.
menudear, *v.t.* do frequently; detail; (*S.A.*) sell retail.—*v.i.* happen frequently; abound; go into detail.

menudencia, *n.f.* minuteness; trifle.—*pl.* offal.
menudeo, *n.m.* frequent repetition; great detail; retail.
menudillos, *n.m. pl.* giblets.
menudo, -da, *a.* tiny; worthless; common, vulgar; petty; (*fam.*) many a.—*adv. a* —, often; *por* —, in detail; at retail.—*n.m.pl.* small change; offal, giblets.
menuzo, *n.m.* fragment.
meñique, *a.* little (*finger*); (*fam.*) tiny.
meollo, *n.m.* (*anat.*) marrow; (*bot.*) pith; brains; gist.
mequetrefe, *n.m.* offensive meddler.
merca, *n.f.* (*fam.*) buy.
mercader, -ra, *n.m.f.* merchant.
mercadería, *n.f.* merchandise.
mercado, *n.m.* market; —**Común,** Common Market.
mercancía, *n.f.* trade; merchandise.—*pl.* goods, merchandise.
mercancías, *n.m. sg.* (*rail.*) freight train.
mercante, *a.* merchant (*naut.*) —*n.m.f.* merchant.
mercantil, *a.* mercantile; mercenary.
mercantilismo, *n.m.* mercantilism; commercialization.
mercar [A], *v.t.* (*obs., dial.*) buy.
merced, *n.f.* favour, grace; mercy, pleasure; *a merced*(*es*), voluntarily, without stipend; *vues*(*tr*)*a* —, (*obs.*) sire, your honour; — *a,* thanks to.
mercedario, -ria, *a., n.m.f.* (*eccl.*) Mercedarian.
mercenario, -ria, *a., n.m.f.* mercenary; Mercedarian.
mercería, *n.f.* haberdashery; (*S.A.*) draper's.
mercurial, *a.* mercurial.
Mercurio, *n.m.* Mercury; **mercurio,** *n.m.* (*chem.*) mercury.
merecedor, -ra, *a.* deserving.
merecer [9], *v.t.* deserve, merit.—*v.i.* be worth. — *la pena,* be worthwhile.
merecido, *n.m.* deserts.
merecimiento, *n.m.* worth, value; merit.
merendar [1], *v.t.* have for lunch. —*v.i.* have lunch *or* a snack.
merendero, *n.m.* open-air snack shop *or* stall.
merengue, *n.m.* meringue.
meretriz, *n.f.* (*pl.* -ices) harlot.
meridiano, -na, *a.* meridian; clear, bright.—*n.m.* meridian.—*n.f.* midday nap; *a la meridiana,* at noon.
meridional, *a.* southern.—*n.m.f.* southerner.
merienda, *n.f.* afternoon snack; light lunch; *juntar meriendas,* (*fam.*) join forces.
merino, -na, *a., n.m.f.* merino (*sheep*).—*n.m.* (*hist.*) royal magistrate.
mérito, *n.m.* merit; worth; *hacer — de,* mention.
meritorio, -ria, *a.* meritorious.—*n.m.f.* volunteer; emeritus.
merluza, *n.f.* (*ichth.*) hake; *coger una* —, (*fam.*) get blotto, drunk.
merma, *n.f.* decrease, leakage, waste.
mermar, *v.t.* cut, decrease.—*v.i., v.r.* dwindle.
mermelada, *n.f.* marmalade; jam (*esp. apricot*).
mero (1), **-ra,** *a.* mere.
mero (2), *n.m.* (*ichth.*) Red Sea bass.
merodear, *v.i.* maraud.

merodeo, *n.m.* marauding.
mes, *n.m.* month; monthly pay.
mesa, *n.f.* table; counter; desk; facet; plateau.
mesar, *v.t.* pluck (*hair, beard*).
meseta, *n.f.* plateau, table-land, meseta.
mesiánico, -ca, *a.* Messianic.
Mesías, *n.m.* Messiah.
mesilla, *n.f.* small table; (*fam.*) dressing-down.
mesmerismo, *n.m.* mesmerism.
mesnada, *n.f.* retinue; band.
mesón, *n.m.* inn.
mesonero, -ra, *a.* rel. to inns.—*n.m.f.* innkeeper.
mesta, *n.f.* (*hist.*) stockmen's guild.
mestizo, -za, *a., n.m.f.* half-breed; mongrel; mestizo.
mesura, *n.f.* gravity, restraint, civility.
mesurado, -da, *a.* moderate; circumspect; grave; restrained.
mesurar, *v.t.* moderate.—*v.r.* act with restraint.
meta, *n.f.* goal.
metabolismo, *n.m.* metabolism.
metafísico, -ca, *a.* metaphysical.—*n.m.f.* metaphysician.—*n.f.* metaphysics.
metáfora, *n.f.* metaphor.
metafórico, -ca, *a.* metaphorical.
metal, *n.m.* metal; brass, bronze; mettle, quality.
metálico, -ca, *a.* metallic.—*n.m.* metalworker; hard cash.—*n.f.* metallurgy.
metalífero, -ra, *a.* metalliferous.
metalurgia, *n.f.* metallurgy.
metalúrgico, -ca, *a.* metallurgic(al).—*n.m.* metallurgist.
metamorfosi(**s**)**,** *n.f.* (*pl.* -fosis) metamorphosis.
metano, *n.m.* methane.
metedor (1), **-ra,** *n.m.f.* smuggler.
metedor (2), *n.m.* napkin; (*U.S.*) diaper.
meteórico, -ca, *a.* meteoric.
meteorito, *n.m.* meteorite.
meteoro, metéoro, *n.m.* meteor, metereological phenomenon.
meteorología, *n.f.* meteorology.
meteorológico, -ca, *a.* meterological.
meteorologista, *n.m.f.* meteorologist.
meter, *v.t.* put; smuggle; cause; make (*noise etc.*); start (*rumours*).—*v.r.* project; butt in; get (*en,* into); meddle; *meterse a,* pass oneself off as; start to; *meterse con,* pick a quarrel with.
metesillas, *n.m. inv.* stage-hand.
meticuloso, -sa, *a.* timid, shy; meticulous.
metido, -da, *a.* rich, full, heavy; tight; involved; intimate.—*n.m.* punch, blow; (*sewing*) seam; napkin.
metilo, *n.m.* methyl.
metimiento, *n.m.* insertion; influence, sway.
metódico, -ca, *a.* methodic(al).
metodismo, *n.m.* Methodism.
metodista, *a., n.m.f.* Methodist.
método, *n.m.* method.
metomentodo, *n.m.f.* (*fam.*) busybody.
metonimia, *n.f.* metonymy.
metraje, *n.m.* length (*of cinema films*).
metralla, *n.f.* grape-shot; shrapnel.
métrico, -ca, *a.* metric(al).—*n.f.* prosody.
metro (1), *n.m.* metre.

metro (2), *n.m.* (*rail.*) Metro, (*U.S.*) subway, (*rail.*) Underground, (*coll.*) tube.
metrópoli, *n.f.* metropolis.
metropolitano, -na, *a.* metropolitan.—*n.m.* metropolitan; (*rail.*) Underground, (*U.S.*) subway.
México, *n.m.* (*S. & C.A.*) Mexico (*Sp.* MÉJICO).
mezcla, *n.f.* mixture.
mezclar, *v.t.*, *v.r.* mix, blend, mingle; *v.r.* meddle.
mezcolanza, *n.f.* jumble, mix-up.
mezquindad, *n.f.* wretchedness; smallness.
mezquino, -na, *a.* poor; mean; tiny.
mezquita, *n.f.* mosque.
mi (1), *n.m.* (*mus.*) (key of) E.
mi (2), *a. poss.* my.
mí, *pron.* (*used after preps.*) me, myself.
miar [L], *v.t.*, *v.i.* miaow.
miasma, *n.m.* miasma.
miau, *n.m.* miaow.
microanálisis, *n.m.* microanalysis.
microbio, *n.m.* microbe.
microcosmo, *n.m.* microcosm.
microfilm, *n.m.* microfilm.
micrófono, *n.m.* microphone.
microgramo, *n.m.* microgram.
micrómetro, *n.m.* micrometer.
microscópico, -ca, *a.* microscopic.
microscopio, *n.m.* microscope.
micho, -cha, *n.m.f.* puss, pussy.
miedo, *n.m.* fear; *dar — a,* frighten; *tener —,* be afraid (*de,* of).
miedoso, -sa, *a.* (*fam.*) windy, scared, afraid.
miel, *n.f.* honey; molasses.
miembro, *n.m.* member; limb.
mientes, *n.f.pl.* (*obs.*) mind; *caer en (las) —,* come to mind; *parar* or *poner — en,* reflect on, consider.
mientras, *adv.* while.—*conj.* (*also — que* or *— tanto*); while, whilst; whereas; *— más ...más,* the more ... the more; *— tanto,* meanwhile.
miércoles, *n.m.* Wednesday; *— corvillo* or *de ceniza,* Ash Wednesday.
mierda, *n.f.* (*low*) dung; excrement.
mies, *n.f.* grain; harvest.
miga, *n.f.* crumb; (*fig.*) substance; bit, fragment; *hacer buenas (malas) migas con,* get on well (badly) with.
migaja, *n.f.* crumb, scrap, bit; smattering.
migar [B], *v.t.* crumble, crumb; add crumbs to.
migración, *n.f.* migration.
migraña, *n.f.* migraine, megrim.
migratorio, -ria, *a.* migratory.
Miguel, *n.m.* Michael.
mijo, *n.m.* millet; (*dial.*) maize, (*U.S.*) corn.
mil, *a.*, *n.m.* a thousand; *hasta las — y monas,* (*fam.*) until the cows come home.
milagrero, -ra, *n.m.f.* miracle-monger, superstitious person.
milagro, *n.m.* miracle.
milagroso, -sa, *a.* miraculous.
milano (1), *n.m.* (*orn.*) kite.
milano (2), *n.m.* thistledown.
milenario, -ria, *a.* millennial.—*n.m.* millennium.
milenio, *n.m.* millennium.
milésimo, -ma, *a.*, *n.m.* thousandth.
mili, *n.f.* (*fam.*) national service, conscription.
milicia, *n.f.* militia; soldiery; warfare.

miliciano, *n.m.* militiaman.
miligramo, *n.m.* milligram.
milímetro, *n.m.* millimetre.
militante, *a.* militant.
militar, *a.* military.—*n.m.* soldier, military man.—*v.i.* serve under arms; militate.
militarismo, *n.m.* militarism.
militarista, *a.*, *n.m.f.* militarist.
militarizar [C], *v.t.* militarize.
milocha, *n.f.* kite (*toy*).
milor(d), *n.m.* milord; (*fam.*) lord. (*pl.*-**lores**)
milla, *n.f.* mile.
millar, *n.m.* thousand; *a millares,* in thousands.
millo, *n.m.* millet; (*S.A.*) maize, (*U.S.*) corn.
millón, *n.m.* million.
millonario, -ria, *a.*, *n.m.f.* millionaire.
millonésimo, -ma, *a.*, *n.m.* millionth.
mimar, *v.t.* fondle; pamper, spoil.
mimbre, *n.m.* or *f.* wicker, osier.
mimbrear, *v.i.*, *v.r.* sway, bend.
mimbreño, -ña, *a.* willowy.
mimbrera, *n.f.*, **mimbrón,** *n.m.* (*bot.*) osier.
mimeografiar [L], *v.t.* mimeograph.
mímico, -ca, *a.* mimic; rel. to mimes.—*n.f.* mimicry; sign language.
mimo, *n.m.* mime; pampering; caress.
mimosa, *n.f.* (*bot.*) mimosa.
mimoso, -sa, *a.* pampered; finicky.
mina, *n.f.* (*min.*, *mil.*) mine; *volar la —,* let the cat out of the bag.
minador, -ra, *a.* mining.—*n.m.* miner; minelayer.
minar, *v.t.* mine; undermine; strive for.
minarete, *n.m.* minaret.
mineraje, *n.m.* mining.
mineral, *a.* mineral.—*n.m.* mineral; ore; source.
minería, *n.f.* mining; miners.
minero, -ra, *a.* rel. to mines.—*n.m.* miner; (*fig.*) source, origin.
Minerva, *n.f.* Minerva; **minerva,** *n.f. de su propia minerva,* out of his own head.
miniar, *v.t.* illuminate, paint in miniature.
miniatura, *n.f.* miniature.
miniaturista, *n.m.* miniaturist.
mínimo, -ma, *a.* least; minimal; minimum; tiny.—*n.m.* minimum.
minimum, *n.m.* minimum.
ministerial, *a.* ministerial.
ministerio, *n.m.* ministry.
ministrar, *v.t.* minister to; administer; supply.
ministro, *n.m.* minister; bailiff; *— de la hacienda,* Chancellor of the Exchequer; *— sin cartera,* minister without portfolio; *primer —,* prime minister.
¡mino! *interj.* puss!
minorar, *v.t.* diminish.
minoría, *n.f.* minority.
minoridad, *n.f.* minority (*age*).
minoritario, -ria, *a.* rel. to a minority.
minucia, *n.f.* mite.—*pl.* minutiae.
minucioso, -sa, *a.* meticulous; detailed.
minué, minuete, *n.m.* minuet.
minúsculo, -la, *a.* tiny; small (*letter*).—*n.f.* small letter.
minuta, *n.f.* draft; list; memorandum; menu.
minutar, *v.t.* make a first draft of.
minutero, *n.m.* minute-hand (*of clock*).
minuto, -ta, *a.*, *n.m.* minute.

147

miñoneta, *n.f.* (*bot.*) mignonette.
mío, mía, *a., pron. m./f.* mine; **de —,** of my own accord.
miope, *a.* myopic.—*n.m.f.* myope.
miopía, *n.f.* myopia, short-sightedness.
mira, *n.f.* sight (*of gun*); target; aim, object; **a la —,** on the look-out.
mirada, *n.f.* look, glance.
miradero, *n.m.* look-out; cynosure.
mirado, -da, *a.* circumspect, cautious; viewed.
mirador, -ra, *n.m.f.* spectator, looker-on.—*n.m.* balcony; watch-tower; bay window.
miramiento, *n.m.* look; care; regard.—*pl.* fussiness.
mirar, *v.t.* look at, watch; look to; — *por,* look after; — *por encima,* glance at. — *v.r.* take care; take an example (*en,* from).
miríada, *n.f.* myriad.
mirilla, *n.f.* peep-hole.
miriñaque, *n.m.* bauble, trinket; crinoline.
mirlar, *v.r.* (*fam.*) put on airs.
mirlo, *n.m.* (*orn.*) blackbird; (*fam.*) airs, affectedness.
mirón, -rona, *a.* watching; nosy, prying.—*n.m.f.* onlooker; busybody.
mirra, *n.f.* myrrh.
mirto, *n.m.* (*bot.*) myrtle.
¡mis! *interj.* puss!
misa, *n.f.* (*eccl.*) Mass.
misacantano, *n.m.* (*eccl.*) priest, celebrant.
misal, *n.m.* missal.
misantrópico, -ca, *a.* misanthropic.
misántropo, *n.m.* misanthrope, misanthropist.
misar, *v.i.* (*fam.*) say *or* hear Mass.
misceláneo, -nea, *a.* miscellaneous.—*n.f.* miscellany.
miserable, *a.* wretched, miserable, niggardly.—*n.m.f.* wretch.
miserando, -da, *a.* pitiable.
miseria, *n.f.* misery, wretchedness, poverty; stinginess; (*fam.*) trifle, bit.
misericordia, *n.f.* compassion; mercy.
misericordioso, -sa, *a.* compassionate, merciful.
mísero, -ra, *a.* (*sup.* **misérrimo, -ma**) miserable.
misión, *n.m.* mission; sending.
misionar, *v.t.* to preach, to spread.
misionario, *n.m.* envoy; missionary.
misionero, *a., n.m.f.* (*eccl.*) missionary.
Misisipí, *n.m.* Mississippi.
misivo, -va, *a., n.f.* missive.
mismamente, *adv.* (*fam.*) exactly; likewise.
mismo, -ma, *a.* same; own; self.—*n.m.* same; self.—*adv.* right; **aquí —,** right here; **así —,** likewise; **da lo —,** it's all the same; **lo —,** the same, the same thing; **por lo —,** for that same reason; **ella misma,** herself, she herself.
misógino, *n.m.* misogynist.
mistar, *v.i.* to mumble.
misterio, *n.m.* mystery.
misterioso, -sa, *a.* mysterious.
misticismo, *n.m.* mysticism.
místico, -ca, *a.* mystic(al).—*n.m.f.* mystic.—*n.f.* mysticism.
mistificar [A], *v.t.* hoax, deceive; mystify.
mistura [MIXTURA].
Misurí, *n.m.* Missouri.

mitad, *n.f.* half; middle; **cara —,** (*fam.*) better half, wife.
mítico, -ca, *a.* mythical.
mitigación, *n.f.* mitigation.
mitigar [B], *v.t.* mitigate.
mitin, *n.m.* (*pl.* **mítines**) meeting.
mito, *n.m.* myth.
mitología, *n.f.* mythology.
mitológico, -ca, *a.* mythological.
mitón, *n.m.* mitten.
mitra, *n.f.* mitre.
mixtif- [MISTIF-].
mixto, -ta, *a.* mixed.—*n.m.* compound; match; explosive mixture.
mixtura, *n.f.* mixture.
mixturar, *v.t.* mix.
¡miz! *interj.* puss!
mnemónico, -ca, *a.* mnemonic.—*n.f.* mnemonics.
mobiliario, moblaje, *n.m.* furnishings.
moblar [4], *v.t.* furnish.
mocasín, *n.m.,* **mocasina,** *n.f.* mocassin.
mocear, *v.i.* be a wild youth.
mocedad, *n.f.* youth; wild oats; frolic.
mocetón, *n.m.* strapping youth.
mocetona, *n.f.* buxom lass.
moción, *n.f.* motion; leaning, bent.
moco, *n.m.* mucus; drippings; slag; **a — de candil,** by candlelight.—*pl.* (*fam.*) nose.
mocoso, -sa, *a.* snivelly; rude; cheeky; mean.—*n.m.f.* brat.
mochila, *n.f.* knapsack.
mocho, -cha, *a.* lopped, shorn.—*n.m.* butt-end.
mochuelo, *n.m.* (*orn.*) little owl; (*fam.*) the rough end.
moda, *n.f.* fashion; mode; **a la —** or **de —** in fashion.
modal, *a.* modal.—*n.m.pl.* manners.
modalidad, *n.f.* way, manner, modality.
modelar, *v.t.* model.—*v.r.* model oneself (*sobre,* on).
modelo, *n.m.* model; pattern.—*n.m.f.* model, mannequin.
moderación, *n.f.* moderation.
moderado, -da, *a., n.m.f.* moderate.
moderador, -ra, *a.* moderating.—*n.m.f.* moderator.
moderantismo, *n.m.* moderation; (*pol.*) moderates.
moderar, *v.t.* moderate.
modernidad, *n.f.* modernity.
modernismo, *n.m.* modernism.
modernista, *a.* modernist(ic).—*n.m.f.* modernist.
modernización, *n.f.* modernization.
modernizar [C], *v.t.* modernize.
moderno, -na, *a., n.m.f.* modern.
modestia, *n.f.* decency, modesty.
modesto, -ta, *a.* decent, modest.
módico, -ca, *a.* moderate.
modificación, *n.f.* modification.
modificar [A], *v.t.* modify.
modismo, *n.m.* idiom.
modistilla, *n.f.* seamstress.
modisto, -ta, *n.m.f.* ladies' tailor.
modo, *n.m.* mode, manner, way; (*gram.*) mood; **de — que,** so that; **sobre —,** extremely; **de todos modos,** anyhow, anyway.

montañoso

modorro, -rra, a. drowsy; stupid.—n.f. drowsiness.
modoso, -sa, a. well-behaved.
modulación, n.f. modulation.
modular, v.t. modulate.
mofa, n.f. mockery.
mofar, v.i., v.r. jeer (de, at).
mogol, -la, a., n.m.f. Mongol.
Mogolia, n.f. Mongolia.
mogollón, n.m. intrusion.
mogote, n.m. hummock, knoll.
mohatra, n.f. fraudulent sale; swindle.
mohatrero, -ra, n.m.f. confidence-trickster.
mohiento, -ta, a. musty, mouldy.
mohin, n.m. grimace.
mohino, -na, a. gloomy; peevish.
moho, n.m. (bot.) moss; mould; rust.
mohoso, -sa, a. mossy; rusty; mouldy.
Moisés, n.m. Moses.
mojama, n.f. salted tunny.
mojar, v.t. wet, soak.—v.r. get wet.
moje, n.m. gravy.
mojiganga, n.f. mummery; (fam.) hypocrisy.
mojigato, -ta, a. sanctimonious, prudish.—n.m.f. prude.
mojón, n.m. boundary stone; heap; milestone.
moldar, v.t. mould, shape.
molde, n.m. mould, matrix; form; good example; de —, just right.
moldear, v.t. cast, mould.
moldura, n.f. moulding, beading.
mole, a. soft.—n.f. mass, bulk.
molécula, n.f. molecule.
molecular, a. molecular.
moler [5], v.t. grind, mill; weary.
molestar, v.t. bother, disturb; annoy.—v.r. be vexed; bother (con, with).
molestia, n.f. bother; annoyance.
molesto, -ta, a. annoying; annoyed.
molicie, n.f. softness flabbiness.
molificar [A], v.t. soften, mollify.
molinero, -ra, n.m.f. miller.
molinete, n.m. small mill; air-vent; turnstile; windlass.
molinillo, n.m. hand-mill (for coffee, pepper etc.).
molino, n.m. mill; (fig.) power-house (person).
molusco, n.m. (zool.) mollusc.
mollear, v.i. give, be soft.
mollera, n.f. crown of head; (fig.) brains.
momentáneo, -nea, a. momentary.
momento, n.m. moment; momentum; importance; al —, at once; de —, suddenly.
momificar [A], v.t., v.r. mummify.
momio, -mia, a. meagre, lean.—n.m. (fam.) bargain, gift.—n.f. mummy.
momo, n.m. grimace, pulled face.
mona [MONO].
monacal, a. monastic, monkish.
monacato, n.m. monkhood, monasticism.
monada, n.f. wry face; fawning; (fam.) pet, dear, pretty thing.
monaguillo, n.m. altar-boy, acolyte.
monarca, n.m. monarch.
monarquía, n.f. monarchy.
monárquico, -ca, a. monarchic(al).
monarquismo, n.m. monarchism.
monarquista, a., n.m.f. monarchist.
monasterio, n.m. monastery.
monasticismo, n.m. monasticism.
monástico, -ca, a. monastic.
mondadientes, n.m. inv. tooth-pick

mondadura, n.f. cleaning.—pl. trimmings.
mondar, v.t. clean; trim; peel; (fam.) fleece.
mondo, -da, a. clean, pure; — y lirondo, (fam.) pure; ser la monda, be ridiculously funny.
monear, v.i. act the goat.
moneda, n.f. coin; money; casa de la —, mint.
monedero, n.m. coiner, minter; money-bag, purse.
monería, n.f. wry face; charming antics; bauble.
monetario, -ria, a. monetary.
mongol- [MOGOL-].
monigote, n.m. lay brother; (fam.) booby.
monipodio, n.m. cabal, crooked plot.
monis, n.m. trinket.—pl. (fam.) cash.
monismo, n.m. monism.
monista, a., n.m.f. monist.
monitor, n.m. monitor.
monja, n.f. nun.
monje, n.m. monk.
monjil, a. monkish, nunnish.—n.m. nun's habit.
mono, -na, a. pretty, nice, cute.—n.m. monkey, ape; mimic, copycat; overalls; nitwit.—n.f. female monkey; Barbary ape; mimic; (fam.) coger una mona, get tipsy.
monocarril, n.m. monorail.
monocromo, -ma, a., n.m. monochrome.
monóculo, -la, a. monocular.—n.m. monacle.
monogamia, n.f. monogamy.
monógamo, -ma, a. monogamous.—n.m.f. monogamist.
monografía, n.f. monograph.
monograma, n.m. monogram.
monólogo, n.m. monologue.
monomanía, n.f. monomania.
monomaníaco, -ca, monómano, -na, a. n.m.f. monomaniac.
monoplano, n.m. (aer.) monoplane.
monopolio, n.m. monopoly.
monopolista, n.m.f. monopolist, monopolizer.
monopolizar [C], v.t. monopolize.
monorriel, n.m. monorail.
monosílabo, -ba, a. monosyllabic.—n.m. monosyllable.
monoteísmo, n.m. monotheism.
monoteísta, n.m.f. monotheist.
monotonía, n.f. monotony.
monótono, -na, a. monotonous.
monseñor, n.m. monseigneur; monsignor.
monserga, n.f. (fam.) gibberish.
monstruo, n.m. monster; prodigy.
monstruoso, -sa, a. monstrous.
monta, n.f. sum; mounting; account, importance.
montadura, n.f. mounting; harness.
montaje, n.m. mounting; installing; setting; assembly.
montantada, n.f. boast; crowd.
montante, n.m. upright, post; amount.
montaña, n.f. mountain; (S.A.) woodland, forest.
montañ(er)ismo, n.m. mountaineering.
montañero, -ra, n.m.f. mountaineer.
montañés, -ñesa, a. highland mountain.—n.m.f. highlander.
montañoso, -sa, a. mountainous.

149

montar, *v.t.* mount; ride; set up, install; amount to.—*v.i.* ride; matter.

montaraz, *a.* (*pl.* -aces) wild, untamed.—*n.m.* forester.

monte, *n.m.* hill, mountain; woodlands, woods; brush, scrub; (*fig.*) snag, obstacle; — *de piedad,* pawnshop; — *pío,* fund for widows *etc.*

montera, *n.f.* cap (*esp. bull-fighter's*).

montería, *n.f.* hunting, the chase.

montero, *n.m.* hunter, huntsman.

montés (*poet.*, *f.* **-tesa**), **montesino, -na,** *a.* wild, feral.

montón, *n.m.* heap, pile; crowd, mass; (*fam.*) lots; *del* —, (*fam.*) ordinary; *a montones,* (*fam.*) by the hundred.

montura, *n.f.* mount; mounting.

monumental, *a.* monumental.

monumento, *n.m.* monument; (*eccl.*) altar of repose.

monzón, *n.m. or f.* monsoon.

moña, *n.f.* doll; hair ribbon.

moño, *n.m.* chignon, top-knot; tuft; airs and graces; whim.

moñudo, -da, *a.* crested, tufted.

moque(te)ar, *v.i.* snivel.

mora (1), *n.f.* delay.

mora (2), *n.f.* (*bot.*) blackberry; mulberry.

mora (3) [MORO].

morada, *n.f.* abode, dwelling; sojourn.

morado, -da, *a.* purple.

moral, *a.* moral.—*n.m.* (*bot.*) mulberry bush. —*n.f.* morals; morale.

moraleja, *n.f.* moral (*of story*).

moralidad, *n.f.* morality; [MORALEJA].

moralista, *n.m.f.* moralist.

moralizar [C], *v.t.*, *v.i.* moralize.

morar, *v.i.* dwell.

mórbido, -da, *a.* morbid; (*art.*) soft, gentle.

morbo, *n.m.* disease.

morboso, -sa, *a.* morbid, diseased.

morcilla, *n.f.* black sausage *or* pudding; (*fam.*) crack, gag; (*theat.*) actor's ad-libbing.

mordacidad, *n.f.* mordacity.

mordaz, *a.* (*pl.* -aces) mordant, mordacious.

mordaza, *n.f.* gag; grab, check.

mordedura, *n.f.* bite.

morder [5], *v.t.* bite; erode; backbite.

mordimiento, *n.m.* bite, biting.

mordiscar [A], *v.t.* nibble.

mordisco, *n.m.* nibble, bite.

moreno, -na, *a.* brown; dark-skinned; suntanned; (*S.A.*) mulatto.—*n.m.f.* dark-skinned person.—*n.f.* brunette.

morería, *n.f.* Moorish quarter; Moors.

Morfeo, *n.m.* (*myth.*) Morpheus.

morfina, *n.f.* morphine.

morfinómano, -na, *n.m.f.* drug addict.

morfología, *n.f.* morphology.

morfológico, -ca, *a.* morphological.

moribundo, -da, *a.*, *n.m.f.* moribund.

morigerar, *v.t.* moderate.

morir [7, *p.p.* **muerto**], *v.t.* (*fam.*) kill.—*v.i.* die.—*v.r.* die; be dying.

morisco, -ca, *a.* Moorish.—*n.m.f.* Morisco; converted Moor.

morisma, *n.f.* Moordom, Mohammedanism.

morlaco, -ca, *a.* playing possum, feigning ignorance.—*n.m.* (*taur.*, *fam.*) bull.

mormón, -mona, *n.m.f.* Mormon.

mormonismo, *n.m.* Mormonism.

moro, -ra (3), *a.* Moorish; Muslim; unwatered

(*wine*).—*n.m.* Moor; Muslim; — *de paz,* peaceful person; *moros en la costa,* fly in the ointment, snag.—*n.f.* Mooress.

morón, *n.m.* mound.

morosidad, *n.f.* tardiness, slowness.

moroso, -sa, *a.* tardy, slow.

morral, *n.m.* nose-bag; kit-bag; game-bag.

morriña, *n.f.* (*vet.*) murrain; (*fam.*) blues, nostalgia.

morriñoso, -sa, *a.* rachitic; (*fam.*) blue, nostalgic.

morro, *n.m.* snout, thick lips; knob; knoll; pebble.

morrocotudo, -da, *a.* (*fam.*) thorny, tricky; whopping, massive.

morsa, *n.f.* (*zool.*) walrus.

mortadela, *n.f.* Bologna sausage.

mortaja, *n.f.* shroud; (*carp.*) mortise.

mortal, *a.* mortal; deadly; dying; certain; definite.—*n.m.f.* mortal.

mortalidad, *n.f.* mortality.

mortandad, *n.f.* mortality; massacre, slaughter.

mortecino, -na, *a.* dead; dying; weak.

mortero, *n.m.* (*cul.*, *mil.*, *arch.*) mortar.

mortífero, -ra, *a.* lethal, deadly.

mortificación, *n.f.* mortification.

mortificar [A], *v.t.* mortify.

mortuorio, -ria, *a.*, *n.m.* funeral.

moruno, -na, *a.* Moorish.

mosaico, -ca, *a.* Mosaic; mosaic.—*n.m.* mosaic.

mosca, *n.f.* fly; (*fam.*) pest, bother; (*fam.*) cash.—*pl.* sparks.

moscardón, *n.m.* horse-fly; hornet; bumble-bee; (*fam.*) pesterer.

moscatel, *n.m.* muscatel; (*fam.*) bore.

mosco, *n.m.* mosquito.

moscón, *n.m.* big fly; (*fam.*) sly person; (*bot.*) maple.

moscovita, *a.*, *n.m.f.* Muscovite.

Moscú, *n.f.* Moscow.

mosquear, *v.t.* swat (*flies*); retort; whip.—*v.r.* shake off impediments; take offence.

mosquero, *n.m.* fly-swatter; fly-paper.

mosquetazo, *n.m.* musket shot *or* wound.

mosquete, *n.m.* musket.

mosquetero, *n.m.* musketeer.

mosquitero, -ra, *n.m. or f.* mosquito-net.

mosquito, *n.m.* mosquito, gnat; (*fam.*) boozer.

mostacero, -ra, *n.m.f.* mustard-pot.

mostacho, *n.m.* moustache; (*fam.*) spot on one's face.

mostaza, *n.f.* mustard.

mosto, *n.m.* must, fresh juice.

mostrado, -da, *a.* accustomed.

mostrador, -ra, *a.* showing, pointing.—*n.m.* counter (*of shop*); clock-face.

mostrar [4], *v.t.* show.—*v.r.* show oneself; appear.

mostrenco, -ca, *a.* stray, homeless; (*fam.*) thick, stupid; (*fam.*) bulky, fat.—*n.m.f.* dolt; stray.

mota, *n.f.* speck, mote; knoll.

mote, *n.m.* nickname; riddle; motto, device.

motear, *v.t.* speckle.

motejar, *v.t.* call names, ridicule (*de,* for, as).

motete, *n.m.* (*mus.*) motet, anthem.

motilar, *v.t.* crop (*hair*).

motín, *n.m.* mutiny, insurrection.

motivar, *v.t.* substantiate; motivate.

motivo, -va, *a., n.m.* motive; **con — de,** on the occasion of; because of; **de su —,** of his own accord.
moto, *n.f.* (*fam.*) motor-bike.
moto-, *prefix.* motor-.
motocicleta, *n.f.* motorcycle.
motociclista, *n.m.f.* motorcyclist.
motor, -ra (*f. also* **motriz**), *a.* motor, motive. —*n.m.* motor engine; mover, author; **— a chorro,** jet engine; **— de combustión interna** or **de explosión,** internal-combustion engine; **— de reacción** or **— cohete,** rocket motor; **— diesel,** Diesel motor.—*n.f.* motor boat.
motorismo, *n.m.* motoring; motor cycling.
motorista, *n.m.f.* motorist, driver.
motorización, *n.f.* motorization.
motorizar [C], *v.t.* motorize.
motril, *n.m.* errand-boy.
motriz (*pl.* **-ices**) [MOTOR].
movedizo, -za, *a.* movable, moving; shaky; fickle.
mover [5], *v.t.* move; wag, shake; stir up.—*v.r.* move.
movible, *a.* movable; fickle.
móvil, *a.* moving, mobile; fickle.—*n.m.* motive; moving body; revenue stamp.
movilidad, *n.f.* mobility.
movilización, *n.f.* mobilization.
movilizar [C], *v.t., v.i., v.r.* mobilize.
movimiento, *n.m.* movement; motion.
mozalbete, *n.m.* lad, stripling.
mozárabe, *a.* Mozarabic.—*n.m.f.* Mozarab.
mozo, -za, *a.* youthful; single.—*n.m.* lad; servant; porter; waiter; **— de cordel** or **de cuerda** or **de requina,** carrier, odd-jobber.—*n.f.* lass; servant, maid; wench.
mu, *n.m.* moo, bellow.—*n.f.* bye-byes, sleep (*infants' word*).
muchachada, muchachería, *n.f.* child's trick.
muchachez, *n.f.* childhood; childishness.
muchacho, -cha, *a.* (*fam.*) boyish, girlish.—*n.m.* boy.—*n.f.* girl; maid.
muchedumbre, *n.f.* crowd; mass.
mucho, -cha, *a.* much, a lot of.—*pl.* many.—*pron.* much.—*adv.* much, a lot, a great deal; hard; a long time; **con —,** by far; **ni con —,** not by a long shot; **ni — menos,** far from it; **por — que,** however much.
muda, *n.f.* change; moult; breaking of voice.
mudable, mudadizo, -za, *a.* changeable.
mudanza, *n.f.* change; house-moving; fickleness.
mudar, *v.t.* change; move (*house*).—*v.i.* change (*de*); moult.—*v.r.* change; (*fam.*) get changed (*change one's clothes*); move.
mudéjar, *a., n.m.f.* Mudejar.
mudez, *n.f.* dumbness; silence.
mudo, -da, *a.* dumb, mute, silent.—*n.m.f.* mute.
mueblaje, *n.m.* furnishings, furniture.
mueble, *a.* (*jur.*) movable.—*n.m.* piece of furniture.—*pl.* furniture.
mueca, *n.f.* pulled face, grimace; **hacer muecas,** make faces.
muela, *n.f.* grindstone; hillock; (*anat.*) molar.
muelle, *a.* soft; luxurious, voluptuous.—*n.m.* (*mech.*) spring; (*naut.*) jetty, quay.
muérdago, *n.m.* mistletoe.
muerte, *n.f.* death; **a —,** to the death; **de mala —,** (*fam.*) lousy, worthless; **de —,** implacably; dangerously (*ill*); **— chiquita,** (*fam.*) nervous shiver.
muerto, -ta, *a.* dead; languid; lifeless; dull; slaked.—*n.m.* corpse; deceased.—*p.p.* MORIR.
muesca, *n.f.* mortise, socket.
muestra, *n.f.* sample; sign (*shop, inn etc.*); dial, face; indication, sign; **pasar —,** review; **feria de muestras,** trade fair.
muestro *etc.* [MOSTRAR].
muevo *etc.* [MOVER].
mugido, *n.m.* moo, bellow, lowing.
mugir [E], *v.i.* low; bellow; roar.
mugre, *n.f.* filth, grime, dirt.
mugriento, -ta, *a.* filthy, grimy.
mujer, *n.f.* woman; wife.
mujerero, -ra (*S.A.*), **mujeriego, -ga** (*Sp.*), *a.* womanly, womanish; womanizing.
mujeril, *a.* womanly; womanish.
mujerío, *n.m.* women; female population.
mujerona, *n.f.* matron, beefy woman.
mújol, *n.m.* (*ichth.*) mullet.
mula, *n.f.* mule; (*C.A.*) junk; **en (la) — de San Francisco,** on Shanks's mare; **hacer la —,** shirk.
muladar, *n.m.* dungheap; filth.
mular, *a.* rel. to mules.
mul(at)ero, *n.m.* muleteer.
mulato, -ta, *a., n.m.f.* mulatto.
muleta, *n.f.* crutch; (*fam.*) snack; (*taur.*) matador's red cape.
muletilla, *n.f.* (*taur.*) muleta; crutch; (*fam.*) theme-song, pet phrase.
mulo, *n.m.* mule.
multa, *n.f.* fine.
multar, *v.t.* fine.
multicolor, *a.* multicoloured.
multicopista, *n.m.* duplicating machine.
multiforme, *a.* multiform.
multilátero, -ra, *a.* multilateral.
multimillonario, -ria, *a. n.m.f.* multi-millionaire.
múltiple, *a.* multiple, manifold.—*n.m.* (*mech.*) manifold.
multiplicación, *n.f.* multiplication.
multiplicar [A], *v.t., v.r.* multiply.
multiplice, *a.* multiple.
multiplicidad, *n.f.* multiplicity.
múltiplo, -la, *a., n.m.* (*elec., math.*) multiple.
multitud, *n.f.* multitude.
mullido, -da, *a.* soft, fluffy.
mullir [J], *v.t.* fluff up; shake up (*beds*); soften; get ready.
mundanal, mundano, -na, *a.* wordly, mundane.
mundial, *a.* world-wide, international.
mundo, *n.m.* world; large trunk; (*fam.*) vast crowd; **tener (mucho) —,** be canny and experienced; **todo el —,** everybody.
munición, *n.f.* munition; supplies; charge (*of gun*); small shot.
municionar, *v.t.* (*mil.*) supply.
municipal, *a.* municipal.—*n.m.* policeman.
municipalizar [C] *v.t.* municipalize.
municipio, *n.m.* municipality; town council.
munificencia, *n.f.* magnificence.
munificente, munífico, -ca, *a.* (*sup.* **munificentísimo, -ma**) munificent.
muñeca, *n.f.* wrist; doll.
muñeco, *n.m.* doll; puppet; (*fam.*) sissy.
muñequera, *n.f.* wrist-watch strap.
muñidor, *n.m.* beadle; activist.

muñir [K], *v.t.* summon; (*fig.*) rig.
muñón, *n.m.* stump (*of amputated limb*); (*mech.*) swivel, gudgeon.
mural, *a., n.m.* mural.
muralla, *n.f.* city wall, rampart.
murciano, -na, *a., n.m.f.* Murcian.
murciégalo, murciélago, *n.m.* (*zool.*) bat.
murga, *n.f.* (*fam.*) street band; (*fam.*) pest.
murmullar, *v.i.* murmur.
murmullo, *n.m.* murmur; rustle; ripple.
murmuración, *n.f.* gossip, backbiting.
murmurar, *v.t., v.i.* murmur; mutter (*de,* against, about).
muro, *n.m.* wall.
murria, *n.f.* melancholy; blues.
murrio, -rria, *a.* dejected, morose.
Musa, *n.f.* Muse.
musaraña, *n.f.* (*zool.*) shrew; spot (*speck in eye*).
muscular, *a.* muscular.
músculo, *n.m.* (*anat.*) muscle.
musculoso, -sa, *a.* muscular.
muselina, *n.f.* muslin.
museo, *n.m.* museum.
musgaño, *n.m.* (*zool.*) shrew.
musgo, *n.m.* (*bot.*) moss.
musgoso, -sa, *a.* mossy.
música, *n.f.* music; band; — **celestial,** (*fam.*) eyewash, nonsense.
musical, *a.* musical.
músico, -ca, *a.* musical.—*n.m.f.* musician.
musitar, *v.i.* mumble, whisper.
muslime, *a., n.m.f.* Muslim, Moslem.
muslo, *n.m.* thigh.
mustela, *n.f.* (*zool.*) weasel.
mustio, -tia, *a.* gloomy, sad; withered.
musulmán, -mana, *a.,n.m.f.* Mussulman, Moslem.
mutabilidad, *n.f.* mutability.
mutación, *n.f.* change; (*biol.*) mutation.
mutante, *n.m.* (*biol.*) mutant.
mutilación, *n.f.* mutilation.
mutilado, -da, *a.* crippled.—*n.m.f.* cripple.
mutilar, *v.t.* cripple; mutilate.
mútilo, -la, *a.* mutilated; defective.
mutis, *n.m.* (*theat.*) exit; **hacer** —, say nothing.
mutismo, *n.m.* mutism; silence.
mutual, *a.* mutual.
mutualidad, *n.f.* mutuality; cooperative.
mutuo, -tua, *a.* mutual.—*n.m.* (*jur.*) loan.
muy, *adv.* very; very much of a; — ... **para,** too ... to; — **de noche,** very late at night.

N

N, n, *n.f.* sixteenth letter of the Spanish alphabet.
nabo, *n.m.* (*bot.*) turnip.
nácar, *n.m.* mother-of-pearl.
nacencia, *n.f.* tumour, growth.
nacer [9], *v.i.* be born; rise.—*v.r.* sprout; split.
nacido, -da, *a.* inborn, innate; apt.—*n.m.* offspring; tumour.

naciente, *a.* recent; incipient; rising (*sun*).
nacimiento, *n.m.* birth; origin; spring; crib.
nación, *n.f.* nation.
nacional, *a., n.m.f.* national.
nacionalidad, *n.f.* nationality.
nacionalismo, *n.m.* nationalism.
nacionalista, *a., n.m.f.* nationalist.
nacionalización, *n.f.* nationalization.
nacionalizar [C], *v.t.* nationalize; naturalize.
nacista, *a., n.m.f.* Nazi.
nada, *n.f.* nothingness, void.—*pron.* nothing. —*adv.* not very, not at all; **de** —, don't mention it, you are welcome.
nadar, *v.i.* swim; float.
nadería, *n.f.* trifle.
nadie, *n.m., pron.* nobody, no one.
nadir, *n.m.* nadir.
a nado, *adv. phr.* swimming; floating.
nafta, *n.f.* naphtha.
naipe, *n.m.* playing card.
nalga, *n.f.* buttock.
nana, *n.f.* lullaby; (*fam.*) granny.
nao, *n.f.* (*poet.*) ship.
Napoleón, *n.m.* Napoleon.
napoleónico, -ca, *a.* Napoleonic.
Nápoles, *n.f.* Naples.
napolitano, -na, *a., n.m.f.* Neapolitan.
naranja, *n.f.* orange; **media** —, (*fam.*) wife; bosom friend.
naranjado, -da, *a.* orange.—*n.f.* orangeade; (*fig.*) vulgarity.
naranjal, *n.m.* orange grove.
naranjo, *n.m.* orange-tree.
narciso, *n.m.* narcissus; fop.
narcótico, -ca, *a., n.m.* narcotic.
narcotizar [C], *v.t.* drug.
narigón, -gona, *a.* big-nosed.—*n.m.* big nose.
narigudo, -da, *a.* [NARIGÓN].
nariz, *n.f.* (*pl.* **-ices**) nose; nostril.
narración, *n.f.* narration; telling.
narrar, *v.t.* narrate.
narrativo, -va, *a., n.f.* narrative.
nasal, *a., n.f.* nasal.
nasalizar [C], *v.t.* nasalize.
naso, *n.m.* (*fam.*) big nose.
nata, *n.f.* cream; (*la*) **flor y** (*la*) —, the cream, élite.
natación, *n.f.* swimming.
natal, *a.* native; natal.—*n.m.* birth; birthday.
natalicio, -cia, *a.* natal.—*n.m.* birthday.
natalidad, *n.f.* birth-rate.
natillas, *n.f.pl.* custard.
natío, -tía, *a.* native; **de su** —, naturally.
natividad, *n.f.* nativity.
nativo, -va, *a.* native.
nato, -ta, *a.* born.
natura, *n.f.* nature; genitalia.
natural, *a.* natural; native.—*n.m.f.* native.— *n.m.* disposition, nature.
naturaleza, *n.f.* nature; nationality.
naturalidad, *n.f.* naturalness; nationality.
naturalizar [C], *v.t.* naturalize.
naufragar [B], *v.i.* be (ship)wrecked; fail.
naufragio, *n.m.* shipwreck; failure.
náufrago, -ga, *a.* shipwrecked.—*n.m.f.* shipwrecked person.
náusea, *n.f.* nausea.
nauseabundo, -da, *a.* nauseating, loathsome.
nauseativo, -va, nauseoso, -sa, *a.* nauseating.
náutico, -ca, *a.* nautical.—*n.f.* nautics, navigation.

nava, *n.f.* plain between mountains.
navaja, *n.f.* razor; clasp-knife.
navajada, *n.f.*, **navajazo,** *n.m.* gash, cut.
naval, *a.* naval.
Navarra, *n.f.* Navarre.
navarro, -rra, *a.*, *n.m.f.* Navarrese.
nave, *n.f.* ship; (*arch.*) nave.
navegable, *a.* navigable (*water*).
navegación, *n.f.* navigation; voyage.
navegador, navegante, *n.m.* navigator.
navegar [B], *v.t.* sail, navigate.
Navidad, *n.f.* Christmas.
navi(da)deño, -ña, *a.* Christmas.
naviero, -ra, *a.* shipping.—*n.m.* ship-owner.
navío, *n.m.* ship, vessel.
nazareno, -na, *a.*, *n.m.f.* Nazarene.
nazi, *a.*, *n.m.f.* Nazi.
nazismo, *n.m.* Naz(i)ism.
neblina, *n.f.* mist, haze.
nebulosa, *n.f.* (*astr.*) nebula.
nebuloso, -sa, *a.* nebulous; cloudy; gloomy.
necedad, *n.f.* foolishness.
necesario, -ria, *a.* necessary.—*n.f.* lavatory.
neceser, *n.f.* sewing basket; toilet bag.
necesidad, *n.f.* necessity; need, want.
necesitado, -da, *a.* needy.
necesitar, *v.t.* need, require.—*v.i.* be in need (*de,* of).
necio, -cia, *a.* foolish, stupid.—*n.m.f.* fool.
necrología, *n.f.* obituary, necrology.
necrópolis, *n.f. inv.* necropolis.
néctar, *n.m.* nectar.
nefando, -da, *a.* abominable.
nefario, -ria, *a.* nefarious.
nefasto, -ta, *a.* ominous, ill-omened.
negar [IB], *v.t.* deny; refuse; disown; hide.—*v.r.* pretend to be out; refuse (*a,* to).
negativo, -va, *a.*, *n.m.* negative.—*n.f.* refusal, denial; negative.
negligencia, *n.f.* negligence.
negligente, *a.* negligent.
negociable, *a.* negotiable.
negociación, *n.f.* negotiation.
negociador, -ra, *n.m.f.* negotiator.
negociante, *n.m.* dealer; business-man.
negociar, *v.t.* negotiate; arrange.—*v.i.* trade.
negocio, *n.m.* business; transaction.
negocioso, -sa, *a.* diligent, business-like.
negra, *n.f.* Negro woman *or* girl.
negrear, *v.i.* show black; be blackish.
negrecer [9], *v.i.* turn black(ish).
negrero, -ra, *a.* slaving, slave-driving.—*n.m.* slaver, slave-driver.
negrilla, -negrita, *n.f.* (*print.*) bold-face.
negro, -ra, *a.* black; dismal; evil; Negro; (*fam.*) penniless.—*n.m.* Negro; *pasar las negras,* (*fam.*) have a bad time of it.
negroide, *a.* Negroid.
negror, *n.m.*, **negrura,** *n.f.* blackness.
negruzco, -ca, *a.* blackish.
nene, nena, *n.m.f.* (*fam.*) baby.
nenúfar, *n.m.* (*bot.*) water-lily.
neocelandés, -desa, *a.* New Zealand.—*n.m.f.* New Zealander.
neoclásico, -ca, *a.* neoclassic(al).—*n.m.f.* neoclassicist.
neolatino, -na, *a.* Neo-Latin; Romance.
neolítico, -ca, *a.* neolithic.
neologismo, *n.m.* neologism.
neón, *n.m.* (*chem.*) neon.

neoyorquino, -na, *a.*, *n.m.f.* rel. to *or* native of New York.
Nepal, *n.m.* Nepal.
nepalés, -lesa, *a.*, *n.m.f.* Nepalese.
nepotismo, *n.m.* nepotism.
Nerón, *n.m.* Nero.
nervio, *n.m.* nerve; mettle; ribbing.
nerviosidad, *n.f.*, **nerviosismo,** *n.m.* nervousness.
nervioso, -sa, nervoso, -sa, *a.* nervous; vigorous; sinewy.
nervudo, -da, *a.* sinewy; robust, vigorous.
neto, -ta, *a.* pure; (*com.*) net.
neumático, -ca, *a.* pneumatic.—*n.m.* tyre.
neumonía, *n.m.* pneumonia.
neuralgia, *n.f.* neuralgia.
neurólogo, *n.m.* neurologist.
neurosis, *n.f. inv.* neurosis.
neurótico, -ca, *a.*, *n.m.f.* neurotic.
neutral, *a.*, *n.m.f.* neutral.
neutralidad, *n.f.* neutrality.
neutralizar [C], *v.t.* neutralize.
neutro, -ra, *a.* neuter; (*chem., elec. etc.*) neutral.
nevada, *n.f.* snowfall.
nevado, -da, *a.* snow-covered; snowy.
nevar [I], *v.i.* snow.—*v.t.* whiten.
nevasca, *n.f.*, **nevazo,** *n.m.* snowstorm.
nevera, *n.f.* refrigerator, ice-box.
nevisca, *n.f.* fine snow.
neviscar [A], *v.i.* snow lightly.
nevoso, -sa, *a.* snowy.
nexo, *n.m.* nexus.
ni, *conj.* neither, nor; *ni . . . ni,* neither . . . nor; — *siquiera,* not even.
nicaragüense, nicaragüeño, -ña, *a.*, *n.m.f.* Nicaraguan.
Nicolás, *n.m.* Nicholas.
nicotina, *n.f.* nicotine.
nicho, *n.m.* niche.
nidada, *n.f.* brood.
nido, *n.m.* nest.
niebla, *n.f.* fog, mist.
nieto, -ta, *n.m.f.* grandchild.—*n.m.* grandson. —*n.f.* grand-daughter.
nieva *etc.* [NEVAR].
nieve, *n.f.* snow.
Níger, *n.m.* **la República del —,** Niger.
nihilismo, *n.m.* nihilism.
nihilista, *a.*, *n.m.f.* nihilist.
Nilo, *n.m.* Nile.
nilón, *n.m.* nylon.
nimbo, *n.m.* halo, nimbus.
nimiedad, *n.f.* prolixity; sparingness.
nimio, -mia, *a.* excessive; stingy.
ninfa, *n.f.* (*ent., myth.*) nymph.
ninfea, *n.f.* (*bot.*) water-lily.
ningún, *a.m. contracted form of* NINGUNO *before n.m. sg.*
ninguno, -na, *a.* no, not any.—*pron. m.f.* none; no one.
niña, *n.f.* girl, child; (*anat.*) pupil; — *del ojo,* apple of one's eye.
niñada, *n.f.* childishness.
niñera, *n.f.* nursemaid.
niñería, *n.f.* trifle; childishness.
niñez, *n.f.* childhood, infancy.
niño, -ña, *a.* young; child-like.—*n.m.f.* child. —*n.m.* boy; *desde —,* from childhood.—*n.f.* girl.
nipón, -pona, *a.*, *n.m.f.* Japanese.
níquel, *n.m.* nickel.

niquelar, *v.t.* nickel-plate.
níspero, *n.m.* (*bot.*) medlar.
nitidez, *n.f.* clearness, sharpness.
nítido, -da, *a.* bright, clear, sharp.
nitrato, *n.m.* (*chem.*) nitrate.
nitro, *n.m.* nitre, salpetre.
nitrógeno, *n.m.* nitrogen.
nivel, *n.m.* level; — **de vida,** standard of living.
nivelar, *v.t.* level; survey.—*v.r.* come level.
Niza, *n.f.* Nice.
no, *adv.* no; not; ¿*a que* — ? (*fam.*) I bet it isn't! ¿*cómo* — ? why not ? (*S.A.*) sure! — *bien,* no sooner.
nobilísimo, -ma, *a. sup. of* NOBLE.
noble, *a., n.m.f.* noble.—*n.m.* nobleman.
nobleza, *n.f.* nobility.
nocente, *a.* noxious; guilty.
noción, *n.f.* notion; rudiment.
nocivo, -va, *a.* harmful.
noctámbulo, -la, *a.* sleepwalking; night-wandering.—*n.m.f.* sleep-walker; night-bird.
nocturno, -na, *a.* nocturnal.—*n.m.* (*mus.*) nocturne.
noche, *n.f.* night; darkness; *de* —, at night; *de la* — *a la mañana,* all of a sudden; *Noche buena,* Christmas Eve ;— *toledana* or *en blanco,* sleepless night; *Noche vieja,* New Year's Eve; *buenas noches,* good night!
nodriza, *n.f.* wet nurse; reserve tank (*in car*).
Noé, *n.m.* Noah.
nogal, *n.m.* walnut (*tree, wood*).
noguera, *n.f.* walnut tree.
nómada, *a.* nomadic.—*n.m.f.* nomad.
nombradía, *n.f.* renown, fame.
nombrado, -da, *a.* renowned.
nombramiento, *n.m.* naming, appointment.
nombrar, *v.t.* name; appoint.
nombre, *n.m.* name; noun; password; *no tener* —, be unmentionable; — *de pila,* Christian name; — *propio,* proper noun; — *de soltera,* maiden name.
nomenclatura, *n.f.* nomenclature.
nomeolvides, *n.f.* (*bot.*) forget-me-not.
nómina, *n.f.* list, roll.
nominación, *n.f.* nomination.
nominal, *a.* nominal; substantival.
nominar, *v.t.* name; nominate.
nominativo, -va, *a., n.m.* nominative.
nominilla, *n.f.* voucher.
non, *a.* (*math.*) odd, uneven.—*n.m.* odd number; *decir que nones,* say no, refuse.
nona, *n.f.* (*eccl.*) nones.
nonada, *n.f.* trifle, nothing.
nonagenario, -ria, *a., n.m.f.* nonagenarian.
nonagésimo, -ma, *a., n.m.* ninetieth.
nono, -na, *a., n.m.* ninth.
nopal, *n.m.* (*bot.*) prickly pear.
norabuena, *n.f.* congratulation(s).—*adv.* fortunately.
noramala, nora tal, *adv.* [ENHORAMALA].
nordeste, *a., n.m.* north-east.
nórdico, -ca, *a., n.m.f.* Nordic. — *a., n.m.* Norse.
noria, *n.f.* draw-well; (*fam.*) chore.
norma, *n.f* standard, norm; (*carp.*) square.
normal, *a.* normal; perpendicular; *según la* —, at right angles.
normalidad, *n.f.* normality.
normalizar [C], *v.t.* normalize; standardize.

Normandia, *n.f.* Normandy.
normando, -da, normano, -na, *a., n.m.f.* Norman.
noroeste, *a.* north-western.—*n.m.* north-west.
norte, *n.m.* north; (*fig.*) pole-star.
Norteamérica, *n.f.* North America.
norteamericano, -na, *a., n.m.f.* North American, American.
norteño, -ña, *a.* northern.—*n.m.f.* northerner.
Noruega, *n.f.* Norway.
noruego, -ga, *a., n.m.f.* Norwegian.
nos, *pron.* us, to us; (to) ourselves; (*obs.*) we.
nosotros, -ras, *pron.* we; (*with prep.*) us.
nostalgia, *n.f.* nostalgia, homesickness.
nostálgico, -ca, *a.* nostalgic, homesick.
nota, *n.f.* note; (*educ.*) mark.
notabilidad, *n.f.* notability.
notable, *a., n.m.f.* notable.
notación, *n.f.* notation.
notar, *v.t.* note; notice; dictate.—*v.r.* be noticeable.
notario, *n.m.* notary.
noticia, *n.f.* piece of news; information; notion; knowledge.—*pl.* news.
noticiar, *v.t.* notify.
noticiario, -ria, *a., n.m.* news.
noticiero, *n.m.* news editor.
notición, *n.m.* (*fam.*) big news.
notificación, *n.f.* notification.
notificar [A], *v.t.* notify.
noto, -ta, *a.* noted; illegitimate.
notoriedad, *n.f.* fame.
notorio, -ria, *a.* widely known, well-known.
novador, -ra, *a.* innovating.
novato, -ta, *a.* new, green.—*n.m.f.* newcomer; novice; freshman.
novecientos, -tas, *a., n.m.pl.* nine hundred.
novedad, *n.f.* novelty; news; trouble; change; *sin* —, as usual; (*mil.*) all quiet.
novel, *a., n.m.* novice.
novela, *n.f.* novel.
novelar, *v.i.* romance; write novels.
novelero, -ra, *a.* fond of novel(tie)s; fickle; (*fam.*) gossiping.
novelesco, -ca, *a.* novelesque.
novelista, *n.m.f.* novelist.
noveno, -na, *a.* ninth.—*n.f.* (*eccl.*) novena.
noventa, *a., n.m.* ninety.
noventón, -tona, *n.m.f.* (*fam.*) nonagenarian.
novia, *n.f.* fiancée; bride.
noviazgo, *n.m.* betrothal, engagement.
novicio, -cia, *a., n.m.f.* novice; apprentice.
noviembre, *n.m.* November.
novilla, *n.f.* heifer.
novillada, *n.f.* bullfight (*of young bulls*).
novillero, *n.m.* (*taur.*) trainee bullfighter; (*fam.*) truant.
novillo, *n.m.* young bull; *hacer novillos,* (*fam.*) play truant.
novio, *n.m.* fiancé; bridegroom; suitor.—*pl.* couple (*engaged or newly-wed*).
novísimo, -ma, *a. sup.* newest, latest.
nuba(rra)do, -da, *a.* cloudy.—*n.f.* shower.
nubarrón, *n.m.* dense, black cloud.
nube, *n.f.* cloud; *andar por las nubes,* cost a fortune; *ponerle por las nubes* or *subirle a las nubes,* praise him to the skies.
núbil, *a.* nubile.
nublado, -da, *a.* cloudy.—*n.m.* storm cloud; gloom; mass.

nubloso, -sa, *a.* cloudy; gloomy.
nuca, *n.f.* (*anat.*) nape; scruff.
nuclear, *a.* nuclear.
núcleo, *n.m.* nucleus; kernel; (*elec.*) core.
nudillo, *n.m.* knuckle; nodule; knot.
nudismo, *n.m.* nudism.
nudista, *n.m.f.* nudist.
nudo, -da, *a.* naked, nude.—*n.m.* knot, bond; snag; node; crisis of drama; lump (*in throat*).
nudoso, -sa, *a.* knotty, knotted.
nuera, *n.f.* daughter-in-law.
nuestro, -tra, *a.* our.—*pron.* ours.
nueva, *n.f.* piece of news.
Nueva York, *n.f.* New York.
Nueva Zelandia, *n.f.* New Zealand.
nueve, *a.,* *n.m.* nine.
nuevo, -va, *a.* new; *de* —, anew, again.
nuez, *n.f.* (*pl.* **nueces**) walnut; nut; kernel; Adam's apple.
nulidad, *n.f.* nullity; incompetence.
nulo, -la, *a.* null, void; useless.
numeración, *n.f.* numeration.
numeral, *a.* numeral.
numerar, *v.t.* number; calculate.
numerario, -ria, *a.* numerary.—*n.m.* coin, hard cash.
numérico, -ca, *a.* numerical.
número, *n.m.* number; *sin* —, countless; unnumbered.
numeroso, -sa, *a.* numerous.
numismático, -ca, *n.m.f.* numismatist.—*n.f.* numismatics.—*a.* numismatic.
nunca, *adv.* never; — *jamás,* never ever.
nuncio, *n.m.* nuncio; forerunner.
nupcial, *a.* nuptial.
nupcias, *n.f.* nuptials; *casarse en segundas* —, remarry.
nutr(i)a, *n.f.* (*zool.*) otter.
nutricio, -cia, *a.* nutritious.
nutrición, *n.f.* nutrition.
nutrido, -da, *a.* full (*of*), rich (*in*) (*de*).
nutrim(i)ento, *n.m.* nutriment, nourishment.
nutrir, *v.t.* nourish; enrich.
nutritivo, -va, *a.* nutritious.

Ñ

Ñ, ñ, *n.f.* seventeenth letter of the Spanish alphabet.
ñapa, *n.f.* (*S.A.*) extra, bonus.
ñaque, *n.m.* junk, rubbish.
ñeque, *n.m.* (*S.A.*) vim, pep, zest.
ñiqueñaque, *n.m.* (*fam.*) good-for-nothing; trash, bunk.
ñoñería, *n.f.* shyness; drivel.
ñoñez, *n.f.* sloppiness; timidity.
ñoño, -ña, *a.* (*fam.*) sloppy, feeble; (*S.A.*) doting.
ñu, *n.m.* (*zool.*) gnu.
ñubl- [NUBL-].
ñud- [NUD-].

O

O, o (1), *n.f.* eighteenth letter of the Spanish alphabet.
o (2), *conj.* or; **o . . . o . . .,** either . . . or . . .; **o sea,** that is to say.
¡o! (3), *interj.* oh!
oasis, *n.m.* oasis.
obcecación, *n.f.* obfuscation.
obedecer [9], *v.t., v.i.* obey; respond.
obediencia, *n.f.* obedience.
obediente, *a.* obedient.
obelisco, *n.m.* obelisk; (*print.*) dagger (†).
obertura, *n.f.* (*mus.*) overture.
obesidad, *n.f.* obesity.
obeso, -sa, *a.* obese.
óbice, *n.m.* obstacle, hindrance.
obispado, *n.m.* bishopric.
obispillo, *n.m.* boy bishop; rump (*of a fowl*), parson's nose; large black pudding.
obispo, *n.m.* bishop.
óbito, *n.m.* (*jur.*) demise.
obituario, *n.m.* obituary.
objetar, *v.t.* object.
objetividad, *n.f.* objectivity.
objetivo, -va, *a.,* *n.m.* objective.
objeto, *n.m.* object; aim, end.
oblación, *n.f.* oblation.
oblato, -ta, *a.,* *n.m.* oblate.
oblea, *n.f.* wafer.
oblicuángulo, -la, *a.* oblique-angled.
oblicuar, *v.t., v.i.* slant.
oblicuidad, *n.f.* obliquity.
oblicuo, -cua, *a.* oblique.
obligación, *n.f.* obligation; bond, debenture.
obligacionista, *n.m.f.* bond-holder.
obligado, -da, *a.* grateful.—*n.m.* (*mus.*) obbligato; public contractor.
obligar [B], *v.t.* oblige, force (*a,* to).—*v.r.* bind oneself (*a,* to).
obligatorio, -ria, *a.* obligatory.
obliteración, *n.f.* (*med.*) failing of memory; cancellation.
obliterar, *v.t.* obliterate.
oblongo, -ga, *a.* oblong.
oboe, *n.m.* oboe; oboist.
óbolo, *n.m.* (widow's) mite.
obra, *n.f.* work; — *maestra,* masterpiece; *en obras,* under repair *or* construction.
obrador, -ra, *a.* working.—*n.m.f.* worker.
obrar, *v.t.* work; act; construct; *obra en mi poder,* (*com.*) I have to hand.
obrerismo, *n.m.* Labour movement.
obrerista, *a.* rel. to Labour.—*n.m.f.* Labour supporter, (*U.S.*) laborite.
obrero, -ra, *a.* working; rel. to labour.— *n.m.f.* worker.
obscenidad, *n.f.* obscenity.
obsceno, -na, *a.* obscene.
obscurantismo, *n.m.* obscurantism.
obscuro, -ra [OSCURO].
obsecuente, *a.* submissive.
obsequiante, *a.* fawning, flattering.
obsequiar, *v.t.* pay attentions to; flatter, court.
obsequio, *n.m.* civility, attention; gift.
obsequioso, -sa, *a.* obliging; attentive.
observable, *a.* observable.
observación, *n.f.* observation.

observador, -ra, a. observant.—n.m.f. observer.
observancia, n.f. observance; regard, reverence.
observante, a. observant.
observar, v.t. observe.
observatorio, n.m. observatory.
obsesión, n.f. obsession.
obsesionante, n.m. a haunting.
obsesionar, v.t. obsess.
obsesivo, -va, a. obsessive.
obstáculo, n.m. obstacle.
obstante, a. standing in the way; no —, notwithstanding; in spite of.
obstar, v.i. obstruct, stand in the way.
obstetricia, n.f. (med.) obstetrics.
obstétrico, -ca, a. obstetrical.—n.m. obstetrician.—n.f. obstetrics.
obstinación, n.f. obstinacy.
obstinado, -da, a. obstinate.
obstinar, v.r. be obstinate; persist.
obstrucción, n.f. obstruction.
obstructivo, -va, a. obstructive.
obstruir [O], v.t. obstruct.
obtener [33], v.t. obtain.
obtenible, a. obtainable.
obturador, -triz, a. stopping, plugging.—n.m. plug, stopper; (aut.) choke; (phot.) shutter.
obturar, v.t. obturate, plug.
obtusángulo, -la, a. obtuse-angled.
obtuso, -sa, a. obtuse (also fig.).
obtuve, etc. [OBTENER].
obué, n.m. [OBOE].
obús, n.m. howitzer.
obvención, n.f. perquisite(s), (fam.) perks.
obviar, v.t. obviate.—v.i. hinder.
obvio, -via, a. obvious.
oca, n.f. goose.
ocasión, n.f. occasion, opportunity; de —, second-hand.
ocasional, a. chance, casual.
ocasionar, v.t. occasion.
ocaso, n.m. west, occident; setting (of a star); decline.
occidental, a. occidental, western.—n.m.f. Occidental, westerner.
occidentalización, n.f. westernization.
occidentalizar [C], v.t. westernize.
occidente, n.m. occident, west.
occipucio, n.m. (anat.) occiput.
occisión, n.f. violent death.
Oceanía, n.f. Oceania.
oceánico, -ca, a. oceanic.—n.m.f. South Sea Islander.
océano, n.m. ocean.
oceanógrafo, n.m. oceanographer.
ocelote, n.m. (zool.) ocelot.
ocio, n.m. idleness; leisure.
ociosidad, n.f. idleness.
ocioso, -sa, a. idle.
oclusión, n.f. occlusion.
oclusivo, -va, a., n.f. occlusive.
ocre, n.m. ochre.
octagonal, a. octagonal.
octágono, -na, a. octagonal.—n.m. octagon.
octano, n.m. (chem.) octane.
octavín, n.m. (mus.) piccolo.
octavo, -va, a., n.m. eighth.—a., n.f. octave; en —, octavo.
octogenario, -ria, a., n.m.f. octogenarian.
octogésimo, -ma, a., n.m. eightieth.

octubre, n.m. October.
ocular, a. ocular.—n.m. eyepiece.
oculista, n.m.f. oculist.
ocultante, a. dense (smoke).
ocultar, v.t. hide, conceal (a, de, from).
ocultismo, n.m. occultism.
oculto, -ta, a. hidden; occult; clandestine.
ocupación, n.f. occupation.
ocupado, -da, a. busy.
ocupador, -ra, a. occupying.—n.m.f. occupier.
ocupante, a. occupying.—n.m.f. occupant.
ocupar, v.t. occupy; keep busy.—v.r. be busy (con, de, en, with).
ocurrencia, n.f. occurrence; witticism; bright idea.
ocurrente, a. witty.
ocurrir, v.i. occur; have recourse (a, to).—v.r. come to mind.
ochavón, -vona, n.m.f. octoroon.
ochenta, a., n.m. eighty.
ocho, a., n.m. eight.
ochocientos, -tas, a., n.m. eight hundred.
oda, n.f. ode.
odiar, v.t. hate.
odio, n.m. hatred, odium.
odioso, -sa, a. odious.
odontología, n.f. (med.) odontology.
odontólogo, -ga, n.m.f. odontologist, dentist.
odorante, a. fragrant.
odorífero, -ra, a. odoriferous.
odre, n.m. wine-skin.
odrina, n.f. wineskin made of cowhide.
oeste, n.m. west.
ofender, v.t., v.i. offend.—v.r. take offence.
ofensa, n.f. offence.
ofensivo, -va, a. offensive.—n.f. offensive.
ofensor, -ra, a. offensive.—n.m.f. offender; attacker.
oferta, n.f. offer; — y demanda, supply and demand.
ofertorio, n.m. offertory.
oficial, a. official.—n.m. clerk; tradesman; office-holder; (mil.) officer.
oficiala, n.f. workwoman, craftswoman.
oficialidad, n.f. official nature; body of officers.
oficiar, v.t. communicate officially.—v.i. officiate.
oficina, n.f. office; laboratory.
oficinista, n.m.f. office-worker.
oficio, n.m. occupation, work; (eccl.) office.
oficiosidad, n.f. officiousness.
oficioso, -sa, a. diligent; officious; unofficial; periódico —, government newspaper.
ofrecer [9], v.t., v.i., v.r. offer.
ofrecimiento, n.m. offer.
ofrenda, n.f. gift, offering, oblation.
oftálmico, -ca, a. ophthalmic.
oftalmología, n.f. ophthalmology.
ofuscar [A], v.t. obfuscate; confuse.
ogaño, adv., (obs.) this year.
ogro, n.m. ogre.
¡oh! interj. oh!
ohmio, n.m. (phys.) ohm.
oíble, a. audible.
oída, n.f. hearing.
oído, n.m. (sense of) hearing; ear; inlet, vent.
oidor, -ra, n.m.f. hearer.—n.m.(obs.) judge.
oigo [OÍR].
oír [22], v.t. hear.
ojal, n.m. button-hole.

¡ojalá! *interj.* God grant!
ojeada, *n.f.* glance.
ojear, *v.t.* eye, stare at; beat (*game*).
ojén, *n.m.* anisette (*liqueur*).
ojera, *n.f.* eye-bath; rings under the eyes.
ojeriza, *n.f.* grudge.
ojeroso, -sa, ojerudo, -da, *a.* with rings under the eyes.
ojete, *n.m.* eyelet.
ojinegro, -ra, *a.* black-eyed.
ojituerto, -ta, *a.* cross-eyed.
ojiva, *n.f.* (*arch.*) ogive.
ojival, *a.* ogival.
ojizaino, -na, *a.* (*fam.*) squint-eyed.
ojo, *n.m.* eye; span (*of bridge*); **hacer del —,** wink; **— con . . .,** beware (of) . . . .
ola, *n.f.* wave.
¡ole! or ¡olé! *interj.* bravo!
oleada, *n.f.* wave (*esp. fig.*).
oleaginoso, -sa, *a.* oleaginous, oily.
óleo, *n.m.* oil (*painting*); oil.
oleoducto, *n.m.* (oil) pipeline.
oleoso, -sa, *a.* oily, oleaginous.
oler [5: **huelo** *etc.*], *v.t.* smell.—*v.i.* smell (*a*, of).
olfatear, *v.t.* smell, scent.
olfato, *n.m.* (*sense of*) smell; flair.
olíbano, *n.m.* frankincense.
oligarca, *n.m.* oligarch.
oligárquico, -ca, *a.* oligarchic.
olimpíada, *n.f.* Olympiad; Olympic Games.
olímpico, -ca, *a.* Olympian; Olympic; haughty.
oliscar [A], *v.t.* smell (out).—*v.i.* smell (*high*).
oliva, *n.f.* olive (*fruit, colour*).
olivar, *a.* olive.—*n.m.* olive grove.
olivera, *n.f.* olive-tree.
olivo, *n.m.* olive-tree.
olmedo, *n.m.*, olmeda, *n.f.* elm-grove.
olmo, *n.m.* elm.
olor, *n.m.* odour; smell; stench; hope.
oloroso, -sa, *a.* fragrant; sweet (*sherry*).
olvidadizo, -za, *a.* forgetful.
olvidar, *v.t.* forget.
olvido, *n.m.* forgetfulness; oblivion.
olla, *n.f.* saucepan, stewpot, kettle; stew; whirlpool; **— podrida,** (sort of) Spanish stew; **— exprés, — de** or **a presión,** pressure cooker.
ollería, *n.f.* pottery.
ollero, -ra, *n.m.f.* potter; dealer in earthen-ware.
olluela, *n.f.* small pot.
ombligo, *n.m.* navel; umbilical cord; (*fig.*) centre.
ombría, *n.f.* shady place.
omega, *n.f.* omega.
ómicron, *n.f.* (*pl.* **omícrones**) omicron.
ominoso, -sa, *a.* ominous.
omisión, *n.f.* omission.
omiso, -sa, *a.* neglectful; remiss.
omitir, *v.t.* omit; overlook.
ómnibus, *n.m. inv.* (omni)bus; local train.
omnímodo, -da, *a.* all-embracing.
omnipotencia, *n.f.* omnipotence.
omnipotente, *a.* omnipotent.
omnisciencia, *n.f.* omniscience.
omniscio, -cia, *a.* omniscient.
omnívoro, -ra, *a.* omnivorous.
onagro, *n.m.* (*zool.*) onager, wild **ass.**
onanismo, *n.m.* onanism.

once, *a.*, *n.m.* eleven.
onceno, -na, *a.* eleventh.
onda, *n.f.* wave.
ondatra, *n.m.* (*zool.*) musk-rat.
ondeante, *a.* undulating.
ondear, *v.t.* wave (*hair*).—*v.i.* wave, undulate.
ondoso, -sa, *a.* wavy.
ondulación, *n.f.* undulation; **— permanente,** permanent wave.
ondulado, -da, *a.* wavy; rolling (*country*).—*n.m.* wave (*in one's hair*).
ondulante, *a.* undulating.
ondular, *v.t.* wave (*hair*).—*v.i.* undulate.
ónice, ónique, ónix, *n.m.* onyx.
onomástico, -ca, *a.* onomastic.
onomatopeya, *n.f.* onomatopeia.
ontología, *n.f.* ontology.
onza (1), *n.f.* ounce; square (*of chocolate*).
onza (2), *n.f.* (*zool.*) snow-leopard, ounce.
opacidad, *n.f.* opacity.
opaco, -ca, *a.* opaque; gloomy, dark.
ópalo, *n.m.* (*min.*) opal.
ópera, *n.f.* opera.
operable, *a.* operable.
operación, *n.f.* operation (*also mil., med.*).
operacional, *a.* operational.
operador, -ra, *a.* operating.—*n.m.f.* operator.
operante, *a.* operating, active.
operar, *v.t.* (*med.*) operate (**a uno de algo,** on s.o. for s.th.).—*v.i.* operate (*com., mil., med.*).
operario, -ria, *n.m.f.* operative.
operativo, -va, *a.* operative.
opereta, *n.f.* operetta.
operista, *n.m.f.* opera singer.
operoso, -sa, *a.* hard-working; wearisome.
opiado, -da, opiato, -ta, *a.*, *n.m.* opiate.
opinable, *a.* problematical.
opinar, *v.i.* opine.
opinión, *n.f.* opinion.
opio, *n.m.* opium.
oponer [25], *v.t.* oppose; set up against.—*v.r.* oppose; compete (*a*, for).
oporto, *n.m.* port (*wine*).
oportunidad, *n.f.* opportuneness; opportunity.
oportunismo, *n.m.* opportunism.
oportuno, -na, *a.* opportune.
oposición, *n.f.* opposition; competitive examination (*esp. pl.*).
opositor, -ra, *n.m.f.* competitor, candidate.
opresión, *n.f.* oppression.
opresor, -ra, *a.* oppressive.—*n.m.f.* oppressor.
oprimir, *v.t.* oppress.
oprobio, *n.m.* opprobrium.
optar, *v.t.* choose.—*v.i.* opt (**por,** to).
optativo, -va, *a.*, *n.m.* optative.
óptico, -ca, *a.* optic.—*n.m.* optician.—*n.f.* optics.
optimismo, *n.m.* optimism.
optimista, *a.* optimistic.—*n.m.f.* optimist.
óptimo, -ma, *a.* optimum.
opuesto, -ta, *a.* opposite; contrary.—*p.p.* [OPONER].
opulencia, *n.f.* opulence.
opulento, -ta, *a.* opulent.
opúsculo, *n.m.* short work, opuscule.
de oque, *adv. phr.* (*fam.*) gratis.
oquedad, *n.f.* hollow; hollowness.
ora, *conj.* **ora . . . ora . . .,** now . . . then . . . .

oración, *n.f.* oration, speech; prayer; (*gram.*) clause.
oráculo, *n.m.* oracle.
orador, *n.m.* orator.
oral, *a.* oral, vocal.
orangután, *n.m.* orang-outang.
orar, *v.i.* pray; speak.
orate, *n.m.f.* lunatic.
oratorio, -ria, *a.* oratorical.—*n.m.* (*eccl.*) oratory; (*mus.*) oratorio.—*n.f.* oratory, eloquence.
orbe, *n.m.* orb, sphere.
órbita, *n.f.* orbit; eye-socket.
orbital, *a.* orbital.
las Órcadas, *n.f.pl.* Orkneys.
órdago, *n.m.* **de —,** (*fam.*) first class.
ordalías, *n.f.pl.* (*hist.*) (trial by) ordeal.
orden, *n.m.* (*pl.* **órdenes**) order (*sequence*); order (*peace*); order (*zool.*); **— de batalla,** battle array.—*n.f.* order (*command*); (*religious*) order.
ordenanza, *n.f.* method, order, ordinance.—*n.m.* (*mil.*) orderly.
ordenar, *v.t.* arrange; ordain.
ordeñador, -ra, *a., n.m.f.* milker.
ordeñar, *v.t.* milk.
ordinal, *a.* ordinal.
ordinariez, *n.f.* rude manners.
ordinario, -ria, *a.* ordinary; coarse.
orear, *v.t.* air.—*v.r.* become aired; take an airing.
orégano, *n.m.* (*bot.*) wild marjoram.
oreja, *n.f.* ear; tongue (*of a shoe*); (*cng.*) flange.
orejano, -na, *a.* unbranded.
orejera, *n.f.* earflap.
orejeta, *n.f.* lug.
orejón, *n.m.* dried peach; tug on the ear; dog-ear (*page*).
orfandad, *n.f.* orphanage; orphanhood.
orfebre, *n.m.* goldsmith, silversmith.
orfebrería, *n.f.* gold *or* silver work.
orgánico, -ca, *a.* organic.
organillo, *n.m.* barrel organ.
organismo, *n.m.* organism.
organista, *n.m.f.* organist.
organización, *n.f.* organization.
organizar [C], *v.t.* organize.
órgano, *n.m.* organ.
orgasmo, *n.m.* orgasm.
orgía, orgia, *n.f.* orgy.
orgullo, *n.m.* pride.
orgulloso, -sa, *a.* proud; haughty.
orientación, *n.f.* orientation.
oriental, *a.* oriental; eastern.—*n.m.f.* Oriental.
orientalista, *a., n.m.f.* Orientalist.
orientar, *v.t.* orientate, orient.—*v.r.* get one's bearings.
oriente, *n.m.* east; orient; origin.
orífice, *n.m.* goldsmith.
orificio, *n.m.* orifice.
origen, *n.m.* (*pl.* **orígenes**) origin; datum line *or* point.
original, *a.* original; odd.—*n.m.* original.
originalidad, *n.f.* originality.
originar, *v.t., v.r.* originate.
originario, -ria, *a.* original, primitive.
orilla, *n.f.* border, edge; selvedge; sidewalk; shoulder (*of road*); **a orillas de,** on the banks of.

orillar, *v.t.* border, trim; (*fig.*) settle, tie up.—*v.i., v.r.* skirt, come to the shore.
orillo, *n.m.* selvedge.
orín (I), *n.m.* rust.
orín (2), *n.m.* urine (*esp. pl.*).
orina, *n.f.* urine.
orinal, *n.m.* chamber pot.
orinar, *v.i.* urinate.
oriol, *n.m.* (*orn.*) oriole.
oriundez, *n.f.* origin.
oriundo, -da, *a.* originating (*de,* from) native (*de,* of).
orla, *n.f.* border; fringe.
orlar, *v.t.* border.
orlo, *n.m.* (*mus.*) Alpine horn.
ornamento, *n.m.* ornament.
ornato, *n.m.* adornment.
ornitología, *n.f.* ornithology.
oro, *n.m.* gold; suit of the Spanish card pack; **— batido,** gold-leaf; **— de ley,** hall-marked gold; **— mate,** mat gold.
orondo, -da, *a.* bulging; pompous.
oropel, *n.m.* tinsel (*also fig.*); imitation gold-leaf.
oropéndola, *n.f.* (*orn.*) golden oriole.
oroya, *n.f.* (*S.A.*) hanging basket for carrying people over a rope bridge.
orozuz, *n.m.* (*bot.*) liquorice plant.
orquesta, *n.f.* orchestra.
orquestación, *n.f.* orchestration.
orquestal, *a.* orchestral.
órquide, *n.m.* (*bot.*) orchis.
orquidea, *n.f.* (*bot.*) orchid.
en orre, *adv. phr.* in bulk.
ortega, *n.f.* sand grouse.
ortiga, *n.f.* nettle.
orto, *n.m.* rise (*of star*).
ortodoxia, *n.f.* orthodoxy.
ortodoxo, -xa, *a.* orthodox.
ortopédico, -ca, *a.* orthopaedic.
oruga, *n.f.* caterpillar; (caterpillar) track; (*bot.*) rocket.
orujo, *n.m.* oil greaves; marc.
orza, *n.f.* gallipot; preserve jar; (*naut.*) luff.
orzar, *v.i.* (*naut.*) luff.
orzuelo, *n.m.* (*med.*) sty; trap, snare.
os, *pron. pers. & r. pl.* (*obs. sg.*) you; yourselves.
osa, *n.f.* (*zool.*) she-bear.
osadía, *n.f.* boldness.
osado, -da, *a.* bold.
osambre, *n.m.,* **osamenta,** *n.f.* skeleton.
osar (I), *v.i.* dare.
osar (2), **osario,** *n.m.* ossuary; charnel house.
oscilación, *n.f.* oscillation.
oscilador, -ra, *a.* oscillating.—*n.m.* oscillator.
oscilante, *a.* oscillating.
oscilar, *v.i.* oscillate.
oscurantismo, *n.m.* obscurantism.
oscurecer [9], *v.t., v.i.* darken.
oscuridad, *n.f.* obscurity.
oscuro, -ra, *a.* dark; obscure.
óseo, -sea, *a.* osseous.
osera, *n.f.* bear's den.
osezno, *n.m.* bear cub.
osificación, *n.f.* ossification.
osificar, *v.r.* become ossified.
osmio, *n.m.* (*chem.*) osmium.
oso, *n.m.* bear; **— blanco,** polar bear; **— marino,** fur seal.
ososo, -sa, *a.* osseous.
ostensible, *a.* ostensible.

ostensivo, -va, *a.* ostensive, on show.
ostentación, *n.f.* ostentation.
ostentar, *v.t.* show, display.
ostento, *n.m.* spectacle; prodigy, portent.
ostentoso, -sa, *a.* ostentatious.
osteópata, *n.m.f.* osteopath.
ostra, *n.f.* oyster.
ostral, *n.m.* oyster bed.
ostro (1), *n.m.* south wind.
ostro (2), *n.m.* large oyster.
osudo, -da, *a.* bony.
osuno, -na, *a.* bearish.
otalgia, *n.f.* (*med.*) otalgia, earache.
otear, *v.t.* survey.
otero, *n.m.* hillock; knoll.
otomano, -na, *a.*, *n.m.f.* Ottoman.—*n.f.* ottoman.
Otón, *n.m.* Otto.
otoñada, *n.f.* autumn season.
otoñal, *a.* autumn.
otoñar, *v.i.* spend the autumn.
otoño, *n.m.* autumn, (*U.S.*) fall.
otorgador, -ra, *a.* granting.—*n.m.f.* grantor.
otorgamiento, *n.m.* granting; approval; (*jur.*) execution (*of a document*).
otorgar [B], *v.t.* grant, consent; (*jur.*) execute (*a deed*).
otro, otra, *a.* other, another.—*pron.* other one, another one; **al — día,** on the next day; **otra vez,** again; another time.
otrosí, *adv.* (*obs., joc.*) furthermore.
ova, *n.f.* seawrack, seaweed.
ovación, *n.f.* ovation.
ovado, -da, oval, *a.* oval.
óvalo, *n.m.* oval.
ovar, *v.i.* lay eggs.
oveja, *n.f.* ewe, sheep.
overa, *n.f.* ovary (*of a bird*).
ovetense, *a.* rel. to Oviedo.—*n.m.f.* inhabitant of Oviedo.
Ovidio, *n.m.* Ovid.
óvido, -da, *a.* ovine.
ovil, *n.m.* sheep-cote.
ovillar, *v.t.* roll into balls.
ovillo, *n.m.* ball (*wool, yarn etc.*).
ovino, -na, *a.*, *n.m.f.* ovine.
ovíparo, -ra, *a.* oviparous.
ovoso, -sa, *a.* full of roe.
ovulación, *n.f.* ovulation.
ovulo, *n.m.* (*med.*) ovum.
¡ox! *interj.* shoo!
oxálico, -ca, *a.* oxalic.
oxidable, *a.* oxidizable.
oxidación, *n.f.* oxidation.
oxidante, *a.* oxidizing.—*n.m.* oxidizer.
oxidar, *v.t.*, *v.r.* oxidize; rust.
óxido, *n.m.* oxide; **— de cinc,** zinc oxide.
oxígeno, *n.m.* oxygen.
¡oxte! *interj.* keep off! shoo! **sin decir — ni moxte,** without a word; without so much as a by-your-leave.
oyente, *a.* hearing.—*n.m.f.* listener.
ozono, *n.m.*, ozona, *n.f.* ozone.

P

P, p, *n.f.* nineteenth letter of the Spanish alphabet.

pabellón, *n.m.* pavilion; flag.
pábilo, pabilo, *n.m.* wick.
pacer [9], *v.t.*, *v.i.* graze.
paciencia, *n.f.* patience.
paciente, *a.*, *n.m.f.* patient.
pacificar [A], *v.t.* pacify.—*v.r.* calm down.
pacifico, -ca, *a.* pacific, peaceful.—*n.m.* **el Pacífico,** the Pacific (Ocean).
Paco, *n.m.* (*fam. form of* FRANCISCO) Frank.
pacotilla, *n.f.* trash, gewgaws.
pactar, *v.t.* agree to.—*v.i.* come to an agreement.
pacto, *n.m.* pact, covenant.
pachorra, *n.f.* sluggishness.
padecer [9], *v.t.* suffer; endure.—*v.i.* suffer (*con, de,* from).
padecimiento, *n.m.* suffering.
padrasto, *n.m.* stepfather; obstacle.
padre, *n.m.* father; stallion; (*eccl.*) father; **— político,** father-in-law.
padrenuestro, *n.m.* (*pl.* **padrenuestros**) Lord's Prayer, paternoster.
padrino, *n.m.* godfather.—*pl.* godparents.
padrón, *n.m.* census; pattern, model.
paella, *n.f.* (*cul.*) rice with meat etc.
¡paf! *interj.* bang! wham!
paga, *n.f.* pay.
pagable, pagadero, -ra, *a.* payable.
pagam(i)ento, *n.m.* payment.
pagano, -na, *a.* pagan.
pagar [B], *v.t.* pay.
pagaré, *n.m.* (*com.*) I.O.U.
página, *n.f.* page.
pago, *a. inv.* (*fam.*) paid.—*n.m.* payment; district.
painel, *n.m.* panel.
país, *n.m.* country, land; landscape; **País de Gales,** Wales; **Países Bajos,** Low Countries, Netherlands.
paisaje, *n.m.* landscape.
paisano, -na, *a.* of the same country.—*n.m.f.* compatriot; **de —,** in civilian clothes.
paja, *n.f.* straw; (*fig.*) padding.
pajar, *n.m.* straw-rick; straw-loft.
pajarero, -ra, *a.* gaudy, gay.—*n.m.f.* bird dealer.—*n.f.* aviary.
pájaro, *n.m.* bird.
pajarota, *n.f.* canard; hoax.
paje, *n.m.* page (boy); cabin boy.
pajizo, -za, *a.* straw-coloured.
pakistano, -na, *a.*, *n.m.f.* Pakistani.
pala, *n.f.* shovel; blade; racket.
palabra, *n.f.* word.
palabrería, *n.f.*, palabrerío, *n.m.* wordiness.
palabrero, -ra, *a.* wordy.
palabrota, *n.f.* coarse word *or* expression.
palaciego, -ga, *a.* palatial, palace.—*n.m.* courtier.
palacio, *n.m.* palace; mansion.
palacra, palacrana, *n.f.* (gold) nugget.
paladar, *n.m.* palate.
paladear, *v.t.*, *v.r.* taste, relish.
paladeo, *n.m.* tasting, relishing.
paladino, -na, *a.* public.—*n.m.* paladin.
palafrén, *n.m.* palfrey.
palanca, *n.f.* lever, crowbar; **— de mayúsculas,** shift-key (*of typewriter*).
palancana, palangana, *n.f.* (wash-)basin.
palanqueta, *n.f.* small lever; dumb-bell.
palastro, *n.m.* sheet-iron.
palatal, *a.*, *n.f.* palatal.
palco, *n.m.* (*theat.*) box.

palenque, *n.m.* palisade; enclosure.
palero, *n.m.* shoveller; (*mil.*) pioneer.
Palestina, *n.f.* Palestine.
palestino, -na, *a.* Palestinian.
paleta (1), *n.f.* fire shovel; paddle (*of a propeller etc.*); (*S.A.*) lollipop; *de* —, opportunely.
paleto, -ta (2), *n.m.f.* (*fam.*) bumpkin, yokel.
paliar, *v.t.* palliate.
paliativo, -va, *a.* palliative.
palidecer [9], *v.i.* turn pale.
palidez, *n.f.* pallor.
pálido, -da, *a.* pallid.
palillo, *n.m.* toothpick; drumstick; cocktail-stick; bobbin.—*pl.* chopsticks; castanets; trifles.
palinodia, *n.f.* recantation, palinode.
palio, *n.m.* (*eccl., hist.*) canopy; cloak.
palique, *n.m.* chit-chat.
paliza, *n.f.* beating, drubbing.
palizada, *n.f.* stockade.
palma, *n.f.* palm (*hand, tree*).—*pl.* clapping.
palmada, *n.f.* slap; clap.
palmario, -ria, *a.* obvious.
palmatoria, *n.f.* small candlestick.
palmeado, -da, *a.* web-footed.
palmera, *n.m.* palm-tree.
palmo, *n.m.* palm, span.
palo, *n.m.* stick; wood; hook (*of a letter*); (*naut.*) mast.—*pl.* beating, drubbing.
paloma, *n.f.* pigeon, dove.
palomar, *n.m.* dovecote.
palomilla, *n.f.* young pigeon; (*mech.*) journal bearing; wall bracket.
palomo, *n.m.* cock pigeon.
palor, *n.m.* pallor.
palpable, *a.* palpable.
palpar, *v.t.* feel.—*v.i.* grope.
pálpebra, *n.f.* eyelid.
palpitación, *n.f.* palpitation.
palpitante, *a.* palpitating.
palpitar, *v.i.* throb, palpitate.
palúdico, -ca, *a.* marshy; malarial.
paludismo, *n.m.* (*med.*) malaria.
palurdo, *n.m.* rustic, boor.
palustre, *a.* marshy.—*n.m.* trowel.
pallete, *n.m.* (*naut.*) fender.
pampa, *n.f.* (*S.A.*) wide plain, pampas.
pampanilla, *n.f.* loin-cloth.
pámpano, *n.m.* vine-tendril.
pampeano, -na, *a.* (*S.A.*) rel. to the pampas.
pampero, -ra, *n.m.f.* (*S.A.*) dweller on the pampas.
pamplemusa, *n.f.* (*S.A.*) grapefruit (*tree, fruit*).
pamplina, *n.f.* chickweed.—*pl.* (*interj.*) nonsense! fiddlesticks!
pampringada, *n.f.* bread and drippings; (*fam.*) nonsense, frivolity.
pan, *n.m.* bread; loaf; cake (*of soap etc.*); piecrust.
pana, *n.f.* velveteen, corduroy; (*S.A.*) breakdown.
panadería, *n.f.* bakery; baker's shop.
panadero, -ra, *n.m.f.* baker.
panadizo, *n.m.* whitlow.
panado, -da, *a.* covered with bread-crumbs, pané.
panal, *n.m.* honeycomb.
Panamá, *n.m.* Panama.
panameño, -ña, *a.* Panamanian.
panamericano, -na, *a.* Pan-American.

panarra, *n.m.,* (*fam.*) blockhead.
pancada, *n.f.* bulk sale.
pancarta, *n.f.* (*S.A.*) placard.
Pancho, *n.m.* (*S.A.*) Frank; **pancho,** *n.m.* paunch.
panda, *n.f.,* (*zool.*) panda.
pandear, *v.i., v.r.* warp.
pandectas, *n.f.pl.* (*com.*) index-book.
pandeo, *n.m.* warping.
pandereta, *n.f.* tambourine.
pandero, *n.m.* tambourine; paper-kite.
pandilla, *n.f.* party, gang.
pando, -da, *a.* bulging; deliberate.
panecillo, *n.m.* roll.
panera, *n.f.* granary; bread-basket.
panfleto, *n.m.* (*S.A.*) pamphlet.
paniaguado, *n.m.* (*fam.*) protégé.
pánico, -ca, *a.* panicky.—*n.m.* panic.
panificación, *n.f.* bread-making.
panique, *n.m.* (*zool.*) flying-fox.
panizo, *n.m.* panic-grass; foxtail millet.
panocha, *n.f.* ear of corn.
pantalón, *n.m.* (*esp. pl.* **-lones**) trousers.
pantalla, *n.f.* screen (*film, T.V.*); lampshade.
pantano, *n.m.* marsh; reservoir; dam.
pantanoso, -sa, *a.* marshy.
panteísmo, *n.m.* pantheism.
pantera, *n.f.* (*zool.*) panther.
pantoque, *n.m.* (*naut.*) bilge.
pantorrilla, *n.f.* (*anat.*) calf.
pantuflo, -la, *n.m.f.* slipper.
panza, *n.f.* paunch.
panzudo, -da, *a.* paunchy.
pañal, *n.m.* napkin, (*U.S.*) diaper; shirt-tail.
pañería, *n.f.* draper's shop, (*U.S.*) dry-goods store.
pañero, *n.m.* draper, (*U.S.*) clothier.
paño, *n.m.* cloth; *al* —, (*theat.*) off-stage.
pañoso, -sa, *a.* ragged.
pañuelo, *n.m.* handkerchief; headscarf.
papa (1), *n.m.* pope.
papa (2), *n.f.* (*esp. S.A.*) potato; (*fam.*) food; fib.—*pl.* gruel, baby-food.
papá, *n.m.* papa, daddy.
papada, *n.f.* double chin, dewlap.
papado, *n.m.* papacy.
papafigo, *n.m.* (*orn.*) ortolan.
papagayo, *n.m.* parrot.
papal, *a.* papal.—*n.m.* (*S.A.*) potato patch.
papamoscas, *n.m. inv.* (*orn.*) fly-catcher; ninny.
papar, *v.t.* gulp down; gape.
páparo, *n.m.* gawk, churl.
paparrucha, *n.f.,* (*fam.*) hoax.
papaya, *n.f.* papaw (*fruit*).
papayo, *n.m.* papaw (*tree*).
papel (1), *n.m.* paper; piece of paper.
papel (2), *n.m.* rôle, character.
papelería, *n.f.* stationery; stationer's shop.
papelero, -ra, *a.* boastful; rel. to paper.—*n.m.* stationer.
papeleta, *n.f.* slip (*of paper*), file card.
papelón, -lona, *a.* (*fam.*) bluffing.
papera, *n.f.* mumps.
papilla, *n.f.* pap; guile.
papillote, *n.m.* curl-paper.
papiro, *n.m.* papyrus.
papo, *n.m.* dewlap.
paquebote, *n.m.* packet (*boat*).
paquete, *n.m.* parcel, packet; (*S.A.*) dandy.
paquetería, *n.f.* retail trade.
el Paquistán, *n.m.* Pakistan.

par, *a.* equal; even.—*n.m.* pair, couple; peer; even number; **al —,** jointly; **de — en —,** wide open; **sin —,** peerless; **pares o nones,** odds or evens.—*n.f.* par; **a la —,** jointly; **at par.**

para, *prep.* to, for; towards; by (*a time*); in order to; **— con,** towards; **— que,** in order that; **¿ — qué?** for what reason?

parabién, *n.m.* congratulations.

parábola, *n.f.* parable; parabola.

parabrisas, *n.m. inv.* windscreen, (*U.S.*) windshield.

paracaídas, *n.m. inv.* parachute.

paracaidista, *n.m.f.* parachutist.

paracleto, paráclito, *n.m.* Paraclete.

parachoques, *n.m. inv.* bumper.

parada, *n.f.* halt, stop; (*mil.*) parade; (*mus.*) pause.

paradero, *n.m.* whereabouts.

paradigma, *n.m.* paradigm.

parado, -da, *a.* stopped; idle; listless.

paradoja, *n.f.* paradox.

paradójico, -ca, paradojo, -ja, *a.* paradoxical.

parador, *n.m.* inn, hostelry.

parafina, *n.f.* paraffin (*wax*).

parafrasear, *v.t.* paraphrase.

paráfrasis, *n.f.* paraphrase.

paraguas, *n.m. inv.* umbrella.

paraguayano, -na, paraguayo, -ya, *a. n.m.f.* Paraguayan.

paraíso, *n.m.* paradise.

paraje, *n.m.* place; condition.

paralelismo, *n.m.* parallelism.

paralelo, -la, *a., n.m.* parallel.

parálisis, *n.f. inv.* paralysis.

paralítico, -ca, *a.* paralytic.

paralizar [C], *v.t.* paralyze.

paramento, *n.m.* embellishment.

páramo, *n.m.* bleak wilderness.

parangón, *n.m.* paragon; comparison.

parangonar, *v.t.* compare.

paraninfo (1), *n.m.* assembly hall.

paraninfo (2), *n.m.* best man, groomsman.

parapeto, *n.m.* parapet.

parar, *v.t.* stop; stake; prepare; parry.—*v.i.* stop; put up (**en,** at).—*v.r.* stop.

pararrayo, *n.m.,* **pararrayos,** *n.m. inv.* lightning conductor.

parasitario, -ria, *a.* parasitic.

parásito, -ta, *a.* parasitic.—*n.m.* parasite; (*rad. esp. pl.*) atmospherics.

parasol, *n.m.* sunshade, parasol.

paraviento, *n.m.* shield, screen.

parcamente, *adv.* parsimoniously.

parcela, *n.f.* plot (*of land*); particle.

parcelar, *v.t.* parcel out.

parcial, *a.* partial; partisan.

parco, -ca, *a.* frugal.

parche, *n.m.* plaster, sticking plaster; patch.

¡pardiez! *interj.* by Jove!

pardillo, *n.m.* linnet.

pardo, -da, *a.* dark, drab; brown.—*n.m.f.* (*C.A.*) mulatto.

parear, *v.t.* match, pair.

parecer (1) [9], *v.i.* appear.—*v.r.* look alike.

parecer (2), *n.m.* opinion.

parecido, -da, *a.* like, similar.—*n.m.* resemblance.

pared, *n.f.* wall.

paredón, *n.m.* thick wall; (*fig.*) firing squad.

pareja, *n.f.* pair, match, couple.

parejo, -ja, *a.* equal, similar.

parentela, *n.f.* parentage; kinsfolk.

parentesco, *n.m.* relationship.

paréntesis, *n.m. inv.* parenthesis; bracket; **entre —,** by the way.

parezco [PARECER].

paridad, *n.f.* parity.

pariente, -ta, *n.m.f.* relative, relation.

parihuela, *n.f.* barrow; stretcher.

parir, *v.t., v.i.* bring forth, give birth (to).

parisiense, *a., n.m.f.* Parisian.

parlamentario, -ria, *a.* parliamentary.—*n.m.f.* member of parliament.

parlamento, *n.m.* parliament; parley; (*theat.*) speech.

parlanchín, -china, *a.* chattering.—*n.m.f.* chatterbox.

parlante, *a.* talking.

parlatorio, *n.m.* parlour; chat.

paro, *n.m.* stoppage, lockout; unemployment; (*orn.*) tit(mouse).

parodia, *n.f.* parody.

paroxismo, *n.m.* paroxysm.

parpadear, *v.i.* blink; wink.

párpado, *n.m.* eyelid.

parque, *n.m.* park.

parquedad, *n.f.* frugality; parsimony.

parra, *n.f.* (trained) vine; honey jar.

párrafo, *n.m.* paragraph; **echar un —,** (*fam.*) have a natter or chat.

parral, *n.m.* vine arbour.

parranda, *n.f.* revel.

parricida, *n.m.f.* parricide (*person*).

parricidio, *n.m.* parricide (*act*).

parrilla, *n.f.* (*cul.*) grill.

párroco, *n.m.* parish priest.

parroquia, *n.f.* parish; parish church; regular customers, clientele.

parroquial, *a.* parochial.

parroquiano, -na, *a.* parochial.—*n.m.f.* parishioner; regular customer.

parte, *n.f.* part; share; party; direction; (*mus.*) part; (*jur.*) party; **a — de, apart from; de — de,** on behalf of.—*pl.* parts, talent.

partera, *n.f.* midwife.

partición, *n.f.* partition.

participación, *n.f.* participation; notification.

participante, *a.* notifying; participant.

participar, *v.t.* inform.—*v.i.* participate (**en,** in); partake (**de,** of).

partícipe, *a., n.m.f.* participant.

participio, *n.m.* participle.

partícula, *n.f.* particle.

particular, *a.* private; particular; peculiar.—*n.m.* individual; particular subject.

partida, *n.f.* departure; entry (*in accounts*); party; game; certificate.

partidario, -ria, *a., n.m.f.* partisan.

partido, *p.p.* munificent.—*n.m.* game; match; (*pol.*) party; advantage; protection; district; **tomar —,** resolve.

partir, *v.t.* divide; distribute; break; sever, split open.—*v.i.* depart.

parto, *n.m.* childbirth; newborn child.

parturiente, parturienta, *a.* parturient, in childbirth.

parvo, -va, *a.* little, small.

párvulo, -la, *a.* tiny; lowly.—*n.m.f.* child.

pasa, *n.f.* raisin.

pasada, *n.f.* passage; game, trick.

pasadero, -ra, *a.* passable.—*n.f.* stepping-stone; colander.

pasadizo, *n.m.* passage; catwalk.
pasado, -da, *a.* past; out-of-date.—*n.m.* past.
—*pl.* ancestors.
pasador, -ra, *a.* smuggling.—*n.m.f.*
smuggler.—*n.m.* (door) bolt; pin.
pasaje, *n.m.* passage.
pasajero, -ra, *a.* passing, fleeting; frequented.
—*n.m.f.* passenger.
pasamanería, *n.f.* passementerie, lacemaking.
pasamano, *n.m.* lace; (*naut.*) gangway.
pasante, *n.m.* student-teacher; assistant.
pasapasa, *n.m.* legerdemain, hocus-pocus.
pasaporte, *n.m.* passport.
pasar, *v.t.* pass, cross; transfer.—*v.i.* pass,
happen; manage, get along; — *a,* go on
to; — *de,* exceed; — *por,* pass through;
pass as; — *sin,* do without.—*v.r.* pass; take
an examination.
pasatiempo, *n.m.* pastime.
pascua, *n.f.* Passover; — *de Resurrección*
or *florida,* Easter; — *de Navidad,* Christmas; — *del Espíritu Santo,* Whitsun.
pascual, *a.* paschal.
pase, *n.m.* pass; feint.
pasear, *v.t.* walk, promenade.—*v.i.,* *v.r.*
walk, take a stroll; *pasearse en bicicleta*
etc., go cycling *etc.*
paseo, *n.m.* walk; stroll, drive; avenue.
pasillo, *n.m.* passage; short step.
pasión, *n.f.* passion.
pasito, *n.m.* short step.—*adv.* gently.
pasividad, *n.f.* passivity.
pasivo, -va, *a.* passive.—*n.m.* (*gram.*) passive;
(*com.*) debit side.
pasmar, *v.t.* chill; stun.—*v.i., v.r.* be astounded.
pasmo, *n.m.* amazement; spasm; tetanus.
pasmoso, -sa, *a.* astounding.
paso, -sa, *a.* dried (*fruit*).—*n.m.* pace, step;
gait; passage; footprint; pitch (*of screw*);
(*theat.*) sketch.—*adv.* gently.
pasquinar, *v.t.* lampoon.
pasta, *n.f.* paste, dough, batter; pulp; pasteboard; pasta.
pastar, *v.t., v.i.* pasture.
pastel, *n.m.* pie; pastel; plot.
pastelería, *n.f.* pastry shop.
pasterizar [C], *v.t.* pasteurize.
pastinaca, *n.f.* (*ichth.*) sting-ray; (*bot.*) parsnip.
pasto, *n.m.* pasture; food.
pastor, *n.m.* shepherd; pastor.
pastora, *n.f.* shepherdess.
pastoso, -sa, *a.* doughy; mellow (*voice*).
pastura, *n.f.* pasture.
pata, *n.f.* paw, foot; (female) duck; *meter la*
—, put one's foot in it; *quedar pata(s),*
be a draw.
pataco, -ca, *a.* churlish.—*n.m.f.* churl.—*n.f.*
Jerusalem artichoke.
patada, *n.f.* kick.
patagón, -gona, *a., n.m.f.* Patagonian.
patán, -tana, *a.* churlish.—*n.m.f.* churl.
patarata, *n.f.* foolishness; affectation.
patata, *n.f.* potato; bulb, corm; *patatas*
fritas, potato chips *or* crisps; (*U.S.*) French
fries.
patear, *v.t.* trample on.—*v.i.* stamp; (*S.A.*)
kick (*of guns*).
patentar, *v.t.* patent.
patente, *a.* patent, evident.—*n.f.* privilege,
patent.
patentizar [C], *v.t.* render evident.

paternidad, *n.f.* paternity.
paterno, -na, *a.* paternal.
pateta, *n.f.* (*fam.*) lame person; (*fam.*) Old
Nick.
patético, -ca, *a.* pathetic.
patiabierto, -ta, *a.* bow-legged.
patibulario, -ria, *a.* rel. to the scaffold;
horrifying.
patíbulo, *n.m.* scaffold, gallows.
patihendido, -da, *a.* cloven-footed.
patilla, *n.f.* small foot; (*esp. pl.*) (side-)
whisker; tenon; (*S.A.*) water-melon.
patín, *n.m.* skate (*ice, roller*); runner, skid.
patinadero, *n.m.* skating-rink.
patinaje, *n.m.* skating; skidding.
patinar, *v.i.* skate; skid.
patinazo, *n.m.* skid.
patinete, *n.m.* (child's) scooter.
patio, *n.m.* courtyard, patio; campus; (*theat.*)
stalls.
patizambo, -ba, *a.* knock-kneed.
pato, *n.m.* drake, (male) duck.
patochada, *n.f.* (*fam.*) blunder.
patojo, -ja, *a.* waddling.
patología, *n.f.* pathology.
patólogo, *n.m.* pathologist.
patraña, *n.f.* old wives' tale; hoax.
patria, *n.f.* homeland, motherland.
patriarca, *n.m.* patriarch.
patricio, -cia, *a.* patrician; (*S.A.*) American-
born.
patrimonio, *n.m.* patrimony.
patrio, -ria, *a.* native, national.
patriota, *n.m.f.* patriot.
patrocinar, *v.t.* favour; sponsor.
patrocinio, *n.m.* patronage.
patrón, -rona, *n.m.f.* patron; protector.—
n.m. landlord; boss; sample; pattern.—*n.f.*
patroness; landlady; mistress.
patronal, *a.* rel. to employers; patronal.
patronato, *n.m.* association of employers;
patronage.
patrono, *n.m.* patron; protector; employer.
patrulla, *n.f.* patrol.
patullar, *v.i.* tramp about.
paulatino, -na, *a.* gradual.
paupérrimo, -ma, *a.* (*sup. of* POBRE) very
poor.
pausa, *n.f.* pause; (*mus.*) rest.
pausado, -da, *a.* slow; deliberate.
pausar, *v.i.* pause; hesitate.
pauta, *n.f.* guide line; model.
pava, *n.f.* turkey hen; *pelar la* —, court.
pavesa, *n.f.* ember.
pavimentar, *v.t.* pave.
pavimento, *n.m.* pavement.
pavo, *n.m.* turkey; — *real,* peacock.
pavón, *n.m.* peacock.
pavonear, *v.i.* swagger.
pavor, *n.m.* terror.
pavoroso, -sa, *a.* fearful.
pavura, *n.f.* dread.
payaso, *n.m.* clown.
payés, -yesa, *n.m.f.* Catalan peasant.
payo, paya, *n.m.f.* churl.
payuelas, *n.f.pl.* chicken-pox.
paz, *n.f.* (*pl.* paces) peace; *en* —, (*fam.*)
quits.
pazguato, -ta, *n.m.f.* dolt.
pe, *n.f.* name of letter P; *de* — *a pa,* all through.
pea, *n.f.* drunken binge.
peaje, *n.m.* toll.

peana, *n.f.* pedestal.
peatón, *n.m.* pedestrian.
pebete, *n.m.* joss-stick; stench; (*S.A.*) lad.
peca, *n.f.* freckle.
pecado, *n.m.* sin.
pecador, -ra, *a.* sinning.—*n.m.f.* **sinner.**
pecaminoso, -sa, *a.* sinful.
pecar [A], *v.i.* sin.
pecari, *n.m.* (*pl.* **-íes**) peccary.
pecera, *n.f.* goldfish bowl.
pecezuela, *n.f.* small piece.
pecezuelo, *n.m.* small fish.
pecio, *n.m.* flotsam.
pecoso, -sa, *a.* freckled.
peculiar, *a.* peculiar.
pechar, *v.t.* pay as a tax.
pechblenda, *n.f.* pitchblende.
pechero, -ra, *a.* taxable.—*n.m.f.* commoner.
 —*n.m.* bib.—*n.f.* shirt front; stomacher.
pecho, *n.m.* breast, chest; tax.
pechuga, *n.f.* breast (*of a fowl*).
pedagogía, *n.f.* pedagogy, education.
pedal, *n.m.* pedal.
pedazo, *n.m.* piece.
pedernal, *n.m.* flint.
pedestal, *n.m.* pedestal.
pedestre, *a.* pedestrian.
pediatra, *n.m.* pediatrician.
pedido, *n.m.* request; (*com.*) order.
pedigüeño, -ña, *a.* importunate.
pedimento, *n.m.* petition.
pedir [8], *v.t.* ask for; beg.
pedregal, *n.m.* stony patch.
pedregoso, -sa, *a.* stony.
pedrera, *n.f.* quarry.
pedrería, *n.f.* jewelry.
pedriscal, *n.m.* stony patch.
pedrisco, *n.m.* hailstorm; shower of stones.
pega, *n.f.* sticking; (*fam.*) trick; snag; (*orn.*)
 magpie; **de —,** fake.
pegadizo, -za, *a.* sticky; sponging; imitation;
 contagious (*disease*).
pegajoso, -sa, *a.* sticky; catching (*disease*);
 (*fam.*) mushy.
pegar [B], *v.t.* stick; fasten; transmit (*a
 disease*); strike.—*v.i.* stick; cling; match;
 knock; stumble.—*v.r.* fight; stick; be
 catching.
pegote, *n.m.* sticking plaster; (*fig.*) sore
 thumb.
peinado, *n.m.* hair-style.
peinador, -ra, *n.m.f.* hairdresser.—*n.m.*
 dressing-gown.
peinar, *v.t.* comb.—*v.r.* comb one's hair.
peine, *n.m.* comb; instep.
peineta, *n.f.* back-comb.
peladilla, *n.f.* sugared almond; small pebble.
pelado, -da, *a.* bare; barren.
peladura, *n.f.* peeling.
pelapatatas, *n.m.inv.* potato-peeler *or* scraper.
pelar, *v.t.* pluck; peel; cut (*hair*); fleece;
 pelárselas por, crave.
peldaño, *n.m.* step, tread (*of stairs*).
pelea, *n.f.* fight, struggle.
pelear, *v.i.* fight, struggle.
peletería, *n.f.* furrier's shop; fur trade.
peliagudo, -da, *a.* downy; (*fam.*) tricky.
pelicano, -na, *a.* grey-haired.
pelícano, *n.m.* pelican.
pelicorto, -ta, *a.* short-haired.
película, *n.f.* film.

peliculero, -ra, *a.* rel. to films.—*n.m.* film
 actor; script writer.—*n.f.* film actress;
 script writer.
peligro, *n.m.* danger, risk.
peligroso, -sa, *a.* dangerous, perilous.
pelillo, *n.m.* trifle; short hair.
pelirrubio, -bia, *a.* fair-haired.
pelma, *n.m.*, **pelmazo,** *n.m.* (*fam.*) bore.
pelo, *n.m.* hair; down; nap; grain; **al —,**
 (*fam.*) perfectly; **en —,** naked; **tomar el —
 a,** make fun of.
pelón, -lona, *a.* bald; (*fam.*) broke.
peloso, -sa, *a.* hairy.
pelota, *n.f.* ball; ball game; **en —,** naked;
 penniless.
pelotari, *n.m.* pelota player.
pelotear, *v.t.* audit.—*v.i.* knock a ball around;
 wrangle.
pelotilla, *n.f.* pellet.
pelotón, *n.m.* large ball; (*mil.*) section, squad.
peltre, *n.m.* pewter.
peluca, *n.f.* wig.
peluche, *n.m.* plush.
peludo, -da, *a.* hairy.
peluquería, *n.f.* hairdresser's shop.
peluquero, -ra, *n.m.f.* hairdresser; wig-
 maker.
pelusa, *n.f.* down.
pella, *n.f.* pellet; puff-pastry; (*fam.*) unpaid
 loan.
pelleja, *n.f.* hide, skin.
pellejo, *n.m.* skin; pelt.
pellizcar [A], *v.t.* pinch, nip.
pellizco, *n.m.* pinch, nip.
pena, *n.f.* punishment; penalty; grief; **so —
 de,** on pain of.
penable, *a.* punishable.
penachera, *n.f.*, **penacho,** *n.m.* crest;
 panache.
penal, *a.* penal.—*n.m.* penitentiary.
penalidad, *n.f.* suffering; penalty.
penar, *v.t.* chastize.—*v.i.* suffer, be tor-
 mented.—*v.r.* grieve.
penco, *n.m.*, nag.
pendencia, *n.f.* dispute; quarrel, fight.
pender, *v.i.* hang; depend.
pendiente, *a.* hanging; pending.—*n.m.*
 pendant; ear-ring; watch-chain.—*n.f.* slope;
 curve (*of graph*).
péndola, *n.f.* pendulum; quill.
pendón, *n.m.* banner, pennon; (*bot.*) shoot.
péndulo, -la, *a.* pendent.—*n.m.* (*mech.*)
 pendulum.
penicilina, *n.f.* penicillin.
penetración, *n.f.* penetration; insight.
penetrar, *v.t.* penetrate.
península, *n.f.* peninsula.
peninsular, *a.*, *n.m.f.* peninsular.
penique, *n.m.* penny.
penitencia, *n.f.* penitence, penance.
penitente, *a.*, *n.m.f.* penitent.
penoso, -sa, *a.* difficult; suffering; (*S.A.*) shy.
pensamiento, *n.m.* thought; (*bot.*) pansy.
pensar [1], *v.t.* think; think of; feed (*animals*).
 —*v.i.* think; **— de,** think of (*opinion*); **— en,**
 think of (*direct one's thoughts*).
pensativo, -va, *a.* pensive, thoughtful.
penseque, *n.m.* oversight.
pensión, *n.f.* pension; allowance; boarding
 house; encumbrance.
pensionar, *v.t.* pension.
pensionista, *n.m.f.* boarder.

pentágono, -na, *a.* pentagonal.—*n.m.* pentagon.
pentagrama, *n.m.* pentagram; (*mus.*) stave.
Pentecostés, *n.m.* Whitsun, Pentecost.
penúltimo, -ma, *a.* penultimate.
peña, *n.f.* boulder; cliff; club.
peñasco, *n.m.* crag; pinnacle.
peñón, *n.m.* rock, crag; *Peñón de Gibraltar,* Rock of Gibraltar.
peón, *n.m.* pedestrian; infantryman; pawn; man (*in checkers*); (*S.A.*) farm-hand; labourer.
peonia, *n.f.* (*bot.*) peony.
peonza, *n.f.* (whip-)top.
peor, *a., adv.* worse; worst.
Pepe, *n.m.* Joe.
pepinillo, *n.m.* gherkin.
pepino, *n.m.* cucumber.
pepita, *n.f.* pip.
pepitoria, *n.f.* giblet fricassee; hotchpotch.
pequeñez, *n.f.* (*pl.* **-ñeces**) smallness; trifle.
pequeño, -ña, *a.* small, little, tiny.
pequeñuelo, -la, *a.* tiny.—*n.m.f.* baby, tot.
pera, *n.f.* pear; goatee (*beard*).
peral, *n.m.* pear tree.
perca, *n.f.* (*ichth.*) perch.
percance, *n.m.* misfortune; perquisite.
percatar, *v.i., v.r.* be wary (*de,* of).
percebe, *n.m.* goose barnacle.
percepción, *n.f.* perception; (tax-)collection.
perceptor, *n.m.* tax-collector.
percibir, *v.t.* perceive; collect; receive (*pay*).
percibo, *n.m.* collection.
percudir, *v.t., v.r.* tarnish.
percusión, *n.f.* percussion.
percusor, *n.m.* firing-pin.
percutir, *v.t.* percuss.
percutor, *n.m.* firing-pin.
percha, *n.f.* perch, pole; clothes-hanger.
perchero, *n.m.* clothes-rack.
perder [2], *v.t.* lose; waste; miss (*a train*).—*v.i.* lose.—*v.r.* lose one's way; get spoiled.
pérdida, *n.f.* loss; waste.
perdigar [B], *v.t.* (*cul.*) brown.
perdigón, *n.m.* young partridge; shot, pellets; (*fam.*) profligate.
perdiguero, *n.m.* pointer, setter.
perdiz, *n.f.* (*pl.* **-ices**) partridge.
perdón, *n.m.* pardon, forgiveness.
perdonable, *a.* pardonable.
perdonar, *v.t.* pardon.
perdulario, -ria, *a.* careless; vicious.
perdurable, *a.* everlasting.
perdurar, *v.i.* last (*a long time*).
perecedero, -ra, *a.* perishable; mortal.
perecer [9], *v.i.* perish; be in want.—*v.r.* pine (*por,* for, *de,* of).
peregrinación, *n.f.* pilgrimage.
peregrino, -na, *a.* wandering; peregrine; strange.—*n.m.f.* pilgrim.
perejil, *n.m.* parsley; (*fam.*) frippery.
perenal, *a.* perennial.
perendengue, *n.m.* trinket; ear-ring.
perengano, -na, *n.m.f.* so-and-so (*after* FULANO).
perenne, *a.* perennial.
pereza, *n.f.* laziness.
perezoso, -sa, *a.* lazy.
perfección, *n.f.* perfection.
perfeccionar, *v.t.* perfect, improve.
perfecto, -ta, *a.* perfect.—*n.m.* (*gram.*) perfect.

perfil, *n.m.* profile, outline; (cross-) section.
perfilar, *v.t.* profile.—*v.r.* stand sideways.
perforar, *v.t.* perforate, drill, punch.
perfume, *n.m.* scent, perfume.
pergamino, *n.m.* parchment.
pérgola, *n.f.* roof garden, arbour.
pericia, *n.f.* skill; practical experience.
pericial, *a.* expert.
perico, *n.m.* parakeet; periwig; mizzen top-gallant; chamber-pot.
periferia, *n.f.* periphery.
perifollo, *n.m.* (*bot.*) chervil; (*fam.*) finery.
perífrasis, *n.f. inv.* periphrasis.
perilla, *n.f.* small pear; pommel, knob.
perillán, -llana, *a.* knavish.—*n.m.f.* rascal.
perímetro, *n.m.* perimeter.
periódico, -ca, *a.* periodical.—*n.m.* newspaper.
periodista, *n.m.f.* journalist.
período, *n.m.* period.
peripuesto, -ta, *a.* (*fam.*) very spruce.
periquete, *n.m.* jiffy, trice.
periscopio, *n.m.* periscope.
peritaje, *n.m.* expert's fee; expert work.
perito, -ta, *a.* skilled, expert.—*n.m.f.* expert, technician.
perjudicar [A], *v.t.* harm, impair, prejudice.
perjudicial, *a.* harmful, prejudicial.
perjuicio, *n.m.* harm, injury; prejudice.
perjurar, *v.i., v.r.* commit perjury.
perjuro, -ra, *a.* perjured.—*n.m.f.* perjuror.—*n.m.* perjury.
perla, *n.f.* pearl.
perlesía, *n.f.* palsy.
permanecer [9], *v.i.* stay.
permanencia, *n.f.* permanence; stay; (*esp. pl. educ.*) prep., study hours.
permanente, *a.* permanent.—*n.f.* permanent wave.
permisión, *n.f.* permission; leave.
permiso, *n.m.* permission; permit, licence.
permitir, *v.t.* permit, allow.
pernada, *n.f.* kick.
pernear, *v.i.* kick.
pernera, *n.f.* trouser-leg.
pernicioso, -sa, *a.* pernicious.
pernil, *n.m.* leg (*of trousers, pork*).
pernio, *n.m.* hinge.
pernituerto, -ta, *a.* crooked-legged.
perno, *n.m.* bolt, spike.
pernoctar, *v.i.* pass the night.
pero, *conj.* but.
perogrullada, *n.f.* truism, platitude.
peróxido, *n.m.* peroxide.
perpendicular, *a., n.f.* perpendicular.
perpendículo, *n.m.* plumb-bob; pendulum.
perpetuar, *v.t.* perpetuate.
perpetuo, -tua, *a.* perpetual, for life.—*n.f.* everlasting flower.
perplejo, -ja, *a.* perplexed; anxious.
perra [PERRO].
perrera, *n.f.* kennel, (*U.S.*) doghouse.
perrillo, -lla, *n.m.f.* puppy.—*n.m.* trigger.
perro, -rra, *a.* mean, stingy.—*n.m.* dog; (*mech.*) pawl.—*n.f.* bitch; drunkenness; small coin.
perruno, -na, *a.* canine, dog-like.
persa, *a., n.m.f.* Persian.
persecución, *n.f.* persecution; pursuit.
perseguir [8G], *v.t.* persecute; pursue.
perseverancia, *n.f.* perseverance.

persiano, -na, *a., n.m.f.* Persian.—*n.f.* Venetian blind.
persignar, *v.r.* cross oneself.
persistencia, *n.f.* persistency.
persistente, *a.* persistent.
persistir, *v.i.* persist.
persona, *n.f.* person.
personaje, *n.m.* personage; (*theat.*) character.
personal, *a.* personal.—*n.m.* personnel, staff.
personalidad, *n.f.* personality.
personificar [A], *v.t.* personify.
perspectivo, -va, *a.* perspective.—*n.f.* prospect; perspective.
perspicacia, *n.f.* perspicacity.
perspicaz, *a.* (*pl.* -aces) perspicacious.
perspiración, *n.f.* perspiration.
perspirar, *v.i.* perspire.
persuadir, *v.t.* persuade (*a*, to).
persuasible, *a.* credible.
persuasión, *n.f.* persuasion.
persuasivo, -va, *a.* persuasive.
pertenecer [9], *v.i.* belong; pertain.
perteneciente, *a.* pertaining.
pertenencia, *n.f.* property; appurtenance.
pértiga, *n.f.* pole, rod; *salto con —*, pole-vault.
pertinaz, *a.* (*pl.* -aces) pertinacious.
pertinencia, *n.f.* relevance.
pertrechar, *v.t.* provide, equip.
pertrechos, *n.m.pl.* supplies; tools.
perturbar, *v.t.* perturb; disturb.
el Perú, *n.m.* Peru.
peruano, -na, peruviano, -na, *a., n.m.f.* Peruvian.
perversión, *n.f.* perversion.
perverso, -sa, *a.* perverse; profligate.—*n.m.f.* profligate.
pervertido, -da, *a.* perverted.—*n.m.f.* (*med.*) pervert.
pervertir [6], *v.t.* pervert.
pesa, *n.f.* weight.
pesadez, *n.f.* heaviness, weight; tiresomeness.
pesadilla, *n.f.* nightmare.
pesado, -da, *a.* heavy; tiresome, dull.
pesadumbre, *n.f.* grief; weight.
pésame, *n.m.* condolence.
pesantez, *n.f.* weight, gravity.
pesar (1), *n.m.* sorrow.
pesar (2), *v.t.* weigh;—*v.i.* weigh; be important.
pesca, *n.f.* fishing; catch.
pescada, *n.f.* hake.
pescado, *n.m.* fish.
pescador, -ra, *a.* fishing.—*n.m.* fisherman, angler.
pescante, *n.m.* jib, boom; (*theat.*) trap-door.
pescar [A], *v.t.* fish, catch.
pescuezo, *n.m.* neck; haughtiness.
pesebre, *n.m.* manger; crib; (*S.A.*) crèche.
peseta, *n.f.* peseta.
pesimismo, *n.m.* pessimism.
pésimo, -ma, *a.* very bad, abominable.
peso, *n.m.* weight; gravity; peso (*coin*).
pespunte, *n.m.* backstitch.
pesquero, -ra, *a.* fishing (*industry etc.*).—*n.m.* fishing boat.—*n.f.* fishery.
pesquisa, *n.f.* inquiry.—*n.m.* (*S.A. fam.*) cop.
pesquisar, *v.t.* investigate.
pestaña, *n.f.* eyelash; flange.
pestañear, *v.i.* wink, blink.
pestañeo, *n.m.* blinking.
peste, *n.f.* plague; stench; (*fam.*) abundance.

pestillo, *n.m.* bolt; latch.
pesuña [PEZUÑA].
petaca, *n.f.* tobacco-pouch; leather trunk.
pétalo, *n.m.* petal.
petardo, *n.m.* petard, bomb; firework; swindle.
petate, *n.m.* bedding roll; (*fam.*) baggage.
petición, *n.f.* petition.
petimetre, *n.m.* dandy.
peto, *n.m.* breastplate.
pétreo, -a, *a.* petreous, rocky.
petrificar [A], *v.t., v.r.* petrify.
petróleo, *n.m.* petroleum, crude oil.
petrolero, -ra, *a.* rel. to oil.—*n.m.* oil-dealer; oil tanker; incendiary.
petrología, *n.f.* petrology.
petulancia, *n.f.* pertness.
petulante, *a.* pert, insolent.
peyorativo, -va, *a.* pejorative.
pez (1), *n.m.* (*pl.* peces) fish (*live*); — *espada*, swordfish.
pez (2), *n.f.* pitch.
pezón, *n.m.* teat, nipple.
pezpita, *n.f.*, pezpítalo, *n.m.* pipit.
pezuña, *n.f.* hoof.
pi, *n.f.* (*math.*) pi.
piadoso, -sa, *a.* pious; merciful.
piamontés, -tesa, *a., n.m.f.* Piedmontese.
pianista, *n.m.f.* pianist.
piano, *n.m.* (*mus.*) piano; — *de cola*, grand piano.
pianoforte, *n.m.* (*mus.*) pianoforte.
piar [L], *v.i.* chirp.
pica, *n.f.* pike; pica; (*S.A.*) pique.
picado, -da, *a.* perforated; cut (*tobacco*); choppy (*sea*); minced.—*n.m.* mincemeat; (*aer.*) nosedive.—*n.f.* peck; puncture.
picador, *n.m.* (*taur.*) picador.
picadura, *n.f.* bite, prick, sting; puncture; shredded tobacco; (dental) cavity.
picante, *a.* biting; piquant; highly-seasoned.
picaporte, *n.m.* latch; (*S.A.*) door-knocker.
picaposte, *n.m.* (*orn.*) woodpecker.
picar [A], *v.t.* prick; pierce; sting; mince; nibble; (*aer.*) dive.—*v.r.* go sour; get moth-eaten.
picaraza, *n.f.* magpie.
Picardía, *n.f.* Picardy; picardía, *n.f.* roguery.
picaresco, -ca, *a.* roguish.—*n.f.* den of thieves.
pícaro, -ra, *a.* roguish.—*n.m.f.* rogue.
picatoste, *n.m.* fried bread.
picazo, -za, *a.* piebald.—*n.m.* jab.—*n.f.* magpie.
pico, *n.m.* beak; spout; nib; (*orn.*) wood-pecker; pick; *las tres y —*, a little after three.
picoso, -sa, *a.* pock-marked.
picotada, *n.f.*, picotazo, *n.m.* peck.
picotear, *v.t.* peck.
pictórico, -ca, *a.* pictorial.
pichel, *n.m.* pewter tankard; pitcher.
pichón, *n.m.* young pigeon.
pie, *n.m.* foot.
piececillo, *n.m.* little foot.
piecezuela, *n.f.* little piece.
piedad, *n.f.* pity; piety.
piedra, *n.f.* stone.
piel, *n.f.* skin; hide; leather; — *de gallina*, goose-flesh.
piélago, *n.m.* (*lit.*) ocean.
pienso, *n.m.* feed(ing), fodder.

pierna, *n.f.* leg; shank; *a — suelta,* at ease.
pieza, *n.f.* piece; coin; (*mech.*) part; room.
pífano, *n.m.* fife; fifer.
pigmento, *n.m.* pigment.
pigmeo, -mea, *a.,* *n.m.f.* pygmy.
pijama, *n.m.* pyjamas, (*U.S.*) pajamas.
pila, *n.f.* basin; trough; font; (*elec.*) pile, battery; *nombre de —,* Christian name.
pilar, *n.m.* pillar; basin.
Pilatos, *n.m.* Pilate.
píldora, *n.f.* pill.
pileta, *n.f.* basin.
pilón (1), *n.m.* basin, trough; (pounding) mortar.
pilón (2), *n.m.* pylon.
pilongo, -ga, *a.* lean.
pilotaje, *n.m.* pile-work; pilotage.
pilotar, *v.t.* pilot, drive.
pilote, *n.m.* pile.
pilotear, *v.t.* pilot, drive.
piloto, *n.m.* pilot; navigator, mate.
pillar, *v.t.* pillage.
pillo, -lla, *a.* (*fam.*) roguish.—*n.m.f.* rogue.
pimentón, *n.m.* cayenne pepper; paprika.
pimienta, *n.m.* (black) pepper.
pimiento, *n.m.* capsicum, cayenne pepper.
pimpollo, *n.m.* sprout, sucker.
pinacoteca, *n.f.* picture gallery.
pináculo, *n.m.* pinnacle.
pinar, *n.m.* pine grove.
pincel, *n.m.* brush; beam.
pincelada, *n.f.* brush-stroke.
pinciano, -na, *a.,* *n.m.f.* native to Valladolid.
pincha, *n.f.* kitchen-maid.
pinchar, *v.t.* prick; puncture.
pinchazo, *n.m.* puncture; jab.
pincho, *n.m.* prick; thorn.
pingar, *v.i.* drip; jump.
pingo, *n.m.* rag.
pingüe, *a.* oily; rich, plentiful.
pingüino, *n.m.* penguin.
pinguosidad, *n.f.* fatness.
pinito, *n.m.* toddling step.
pino (1), **-na,** *a.* steep.
pino (2), *n.m.* pine (*tree*).
pinocha, *n.f.* pine needle.
pintado, -da, *a.* mottled; (*fam.*) tipsy.—*n.m.f.* guinea fowl.
pintar, *v.t.* paint; (*fam.*) show.
pintarraj(e)ar, *v.t.* daub.
pintiparado, -da, *a.* (*fam.*) perfectly like.
pintor, -ra, *n.m.f.* painter.
pintoresco, -ca, *a.* picturesque.
pintura, *n.f.* painting; paint.
pinza, *n.f.* clothes-peg, (*U.S.*) clothespin; (*esp. pl.*) pincers, tweezers.
pinzón, *n.m.* (*orn.*) chaffinch.
piña, *n.f.* pine-cone; pineapple.
piñón, *n.m.* pine kernel; (*mech.*) pinion.
pío (1), **pía** (1), *a.* pious; merciful.
pío (2), **pía** (2), *a.* pied.
pío (3), *n.m.* chirping.
piojo, *n.m.* louse.
pipa (1), *n.f.* (*tobacco*) pipe; (*wine*) cask; (*mus.*) pipe, reed.
pipa (2), *n.f.* (*orange etc.*) pip.
pipeta, *n.f.* pipette.
pipiar [L], *v.i.* chirp; peep.
pipote, *n.m.* keg.
pique, *n.m.* pique, resentment; (*S.A.*) spade (*at cards*); *a —,* steep; *echar a —,* sink (*of a ship*); *a — de,* on the point of.

piquete, *n.m.* picket.
piquituerto, *n.m.* (*orn.*) crossbill.
piragua, *n.f.* pirogue, canoe, kayak.
pirámide, *n.f.* pyramid.
pirata, *n.m.* pirate.
piratería, *n.f.* piracy.
pirenaico, -ca, pirineo, -nea, *a.* Pyrenean.
los Pirineos, *n.m.pl.* Pyrenees.
pirita, *n.f.* (*min.*) pyrites.
piropear, *v.t.* flatter; compliment.
piropo, *n.m.* compliment; flirtatious remark; garnet.
pisada, *n.f.* tread.
pisapapeles, *n.m. inv.* paperweight.
pisar, *v.t.* trample.
pisaverde, *n.m.* (*fam.*) fop.
piscina, *n.f.* swimming-pool; fishpond; piscina.
piscolabis, *n.m. inv.* (*fam.*) snack.
piso, *n.m.* tread; floor; storey; flat, apartment; *— bajo,* ground floor.
pisonadora, *n.f.* steam-roller, road-roller.
pisotear, *v.t.* trample.
pista, *n.f.* track; runway; trail.
pisto, *n.m.* vegetable stew.
pistola, *n.f.* pistol.
pistolera, *n.f.* holster.
pistolero, *n.m.* gunman; gun-operator.
pistón, *n.m.* piston.
pistonear, *v.i.* knock (*cylinder*).
pistonudo, -da, *a.* (*fam.*) smashing.
pitar, *v.i.* blow a whistle.
pitido, *n.m.* whistling.
pitillera, *n.f.* cigarette-case.
pitillo, *n.m.* cigarette.
pito, *n.m.* whistle; fife; car horn; *no vale un —,* it's not worth a straw.
pitón (1), *n.m.* python.
pitón (2), *n.m.* nozzle; sprout.
pitonisa, *n.f.* pythoness; sorceress.
pitorra, *n.f.* woodcock.
pituso, -sa, *a.* tiny, pretty, cute.
piular, *v.i.* chirp.
pizarra, *n.f.* slate; shale; blackboard.
pizca, *n.f.* (*fam.*) whit, jot.
placa, *n.f.* plaque, plate.
placer (1), *n.m.* pleasure.—*v.t.* [23] please.
placer (2), *n.m.* sandbank, reef.
plácido, -da, *a.* placid.
plaga (1), *n.f.* plague, scourge.
plaga (2), *n.f.* (compass) point.
plagar [B], *v.t.* plague, infest.
plagiar, *v.t.* plagiarize; (*S.A.*) kidnap.
plagio, *n.m.* plagiarism; (*S.A.*) kidnapping.
plan, *n.m.* plan; plane; (*fam.*) date (*appointment*); *en — grande,* on a large scale.
plancha, *n.f.* (flat) iron; sheet (*of metal*); grill-plate; (*fam.*) blunder; gangplank; *a la —,* (*cul.*) grilled.
planchar, *v.t.* iron; press.
planeador, *n.m.* (*aer.*) glider.
planear, *v.t.* plane (*wood*).—*v.i.* glide.
planeo, *n.m.* (*aer.*) gliding.
planeta, *n.m.* planet.
planicie, *n.f.* plain.
planificación, *n.f.* planning.
planificar [A], *v.t.* plan.
plano, -na, *a.* plane, smooth, level.—*n.m.* plan; plane; *de —,* plainly.—*n.f.* trowel; flat country; *plana mayor,* (*mil.*) staff.
planta, *n.f.* (*bot.*) plant; sole (*of foot*); plan; floor plan; storey; stance.

plantar, *v.t.* plant; establish; (*fam.*) jilt.—*v.r.* adopt a stance; stand firm.

planteamiento, *n.m.* planning; framing (*a question*).

plantear, *v.t.* plan; pose (*a question*).

plantilla, *n.f.* insole; template; staff.

plantío, *n.m.* plantation.

plañir [K], *v.t.* lament.—*v.i.* grieve.

plasmar, *v.t.* mould.

plasta, *n.f.* paste, soft mass.

plástico, **-ca,** *a.* plastic.—*n.m.* plastic (*material*).—*n.f.* modelling.

plata, *n.f.* silver; plate; (*S.A.*) money.

plataforma, *n.f.* platform.

platanero, *n.m.* banana boat.

plátano, *n.m.* banana; plantain; plane tree.

platea, *n.f.* (*theat.*) orchestra stalls.

platear, *v.t.* plate with silver.

platero, *n.m.* silversmith.

plática, *n.f.* talk; chat.

platicar [A], *v.t.* talk over.—*v.i.* chat.

platija, *n.f.* (*ichth.*) plaice.

platillo, *n.m.* plate; saucer; — **volante,** flying saucer.

platino, *n.m.* platinum.

plato, *n.m.* dish; plate; course.

Platón, *n.m.* Plato; **platón,** *n.m.* large plate; (*S.A.*) washbowl.

platudo, **-da,** *a.* (*S.A.*) well-to-do.

plausibilidad, *n.f.* praiseworthiness.

plausible, *a.* praiseworthy, commendable.

playa, *n.f.* beach.

plaza, *n.f.* square, piazza; market place; fortified town; space; employment; (*taur.*) ring.

plazo, *n.m.* term, time; credit; **comprar a plazos,** buy on hire-purchase, (*U.S.*) buy on the instalment plan.

pleamar, *n.f.* high tide.

plebe, *n.f.* plebs.

plebeyo, **-ya,** *a.*, *n.m.f.* plebeian.

plebiscito, *n.m.* plebiscite.

plegadamente, *adv.* confusedly.

plegadizo, **-za,** *a.* folding.

plegadura, *n.f.*, **plegamiento,** *n.m.* fold; pleat.

plegar [1B], *v.t.* fold; pleat; crease.—*v.r.* yield.

plegaria, *n.f.* prayer.

pleito, *n.m.* lawsuit; dispute; battle.

plenario, **-ria,** *a.* plenary.

plenilunio, *n.m.* full moon.

plenitud, *n.f.* plenitude.

pleno, **-na,** *a.* full.

pliego, *n.m.* sheet (*of paper*).

pliegue, *n.m.* fold, crease.

plomar, *v.t.* seal (*with lead*).

plomizo, **-za,** *a.* leaden.

plomo, *n.m.* lead (*metal*).

plugo [PLACER].

pluma, *n.f.* feather; pen; — **estilográfica,** fountain pen.

plumaje, *n.m.* plumage.

plumazo, *n.m.* feather bed.

plural, *a.*, *n.m.* plural.

pluralidad, *n.f.* plurality; majority.

plus, *n.m.* bonus.

pluscuamperfecto, **-ta,** *a.*, *n.m.* pluperfect.

plusmarca, *n.f.* (sporting) record.

población, *n.f.* population; town, village.

poblado, *n.m.* town, village.

poblar [4], *v.t.* people, populate; colonize. stock.—*v.r.* settle.

pobre, *a.* poor.—*n.m.f.* pauper.

pobrete, **-ta,** *a.* wretched.

pobreza, *n.f.* poverty.

pocilga, *n.f.* pigsty.

pócima, poción, *n.f.* potion.

poco, **-ca,** *a.* little.—*pl.* few.—*adv.* little, not at all; — **a** —, little by little.—*n.m.* little, bit.

pocho, **-cha,** *a.* discoloured; rotten; (*fam.*) out of sorts.

podagra, *n.f.* (*med.*) gout.

podar, *v.t.* prune.

podenco, *n.m.* hound.

poder, *n.m.* power; **por poderes,** by proxy.—*v.i.* [24] be able (*to*); can, could etc.; — **con,** master, overcome; **no — menos de,** not be able to help.

poderío, *n.m.* power, might.

poderoso, **-sa,** *a.* powerful.

podre, *n.m.* or *f.* pus.

podré [PODER].

podredumbre, *n.f.* corruption; rot.

podrido, **-da,** *a.* rotten; corrupt.

podrir [PUDRIR].

poema, *n.m.* poem.

poesía, *n.f.* poetry; poem.

poeta, *n.m.* poet.

poético, **-ca,** *a.* poetic(al).—*n.f.* poetics.

poetisa, *n.f.* poetess.

polaco, **-ca,** *a.* Polish.—*n.m.f.* Pole.

polaina, *n.f.* legging, puttee.

polea, *n.f.* pulley.

polen, *n.m.* pollen.

policía, *n.f.* police (force); cleanliness.—*n.m.* policeman.

policíaco, **-ca,** *a.* rel. to the police; detective (*story*).

policopiar, *v.t.* duplicate, cyclostyle.

Polichinela, *n.m.* Punch.

poliedro, *n.m.* polyhedron.

polifacético, **-ca,** *a.* versatile.

polifonía, *n.f.* polyphony.

poligamia, *n.f.* polygamy.

polígamo, **-ma,** *a.* polygamous.—*n.m.f.* polygamist.

polígloto, **-ta, poligloto,** **-ta,** *a.*, *n.m.f.* polyglot.

polígono, *n.m.* polygon.

polilla, *n.f.* moth; book-worm.

polisón, *n.m.* bustle (*of a dress*).

politeísta, *a.* polytheistic.—*n.m.f.* polytheist.

político, **-ca,** *a.* political; -in-law; **padre —,** father-in-law.—*n.m.f.* politician.—*n.f.* politics; policy.

póliza, *n.f.* policy, contract.

polizón, *n.m.* tramp.

polizonte, *n.m.* (*pej.*) policeman, cop.

polo, *n.m.* pole; polo; Andalusian song.

Polonia, *n.f.* Poland.

poltrón, **-rona,** *a.* idle; easy.—*n.m.* coward.

poluto, **-ta,** *a.* dirty, filthy.

polvareda, *n.f.* cloud of dust.

polvera, *n.f.* powder compact.

polvo, *n.m.* dust; (*esp. pl.*) face powder; **en —,** powdered; **hecho —,** (*fam.*) worn out, exhausted.

pólvora, *n.f.* gunpowder; fireworks.

polvorear, *v.t.* powder.

polvoriento, **-ta,** *a.* dusty.

polvorizar [C], *v.t.* pulverize.

polvoroso, **-sa,** *a.* dusty.

pollo, *n.m.* chicken.
polluelo, -la, *n.m.f.* chick.
pomez, *n.m.* pumice.
pomo, *n.m.* pommel; knob.
pompa, *n.f.* pomp; bubble; bulge.
pomposidad, *n.f.* pomposity.
pomposo, -sa, *a.* pompous.
pómulo, *n.m.* cheekbone.
pon [PONER].
ponche, *n.m.* punch (*drink*).
poncho, -cha, *a.* lazy; careless.—*n.m.* poncho.
ponderación, *n.f.* weighing; exaggeration.
ponderar, *v.t.* ponder; exaggerate.
ponderoso, -sa, *a.* ponderous; circumspect.
ponedero, -ra, *a.* laying eggs.—*n.m.* nest-egg.
ponencia, *n.f.* report, paper.
ponente, *n.m.* referee, arbitrator.
poner [25], *v.t.* put, place, lay, set; take (*time*); make, turn; — **alguien a hacer,** set s.o. to do; — **a uno de,** set s.o. up as a. —*v.r.* set (*of stars*); put on (*dress*); become, get, turn; **ponerse a hacer,** set about doing; **ponerse bien con,** get in with.
pongo (1), *n.m.* orang-outang.
pongo (2), (*S.A.*) Indian servant; (*S.A.*) gully.
pongo (3) [PONER].
poniente, *n.m.* west; west wind.
ponlevi, *n.m.* (*pl.* -**ies**) high heel; high-heeled shoe.
pontífice, *n.m.* pontiff, pontifex.
pontón, *n.m.* pontoon.
ponzoña, *n.f.* poison.
ponzoñoso, -sa, *a.* poisonous.
popa, *n.f.* stern, poop.
popar, *v.t.* scorn; fondle.
popelina, *n.f.* poplin.
populacho, *n.m.* populace, mob.
popular, *a.* popular, people's.
popularizar [C], *v.t.* popularize.
populoso, -sa, *a.* populous.
poquísimo, -ma, *a.* very little; very few.
poquito, -ta, *a.* very little.
por, *prep.* by; (in exchange) for; through; because of; — **ciento,** per cent; **dos — dos,** two times two; — **la mañana,** in the morning; — **aquí,** this way; — **mayor,** wholesale; **estar — hacer,** remain to be done; be about to do; be ready to do; *¿* — **qué?** why?
porcelana, *n.f.* porcelain.
porcentaje, *n.m.* percentage.
porcino, -na, *a.* rel. to pigs; **fiebre porcina,** swine-fever.
porción, *n.f.* portion; lot; allotment.
porcuno, -na, *a.* hoggish.
porche, *n.m.* porch, portico.
pordiosear, *v.i.* go out begging.
pordiosero, -ra, *a.* begging.—*n.m.f.* beggar.
porfía, *n.f.* stubbornness; dispute.
porfiar, *v.i.* contend; persist, insist.
pormenor, *n.m.* detail, particular.
pormenorizar [C], *v.i.* particularize; give a detailed account.
pornografía, *n.f.* pornography.
poro, *n.m.* pore.
porosidad, *n.f.* porosity.
porque, *conj.* because.
porqué, *n.m.* reason why; (*fam.*) wherewithal.
porquería, *n.f.* filth; trifle.
porqueriza, *n.f.* pigsty.
porquer(iz)o, *n.m.* swineherd.

porqueta, *n.f.* woodlouse.
porra, *n.f.* club, bludgeon; (*fam.*) stupid person.
porrón, *n.m.* wine bottle with long spout.
porta, *n.f.* (*naut.*) porthole.
porta(a)viones, *n.m. inv.* aircraft carrier.
portada, *n.f.* porch, façade; title-page; frontispiece.
portador, -ra, *n.m.f.* carrier; bearer.
portaestandarte, *n.m.* standard-bearer.
portal, *n.m.* porch, portico; vestibule.
portalámparas, *n.m. inv.* lamp-holder, socket.
portalón, *n.m.* (*naut.*) gangway; gate.
portaminas, *n.m. inv.* mechanical pencil.
portamonedas, *n.m. inv.* purse, (*U.S.*) pocket-book.
portañuela, *n.f.* fly (*of trousers*).
portaplumas, *n.m. inv.* pen(holder).
portar, *v.r.* behave.
portátil, *a.* portable.
portavoz, *n.m.* (*pl.* -**oces**) megaphone; spokesman.
portazgo, *n.m.* toll.
portazo, *n.m.* slam (*of a door*).
porte, *n.m.* freight charge; postage; (*naut.*) tonnage; behaviour; nobility; (*S.A.*) birthday present.
portear, *v.t.* carry, transport.—*v.i.* slam.
portento, *n.m.* prodigy, wonder.
portentoso, -sa, *a.* prodigious, marvellous.
porteño, -ña, *a.*, *n.m.f.* rel. to Buenos Aires.
potería, *n.f.* porter's lodge; (*sport*) goalposts.
portero, -ra, *n.m.f.* doorkeeper.—*n.m.* porter, janitor; (*sport*) goalkeeper.—*n.f.* concierge, janitress.
pórtico, *n.m.* portico.
portilla, *n.f.* (*naut.*) porthole.
portillo, *n.m.* gap, aperture; postern.
portuario, -ria, *a.* rel. to port *or* harbour.
Portugal, *n.m.* Portugal.
portugués, -guesa, *a.*, *n.m.f.* Portuguese.
porvenir, *n.m.* future.
en pos de, *adv. phr.* in pursuit of, after.
posada, *n.f.* inn, small hotel; lodging.
posadero, -ra, *n.m.f.* inn-keeper.—*n.f.* (*esp. pl.*) buttocks.
posar, *v.t.* rest (*a load*).—*v.i.* lodge; perch; pose.—*v.r.* settle (*of lees*); alight.
posdata, *n.f.* postscript.
poseer [N], *v.t.* possess, own; master (*a language*).
posesión, *n.f.* possession.
posesionar, *v.t.* give possession to.—*v.r.* take possession (*de,* of).
posesivo, -va, *a.*, *n.m.* possessive.
poseso, -sa, *a.* possessed.
posfechar, *v.t.* postdate.
posguerra, *n.f.* post-war period.
posibilidad, *n.f.* possibility.
posibilitar, *v.t.* render possible.
posible, *a.* possible.
posición, *n.f.* position, standing.
positivo, -va, *a.*, *n.m.* positive.—*n.f.* (*phot.*) positive.
poso, *n.m.* sediment; repose.
a pospelo, *adv. phr.* against the grain.
posponer [25], *v.t.* subordinate; put off.
posta, *n.f.* post house; stage, relay.
postal, *a.* postal.—*n.f.* post-card.
poste, *n.m.* post, pole; **dar — a,** keep waiting.
postema, *n.f.* abscess.

postergar [B], *v.t.* postpone; pass over.
posteridad, *n.f.* posterity.
posterior, *a.* later; posterior, back, rear.
posterioridad, *n.f.* posteriority; **con — a,** subsequent to.
postguerra, *n.f.* post-war period.
postigo, *n.m.* postern, wicket.
postilla, *n.f.* scab.
postillón, *n.m.* postilion.
postizo, -za, *a.* false, artificial; detachable.— *n.m.* toupet, switch.
postor, *n.m.* bidder (*at an auction*).
postración, *n.f.* prostration.
postrar, *v.t.* prostrate.
postre, *a.* last; **al** or **a la —,** in the long run. —*n.m.* dessert.
postremo, -ma, postrero & **postrer, -ra, postrimero** & **postrimer, -ra,** *a.* last.
postulado, *n.m.* postulate.
postular, *v.t.* postulate; nominate.
póstumo, -ma, *a.* posthumous.
postura, *n.f.* posture; bet; laying; transplanting.
potable, *a.* potable, drinking (*water*).
potación, *n.f.* potation.
potaje, *n.m.* broth, soup; (*mixed*) brew; dried vegetables.
potasa, *n.f.* potash.
potasio, *n.m.* potassium.
pote, *n.m.* pot; flower-pot; **a —,** in abundance.
potencia, *n.f.* (*math., phys., pol.*) power.
potencial, *a.,* *n.m.* potential.
potentado, *n.m.* potentate.
potente, *a.* potent, powerful.
potestad, *n.f.* power, dominion.
potra, *n.f.* filly; (*fam.*) hernia.
potro, *n.m.* foal; (gymnastic) horse.
pozal, *n.m.* pail, bucket.
pozo, *n.m.* well; deep hole; (*min.*) pit; (*naut.*) hold; — **negro,** cesspit.
práctica, *n.f.* practice; habit.
practicable, *a.* feasible.
practicante, *n.m.f.* medical assistant.
practicar [A], *v.t.* practise; cut (*a hole*).
práctico, -ca, *a.* practical.—*n.m.* practitioner; (*naut.*) pilot.
pradera, *n.f.* meadow; prairie.
prado, *n.m.* meadow, pasture; promenade.
pragmático, -ca, *a.* pragmatic(al).—*n.f.* decree, pragmatic.
pravedad, *n.f.* depravity.
pravo, -va, *a.* depraved.
precario, -ria, *a.* precarious.
precaución, *n.f.* precaution; vigilance.
precaver, *v.t.* prevent.—*v.r.* be on one's guard (*contra,* against).
precedencia, *n.f.* precedence.
precedente, *a.,* *n.m.* precedent.
preceder, *v.t.,* *v.i.* precede.
precepto, *n.m.* precept.
preceptor, -ra, *n.m.f.* teacher.
preces, *n.f.pl.* prayers.
preciar, *v.t.* estimate.—*v.r.* boast (*de,* of).
precintar, *v.t.* strap; seal.
precinto, *n.m.* strapping; seal.
precio, *n.m.* price; esteem.
preciosidad, *n.f.* value, preciousness; (*fam.*) beautiful thing.
precioso, -a, *a.* precious; (*fam.*) lovely.
precipicio, *n.m.* precipice.
precipitar, *v.t.* precipitate.—*v.r.* hurry.
precipitoso, -sa, *a.* precipitous; rash.

precisamente, *adv.* precisely; just so.
precisar, *v.t.* specify; need; oblige (*a,* to).— *v.i.* be necessary *or* urgent.
precisión, *n.f.* need; obligation; precision.
preciso, -sa, *a.* necessary; precise.
preclaro, -ra, *a.* illustrious.
precocidad, *n.f.* precociousness, precocity.
preconizar [C], *v.t.* proclaim; praise.
precoz, *a.* (*pl.* -oces) precocious.
predecir [17], *v.t.* predict, forecast.
predicción, *n.f.* prediction.
predilección, *n.f.* predilection.
predilecto, -ta, *a.* favourite.
predio, *n.m.* landed property.
predominar, *v.t.* predominate; overlook; prevail.
predominio, *n.m.* superiority; predominance.
preeminente, *a.* pre-eminent.
prefacio, *n.m.* preface.
prefecto, *n.m.* prefect.
preferente, *a.* preferential; preferable.
preferir [6], *v.t.* prefer.
prefijo, *n.m.* (*gram.*) prefix.
pregón, *r*   proclamation (*by crier*).
pregonar, *v.t.* proclaim.
pregonero, *n.m.* town-crier; auctioneer.
pregunta, *n.f.* question.
preguntar, *v.t.* ask.—*v.i.* ask, enquire (*por,* after).—*v.r.* wonder.
prejuicio, *n.m.* prejudice.
prelado, *n.m.* prelate.
preliminar, *a.* preliminary.
preludio, *n.m.* prelude.
prematuro, -ra, *a.* premature.
premeditar, *v.t.* premeditate.
premiar, *v.t.* reward, award a prize to.
premio, *n.m.* prize.
premioso, -sa, *a.* tight; constricting.
premisa, *n.f.* premise.
premura, *n.f.* pressure, urgency.
prenda, *n.f.* pledge; token; garment; article of jewelry; loved one; (*esp. pl.*) talent.
prendar, *v.t.* pawn; charm.—*v.r.* take a fancy (*de,* to).
prender, *v.t.* seize; pin; capture.—*v.i.* catch on; take root.—*v.r.* dress up.
prensa, *n.f.* press.
prensar, *v.t.* press.
preñado, -da, *a.* pregnant.
preñez, *n.f.* pregnancy.
preocupación, *n.f.* preoccupation; worry; prejudice.
preocupado, -da, *a.* preoccupied; prejudiced.
preocupar, *v.t.* preoccupy.—*v.r.* be worried (*con, por,* about); be preoccupied; be prejudiced.
preparación, *n.f.* preparation.
preparado, -da, *a.* prepared.—*n.m.* preparation.
preparar, *v.t.* prepare.
preparativo, -va, *a.* preparative.—*n.m.* preparation.
preparatorio, -ria, *a.* preparatory.
preponderancia, *n.f.* preponderance.
preponderante, *a.* preponderant.
preponderar, *v.i.* preponderate.
preponer [25], *v.t.* put before, prefer.
preposición, *n.f.* preposition.
preposicional, *a.* prepositional.
prepotente, *a.* very powerful.
prepucio, *n.m.* foreskin, prepuce.
prepuesto [PREPONER].

presa, *n.f.* seizure; prey; dam; claw; — *de caldo,* broth.
presbítero, *n.m.* presbyter, priest.
presciencia, *n.f.* prescience, foreknowledge.
prescindible, *a.* dispensable.
prescindir, *v.i.* dispense (*de,* with).
prescribir [*p.p.* **prescrito**], *v.t., v.i.* prescribe; acquire prescriptive rights over.
prescripción, *n.f.* prescription.
prescripto [PRESCRITO].
presencia, *n.f.* presence; physique.
presenciar, *v.t.* witness.
presentación, *n.f.* presentation.
presentar, *v.t.* present; offer.—*v.r.* offer one's services.
presente, *a.* present, actual, current.—*n.m.* present, gift.
presentemente, *adv.* at present.
presentimiento, *n.m.* presentiment.
presentir [6], *v.t.* have a presentiment of.
preservar, *v.t.* save, guard.
presidencia, *n.f.* presidency; president's residence.
presidente, *n.m.* president; chairman.
presidiario, *n.m.* convict.
presidio, *n.m.* garrison; prison; praesidium.
presidir, *v.t.* preside.
presilla, *n.f.* loop, clip.
presión, *n.f.* pressure.
preso, -sa, *a.* imprisoned.—*n.m.f.* prisoner.
prestación, *n.f.* loan.
prestado, -da, *p.p.* lent; **dar —,** lend; **pedir —,** borrow.
prestamista, *n.m.f.* money-lender; pawnbroker.
préstamo, *n.m.* loan.
prestar, *v.t.* lend, loan.
presteza, *n.f.* quickness.
prestidigitación, *n.f.* juggling.
prestigiador, -ra, *a.* fascinating; prestige-winning.—*n.m.f.* imposter.
prestigio, *n.m.* prestige; juggling; fascination.
prestigioso, -sa, *a.* spell-binding; renowned.
presto, -ta, *a.* quick; ready.—*adv.* quickly.
presumir, *v.t.* presume.—*v.i.* presume, boast (*de,* of being).
presunción, *n.f.* presumption.
presuntivo, -va, *a.* presumptive.
presunto, -ta, *a.* presumed, presumptive.
presuntuoso, -sa, *a.* presumptuous.
presuponer [25], *v.t.* presuppose.
presupuesto, *n.m.* motive, pretext; budget, estimate.
presuroso, -sa, *a.* hasty; quick.
pretender, *v.t.* pretend to; claim to; try for.
pretendiente, *n.m.f.* claimant.—*n.m.* suitor.
pretérito, -ta, *a.* past.—*n.m.* (*gram.*) preterit(e).
pretextar, *v.t.* give as a pretext.
pretexto, *n.m.* pretext.
pretil, *n.m.* breastwork, railing.
prevalecer [9], *v.i.* prevail (*sobre,* against); take root.
prevaler [35], *v.i.* prevail.—*v.r.* take advantage (*de,* of).
prevaricar [A], *v.i.* play false; prevaricate.
prevención, *n.f.* foresight; warning; preparation; guard-room.
prevenir [36], *v.t.* prepare; forestall; warn.
prever [37], *v.t.* foresee.
previo, -via, *a.* previous.
previsible, *a.* foreseeable.

previsión, *n.f.* prevision, foresight; — *del tiempo,* weather forecasting.
previsor, -ra, *a.* provident.
previsto [PREVER].
prez, *n.m.* or *f.* honour, fame.
prieto, -ta, *a.* black; tight.
primacía, *n.f.* primacy.
primado, *n.m.* (*eccl.*) primate.
primario, -ria, *a.* primary.
primate, *n.m.* (*zool.*) primate; worthy.
primavera, *n.f.* spring; (*bot.*) primrose.
primaveral, *a.* rel. to spring.
primer [PRIMERO].
primerizo, -za, *a.* first; firstling.
primero, primer, -ra, *a.* first; prime; raw (*materials*).—*adv.* at first.
primicia, *n.f.* (*esp. pl.*) first fruits.
primitivo, -va, *a.* primitive.
primo, -ma (1), *a.* prime; raw (*materials*).
primo, -ma (2), *n.m.f.* cousin.
primogénito, -ta, *a.* first-born.
primor, *n.m.* elegance; care; skill.
primoroso, -sa, *a.* exquisite; elegant; careful.
princesa, *n.f.* princess.
principado, *n.m.* principality.
principal, *a.* principal, main; notable.—*n.m.* chief, head; main floor, first (*U.S.* second) floor.
principalidad, *n.f.* nobility.
príncipe, *n.m.* prince.
principiante, -ta, *n.m.f.* beginner.
principiar, *v.t.* begin.
principio, *n.m.* beginning; principle.
pringar [B], *v.t.* dip in grease; meddle.
pringoso, -sa, *a.* greasy.
pringue, *n.m.* or *f.* grease; grease-spot; greasiness.
prior, *a., n.m.* prior.
priora, *n.f.* prioress.
prioridad, *n.f.* priority.
prisa, *n.f.* hurry; speed; *de —,* in a hurry; *darse —,* hurry; *tener —,* be in a hurry.
prisión, *n.f.* seizure; imprisonment.—*pl.* shackles.
prisionero, *n.m.* (*mil.*) prisoner.
prisma, *n.m.* prism.
pristino, -na, *a.* pristine.
privado, -da, *a.* private.—*n.m.* (court-) favourite.—*n.f.* privy.
privanza, *n.f.* favour (*at court*).
privar, *v.t.* deprive; forbid.—*v.i.* be in favour. —*v.r.* deprive oneself (*de,* of).
privativo, -va, *a.* private; peculiar.
privilegio, *n.m.* privilege; patent.
pro, *n.m.* or *f.* advantage.
proa, *n.f.* bow, prow.
probabilidad, *n.f.* probability.
probable, *a.* probable; provable.
probación, *n.f.* probation.
probanza, *n.f.* proof.
probar [4], *v.t.* try; examine, test; sample; prove.—*v.i.* taste.—*v.r.* try on (*clothes*).
probeta, *n.f.* test specimen; test-glass; pressure gauge.
problema, *n.m.* problem.
probo, -ba, *a.* honest.
procaz, *a.* (*pl.* -aces) impudent; bold.
procedencia, *n.f.* origin.
procedente, *a.* originating. coming (*de,* from).
proceder (1), *n.m.* conduct.
proceder (2), *v.i.* proceed; originate; behave.
procedimiento, *n.m.* proceeding; procedure.

prócer, *a.* lofty.—*n.m.* dignitary.
procesión, *n.f.* procession (*esp. eccl.*).
proceso, *n.m.* law-suit; (*S.A.*) — *verbal*, report.
proclamación, *n.f.* proclamation.
proclamar, *v.t.* proclaim; acclaim.
proclive, *a.* inclined.
procreación, *n.f.* procreation.
procrear, *v.t.* procreate.
procuración, *n.f.* careful management; power of attorney.
procurador, *n.m.* solicitor, attorney; proxy.
procurar, *v.t.* strive for; manage.
prodición, *n.f.* treachery.
prodigalidad, *n.f.* prodigality.
prodigar [B], *v.t.* squander.
prodigio, *n.m.* prodigy; portent.
prodigioso, -sa, *a.* prodigious.
pródigo, -ga, *a.* prodigal; lavish.
producción, *n.f.* production.
producir [16], *v.t.* produce.
producto, *n.m.* product.
proemio, *n.m.* introduction, proem.
proeza, *n.f.* prowess.
profanar, *v.t.* profane.
profano, -na, *a.* profane.
profecía, *n.f.* prophecy.
proferir [6], *v.t.* utter.
profesar, *v.t.* profess.
profesión, *n.f.* profession.
profesional, *a.* professional.
profeso, -sa, *a., n.m.f.* (*eccl.*) professed.
profesor, -ra, *n.m.f.* teacher; professor.
profeta, *n.m.* prophet.
profetisa, *n.f.* prophetess.
profetizar [C], *v.t., v.i.* prophesy.
profundidad, *n.f.* profundity; depth.
profundo, -da, *a.* profound; deep.
profusión, *n.f.* profusion.
profuso, -sa, *a.* profuse.
prognosis, *n.f. inv.* prognosis; forecast (*esp.* weather-).
programa, *n.m.* programme; plan.
progresar, *v.i.* progress.
progreso, *n.m.* progress.
prohibir, *v.t.* prohibit.
prohijar, *v.t.* adopt.
prohombre, *n.m.* top man; (*fam.*) big shot.
prójimo, *n.m.* neighbour, fellow man.
prole, *n.f.* progeny, offspring.
proletariado, *n.m.* proletariat.
proletario, -ria, *a.* proletarian.
prolijo, -ja, *a.* prolix.
prólogo, *n.m.* prologue.
prolongar [B], *v.t.* prolong.—*v.r.* extend.
promediar, *v.t.* average.
promedio, *n.m.* average, mean.
promesa, *n.f.* promise.
prometer, *v.t., v.i.* promise.
prometido, -da, *a.* engaged.—*n.m.* fiancé.—*n.f.* fiancée.
prominente, *a.* prominent.
promiscuidad, *n.f.* promiscuity.
promiscuo, -cua, *a.* promiscuous; indiscriminate.
promisión, *n.f.* promise; *tierra de* —, promised land.
promoción, *n.f.* promotion; graduation, class.
promontorio, *n.m.* promontory.
promover [5], *v.t.* promote.
promulgar [B], *v.t.* promulgate.
pronombre, *n.m.* pronoun.

pronóstico, *n.m.* prognosis; forecast.
pronto, -ta, *a.* quick; ready; prompt.—*adv.* quickly; soon.
pronunciación, *n.f.* pronunciation.
pronunciamiento, *n.m.* insurrection; decree.
pronunciar, *v.t.* pronounce.—*v.r.* rebel.
propaganda, *n.f.* propaganda; advertising.
propagar [B], *v.t.* propagate, spread.
propender, *v.i.* be inclined.
propiciar, *v.t.* propitiate.
propicio, -cia, *a.* propitious.
propiedad, *n.f.* property; ownership.
propietario, -ria, *n.m.* proprietor.—*n.f.* proprietress.
propina, *n.f.* tip.
propinar, *v.t.* treat.
propio, -pia, *a.* proper; peculiar; same; own.
proponer [25], *v.t.* propose; propound.
proporción, *n.f.* proportion.
proporcionar, *v.t.* proportion; furnish, supply.
proposición, *n.f.* proposition.
propósito, *n.m.* aim; intention; subject-matter.
propuesta, *n.f.* proposal.
propuesto [PROPONER].
propulsar, *v.t.* propel.
propulsión, *n.f.* propulsion; — *a chorro*, jet propulsion.
propulsor, -ra, *a.* propellent.
prorrumpir, *v.i.* burst forth.
prosa, *n.f.* prose.
prosaico, -ca, *a.* prosaic.
prosapia, *n.f.* ancestry.
proscribir [*p.p.* **proscrito**], *v.t.* proscribe.
proscripción, *n.f.* proscription, outlawing.
proscrito, -ta, *p.p.* [PROSCRIBIR].—*n.m.f.* exile; outlaw.
proseguir [8G], *v.t., v.i.* continue.
prosélito, *n.m.* proselyte.
prosificar [A], *v.t.* turn poetry into prose.
prosista, *n.m.f.* prose-writer.
prosodia, *n.f.* prosody.
prospecto, *n.m.* prospectus.
prosperar, *v.t., v.i.* prosper.
prosperidad, *n.f.* prosperity.
próspero, -ra, *a.* prosperous.
próstata, *n.f.* (*anat.*) prostate gland.
prosternar, *v.r.* prostrate oneself.
prostitución, *n.f.* prostitution.
prostituir [O], *v.t.* prostitute.
prostituta, *n.f.* prostitute.
protagonista, *n.m.f.* protagonist.
protección, *n.f.* protection.
protector, -ra *or* **-triz** (*pl.* **-trices**), *a.* protective.—*n.m.* protector.—*n.f.* protectress.
protectorado, *n.m.* protectorate.
proteger [E], *v.t.* protect.
protegido, -da, *n.m.f.* protégé(e).
proteína, *n.f.* protein.
protesta, *n.f.* protest.
protestante, *a.* protesting; Protestant.—*n.m.f.* Protestant.
protestantismo, *n.m.* Protestantism.
protestar, *v.t.* protest; asseverate.—*v.i.* protest.
protesto, *n.m.* (*com.*) protest.
protocolo, *n.m.* protocol.
protón, *n.m.* (*phys.*) proton.
prototipo, *n.m.* prototype.
protuberancia, *n.f.* protuberance.
provecho, *n.m.* advantage; benefit.

provechoso, -sa, *a.* advantageous.
proveedor, -ra, *n.m.f.* supplier.
proveer [N, *p.p.* **provisto**], *v.t.* provide (*a,* for *de,* with).
proveimiento, *n.m.* provisioning.
provenir [36], *v.i.* come; originate.
Provenza, *n.f.* Provence.
provenzal, *a., n.m.f.* Provençal.
proverbio, *n.m.* proverb.
providencia, *n.f.* providence.
providencial, *a.* providential.
providente, *a.* provident.
provincia, *n.f.* province.
provincial, *a., n.m.f.* provincial.
provisión, *n.f.* provision.
provisto [PROVEER].
provocación, *n.f.* provocation.
provocante, *a.* provocative.
provocar [A], *v.t.* provoke.
proximidad, *n.f.* proximity.
próximo, -ma, *a.* next; near.
proyección, *n.f.* projection.
proyectar, *v.t.* project, cast.
proyectil, *n.m.* projectile, missile; — *dirigido,* guided missile; — *autodirigido,* homing missile.
proyecto, *n.m.* project, plan; — *de ley,* bill.
proyector, *n.m.* projector; searchlight.
prudencia, *n.f.* prudence.
prudente, *a.* prudent.
prueba, *n.f.* proof; sample; test; *a —,* on approval; *a — de,* proof against.
prurito, *n.m.* itch.
Prusia, *n.f.* Prussia.
prúsico, -ca, *a.* prussic.
pseudónimo, *n.m.* pseudonym.
psicoanálisis, *n.m.* or *f.* psychoanalysis.
psicoanalizar [C], *v.t.* psychoanalyze.
psicología, *n.f.* psychology.
psicológico, -ca, *a.* psychological.
psicólogo, *n.m.* psychologist.
psicópata, *n.m.f.* psychopath.
psicosis, *n.f. inv.* psychosis.
psique, *n.f.* cheval glass; psyche.
psiquiatra, psiquiatra, *n.m.f.* psychiatrist.
psiquiatría, *n.f.* psychiatry.
psíquico, -ca, *a.* psychic.
púa, *n.f.* point; prick; tooth (*of comb*); barb.
púbico, -ca, *a.* pubic.
publicación, *n.f.* publication.
publicar [A], *v.t.* publish.
publicidad, *n.f.* publicity; advertising.
publicitario, -ria, *a.* rel. to advertising.
público, -ca, *a., n.m.* public.
puchero, *n.m.* pot; kettle; stew.—*pl.* pouting.
pude [PODER].
pudibundo, -da, *a.* modest; shy.
pudor, *n.m.* modesty.
pudrimiento, *n.m.* rotting.
pudrir [*var. p.p.* **podrido**], *v.t., v.r.* rot.
pueblo, *n.m.* people; town, village.
puente, *n.m.* bridge; deck.
puerco, -ca, *a.* filthy.—*n.m.* hog; — *espín,* porcupine.—*n.f.* sow; wood-louse; slug.
pueril, *a.* puerile; childish.
puerro, *n.m.* leek.
puerta, *n.f.* door; gate; (*sport*) goal (*posts*).
puerto, *n.m.* port, harbour.
puertorriqueño, -ña, *a., n.m.f.* Puerto Rican.
pues, *adv.* then, well; yes.—*conj.* for; since; because.—*interj.* well, then!

puesta, *n.f.* stake (*at cards*); setting (*of sun*).
puesto (1) [PONER].
puesto (2), *n.m.* shop, stall; post, employment.
puf (1), *n.m.* pouf.
¡puf! (2), *interj.* ugh!
pugilato, *n.m.* pugilism, boxing.
pugna, *n.f.* fight, battle; struggle.
pugnar, *v.i.* fight; struggle.
pugnaz, *a.* (*pl.* -aces) pugnacious.
pujante, *a.* powerful, puissant.
pujanza, *n.f.* might.
pujar, *v.t.* push ahead.—*v.i.* falter; grope; bid.
pulcritud, *n.f.* neatness, tidiness.
pulcro, -ra, *a.* neat; trim; beautiful.
pulga, *n.f.* flea.
pulgada, *n.f.* inch.
pulgar, *n.m.* thumb.
pulidez, *n.f.* cleanliness; neatness.
pulido, -da, *a.* clean; neat; pretty.
pulir, *v.t.* polish.
pulmón, *n.m.* lung.
pulmonía, *n.f.* pneumonia.
pulpa, *n.f.* pulp.
pulpejo, *n.m.* soft part (*of thumb etc.*).
pulpería, *n.f.* (*S.A.*) grocery store.
púlpito, *n.m.* pulpit.
pulpo, *n.m.* octopus.
pulsación, *n.f.* pulsation.
pulsador, -ra, *a.* pulsating.—*n.m.* push-button.
pulsar, *v.t.* touch lightly; feel the pulse of.—*v.i.* puls(at)e.
pulsera, *n.f.* bracelet; watch-strap.
pulso, *n.m.* pulse; tact.
pulular, *v.i.* pullulate.
pulverizar [C], *v.t.* pulverize.
pulla, *n.f.* cutting *or* obscene remark; innuendo.
¡pum! *interj.* bang!
puma, *n.f.* puma, cougar, panther.
pundonor, *n.m.* point of honour.
pungir [E], *v.t.* prick; sting.
punible, *a.* punishable.
punitivo, -va, *a.* punitive.
punta, *n.f.* point, tip; nail; apex; promontory; tartness; *de —,* on tiptoe.
puntada, *n.f.* stitch.
puntapié, *n.m.* kick.
puntear, *v.t.* dot; play (*the guitar*); stitch.—*v.i.* (*naut.*) tack.
puntero, -ra, *a.* sharpshooting.—*n.m.* pointer, hand; chisel.—*n.f.* toe-cap.
puntilla, *n.f.* brad; *de* or *en puntillas,* on tiptoe.
puntillero, *n.m.* (*taur.*) puntillero, dagger man.
puntillo, *n.m.* small point *or* dot; punctilio.
puntilloso, -sa, *a.* punctilious.
punto, *n.m.* point; dot; full stop, (*U.S.*) period; stitch; — *y coma,* semi-colon; — *muerto,* (*auto.*) neutral (*gear*); (*pol.*) deadlock; *dos puntos,* colon.
puntuación, *n.f.* punctuation; (*educ.*) mark; score.
puntual, *a.* punctual; reliable. certain.
puntualidad, *n.f.* punctuality.
puntuar [M], *v.t., v.i.* punctuate.
puntuoso, -sa, *a.* punctilious.
punzada, *n.f.* prick, sudden pain.
punzante, *a.* pricking; sharp.

punzar [C], *v.t.* prick; punch; bore.—*v.i.* sting.
puñada, *n.f.* punch.
puñal, *n.m.* dagger.
puñalada, *n.f.* stab.
puño, *n.m.* fist; grasp; handful.
pupa, *n.f.* pimple; (*fam.*) hurt.
pupilaje, *n.m.* wardship; board and lodging.
pupilo, -la, *n.m.f.* boarder; ward; pupil.—*n.f.* (*anat.*) pupil.
pupitre, *n.m.* desk.
puré, *n.m.* purée; — *de patatas*, mashed potatoes.
pureza, *n.f.* purity.
purga, *n.f.* purge; drainage valve.
purgante, *a.*, *n.m.* purgative.
purgar [B], *v.t.* purge; drain; expiate.—*v.i.* drain; atone.
purgatorio, *n.m.* purgatory.
puridad, *n.f.* purity; secrecy.
purificar [A], *v.t.* purify.
púrpura, *n.f.* purple.
puro, -ra, *a.* pure; sheer.—*n.m.* cigar.
purpurado, -da, purpúreo, -rea, *a.* purple.
purulento, -ta, *a.* purulent.
pus (1), *a.* (*S.A.*) puce.
pus (2), *n.m.* pus.
puse [PONER].
pusilánime, *a.* pusillanimous.
pústula, *n.f.* pustule.
puta, *n.f.* whore, harlot.
putativo, -va, *a.* putative; spurious.
putrefacción, *n.f.* putrefaction.
pútrido, -da, *a.* putrid.
puya, *n.f.* goad.
puyazo, *n.m.* jab.

Q

Q, q, *n.f.* twentieth letter of the Spanish alphabet.
que, *rel. pron.* that, which; who, whom; *el* —, that, the one that, he who *etc.*—*adv.* than.—*conj.* that; for.
¿ qué? *interrog. pron.* what? which? *¿ — más da?* what does it matter? *¿y* —*?* so what?
¡qué! *pron.* what! what a! how! *¡ — de . . . !* how much *or* many! what a lot of. . . .!
quebracho, *n.m.* (*bot.*) quebracho.
quebrada, *n.f.* ravine; (*com.*) failure.
quebradero de cabeza, *n.m.* worry, big problem.
quebradizo, -za, *a.* brittle; frail.
quebradura, *n.f.* break; rupture.
quebrajar, *v.t.* split, crack.
quebrantamiento, *n.m.* breaking; break; rupture; fatigue.
quebrantar, *v.t.* crack; break; break open; break out of; crush; diminish; exhaust.—*v.r.* break, get broken.
quebranto, *n.m.* breaking; break; grief; collapse.
quebrar [1], *v.t.* break, smash; crush; break down.—*v.i.* break; collapse; fail.—*v.r.* break; weaken.

quechua [QUICHUA].
queda, *n.f.* curfew.
quedada, *n.f.* stay.
quedar, *v.i.* stay, remain; be left; be; turn out; — *en*, agree on *or* to; *queda por hacer*, it remains to be done.—*v.r.* stay; *quedarse con*, keep.
quedito, *adv.* gently, quietly.
quedo, -da, *a.* still.—*adv.* quietly, gently.
quehacer, *n.m.* task, job.
queja, *n.f.* complaint; moan.
quejar, *v.r.* complain (*de*, of, about); moan.
quejicoso, -sa, *a.* complaining, moaning.
quejido, *n.m.* complaint; groan.
quejoso, -sa, *a.* complaining.
quejumbre, *n.f.* moan.
quejumbroso, -sa, *a.* moaning.
quema, *n.f.* burning; fire; (*fig.*) danger.
quemado, *n.m.* fire, burning.
quemadura, *n.f.* burn; scald; (*agr.*) blight.
quemante, *a.* burning.
quemar, *v.t.* burn; scorch; blight; sell cheaply.—*v.i.* burn; be hot.—*v.r.* burn, be on fire; fret; be warm (*in search*); *a quema ropa*, point blank.
quemazón, *n.f.* burning; smarting; itch; (*fam.*) anger; (*fam.*) cutting remark.
quepo [CABER].
querella, *n.f.* complaint; plaint.
querellado, -da, *n.m.f.* (*jur.*) defendant.
querellante, *n.m.f.* (*jur.*) plaintiff.
querellar, *v.r.* complain.
querelloso, -sa, *a.* querulous.
querencia, *n.f.* homing instinct; fondness; haunt.
querer [26], *v.t.* love; want, wish; like.—*v.i.* be willing; be about to; — *más*, prefer; *como quiera*, anyhow; *como quiera que*, whereas; *cuando quiera*, any time; *donde quiera*, anywhere; *sin* —, unwillingly; unintentionally.—*n.m.* love; fondness.
querido, -da, *a.* dear.—*n.m.* lover.—*n.f.* mistress.
queso, *n.m.* cheese.
quetzal, *n.m.* (*orn.*) quetzal.
quevedos, *n.m.pl.* pince-nez.
¡quia! *interj.* (*fam.*) not on your life!
quicial, *n.m.* side-post, hinge post.
quicio, *n.m.* hook-hinge, pivot hole.
quichua, *a.*, *n.m.f.* Quechua(n).
quid, *n.m.* gist, main point.
quídam, *n.m.* (*fam.*) who's-it, what's his name; (*fam.*) a nonentity.
quiebra, *n.f.* break; crack; damage; (*com.*) failure, bankruptcy.
quiebro, -bras *etc.* [QUEBRAR].
quien, *rel. pron. sg.* who; whom; he who *etc.*, whoever.
¿quién? *interrog. pron.* who? whom? whoever?
quienquiera, *pron.* anybody.—*rel. pron.* whoever.
quiero [QUERER].
quieto, -ta, *a.* still; orderly.
quietud, *n.f.* calm, peace.
quijada, *n.f.* jaw, jawbone.
quijotada, *n.f.* quixotic enterprise.
quijote, *n.m.* Quixote; cuisse; croup.
quijotería, *n.f.* quixotry.
quijotesco, -ca, *a.* quixotic.
quijotismo, *n.m.* quixotism.

quilate, *n.m.* carat; (*fam.*) tiny bit.
quilo- [KILO-].
quilla, *n.f.* keel; breastbone (*of birds*).
quimera, *n.f.* chimera; quarrel.
quimérico, -ca, *a.* chimerical.
quimerista, *n.m.f.* visionary; brawler.
químico, -ca, *a.* chemical; *productos químicos,* chemicals.—*n.m.f.* chemist.—*n.f.* chemistry.
quimono, *n.m.* kimono.
quina, *n.f.* Peruvian bark.
quincalla, *n.f.* hardware.
quince, *a., n.m.* fifteen.
quincena, *n.f.* fortnight.
quincenal, *a.* fortnightly.
quinceno, -na, *a., n.m.* fifteenth.
quincuagésima, *n.f.* Quinquagesima.
quingentésimo, -ma, *a.* five-hundredth.
quinientos, -tas, *a., n.m.* five hundred.
quinina, *n.f.* quinine.
quinqué, *n.m.* oil lamp; (*fam.*) insight, nous.
quinquenio, *n.m.* quinquennium.
quinta, *n.f.* villa; (*mil.*) draft.
quintacolumnista, *a., n.m.f.* fifth-columnist.
quintaesencia, *n.f.* quintessence.
quintaesenciar, *v.t.* purify.
quintal, *n.m.* hundred-weight (46 *kg.*); — *métrico,* 100 kg.
quintar, *v.t.* (*mil.*) draft.
quinteto, *n.m.* quintet.
quintilla, *n.f.* five-lined stanza.
quintillizo, -za, *n.m.f.* quintuplet.
Quintín, *n.m.* Quentin; *armar la de San —,* raise a shindy.
quinto, -ta, *a., n.m.f.* fifth.—*n.m.* (*mil.*) conscript; piece of land.
quintuplicar [A], *v.t.* quintuple.
quíntuplo, -la, *a.* fivefold.
quinzavo, -va, *a., n.m.f.* fifteenth.
quiñón, *n.m.* share, portion.
quiñonero, *n.m.* part-owner.
quiosco, *n.m.* kiosk, stand.
quirófano, *n.m.* operating theatre.
quiropodista, *n.m.f.* chiropodist.
quirúrgico, -ca, *a.* surgical.
quise [QUERER].
quisicosa, *n.f.* (*fam.*) stumper, puzzle.
quisquilla, *n.f.* quibble; (*ichth.*) shrimp.
quisquilloso, -sa, *a.* quibbling; touchy.
quiste, *n.m.* cyst.
quisto, -ta, *a.* loved; *bien —,* well-liked; *mal —,* disliked, unpopular.
quita, *n.f.* (*jur.*) acquittance, discharge.
quitación, *n.f.* salary; (*jur.*) acquittance.
quitamanchas, *n.m. inv.* spot-remover.
quitamiedos, *n.m. inv.* handrail.
quitanieve, *n.m.* snow-plough.
quitanza, *n.f.* (*jur.*, *com.*) quittance.
quitapesares, *n.m. inv.* (*fam.*) comfort; cheering-up; trip.
quitar, *v.t.* take away, remove; save from (*work etc.*); free; parry.—*v.r.* take off (*clothes*); clear off, go away; abstain; get rid of; *de quita y pon,* detachable; *quitarse de encima,* get rid of, do away with.
quitasol, *n.m.* parasol.
quitasueño, *n.m.* (*fam.*) nagging worry.
quite, *n.m.* hindrance; parry; dodge; (*taur.*) drawing bull away from man in danger.
quito, -ta, *a.* free, exempt; quits.
quizá(s), *adv.* perhaps.
quórum, *n.m. inv.* quorum.

R

R, r, *n.f.* twenty-first letter of the Spanish alphabet.
rábano, *n.m.* radish.
rabear, *v.i.* wag the tail.
rabel, *n.m.* (*mus.*) rebec; (*joc.*) backside.
rabera, *n.f.* tail-end; remains.
rabí, *n.m.* (*pl.* **-íes**) rabbi.
rabia, *n.f.* rage, fury; (*med.*) rabies.
rabiar, *v.i.* rave, rage; long (*por,* for).
rábido, -da, *a.* rabid.
rabieta, *n.f.* (*fam.*) tantrum.
rabillo, *n.m.* stem; mildew; corner (*of eye*).
rabínico, -ca, *a.* rabbinic(al).
rabino, *n.m.* rabbi.
rabioles, rabiolos, *n.m.pl.* ravioli.
rabioso, -sa, *a.* rabid, furious, wild.
rabo, *n.m.* tail; corner (*of eye*); stalk.
rabosear, *v.t.* fray.
raboso, -sa, *a.* frayed, tattered.
racial, *a.* racial.
racimo, *n.m.* bunch (*of grapes*); cluster.
raciocinio, *n.m.* reason; argument.
ración, *n.f.* portion; allowance; pittance; ration; (*eccl.*) prebend.
racional, *a., n.m.* rational.
racionalidad, *n.f.* rationality.
racionalismo, *n.m.* rationalism.
racionalista, *a., n.m.f.* rationalist.
racionamiento, *n.m.* rationing.
racionar, *v.t.* ration.
racismo, *n.m.* racism, racialism.
racista, *a., n.m.f.* racist, racialist.
racha, *n.f.* gust; run of luck; split; big splinter.
radar, *n.m.* radar
radiación, *n.f.* radiation.
radiactividad, *n.f.* radioactivity.
radiactivo, -va, *a.* radioactive.
radiador, *n.m.* radiator.
radial, *a.* radial.
radiante, *a.* radiant.
radiar, *v.t.* broadcast.—*v.t., v.i.* radiate.
radicación, *n.f.* rooting; situation; established practice.
radical, *a., n.m.f.* radical.
radicalismo, *n.m.* radicalism.
radicar [A], *v.i., v.r.* take root; be situated; settle.
radio, *n.m.* radius; spoke; edge; radium.—*n.f.* radio.
radioact- [RADIACT-].
radioaficionado, -da, *n.m.f.* radio fan, (*fam.*) ham.
radiodifundir, *v.t., v.i.* broadcast.
radiodifusión, *n.f.* broadcasting.
radioemisora, *n.f.* broadcasting station.
radioescucha, *n.m.f.* listener.
radiografía, *n.f.* radiography; X-ray (photograph).
radiografiar, *v.t.* X-ray.
radiograma, *n.m.* radiogram.
radioisótopo, *n.m.* radio-isotope.
radiología, *n.f.* radiology.
radiólogo, -ga, *n.m.f.* radiologist.
radio(o)nda, *n.f.* radio-wave.
radiopertubación, *n.f.* (*rad.*) jamming.
radiorreceptor, *n.m.* wireless receiver.

radioso, -sa, *a.* radiant.
radioteléfono, *n.m.* radiotelephone.
radiotelegrafía, *n.f.* radiotelegraphy.
radiotelegrafista, *n.m.f.* wireless operator.
radiotelescopio, *n.m.* radiotelescope.
radioterapia, *n.f.* radiotherapy.
radioyente, *n.m.f.* listener.
raedera, *n.f.* scraper.
raedura, *n.f.* scraping.
raer [27], *v.t.* scrape (off); scratch.—*v.r.*
become worn *or* frayed.
ráfaga, *n.f.* gust; flash; burst.
rafia, *n.f.* raffia.
rahez, *a.* (*pl.* **-eces**) low, vile.
raído, -da, *a.* worn, threadbare; cheeky.
raigambre, *n.f.* root-mass; deep-rootedness.
raigón, *n.m.* root.
rail, *n.m.* (*pl.* **raíles**) (*rail.*) rail.
raimiento, *n.m.* scraping; barefacedness.
raíz, *n.f.* (*pl.* **raíces**) root; *a — de,* immediately after.
raja, *n.f.* chink, crack; chip; slice; *sacar —,*
(*fam.*) gain (*de,* from, by).
rajar, *v.t.* split, crack; slice.—*v.i.* (*fam.*)
boast; (*fam.*) natter, chat.—*v.r.* split;
(*fam.*) back out, break (*word etc.*).
ralea, *n.f.* kind; (*pej.*) breed; prey (*of hawks
etc.*).
ralear, *v.i.* be sparse; reveal one's true nature.
raleza, *n.f.* sparsity.
ralo, -la, *a.* sparse.
rallador, *n.m.* (*cul.*) grater.
rallar, *v.t.* grate; (*fam.*) annoy.
rama, *n.f.* branch; *en —,* raw, crude; (*print.*)
uncut.
ramada, *n.f.* branches; shed.
ramaje, *n.m.* branches.
ramal, *n.m.* strand; (*rail.*) branch.
rambla, *n.f.* dry ravine; boulevard.
ramera, *n.f.* whore.
ramificación, *n.f.* ramification.
ramificar [A], *v.t., v.r.* ramificate.
ramillete, *n.m.* posy, bouquet; cluster.
ramo, *n.m.* branch; bunch (*of flowers*); line;
touch (*of illness*); (*Domingo de*) *Ramos,*
Palm Sunday.
ramojo, *n.m.* brushwood.
Ramón, *n.m.* Raymond.
rampa, *n.f.* ramp.
rampante, *a.* (*her.*) rampant.
ramplón,-plona,*a.* coarse, vulgar.
ramplonería, *n.f.* vulgarity, crudeness.
rana, *n.f.* frog; *no ser —,* (*fam.*) be handy
or skilled.
rancajada, *n.f.* uprooting.
rancajo, *n.m.* splinter.
ranciar, *v.r.* go rancid.
rancidez, rancidad, *n.f.* staleness, rancidness.
rancio, -cia, *a.* stale; rancid; old (*wine*).
ranchear, *v.i., v.r.* settle in huts.
ranchería, *n.f.* hut settlement.
ranchero, *n.m.* mess-steward; (*C.A.*) farmer.
rancho, *n.m.* mess; gathering; hut; (*C.A.*)
farm; (*naut.*) provisions.
rango, *n.m.* class, rank.
rangua, *n.f.* socket.
ranúnculo, *n.m.* (*bot.*) ranunculus; buttercup.
ranura, *n.f.* groove; *a — y lengüeta,*
tongue-and-groove.
ranurar, *v.t.* groove.
rapacería, *n.f.* childish prank.

rapacidad, *n.f.* rapacity.
rapagón, *n.m.* stripling, lad.
rapar, *v.t.* crop; shave; steal.
rapaz, *a.* (*pl.* **-aces**) rapacious; thieving.—
n.m. lad.—*pl.* (*orn.*) raptores.
rapaza, *n.f.* lass.
rape, *n.m.* (*fam.*) scrape, shave; *al —,* close-
cropped (*hair*).
rapé, *n.m.* snuff.
rapidez, *n.f.* rapidity.
rápido, -da, *a.* rapid.—*n.m.* express (*train*).
rapiña, *n.f.* plundering, rapine; *ave de —,*
bird of prey.
raposera, *n.f.* fox-hole.
raposería, *n.f.* foxiness.
raposo, -sa, *n.m.f.* fox; foxy person.
rapsodia, *n.f.* rhapsody.
rapsódico, -ca, *a.* rhapsodic(al).
raptar, *v.t.* abduct.
rapto, *n.m.* rapture, swoon; abduction; rape.
raptor, *n.m.* ravisher.
raque, *n.m.* beachcombing.
Raquel, *n.f.* Rachel.
raquero, -ra, *a.* piratical.—*n.m.* beach-
comber; dock-thief.
raqueta, *n.f.* racket, racquet; snow-shoe.
raquítico, -ca, *a.* rachitic; rickety.
raquitis, *n.f.*, **raquitismo,** *n.m.* rickets.
rarefacción, *n.f.* rarefaction.
rarefacer [20], *v.t.* rarefy.
rarefacto, -ta, *a.* rarefied.
rareza, *n.f.* rarity, rareness; oddity.
raridad, *n.f.* rarity.
rarificar [A], *v.t.* rarefy; make rare.
raro, -ra, *a.* rare; odd, strange; sparse;
rara vez or *raras veces,* rarely.
ras, *n.m.* levelness; *a —,* very close (*de,* to).
rasa, *n.f.* thinness (*in cloth*); plateau.
rasar, *v.t.* level off; graze, skim.—*v.r.* clear.
rascacielos, *n.m. inv.* skyscraper.
rascadera, *n.f.*, **rascador,** *n.m.* scraper.
rascadura, *n.f.* scratch; scraping.
rascar [A], *v.t.* scrape; scratch.—*v.r.*
(*S.A., C.A.*) get drunk.
rascatripas, *n.m. inv.* (*pej.*) scraper, fiddler.
rascazón, *n.f.* itch, itching.
rascón, -cona, *a.* sharp, tart.
rasero, *n.m.* strickle; *medir por un —,* treat
quite impartially.
rasgado, -da, *a.* wide, light (*window*); full,
wide (*mouth*); large (*eyes*).—*n.m.* tear, rip.
rasgadura, *n.f.* tearing; tear.
rasgar [B], *v.t.* tear (up); rip apart.—*v.r.* tear;
get torn.
rasgo, *n.m.* feature, trait; flourish, dash; feat;
flash of wit.
rasgón, *n.m.* rent, rip, tear.
rasguear, *v.t.* strum.
rasgueo, *n.m.* strumming.
rasguñar, *v.t.* scratch; sketch.
rasguño, *n.m.* scratch; outline.
raso, -sa, *a.* smooth, level; flat, plain; clear,
open; skimming the ground.—*n.m.* satin;
flat land; *al —,* in the open air; *soldado —,*
private.
raspadura, *n.f.* scraping.
raspar, *v.t.* scrape (off); bite, be sharp (on);
steal.
raspear, *v.i.* scratch (*pen*).
rastra, *n.f.* sledge; harrow; track; grapnel;
string of onions; anything trailing; *a (la) —,*
a rastras, dragging; unwillingly.

rastrear, *v.t.* trail, trace, track; harrow; drag; fathom out; dredge; skim.—*v.i.* fly very low.

rastreo, *n.m.* dredging; trawling.

rastrero, -ra, *a.* trailing; dragging; skimming the ground; low, abject; creeping; grovelling.—*n.m.* slaughterman.

rastrillar, *v.t.* comb, hackle; (*agr.*) rake (up).

rastrillo, *n.m.* (*agr.*) rake; portcullis, grating; (*rail.*) cow-catcher.

rastro, *n.m.* trace; scent, trail; rake, harrow; street market.

rastrojo, *n.m.* stubble.

rasurar, *v.t., v.r.* shave.

rata (1), *n.f.* (*zool.*) rat.—*n.m.* (*fam.*) [RATERO].

rata (2) **por cantidad,** *adv.* pro rata.

rataplán, *n.m.* drum-beat, rub-a-dub.

ratear, *v.t.* share out; lessen; filch.—*v.i.* creep.

ratería, *n.f.* petty larceny; meanness.

ratero, -ra, *a.* trailing; vile; thievish.—*n.m.f.* petty thief, pickpocket.

ratificación, *n.f.* ratification.

ratificar [A], *v.t.* ratify.

rato, *n.m.* while; moment; **buen —,** quite a while; **pasar el —,** waste one's time; kill time; **a ratos perdidos,** during leisure.

ratón, -tona, *n.m.f.* (*zool.*) mouse; **— de biblioteca,** (*fam.*) book-worm.

ratonero, -ra, *a.* mousy.—*n.f.* mouse-trap; mouse-hole.

rauco, -ca, (*poet.*) [RONCO].

raudal, *n.m.* torrent; abundance.

raudo, -da, *a.* swift.

raya, *n.f.* stripe; dash; line; scratch; crease, pleat; parting (*of hair*); boundary; (*ichth.*) ray; **tener a —,** keep within bounds, keep at bay; **hacer —,** be eminent.

rayado, -da, *a.* striped; scratched.—*n.m.* ruling lines.

rayano, -na, *a.* bordering; borderline.

rayar, *v.t.* line; stripe; scratch; cross out; rifle; underline.—*v.i.* border (**en,** on); begin to appear; shine.

rayo, *n.m.* ray, beam; lightning; thunderbolt; sudden havoc; **echar rayos,** be fuming with rage; **rayos alfa, beta, gama,** alpha, beta, gamma rays; **rayos infrarrojos** (**ultravioletas**), infra-red (ultraviolet) rays; **rayos X,** X-rays. [RAER].

rayón, *n.m.* rayon.

rayoso, -sa, *a.* striped, rayed.

raza, *n.f.* race; breed; quality; cleft, crack; fault (*in cloth*); **de —,** thoroughbred.

rázago, *n.m.* sackcloth.

razón, *n.f.* reason; right; rate; ratio; account, story; **a — de,** at the rate of; **con —,** rightly; **dar la — a,** agree with; **dar — de,** give an account of; **— social,** (*com.*) firm; **tener —,** be right.

razonable, *a.* reasonable.

razonamiento, *n.m.* reasoning.

razonar, *v.t.* reason out, discourse; itemize.

razzia, *n.f.* razzia, raid.

re (1), *n.m.* (*mus.*) (key of) D.

re- (2), *prefix.* **re-** *indicates repetition, as* **releer,** re-read; *prefixed to adjectives & advs.,* very, *as* **rebueno,** very good.

rea, *n.f.* female defendant.

reacción, *n.f.* reaction; **— en cadena,** chain reaction; [MOTOR].

reaccionar, *v.i.* react.

reaccionario, -ria, *a., n.m.f.* reactionary.

reacio, -cia, *a.* stubborn.

reactivo, -va, *a.* reactive.—*n.m.* reagent.

reactor, *n.m.* reactor.

reajuste, *n.m.* readjustment.

real, *a.* real; royal; fine, superb.—*n.m.* army camp; real (25 céntimos).

realce, *n.m.* raised work, relief; enhancement; emphasis.

realengo, -ga, *a.* of royal ownership.

realeza, *n.f.* royalty.

realidad, *n.f.* reality; truth.

realismo, *n.m.* royalism; realism.

realista (1), *a.* realistic.—*n.m.f.* realist.

realista (2), *a., n.m.f.* royalist.

realizable, *a.* realizable; saleable.

realización, *n.f.* realization; carrying out; sale; (*cine.*) production.

realizar [C], *v.t.* realize; carry out; perform; (*cine.*) produce.—*v.r.* be fulfilled; happen.

realzar [C], *v.t.* raise; enhance; emphasize, emboss.

reanimar, *v.t., v.r.* revive; cheer up.

reanudar, *v.t.* resume.

reaparecer [9], *v.i.* reappear.

reaparición, *n.f.* reappearance.

rearmar, *v.t., v.r.* rearm.

rearme, *n.m.* rearmament.

reata, *n.f.* tethered line of horses; single file; **de —,** in single file; (*fam.*) on a piece of string, round one's little finger.

rebaba, *n.f.* burr, rough edge.

rebaja, *n.f.* rebate, discount; price-cut(ting).

rebajamiento, *n.m.* lowering; discounting; humbling.

rebajar, *v.t.* lower, reduce; tone down; humble.—*v.r.* be humbled; humble oneself, condescend (**a,** to); (*mil.*) be discharged.

rebalsar, *v.t.* dam (*a stream*).—*v.i., v.r.* get blocked up; pile up.

rebanada, *n.f.* slice (*esp. of bread*).

rebanar, *v.t.* slice.

rebañar, *v.t.* clean up, pick clean.

rebaño, *n.m.* flock.

rebasar, *v.t.* go beyond.

rebate, *n.m.* encounter, clash.

rebatimiento, *n.m.* refutation; repulsion.

rebatiña, *n.f.* scramble, grabbing.

rebatir, *v.t.* refute; repel, drive off; deduct.

rebato, *n.m.* (*mil.*) surprise; alarm; great excitement.

rebeco, *n.m.* (*zool.*) chamois.

rebelar, *v.r.* rebel, revolt.

rebelde, *a.* rebellious.—*n.m.* rebel; (*jur.*) defaulter.

rebeldía, *n.f.* rebelliousness; (*jur.*) default.

rebelión, *n.f.* rebellion, revolt.

rebién, *adv.* (*fam.*) very well.

reblandecer [9], *v.t., v.r.* soften.

rebocillo, -ciño, *n.m.* shawl.

rebombar, *v.i.* resound.

rebosadero, *n.m.* overflow.

rebosadura, *n.f.,* **rebosamiento,** *n.m.* overflow, overflowing.

rebosar, *v.t.* overflow with.—*v.i., v.r.* overflow, be bursting (**de, en,** with).

rebotadura, *n.f.* rebounding.

rebotar, *v.t.* repel, reject; bend over; alter; (*fam.*) bother.—*v.i.* rebound, bounce (**en,** off).—*v.r.* alter; (*fam.*) get worried.

rebote, *n.m.* bounce; rebound; **de —,** incidentally.

rebozado, -da, a. (cul.) in batter.
rebozar [C], v.t. (cul.) batter; disguise; muffle up.—v.r. muffle oneself up.
rebozo, n.m. disguise; muffler; shawl; de —, secretly; sin —, openly.
rebrotar, v.i. sprout.
rebrote, n.m. (agr.) shoot; (med.) recurrent attack.
rebufar, v.i. blow and snort.
rebujar, v.t. jumble up.—v.r. wrap oneself up.
rebullir [J], v.i., v.r. stir, move.
rebumbar, v.i. whistle (bullet, shell).
rebusca, n.f. careful search; gleaning; remains.
rebuscado, -da, a. recherché; affected.
rebuscamiento, n.m. searching; affectation.
rebuscar [A], v.t. seek; examine; glean.
rebuznar, v.i. bray, hee-haw.
rebuzno, n.m. bray, hee-haw.
recabar, v.t. manage to get.
recadero, -ra, n.m.f. messenger, errand-boy or girl.
recado, n.m. message; errand; gift; outfit; provisions; safety.
recaer [14], v.i. fall again; relapse; devolve (en, upon).
recaída, n.f. relapse.
recalar, v.t. drench.—v.i. (naut.) sight land.
recalcar [A], v.t. press tight; cram; stress.—v.i. (naut.) list.—v.r. sprain; harp on.
recalcitrante, a. recalcitrant.
recalcitrar, v.i. baulk; resist.
recalentar [1], v.t. reheat, warm up; overheat.
recamar, v.t. embroider.
recambio, n.m. re-exchange; de —, spare (part).
recapacitar, v.t., v.i. think out, run over.
recapitulación, n.f. recapitulation.
recapitular, v.t., v.i. recapitulate.
recarga, n.f. recharge, recharging.
recargar [B], v.t. reload; recharge; overload; overcharge; increase (taxes); overdo.
recargo, n.m. new charge or load; extra charge; overload; increase.
recatado, -da, a. cautious; modest.
recatar, v.t. conceal; taste again.—v.r. hide; be reserved or cautious.
recato, n.m. caution, prudence; modesty.
recauchar, v.t. retread (tyres).
recaudación, n.f. tax collecting; tax office.
recaudador, n.m. tax-collector.
recaudamiento, n.m. tax collecting; tax district.
recaudar, v.t. collect, gather; watch over.
recaudo, n.m. tax collecting; caution; bail.
recelar, v.t. fear, distrust; suspect.—v.i., v.r. distrust; be suspicious (de, of).
recelo, n.m. fear, foreboding; distrust.
receloso, -sa, a. distrustful, fearful.
recensión, n.f. review, recension.
recentar [1], v.t. leaven.—v.r. be renewed.
recepción, n.f. reception; admission.
receptáculo, n.m. receptacle; refuge.
receptar, v.t. (jur.) receive (stolen goods); welcome; conceal; abet.
receptivo, -va, a. receptive; susceptible.
receptor, -ra, a. receiving.—n.m. (rad., T.V., tel.) receiver.
recesivo, -va, a. recessive.
receso, n.m. recess(ion); deviation.

receta, n.f. (cul.) recipe; (med.) prescription; schedule.
recetar, v.t. (med.) prescribe.
recibí, n.m. receipt.
recibidor, -ra, n.m. receiver; ante-room.
recibimiento, n.m. reception; hall.
recibir, v.t. receive.—v.r. be received, be admitted (de, as).
recibo, n.m. receipt; salon; reception; at home.
recidiva, n.f. relapse.
recién, adv. (only before p.p.s except in S.A.) recently, newly.
reciente, a. recent.
recinto, n.m. enclosure.
recio, -cia, a. robust, strong; harsh; impetuous.—adv. strongly, harshly.
récipe, n.m. (fam.) prescription; (fam.) displeasure; scolding.
recipiente, a. receiving.—n.m. recipient.
reciprocación, n.f. reciprocation.
reciprocar [A], v.t., v.r. reciprocate.—v.r. match.
recíproco, -ca, a., n.m.f. reciprocal.
recitación, n.f. recitation.
recital, n.m. recital.
recitar, v.t. recite.
reciura, n.f. vigour; rigour.
reclamación, n.f. claim; reclamation; objection.
reclamar, v.t. claim; reclaim; decoy, lure; call.—v.i. cry out.
reclamista, n.m.f. publicity agent.
reclamo, n.m. decoy, lure; reclamation; call; catch-word; advert(isement), blurb.
reclinar, v.t., v.r. recline, lean.
recluir [O], v.t. seclude, intern.
reclusión, n.f. reclusion, seclusion; imprisonment.
recluso, -sa, a. secluded; confined.—n.m.f. prisoner; recluse.
recluta, n.f. recruiting.—n.m. recruit.
reclutamiento, n.m. recruitment; recruiting.
reclutar, v.t. recruit; (S.A.) round up.
recobrar, v.t., v.r. recover.
recobro, n.m. recovery.
recodar, v.i., v.r. lean (on elbow); twist and turn.
recodo, n.m. bend, turn.
recogedero, n.m. gatherer; gathering area.
recogedor, -ra, n.m.f. gatherer, collector.—n.m. rake; gatherer; box.
recoger [E], v.t. pick up; gather; pull or take in; welcome; shelter.—v.r. take shelter; withdraw; go home; cut spending.
recogido, -da, a. secluded, cloistered; modest.—n.m.f. inmate.—n.f. gathering; withdrawal.
recogimiento, n.m. gathering, collection; retreat; shelter.
recolección, n.f. summary, compilation; collection; meditation; retreat; harvest.
recolectar, v.t. harvest.
recoleto, -ta, a., n.m.f. (eccl.) said of strict orders.
recomendable, a. commendable.
recomendación, n.f. recommendation; (fam.) piece of advice or of one's mind.
recomendar [1], v.t. recommend.
recompensa, n.f. recompense, reward.
recompensar, v.t. recompense, reward.
recomponer [25], v.t. repair; recompose.

reconcentrar, *v.t.* gather, concentrate; conceal.—*v.r.* assemble, gather; concentrate.
reconciliable, *a.* reconcilable.
reconciliación, *n.f.* reconciliation.
reconciliar, *v.t.* reconcile; confess (*s.o.*); reconsecrate.—*v.r.* be reconciled.
reconditez, *n.f.* mystery.
recóndito, -ta, *a.* recondite.
reconocedor, -ra, *n.m.f.* inspector.
reconocer [9], *v.t.* recognize; inspect; reconnoitre; admit.—*v.r.* confess; be plain *or* clear.
reconocido, -da, *a.* grateful, obliged.
reconocimiento, *n.m.* recognition; gratitude; inspection; reconnaissance; (*med.*) examination.
reconquista, *n.m.f.* reconquest.
reconquistar, *v.t.* reconquer; recover.
reconstruir [O], *v.t.* reconstruct.
recontar [4], *v.t.* recount, relate.
reconvención, *n.f.* expostulation, charge.
reconvenir [36], *v.t.* reproach, charge.
recopilación, *n.f.* compendium, digest, compilation.
recopilar, *v.t.* compile.
record, *n.m.* (*pl.* **-ds**) record; *batir* or *establecer un* —, break *or* set up a record.
recordable, *a.* memorable.
recordar [4], *v.t.* remember; remind.—*v.i.* remember; wake; come round.
recorrer, *v.t.* cross, travel through; look over, run over.
recorrido, *n.m.* run, path; refit; mileage; (*mech.*) stroke.
recortado, *n.m.* cut-out (*figure*).
recortadura, *n.f.* cutting, clipping.
recortar, *v.t.* cut off; trim; cut out; outline. —*v.r.* stand out.
recorte, *n.m.* cutting.
recostar [4], *v.t., v.r.* recline, lean.
recoveco, *n.m.* turn, bend; trick.
recreación, *n.f.* recreation.
recrear, *v.t.* re-create; amuse, relax.—*v.r.* relax, amuse oneself.
recreativo, -va, *a.* recreative.
recrecer [9], *v.t., v.i.* increase.—*v.i.* recur.— *v.r.* recover one's spirits.
recreo, *n.m.* recreation; place of amusement.
recriminación, *n.f.* recrimination.
recriminar, *v.t., v.i.* recriminate.
recrudecer [9], *v.i., v.r.* recur; get worse.
recrude(s)cencia, *n.f.* **recrudecimiento,** *n.m.* recrudescence.
rectangular, *a.* rectangular.
rectángulo, *n.m.* rectangle.
rectificación, *n.f.* rectification.
rectificar [A], *v.t.* rectify.
rectilíneo, -nea, *a.* rectilinear.
rectitud, *n.f.* rectitude.
recto, -ta, *a.* straight; right; upright; basic. —*n.m.* rectum.—*adv.* straight ahead.
rector, -ra, *a.* governing.—*n.m.f.* principal. —*n.m.* rector.
recua, *n.f.* drove; multitude.
recubrir [*p.p.* **recubierto**], *v.t.* cover; recover.
recudir, *v.t.* pay (*due*).—*v.i.* revert.
recuento, *n.m.* count; re-count.
recuerdo, *n.m.* memory; souvenir.—*pl.* regards; [RECORDAR].
recuero, *n.m.* drover.
recuesta, *n.f.* request.

recuestar, *v.t.* request, require.
reculada, *n.f.* recoil; backing.
recular, *v.i.* fall back; recoil.
recuperable, *a.* recoverable.
recuperación, *n.f.* recuperation.
recuperar, *v.t., v.r.* recuperate, recover.
recurrir, *v.i.* resort; revert.
recurso, *n.m.* resource; recourse; petition.
recusar, *v.t.* decline; (*jur.*) challenge.
rechazamiento, *n.m.* repulsion; rejection.
rechazar [C], *v.t.* repulse; reject; repel.
rechazo, *n.m.* rebound, recoil; rejection.
rechiflar, *v.t.* boo, hiss, deride.
rechinador, -ra, rechinante, *a.* squeaking, creaking.
rechinar, *v.i.* creak, squeak, grate.
rechistar, *v.i.* *sin* —, without a word without protest.
rechoncho, -cha, *a.* (*fam.*) chubby.
de rechupete, *a. phr.* (*fam.*) super. smashing.
red, *n.f.* net; net-work; netting; (*fig.*) trap.
redacción, *n.f.* editing; editorial office.
redactar, *v.t.* edit; draw up, compose.
redactor, -ra, *n.m.f.* editor.—*n.m.f.* compiler.
redar, *v.t.* net, haul.
redargüir [I], *v.t.* refute; impugn.
redecilla, *n.f.* netting; hair-net.
rededor, *n.m.* surroundings; *al* or *en* — (*de*), around.
redención, *n.f.* redemption, salvation.
redentor, -ra, *a.* redeeming.—*n.m.* redeemer.
redición, *n.f.* reiteration.
redil, *n.m.* sheepfold.
redimir, *v.t.* redeem; ransom; rescue.
rédito, *n.m.* (*com.*) yield.
redituar [M], *v.t.* (*com.*) yield.
redivivo, -va, *a.* resuscitated.—*n.m.f.* ghost one back from the dead.
redobladura, *n.f.,* **redoblamiento,** *n.m.* redoubling; doubling.
redoblar, *v.t.* double; redouble; bend over; do again.—*v.i.* roll (*drums*).
redoble, *n.m.* [REDOBLAMIENTO]; roll (*of drums*).
redoblón, *n.m.* rivet.
redolor, *n.m.* after-pain, dull ache.
redoma, *n.f.* phial, flask.
redonda, *n.f.* district; pasture; *a la* — roundabout.
redondel, *n.m.* circle; bull-ring.
redondez, *n.f.* roundness.
redondo, -da, *a.* round; clear; decided; (*print.*) roman.—*n.m.* circle, ring; (*fam.*) cash; *caer* —, fall senseless.
redopelo, *n.m.* scuffle, scrap; *al* —, against the grain; without rhyme or reason.
redro, *adv.* (*fam.*) back(wards).
redropelo [REDOPELO].
reducción, *n.f.* reduction.
reducido, -da, *a.* reduced; small; narrow, close.
reducir [15], *v.t.* reduce.—*v.r.* get into order; come, amount (*a*, to).
reducto, *n.m.* redoubt.
reductor, -ra, *a.* reducing.—*n.m.* reducer.
redundancia, *n.f.* redundancy.
redundante, *a.* redundant.
redundar, *v.i.* overflow; redound (*en*, to).
reduplicar [A], *v.t.* redouble, reduplicate.
reduzco [REDUCIR].
reeditar, *v.t.* reprint, republish.

re(e)mbarcar [A], *v.t.* re-embark.
re(e)mbarco, *n.m.* re-embarkation.
re(e)mbolsar, *v.t.* refund, reimburse.
re(e)mbolso, *n.m.* refund; reimbursement; *contra* —, cash on delivery.
re(e)mplazante, *n.m.f.* substitute (*person*).
re(e)mplazar [C], *v.t.* replace, substitute.
reencarnación, *n.f.* reincarnation.
re(e)ncuentro, *n.m.* clash.
re(e)nganchar, *v.t.* re-enlist; recouple.
re(e)nviar [L], *v.t.* forward, send on.
re(e)xpedir [8], *v.t.* forward, send on.
refacción, *n.f.* refreshment; (*fam.*) extra; (*S.A.*) upkeep.
refección, *n.f.* refreshment; repairs.
refectorio, *n.m.* refectory.
referencia, *n.f.* reference; narrative; report.
referéndum, *n.m.* (*pl.* -ms) referendum.
referente, *a.* referring.
referido, -da, *a., n.m.f.* aforesaid.
referir [6], *v.t.* refer; relate, report.—*v.r.* refer.
refertero, -ra, *a.* quarrelsome.
de refilón, *adv. phr.* askance; in passing.
refinación, *n.f.* refinement; refining.
refinado, -da, *a.* refined; sharp, artful.
refinamiento, *n.m.* refinement; refining.
refinar, *v.t.* refine; polish, improve.
refinería, *n.f.* refinery.
refirmar, *v.t.* ratify.
refitolero, -ra, *n.m.f.* refectioner; (*fam.*) busybody.
reflectar, *v.t.* (*phys.*) reflect.
reflector, -ra, *a.* reflecting.—*n.m.* reflector; (*mil.*) searchlight; head-light.
reflejar, *v.t.* reflect; mirror; show.—*v.r.* be reflected.
reflejo, -ja, *a.* reflected; reflexive.—*n.m.* reflex; reflection; glare, glow.
reflexión, *n.f.* reflection.
reflexionar, *v.t.* think over.—*v.i.* reflect (*en, sobre*, on).
reflexivo, -va, *a.* reflexive.
reflujo, *n.m.* reflux, ebb.
refocilar, *v.t.* exhilarate; cheer.—*v.r.* frolic; find new vigour.
reforma, *n.f.* reform; (*eccl.*) Reformation.
reformación, *n.f.* reformation.
reformador, -ra, *n.m.f.* reformer.
reformar, *v.t.* reform; re-form; revise; mend.—*v.r.* reform.
reformativo, -va, *a.* reformative.
reformatorio, -ria, *a., n.m.* reformatory.
reformista, *n.m.f.* reformist.
reforzar [4C], *v.t.* reinforce; strengthen; boost; cheer.
refracción, *n.f.* refraction.
refractar, *v.t.* refract.
refractario, -ria, *a.* refractive; stubborn, rebellious.
refractivo, -va, *a.* refractive.
refractor, -ra, *a.* refractive.—*n.m.* refractor.
refrán, *n.m.* proverb.
refranero, *n.m.* collection of proverbs.
refregar [1B], *v.t.* rub; (*fam.*) tell off.
refregón, *n.m.* rub, rubbing.
refreír [28, *p.p.* refrito], *v.t.* re-fry; fry well; (*fam.*) bore to tears.
refrenar, *v.t.* restrain, curb.
refrescante, *a.* refreshing; cooling.
refrescar [A], *v.t.* refresh; cool.
refresco, *n.m.* refreshment; cold drink.

refriega, *n.f.* skirmish, affray.
refrigeración, *n.f.* refrigeration; cooling.
refrigerador, *n.m.* refrigerator.
refrigerante, *a.* cooling, refrigerating.
refrigerar, *v.t.* cool; refrigerate.
refrigerio, *n.m.* coolness; refreshment; comfort.
refringir [E], *v.t.* refract.
refrito, -ta, *p.p.* [REFREÍR].—*n.m.* rehash.
refuerzo, *n.m.* reinforcement.
refugiado, -da, *n.m.f.* refugee.
refugiar, *v.t.* shelter.—*v.r.* take refuge.
refugio, *n.m.* refuge; shelter; asylum.
refulgencia, *n.f.* refulgence.
refulgente, *a.* refulgent.
refulgir [E], *v.i.* shine, gleam.
refundición, *n.f.* adaptation; remelting.
refundir, *v.t.* recast; adapt.
refunfuñar, *v.i.* grumble.
refutación, *n.f.* refutation.
refutar, *v.t.* refute.
regadera, *n.f.* watering-can; sprinkler; ditch.
regadío, -ía, *a.* irrigable.—*n.m.* irrigated land.
regajal, regajo, *n.m.* puddle; trickle.
regala, *n.f.* (*naut.*) gunwale.
regalado, -da, *a.* delightful; delicate.
regalar, *v.t.* give; regale; fondle.—*v.r.* live sumptuously.
regalía, *n.f.* privilege; bonus.—*pl.* regalia.
regaliz, *n.m.*, regaliza, *n.f.* licorice.
regalo, *n.m.* present; gift; pleasure; luxury.
regalón, -lona, *a.* (*fam.*) easy, comfortable.
regante, *n.m.* irrigator.
a regañadientes, *adv. phr.* grumblingly, reluctantly.
regañar, *v.t.* (*fam.*) scold.—*v.i.* growl; quarrel.
regaño, *n.m.* snarl; scolding.
regar [1B], *v.t.* water; sprinkle.
regata, *n.f.* regatta; water-course.
regatear, *v.t.* haggle over; sell retail; (*fam.*) duck (*evade*).—*v.i.* haggle.
regateo, *n.m.* haggling.
regatería, *n.f.* retailer's; retail.
regatero, -ra, *a.* retailing; (*fam.*) haggling.—*n.m.f.* retailer.
regatonear, *v.i.* trade retail.
regazar [C], *v.t.* tuck up.
regazo, *n.m.* lap.
regencia, *n.f.* regency.
regeneración, *n.f.* regeneration.
regenerar, *v.t.* regenerate.
regenta, *n.f.* wife of regent *or* professor *etc.*
regentar, *v.t.* govern, rule, boss.
regente, *a.* ruling.—*n.m.f.* regent.—*n.m.* manager; foreman; professor.
regicida, *n.m.f.* regicide (*person*).
regicidio, *n.m.* regicide (*act*).
regidor, *n.m.* alderman; prefect.
régimen, *n.m.* (*pl.* regímenes) regime; regimen; system; rules; normality; (*med.*) regimen, diet; (*gram.*) government.
regimentación, *n.f.* regimentation.
regimental, *a.* regimental.
regimentar [1], *v.t.* regiment.
regimiento, *n.m.* rule, government; council; regiment.
regio, -gia, *a.* royal, regal.
región, *n.f.* region.
regional, *a.* regional.
regir [8E], *v.t.* rule; govern; direct; steer.—*v.i.* be in force.

registrador

registrador, -ra, *a.* registering.—*n.m.f.* registrar, recorder.—*n.f.* till.
registrar, *v.t.* register; record; inspect, search.—*v.r.* register.
registro, *n.m.* register; search, inspection; record; (*mus.*) organ stop; (*med.*) period; pitch.
regla, *n.f.* rule, order; ruler; *por —general,* as a general rule; *— de cálculo,* slide-rule.
reglado, -da, *a.* moderate.
reglamentar, *v.t.* regulate.
reglamentario, -ria, *a.* statutory, regulation.
reglamento, *n.m.* regulation; regulations.
reglar, *a.* (*eccl.*) regular.—*v.t.* line, rule; regulate; guide.
regocijar, *v.t.* gladden, exhilarate.—*v.r.* rejoice.
regocijo, *n.m.* joy, rejoicing.
regodear, *v.r.* (*fam.*) have fun.
regodeo, *n.m.* (*fam.*) fun.
regoldar [10], *v.i.* (*low*) belch.
regraciar, *v.t.* be grateful for.
regresar, *v.i.* return.
regresión, *n.f.* regression.
regresivo, -va, *a.* regressive.
regreso, *n.m.* return.
regüeldo, *n.m.* (*low*) belch.
regulación, *n.f.* control, regulation.
regular, *a.* regular; (*fam.*) so-so, not bad.—*v.t.* control, regulate.
regularidad, *n.f.* regularity.
regularizar [C], *v.t.* regularize.
regurgitación, *n.f.* regurgitation.
regurgitar, *v.i.* regurgitate.
rehabilitación, *n.f.* rehabilitation.
rehabilitar, *v.t.* rehabilitate, restore.
rehacer [20], *v.t.* remake; re-do; repair.—*v.r.* recover.
rehacimiento, *n.m.* remaking; repair; recovery.
rehecho, -cha, *a.* dumpy.—*p.p.* [REHACER].
rehén, *n.m.* hostage.
reherir [6], *v.t.* repel.
rehervir [6], *v.t.* reboil.—*v.i.* boil again; seethe.—*v.r.* ferment.
rehilar, *v.i.* quiver; whiz.
rehuir [O], *v.t.* flee, shun.
rehusar, *v.t.* refuse.
reidero, -ra, *a.* (*fam.*) laughable.—*n.f.pl.* laughing fit.
reimpresión, *n.f.* reprint.
reimprimir [*p.p.* **reimpreso**; *obs.* **reimprimido**], *v.t.* reprint.
reina, *n.f.* queen.
reinado, *n.m.* reign.
reinante, *a.* reigning, prevailing.
reinar, *v.i.* reign; prevail.
reincidencia, *n.f.* relapse.
reincidir, *v.i.* relapse, fall back.
reino, *n.m.* kingdom, realm.
reintegrar, *v.t.* reintegrate; restore.—*v.r.* recover; return (*a,* to).
reír [28], *v.t.* laugh at.—*v.i., v.r.* laugh (*de, at*); (*fam.*) tear, split.
reiteración, *n.f.* reiteration.
reiterar, *v.t.* reiterate.
reiterativo, -va, *a.* reiterative.
reja, *n.f.* grating, grille; ploughshare.
rejería, *n.f.* ironwork.
rejilla, *n.f.* lattice; screen, grating; (*elec.*) grid.
rejo, *n.m.* goad; vigour.

rejón, *n.m.* dagger; spear.
rejoneador, *n.m.* mounted bullfighter.
rejonear, *v.t.* (*taur.*) fight bulls while mounted.
rejuvenecer [9], *v.t., v.i., v.r.* rejuvenate.
rejuvenecimiento, *n.m.* rejuvenation.
relación, *n.f.* relation; tale; report.
relacionar, *v.t.* relate.—*v.r.* be related.
relajación, *n.f.* relaxation, release, slackening; laxity; rupture.
relajante, *a.* relaxing, slackening.
relajar, *v.t.* relax; hand over; debauch.—*v.r.* relax; become lax; get ruptured.
relamer, *v.t.* lick again.—*v.r.* lick one's lips; relish; glory; use make-up.
relamido, -da, *a.* affected, prim.
relámpago, *n.m.* lightning flash.
relampaguear, *v.i.* flash; lighten.
relampagueo, *n.m.* flashing; lightning.
relance, *n.m.* chance.
relapso, -sa, *a.* relapsed.—*n.m.f.* backslider.
relatar, *v.t.* relate, tell, report.
relatividad, *n.f.* relativity.
relativismo, *n.m.* relativism.
relativo, -va, *a.* relative.
relato, *n.m.* story; report.
relator, -ra, *n.m.f.* narrator; reporter.
relegación, *n.f.* relegation; exile.
relegar [B], *v.t.* relegate.
relevación, *n.f.* relief; (*jur.*) remission.
relevante, *a.* outstanding, excellent.
relevar, *v.t.* bring into relief; relieve; release; replace.—*v.i.* stand out.
relevo, *n.m.* (*mil.*) relief.
relicario, *n.m.* reliquary, shrine.
relicto, -ta, *a.* (*jur.*) bequeathed.
relieve, *n.m.* relief; relievo; *bajo —,* bas-relief; *poner de —,* emphasize.—*pl.* leavings, offal.
religión, *n.f.* religion.
religioso, -sa, *a.* religious.—*n.m.* monk.—*n.f.* nun.
relinchar, *v.i.* neigh.
relinch(id)o, *n.m.* neigh.
reliquia, *n.f.* relic; vestige; heirloom.
reloj, *n.m.* watch, clock; meter.
relojería, *n.f.* watchmaker's; watchmaking.
relojero, *n.m.* watchmaker.
reluciente, *a.* shining.
relucir [9], *v.i.* shine.
relumbrante, *a.* dazzling, brilliant.
relumbrar, *v.i.* shine, dazzle, glare.
relumbre, *n.m.* flash, blaze, glare.
relumbrón, *n.m.* flash, bright light; tinsel.
rellanar, *v.t.* level out.—*v.r.* fall flat.
rellano, *n.m.* landing (*stair*); flat place.
rellenar, *v.t.* refill; fill up; stuff.
relleno, -na, *a.* very full, packed tight; stuffed.—*n.m.* stuffing; padding.
remachar, *v.t.* rivet; stress.
remanecer [9], *v.i.* appear suddenly.
remanente, *n.m.* residue, remnant.
remansar, *v.r.* slow, eddy.
remanso, *n.m.* backwater, eddy; slowness.
remar, *v.i.* row (*boat*); toil.
rematar, *v.t.* finish off.—*v.i.* end.—*v.r.* come to an end; *loco rematado,* raving mad.
remate, *n.m.* end; top, crown; *de —,* utterly; *por —,* in the end.
remedar, *v.t.* imitate, mimic.
remediable, *a.* remediable.
remediar, *v.t.* remedy; save; aid.

remedio, *n.m.* remedy; aid; amendment; (*jur.*) action; **no hay (más) —,** it can't be helped.
remedo, *n.m.* copy, imitation.
remellado, -da, *a.* dented; jagged.
remembrar, rememorar, *v.t.* recollect, recall.
remendar [1], *v.t.* patch (up).
remendón, -dona, *a.* mending.—*n.m.f.* mender.
rementir [6], *v.i., v.r.* tell many lies.
remero, -ra, *n.m.f.* rower.—*n.m.* oarsman.
remesar, *v.t.* remit; ship; tear.
remezón, *n.m.* (*S.A.*) earth tremor.
remiendo, *n.m.* patch, repair; mending.
remilgado, -da, *a.* prudish, fussy, affected.
remilgo, *n.m.* primness, affectation, fussiness.
reminiscencia, *n.f.* reminiscence.
remirado, -da, *a.* watchful, careful.
remirar, *v.t.* look at again *or* closely.—*v.r.* delight in watching; take pains (*en,* to).
remisión, *n.f.* remission; remitting; reference.
remiso, -sa, *a.* remiss, lazy.
remisor, -ra, *n.m.f.* (*S.A.*) sender.
remitente, *n.m.f.* sender.
remitir, *v.t.* remit, send; refer.—*v.r.* slacken; refer (*a,* to); submit.
remo, *n.m.* oar; rowing; limb; hard labour.
remoción, *n.f.* removal.
remojar, *v.t.* soak; (*fam.*) drink to.
remojo, *n.m.* soaking.
remolacha, *n.f.* (*bot.*) beet; sugar-beet.
remolcador, *n.m.* (*naut.*) tug; tower.
remolcar [A], *v.t.* tow.
remoler [5], *v.t.* grind up.
remolin(e)ar, *v.t., v.i., v.r.* whirl about.
remolino, *n.m.* whirl, whirlwind, whirlpool; eddy; throng.
remolón, -lona, *a.* shirking.—*n.m.f.* shirker.
remolque, *n.m.* tow, tow-rope, towing; trailer.
remonta, *n.f.* remount; repair.
remontar, *v.t.* scare off; mend; go up; raise. —*v.r.* rise, soar; go back.
remonte, *n.m.* remounting; repair; soaring.
remoquete, *n.m.* punch; gibe; nickname; (*fam.*) flirting.
rémora, *n.f.* hindrance; (*ichth.*) remora.
remorder [5], *v.t.* bite again; prick.—*v.r.* show one's feelings.
remordimiento, *n.m.* remorse; **remordimientos de conciencia,** prick(s) of conscience.
remoto, -ta, *a.* remote; vague.
remover [5], *v.t.* remove; upset; stir, shake. —*v.r.* move away.
remozar [C], *v.t., v.r.* rejuvenate.
rempujar, *v.t.* (*fam.*) jostle; shove.
rempujo, rempujón, *n.m.* (*fam.*) shove.
remudar, *v.t.* change, replace.
remuneración, *n.f.* remuneration.
remunerar, *v.t.* remunerate.
remunerativo, -va, *a.* remunerative.
remusgar [B], *v.t.* suspect.
renacentista, *a.* rel. to Renaissance.—*n.m.f.* Renaissance scholar.
renacer [9], *v.i.* be reborn; recover.
renaciente, *a.* renascent.
renacimiento, *n.m.* rebirth; Renaissance.
renacuajo, *n.m.* tadpole.
renal, *a.* renal.
rencilla, *n.f.* quarrel, bickering.
rencilloso, -sa, *a.* bickering.

rencor, *n.m.* rancour.
rencoroso, -sa, *a.* rancorous.
rencuentro, *n.m.* encounter, clash.
rendajo, *n.m.* (*orn.*) jay.
rendición, *n.f.* surrender; exhaustion.
rendido, -da, *a.* weary; abject.
rendija, *n.f.* crack, crevice.
rendimiento, *n.m.* submission; exhaustion; yield, output.
rendir [8], *v.t.* overcome; yield, produce; render; hand over.—*v.i.* yield.—*v.r.* surrender; become weary.
rene, *n.f.* kidney.
renegado, -da, *a., n.m.f.* renegade.
renegar [1B], *v.t.* deny; detest.—*v.i.* curse; apostatize; deny (*de*).
renegrido, -da, *a.* black-and-blue.
renglera, *n.f.* rank, row.
renglón, *n.m.* line (*print, writing*).
reniego, *n.m.* curse.
renitente, *a.* reluctant.
reno, *n.m.* reindeer.
renombrado, -da, *a.* renowned.
renombre, *n.m.* renown; surname.
renovable, *a.* renewable.
renovación, *n.f.* renewal; renovation.
renovador, -ra, *n.m.f.* renovator.
renovar [4], *v.t.* renew; renovate.
renquear, *v.i.* limp, hobble.
renta, *n.f.* income; **— vitalicia,** life annuity.
rentabilidad, *n.f.* (*com.*) yield.
rentado, -da, *a.* having an income.
rentar, *v.t.* produce, yield.
rentista, *n.m.f.* financier; receiver of income.
renuente, *a.* reluctant.
renuevo, *n.m.* renewal; new shoot.
renuncia, *n.f.* renunciation; resignation.
renunciación, *n.f.* renunciation.
renunciamiento, *n.m.* renouncement.
renunciar, *v.t.* renounce; resign; abandon; give (*a,* up).
renuncio, *n.m.* error, slip; (*fam.*) fib.
reñido, -da, *a.* at variance; bitter.
reñir [8K], *v.t.* scold; argue about.—*v.i., v.r.* quarrel, fall out.
reo, rea, *a.* guilty.—*n.m.f.* criminal, offender.
de reojo, *adv. phr.* askance.
reorganizar [C], *v.t., v.r.* reorganize.
reparable, *a.* reparable; remarkable.
reparación, *n.f.* repair; reparation.
reparar, *v.t.* repair; remedy; observe; stop. —*v.i.* halt; spot, take note (*en,* of).—*v.r.* stop; refrain.
reparo, *n.m.* repair; remark; objection, doubt; shelter; parry.
repartición, *n.f.* dealing; distribution.
repartimiento, *n.m.* distribution; assessment, allotment.
repartir, *v.t.* distribute; allot.
reparto, *n.m.* distribution; (*theat.*) cast.
repasar, *v.t.* retrace; revise; mend.
repaso, *n.m.* review; (*fam.*) scolding.
repatriación, *n.f.* repatriation.
repatriado, -da, *n.m.f.* repatriate.
repatriar [L], *v.t.* repatriate.
repecho, *n.m.* incline.
repelente, *a.* repellent.
repeler, *v.t.* repel.
repelo, *n.m.* twist, irregularity; (*fam.*) squabble; aversion.
repelón, *n.m.* tug, snatch; spurt.
repente, *n.m.* sudden start; **de —,** suddenly.

repentino, -na, *a.* sudden.
repentista, *n.m.f.* improviser; (*mus.*) sight-reader.
repercusión, *n.f.* repercussion; reflection.
repercutir, *v.i.* rebound; reverberate; have repercussions (**en,** on).
repertorio, *n.m.* repertoire; repertory.
repetición, *n.f.* repetition.
repetir [8], *v.t.* repeat.
repicar [A], *v.t.* hash, mince; ring.—*v.i.* resound.—*v.r.* boast.
repinar, *v.r.* rise.
repipi, *a., n.m.f.* (*fam.*) show-off, know-all.
repique, *n.m.* mincing; ringing; (*fam.*) squabble.
repiquete, *n.m.* peal; rapping; clash.
repiquetear, *v.t.* ring, chime; rap on.—*v.i.* peal; clatter.—*v.r.* (*fam.*) wrangle.
repisa, *n.f.* shelf; sill; mantelpiece.
repisar, *v.t.* trample on; fix in one's mind.
repizcar [C], *v.t.* pinch.
replegar [B], *v.t.* fold back.—*v.r.* fall back.
repleto, -ta, *a.* replete, packed, full.
réplica, *n.f.* reply, retort; replica.
replicar [A], *v.t.* reply to.—*v.i.* retort.
repliegue, *n.m.* fold; falling back.
repoblación, *n.f.* repopulation; restocking.
repoblar [4], *v.t.* repopulate, restock.
repollo, *n.m.* white cabbage.
reponer [25], *v.t.* replace; restore; reply.—*v.r.* recover; become calm.
reportaje, *n.m.* report, reporting.
repórter, *n.m.* reporter.
reporterismo, *n.m.* newspaper reporting.
reportero, -ra, *n.m.f.* reporter.
reposado, -da, *a.* restful; solemn.
reposar, *v.i., v.r.* rest.
reposición, *n.f.* replacement; recovery.
reposo, *n.m.* repose, rest.
repostería, *n.f.* pastry-shop; pantry.
repostero, *n.m.* pastry-cook; royal butler.
repregunta, *n.f.* cross-examination.
repreguntar, *v.t.* cross-examine.
reprender, *v.t.* reprehend.
reprensible, *a.* reprehensible.
reprensión, *n.f.* censure.
reprensor, -ra, *a.* reproving.—*n.m.f.* reproacher.
represa, *n.f.* dyke; recapture; check.
represalia, *n.f.* reprisal.
represaliar, *v.t.* retaliate against.
represar, *v.t.* dyke; check; recapture.
representación, *n.f.* performance; representation; dignity.
representanta, *n.f.* actress.
representante, *n.m.f.* representative, agent; actor.
representar, *v.t.* represent; show; perform; declare.—*v.r.* imagine.
representativo, -va, *a.* representative.
represión, *n.f.* repression.
represivo, -va, *a.* repressive.
represor, -ra, *n.m.f.* represser.
reprimenda, *n.f.* reprimand.
reprimir, *v.t.* repress.
reprobar [4], *v.t.* reprove.
réprobo, -ba, *a., n.m.f.* reprobate.
reprochar, *v.t.* reproach.
reproche, *n.m.* reproach.
reproducción, *n.f.* reproduction.
reproducir [16], *v.t., v.r.* reproduce.

reproductivo, -va, reproductor, -ra, *a.* reproductive.
reptar, *v.i.* crawl.
reptil, *a., n.m.* reptile.
república, *n.f.* republic; *República Arabe Unida,* United Arab Republic.
republicanismo, *n.m.* republicanism.
republicano, -na, *a., n.m.f.* republican.
repudiación, *n.f.* repudiation.
repudiar, *v.t.* repudiate.
repuesto, -ta, *a.* secluded.—*n.m.* spare; *de* — spare.—*p.p.* [REPONER].
repugnancia, *n.f.* repugnance.
repugnante, *a.* repugnant.
repugnar, *v.t.* contradict; avoid.—*v.i.* repel.
repulgo, *n.m.* hem; (*fig.*) silly scruple.
repulir, *v.t.* polish highly.—*v.t., v.r.* doll up.
repulsa, *n.f.* refusal, rejection.
repulsar, *v.t.* reject.
repulsión, *n.f.* repulsion; rejection.
repulsivo, -va, *a.* repulsive.
repullo, *n.m.* bound, start.
repuntar, *v.i.* move (*tide*).—*v.r.* go sour; (*fam.*) have a tiff.
repuse [REPONER].
reputación, *n.f.* reputation.
reputar, *v.t.* repute; appraise.
requebrar [1], *v.t.* flatter; flirt with; re-break.
requemazón, *n.f.* pungency; burn.
requerimiento, *n.m.* request; summons.
requerir [6], *v.t.* require; examine; woo; notify.
requesón, *n.m.* curds.
requetebién, *adv.* (*fam.*) fine, well.
requiebro, *n.m.* flattery; flirting; compliment.
réquiem *n.m.* (*pl.* **-ms**) requiem.
requilorios, *n.m.pl.* (*fam.*) wasting time.
requisa, *n.f.* inspection; (*mil.*) requisition.
requisar, *v.t.* inspect; (*mil.*) requisition.
requisición, *n.f.* requisition.
requisito, -ta, *a., n.m.* requisite; — *previo,* prerequisite.
res, *n.f.* head of cattle, beast.
resaber [30], *v.t.* know completely.
resabiar, *v.t.* lead into evil ways.—*v.r.* contract vices; relish; leave aftertaste.
resabido, -da, *a.* well-known; pedantic.
resabio, *n.m.* nasty aftertaste; vice.
resaca, *n.f.* surge; backwash; (*fam.*) hangover.
resalir [31], *v.i.* jut out.
resaltar, *v.i.* rebound; stand out.
resalte, *n.m.* projection.
resalto, *n.m.* rebound; projection.
resaludar, *v.t.* return the greeting of.
resarcir [D], *v.t.* compensate.
resbaladero, -ra, *n.m.f.* chute, slide; slipp(er)y place.
resbaladizo, -za, *a.* slipp(er)y.
resbaladura, *n.f.* slip *or* skid mark.
resbalar, *v.i.* slide; skid.—*v.r.* slip.
resbalón, *n.m.* slip.
rescatar, *v.t.* redeem; ransom; rescue.
rescate, *n.m.* ransom; rescue.
rescindir, *v.t.* rescind.
rescoldo, *n.m.* embers; smouldering; scruple.
rescontrar [4], *v.t.* (*com.*) offset.
resé [RESABER].
resecar [A], *v.t., v.r.* dry thoroughly.
reseco, -ca, *a.* very dry; skinny.
resellar, *v.t.* re-stamp; reseal.—*v.r.* turncoat.

resentido, -da, *a.* resentful.
resentimiento, *n.m.* resentment; grudge.
resentir [6], *v.r.* resent (*por*); weaken;
suffer (*de*, from).
reseña, *n.f.* review; outline.
reseñar, *v.t.* review; outline.
resequido, -da, *a.* dried up.
resero, *n.m.* stockman, rancher.
reserva, *n.f.* reserve, reservation.
reservación, *n.f.* reservation.
reservar, *v.t.* reserve; defer; conceal;
exempt.—*v.r.* be wary.
reservista, *n.m.* (*mil.*) reservist.
reservón, -vona, *a.* (*fam.*) distant, reserved.
reservorio, *n.m.* reservoir.
resfriado, *n.m.* (*med.*) chill, cold.
resfriante, *a.* cooling.—*n.m.* cooler.
resfriar [L], *v.t.*, *v.i.* cool.—*v.r.* cool off;
catch cold.
resfrío, *n.m.* cold.
resguardar, *v.t.* protect, shield.
resguardo, *n.m.* shield, guard, protection;
(*com.*) surety.
residencia, *n.f.* residence; hostel; (*jur.*)
impeachment.
residencial, *a.* residential.
residenciar, *v.t.* impeach.
residente, *a.*, *n.m.f.* resident.
residir, *v.i.* reside.
residual, *a.* residual, residuary.
residuo, *n.m.* residue; residuum.—*pl.* by-
products.
resignación, *n.f.* resignation.
resignar, *v.t.* resign.
resina, *n.f.* resin, rosin.
resinoso, -sa, *a.* resinous.
resistencia, *n.m.f.* resistance; stamina.
resistente, *a.* resistant.
resistir, *v.t.* resist, withstand.—*v.i.*, *v.r.*
resist; refuse (*a*, to).
resistor, *n.m.* (*elec.*) resistor.
resma, *n.f.* ream.
resolución, *n.f.* resolution.
resoluto, -ta, *a.* resolute; skilled; brief.
resolver [5, *p.p.* **resuelto**], *v.t.* decide on;
solve; resolve.—*v.r.* resolve (*a*, to); turn,
dissolve (*en*, into); decide (*por*, on).
resollar [4], *v.i.* pant; take a rest; **no —**,
not breathe a word.
resonancia, *n.f.* resonance; (*fig.*) repercussion.
resonante, *a.* resonant.
resonar [4], *v.i.* resound.
resoplar, *v.i.* puff; snort.
resopl(id)o, *n.m.* panting, puff.
resorte, *n.m.* (*mech.*) spring; motive; means;
springiness; (*S.A.*) field, province.
respaldar, *n.m.* back (*of seat*).—*v.t.* endorse;
back.—*v.r.* lean.
respaldo, *n.m.* back (*of seat*).
respectar, *v.t.* concern.
respectivo, -va, *a.* respective.
respecto, *n.m.* respect, reference; **— a,**
with regard to.
respetabilidad, *n.f.* respectability.
respetable, *a.* respectable; (*fam.*) audience,
spectators.
respetador, -ra, *a.* respectful.
respetar, *v.t.* respect.
respeto, *n.m.* respect, veneration; *campar*
por su **—,** be one's own master; *de* **—,**
spare; on ceremony.

respetuoso, -sa, *a.* respectful; awesome.
respigar [B], *v.t.* glean.
respingado, -da, *a.* turned-up (*nose*).
respingar [B], *v.i.* kick, baulk; fit badly.
respiración, *n.f.* respiration, breathing.
respiradero, *n.m.* vent.
respirador, *n.m.* respirator.
respirar, *v.t.*, *v.i.* breathe; breathe again;
feel respite; smell (*a*, of).
respiratorio, -ria, *a.* respiratory.
respiro, *n.m.* breathing; respite.
resplandecer [9], *v.i.* shine.
resplandeciente, *a.* brilliant, gleaming.
resplandor, *n.m.* brilliance, radiance.
responder, *v.t.* answer; reply to.—*v.i.*
answer (*de*, for); harmonize; respond.
responsabilidad, *n.f.* responsibility.
responsable, *a.* responsible (*de*, for).
responsivo, -va, *a.* responsive.
responso, *n.m.* (*eccl.*) response; (*fam.*)
telling-off.
respuesta, *n.f.* answer, reply.
resquebra(ja)dura, *n.f.* split, cleft.
resquebrajadizo, -za, *a.* brittle.
resquebrajar, *v.t.*, *v.r.* split.
resquebrar [1], *v.t.*, *v.r.* crack.
resquemar, *v.t.* sting, parch, bite.
resquemazón, *n.f.* bite, sting; burn.
resquemor, *n.m.* anguish; sting.
resquicio, *n.m.* chink, crack; chance.
resta, *n.f.* subtraction; remainder.
restablecer [9], *v.t.* re-establish, restore.—
v.r. recover.
restablecimiento, *n.m.* re-establishment,
restoration; recovery.
restallar, *v.i.* crack, smack.
restante, *a.* remaining.—*n.m.* remainder, rest.
restañar, *v.t.* stanch; re-tin.
restar, *v.t.* subtract.—*v.i.* be left.
restauración, *n.f.* restoration.
restaurán, *n.m.* restaurant.
restaurante, *a.* restoring.—*n.m.* restaurant.
restaurar, *v.t.* restore.
restaurativo, -va, *a.* restorative.
restitución, *n.f.* restitution.
restituir [O], *v.t.* return, restore.
resto, *n.m.* rest, remainder.—*pl.* remains.
restorán, restorante, *n.m.* restaurant.
restregar [1B], *v.t.* scrub.
restricción, *n.f.* restriction; reservation.
restrictivo, -va, *a.* restrictive.
restringir [E], *v.t.* restrict; limit.
restriñir, *v.t.* restrain; bind.
resucitación, *n.f.* resuscitation.
resucitar, *v.t.* resurrect, resuscitate.—*v.i.*
rise from the dead, revive.
resudar, *v.i.* sweat; seep; dry out.
resuelto, -ta, *a.* resolute; swift.—*p.p.*
[RESOLVER].
resuello, *n.m.* heavy breathing.
resulta, *n.m.* outcome, effect; vacancy.
resultado, *n.m.* result.
resultando, *n.m.* (*jur.*) finding.
resultar, *v.i.* result (*en*, in); turn out to be.
resumen, *n.m.* résumé; *en* **—,** in short.
resumidamente, *adv.* in short.
resumir, *v.t.* sum up.—*v.r.* be converted
(*en*, into).
resurgimiento, *n.m.* resurgence.
resurgir, *v.i.* re-arise; revive.
resurrección, *n.f.* resurrection.
resurtir, *v.i.* rebound.

retablo, *n.m.* (*eccl.*) altar-piece.
retaguardia, *n.f.* (*mil.*) rearguard.
retahila, *n.f.* file, line.
retama, *n.f.* (*bot.*) broom; furze.
retar, *v.t.* challenge.
retardar, *v.t.* retard.
retardo, *n.m.* delay.
retazo, *n.m.* scrap, piece.
retén, *n.m.*, store; reserve.
retención, *n.f.* retention.
retener [33], *v.t.* retain; detain.
retentivo, -va, *a.* retentive.—*n.f.* memory.
retina, *n.f.* (*anat.*) retina.
retintín, *n.m.* jingle, ringing.
retiñir [K], *v.i.* jingle, ring.
retirada, *n.f.* withdrawal, retreat.
retirar, *v.t.*, *v.r.* retire; withdraw.
retiro, *n.m.* retreat (*place*).
reto, *n.m.* challenge; threat.
retocar [A], *v.t.* retouch, touch up.
retoño, *n.m.* shoot, sprout.
retoque, *n.m.* retouching, touching-up.
retorcer [5D], *v.t.* twist; wring.—*v.r.* twist, writhe.
retórico, -ca, *a.* rhetorical.—*n.f.* rhetoric.
retornar, *v.t.*, *v.i.*, *v.r.* return.
retorno, *n.m.* return; reward; barter.
retortero, *n.m.* turn, twist.
retortijar, *v.t.* twist, curl.
retortijón, *n.m.* stomach-pain.
retozar [C], *v.i.* frolic; seethe.
retozón, -zona, *a.* frisky.
retracción, *n.f.* retraction.
retractación, *n.f.* retractation.
retractar, *v.t.* retract.
retráctil, *a.* retractile.
retraer [34], *v.t.* bring back; withdraw.—*v.r.* withdraw (*de*, from).
retrasar, *v.t.* delay; put back (*clock*).—*v.i.* be late *or* behind.—*v.r.* delay; be behind; be late.
retraso, *n.m.* delay; lateness.
retratar, *v.t.* portray; copy; photograph.
retrato, *n.m.* portrait; copy; photograph.
retrechero, -ra, *a.* (*fam.*) cunning.
retreta, *n.f.* (*mil.*) retreat; tattoo.
retrete, *n.m.* closet; lavatory.
retribución, *n.f.* payment, fee.
retribuir [O], *v.t.* reward, pay for.
retroceder, *v.i.* recede; recoil.
retroceso, *n.m.* backing; recoil (*of gun*); retrocession.
retrógrado, -da, *a.*, *n.m.f.* retrograde; reactionary.
retrogressión, *n.f.* retrogression.
retropropulsión, *n.f.* jet-propulsion.
retrospección, *n.f.* retrospect(ion).
retrospectivo, -va, *a.* retrospective.
retrovisor, *n.m.* (*auto.*) rear-view mirror.
retruécano, *n.m.* pun.
setumbante, *a.* high-flown; resounding.
retumbar, *v.i.* resound, re-echo.
reuma, *n.m.* rheumatism.—*n.m. or f.* (*med.*) rheum.
reumático, -ca, *a.* rheumatic.
reumatismo, *n.m.* rheumatism.
reunión, *n.f.* meeting, reunion.
reunir [P], *v.t.* assemble; unite; reunite.—*v.r.* meet, assemble.
revalidar, *v.t.* confirm, ratify.
revaloración, *n.f.* revaluation.
revalorar, revalorizar [C], *v.t.* revalue.

revancha, *n.f.* revenge, (*fam.*) evening the score.
revejecer [9], *v.i.*, *v.r.* age prematurely.
revelación, *n.f.* revelation.
revelar, *v.t.* reveal; (*phot.*) develop.
revenir [36], *v.i.* come back.—*v.r.* turn sour; shrivel; cave in; weaken.
reventar [1], *v.t.* smash up *or* open; burst; work to death; annoy.—*v.i.* burst; (*fam.*) peg out, die.—*v.r.* burst, explode.
reventón, *n.m.* burst; toil; steep hill.
rever [37], *v.t.* review, revise.
reverberar, *v.i.* reverberate.
reverbero, *n.m.* reverberation; reflector; street lamp; (*S.A.*) chafing dish.
reverdecer [9], *v.t.*, *v.i.* turn green again; rejuvenate.
reverencia, *n.f.* reverence; bow, curtsy.
reverenciar, *v.t.* revere.—*v.i.* bow, curtsy.
reverendo, -da, *a.* reverend.—*n.f.pl.* great qualities.
reverente, *a.* reverent.
reversible, *a.* reversible.
reversión, *n.f.* reversion.
reverso, *n.m.* reverse, back.
revés, *n.m.* reverse; back; setback; **al —,** the wrong way round; upside down; quite the opposite.
revesado, -da, *a.* complicated; wayward.
revestir [8], *v.t.* coat, cover; don; assume (*an air*); bedeck; invest (*con, de,* with).
revezar [C], *v.i.* work in shifts.
revezo, *n.m.* shift, turn.
revisar, *v.t.* revise, review, look over.
revisión, *n.f.* revision, revisal.
revisor, -ra, *a.* revisory.—*n.m.f.* reviser; (*rail.*) ticket inspector.
revista, *n.f.* inspection; (*mil.*) review; (*theat.*) revue; magazine; **pasar —,** inspect, review.
revivificar [C], *v.t.* revive, revivify.
revivir, *v.i.* revive; be renewed.
revocar [A], *v.t.* revoke; whitewash.
revolar [4], *v.i.* fly about.
revolcar [4A], *v.t.* overturn, knock down.—*v.r.* overturn; wallow.
revolcón, *n.m.* (*fam.*) upset.
revol(ot)ear, *v.t.* fling up.—*v.i.* flutter.
revoltijo, revoltillo, *n.m.* mess, jumble.
revoltoso, -sa, *a.* rebellious; trouble-making; involved; winding.—*n.m.f.* rebel; trouble-maker.
revolución, *n.f.* revolution.
revolucionar, *v.t.* revolutionize; incite to rebellion.—*v.r.* rebel.
revolucionario, -ria, *a.*, *n.m.f.* revolutionary.
revolver [5, *p.p.* **revuelto**], *v.t.* turn over; shake; revolve; retrace.—*v.i.* retrace one's steps.—*v.r.* turn; toss and turn.
revólver, *n.m.* revolver.
revolvimiento, *n.m.* revolving; upset(ting); commotion.
revuelco, *n.m.* upset; wallowing.
revuelo, *n.m.* (second) flight; upset.
revuelto, -ta, *a.* complex; messy; naughty; changeable; boisterous.—*n.f.* return; revolt; fight; change; upset.—*p.p.* [REVOLVER].
rey, *n.m.* king; **— de zarza,** (*orn.*) wren; **Reyes Magos,** the Three Wise Men (*in Spain, the equivalent of Santa Claus*); **(Día de) Reyes,** Epiphany.

reyerta, *n.f.* wrangle.
reyezuelo, *n.m.* petty king; (*orn.*) goldcrest.
rezagado, -da, *a.* laggardly.—*n.m.f.* laggard, straggler.
rezagar [B], *v.t.* leave behind, outstrip; postpone.—*v.r.* lag behind.
rezar [C], *v.t.* pray; say.—*v.i.* pray; (*fam.*) have to do (**con**, with).
rezo, *n.m.* prayer; devotions.
rezongar [B], *v.i.* grumble.
rezumar, *v.t., v.i., v.r.* ooze, seep.
ria, *n.f.* inlet, estuary; fjord.
riachuelo, *n.m.* brook, rivulet.
riada, *n.f.* flood.
ribaldo, -da, *a.* (*obs.*) knavish.
ribazo, *n.m.* embankment.
ribera, *n.f.* bank, shore; riverside.
ribero, *n.m.* dyke.
ribete, *n.m.* trimming; sign.
ribetear, *v.t.* trim.
ricacho, -cha, *a.* (*fam.*) very rich.
Ricardo, *n.m.* Richard.
rico, -ca, *a.* rich; (*fam.*) superb; (*pej.*) cheeky. —*n.m.* rich man; **nuevo —**, nouveau riche. —*n.m.f.* love, dear.
ridiculez, *n.f.* ridiculousness.
ridiculizar [C], *v.t.* ridicule.
ridiculo, -la, *a.* ridiculous; touchy.—*n.m.* ridicule; **poner en —**, make a fool of.
riego, *n.m.* irrigation; watering.
riel, *n.m.* rail; ingot.
rienda, *n.f.* rein.
riente, *a.* laughing, cheerful.
riesgo, *n.m.* risk, peril.
rifa, *n.f.* wrangle, fight; raffle.
rifar, *v.t.* raffle.
rifle, *n.m.* rifle.
rigidez, *n.f.* rigidity.
rigido, -da, *a.* rigid.
rigor, *n.m.* rigour; **ser de —**, be indispensable; **en —**, to be precise.
rigorista, *n.m.f.* stickler, rigorist.
rigoroso, riguroso, -sa, *a.* rigorous.
rija, *n.f.* squabble.
rima, *n.f.* rhyme; pile.
rimar, *v.t., v.i.* rhyme.
rimbombante, *a.* high-flown; resounding.
rimbombar, *v.i.* resound.
rimero, *n.m.* pile.
Rin, *n.m.* Rhine.
rincón, *n.f.* corner, nook; patch.
rinconada, *n.f.* corner.
ringla, ringlera, *n.f.* row, tier.
ringorrango, *n.m.* (*fam.*) fancy flourish, frippery.
rinoceronte, *n.m.* (*zool.*) rhinoceros.
riña, *n.f.* quarrel; scuffle, fight.
riñon, *n.m.* (*anat.*) kidney.—*pl.* back; loins.
río, *n.m.* river.
rioplatense, *a., n.m.f.* rel. to or native of River Plate area.
ripio, *n.m.* debris, rubble; doggerel; padding; (*fam.*) chance.
riqueza, *n.f.* riches, wealth; richness.
risa, *n.f.* laugh; laughter.
risco, *n.m.* crag, cliff.
riscoso, -sa, *a.* craggy, rugged.
risible, *a.* laughable.
risica, risilla, risita, *n.f.* giggle, titter.
risotada, *n.f.* guffaw.
risotear, *v.i.* guffaw.

ristra, *n.f.* string, line; lance-rest.
risueño, -ña, *a.* smiling.
ritmico, -ca, *a.* rhythmic(al).
ritmo, *n.m.* rhythm.
rito, *n.m.* rite.
ritual, *a., n.m.* ritual.
rival, *a., n.m.f.* rival.
rivalidad, *n.f.* rivalry.
rivalizar [C], *v.i.* vie, rival.
rizado, -da, *a.* curly.
rizar [C], *v.t., v.r.* curl; frizzle.
rizo, -za, *a.* curly.—*n.m.* curl; (*aer.*) loop.
rizoma, *n.f.* rhizome.
rizoso, *a.* curly.
robar, *v.t.* rob; steal; carry off.
roble, *n.m.* oak.
robledal, robledo, *n.m.* oak-wood *or* forest.
roblón, *n.m.* rivet; tile-ridge.
roborar, *v.t.* reinforce; corroborate.
robot, *n.m.* robot.
robustecer [9], *v.t., v.r.* strengthen.
robustez(a), *n.f.* robustness.
robusto, -ta, *a.* robust.
roca, *n.f.* rock.
rocalla, *n.f.* pebbles, gravel.
roce, *n.m.* rubbing; social contact.
rociada, *n.f.* sprinkling; spray; dew.
rociar [L], *v.t.* sprinkle, spray; dew.—*v.i.* drizzle.
rocín, *n.m.* nag; work-horse.
rocío, *n.m.* dew; drizzle.
rococó, *a., n.m.* rococo.
rocoso, -sa, *a.* rocky.
rodaje, *n.m.* making (*of film*); wheels; **en —**, (*auto.*) being broken in.
rodamiento, *n.m.* (*mech.*) bearing; tyre-tread.
Ródano, *n.m.* Rhone.
rodante, *a.* rolling.
rodar [4] *v.t.* roll, rotate; make (*a film*); film. —*v.i.* roll; roam; **echar a —**, ruin.
rodear, *v.t.* surround; go round.—*v.i.* wander about.—*v.r.* twist about.
rodeo, *n.m.* winding; roundabout way; round-up, rodeo.
rodera, *n.f.* rut, track.
rodilla, *n.f.* knee; **de rodillas**, kneeling down.
rodillo, *n.m.* roller; rolling-pin.
Rodrigo, *n.m.* Roderick.
roedor, -ra, *a.* gnawing.—*a., n.m.* (*zool.*) rodent.
roer [29], *v.t.* gnaw; gnaw away.
rogación, *n.f.* petition; rogation.
rogar [4B], *v.t., v.i.* request; beg; plead.
rogativo, -va, *a.* supplicatory.—*n.f.* rogation.
roído, -da, *a.* (*fam.*) stingy. [ROER].
rojear, *v.i.* redden.
rojete, *n.m.* rouge (*make-up*).
rojizo, -za, *a.* reddish.
rojo, -ja, *a., n.m.* red; (*pol.*) Red.
rol, *n.m.* roll, list.
Rolando, Roldán, *n.m.* Roland.
rollar, *v.t.* roll up.
rollizo, -za, *a.* chubby; sturdy; round.
rollo, *n.m.* roll; scroll; roller; log; (*fam.*) mess; (*fam.*) bore.
Roma, *n.f.* Rome.
romana, *n.f.* steelyard; (*fig.*) balance.
romance, *a.* Romance.—*n.m.* Romance; Spanish; traditional ballad; (*fig.*) plain language.—*pl.* romancing.

romancear, *v.t.* translate.
romancero, *a.* romancing.—*n.m.* corpus *or* collection of ballads.
romanesco, -ca, *a.* novelesque; Roman.
románico, -ca, *a., n.m.* Romanic; Romanesque; Romance.
romanilla, *n.f.* (*print.*) roman.
romanizar [C], *v.t., v.r.* Romanize.
romano, -na, *a., n.m.f.* Roman.
romanticismo, *n.m.* romanticism; Romanticism.
romántico, -ca, *a., n.m.f.* romantic; Romantic.
romería, *n.f.* pilgrimage.
romero (1), **-ra,** *n.m.f.* pilgrim.
romero (2), *n.m.* (*bot.*) rosemary.
romo, -ma, *a.* dull, blunt.
rompecabezas, *n.m. inv.* puzzle.
rompehielos, *n.m. inv.* ice-breaker.
rompeolas, *n.m. inv.* breakwater.
romper [*p.p.* roto], *v.t.. v.i.* break; — *a,* begin suddenly to.
rompimiento, *n.m.* break; breakage.
Rómulo, *n.m.* Romulus.
ron, *n.m.* rum.
ronca, *n.f.* (*fam.*) menace, bullying.
roncar [A], *v.i.* snore; roar.
roncear, *v.i.* dawdle; wheedle.
ronco, -ca, *a.* hoarse; raucous; husky.
ronchar, *v.t., v.i.* crunch.
ronda, *n.f.* night-patrol; (*fam.*) round (*of drinks*); serenaders.
rondalla, *n.f.* yarn, tale.
rondar, *v.t.* go round; menace; patrol; roam (*esp. at night*).
de rondón, *adv. phr.* rashly, brashly.
ronquedad, *n.f.* hoarseness.
ronquido, *n.m.* snore; harsh sound.
ronronear, *v.i.* purr.
roña, *n.f.* manginess; filth.
roñería, *n.f.* stinginess.
roñoso, -sa, *a.* mangy; filthy; mingy, stingy.
ropa, *n.f.* clothes, clothing.
ropaje, *n.m.* garment(s); adornment.
ropavejero, -ra, *n.m.f.* old-clothes dealer.
ropero, -ra, *n.m.f.* clothier.—*n.m.* wardrobe.
roque, *n.m.* rook (*chess*).
rorro, *n.m.* (*fam.*) baby.
rosa, *n.f.* rose.
rosada, *n.f.* frost, rime.
rosado, -da, *a.* rose, rosy, pink; rosé (*wine*).
rosal, *n.m.* rose-bush.
rosario, *n.m.* rosary.
rosbif, *n.m.* roast-beef.
rosca, *n.f.* spiral; screw-thread.
roscar [A], *v.t.* thread, spiral.
rosco, *n.m.* bun.
róseo, -sea, *a.* rosy.
roseta, *n.f.* red spot; rose (*of pipe*); rosette.— *pl.* pop-corn.
rosicler, *n.m.* dawn-pink.
rosmarino, -na, *a.* pink.—*n.m.* rosemary.
rosquilla, *n.f.* dough-nut.
rostro, *n.m.* face; beak; *hacer — a,* face up to.
rostropálido, -da, *a., n.m.f.* pale-face (*white man*).
rota, *n.f.* rout; course, route.
rotación, *n.f.* rotation.
rotativo, -va, rotatorio, -ria, *a.* rotary.

roto, -ta, *a.* broken; dissolute; torn.—*p.p.* [ROMPER].
rotular, *v.t.* label.
rótulo, *n.m.* label; poster.
rotundo, -da, *a.* rotund.
rozagante, *a.* showy; sweeping (*dress*).
rozar [C], *v.t.* clear, clean; rub down; graze. —*v.i.* brush (*con,* against).—*v.r.* rub shoulders; falter.
rubéola, *n.f.* German measles.
rubí, *n.m.* (*pl.* -ies) ruby.
rubicundo, -da, *a.* rubicund.
rubio, -bia, *a.* blond(e), fair.—*n.m.f.* blond(e).
rublo, *n.m.* rouble.
rubor, *n.m.* redness; blush; shame.
ruborizar [C], *v.r.* redden.
rúbrica, *n.f.* rubric; heading; flourish.
rubricar [A], *v.t.* sign and seal; endorse.
rubro, -ra, *a.* red.—*n.m.* (*S.A.*) title.
rucio, -cia, *a.* gray, hoary.
rudeza, *n.f.* coarseness; roughness.
rudimentario, -ria, *a.* rudimentary.
rudimento, *n.m.* rudiment.
rudo, -da, *a.* rough; crude; harsh.
rueca, *n.f.* distaff; turn, twist.
rueda, *n.f.* wheel; ring; *hacer la —,* flatter; *— de presos,* identification parade.
ruedo, *n.m.* bull-ring; turn; circle; arena.
ruego, *n.m.* request, petition.
rufián, *n.m.* pimp; thug.
rugido, *n.m.* roar, bellow.
rugir [E], *v.i.* roar; leak out.
rugoso, -sa, *a.* wrinkled; corrugated.
ruibarbo, *n.m.* rhubarb.
ruido, *n.m.* noise.
ruidoso, -sa, *a.* noisy.
ruin, *a.* vile; wretched; nasty.—*n.m.* rogue.
ruina, *n.f.* ruin; ruination.
ruindad, *n.f.* vileness; pettiness; nastiness.
ruinoso, -sa, *a.* ruinous; harmful; collapsing.
ruiseñor, *n.m.* nightingale.
ruleta, *n.f.* roulette.
Rumania, *n.f.* Romania.
rumano, -na, *a., n.m.f.* Romanian.
rumba, *n.f.* rumba.
rumbático, -ca, *a.* showy, flashy.
rumbo, *n.m.* course; (*fam.*) flashiness.
rumboso, -sa, *a.* flashy, showy; (*fam.*) generous.
rumiante, *a., n.m.* (*zool.*) ruminant.
rumiar, *v.i.* ruminate; muse; fret.
rumor, *n.m.* rumour; murmur.
rumorear, *v.t.* rumour.—*v.i.* murmur.
runrún, *n.m.* (*fam.*) murmur; rumour; noise.
rupestre, *a.* rock, cave (*paintings etc.*).
rupia, *n.f.* rupee.
ruptura, *n.f.* break; rupture; crack.
rural, *a.* rural.
Rusia, *n.f.* Russia.
ruso, -sa, *a., n.m.f.* Russian.
rústico, -ca, *a., n.m.f.* rustic; *en rústica,* paper-bound (*book*).
rustiquez(a), rusticidad, *n.f.* rusticity.
Rut, *n.f.* Ruth.
ruta, *n.f.* route.
rutilar, *v.i.* (*poet.*) shine.
rutina, *n.f.* routine.
rutinario, -ria, rutinero, -ra, *a.* routine. —*n.m.f.* slave of routine; routinist.

S

S, s, *n.f.* twenty-second letter of the Spanish alphabet.
sábado, *n.m.* Saturday.
sabana, *n.f.* savanna(h).
sábana, *n.f.* sheet.
sabandija, *n.f.* vermin; bug.
sabañón, *n.m.* chilblain.
sabático, -ca, *a.* sabbatical.
sabatino, -na, *a.* rel. to Saturday.
sabedor, -ra, *a.* well-informed.
sabelotodo, *n.m.f. inv.* know-all.
saber, *n.m.* knowledge.—*v.t., v.i.* [30] know; taste (*a*, of); know how to; *a* —, to wit, namely; — *de*, know of; hear from.—(*S.A.*) [SOLER].
sabidillo, -lla, *a., n.m.f.* (*pej.*) know-all.
sabiduría, *n.f.* wisdom, learning.
a sabiendas, *adv. phr.* knowingly.
sabihondo, -da, *a., n.m.f.* know-all.
sabio, -bia, *a.* wise, learned.—*n.m.f.* wise person, sage; scholar; scientist.
sablazo, *n.m.* sabre blow *or* wound; (*fam.*) sponging, touch.
sable, *n.m.* sabre, cutlass; (*her.*) sable.
sabor, *n.m.* flavour; *a* —, to one's liking.
saborear, *v.t.* savour; flavour; entice.—*v.r.* relish, savour, delight (*con*, in).
sabotaje, *n.m.* sabotage.
saboteador, -ra, *n.m.f.* saboteur.
sabotear, *v.t.* sabotage.
sabroso, -sa, *a.* delicious, tasty; (*fam.*) salty.
sabuco, sabugo, *n.m.* (*bot.*) elder.
sabueso, *n.m.* bloodhound.
saca, *n.f.* extraction; draft.
sacabocado(s), *n.m.* (*pl.* **-dos**) ticket-punch.
sacacorchos, *n.m. inv.* corkscrew.
sacacuartos, *n.m. inv.* (*fam.*), **sacadinero(s),** *n.m.* (*pl.* **-ros**) (*fam.*) catch-penny.
sacaliña, *n.f.* goad; cunning.
sacamanchas, *n.m. inv.* stain-remover.
sacamuelas, *n.m. inv.* (*fam.*) dentist, tuggem.
sacaperras, *n.m. inv.* (*fam.*) one-armed bandit, gambling machine.
sacapuntas, *n.m. inv.* pencil sharpener.
sacar [A], *v.t.* take *or* pull *or* draw out; remove; bring out; solve; (*phot.*) take; get, win; book (*tickets*); — *a luz*, publish.
sacarina, *n.f.* saccharine.
sacerdocio, *n.m.* priesthood.
sacerdotal, *a.* priestly.
sacerdote, *n.m.* priest.
saciar, *v.t.* satiate.
saciedad, *n.f.* satiety.
saco, *n.m.* sack, bag; pillage, sacking.
sacramental, *a., n.m.f.* sacramental.
sacramentar, *v.t.* administer the sacrament to.
sacramento, *n.m.* sacrament.
sacratísimo, *sup. of* SACRO.
sacrificar [A], *v.t.* sacrifice.
sacrificio, *n.m.* sacrifice.
sacrilegio, *n.m.* sacrilege.
sacrílego, -ga, *a.* sacrilegious.
sacrista, sacristán, *n.m.* sacristan, sexton.
sacristía, *n.f.* sacristy.
sacro, -ra, *a.* sacred, holy.
sacrosanto, -ta, *a.* sacrosanct.

sacudido, -da, *a.* determined; indocile.—*n.f.* jolt, shake.
sacudir, *v.t.* shake, jar; beat.
sádico, -ca, *a.* sadistic.
sadismo, *n.m.* sadism.
saeta, *n.f.* arrow; finger (*of clock*); song to the Virgin.
saetera, *n.f.* loophole.
saetero, *n.m.* bowman, archer.
saetilla, *n.f.* finger (*of clock*); magnetic needle.
safari, *n.m.* safari.
sáfico, -ca, *a.* Sapphic.
sagacidad, *n.f.* sagacity.
sagaz, *a.* (*pl.* **-aces**) sagacious; sharp, keen.
sagrado, -da, *a.* sacred.—*n.m.* asylum sanctuary.
sagú, *n.m.* (*pl.* **-úes**) sago.
sahorno, *n.m.* scratch, graze.
sahumar, *v.t.* smoke, incense.
saín, *n.m.* grease, fat, oil.
sainete, *n.m.* one-act farce; zest; tit-bit.
sajar, *v.t.* cut, tap.
sajón, -jona, *a., n.m.f.* Saxon.
sal, *n.f.* salt; wit; charm.
sala, *n.f.* hall, drawing-room; court; room.
salacidad, *n.f.* salacity.
saladar, *n.m.* salt-marsh.
salado, -da, *a.* salt, salty; briny; witty; charming; (*S.A.*) dear, high-priced.
salamandra, *n.f.* (*zool.*) salamander; newt.
salar, *v.t.* salt.
salariar, *v.t.* salary.
salario, *n.m.* salary, pay.
salaz, *a.* (*pl.* **-aces**) salacious.
salazón, *n.f.* salting, curing; salted meat.
salchicha, *n.f.* sausage.
saldar, *v.t.* settle, liquidate; sell out.
saldo, *n.m.* liquidation, settlement; sale.
saldré [SALIR].
saledizo, -za, *a.* projecting.—*n.m.* projection.
salero, *n.m.* salt-cellar; salt-mine; wit, charm.
salgo [SALIR].
sálico, -ça, *a.* Salic.
salida, *n.f.* exit; departure; result; sally; outlet; success.
salidizo, *n.m.* projection.
salido, -da, *a.* projecting.
saliente, *a.* projecting; outstanding; rising (*sun*).
salino, -na, *a.* saline.—*n.f.* salt-mine; salt-pit.
salir [31], *v.i.* go *or* come out; leave, depart; appear; start; turn out; — *con bien*, succeed; *salirse con la suya*, have one's way.
salitre, *n.m.* saltpetre.
saliva, *n.f.* saliva.
salmantino, -na, *a., n.m.f.* rel. to *or* native of Salamanca.
salmo, *n.m.* psalm.
salmodia, *n.f.* psalmody; (*fam.*) singsong.
salmón, *n.m.* salmon.
salmuera, *n.f.* brine.
salobre, *a.* brackish.
saloma, *n.f.* (*naut.*) shanty.
Salomón, *n.m.* Solomon.
salón, *n.m.* saloon; hall, room.
salpicadura, *n.f.* splash, spatter.
salpicar [A], *v.t.* splash, splatter; skimp.
salpicón, *n.m.* splash; mince, hodge-podge.

salpimentar

salpimentar [1], *v.t.* salt and pepper; (*fam.*) sugar the pill.
salpresar, *v.t.* salt, cure.
salpreso, -sa, *a.* salt, cured.
salpullido, *n.m.* rash.
salsa, *n.f.* sauce; — *de San Bernado*, (*fam.*) hunger.
saltabanco(s), *n.m.* (*pl.* -cos) mountebank.
saltadizo, -za, *a.* brittle.
saltamontes, *n.m. inv.* grasshopper.
saltar, *v.t., v.i.* jump.—*v.i.* leap, bound, spurt; — *a la vista*, be obvious.—*v.r.* skip, omit.
saltarín, -rina, *n.m.f.* dancer; restless person.
salteador, *n.m.* highwayman.
saltear, *v.t.* hold up, waylay; take by surprise; skip through.
salterio, *n.m.* psaltery; Psalter.
saltimbanco [SALTABANCO].
salto, *n.m.* leap, jump; jolt, sudden change; skipping; dive.
saltón, -tona, *a.* jumping.—*n.m.* grasshopper; worm.
salubre, *a.* salubrious.
salud, *n.f.* health; salvation; welfare.—*interj.* good health!
saludable, *a.* salutary, wholesome.
saludar, *v.t.* greet; salute.
saludo, *n.m.* greeting; salute.
salutación, *n.f.* salutation.
salva, *n.f.* salvo; great applause; greeting.
salvación, *n.f.* salvation.
salvado, *n.m.* bran.
el Salvador, *n.m.* the Saviour; **salvador, -ra**, *n.m.f.* saver; saviour.
salvaguardar, *v.t.* safeguard.
salvaguardia, *n.m.* guard.—*n.f.* safeguard; safe-conduct.
salvajada, *n.f.* savagery.
salvaje, *a.* savage; wild.—*n.m.f.* savage.
salvajería, *n.f.*, **salvajismo**, *n.m.* savagery.
a salvamano, *adv. phr.* without risk.
salvam(i)ento, *n.m.* saving; salvage.
salvar, *v.t.* save; salvage; overcome, get round; jump over.—*v.r.* be saved.
salvavidas, *n.m. inv.* life-buoy; guard; (*rail.*) cow-catcher; traffic island.
salvedad, *n.f.* reservation.
salvo, -va, *a.* safe; excepted.—*prep.* except for, save; — *que*, unless; *a* —, safe (*de*, from); *en* —, safe; at liberty.
salvoconducto, *n.m.* safe-conduct.
samaritano, -na, *a., n.m.f.* Samaritan.
sambenito, *n.m.* sanbenito; infamy.
samblaje, *n.m.* joint; joinery.
San, (*contraction of* SANTO) Saint (*used before masc. names, except those beginning with* To- *or* Do-).
sanar, *v.t., v.i.* heal.
sanatorio, *n.m.* sanatorium.
sanción, *n.f.* sanction.
sancionar, *v.t.* sanction.
sandalia, *n.f.* sandal.
sandez, *n.f.* (*pl.* -eces) folly, nonsense.
sandía, *n.f.* water-melon.
sandio, -dia, *a.* silly, foolish.
sanear, *v.t.* indemnify; guarantee; drain.
sangradura, *n.f.* (*med.*) bleeding; outlet.
sangrante, *a.* bleeding.
sangrar, *v.t.* bleed; drain; indent.—*v.i.* bleed; be new *or* evident.
sangre, *n.f.* blood; — *azul* or *goda*, blue

blood; — *fría*, sang-froid, presence of mind.
sangría, *n.f.* (*med.*) bleeding, blood-letting; drain, tap; (*cul.*) wine-cup.
sangriento, -ta, *a.* bloody.
sanguijuela, *n.f.* (*zool.*) leech.
sanguinario, -ria, *a.* sanguinary.
sanguíneo, -nea, *a.* sanguineous; sanguine.
sanguino, -na, *a.* sanguine; sanguineous.
sanidad, *n.f.* health, healthiness; sanitation.
sano, -na, *a.* healthy; sound; safe; — *y salvo*, safe and sound.
sánscrito, -ta, *a., n.m.* Sanskrit.
sanseacabó, *interj.* (*fam.*) that's it! all done!
Sansón, *n.m.* Samson.
santabárbara, *n.f.* (*naut.*) magazine.
santanderino, -na, *a., n.m.f.* rel. to *or* native of Santander.
santero, -ra, *a.* devoted to saints.—*n.m.* sexton; beggar.
Santiago, *n.m.* St. James.
santiamén, *n.m.* (*fam.*) jiffy.
santidad, *n.f.* holiness.
santiguar [H], *v.t.* bless, cross.—*v.r.* cross oneself.
Santo, -ta, *a.* Saint; **santo, -ta**, *a.* holy, blessed, sacred; saintly; (*fam.*) simple.— *n.m.f.* saint.—*n.m.* (*mil.*) password; (*fam.*) onomastic day.
santón, *n.m.* dervish; hypocrite.
santoral, *n.m.* saints' calendar.
santuario, *n.m.* sanctuary.
santurrón, -rrona, *a.* sanctimonious.
saña, *n.f.* fury; — *vieja*, old score, vendetta.
sañoso, -sa, **sañudo, -da**, *a.* furious; irascible.
Sapiencia, *n.f.* (*Bib.*) Wisdom of Solomon.
sapiencia, *n.f.* sapience, wisdom.
sapiente, *a.* sapient.
sapo, *n.m.* (*zool.*) toad.
saquear, *v.t.* loot, plunder, sack.
saqueo, *n.m.* plundering, sacking.
sarampión, *n.m.* (*med.*) measles.
sarao, *n.m.* soirée.
sarcasmo, *n.m.* sarcasm.
sarcástico, -ca, *a.* sarcastic.
sarcia, *n.f.* burden.
sarcófago, *n.m.* sarcophagus.
sardana, *n.f.* sardana (*Catalan dance*).
sardina, *n.f.* (*ichth.*) sardine.
sardo, -da, *a., n.m.f.* Sardinian.
sardónico, -ca, *a.* sardonic.
sargento, *n.m.* sergeant.
sarmiento, *n.m.* vine shoot.
sarna, *n.f.* mange, itch.
sarnoso, -sa, *a.* mangy.
sarraceno, -na, *a., n.m.f.* Saracen.
sarracina, *n.f.* scuffle, fight.
sarro, *n.m.* sediment; tartar; crust.
sarta, *n.f.* string (*of beads*); file, line.
sartal, *n.m.* string (*of beads*).
sartén, *n.f.* frying-pan.
sastre, *n.m.* tailor.
Satán, Satanás, *n.m.* Satan.
satánico, -ca, *a.* satanic, devilish.
satélite, *n.m.* satellite; (*fam.*) henchman.
sátira, *n.f.* satire.
satírico, -ca, *a.* satirical.—*n.m.f.* satirist.
satirizar [C], *v.t.* satirize.
sátiro, *n.m.* satyr.
satisfacción, *n.f.* satisfaction.

satisfacer [20], *v.t.* satisfy.—*v.r.* be satisfied (*de*, with).
satisfactorio, -ria, *a.* satisfactory.
satisfecho, -cha, *a.* conceited.—*p.p.* [SATIS-FACER].
sativo, -va, *a.* tilled (*land*).
saturación, *n.f.* saturation.
saturar, *v.t.* saturate; glut.
saturnal, *n.f.* saturnalia.
Saturno, *n.m.* Saturn.
sauce, *n.m.* (*bot.*) willow.
saúco, *n.m.* (*bot.*) elder.
Saúl, *n.m.* Saul.
savia, *n.f.* sap.
saxófono, *n.m.* saxophone.
saya, *n.f.* petticoat; skirt; tunic.
sayal, *n.m.* sackcloth, serge.
sayo, *n.m.* smock.
sayón, *n.m.* executioner; lout.
sazón, *n.f.* season; time; ripeness; *a la —,* at that time; *en —,* in season, ripe.
sazonar, *v.t.* ripen; season.
se, *inv. pron. m. & f.* himself; herself; itself; yourself; themselves; *also renders the English passive: — dice,* it is said; *aquí — habla español,* Spanish (is) spoken here. —*pron. dat.* (*replaces* LE, LES, *when these are followed by another pronoun*).
sé [SABER].
sebo, *n.m.* tallow.
seca, *n.f.* drought.
secano, -na, *a.* dry, waterless.—*n.m.* dry, arid land.
secante, *a.* drying.—*n.m.* blotting paper.—*n.f.* secant.
secar [A], *v.t.* dry, dry out; bore, annoy.—*v.r.* dry out, dry up.
sección, *n.f.* section; (*mil.*) platoon.
seccionar, *v.t.* section.
secesión, *n.f.* secession.
secesionismo, *n.m.* secessionism.
seco, -ca, *a.* dry, dried up, dried out; lean, meagre; hard; *en —,* high and dry; for no reason; suddenly.
secreción, *n.f.* secretion; segregation.
secretaría, *n.f.* secretary's office; secretariat.
secretario, -ria, *n.m.f.* secretary.
secretear, *v.i.* (*fam.*) whisper.
secreto, -ta, *a.* secret; secretive.—*n.m.* secret; — *a voces,* open secret.
secta, *n.f.* sect.
sectario, -ria, *a.*, *n.m.f.* sectarian.
sector, *n.m.* sector.
secuaz, *a.* (*pl.* -aces) following, attendant. —*n.m.f.* follower.
secuela, *n.f.* sequel, result.
secuestrar, *v.t.* kidnap; sequestrate.
secuestro, *n.m.* kidnapping; sequestration.
secular, *a.* secular; century-long.
secularismo, *n.m.* secularism.
secularizar [C], *v.t.*, *v.r.* secularize.
secundar, *v.t.* second.
secundario, -ria, *a.* secondary.
sed, *n.f.* thirst; *tener —,* be thirsty (*de*, for).
seda, *n.f.* silk.
sedal, *n.m.* fishing-line.
sedán, *n.m.* sedan.
sedante, *a.*, *n.m.* sedative.
sedar, *v.t.* allay, soothe.
sede, *n.f.* (*eccl.*) see; seat; (*com.*) head office.
sedentario, -ria, *a.* sedentary.
sedicente, *a.* self-styled.

sedición, *n.f.* sedition.
sedicioso, -sa, *a.* seditious.
sediento, -ta, *a.* thirsty.
sedimentar, *v.t.*, *v.r.* sediment.
sedimento, *n.m.* sediment.
sedoso, -sa, *a.* silken, silky.
seducción, *n.f.* attraction, charm; enticement; seduction.
seducir [15], *v.t.* deceive; captivate; seduce.
seductor, -ra, *a.* captivating; attractive.—*n.m.f.* seducer; enticer.
seduje, seduzco [SEDUCIR].
sefardí, *a.* (*pl.* -íes) Sephardic.—*n.m.f.* Sephardi.
segador, -ra, *a.* harvesting.—*n.m.f.* harvester.
segar [1B], *v.t.* mow, reap; mow down.
seglar, *a.* lay; secular.—*n.m.* layman.—*n.f.* laywoman.
segmento, *n.m.* segment.
segregación, *n.f.* segregation; secretion.
segregar [B], *v.t.* segregate; secrete.
seguida, *n.f.* continuation; *en —,* at once.
seguidamente, *adv.* successively; at once.
seguidilla, *n.f.* Spanish metre and tune.
seguido, -da, *a.* continuous, successive; direct; running in a row.
seguidor, -ra, *n.m.f.* follower.
seguir [8G], *v.t.* follow; pursue; carry on, continue.—*v.i.* carry on, go on.—*v.r.* ensue; follow, issue.
según, *adv.* it depends.—*prep.* according to.—*conj.* according to what.
segundo, -da, *a.* second; *de segunda mano,* second-hand.—*n.m.* second (*time*).
segur, *n.f.* axe, sickle.
seguridad, *n.f.* security; surety, certainty; safety.
seguro, -ra, *a.* sure, certain; safe, secure; steady.—*n.m.* safe place; insurance; *de —,* assuredly; *sobre —,* without risk.
seis, *a.*, *n.m.* six.
seisavo, -va, *a.*, *n.m.* sixth; hexagon(al).
seísm- [SISM-].
selección, *n.f.* selection.
seleccionar, *v.t.* select.
selectivo, -va, *a.* selective.
selecto, -ta, *a.* select.
selector, -ra, *a.* selecting.—*n.m.* selector.
selva, *n.f.* forest; jungle.
selvicultura, *n.f.* forestry.
selvoso, -sa, *a.* wooded.
sellar, *v.t.* seal; stamp.
sello, *n.m.* seal; stamp.
semáforo, *n.m.* semaphore; traffic light.
semana, *n.f.* week; *entre —,* during midweek.
semanal, *a.* weekly.
semanario, -ria, *a.*, *n.m.* weekly.
semántico, -ca, *a.* semantic.—*n.f.* semantics.
semblante, *n.m.* face, mien; look, aspect; *hacer — de,* feign.
sembrado, *n.m.* corn-field, (*U.S.*) grainfield.
sembrar [1], *v.t.* sow; scatter.
semejante, *a.* similar, like, alike.—*n.m.* fellow, equal; likeness.
semejanza, *n.f.* likeness, resemblance; *a — de,* like.
semejar, *v.i.*, *v.r.* be alike; — (*a*), be like, resemble.
semen, *n.m.* semen.
sementar [1], *v.t.* sow, seed.
sementera, *n.f.* seed-bed; sowing; hot-bed.

semestre, *n.m.* six months; semester.
semicírculo, *n.m.* semicircle.
semiconsciente, *a.* semiconscious.
semidiós, *n.m.* demigod.
semidormido, -da, *a.* half-asleep.
semilla, *n.f.* seed.
semillero, *n.m.* seed-bed.
seminal, *a.* seminal.
seminario, *n.m.* seminary; seed-bed; seminar.
seminarista, *n.m.* seminarist.
semita, *a.* Semitic.—*n.m.f.* Semite.
semítico, -ca, *a.* Semitic.
semivivo, -va, *a.* half-alive.
sémola, *n.f.* semolina.
sempiterno, -na, *a.* everlasting, sempiternal.
Sena, *n.m.*Seine; **sena,** *n.f.* senna.
senado, *n.m.* senate.
senador, *n.m.* senator.
sencillez, *n.f.* simplicity.
sencillo, -lla, *a.* simple.
senda, *n.f.,* **sendero,** *n.m.* path.
sendos, -das, *a.* one each, sundry; (*fam.*) great.
senectud, *n.f.* old age.
el Senegal, *n.m.* Senegal.
senegalés, -lesa, *a., n.m.f.* Senegalese.
senil, *a.* senile.
senilidad, *n.f.* senility.
senilismo, *n.m.* senile decay.
seno, *n.m.* bosom; lap; bay; (*math.*) sine.
sensación, *n.f.* sensation.
sensacional, *a.* sensational.
sensacionalismo, *n.m.* sensationalism.
sensatez, *n.f.* (good) sense.
sensato, -ta, *a.* sensible, wise.
sensibilidad, *n.f.* sensitiveness, sensibility.
sensibilizar [C], *v.t.* sensitize.
sensible, *a.* perceptible; sensitive; grievous.
sensiblería, *n.f.* sentimentality.
sensiblero, -ra, *a.* sentimental, mawkish.
sensitivo, -va, *a.* sensitive; sensual.
sensorio, -ria, *a.* sensory.
sensual, *a.* sensuous, sensual.
sensualidad, *n.f.* sensuality.
sensualismo, *n.m.* sensualism.
sentada, *n.f.* sitting.
sentadero, *n.m.* place to sit.
sentado, -da, *a.* settled, stable; grave, sedate; **dar por —,** take for granted.
sentar [1], *v.t.* seat; fit, suit; settle; set down. —*v.r.* sit down; mark.
sentencia, *n.f.* sentence.
sentenciar, *v.t.* sentence.
sentencioso, -sa, *a.* sententious.
sentido, -da, *a.* felt; feeling; touchy.—*p.p.* [SENTIR].—*n.m.* sense; meaning; **sin —,** senseless.
sentimental, *a.* sentimental.
sentimiento, *n.m.* feeling; sentiment; sorrow.
sentina, *n.f.* bilge; den of vice.
sentir, *n.m.* feeling; opinion.—*v.t.* [6] feel; regret; be sorry about; perceive; hear.—*v.r.* feel; complain; have a pain (*de,* in, from); split; decay.
seña, *n.f.* sign, mark, token; vestige; password.—*pl.* address; **señas mortales,** clear indication.
señá, *n.f.* (*fam.*) [SEÑORA].
señal, *n.f.* sign, token; signal; marker; scar; trace; road-sign; traffic light; symptom; pledge; **en — de,** as a token of.—*pl.* **señales acústicas,** (*auto.*) horn.

señalado, -da, *a.* noted.
señalar, *v.t.* point out, indicate; mark; designate.—*v.r.* excel.
el Señor, *n.m.* the Lord; **señor, -ra,** *a.* master; (*fam.*) fine, great.—*n.m.* sir (*in voc.*); mister, Mr.; lord; owner, master.— *n.f.* lady; mistress; Mrs.; madam (*in voc.*); wife; **nuestra Señora,** Our Lady.
señorear, *v.t.* rule, lord, control; tower above.—*v.r.* lord it; take control (*de,* of).
señorío, *n.m.* mastery; dominion, rule; gentry; manor; gravity.
señorita, *n.f.* Miss; young lady.
señorito, *n.m.* Master; young master; (*fam.*) dandy; (*pej.*) whippersnapper.
señuelo, *n.m.* decoy, lure.
sepa [SABER].
separación, *n.f.* separation.
separado, -da, *a.* separate; **por —,** separately.
separar, *v.t., v.r.* separate.
separata, *n.f.* off-print.
separatismo, *n.m.* separatism.
separatista, *a., n.m.f.* separatist.
sepia, *n.f.* (*zool.*) sepia.—*n.m.* sepia (*colour*).
septentrional, *a.* northern.
séptico, -ca, *a.* septic.
septiembre, *n.m.* September.
séptimo, -ma, *a., n.m.* seventh.
sepulcro, *n.m.* tomb, sepulchre.
sepultar, *v.t.* bury, inter; hide.
sepultura, *n.f.* burial; grave.
sequedad, *n.f.* dryness, aridity.
sequero, *n.m.* arid land, dry place.
sequía, *n.f.* drought.
séquito, *n.m.* retinue, suite; following.
ser, *n.m.* being; essence.—*v.i.* [32] be; belong (*de,* to); become (*de,* of); **es de,** it is to be; **a no — por,** but for; **a no — que,** unless; **o sea,** that is; **— para,** suit; be fit for.
serafín, *n.m.* seraph.
serenar, *v.t.* calm.—*v.i., v.r.* calm down, clear up, settle.
serenata, *n.f.* serenade.
serenidad, *n.f.* serenity.
sereno, -na, *a.* calm, serene, cloudless.—*n.m.* night watchman; evening dew; **al —,** in the night air.
serie, *n.f.* series; **en —,** in series; mass (*production*).
seriedad, *n.f.* seriousness, gravity; sincerity.
serio, -ria, *a.* serious; grave; reliable; solemn; **en —,** seriously; in earnest.
sermón, *n.m.* sermon.
sermonear, *v.t., v.i.* sermonize.
seroja, *n.f.,* **serojo,** *n.m.* firewood; dry leaves.
serpentear, *v.i.* wind, meander, twist; wriggle.
serpenteo, *n.m.* winding, twisting; wriggling.
serpiente, *n.f.* snake, serpent.
serranil, *n.m.* knife.
serrano, -na, *a.* highland, mountain; **jamón —,** smoked ham.—*n.m.f.* highlander.
serrar [1], *v.t.* saw.
serrín, *n.m.* sawdust.
servible, *a.* serviceable.
servicio, *n.m.* service.
servidero, -ra, *a.* serviceable; demanding.
servidor, -ra, *n.m.f.* servant.
servidumbre, *n.f.* servants; servitude; (*jur.*) right.

servil, *a.* servile.
servilleta, *n.f.* napkin, serviette.
Servia, *n.f.* Serbia; **servio, -via**, *a., n.m.f.* Serbian.
servir [8], *v.t.* serve; wait on.—*v.i.* be of use; serve (*de*, as, for).—*v.r.* serve oneself; be pleased to; make use (*de*, of); *sírvase* ..., please. ...
servocroata, *a., n.m.f.* Serbo-Croat.
sesear, *v.i.* pronounce *z* and *c* as *s* in Spanish.
sesenta, *a., n.m.* sixty.
sesentón, -tona, *n.m.f.* (*fam.*) sexagenarian.
sesgar, *v.t.* slant.
sesgo, -ga, *a.* slanting; oblique.—*n.m.* slope, slant; bevel; means; *al* —, aslant.
sesión, *n.f.* session.
seso, *n.m.* brain; brains; sense, wisdom.
sesquipedal, *a.* sesquipedalian.
sestear, *v.i.* take a siesta.
sesudo, -da, *a.* wise, prudent.
seta, *n.f.* edible fungus; bristle.
setecientos, -tas, *a., n.m.pl.* seven hundred.
setenta, *a., n.m.* seventy.
setentón, -tona, *a., n.m.f.* (*fam.*) seventy-year-old.
setiembre [SEPTIEMBRE].
seto, *n.m.* fence; — *vivo*, hedge.
seudónimo, *n.m.* pseudonym.
severidad, *n.f.* severity.
severo, -ra, *a.* severe; strict.
sexo, *n.m.* sex.
sextante, *n.m.* sextant.
sexto, -ta, *a., n.m.* sixth.
sexual, *a.* sexual.
si (1), *conj.* if; whether; *por* — *acaso*, just in case.
si (2), *n.m.* (*mus.*) (key of) B.
sí (1), *adv.* yes; indeed.
sí (2), *r. pron.* (*used after preps.*) himself; herself; oneself; yourself; itself; themselves.
siamés, -mesa, *a., n.m.f.* Siamese.
sibarita, *a., n.m.f.* Sybarite.
siberiano, -na, *a.* Siberian.
sibilante, *a., n.f.* sibilant.
Sicilia, *n.f.* Sicily.
siciliano, -na, *a., n.m.f.* Sicilian.
sico- [PSICO-].
sicómoro, *n.m.* sycamore.
siderurgia, *n.f.* siderurgy; iron and steel manufacture.
siderúrgico, -ca, *a.* siderurgical; rel. to iron and steel manufacture.
sidra, *n.f.* cider.
siembra, *n.f.* sowing; sown land.
siempre, *adv.* always; *de* —, usual; — *que*, whenever; provided that.
sien, *n.f.* (*anat.*) temple.
sienta, -te, -to [SENTAR, SENTIR].
sierpe, *n.f.* snake, serpent.
sierra, *n.f.* jagged mountain range; saw.
siervo, -va, *n.m.f.* slave; servant; serf.
siesta, *n.f.* siesta, nap; hottest part of day.
siete, *a., n.m.* seven.
sífilis, *n.f.* syphilis.
sifón, *n.m.* soda-syphon; soda-water; syphon.
sigilo, *n.m.* seal, signet; secrecy; concealment.
sigiloso, -sa, *a.* silent, tight-lipped.
sigla, *n.f.* abbreviation, symbol.
siglo, *n.m.* century; age; the world.
signar, *v.t.* sign; cross; mark.

signatura, *n.f.* sign; reference number; signature.
significación, *n.f.* significance, import.
significado, -da, *a.* well-known, important. —*n.m.* meaning.
significar [A], *v.t.* mean, signify; make known. —*v.i.* matter.
significativo, -va, *a.* significant.
signo, *n.m.* sign; cross; destiny.
siguiente, *a.* following, next.
sílaba, *n.f.* syllable.
silábico, -ca, *a.* syllabic.
silbante, *a.* whistling.
silbar, *v.t., v.i.* whistle; hiss, boo.
silbato, silbido, silbo, *n.m.* whistle; hiss.
silenciador, *n.m.* silencer; (*auto.*) muffler.
silenciar, *v.t.* silence; keep quiet, not reveal.
silencio, *n.m.* silence.
silencioso, -sa, *a.* silent, quiet.
silero, *n.m.* (*agr.*) silo.
sílice, *n.f.* silica.
silicio, *n.m.* silicon.
silo, *n.m.* (*agr.*) silo; cavern.
silogismo, *n.m.* syllogism.
silueta, *n.f.* silhouette.
silvestre, *a.* wild.
silvicultura, *n.f.* forestry.
silla, *n.f.* chair; saddle.
sillín, *n.m.* light saddle; cycle saddle.
sillón, *n.m.* arm-chair.
simbiosis, *n.f.* symbiosis.
simbólico, -ca, *a.* symbolic(al).
simbolismo, *n.m.* symbolism.
simbolizar [C], *v.t.* symbolize.
símbolo, *n.m.* symbol; emblem, device; (*eccl.*) creed.
simetría, *n.f.* symmetry.
simétrico, -ca, *a.* symmetrical.
simiente, *n.f.* seed, germ; semen.
símil, *a.* similar.—*n.m.* similarity; simile.
similar, *a.* similar.
similitud, *n.f.* similitude.
simonía, *n.f.* simony.
simpatía, *n.f.* liking, fellow-feeling; sympathy; *tener* — *por*, like (*s.o.*) very much.
simpático, -ca, *a.* nice, likeable, pleasant; sympathetic.
simpatizar [C], *v.i.* get on well (*con*, with).
simple, *a.* simple; mere; *a* — *vista*, at first sight.
simpleza, simplicidad, *n.f.* simplicity.
simpli(ci)sta, *a., n.m.f.* simpliste.
simplificar [A], *v.t.* simplify.
simposio, *n.m.* symposium.
simulación, *n.f.* simulation.
simulacro, *n.m.* simulacrum; sham.
simular, *v.t.* simulate, feign.
simultáneo, -nea, *a.* simultaneous.
sin, *prep.* without.
sinagoga, *n.f.* synagogue.
sinalefa, *n.f.* synal(o)epha.
sinapismo, *n.m.* mustard-plaster; (*fam.*) bore.
sincerar, *v.t.* vindicate, justify.
sinceridad, *n.f.* sincerity.
sincero, -ra, *a.* sincere; ingenuous.
sincopar, *v.t.* syncopate.
síncope, *n.m.* syncope; (*med.*) faint, swoon.
sincronizar [C], *v.t.* synchronize.
sindical, *a.* syndical; trade unionist.
sindicalismo, *n.m.* trade unionism.

191

sindicato, *n.m.* trade union; syndicate.
sinecura, *n.f.* sinecure.
sinéresis, *n.f.* synaeresis.
sinfín, *n.m.* great number.
sinfonía, *n.f.* symphony.
singlar, *v.i.* (*naut.*) follow a course.
singular, *a.*, *n.m.* singular.
singularidad, *n.f.* singularity.
singularizar [C], *v.t.* distinguish, singularize.
singulto, *n.m.* sob; hiccup.
siniestro, -ra, *a.* sinister; left.—*n.m.* malice; disaster.
sinnúmero, *n.m.* endless number.
sino (1), *n.m.* destiny, fate.
sino (2), *conj.* but, if not; **no . . . —**, not . . . but.
sínodo, *n.m.* synod.
sinonimia, *n.f.* synonymy.
sinónimo, -ma, *a.* synonymous.—*n.m.* synonym.
sinóptico, -ca, *a.* synoptic(al).
sinrazón, *n.f.* wrong, injustice.
sinsabor, *n.m.* displeasure; sorrow.
sintáctico, -ca, *a.* syntactic(al).
sintaxis, *n.f.* syntax.
síntesis, *n.f. inv.* synthesis.
sintético, -ca, *a.* synthetic(al).
sintetizar [C], *v.t.* synthesize.
síntoma, *n.m.* symptom.
sintomático, -ca, *a.* symptomatic.
sintonizar [C], *v.t.*, *v.i.* (*rad.*) tune (in).
sinuoso, -sa, *a.* sinuous, twisting.
sinvergüenza, *a.* (*fam.*) brazen.—*n.m.f.* (*fam.*) shameless rogue.
sionismo, *n.m.* Zionism.
siqu- [PSIQU-].
siquiera, *adv.* even.—*conj.* even though.
sirena, *n.f.* siren.
sirga, *n.f.* tow-rope.
Siria, *n.f.* Syria.
sirio, -ria, *a.*, *n.m.f.* Syrian.
sirle, *n.m.* dung.
siroco, *n.m.* sirocco.
sirte, *n.f.* sandbank, rock; peril.
sirvienta, *n.f.* servant.
sirviente, *a.* serving. —*n.m.* servant.
sisa, *n.f.* pilfering; (*obs.*) excise.
sisar, *v.t.* filch.
sisear, *v.t.*, *v.i.* hiss; boo.
siseo, *n.m.* hiss; sizzle.
sísmico, -ca, *a.* seismic.
sismografía, *n.f.* seismography.
sismómetro, *n.m.* seismometer.
sisón, *n.m.* filcher; (*orn.*) little bustard.
sistema, *n.m.* system.
sistemático, -ca, *a.* systematic(al).
sistematizar [C], *v.t.* systematize.
sitiar, *v.t.* besiege.
sitio, *n.m.* place, spot; siege.
sito, -ta, *a.* situate.
situación, *n.f.* situation.
situar [M], *v.t.* situate, place.
smoking, *n.m.* (*pl.* **-gs**) dinner jacket.
so, *n.m.* (*mus.*) (key of) G.
sobaco, *n.m.* armpit.
sobajar, *v.t.* crumple; (*S.A.*) humble.
sobar, *v.t.* knead, pummel; paw.
sobarbada, *n.f.* jerk; reprimand.
sobarcar [A], *v.t.* tuck under the arm.
soberanía, *n.f.* sovereignty; dominion.
soberano, -na, *a.*, *n.m.f.* sovereign.

soberbio, -bia, *a.* vain, proud; superb.—*n.f.* pride.
sobordo, *n.m.* (*naut.*) cargo list.
sobornar, *v.t.* bribe.
soborno, *n.m.* bribe; bribery.
sobra, *n.f.* excess; **de —**, in excess; left over; superfluous.—*pl.* left-overs.
sobrado, -da, *a.* overmuch, too many; daring; rich.—*n.m.* attic.
sobrancero, -ra, *a.* unemployed.
sobrante, *a.*, *n.m.* surplus.
sobrar, *v.t.* surpass.—*v.i.* be left over; be too much *or* many.
sobre, *n.m.* envelope.—*prep.* on, upon, above, over.—*prefix* over-, super-.
sobreaguar [H], *v.t.*, *v.i.* float (*on*).
sobrecama, *n.f.* bedspread.
sobrecarga, *n.f.* overload; further trouble; surcharge.
sobrecargar [B], *v.t.* overload; surcharge.
sobreceja, *n.f.* brow.
sobrecejo, *n.m.* frown.
sobrecoger [E], *v.t.* surprise, take aback.
sobrecomida, *n.f.* dessert.
sobrecomprimir, *v.t.* (*aer.*) pressurize.
sobrecubierta, *n.f.* wrapper; (*naut.*) upper deck.
sobredicho, -cha, *a.* above-mentioned.
sobredorar, *v.t.* gild; gloss over.
sobreen- [SOBREN-].
sobreexponer [25], *v.t.* over-expose.
sobrefaz, *n.f.* (*pl.* **-aces**) surface.
sobrehombre, *n.m.* superman.
sobrehueso, *n.m.* bother, bore.
sobrehumano, -na, *a.* superhuman.
sobreintendencia, *n.f.* superintendance.
sobrellevar, *v.t.* bear; ease, share; overlook.
sobremanera, *adv.* exceedingly.
sobremesa, *n.f.* table cloth; dessert; **de —**, after dinner.
sobremodo, *adv.* exceedingly.
sobremundano, -na, *a.* supermundane; other-worldly.
sobrenadar, *v.i.* float.
sobrenatural, *a.* supernatural.
sobrenombre, *n.m.* added name, epithet.
sobrentender [2], *v.t.* gather, read between the lines.
sobrepaga, *n.f.* pay-increase.
sobreparto, *n.m.* (*med.*) confinement.
sobrepasar, *v.t.* surpass.
sobrepelliz, *n.f.* (*pl.* **-ices**) surplice.
sobreponer [25], *v.t.* super(im)pose.—*v.r.* overcome (*a*).
sobrepujar, *v.t.* surpass, exceed.
sobrero, -ra, *a.* extra; spare.
sobresaliente, *a.* outstanding; (*educ.*) excellent, First Class.—*n.m.f.* understudy.
sobresalir [31], *v.i.* stand out, excel.
sobresaltar, *v.t.* assail; startle.—*v.i.* stand out, be noticeable.
sobresalto, *n.m.* sudden attack; start, fright.
sobresanar, *v.t.* heal superficially; cover up, conceal (*defects*).
sobresano, *adv.* feignedly.
sobrescribir, *v.t.* superscribe.
sobrescrito, *n.m.* superscript(ion).
sobreseer [N], *v.t.*, *v.i.* stay.
sobreseguro, *adv.* without risk.
sobrestadía, *n.f.* (*naut.*) extra lay days.
sobrestante, *n.m.* foreman, supervisor.
sobretarde, *n.f.* late evening.

soluble

sobretodo, *n.m.* overcoat.—*adv.* above all.
sobrevenida, *n.f.* surprise coming.
sobrevenir [36], *v.i.* happen, supervene.
sobrevienta, *n.f.* gust; onslaught; surprise.
sobreviento, *n.m.* gust of wind.
sobreviviente, *a.* surviving.—*n.m.f.* survivor.
sobrevivir, *v.i.* survive (*a*).
sobrexceder, *v.t.* exceed.
sobrexcitar, *v.t.* overexcite.
sobriedad, *n.f.* sobriety, frugality.
sobrino, -na, *n.m.* nephew.—*n.f.* niece.
sobrio, -ria, *a.* sober, moderate.
socaire, *n.m.* (*naut.*) lee; (*fam.*) safety.
socaliña, *n.f.* swindle.
socaliñar, *v.t.* swindle out of.
socapa, *n.f.* pretext, pretence.
socarrar, *v.t.* scorch.
socarrén, *n.m.* eaves.
socarrena, *n.f.* cavity.
socarrón, -rrona, *a.* crafty, sly.
socarronería, *n.f.* slyness.
socavar, *v.t.* undermine.
sociabilidad, *n.f.* sociability.
sociable, *a.* sociable.
social, *a.* social; rel. to a firm.
socialismo, *n.m.* socialism.
socialista, *a., n.m.f.* socialist.
socializar [C], *v.t.* socialize.
sociedad, *n.f.* society; (*com.*) company, firm.
societario, -ria, *a.* rel. to union(s).—*n.m.f.* member.
socio, -cia, *n.m.f.* member; partner; (*pej.*) person.
sociología, *n.f.* sociology.
sociológico, -ca, *a.* sociological.
sociólogo, -ga, *n.m.f.* sociologist.
socolor, *n.m.* pretext, cover.
socorrer, *v.t.* aid, succour.
socorrido, -da, *a.* helpful; well-stocked; trite.
socorro, *n.m.* help, aid; part payment.—*interj.* help!
soda, *n.f.* soda.
sódico, -ca, *a.* rel. to sodium.
sodio, *n.m.* sodium.
soez, *a.* (*pl.* **soeces**) vile, crude.
sofá, *n.m.* (*pl.* **sofás**) sofa.
sofión, *n.m.* snort; blunderbuss.
sofisma, *n.m.* sophism.
sofista, *a.* sophistic(al).—*n.m.f.* sophist.
sofistería, *n.f.* sophistry.
sofisticar [A], *v.t.* falsify.
sofístico, -ca, *a.* sophistic(al).
soflama, *n.f.* glow; blush; cheating; speech.
soflamar, *v.t.* make blush; cheat; char.
soflamero, -ra, *a., n.m.f.* hypocrite.
sofocación, *n.f.* suffocation.
sofocar [A], *v.t.* choke; stifle; smother; embarrass.
sofoco, *n.m.* anguish; embarrassment.
sofocón, *n.m.*, **sofoquina,** *n.f.* (*fam.*) disappointment.
sofrenada, *n.f.* restraint; check(ing).
sofrenar, *v.t.* check; restrain.
soga, *n.f.* rope; (*fam.*) mocking; **hacer —,** linger, lag.
soguero, *n.m.* rope-maker.
soguilla, *n.f.* cord; braid.—*n.m.* errand-boy.
soja, *n.f.* soya bean.
sojuzgar [B], *v.t.* conquer, subdue.
sol (1), *n.m.* sun; sunshine; **hace —,** it is sunny.

sol (2), *n.m.* (*mus.*) (key of) G.
solana, *n.f.* sunny place; sun-porch *or* -room.
solanera, *n.f.* sunburn; sunny place.
solapa, *n.f.* lapel; pretext, cover.
solapado, -da, *a.* under-hand, sly.
solapar, *v.t.* overlap; conceal, cloak.
solape, solapo, *n.m.* lapel; pretext.
solar, *a.* solar, sun.—*n.m.* plot of ground; family seat, mansion.—*v.t.* [4] pave; sole.
solariego, -ga, *a.* ancestral.
solazar [C], *v.t.* amuse, divert.
solazo, *n.m.* (*fam.*) burning sun.
soldadesco, -ca, *a.* soldierly, soldiers'.—*n.f.* soldiery.
soldado, *n.m.* soldier; **— raso,** private.
soldador, *n.m.* solderer; welder; soldering iron.
soldadura, *n.f.* solder(ing); weld(ing).
soldán, *n.m.* sultan.
soldar [4], *v.t.* solder; weld; join; repair.
solear, *v.t.* sun.
soledad, *n.f.* solitude; loneliness; wilderness.
solemne, *a.* solemn; (*fam.*) downright.
solemnidad, *n.f.* solemnity.
solemnizar, *v.t.* solemnize.
soler [5, *only pres. & imperf. indic.*], *v.t.* be used to, be accustomed to; **suele venir hoy,** he usually comes today.
solera, *n.f.* beam; floor, bottom; mother-wine; **de —,** fine, long-established.
solevamiento, *n.m.* upheaval.
solev(ant)ar, *v.t.* raise; incite.—*v.r.* rise up; rebel.
solfa, *n.f.* (*mus.*) sol-fa; notation; (*fam.*) beating; **poner en —,** make fun of.
solfear, *v.t.* (*mus.*) sol-fa; sight-read; (*fam.*) thrash.
solfeo, *n.m.* (*mus.*) sol-fa; sight-reading; (*fam.*) thrashing.
solicitación, *n.f.* request; wooing.
solicitante, *n.m.f.* applicant; petitioner.
solicitar, *v.t.* request; attract; court; see to.
solícito, -ta, *a.* diligent; (*fam.*) affectionate.
solicitud, *n.f.* request; application; care.
solidar, *v.t.* make firm; prove.
solidaridad, *n.f.* solidarity.
solidario, -ria, *a.* solidary; joint; integral.
solidarizar, *v.r.* unite, join resources.
solidez, *n.f.* solidity.
solidificación, *n.f.* solidification.
solidificar [A], *v.t., v.r.* solidify.
sólido, -da, *a., n.m.* solid.
soliloquio, *n.m.* soliloquy.
solista, *n.m.f.* soloist.
solitario, -ria, *a.* solitary.—*n.m.f.* recluse.
sólito, -ta, *a.* wont.
soliviantar, *v.t.* incite, stir up.
soliviar, *v.t.* lift, raise slightly.
solo, -la, *a.* alone; lonely; sole, only; **a solas,** on his own.—*n.m.* solo.
sólo, *adv.* only, solely.
solom(ill)o, *n.m.* sirloin.
solsticio, *n.m.* solstice.
soltar [4], *v.t.* release; let go (of); let out; explain.—*v.i.* begin, burst out (*a*).—*v.r.* come loose *or* off; come undone; loosen up.
soltero, -ra, *n.m.* bachelor.—*n.f.* spinster.
solterón, -rona, (*fam.*) *n.m.* confirmed bachelor.—*n.f.* old maid.
soltura, *n.f.* ease; freedom; release; fluency.
solubilidad, *n.f.* solubility.
soluble, *a.* soluble.

193

solución, n.f. solution.
solucionar, v.t. solve; settle.
solvencia, n.f. settlement; solvency.
solventar, v.t. settle (debts); solve.
solvente, a., n.m. solvent.
sollamar, v.t. singe.
sollastre, n.m. scullion.
sollozar [C], v.i. sob.
sollozo, n.m. sob.
somalí, a., n.m.f. Somali.
la Somalia, n.f. Somalia.
somatén, n.m. vigilantes; (fam.) hubbub.
sombra, n.f. shade, shadow; (fam.) luck; wit.
sombr(e)ar, v.t. shade.
sombrerero, -ra, n.m. hatter.—n.f. milliner.
sombrero, n.m. hat.
sombrilla, n.f. shade; sun-shade.
sombrío, - a, a. gloomy, sombre, sullen.
sombroso, -sa, a. shadowy.
somero, -ra, a. superficial, shallow.
someter, v.t. subdue.—v.i., v.r. submit.
sometido, -da, a. submissive.
sometimiento, n.m. submission.
somnambulismo, n.m. somnambulism.
somnámbulo, -la, a., n.m.f. somnambulist.
somnolencia, n.f. somnolence.
de somonte, a. phr. rough, coarse.
somorgujar, v.t., v.i., v.r. dive, duck.
somorgujo, n.m. (orn.) dabchick, grebe; **a** (lo) —, under water; on the quiet.
somos [SER].
son, n.m. sound; news; pretext; reason. [SER].
sonadero, n.m. [PAÑUELO].
sonado, -da, a. famous; talked-about.
sonaja, n.f. jingle; timbrel.
sonajero, n.m. baby's rattle.
sonam- [SOMNAM-].
sonante, a. sounding; jingling.
sonar [4], v.t. sound; ring; blow (nose).—v.i. sound; jingle; sound familiar or right; be rumoured.—v.r. blow one's nose.
sonata, n.f. sonata.
sonda, n.f. sounding; plummet; borer.
sond(e)ar, v.t. sound (out); fathom.
soneto, n.m. sonnet.
sónico, -ca, a. sonic.
sonido, n.m. sound; literal meaning; rumour.
sonochada, n.f. late evening; sunset watch.
sonoro, -ra, a. sonorous; sounding.
sonreír [28], v.i., v.r. smile.
sonriente, a. smiling.
sonrisa, n.f. smile.
sonroj(e)ar, v.t. make blush.—v.r. blush.
sonrojo, n.m. blush.
sonrosado, -da, a. rosy.
sonros(e)ar [SONROJEAR].
sonsaca, n.f. pilfering; wheedling.
sonsacar [A], v.t. pilfer; wheedle.
sonsonete, n.m. sing-song tone; tapping.
soñador, -ra, a. dreaming.—n.m.f. dreamer.
soñar [4], v.t., v.i. dream (con, en, about).
soñ(arr)era, n.f. sleepiness.
soñolencia, n.f. somnolence.
soñoliento, -ta, a. sleepy, drowsy.
sopa, n.f. soup; sops.
sopapo, n.m. chuck under the chin; slap.
sop(e)ar, v.t. steep; trample on.
sopero, -ra, n.m. soup-dish.—n.f. tureen.
sopesar, v.t. try the weight of.
sopetón, n.m. slap; **de** —, suddenly, in a flash.

sopista, n.m.f. person living on charity.
soplar, v.t. blow, blow away or up; pinch, steal; (fam.) split or squeal on; tip off; whisper.—v.i. blow.—v.r. get puffed-up or vain.
soplete, n.m. blow-pipe; torch.
soplido, n.m. blast, puff.
soplo, n.m. blast, blowing; breath; (fam.) tip-off; squeal, give-away.
soplón, -plona, n.m.f. (fam.) tattler, squealer.
soponcio, n.m. swoon, faint.
sopor, n.m. stupor, drowsiness.
soporífero, -ra, soporífico, -ca, a., n.m. soporific.
soportable, a. bearable.
soportar, v.t. bear; endure.
soporte, n.m. support, stand.
soprano, n.m.f. soprano.
Sor, n.f. Sister . . . (nun).
sorber, v.t. sip; soak up.—v.r. swallow.
sorbete, n.m. sherbet.
sorbo, n.m. sip; gulp.
Sorbona, n.f. Sorbonne.
sordera, n.f. deafness.
sordidez, n.f. sordidity, sordidness.
sórdido, -da, a. sordid.
sordo, -da, a. deaf; silent; dull.
sordomudo, -da, a., n.m.f. deaf-mute.
sorna, n.f. sloth; malice.
soroche, n.m. (S.A.) mountain sickness.
sóror, n.f. (eccl.) sister.
sorprendente, a. surprising.
sorprender, v.t. surprise.—v.r. be surprised.
sorpresa, n.f. surprise.
sortear, v.t. raffle off; cast lots for; evade; (taur.) fight well.
sorteo, n.m. raffle, draw; evasion.
sortero, -ra, n.m.f. fortune-teller.
sortija, n.f. ring; curl.
sortilegio, n.m. sorcery.
sosa, n.f. soda.
sosegado, -da, a. peaceful, calm.
sosegar [1B], v.t. calm.—v.i., v.r. calm down.
sosera, sosería, n.f. insipidity; dullness, inanity.
sosiego, n.m. calm, peace.
soslayar, v.t. slant; evade; ward off.
soslayo, -ya, a. slanting; **de** —, askance; aslant.
soso, -sa, a. insipid; dull; inane.
sospecha, n.f. suspicion.
sospechable, a. suspect.
sospechar, v.t. suspect; be suspicious (de, of).
sospechoso, -sa, a. suspicious.—n.m.f. suspect.
sostén, n.m. support.
sostener [33], v.t. sustain.
sostenido, n.m. (mus.) sharp.
sostenimiento, n.m. sustenance; support.
sota, n.f. jack (cards); hussy.
sotabarba, n.f. fringe-beard.
sotana, n.f. cassock; (fam.) beating.
sótano, n.m. cellar; basement.
sotavento, n.m. leeward.
soterraño, -ña, a. underground.
soterrar [1], v.t. bury.
sotileza, n.f. fishing gut.
soto, n.m. copse; thicket.
sotreta, n.f. (S.A.) broken-down horse.
sotrozo, n.m. linch- or axle-pin.
soviético, -ca, a. soviet.
soy [SER].

su, *poss. pron.* his, her, its, their, your.
suave, *a.* suave, smooth, gentle.
suavidad, *n.f.* suavity; gentleness.
suavizar [C], *v.t.* smooth; sweeten; mellow; strop.
sub-, *prefix.* sub- under-.
subacuático, -ca, *a.* underwater.
subalterno, -na, *a., n.m.f.* subordinate.
subarrendar [1], *v.t.* sub-let.
subasta, *n.f.* auction.
subastar, *v.t.* auction.
subconsciencia, *n.f.* subconscious(ness).
subconsciente, *a., n.m.* subconscious.
subcontratista, *n.m.f.* subcontractor.
súbdito, -ta, *a., n.m.f.* (*pol.*) subject.
subentender [SOBRENTENDER].
subida, *n.f.* ascent; rise.
subido, -da, *a.* high; strong; bright.
subir, *v.t.* bring or take up; lift; go up; raise. —*v.i.* go or come up; rise.—*v.r.* rise.
subitáneo, -nea, *a.* sudden.
súbito, -ta, *a.* sudden.—*adv.* suddenly.
subjetividad, *n.f.* subjectivity.
subjetivo, -va, *a.* subjective.
subjuntivo, -va, *a., n.m.* subjunctive.
sublevación, *n.f.* revolt, uprising.
sublevar, *v.t.* incite.—*v.r.* revolt.
sublimación, *n.f.* sublimation.
sublimar, *v.t.* sublimate, exalt.
sublime, *a.* sublime.
sublimidad, *n.f.* sublimity.
subliminar, *a.* subliminal.
submarino, -na, *a., n.m.* submarine.
subordinado, -da, *a., n.m.* subordinate.
subordinar, *v.t.* subordinate.
subrayar, *v.t.* underline; stress.
subrogar [B], *v.t.* subrogate, substitute.
subsanar, *v.t.* excuse; amend.
subscribir [*p.p.* subscrito], *v.t., v.r.* subscribe.
subscripción, *n.f.* subscription.
subsecuente, *a.* subsequent.
subseguir [8G], *v.i., v.r.* follow next.
subsidiar, *v.t.* subsidize.
subsidiario, -ria, *a.* subsidiary.
subsidio, *n.m.* subsidy; pension; relief.
subsistencia, *n.f.* subsistence.
subsistir, *v.i.* subsist.
substancia, *n.f.* substance.
substancial, *a.* substantial.
substanciar, *v.t.* condense; (*jur.*) try.
substancioso, -sa, *a.* substantial.
substantivo, -va, *a.* substantival.—*n.m.* noun.
substitución, *n.f.* substitution.
substituir [O], *v.t.* substitute.
substituto, -ta, *n.m.f.* substitute.
substracción, *n.f.* subtraction.
substraer [34], *v.t.* withhold; subtract.—*v.r.* withdraw (*a*, from).
substrato, *n.m.* substratum.
subsuelo, *n.m.* subsoil.
subteniente, *n.m.* second lieutenant.
subterfugio, *n.m.* subterfuge.
subterráneo, -nea, *a.* subterranean.
suburbano, -na, *a.* suburban.—*n.m.f.* suburbanite.
suburbio, *n.m.* suburb; slum.
subvención, *n.f.* subsidy.
subvencionar, *v.t.* subsidize.
subvenir [36], *v.t.* defray; provide.
subversión, *n.f.* subversion.

subversivo, -va, *a.* subversive.
subyugación, *n.f.* subjugation.
subyugar [B], *v.t.* subjugate.
succión, *n.f.* suction.
succionar, *v.t.* (*mech.*) suck.
suceder, *v.t.* succeed, follow.—*v.i.* happen.
sucesión, *n.f.* succession; estate.
sucesivo, -va, *a.* successive; *en lo —,* henceforth; *y así sucesivamente,* and so on or forth.
suceso, *n.m.* event, incident; (*obs.*) outcome; lapse.
sucesor, -ra, *n.m.f.* successor.
suciedad, *n.f.* filth, dirt.
sucinto, -ta, *a.* succint.
sucio, -cia, *a.* dirty, filthy, foul.—*adv.* unfairly.
suco, *n.m.* juice.
sucucho, *n.m.* nook.
suculento, -ta, *a.* succulent.
sucumbir, *v.i.* succumb.
sucursal, *a., n.f.* (*com.*) branch.
Sudáfrica, *n.f.* South Africa.
sudafricano, -na, *a., n.m.f.* South African.
Sudamérica, *n.f.* South America.
sudamericano, -na, *a., n.m.f.* South American.
Sudán, *n.m.* Sudan.
sudanés, -nesa, *a., n.m.f.* Sudanese.
sudante, *a.* sweating.
sudar, *v.t., v.i.* sweat; ooze.
sudario, *n.m.* shroud.
sudeste, *n.m.* south-east.
sudoeste, *n.m.* south-west.
sudor, *n.m.* sweat.
sudoriento, -ta, **sud(or)oso, -sa,** *a.* sweaty, sweating.
sudueste [SUDOESTE].
Suecia, *n.f.* Sweden.
sueco, -ca, *a., n.m.* Swedish.—*n.m.f.* Swede; *hacer(se) el —,* pretend not to notice.
suegro, -gra, *n.m.* father-in-law.—*n.f.* mother-in-law; crust.
suela, *n.f.* sole; *de siete suelas,* (*fam.*) downright.
sueldo, *n.m.* pay, salary; [SOLDAR].
suelo, *n.m.* ground; land; soil; floor; *medir el —,* fall flat; [SOLER].
suelto, -ta, *a.* loose; free; odd, single; fluent, agile.—*n.m.* small change; item of news; chapbook.—*n.f.* release; fetters, tie.
sueño, *n.m.* dream; sleep; *en(tre) sueños,* while dreaming; *tener —,* be sleepy.
suero, *n.m.* whey; serum.
suerte, *n.f.* chance; fortune, luck; fate; sort; feat; way; *de — que,* so that; *echar suertes,* cast lots.
suficiencia, *n.f.* sufficiency, adequacy.
suficiente, *a.* sufficient, enough; competent.
sufijo, -ja, *a.* suffixed.—*n.m.* suffix.
sufragáneo, -nea, *a., n.m.* suffragan.
sufragar [B], *v.t.* aid; defray.—*v.i.* (*S.A.*) vote (*por,* for).
sufragio, *n.m.* suffrage.
sufragista, *n.m.* suffragist.—*n.f.* suffragette.
sufrible, *a.* sufferable.
sufridero, -ra, *a.* sufferable.
sufrido, -da, *a.* long-suffering.
sufridor, -ra, *a.* suffering.—*n.m.f.* sufferer.
sufriente, *a.* suffering.
sufrimiento, *n.m.* suffering; sufferance.
sufrir, *v.t., v.i.* suffer; undergo.

sugerencia, *n.f.* suggestion.
sugerente, *a.* suggestive.
sugerir [6], *v.t.* suggest.
sugestión, *n.f.* suggestion, hint; influence.
sugestionable, *a.* easily suggested *or* influenced.
sugestionar, *v.t.* influence; inveigle.
sugestivo, -va, *a.* suggestive.
suicida, *a.* suicidal.—*n.m.f.* suicide (*person*).
suicidar, *v.r.* commit suicide.
suicidio, *n.m.* suicide (*act*).
Suiza, *n.f.* Switzerland.
suizo, -za, *a., n.m.f.* Swiss.—*n.m.* bun.—*n.f.* brawl.
sujeción, *n.f.* subjection.
sujetar, *v.t.* hold firm, fasten; subject.
sujeto, -ta, *a.* subject, liable; firm, fastened.—*n.m.* (*pej.*) fellow, individual; (*gram.*) subject.
sulfato, *n.m.* sulphate.
sulfurar, *v.t.* sulphurize; enrage.
sulfúreo, -rea, sulfúrico, -ca, *a.* sulphuric.
sulfuro, *n.m.* sulphur.
sulfuroso, -sa, *a.* sulphurous.
sultán, *n.m.* sultan.
suma, *n.f.* sum; total; addition; compendium; summa; *en* —, in short.
sumamente, *adv.* extremely.
sumar, *v.t.* add up; amount to.—*v.r.* add up (*a,* to); adhere.
sumario, -ria, *a., n.m.* summary.—*n.m.* (*jur.*) indictment.
sumergible, *a.* submersible.—*n.m.* submarine.
sumergir [E], *v.t., v.r.* submerge.
sumersión, *n.f.* submersion.
sumidad, *n.f.* apex, summit.
sumidero, *n.m.* drain; sump.
suministración, *n.f.* supply.
suministrar, *v.t.* supply.
suministro, *n.m.* provision, supply.
sumir, *v.t., v.r.* sink.—*v.t.* (*eccl.*) receive (*Holy Communion*).
sumisión, *n.f.* submission.
sumiso, -sa, *a.* submissive; humble.
sumo, -ma, *a.* highest, greatest, supreme.
suntuosidad, *n.f.* sumptuousness.
suntuoso, -sa, *a.* sumptuous, gorgeous.
supe [SABER].
supeditar, *v.t.* oppress; subject.
super-, *prefix.* super-, over-.
superable, *a.* superable.
superar, *v.t.* surpass; overcome.
superávit, *n.m.* surplus, residue.
superchería, *n.f.* fraud, swindle.
superchero, -ra, *a.* deceitful.
superentender [2], *v.t.* superintend.
superestructura, *n.f.* superstructure.
superficial, *a.* superficial.
superficie, *n.f.* surface; exterior.
superfluo, -flua, *a.* superfluous.
superhombre, *n.m.* superhuman.
superintendencia, *n.f.* superintendence.
superintendente, *n.m.f.* superintendent.
superior, *a.* superior; upper.—*n.m.* superior.
superiora, *n.f.* mother superior.
superioridad, *n.f.* superiority.
superlativo, -va, *a., n.m.* superlative.
supernumerario, -ria, *a., n.m.f.* supernumerary.
superponer [25], *v.t.* superpose.

supersensible, *a.* hypersensitive.
supersónico, -ca, *a.* supersonic.
superstición, *n.f.* superstition.
supersticioso, -sa, *a.* superstitious.
supérstite, *a., n.m.f.* (*jur.*) survivor.
supervenir [SOBREVENIR].
supervisión, *n.f.* supervision.
supervivencia, *n.f.* survival.
superviviente, *a.* surviving.
supino, -na, *a., n.m.* supine.
súpito, -ta [SÚBITO].
suplantar, *v.t.* supplant; falsify.
supleausencias, *n.m.f. inv.* substitute.
suplefaltas, *n.m.f. inv.* scapegoat.
suplementario, -ria, *a.* supplementary.
suplemento, *n.m.* supplement.
súplica, *n.f.* petition, request.
suplicación, *n.f.* supplication; cone wafer.
suplicante, *a., n.m.f.* suppli(c)ant.
suplicar [A], *v.t.* implore; (*jur.*) appeal.
suplicio, *n.m.* torture; execution, death penalty.
suplir, *v.t.* supply, furnish; make up for; substitute; excuse; (*gram.*) understand.
suponer, *n.m.* (*fam.*) conjecture.—*v.t.* [25] suppose; imply.—*v.i.* matter.
suposición, *n.f.* surmise supposition; authority; imposture.
supositivo, -va, *a.* suppositional.
supradicho [SOBREDICHO].
supremacía, *n.f.* supremacy.
supremo, -ma, *a.* supreme.
supresión, *n.f.* suppression.
supresor, -ra, *n.m.f.* suppressor.
suprimir, *v.t.* suppress; omit.
supuesto, -ta, *a.* supposed; so-called.—*n.m.* assumption; — *que,* since; *por* —, of course.
supurar, *v.t.* suppurate.
supuse [SUPONER].
suputar, *v.t.* compute.
sur, *n.m.* south.
surcar [A], *v.t.* plough, furrow.
surco, *n.m.* furrow; groove.
surgir [E], *v.i.* spurt; arise; anchor.
suripanta, *n.f.* hussy.
suroeste [SUDOESTE].
surrealismo, *n.m.* surrealism.
surrealista, *a., n.m.f.* surrealist.
surtidero, *n.m.* outlet; jet.
surtido, *n.m.* stock, supply; jet; *de* —, stock.
surtidor, -ra, *n.m.f.* supplier.—*n.m.* spout; fountain; pump (*gas etc.*).
surtir, *v.t.* supply, provide.—*v.i.* spout.
¡sus! *interj.* hurry! cheer up!
sus- [SUBS-].
susceptible, susceptivo, -va, *a.* susceptible.
suscitar, *v.t.* provoke.
susidio, *n.m.* anxiety..
susodicho, -cha, *a.* above-mentioned.
suspender, *v.t.* suspend; astound; (*educ.*) fail.
suspendido, *a.* (*educ.*) fail(ed).
suspense, *n.m.* suspense.
suspensión, *n.f.* suspension; amazement; (*educ.*) failure.
suspensivo, -va, *a.* suspensive.
suspenso, -sa, *a.* suspended; astounded; baffled.
suspensores, *n.m. pl.* (*S.A.*) braces, (*U.S.*) suspenders.
suspicacia, *n.f.* suspicion.

suspicaz, *a.* (*pl.* **-aces**) suspicious.
suspirar, *v.i.* sigh (*por,* for).
suspiro, *n.m.* sigh; (*cul.*) meringue.
sustentáculo, *n.m.* prop, support.
sustentar, *v.t.* sustain, maintain.
sustento, *n.m.* sustenance.
susto, *n.m.* scare, fright.
susurrar, *v.i.* whisper, murmur.—*v.r.* be rumoured.
susurr(id)o, *n.m.* murmur, whisper.
sutil, *a.* subtle; fine.
sutileza, *n.f.* subtlety; dexterity.
sutilizar [C], *v.t.* make subtle *or* fine.—*v.i.* quibble.
suyo, -ya, *a. poss. & pron.* his, hers, its, yours, theirs; *de —,* of his (her *etc.*) accord; *salirse con la suya,* have one's way.

T

T, t, *n.f.* twenty-third letter of the Spanish alphabet.
tabacalero, -ra, *a.* tobacco.—*n.m.* tobacconist.—*n.f.* tobacco works *or* firm *or* shop.
tabaco, *n.m.* tobacco.
tabalear, *v.t., v.r.* rock.—*v.i.* drum.
tábano, *n.m.* gadfly.
tabaola, *n.f.* uproar.
taberna, *n.f.* tavern.
tabernáculo, *n.m.* tabernacle.
tabernario, -ria, *a.* vulgar, low.
tabernero, *n.m.* innkeeper.
tabica, *n.f.* panel.
tabicar [A], *v.t.* wall up.
tabique, *n.m.* partition, partition-wall.
tabla, *n.f.* board, plank; table, list; plate, sheet; strip of land; ski; *a raja —,* sweeping all before.—*pl.* boards, stage; *hacer tablas,* reach a deadlock.
tablado, *n.m.* stage; scaffold; flooring; boarding.
tablaje, *n.m.* planking.
tablazón, *n.f.* boarding; deck.
tablear, *v.t.* saw up (*timber*); lay out.
tablero, *n.m.* panel; board; gambling table; chess-board.
tableta, *n.f.* plank; tablet; lozenge; clapper.
tabletear, *v.i.* rattle.
tablilla, *n.f.* lath; notice-board.
tablón, *n.m.* beam, board; *coger un —,* (*fam.*) get tipsy.
tabú, *n.m.* taboo.
tabuco, *n.m.* hovel.
tabular, *a.* tabular.—*v.t.* tabulate.
taburete, *n.m.* stool.
tac, *n.m.* tick (*sound*).
tacaño, -ña, *a.* stingy, mean.—*n.m.f.* miser.
tacar [A], *v.t.* mark, scar.
tacita, *n.f.* small cup.
tácito, -ta, *a.* tacit.
taciturno, -na, *a.* taciturn.
taco, *n.m.* plug, wad, bung; billiard-cue; pad; (*fam.*) curse; (*fam.*) bite, snack; sip.
tacón, *n.m.* heel (*of shoe*).

taconear, *v.i.* drum the heels.
táctico, -ca, *a.* tactical.—*n.m.* tactician.—*n.f.* tactics.
tacto, *n.m.* touch; tact.
tacha, *n.f.* flaw; tack.
tachadura, *n.f.* erasure.
tachar, *v.t.* cross out; accuse, blame.
tacho, *n.m.* (*S.A.*) bin; pan; pot.
tachón, *n.m.* erasure; gilded tack.
tafetán, *n.m.* taffeta.—*pl.* colours, flag.
tafilete, *n.m.* morocco leather.
tagarote, *n.m.* (*orn.*) hawk; (*fam.*) has-been.
taheño, -ña, *a.* red (*hair*).
tahona, *n.f.* bakery; mill.
tahur, -ra, *n.m.f.* gambler; cheat.
taifa, *n.f.* faction; (*fam.*) gang.
Tailandia, *n.f.* Thailand.
tailandés, -desa, *a., n.m.f.* Thai.
taimado, -da, *a.* sly, crafty.
taita, *n.m.* (*fam.*) papa, daddy.
taja, *n.f.* cut; tally.
tajado, -da, *a.* steep, sheer.—*n.f.* slice; cut.
tajante, *a.* cutting, sharp; utter.
tajar, *v.t.* cut, slice; sharpen.
Tajo, *n.m.* Tagus; **tajo,** *n.m.* cut; drop; trench; block; work.
tal, *a.* such, such a.—*pron.* such a one *or* thing.—*adv.* thus, so; *con — que,* provided that; *¿qué —?* how goes it? *un —,* a certain.
tala, *n.f.* felling; havoc; tip-cat.
taladrar, *v.t.* drill, bore; pierce.
taladro, *n.m.* drill; bit, auger; hole.
tálamo, *n.m.* bridal bed; thalamus.
talán, *n.m.* ding-dong.
talanquera, *n.f.* parapet; (*fig.*) safety.
talante, *n.m.* mien; mode; will.
talar (1), *a.* full-length (*robe*).
talar (2), *v.t.* fell; lay waste.
talco, *n.m.* talc, talcum; tinsel.
talcual, talcualillo, -lla, *a.* (*fam.*) so-so, middling.
talego, -ga, *n.m.f.* bag, sack.
talento, *n.m.* talent.
talentoso, -sa, talentudo, -da, *a.* talented.
talismán, *n.m.* talisman.
talón, *n.m.* heel; counterfoil, coupon.
talla, *n.f.* carving; size; stature; reward.
tallado, -da, *a.* shaped.
tallar, *n.m.* timber-land(s).—*v.t.* carve; cut; measure.
talle, *n.m.* figure, shape; size; waist; outline.
taller, *n.m.* workshop; studio.
tallo, *n.m.* stalk; shoot.—*pl.* (*S.A.*) (*cul.*) greens.
tallón, *n.m.* reward.
talludo, -da, *a.* lanky; ageing.
tamaño, -ña, *a.* so big; such a big.—*n.m.* size.
tambalear, *v.i., v.r.* totter.
tambaleo, *n.m.* tottering.
también, *adv.* also, too, as well.
tambo, *n.m.* (*S.A.*) inn; cow-shed.
tambor, *n.m.* drum.
tamborear, *v.i.* drum.
tamboril, *n.m.* timbrel.
tamborilear, *v.t.* extol.—*v.i.* drum.
Támesis, *n.m.* the Thames.
tamiz, *n.m.* (*pl.* **-ices**) sieve.
tamizar [C], *v.t.* sift.
tamo, *n.m.* fluff, dust.
tampoco, *adv.* neither, not either.
tan, *adv.* so.

tanda, *n.f.* turn; relay, shift; batch; series; task; match.
en tanganillas, *a., adv. phr.* wobbly.
tanganillo, *n.m.* prop.
tangente, *a., n.f.* tangent.
Tánger, *n.f.* Tangier.
tangerino, -na, *a., n.m.f.* Tangerine.—*n.f.* tangerine (*fruit*).
tangible, *a.* tangible.
tango, *n.m.* tango.
tanque, *n.m.* tank.
tantán, *n.m.* ding-dong.
tantarantán, *n.m.* beating of drum.
tantear, *v.t.* size up, test; outline; score.—*v.i.* feel one's way.
tanteo, *n.m.* trial and error; sizing-up; score.
tanto, -ta, *a.* so much, as much.—*pl.* so many, as many.—*n.m.* copy; goal, score.—*adv.* so much, so often; *algún —,* somewhat; *al — de,* because of; aware of; *en(tre) —,* meanwhile; *por (lo) —,* therefore; *— mejor,* so much the better; *treinta y tantos,* thirty odd.
tañer [K], *v.t., v.i.* play; ring.
tapa, *n.f.* lid, cover, cap; book cover; titbit, snack.
tapadera, *n.f.* cover, lid.
tapadero, *n.m.* stopper.
tapador, *n.m.* cover; stopper.
tapaporos, *n.m. inv.* filler, primer.
tapar, *v.t.* cover; plug; conceal; stop up.
taparrabo, *n.m.* loincloth; trunks.
tapete, *n.m.* rug, carpet; *sobre el —,* (*fig.*) under discussion.
tapia, *n.f.,* **tapial,** *n.m.* (*S.A.*) mud or adobe wall; garden wall.
tapiar, *v.t.* wall up or in; block.
tapicería, *n.f.* upholstery; tapestries.
tapiz, *n.m.* (*pl.* **-ices**) tapestry.
tapizar [C], *v.t.* upholster; carpet; tapestry.
tapón, *n.m.* cork, stopper; plug; cap.
taponar, *v.t.* plug; stopper.
tapujo, *n.m.* muffler; cover.
taque, *n.m.* click, rap.
taquigrafía, *n.f.* shorthand.
taquígrafo, -fa, *n.m.f.* stenographer.
taquimecanógrafo, -fa, *n.m.f.* shorthand-typist.
taquilla, *n.f.* ticket- or box-office; rack, file.
tara, *n.f.* tare; tally; (*fam.*) exaggeration.
tarabilla, *n.f.* clapper; latch.
taracea, *n.f.* marquetry.
tarántula, *n.f.* (*zool.*) tarantula.
tarara, tarará, *n.f.* trumpet-sound.
tararear, *v.t., v.i.* hum.
tarasca, *n.f.* huge dragon carried in Corpus Christi processions; (*fam.*) slut.
tarascar [A], *v.t.* bite (*dogs*).
tarazar [C], *v.t.* bite; bother.
tarazón, *n.m.* chunk.
tardanza, *n.f.* tardiness, delay.
tardar, *v.i.* be late or long (*en,* in); *a más —,* at the latest.
tarde, *n.f.* afternoon, evening.—*adv.* (too) late.
tardecer [9], *v.i.* get late, go dark.
tardío, -día, *a.* late; slow.
tardo, -da, *a.* late; slow, backward.
tarea, *n.f.* job, task; toil.
tarifa, *n.f.* tariff; price-list; fare.
tarja, *n.f.* buckler; tally; *sobre —,* (*fam.*) on tick.
tarjeta, *n.f.* card; tablet; legend (*of maps*).

tarquín, *n.m.* mud, silt.
tarro, *n.m.* jar; (*S.A.*) top hat.
tarta, *n.f.* tart, gâteau.
tártago, *n.m.* (*bot.*) spurge; (*fam.*) tough luck; (*fam.*) mean joke.
tartajoso, -sa, *a.* stuttering.
tartalear, *v.i.* stagger.
tartamudear, *v.i.* stammer.
tartamudez, *n.f.* stutter, stammer.
tartamudo, -da, *a.* stammering.—*n.m.f.* stutterer.
tártaro, -ra, *a., n.m.f.* Tartar.—*n.m.* tartar.
tartufo, *n.m.* hypocrite.
tarugo, *n.m.* wooden peg or block.
tarumba, *a. inv.* (*fam.*) rattled.
tasa, *n.f.* rate; valuation; standard.
tasador, -ra, *n.m.f.* (*com.*) valuer.
tasar, *v.t.* value; appraise; grant within limits.
tasca, *n.f.* (*fam.*) pub, bar.
tascar [B], *v.t.* champ, nibble.
tasquera, *n.f.* (*fam.*) scuffle, row.
tasquil, *n.m.* flake, chip.
tasto, *n.m.* tang, bad taste.
tata, *n.f.* (*fam.*) nurse; (*S.A.*) sis.—*n.m.* (*S.A.*) daddy.
tatar(a)-, *prefix.* great-great- (*relative*); *tatarabuelo,* great-great-grandfather.
¡tate! *interj.* look out! I see!
tato, -ta, *a.* stuttering.
tatuaje, *n.m.* tattoo(ing).
tatuar [M], *v.t.* tattoo.
taumaturgo, -ga, *n.m.f.* miracle-worker.
taurino, -na, *a.* rel. to bulls or bull-fighting.
taurófilo, -la, *n.m.f.* bull-fighting fan.
tauromaquia, *n.f.* (*fam.*) bull-fighting.
taxear, *v.i.* (*aer.*) taxi.
taxi, *n.m.* (*pl.* **taxis**) taxi.
taxidermia, *n.f.* taxidermy.
taxímetro, *n.m.* taximeter; taxi.
taxista, *n.m.f.* taxi-driver.
taz a taz, *adv.phr.* without added cost.
taza, *n.f.* cup; basin.
tazar [C], *v.t.* fray.
te (1), *n.f.* name of letter T.
te (2), *pron. fam.* you, to you.
té, *n.m.* tea.
tea, *n.f.* firebrand, torch.
teatral, *a.* theatrical.
teatro, *n.m.* theatre.
teca (1), *n.f.* teak.
teca (2), *n.f.* locket.
tecla, *n.f.* key (*piano, typing etc.*); delicate matter.
teclado, *n.m.* keyboard.
teclear, *v.t.* (*fam.*) feel one's way to.—*v.i.* strum the keys; type; drum.
tecleo, *n.m.* fingering; clatter (*of typing*).
técnica, *n.f.* technique; technic(s).
tecnicidad, *n.f.* technicality.
tecnicismo, *n.m.* technical term.
técnico, -ca, *a.* technical.—*n.m.f.* technician.
tecnicolor, *n.m.* Technicolor (*reg. trade mark*).
tecnología, *n.f.* technology.
tecnológico, -ca, *a.* technological.
tecnólogo, -ga, *n.m.f.* technologist.
techado, *n.m.* roof.
techar, *v.t.* roof.
techo, *n.m.* roof; ceiling; *bajo —,* indoors.
techumbre, *n.f.* roofing; ceiling.
tediar, *v.t.* loathe.
tedio, *n.m.* tedium; loathing.

tedioso, -sa, *a.* tedious.
teísta, *a., n.m.f.* theist.
teja, *n.f.* roof-tile.
tejado, *n.m.* roof.
tejar, *v.t.* tile.
tejaroz, *n.m.* eaves.
tejedor, -ra, *n.m.f.,* **tejedera,** *n.f.* weaver.
tejer, *v.t., v.i.* weave; — **y destejer,** chop and change, vacillate.
tejido, *n.m.* fabric, textile; weave, tissue.
tejo (1), *n.m.* quoit.
tejo (2), *n.m.* (*bot.*) yew.
tejón, *n.m.* (*zool.*) badger.
tela, *n.f.* cloth; skin; subject, matter; (*art*) canvas; **poner en — de juicio,** question, doubt; — **metálica,** wire netting.
telar, *n.m.* loom; frame.
telaraña, *n.f.* cobweb.
tele-, *prefix.* tele-; remote.
telecomunicación, *n.f.* telecommunication.
telecontrol, *n.m.* remote control.
teledifundir, *v.t.* televise; telecast.
telefonazo, *n.m.* (*fam.*) telephone-call.
telefon(e)ar, *v.t., v.i.* telephone.
telefonema, *n.m.* telephone message.
telefonía, *n.f.* telephony.
telefónico, -ca, *a.* telephonic.
telefonista, *n.m.f.* telephonist.
teléfono, *n.m.* telephone.
telegrafía, *n.f.* telegraphy.
telegrafiar [L], *v.t.* telegraph.
telégrafo, *n.m.* telegraph; (*fam.*) sign.
telegrama, *n.m.* telegram.
teleguiado, -da, *a.* remote-controlled, guided.
teleobjetivo, *n.m.* telephoto lens.
telepatía, *n.f.* telepathy.
telerreceptor, *n.m.* T.V. set.
telescopar, *v.t., v.r.* telescope.
telescópico, -ca, *a.* telescopic.
telescopio, *n.m.* telescope.
teleta, *n.f.* blotting-paper.
teletipia, teletipiadora, *n.f.,* **teletipo,** *n.m.* teletype.
teletubo, *n.m.* (T.V.) tube.
televidente, *n.m.f.* television viewer.
televisar, *v.t.* televise.
televisión, *n.f.* television.
televisor, -ra, *a.* rel. to television.—*n.m.* T.V. set.—*n.f.* T.V. transmitter.
telón, *n.m.* (*theat.*) curtain; — **de acero,** Iron Curtain.
telliza, *n.f.* quilt.
tema, *n.m.* subject, theme; exercise; (*gram.*) stem.—*n.m.* or *f.* mania; obstinacy; grudge.
temático, -ca, *a.* thematic; obsessed.
tembladero, -ra, *a.* quaking.—*n.m.* quagmire.
temblador, -ra, *n.m.f.* trembler; (*relig.*) Quaker.
temblante, *a.* trembling.—*n.m.* bracelet.
temblar [1], *v.i.* tremble, quake, quiver; shiver.
temblón, -blona, *a.* quaking, shaking.
temblor, *n.m.* tremor; shiver; trembling.
tembl(or)oso, -sa, *a.* tremulous; quivering.
temedero, -ra, *a.* dread.
temer, *v.t.* fear, be afraid of.
temerario, -ria, *a.* rash.
temeridad, *n.f.* temerity, rashness.
temeroso, -sa, *a.* timid; fearful.
temible, *a.* terrible, dreaded.
temor, *n.m.* fear, dread.

témpano, *n.m.* flitch; drum; iceberg.
temperamento, *n.m.* temperament; climate; compromise.
temperar [TEMPLAR].
temperatura, *n.f.* temperature.
temperie, *n.f.* weather.
tempestad, *n.f.* storm.
tempestear, *v.i.* storm.
tempestivo, -va, *a.* timely.
tempestuoso, -sa, *a.* stormy.
templado, -da, *a.* temperate; medium; firm.
templanza, *n.f.* temperance; mildness.
templar, *v.t.* temper, moderate; cool, calm; tune.—*v.r.* be moderate.
temple, *n.m.* weather; temper; humour; tuning.
templo, *n.m.* temple.
temporada, *n.f.* season; space of time.
temporal, *a.* temporal; temporary.—*n.m.* storm; (bad) weather.
temporáneo, -nea, temporario, -ria, *a.* temporary.
témporas, *n.f.pl.* Ember Days.
temporero, -ra, *a., n.m.f.* temporary.
temporizar [C], *v.i.* temporize.
temprano, -na, *a., adv.* early.
tenacidad, *n.f.* tenacity.
tenacillas, *n.f.pl.* tongs; tweezers.
tenaz, *a.* (*pl.* **-aces**) tenacious.
tenazas, *n.f.pl.* tongs; pliers, pincers.
tenca, *n.f.* (*ichth.*) tench.
tención, *n.f.* possession.
tendal, *n.m.* awning; tent.
tendejón, *n.m.* tiny shop; shed.
tendencia, *n.f.* tendency.
tendencioso, -sa, *a.* tentitious.
tender [2], *v.t.* spread (out); tender, offer; extend; hang out; set (*traps*).—*v.i.* tend (*a,* to).—*v.r.* lie down; slacken; stretch.
ténder, *n.m.* (rail.) tender.
tendero, -ra, *n.m.f.* shopkeeper.
tendido, -da, *n.m.* batch; laying; coat; slope.
tendón, *n.m.* tendon.
tendré [TENER].
tenducho, -cha, *n.m.f.* shabby shop.
tenebrosidad, *n.f.* darkness, gloom.
tenebroso, -sa, *a.* dark, gloomy.
tenedor, *n.m.* fork; holder.
teneduría, *n.f.* book-keeping.
tenencia, *n.f.* tenure; holding; lieutenancy.
tener [33], *v.t.* have, own; hold; consider; detain; — **por,** consider to be; — **que,** have to.—*v.r.* hold back; hold oneself.
tenería, *n.f.* tannery.
tengo [TENER].
tenida, *n.f.* session.
teniente, *a.* having, holding; mean; deafish.—*n.m.* lieutenant.
tenis, *n.m.* tennis.
tenisista, *n.m.f.* tennis-player.
tenor, *n.m.* tenor; purport; kind; (*mus.*) tenor.
tenorio, *n.m.* lady-killer.
tensión, *n.f.* tension.
tenso, -sa, *a.* taut, tense.
tentación, *n.f.* temptation.
tentáculo, *n.m.* tentacle.
tentador, -ra, *a.* tempting.—*n.m.* tempter.—*n.f.* temptress.
tentalear, *v.t.* (*fam.*) feel over.
tentar [2], *v.t.* tempt; touch, feel; try.
tentativo, -va, *a.* tentative.—*n.f.* attempt.
a tente bonete, *adv. phr.* (*fam.*) doggedly.

tentemozo, *n.m.* prop; tumbler (*toy*).
tentempié, *n.m.* (*fam.*) snack.
tenue, *a.* slight; fine, light.
tenuidad, *n.f.* tenuousness; triviality.
teñido, *n.m.,* **teñidura,** *n.f.* dyeing.
teñir [8K], *v.t.* dye; stain.
teocrático, -ca, *a.* theocratic.
teodolito, *n.m.* theodolite.
teología, *n.f.* theology.
teológico, -ca, *a.* theological.
teólogo, *n.m.* theologian.
teorema, *n.m.* theorem.
teoría, *n.f.* theory.
teórico, -ca, *a.* theoretic(al).—*n.m.f.* theorist.
 —*n.f.* theory.
teorizar [C], *v.t., v.i.* theorize (on).
teosofía, *n.f.* theosophy.
tequila, *n.f.* tequila (*drink*).
terapéutico, -ca, *a.* therapeutic(al).
terapia, *n.f.* therapy.
tercena, *n.f.* state tobacco store.
tercer, *a.m. contracted form of* TERCERO *before n.m.sg.*
tercería, *n.f.* mediation.
tercero, -ra, *a., n.m.f.* third.—*n.m.f.* mediator;
 bawd; umpire; middleman.
terciado, *n.m.* cutlass.
terciana, *n.f.* tertian ague.
terciar, *v.t.* slant; divide into three.—*v.i.*
 mediate; take part.—*v.r.* be all right.
tercio, -cia, *a., n.m.* third.—*n.m.* troop,
 corps, regiment; turn, favour.—*pl.* strong
 limbs.
terciopelo, *n.m.* velvet.
terco, -ca, *a.* stubborn; hard.
tergiversar, *v.t.* falsify, twist.
terma, *n.f.* power station.
termal, *a.* thermal.
termas, *n.f.pl.* hot baths.
térmico, -ca, *a.* thermic.
terminable, *a.* terminable.
terminación, *n.f.* termination.
terminal, *a., n.m.* (*elec.*) terminal.
terminante, *a.* final, definite.
terminar, *v.t., v.i., v.r.* finish, end.
término, *n.m.* end; boundary; aim; district;
 manner; term, word; terminus; — *medio,*
 average; compromise.
terminología, *n.f.* terminology.
termio, *n.m.* therm.
termo-, *prefix.* thermo-; [TERMOS].
termómetro, *n.m.* thermometer.
termonuclear, *a.* thermonuclear.
termos, *n.m. inv.* thermos.
termóstato, *n.m.* thermostat.
terna, *n.f.* set of three.
terne, *a., n.m.f.* (*fam.*) tough.
ternero, -ra, *n.m.f.* calf.
ternerón, -rona, *a.* soppy, mawkish.
terneza, *n.f.* tenderness.
ternilla, *n.f.* gristle.
terno, *n.m.* suit; set of three; curse; — *seco,*
 (*fam.*) windfall.
ternura, *n.f.* tenderness.
terquedad, *n.f.* stubbornness.
Terranova, *n.f.* Newfoundland.
terraplén, *n.m.* embankment.
terrateniente, *n.m.f.* land-owner.
terraza, *n.f.* terrace; pitcher.
terremoto, *n.m.* earthquake.
terrenal, *a.* earthly.

terreno, -na, *a.* worldly.—*n.m.* ground, land,
 field.
terrero, -ra, *a.* earthly; humble.—*n.m.*
 mound; dump; terrace; target.—*n.f.* steep
 land; (*orn.*) lark.
terrestre, *a.* terrestrial.
terrible, *a.* terrible.
territorial, *a.* territorial; regional.
territorio, *n.m.* territory.
terrón, *n.m.* clod; lump.—*pl.* farmland.
terror, *n.m.* terror.
terr(or)ífico, -ca, *a.* terrifying.
terrorismo, *n.m.* terrorism.
terrorista, *a., n.m.f.* terrorist.
terroso, -sa, *a.* earthy.
terruño, *n.m.* field; native region.
tersar, *v.t.* polish, smooth.
terso, -sa, *a.* smooth, polished.
tersura, *n.f.* smoothness, polish.
tertulia, *n.f.* party; meeting.
tertuliano, -na, tertuliante, *n.m.f.* party-
 goer; habitué; member.
tesauro, *n.m.* thesaurus.
tesis, *n.f. inv.* thesis.
tesitura, *n.f.* attitude.
teso, -sa, *a.* taut.—*n.m.* lump.
tesón, *n.m.* grit, tenacity.
tesonería, *n.f.* obstinacy.
tesorería, *n.f.* treasury.
tesorero, -ra, *n.m.f.* treasurer.
tesoro, *n.m.* treasure.
testa, *n.f.* head; (*fam.*) nous, brains.
testado, -da, *a.* testate.
testaférrea, testaferro, *n.m.* figurehead,
 front-man.
testamentario, -ria, *a.* testamentary.—*n.m.f.*
 executor.
testamento, *n.m.* will; testament.
testar, *v.i.* make a will.
testarada, *n.f.* butt; pig-headedness.
testarudo, -da, *a.* pig-headed.
testificar [A], *v.t., v.i.* testify.
testigo, -ga, *n.m.f.* witness.
testimoniar, *v.t.* attest, vouch for.
testimoniero, -ra, *a.* bearing false witness.
testimonio, *n.m.* testimony; false witness.
teta, *n.f.* teat; breast.
tétano(s), *n.m.* (*med.*) tetanus.
tetar, *v.t.* suckle.
tetera, *n.f.* tea-pot; kettle.
tetilla, *n.f.* nipple.
tetrarca, *n.m.* tetrarch.
tétrico, -ca, *a.* dismal, gloomy.
teutón, -tona, *a., n.m.f.* Teuton.
teutónico, -ca, *a., n.m.* Teutonic.
textil, *a., n.m.* textile.
texto, *n.m.* text; *fuera de —,* full-page
 (*illustration*).
textual, *a.* textual.
textura, *n.f.* texture.
tez, *n.f.* complexion.
ti, *pron.* (*used after preps.*) you.
tía, *n.f.* aunt(ie); (*fam.*) whore; *no hay tu —,*
 (*fam.*) you've had it.
Tíber, *n.m.* Tiber.
tiberio, *n.m.* (*fam.*) racket, uproar.
tibetano, -na, *a., n.m.f.* Tibetan.
tibieza, *n.f.* lukewarmness.
tibio, -bia (1), *a.* lukewarm.
tibia (2), *n.f.* (*anat.*) tibia.
tiburón, *n.m.* shark.
tic, *n.m.* (*pl.* tiques) (*med.*) tic.

tictac, *n.m.* tick-tack.
tiemblo, *n.m.* (*bot.*) aspen.
tiempo, *n.m.* time; weather; (*gram.*) tense; tempo; (*mus.*) movement; (*sport*) half; **hace buen (mal) —,** the weather is fine (bad).
tienda, *n.f.* shop; tent, awning.
tienta, *n.f.* probe; cunning; **andar a tientas,** grope.
tiento, *n.m.* touch; blind-man's stick; care; try-out.
tierno, -na, *a.* tender; weepy.
tierra, *n.f.* earth; land, soil; country; **echar por —,** destroy, ruin; **echar — a,** (*fig.*) hush up; **— adentro,** inland.
tieso, -sa, *a.* taut, tight; stiff.
tiesto, *n.m.* flowerpot; crack.
tífico, -ca, *a.* rel. to typhus.
tifo (1), **-fa,** *a.* (*fam.*) fed-up, sated.
tifo (2), *n.m.* (*med.*) typhus.
tifoideo, -ea, *a.* typhoid.
tifón, *n.m.* typhoon.
tifus, *n.m.* typhus; **de —,** (*S.A.*, *low*) free, gratis.
tigra, *n.f.* (*S.A.*) jaguar.
tigre, *n.m.* tiger; jaguar.
tigresa, *n.f.* tigress.
tijera, *n.f.* scissors (*usually* **tijeras**); (*fam.*) gossip; big eater.
tijereta, *n.f.* earwig.
tijeretear, *v.t.* snip; meddle in.
tila, *n.f.* (*bot.*) linden blossom; **infusión de —,** tisane.
tildar, *v.t.* put a tilde on; brand.
tilde, *n.m.* or *f.* tilde (˜); jot, tittle; flaw.
tilín, *n.m.* ting-a-ling; (*fam.*) trice; winsomeness.
tilo, *n.m.* linden, lime-tree.
tillado, *n.m.* plank floor.
timar, *v.t.* swindle; (*fam.*) ogle.
timba, *n.f.* (*fam.*) gamble.
timbal, *n.m.* kettle-drum.—*pl.* (*mus.*) tympani.
timbre, *n.m.* stamp; (door-)bell, buzzer; timbre.
timidez, *n.f.* timidity.
tímido, -da, *a.* timid.
timo, *n.m.* (*fam.*) swindle.
timón, *n.m.* rudder, helm.
timonel, *n.m.* helmsman.
timorato, -ta, *a.* God-fearing; timid.
tímpano, *n.m.* timpano; tympanum.
tina, *n.f.* large jar; vat, tub.
tinglado, *n.m.* shed; boarding; trick.
tiniebla(s), *n.f.* (*pl.*) darkness.
tino (1), *n.m.* knack; good sense; good aim; **a buen —,** at a guess.
tino (2), *n.m.* vat.
tinta, *n.f.* ink; hue; **de buena —,** on good authority.
tintar, *v.t.* tinge.
tinte, *n.m.* colour, dye; tint; dyeing; dry cleaner's.
tinterillo, *n.m.* (*fam.*) pen-pusher; (*S.A.*) pettifogger.
tintero, *n.m.* inkwell; **dejar en el —,** (*fam.*) forget about.
tintín, *n.m.* clink; tinkle.
tintirintín, *n.m.* tarara (*trumpeting*).
tinto, -ta, *a.* red.—*n.m.* red wine.
tintorero, -ra, *n.m.f.* dyer.
tintura, *n.f.* tincture; make-up; dyeing.

tiña, *n.f.* ringworm; (*fam.*) meanness.
tiñe [TEÑIR].
tiñoso, -sa, *a.* mangy; (*fam.*) stingy.
tío, *n.m.* uncle; (*fam.*) fellow, chap.
tiovivo, *n.m.* merry-go-round.
tipiadora, *n.f.* (*S.A.*) typewriter; typist.
tipiar, *v.t., v.i.* (*S.A.*) type.
típico, -ca, *a.* typical.
tiple, *n.m.f.* treble.
tipo, *n.m.* type; (*fam.*) chap.
tipografía, *n.f.* typography.
tiquismiquis, *n.m.pl.* (*fam.*) faddiness; bowing and scraping.
tira, *n.f.* strip.
tirabuzón, *n.m.* corkscrew.
tirada, *n.f.* throw; pull; issue, edition; period; distance; **— aparte,** off-print, separate.
tirado, -da, *a.* dirt-cheap; long; tall.—*n.m.* pulling, drawing.
tirador, -ra, *n.m.f.* puller; good shot.—*n.m.* knob, chain, cord (*to be pulled*).
tiranía, *n.f.* tyranny.
tiránico, -ca, *a.* tyrannical.
tiranizar [C], *v.t., v.i.* tyrannize.
tirano, -na, *a.* tyrannous.—*n.m.f.* tyrant.
tirante, *a.* tight, strained.—*n.m.* brace, tie.—*pl.* braces, (*U.S.*) suspenders.
tirantez, *n.f.* strain, tension;(full)length.
tirar, *v.t.* throw (away); fire, shoot; stretch; draw; pull; waste; attract; print.—*v.i.* last; be appealing; shoot; tend; boast; turn.—*v.r.* rush; lie down; **a todo** *or* **más—,** the utmost; **— a,** shoot at; turn to; aspire to.
tiritar, *v.i.* shiver.
tiritón, *n.m.* shiver.
tiro, *n.m.* throw; shot; charge; length; stretch; range; shooting; theft; depth; **a —,** within range *or* reach; **al —,** at once; **de tiros largos,** all dressed-up.
tirón, *n.m.* tug; novice.
tirotear, *v.t., v.i.* snipe (at).
tiroteo, *n.m.* sniping; shooting.
tirria, *n.f.* (*fam.*) dislike.
tísico, -ca, *a.*, *n.m.f.* consumptive.
tisis, *n.f.* (*med.*) consumption.
tisú, *n.m.* (*pl.* **tisúes**) tissue (*gold, silver*).
Titán, *n.m.* Titan; **titán,** *n.m.* titan.
titánico, -ca, *a.* titanic.
títere, *n.m.* puppet.
titilación, *n.f.* titillation; twinkling.
titilar, *v.t.* titillate.—*v.i.* twinkle.
titiritar, *v.i.* shiver.
titiritero, *n.m.* puppeteer; juggler.
titubeante, *a.* hesitant; tottering.
titubear, *v.i.* waver.
titubeo, *n.m.* tottering; hesitation.
titular, *a.* titulary.—*v.t.* title, call.
título, *n.m.* title; diploma; degree; right; reason; **¿a qué —?** what for? with what right? **a — de,** by way of, as; **a — personal,** speaking for oneself.
tiza, *n.f.* chalk.
tizna, *n.f.* blacking; grime.
tiznadura, *n.f.* (*fam.* **tiznajo,** *n.m.*) smudge, smut.
tiznar, *v.t.* smudge; mark; blacken.—*v.r.* get smudged; (*S.A.*) get drunk.
tizne, *n.m.* smudge; smut, soot.
tizón, *n.m.* firebrand; (*fig.*) disgrace.
tizonear, *v.t.* stir (*fire*).
tizonero, *n.m.* poker.
toalla, *n.f.* towel.

toar, *v.t.* tow.
tobillo, *n.m.* ankle.
toca, *n.f.* coif, hood, wimple.
tocadiscos, *n.m. inv.* record player.
tocado, *n.m.* coiffure, hair-do.
tocador, -ra, *n.m.f.* (*mus.*) player.—*n.m.* dressing-table; boudoir.
tocante, *a.* touching; concerning (*a*).
tocar [A], *v.t.* touch; feel; (*mus.*) play; do up (hair).—*v.i.* touch; concern (*a*); be the turn (*a*, of); knock; fall to; be close.—*v.r.* touch; be related: put on one's hat; (*fam.*) be touched (*daft, crazy*).
tocayo, -ya, *n.m.f.* namesake.
tocino, *n.m.* bacon; salt pork.
tocón, *n.m.* stump.
tocho, -cha, *a.* uncouth.—*n.m.* ingot; brick.
todavía, *adv.* still, yet.
todo, -da, *a.* all; whole; any; every.—*n.m.* everything; all; *con* —, all the same; *del* —, quite; *sobre* —, above all.—*pl.* everybody, all.
todopoderoso, -sa, *a.* almighty.
toga, *n.f.* toga; (*educ., jur.*) gown.
toisón (de oro), *n.m.* Golden Fleece.
tojo, *n.m.* (*bot.*) furze.
toldar, *v.t.* cover with awning.
toldo, *n.m.* awning; pride, pomp.
tole, *n.m.* uproar; outcry.
toledano, -na, *a., n.m.f.* Toledan.
tolerable, *a.* tolerable.
tolerancia, *n.f.* tolerance, toleration.
tolerante, *a.* tolerant.
tolerar, *v.t.* tolerate.
tolondro, -dra, *a., n.m.f.* fool.—*n.m.* lump, bump.
tolva, *n.f.* chute.
tolvanera, *n.f.* dust-storm.
toma, *n.f.* taking; (*elec.*) main; outlet.
tomada, *n.f.* conquest.
tomar, *v.t.* take; grip; catch; get.—*v.r.* rust; — *a bien* (*mal*), take well (badly); — *prestado*, borrow.
Tomás, *n.m.* Thomas.
tomate, *n.m.* tomato.
tomavistas, *n.m. inv.* camera.
tómbola, *n.f.* raffle.
tomillo, *n.m.* (*bot.*) thyme.
tomo, *n.m.* volume, tome; bulk, importance.
tonada, *n.f.* tune, air.
tonel, *n.m.* barrel.
tonelada, *n.f.* ton.
tonga(da), *n.f.* layer, coat.
tónico, -ca, *a., n.m.* tonic.
tonificar [A], *v.t.* tone up.
tonillo, *n.m.* lilt.
tono, *n.m.* tone; (*fam.*) airs; style; (*mus.*) pitch, key.
tonsura, *n.f.* tonsure; shearing.
tontada, *n.f.* silliness.
tontear, *v.i.* fool about.
tontería, *n.f.* (piece of) foolery, stupidity; worthless object.
tonto, -ta, *a.* silly, stupid.—*n.m.f.* fool, numskull; *hacer el* —, play the fool.
topar, *v.t.* butt, run into; — *con*, bump into; come across.—*v.i.* crop up; succeed.
tope, *n.m.* butt; collision; buffer; encounter; clash; snag; top, brim.
topetada, *n.f.*, **topetón, topetazo**, *n.m.* butt, bump.
tópico, -ca, *a.* topical.—*n.m.* topic.

topinada, *n.f.* blunder(ing).
top(in)era, *n.f.* mole-hill.
topo, *n.m.* (*zool.*) mole; (*fam.*) blunderer.
topográfico, -ca, *a.* topographic(al).
toponimia, *n.f.* toponymy.
topónimo, *n.m.* place-name.
toque, *n.m.* touch; contact; ring, knock; check, try; beat; tap; gist; (*naut.*) call; — *de queda*, curfew (*bell*); *dar un* — *a*, try out, sound out; (*fam.*) pump.
torbellino, *n.m.* whirlwind.
torca, *n.f.* cavern.
torcaz, -za, *n.m.f.* woodpigeon.
torcedura, *n.f.* twist; sprain.
torcer [5D], *v.t.* twist; turn; hurt.—*v.i.* turn. —*v.r.* warp; twist; turn; go wrong.
torcido, -da, *a.* twisted; crooked; bent; on bad terms; cross (*eyes*).—*n.m.* twist.
torcimiento, *n.m.* twist(ing); wordiness.
tordo, *a.* dappled.—*n.m.* (*orn.*) thrush; starling.
torear, *v.t., v.i.* fight (*bulls*); tease.
toreo, *n.m.* bull-fighting.
torero, -ra, rel. to bull-fighting.—*n.m.* bull-fighter.
torete, *n.m.* puzzle, baffling thing; current topic.
toril, *n.m.* bull-pen.
tormenta, *n.f.* storm, tempest; turmoil; adversity.
tormento, *n.m.* torture; torment, anguish.
tormentoso, -sa, *a.* stormy.
torna, *n.f.* return; sluice.
tornada, *n.f.* return; (*poet.*) envoi.
tornadizo, -za, *a., n.m.f.* turncoat.
tornado, *n.m.* tornado.
tornar, *v.t., v.i.* return.—*v.r.* turn, become; — *a hacer*, do again.
tornasol, *n.m.* sunflower; litmus.
tornasolar, *v.t.* iridesce.
tornátil, *a.* fickle; lathe-turned.
tornear, *v.t.* turn (*on lathe*).—*v.i.* turn round; joust; muse.
torneo, *n.m.* tournament, tourney.
tornillero, *n.m.* (*mil.*) deserter.
tornillo, *n.m.* screw; vice, clamp.
torniquete, *n.m.* tourniquet; swivel; turn-stile.
torno, *n.m.* turn; lathe; winch; spindle; wheel; *en* — *de*, around.
toro, *n.m.* bull; — *corrido*, wily experienced person; — *de lidia* or *de muerte*, fighting bull.—*pl.* bull-fight(ing).
toronja, *n.f.* grapefruit.
toroso, -sa, *a.* robust.
torpe, *a.* heavy, clumsy, stupid; crude, lewd; foul.
torpedear, *v.t.* torpedo.
torpedero, *n.m.* torpedo-boat.
torpedo, *n.m.* torpedo.
torpeza, *n.f.* heaviness, clumsiness, stupidity; crudeness, foulness.
torrar, *v.t.* toast.
torre, *n.f.* tower; turret; rook (*chess*).
torrencial, *a.* torrential.
torrente, *n.m.* torrent.
torrentera, *n.f.* ravine, gully.
torreón, *n.m.* turret.
torrezno, *n.m.* bacon rasher.
tórrido, -da, *a.* torrid.
torsión, *n.f.* torsion, sprain.
torso, *n.m.* trunk, torso.

torta, *n.f.* tart, pie; (*fam.*) biff, blow.
tortilla, *n.f.* omelet; flop.
tórtola, *n.f.* turtle-dove.
tortuga, *n.f.* tortoise; turtle.
tortuoso, -sa, *a.* tortuous.
tortura, *n.f.* twist; torture.
torturar, *v.t.* put to torture.
torvo, -va, *a.* grim, stern.
tos, *n.f.* cough.
Toscana, *n.f.* Tuscany.
toscano, -na, *a., n.m.f.* Tuscan.
tosco, -ca, *a.* rough, crude.
toser, *v.t.* (*fam.*) defy, beat.—*v.i.* cough.
tósigo, *n.m.* poison; grief.
tosquedad, *n.f.* coarseness.
tostada, *n.f.* toast.
tostado, *n.m.* toasting.
tostar [4], *v.t.. v.r.* toast; roast; tan.
tostón, *n.m.* roast piglet; toast.
total, *a., n.m.* total.—*adv.* in a word.
totalidad, *n.f.* totality; whole
totalitario, -ria, *a.* totalitarian.
totalitarismo, *n.m.* totalitarianism.
totalizar [C], *v.t.* total, add up.—*v.r.* total (*en*).
tótem, *n.m.* (*pl.* -ms) totem.
totuma, *n.f.* (*S.A.*) calabash.
toxicar [A], *v.t.* poison.
tóxico, -ca, *a.* toxic.
toxicomanía, *n.f.* drug-addiction.
toxicómano, -na, *n.m.f.* drug-addict.
toxina, *n.f.* toxin.
tozudo, -da, *a.* stubborn.
traba, *n.f.* bond; trammel.
trabacuenta, *n.f.* mistake; quarrel.
trabajado, -da, *a.* laboured; weary.
trabajador, -ra, *a.* hard-working.—*n.m.f.* worker.
trabajar, *v.t.* work; till; harass.—*v.i.* work; labour; strain.—*v.i., v.r.* strive (*en, por, to*).
trabajo, *n.m.* work, labour; travail.—*pl.* tribulations; **trabajos forzados**, (*jur.*) hard labour.
trabajoso, -sa, *a.* laborious; ailing; laboured.
trabalenguas, *n.m. inv.* tongue-twister.
trabar, *v.t.* join; tie; grasp; shackle; begin.—*v.r.* tangle; get stuck.
trabazón, *n.f.* bond, connexion.
trabuca, *n.f.* fire-cracker.
trabucar [A], *v.t.* upset; mix up.
trabuco, *n.m.* blunderbuss.
tracción, *n.f.* traction; drive.
tracista, *n.m.f.* designer.
tracto, *n.m.* tract.
tractor, *n.m.* tractor.
tradición, *n.f.* tradition.
tradicional, *a.* traditional.
traducción, *n.f.* translation.
traducir [16], *v.t.* translate.
traductor, -ra, *n.m.f.* translator.
traer [34], *v.t.* bring; draw; be wearing; have (*consigo*, on one).
traeres, *n.m.pl.* finery.
tráfago, *n.m.* traffic; drudgery.
traficante, *n.m.f.* dealer.
traficar [A], *v.i.* travel; deal, trade.
tráfico, *n.m.* traffic.
tragaderas, *n.f.pl.* gullet; **tener buenas —**, be credulous.
tragadero, *n.m.* abyss; pit; throat.
tragaluz, *n.f.* (*pl.* -uces) skylight.

tragaperras, *n.m. inv.* slot-machine.
tragar [B], *v.t.* swallow; omit.
tragazón, *n.f.* (*fam.*) gluttony.
tragedia, *n.f.* tragedy.
trágico, -ca, *a.* tragic(al).—*n.m.* tragedian.
tragicomedia, *n.f.* tragicomedy.
trago, *n.m.* swallow; bad luck; **a tragos**, slowly.
tragón, -gona, *a.* gluttonous.—*n.m.f.* glutton.
traición, *n.f.* betrayal; treachery; treason.
traicionar, *v.t.* betray.
traicionero, -ra, traidor, -ra, *a.* treacherous; treasonous.—*n.m.f.* traitor; villain; betrayer.
traigo [TRAER].
traílla, *n.f.* lead, leash; scraper.
traje, *n.m.* suit; costume. [TRAER].
trajín, *n.m.* carrying, fetching; coming and going.
trama, *n.f.* weft, woof; plot.
tramar, *v.t.* weave; plot, contrive.
tramitación, *n.f.* procedure; transaction.
tramitar, *v.t.* transact.
trámite, *n.m.* transit; procedure; step.
tramo, *n.m.* tract, parcel; flight (*stairs*); span; piece.
tramontar, *v.t.* pass *or* sink behind mountains.—*v.r.* flee, escape.
tramoya, *n.f.* stage machinery; artifice.
trampa, *n.f.* trap; trap-door; pitfall; cheating, fraud.
trampantojo, *n.m.* deception, sleight.
trampear, (*fam.*) *v.t., v.i.* cheat; manage somehow.
trampolín, *n.m.* spring-board.
tramposo, -sa, *a.* cheating.—*n.m.f.* cheat; trickster.
tranca, *n.f.* bar; club; **coger una —**, (*fam.*) get canned *or* drunk.
trancada, *n.m.* huge stride; (*fam.*) trice.
trancar, *v.t.* bar.—*v.i.* stride along.
trancazo, *n.m.* club-blow; (*fam.*) flu.
trance, *n.m.* critical moment; (*jur.*) seizure for debt; **a todo —**, at any price; **en — de muerte**, at death's door.
tranco, *n.m.* big stride; threshold; **a trancos**, in a dash, pell-mell.
tranquilidad, *n.f.* tranquillity, peace.
tranquilizar [C], *v.t., v.r.* calm.
tranquilo, -la, *a.* calm; (*fam.*) in peace.
tranquilla, *n.f.* pin, bar; trick question.
trans-, *prefix.* trans- [TRAS].
transacción, *n.f.* settlement; transaction.
transaéreo, *n.m.* air-liner.
transar, *v.i.* (*S.A.*) compromise.
transatlántico, -ca, *a.* transatlantic.—*n.m.* liner; steamer.
transbordador, *n.m.* ferry.
transbordar, *v.t.* trans-ship, transfer.
transbordo, *n.m.* trans-shipment, transfer.
transcendencia, *n.f.* importance, consequence; acumen; transcendence.
transcendental, *a.* far-reaching, highly important; transcendental.
transcendente, *a.* acute; vital; transcendent.
transcender [2],*v.t.* analyse, sift.—*v.i.* spread; leak out; smell sweet.
transcribir [*p.p.* transcri(p)to], *v.t.* transcribe.
transcripción, *n.f.* transcription.
transcriptor, -ra, *n.m.f.* transcriber.
transcurrir, *v.i.* elapse.

transcurso, *n.m.* passage, course (*time*).
transeúnte, *a.* transient.—*n.m.f.* passer-by; temporary guest.
transferencia, *n.f.* transfer(ence).
transferir [6], *v.t.* transfer; convey; postpone.
transfiguración, *n.f.* transfiguration.
transfigurar, *v.t.* transfigure.—*v.r.* become transfigured.
transfijo, -ja, *a.* transfixed.
transformación, *n.f.* transformation.
transformador, *n.m.* (*elec.*) transformer.
transformar, *v.t.* transform.
transfretano, -na, *a.* across the straits.
transfretar, *v.t.* cross (*seas*).—*v.i.* spread.
tránsfuga, *n.m.f.,* **tránsfugo,** *n.m.* fugitive; turncoat.
transfundir, *v.t.* transmit; transfuse.
transfusión, *n.f.* transfusion.
transgredir [Q], *v.t.* transgress.
transgresión, *n.f.* transgression.
transgresor, -ra, *a.* transgressing.—*n.m.f.* transgressor.
transición, *n.f.* transition.
transido, -da, *a.* worn out; mean.
transigir [E], *v.t., v.i.* compromise, settle (*en, con*).
transistor, *n.m.* (*elec.*) transistor; (*fam.*) transistor radio.
transitable, *a.* passable.
transitar, *v.i.* journey.
transitivo, -va, *a.* transitive.
tránsito, *n.m.* transit; stop; passing-on (*of saints*); transfer; **de —,** on the way; passing through.
translucidez, *n.f.* translucence.
translúcido, -da, *a.* translucent.
transmisión, *n.f.* transmission.
transmisor, -ra, *n.m.f.* transmitter.
transmitir, *v.t., v.i.* transmit.
transmutación, *n.f.* transmutation.
transmutar, *v.t., v.r.* transmute.
transparencia, *n.f.* transparency; (*photo.*) slide.
transparentar, *v.r.* be(come) transparent; show through.
transparente, *a.* transparent.—*n.m.* stained-glass window.
transpirar, *v.t., v.i.* perspire.
transponer [25], *v.t.* transpose; turn, go round (*corner*); transfer.—*v.r.* get sleepy; set (*sun*).
transportación, *n.f.* transport(ation).
transportamiento, *n.m.* (*lit. fig.*) transport.
transportar, *v.t.* transport; transfer.—*v.r.* go into ecstasies.
transporte, *n.m.* transport.
transpu- [TRANSPONER].
transversal, *a.* transversal, crossing.—*n.f.* side-street.
tranvía, *n.m.* tram, (*U.S.*) streetcar.
tranviario, -ria, *a.* rel. to trams.—*n.m.f.* tram-worker.
tranzar [C], *v.t.* truncate.
trapa, *n.f.* tramping: uproar; (*naut.*) line.
trapacear, *v.i.* cheat.
trapacero, -ra, *n.m.f.* cheat.
trapajo, *n.m.* tatter.
trápala, *n.f.* stamping, tramping; clopping; (*fam.*) swindle.—*n.m.f.* (*fam.*) twister, cheat.
trapaza, *n.f.* swindle, fraud.

trapecio, *n.m.* trapezium; trapeze.
trapense, *a., n.m.f.* Trappist.
trapero, *n.m.* rag-and-bone man.
trapío, *n.m.* spirit, mettle; (*fam.*) nerve, cheek.
trapisonda, *n.f.* (*fam.*) din, clatter; deception.
trapista, *a., n.m.f.* Trappist; (*S.A.*) [TRAPERO].
trapo, *n.m.* rag; sails; (*taur.*) red cape.—*pl.* (*fam.*) rags, togs.
traque, *n.m.* bang; crack; fuse, touch paper.
traquear, *v.t.* shake; (*fam.*) fool with.—*v.t., v.i.* rattle; bang.
traquido, *n.m.* bang, crack.
tras, *prep.* after, behind.—*n.m.* rap knock. [TRANS].
trascendido, -da, *a.* keen, acute.
trascocina, *n.f.* back kitchen.
trascuenta, *n.f.* mistake.
trasegar [1B], *v.t.* upset; decant.
trasero, -ra, *a.* rear, hind.—*n.m.* rump.—*pl.* (*fam.*) ancestors.—*n.f.* back (part).
trasfondo, *n.m.* background.
trasgo, *n.m.* imp; goblin.
trashoguero, -ra, *a., n.m.f.* stay-at-home, idler.—*n.m.* log.
trashojar, *v.t.* glance through (*a book*).
trashumante, *a.* seasonally nomadic (*shepherds and flocks*).
trashumar, *v.t., v.i.* move to seasonal pastures.
trasiego, *n.m.* removal; upset; decanting.
traslación, *n.f.* transfer, move; deferment; copy.
trasladar, *v.t.* (re)move; copy; postpone; transfer.—*v.r.* move (*house, from job etc.*).
traslado, *n.m.* copy, transcript; transfer.
traslapar, *v.t., v.i.* overlap.
traslaticio, -cia, *a.* figurative.
traslucir [9], *v.t.* infer.—*v.r.* leak out; be translucent.
traslumbrar, *v.t.* dazzle.—*v.r.* vanish.
trasluz, *n.m.* reflected light; **a(l) —,** against the light.
trasmano, *n.m.* second hand (*at cards*); **a —,** out of reach; off the beaten track.
trasmañanar, *v.t.* leave for the morrow.
trasmatar, *v.t.* (*fam.*) bury (*consider dead*).
trasminar, *v.t.* undermine.—*v.r.* seep.
trasnochado, -da, *a.* stale; haggard; trite.—*n.f.* sleepless night; last night; night attack.
trasnochar, *v.t.* sleep on (*a problem*).—*v.i.* stay up all night.
trasoñar [4], *v.t.* dream up, muddle.
traspapelar, *v.t.* mislay.—*v.r.* get mislaid.
traspasar, *v.t.* cross (over); transfer; transfix, run through; break (*law*); pain.—*v.r.* overstep the mark.
traspaso, *n.m.* transfer; trespass; anguish.
traspié, *n.m.* stumble, tripping.
trasplantar, *v.t.* transplant.
traspuesta, *n.f.* removal; nook; disappearance; flight.
traspunte, *n.m.* (*theat.*) prompter.
trasquila, *n.f.* shearing.
trasquilar, *v.t.* shear; crop; (*fam.*) lop off.
traste, *n.m.* (*mus.*) fret; **dar al — con,** spoil; give up as a bad job; **sin trastes,** (*fam.*) messily, messy.
trastera, *n.f.* lumber-room, loft, attic.
trastienda, *n.f.* back-room (*of shop*); (*fam.*) wariness.

trasto, *n.m.* piece, thing, luggage.—*pl.* gear tackle.
trastornar, *v.t.* upset; overturn.
trastorno, *n.m.* upset; disorder.
trastrocar [4A], *v.t.* interchange; reverse.
trastulo, *n.m.* plaything; fun.
trasunto, *n.m.* copy, transcript.
trata, *n.f.* — *de negros,* slave trade; — *de blancas,* white-slave trade.
tratable, *a.* tractable, sociable.
tratado, *n.m.* treatise; treaty.
tratamiento, *n.m.* treatment; title.
tratante, *n.m.* dealer.
tratar, *v.t.* treat; deal with; address (*de,* as); —*v.i.* try (*de,* to); deal.—*v.r.* deal; behave; be a matter (*de,* of).
trato, *n.m.* treatment, conduct; usage; address; pact; trade; social intercourse.
trauma, *n.m.* trauma.
traumático, -ca, *a.* traumatic.
través, *n.m.* slant; reverse; *a(l)* — *de,* through, across; *dar al* — *con,* do away with.
travesaño, *n.m.* cross-bar; bolster.
travesar [1], *v.t.* cross.
travesía, *n.f.* crossing.
travestido, -da, *a.* disguised.
travesura, *n.f.* prank, mischief.
travieso, -sa, *a.* cross; sharp; naughty; lewd.—*n.f.* crossing; cross-beam; (*rail.*) sleeper.
trayecto, *n.m.* journey, distance.
trayectoria, *n.f.* trajectory.
traza, *n.f.* design; looks; mode; sign.
trazado, -da, *a.* outlined; formed.—*n.m.* plan, design; sketch; route.
trazar [C], *v.t.* design; outline; draw; trace.
trazo, *n.m.* outline; tracing; stroke.
trebejo, *n.m.* plaything; chess piece.—*pl.* implements.
trébol, *n.m.* (*bot.*) clover; (*cards*) club.
trece, *a., n.m.* thirteen; *seguir en sus* —, (*fam.*) not budge in one's ideas.
treceno, -na, *a.* thirteenth.
trecho, *n.m.* space, stretch; while, time.
tregua, *n.f.* truce; respite.
treinta, *a., n.m.* thirty.
tremebundo, -da, *a.* dreadful.
tremedal, *n.m.* quagmire.
tremendo, -da, *a.* tremendous.
tremer, *v.i.* tremble.
tremolar, *v.t.i., v.i.* wave.
tremolina, *n.f.* rustling; (*fam.*) fuss.
tremor, *n.m.* tremor.
trémulo, -la, *a.* quivering.
tren, *n.m.* train; retinue; (*sport*) pace; pomp; (*mech.*) gears; — *de aterrizaje,* (*aer.*) undercarriage.
trencilla, *n.f.* braid, plait.
treno, *n.m.* dirge.
trenza, *n.f.* plait; tress.
trenzar [C], *v.t.* plait.—*v.i.* caper.
trepa, *n.f.* climb(ing); drill(ing); (*fam.*) fraud; (*fam.*) flogging.
trepadora, *n.f.* climbing plant; rambler.
trepanar, *v.t.* (*med.*) trepan.
trepar, *v.t.* climb; drill.—*v.i.* climb (*por,* up).
trepe, *n.m.* (*fam.*) telling-off.
trepidar, *v.i.* shake, tremble.
tres, *a., n.m.* three.
trescientos, -tas, *a., n.m.pl.* three hundred.

tresillo, *n.m.* ombre (*cards*); set of three; settee.
treta, *n.f.* trick; feint.
triángulo, *n.m.* triangle.
triar [L], *v.t.* sort, select.
trib(u)al, *a.* tribal.
tribu, *n.f.* tribe.
tribulación, *n.f.* tribulation.
tribuna, *n.f.* tribune; rostrum.
tribunal, *n.m.* tribunal, court; board.
tributación, *n.f.* taxation; tribute.
tributar, *v.t.* pay (*taxes, homage*).
tributario, -ria, *a., n.m.f.* tributary; tax-payer.
tributo, *n.m.* tax; contribution; tribute.
tricolor, *a.* tricolour.
tricornio, -nia, *a.* three-cornered *or* -horned. —*n.m.* three-cornered hat.
tridente, *a., n.m.* trident.
trienio, *n.m.* triennium.
trigo, *n.m.* wheat; (*low*) loot, money.
trigonometría, *n.f.* trigonometry.
trilátero, -ra, *a.* trilateral.
trilingüe, *a.* trilingual.
trilogía, *n.f.* trilogy.
trillado, -da, *a.* trite, stale; beaten (*track*).
trillar, *v.t.* thresh; frequent.
trillón, *n.m.* trillion (10^{18}), (*U.S.*) quintillion.
trimestral, *a.* quarterly.
trimestre, *n.m.* term; quarter.
trinar, *v.i.* trill; (*fam.*) rave.
trincar [A], *v.t.* tie, bind; smash; (*fam.*) do in, kill.—*v.i.* (*fam.*) have a drink.
trinchante, *n.m.* carving-knife; carver.
trinchar, *v.t.* carve; (*fam.*) settle.
trinchera, *n.f.* trench.
trineo, *n.m.* sledge, sleigh.
Trinidad, *n.f.* Trinity.
trino, -na, *a.* trinal.—*n.m.* trill.
trinquete, *n.m.* (*mech.*) pawl, ratchet; fore-sail.
trinquis, *n.m. inv.* (*fam.*) drop, drink.
trío, *n.m.* trio.
tripa, *n.f.* bowel, gut; belly; *hacer de tripas corazón,* pluck up courage.
tripartito, -ta, *a.* tripartite.
tripicallos, *n.m.pl.* (*cul.*) tripe.
triple, *a., n.m.* triple, treble.
triplicado, *a.* triplicate.
triplicar [A], *v.t.i., v.r.* treble.
tríplice, *a.* triple.
tríptico, *n.m.* triptych.
tripudo, -da, *a.* pot-bellied.
tripulación, *n.f.* crew.
tripulante, *n.m.* member of crew.
tripular, *v.t.* man, fit out.
trique, *n.m.* crack, snap.
triquiñuela, *n.f.* hoodwinking.
triquitraque, *n.m.* crack; clatter; cracker.
tris, *n.m.* tinkle, crack; instant; *en un* —, within an ace.
triscar [A], *v.t.* mingle; set.—*v.i.* stamp; frisk.
trisecar [A], *v.t.* trisect.
triste, *a.* sad; gloomy; wretched.
tristeza, *n.f.* sadness.
triturar, *v.t.* triturate; crush.
triunfal, *a.* triumphal.
triunfante, *a.* triumphant.
triunfar, *v.i.* triumph (*de,* over); trump.
triunfo, *n.m.* triumph; trump.
trivial, *a.* ordinary; well-trodden; trivial.

205

trivialidad, *n.f.* triviality.
triza, *n.f.* fragment, smithereen.
a la trocada, *adv. phr.* in exchange; in the opposite way.
trocamiento, *n.m.* (ex)change.
trocar [4A], *v.t.* exchange, barter; change; confuse.—*v.r.* change over.
trocatinta, *n.f.* (*fam.*) mix-up.
trocla, tróclea, *n.f.* pulley.
trocha, *n f.* path, trail.
a trochemoche, *adv. phr.* pell-mell.
trofeo, *n.m.* trophy.
troglodita, *a.,* *n.m.f.* troglodyte; (*fig.*) brute.
troj(e), *n.f.* granary, barn.
trola, *n.f.* (*fam.*) fib.
trolebús, *n.m.* trolley-bus.
tromba, *n.f.* whirl, water-spout.
trombón, *n.m.* trombone.
trombosis, *n.f.* thrombosis.
trompa, *n.f.* (*mus.*) horn; trunk, proboscis; (*anat.*) tube.
trompazo, *n.m.* horn-blast; hard bump.
trompeta, *n.f.* trumpet.—*n.m.* trumpeter.
trompetazo, *n.m.* trumpet-call; (*fam.*) silly remark.
trompetero, *n.m.* trumpeter.
trompicar [A], *v.t.* trip; (*fam.*) promote over s.o.'s head.—*v.i.* stumble.
trompicón, *n.m.* stumble; **a trompicones,** stumbling(ly).
trompo, *n.m.* top (*toy*); chess-man.
trompón, *n.m.* bump; (*bot.*) daffodil.
tronada, *n.f.* thunder-storm.
tronante, *a.* thunderous.
tronar [4], *v.i.* thunder; (*fam.*) flop; (*fam.*) quarrel (*con,* with).
troncar [A], *v.t.* truncate.
tronco, *n.m.* (*bot., anat.*) trunk; log.
troncha, *n.f.* (*S.A.*) slice.
tronchar, *v.t.* split.
troncho, *n.m.* stem.
tronera, *n.f.* port-hole; embrasure.
tronido, *n.m.* thunder-clap.
trono, *n.m.* throne.
tronzar [C], *v.t.* shatter, smash.
tropa, *n.f.* troop, crowd.—*pl.* (*mil.*) troops.
tropel, *n.m.* tumult; rush.
tropelía, *n.f.* mad rush; outrage.
tropezar [C], *v.i.* stumble (*con, en,* on).
tropezón, -zona, *a.* stumbling.—*n.m.* trip, stumble; obstacle; tit-bit.
tropical, *a.* tropic(al).
trópico, *n.m.* tropic.
tropiezo, *n.m.* stumble; slip; hitch.
troquel, *n.m.* die, stamp.
troqueo, *n.m.* trochee.
trotaconventos, *n.f. inv.* procuress.
trotamundos, *n.m.f. inv.* globe-trotter.
trotar, *v.i.* trot.
trote, *n.m.* trot; **al —,** on the trot.
trotón, -tona, *a.* trotting.—*n.f.* chaperone.
trova, *n.f.* lay, lyric; (*S.A.*) fib.
trovador, -ra, *a., n.m.* troubadour.
trovar, *v.t.* parody.—*v.i.* write verse.
Troya, *n.f.* Troy.
troyano, -na, *a., n.m.f.* Trojan.
trozo, *n.m.* piece; extract; log.
truco, *n.m.* trick; (*fam.*) wrinkle, knack.
truculento, -ta, *a.* truculent.
trucha, *n.f.* trout.
truchimán, -mana, *a.* shrewd, slick.—*n.m.f.* interpreter.

trueco [TRUEQUE, TROCAR].
trueno, *n.m.* thunder; bang; harum-scarum; scandal.
trueque, *n.m.* barter, exchange; *a — de,* in exchange for.
trufa, *n.f.* truffle; lie.
trufar, *v.i.* stuff with truffles; fib.
truhán, -hana, *n.m.f.* crook; buffoon.
truismo, *n.m.* truism.
trujimán, -mana, *n.m.f.* interpreter.
trulla, *n.f.* trowel; hurly-burly.
truncar [A], *v.t.* truncate; maim; cut short.
tu, *a. poss.* thy, your.
tú, *pron. pers.* thou; you; *tratar de — a,* [TUTEAR].
tuáutem, *n.m.f. inv.* (*fam.*) king pin; vital factor.
tubérculo, *n.m.* tubercle.
tuberculosis, *n.f.* tuberculosis.
tuberculoso, -sa, *a.* tuberculous, tubercular. —*n.m.f.* tuberculosis sufferer.
tubería, *n.f.* piping, pipes.
tubo, *n.m.* pipe; tube; gun-barrel.
tubular, *a.* tubular.
tudesco, -ca, *a., n.m.f.* German.
tueco, *n.m.* stump; worm-hole.
tuerca, *n.f.* (*mech.*) nut.
tuerce, *n.m.* twist; sprain.
tuerto, -ta, *a.* twisted; one-eyed.—*n.m.* wrong, tort.
tuétano, *n.m.* marrow; pith.
tufo, *n.m.* vapour, fume; stench.—*pl.* airs, graces.
tufoso, -sa, *a.* foul; cocky, vain.
tugurio, *n.m.* hut.
tuitivo, -va, *a.* protective.
tul, *n.m.* tulle.
tulipán, *n.m.* (*bot.*) tulip.
tullido, -da, *a.* crippled.—*n.m.f.* cripple.
tullir [J], *v.t.* cripple; harm.
tumba, *n.f.* grave, tomb.
tumbar, *v.t.* knock down; (*fam.*) knock out. —*v.i.* fall down.—*v.r.* (*fam.*) lie down; give up.
tumbo, *n.m.* tumble, fall; rumble; important matter; **— de dado,** imminent peril.
tumbón, -bona, *a.* (*fam.*) sly; lazy.—*n.m.f.* idler.—*n.f.* air-bed.
tumefacer [20], *v.t., v.r.* swell.
tumescente, *a.* tumescent.
túmido, -da, *a.* tumid.
tumor, *n.m.* tumour.
túmulo, *n.m.* tumulus.
tumulto, *n.m.* tumult.
tumultuoso, -sa, *a.* tumultuous.
tuna (1), *n.f.* (*bot.*) prickly pear.
tuna (2), *n.f.* band of serenaders; (*fam.*) loose living.
tunante, *a.* crafty, dishonest.—*n.m.f.* (*also* **tunanta**) crook; idler.
tunda, *n.f.* (*fam.*) beating.
tundente, *a.* blunt, bruising.
tunecino, -na, *a., n.m.f.* Tunisian.
túnel, *n.m.* tunnel.
Túnez, *n.f.* Tunis; Tunisia.
tungsteno, *n.m.* tungsten.
túnica, *n.f.* tunic.
tuno, -na, *a.* crooked.—*n.m.f.* crook; serenader.
al (buen) tuntún, *adv. phr.* (*fam.*) wildly, irresponsibly.
tupa, *n.f.* stuffing.

tupé, *n.m.* toupee; (*fam.*) cheek.
tupido, -da, *a.* dense, thick; blocked.
tupir, *v.t.* block up; press close.—*v.r.* over-eat.
turba, *n.f.* crowd; peat.
turbamulta, *n.f.* rabble.
turbante, *n.m.* turban.
turbar, *v.t.* disturb.
turbieza, *n.f.* obscurity; bewilderment.
turbina, *n.f.* turbine.
turbio, -bia, *a.* muddy. clouded; obscure.
turbión, *n.m.* squall; storm; rush.
turborreactor, *n.m.* turbo-jet.
turbulencia, *n.f.* turbulence.
turbulento, -ta, *a.* turbulent.
turco, -ca, *a.* Turkish.—*n.m.f.* Turk; *coger una turca,* (*fam.*) get canned *or* drunk.
turgente, *a.* turgid.
turismo, *n.m.* tourism; (*auto.*) tourer.
turista, *a.,* *n.m.f.* tourist.
turístico, -ca, *a.* tourist.
turnar, *v.i.* take turns.
turnio, -nia, *a.* cross-eyed.
turno, *n.m.* turn; shift; *de* —, on duty.
turquesa, *n.f.* turquoise.
Turquía, *n.f.* Turkey.
turrar, *v.t.* roast.
turrón, *n.m.* nut-brittle, nougat.
turulato, -ta, *a.* (*fam.*) staggered.
turuta, *n.f.* (*fam.*) [TURCA].
tus, *interj. sin decir* — *ni mus,* (*fam.*) keeping mum.
tutear, *v.t.* speak to familiarly [TÚ]; be on intimate terms with.
tutela, *n.f.* tutelage; guardianship.
tuteo, *n.m.* act of TUTEAR.
a tutiplén, *adv. phr.* (*fam.*) more than enough.
tutor, -tora (*f. also* -triz), *n.m.f.* guardian.
tuve [TENER].
tuyo, -ya, *poss. a., pron.* yours; (*obs., eccl.*) thine.

U

U, u, *n.f.* twenty-fourth letter of the Spanish alphabet.
U. [USTED].
u, *conj.* or (*before following* o *or* ho). [O].
ubérrimo, -ma, *a. sup.* very fruitful; abundant.
ubicar [A], *v.t.* (*S.A.*) situate, place.—*v.i., v.r.* be situated.
ubicuo, -cua, *a.* ubiquitous.
ubre, *n.f.* udder.
Ucrania, *n.f.* Ukraine.
ucranio, -nia, *a., n.m.f.* Ukrainian.
ues- [OES-].
¡uf! *interj.* ugh!
ufanar, *v.r.* pride oneself (*de, con,* on).
ufanía, *n.f.* pride; mastery.
ufano, -na, *a.* proud; vain; masterly.

a ufo, *adv. phr.* [DE GORRA].
ujier, *n.m.* usher.
úlcera, *n.f.* ulcer; sore.
ulcerar, *v.t., v.r.* ulcerate.
ulceroso, -sa, *a.* ulcerous.
Ulises, *n.m.* Ulysses.
ulterior, *a.* farther; subsequent.
ultimamente, *adv.* finally; recently.
ultimar, *v.t.* terminate, finish.
ultimátum, *n.m.* ultimatum; final word.
ultimidad, *n.f.* finality; recentness.
último, -ma, *a.* final, last; latest, (most) recent; furthest; best; *por* —, finally; *a últimos de,* towards the end of.
ultra, *prep., adv.* besides, beyond.
ultra- *prefix.* ultra-, extra-.
ultrajar, *v.t.* offend against, insult.
ultraje, *n.m.* insult, offence, outrage.
ultrajoso, -sa, *a.* outrageous, offensive.
ultramar, *n.m.* overseas.
ultramarino, -na, *a.* overseas.—*n.m.* ultramarine (blue).—*pl.* imported groceries.
a ultranza, *adv. phr.* to death; at any cost.
ultrarrojo, -ja, *a.* infra-red.
ultrasónico, -ca, *a.* supersonic.
ultratumba, *adv.* beyond the grave.
ultraviolado, -da, *a.* ultravioleta, *a.* ultraviolet.
úlula, *n.f.* (*orn.*) tawny owl.
ulular, *v.i.* hoot, shriek.
ululato, *n.m.* hoot, shriek.
umbral, *n.m.* threshold (*often pl.*).
umbrío, -bría, *a.* shady.—*n.f.* shady place.
umbro, -bra, *a., n.m.f.* Umbrian.
umbroso, -sa, *a.* shady.
un, una, *indef. art.* a, an.
unánime, *a.* unanimous.
unanimidad, *n.f.* unanimity.
unción, *n.f.* unction.
uncir [D], *v.t.* yoke.
undécimo, -ma, *a., n.m.* eleventh.
undoso, -sa, *a.* wavy, undulating.
undular [ONDULAR].
ungir [E], *v.t.* anoint.
ungüento, *n.m.* ointment, salve.
únicamente, *adv.* solely, only.
único, -ca, *a.* sole, single, only; unique.
unicornio, *n.m.* unicorn.
unidad, *n.f.* unity; unit.
unidireccional, *a.* one-way.
unificación, *n.f.* unification.
unificar [A], *v.t.* unify.—*v.r.* unite.
uniformar, *v.t.* uniform; make uniform.
uniforme, *a., n.m.* uniform.
uniformidad, *n.f.* uniformity.
unigénito, -ta, *a.* only-begotten.
unilateral, *a.* unilateral.
unión, *n.f.* union; *Unión de Repúblicas Socialistas Soviéticas,* Union of Soviet Socialist Republics.
unionista, *a., n.m.f.* unionist.
unir, *v.t., v.r.* unite.
unísón, *n.m.* (*mus.*) unison.
unisonancia, *n.f.* monotony.
unísono, -na, *a.* in unison; *al* —, unanimously.
unitario, -ria, *a., n.m.f.* unitarian.
universal, *a., n.m.* universal.
universidad, *n.f.* university.
universitario, -ria, *a.* university.—*n.m.f.* university teacher *or* student.
universo, -sa, *a.* universal.—*n.m.* universe.

uno, una, *a., pron.* one. — *y otro,* both; —*pl.* some; **uno — (s) a otro(s),** each *or* one another; — *que otro, unos cuantos,* a few; [UN].

untar, *v.t.* grease; anoint; smear; (*fam.*) bribe.

unto, *n.m.* grease; ointment; polish; bribe.

unt(u)oso, -sa, *a.* greasy; unctuous.

untura, *n.f.* anointing; ointment; greasing.

uña, *n.f.* (*anat.*) nail; talon, claw; hoof; thorn; *a — de caballo,* at full speed; *ser — y carne,* be very close, intimate; *ser largo de uñas,* be light-fingered.

uña(ra)da, *n.f.,* **uñetazo,** *n.m.* scratch.

uñero, *n.m.* ingrown nail.

uñoso, -sa, *a.* long-nailed.

¡upa! *interj.* hoop-la! up!

uranio, *n.m.* uranium.

urbanidad, *n.f.* urbanity, courtesy.

urbanismo, *n.m.* town-planning.

urbanista, *n.m.f.* town-planner.

urbanización, *n.f.* urbanization.

urbanizar [C], *v.t.* urbanize.

urbano, -na, *a.* urbano; urbane.

urbe, *n.f.* metropolis.

urdimbre, *n.f.* warp.

urdir, *v.t.* warp (*yarn*); (*fig.*) plot, contrive.

urea, *n.f.* urea.

urgencia, *n.f.* emergency; urgency.

urgente, *a.* urgent; express (*mail*).

urgir [E], *v.i.* be urgent.

urinal, urinario, *n.m.* urinal.

urraca, *n.f.* (*orn.*) magpie.

el Uruguay, *n.m.* Uruguay.

uruguayo, -ya, *a., n.m.f.* Uruguayan.

usado, -da, *a.* used; second-hand; worn; usual.

usagre, *n.m.* (*med.*) impetigo; distemper.

usanza, *n.f.* usage, custom.

usar, *v.t.* use; wear; enjoy; follow (*profession*). —*v.i.* make use (*de,* of), employ; be accustomed.—*v.r.* be in use *or* the custom.

usarcé (*obs.*), [USTED].

usgo, *n.m.* loathing.

usía, *pron., m.f.* your excellency.

usina, *n.f.* (S.A.) factory; power-station.

uso, *n.m.* use; custom; wear; practice; condition; *al —,* according to custom.

uste [OXTE].

usted, *pron. pers.* you (*polite form*); *pl.* **ustedes.**

usual, *a.* usual; usable; sociable.

usufructo, *n.m.* usufruct.

usura, *n.f.* usury; profit; interest; profiteering.

usurear, *v.i.* profiteer.

usurero, -ra, *n.m.f.* usurer; profiteer.

usurpar, *v.t.* usurp.

utensilio, *n.m.* utensil; tool.

útil, *a.* useful; (*jur.*) legal (*day*).—*n.m.* use.— *pl.* tools.

utilidad, *n.f.* usefulness; use; profit.

utilitario, -ria, *a.* utilitarian.

utilizar [C], *v.t.* use, utilize; employ.

utillería, *n.f.* equipment; tools.

utopia, utopía, *n.f.* utopia.

utópico, -ca, *a.* utopian.

UU. [USTEDES].

uva, *n.f.* grape; grapes; — *espina,* gooseberry; — *pasa,* raisin; *hecho una —,* drunk as a lord; *uvas verdes,* (*fig.*) sour grapes.

V

V, v, *n.f.* twenty-fifth letter of the Spanish alphabet.

va [IR].

vaca, *n.f.* cow; beef.

vacación, *n.f.* vacation; vacancy.—*pl.* holiday(s); vacation.

vacancia, *n.f.* vacancy.

vacante, *a.* vacant.—*n.f.* vacation; vacancy.

vacar [A], *v.i.* be vacant *or* idle; lack (*de*); attend (*a,* to).

vaciado, *n.m.* cast; excavation.

vaciante, *n.m.* ebb-tide.

vaciar [L], *v.t., v.i.* empty; drain; hollow out; cast.

vaciedad, *n.f.* frothy nonsense.

vacilación, *n.f.* vacillation.

vacilar, *v.i.* vacillate; waver (*en,* to).

vacío, -cía, *a.* hollow, empty.—*n.m.* emptiness; hollow; void; *en —,* in vacuo.

vacuidad, *n.f.* vacuity.

vacuna, *n.f.* vaccine.

vacunación, *n.f.* vaccination.

vacunar, *v.t.* vaccinate.

vacuno, -na, *a.* bovine.

vacuo, -cua, *a.* empty.—*n.m.* vacuum.

vadear, *v.t.* ford; sound out; overcome.—*v.r.* behave.

vado, *n.m.* ford; way out, solution.

vagabundear, vagamundear, *v.i.* roam; idle.

vagabundo, -da, vagamundo, -da, *a., n.m.f.* vagabond.

vagancia, *n.f.* vagrancy.

vagar, *n.m.* leisure.—*v.i.* [B] wander, roam; idle.

vagaroso, -sa, *a.* wandering.

vago, -ga, *a.* vagrant; lazy; vague; wavering. —*n.m.* loafer.

vagón, *n.m.* wagon; (*rail.*) coach.

vaguear, *v.i.* roam; loaf.

vaguedad, *n.f.* vagueness.

vaguido, -da, *a.* dizzy.—*n.f.* dizziness.

vah(e)ar, *v.i.* emit vapour, exhale.

vahído, *n.m.* dizziness, giddiness.

vaho, *n.m.* fume, vapour; breath.

vaina, *n.f.* sheath; pod; (S.A.) bother.

vainilla, *n.f.* vanilla.

vais [IR].

vaivén, *n.m.* seesawing, wavering; risk.

vajilla, *n.f.* crockery, ware.

val [VALLE].

valdré [VALER].

vale, *n.m.* voucher; adieu; receipt; (S.A. *low*) mate, chum.

valedero, -ra, *a.* valid.

valedor, -ra, *n.m.f.* protector; (S.A.) chum.

valenciano, -na, *a., n.m.f.* Valencian.

valentía, *n.f.* valour; exploit; boast.

Valentín, *n.m.* Valentine.

valentón, -tona, *a., n.m.f.* braggart.

valentona(da), *n.f.* bragging.

valer, *n.m.* worth.—*v.t.* [36] be worth; avail; produce.—*v.i.* be valuable; be valid; prevail; matter.—*v.r.* make use of, avail oneself of (*de*); *más vale . . . ,* it is better to . . . ; — *para,* serve to; — *por,* be as good as, equal.

valeroso, -sa, *a.* valiant; effective.
valgo [VALER].
valía, *n.f.* worth, value; credit; faction.
validar, *v.t.* validate.
validez, *n.f.* validity; efficacy.
valido, -da, *a.* valued.—*n.m.* favourite, minister.
válido, -da, *a.* valid; sound.
valiente, *a.* brave; superb; strong.—*n.m.* brave man; bully.
valija, *n.f.* valise; mail-bag.
valimiento, *n.m.* protection; (*pol.*) favouritism.
valioso, -sa, *a.* valuable; wealthy.
valón, -lona, *a., n.m.f.* Walloon.—*n.m. pl.* bloomers.—*n.f.* Vandyke collar.
valor, *n.m.* value, worth; valour; validity; import(ance).—*pl.* securities, bonds.
valoración, *n.f.* valuation.
valor(e)ar, *v.t.* value, evaluate.
valoría, *n.f.* worth.
valorizar [C], *v.t.* value.
vals, *n.m.* waltz.
vals(e)ar, *v.i.* waltz.
valuación, *n.f.* valuation.
válvula, *n.f.* valve.
valla, *n.f.* barricade; hurdle; barrier.
valladar, vallado, *n.m.* barrier, fence.
vallar, *v.t.* barricade.
valle, *n.m.* valley; vale.
vallisoletano, -na, *a., n.m.f.* rel. to *or* native of Valladolid.
vamos [IR].
vampiro, *n.m.* vampire.
van [IR].
vanagloria, *n.f.* vainglory.
vanagloriar, *v.r.* boast (*de*, of).
vanaglorioso, -sa, *a.* vainglorious.
vandalismo, *n.m.* vandalism.
vándalo, -la, *a., n.m.f.* Vandal, vandal.
vanear, *v.i.* talk rubbish.
vanguardia, *n.f.* vanguard; lead.
vanidad, *n.f.* vanity.
vanidoso, -sa, *a.* vain, conceited.
vanistorio, *n.m.* (*fam.*) stuck-up person.
vano, -na, *a.* vain.—*n.m.* opening.
vapor, *n.m.* steam; mist; vapour; (*naut.*) steamer.
vaporar [EVAPORAR].
vaporizar [C], *v.t.* vaporize.
vaporoso, -sa, *a.* steamy; vaporous.
vapular, *v.t.* flog.
vaquería, *n.f.* dairy; herd.
vaquerizo, -za, *a.* rel. to cattle.—*n.m.* cowman.—*n.f.* cowshed.
vaquero, -ra, *a.* rel. to cattle.—*n.m.* cowherd, cowboy.
vaqueta, *n.f.* leather.
vara, *n.f.* rod; twig; measure of length (2 *ft.* 9 *ins.*); — **alta,** authority.
varar, *v.t.* beach (*boats*).—*v.i.* run aground.
varear, *v.t.* knock down; measure; prod.
vareta, *n.f.* twig; stripe; sharp hint.
varga, *n.f.* steep slope.
variable, *a.* variable.
variación, *n.f.* variation.
variante, *a., n.f.* variant.
variar [L], *v.t., v.i.* vary.
várice, *n.f.* varicose vein.
varicoso, -sa, *a.* varicose.
variedad, *n.f.* variety; odd item.
varilla, *n.f.* wand; twig; stem; spoke.

vario, -ria, *a.* various; variegated; fickle.—*pl.* various, several.—*n.m.pl.* miscellanea.
varón, *a., n.m.* male; *santo* —, simple soul.
varonil, *a.* manly, virile.
Varsovia, *n.f.* Warsaw.
vas [IR].
vasallo, -lla, *a., n.m.f.* vassal.
vasco, -ca, *a., n.m.f.* Basque.
vascongado, -da, *a., n.m.f.* Spanish Basque.
vascuence, *a., n.m.* Basque (*language*).
vaselina, *n.f.* (*reg. trade mark*) Vaseline.
vasija, *n.f.* vessel; dish; cask.
vaso, *n.m.* tumbler, glass; vase.
vástago, *n.m.* shoot; offspring; (*mech.*) rod.
vastedad, *n.f.* vastness.
vasto, -ta, *a.* vast.
vate, *n.m.* bard, poet; seer.
váter, *n.m.* [WATER].
vaticano, -na, *a.* Vatican; *el Vaticano*, the Vatican.
vaticinar, *v.t.* foretell, predict.
vatio, *n.m.* (*elec.*) watt.
vaya, *n.f.* scoff.—*v.* [IR.]
Vd., Vds. [USTED(ES)].
ve [IR, VER].
vecero, -ra, *a.* alternating.—*n.m.f.* customer.—*n.f.* herd.
vecinal, *a.* local.
vecindad, *n.f.* neighbourhood.
vecindario, *n.m.* neighbours; population.
vecino, -na, *a.* neighbouring.—*n.m.f.* neighbour; native.
veda, *n.f.* close season; prohibition.
vedado, *n.m.* game reserve.
vedar, *v.t.* forbid; veto; hinder.
vedija, *n.f.* tuft.
veedor, -ra, *a.* prying.
vega, *n.f.* fertile plain.
vegetación, *n.f.* vegetation.
vegetal, *a., n.m.* vegetable.
vegetar, *v.i.* vegetate.
vegetariano, -na, *a., n.m.f.* vegetarian.
vegetativo, -va, *a.* vegetative.
vehemencia, *n.f.* vehemence.
vehemente, *a.* vehement.
vehículo, *n.m.* vehicle.
veía [VER].
veintavo, -va, *a., n.m.* twentieth.
veinte, *a., n.m.* twenty.
veinteno, -na, *a.* twentieth.—*n.f.* score.
veinti- [VEINTE Y -].
vejación, *n.f.* vexation.
vejamen, *n.m.* taunt; vexation.
vejar, *v.t.* annoy, vex; jibe at.
vejestorio, *n.m.* (*fam.*) dotard.
vejez, *n.f.* old age; old story.
vejiga, *n.f.* bladder; blister.
vejigoso, -sa, *a.* blistered.
vela (1), *n.f.* watchfulness, vigil; pilgrimage.
vela (2), *n.f.* candle.
vela (3), *n.f.* sail.
velado, -da, *a.* veiled.—*n.m.* husband.—*n.f.* wife; vigil; soirée.
velador, -ra, *a.* watchful.—*n.m.* watchman.
velaje, velamen, *n.m.* sails.
velar, *v.* velar.—*v.t.* veil; watch (over).—*v.i.* stay awake; work at night; take care; watch (*por, sobre,* over).—*v.r.* (*phot.*) fog.
velatorio, *n.m.* (*eccl.*) wake.
veleidad, *n.f.* levity; whim; feebleness.
veleidoso, -sa, *a.* fickle, giddy.

209

velero (1), *n.m.* chandler.
velero (2), *n.m.* sail-maker; sailing boat.
veleta, *n.f.* weather-vane; float; streamer.
velo, *n.m.* veil; (*anat.*) velum.
velocidad, *n.f.* speed, velocity; (*mech.*) gear.
velocímetro, *n.m.* speedometer.
velón, *n.m.* oil-lamp.
velorio, *n.m.* wake; night party; (*eccl.*) taking
of the veil.
veloz, *a.* (*pl.* **-oces**) swift, fast, fleet.
vello, *n.m.* down.
vellocino, *n.m.* fleece.
vellón, *n.m.* fleece; copper alloy.
velloso, -sa, *a.* downy.
velludo, -da, *a.* shaggy.—*n.m.* velvet, plush.
ven [VENIR].
vena, *n.f.* vein; dash, streak; inspiration.
venablo, *n.m.* javelin.
venado, *n.m.* deer, stag.
venal, *a.* venal; venous.
venalidad, *n.f.* venality.
venático, -ca, *a.* (*fam.*) cranky.
vencedor, -ra, *n.m.f.* conqueror.
vencejo, *n.m.* band; (*orn.*) swift.
vencer [D], *v.t.* conquer.—*v.i.* mature, fall
due.
vencible, *a.* superable.
vencimiento, *n.m.* victory, conquest; (*com.*)
maturity.
venda, *n.f.* bandage; blindfold.
vendaje, *n.m.* bandaging.
vendar, *v.t.* bandage; blindfold.
vendaval, *n.m.* violent wind.
vendedor, -ra, *n.m.f.* seller.
vendeja, *n.f.* public sale.
vender, *v.t.* sell.—*v.r.* pretend (*por*, to be);
se vende caro, it is dear; it *or* he is rarely
seen.
vendible, *a.* sellable, saleable.
vendimia, *n.f.* vintage.
vendimiar, *v.t.* gather (*grapes*); reap unjust
benefit; (*fam.*) bump off, kill.
vendré [VENIR].
venduta, *n.f.* (*S.A.*) sale; greengrocer's.
Venecia, *n.f.* Venice; Venetia.
veneciano, -na, *a.* Venetian.
veneno, *n.m.* poison.
venenoso, -sa, *a.* poisonous.
venera, *n.f.* spring; pilgrim's scallop.
venerable, *a.* venerable.
veneración, *n.f.* veneration.
venerando, -da, *a.* reverend.
venerar, *v.t.*, *v.i.* venerate.
venéreo, -rea, *a.* venereal.
venero, *n.m.* spring, source, origin.
venezolano, -na, *a.*, *n.m.f.* Venezuelan.
vengador, -ra, *a.* avenging.—*n.m.f.* avenger.
venganza, *n.f.* revenge, vengeance.
vengar [B], *v.t.* avenge.—*v.r.* take revenge
(*de*, for, *en*, on).
vengativo, -va, *a.* revengeful.
vengo, -ga [VENIR].
venia, *n.f.* forgiveness; leave.
venial, *a.* venial.
venida, *n.f.* coming, arrival; rush.
venidero, -ra, *a.* future, coming.—*n.m.pl.*
posterity
venir [36], *v.t.* fit, suit.—*v.i.* come; *venirse
abajo*, collapse.
venta, *n.f.* sale; inn; *de or en —*, for (on) sale.
ventada, *n.f.* gust.
ventaja, *n.f.* advantage.

ventajoso, -sa, *a.* advantageous.
ventana, *n.f.* window.
ventanal, *n.m.* church window; large window.
ventanero, -ra, *a.* window-gazing.—*n.m.f.*
window-gazer.
ventanilla, *n.f.* window (*ticket-, car- etc.*).
ventanillo, *n.m.* peep-hole.
ventarrón, *n.m.* strong wind.
vent(e)ar, *v.t.* sniff, smell out; air.—*v.i.*
blow (*wind*).—*v.r.* split.
ventero, -ra, *n.m.f.* inn-keeper.
ventilación, *n.f.* ventilation.
ventilador, *n.m.* ventilator.
ventilar, *v.t.* ventilate; (*fig.*) air.
ventisco, -ca, *n.m.f.* blizzard; snow-drift.
ventiscar [A], **ventisquear**, *v.i.* snow; drift.
ventisquero, *n.m.* blizzard; snow-drift;
glacier; snow-cap.
ventorro, ventorrillo, *n.m.* wretched inn.
ventoso, -sa, *a.* windy; flatulent.
ventrílocuo, -cua, *n.m.f.* ventriloquist.
ventriloquia, *n.f.* ventriloquy, ventriloquism.
ventura, *n.f.* chance, luck; happiness; risk;
a la —, at random.
venturado, -da, *a.* fortunate.
venturero, -ra, *a.* adventurous.—*n.m.f.*
adventurer.
venturo, -ra, *a.* coming, future.
venturoso, -sa, *a.* lucky.
venusto, -ta, *a.* beautiful.
veo [VER].
ver, *n.m.* sight; opinion.—*v.t.* [37] see; (*jur.*)
try.—*v.r.* find oneself, be; be obvious; *a
mi —*, to my mind; *a más —*, so long;
a —, let's see; *tener que — con*, have to
do with; *ya se ve*, of course.
vera, *n.f.* edge.
veracidad, *n.f.* veracity.
veranda, *n.f.* veranda.
veraneante, *a.* summering.—*n.m.f.* summer
holiday-maker.
veranear, *v.i.* spend the summer.
veraneo, *n.m.* summering; summer holiday.
veraniego, -ga, *a.* summer(y); ailing; slight.
verano, *n.m.* summer
veras, *n.f.pl.* truth; *de —*, really; in earnest.
veraz, *a.* (*pl.* **-aces**) veracious.
verbal, *a.* verbal.
verbena, *n.f.* soirée; verbena.
verberación, *n.f.* pounding.
verberar, *v.t.* beat (against).
verbigracia, verbi gratia, e.g.
verbo, *n.m.* verb; (*eccl.*) Word.
verborrea, *n.f.* (*fam.*) wordiness.
verbosidad, *n.f.* verbosity.
verboso, -sa, *a.* verbose.
verdad, *n.f.* truth; *cuatro verdades*,
home truths; *¿ (no es) —?* is it not so ? *es
—*, it is true.
verdadero, -ra, *a.* true, real.
verdal, *a.* green.
verde, *a.* green; young; smutty.—*n.m.* green;
(*fam.*) fling; *poner —*, (*fam.*) tell off
strongly.
verdear, *v.i.* look greenish.
verdecer [9], *v.i.* turn green.
verdegal, *n.m.* green field.
verdegay, *a.*, *n.m.* light green.
verdemar, *n.m.* sea-green.
verderón, *n.m.* (*orn.*) greenfinch; (*zool.*)
cockle.
verdín, *n.m.* pond-scum; mildew; verdure.

verdinegro, -ra, *a.* dark green.
verdino, -na, *a.* bright green.
verdor, *n.m.* verdure; vigour.
verdoso, -sa, *a.* greenish.
verdugo, *n.m.* shoot, sucker; rod; lash; executioner; (*orn.*) shrike.
verdulero, -ra, *n.m.f.* greengrocer.—*n.f.* vulgar fishwife.
verdura, *n.f.* verdure.—*pl.* greens.
verdusco, -ca, *a.* darkish green.
vereda, *n.f.* path; route; (*S.A.*) pavement, (*U.S.*) sidewalk.
veredicto, *n.m.* verdict.
verga, *n.f.* (*naut.*) yard, boom; penis; bow.
vergel, *n.m.* orchard garden.
vergonzante, *a.* bashful.
vergonzoso, -sa, *a.* shameful; bashful.
verguear, *v.t.* flog.
vergüenza, *n.f.* shame; bashfulness; disgrace; dignity; **tener** —, be ashamed (**de,** of).
verídico, -ca, *a.* truthful.
verificable, *a.* verifiable.
verificación, *n.f.* verification; checking.
verificar [A], *v.t.* verify; check.—*v.r.* prove true; take place.
verisímil [VEROSÍMIL].
verismo, *n.m.* realism; truth.
verja, *n.f.* grill.
verminoso, -sa, *a.* verminous.
vermut, *n.m.* vermouth.
vernáculo, -la, *a.* vernacular.
verónica, *n.f.* (*taur.*) pass with open cape.
verosímil, *a.* likely, probable.
verosimilitud, *n.f.* verisimilitude.
verraco, *n.m.* hog, boar.
verriondo, -da, *a.* rutting; withered.
verruga, *n.f.* wart; (*fam.*) pest.
verrugo, *n.m.* (*fam.*) miser.
versado, -da, *a.* versed (**en,** in).
versal, *a.,* *n.f.* capital (*letter*).
versalilla, versalita, *n.f.* small capital.
versar, *v.i.* turn; deal with, treat of (**sobre**).—*v.r.* become versed (**en,** in).
versátil, *a.* versatile, fickle.
versicolor, *a.* many-coloured.
versículo, *n.m.* verse, versicle.
versificar [A], *v.t.* versify.
versión, *n.f.* version; translation.
versista, *n.m.f.* versifier.
verso, *n.m.* verse; line of verse; verso.
vértebra, *n.f.* vertebra.
vertebrado, -da, *a.* vertebrate.
vertebral, *a.* vertebral.
vertedero, *n.m.* dump; weir.
verter [2], *v.t.* pour; spill; dump; translate.
vertible, *a.* changeable.
vertical, *a.,* *n.m.* or *f.* vertical.
vértice, *n.m.* vertex.
vertiente, *n.m.* or *f.* slope; (*S.A.,* *f.*) spring.
vertiginoso, -sa, *a.* vertiginous.
vértigo, *n.m.* vertigo.
vesania, *n.f.* insanity.
vesánico, -ca, *a.* insane.
vesícula, *n.f.* vesicle, sac, cell.
vespertino, -na, *a.* evening.—*n.m.* or *f.* evening class *or* sermon.
vestíbulo, *n.m.* foyer, lobby, vestibule.
vestido, *n.m.* clothing; dress; suit.
vestidura, *n.f.* vestment.
vestigial, *a.* vestigial.
vestigio, *n.m.* vestige.

vestiglo, *n.m.* monster, bogey.
vestimenta, *n.f.* clothes.
vestir [8], *v.t.,* *v.r.* dress (**de,** in, as); cover.
vestuario, *n.m.* uniform; wardrobe.
Vesubio, *n.m.* Vesuvius.
veta, *n.f.* vein; stripe; seam.
vetar, *v.t.* veto.
vetear, *v.t.* grain.
veterano, -na, *a.,* *n.m.f.* veteran.
veterinario, -ria, *a.,* *n.m.f.* veterinary.
veto, *n.m.* veto.
vetustez, *n.f.* antiquity.
vetusto, -ta, *a.* ancient, age-old.
vez, *n.f.* (*pl.* **veces**) time; turn; herd; **a la** —, at once, at the same time; **a su** —, in turn; for his part; **de** — **en cuando,** from time to time; **en** — **de,** instead of; **tal** —, perhaps; **hacer las veces de,** act for, take the place of.
vezar [C], *v.t.* accustom.
vía, *n.f.* way; route; (*rail.*) track; (*naut.*) leak; — **muerta,** (*rail.*) siding.—*prep.* vía.
viabilidad, *n.f.* viability.
viable, *a.* viable.
viaducto, *n.m.* viaduct.
viajante, *a.* travelling.—*n.m.* (*com.*) traveller.
viajar, *v.i.* travel.
viajata, *n.f.* (*fam.*) trip.
viaje, *n.m.* journey; voyage; way; load; supply; **¡buen** — **!** bon voyage!
viajero, -ra, *n.m.f.* passenger, traveller.
vial, *a.* rel. to roads.
vialidad, *n.f.* highways department.
vianda, *n.f.* viand, victuals.
viandante, *n.m.f.* traveller, tramp.
viático, *n.m.* (*eccl.*) viaticum; travelling expenses.
víbora, *n.f.* (*zool.*) viper.
vibración, *n.f.* vibration.
vibrante, *a.* vibrant.
vibrar, *v.t.,* *v.i.* vibrate.—*v.t.* brandish; hurl; shake.
vicaria, *n.f.* under-abbess.
vicaría, *n.f.* vicarage; vicarship.
vicario, -ria, *a.* vicarious.—*n.m.* vicar.
vice-, *prefix.* vice-, deputy-.
Vicente, *n.m.* Vincent.
viciar, *v.t.* vitiate.
vicio, *n.m.* vice; defect; bad habit; luxuriance; **de** —, through habit.
vicioso, -sa, *a.* corrupt(ed); unruly; luxuriant; robust.
vicisitud, *n.f.* vicissitude.
vict- [VIT-].
víctima, *n.f.* victim.
victimar, *v.t.* (*S.A.*) murder.
victo, *n.m.* daily bread.
victoria, *n.f.* victory; victoria (*carriage*).
victorioso, -sa, *a.* victorious.
vicuña, *n.f.* (*zool.*) vicunia.
vid, *n.f.* (*bot.*) vine.
vida, *n.f.* life; living; **con** —, alive; **en la** —, never; **hacer** —, live together; — **airada** *or* **ancha,** loose living.
vidente, *a.* seeing.—*n.m.f.* seer.
vidriado, -da, *a.* glazed; brittle.—*n.m.* glazed ware.
vidriar [L], *v.t.* glaze.
vidriera, *n.f.* glass window; (*S.A.*) shop-window.
vidriería, *n.f.* glass-work(s) *or* -shop.
vidriero, *n.m.* glass-worker; glazier.

vidrio, *n.m.* glass.
vidrioso, -sa, *a.* vitreous; glassy; brittle; slippery; peevish.
viejo, -ja, *a.* old.—*n.m.* old man.—*n.f.* old woman.
vienés, -nesa, *a., n.m.f.* Viennese.
vientecillo, *n.m.* breeze.
viento, *n.m.* wind; *ir — en popa,* run smoothly.
vientre, *n.m.* belly; womb.
viernes, *n.m.* Friday.
viga, *n.f.* beam; girder.
vigencia, *n.f.* operation, force; vogue.
vigente, *a.* in force, prevailing.
vigesimal, *a.* vigesimal.
vigésimo, -ma, *a., n.m.* twentieth.
vigía, *n.f.* watch.—*n.m.* look-out.
vigilancia, *n.f.* vigilance.
vigilante, *a.* vigilant.—*n.m.* watchman, guard.
vigilar, *v.t., v.i.* watch, guard.
vigilia, *n.f.* vigil, eve; (*mil.*) watch; night-work.
vigor, *n.m.* vigour; *en —,* into effect.
vigorizar [C], *v.t.* invigorate.
vigoroso, -sa, *a.* vigorous.
vil, *a.* base, vile, low.
vilano, *n.m.* thistledown.
vileza, *n.f.* vileness; disgrace.
vilipendiar, *v.t.* revile.
vilipendio, *n.m.* scorn.
en vilo, *adv. phr.* suspended, in the air.
vilordo, -da, *a.* slothful.
viltrotera, *n.f.* (*fam.*) gad-about.
villa, *n.f.* town; villa.
Villadiego, *tomar las de —,* beat it, run off.
villancete, villancico, *n.m.* carol.
villanchón, -chona, *a.* yokelish.
villanesco, -ca, *a.* rustic; boorish.
villanía, *n.f.* low birth; villainy.
villano, -na, *a.* coarse; wicked.—*n.m.f.* peasant; villain.
villoría, *n.f.* hamlet; farm.
villorio, *n.m.* one-horse town.
vimbre, *n.m.* osier.
vinagre, *n.m.* vinegar.
vinagroso, -sa, *a.* vinegary.
vinajera, *n.f.* (*eccl.*) wine-vessel, cruet.
vinario, -ria, *a.* rel. to wine.
vinatero, *n.m.* vintner.
vincular, *v.t.* (*jur.*) entail; (*fig.*) base; continue.
vindicación, *n.f.* vindication.
vindicar [A], *v.t.* vindicate.
vindicta, *n.f.* vengeance.
vine [VENIR].
vínico, -ca, *a.* vinic, rel. to wine.
vinícola, *a.* wine-growing.—*n.m.f.* vine-grower.
vinicultor, -ra, *n.m.f.* wine-grower.
vinicultura, *n.f.* vine-growing.
vinilo, *n.m.* vinyl.
vino, *n.m.* wine; *tener mal —,* be fighting drunk. [VENIR].
vinolento, -ta, *a.* too fond of wine.
vinoso, -sa, *a.* vinous.
viña, *n.f.* vineyard; (*fig.*) gold-mine.
viñador, *n.m.* vine-grower.
viñedo, *n.m.* vineyard.
viñero, -ra, *n.m.f.* owner of vineyard.
viñeta, *n.f.* vignette.
viola (1), *n.f.* (*mus.*) viola.

viola (2), *n.f.* (*bot.*) viola.
violación, *n.f.* violation.
violado, -da, *a., n.m.* violet.
violar, *v.t.* violate.
violencia, *n.f.* violence.
violentar, *v.t.* violate; force; break down.
violento, -ta, *a.* violent; embarrassed.
violeta, *a. inv., n.f.* (*bot.*) violet.—*n.m.* (*colour*) violet.
violín, *n.m.* violin.
violinista, *n.m.f.* violinist.
violón, *n.m.* (*mus.*) double bass.
violonc(h)elo, *n.m.* (violon)cello.
viperino, -na, *a.* viperous.
vira, *n.f.* dart; shoe-welt.
virada, *n.f.* turn, tacking.
virago, *n.f.* virago.
viraje, *n.m.* turn, bend.
virar, *v.t., v.r.* (*naut.*) tack, veer, turn.
virgen, *n.f.* virgin.
Virgilio, *n.m.* Vergil.
virginal, *a., n.m.* virginal.
virginidad, *n.f.* virginity.
vírgula, *n.f.* dash; comma.
viril, *a.* virile; manly.
virilidad, *n.f.* virility.
virolento, -ta, *a.* having small-pox; pock-marked.
virote, *n.m.* dart, bolt; (*fam.*) young blood; stuffed-shirt.
virreinato, *n.m.* viceroyalty.
virrey, *n.m.* viceroy.
virtual, *a.* virtual.
virtud, *n.f.* virtue.
virtuoso, -sa, *a.* virtuous.—*n.m.* virtuoso.
viruela, *n.f.* small-pox; pock-mark.
virulento, -ta, *a.* virulent.
virus, *n.m.inv.* virus.
viruta, *n.f.* shaving, sliver.
visado, *n.m.* visa.
visaje, *n.m.* grimace.
visar, *v.t.* visa; countersign; (*mil.*) sight.
vísceras, *n.f.pl.* viscera.
visco, *n.m.* bird-lime.
viscoso, -sa, *a.* viscous.
visera, *n.f.* visor; cap-peak.
visibilidad, *n.f.* visibility.
visible, *a.* visible; conspicuous.
visigodo, -da, *a.* Visigoth.
visigótico, -ca, *a.* Visigothic.
visillo, *n.m.* window-curtain.
visión, *n.f.* vision.
visionario, -ria, *a., n.m.f.* visionary.
visir, *n.m.* vizier.
visita, *n.f.* visit; visitor; inspection.
visitación, *n.f.* visitation.
visitador, -ra, *n.m.f.* visitor; inspector.
visitante, *a.* visiting.—*n.m.f.* visitor.
visitar, *v.t.* visit; inspect.
visitero, -ra, *n.m.f.* (*fam.*) visitor.
vislumbrar, *v.t.* glimpse.—*v.r.* glimmer.
vislumbre, *n.m.* glimpse; inkling.
viso, *n.m.* sheen, lustre; pretext; semblance; *de —,* important; *a dos visos,* dual-purpose;
visón, *n.m.* mink.
visor, *n.m.* view-finder; bomb-sight.
visorio, -ria, *a.* optic.—*n.m.* expert examination.
víspera, *n.f.* eve.—*pl.* vespers.
vista, *n.f.* sight; view, vista; (*jur.*) trial; look.
vistazo, *n.m.* glance.

212

vistillas, *n.f.pl.* vantage point.
visto, -ta, *a.* evident; seen; **bien (mal)** —, well (ill) regarded; — **bueno,** approved; — **que,** seeing that. [VER].
vistoso, -sa, *a.* showy; flashy.
visual, *a.* visual.—*n.f.* line of sight.
visualizar [C], *v.t.* visualize.
visura, *n.f.* examination.
vital, *a.* vital; life.
vitalicio, -cia, *a.* life-long.—*n.m.* life policy; life annuity.
vitalidad, *n.f.* vitality.
vitalizar [C], *v.t.* vitalize.
vitamina, *n.f.* vitamin.
vitando, -da, *a.* to be avoided, taboo.
vitela, *n.f.* vellum, calf.
viti- [VINI-].
vito, *n.m.* Andalusian dance.
vitor, *n.m.* triumphal pageant; memorial.—*interj.* hurrah!
vitorear, *v.t.* cheer, acclaim.
vitreo, -trea, *a.* vitreous.
vitrificar [A], *v.t.*, *v.r.* vitrify.
vitrina, *n.f.* glass case.
vitriolo, *n.m.* vitriol.
vitualla, *n.f.* provisions; vegetables.
vituperar, *v.t.* vituperate.
vituperio, *n.m.* vituperation.
viuda, *n.f.* widow.
viudez, *n.f.* widowhood.
viudo, -da, *a.* widowed.—*n.m.* widower.
viva, *n.m.* (*obs.*) huzza.—*interj.* hurrah! long live!
vivacidad, *n.f.* vigour; brilliance.
vivaque, *n.m.* bivouac.
vivar, *n.m.* warren; fish-pond.—*v.t.* (*S.A.*) acclaim.
vivaracho, -cha, *a.* (*fam.*) frisky, lively.
vivaz, *a.* (*pl.* **-aces**) lively; keen; perennial.
víveres, *n.m.pl.* provisions, food.
vivero, *n.m.* nursery; fish-pond; shell-fish beds.
viveza, *n.f.* liveliness; gaiety; ardour; keenness; lustre; thoughtlessness.
vivido, -da, *a.* lived-through.
vívido, -da, *a.* vivid.
vividor, -ra, *a.* living; thrifty.—*n.m.f.* hard-liver; saver; (*fam.*) crook; sponger.
vivienda, *n.f.* dwelling; housing.
viviente, *a.* living.
vivificar [A], *v.t.* vivify.
vivir, *n.m.* life; living.—*v.t.*, *v.i.* live (**de,** on); ¿**quién vive?** who goes there?
vivisección, *n.f.* vivisection.
vivo, -va, *a.* alive, living; smart; nimble; quick, raw; acute, keen; expressive.—*n.m.* edge; the quick; **en lo** —, to the quick.
vizcaíno, -na, *a.*, *n.m.f.* Biscayan.
Vizcaya, *n.f.* Biscay.
vizconde, *n.m.* viscount.
vocablo, *n.m.* word, term; pun.
vocabulario, *n.m.* vocabulary.
vocación, *n.f.* vocation; dedication.
vocal, *a.* vocal.—*n.m.f.* committee member.—*n.f.* vowel.
vocálico, -ca, *a.* vocalic.
vocalizar [C], *v.t.* vocalize.
vocativo, -va, *a.*, *n.m.* vocative.
vocear, *v.t.* shout; hail.
vocería, *n.f.*, **vocerío,** *n.m.* shouting.
vocero, *n.m.* spokesman.
vociferar, *v.t.* vociferate; boast of.

vocinglero, -ra, *a.* bawling; babbling.—*n.m.f.* bawler; babbler.
volada, *n.f.* short flight.
voladero, -ra, *a.* flying; fleeting.—*n.m.* precipice.
volado, *n.m.* (*cul.*) meringue.
voladura, *n.f.* explosion, blast; flight.
volandero, -ra, *a.* fledgling; dangling; casual chance; unsettled.—*n.f.* (*mech.*) washer.
volante, *a.* flying.—*n.m.* steering-wheel; fly-wheel; shuttlecock; balance wheel; frill.
volantín, -tina, *a.* flying.—*n.m.* fishing-line; (*S.A.*) kite.
volantón, -tona, *a.*, *n.m.f.* fledgling.
volar [4], *v.t.* blow up; flush; enrage.—*v.i.* fly; jut out; vanish; spread rapidly.
volatería, *n.f.* birds; bird hunting; (*fig.*) wool-gathering; **de** —, by pure chance.
volátil, *a.* volatile.
volati(li)zar [C], *v.t.*, *v.r.* volatilize, evaporate.
volatín, *n.m.*, **volatinero, -ra,** *n.m.f.* tight-rope walker.
volcán, *n.m.* volcano.
volcánico, -ca, *a.* volcanic.
volcar [4A], *v.t.* upset, overturn; daze; change the mind of; irritate.—*v.i.* capsize.
volea, *n.f.*, **voleo,** *n.m.* volley; punch.
volición, *n.f.* volition.
volitar, *v.i.* flutter.
volquear, *v.r.* roll over.
volquete, *n.m.* tipping-truck, dump truck.
voltaje, *n.m.* voltage.
voltario, -ria, *a.* fickle.
voltear, *v.t.* roll; turn upside down; upset.—*v.i.* roll over, tumble.
voltereta, *n.f.* somersault.
volteriano, -na, *a.* Voltairean.
voltio, *n.m.* volt.
voltizo, -za, *a.* twisted; fickle.
voluble, *a.* fickle; voluble.
volumen, *n.m.* volume (*mass, tome*).
voluminoso, -sa, *a.* voluminous.
voluntad, *n.f.* will; free-will; love.
voluntariedad, *n.f.* voluntariness; wilfulness.
voluntario, -ria, *a.* voluntary; wilful.—*n.m.f.* volunteer.
voluntarioso, -sa, *a.* wilful, self-willed; determined.
voluptuoso, -sa, *a.* voluptuous.—*n.m.f.* voluptuary.
voluta, *n.f.* volute.
volver [5, *p.p.* **vuelto**], *v.t.* turn; turn over; send back; close; vomit.—*v.i.* come back, return; turn; — **a,** do again; — **en sí,** come round; — **por,** defend; — **sobre,** change (*opinions*); — **sobre sí,** retain self-control.—*v.r.* return; turn; become.
vomitar, *v.t.*, *v.i.* vomit, spew.
vómito, *n.m.* vomit.
voracidad, *n.f.* voracity.
vorágine, *n.f.* vortex, whirlpool.
voraz, *a.* (*pl.* **-aces**) voracious; savage.
vórtice, *n.m.* vortex.
vos, *pron. pers. pl.* (*obs.*, *eccl.*, *poet.*) ye, you; (*S.A.*, *fam.*) you, thou (*sing. with pl. v.*); [VOSOTROS, TÚ].
vosear, *v.t.* address as VOS; (*S.A.*) [TUTEAR].
voseo, *n.m.* use of VOS; (*S.A.*) [TUTEO].
vosotros, -tras, *pron. pers. m.f.* you (*pl. of* TÚ).
votación, *n.f.* voting; ballot.

votador, -ra, *n.m.f.* voter; swearer.
votante, *n.m.f.* voter.
votar, *v.t.* vote for; vow to; vote on.—*v.i.* vote; vow; swear.
votivo, -va, *a.* votive.
voto, *n.m.* vow; vote; oath.—*pl.* wishes.
voy [IR].
voz, *n.f.* (*pl.* **voces**) voice; word; cry, shout; rumour; **en — alta,** aloud; **dar voces,** shout.
vuece(le)ncia, *pron. pers.* (*obs.*) [VUESTRA EXCELENCIA].
vuelco, *n.m.* overturning; upset; start, jump.
vuelo, *n.m.* flight; flare, fullness; lace frill; projection; **al —,** in flight; quickly; by chance.
vuelta, *n.f.* turn; change; return; reverse; stroll; roll.
vuelto, *n.m.* verso; (*S.A.*) change (*money*). [VOLVER].
vuesamerced, vuesarced, *pers., pron.* (*obs.*) [USTED].
vuestro, -ra, *a., poss. pron.* your, yours.
vulcanita, *n.f.* vulcanite.
vulcanizar [C], *v.t.* vulcanize.
vulgacho, *n.m.* rabble.
vulgar, *a.* vulgar, popular, vernacular.
vulgaridad, *n.f.* vulgarity; commonplace.
vulgarizar [C], *v.t.* vulgarize; popularize.—*v.r.* become vulgar, popular *or* common.
Vulgata, *n.f.* Vulgate.
vulgo, *n.m.* populace, common people, mob.
vulnerable, *a.* vulnerable.
vulnerar, *v.t.* harm, damage.
vulpeja, *n.f.* vixen.

W

W, w, *n.f. this letter does not belong to the Spanish alphabet. It is replaced by* **V, v,** *and pronounced as such.*
wat, *n.m.* (*pl.* **wats**) [VATIO].
wáter, *n.m.* lavatory, toilet, W.C.

X

X, x, *n.f.* twenty-sixth letter of the Spanish alphabet.
xenofobia, *n.f.* xenophobia.
xenófobo, -ba, *a., n.m.f.* xenophobe.
xilófono, *n.m.* xylophone.
xilografía, *n.f.* xylography; wood-cut.

Y

Y, y (1), *n.f.* twenty-seventh letter of the Spanish alphabet.
y (2), *conj.* and. [E].

ya, *adv.* already; now; finally; at once; **— no,** no longer; **— que,** since, as; **ya. . . . ya,** whether . . . or; now . . . . now; *¡ya ya!* yes, of course.
yacer [38], *v.i.* lie.
yacija, *n.f.* bed, couch; grave.
yacimiento, *n.m.* (*min.*) deposit, bed.
yaguar [JAGUAR].
yanqui, *a., n.m.f.* Yankee.
yapa, *n.f.* (*S.A.*) extra, bonus.
yarda, *n.f.* yard (*measure*).
yate, *n.m.* yacht.
yedra, *n.f.* ivy.
yegua, *n.f.* mare.
yeísmo, *n.m.* pronunciation of Spanish **ll** as **y.**
yelmo, *n.m.* helmet.
yema, *n.f.* egg-yolk; bud; middle; best.
yendo [IR].
yerba [HIERBA].
yerbajo, *n.m.* weed.
yermar, *v.t.* lay waste; abandon.
yermo, -ma, *a.* waste, deserted.—*n.m.* wilderness, desert.
yerno, *n.m.* son-in-law.
yerro, *n.m.* error, mistake. [ERRAR].
yerto, -ta, *a.* stiff, rigid.
yesca, *n.f.* tinder.
yeso, *n.m.* gypsum; plaster of Paris.
yo, *pron. pers.* I.
yodo, *n.m.* iodine.
yuca, *n.f.* (*bot.*) yucca, cassava.
yugo, *n.m.* yoke.
Yugo(e)slavia, *n.f.* Yu- *or* Jugoslavia.
yugo(e)slavo, -va, *a., n.m.f.* Yu- *or* Jugoslav(ian).
yugular, *a.* jugular.
yunque, *n.m.* anvil; drudge.
yunta, *n.f.* yoke, pair.
yusión, *n.f.* (*jur.*) order; precept.
yute, *n.m.* jute.
yuxtaponer [25], *v.t.* juxtapose.

Z

Z, z, *n.f.* twenty-eighth letter of the Spanish alphabet.
¡za! *interj.* get away! go!
zabordar, *v.i.* (*naut.*) run aground.
zabu- [ZAMBU-].
zabucar [A], *v.t.* shake up.
zacapel(l)a, *n.f.* shindy.
zacear, *v.t.* shoo.—*v.i.* lisp.
zafacoca, *n.f.* (*S.A.*) shindy.
zafrado, -da, *a.* (*S.A.*) cheeky.
zafar (1), *v.t.* deck; adorn.
zafar (2), *v.t.* loosen; clear.—*v.r.* run away; rid oneself.
zafarrancho, *n.m.* (*naut.*) clearing for action; (*fam.*) rumpus.
zafio, -fia, *a.* crude, boorish.
zafir(o), *n.m.* sapphire.
zaga, *n.f.* rear.
zagal (1), *n.m.* youth; swain.
zagal (2), *n.m.* skirt.

zagala, *n.f.* lass; shepherdess.
zaguán, *n.m.* porch, hall.
zaguero, -ra, *a.* hind, rear; loitering.—*n.m.* (*sport*) back.
zahareño, -ña, *a.* wild, haggard.
zaherir [6], *v.t.* reproach.
zahones, *n.m.pl.* chaps, breeches.
zahorí, *n.m.* (*pl.* -íes) seer, diviner.
zahurda, *n.f.* pig-sty.
zaino, -na, *a.* chestnut (*horse*); black (*bull*); wicked; *de* —, askance.
zalagarda, *n.f.* ambush; trap; shindy.
zalamero, -ra, *a.* wheedling.—*n.m.f.* wheedler.
zamarra, *n.f.* sheepskin jerkin.
zambo, -ba, *a.* knock-kneed.
zambucar [A], *v.t.* hide away.
zambullid(ur)a, *n.f.* dive, plunge.
zambullir [J], *v.t.* duck.—*v.r.* dive.
zampa, *n.f.* pile.
zampar, *v.t.* hide; gobble up.—*v.r.* rush off.
zampoña, *n.f.* shepherd's pipe; rubbish.
zanahoria, *n.f.* carrot.
zanca, *n.f.* shank.
zancada, *n.f.* big stride.
zancadilla, *n.f.* tripping up.
zancajo, *n.m.* heel.
zancajoso, -sa, *a.* pigeon-toed.
zanco, *n.m.* stilt.
zancudo, -da, *a.* long-legged.—*n.f.* (*orn.*) wader.
zanganear, *v.i.* (*fam.*) loaf around.
zángano, -na, *n.m.f.* idler, loafer.—*n.m.* drone.
zangolotino, -na, *a.* babyish (*youth*).
zanguango, -ga, *a.* (*fam.*) shiftless, malingering.
zanja, *n.f.* trench; gully; *abrir las zanjas,* lay the foundations.
zanjar, *v.t.* trench; settle.
zanquear, *v.i.* waddle; trot.
zanquituerto, -ta, *a.* bandy-legged.
zapa, *n.f.* spade; trench; shagreen.
zapador, *n.m.* (*mil.*) sapper.
zapapico, *n.m.* pick-axe.
zapar, *v.t.* mine, sap.
zapateado, *n.m.* tap-dance.
zapatería, *n.f.* shoe-maker's shop.
zapatero, *n.m.* shoe-maker, cobbler.
zapatilla, *n.f.* slipper; (*mech.*) soft washer.
zapato, *n.m.* shoe.
zapear, *v.t.* shoo; scare.
zaque, *n.m.* wine-bag; drunk.
zaquizamí, *n.m.* (*pl.* -míes) garret.
zar, *n.m.* tsar.
zarabanda, *n.f.* saraband; uproar.
zaragatero, -ra, *a.* rowdy.
Zaragoza, *n.f.* Saragossa.
zaragüelles, *n.m.pl.* breeches.
zarandar, *v.t.* sieve, sift.
zarandillo, *n.m.* sieve; (*fam.*) live wire.
zarapito, *n.m.* (*orn.*) curlew.
zarista, *a.*, *n.m.f.* tsarist.
zarpa, *n.f.* paw; claw; mud-splash.
zarpar, *v.t.*, *v.i.* (*naut.*) weigh anchor.
zarcillo (1), *n.m.* drop earring; tendril.
zarcillo (2), *n.m.* hoe.
zarracatería, *n.f.* (*fam.*) soft soap.
zarramplín, *n.m.* botcher.
zarrapastra, *n.f.* mud-splash.

zarria (1), *n.f.* mud-splash; tatter.
zarria (2), *n.f.* thong.
zarza, *n.f.* bramble.
zarzal, *n.m.* bramble patch.
zarzamora, *n.f.* blackberry.
zarzaparrilla, *n.f.* sarsaparilla.
zarzaperruna, *n.f.* dog-rose.
zarzuela, *n.f.* musical comedy.
¡zas! *interj.* bang!
zascandil, *n.m.* (*fam.*) busybody, meddler.
zazo, -za, *a.* stammering.
zedilla, *n.f.* cedilla (ç).
Zeland(i)a, *n.f.* Zealand.
zigzag, *n.m.* zigzag.
zigzaguear, *v.i.* zigzag.
zinc, *n.m.* zinc.
¡zis zas! *interj.* bang bang!
ziszás [ZIGZAG].
zócalo, *n.m.* socle; skirting.
zoclo, *n.m.* clog.
zoco, -ca, *a.* (*fam.*) left-handed. —*n.m.* clog; Moorish market.
zodíaco, *n.m.* zodiac.
zoilo, *n.m.* carping critic.
zona, *n.f.* zone.
zonzo, -za, *a.* stupid; insipid.
zoología, *n.f.* zoology.
zoológico, -ca, *a.* zoological.
zoólogo, -ga, *n.m.f.* zoologist.
zopenco, -ca, *a.* (*fam.*) doltish.—*n.m.f.* dolt.
zop(it)as, *n.m. inv.* lisper.
zoquete, *n.m.* chunk; dolt.
zorra, *n.f.* vixen, fox; whore; *pillar una —,* get tipsy.
zorrero, -ra, *a.* foxy.—*n.f.* fox-hole.
zorrillo, *n.m.* skunk.
zorro, *n.m.* fox; *hecho un —,* dog-tired.
zorruno, -na, *a.* foxy.
zorzal, *n.m.* (*orn.*) fieldfare; slyboots; (*S.A.*) clot.
zozobra, *n.f.* upset; worry.
zozobrar, *v.t.* upset.—*v.r.* capsize.
zozobroso, -sa, *a.* anxious.
zuavo, *n.m.* Zouave.
zueco, *n.m.* clog.
zulaque, *n.m.* bitumen; oakum.
zumaque, *n.m.* sumach; (*fam.*) wine.
zumaya, *n.f.* (*orn.*) night-heron; nightjar.
zumba, *n.f.* mule-bell; whistle; *hacer — a,* poke fun at.
zumbar, *v.t.* poke fun at; swing (*a blow at*).—*v.i.* buzz, hum.
zumbido, *n.m.* hum, buzz; (*fam.*) slap.
zumbón, -bona, *a.* waggish.—*n.m.f.* wag.
zumo, *n.m.* juice; gain; *— de cepas* or *parras,* (*fam.*) vine-milk, wine.
zupia, *n.f.* dregs, scum.
zurcir [D], *v.t.* darn; join; (*fam.*) cook up (*lies*).
zurdo, -da, *a.* left(-handed).
zurear, *v.i.* coo.
zureo, *n.m.* cooing.
zurra, *n.f.* drudgery; beating; set-to.
zurrar, *v.t.* tan curry; flog.—*v.r.* be scared.
zurriaga, *n.f.*, **zurriago**, *n.m.* whip.
zurribanda, *n.f.* (*fam.*) beating; shindy.
zurrir, *v.i.* hum; rattle.
zurrón, *n.m.* shepherd's bag; husk.
zutano, -na, *n.m.f.* (*fam.*) who's-it, so-and-so.
zuzón, *n.f.* (*bot.*) groundsel.

A, a (1) [ei], *n.* primera letra del alfabeto inglés; *A*, (*mus.*) la; *AI*, de primera clase; *A-bomb*, bomba atómica.
a (2) [ə], *art. indef.* un, una; por, cada; — *pound* — *month*, una libra al *o* por mes; — *penny an ounce*, un penique la *o* por onza.
aback [ə'bæk], *adv.* (*naut.*) en facha; *to take* —, azorar, desconcertar.
abandon [ə'bændən], *n.* abandono.—*v.t.* abandonar.
abase [ə'beis], *v.t.* degradar.
abasement [ə'beismənt], *n.* degradación, *f.*
abash [ə'bæʃ], *v.t.* amilanar; avergonzar.
abate [ə'beit], *v.t.* calmar, disminuir.—*v.i.* decrecer, caer, amainar.
abattoir ['æbətwɑː], *n.* matadero.
abbacy ['æbəsi], *n.* abadía.
abbess ['æbis], *n.* abadesa.
abbey ['æbi], *n.* abadía.
abbot ['æbət], *n.* abad, *m.*
abbreviate [ə'briːvieit], *v.t.* abreviar.
abbreviation [əbriːvi'eiʃən], *n.* abreviatura (*signo*); abreviación (*hecho*), *f.*
abdicate ['æbdikeit], *v.t.*, *v.i.* abdicar.
abdomen [æb'doumən], *n.* abdomen, *m.*
abduct [æb'dʌkt], *v.t.* raptar, secuestrar.
abduction [æb'dʌkʃən], *n.* rapto, secuestro; abducción, *f.*
abed [ə'bed], *adv.* (*obs.*) en cama.
aberration [æbə'reiʃən], *n.* aberración, *f.*
abet [ə'bet], *v.t.* instigar; auxiliar.
abettor [ə'betə], *n.* (*jur.*) cómplice, *m.f.*
abeyance [ə'beiəns], *n.* desuetud; cesación, *f.*; *in* —, en suspenso.
abhor [əb'hɔː], *v.t.* abominar, aborrecer.
abhorrent [əb'hɔrənt], *a.* aborrecible.
abide [ə'baid], *v.t.* tolerar, aguantar; *to* — *by*, atenerse a.—*v.i. irr.* (*obs.*) morar.
abiding [ə'baidin], *a.* (*lit.*) eternal, perdurable.
ability [ə'biliti], *n.* capacidad, habilidad, *f.*; talento.
abject ['æbʒekt], *a.* abyecto, abatido.
abjure [əb'dʒuə], *v.t.* abjurar.
ablative ['æblətiv], *a.*, *n.* ablativo.
ablaze [ə'bleiz], *a.* encendido, llameante; en llamas.
able [eibl], *a.* capaz, hábil; *to be* — *to*, poder.
able-bodied ['eibl'bɔdid], *a.* sano, entero; (*naut.*) de primera clase.
ablution [æb'luːʃən], *n.* ablución, *f.*
ably ['eibli], *adv.* hábilmente, con acierto.
abnegation [æbni'geiʃən], *n.* abnegación, *f.*
abnormal [æb'nɔːməl], *a.* anormal; deforme.
abnormality [æbnɔː'mæliti], *n.* anormalidad; deformidad, *f.*
aboard [ə'bɔːd], *adv.* (*naut.*) a bordo.—*prep.* al bordo de; en (*trenes*); *all* — *!* ¡al tren!
abode [ə'boud], *n.* (*obs.*) albergue, *m.*, morada. [ABIDE]
abolish [ə'bɔliʃ], *v.t.* anular, abolir, suprimir.
abolition [æbə'liʃən], *n.* anulación, supresión; abolición, *f.*

abominable [æ'bɔminəbl], *a.* abominable.
abominate [æ'bɔmineit], *v.t.* abominar de.
abomination [æbɔmi'neiʃən], *n.* abominación, *f.*
aborigines [æbə'ridʒiniːz], *n.pl.* aborígenes, *m.pl.*
abort [ə'bɔːt], *v.t.*, *v.i.* abortar.
abortion [ə'bɔːʃən], *n.* aborto.
abortive [ə'bɔːtiv], *a.* abortivo.
abound [ə'baund], *v.i.* abundar (*with*, *in*, en).
about [ə'baut], *adv.* casi; por aquí, por ahí.— *prep.* alrededor de; cerca de; acerca de; hacia, a eso de; — *to*, a punto de; *what is it* — ? ¿ de qué se trata ?
above [ə'bʌv], *adv.* arriba, encima, en lo alto. —*prep.* (por) encima de; superior a; más de *o* que; más alto que; — *all*, sobre todo.
above-board [ə'bʌv'bɔːd], *a.* abierto, franco. — *adv.* abiertamente.
Abraham ['eibrəhæm], *n.* Abrahán, *m.*
abrasion [ə'breiʒən], *n.* abrasión, *f.*
abrasive [ə'breiziv], *a.*, *n.* abrasivo.
abreast [ə'brest] *adv.* de frente; de costado; — *of*, al corriente de.
abridge [ə'bridʒ], *v.t.* abreviar, compendiar.
abridg(e)ment [ə'bridʒmənt], *n.* abreviación, *f.*; compendio.
abroad [ə'brɔːd], *adv.* en el *o* al extranjero; en *o* por todas partes; fuera de casa.
abrogate ['æbrougeit], *v.t.* abrogar.
abrupt [ə'brʌpt], *a.* brusco; repentino; abrupto, escarpado.
abscess ['æbses], *n.* absceso.
abscessed ['æbsest], *a.* apostemado.
abscond [əb'skɔnd], *v.i.* evadirse.
absconder [əb'skɔndə], *n.* prófugo; contumaz, *m.f.*
absence ['æbsəns], *n.* ausencia; falta.
absent ['æbsənt], *a.* ausente.—[æb'sent], *v.r.* ausentarse.
absentee [æbsən'tiː], *n.* ausente; absentista, *m.f.*
absenteeism [æbsən'tiːizm], *n.* absentismo.
absent-minded ['æbsənt'maindid], *a.* distraído.
absinthe ['æbsinθ], *n.* ajenjo; absenta.
absolute ['æbsəluːt], *a.*, *n.* absoluto.
absolution [æbsə'luːʃən], *n.* absolución, *f.*
absolutism ['æbsəluːtizm], *n.* absolutismo.
absolutist ['æbsəluːtist], *a.*, *n.* absolutista, *m.f.*
absolve [əb'zɔlv], *v.t.* absolver.
absorb [əb'zɔːb], *v.t.* absorber.
absorbed [əb'zɔːbd], *a.* absorto.
absorbent [əb'zɔːbənt], *a.* absorbente.
absorbing [əb'zɔːbin], *a.* absorbente (*interesante*).
absorption [əb'zɔːpʃən], *n.* absorción, *f.*
abstain [æb'stein], *v.i.* abstenerse (*from*, de).
abstainer [æb'steinə], *n.* abstinente.
abstemious [æb'stiːmiəs], *a.* abstemio.
abstention [æb'stenʃən], *n.* abstención, *f.*
abstinence ['æbstinəns], *n.* abstinencia.
abstinent ['æbstinənt], *a.* abstinente.

abstract ['æbstrækt], *a.*, *n.* abstracto.— [æb'strækt], *v.t.* abstraer.
abstraction [æb'strækʃen], *n.* abstracción, *f.*
abstruse [æb'stru:s], *a.* abstruso.
absurd [əb'sə:d], *a.* absurdo.
absurdity [əb'sə:diti], *n.* absurdo; absurdidad, *f.*
abundance [ə'bʌndəns], *n.* abundancia.
abundant [ə'bʌndənt], *a.* abundante.
abuse [ə'bju:s], *n.* abuso; injuria; maltrato.— [ə'bju:z], *v.t.* abusar de; injuriar; maltratar.
abusive [ə'bju:siv], *a.* abusivo; injurioso.
abut [ə'bʌt], *v.t.* lindar con.
abysm [ə'bizm] [ABYSS].
abysmal [ə'bizməl], *a.* abismal.
abyss [ə'bis], *n.* abismo.
acacia [ə'keiʃə], *n.* acacia.
academic [ækə'demik], *a.*, *n.* académico.
academician [əkædə'miʃən], *n.* académico.
academy [ə'kædəmi], *n.* academia.
accede [æk'si:d], *v.i.* acceder.
accelerate [æk'seləreit], *v.t.* acelerar.—*v.i.* -se.
acceleration [ækselə'reiʃən], *n.* aceleración, *f.*
accelerator [ak'seləreitə], *n.* acelerador, *m.*
accent ['æksənt], *n.* acento.—[æk'sent], *v.t.* acentuar.
accentuate [æk'sentjueit], *v.t.* acentuar; recalcar.
accept [ək'sept], *v.t.* aceptar.
acceptable [ək'septəbl], *a.* aceptable.
acceptance [ək'septəns], *n.* aceptación, *f.*
acceptation [æksep'teiʃən], *n.* acepción; aceptación, *f.*
access ['ækses], *n.* acceso.
accessible [ək'sesibl], *a.* accesible.
accession [æk'seʃən], *n.* accesión, *f.*; advenimiento; ascenso; adición, *f.*
accessory [æk'sesəri], *a.*, *n.* accesorio.—*n.* (*jur.*) instigador; encubridor, *m.*
accident ['æksidənt], *n.* accidente, *m.*
accidental [æksi'dentəl], *a.* accidental.
acclaim [ə'kleim], *n.* aclamación, *f.*—*v.t.* aclamar, ovacionar.
acclamation [æklə'meiʃən], *n.* aclamación, *f.*
acclimatize [ə'klaimətaiz] (*U.S.* **acclimate** ['æklimeit]), *v.t.* aclimatar.
accolade ['ækəleid], *n.* acolada.
accommodate [ə'kɔmədeit], *v.t.* acomodar; alojar.
accommodating [ə'kɔmədeitiŋ], *a.* acomodadizo; acomodaticio.
accommodation [əkɔmə'deiʃən], *n.* alojamiento; acomodamiento; vivienda.
accompaniment [ə'kʌmpnimənt], *n.* acompañamiento.
accompanist [ə'kʌmpənist], *n.* acompañante, *m.f.*
accompany [ə'kʌmpəni], *v.t.* acompañar.
accomplice [ə'kʌmplis], *n.* cómplice, *m.f.*
accomplish [ə'kʌmpliʃ], *v.t.* realizar, cumplir.
accomplished [ə'kʌmpliʃt], · *a.* consumado, acabado; culto.
accomplishment [ə'kʌmpliʃmənt], *n.* consumación, *f.*; talento, prenda.
accord [ə'kɔ:d], *n.* acuerdo; armonía; convenio; *of his own* —, de su querer.—*v.t.* acordar; otorgar.—*v.i.* avenirse.
accordance [ə'kɔ:dəns], *n.* conformidad, *f.*; *in* — *with*, de acuerdo con, con arreglo a.
according [ə'kɔ:diŋ], *adv.* según (*to*).

accordingly [ə'kɔ:diŋli], *adv.* en conformidad; en consecuencia.
accordion [ə'kɔ:djən], *n.* acordeón, *m.*
accost [ə'kɔst], *v.t.* abordar.
account [ə'kaunt] *n.* cuenta; monta, importancia; informe, *m.*, narración, *f.*; *on* — *of*, a causa de, por motivo de; *on no* —, de ninguna manera; *on* —, a cuenta. —*v.t.* tener por, juzgar; *to take into* —, tomar en cuenta; *to turn to* (*good*) —, sacar provecho de.—*v.i.* dar razón de, explicar (*for*).
accountable [ə'kauntəbl], *a.* responsable; explicable.
accountancy [ə'kauntənsi], *n.* contabilidad, *f.*
accountant [ə'kauntənt], *n.* contador, *m.*
accoutre [ə'ku:tə], *v.t.* equipar, aviar.
accoutrements [ə'ku:trəmənts], *n.pl.* equipo, pertrechos, *m.pl.*
accredit [ə'kredit], *v.t.* acreditar.
accretion [ə'kri:ʃən], *n.* acrecimiento; acreción, *f.*
accrue [ə'kru:], *v.i.* resultar; aumentar.
accumulate [ə'kju:mjuleit], *v.t.* acumular.—*v.i.* -se.
accumulation [əkju:mju'leiʃən], *n.* acumulación, *f.*
accumulator [ə'kju:mjuleitə], *n.* (*elec.*) acumulador, *m.*
accuracy ['ækjurəsi], *n.* exactitud, corrección, *f.*
accurate ['ækjurit], *a.* exacto, puntual, fiel.
accursed [ə'kə:sid], *a.* maldito, malvado.
accusation [ækju'zeiʃən], *n.* acusación, *f.*
accusative [ə'kju:zətiv], *a.*, *n.* acusativo.
accuse [ə'kju:z], *v.t.* acusar, denunciar.
accused [ə'kju:zd], *n.* acusado, procesado.
accuser [ə'kju:zə], *n.* acusador.
accustom [ə'kʌstəm], *v.t.* acostumbrar, avezar.
accustomed [ə'kʌstəmd], *a.* acostumbrado.
ace [eis], *n.* as, *m.*; *within an* — *of*, a dos dedos de.
acetic [ə'si:tik], *a.* acético.
acetone ['æsitoun], *n.* acetona.
acetylene [ə'setili:n], *n.* acetileno.
ache [eik], *n.* tʃi:v], *v.t.* doler.
achieve [ə'tʃi:v], *v.t.* alcanzar, lograr, obtener.
achievement [ə'tʃi:vmənt], *n.* logro, realización, *f.*; proeza.
Achilles [ə'kili:z], *n.* Aquiles, *m.*
aching ['eikiŋ], *a.* dolorido, doliente.—*n.* pena, dolor, *m.*
acid ['æsid], *a.*, *n.* ácido.
acidity [ə'siditi], *n.* acidez, *f.*
ack-ack [æk'æk], *n.* (*mil.*) artillería antiaérea.
acknowledge [ək'nɔlidʒ], *v.t.* reconocer; acusar (*recibimiento*).
acknowledg(e)ment [ək'nɔlidʒmənt], *n.* reconocimiento; acuse, *m.*
acme ['ækmi], *n.* cumbre, *f.*; (*med.*) acmé, *f.*
acolyte ['ækəlait], *n.* monaguillo, acólito.
aconite ['ækənait], *n.* acónito.
acorn ['eikɔ:n], *n.* bellota.
acoustic [ə'ku:stik], *a.* acústico.—*n.pl.* acústica.
acquaint [ə'kweint], *v.t.* familiarizar; poner al corriente (*with*, de); *to be(come)* *acquainted with*, conocer; ponerse al corriente de.

acquaintance [ə'kweintəns], n. conocimiento; conocido.
acquaintanceship [ə'kweintənsʃip], n. conocimiento, relaciones, f.pl., trato.
acquiesce [ækwi'es], v.i. consentir, tolerar (in).
acquiescence [ækwi'esəns], n. consentimiento, transigencia.
acquire [ə'kwaiə], v.t. adquirir.
acquirement [ə'kwaiəmənt], n. adquisición, f.—pl. dotes, m.pl., prendas, f.pl.
acquisition [ækwi'ziʃən], n. adquisición, f.
acquisitive [ə'kwizitiv], a. adquisidor, codicioso.
acquit [ə'kwit], v.t. absolver.—v.r. conducirse.
acquittal [ə'kwitəl], n. absolución, f.
acre ['eikə], n. acre, m.
acreage ['eikəridʒ], n. área.
acrid ['ækrid], a. acre, picante.
acrimonious [ækri'mounjəs], a. acrimonioso.
acrimony ['ækriməni], n. acrimonia.
acrobat ['ækrəbæt], n. acróbata, m.f., volatinero.
acrobatic [ækrə'bætik], a. acrobático.—n.pl. acrobacia.
acropolis [ə'krɔpəlis], n. acrópolis, f.
across [ə'krɔs], adv. a través; al otro lado.—prep. a(l) través de; al otro lado de.
acrostic [ə'krɔstik], a., n. acróstico.
act [ækt], n. acto, obra; acción, f.; in the —, en flagrante; (jur.) ley, f.; (theat.) acto, jornada.—v.t. (theat.) representar; desempeñar (un papel); aparentar, simular.—v.i. tener efecto; actuar; fingir; comportarse.
acting ['æktiŋ], a. interino; teatral.—n. histrionismo, arte histriónico; representación, f.
action ['ækʃən], n. acción, f.; expediente, m.
actionable ['ækʃənəbl], a. (jur.) procesable.
active ['æktiv], a. activo.
activity [æk'tiviti], n. actividad, f.
actor ['æktə], n. actor, m.
actress ['æktris], n. actriz, f.
actual ['æktjuəl], a. efectivo, real; actual.
actuality [æktju'æliti], n. realidad; actualidad, f.
actually ['æktjuəli], adv. verdaderamente, en efecto.
actuary ['æktjuəri], n. actuario.
actuate ['æktjueit], v.t. poner en acción; impulsar.
acumen [ə'kju:men], n. agudeza.
acute [ə'kju:t], a. agudo.
acuteness [ə'kju:tnis], n. agudeza.
adage ['ædidʒ], n. adagio.
Adam ['ædəm], n. Adán, m.; **Adam's apple**, nuez (f.) de la garganta.
adamant ['ædəmənt], a. muy duro; inexorable.
adapt [ə'dæpt], v.t. adaptar, ajustar; (lit.) refundir.
adaptable [ə'dæptəbl], a. adaptable.
adaptation [ædæp'teiʃən], n. adaptación, f.; (lit.) arreglo, refundición, f.
add [æd], v.t. añadir; sumar, adicionar.—v.i. sumar.
addendum [ə'dendəm], n. (pl. -da) addenda, m., adición, f.
adder ['ædə], n. víbora.
addict ['ædikt], n. (en)viciado; adicto;

morfinómano. — [ə'dikt], v.t. enviciar; entregar.
addiction [ə'dikʃən], n. enviciamiento; abandono.
addition [ə'diʃən], n. adición, f.; suma; in — (to), además (de).
additional [ə'diʃənəl], a. adicional.
addle [ædl], v.t. enhuerar.
addled [ædld], a. huero.
addle-headed ['ædl'hedid], **addle-brained** ['ædl'breind], a. cabeza de chorlito.
address [ə'dres], n. dirección, f., señas, f.pl.; alocución; destreza; atención, f.—v.t. dirigirse a; dirigir (carta).
addressee [ædre'si:], n. destinatario.
adduce [ə'dju:s], v.t. aducir.
adept ['ædept], a., n. perito; adepto.
adequate ['ædikwit], a. suficiente; adecuado.
adhere [əd'hiə], v.i. adherir(se).
adherent [əd'hiərənt], a., n. adherente, m.f.
adhesion [əd'hi:ʒən], n. adhesión, f.; adherencia.
adhesive [əd'hi:siv], a., n. adhesivo.
adieu [ə'dju:], n. interj. (lit.) adiós, m.
adjacent [ə'dʒeisənt], a. contiguo, adyacente.
adjectival [ædʒik'taivəl], a. adjetival.
adjective ['ædʒiktiv], n. adjetivo.
adjoin [ə'dʒɔin], v.t. lindar con.
adjoining [ə'dʒɔiniŋ], a. colindante; contiguo.
adjourn [ə'dʒə:n], v.t. prorrogar.—v.i. -se.
adjournment [ə'dʒə:nmənt], n. suspensión, f., prórroga.
adjudicate [ə'dʒu:dikeit], v.t., v.i. juzgar.
adjunct ['ædʒʌŋkt], a., n. adjunto.
adjure [ə'dʒuə], v.t. juramentar; conjurar.
adjust [ə'dʒʌst], v.t. ajustar; tasar; verificar.
adjustable [ə'dʒʌstəbl], a. ajustable.
adjustment [ə'dʒʌstmənt], n. ajuste, m.; arreglo.
adjutant ['ædʒutənt], n. ayudante, m.f.
ad lib [æd'lib], v.t., v.i. (fam.) repentizar.
administer [əd'ministə], v.t. administrar.
administration [ədminis'treiʃən], n. administración, dirección, f.
administrator [əd'ministreitə], n. administrador, m.
admirable ['ædmərəbl], a. admirable.
admiral ['ædmərəl], n. almirante, m.
Admiralty ['ædmərəlti], n., Ministerio de la Marina; **admiralty**, n. almirantazgo.
admiration [ædmə'reiʃən], n. admiración, f.
admire [əd'maiə], v.t. admirar.
admirer [əd'maiərə], n. admirador, m.
admiring [əd'maiəriŋ], a. admirativo.
admissible [əd'misibl], a. admisible.
admission [əd'miʃən], n. admisión; recepción, f.; entrada; confesión, f.
admit [əd'mit], v.t. admitir; confesar.
admittance [əd'mitəns], n. admisión, f.; entrada; no —, se prohíbe entrar.
admixture [əd'mikstʃə], n. adición, f.
admonish [əd'mɔniʃ], v.t. amonestar, prevenir.
admonition [ædmə'niʃən], n. admonición, f.
ado [ə'du:], n. bullicio; **without more —**, sin más ni más.
adobe [ə'doubi], n. adobe, m.
adolescence [ædə'lesəns], n. adolescencia.
adolescent [ædə'lesənt], a., n. adolescente m.f.

219

adopt [ə'dɔpt], *v.t.* adoptar; prohijar.
adoption [ə'dɔpʃən], *n.* adopción, *f.*
adoptive [ə'dɔptiv], *a.* adoptivo.
adorable [ə'dɔːrəbl], *a.* adorable.
adoration [ædɔː'reiʃən], *n.* adoración, *f.*
adore [ə'dɔː], *v.t.* adorar.
adorn [ə'dɔːn], *v.t.* adornar.
adornment [ə'dɔːnmənt], *n.* adorno, gala.
Adriatic [eidri'ætik], *a.*, *n.* Adriático.
adrift [ə'drift], *adv.* a la deriva.
adroit [ə'drɔit], *a.* diestro.
adroitness [ə'drɔitnis], *n.* destreza.
adulation [ædju'leiʃən], *n.* adulación, *f.*
adult [ə'dʌlt], *a.*, *n.* adulto.
adulterate [ə'dʌltəreit], *v.t.* adulterar.
adulteration [ədʌltə'reiʃən],*n.* adulteración,*f.*
adulterer [ə'dʌltərə], *n.* adúltero.
adulteress [ə'dʌltəris], *n.* adúltera.
adulterous [ə'dʌltərəs], *a.* adúltero.
adumbrate ['ædʌmbreit], *v.t.* esbozar; presagiar, indicar.
advance [əd'vɑːns], *n.* adelanto, avance, *m.*; progreso; — *payment*, anticipo; *in* —, delante; de antemano; por adelantado.— *pl.* requerimientos, *m.pl.*—*v.t.* adelantar; avanzar.—*v.i.* adelantar(se).
advancement [əd'vɑːnsmənt], *n.* progreso; ascenso; anticipo.
advantage [əd'vɑːntidʒ], *n.* ventaja; *to take* — *of*, aprovecharse de.—*v.t.* (*obs.*) aventajar.
advantageous [ædvən'teidʒəs], *a.* ventajoso.
Advent ['ædvənt], *n.* (*eccl.*) Adviento; **advent**, *n.* advenimiento.
adventitious [ædvən'tiʃəs], *a.* adventicio.
adventure [əd'ventʃə], *n.* aventura.—*v.t.* aventurar.—*v.i.* -se.
adventurer [əd'ventʃərə], *n.* aventurero.
adventuress [əd'ventʃəris], *n.* aventurera.
adventurous [əd'ventʃərəs], *a.* aventurero, atrevido.
adverb ['ædvəːb], *n.* adverbio.
adverbial [əd'vəːbjəl], *a.* adverbial.
adversary ['ædvəsəri], *n.* adversario.
adverse ['ædvəːs], *a.* adverso.
adversity [əd'vəːsiti], *n.* adversidad, *f.*
advert ['ædvəːt], *n.* (*fam.*) anuncio.
advertise ['ædvətaiz], *v.t.* anunciar; pregonar.
advertisement [əd'vəːtizmənt], *n.* anuncio, reclamo.
advertiser ['ædvətaizə], *n.* anunciador, *m.*, anunciante, *m.f.*; diario publicitario.
advertising ['ædvətaiziŋ], *a.* publicitario.— *n.* publicidad, *f.*; anuncios, *m.pl.*
advice [əd'vais], *n.* consejo; aviso.
advisable [əd'vaizəbl], *a.* conveniente, aconsejable.
advise [əd'vaiz], *v.t.* aconsejar; avisar.
advisedly [əd'vaizidli], *adv.* con intención.
adviser, advisor [əd'vaizə], *n.* consejero.
advisory [əd'vaizəri], *a.* consultativo.
advocate ['ædvəkit], *n.* abogado; defensor, *m.* ['ædvəkeit], *v.t.* abogar por.
adze [ædz], *n.* azuela.
Aegean [iː'dʒiːən], *a.* egeo.—*n.* Mar Egeo.
aerate ['ɛəreit], *v.t.* airear; hacer efervescente.
aerial ['ɛəriəl], *a.* aéreo.—*n.* antena.
aerie, aery ['ɛəri, 'iəri], *n.* aguilera.
aerodrome ['ɛərədroum], *n.* aeródromo.
aerodynamic [ɛəroudai'næmik], *a.* aerodinámico.—*n.pl.* aerodinámica.

aeronaut ['ɛərənɔːt], *n.* aeronauta, *m.f.*
aeronautic [ɛərə'nɔːtik], *a.* aeronáutico.— *n.pl.* aeronáutica.
aeronautical [ɛərə'nɔːtikəl], *a.* aeronáutico.
aeroplane ['ɛərəplein], *n.* avión, *m.*; aeroplano.
aesthete ['iːsθiːt], *n.* esteta, *m.f.*
aesthetic [iːs'θetik], *a.* estético.—*n.pl.* estética.
afar [ə'fɑː], *adv.* lejos; *from* —, desde lejos.
affable ['æfəbl], *a.* afable.
affair [ə'fɛə], *n.* negocio, asunto; lance, *m.*; cuestión, *f.*, amorío.
affect [ə'fekt], *v.t.* influir en; afectar; fingir; impresionar.
affectation [æfek'teiʃən], *n.* afectación, *f.*
affected [ə'fektid], *a.* afectado.
affection [ə'fekʃən], *n.* cariño; (*med.*) afección, *f.*
affectionate [ə'fekʃənit], *a.* afectuoso, cariñoso.
affidavit [æfi'deivit], *n.* (*jur.*) declaración jurada.
affiliate [ə'filieit], *v.t.* afiliar.—*v.i.* -se (*with*, a).
affiliation [əfili'eiʃən], *n.* afiliación, *f.*
affinity [ə'finiti], *n.* afinidad, *f.*
affirm [ə'fəːm], *v.t.* afirmar.
affirmation [æfə'meiʃən], *n.* afirmación, *f.*
affirmative [ə'fəːmətiv], *a.* afirmativo.—*n.* afirmativa.
affix [ə'fiks], *v.t.* añadir, poner.
afflict [ə'flikt], *v.t.* afligir.
affliction [ə'flikʃən], *n.* aflicción, *f.*
affluence ['æfluəns], *n.* afluencia.
affluent ['æfluənt], *a.* afluente; opulento (*rico*).
afford [ə'fɔːd], *v.t.* proporcionar; *to be able to* —, poder comprar; tener los medios para; tener con que . . .
afforest [ə'fɔrist], *v.t.* plantar, repoblar.
afforestation [æfɔris'teiʃən], *n.* aforestación, *f.*
affray [ə'frei], *n.* refriega.
affront [ə'frʌnt], *n.* afrenta.—*v.t.* denostar, afrentar.
Afghan ['æfgæn], *a.*, *n.* afgano.
Afghanistan [æf'gænistæn], *n.* el Afganistán.
afield [ə'fiːld], *adv.* fuera; *far* —, muy lejos.
afire [ə'faiə], *adv.* ardiendo.
aflame [ə'fleim], *adv.* en llamas.
afloat [ə'flout], *adv.* a flote; corriente.
afoot [ə'fut], *adv.* a pie; en movimiento; *what's* — ? ¿ qué pasa ?
aforesaid [ə'fɔːsed], *a.* ya citado, dicho.
aforethought [ə'fɔːθɔːt], *a. with malice* —, con premeditación.
afraid [ə'freid], *a.* medroso, espantado; *to be* —, tener miedo (*of, to,* a, de).
afresh [ə'freʃ], *adv.* de nuevo.
Africa ['æfrikə], *n.* África.
African ['æfrikən], *a.*, *n.* africano.
aft [ɑːft], *adv.* (*naut.*) a en popa.
after ['ɑːftə], *a.* posterior; *the day* —, el día siguiente; *to be* —, buscar, ir en busca de.—*adv.* después.—*prep.* después de; según; en pos de.—*conj.* después (de) que.
after-birth [ɑ:ftəbə:θ], *n.* secundinas.
after-care ['ɑːftəkɛə], *n.* cura postoperatoria.
after-dinner ['ɑːftədinə], *a.* de sobremesa.
after-effect ['ɑːftəifekt], *n.* efecto posterior.

afterglow [ɑ:ftəglou], *n.* resplendor crepuscular, *m.*

after-hours [ɑ:ftərauəz], *n.* horas extraordinarias.—*adv.* después de las horas ordinarias.

after-life [ɑ:ftəlaif], *n.* resto de la vida; trasmundo.

aftermath [ɑ:ftəmæθ], *n.* secuela, consecuencia.

aftermost [ɑ:ftəmoust], *a.* último; trasero.

afternoon [ɑ:ftə'nu:n], *n.* tarde, *f.*

after-taste [ɑ:ftəteist], *n.* resabio, gustillo.

afterthought [ɑ:ftəθɔ:t], *n.* idea tardía; idea posterior.

afterwards [ɑ:ftəwədz], *adv.* después, más tarde.

after-world [ɑ:ftəwə:ld], *n.* ultramundo.

again [ə'gein], *adv.* de nuevo, otra vez; además; **now and —**, de vez en cuando; **to do —**, volver a hacer.

against [ə'genst], *prep.* contra; cerca de; tocante.

agape [ə'geip], *a.*, *adv.* con la boca abierta, boquiabierto.

agate [ægət], *n.* ágata.

agave [ægeiv], *n.* (*bot.*) pita.

age [eidʒ], *n.* edad; época; vejez, *f.*; (*fam.*) eternidad, *f.*; **of —**, mayor de edad; **under —**, menor de edad.—*pl.* (*fam.*) horas y horas; siglos.—*v.t.* envejecer; madurar.—*v.i.* envejecer(se).

aged [eidʒd], *a.* de la edad de; [eidʒid] anciano, viejo, envejecido.

ageless [eidʒlis], *a.* siempre joven.

agency [eidʒənsi], *n.* agencia; oficio, acción, *f.*

agenda [ə'dʒendə], *n.* agenda.

agent [eidʒənt], *n.* agente; representante, *m.*

agglomeration [əgləmə'reiʃən], *n.* aglomeración, *f.*

aggrandizement [ə'grændizmənt], *n.* engrandecimiento.

aggravate [ægrəveit], *v.t.* agravar; (*fam.*) enfadar.

aggravation [ægrə'veiʃən], *n.* agravamiento; (*fam.*) vejación, *f.*

aggregate [ægrigit], *a.*, *n.* agregado.— [ægrigeit], *v.t.* agregar, juntar.

aggression [ə'greʃən], *n.* agresión, *f.*

aggressive [ə'gresiv], *a.* agresivo.

aggressor [ə'gresə], *n.* agresor.

aggrieve [ə'gri:v], *v.t.* acongojar, vejar; ofender.

aghast [ə'gɑ:st], *a.* despavorido.

agile [ædʒail], *a.* ágil, ligero.

agility [ə'dʒiliti], *n.* agilidad, *f.*

agitate [ædʒiteit], *v.t.*, *v.i.* agitar.

agitation [ædʒi'teiʃən], *n.*agitación, *f.*

agitator [ædʒiteitə], *n.* agitador; provocador, *m.*

aglow [ə'glou], *a.* encendido.

agnostic [æg'nɔstik], *a.*, *n.* agnóstico.

ago [ə'gou], *adv.* hace, ha; **two days —**, hace dos días; **long —**, hace mucho.

agog [ə'gɔg], *a.*, *adv.* ansioso; curioso.

agonize [ægənaiz], *v.t.* atormentar, martirizar.—*v.i.* agonizar.

agony [ægəni], *n.* agonía; angustia.

agrarian [ə'grɛəriən], *a.* agrario.

agree [ə'gri:], *v.i.* estar de acuerdo; quedar(se) en; concordar; convenir (**to**, en).

agreeable [ə'gri:əbl], *a.* agradable; dispuesto, conforme.

agreement [ə'gri:mənt], *n.* acuerdo; concordancia.

agricultural [ægri'kʌltʃərəl], *a.* agrícola.

agriculture [ægrikʌltʃə], *n.* agricultura.

aground [ə'graund], *a.*, *adv.* encallado; **to run —**, encallar.

ague [eigju:], *n.* escalofrío; fiebre.

ahead [ə'hed], *adv.* delante, al frente; por delante; **— of**, antes de; **to get —**, adelantarse.

ahem! [hm], *interj.* ¡eh! ¡pues!

ahoy! [ə'hɔi], *interj.* (*naut.*) **ship —!** ¡ah del barco! **— there !** ¡huloa!

aid [eid], *n.* auxilio, ayuda.—*v.t.* ayudar.

aide (-de-camp) [eid(də'kã)], *n.* (*mil.*) ayudante de campo, edecán, *m.*

ail [eil], *v.t.* doler, afligir.—*v.i.* enfermar, sufrir.

aileron [eilərɔn], *n.* alerón, *m.*

ailing [eilin], *a.* enfermizo, doliente.

ailment [eilmənt], *n.* achaque, *m.*; dolencia.

aim [eim], *n.* hito, blanco; mira; puntería.— *v.t.*, *v.i.* apuntar; **to — to**, tratar de, mirar a.

aimless [eimlis], *a.* sin objeto, a la ventura.

ain't [eint], (*dial.*, *low*) [AM NOT; IS NOT; ARE NOT].

air [ɛə], *n.* aire, *m.*; (*fig.*) radio, *f.*—*v.t.* ventilar; **— force**, fuerza aérea, ejército del aire; **— liner**, transaéreo; **— mail**, correo aéreo. correo por avión.

air- [ɛə], *prefix.* aéreo.

airborne [ɛəbɔ:n], *a.* aéreo, por aire.—*adv.* en vuelo.

air-conditioning [ɛəkən'diʃənin], *n.* aire acondicionado.

aircraft [ɛəkrɑ:ft], *n.* avión, *m.*

aircraft-carrier [ɛəkrɑ:ft'kæriə], *n.* portaviones, *m.sg.*

airfield [ɛəfi:ld], *n.* campo de aviación.

air-gun [ɛəgʌn], *n.* escopeta de aire comprimido.

air-hostess [ɛəhoustes], *n.* azafata.

airing [ɛərin], *n.* ventilación, *f.*; oreo; paseata.

air-lane [ɛəlein], *n.* ruta aérea.

air-lift [ɛəlift], *n.* puente aéreo.

airman [ɛəmən], *n.* aviador, *m.*; soldado aéreo.

airplane [ɛəplein], (*U.S.*) [AEROPLANE].

air-pocket [ɛəpɔkit], *n.* bache aéreo.

airport [ɛəpɔ:t], *n.* aeropuerto.

air-raid [ɛəreid], *n.* bombardeo aéreo; **— shelter**, refugio antiaéreo.

airship [ɛəʃip], *n.* aeronave, *f.*

airstrip [ɛəstrip], *n.* pista de aterrizaje.

airtight [ɛətait], *a.* hermético, herméticamente cerrado.

airworthy [ɛəwə:ði], *a.* en condiciones de vuelo.

airy [ɛəri], *a.* airoso; alegre.

aisle [ail], *n.* pasillo.

aitch [eitʃ], *n.* H, hache, *f.*

ajar [ə'dʒɑ:], *a.*, *adv.* entornado, entreabierto.

akimbo [ə'kimbou], *a.*, *adv.* **arms —**, en jarras.

akin [ə'kin], *a.* semejante; emparentado.

alabaster [æləbɑ:stə], *a.* alabastrino.—*n.* alabastro.

alacrity [ə'lækriti], *n.* alacridad, *f.*

alarm [ə'lɑ:m], *n.* alarma; rebato.—*v.t.* alarmar.

alarm-clock

alarm-clock [ə'lɑ:mklɔk], *n.* despertador, *m.*
alarming [ə'lɑ:miŋ], *a.* alarmante.
alas! [ə'læs], *interj.* ¡ay! ¡guay!
alb [ælb], *n. (eccl.)* alba.
Albanian [æl'beinjən], *a., n.* albanés, *m.*
albatross ['ælbətrɔs], *n.* albatros, *m.*
albeit [ɔ:l'bi:it], *conj. (lit.)* bien que, aunque.
albino [æl'bi:nou], *a., n. (pl. -nos)* albino.
Albion ['ælbjən], *n.* Albión, *f.*
album ['ælbəm], *n.* álbum, *m.*
albumen [æl'bju:min], *n.* albúmina; albumen, *m.*
alchemist ['ælkimist], *n.* alquimista.
alchemy ['ælkimi], *n.* alquimia.
alcohol ['ælkəhɔl], *n.* alcohol, *m.*
alcoholic [ælkə'hɔlik], *a., n.* alcohólico, alcoholizado.
alcove ['ælkouv], *n.* nicho, hueco.
alder ['ɔ:ldə], *n. (bot.)* aliso.
alderman ['ɔ:ldəmən], *n.* concejal, *m.*
ale [eil], *n.* cerveza.
alert [ə'lə:t], *a.* vigilante, listo, vivo.—*n.* alerta, *m.*; **on the —,** alerta, sobre aviso.—*v.t.* alertar.
Alexander [ælig'zɑ:ndə], *n.* Alejandro.
alga ['ælgə], *n. (pl. algae) (bot.)* alga.
algebra ['ældʒibrə], *n.* álgebra.
Algeria [æl'dʒiəriə], *n.* Argelia.
Algerian [æl'dʒiəriən], *a., n.* argelino.
Algiers [æl'dʒiəz], *n.* Argel, *f.*
alias ['eiliəs], *adv., n.* alias, *m.*
alibi ['ælibai], *n.* coartada.
alien ['eiljən], *a.* ajeno, extraño.—*n.* extranjero.
alienate ['eiljəneit], *v.t.* enajenar; malquistar.
alight (1) [ə'lait], *a.* encendido, en llamas.
alight (2) [ə'lait], *v.i.* bajar, apearse; posarse.
align [ə'lain], *v.t.* alinear.
alignment [ə'lainmənt], *n.* alineación, *m.*
alike [ə'laik], *a.* igual, parecido.—*adv.* igualmente, lo mismo.
alimentary [æli'mentəri], *a.* alimenticio.
alimony ['æliməni], *n.* alimentos, *m.pl.*
aline [ALIGN].
alive [ə'laiv], *a.* vivo, con vida; activo; sensible (*to, a*); hormigueante (*with,* en).
alkali ['ælkəlai], *n. (pl. -lis, -lies)* álcali, *m.*
alkaline ['ælkəlain], *a.* alcalino.
all [ɔ:l], *pron.* todo, todos, todo el mundo.—*a., adv.* todo; *at —,* de algún modo; *not at —,* de ningún modo; de nada; — *along,* todo el tiempo; — *but,* casi; — *the better,* tanto mejor; — *in,* todo incluído; *(fam.)* hecho polvo; — *off, (fam.)* abandonado; — *over,* acabado; general; — *right,* está bien; regular; — *told,* en total; — *too,* ya demasiado.
Allah ['ælɑ:], *n.* Alá, *m.*
allay [ə'lei], *v.t.* aliviar, calmar.
allegation [æle'geiʃən], *n.* alegación, *f.,* alegato.
allege [ə'ledʒ], *v.t.* alegar.
allegiance [ə'li:dʒəns], *n.* fidelidad, lealtad, *f.*
allegoric(al) [æli'gɔrik(əl)], *a.* alegórico.
allegory ['æligəri], *n.* alegoria.
alleluia [æli'lu:jə], *n., interj.* aleluya.
allergic [ə'lə:dʒik], *a.* alérgico.
allergy ['ælədʒi], *n.* alergia.
alleviate [ə'li:vieit], *v.t.* aliviar.
alley ['æli], *n.* callejuela; pasadizo.
alley-way ['æliwei], *n.* pasadizo.

All Fools' Day [ɔ:l'fu:lzdei], *n.* dia (*m.*) de inocentadas (1 *de abril*).
alliance [ə'laiəns], *n.* alianza.
allied ['ælaid], *a.* afín; aliado.
alligator ['æligeitə], *n.* caimán, *m.*
all-in wrestling ['ɔ:lin'resliŋ], *n.* lucha libre.
alliteration [əlitə'reiʃən], *n.* aliteración, *f.*
allocate ['æləkeit], *v.t.* asignar.
allocation [ælə'keiʃən], *n.* asignación, *f.* cuota.
allot [ə'lɔt], *v.t.* asignar.
allotment [ə'lɔtmənt], *n.* asignación, *f.*; lote, *m.*; porción, *f.*; huerto alquilado.
allow [ə'lau], *v.t.* permitir; admitir, conceder. —*v.i. (for)* tener en cuenta.
allowable [ə'lauəbl], *a.* admisible, permisible.
allowance [ə'lauəns], *n.* permiso; ración; rebaja; pensión, *f.*; tolerancia.
alloy ['ælɔi], *n.* liga, aleación, *f.*—[ə'lɔi], *v.t.* ligar, alear; adulterar.
all-powerful ['ɔ:lpauəful], *a.* todopoderoso.
all-round ['ɔ:lraund], *a.* hábil para todo, universal.
allude [ə'l(j)u:d], *v.i.* aludir.
allure [ə'ljuə], *v.t.* halagar, fascinar.
allurement [ə'ljuəmənt], *n.* fascinación, *f.*; halago.
alluring [ə'ljuəriŋ], *a.* seductor, fascinante.
allusion [ə'l(j)u:ʒən], *n.* alusión, *f.*
alluvium [ə'lu:viəm], *n. (pl. -via)* aluvión, *f.*
ally ['ælai], *n.* aliado.—[ə'lai], *v.t.* aliar.—*v.r.* -se.
almanac(k) ['ɔ:lmənæk], *n.* almanaque, *m.*
Almighty [ɔ:l'maiti], *n.* Todopoderoso; **almighty,** *a.* todopoderoso; *(fam.)* tremendo, gordo, grave.
almond ['ɑ:mənd], *n.* almendra.
almond-tree ['ɑ:mənd'tri:], *n.* almendro.
almoner ['ɑ:mənə], *n.* limosnero.
almost ['ɔ:lmoust], *adv.* casi.
alms [ɑ:mz], *n.inv.* limosna.
almshouse [ɑ:mzhaus], *n.* hospicio, asilo de pobres.
aloe ['ælou], *n. (bot.)* áloe(s), *m.*; — *pl.* acíbar, *m.*
aloft [ə'lɔft], *adv.* en alto.
alone [ə'loun], *a.* solo; *let —,* sin contar.— *adv.* solamente; *to let o leave —,* no tocar, no molestar.
along [ə'lɔŋ], *adv.* a lo largo; junto (*with,* con); adelante.—*prep.* a lo largo de; *to get —,* medrar; quedar bien.
alongside [ələŋ'said], *adv. (naut.)* al costado, bordo con bordo.—*prep.* al costado de.
aloof [ə'lu:f], *a.* apartado; frío.
aloud [ə'laud], *adv.* en voz alta.
alphabet ['ælfəbet], *n.* alfabeto.
alphabetic(al) ['ælfə'betik(əl)], *a.* alfabético.
alpine ['ælpain], *a.* alpino; alpestre.
Alps [ælps], *n.pl.* Alpes, *m.pl.*
already [ɔ:l'redi], *adv.* ya.
also ['ɔ:lsou], *adv.* también.
altar ['ɔ:ltə], *n.* altar, *m.*; ara.
altar-boy ['ɔ:ltəbɔi], *n.* monaguillo.
altar-piece ['ɔ:ltəpi:s], *n.* retablo.
alter ['ɔ:ltə], *v.t.* alterar; cambiar.—*v.i.* -se.
alteration [ɔ:itə'reiʃən], *n.* cambio, alteración, *f.*
altercation [ɔ:ltə'keiʃən], *n.* altercación, *f.* altercado.

222

alternate [ɔ:l'tə:nit], *a.* alterno.—['ɔ:ltəneit], *v.t., v.i.* alternar.
alternation [ɔ:ltə:'neiʃən], *n.* alternación, *f.*; alternancia.
alternative [ɔ:l'tə:nətiv], *a.* alternativo.—*n.* alternativa.
although [ɔ:l'ðou], *conj.* aunque.
altimeter ['æltimi:tə], *n.* altímetro.
altitude ['æltitju:d], *n.* altitud, *f.*, altura.
altogether [ɔ:ltə'geðə], *adv.* en conjunto; del todo, totalmente; todos juntos.
altruist ['æltruist], *n.* altruista, *m.f.*
alum ['æləm], *n.* alumbre, *m.*
aluminium [ælju'minjəm], *n.* (*U.S.* **aluminum**) aluminio.
always ['ɔ:lweiz], *adv.* siempre.
am [æm] [BE].
amalgam [ə'mælgəm], *n.* amalgama.
amalgamate [ə'mælgəmeit], *v.t.* amalgamar.—*v.i.* -se.
amanuensis [əmænju'ensis], *n.* (*pl.*-**ses**) amanuense, *m.f.*
amass [ə'mæs], *v.t.* acumular.
amateur ['æmətə], *a., n.* aficionado; chapucero.
amatory ['æmətəri], *a.* amatorio.
amaze [ə'meiz], *v.t.* pasmar, asombrar; *to be amazed,* asombrarse (*at, by,* de).
amazement [ə'meizmənt], *n.* asombro.
amazing [ə'meiziŋ], *a.* asombroso, maravilloso.
Amazon ['æməzən], *n.* Amazonas, *m.sg.*; **amazon,** *n.* amazona.
ambassador [æm'bæsədə], *n.* embajador, *m.*
ambassadress [æm'bæsədris], *n.* embajadora.
amber ['æmbə], *a.* ambarino.—*n.* ambar, *m.*
ambidextrous [æmbi'dekstrəs], *a.* ambidextro; (*fig.*) venal.
ambient ['æmbiənt], *a.* ambiente.
ambiguity [æmbi'gju:iti], *n.* ambigüedad, *f.*
ambiguous [æm'bigjuəs], *a.* ambiguo.
ambit ['æmbit], *n.* ámbito.
ambition [æm'biʃən], *n.* ambición, *f.*
ambitious [æm'biʃəs], *a.* ambicioso.
amble [æmbl], *n.* portante, *m.*; paso de ambladura.—*v.i.* amblar.
ambrosia [æm'brouzjə], *n.* ambrosia.
ambulance ['æmbjuləns], *n.* ambulancia.
ambush ['æmbuʃ], *n.* emboscada.—*v.t.* emboscar, asechar.
ameliorate [ə'mi:ljəreit], *v.t., v.i.* mejorar.
amen ['ɑ:'men,'ei'men], *n., interj.* amén, *m.*
amenable [ə'mi:nəbl], *a.* tratable, dócil.
amend [ə'mend], *v.t.* enmendar; *to make amends for,* indemnizar; enmendar.
amendment [ə'mendmənt], *n.* enmienda.
amenity [ə'mi:niti], *n.* amenidad; comodidad, *f.*
America [ə'merikə], *n.* América; Estados Unidos, *m.pl.*
American [ə'merikən], *a., n.* americano; norteamericano, estadounidense, *m.f.*; — **plan,** (*U.S.*) pensión completa.
Americanize [ə'merikənaiz], *v.t.* americanizar.
amethyst ['æmiθist], *n.* amatista.
amiable ['eimjəbl], *a.* amigable, amistoso.
amicable ['æmikəbl], *a.* amigable.
amid(st) [ə'mid(st)], *prep.* en medio de.
amiss [ə'mis], *a.* errado, malo.—*adv.* mal, erradamente; *to take —,* tomar en mala parte.

amity ['æmiti], *n.* bienquerencia.
ammonia [ə'mounjə], *n.* amoníaco, *m.*
ammunition [æmju'niʃən], *n.* municiones, *f.pl.*
amnesty ['æmnisti], *n.* amnistía.—*v.t.* amnistiar.
amok [AMUCK].
among(st) [ə'mʌŋ(st)], *prep.* entre, en medio de.
amoral [æ'mɔrəl], *a.* amoral.
amorous ['æmərəs], *a.* amoroso.
amount [ə'maunt], *n.* importe, *m.*, cantidad, *f.*—*v.i.* ascender, subir a; *to — to,* significar.
amour [ə'muə], *n.* amorio.
amour-propre [ə'muə'propr], *n.* amor propio.
ampere ['æmpɛə], *n.* amperio.
ampersand ['æmpəsænd], *n.* el signo &.
amphibian [æm'fibiən], *a., n.* anfibio.
amphibious [æm'fibiəs], *a.* anfibio.
amphitheatre ['æmfiθiətə], *n.* (*U.S.* **amphitheater**) anfiteatro.
amplifier ['æmplifaiə], *n.* amplificador, *m.*
amplify ['æmplifai], *v.t.* amplificar, desarrollar.
amply ['æmpli], *adv.* ampliamente; bastante.
amputate ['æmpjuteit], *v.t.* amputar.
amputation [æmpju'teiʃən], *n.* amputación, *f.*
amuck [ə'mʌk], *adv.* furiosamente; *to run —,* correr lleno de furia homicida.
amulet ['æmjulet], *n.* amuleto.
amuse [ə'mju:z], *v.t.* divertir; entretener.
amusement [ə'mju:zmənt], *n.* diversión; recreación, *f.*
amusing [ə'mju:ziŋ], *a.* divertido.
an [æn, ən], *indef. art.* se emplea en lugar de **a** cuando la voz siguiente empieza con vocal o H muda.
anachronism [ə'nækrənizm], *n.* anacronismo.
anaemia [ə'ni:mjə], *n.* anemia.
anaemic [ə'ni:mik], *a.* anémico.
anaesthetic [ænis'θetik], *a., n.* anestético.
anagram ['ænəgræm], *n.* anagrama, *m.*
analogous [ə'næləgəs], *a.* análogo.
analogy [ə'nælədʒi], *n.* analogía.
analyse ['ænəlaiz], *v.t.* analizar.
analysis [ə'næləsis], *n.* análisis, *m.* o *f.* *inv.*
analyst ['ænəlist], *n.* analista, *m.f.*
analytic(al) [ænə'litik(əl)], *a.* analítico.
anarchic(al) [æ'na:kik(əl)], *a.* anárquico.
anarchist ['ænəkist], *n.* anarquista, *m.f.*
anarchy ['ænəki], *n.* anarquía.
anathema [ə'næθimə], *n.* anatema, *m.* o *f.*
anatomical [ænə'tɔmikəl], *a.* anatómico.
anatomist [ə'nætəmist], *n.* anatómico, anatomista, *m.f.*
anatomy [ə'nætəmi], *n.* anatomía.
ancestor ['ænsestə], *n.* antepasado, antecesor, *m.*
ancestral [æn'sestrəl], *a.* hereditario; solariego (casa).
ancestry ['ænsestri], *n.* prosapia; estirpe, *f.*; abolengo.
anchor ['æŋkə], *n.* ancla, áncora, *at —,* anclado.—*v.t.* poner al ancla; sujetar.—*v.i.* anclar.
anchorage ['æŋkəridʒ], *n.* anclaje, *m.*, fondeadero.
anchovy ['æntʃəvi], *n.* anchoa; boquerón, *m.*
ancient ['einʃənt], *a., n.* antiguo.
and [ænd, ənd], *conj.* y, e.

Andalusia [ændə'lu:zjə], *n.* Andalucía.
Andalusian [ændə'lu:zjən], *a.*, *n.* andaluz, *m.*
Andrew ['ændru:], Andrés, *m.*
anecdote ['ænikdout], *n.* anécdota.
anemone [ə'neməni], *n.* anémona.
anew [ə'nju:], *adv.* de nuevo.
angel ['eindʒəl], *n.* ángel, *m.*
angelic [æn'dʒelik], *a.* angélico.
angelus ['ændʒiləs], *n.* ángelus, *m.*
anger ['æŋgə], *n.* ira, cólera, enojo.—*v.t.* enojar, encolerizar.
angle [æŋgl], *n.* ángulo.—*v.t.* inclinar.—*v.i.* pescar con caña (*for*).
angler ['æŋglə], *n.* pescador con caña.
Anglican ['æŋglikən], *a.*, *n.* anglicano.
Anglicism ['æŋglisizm], *n.* anglicismo.
Anglicize ['æŋglisaiz], *v.t.* inglesar.
angling ['æŋgliŋ], *n.* pesca con caña.
Anglo-Saxon ['æŋglou'sæksən], *a.*, *n.* anglosajón, *m.*
angry ['æŋgri], *a.* enojado, encolerizado, colérico; **to get —**, enfadarse, enojarse (*at*, de, *with*, con).
anguish ['æŋgwiʃ], *n.* congoja, angustia.—*v.t.* acongojar.
angular ['æŋgjulə], *a.* angular; anguloso.
anil ['ænil], *n.* añil, *m.*
aniline ['ænili:n, 'ænilain], *n.* anilina.
animal ['æniməl], *a.*, *n.* animal, *m.*
animate ['ænimeit], *a.* animado, viviente.—['ænimeit], *v.t.* animar, vivificar.
animation [æni'meiʃən], *n.* animación, *f.*
animosity [æni'mɔsiti], *n.* animosidad, *f.*
anise ['ænis], *n.* anís, *m.*
aniseed ['ænisi:d], *n.* grano de anís.
anisette [æni'zet], *n.* licor (*m.*) de anís.
ankle [æŋkl], *n.* tobillo.
anklet ['æŋklit], *n.* ajorca.
annals ['ænlz], *n.pl.* anales, *m.pl.*
anneal [ə'ni:l], *v.t.* recocer, templar.
annexe ['æneks], *n.* anexo, anejo; dependencia. —[ə'neks], *v.t.* anexar, anexionar.
annexation [ænek'seiʃən], *n.* anexión, *f.*
annihilate [ə'naialeit], *v.t.* aniquilar.
annihilation [ənaiə'leiʃən], *n.* aniquilación, *f.*
anniversary [æni'və:səri], *a.*, *n.* aniversario.
anno Domini ['ænou'dɔminai] (*abbrev.* A.D.) *n.* año de Cristo.
annotate ['ænouteit], *v.t.* anotar, glosar.
announce [ə'nauns], *v.t.* anunciar.
announcement [ə'naunsmənt], *n.* aviso, anuncio.
announcer [ə'naunsə], *n.* anunciador; (*rad.*) locutor, *m.*
annoy [ə'nɔi], *v.t.* molestar, enfadar.
annoyance [ə'nɔiəns], *n.* molestia; enfado.
annoying [ə'nɔiiŋ], *a.* molesto.
annual ['ænjuəl], *a.* anual.—*n.* anuario.
annuity [ə'nju:iti], *n.* renta vitalicia, anualidad, *f.*
annul [ə'nʌl], *v.t.* anular, invalidar.
annulment [ə'nʌlmənt], *n.* anulación; revocación, *f.*
annunciation [ənʌnsi'eiʃən], *n.* anunciación, *f.*
anode ['ænoud], *n.* (*elec.*) ánodo.
anoint [ə'nɔint], *v.t.* ungir, untar.
anomalous [ə'nɔmələs], *a.* anómalo.
anomaly [ə'nɔməli], *n.* anomalía.
anon [ə'nɔn], *adv.* (*obs.*) luego, presto.

anonymity [ænɔ'nimiti], *n.* anonimidad, *f.*, anónimo.
anonymous [ə'nɔniməs], *a.* anónimo.
another [ə'nʌðə], *pron.* otro, uno más; **one —**, uno(s) a otro(s).—*a.* otro.
answer ['a:nsə], *n.* respuesta, contestación, *f.* —*v.t.* contestar a; resolver (*problemas*); convenir a (*fin*); responder (*for*, de).
answerable ['a:nsərəbl], *a.* contestable; responsable; determinable.
ant [ænt], *n.* hormiga.
antagonism [æn'tægənizm], *n.* antagonismo.
antagonist [æn'tægənist], *n.* antagonista, *m.f.*
antagonistic, [æntægə'nistik], *a.* antagónico.
antagonize [æn'tægənaiz], *v.t.* enemistar; oponerse a.
Antarctic [ænt'a:ktik], *a.* antártico.—*n.* Antártica, *f.*
ante- [ænti-], *prefix.* ante-.
antecedent [ænti'si:dənt], *a.*, *n.* antecedente, precedente, *m.*
antechamber ['æntitʃeimbə], *n.* antecámara.
antedate ['æntideit], *v.t.* antedatar; preceder.
antediluvian [æntidi'lu:vjən], *a.* antediluviano.
antelope ['æntiloup], *n.* antílope, *m.*
antenatal ['ænti'neitl], *a.* antenatal.
antenna [æn'tenə], *n.* (*pl.* **-nae, -nas**) antena.
antepenultimate [æntipen'ʌltimit], *a.*, *n.* antepenúltimo.
anterior [æn'tiəriə], *a.* anterior.
anteroom ['æntirum], *n.* antecámara.
anthem ['ænθəm], *n.* himno; (*eccl.*) antífona, *f.*, motete, *m.*
anthill ['ænθil], *n.* hormiguero.
anthology [æn'θɔlədʒi], *n.* antología.
anthracite ['ænθrəsait], *n.* antracita.
anthrax ['ænθræks], *n.* ántrax, *m.*
anthropoid ['ænθrəpɔid], *a.*, *n.* antropoide, *m.*
anthropologist [ænθrə'pɔlədʒist], *n.* antropólogo.
anthropology [ænθrə'pɔlədʒi], *n.* antropología.
anti- ['ænti], *prefix.* anti-, contra.
anti-aircraft [ænti'εəkra:ft], *a.* antiaéreo.
antibody ['æntibɔdi], *n.* anticuerpo.
antics ['æntiks], *n. pl.* cabriola, travesura.
Antichrist ['æntikraist], *n.* Anticristo.
anticipate [æn'tisipeit], *v.t.* prever; esperar, prometerse; anticipar(se a).
anticipation [æntisi'peiʃən], *n.* expectación, *f.*; anticipación, *f.*
antidote ['æntidout], *n.* antídoto, contraveneno.
antifreeze ['æntifri:z], *n.* anticongelante, *m.*
Antilles [æn'tili:z], *n. pl.* Antillas, *f.pl.*
antimony ['æntiməni], *n.* antimonio.
antinomy ['æntinəmi], *n.* antinomia.
antipathy [æn'tipəθi], *n.* antipatía; aversión, *f.*
antipodes [æn'tipədi:z], *n.pl.* antípoda, *m.sg.*
antipope ['æntipoup], *n.* antipapa, *m.*
antiquarian [ænti'kwεəriən], *a. n.* anticuario.
antiquated ['æntikweitid], *a.* anticuado; arcaizante.
antique [æn'ti:k], *a.* antiguo.—*n.* antigualla; **— dealer**, anticuario.
antiquity [æn'tikwiti], *n.* antigüedad, *f.*
anti-Semitism [ænti'semitizm], *n.* antisemitismo.
antiseptic [ænti'septik], *a.*, *n.* antiséptico.

antisocial [ænti'souʃəl], *a.* antisocial.

antitank [ænti'tæŋk], *a.* antitanque, contra-carro.

antithesis [æn'tiθisis], *n.* antítesis, *f.*

antlers ['æntləz], *n. pl.* cornamenta.

Antwerp ['æntwɔːp], *n.* Amberes, *f.sg.*

anvil ['ænvil], *n.* yunque, *m.*

anxiety [æŋ'zaiəti], *n.* inquietud, ansiedad, *f.*

anxious ['æŋkʃəs], *a.* inquieto, ansioso.

any ['eni], *a.* cualquier; todo; alguno; *not — more,* no . . . más; ya no.

anybody [enibodi], *pron.* alguien, alguno; cualquiera, cualquier persona; todo el mundo; *not —,* nadie.

anyhow ['enihau], *adv.* de cualquier modo; como quiera que sea; de todos modos; con todo.

anyone ['eniwʌn] [ANYBODY].

anyplace ['enipleis] (*U.S.*) [ANYWHERE].

anything ['eniθiŋ], *pron.* cualquier cosa; todo lo que; *not —,* nada.

anyway ['eniwei] [ANYHOW].

anywhere ['eni(h)wɛə], *adv.* dondequiera; en *o* a cualquier parte; *not —,* en *o* a ninguna parte.

apace [ə'peis], *adv.* presto, aína (*poet., obs.*).

Apache [ə'pætʃi], **apache** [ə'paːʃ], *n.* apache, *m.*

apart [ə'paːt], *adv.* aparte; roto; — *from,* aparte de; separado de; *to take —,* des-montar, desarmar; *to tear —,* despedazar; *to come —,* deshacerse, romperse.

apartheid [ə'paːteit, ə'paːtaid], *n.* apartheid, *m.*

apartment [ə'paːtmənt], *n.* aposento; (*U.S.*) piso.—*pl.* estancia.

apathetic [æpə'θetik], *a.* apático.

apathy ['æpəθi], *n.* apatía.

ape [eip], *n.* mono, simio.—*v.t.* remedar.

aperient [ə'piəriənt], *a., n.* laxante, *m.*

aperitive [ə'peritiv], *n.* aperitivo.

aperture ['æpətjuə], *n.* abertura; boquete, *m.*; resquicio.

apex ['eipeks], *n.* (*pl.* **apices, apexes**) ápice, *m.*

aphorism ['æfərism], *n.* aforismo.

apiary ['eipiəri], *n.* colmenar, *m.*

apiece [ə'piːs], *adv.* cada uno; por cabeza.

apish ['eipiʃ], *a.* monesco; fatuo.

aplomb [ə'plom], *n.* aplomo, serenidad, *f.*

apocalypse [ə'pokəlips], *n.* apocalipsis, *m.*; revelación, *f.*

apocope [ə'pokəpi], *n.* apócope, *f.*

apocrypha [ə'pokrifə], *n.* libros apócrifos, *m.pl.*

apocryphal [ə'pokrifəl], *a.* apócrifo.

apogee ['æpodʒiː], *n.* apogeo.

Apollo [ə'polou], *n.* Apolo.

apologetic [əpolə'dʒetik], *a.* que pide perdón, arrepentido; apologético.

apologize [ə'polədʒaiz], *v.i.* disculparse (*to,* con, *for,* de).

apology [ə'polədʒi], *n.* excusa, disculpa; apología, *f.*

apoplexy ['æpəpleksi], *n.* apoplejía.

apostasy [ə'postəsi], *n.* apostasía.

apostate [ə'postət], *n.* apóstata, *m.f.*, rene-gado.

apostle [ə'posl], *n.* apóstol, *m.*

apostolic ['æpəs'tolik], *a.* apostólico.

apostrophe [ə'postrəfi], *n.* (*gram.*) apóstrofo ('), apóstrofe, *m. o f.*

apothecary [ə'poθikəri], *n.* boticario; *apoth-ecary shop,* botica.

apotheosis [əpoθi'ousis], *n.* apoteosis, *f.*

appal [ə'poːl], *v.t.* amendrentar, espantar; arredrar.

appalling [ə'poːliŋ], *a.* espantoso; descon-certante.

apparatus [æpə'reitəs], *n.* aparato.

apparel [ə'pærəl], *n.* vestidura.

apparent [ə'pærənt], *a.* aparente; evidente, manifiesto.

apparently [ə'pærəntli], *adv.* según parece, por lo visto.

apparition [æpə'riʃən], *n.* aparición, *f.*

appeal [ə'piːl], *n.* súplica; atracción, *f.*; (*jur.*) apelación, *f.—v.i.* suplicar (*to*); atraer (*to*); (*jur.*) apelar.

appealing [ə'piːliŋ], *a.* suplicante; atractivo.

appear [ə'piə], *v.i.* aparecer; parecer (*impers.*); (*jur.*) comparecer.

appearance [ə'piərəns], *n.* apariencia, aspecto; aparecimiento; (*jur.*) compare-cencia.

appease [ə'piːz], *v.t.* aplacar, apaciguar.

appeasement [ə'piːzmənt], *n.* aplacamiento, apaciguamiento.

appellant [ə'pelənt], *n.* apelante, *m.f.*

appellation [æpə'leiʃən], *n.* estilo, título, trato.

append [ə'pend], *v.t.* añadir, anexar.

appendage [ə'pendidʒ], *n.* apéndice, *m.*

appendicitis [əpendi'saitis], *n.* apendicitis, *f.*

appendix [ə'pendiks], *n.* (*pl.* **-dices, -dixes**) apéndice, *m.*

appertain [æpə'tein], *v.i.* atañer, relacionarse con (*to*).

appetite ['æpitait], *n.* apetito.

appetizer ['æpitaizə], *n.* aperitivo, apetite, *m.*

appetizing ['æpitaiziŋ], *a.* apetitoso, tentador.

applaud [ə'ploːd], *v.t., v.i.* aplaudir.

applause [ə'ploːz], *n.* aplauso(s).

apple [æpl], *n.* manzana; — *of his eye,* niña de su ojo; *in apple-pie order,* bien regladito.

apple-tree ['æpl'triː], *n.* manzano.

appliance [ə'plaiəns], *n.* dispositivo, meca-nismo; utensilio; aplicación, *f.*

applicable ['æplikəbl, ə'plikəbl], *a.* apli-cable.

applicant ['æplikənt], *n.* solicitante, candi-dato, *m.*

application [æpli'keiʃən], *n.* solicitud, *f.*, candidatura; aplicación, *f.*

apply [ə'plai], *v.t.* aplicar.—*v.i.* aplicarse (*to,* a); dirigirse; solicitar (*for*).

appoint [ə'point], *v.t.* nombrar, señalar, elegir; establecer; surtir.

appointment [ə'pointmənt], *n.* puesto, em-pleo; nombramiento; cita, compromiso.

apportion [ə'poːʃən], *v.t.* repartir, prorratear.

apposite ['æpəzit], *a.* conveniente, oportuno.

apposition [æpə'ziʃən], *n.* aposición, *f.*

appraisal [ə'preizəl], *n.* apreciación; valua-ción, *f.*

appraise [ə'preiz], *v.t.* valorizar, tasar.

appreciable [ə'priːʃiəbl], *a.* sensible; apre-ciable.

appreciate [ə'priːʃieit], *v.t.* apreciar; valori-zar.—*v.i.* subir en valor.

appreciation [əpriːʃi'eiʃən], *n.* tasa, valua-ción, *f.*; aprecio; aumento de precio *o* valor.

appreciative [ə'priːʃjətiv], *a.* apreciativo; reconocido.

apprehend [æpri'hend], *v.t.* aprehender; recelar; comprender.

apprehension [æpri'henʃən], *n.* aprehensión, *f.*, captura; aprensión, *f.*, recelo.

apprehensive [æpri'hensiv], *a.* aprensivo, remirado.

apprentice [ə'prentis], *n.* aprendiz, *m.*— *v.t.* poner de aprendiz (*to*, a).

apprenticeship [ə'prentisʃip], *n.* aprendizaje, *m.*

apprise [ə'praiz], *v.t.* informar.

approach [ə'proutʃ], *n.* acercamiento; acceso, entrada; propuesta.—*pl.* (*mil.*) aproches, *m.pl.*—*v.t.* acercarse a; acercar, arrimar; parecerse a.—*v.i.* acercarse, aproximarse.

approachable [ə'proutʃəbl], *a.* abordable, accesible, tratable.

approbation [æprə'beiʃən], *n.* anuencia; aprobación, *f.*

appropriate [ə'prouprieit], *a.* apropiado.—*v.t.* apropiarse; asignar.

approval [ə'pruːvəl], *n.* aprobación, *f.*; **on** —, a prueba.

approve [ə'pruːv], *v.t.* aprobar (*of*).

approximate [ə'prɔksimət], *a.* aproximado.—*v.t.* [ə'prɔksimeit] aproximar.—*v.i.* aproximarse (*to*, a).

approximation [əprɔksi'meiʃən], *n.* aproximación, *f.*

appurtenance [ə'pəːtinəns], *n.* pertenencia.

apricot ['eiprikɔt], *n.* albaricoque, *m.*

apricot-tree ['eiprikɔt'triː], *n.* albaricoquero.

April ['eipril], *n.* abril, *m.*; — **fool's day**, el 1° de abril.

apron ['eiprən], *n.* delantal, *m.*; mandil (*blusa*), *m.*; (*arch.*) batiente, *m.* antepecho.

apropos ['æprəpou], *adv.* a propósito (*of*, de).

apse [æps], *n.* ábside, *m.*

apt [æpt], *a.* apto; propenso; capaz.

aptitude ['æptitjuːd], *n.* aptitud, *f.*

aptness ['æptnis], *n.* aptitud, *f.*; conveniencia.

aquamarine [ækwəmə'riːn], *n.* aguamarina.

aquarium [ə'kweəriəm], *n.* (*pl.* **-riums, -ria**) acuario.

aquatic [ə'kwætik], *a.* acuático.

aquatint ['ækwətint], *n.* acuatinta.

aqueduct ['ækwidʌkt], *n.* acueducto.

aqueous ['eikwiəs], *a.* ácueo, acuoso.

aquiline ['ækwilain], *a.* aguileño.

Aquinas [ə'kwainæs], *n.* Aquino.

Arab ['ærəb], *a.*, *n.* árabe.

arabesque [ærə'besk], *a.*, *n.* arabesco.

Arabian [ə'reibjən], *a.* árabe, arábigo.—*n.* árabe.

Arabic ['ærəbik], *a.*, *n.* árabe; arábigo.

arable ['ærəbl], *a.* de labrantío, arable.

Aragon ['ærəgən], *n.* Aragón, *m.*

Aragonese [ærəgə'niːz], *a.*, *n.* aragonés.

arbiter ['aːbitə], *n.* árbitro.

arbitrary ['aːbitrəri], *a.* arbitrario.

arbitrate ['aːbitreit], *v.t.*, *v.i.* arbitrar.

arbitration [aːbi'treiʃən], *n.* arbitraje, *m.*

arbitrator ['aːbitreitə], *n.* árbitro, componedor, *m.*

arbour ['aːbə], *n.* emparrado, glorieta, cenador, *m.*

arbutus [aː'bjuːtəs], *n.* (*bot.*) madroño.

arc [aːk], *n.* arco.

arcade [aː'keid], *n.* arcada; pasaje, *m.*, galería.

Arcadian [aː'keidjən], *a.*, *n.* árcade, arcadio.

arcane [aː'kein], *a.* arcano.

arcanum [aː'keinəm], *n.* arcano.

arch [aːtʃ], *a.* insigne; socarrón.—*n.* arco.—*v.t.* arquear, combar.—*prefix.* principal.

archaeological [aːkiə'lɔdʒikəl], *a.* arqueológico.

archaeologist [aːki'ɔlədʒist], *n.* arqueólogo.

archaeology [aːki'ɔlədʒi], *n.* arqueología.

archaic [aː'keiik], *a.* arcaico, arcaizante.

archaism ['aːkeiizm], *n.* arcaísmo.

archangel ['aːkeindʒəl], *n.* arcángel, *m.*

archbishop [aːtʃ'biʃəp], *n.* arzobispo.

archdeacon [aːtʃ'diːkən], *n.* arcediano.

archduke [aːtʃ'djuːk], *n.* archiduque, *m.*

archer ['aːtʃə], *n.* arquero, saetero; ballestero.

archery ['aːtʃəri], *n.* tiro de arco; ballestería.

archetype ['aːkitaip], *n.* arquetipo.

archipelago [aːki'peligou], *n.* archipiélago.

architect ['aːkitekt], *n.* arquitecto.

architecture ['aːkitektʃə], *n.* arquitectura.

archive ['aːkaiv], *n.* archivo.

archway ['aːtʃwei], *n.* arco (*de entrada*), portal, *m.*; arcada.

Arctic ['aːktik], *n.* el polo ártico; **arctic,** *a.* ártico.

ardent ['aːdənt], *a.* férvido, fogoso.

ardour ['aːdə], *n.* fervor, ardor, *m.*, pasión, *f.*

arduous ['aːdjuəs], *a.* arduo, dificultoso.

are [aː] [BE].

area ['eəriə], *n.* área, superficie; comarca; extensión, *f.*

arena [ə'riːnə], *n.* arena, liza; ruedo.

aren't [aːnt] [ARE NOT].

argent ['aːdʒənt], *a.* (*poet.*) argento.—*n.* (*her.*) argén, *m.*

Argentina [aːdʒən'tiːnə], *n.* Argentina.

Argentine ['aːdʒəntain], *a.*, *n.* argentino. [ARGENTINA].

argon ['aːgɔn], *n.* argo, argón, *m.*

argosy ['aːgəsi], *n.* bajel rico; cosa de gran valor.

argot ['aːgou], *n.* jerga; argot, *m.*

argue ['aːgjuː], *v.t.* debatir; argumentar; argüir; disputar; probar.—*v.i.* disputar, discutir.

argument ['aːgjumənt], *n.* argumento; disputa.

argumentative [aːgju'mentətiv], *a.* argumentador; disputador.

aria ['aːriə], *n.* (*mus.*) aria.

arid ['ærid], *a.* árido.

aridness ['æridnis], **aridity** [æ'riditi], *n.* aridez, *f.*

aright [ə'rait], *adv.* justamente, con acierto.

arise [ə'raiz], *v.i.* (*conjug.* like RISE) surgir, provenir; levantarse.

aristocracy [æris'tɔkrəsi], *n.* aristocracia, *f.*

aristocrat ['æristəkræt], *n.* aristócrata, *m.f.*

aristocratic [æristə'krætik], *a.* aristocrático.

Aristotelian [ærisə'tiːljən], *a.* aristotélico.

Aristotle ['æristɔtl], *n.* Aristóteles. *m.*

arithmetic [ə'riθmətik], *n.* aritmética.

ark [aːk], *n.* arca.

arm [aːm], *n.* brazo; (*mil.*) arma.—*v.t.* armar; blindar, acorazar.—*v.i.* armarse.

armament ['aːməmənt], *n.* armamento; **armaments race,** carrera armamentista.

armature ['aːmətjuə], *n.* armadura.

armchair [aːm'tʃeə], *n.* sillón, *m.*

armful ['ɑ:mful], *n.* brazado.
arm-in-arm ['ɑ:min'ɑ:m], *adv.* de bracero.
armistice ['ɑ:mistis], *n.* armisticio.
armless ['ɑ:mlis], *a.* sin brazos *o* armas.
armlet ['ɑ:mlit], *n.* brazal, *m.*
armorial [ɑ:'mɔːriəl], *a.* héraldico.
armour ['ɑ:mə], *n.* armadura; blindaje, *m.*—*v.t.* blindar.
armourer ['ɑ:mərə], *n.* armero.
armour-plating [ɑ:mə'pleitiŋ], *n.* corazas, *f.pl.*; blindaje, *m.*
armoury ['ɑ:məri], *n.* armería; arsenal, *m.*
armpit ['ɑ:mpit], *n.* sobaco.
army ['ɑ:mi], *a.* castrense.—*n.* ejército.
aroma [ə'roumə], *n.* aroma, *m.*
aromatic [ærou'mætik], *a.* aromático.
around [ə'raund], *adv.* a la redonda; a la vuelta.—*prep.* a la vuelta de; hacia, cerca de; alrededor de. [ROUND].
arouse [ə'rauz], *v.t.* excitar, despertar.
arraign [ə'rein], *v.t.* acusar, denunciar.
arrange [ə'reindʒ], *v.t.* arreglar, ordenar; disponer; refundir.
arrangement [ə'reindʒmənt], *n.* arreglo, orden, *m.*; disposición, *f.*; medida.
arrant ['ærənt], *a.* consumado, de siete suelas.
array [ə'rei], *n.* haz, *m.*, orden (*m.*) de batalla; gala, atavío.—*v.t.* ataviar, engalanar.
arrears [ə'riəz], *n.pl.* atrasos, *m.pl.*
arrest [ə'rest], *n.* detención, *f.*, arresto.—*v.t.* detener, arrestar; impresionar.
arrival [ə'raivəl], *n.* llegada; llegado (*persona*).
arrive [ə'raiv], *v.i.* llegar (*at*, a).
arrogance ['ærəgəns], *n.* arrogancia, altanería.
arrogant ['ærəgənt], *a.* arrogante, altanero.
arrow ['ærou], *n.* flecha, saeta.
arrow-head ['ærouhed], *n.* punta de flecha.
arrow-root ['ærouru:t], *n.* arrurruz, *m.*
arsenal ['ɑ:sinl], *n.* arsenal, *m.*
arsenic ['ɑ:sənik], *a., n.* arsénico.
arson [ɑ:sn], *n.* incendiarismo, delito de incendio.
art (1) [ɑ:t], *n.* arte, *usually f.*
art (2) [ɑ:t], *v.i.(obs.)* eres [BE].
arterial [ɑ:'tiəriəl], *a., n.* arterial.
artery ['ɑ:təri], *n.* arteria.
artesian [ɑ:'ti:zjən], *a.* artesiano.
artful ['ɑ:tful], *a.* artero, mañoso.
Arthur ['ɑ:θə], *n.* Arturo, (*obs.*) Artús. *m.*
Arthurian [ɑ:'θjuəriən], *a.* artúrico, de Artús.
artichoke ['ɑ:titʃouk], *n.* alcachofa.
article ['ɑ:tikl], *n.* artículo.
articulate [ɑ:'tikjulit], *a.* articulado; claro, distinto; que sabe hablar.—[ɑ:'tikjuleit], *v.t.* articular.
artifact ['ɑ:rtifækt], *n.* artefacto.
artifice ['ɑ:tifis], *n.* artificio.
artificial [ɑ:ti'fiʃəl], *a.* artificial.
artificiality [ɑ:tifiʃi'æliti], *n.* cosa *o* carácter (*m.*) artificial.
artillery [ɑ:'tiləri], *n.* artillería.
artisan ['ɑ:tizæn], *n.* artesano.
artist ['ɑ:tist], *n.* artista.
artiste [ɑ:'ti:st], *n.* (*theat.*) artista, *m.f.*
artistic [ɑ:'tistik], *a.* artístico.
artistry ['ɑ:tistri], *n.* destreza, maestría; arte, *m.* o *f.*
artless ['ɑ:tləs], *a.* sin arte, chabacano; sincero, sencillo.
Aryan ['ɛəriən], *a., n.* ario.

as [æz, əz], *adv.* tan.—*prep.* como; por.—*conj.* como; ya que; según; a medida que; *as ... as,* tan ... como; — *if to,* como para; — *for,* — *to,* en cuanto a; — *well,* también; — *well* —, además de, así como; — *yet,* hasta ahora; *the same* —, el mismo que.
asbestos [æz'bestəs], *n.* asbesto.
ascend [ə'send], *v.t., v.i.* ascender, subir.
ascendency [ə'sendənsi], *n.* ascendiente, *m.*; dominio.
ascendent [ə'sendənt], *a.* ascendente.—*n.* ascendiente, *m.*; *in the* —, predominante; ganando poder.
Ascension [ə'senʃən], *n.* (*eccl.*) Ascensión, *f.*
ascent [ə'sent], *n.* subida; ascenso.
ascertain [æsə'tein], *v.t.* averiguar.
ascetic [ə'setik], *a.* ascético.—*n.* asceta, *m.f.*
asceticism [ə'setisizm], *n.* ascetismo.
ascribe [əs'kraib], *v.t.* atribuir, achacar.
ash (1) [æʃ], *n.* ceniza; *Ash Wednesday,* *n.* miércoles de ceniza.
ash (2) [æʃ], *n.* (*bot.*) fresno.
ashamed [ə'ʃeimd], *a.* avergonzado; *to be* — (*of*), tener vergüenza (de); avergonzarse (de, por).
ashen [æʃn], *a.* ceniciento; pálido; de fresno.
ashore [ə'ʃɔː], *adv.* a *o* en tierra; *to go* —, desembarcar.
ashtray ['æʃtrei], *n.* cenicero.
ashy ['æʃi], *a.* cenizoso.
Asia ['eiʃə], *n.* Asia.
Asian ['eiʃən], **Asiatic** [eiʃi'ætik], *a., n.* asiático.
aside [ə'said], *n.* aparte, *m.*—*adv.* aparte, a un lado; además (*from,* de).
asinine ['æsinain], *a.* necio, burro.
ask [ɑ:sk], *v.t.* pedir; preguntar; invitar; *to* — *for,* pedir; *to* — *in,* rogar que entre (*alguien*).
askance [əs'kæns], *adv.* de soslayo; de reojo.
askew [əs'kju:], *a.* de través; al sesgo.
asking ['ɑ:skiŋ], *n.* petición, *f.*; (*eccl.*) amonestación, *f.*; *for the* —, con sólo pedirlo.
asleep [ə'sli:p], *a.* dormido; *to fall* —, dormirse.
asp [æsp], *n.* áspid, *m.*
asparagus [əs'pærəgəs], *n.* espárrago(s).
aspect ['æspekt], *n.* aspecto.
asperity [æs'periti], *n.* aspereza.
aspersion [əs'pɔː.ʃən], *n.* calumnia; aspersión, *f.*
asphalt ['æsfælt], *n.* asfalto.—*v.t., v.i.* asfaltar.
asphyxiate [æs'fiksieit], *v.t.* asfixiar.
aspic ['æspik], *n.* áspid, *m.*; jalea de carne *etc.*
aspidistra [æspi'distrə], *n.* aspidistra.
aspirate ['æspəreit], *a.* aspirado.—*v.t.* aspirar.
aspiration [æspə'reiʃən], *n.* aspiración, *f.*
aspire [əs'paiə], *v.i.* aspirar (*to,* a).
aspirin ['æspərin], *n.* aspirina.
ass [æs], *n.* asno.
assail [ə'seil], *v.t.* agredir.
assailant [ə'seilənt], *n.* agresor, asaltador, *m.*
assassin [ə'sæsin], *n.* asesino.
assassinate [ə'sæsineit], *v.t.* asesinar.
assassination [əsæsi'neiʃən], *n.* asesinato.
assault [ə'sɔ:lt], *n.* asalto.—*v.t.* asaltar.
assay [ə'sei], *n.* ensaye, *m.*—*v.t.* ensayar; aquilatar.

assemble [ə'sembl], *v.t.* reunir; (*mech.*) montar.—*v.i.* reunirse.
assembly [ə'sembli], *n.* asamblea; (*mech.*) montaje, *m.*; — **hall,** salón (*m*). de sesiones.
assent [ə'sent], *n.* asentimiento, asenso.—*v.i.* asentir (*to,* a).
assert [ə'sə:t], *v.t.* afirmar, hacer valer, aseverar.—*v.r.* imponerse, sostener su dignidad *o* sus derechos.
assertion [ə'sə:ʃən], *n.* afirmación, *f.*, aserto.
assertive [ə'sə:tiv], *a.* asertivo; agresivo.
assess [ə'ses], *v.t.* tasar, fijar; amillarar.
assessment [ə'sesmənt], *n.* prorrateo; fijación, *f.*; tasa.
assessor [ə'sesə], *n.* tasador, *m.*
asset ['æset], *n.* ventaja.—*pl.* (*com.*) activo; bienes, *m.pl.*; haber, *m.*
assiduous [ə'sidjuəs], *a.* asiduo.
assign [ə'sain], *v.t.* asignar; ceder.
assignation [æsig'neiʃən], *n.* asignación, *f.*; cita, compromiso.
assignment [ə'sainmənt], *n.* asignación, cesión, *f.*; tarea.
assimilate [ə'simileit], *v.t.* asimilar(se).
Assisi [ə'si:zi], *n.* Asís, *m.*
assist [ə'sist], *v.t.* asistir, auxiliar.
assistance [ə'sistəns], *n.* ayuda, asistencia.
assistant [ə'sistənt], *n.* ayudante; empleado, dependiente (*tiendas*), *m.f.*
assizes [ə'saiziz], *n.pl.* alto tribunal inglés que suele reunirse dos veces al año en cada condado.
associate [ə'souʃieit], *a.*, *n.* asociado, adjunto.—*v.t.* asociar.—*v.i.* asociarse (*with,* con).
association [əsousi'eiʃən], *n.* asociación, *f.*
assonance ['æsənəns], *n.* asonancia; asonante, *m.*
assorted [ə'sɔ:tid], *a.* surtido, variado; seleccionado.
assortment [ə'sɔ:tmənt], *n.* surtido; selección variada.
assuage [ə'sweidʒ], *v.t.* suavizar, templar.
assume [ə'sju:m], *v.t.* asumir; arrogarse; suponer, presumir.
assumed [ə'sju:md], *a.* supuesto; fingido, falso.
Assumption [ə'sʌmpʃən], *n.* (*eccl.*) Asunción, *f.*
assumption [ə'sʌmpʃən], *n.* arrogación; adopción; suposición, *f.*
assurance [ə'ʃuərəns], *n.* aseguramiento; confianza, intrepidez, *f.*; (*com.*) seguro.
assure [ə'ʃuə], *v.t.* asegurar.
assured [ə'ʃuəd], *a.* confiado; descarado.
aster ['æstə], *n.* (*bot.*) áster, *m.*
asterisk ['æstərisk], *n.* asterisco (*).
astern [əs'tə:n], *adv.* a *o* en popa.
asteroid ['æstərɔid], *a.*, *n.* asteroide, *m.*
asthma ['æsθmə], *n.* asma.
asthmatic [æs'θmætik], *a.*, *n.* asmático.
astir [ə'stə:], *a.*, *adv.* en movimiento, activo.
astonish [əs'toniʃ], *v.t.* pasmar, asombrar.
astonishing [əs'toniʃiŋ], *a.* asombroso.
astonishment [əs'toniʃmənt], *n.* asombro.
astound [əs'taund], *v.t.* asombrar, aturdir.
astounding [əs'taundiŋ], *a.* pasmoso.
astral ['æstrəl], *a.* astral, sidereal.
astray [əs'trei], *a.*, *adv.* depistado, errado de camino; **to lead** —, extraviar.
astride [əs'traid], *adv.* a horcajadas.—*prep.* a horcajadas en.

astringent [əs'trindʒənt], *a.*, *n.* astringente *m.*
astrologer [əs'trolədʒə], *n.* astrólogo.
astrology [əs'trolədʒi], *n.* astrología.
astronaut ['æstrənɔ:t], *n.* astronauta, *m.*
astronautics [æstrə'nɔ:tiks], *n.* astronáutica.
astronomer [əs'tronəmə], *n.* astrónomo.
astronomic(al) [æstrə'nomik(əl)], *a.* astronómico.
astronomy [əs'tronəmi], *n.* astronomía.
astrophysics [æstrou'fiziks], *n.* astrofísica.
astute [əs'tju:t], *a.* astuto, agudo.
astuteness [əs'tju:tnis], *n.* astucia, sagacidad, *f.*
asunder [ə'sʌndə], *adv.* en dos, en pedazos.
asylum [ə'sailəm], *n.* asilo; **lunatic** —, manicomio.
at [æt], *prep.* a, en; — **X's,** en casa de X.
atavism ['ætəvizm], *n.* atavismo.
ate [eit] [EAT].
atheism ['eiθiizm], *n.* ateísmo.
atheist ['eiθiist], *a.*, *n* ateo.
atheistic [eiθi'istik], *a.* ateo.
Athens ['æθinz], *n.* Atenas. *f.sg.*
athlete ['æθli:t], *n.* atleta, *m.f.*
athletic [æθ'letik], *a.* atlético. — *n.pl.* atletismo; atlética.
at-home [ət'houm], *n.* recepción, *f.*, guateque, *m.*
Atlantic [ət'læntik], *a.*, *n.* Atlántico.
Atlas ['ætləs], *n.* Atlante, Atlas *m.*; **atlas,** *n.* atlas, *m.*
atmosphere ['ætməsfiə], *n.* atmósfera.
atmospheric [ætməs'ferik], *a.* atmosférico.— *n.pl.* perturbaciones atmosféricas, *f.pl.*
atoll ['ætol], *n.* atolón, *m.*
atom ['ætəm], *n.* átomo; — **bomb,** bomba atómica.
atomic [ə'tomik], *a.* atómico.
atomize ['ætəmaiz], *v.t.* atomizar.
atone [ə'toun], *v.i.* expiar (*for*).
atonement [ə'tounmənt], *n.* expiación, (*eccl.*) redención, *f.*
atrocious [ə'trouʃəs], *a.* atroz.
atrocity [ə'trositi], *n.* atrocidad, *f.*
atrophy ['ætrəfi], *v.t.* atrofiar.—*v.i.* -se.
attach [ə'tætʃ], *v.t.* ligar, pegar, juntar; dar, conceder (*importancia*); (*jur.*) embargar; **to be attached to,** tener cariño a.
attaché [ə'tæʃei], *n.* agregado.
attachment [ə'tætʃmənt], *n.* accesorio; unión, *f.*; apego; (*jur.*) embargo.
attack [ə'tæk], *n.* ataque, *m.*—*v.t.*, *v.i.* atacar.
attacker [ə'tækə], *n.* agresor, *m.*
attain [ə'tein], *v.t.* lograr, alcanzar, merecer.
attainment [ə'teinmənt], *n.* consecución, *f.*— *pl.* dotes, *f.pl.*, talento.
attar ['ætə], *n.* esencia fragrante.
attempt [ə'tempt], *n.* tentativa; conato.—*v.t.* intentar.
attend [ə'tend], *v.t.* asistir a; atender; auxiliar; **to — to,** atender a.
attendance [ə'tendəns], *n.* asistencia, concurrencia; **to dance — on,** bailar el agua a.
attendant [ə'tendənt], *a.* concomitante.—*n.* encargado.
attention [ə'tenʃən], *n.* atención, *f.*; **to call to,** hacer presente, destacar.
attentive [ə'tentiv], *a.* atento.
attenuate [ə'tenjueit], *v.t.* atenuar.

attest [ə'test], v.t. atestiguar, deponer; *to — to,* dar fe de.
attestation [ætes'teiʃən], n. atestación, f.
attic ['ætik], n. desván, m., buharda.
attire [ə'taiə], n. atavío, ropaje, m.—v.t. ataviar, engalanar.
attitude ['ætitjuːd], n. actitud, f.; ademán, m., postura.
attitudinize [æti'tjuːdinaiz], v.i. fachendear.
attorney [ə'təːni], n. procurador, m., apoderado; (U.S.) abogado.
attract [ə'trækt], v.t. atraer; llamar (atención).
attraction [ə'trækʃən], n. atracción, f.; atractivo, aliciente, m.
attractive [ə'træktiv], a. atractivo, llamativo.
attribute ['ætribjuːt], n. atributo.—[ə'tribjut], v.t. atribuir.
attribution [ætri'bjuːʃən], n. atribución, f.
attrition [ə'triʃən], n. atrición, f.; agotamiento, degaste, m.
attune [ə'tjuːn], v.t. afinar, acordar.
auburn ['ɔːbən], a. castaño, rojizo.
auction ['ɔːkʃən], n. subasta.—v.t. subastar.
audacious [ɔː'deiʃəs], a. audaz.
audacity [ɔː'dæsiti], n. audacia.
audible ['ɔːdibl], a. oíble, audible.
audience ['ɔːdiəns], n. público, auditorio; audiencia.
audio-visual ['ɔːdiouviʒuəl], a. audiovisual.
audit ['ɔːdit], n. intervención, f.—v.t. intervenir.
audition [ɔː'diʃən], n. audición, f.
auditor ['ɔːditə], n. interventor, m.
auditorium [ɔːdi'tɔːriəm], n. (pl. -ums, -ria) auditorio; paraninfo.
auger ['ɔːgə], n. barrena.
aught [ɔːt], pron. (obs.) algo; nada.
augment [ɔːg'ment], v.t., v.i. aumentar.—v.i. aumentarse.
augur ['ɔːgə], n. agorero.—v.t. augurar, agorar.
augury ['ɔːgjuri], n. augurio.
August ['ɔːgəst], n. agosto.
august [ɔː'gʌst], a. augusto.
Augustine [ɔː'gʌstin], **Augustinian** [ɔːgəs-'tiniən], a., n. Agustín, agustino.
auk [ɔːk], n. (orn.) alca.
aunt [ɑːnt], n. tía.
aunty ['ɑːnti], tiíta.
aura ['ɔːrə], n. aura.
aurora [ɔː'rɔːrə], n. aurora.
auspice ['ɔːspis], n. auspicio.
auspicious [ɔːs'piʃəs], a. propicio.
austere [ɔːs'tiə], a. austero.
austerity [ɔːs'teriti], n. austeridad, f.
Australian [ɔs'treiliən], a., n. australiano.
Austrian ['ɔstriən], a., n. austríaco.
authentic [ɔː'θentik], a. auténtico.
authenticate [ɔː'θentikeit], v.t. autenticar.
authenticity [ɔːθen'tisiti], n. autenticidad, f.
author ['ɔːθə], n. autor, m.
authoress ['ɔːθəres], n. autora.
authoritarian [ɔː'θɔri'teəriən], a. autoritario.
authoritative [ɔː'θɔritətiv], a. autorizado.
authority [ɔː'θɔriti], n. autoridad; *to have on good —,* saber de buena tinta.
authorize ['ɔːθəraiz], v.t. autorizar.
authorship ['ɔːθəʃip], n. paternidad literaria, autoría; profesión (f.) de autor.
autobiography [ɔːtoubai'ɔgrəfi], n. autobiografía.

autocade ['ɔːtoukeid], n. (U.S.) desfile (m.) de coches.
autocracy [ɔː'tɔkrəsi], n. autocracia.
autograph ['ɔːtəgrɑːf], n. autógrafo.
autogyro [ɔːtou'dʒairou], n. autogiro.
automat ['ɔːtoumæt], n. restaurante automático.
automatic [ɔːtə'mætik], a. automático.
automation [ɔːtə'meiʃən], n. automatización, f.
automaton [ɔː'tɔmətən], n. autómata, m.f.
automobile ['ɔːtəməbiːl], a., n. automóvil, m.
autonomous [ɔː'tɔnəməs], a. autónomo.
autonomy [ɔː'tɔnəmi], n. autonomía.
autopsy ['ɔːtɔpsi]. n. autopsia.
autumn ['ɔːtəm], n. otoño.
autumnal [ɔː'tʌmnəl], a., otoñal, autumnal.
auxiliary [ɔːg'ziljəri], a., n. auxiliar.
avail [ə'veil], n. provecho, ventaja.—v.t. valer a, aprovechar, beneficiar.—v.r. aprovecharse (of, de).
available [ə'veiləbl], a. disponible, aprovechable; en venta.
avalanche ['ævəlɑːnʃ], n. alud, m., avalancha.
avarice ['ævəris], n. avaricia, codicia.
avaricious [ævə'riʃəs], a. avariento.
avenge [ə'vendʒ], v.t. vengar.
avenue ['ævənjuː], n. avenida.
aver [ə'vəː], v.t. afirmar, aseverar.
average ['ævəridʒ], a. mediano; ordinario, regular.—n. término medio, promedio.—v.t. producir o recibir por término medio.
averse [ə'vəːs], a. opuesto, renuente.
aversion [ə'vəːʃən], n. aversión, f.; antipatía.
avert [ə'vəːt], v.t. alejar, apartar, evitar.
aviary ['eivjəri], n. avería.
aviation [eivi'eiʃən], n. aviación, f.
aviator ['eivieitə], n. aviador, m.
avid ['ævid], a. ávido, voraz, codicioso.
avidity [ə'viditi], n. avidez, f., codicia.
avoid [ə'vɔid], v.t. evitar; esquivar, rehuir.
avoidable [ə'vɔidəbl], a. evitable.
avoidance [ə'vɔidəns], n. evitación, f.
avoirdupois [ævədə'pɔiz], n. sistema (m.) de peso inglés.
avow [ə'vau], v.t. confesar, declarar.
await [ə'weit], v.t. aguardar, esperar.
awake [ə'weik], a. despierto.—v.t., v.i. (conjug. like WAKE) despertar.
awaken [ə'weikən], v.t.,v.i. despertar.
awakening [ə'weikəniŋ], n. despertamiento; (fig.) alba.
award [ə'wɔːd], n. premio; recompensa.—v.t. conceder; conferir.
aware [ə'wɛə], a. enterado.
away [ə'wei], a. ausente.—adv. fuera, lejos; mucho; de en medio.—interj. ¡fuera!
awe [ɔː], n. temor, pasmo.—v.t. pasmar, atemorizar.
awesome ['ɔːsəm], a. pasmoso.
awe-struck ['ɔːstrʌk], a. pasmado.
awful ['ɔːful], a. espantoso, atroz.
awfully ['ɔːf(u)li], adv. (fam.) hasta más no poder, muy.
awhile [ə'hwail], adv. algún tiempo.
awkward ['ɔːkwəd], a. desmañado; desgarbado; peliagudo.
awl [ɔːl], n. alesna, lezna, subilla.
awning ['ɔːniŋ], n. toldo.
awoke [ə'wouk] [AWAKE].
axe [æks], n. hacha; *an — to grind,* un fin interesado.

229

axis ['æksis], *n.* (*pl.* **axes**) eje, *m.*
axle [æksl], *n.* eje, árbol, *m.*
aye (1) [ai], *adv.* (*prov.*) [ai], sí.
aye (2) [ei], *adv.* (*poet.*) siempre.
Aztec ['æztek], *a.*, *n.* azteca, *m.f.*
azure ['æʒjuə], *a.*, *n.* azul, *m.*; (*her.*) blao.

B

B, b [bi:], *n.* segunda letra del alfabeto inglés; **B,** (*mus.*) si.
baa [ba:], *n.* balido, be, *m.—v.i.* balar.
babble [bæbl], *n.* murmullo; cháchara.— *v.t.* barbotar.—*v.i.* parlotear, murmurar.
babe [beib], *n.* (*poet.*) criatura.
baboon [bə'bu:n], *n.* babuino.
baby ['beibi], *n.* bebé, nene, *m.* criatura; crío (*animal*).
babyish ['beibiiʃ], *a.* aniñado, pueril.
Babylonian [bæbi'lounjən], *a.*, *n.* babilonio.
Bacchus ['bækəs], *n.* Baco.
bachelor ['bætʃələ], *n.* soltero; (*educ.*) licenciado, bachiller, *m.*
back [bæk], *a.* trasero, posterior; apartado.— *n.* espalda; dorso, reverso, revés, *m.*; lomo espinazo; respaldo; fondo.—*v.t.* apoyar; mover hacia atrás; apostar sobre.—*v.i.* moverse hacia atrás; **to — out of,** desdecirse de. **—adv.** de vuelta; hacia atrás, para atrás; hace [AGO]; de nuevo; **to go** o **come —,** volver; **to go — on,** no cumplir.
backbite ['bækbait], *v.t.* (*conjug. like* BITE) cortar un traje a.—*v.i.* chismear.
backbone ['bækboun], *n.* espinazo; (*fig.*) firmeza.
back-door ['bæk'dɔ:], *n.* puerta trasera, postigo.
backer ['bækə], *n.* impulsor; apostador, *m.*
backfire ['bækfaiə], *n.* petardeo.—*v.i.* petardear; fracasar.
background ['bækgraund], *n.* fondo, último término; educación, *f.*, antecedentes, *m.pl.*
backing ['bækiŋ], *n.* apoyo; refuerzo.
backslide ['bæk'slaid], *v.i.* (*conjug. like* SLIDE) reincidir, apostatar.
backward ['bækwəd], *a.* atrasado; retraído.— *adv.* (*also* **backwards** ['bækwədz]) atrás, hacia atrás; al revés.
backwardness ['bækwədnis], *n.* atraso; tardanza; timidez, *f.*
backwater ['bækwɔ:tə], *n.* remanso, rebalsa.
backwoods ['bækwudz], *n.pl.* región apartada; monte, *m.*
back-yard [bæk'ja:d], *n.* patio, corral, *m.*
bacon ['beikən], *n.* tocino.
bacterium [bæk'ti:riəm], *n.* (*pl.*-**ria**)bacteria, microbio.
bad [bæd], *a.* malo; podrido; falso; enfermo. **—n.** mal, *m.*; **from — to worse,** de mal en peor; **not —,** regular.
bade [bæd, beid] [BID].
badge [bædʒ], *n.* divisa; insignia; señal, *f.*; emblema, *m.*

badger ['bædʒə], *n.* (*zool.*) tejón, *m.—v.t.* fastidiar.
badly ['bædli], *adv.* mal; mucho, con urgencia; **— off,** maltrecho.
badness ['bædnis], *n.* maldad, *f.*
baffle [bæfl], *v.t.* trabucar.
bag [bæg], *n.* saco; bolsa; caza, piezas cobradas.—*v.t.* ensacar; (*fam.*) cazar, pescar.
baggage ['bægidʒ], *n.* bagaje, *m.*; (*U.S.*) equipaje, *m.*; (*fam.*) descarada.
bagpipe ['bægpaip], *n.* gaita.
bail [beil], *n.* fianza.—*v.t.* salir fiador (**out,** por); (*naut.*) achicar; **to — out,** (*aer.*) saltar en paracaídas.
bailiff ['beilif], *n.* corchete; guardián, *m.*
bairn [bɛən], *n.* (*Scot.*) nene, *m.f.*, niño,-ña.
bait [beit], *n.* cebo, anzuelo; añagaza.—*v.t.* cebar; hostigar.
baize [beiz], *n.* bayeta.
bake [beik], *v.t.*, *v.i.* cocer al horno.
bakelite ['beikəlait], *n.* baquelita.
baker ['beikə], *n.* panadero; **baker's dozen,** docena del fraile (13).
bakery ['beikəri], *n.* panadería.
baking ['beikiŋ], *n.* hornada, cochura; **— powder,** levadura química.
balance ['bæləns], *n.* equilibrio, balanza; (*com.*) balance, *m.*; resto.—*v.t.* equilibrar, balancear.—*v.i.* equilibrarse.
balcony ['bælkəni], *n.* balcón, *m.*; (*theat.*) galería.
bald [bɔ:ld], *a.* calvo; directo, escueto.
balderdash ['bɔ:ldədæʃ], *n.* galimatías, *m.sg.*, disparates, *m.pl.*
baldness ['bɔ:ldnis], *n.* calvicie, *f.*
bale [beil], *n.* bala, fardo (*de papel etc.*). —*v.t.* embalar.
baleful ['beilful], *a.* funesto, pernicioso.
balk [bɔ:k], *n.* viga; contratiempo.—*v.t.* frustrar.—*v.i.* rebelarse (**at,** contra). [BAULK].
ball (1) [bɔ:l], *n.* pelota, balón, *m.*; globo; ovillo; bola; bala (*cañon*); **— bearings,** juego de bolas.
ball (2) [bɔ:l], *n.* baile (*danza*), *m.*
ballad ['bæləd], *n.* balada; romance, *m.*
ballast ['bæləst], *n.* lastre, *m.*; (*rail.*) balasto. —*v.t.* lastrar; balastar.
ballerina [bælə'ri:nə], *n.* bailarina.
ballet ['bælei], *n.* ballet, *m.*
ballistics [bə'listiks], *n. pl.* balística.
balloon [bə'lu:n], *n.* globo.
ballot ['bælət], *n.* votación, *f.*; bolita para votar; escrutinio.—*v.i.* votar.
bally ['bæli], *a.* (*fam.*) dichoso, santo.
ballyhoo [bæli'hu:], *n.* bombo; bullanga.
balm [ba:m], *n.* bálsamo.
balmy ['ba:mi], *a.* balsámico, suave.
balsam ['bɔ:lsəm], *n.* bálsamo.
Baltic ['bɔ:ltik], *a.* báltico.—*n.* Báltico.
balustrade [bæləs'treid], *n.* balaustrada.
bamboo [bæm'bu:], *n.* bambú, *m.*
bamboozle [bæm'bu:zl], *v.t.* (*fam.*) embaucar.
ban [bæn], *n.* prohibición, *f.*; entredicho; bando de destierro.—*v.t.* prohibir, proscribir.
banal [bæ'na:l], *a.* trillado, trivial.
banana [bə'na:nə], *n.* plátano; (*S.A.*) banana; banano (*planta*).
band [bænd], *n.* faja, cinta; lista; banda; cuadrilla; correa.—*v.t.* abanderizar.
bandage ['bændidʒ], *n.* venda.—*v.t.* vendar.

bandit ['bændit], *n.* bandolero, bandido.
banditry ['bænditri], *n.* bandolerismo.
bandy ['bændi], *a.* estevado.—*v.t.* trocar.
bane [bein], *n.* tósigo; (*fig.*) azote, *m.*
baneful ['beinful], *a.* venenoso; nocivo, mortal.
bang [bæŋ], *n.* golpazo; estallido.—*v.t.* golpear con violencia.—*v.i.* saltar, estallar; *to — the door,* dar un portazo; *to — into,* dar contra, topar con.
bangle [bæŋgl], *n.* ajorca.
banish ['bæniʃ], *v.t.* desterrar; despedir.
banishment ['bæniʃmənt], *n.* destierro.
banister ['bænistə], *n.* baranda, pasamano.
bank [bæŋk], *n.* orilla, ribera (*de un río etc.*); banco, montón (*pila*), *m.*; batería; hilera; (*com.*) banco; cuesta.—*v.t.* amontonar; apresar; depositar en el banco.—*v.i.* tener banco; (*aer.*) ladearse; *to — on,* contar con.
banker ['bæŋkə], *n.* banquero.
banking ['bæŋkiŋ], *a.* bancario.—*n.* (*com.*) banca.
bankrupt ['bæŋkrʌpt], *a.* quebrado.—*n.* quebrado; bancarrotero.—*v.t., v.i.* quebrar.
bankruptcy ['bæŋkrʌptsi], *n.* quiebra; bancarrota.
banner ['bænə], *n.* bandera; estandarte, *m.*
banns ['bænz], *n.pl.* (*eccl.*) amonestaciones, *f.pl.*
banquet ['bæŋkwit], *n.* banquete, *m.*—*v.i.* banquetear.
banter ['bæntə], *n.* chanza, vaya.—*v.t.* mofarse de.—*v.i.* chancear.
Bantu ['bæntu:], *a., n.* bantú, *m.f.*
baptism ['bæptizm], *n.* bautizo; bautismo.
Baptist ['bæptist], *n.* baptista (*denominación*), *m.f.*; **baptist**, *n.* bautista, *m.*
baptize [bæp'taiz], *v.t.* bautizar.
bar [ba:], *n.* barra; bar (*para bedidas*), mostrador, *f.*; lingote, *m.*; raya; (*jur.*) foro; reja (*en una ventana*).—*v.t.* atrancar; barrear; impedir; exceptuar.—*prep.* excepto. **[pub]**
barb [ba:b], *n.* lengüeta, púa.
barbarian [ba:'beəriən], *a., n.* bárbaro.
barbaric [ba:'bærik], *a.* barbárico.
barbarism ['ba:bərizm], *n.* barbaridad, *f.*; (*gram.*) barbarismo.
barbarity [ba:'bæriti], *n.* barbarie, *f.*
barbarous ['ba:bərəs], *a.* bárbaro.
barbecue ['ba:bikju:], *n.* (*S.A.*) churrasco, barbacoa.
barbed [ba:bd], *a.* armado con lengüetas; — *wire,* alambre espinoso *o* de púas.
barbel ['ba:bəl], *n.* (*ichth.*) barbo.
barber ['ba:bə], *n.* barbero, peluquero.
bard [ba:d], *n.* bardo.
bare [bɛə], *a.* desnudo; mero, solo; *to lay —,* poner a descubierto.—*v.t.* desnudar; exponer.
barefaced ['bɛəfeisd], *a.* descarado.
barefooted [bɛə'futid], *a.* descalzo.
barely ['bɛəli], *adv.* apenas.
bareness ['bɛənis], *n.* desnudez, *f.*
bargain ['ba:gin], *n.* (buen) negocio; ganga; *into the —,* de añadidura.—*v.i.* negociar; contratar; regatear.
bargaining ['ba:giniŋ], *n.* trato; regateo.
barge [ba:dʒ], *n.* barcaza, gabarra.—*v.i. to — in,* entrar atropelladamente, *o* sin permiso.
baritone ['bæritoun], *n.* barítono.
bark (1) [ba:k], *n.* corteza (*árbol*).
bark (2) [ba:k], *n.* raya; (*jur.*) foro.—*v.t.* ladrar (*perros*).
bark (3) [ba:k], *n.* (*poet.*) nao, *f.*
barley ['ba:li], *n.* cebada.

barmaid ['ba:meid], *n.* moza de bar.
barman ['ba:mən], *n.* barman, *m.*
barmy ['ba:mi], *a.* (*fam.*) guillado, gilí.
barn [ba:n], *n.* granero, hórreo; pajar, *m.*
barnacle ['ba:nəkl], *n.* (*zool.*) percebe, *m.*
barn-owl ['ba:naul], *n.* lechuza.
barometer [bə'rɒmitə], *n.* barómetro.
baron ['bærən], *n.* barón, *m.*
baroness ['bærənes], *n.* baronesa.
baroque [bə'rɒk], *a., n.* barroco.
barrack ['bærək], *v.t.* (*fam.*) silbar, pitar.
barracks ['bærəks], *n.pl.* cuartel, *m.,* caserna.
barrage ['bæra:ʒ], *n.* presa; bombardeo.
barrel ['bærəl], *n.* barril, tonel, *m.*; (*mil.*) tubo de cañón.—*v.t.* embarrilar.
barren ['bærən], *a.* yermo; estéril.
barricade [bæri'keid], *n.* empalizada, barricada.—*v.t.* barrear.
barrier ['bæriə], *n.* barrera.
barring ['ba:riŋ], *prep.* salvo; amén de.
barrister ['bæristə], *n.* abogado.
barrow ['bærou], *n.* carretilla; túmulo.
barter ['ba:tə], *n.* trueque, *m.*, barata.—*v.t.* trocar, baratar.
Bartholomew [ba:'θɒləmju:], *n.* Bartolomé, *m.*
base (1) [beis], *a.* vil, bajo; bajo de ley.
base (2) [beis], *n.* base, *f.*, fundamento; (*arch.*) basa.—*v.t.* basar (*on,* en).
baseball ['beisbo:l], *n.* beisbol, *m.*
basement ['beismənt], *n.* sótano.
baseness ['beisnis], *n.* bajeza, vileza.
bash [bæʃ], *v.t.* (*fam.*) golpear.
bashful ['bæʃful], *a.* encogido, tímido, corto.
bashfulness ['bæʃfulnis], *n.* timidez, cortedad, *f.*
basil ['bæz(i)l], *n.* (*bot.*) albahaca.
basilica [bə'zilikə], *n.* basílica.
basin ['beisən], *n.* jofaina; bacía; cuenca (*de un río*); dársena (*puerto*).
basis ['beisis], *n.* (*pl.* **bases**) base, *f.*; fundamento.
bask [ba:sk], *v.i.* asolearse; calentarse.
basket ['ba:skit], *n.* cesta; cesto (*grande*), canasta.
basket-work ['ba:skitwə:k], *n.* cestería.
Basque [bæsk], *a., n.* vasco, vascongado.—*n.* vascuence (*idioma*), *m.*
bas-relief ['bæsrili:f], *n.* bajo relieve, *m.*
bass (1) [beis], *a., n.* (*mus.*) bajo.
bass (2) [bæs], *n.* (*ichth.*) lobina.
bassoon [bə'su:n], *n.* bajón, *m.*
bastard ['ba:stəd], *a., n.* bastardo.
bastardy ['bæstədi], *n.* bastardía.
baste [beist], *v.t.,* (*cul.*) pringar, enlardar.
bastion ['bæstiən], *n.* baluarte, bastión, *m.*
bat (1) [bæt], *n.* palo; ladrillo roto.—*v.t.* golpear.—*v.i.* jugar con el palo (*cricket etc.*).
bat (2) [bæt], *n.* (*zool.*) murciélago.
batch [bætʃ], *n.* hornada; grupo.
bath [ba:θ], *n.* baño; bañera (*cosa*).—*v.t.* bañar; *to take a —,* bañarse.
bathe [beið], *n.* baño.—*v.t.* bañar(*herida etc.*). — *v.i.* bañarse (*nadar*).
bather ['beiðə], *n.* bañista, *m.f.*
bathing ['beiðiŋ], *a.* de baño(s), — *n.* baño; — *suit,* traje de baño, bañador, *m.*
bathos ['beiθɒs], *n.* anticlímax, *m.*; sensiblería.
bathroom ['ba:θrum], *n.* cuarto de baño.
bath-tub ['ba:θtʌb], *n.* bañera.

batman ['bætmən], *n.* (*mil.*, *Brit.*) ordenanza, *m.*
baton ['bætən], *n.* (*mus.*) batuta; (*mil.*) bastón, *m.*
batsman ['bætsmən], *n.* el que BATS en CRICKET.
battalion [bə'tæljən], *n.*, (*mil.*) batallón, *m.*
batten [bætn], *n.* (*carp.*) listón, *m.*; tablilla.
batter ['bætə], *n.*, (*cul.*) pasta, batido; (*cul.*) *in* —, rebozado en gabardina. — *v.t.* golpear; magullar; *to* — *down*, derribar.
battering-ram ['bætəriŋ'ræm], *n.* ariete, *m.*
battery ['bætəri], *n.* (*mil.*, *elec.*) batería; (*elec.*) pila (*para una lámpara eléctrica*); (*jur.*) agresión, *f.* [ACCUMULATOR]
battle [bætl], *n.* batalla.—*v.i.* batallar.
battle-axe ['bætlæks], *n.* hacha de combate; (*fam.*) marimacho.
battlement ['bætlmənt], *n.* almenas, *f.pl.*
battleship ['bætlʃip], *n.* acorazado.
bauble ['bɔ:bl], *n.* friolera.
bauxite ['bɔ:ksait], *n.* bauxita.
Bavarian [bə'vɛəriən], *a.*, *n.* bávaro.
bawd [bɔ:d], *n.* alcahueta.
bawdy ['bɔ:di], *a.* verde, obsceno.
bawl [bɔ:l], *v.t.*, *v.i.* vocear, chillar; (*fam.*) lloriquear.
bay (1) [bei], *n.* bahía (*mar*); — *window*, mirador; ventana cimbrada.
bay (2) [bei], *n.* bayo (*caballo*).
bay (3) [bei], *n.* (*bot.*) laurel, *m.*
bay (4) [bei], *v.i.* aullar (*perros*); *at* —, acorralado.
bayonet ['beiənit], *n.* bayoneta.—*v.t.* dar un bayonetazo a.
bazaar [bə'zɑ:], *n.* bazar, *m.*
be [bi:], *irreg.* *v.i.*, *auxiliary.* ser; estar; *there is* o *are*, hay; *he is to go*, ha de ir; *wife to* —, futura.
beach [bi:tʃ], *n.* playa.—*v.t.* encallar.
beacon ['bi:kən], *n.* faro, fanal, *m.*
bead [bi:d], *n.* abalorio, cuenta; gota; botón, *m.*; puntería.
beadle [bi:dl], *n.* bedel, *m.*
beagle ['bi:gl], *n.* sabueso.
beak [bi:k], *n.* pico; (*fam.*) juez, *m.*
beaker ['bi:kə], *n.* vaso, tazón, *m.*
beam [bi:m], *n.* (*carp.*) viga; (*naut.*) bao; rayo. —*v.t.* radiar.—*v.i.* brillar; sonreír.
beaming ['bi:miŋ], *a.* radiante; risueño.
bean [bi:n], *n.* haba (*broad*); habichuela, judía, alubia.
bean-feast ['bi:nfi:st], *n.* comilona.
beano ['bi:nou], *n.* juego casero.
bear (1) [bɛə], *n.* (*zool.*) oso; (*com.*) bajista, *m.f.*
bear (2) [bɛə], *v.t. irr.* llevar; aguantar; permitir; producir; parir.—*v.i.* dirigirse; *to* — *out*, apoyar; *to* — *with*, conllevar; *to* — *in mind*, tener presente o en cuenta.
bearable ['bɛərəbl], *a.* soportable.
beard [biəd], *n.* barba.—*v.t.* mesar la barba a, enfrentarse con.
bearded ['biədid], *a.* barbudo.
beardless ['biədlis], *a.* imberbe; afeitado.
bearer ['bɛərə], *n.* portador, *m.*
bear-garden ['bɛəgɑ:dn], *n.* (*fig.*) bullicio, babel, *m.* or *f.*
bearing ['bɛəriŋ], *n.* porte, *m.*; paciencia; (*mech.*) cojinete, *m.*; orientación, *f.*; *to lose one's bearings*, desorientarse.
beast [bi:st], *n.* bestia.
beastly ['bi:stli], *a.* bestial.

beat [bi:t], *n.* latido; golpe; compás, *m.*; ronda (*patrulla*).—*v.t. irr.* batir; vencer; tocar (*tambor*).—*v.i.* latir.
beatific [bi:ə'tifik], *a.* beatífico.
beating ['bi:tiŋ], *a.* palpitante, latiente.—*n.* paliza; derrota; golpeo; pulsación, *f.*
beau [bou], *n.* (*pl.* **-us** o **-ux**) guapo.
beautiful ['bju:təful], *a.* hermoso.
beauty ['bju:ti], *n.* belleza, hermosura, beldad, *f.*; (*fam.*) lo mejor.
beaver ['bi:və], *n.* (*zool.*) castor, *m.*
becalm [bi'kɑ:m], *v.t.* encalmar.
became [bi'keim] [BECOME].
because [bi'kɔz], *conj.* porque; — *of*, a causa de.
beckon ['bekən], *v.i.* llamar con señas.
become [bi'kʌm], *v.t.* (*conjug. like* COME) convenir.—*v.i.* hacerse, ponerse, volverse; convertirse en; llegar a ser; *to* — *of*, ser de, hacerse de; *to* — *cross*, enfadarse; *to* — *conceited*, envanecerse etc.
becoming [bi'kʌmiŋ], *a.* conveniente.
bed [bed], *n.* cama, lecho; mesa (*jardín*); madre, lecho (*río*); (*min.*) yacimiento.
bedding ['bediŋ], *n.* ropa de cama.
bedevil [bi'devəl]. *v.t.* endiablar; obstaculizar.
bedlam ['bedləm], *n.* manicomio.
bedraggle [bi'drægl], *v.t.* hacer cazcarriento.
bedroom ['bedrum], *n.* dormitorio, alcoba.
bedspread ['bedspred], *n.* cubrecama, *m.*, colcha.
bedstead ['bedsted], *n.* cuja.
bee [bi:], *n.* abeja.
beech [bi:tʃ], *n.* haya.
beef [bi:f], *n.* carne (*f.*) de vaca; (*fam.*) carnadura.
beefy ['bi:fi], *a.* (*fam.*) forzudo.
beeline ['bi:lain], *n.* línea recta.
been [bi:n, bin] [BE].
beer [biə], *n.* cerveza.
beet, beetroot [bi:t(ru:t)], *n.* remolacha.
beetle [bi:tl], *n.* escarabajo.
befall [bi'fɔ:l], *v.t.* (*conjug. like* FALL) ocurrir a, suceder a.—*v.i.* acontecer.
befit [bi'fit], *v.t.* convenir a.
before [bi'fɔ:], *adv.* antes; delante.—*prep.* antes de; delante de.—*conj.* antes (de) que.
beforehand [bi'fɔ:hænd], *adv.* con anticipación, de antemano.
befriend [bi'frend], *v.t.* hacerse amigo de, amparar.
beg [beg], *v.t.* rogar, pedir, mendigar.—*v.i.* mendigar, pordiosear.
beget [bi'get], *v.t. irr.* engendrar.
beggar ['begə], *n.* mendigo, pordiosero; (*fam.*) tío, tipo.—*v.t.* arruinar; imposibilitar.
beggarly ['begəli], *a.* miserable, mezquino.
begin [bi'gin], *v.t.*, *v.i. irr.* empezar, comenzar (*by*, por).
beginner [bi'ginə], *n.* principiante; iniciador, *m.*
beginning [bi'giniŋ], *n.* principio; origen, *m.*
begone! [bi'gɔn], *interj.* (*obs.*) ¡fuera!
begot [bi'gɔt] [BEGET].
begrudge [bi'grʌdʒ], *v.t.* escatimar; envidiar; dar de mala gana.
beguile [bi'gail], *v.t.* engañar; engatusar; distraer.
begun [bi'gʌn] [BEGIN].

behalf [bi'hɑ:f], *n.* favor, lugar; **on — of,** por cuenta de, a favor de; **to act on — of,** hacer las veces de.
behave [bi'heiv], *v.i.* portarse, conducirse; actuar; (*fam.*) portarse bien.
behaviour [bi'heivjə], *n.* conducta; porte, *m.*; operación, *f.*
behead [bi'hed], *v.t.* descabezar.
behind [bi'haind], *n.* (*low.*) trasero, culo.— *adv.* detrás; atrás; con retraso.—*prep.* detrás de.
behindhand [bi'haindhænd], *adv.* atrasado.
behold [bi'hould], *v.t.* (*conjug. like* HOLD) (*obs.*) catar, contemplar.
beholden [bi'houldən], *a.* deudor, obligado.
behoove [bi'houv], *v.t.,* incumbir.
beige [beiʒ], *a.* beige, color (*m.*) de arena. —*n.* sarga.
being ['bi:iŋ], *a.* existente; **for the time —,** por el momento.—*n.* ser, *m.*
belabour [bi'leibə], *v.t.* elaborar con afán; apalear.
belated [bi'leitid], *a.* atrasado, tarde.
belch [beltʃ], *n.* eructo.—*v.t.* vomitar.—*v.i.* eructar.
beleaguer [bi'li:gə], *v.t.* sitiar, bloquear.
belfry ['belfri], *n.* campanario.
Belgian ['beldʒən], *a.*, *n.* belga, *m.f.*
Belgium ['beldʒəm], *n.* Bélgica.
belie [bi'lai], *v.t.* desmentir; falsear; calumniar.
belief [bi'li:f], *n.* creencia.
believable [bi'li:vəbl], *a.* creíble.
believe [bi'li:v], *v.t., v.i.* creer (**in,** en).
believer [bi'li:və], *n.* creyente; (*eccl.*) fiel, *m.f.*
belittle [bi'litl], *v.t.* empequeñecer, achicar.
bell [bel], *n.* campana; timbre, cascabel, *m.*; cencerro.
belladonna [belə'dɒnə], *n.* belladona.
belle [bel], *n.* beldad, mujer bella, *f.*
belles-lettres ['bel'letr], *n.* bellas letras, *f.pl.*
bellhop ['belhɒp], *n.* (*U.S.*) botones, *m.sg.*
bellicose ['belikous], *a.* belicoso.
belligerence [bə'lidʒərəns], *n.* beligerancia.
belligerent [bə'lidʒərənt], *a., n.* beligerante, *m.*
bellow ['belou], *n.* bramido.—*pl.* fuelle, *m.*— *v.t.* vociferar.—*v.i.* bramar.
belly ['beli], *n.* barriga, panza.
belong [bi'lɒŋ], *v.i.* pertenecer (**to,** a).
belongings [bi'lɒŋiŋz], *n.pl.* pertenencias, *f.pl.*; (*fam.*) bártulo, *m.pl.*
beloved [bi'lʌv(i)d], *a.*, *n.* dilecto, amado.
below [bi'lou], *adv.* abajo.—*prep.* bajo, debajo de.
belt [belt], *n.* cinturón, *m.*; correa; zona.
bemoan [bi'moun], *v.t.* plañir, lamentar.
bemuse [bi'mju:z], *v.t.* pasmar, atontar.
bench [bentʃ], *n.* banco; (*jur.*) tribunal, *m.*
bend [bend], *n.* curva, recodo; inclinación, *f.* —*v.t. irr.* inclinar; torcer; encorvar; dirigir. —*v.i. irr.* encorvarse; inclinarse; doblarse.
beneath [bi'ni:θ], *adv.* debajo, abajo.—*prep.* debajo de.
Benedict ['benidikt], *n.* Benito; Benedicto.
Benedictine [beni'diktin], *a., n.* benedictino.
benediction [beni'dikʃən], *n.* bendición, *f.*; (*eccl.*) Exposición (*f.*) del Santísimo.
benefactor ['benifæktə], *n.* bienhechor, *m.*
benefactress ['benifæktres], *n.* bienhechora.
benefice ['benifis], *n.* (*eccl.*) beneficio.
beneficent [bi'nefisənt], *a.* benéfico.
beneficial [beni'fiʃəl], *a.* beneficioso.

beneficiary [beni'fiʃəri], *n.* beneficiario.
benefit ['benifit], *n.* beneficio.—*v.t., v.i.* aprovechar.
benevolence [bi'nevələns], *n.* benevolencia.
benevolent [bi'nevələnt], *a.* benévolo.
benighted [bi'naitid], *a.* sumido en ignorancia.
benign [bi'nain], *a.* benigno.
bent [bent], *a.* resuelto (**on,** a).—*n.* propensión *f.*; tendencia. [BEND].
benumb [bi'nʌm], *v.t.* entorpecer.
benzedrine ['benzidri:n], *n.* bencedrina.
benzine ['benzi:n], *n.* bencina.
bequeath [bi'kwi:ð], *v.t.* legar.
bequest [bi'kwest], *n.* legado, manda.
bereave [bi'ri:v], *v.t. irr.* despojar; desolar.
bereavement [bi'ri:vmənt], *n.* privación, *f.*; duelo.
beret ['berei, 'beri], *n.* boina.
Berlin [bə:'lin], *n.* Berlín, *m.*
berry ['beri], *n.* baya; grano.
berserk [bə:'sə:k], *a.* demente, frenético.
berth [bə:θ], *n.* (*naut.*) camarote, *m.*; amarradero.
beseech [bi'si:tʃ], *v.t. irr.* impetrar, instar.
beset [bi'set], *v.t.* (*conjug. like* SET) sitiar, acosar.
beside [bi'said], *adv.* además.—*prep.* al lado de, cerca de; además de; — **oneself,** fuera de sí; **to be — the point,** no venir al caso.
besides [bi'saidz], *adv., prep.* además (de).
besiege [bi'si:dʒ], *v.t.* sitiar, asediar.
besot [bi'sɒt], *v.t.* embelañar, entontecer.
bespeak [bi'spi:k], *v.t.* (*conjug. like* SPEAK, *p.p. also* BESPOKE) encomendar, encargar.
best [best], *a., adv. superl. of* GOOD, WELL. mejor; **the —,** lo mejor; **at —,** a lo más; **to like —,** preferir; **to get the —,** vencer, llevar ventaja a.
bestial ['bestjəl], *a.* bestial, embrutecido.
bestir [bis'tə:], *v.t.* mover, incitar.
bestow [bis'tou], *v.t.* otorgar, conceder; dedicar.
bet [bet], *n.* apuesta.—*v.t., v.i.* (*conjug. like* WET) apostar (**on,** sobre, por); **I —,** a que.
betake [bi'teik], *v.r.* (*conjug. like* TAKE) acudir, dirigirse.
betide [bi'taid], *v.i. woe — . . . !* ¡ay de. . . . !
betoken [bi'toukən], *v.t.* presagiar, indicar.
betray [bi'trei], *v.t.* traicionar; descubrir.
betrayal [bi'treiəl], *n.* traición; revelación, *f.*
betroth [bi'trouð], *v.t.* dar en matrimonio.— *v.r.* desposarse.
betrothal [bi'trouðəl], *n.* desposorio, noviazgo.
betrothed [bi'trouðd], *n.* prometido, novio.
better ['betə], *a. compar. of* GOOD, *n.* superior. —*a., adv. compar. of* GOOD, WELL, mejor; **to be —,** valer más; estar mejor; **— half,** (*fam.*) cara mitad (*mujer*).—*v.t.* mejorar; **to get —,** mejorarse; **to think — of,** cambiar de idea sobre, cambiar de decisión acerca de.
betterment ['betəmənt], *n.* mejoramiento.
between [bi'twi:n], *adv.* en medio.—*prep.* entre.
betwixt [bi'twikst], *prep.* (*obs.*) entre.
bevel ['bevəl], *n.* bisel, *m.*—*v.t.* biselar.
beverage ['bevəridʒ], *n.* potación, *f.*
bevy ['bevi], *n.* bandada; hato; corrillo.
bewail [bi'weil], *v.t.* (*naut.*) lamentar.
beware [bi'wɛə], *v.t., v.i.* recatarse (**of,** de); **— of. . . . !** ¡atención a. . . . ! ¡ojo con . . . !

bewilder [bi'wildə], *v.t.* dejar perplejo, aturrullar.
bewilderment [bi'wildəmənt], *n.* aturdimiento.
bewitch [bi'witʃ], *v.t.* embrujar, hechizar.
bewitching [bi'witʃiŋ], *a.* encantador.
beyond [bi'jɔnd], *adv., prep.* más allá (de), fuera (de); *he is — doing that*, es incapaz de eso; *the —*, el más allá.
bias ['baiəs], *n.* sesgo; prejuicio.—*v.t.* predisponer.
bib [bib], *n.* babero, babador *m.*; pechero.
Bible [baibl], *n.* Biblia.
Biblical ['biblikəl], *a.* bíblico.
bibliography [bibli'ɔgrəfi], *n.* bibliografía.
bibulous ['bibjuləs], *a.* avinado, bebido.
bicarbonate [bai'kɑ:bənit], *n.* bicarbonato.
biceps ['baiseps], *n.pl.* bíceps, *m.pl.*
bicker ['bikə], *v.i.* andarse en cojijos.
bicycle ['baisikl], *n.* bicicleta.
bid (1) [bid], *n.* oferta, puja, postura.—*v.i.* hacer una oferta, pujar.
bid (2) [bid],*v.t. irr.* mandar; dar (*la bienvenida*); decir (*adiós*).
bidder ['bidə], *n.* postor, licitador, *m.*
bidding ['bidiŋ], *n.* mandato; oferta, licitación, *f.*
bide [baid], *v.t., v.i.* aguardar(se); *to — one's time*, esparar el momento oportuno.
biennial [bai'eniəl], *a., n.* bienal, *m.*
bier [biə], *n.* féretro.
biff [bif], *n.* (*fam.*) torta, golpe, *m.*—*v.t.* (*fam.*) dar una torta a.
big [big], *a.* grande; abultado; adulto; crecido; *to talk —*, (*fam.*) entonarse; decir cosas de gran monta.
bigamist ['bigəmist], *n.* bígamo.
bigamous ['bigəməs], *a.* bígamo.
bigamy ['bigəmi], *n.* bigamia.
big-end ['big'end], *n.* (*mech.*) cabeza de biela.
biggish ['bigiʃ], *a.* grandote, grandecillo.
big-hearted [big'hɑ:tid], *a.* generoso.
bight [bait], *n.* ensenada; recodo.
bigness ['bignis], *n.* grandeza; tamaño.
bigot ['bigət], *n.* beatón, *m.*
bigoted ['bigətid], *a.* fanático.
bike [baik], *n.* (*fam.*) bicicleta.
bile [bail], *n.* bilis, *f.*
bilge [bildʒ], *n.* (*naut.*) pantoque, *m.*; agua de pantoque; (*fam.*) bobería.
bilingual [bai'liŋgwəl], *a.* bilingüe.
bilious ['biljəs], *a.* bilioso; (*fam.*) enfermizo.
bill [bil], *n.* cuenta; (*U.S.*) billete de banco, cartel, *m.*, anuncio; proyecto de ley; (*orn.*) pico; *— of health*, patente (*f.*) de sanidad; (*com.*) letra; giro;—*of exchange*, letra de cambio; —*of lading*, conocimiento de carga; *— of sale*, escritura de venta.
billet ['bilit], *n.* (*mil.*) alojamiento; boleta.—*v.t.* (*mil.*) alojar.
billiards ['biljədz], *n.pl.* billar, *m.*
billion ['biljən], *n.* billón, *m.*, (*U.S.*) mil millones.
billow ['bilou], *n.* oleada.—*v.i.* hincharse.
billy-goat ['biligout], *n.* macho cabrío; (*fig.*) bobo.
bin [bin], *n.* hucha; arcón, *m.*
bind [baind], *n.* (*fam.*) pega, lata.—*v.t. irr.* ligar, atar, encuadernar; vendar; obligar.—*v.i. irr.* endurecerse, pegarse.
binding ['baindiŋ], *a.* obligatorio.—*n.* encuadernación, *f.*

bindweed ['baindwi:d], *n.* corregüela, enredadera, *f.*
binge [bindʒ], *n.* (*fam.*) juerga.
binoculars [bi'nɔkjuləz], *n.pl.* prismáticos *m.pl.*
biographer [bai'ɔgrəfə], *n.* biógrafo.
biography [bai'ɔgrəfi], *n.* biografía.
biological [baiə'lɔdʒikl], *a.* biológico.
biologist [bai'ɔlədʒist], *n.* biólogo.
biology [bai'ɔlədʒi], *n.* biología.
biplane ['baiplein], *n.* biplano.
birch [bə:tʃ], *n.* (*bot.*) abedul, *m.*; palmeta férula.—*v.t.* (*jur.*) azotar.
bird [bə:d], *n.* pájaro; ave, *f.*; (*fam.*) sujeto.
bird-cage ['bə:dkeidʒ], *n.* jaula.
bird-lime ['bə:dlaim], *n.* liga.
bird's-eye view ['bə:dzai'vju:], *n.* vista de pájaro.
birth [bə:θ], *n.* nacimiento; parto; cuna alcurnia; origen, *m.*; *to give — to*, dar a luz parir.
birthday ['bə:θdei], *n.* cumpleaños, *m.sg.*
birthplace ['bə:θpleis], *n.* lugar (*m.*) de nacimiento, suelo nativo.
birth-rate ['bə:θreit], *n.* natalidad, *f.*
birthright ['bə:θrait], *n.* primogenitura mayorazgo; derechos (*m.pl.*) de nacimiento.
biscuit ['biskit], *n.* galleta.
bisect [bai'sekt], *v.t.* dividir en dos partes bisecar.
bishop ['biʃəp], *n.* obispo; alfil (*ajedrez*), *m.*
bison ['baisən], *n.* (*zool.*) bisonte, *m.*
bit [bit], *n.* trozito, pedacito; ratito; bocado barrena (*taladro*); *not a —*, nada de eso; *— tired*, algo cansado. [BITE].
bitch [bitʃ], *n.* perra; (*low*) zorra.
bite [bait], *n.* mordedura, mordisco; picadura resquemo; bocado; (*fig.*) impresión, *f.*—*v.t. v.i. irr.* morder; picar; tragar el anzuelo.
biting ['baitiŋ], *a.* mordaz; picante; cáustico
bitter ['bitə], *a.* amargo; enconado.—*pl.* cerveza amarga.—*pl.* bíter, *m.*; *it i bitterly cold*, hace un frío criminal cortante.
bitterness ['bitənis], *n.* amargura; amargor *m.*; encono.
bitumen ['bitjumən], *n.* betún, *m.*
bivouac ['bivuæk], *n.* vivaque, vivac, *m.*—*v.i (past tense and p.p.* **bivouacked**) vivaquear
bizarre [bi'zɑ:], *a.* estrambótico.
blab [blæb], *n.* lenguaraz, *m.*—*v.t., v.i.* chismear.
black [blæk], *a., n.* negro.—*v.t.* ennegrecer limpiar (*zapatos*); *to — out*, apagar la luces; desmayarse (*persona*).
blackball ['blækbɔ:l], *n.* bola negra.—*v.t* votar en contra de.
blackberry ['blækbəri], *n.* mora; *— bush* zarzamora.
blackbird ['blækbə:d], *n.* mirlo.
blackboard ['blækbɔ:d], *n.* pizarra.
blacken ['blækən], *v.t.* ennegrecer; difamar denigrar.
blackguard ['blægɑ:d], *n.* tunante, *m.*
blacklead ['blækled], *n.* grafito, plombagina
blackleg ['blækleg], *n.* esquirol, *m.*; fullero.
black-letter ['blækletə], *n.* negrilla, negrita letra gótica.
blackmail ['blækmeil], *n.* chantaje, *m.*—*v.i* hacer chantaje a.
blackness ['blæknis], *n.* negrura.
black-out ['blækaut], *n.* apagón; síncope, *m.*

blacksmith ['blæksmiθ], *n.* herrero, herrador, *m.*
bladder ['blædə], *n.* vejiga.
blade [bleid], *n.* hoja; brizna, tallo; (*aer.*) aleta; pala.
blame [bleim], *n.* culpa.—*v.t.* culpar, echar la culpa a (*for*, de); *I am to* —, yo tengo la culpa.
blameless ['bleimlis], *a.* intachable, inocente.
blameworthy ['bleimwə:ði], *a.* culpable, censurable.
blanch [blɑ:ntʃ], *v.t.* emblanquecer; (*cul.*) blanquear.—*v.i.* palidecer.
blancmange [blə'mɒnʒ], *n.* manjar blanco natillas.
bland [blænd], *a.* blando; lisonjero.
blandishment ['blændiʃmənt], *n.* zalamería, lisonja.
blank [blæŋk], *a.* blanco, en blanco; ciego; vago.—*n.* blanco; (*mil.*) cartucho sin bala.
blanket ['blæŋkit], *n.* manta.
blare [blɛə], *n.* fragor, *m.*—*v.t.* vociferar.—*v.i.* bramar, resonar.
blarney ['blɑ:ni], *n.* zalamería, bola.
blaspheme [blæs'fi:m], *v.i.* blasfemar.
blasphemous ['blæsfəməs], *a.* blásfemo.
blasphemy ['blæsfəmi], *n.* blasfemia.
blast [blɑ:st], *n.* ráfaga; rebufo; explosión, *f.*; (*mus.*) toque, *m.*; *full* —, en plena marcha, a pleno tiro.—*v.t.* volar; maldecir.
blast-furnace ['blɑ:stfə:nis], *n.* alto horno.
blatant ['bleitənt], *a.* vociglero, chillón, llamativo.
blaze [bleiz], *n.* incendio; hoguera; llamarada; señal, *f.*—*v.i.* arder con violencia; *to* — *a trail*, abrir un camino.
blazer ['bleizə], *n.* chaqueta de franela.
blazon ['bleizən], *n.* blasón, *m.*—*v.t.* blasonar.
bleach [bli:tʃ], *n.* blanqueo.—*v.t., v.i.* blanquear.
bleak [bli:k], *a.* desabrigado; sombrío.
bleary ['bliəri], *a.* legañoso.
bleed [bli:d], *v.t., v.i. irr.* sangrar; *to* — *white*, desangrar.
blemish ['blemiʃ], *n.* tacha, mancilla.—*v.t.* manchar.
blench [blentʃ], *v.i.* palidecer de miedo.
blend [blend], *n.* mezcla, combinación, *f.*—*v.t.* mezclar, combinar, casar.—*v.i.* -se.
bless [bles], *v.t. irr.* bendecir.
blessed ['blesid, blesd], *a.* bendito, bienaventurado; santo.
blessing ['blesiŋ], *n.* bendición, *f.*
blest [blest], *p.p.* [BLESS].
blew [blu:] [BLOW].
blight [blait], *n.* tizón, añublo; pulgón, *m.*; ruina.—*v.t.* atizonar.
blind [blaind], *a.* ciego; — *alley*, callejón (*m.*) sin salida.—*n.* velo, venda; pretexto; celosia, persiana.—*v.t.* cegar.
blindfold ['blaindfould], *a.* con los ojos vendados.—*n.* venda.—*v.t.* vendar los ojos a.
blindness ['blaindnis], *n.* ceguera; ceguedad, *f.*
blink [bliŋk], *n.* guiñada.—*v.t. v.i.* guiñar; parpadear.
blinker ['bliŋkə], *n.* anteojera.
bliss [blis], *n.* bienaventuranza, beatitud, *f.*; dicha.
blissful ['blisful], *a.* bienaventurado, dichoso.
blister ['blistə], *n.* ampolla.—*v.t.* ampollar.
blithe [blaið], *a.* ledo.

blitz [blits], *n.* bombardeo aéreo.—*v.t.* bombardear.
blizzard ['blizəd], *n.* nevasca, ventisca.
bloat [blout], *v.t.* hinchar.—*v.i.* abotagarse.
bloater ['bloutə], *n.* arenque ahumado.
blob [blɒb], *n.* gota; goterón, *m.*; burujo, gurullo.
block [blɒk], *n.* bloque, *m.*; tajo; (*arch.*) manzana; (*fig.*) obstáculo; cubo de madera.—*v.t.* bloquear; obstruir; parar; tapar.
blockade [blɒ'keid], *n.* bloqueo.—*v.t.* bloquear.
blockage ['blɒkidʒ],*n.* obstáculo; obturación,*f.*
blockhead ['blɒkhed], *n.* zoquete,*m.*,zopenco.
bloke [blouk], *n.* (*low*) tío, fulano.
blond(e) [blɒnd], *a.,n.* rubio.
blood [blʌd], *n.* sangre, *f.*; valentón, *m.*; *blue* —, sangre azul *o* goda.
bloodcurdling ['blʌdkə:dliŋ], *a.* horripilante.
bloodhound ['blʌdhaund], *n.* sabueso.
bloodless ['blʌdlis], *a.* exangüe; sin derramar sangre.
blood-letting ['blʌdletiŋ], *n.* sangría.
bloodshed ['blʌdʃed], *n.* efusión (*f.*) de sangre; matanza, mortandad, *f.*
blood-sucker ['blʌdsʌkə], *n.* sanguijuela; (*fig.*) usurero.
bloodthirsty ['blʌdθə:sti], *a.* sanguinario sangriento.
bloody ['blʌdi], *a.* sangriento; (*low*) maldito; la mar de, muy.—*v.t.* esangrentar.
bloom [blu:m], *n.* flor, *f.*; florescencia, belleza, lozanía; pelusilla; changote, *m.*—*v.i.* florecer, florar.
bloomer ['blu:mə], *n.*, (*fam.*) gazapatón, *m.*—*pl.* bragas, *f.pl.*
blossom ['blɒsəm], *n.* flor, florescencia; *in* —, en cierne, en flor.—*v.i.* [BLOOM].
blot [blɒt], *n.* borrón, *m.*, mancha.—*v.t.* manchar; emborronar; borrar; secar.
blotch [blɒtʃ], *n.* pústula; manchón, *m.*
blotter ['blɒtə], *n.* borrador; papel secante, *m.*
blotting-paper ['blɒtiŋpeipə], *n.* papel secante, *m.*
blouse [blauz], *n.* blusa.
blow [blou], *n.* golpe, choque, revés, *m.*, soplido; *to come to blows*, venir a las manos.—*v.t. irr.* soplar; sonar; (*fam.*) maldecir; volar.—*v.i. irr.* soplar; jadear; estallar; *to* — *up*, volar; inflar; *to* — *over*, pasar, olvidarse.
blow-out ['blouaut], *n.* (*U.S.*) pinchazo, reventón, *m.*; (*fam.*) comilona.
blow-pipe ['bloupaip],*n.* cerbatana; soplete,*m.*
blubber ['blʌbə], *n.* grasa (de ballena).—*v.i.* lloriquear.
bludgeon ['blʌdʒən], *n.* cachiporra.—*v.t.* aporrear.
blue [blu:], *a.* azul; (*fig.*) triste; verde (*obsceno*); *true* —, leal.—*n.* azul, *m.*—*pl.* (*fam.*) morriña.
blue-bell ['blu:bel], *n.* (*bot.*) jacinto silvestre.
blue-bottle ['blu:bɒtl], *n.* (*ent.*) moscarda.
bluestocking ['blu:stɒkiŋ], *n.* marisabidilla.
bluff [blʌf], *a.* áspero.—*n.* risco, peñasco; finta, farol, *m.*—*v.i.* farolear, blufar.
blunder ['blʌndə], *n.* desatino, despropósito, patochada.—*v.i.* desatinar; tropezar.
blunderbuss ['blʌndəbʌs], *n.* trabuco.
blunt [blʌnt], *a.* embotado, romo; brusco, directo.—*v.t.* embotar.

blur

blur [blə:], *n.* borrón, *m.*; forma confusa.—*v.t.* hacer borroso.

blurb [blə:b], *n.* reclamo retumbante.

blurred [blə:d], *a.* borroso.

blurt [blə:t], *v.i.* descolgarse (*out*, con).

blush [blʌʃ], *n.* sonrojo; color (*m.*) de rosa.—*v.i.* sonrojarse.

bluster ['blʌstə], *n.* fanfarria; tempestad, *f.*—*v.i.* fanfarrear.

blustering ['blʌstəriŋ], *a.* fanfarrón; tempestuoso.

boa [bouə], *n.* boa.

boar [bɔ:], *n.* (*zool.*) jabalí, *m.*; (*agr.*) verraco.

board [bɔ:d], *n.* tabla; tablero; hospedaje, *m.*, mesa; consejo (*de directores*); cartón, *m.*; — **and lodging**, pensión completa; **on** —, a bordo; en el vehículo.—*v.t.* hospedar; subir a; (*naut.*) abordar; entablar.

boarder ['bɔ:də], *n.* huésped, *m.*; (*educ.*) interno.

boarding house ['bɔ:diŋhaus], *n.* casa de huéspedes.

boast [boust], *n.* jactancia.—*v.i.* jactarse.

boastful ['boustful], *a.* jactancioso.

boat [bout], *n.* barco; barca.

boating ['boutiŋ], *n.* paseo en barco.

boatman ['boutmən], *n.* barquero.

boatswain [bousn, 'boutswein], *n.* contramaestre, *m.*

bob [bɔb], *n.* balanceo; borla, colgajo; lenteja; (*fam.*) chelín (12 *peniques*), *m.*—*v.t.* desmochar, cortar; (*fam.*) soslayar.—*v.i.* menearse; **to** — **up**, aparecer de repente.

bobbin ['bɔbin], *n.* carrete, *m.*; broca.

bobby ['bɔbi], *n.* (*fam.*) polizonte, *m.*

bode [boud], *v.t., v.i.* presagiar, prometer.

bodice ['bɔdis], *n.* corpiño.

bodily ['bɔdili], *a.* corpóreo.—*adv.* todos juntos; el cuerpo entero; en persona.

body ['bɔdi], *n.* (*anat.*) cuerpo; carrocería (*de un coche*); masa; entidad, *f.*; (*fam.*) uno, persona.

bodyguard ['bɔdiga:d], *n.* guardia de corps.

Boer [bouə], *a., n.* bóer, *m.f.*

bog [bɔg], *n.* pantano, ciénaga; **to** — **down**, atascar; **to get bogged down**, atascarse.

bog(e)y ['bougi], *n.* espantajo, duende, *m.*

boggy ['bɔgi], *a.* pantanoso.

bogus ['bougəs], *a.* espurio, fingido.

Bohemian [bou'hi:mjən], *a., n.* bohemio.

boil [bɔil], *n.* hervor, *m.*, cocción, *f.*; (*med.*) grano, divieso.—*v.t.* hacer hervir, calentar.—*v.i.* hervir, cocer.

boiler ['bɔilə], *n.* caldera.

boiler-maker ['bɔiləmeikə], *n.* calderero.

boisterous ['bɔistərəs], *a.* borrascoso, alborotado.

bold [bould], *a.* osado, arrojado; impudente; **to make** — **to**, tomar la libertad de.

boldness ['bouldnis], *n.* osadía.

Bolivian [bə'livjən], *a., n.* boliviano.

Bolshevik ['bɔlʃivik], *a., n.* bolchevique, *m.f.*

bolster ['boulstə], *n.* travesaño; soporte, sostén, *m.*—*v.t.* reforzar; sostener; animar.

bolt [boult], *n.* cerrojo, pestillo; cuadrillo; rayo; — **upright**, derecho, rígido.—*v.t.* acerrojar; comer vorazmente.—*v.i.* desbocarse; fugarse; lanzarse.

bomb [bɔm], *n.* bomba.—*v.t.* bomb(ard)ear.

bombard [bɔm'ba:d], *v.t.* bombardear.

bombast ['bɔmbæst], *n.* bombo, ampulosidad, *f.*

bombastic [bɔm'bæstik], *a.* bombástico, ampuloso.

bomber ['bɔmə], *n.* (*aer.*) bombardero.

bombing ['bɔmiŋ], *n.* bomb(ard)eo.

bombshell ['bɔmʃel], *n.* bomba; (*fig.*) mala sorpresa.

bonanza [bə'nænzə], *n.* bonanza.

bond [bɔnd], *n.* lazo; unión, *f.*, vínculo; obligación, *f.*; almacén aduanero; trabazón, *f.*; pagaré, valor, *m.*; divisa.—*pl.* atadura, cadenas, *f.pl.*

bondage ['bɔndidʒ], *n.* servidumbre, *f.*

bondman ['bɔndmən], *n.* esclavo, siervo.

bondsman ['bɔndzmən], *n.* fiador, *m.*

bone [boun], *n.* hueso; espina (*de pez*).—*v.t.* desosar; (*U.S. fam.*) empollar.

bonfire ['bɔnfaiə], *n.* hoguera.

bonhomie ['bɔnəmi], *n.* afabilidad, *f.*

bonnet ['bɔnit], *n.* toca, sombrero de mujer; capota; (*mech.*) cubierta; (*eccl., educ.*) bonete, *m.*

bonny ['bɔni], *a.* (*dial.*) lindo, bonito; regordete.

bonus ['bounəs], *n.* bonificación, *f.*, adehala.

bony ['bouni], *a.* huesudo; huesoso; descarnado.

boo [bu:], *n.* silba, pitada.—*v.t., v.i.* silbar, pitar.

booby ['bu:bi], *n.* zoquete, *m.*, marmolillo.

booby-prize ['bu:bipraiz], *n.* premio dado con ironía al último.

booby-trap ['bu:bitræp], *n.* armadijo, trampa explosiva.

book [buk], *n.* libro; libreta, librillo; **to bring to** —, pedir cuentas a; **by the** —, según las reglas.—*v.t.* sacar (*billetes*), reservar; notar; (*fam.*) acusar.

bookbinder ['bukbaində], *n.* encuadernador, *m.*

bookbinding ['bukbaindiŋ], *n.* encuadernación, *f.*

bookcase ['bukkeis], *n.* estantería, armario, *m.*

booking ['bukiŋ], *n.* reservación, *f.*; — **office**, taquilla, despacho de billetes.

bookish ['bukiʃ], *a.* libresco.

booklet ['buklit], *n.* folleto, librete, *m.*

bookmaker ['bukmeikə], *n.* corredor (*m.*) de apuestas.

bookmark ['bukma:k], *n.* señal, *f.*

bookseller ['bukselə], *n.* librero.

book-shop ['bukʃɔp], *n.* librería.

bookworm ['bukwə:m], *n.* polilla; (*fam.*) ratón (*m.*) de biblioteca.

boom [bu:m], *n.* trueno; (*mech.*) aguilón, *m.*; (*naut.*) barrera; botalón, *m.*; auge, *m.*; (*com.*) prosperidad repentina.—*v.i.* medrar, prosperar mucho.

boomerang ['bu:məræŋ], *n.* bumerang, *m.*; (*fig.*) repercusión, (*f.*) que causa efecto en el autor de una acción.—*v.i.* repercutir los efectos de una acción en su autor.

boon [bu:n], *n.* favor, *m.*, gracia; dicha, bendición, *f.*; — **companion**, buen compañero, compañero inseparable.

boor [buə], *n.* patán, *m.*, pataco.

boorish ['buəriʃ], *a.* chabacano; batueco.

boost [bu:st], *n.* empujón, *m.*; ayuda.—*v.t.* empujar; ayudar; reforzar.

booster ['bu:stə], *n.* (*mech.*) elevador, aumentador, *m.*

236

boot (I) [bu:t], *n.* bota; (*Brit.*) portaequipaje (*de un coche*), *m.*; —*v.t.* dar un puntapié a.
boot (2) [bu:t], *n.* garancia.
bootblack ['bu:tblæk], *n.* limpiabotas, *m.sg.*
bootee [bu:'ti:], *n.* bota de mujer *o* de niños.
booth [bu:ð], *n.* quiosco, cabina; puesto.
bootlegging ['bu:tlegiŋ], *n.* contrabanda de licores.
boot-licker ['bu:tlikə], *n.* (*fam.*) lameculos, *m.f. inv.*
booty ['bu:ti], *n.* botín, *m.*
booze [bu:z], *n.* (*fam.*) zumo de cepas, bebidas.—*v.i.* (*fam.*) beber mucho, coger una turca.
borax ['bɔ:ræks], *n.* bórax, *m.*
Bordeaux [bɔ:'dou], *n.* Burdeos, *m.*
border ['bɔ:də], *n.* confín, *m.*; frontera; margen, *m.* o *f.*; dobladillo; orla; borde, *m.*; franja; arriata (*jardín*).—*v.t.* orlar, dobladillar.—*v.i.* lindar, confinar (con), rayar en (*on, upon*).
borderline ['bɔ:dəlain], *a.* fronterizo; incierto.—*n.* región fronteriza.
bore [bɔ:], *n.* taladro, barreno; calibre, *m.*; (*fam.*) lata; pelmazo, machacón (*persona*), *m.*—*v.t.* taladrar, barrenar; aburrir, fastidiar. [BEAR].
boredom ['bɔ:dəm], *n.* aburrimiento.
boring ['bɔ:riŋ], *a.* aburrido.
born [bɔ:n], *a.* nacido; nato; *to be —,* nacer.
borne [bɔ:n], [BEAR].
borough ['bʌrə], *n.* municipio.
borrow ['bɔrou], *v.t.* pedir *o* tomar prestado.
bosh [bɔʃ], *n.* (*fam.*) bobada, tontería.
bosom ['buzəm], *n.* seno; — *friend,* amigo íntimo.
boss (I) [bɔs], *n.* jefe, *m.,* amo; (*pol.*) cacique, *m.*—*v.t.* dominar, ser muy mandamás.
boss (2) [bɔs], *n.* protuberancia.
bossy ['bɔsi], *a.* mandón.
bo'sun [BOATSWAIN].
botanical [bə'tænikəl], *a.* botánico.
botanist ['bɔtənist], *n.* botánico.
botany ['bɔtəni], *n.* botánica.
botch [bɔtʃ], *n.* chapucería.—*v.t.* chapucear.
both [bouθ], *a., pron.* ambos, los dos; — ... *and,* tanto ... como.
bother ['bɔðə], *n.* molestia.—*v.t.* molestar.—*v.i.* molestarse (*with, about,* con).
bothersome ['bɔðəsəm], *a.* molesto.
bottle [bɔtl], *n.* botella.—*v.t.* embotellar.
bottom ['bɔtəm], *n.* fondo; base, *f.*; pie, *m.*; (*fam.*) asentaderas, *f.pl.*; *at —,* en el fondo.
bottomless ['bɔtəmlis], *a.* insondable.
boudoir ['bu:dwa:], *n.* tocador, gabinete, *m.*
bough [bau], *n.* rama.
bought [bɔ:t] [BUY].
boulder ['bouldə], *n.* canto.
bounce [bauns], *n.* bote, *m.*—*v.t.* hacer botar.—*v.i.* botar; dar saltitos.
bouncing ['baunsiŋ], *a.* rollizo, frescachón.
bound (I) [baund], *a.* forzado, obligado; encuadernado; resuelto; relacionado. [BIND].
bound (2) [baund], *a.* — *for,* con rumbo a.
bound (3) [baund], *n.* salto; bote, *m.*—*v.i.* saltar.
bound (4) [baund], *n.* límite, *m.*—*v.t.* confinar.
boundary ['baundəri], *n.* término, límite, confín, *m.*
boundless ['baundlis], *a.* infinito.
bountiful ['bauntiful], *a.* largo, dadivoso; copioso.
bounty ['baunti], *n.* munificencia; prima.

bouquet [bu'kei], *n.* ramillete, *m.*; aroma del vino.
Bourbon ['buəbən], *n.* Borbón, *m.*
bourgeois ['buəʒwa:], *a., n. inv.* burgués (*n. m.*).
bourgeoisie [buəʒwa:'zi:], *n.* burguesía.
bout [baut], *n.* partida; ataque, *m.*
bovine ['bouvain], *a.* bovino, vacuno.
bow (I) [bou], *n.* arco; nudo, lazo.
bow (2) [bau], *n.* reverencia, cortesía; (*naut.*) proa.—*v.t.* inclinar; someter.—*v.i.* inclinarse; doblarse, ceder.
bowdlerize ['baudləraiz], *v.t.* expurgar.
bowels [bauəlz], *n.pl.* entrañas, *f.pl.,* intestinos, *m.pl.*
bower [bauə], *n.* emparrado, cenador, *m.*
bowl (I) [boul], *n.* escudilla, taza; tazón, *m.*; cuenco. bola (*sport*).—*pl.* bolos (*juego*).—*v.t.* hacer rodar; bolear; *to — over,* derribar; atropellar; desconcertar.—*v.i.* jugar a los bolos.
bow-legged ['bou'legid], *a.* (pati)estevado.
bowman ['boumən], *n.* arquero.
bowsprit ['bousprit], *n.* bauprés, *m.*
box [bɔks], *n.* caja; (*theat.*) palco; (*bot.*) boj, *m.*; manotada.—*v.t.* encajonar; abofetear.—*v.i.* boxear.
boxer ['bɔksə], *n.* boxeador, *m.*
boxing ['bɔksiŋ], *a.* de boxeo.—*n.* boxeo.
Boxing-day ['bɔksiŋdei], *n.* día (*m.*) de los aguinaldos (26 *de diciembre*).
box-office ['bɔksɔfis], *n.* taquilla; despacho de entradas.
boy [bɔi], *n.* muchacho; chico; niño; mozo; — *scout,* explorador, *m.*
boycott ['bɔikɔt], *n.* boicot(eo), *m.*—*v.t.* boicotear.
bra [bra:], *n.* (*fam.*) sostén, ajustador, *m.*
brace [breis], *n.* tirante, *m.*; par (*dos*), *m.*; (*carp.*) berbiquí, *m.*; — *pl.* (*Brit.*) tirantes.—*v.t.* arriostrar; asegurar; atesar.—*v.r.* prepararse.
bracelet ['breislit], *n.* pulsera; brazalete, *m.*
bracing ['breisiŋ], *a.* fortificante. [BRACE].
bracken ['brækən], *n.* helecho.
bracket ['brækit], *n.* soporte, *m.,* repisa; (*print.*) corchete, paréntesis, *m.*
brackish ['brækiʃ], *a.* salobre.
bradawl ['brædɔ:l], *n.* (a)lesna, (a)lezna.
brag [bræg], *n.* bravata.—*v.i.* jactarse.
braggart ['brægət], *n.* bravucón, *m.*
bragging ['brægiŋ], *n.* jactancia.
braid [breid], *n.* galón, *m.*; trenza.
brain [brein], *n.* cerebro, seso; — *pl.* inteligencia; (*cul.*) sesos, *m.pl.*; *to rack one's brains,* devanarse los sesos.—*v.t.* descalabrar.
brainless ['breinlis], *a.* insensato, lelo, tonto.
brain-wave ['breinweiv], *n.* inspiración genial, *f.*
brainy ['breini], *a.* sesudo, inteligente.
brake [breik], *n.* freno; (*bot.*) helecho; matorral, *m.*—*v.t.* frenar.
bramble ['bræmbl], *n.* zarza.
bran [bræn], *n.* salvado.
branch [bra:ntʃ], *n.* rama; ramo; (*com.*) sucursal, *f.*; ramal, *m.*—*v.i.* ramificarse; *to — out,* extenderse.
brand [brænd], *n.* (*com.*) marca; hierro; tizón, *m.*; — *-new,* nuevo flamante.—*v.t.* marcar; herrar; tiznar.

brandish ['brændiʃ], *v.t.* blandir, blandear.
brandy ['brændi], *n.* coñac, *m.*
brasier [BRAZIER].
brass [brɑ:s], *n.* latón, *m.*; (*fam.*) parné, *m.*, dinero; (*fam., mil.*) jefotes, *m.pl.*
brass band ['brɑ:s'bænd], *n.* charanga.
brassière ['bræsiǝ], *n.* sostén, ajustador, *m.*
brassy ['brɑ:si], *a.* de latón; descarado; metálico.
brat [bræt], *n.* (*pej.*) mocoso.
bravado [brǝ'vɑ:dou], *n.* bravata.
brave [breiv], *a.* valiente, valeroso.—*n.* guerrero pelirrojo.—*v.t.* arrostrar; retar.
bravery ['breivǝri], *n.* valentía, valor, *m.*
bravo! ['brɑ'vou], *interj.* ¡bravo!
brawl [brɔ:l], *n.* reyerta.—*v.i.* armar camorra.
brawn [brɔ:n], *n.* embutido; fuerza, músculos, *m.pl.*
brawny ['brɔ:ni], *a.* forzudo, fuertote.
bray [brei], *n.* rebuzno.—*v.i.* rebuznar.
brazen ['breizǝn], *a.* de latón; de bronce; descarado (*persona*).
brazier ['breiziǝ], *n.* brasero.
Brazil [brǝ'zil], *n.* Brasil, *m.*
Brazilian [brǝ'ziljǝn], *a., n.* brasileño.
breach [bri:tʃ], *n.* brecha, abertura; abuso, violación, *f.*—*v.t.* batir en brecha.
bread [bred], *n.* pan, *m.*
breadth [bredθ], *n.* anchura.
break [breik], *n.* rotura; rompimiento; grieta, raja; interrupción, *f.*; recreo, descanso; ruptura.—*v.t.* *irr.* quebrar, quebrantar; romper; cortar; comunicar (*noticias*); faltar a (*palabra*); batir (*un 'record'*).—*v.i. irr.* romper(se); quebrar(se); **to — down,** analizar; desquiciar; averiarse; deshacerse; **to — in,** domar (*caballos*); entrar para robar; forzar; **to — out,** declararse, estallar; evadirse.
breakage ['breikidʒ], *n.* rotura; fractura.
breakdown ['breikdaun], *n.* avería; colapso; análisis, *m. inv.*
breakfast ['brekfǝst], *n.* desayuno.—*v.i.* desayunar.
break-through ['breikθru:], *n.* brecha; avance sensacional, *m.*
breakwater ['breikwɔ:tǝ], *n.* rompeolas, *m.sg.*
breast [brest], *n.* pecho; (*orn.*) pechuga; pechera (*ropa*); **to make a clean — of,** confesar francamente.
breast-plate ['brestpleit], *n.* peto, coraza.
breastwork ['brestwǝ:k], *n.* parapeto.
breath [breθ], *n.* aliento, respiración, *f.*; sollo; **— of wind,** soplo de viento; **under one's —,** en voz baja; **out of —,** sin aliento.
breathe [bri:ð], *v.t.* respirar; infundir.—*v.i.* respirar; soplar; **to — in,** aspirar; **to — out,** espirar.
breather ['bri:ðǝ], *n.* respiro, descansito.
breathing ['bri:ðiŋ], *n.* respiración, *f.*; **— space,** descanso.
breathless ['breθlis], *a.* jadeante; sin aliento.
breath-taking ['breθteikiŋ], *a.* pasmoso.
bred [bred] [BREED].
breech [bri:tʃ], *n.* culata (*fusil*); trasero.—*pl.* calzones, *m.pl.*
breed [bri:d], *n.* raza.—*v.t. irr.* criar.—*v.i. irr.* criarse.
breeder ['bri:dǝ], *n.* criador, *m.*
breeding ['bri:diŋ], *n.* cria; crianza; educación, *f.*; linaje, *m.*
breeze [bri:z], *n.* brisa.

breezy ['bri:zi], *a.* airoso; vivaracho.
brethren ['breðrin], *n.pl.* (*eccl. etc.*) hermanos, *m.pl.*
Breton ['bretǝn], *a., n.* bretón, *m.*
breve [bri:v], *n.* (*mus.*) breve, *f.*
breviary ['bri:vjǝri], *n.* breviario.
brevity ['breviti], *n.* brevedad, *f.*
brew [bru:], *n.* mezcla; infusión, *f.*—*v.t.* bracear (*cerveza*), preparar, hacer (*té etc.*); urdir.—*v.i.* elaborar cerveza; amenazar, urdirse.
brewer [bru:ǝ], *n.* cervecero.
brewery ['bru:ǝri], *n.* cervecería.
brewing ['bru:iŋ], *a.* cervecero.
briar [braiǝ], *n.* rosal silvestre, *m.*; zarza.
bribe [braib], *n.* soborno.—*v.t.* sobornar.
bribery ['braibǝri], *n.* cohecho, soborno.
bric-à-brac ['brikǝbræk], *n.* fruslerías, curiosidades, *f.pl.*
brick [brik], *n.* ladrillo; (*fam.*) buen tipo.
brickbat ['brikbæt], *n.* pedazo de ladrillo.
bricklayer ['brikleiǝ], *n.* albañil, *m.*
brickwork ['brikwɔ:k], *n.* enladrillado.
brickyard ['brikja:d], *n.* ladrillar, *m.*
bridal [braidl], *a.* de novia, nupcial.
bride [braid], *n.* novia.
bridegroom ['braidgrum], *n.* novio.
bridesmaid ['braidzmeid], *n.* madrina de boda.
bridge [bridʒ], *n.* puente, *m.*—*v.t.* pontear; salvar.
bridle [braidl], *n.* brida, freno.—*v.t.* refrenar; embridar.
brief [bri:f], *a.* breve.—*n.* (*jur.*) escrito, causa; (*eccl.*) breve, *m.*—*v.t.* (*jur.*) alegar; dar instrucciones a.
brier [BRIAR].
brig(antine) ['brig(ǝnti:n)], *n.* bergantín, *m.*
brigade [bri'geid], *n.* brigada.
brigadier [brigǝ'diǝ], *n.* general (*m.*) de brigada.
brigand ['brigǝnd], *n.* bandolero.
bright [brait], *a.* claro, brillante; subido; listo.
brighten [braitn], *v.t.* abrillantar; avivar.—*v.i.* despejarse; avivarse.
brightness ['braitnis], *n.* claridad, brillantez, *f.*; viveza.
brilliance ['briljǝns], *n.* brillantez, *f.*, brillo.
brilliant ['briljǝnt], *a.* brillante.
brim [brim], *n.* orilla; labio (*de vaso*); ala (*de sombrero*).—*v.i.* estar lleno; desbordarse.
brimful ['brimful], *a.* rebosante.
brimstone ['brimstǝn], *n.* azufre, *m.*
brine [brain], *n.* salmuera.
bring [briŋ], *v.t. irr.* traer; llevar; hacer venir; acarrear; reducir.—*v.r.* resignarse (**to,** a); **to — about,** causar; efectuar; **to — forth,** parir; producir; **to — off,** lograr; **to — on,** ocasionar; acarrear; **to — out,** sacar; publicar; **to — over,** persuadir; **to — up,** subir; educar, criar; **to — to light,** descubrir, sacar a luz.
brink [briŋk], *n.* borde, *m.*, margen, *m.* o *f.*; **on the — of,** a dos dedos de.
brinkmanship ['briŋkmǝnʃip], *n.* (*pol.*) política de riesgos calculados.
briny ['braini], *a.* salado, salobre.—*n.* (*fam.*) el mar.
brisk [brisk], *a.* animado; vivo, rápido.
bristle [brisl], *n.* cerda.—*v.i.* erizarse.
bristly ['brisli], *a.* erizado.

Britain ['britən], *n*. Gran Bretaña.
Britannia [bri'tænjə], *n*. dama simbólica de la Gran Bretaña.
British ['britiʃ], *a*. británico; **the —**, los británicos.
Briton ['britən], *n*. britano, británico.
Brittany ['britəni], *n*. Bretaña.
brittle [britl], *a*. quebradizo.
broach [broutʃ], *v.t*. encentar; abrir, empezar.
broad [brɔ:d], *a*. ancho; (*fig*.) lato; amplio; claro; indecente; pleno; grosero; fuerte (*dialecto*).
broadcast ['brɔ:dkɑ:st], *n*. (*rad*.) emisión, *f*.—*v.t*. (*conjug. like* CAST) (*rad*.) emitir, radiar; esparcir.
broadcasting ['brɔ:dkɑ:stiŋ], *n*. radio, *f*.
broaden [brɔ:dn], *v.t*. ensanchar.—*v.i.* -se.
broad-minded [brɔ:d'maindid], *a*. de manga ancha, de amplias miras.
broad-shouldered [brɔ:d'ʃouldəd], *a*. ancho de espaldas.
broadsheet ['brɔ:dʃi:t], *n*. pasquín, *m*.
broadside ['brɔ:dsaid], *n*. andanada.
brocade [bro'keid], *n*. brocado.
broccoli ['brɔkəli], *n*. brécol(es), *m.(pl.)*.
brochure ['brouʃə], *n*. folleto.
brogue [broug], *n*. zapato fuerte; acento irlandés.
broil [brɔil], *n*. camorra.—*v.t*. soasar.
broiler ['brɔilə], *n*. pollo para asar.
broke [brouk], *a*. (*fam*.) pelado, sin blanca. [BREAK].
broken [broukn], *a*. roto; accidentado, [BREAK].
broken-down ['broukndaun], *a*. descompuesto; destartalado, desvencijado.
broker ['broukə], *n*. corredor, cambista, *m*.
brokerage ['broukəridʒ], *n*. corretaje, *m*.
brolly ['brɔli], *n*. (*fam*.) paraguas, *m.sg*.
bromine ['broumi:n], *n*. bromo.
bronchitis [brɔŋ'kaitis], *n*. bronquitis, *f*.
bronco ['brɔŋkou], *n*. caballo cerril.
bronze [brɔnz], *n*. bronce, *m*.—*v.t.* broncear.
brooch [broutʃ], *n*. broche, alfiler (*m*.) de pecho.
brood [bru:d], *n*. nidada, camada; casta.—*v.t*. empollar.—*v.i*. enclocar; **to — (over),** rumiar, meditar melancólicamente.
broody ['bru:di], *a*. clueco; melancólico.—*n*. clueca.
brook [bruk], *n*. arroyo.—*v.t*. tolerar.
brooklet ['bruklit], *n*. arroyuelo.
broom (I) [bru:m], *n*. escoba.
broom (2) [bru:m], *n*. (*bot*.) hiniesta, retama.
broth [brɔθ], *n*. caldo.
brothel [brɔθl], *n*. burdel, *m*.
brother ['brʌðə], *n*. hermano.
brotherhood ['brʌðəhud], *n*. hermandad, *f*.
brother-in-law ['brʌðərinlɔ:], *n*. (*pl*. **brothers-in-law**) cuñado.
brotherly ['brʌðəli], *a*. fraternal.
brought [brɔ:t] [BRING].
browbeat ['braubi:t], *v.t*. (*conjug. like* BEAT) conminar.
brown [braun], *a*. castaño, pardo; moreno; tostado; dorado; **— bread,** pan bazo; **— study,** ensimismamiento; **— sugar,** azúcar moreno.—*v.t*. dorar; tostar.
brownish ['brauniʃ], *a*. pardusco.
browse [brauz], *v.i*. pacer; ramonear; hojear libros.

bruin ['bru:in], *n*. (*fam*.) oso.
bruise [bru:z], *n*. contusión, *f*., cardenal, *m*.—*v.t*. magullar, contundir; majar.
brunette [bru:'net], *n*. morena.
brunt [brʌnt], *n*. choque, *m*.; (*fig*.) lo más fuerte.
brush [brʌʃ], *n*. cepillo; brocha; (*art*.) pincel, *m*.; escaramuza; roce, *m*.; broza, mata.—*v.t*. cepillar; barrer; **to — against,** rozar con; **to — up,** repasar.
brushwood ['brʌʃwud], *n*. broza; matorral, *m*.
brusque [brusk], *a*. rudo, brusco.
Brussels [brʌslz], *n*. Bruselas, *f.sg*.; **— sprouts,** bretones, *m.pl*., coles (*f.pl*.) de Bruselas.
brutal [bru:tl], *a*. brutal, bestial.
brutality [bru:'tæliti], *n*. brutalidad, *f*.
brute [bru:t], *a*., *n*. bruto.
bubble [bʌbl], *n*. burbuja; ampolla; engañifa.—*v.i*. burbujear; **to — over,** rebosar.
bubonic plague [bju:'bɔnik'pleig], *n*. peste bubónica.
buccaneer [bʌkə'niə], *n*. filibustero, bucanero.
buck [bʌk], *n*. conejo; ciervo, gamo; macho cabrío; petimetre, *m*.; (*U.S. fam*.) dólar, *m*.—*v.i*. encorvarse; **to — up,** (*fam*.) animarse.
bucket ['bʌkit], *n*. cubo.
buckle [bʌkl], *n*. hebilla.—*v.t*. abrochar.
bucolic [bju:'kɔlik], *a*. bucólico.—*n*. bucólica.
bud [bʌd], *n*. botón, *m*.; yema; brote, *m*., pimpollo; **to nip in the —,** atajar lo apenas empezado.—*v.i*. brotar.
Buddha ['budə], *n*. Buda, *m*.
buddhist ['budist], *a*., *n*. budista, *m.f*.
buddy ['bʌdi], *n*. (*U.S., fam*.) compañero.
budge [bʌdʒ], *v.t*. remover.—*v.i*. removerse.
budgerigar ['bʌdʒərigɑ:], *n*. periquito.
budget ['bʌdʒit], *n*. presupuesto.—*v.t*. presuponer.
buff [bʌf], *a*., *n*. color (*m*.) de ante.
buffalo ['bʌfəlou], *n*. búfalo.
buffer ['bʌfə], *n*. tope, *m*., paragolpes, *m.sg*.; **— state,** estado tapón.
buffet (I) ['bʌfit], *n*. bofetada; alacena.—*v.t*. abofetear; golpear.
buffet (2) ['bufit], *n*. fonda; bar, *m*.; **— supper,** cena en frío.
buffoon [bə'fu:n], *n*. bufón, *m*.
buffoonery [bə'fu:nəri], *n*. bufonada.
bug [bʌg], *n*. (*Brit*.) chinche, *m*.; (*U.S*.) bicho, insecto.
bugbear ['bʌgbeə], *n*. espantajo.
bugle [bju:gl], *n*. corneta.
bugler ['bju:glə], *n*. corneta, *m*.
build [bild], *n*. talle, *m*.—*v.t. irr*. edificar, construir.
builder ['bildə], *n*. constructor, *m*., maestro de obras.
building ['bildiŋ], *n*. edificio; construcción, *f*.
build-up ['bildʌp], *n*. propaganda preparativa, bombo.
built [bilt], [BUILD].
built-in [bilt'in], *a*. incorporado; empotrado.
built-up area ['biltʌp'eəriə], *n*. aglomeración urbana.
bulb [bʌlb], *n*. (*elec*.) bombilla; (*bot*.) patata, bulbo; ampoll(et)a.
bulbous ['bʌlbəs], *a*. bulboso.
Bulgarian [bʌl'geəriən], *a*., *n*. búlgaro.

bulge

bulge [bʌldʒ], *n.* pandeo, comba.—*v.i.* combarse, bombearse.
bulk [bʌlk], *n.* bulto, masa, volumen, *m.*
bulky ['bʌlki], *a.* grueso, abultado.
bull (1) [bul], *n.* toro; (*com.*) alcista, *m.*; (*low*) música celestial.
bull (2) [bul], *n.* (*eccl.*) bula.
bulldog ['buldɔg], *n.* alano inglés, dogo.
bulldozer ['buldouzə], *n.* empujadora.
bullet ['bulit], *n.* bala.
bulletin ['bulitin], *n.* boletín, *m.*; (*U.S.*) anuncio. [**notice-board**]
bullfight ['bulfait], *n.* corrida de toros.
bullfighter ['bulfaitə], *n.* torero.
bullfighting ['bulfaitiŋ], *n.* toreo, tauromaquia.
bullfinch ['bulfintʃ], *n.* (*orn.*) camachuelo.
bullion ['buljən], *n.* oro *o* plata en lingotes.
bullock ['bulək], *n.* buey, *m.*, novillo.
bull-ring ['bulriŋ], *n.* plaza de toros; ruedo.
bull's-eye ['bulzai], *n.* blanco, centro del blanco.
bully ['buli], *n.* matón, matasiete, *m.*—*v.t.* intimidar, amenazar.
bulrush ['bulrʌʃ], *n.* junco.
bulwark ['bulwək], *n.* baluarte, *m.*
bumble-bee ['bʌmblbi:], *n.* abejarrón, *m.*
bump [bʌmp], *n.* tope, topetón, golpe, *m.*; comba; rebote, golpe, *m.*, hinchazón, *f.*—*v.t.* dar contra; golpear.—*v.i.* chocar; dar sacudidas.
bumper ['bʌmpə], *n.* parachoques, *m.sg.*
bumpkin ['bʌmpkin], *n.* patán, *m.*, paleto.
bumptious ['bʌmpʃəs], *a.* fantasmón.
bun [bʌn], *n.* bollo.
bunch [bʌntʃ], *n.* manojo; racimo (*de uvas*); ristra; ramo, ramillete (*de flores*), *m.*, grupo.—*v.t.* juntar.
bundle [bʌndl], *n.* lío; atado; fardo.—*v.t.* liar; mandar.
bung [bʌŋ], *n.* bitoque, tapón, *m.*
bungle [bʌŋgl], *v.t., v.i.* chapucear.
bungler ['bʌŋglə], *n.* chapucero.
bunion ['bʌnjən], *n.* juanete, *m.*
bunk [bʌŋk], *n.* tarima; (*fam.*) música celestial, disparates, *m.pl.*
bunker ['bʌŋkə], *n.* carbonera; fortín, *m.*; hoya.
bunkum ['bʌŋkəm], *n.* (*fam.*) [BUNK].
bunny ['bʌni], *n.* (*fam.*) conejito.
bunsen burner ['bʌnsn'bə:nə], *n.* mechero Bunsen.
bunting (1) ['bʌntiŋ], *n.* banderas (*f.pl.*) de adorno, lanilla.
bunting (2) ['bʌntiŋ], *n.* (*orn.*) escribano.
buoy [bɔi], *n.* boya.
buoyant ['bɔiənt], *a.* boyante; vivaz.
burden ['bə:dn], *n.* carga; tema, *m.*; importe, *m.*; estribillo.—*v.t.* cargar; gravar.
bureau [bjuə'rou], *n.* agencia, oficina; escritorio.
bureaucracy [bjuə'rɔkrəsi], *n.* burocracia.
bureaucrat ['bjuəroukræt], *n.* burócrata, *m.f.*
burgess ['bə:dʒis], *n.* ciudadano, burgués, *m.*
burglar ['bə:glə], *n.* ladrón, escalador, *m.*
burglary ['bə:gləri], *n.* robo de una casa.
burgle [bə:gl], *v.t.* robar (*una casa*).
Burgundy ['bə:gəndi], *n.* Borgoña; borgoña (*vino*), *m.*
burial ['beriəl], *n.* entierro.
burlesque [bə:'lesk], *a.* festivo, burlesco.—*n.* parodia.

burly ['bə:li], *a.* fornido.
Burma ['bə:mə], *n.* Birmania.
Burmese ['bə:'mi:z], *a., n.* birmano.
burn [bə:n], *n.* quemadura; (*dial.*) arroyo.—*v.t. irr.* quemar; incendiar.—*v.i. irr.* arder; quemarse; escocer (*dolor*).
burnish ['bə:niʃ], *v.t.* bruñir.
burnt [bə:nt] [BURN].
burrow ['bʌrou], *n.* madriguera.—*v.i.* amadrigarse.
bursar ['bə:sə], *n.* tesorero.
bursary ['bə:səri], *n.* beca; tesorería.
burst [bə:st] *n.* reventón, *m.*; ráfaga.—*v.t. irr.* reventar, quebrar.—*v.i. irr.* reventar(se); arrojarse; romper (*out, into,* a).
bury ['beri], *v.t.* enterrar.
bus [bʌs], *n.* autobús, *m.*
bush [buʃ], *n.* arbusto; matorral, *m.*; mata; (*mech.*) buje, *m.*
bushel [buʃl], *n.* medida de capacidad de unos 36, 35 litros; (*U.S.*) 35, 23 litros.
bushy ['buʃi], *a.* espeso; matoso.
business ['biznis], *n.* negocio(s); comercio; asunto; *you have no — to do that,* Vd. no tiene derecho a hacer eso; *meaning* —, en serio.
businesslike ['biznislaik], *a.* serio, metódico.
businessman ['biznismən], *n.* hombre (*m.*) de negocios.
buskin ['bʌskin], *n.* borceguí, *m.*
bust [bʌst], *n.* busto; pecho de mujer.
bustle [bʌsl], *n.* bullicio; polisón (*vestido*), *m.*—*v.i.* apresurarse.
busy ['bizi], *a.* ocupado; atareado.—*v.t.* ocupar.
busybody ['bizibɔdi], *n.* bullebulle, *m.*, entremetido.
but [bʌt], *prep.* excepto, sino.—*conj.* pero, mas; (*after neg.*) sino que; *all* —, casi; *nothing* —, nada más que.
butcher ['butʃə], *n.* carnicero.—*v.t.* matar.
butchery ['butʃəri], *n.* carnicería.
butler ['bʌtlə], *n.* mayordomo, repostero.
butt [bʌt], *n.* blanco, hito; cabezada; hazmerreír; tonel, *m.*; colilla; culata.—*v.t.* top(et)ar; dar cabezadas a.
butter ['bʌtə], *n.* mantequilla.—*v.t.* (*fam.*) lisonjear.
butterfly ['bʌtəflai], *n.* mariposa.
buttocks ['bʌtəks], *n.pl.* nalgas, *f.pl.*
button [bʌtn], *n.* botón, *m.*—*v.t.* abotonar.
button-hole ['bʌtnhoul], *n.* ojal, *m.*—*v.t.* detener (*persona*).
buttress ['bʌtris], *n.* contrafuerte, *m.*; apoyo.—*v.t.* reforzar; apoyar.
buxom ['bʌksəm], *a.f.* regordeta, rolliza.
buy [bai], *v.t.* (*fam.*) compra.—*v.t. irr.* comprar.
buzz [bʌz], *n.* zumbido.—*v.i.* zumbar; — *off!* (*fam.*) ¡lárgate!
buzzard ['bʌzəd], *n.* (*orn.*) ratonero.
buzz saw ['bʌzsɔ:], *n.* (*U.S.*) sierra circular.
by [bai], *adv.* cerca; por aquí *o* ahí.—*prep.* por; de; para (*cierto tiempo*); — *and* —, dentro de poco; — *and large,* en general; — *far,* con mucho.
'bye! [bai], *interj.* ¡hasta luego!
by-election ['baiilekʃn], *n.* (*Brit.*) elección (*f.*) para llenar una vacante parlamentaria.
Byelorussian ['bjelou'rʌʃən], *a.* bielorruso.
bygone ['baigɔn], *a., a.* pasado; *let bygones be bygones,* lo pasado pasado.

by-law [ˈbailɔ:], *n.* ley local *o* secundaria, *f.*
by-pass [ˈbaipɑ:s], *n.* desviación, *f.—v.t.* evitar.
by-product [ˈbaiprɔdʌkt], *n.* derivado.
bystander [ˈbaistændə], *n.* circunstante, *m.f.*
by-street [ˈbaistri:t], *n.* callejuela.
by-ways [ˈbaiweiz], *n.pl.* andurriales, *m.pl.*
by-word [ˈbaiwə:d], *n.* apodo; oprobio; dicho, refrán, *m.*

C

C, c [si:], *n.* tercera letra del alfabeto inglés; **C,** (*mus.*) do.
cab [kæb], *n.* cabriolé; taxi, *m.*; casilla (*del maquinista*).
cabal [kəˈbæl], *n.* cábala.
cabbage [ˈkæbidʒ], *n.* col, *f.*, berza.
cabby [ˈkæbi], *n.* (*fam.*) taxista, *m.*
cabin [ˈkæbin], *n.* cabaña; (*naut.*) camarote, *m.*; (*aer.*) cabina.
cabin-boy [ˈkæbinbɔi], *n.* mozo de cámara.
cabinet [ˈkæbinit], *a.* (*pol.*) ministerial.—*n.* gabinete; escaparate, *m.*, vitrina (*de vidrio*); armario.
cabinet-maker [ˈkæbinitˈmeikə] *n.* ebanista, *m.*
cable [keibl], *n.* cable; cablegrama, *m.—v.t., v.i.* cablegrafiar.
cache [kæʃ], *n.* escondite, *m.—v.t.* esconder.
cachet [ˈkæʃei], *n.* sello particular.
cackle [kækl], *n.* cacareo; cháchara.—*v.i.* cacarear; reírse; chacharear.
cacophonous [kəˈkɔfənəs], *a.* cacofónico.
cacophony [kəˈkɔfəni], *n.* cacofonía.
cactus [ˈkæktəs], *n.* cacto.
cad [kæd], *n.* canalla, *m.*; persona mal educada.
cadaverous [kəˈdævərəs], *a.* cadavérico.
caddie [ˈkædi], *n.* muchacho (*golf*).
caddish [ˈkædiʃ], *a.* mal educado.
caddy [ˈkædi], *n.* cajita (*para té*).
cadence [ˈkeidəns], *n.* cadencia.
cadet [kəˈdet], *n.* (*mil.*) cadete, *m.*; (*lit.*) hermano menor.
cadge [kædʒ], *v.t.* (*fam.*) obtener mendigando.—*v.i.* (*fam.*) gorronear.
cadmium [ˈkædmiəm], *n.* cadmio.
caesura [siˈzjuərə], *n.* cesura.
café [ˈkæfei], *n.* café (*sitio*), *m.*
cafeteria [kæfiˈtiəriə], *n.* restaurante, café, *m.*
cafein(e) [ˈkæfi:n], *n.* cafeína.
cage [keidʒ], *n.* jaula.—*v.t.* enjaular.
cag(e)y [ˈkeidʒi], *a.* (*fam.*) zorro, cauteloso.
Cain [kein] *n.* (*Bib.*) Caín, *m.*
Cairo [ˈkaiərou], *n.* el Cairo, *m.*
cajole [kəˈdʒoul], *v.t.* halagar.
cajolery [kəˈdʒouləri], *n.* halago, zalamería.
cake [keik], *n.* bollo, pastel, *m.*; pastilla (*jabón etc.*).—*v.i.* pegarse.
calabash [ˈkæləbæʃ], *n.* calabaza.
calamitous [kəˈlæmitəs], *a.* calamitoso.
calamity [kəˈlæmiti], *n.* calamidad, *f.*
calcium [ˈkælsiəm], *n.* calcio.
calculate [ˈkælkjuleit], *v.t.* calcular; *calculated to,* aprestado para.

calculation [ˈkælkjuˈleiʃən], **calculus** [ˈkælkjuləs], *n.* cálculo.
caldron [CAULDRON].
Caledonian [kæliˈdounjən], *a.* caledonio escocés.
calendar [ˈkælində], *n.* calendario.
calends [ˈkælindz], *n.pl.* calendas, *f.pl.*
calf (1) [kɑ:f], *n.* (*pl.* **calves**) ternero; (piel de) becerro; pasta española.
calf (2) [kɑ:f], *n.* (*anat.*) pantorrilla.
calibrate [ˈkælibreit], *v.t.* calibrar.
calibre [ˈkælibə], *n.* calibre, *m.*; (*fig.*) calaña.
calico [ˈkælikou], *n.* calicó.
calipers [ˈkælipəz], *n.pl.* calibrador, *m.*
caliph [ˈkeilif], *n.* califa, *m.*
caliphate [ˈkælifeit], *n.* califato.
calix [ˈkeiliks], *n.* (*bot.*) cáliz, *m.*
calk [CAULK].
call [kɔ:l], *n.* llamada; grito; visita; **on —,** disponible; de guardia; (*com.*) a solicitud.—*v.t.* llamar; despertar; llamar (por teléfono); **to — back,** (*tel.*) volver a llamar; **to — off,** aplazar; disuadir; **to — together,** convocar; **to — up,** reclutar; llamar (por teléfono).—*v.i.* gritar; hacer una visita.
call-boy [ˈkɔ:lbɔi], *n.* botones, *m.sg.*; (*theat.*) avisador, *m.*
caller [ˈkɔ:lə], *n.* llamador, *m.*; visita.
calligraphy [kæˈligrəfi], *n.* caligrafía.
calliper(s) [CALIPERS].
callous [ˈkæləs], *a.* duro, insensible; calloso.
callousness [ˈkæləsnis], *n.* (*fig.*) dureza; callosidad, *f.*
callow [ˈkælou], *a.* joven e inexperto.
callus [ˈkæləs], *n.* callo.
calm [kɑ:m], *a.* tranquilo, quieto.—*n.* calma; sosiego, serenidad, *f.—v.t.* calmar, tranquilizar.—*v.i.* calmarse (**down**).
calmly [ˈkɑ:mli], *adv.* sosegadamente.
calmness [ˈkɑ:mnis], *n.* tranquilidad, *f.*
calorie, calory [ˈkæləri], *n.* caloría.
calumniate [kəˈlʌmnieit], *v.t.* calumniar.
calumny [ˈkæləmni], *n.* calumnia.
Calvary [ˈkælvəri], *n.* Calvario.
calve [ˈkɑ:v], *v.t., v.i.* parir (*dícese de la vaca*).—*n.pl.* [CALF].
Calvinist [ˈkælvinist], *a., n.* calvinista, *m.f.*
calypso [kəˈlipsou], *n.* calipso.
calyx [CALIX].
cam [kæm], *n.* leva.
camber [ˈkæmbə], *n.* comba; convexidad (*del camino*), *f.*
Cambodia [kæmˈboudjə], *n.* Camboya.
Cambodian [kæmˈboudjən], *a., n.* camboyano.
cambric [ˈkæmbrik], *n.* batista, holán, *m.*
came [keim] [COME].
camel [ˈkæməl], *n.* camello.
camellia [kəˈmi:ljə], *n.* camelia.
cameo [ˈkæmiou], *n.* camafeo.
camera [ˈkæmərə], *n.* máquina (fotográfica); **in —** (*jur.*) en secreto.
cameraman [ˈkæmərəmæn], *n.* (*cin.*) operador.
Cameroons [kæməˈru:nz], *n.pl.* Camerón, *m.*
camomile [ˈkæməmail], *n.* manzanilla, camomila.
camouflage [ˈkæməflɑ:ʒ], *n.* (*mil.*) camuflaje *m.*; enmascaramiento.—*v.t.* camuflar.
camp [kæmp], *n.* campamento; campo.—*v.i.* acampar.
campaign [kæmˈpein], *n.* campaña.

camp-follower ['kæmp'fɒlouə], *n.* vivandero.
camphor ['kæmfə], *n.* alcanfor, *m.*
camphorate ['kæmfəreit], *v.t.* alcanforar.
campus ['kæmpəs], *n.* (*esp.* *U.S.*) recinto (*de la universidad*).
cam-shaft ['kæmʃɑːft], *n.* árbol (*m.*) de levas.
can (1) [kæn], *n.* lata, envase, *m.—v.t.* enlatar. (TIN).
can (2) [kæn], *v. aux. irr.* poder.
Canaan ['keinən], *n.* (*Bib.*) Tierra de Canaán *o* de promisión.
Canada ['kænədə], *n.* Canadá, *m.*
Canadian [kə'neidjən], *a., n.* canadiense, *m.f.*
canal [kə'næl], *n.* canal, *m.*; acequia (*riego*).
canard [kæ'nɑːd], *n.* noticia falsa; embuste, *m.*
Canaries [kə'neəriz], **Canary Islands** [kə'neəri ailəndz], *n.pl.* Canarias, *f.pl.*
canary [kə'neəri], *n.* (*orn.*) canario.
cancan ['kænkæn], *n.* cancán, *m.*
cancel ['kænsəl], *v.t.* suprimir; cancelar; matasellar (*correo*).
cancellation [kænsə'leiʃən], *n.* supresión; cancelación, *f.*; matasello (*correo*).
cancer ['kænsə], *n.* cáncer, *m.*; (*astr.*) Cáncer, *m.*
cancerous ['kænsərəs], *a.* canceroso.
candelabrum [kændi'lɑːbrəm], *n.* (*pl.* **-bra**) candelabro.
candid ['kændid], *a.* franco; cándido.
candidate ['kændidit], *n.* candidato.
candidature ['kændiditʃə], *n.* candidatura.
candle [kændl], *n.* vela, bujía, candela.
candlepower ['kændlpauə], *n.* bujía.
candlestick ['kændlstik], *n.* palmatoria; candelero.
candour ['kændə], *n.* franqueza; candor, *m.*
candy ['kændi], *n.* (*esp.* *U.S.*) dulce, confite, bonbón, *m.*
cane [kein], *n.* bastón, *m.*; caña; mimbre, *m.—v.t.* apalear, bastonear.
canine ['keinain], *a.* canino.—*n.* colmillo (*diente*).
canister ['kænistə], *n.* lata, bote, *m.*
canker ['kæŋkə], *n.* (*bot.*) cancro; (*med.*) gangrena; corrosión, *f.—v.t.* gangrenar.—*v.i.* -se.
cankerous ['kæŋkərəs], *a.* gangrenoso.
cannery ['kænəri], *n.* fábrica de conservas.
cannibal ['kænibəl], *a., n.* caníbal, *m.f.*, antropófago.
canning ['kæniŋ], *a.* conservero.—*n.* envase (*en latas*). *m.*
cannon ['kænən], *n.* cañón, *m.*
cannon-ball ['kænənbɔːl], *n.* bala de cañón.
cannon-fodder ['kænən'fɔdə], *n.* carne (*f.*) de cañón.
cannon-shot ['kænən'ʃɔt], *n.* tiro de cañón; alcance (*m.*) de cañón.
cannot ['kænɔt] [CAN NOT].
canny ['kæni], *a.* astuto.
canoe [kə'nuː], *n.* piragua, canoa.
canon ['kænən], *n.* canon (*regla*), *m.*; canónigo (*señor*).
canonical [kə'nɒnikəl], *a.* canónico.
canonize ['kænənaiz], *v.t.* canonizar.
canonry ['kænənri], *n.* canonjía.
can-opener ['kænoupənə], *n.* (*U.S.*) abrelatas, *m.sg.*
canopy ['kænəpi], *n.* dosel, *m.*; (*elec.*) campana.—*v.t.* endoselar.
cant [kænt], *n.* hipocresía; jerga; sesgo.—*v.t.* inclinar.—*v.i.* -se; hablar con hipocresía.

can't [kɑːnt] [CAN NOT].
cantankerous [kæn'tæŋkərəs], *a.* pendenciero, avieso.
canteen [kæn'tiːn], *n.* cantina; (*mil.*) cantimplora.
canter ['kæntə], *n.* medio galope.—*v.i.* andar (a caballo) a medio galope.
Canterbury ['kæntəbəri], *n.* Cantórbery, *m.*
cantharides [kæn'θæridiːz], *n.pl.* polvo de cantárida.
canticle ['kæntikl], *n.* cántico.
cantilever ['kæntiliːvə], *n.* viga voladiza; — *bridge,* puente (*m.*) de contrapeso.
canton ['kæntɔn], *n.* cantón, *m.*
cantonment [kæn'tuːnmənt], *n.* acantonamiento.
cantor ['kæntɔː], *n.* chantre, *m.*; cantor principal, *m.*
canvas ['kænvəs], *n.* cañamazo, lona; *under* —, (*mil.*) en tiendas, (*naut.*) con las velas izadas.
canvass ['kænvəs], *n.* solicitación (*f.*) de votos *o* opiniones; escrutinio.—*v.i.* solicitar votos.
canyon ['kænjən], *n.* cañón, *m.*
cap [kæp], *n.* gorra (*sombrero*); tapa, tapón (*de una lata etc.*), *m.*; bonete (*universidad*) *m.*; cápsula (*percusión*).—*v.t.* poner tapa a saludar; acabar, rematar.
capability [keipə'biliti], *n.* habilidad, *f.*
capable ['keipəbl], *a.* capaz, hábil.
capacious [kə'peiʃəs], *a.* capaz, espacioso.
capacity [kə'pæsiti], *n.* capacidad; aptitud *f.*
caparison [kə'pærisn], *n.* caparazón, *m.* paramento.
cape (1) [keip], *n.* capa, esclavina (*ropa*).
cape (2) [keip], *n.* (*geog.*) cabo; *Cape Horn* Cabo de Hornos; *Cape of Good Hope* Cabo de Buena Esperanza.
caper (1) ['keipə], *n.* cabriola.—*v.i.* cabriolar
caper (2) ['keipə], *n.* (*bot.*) alcaparra.
capillary [kə'piləri], *a.* capilar.
capital ['kæpitl], *a.* capital; mayúsculo.—*n* capital (*dinero*), *m.*; capital (*ciudad*), *f.*
capitalism ['kæpitəlizəm], *n.* capitalismo.
capitalize ['kæpitəlaiz], *v.t.* capitalizar escribir con mayúscula; aprovechar.
capitol ['kæpitl], *n.* capitolio.
capitulate [kə'pitjuleit], *v.i.* capitular, ren dirse.
capon ['keipən], *n.* capón, *m.*
caprice [kə'priːs], *n.* capricho; veleidad, *f.*
capricious [kə'priʃəs], *a.* caprichoso, anto jadizo.
Capricorn ['kæprikɔːn], *n.* Capricornio.
capsize [kæp'saiz], *v.t., v.i.* volcar.
capstan ['kæpstən], *n.* cabrestante, *m.*
capsule ['kæpsjuːl], *n.* cápsula.
captain ['kæptin], *n.* capitán, *m.*
caption ['kæpʃən], *n.* título; subtítulo.—*v.t* intitular.
captious ['kæpʃəs], *a.* caviloso.
captivate ['kæptiveit], *v.t.* encautivar; fas cinar, encantar.
captive ['kæptiv], *a., n.* cautivo.
captivity [kæp'tiviti], *n.* cautiverio.
capture ['kæptʃə], *n.* toma, presa; botín, *m.* *v.t.* apresar; (*mil.*) tomar.
car [kɑː], *n.* coche, *m.*; carro. [**van** (2)]
carafe [kə'ræf], *n.* garafa.
caramel ['kærəməl], *n.* caramelo.
carat ['kærət], *n.* quilate, *m.*

caravan ['kærəvæn], *n.* caravana, recua; remolque, *m.*
caraway ['kærəwei], *n.* alcaravea; carvi, *m.*
carbide ['kɑ:baid], *n.* carburo.
carbine ['kɑ:bain], *n.* carabina.
carbolic [kɑ:'bɔlik], *a.* fénico.—*n.* fenol, *m.*
carbon ['kɑ:bən], *n.* (*chem.*) carbono; (*elec.*) carbón, *m.*; — *paper,* papel carbón, *m.*
carbuncle ['kɑ:bʌnkl], *n.* (*med., gem.*) carbunclo.
carburettor [kɑ:bju'retə], *n.* carburador, *m.*
carcass ['kɑ:kəs], *n.* res muerta; (*fig.*) armazón, *m.*
card [kɑ:d], *n.* tarjeta; naipe, *m.*, carta; ficha.
cardboard ['kɑ:dbɔ:d], *n.* cartón, *m.*
cardiac ['kɑ:diæk], *a.* cardíaco.
cardigan ['kɑ:digən], *n.* rebeca.
cardinal ['kɑ:dinəl], *a.* cardinal.—*n.* cardenal, *m.*
care [kɛə], *n.* cuidado; inquietud (*ansiedad*), *f.*; esmero (*atención*); cargo; — *of Mr. X,* en casa del Sr. X.—*v.i.* cuidar; tener cuidado; *to — to,* tener ganas de; *to — for something,* gustar de algo.
career [kə'riə], *n.* carrera.—*v.i.* correr a todo galope.
careful ['kɛəful], *a.* cuidadoso; ansioso; atento.
carefully ['kɛəfuli], *adv.* esmeradamente.
carefulness ['kɛəfulnis], *n.* cuidado.
careless ['kɛəlis], *a.* descuidado; inconsiderado.
carelessness ['kɛəlisnis], *n.* descuido; inconsideración, *f.*
caress [kə'res], *n.* caricia.—*v.t.* acariciar.
caretaker ['kɛəteikə], *n.* conserje, portero; curador, *m.*
cargo ['kɑ:gou], *n.* cargamento, carga.
Caribbean [kæri'bi:ən], *a.* caribe.—*n.* mar Caribe, *m.*
caricature ['kærikətjuə], *n.* caricatura.—*v.t.* ridiculizar.
carillon [kə'riljən], *n.* repique, *m.*; carillón, *m.*
carman ['kɑ:mən], *n.* carretero.
carmine ['kɑ:main], *a.* de carmín.—*n.* carmín, *m.*
carnage ['kɑ:nidʒ], *n.* matanza, mortandad, *f.*
carnal ['kɑ:nəl], *a.* carnal.
carnality [kɑ:'næliti], *n.* carnalidad, *f.*
carnation [kɑ:'neiʃən], *n.* clavel, *m.*
carnival ['kɑ:nivəl], *n.* carnaval, *m.*, carnestolendas, *f.pl.*
carnivorous [kɑ:'nivərəs], *a.* carnívoro.
carob ['kærəb], *n.* algarroba (*judia*); algarrobo (*árbol*).
carol ['kærəl], *n.* villancico.—*v.i.* cantar, gorjear.
carousal [kə'rauzəl], *n.* francachela; jarana.
carouse [kə'rauz], *v.i.* embriagarse, jaranear.
carp (1) [kɑ:p], *n.* (*ichth.*) carpa.
carp (2) [kɑ:p], *v.i.* regañar, cavilar.
carpenter ['kɑ:pintə], *n.* carpintero.
carpentry ['kɑ:pintri], *n.* carpintería.
carpet ['kɑ:pit], *n.* alfombra.—*v.t.* alfombrar; (*fig.*) felpar; — *sweeper,* escoba mecánica.
carpet-bagger ['kɑ:pitbægə], *n.* (*U.S.*) politicastro.
carping ['kɑ:piŋ], *a.* caviloso.—*n.* censura inmotivada.
carriage ['kæridʒ], *n.* transporte, *m.*; coche (*vehículo*); porte (*manera de andar etc.*), *m.*;

carro (*de una máquina de escribir*); — *paid,* porte pagado. [**perambulator**]
carrier ['kæriə], *n.* portador, *m.*; arriero.
carrion ['kæriən], *n.* carroña.
carrot ['kærət], *n.* zanahoria.
carroty ['kærəti], *a.* (*fam.*) amarillo rojizo.
carry ['kæri], *v.t.* llevar, traer; transportar; incluir; acarrear.—*v.i.* alcanzar, llegar; *to — off* o *away,* llevarse; *to — on,* continuar; *to — out,* llevar a cabo; *to — forward,* (*com.*) pasar a la vuelta o al frente.
cart [kɑ:t], *n.* carro, carreta.—*v.t.* acarrear.
cartage ['kɑ:tidʒ], *n.* acarreo.
carte-blanche [kɑ:t'blɑ:nʃ], *n.* carta blanca.
cartel [kɑ:'tel], *n.* cartel, *m.*
Carthusian [kɑ:'θju:zjən], *a., n.* cartuj(an)o.
cartilage ['kɑ:tilidʒ], *n.* cartílago.
cartographer [kɑ:'tɔgrəfə], *n.* cartógrafo.
carton ['kɑ:tən], *n.* caja de cartón.
cartoon [kɑ:'tu:n], *n.* caricatura; (*cine.*) dibujo animado; (*art.*) cartón, *m.*
cartridge ['kɑ:tridʒ], *n.* cartucho.
carve [kɑ:v], *v.t.* (*art.*) tallar, esculpir; (*cul.*) trinchar.
carver ['kɑ:və], *n.* tallista, *m.f.*; trinchante (*cuchillo*), *m.*
carving ['kɑ:viŋ], *n.* (obra de) talla, escultura.
cascade [kæs'keid], *n.* cascada.
cascara [kæs'kɑ:rə], *n.* (*med.*) cáscara sagrada.
case [keis], *n.* (*gram., med.*) caso; (*jur.*) causa, pleito; caja; estuche, *m.*, funda; (*just*) *in —,* por si acaso; *in any —,* de todos modos.
casement ['keismənt], *n.* ventana a bisagra.
cash [kæʃ], *n.* dinero contante; pago al contado; metálico; (*com.*) caja.—*v.t.* cobrar, hacer efectivo; *to — in on,* (*fam.*) aprovechar.
cashbox ['kæʃbɔks], *n.* caja.
cashew [kæ'ʃu:], *n.* anacardo.
cashier [kæ'ʃiə], *n.* cajero, contador, *m.*—*v.t.* (*mil.*) destituir.
Cashmere [kæʃ'miə], *n.* cachemira; casimir, *m.*
cask [kɑ:sk], *n.* barril, tonel, *m.*, pipa.
casket ['kɑ:skit], *n.* cajita (*para joyas*), cofrecito; (*U.S.*) ataúd, *m.*
Caspian ['kæspiən], *a.* caspio.—*n.* mar Caspio.
casserole ['kæsəroul], *n.* cacerola.
cassock ['kæsək], *n.* sotana.
cassowary ['kæsəweəri], *n.* (*orn.*) casuario.
cast [kɑ:st], *n.* echada; (*theat.*) reparto, distribución, *f.*; semblante, *m.*—*v.t. irr.* tirar, arrojar, lanzar; echar; fundir; *to — aside,* desechar; *to — down,* derribar; *to — forth,* despedir; *to — loose,* soltar; *to — lots,* echar a la suerte; *to — off,* echar; hacer la última hilera (*de puntadas*); (*naut.*) desmarrar.
castanet [kæstə'net], *n.* castañuela.
castaway ['kɑ:stəwei], *n.* náufrago.
caste [kɑ:st], *n.* casta; grupo privilegiado.
castellated ['kæstileitid], *a.* encastillado.
castigate ['kæstigeit], *v.t.* castigar.
Castile [kæs'ti:l], *n.* Castilla.
Castilian [kəs'tiliən], *a., n.* castellano.
casting ['kɑ:stiŋ], *n.* fundición; pieza fundida; (*theat.*) distribución, *f.*; — *vote,* voto de calidad, voto decisivo.
cast-iron ['kɑ:st'aiən], *a.* hecho de hierro colado; fuerte.—*n.* hierro colado.

castle

castle [kɑːsl], *n.* castillo; torre (*ajedrez*), *f.—v.i.* enrocar (*ajedrez*).
castor (1) ['kɑːstə], *n.* (*zool.*) castor, *m.*
castor (2) ['kɑːstə], *n.* rodaja; vinagreras, *f.pl.*
castor-oil ['kɑːstərɔil], *n.* aceite (*m.*) de ricino.
castrate [kæs'treit], *v.t.* castrar.
casual ['kæʒuəl], *a.* casual, fortuito; informal; poco formal, negligente.
casualness ['kæʒuəlnis], *n.* falta de aplicación *o* de formalidad, despreocupación, *f.*
casualty ['kæʒuəlti], *n.* (*mil.*) baja; víctima; herido; accidente, *m.*
casuistry ['kæzjuistri], *n.* (*theol.*) casuística; (*fig.*) sofisma, *m.*
cat [kæt], *n.* gato; azote, *m.*
cataclysm ['kætəklizm], *n.* cataclismo.
catacomb ['kætəkuːm], *n.* catacumba.
Catalan [kætə'læn], *a., n.* catalán.
catalogue ['kætəlɔg], *n.* catálogo.
Catalonia [kætə'louniə], *n.* Cataluña.
catapult ['kætəpʌlt], *n.* catapulta; honda.
cataract ['kætərækt], *n.* (*geog., med.*) catarata.
catarrh [kə'tɑː], *n.* (*med.*) catarro.
catastrophe [kə'tæstrəfi], *n.* catástrofe, *m.*
catcall ['kætkɔːl], *n.* rechifla.
catch [kætʃ], *n.* broche, presa; lo pescado *o* cogido; trampa; buen partido; rondó, *m.—v.t.* coger, asir; capturar; alcanzar; enganchar; *to — cold,* coger un resfriado; *to — out,* cazar; *to — up,* alcanzar; ponerse al corriente.
catching ['kætʃiŋ], *a.* contagioso.
catchword ['kætʃwəːd], *n.* (*print.*) reclamo; (*fig.*) lema, *m.*
catechise ['kætəkaiz], *v.t.* catequizar.
catechism ['kætəkizm], *n.* catecismo.
categoric(al) [kæti'gɔrikl], *a.* categórico; terminante.
category ['kætigəri], *n.* categoría.
cater ['keitə], *v.i.* abastecer; *to — for,* abastecer; *to — to,* proveer a.
caterer ['keitərə], *n.* abastecedor, *m.*
caterpillar ['kætəpilə], *n.* oruga, gusano.
catfish ['kætfiʃ], *n.* bagre, *m.*
catgut ['kætgʌt], *n.* cuerda de tripa.
cathedral [kə'θiːdrəl], *a.* catedralicio.—*n.* catedral, *f.*
cathode ['kæθoud], *n.* cátodo; *— ray,* rayo catódico.
catholic ['kæθəlik], *a., n.* católico.
catholicism [kə'θɔlisizm], *n.* catolicismo.
catholicity [kæθə'lisiti], *n.* catolicidad, *f.*
catkin ['kætkin], *n.* candelilla, amento.
Cato ['keitou], *n.* Catón, *m.*
cat's-paw ['kætspɔː], *n.* (*fig.*) hombre (*m.*) de paja.
catsup ['kætsʌp], *(U.S.)* [KETCHUP].
cattiness ['kætinis], *n.* chismería; malicia.
cattle [kætl], *n.* ganado, ganado vacuno.
cattleman ['kætlmən], *n.* ganadero; vaquero.
catty ['kæti], *a.* chismoso; rencoroso; gatuno.
catwalk ['kætwɔːk], *n.* pasadizo, pasarela.
Caucasian [kɔː'keiziən], *a.* caucásico; de la raza blanca.
Caucasus ['kɔːkəsəs], *n.* Cáucaso.
caucus ['kɔːkəs], *n.* (*esp. U.S.*) camarilla.
caught [kɔːt] [CATCH].
cauldron ['kɔːldrən], *n.* calderón, *m.*
cauliflower ['kɔliflauə], *n.* coliflor, *m.*
caulk [kɔːk], *v.t.* calafatear.
causal ['kɔːzəl], *a.* causal.

244

cause [kɔːz], *n.* causa; origen, *m.—v.t.* causar.
causeway ['kɔːzwei], *n.* calzada, terraplén, *m.*
caustic ['kɔːstik], *a.* cáustico; (*fig.*) mordaz.
cauterize ['kɔːtəraiz], *v.t.* cauterizar.
caution ['kɔːʃən], *n.* cautela; amonestación, *f.—v.t.* amonestar.
cautionary ['kɔːʃnəri], *a.* amonestador.
cautious ['kɔːʃəs], *a.* cauteloso; prudente.
cautiousness ['kɔːʃnis], *n.* cautela.
cavalcade [kævəl'keid], *n.* cabalgata.
cavalier [kævə'liə], *a.* altivo.—*n.* caballero; galán, *m.*
cavalry ['kævəlri], *n.* caballería.
cave [keiv], *n.* cueva.—*v.i. to — in,* derrumbarse.
cavern ['kævən], *n.* caverna.
caviare ['kæviɑː], *n.* caviar, *m.*
cavil ['kævil], *v.i.* cavilar.
cavity ['kæviti], *n.* cavidad, *f.*, hueco.
caw [kɔː], *n.* graznido.—*v.i.* graznar.
cease [siːs], *v.t.* parar.—*v.i.* parar, cesar.
ceaseless ['siːslis], *a.* incesante.
cedar ['siːdə], *n.* cedro.
cede [siːd], *v.t.* ceder, traspasar.
ceiling ['siːliŋ], *n.* techo, cielo raso.
celandine ['seləndain], *n.* (*bot.*) celidonia.
celebrate ['selibreit], *v.t., v.i.* celebrar.
celebrated ['selibreitid], *a.* célebre.
celebration [seli'breiʃən], *n.* celebración, *f.*, fiesta.
celebrity [si'lebriti], *n.* celebridad, *f.*
celerity [si'leriti], *n.* celeridad, *f.*
celery ['seləri], *n.* apio.
celestial [si'lestjəl], *a.* celestial.
celibacy ['selibəsi], *n.* celibato.
celibate ['selibət], *a., n.* célibe.
cell [sel], *n.* celda; (*elec. etc.*) célula.
cellar ['selə], *n.* sótano; bodega.
cello ['tʃelou], *n.* (violon)celo.
cellophane ['seləfein], *n.* celofán, *m.*
cellular ['seljulə], *a.* celular.
celluloid ['seljuloid], *n.* celuloide, *m.*
cellulose ['seljulouz], *n.* celulosa.
Celt [kelt, selt], *n.* Celta, *m.f.*
Celtiberian [keltai'biːriən], *a., n.* Celtíbero.
Celtic ['keltik, 'seltik], *a.* céltico.
cement [si'ment], *n.* cemento, argamasa.—*v.t.* unir (con cemento).
cemetery ['semitri], *n.* cementerio, camposanto.
censor ['sensə], *n.* censor, *m.—v.t.* censurar.
censorship ['sensəʃip], *n.* censura.
censure ['senʃə], *n.* reprobación, *f.—v.t.* criticar, censurar.
census ['sensəs], *n.* censo.
cent [sent], *n.* céntimo, centavo; *per —,* por ciento.
centaur ['sentɔː], *n.* centauro.
centenary [sen'tiːnəri], *n.* centenario.
center (*U.S.*) [CENTRE].
centigrade ['sentigreid], *a.* centígrado.
centigramme ['sentigræm], *n.* centigramo.
centime ['sɑːntiːm], *n.* céntimo.
centimetre ['sentimiːtə], *n.* centímetro.
centipede ['sentipiːd], *n.* ciempiés, *m. inv.*
central ['sentrəl], *a.* central, céntrico.—*n.* (*U.S. tel.*) central, *f.*
centralize ['sentrəlaiz], *v.t.* centralizar.
centre ['sentə], *n.* centro.
centrifugal [sen'trifjugəl], *a.* centrífugo.
centripetal [sen'tripitl], *a.* centrípeto.
centurion [sen'tjuəriən], *n.* centurión, *m.*

century ['sentʃuri], n. siglo, centuria.
ceramic [si'ræmik], a. cerámico.—n.pl.
cerámica.
cereal ['siəriəl], a., n. cereal.—n. grano,
cereal, m.
cerebral ['seribrəl], a. cerebral.
ceremonial [seri'mounjəl], a. ceremonioso,
ceremonial.—n. ceremonial, m., aparato.
ceremony ['seriməni], n. ceremonia.
certain ['sə:tin], a. cierto, seguro; a —,
cierto.
certainness ['sə:tinnis], certainty ['sə:tinti],
n. certeza, certidumbre, f.
certificate [sə:'tifikeit], n. certificado; (com.)
título; partida.
certify ['sə:tifai], v.t. certificar.
certitude ['sə:titju:d], n. certidumbre, f.
Cesarean [si'zɛəriən], a. (med.) cesáreo.
cessation [se'seiʃən], n. cesación, f.
cession ['seʃən], n. cesión, f., traspaso.
cesspit ['sespit], cesspool ['sespu:l], n.
pozo negro.
Ceylon [si'lɔn], n. Ceilán, m.
Ceylonese [silə'ni:z], a., n.inv. ceilanés, m.
chafe [tʃeif], n. frotamiento.—v.t. frotar;
irritar.
chaff [tʃɑ:f], n. barcia; paja menuda; chanza.
v.t. chancear (con), burlarse (de).
chaffinch ['tʃæfintʃ], n. pinzón, m.
chafing ['tʃeifiŋ], n. frotamiento; irritación, f.
chagrin ['ʃægrin], n. desazón, m.; pesadumbre, f.—v.t. apesadumbrar.
chain [tʃein], n. cadena.—v.t. encadenar.
chair [tʃɛə], n. silla; silla de manos; (educ.)
cátedra.
chairman ['tʃɛəmən], n. presidente, m.
chaise [ʃeiz], n. silla volante; calesín, m.
chalet ['ʃælei], n. chalet, m., casita de campo.
chalice ['tʃælis], n. cáliz, m.
chalk [tʃɔ:k], n. creta; (educ.) tiza.—v.t.
escribir etc. con tiza.
chalky ['tʃɔ:ki], a. gredoso; pálido.
challenge ['tʃælənd3], n. desafío; (mil.) quién
vive, m.—v.t. desafiar; disputar.
challenger ['tʃælind3ə], n. desafiador, m.;
aspirante, m f.
chamber ['tʃeimbə], n. cámara; aposento.
chamberlain ['tʃeimbəlin], n. chambelán, m.,
tesorero, camarlengo.
chamber-maid ['tʃeimbəmeid], n. camarera.
chameleon [kə'mi:ljən], n. camaleón, m.
chamfer ['tʃæmfə], n. (carp.) chaflán, m.—
v.t. chaflanar.
chamois ['ʃæmwɑ:], n. gamuza.
champ [tʃæmp], n. mordisco.—v.t., v.i.
mordiscar.
champagne [ʃæm'pein], n. champaña.
champion ['tʃæmpjən], n. campeón, m.;
paladín, m.—v.t. defender; abogar por.
chance [tʃɑ:ns], n. fortuna, accidente, m.
chancel ['tʃɑ:nsəl], n. (eccl.) santuario.
chancellor ['tʃɑ:nsələ], n. canciller, m.
chancery ['tʃɑ:nsəri], n. (jur.) cancillería.
chancy ['tʃɑ:nsi], a. (fam.) arriesgado.
chandelier [ʃændə'liə], n. araña de luces.
change [tʃeind3], n. cambio; variedad, f.
—v.t., v.i. cambiar, mudar.
changeable ['tʃeind3əbl], a. variable, mudable.
changeless ['tʃeind3lis], a. constante, inmutable.

changeling ['tʃeind3liŋ], n. niño cambiado
en secreto por otro.
channel ['tʃænəl], n. canal, m.; acequia;
English Channel, Canal de la Mancha.—
v.t. encauzar.
chant [tʃɑ:nt], n. canto; sonsonete, m.—v.t.
v.i. cantar.
chantry ['tʃɑ:ntri], n. capilla.
chaos ['keiɔs], n. caos, m.sg.
chaotic [kei'ɔtik], a. caótico.
chap (1) [tʃæp], n. (fam.) tipo, tío.
chap (2) [tʃæp], n. grieta.—v.t. agrietar,
hender.—v.i. agrietarse.
chapel ['tʃæpəl], n. capilla.
chaperon ['ʃæpəroun], n. dueña, señora de
compañía.—v.t. acompañar, vigilar.
chaplain ['tʃæplin], n. capellán, m.
chapter ['tʃæptə], n. capítulo; categoría;
(eccl.) cabildo.
char (1) [tʃɑ:], n. (ichth.) umbra.
char (2) [tʃɑ:], n. [CHARWOMAN].—v.t.
limpiar.
char (3) [tʃɑ:], v.t. carbonizar.
character ['kærəktə], n. carácter, m.; (theat.)
papel, personaje, m.; (fam.) original.
characteristic [kærəktə'ristik], a. característico, típico.—n. rasgo.
characterize ['kærəktəraiz], v.t. caracterizar.
charade [ʃə'rɑ:d], n. charada.
charcoal ['tʃɑ:koul], n. carbón (de leña), m.
charge [tʃɑ:d3], n. carga (de un fusil, un
cañón etc.); cargo (responsabilidad);
precio; in — of, a cargo de.—v.t. cargar;
cobrar; to — with, cargar de, acusar de.
chargé d'affaires [ʃɑ:3eidæ'fɛə], n. encargado de negocios.
charger ['tʃɑ:d3ə], n. fuente, f., azafate;
caballo de guerra; cargador, m.
chariot ['tʃæriət], n. carro; carroza.
charioteer [tʃæriə'tiə], n. auriga, m.
charitable ['tʃæritəbl], a. caritativo.
charity ['tʃæriti], n. caridad, f.
charlatan ['ʃɑ:lətən], n. embaidor; curandero.
charm [tʃɑ:m], n. encanto; maleficio;
amuleto.—v.t. encantar; hechizar.
charming ['tʃɑ:miŋ], a. encantador.
charnel-house ['tʃɑ:nəlhaus], n. carnero.
chart [tʃɑ:t], n. carta, mapa, m.; cuadro.—v.t.
trazar en una carta.
charter ['tʃɑ:tə], n. carta, fuero; fletamiento.
—v.t. estatuir; fletar; alquilar (un avión).
charwoman ['tʃɑ:wumən], n. asistenta.
chary ['tʃɛəri], a. cauteloso; circunspecto.
chase [tʃeis], n. caza; seguimiento; ranura.—
v.t. cazar; perseguir; grabar.
chasm [kæzm], n. abismo, desfiladero.
chaste [tʃeist], a. casto.
chasten ['tʃeisn], v.t. corregir, castigar.
chasteness ['tʃeistnəs], n. castidad, f.
chastise [tʃæs'taiz], v.t. castigar.
chastisement [tʃæs'taizmənt], n. castigo.
chastity ['tʃæstiti], n. castidad, f.
chat [tʃæt], n. charla.—v.i. charlar, platicar.
chateau ['ʃætou], n. casa solariega, castillo.
chatelaine ['ʃætəlein], n. castellana; llavero
con dijes.
chattels ['tʃætlz], n.pl. bienes muebles,
enseres, m.pl.
chatter ['tʃætə], n. charla.—v.i. charlar;
castañetear (los dientes).

chatterbox

chatterbox ['tʃætəbɔks], *n.* tarabilla, parlanchín, *m.*
chauffeur ['ʃoufə], *n.* chófer, (*S.A.*) chofer, *m.*
cheap [tʃiːp], *a.* barato; (*fig.*) ordinario; vil, ruin.
cheapen ['tʃiːpən], *v.t.* rebajar, abaratar.— *v.i.* abaratarse.
cheapness ['tʃiːpnis], *n.* baratura.
cheat [tʃiːt], *n.* timador, *m.*; trampa, engaño. —*v.t.* trampear; *to — someone out of something,* defraudar algo a alguien.
check [tʃek], *a.* de cuadros.—*n.* resistencia, freno; (*com.*) talón, *m.*; contraseña; (*U.S.*) cuenta; (*U.S.*) cheque; jaque (*ajedrez*), *m.*; comprobación, *f.*, visita.—*v.t.* parar; trabar; facturar; (*U.S.*) depositar (*equipaje*); comprobar, verificar; marcar con cuadros; dar jaque a.—*v.i.* pararse; *to — in,* (*U.S.*) llegar (a un hotel); *to — up,* verificar.
checker ['tʃekə], *n.* inspector, *m.*; cuadro (*de una tela tejida*); ficha (*damas*).—*pl.* damas, *f.pl.*—*v.t.* cuadricular.
checkerboard ['tʃekəbɔːd], *n.* (*esp. U.S.*) tablero (de damas).
checkered ['tʃekəd], *a.* (*fig.*) accidentado, irregular.
checkmate ['tʃekmeit], *n.* jaque mate, *m.*— *v.t.* dar mate a.
cheek [tʃiːk], *n.* mejilla, carrillo; (*fam.*) frescura, descaro.
cheeky ['tʃiːki], *a.* insolente, descarado.
cheep [tʃiːp], *n.* pío.—*v.i.* piar.
cheer [tʃiə], *n.* aplauso; alegría; alimento.— *v.t.* aplaudir, animar.—*v.i.* alegrarse; — *up!* ¡ánimo!
cheerful ['tʃiəful], *a.* alegre.
cheerfulness ['tʃiəfulnis], *n.* alegría, buen humor, *m.*
cheerless ['tʃiəlis], *a.* triste.
cheese [tʃiːz], *n.* queso.
cheetah ['tʃiːtə], *n.* (*zool.*) leopardo cazador (de la India).
chef [ʃef], *n.* cocinero; jefe (*m.*) de cocina.
chemical ['kemikəl], *a.* químico.—*n.* producto químico.
chemist ['kemist], *n.* químico; (*Brit.*) boticario, farmacéutico; *chemist's,* farmacia.
chemistry ['kemistri], *n.* química.
cheque [tʃek], *n.* cheque, *m.*
cheque-book ['tʃekbuk], *n.* talonario de cheques.
chequered [CHECKERED].
cherish ['tʃeriʃ], *v.t.* acariciar; tratar con ternura; abrigar (*esperanzas*).
cherry ['tʃeri], *n.* cereza, guinda; — *tree,* cerezo.
cherub ['tʃerəb], *n.* (*Bib.*) (*pl.* **cherubim**) querubín, *m.*; (*fig.*) (*pl.* **cherubs**) niño angelical.
chess [tʃes], *n.* ajedrez, *m.*
chessboard ['tʃesbɔːd], *n.* tablero (de ajedrez).
chest [tʃest], *n.* (*anat.*) pecho; arca, cofre (*caja*), *m.*; — *of drawers,* cómoda.
chestnut ['tʃesnʌt], *n.* castaña (*fruta*); castaño (*árbol*); (*fig.*) chiste viejo.
chevron ['ʃevrən], *n.* (*her.*) cheurón, *m.*; (*mil.*) galón, *m.*
chew [tʃuː], *v.t.* mascar, masticar.
chiaroscuro [kiɑːrəˈskjuərou], *n.* (*art.*) claroscuro.
chic [ʃiːk], *a.* elegante.—*n.* chic, elegancia.
chicanery [ʃiˈkeinəri], *n.* embuste, *m.*

chick [tʃik], *n.* polluelo.
chicken ['tʃikin], *n.* pollo; gallina, gallo.
chicken-hearted ['tʃikinˈhaːtid], *a.* cobarde.
chicken-pox ['tʃikinpɔks], *n.* (*med.*) varicela.
chickpea ['tʃikpiː], *n.* garbanzo.
chickweed ['tʃikwiːd], *n.* (*bot.*) morgelina, pamplina.
chicory ['tʃikəri], *n.* (*bot.*) achicoria.
chide [tʃaid], *v.t. irr.* regañar.
chief [tʃiːf], *a.* principal.—*n.* jefe, *m.*, caudillo; cacique, *m.*
chiefly ['tʃiːfli], *adv.* principalmente.
chiffon ['ʃifɔn], *n.* gasa, chifón, *m.*
chilblain ['tʃilblein], *n.* sabañón, *m.*
child [tʃaild], *n.* (*pl.* **children**) niño; descendiente, *m.f.*; *to be with —,* estar encinta; *child's play,* (*fig.*) cosa facilísima.
childbirth ['tʃaildbɔːθ], *n.* parto, alumbramiento.
childhood ['tʃaildhud], *n.* infancia, niñez, *f.*
childish ['tʃaildiʃ], *a.* pueril, infantil.
children ['tʃildrən] [CHILD].
Chile ['tʃili], *n.* Chile, *m.*
Chilean ['tʃilian], *a., n.* chileno.
chill [tʃil], *a.* frío, glacial.—*n.* frío; resfriado; escalofrío.—*v.t.* helar, enfriar.
chilly ['tʃili], *a.* frío; friolento.
chimera [kaiˈmiərə], *n.* quimera.
chime [tʃaim], *n.* juego de campanas; repique, *m.*—*v.t., v.i.* repicar; *to — in,* (*fig.*) hacer coro; · entremeterse.
chimerical [kiˈmerikəl], *a.* quimérico.
chimney ['tʃimni], *n.* chimenea; — *pot,* cañón (*m.*) de chimenea; —*sweep,* deshollinador, *m.*
chimpanzee [tʃimpænˈziː], *n.* (*zool.*) chimpancé, *m.*
chin [tʃin], *n.* barbilla, mentón, *m.*
China ['tʃainə], *n.* China; **china,** *n.* porcelana.
Chinese [tʃaiˈniːz], *a., n.* chino.
chink [tʃiŋk], *n.* grieta, hendedura; sonido metálico.—*v.i.* sonar metálicamente.
chintz [tʃints], *n.* quimón, *m.*, zaraza.
chip [tʃip], *n.* astilla.—*v.t.* patatas fritas.— *v.t.* descantillar.—*v.i.* romperse.
chirp [tʃəːp], *v.i.* piar.
chisel ['tʃizəl], *n.* (*carp.*) escoplo; (*art., metal.*) cincel, *m.*
chit (1) [tʃit], *n.* (*fam.*) chiquillo.
chit (2) [tʃit], *n.* (*Brit.*) esquela; vale, *m.*
chit-chat ['tʃittʃæt], *n.* (*fam.*) hablilla, chismes, *m.pl.*
chivalrous ['ʃivəlrəs], *a.* caballeresco; caballeroso.
chivalry ['ʃivəlri], *n.* caballerosidad, *f.*; caballería.
chive [tʃaiv], *n.* (*bot.*) cebollana.
chloral ['klɔːrəl], *a.* (*chem.*) cloral.
chlorate ['klɔːreit], *n.* (*chem.*) clorato.
chloride ['klɔːraid], *n.* (*chem.*) cloruro.
chlorine ['klɔːriːn], *n.* (*chem.*) cloro.
chlorinate ['klɔːrineit], *v.t.* desinfectar con cloro.
chloroform ['klɔrəfɔːm], *n.* cloroformo.
chlorophyll ['klɔrəfil], *n.* clorofila.
chock [tʃɔk], *n.* cuna.
chock-full [tʃɔkful], *a.* colmado.
chocolate ['tʃɔklit], *n.* chocolate, *m.*
choice [tʃɔis], *a.* escogido.—*n.* selección, *f.*; preferencia; (*cosa*) escogida.
choicely ['tʃɔisli], *adv.* primorosamente.
choir [kwaiə], *n.* coro.

246

choke [tʃouk], *n.* estrangulación, *f.*; (*mech.*) obturador, *m.—v.t.* estrangular; atascar.— *v.i.* sofocarse; obstruirse; atragantarse.
cholera ['kɔlərə], *n.* (*med.*) cólera.
choose [tʃu:z], *v.t. irr.* escoger, elegir.—*v.i. irr.* optar.
chop [tʃɔp], *n.* (*cul.*) chuleta; tajada; mejilla.— *v.t.* cortar, tajar.
chopper ['tʃɔpə], *n.* hacha; cuchillo de carnicero.
choppy ['tʃɔpi], *a.* agitado (*mar*).
chopsticks ['tʃɔpstiks] *n.pl.* palitos, *m. pl.*
choral ['kɔ:rəl], *a.* coral.
chord [kɔ:d], *n.* (*mus.*) acorde, *m.*; (*eng., math.*) cuerda.
chore [tʃɔ:], *n.* tarea.
chorus ['kɔ:rəs], *n.* coro (*grupo*); estribillo (*de una canción*); — *girl,* corista, *f.*; *in* —, en coro, a una voz.
chose(n) ['tʃouʒ(n)], [CHOOSE].
christen [krisn], *v.t.* bautizar.
Christendom ['krisndəm], *n.* cristiandad, *f.*
christening ['krisniŋ], *n.* bautismo, bautizo.
Christian ['kristʃən], *a., n.* cristiano;—*name,* nombre (de pila).
Christianity [kristi'æniti], *n.* cristianismo.
Christmas ['krisməs], *n.* Navidad, *f.*, pascuas de Navidad; — *box,* aguinaldo; *Merry* —, Felices Pascuas.
chromium ['kroumjəm], *n.* cromo.
chronicle ['krɔnikl], *n.* crónica.
chronology [krə'nɔlədʒi], *n.* cronología.
chrysalis ['krisəlis], *n.* crisálida.
chrysanthemum [kri'zænθəməm], *n.* (*bot.*) cristantemo.
chub [tʃʌb], *n.* (*ichth.*) coto, cacho.
chubby ['tʃʌbi], *a.* gordo, gordiflón.
chuck [tʃʌk], *v.t.* (*fam.*) arrojar.
chuckle [tʃʌkl], *n.* risa ahogada.—*v.i.* reír entre dientes.
chum [tʃʌm], *n.* (*fam.*) compinche, *m.*, compañero.
chump [tʃʌmp], *n.* zoquete, *m.*
chunk [tʃʌŋk], *n.* pedazo grueso.
church [tʃə:tʃ], *n.* iglesia.
churchyard ['tʃə:tʃja:d], *n.* cementerio.
churl [tʃə:l], *n.* palurdo.
churlish ['tʃə:liʃ], *a.* grosero, palurdo.
churn [tʃə:n], *n.* mantequera.—*v.t.* batir (en una mantequera); *to* — *out,* (*fig.*) fabricar en gran serie.
chute [ʃu:t], *n.* conducto.
cicada [si'keidə], *n.* (*ent.*) cigarra.
cider ['saidə], *n.* sidra.
cigar [si'ga:], *n.* puro, cigarro (puro).
cigarette [sigə'ret], *n.* cigarrillo, pitillo; — *holder,* boquilla; — *lighter,* encendedor (*m.*) de cigarrillos, mechero; — *paper,* papel (*m.*) de fumar.
cinder ['sində], *n.* ceniza.
Cinderella [sində'relə], *n.* Cenicienta.
cine-camera ['sinikæmərə], *n.* cámara.
cinema ['sinəma:], *n.* cine, *m.*
cinnamon ['sinəmən], *a.* acanelado.—*n.* canela.
cipher ['saifə], *n.* cifra; cero; clave (*de una cifra*), *f.—v.t.* cifrar.—*v.i.* calcular.
circa ['sə:kl], *prep.* (*Lat.*) hacia.
circle [sə:kl], *n.* círculo.—*v.t.* dar la vuelta a. —*v.i.* dar vueltas.
circuit ['sə:kit], *n.* circuito.
circuitous [sə'kjuitəs], *a.* tortuoso, indirecto.

circular ['sə:kjulə], *a.* circular, redondo.—*n.* carta circular.
circulate ['sə:kjuleit], *v.t.* diseminar, propagar.—*v.i.* propagarse.
circulation [sə:kju'leiʃən], *n.* circulación, *f.*; tirada.
circumcise ['sə:kʌmsaiz], *v.t.* circuncidar.
circumcision [sə:kəm'siʒən], *n.* circuncisión, *f.*
circumference [sə'kʌmfərəns], *n.* circunferencia, periferia.
circumspect ['sə:kəmspekt], *a.* circunspecto, prudente.
circumstance ['sə:kəmstæns], *n.* circunstancia.
circumstantial [sə:kəm'stænʃl], *a.* circunstanciado; casual.
circumvent [sə:kəm'vent], *v.t.* soslayar.
circumvention [sə:kəm'venʃən], *n.* evitación, *f.*; rodeo.
circus ['sə:kəs], *n.* circo; plaza circular.
Cistercian [sis'tə:ʃən], *a.* cisterciense.
cistern ['sistən], *n.* cisterna, aljibe, *m.*; depósito.
citadel ['sitədəl], *n.* ciudadela.
citation [sai'teiʃən], *n.* citación; (*mil.*) mención, *f.*
cite [sait], *v.t.* citar; (*mil.*) mencionar.
citizen ['sitizən], *n.* ciudadano; súbdito.
citizenship ['sitizənʃip], *n.* ciudadanía, nacionalidad, *f.*
citric ['sitrik], *a.* cítrico.
citron ['sitrən], *n.* cidra, toronja; — *tree,* cidro, toronjal, *m.*, toronjo.
citrus ['sitrəs], *a.* auranciáceo; — *fruits,* agrios, frutas agrias.
city ['siti], *n.* ciudad, *f.*; — *council,* ayuntamiento.
civic ['sivik], *a.* cívico. — *n.pl.* educación política.
civil ['sivəl], *a.* cortés; civil; — *defence,* defensa pasiva; — *servant,* funcionario.
civilian [si'viljən], *a., n.* (*mil.*) paisano.
civilization [sivilai'zeiʃən], *n.* civilización, *f.*
civilize ['sivilaiz], *v.t.* civilizar.
clad [klæd], *pret., p.p.* (*obs.*) [CLOTHE].
claim [kleim], *n.* demanda; reclamación, *f.*; (*min.*) pertenencia.—*v.t.* reclamar; demandar; declarar; *to* — *to be,* pretender ser.
claimant ['kleimənt], *n.* demandante, *m.f.*
clairvoyant [kleə'vɔiənt], *a., n.* clarividente, *m.f.*
clam [klæm], *n.* almeja, tellina.
clamber ['klæmbə], *v.i.* subir gateando.
clammy ['klæmi], *a.* frío y húmedo; pegajoso.
clamour ['klæmə], *n.* clamor, *m.—v.i.* gritar, clamorear.
clamp [klæmp], *n.* abrazadera.—*v.t.* asegurar; *to* — *down on,* apretar los tornillos a.
clandestine [klæn'destin], *a.* clandestino.
clang [klæŋ], *n.* sonido metálico, tantán, *m.* [CLANK].
clank [klæŋk], *n.* sonido metálico, más profundo que el CLINK y menos resonante que el CLANG.
clap [klæp], *n.* palmoteo.—*v.t.* aplaudir.—*v.i.* dar palmadas; *to* — *eyes on,* (*fam.*) echar la vista a.
claret ['klærət], *n.* vino de Burdeos; clarete, *m.*
clarify ['klærifai], *v.t.* aclarar; clarificar (*azúcar etc.*).

clarinet [klæri'net], *n.* clarinete, *m.*
clarity ['klæriti], *n.* claridad, *f.*
clash [klæʃ], *n.* choque, *m.*; estruendo.—*v.i.* chocar.
clasp [klɑ:sp], *n.* hebilla; agarro.—*v.t.* abrochar; agarrar.
class [klɑ:s], *n.* clase, *f.*—*v.t.* clasificar.
classic ['klæsik], *a.*, *n.* clásico.
classify ['klæsifai], *v.t.* clasificar.
clatter ['klætə], *n.* estruendo; martilleo.—*v.i.* chocar ruidosamente.
clause [klɔ:z], *n.* cláusula; (*gram.*) oración, *f.*
claw [klɔ:], *n.* garra; uña; pinza.—*v.t.* despedazar; arañar.
clay [klei], *n.* arcilla.
clean [kli:n], *a.* limpio.—*adv.* (*fam.*) completamente.—*v.t.* limpiar.
cleaning ['kli:niŋ], *n.* limpieza, limpiadura.
cleanliness ['klenlinis], *n.* limpieza, aseo.
cleanly (1) ['klenli], *a.* habitualmente limpio.
cleanly (2) ['kli:nli], *adv.* limpiamente.
cleanness ['kli:nnis], *n.* limpieza.
cleanse [klenz], *v.t.* limpiar, purificar.
clear [kliə], *a.* claro; completo; evidente; — **of,** libre de.—*adv.* completamente.—*v.t.* limpiar; aclarar; clarificar; saltar por encima de; absolver; **to — away,** quitar; **to — one's throat,** carraspear; **to — the way,** abrir camino.—*v.i.* aclararse; despejarse.
clearance ['kliərəns], *n.* espacio libre (*entre dos cosas*), espacio muerto; — **sale,** liquidación, *f.*
clearing ['kliəriŋ], *n.* claro (*de un bosque*); vindicación, *f.*
cleave (1) [kli:v], *v.t. irr.* hender; dividir.—*v.i.* henderse.
cleave (2) [kli:v], *v.i.* pegarse; ser fiel.
cleft [kleft], *p.p.*, *a.* hendido.—*n.* grieta.
clematis ['klemətis], *n.* (*bot.*) clemátide, *f.*
clench [klentʃ], *v.t.* apretar; agarrar.
clergy ['klə:dʒi], *n.* clero, clerecía.
clergyman ['klə:dʒimən], *n.* clérigo; cura, *m.*
cleric ['klerik], *n.* clérigo.
clerical ['klerikəl], *a.* eclesiástico, clerical; oficinesco; — **error,** error (*m.*) de pluma.
clerk [klɑ:k], *n.* oficinista, *m.f.*; (*U.S.*) dependiente de tienda; eclesiástico; escribiente, *m.*; archivero; escribano.
clever ['klevə], *a.* diestro, mañoso; inteligente, hábil.
cleverness ['klevənis], *n.* destreza; inteligencia.
cliché ['kliʃei], *n.* (*print.*) clisé; (*fig.*) cliché, *m.*
click [klik], *n.* golpecito; tecleo; chasquido.—*v.t.* chascar (*la lengua*).—*v.i.* hacer tictac.
client ['klaiənt], *n.* cliente, *m.f.*, parroquiano.
cliff [klif], *n.* acantilado, escarpa, precipicio.
climate ['klaimət], *n.* clima, *m.*
climax ['klaimæks], *n.* colmo, culminación, *f.*
climb [klaim], *n.* subida.—*v.t.*, *v.i.* trepar, escalar, subir.
climber ['klaimə], *n.* escalador, trepador, *m.*; (*bot.*) trepadora.
clime [klaim], *n.* (*poet.*) clima, *m.*; región, *f.*
clinch [klintʃ], *n.* agarro.—*v.t.* agarrar; resolver decisivamente.—*v.i.* luchar cuerpo a cuerpo.
cling [kliŋ], *v.i. irr.* adherirse, pegarse.
clinic ['klinik], *n.* clínica.
clink [kliŋk], *n.* tintín, *m.*, sonido metálico. [CLANK].

clinker ['kliŋkə], *n.* escoria.
clip [klip], *n.* presilla; tijereteo, trasquila; pinza; (*fam.*) golpe seco.—*v.t.* esquilar; recortar.
clipper ['klipə], *n.* (*naut.*) clíper, *m.*—*pl.* tijeras, *f.pl.*; cizalla.
clique [kli:k], *n.* pandilla.
cloak [klouk], *n.* capa; (*fig.*) disimulo.—*v.t.* encubrir.
cloakroom ['kloukrum], *n.* guardarropa.
clock [klɔk], *n.* reloj, *m.*; **it is four o'clock,** son las cuatro.
clockwise ['klɔkwaiz], *adv.* en el sentido de las agujas de reloj.
clockwork ['klɔkwə:k], *n.* aparato de relojería; movimiento de reloj.
clod [klɔd], *n.* terrón, *m.*; palurdo.
clog [klɔg], *n.* zueco; (*fig.*) embarazo.—*v.t.* estorbar; atascar.
cloister ['klɔistə], *n.* claustro.
close (1) [klous], *a.* cercano; cerrado.—*n.* recinto.—*adv.* de cerca.
close (2) [klouz], *n.* fin, terminación, *f.*—*v.t.* cerrar; terminar; **to — in,** acercarse.
closely ['klousli], *adv.* estrechamente; de cerca.
closet ['klɔzit], *n.* gabinete; retrete, *m.*
closure ['klouʒə], *n.* clausura, fin, *m.*
clot [klɔt], *n.* grumo; cuajarón, *m.*; (*fam.*) imbécil.—*v.i.* engrumecerse, cuajarse.
cloth [klɔθ], *n.* (*pl.* **cloths** [klɔðz]) tela, paño; género.
clothe [klouð], *v.t. irr.* vestir; cubrir.
clothes [klouðz], *n.pl.* ropa, vestidos; **bed —,** ropa de cama.
clothes-brush ['klouðzbrʌʃ], *n.* cepillo de ropa.
clothes-hanger ['klouðzhæŋə], *n.* percha.
clothes-horse ['klouðzhɔ:s], *n.* enjugador, *m.*
clothing ['klouðiŋ], *n.* vestidos, ropa.
cloud [klaud], *n.* nube, *f.*—*v.t.* nublar; entristecer.—*v.i.* nublarse; entristecerse.
cloud-burst ['klaudbə:st], *n.* chaparrón, *m.*
cloudy ['klaudi], *a.* nublado; velado; oscuro.
clout [klaut], *n.* (*fam.*) golpe, *m.*; trapo.
clove [klouv], *n.* clavo (*de especia*).
cloven ['klouvən], *p.p.* [CLEAVE].— *a.* hendido.
clover ['klouvə], *n.* trébol, *m.*
clown [klaun], *n.* payaso; palurdo.
cloy [klɔi], *v.t.*, *v.i.* empalagar, hastiar.
club [klʌb], *n.* porra, cachiporra; club, *m.*; círculo; trébol (*naipes*), *m.*—*v.t.* aporrear.—*v.i.* contribuir.
cluck [klʌk], *n.* cloqueo.—*v.i.* cloquear.
clue [klu:], *n.* indicio; guía.
clump [klʌmp], *n.* grupo; pisada fuerte.—*v.i.* andar torpemente.
clumsy ['klʌmzi], *a.* torpe.
clung [klʌŋ] [CLING].
Cluniac ['klu:niæk], *a.* cluniacense.
cluster ['klʌstə], *n.* racimo; grupo.—*v.i.* agruparse, juntarse.
clutch [klʌtʃ], *n.* agarro; nidada; (*aut.*) embrague, *m.*—*v.t.* agarrar, asir.
clutter ['klʌtə], *n.* confusión, *f.*; baraúnda.—*v.t.* poner en desorden.
coach (1) [koutʃ], *n.* coche, *m.*; diligencia.
coach (2) [koutʃ], *n.* (*sport*) preparador, entrenador, *m.*; (*educ.*) profesor particular, *m.*—*v.t.* preparar.

coachman ['koutʃmæn], n. cochero, mayoral, m.
coagulate ['kouægjuleit], v.i. coagular, cuajar.
coal [koul], n. carbón (de piedra), m.; ascua, brasa.
coalesce [kouə'les], v.i. unirse.
coalition [kouə'liʃən], n. coalición, f.; alianza.
coal-mine ['koulmain], n. mina de carbón, mina hullera.
coal-miner ['koulmainə], n. minero, hullero.
coarse [kɔ:s], a. basto; grueso; soez.
coast [koust], n. costa, orilla.—v.i. (naut.) costear; (mech.) andar en punto muerto.
coat [kout], n. hábito; chaqueta, americana; abrigo; capa, mano (de pintura), f.; — of arms, escudo de armas.—v.t. cubrir.
coax [kouks], v.t. halagar, engatusar.
cob (1) [kɔb], n. mazorca.
cob (2) [kɔb], n. jaca.
cobalt ['koubɔ:lt], n. cobalto.
cobbler ['kɔblə], n. zapatero de viejo.
cobblestone ['kɔbəlstoun], n. guijarro.
cob-nut ['kɔbnʌt], n. avellana.
cobweb ['kɔbweb], n. telaraña.
cocaine [ko'kein], n. cocaína.
cochineal [kɔtʃi'ni:l], n. cochinilla.
cock [kɔk], n. gallo; macho (de una ave); grifo; veleta.—v.t. erguir, levantar.
cockerel ['kɔkərəl], n. gallo.
cockle ['kɔkəl], n. coquina.
Cockney ['kɔkni], a., n. londinense.
cockpit ['kɔkpit], n. gallera, valla; (aer.) carlinga.
cockroach ['kɔkroutʃ], n. cucaracha.
cockscomb ['kɔkskoum], n. cresta de gallo; fanfarrón, m.
cocktail ['kɔkteil], n. cóctel, m., combinado; cualquier mezcla.
cocoa ['koukou], n. cacao (árbol, fruto); chocolate (bebida), m.
coconut ['koukənʌt], n. coco.
cocoon [kə'ku:n], n. capullo.
cod [kɔd], n. (ichth.) bacalao, abadejo.
code [koud], n. código; cifra.
codex ['koudeks], n. códice, m.
codify ['koudifai], v.t. codificar.
coexistence [kouig'zistəns], n. coexistencia, convivencia.
coffee ['kɔfi], n. café, m.; black —, café solo; white —, café con leche.
coffee-mill ['kɔfimil], n. molinillo.
coffee-pot ['kɔfipɔt], n. cafetera.
coffer ['kɔfə], n. arca, cofre, m.
coffin ['kɔfin], n. ataúd, m.
cog [kɔg], n. diente (de rueda), m.
cogent ['koudʒənt], a. convincente, fuerte.
cogitate ['kɔdʒiteit], v.i. meditar.
cognac ['kɔnjæk], n. coñac, m.
cognate ['kɔgneit], a. cognado; análogo.
cognizance ['kɔgnizəns], n. conocimiento.
cohabit [kou'hæbit], v.i. cohabitar.
co-heir ['kou'ɛə], n. coheredero.
coherence [kou'hiərəns], n. consecuencia; cohesión, f., coherencia, f.
coherent [kou'hiərənt], a. coherente.
cohesion [kou'hi:ʒən], n. cohesión, f.
cohort ['kouhɔ:t], n. cohorte, f.
coiffure [kwa'fjuə], n. peinado, tocado.
coil [kɔil], n. rollo, espiral, m.; (elec.) carrete, m.; rizo (de cabellos).—v.t. arrollar.—v.i. -se.

coin [kɔin], n. moneda; dinero.—v.t. acuñar.
coinage ['kɔinidʒ], n. sistema monetario, m.; acuñación, f.
coincide [kouin'said], v.i. coincidir.
coincidence [kou'insidəns], n. coincidencia, casualidad, f.
coincidental [kouinsi'dentl], a. coincidente.
coiner ['kɔinə], n. acuñador, m.; monedero falso.
coke [kouk], n. coque, m.
colander ['kʌləndə], n. colador, pasador, m.
cold [kould], a. frío.—n. frío; resfriado, constipado; to catch —, constiparse, resfriarse.
cold-chisel [kould'tʃizl], n. cortafrío.
coldness ['kouldnis], n. frialdad, f.
collaborate [kə'læbəreit], v.i. colaborar.
collapse [kə'læps], n. derrumbamiento; ruina.—v.i. derrumbarse; fracasar.
collar ['kɔlə], n. cuello; collar (de perro), m. —v.t. (fam.) coger.
collar-bone [kɔləboun], n. clavícula.
collate [kə'leit], v.t. cotejar, comparar.
collateral [kə'lætərəl], a. colateral; paralelo. —n. (com.) resguardo.
collation [kə'leiʃən], n. contejo.
colleague ['kɔli:g], n. colega, m.
collect [kə'lekt], v.t. recoger; coleccionar; cobrar; to — oneself, reponerse.
collection [kə'lekʃən], n. colección; recaudación, f.; (eccl.) colecta.
collective [kə'lektiv], a. colectivo.
collector [kə'lektə], n. coleccionador; recaudador, m.
college ['kɔlidʒ], n. colegio.
collide [kə'laid], v.i. chocar.
collier ['kɔljə], n. hullero, minero; barco carbonero.
colliery ['kɔljəri], n. mina de carbón.
collision [kə'liʒən], n. colisión, f., choque, m.
colloquial [kə'loukwiəl], a. familiar.
colloquy ['kɔləkwi], n. coloquio.
collusion [kə'lu:ʒən], n. confabulación, conclusión, f.
Colombia [kə'lɔmbiə], n. Colombia.
Colombian [kə'lɔmbiən], a., n. colombiano.
colon (1) ['koulən], n. (anat.) colon, m.
colon (2) ['koulən], n.(gram.) dos puntos.
colonel ['kə:nəl], n. coronel, m.
colonial [kə'lounjəl], a. colonial.
colonist ['kɔlənist], n. colono, colonizador, m.
colonization [kɔlənai'zeiʃən], n. colonización, f.
colonize ['kɔlənaiz], v.t. colonizar.
colony ['kɔləni], n. colonia.
colossal [kə'lɔsəl], a. colosal.
colour ['kʌlə], n. color, m.—v.t. colorar.
coloured ['kʌləd], a. colorado; exagerado; de color, de raza negra.
colouring ['kʌlərin], n. color, m., colorido.
colt [koult], n. potro.
columbine ['kɔləmbain], n. aguileña.
Columbus [kə'lʌmbəs], n. Colón, m.
column ['kɔləm], n. columna.
comb [koum], n. peine, m.—v.t. peinar.
combat ['kɔmbæt], n. combate, m., batalla.
combine (1) ['kɔmbain], n. monopolio; (agr.) segadora trilladora.
combine (2) [kəm'bain], v.t. combinar.—v.i. unirse.
combustible [kəm'bʌstəbl], a. combustible.
combustion [kəm'bʌstʃən], n. combustión, f.

come [kʌm], *v.i. irr.* venir; ir; — *along !* ¡vamos!; *coming !* ¡ya voy! *to — about,* suceder; *to — across,* encontrar; *to — between,* desunir; *to — by,* obtener; *to — off,* tener lugar; despegarse; *to — out,* salir; *to — to,* volver en sí; llegar a; *to — upon,* encontrar, dar con.

comedian [kə'miːdjən], *n.* cómico.

comedy ['kɔmədi], *n.* comedia.

comeliness ['kʌmlinis] *n.* hermosura; donaire, *m.*

comely ['kʌmli], *a.* gentil, hermoso, bien parecido.

comet ['kɔmit], *n.* cometa, *m.*

comfort ['kʌmfət], *n.* comodidad, *f.*; confort, *m.*, alivio, consuelo.—*v.t.* confortar.

comfortable ['kʌmfətəbl], *a.* cómodo, confortable.

comic ['kɔmik], *a., n.* cómico; gracioso; — (*paper*), tebeo; — *strip,* tira cómica.

comical ['kɔmikl], *a.* cómico.

coming ['kʌmiŋ], *n.* venida, llegada, (*eccl.*) advenimiento.

comma ['kɔmə], *n.* coma.

command [kə'maːnd], *n.* mando; orden, *f.*; dominio.—*v.t., v.i.* mandar.

commandant ['kɔməndænt], *n.* comandante, *m.*

commander [kə'maːndə], *n.* comandante; comendador (*de una orden militar*), *m.*

commander-in-chief [kə'maːndərintʃiːf], *n.* (*pl.* **commanders-in-chief**) generalísimo, jefe supremo.

commandment [kə'maːndmənt], *n.* (*Bibl.*) mandamiento.

commemoration [kəmemə'reiʃən], *n.* conmemoración, *f.*

commence [kə'mens], *v.t., v.i.* comenzar, empezar.

commencement [kə'mensmənt], *n.* principio, comienzo; (*U.S.*) graduación, *f.*

commend [kə'mend], *v.t.* recomendar; alabar; encomendar.

commendable [kə'mendəbl], *a.* loable.

comment ['kɔment], *n.* observación, *f.*; comentario.—*v.t.* comentar, glosar (*on*).—*v.i.* comentar.

commerce ['kɔməːs], *n.* comercio, negocios, *m.pl.*; trato familiar.

commercial [kə'məːʃəl], *a.* comercial; — *traveller,* viajante, *m.*

commiserate [kə'mizəreit], *v.i.* condolerse (*with,* de).

commissar [kɔmi'saː], *n.* comisario.

commissariat [kɔmi'seəriæt], *n.* comisaría; administración militar, *f.*

commission [kə'miʃən], *n.* comisión, *f.*—*v.t.* comisionar, apoderar, encargar.

commit [kə'mit], *v.t.* cometer; entregar; *to — oneself,* comprometerse.

committee [kə'miti], *n.* comité, *m.*

commode [kə'moud], *n.* cómoda; lavabo.

commodious [kə'moudiəs], *a.* espacioso.

commodity [kə'mɔditi], *n.* mercancía, género, comodidad, *f.*

commodore ['kɔmədɔː], *n.* comodoro.

common ['kɔmən], *a.* común; vulgar, ordinario.—*n.* pastos comunes; (*pol.*) *the Commons,* la Cámara de los Comunes.

commoner ['kɔmənə], *n.* plebeyo.

commonwealth ['kɔmənwelθ], *n.* república;

federación, mancomunidad, *f.*, commonwealth, *m.*

commotion [kə'mouʃən], *n.* alboroto; conmoción, *f.*

communal ['kɔmjunəl], *a.* comunal.

commune ['kɔmjuːn], *n.* (*pol.*) comuna.— [kə'mjuːn], *v.i.* conversar; comulgar.

communicant [kə'mjuːnikənt], *n.* (*eccl.*) comulgante, *m.f.*

communicate [kə'mjuːnikeit], *v.t., v.i.* comunicar; (*eccl.*) comulgar.

communication [kəmjuːni'keiʃən], *n.* comunicación, *f.*

communion [kə'mjuːnjən], *n.* comunión, *f.*

communiqué [kə'mjuːnikei], *n.* comunicado, parte, *m.*

communism ['kɔmjunizm], *n.* comunismo.

communist ['kɔmjunist], *n.* comunista, *m.f.*

community [kə'mjuːniti], *n.* comunidad, *f.*; vecindario; — *chest,* (*U.S.*) caja de beneficencia.

commute [kə'mjuːt], *v.t., v.i.* conmutar.—*v.i.* viajar cada día entre su lugar de trabajo y el barrio (lejano) en que vive.

commuter [kə'mjuːtə], *n.* abonado al ferrocarril que viaja cada día a su lugar de trabajo.

compact [kəm'pækt], *a.* compacto.— ['kɔmpækt], *n.* estuche, *m.*; convenio.—*v.t.* comprimir.

companion [kəm'pænjən], *n.* compañero.

companion-way [kəm'pænjənwei], *n.* (*naut.*) escalera de cámara.

company ['kʌmpəni], *n.* (*com.*) compañía, sociedad, *f.*, empresa; (*mil.*) compañía; (*naut.*) tripulación, *f.*; (*fam.*) invitados, *m.pl.*, visitas, *f. pl.*

compare [kəm'peə], *v.t.* comparar. — *n.* (*only in*) *beyond —,* sin comparación.

comparison [kəm'pærisən], *n.* comparación, *f.*; *in — with,* comparado con.

compartment [kəm'paːtmənt], *n.* compartimiento; (*rail.*) departamento.

compass ['kʌmpəs], *n.* (*naut.*) brújula; alcance; *pair of compasses,* compás, *m.sg.* —*v.t.* alcanzar; rodear.

compatriot [kəm'peitriət], *n.* compatriota, *m.f.*, paisano.

compel [kəm'pel], *v.t.* compeler, obligar, forzar.

compendium [kəm'pendiəm], *n.* compendio.

compensate ['kɔmpənseit], *v.t.* indemnizar, compensar.—*v.i.* compensarse.

compensation [kɔmpən'seiʃən], *n.* compensación, (*jur.*) indemnización, *f.*

compete [kəm'piːt], *v.i.* rivalizar; competir concurrir.

competence ['kɔmpitəns], *n.* suficiencia; capacidad, *f.*, competencia.

competent ['kɔmpitənt], *a.* competente.

competition [kɔmpi'tiʃən], *n.* concurrencia; competencia; concurso.

competitive [kəm'petitiv], *a.* de concurso, de oposición.

competitor [kəm'petitə], *n.* concurrente, *m.f.*, competidor, *m.*

compile [kəm'pail], *v.t.* recopilar, compilar.

complacency [kəm'pleisensi], *n.* satisfacción (*f.*) de sí mismo; complacencia.

complacent [kəm'pleisənt], *a.* satisfecho de sí mismo, engreído.

complain [kəm'plein], *v.i.* quejarse.

complaint [kəm'pleint], *n.* queja; querella; enfermedad (*falta de salud*), *f.*
complaisant [kəm'pleizənt], *a.* complaciente.
complement ['kɔmplimənt], *n.* complemento; personal, *m.*
complementary [kɔmpli'mentəri], *a.* complementario.
complete [kəm'pli:t], *a.* completo; cabal.— *v.t.* completar, acabar.
completion [kəm'pli:ʃən], *n.* terminación, *f.*
complex ['kɔmpleks], *a., n.* complejo.
complexion [kəm'plekʃən], *n.* tez (*de la cara*), *f.*; carácter, *m.*
compliance [kəm'plaiəns], *n.* sumisión, *f.*, complacencia; obediencia.
compliant [kəm'plaiənt], *a.* sumiso; obediente.
complicate ['kɔmplikeit], *v.t.* complicar.
complicated ['kɔmplikeitid], *a.* complicado.
complication [kɔmpli'keiʃən], *n.* complicación, *f.*
compliment ['kɔmplimənt], *n.* cumplido, alabanza; saludo.—*v.t.* cumplimentar, felicitar.
complimentary [kɔmpli'mentəri], *a.* de cortesía, gratuito; galante, lisonjero.
complin(e) ['kɔmplin], *n.* completas, *f.pl.*
comply [kəm'plai], *v.i.* conformarse (*with*, con).
component [kəm'pounənt], *a., n.* componente, *m.* o *f.*
compose [kəm'pouz], *v.t.* componer.
composed [kəm'pouzd], *a.* sosegado; compuesto (*of*, de).
composer [kəm'pouzə], *n.* compositor, *m.*
composite [kəm'pɔzit], *a.* compuesto.
composition [kɔmpə'ziʃən], *n.* composición, *f.*
compositor [kəm'pɔzitə], *n.* (*print.*) cajista, *m.*
compost ['kɔmpɔst], *n.* abono compuesto.
composure [kəm'pouʒə], *n.* serenidad, *f.*, calma.
compound ['kɔmpaund], *a., n.* compuesto.— [kəm'paund]. *v.t.* componer ; (*jur.*) encubrir.
comprehend [kɔmpri'hend], *v.t.* comprender.
comprehension [kɔmpri'henʃən], *n.* comprensión, *f.*
comprehensive [kɔmpri'hensiv]. *a.* comprensivo; amplio.
compress ['kɔmpres], *n.* compresa.— [kəm'pres], *v.t.* comprimir.
compressor [kəm'presə], *n.* compresor, *m.*
comprise [kəm'praiz], *v.t.* comprender, constar de.
compromise ['kɔmprəmaiz], *n.* compromiso. —*v.t.* comprometer.—*v.i.* transigir.
comptroller [kən'troulə], *n.* interventor, *m.*
compulsory [kəm'pʌlsəri], *a.* obligatorio.
compute [kəm'pju:t], *v.t.* computar, calcular.
computer [kəm'pju:tə], *n.* calculadora; calculista (*persona*), *m.f.*
comrade ['kɔmrid], *n.* camarada, *m.f.*
comradeship ['kɔmridʃip], *n.* camaradería, compañerismo.
con (1) [kɔn], *n.* contra.
con (2) [kɔn], *v.t.* estudiar, aprender.
concatenate [kɔn'kætineit], *v.t.* concatenar.
concave ['kɔnkeiv], *a.* cóncavo.
conceal [kən'si:l], *v.t.* ocultar.
concede [kən'si:d], *v.t.* conceder.
conceit [kən'si:t], *n.* presunción, *f.*, engreimiento; concepto.

conceited [kən'si:tid], *a.* vanidoso, engreído.
conceive [kən'si:v], *v.t.* concebir.
concentrate ['kɔnsəntreit], *v.t.* concentrar.— *v.i.* -se.
concentration [kɔnsən'treiʃən], *n.* concentración, *f.*
concentric [kɔn'sentrik], *a.* concéntrico.
concept ['kɔnsept], *n.* concepto.
conception [kən'sepʃən], *n.* concepción, *f.*
concern [kən'sə:n], *n.* empresa, compañía; interés, *m.*; preocupación, inquietud, *f.*— *v.t.* preocupar; atañer, tocar a; interesar; *as concerns*, respecto a.
concerning [kən'sə:niŋ], *prep.* respecto a; sobre.
concert ['kɔnsət], *n.* concierto.—[kən'sə:t], *v.t.* concertar.
concerto [kən'tʃə:tou], *n.* conc(i)erto.
concession [kən'seʃən], *n.* concesión, *f.*
conch [kɔntʃ], *n.* concha.
concierge [kɔnsi'ɛəʒ], *n.* conserje, *m.*, portero.
conciliate [kən'silieit], *v.t.* conciliar.
concise [kən'sais], *a.* sucinto, conciso.
concision [kən'siʒən], *n.* concisión, *f.*
conclave [kɔnkleiv], *n.* conclave, *m.*
conclude [kən'klu:d], *v.t., v.i.* concluir.
conclusion [kən'klu:ʒən], *n.* conclusión, *f.*
conclusive [kən'klu:siv], *a.* concluyente.
concoct [kən'kɔkt], *v.t.* confeccionar; forjar, urdir.
concoction [kən'kɔkʃən], *n.* confección, *f.*; forja, trama.
concomitant [kən'kɔmitənt], *a., n.* concomitante, *m.*
concord ['kɔnkɔ:d], *n.* concord(anc)ia.— [kən'kɔ:d], *v.i.* concordar.
concordat [kən'kɔ:dæt], *n.* concordato.
concourse ['kɔnkɔ:s], *n.* concurso; confluencia.
concrete ['kɔnkri:t], *a.* concreto; sólido; de hormigón.—*n.* hormigón, *m.*
concubine ['kɔŋkjubain], *n.* concubina.
concur [kən'kə:], *v.i.* concurrir.
concussion [kən'kʌʃən], *n.* concusión, *f.*
condemn [kən'dem], *v.t.* condenar.
condemnation [kɔndem'neiʃən], *n.* condenación, *f.*
condensation [kɔnden'seiʃən], *n.* condensación, *f.*
condense [kən'dens], *v.t.* condensar.—*v.i.* -se.
condescend [kɔndi'send], *v.i.* dignarse (*to*, a).
condescending [kɔndi'sendiŋ], *a.* arrogante, condescendente.
condescension [kɔndi'senʃən], *n.* aire (*m.*) protector o de superioridad.
condiment ['kɔndimənt], *n.* condimento.
condition [kən'diʃən], *n.* condición, *f.* — *v.t.* (a)condicionar.
conditional [kən'diʃənəl], *a.* condicional.
condolence [kən'douləns], *n.* condolencia.
condone [kən'doun], *v.t.* condonar.
condor ['kɔndɔ:], *n.* cóndor, *m.*
conducive [kən'dju:siv], *a.* conducente.
conduct ['kɔndʌkt], *n.* conducta.—[kən'dʌkt], *v.t., v.i.* conducir; (*mus.*) dirigir.
conduction [kən'dʌkʃən], *n.* conducción, *f.*
conductor [kən'dʌktə], *n.* (*elec.*) conductor; (*mus.*) director de orquesta; (*U.S., rail.*) revisor; cobrador (*de autobus*), *m.*
conduit ['kʌndit], *n.* conducto, canal, *m.*

cone [coun], *n.* cono; cucurucho; barquillo (*para helados*).
coney ['kouni], *n.* conejo.
confab ['kɔnfæb], (*fam. abbr.* **confabulation** [kɔnfæbju'leiʃən]), *n.* confabulación, *f.*
confection [kɔn'fekʃən], *n.* confite, *m.*; confección, *f.*
confectionery [kən'fekʃənri], *n.* confitería; confites, *n.pl.*
confederate [kən'fedərit], *a.*, *n.* confederado, cómplice, *m.*—[kən'fedəreit], *v.t.* confederar.—*v.i.* -se.
confederation [kɔnfedə'reiʃən], *n.* confederación, *f.*
confer [kən'fɔ:], *v.t.* conferir, otorgar.—*v.i.* conferenciar.
conference ['kɔnfərəns], *n.* congreso; conferencia.
confess [kən'fes], *v.t.*, *v.i.* confesar(se).
confessedly [kən'fesidli], *adv.* manifiestamente.
confession [kən'feʃən], *n.* confesión, *f.*
confessional [kən'feʃənl], *n.* confesionario.
confessor [kən'fɔsə], *n.* confesor, *m.*; penitente, *m.*
confidant(e) ['kɔnfidænt], *n.m.f.* confidente, confidenta.
confide [kən'faid], *v.t.* confiar.—*v.i.* confiar; *to — in,* decir confidencias a.
confidence ['kɔnfidəns], *n.* confianza; confidencia; *— trickster,* timador, *m.*
confident ['kɔnfidənt], *a.* confiado, seguro.
confidential [kɔnfi'denʃəl], *a.* confidencial, en confianza.
confine ['kɔnfain], *n.* confín, límite, *m.*— [kən'fain], *v.t.* limitar; encerrar; *to be confined,* estar de parto; *to be confined to bed,* guardar la cama.
confinement [kən'fainmənt], *n.* parto; limitación; prisión, *f.*
confirm [kən'fɔ:m], *v.t.* confirmar.
confirmation [kɔnfə'meiʃən], *n.* confirmación, *f.*
confiscate ['kɔnfiskeit], *v.t.* comisar, confiscar.
conflagration [kɔnflə'greiʃən], *n.* conflagración, *f.*
conflict ['kɔnflikt], *n.* conflicto.—[kən'flikt], *v.i.* contradecirse; chocar; combatir.
conform [kən'fɔ:m], *v.i.* conformarse.
conformist [kən'fɔ:mist], *n.* conformista, *m.f.*
conformity [kən'fɔ:miti], *n.* conformidad, *f.*
confound [kən'faund], *v.t.* confundir; condenar.
confront [kən'frʌnt], *v.t.* arrostrar; confrontar; confrontarse con.
confuse [kən'fju:z], *v.t.* confundir.
confused [kən'fju:zd], *a.* confuso.
confusion [kən'fju:ʒən], *n.* confusión, *f.*
confute [kən'fju:t], *v.t.* confundir.
congeal [kən'dʒi:l], *v.t.* congelar.—*v.i.* -se.
congenial [kən'dʒi:niəl], *a.* congenial, simpático; compatible.
conger eel ['kɔŋgər'i:l], *n.* congrio.
congest [kən'dʒest], *v.t.* apiñar, congestionar.
congestion [kən'dʒestʃən], *n.* congestión, obstrucción, *f.*
conglomerate [kən'glɔməreit], *v.t.* conglomerar.—*v.i.* -se.
conglomeration [kənglɔmə'reiʃən], *n.* conglomeración, *f.*

Congolese [kɔŋgə'li:z], *a.*, *n.* congolés, congoleño.
congratulate [kən'grætjuleit], *v.t.* felicitar.
congratulation [kəngrætju'leiʃən], *n.* felicitación, *f.*
congregate ['kɔŋgrigeit], *v.i.* congregarse.
congregation [kɔŋgri'geiʃən], *n.* congregación, *f.*; (*eccl.*) fieles, *m.pl.*
congress ['kɔŋgres], *n.* congreso.
congressional [kən'greʃənəl], *a.* congresional.
congressman ['kɔŋgresmən], *n.* congresista, *m.*; (*U.S.*) diputado.
congruent ['kɔŋgruənt], *a.* congruente.
conical ['kɔnikəl], *a.* cónico.
conifer ['kɔnifə], *n.* conífera.
coniferous [kə'nifərəs], *a.* conífero.
conjecture [kən'dʒektʃə], *n.* conjetura.—*v.t.* conjeturar.
conjoint [kən'dʒɔint], *a.* aliado, conjunto.
conjugal ['kɔndʒugəl], *a.* conyugal.
conjugate ['kɔndʒugeit], *v.t.* conjugar.
conjugation [kɔndʒu'geiʃən], *n.* conjugación, *f.*
conjunction [kən'dʒʌŋkʃən], *n.* conjunción, *f.*
conjuncture [kən'dʒʌŋktʃə], *n.* coyuntura.
conjure [kən'dʒuə], *v.t.* conjurar; ['kʌndʒə], conjurar; realizar por arte mágica; *to — up,* evocar; *to — away,* exorcizar.
conjurer, conjuror ['kʌndʒərə], *n.* prestidigitador, *m.*
connect [kə'nekt], *v.t.* conectar, enlazar.— *v.i.* -se.
connection, connexion [kə'nekʃən], *n.* conexión, *f.*; (*rail.*) combinación, *f.*; enlace; empalme, *m.*
conning-tower ['kɔniŋtauə], *n.* torreta.
connivance [kə'naivəns], *n.* connivencia.
connive [kə'naiv], *v.i.* tolerar, hacer la vista gorda (*at,* a).
connoisseur [kɔni'sə:], *n.* conocedor, perito; catador, *m.*
connotation [kɔnə'teiʃən], *n.* connotación, *m.*
conquer ['kɔŋkə], *v.t.* conquistar; vencer.
conqueror ['kɔŋkərə], *n.* conquistador; vencedor, *m.*
conquest ['kɔŋkwest], *n.* conquista.
conscience ['kɔnʃəns], *n.* conciencia.
conscientious [kɔnʃi'enʃəs], *a.* concienzudo; *— objector,* pacifista, *m.f.*
conscious ['kɔnʃəs], *a.* consciente; *to be — of,* tener conocimiento de.
consciousness ['kɔnʃəsnis], *n.* conciencia; *to lose —,* perder el conocimiento.
conscript ['kɔnskript], *n.* recluta, *m.*, quinto, conscripto.—[kən'skript], *v.t.* reclutar.
conscription [kən'skripʃən], *n.* conscripción, *f.*, reclutamiento.
consecrate ['kɔnsikreit], *v.t.* consagrar.
consecutive [kən'sekjutiv], *a.* consecutivo, seguido.
consensus [kən'sensəs], *n.* consenso.
consent [kən'sent], *n.* consentimiento.—*v.i.* consentir (*to,* en).
consequence ['kɔnsikwəns], *n.* consecuencia.
consequently ['kɔnsikwəntli], *a.* por consiguiente.
conservation [kɔnsə'veiʃən], *n.* conservación, *f.*
conservatism [kən'sə:vətizm], *n.* conservadurismo.

conservative [kən'sə:vətiv], *a.*, *n.* conservativo; (*pol.*) conservador, *m.*

conservatoire [kən'sə:vətwa:], *n.* conservatorio.

conservatory [kən'sə:vətəri], *n.* conservatorio; invernáculo.

conserve [kən'sə:v], *n.* conserva.—*v.t.* conservar.

consider [kən'sidə], *v.t.* considerar.

considerable [kən'sidərəbl], *a.* considerable.

considerate [kən'sidərit], *a.* considerado, atento.

consideration [kənsidə'reiʃən], *n.* consideración, *f.*

consign [kən'sain], *v.t.* encomendar; consignar.

consignment [kən'sainmənt], *n.* consignación, *f.*; envío.

consist [kən'sist], *v.i.* consistir en, constar de (*of*).

consistency [kən'sistənsi], *n.* consecuencia; consistencia.

consistent [kən'sistənt], *a.* consistente, consecuente.

consolation [kənsə'leiʃən], *n.* consolación, *f.*, consuelo.

console (1) ['kɔnsoul], *n.* consola.

console (2) [kən'soul], *v.t.* consolar.

consolidate [kən'sɔlideit], *v.t.* consolidar.—*v.i.* -se.

consoling [kən'soulin], *a.* consolador.

consols ['kɔnsoulz], *n.pl.* (*com.*) consolidados, *m.pl.*

consonant ['kɔnsənənt], *a.*, *n.* consonante, *f.*

consort ['kɔnsɔ:t], *n.* consorte, *m.f.*—[kən'sɔ:t], *v.t.* asociarse.

consortium [kən'sɔ:tjəm], *n.* consorcio.

conspectus [kən'spektəs], *n.* sumario, compendio.

conspicuous [kən'spikjuəs], *a.* conspícuo.

conspiracy [kən'spirəsi], *n.* conjuración, conspiración, *f.*

conspirator [kən'spirətə], *n.* conspirador, *m.*, conjurado.

conspire [kən'spaiə], *v.i.* conspirar, conjurarse, maquinar.

constable ['kʌnstəbl], *n.* condestable, *m.*; policía, *m.*, guardia, *m.*

constabulary [kən'stæbjuləri], *n.* policía regional, *f.*

constancy ['kɔnstənsi], *n.* constancia.

constant ['kɔnstənt], *a.* constante.

constellation [kɔnstə'leiʃən], *n.* constelación, *f.*

consternation [kɔnstə'neiʃən], *n.* consternación, *f.*

constipate ['kɔnstipeit], *v.t.* estreñir.

constipation [kɔnsti'peiʃən], *n.* estreñimiento.

constituency [kən'stitjuənsi], *n.* distrito electoral.

constituent [kən'stitjuənt], *a.*, *n.* constitutivo, constituyente, *m.*; (*pol.*) constituyente; votante, *m.f.*

constitute ['kɔnstitju:t], *v.t.* constituir.

constitution [kɔnsti'tju:ʃən], *n.* constitución, *f.*

constitutional [kɔnsti'tju:ʃənəl], *a.* constitucional.

constitutive [kən'stitjutiv], *a.* constitutivo, constituyente.

constraint [kən'streint], *n.* coacción, *f.*, constreñimiento.

constrict [kən'strikt], *v.t.* estrechar, constreñir.

constriction [kən'strikʃən], *n.* constricción, *f.*

constringent [kən'strindʒənt], *a.* constringente.

construct [kən'strʌkt], *v.t.* construir.

construction [kən'strʌkʃən], *n.* construcción; interpretación, *f.*

constructive [kən'strʌktiv], *a.* constructivo.

constructor [kən'strʌktə], *n.* constructor, *m.*

construe [kən'stru:], *v.t.* construir; interpretar.

consul ['kɔnsəl], *n.* cónsul, *m.*

consular ['kɔnsjulə], *a.* consular.

consulate ['kɔnsjulit], *n.* consulado.

consult [kən'sʌlt], *v.t.*, *v.i.* consultar.

consultant [kən'sʌltənt], *n.* consultor, *m.*; especialista, *m.f.*

consultation [kɔnsəl'teiʃən], *n.* consulta(ción), *f.*

consultative [kən'sʌltətiv], *a.* consult(at)ivo.

consume [kən'sju:m], *v.t.* consumir.—*v.i.* -se.

consumer [kən'sju:mə], *n.* consumidor, *m.*

consummate [kən'sʌmit], *a.* consumado.— ['kɔnsəmeit], *v.t.* consumar.

consumption [kən'sʌmpʃən], *n.* consumo; (*med.*) consunción, *f.*

consumptive [kən'sʌmptiv], *a.*, *n.* tísico.

contact ['kɔntækt], *n.* contacto.—*v.t.* ponerse en contacto con.

contagious [kən'teidʒəs], *a.* contagioso.

contain [kən'tein], *v.t.* contener.

container [kən'teinə], *n.* continente; envase *m.*

contaminate [kən'tæmineit], *v.t.* contaminar.

contamination [kəntæmi'neiʃən], *n.* contaminación, *f.*

contemplate ['kɔntəmpleit], *v.t.* contemplar; proponerse.

contemplation [kɔntəm'pleiʃən], *n.* contemplación, *f.*

contemplative [kən'templətiv], *a.* contemplativo.

contemporary [kən'tempərəri], *a.*, *n.* contemporáneo, coetáneo.

contempt [kən'tempt], *n.* desprecio; (*jur.*) contumacia.

contemptible [kən'temptibl], *a.* despreciable.

contemptuous [kən'temptjuəs], *a.* despreciativo, desdeñoso, altivo.

contend [kən'tend], *v.t.* sostener.—*v.i.* contender.

contender [kən'tendə], *n.* competidor, *m.*, contendiente, *m.f.*

contending [kən'tendin], *a.* contrario, opuesto.

content [kən'tent], *a.* contento, satisfecho.— ['kɔntent], *n.* contenido; cabida.—[kən'tent], *v.t.* contentar, satisfacer.

contented [kən'tentid], *a.* contento, satisfecho.

contention [kən'tenʃən], *n.* contención, *f.*; contienda.

contentious [kən'tenʃəs], *a.* contencioso.

contentment [kən'tentmənt], *n.* contentamiento.

contest ['kɔntest], *n.* contienda, lucha, concurso.—[kən'test], *v.t.* disputar, competir por.

context ['kɔntekst], *n.* contexto.
contiguous [kən'tigjuəs], *a.* contiguo.
continence ['kɔntinəns], *n.* continencia.
continent ['kɔntinənt], *a.*, *n.* continente, *m.*
continental [kɔnti'nentəl], *a.*, *n.* continental, *m.f.*
contingency [kən'tindʒənsi], *n.* contingencia.
contingent [kən'tindʒənt], *a.*, *n.* contingente, *m.*
continual [kən'tinjuəl], *a.* continuo.
continually [kən'tinjuəli], *adv.* continua(da)mente.
continuation [kəntinju'eiʃən], *n.* continuación, prolongación, *f.*
continue [kən'tinju:], *v.t.*, *v.i.* continuar.
continuity [kɔnti'nju:iti], *n.* continuidad, *f.*
continuous [kən'tinjuəs], *a.* continuo.
contorted [kən'tɔ:tid], *a.* torcido, contorsionado.
contortion [kən'tɔ:ʃən], *n.* contorsión, *f.*
contour ['kɔntuə], *n.* contorno; curva de nivel (*sobre un mapa*).
contraband ['kɔntrəbænd], *n.* contrabando.
contract ['kɔntrækt], *n.* contrato; [kɔn'trækt], *v.t.* contraer.—*v.i.* contraerse.
contraction [kən'trækʃən], *n.* contracción, *f.*
contractor [kən'træktə], *n.* contratista, *m.f.*; empresario.
contradict [kɔntrə'dikt], *v.t.* contradecir.
contradiction [kɔntrə'dikʃən], *n.* contradicción, *f.*
contradictory [kɔntrə'diktəri], *a.* contradictorio.
contralto [kən'træltou], *n.* contralto.
contraption [kən'træpʃən], *n.* (*fam.*) cachivache, *m.*, dispositivo, artefacto.
contrary ['kɔntrəri], *a.*, *n.* contrario; **on the** —, al contrario; [kɔn'treəri], *a.* terco (*persona*).
contrast ['kɔntra:st], *n.* contraste, *m.* —[kən'tra:st], *v.t.* poner en contraste.—*v.i.* contrastar.
contravene [kɔntrə'vi:n], *v.t.* infringir, contravenir.
contribute [kən'tribju:t], *v.t.* contribuir.
contribution [kɔntri'bju:ʃən], *n.* contribución; cooperación, *f.*
contributor [kən'tribjutə], *n.* contribuyente, *m.f.*
contrite ['kɔntrait], *a.* contrito.
contrivance [kən'traivəns], *n.* aparato, artefacto; invención, *f.*
contrive [kən'traiv], *v.t.* idear, maquinar, fraguar.—*v.i.* ingeniarse (**to**, para).
control [kən'troul], *n.* gobierno, dirección, *f.*; mando; freno; manejo; dominio; **under** —, dominado.—*v.t.* gobernar, mandar; dominar; dirigir; regular; manejar.—*v.r.* dominarse.
controller [kən'troulə], *n.* interventor; regulador, *m.*
controversial [kɔntrə'və:ʃəl], *a.* debatido, batallón.
controversy ['kɔntrəvə:si], *n.* controversia, debate, *m.*
contusion [kən'tju:ʒən], *n.* contusión, *f.*
conundrum [kə'nʌndrəm], *n.* rompecabezas, *m. inv.*
convalesce [kɔnvə'les], *v.i.* reponerse, convalecer.
convalescent [kɔnvə'lesənt], *a.*, *n.* convaleciente, *m.f.*; — **home**, clínica de reposo.
convection [kən'vekʃən], *n.* convección, *f.*

convene [kən'vi:n], *v.t.* convocar.—*v.i.* reunirse.
convenience [kən'vi:niəns], *n.* comodidad, *f.*; retrete, *m.* (*W.C.*).
convenient [kən'vi:niənt], *a.* cómodo, oportuno, conveniente.
convent ['kɔnvent], *n.* convento (de monjas).
convention [kən'venʃən], *n.* congreso; convención, *f.*, conveniencia.
conventional [kən'venʃənəl], *a.* convencional.
converge [kən'və:dʒ], *v.i.* convergir.
convergence [kan'və:dʒəns], *n.* convergencia.
conversant [kən'və:sənt], *a.* versado (**with**, en).
conversational [kɔnvə'seiʃənəl], *a.* de la conversación; conversacional.
converse ['kɔnvə:s], *a.*, *n.* inverso, contrario.— [kən'və:s], *v.i.* conversar.
conversion [kən'və:ʃən], *n.* conversión, *f.*
convert ['kɔnvə:t], *n.* convertido, converso.— [kən'və:t], *v.t.* convertir.
convertible [kən'və:təbl], *a.* convertible.—*n.* descapotable (*coche*), *m.*
convex ['kɔnveks], *a.* convexo.
convey [kən'vei], *v.t.* transportar; comunicar, participar; transferir.
conveyance [kən'veiəns], *n.* transporte, *m.*, comunicación, *f.*; vehículo; traspaso.
conveyor [kən'veiə], *n.* conductor, *m.*; (*mech.*) correa transportadora.
convict ['kɔnvikt], *n.* reo, preso, presidiario. —[kən'vikt], *v.t.* sentenciar, condenar.
conviction [kən'vikʃən], *n.* convicción, *f.*; (*jur.*) sentencia, condena.
convince [kən'vins], *v.t.* convencer.
convincing [kən'vinsin], *a.* convincente.
convivial [kən'viviəl], *a.* festivo, jovial.
convocation [kɔnvə'keiʃən], *n.* convocación, *f.*, asamblea.
convoke [kən'vouk], *v.t.* convocar.
convoy ['kɔnvɔi], *n.* convoy, *m.*, escolta.— [kən'vɔi], *v.t.* convoyar.
convulse [kən'vʌls], *v.t.* convulsionar, crispar, agitar.
convulsion [kən'vʌlʃən], *n.* convulsión, *f.*, espasmo.
cony ['kouni], *n.* conejuna (*piel*), [CONEY].
coo [ku:], *n.* arrullo.—*v.i.* arrullar.
cook [kuk], *n.* cocinero.—*v.t.* cocinar, cocer; (*fam.*) falsificar; arruinar.—*v.i.* cocer; cocinar, guisar (*persona*).
cookery ['kukəri], *n.* cocina, arte (*f.*) de cocina.
cookie ['kuki], *n.* (*U.S.*) galleta, pastelito.
cool [ku:l], *a.* fresco; sereno.—*n.* fresco.—*v.t.* refrescar, enfriar; calmar.—*v.r.* -se.
cooler ['ku:lə], *n.* enfriadera; (*low*) chirona, cárcel, *f.*
coolie ['ku:li], *n.* culí, *m.*
coolness ['ku:lnis], *n.* fresco; frío; frialdad, *f.*; calma.
coop [ku:p], *n.* gallinero.—*v.t.* encerrar (**up**).
cooper ['ku:pə], *n.* tonelero.
co-operate [kou'ɔpəreit], *v.i.* cooperar (**in**, a).
co-operation [kouɔpə'reiʃən], *n.* cooperación, *f.*
co-operative [kou'ɔpərətiv], *a.* cooperativo. —*n.* cooperativa.
co-operator [kou'ɔpəreitə], *n.* cooperador, *m.*
co-ordinate [kou'ɔ:dineit], *v.t.* coordinar.
coot [ku:t], *n.* focha, foja.
cop [kɔp], *n.* (*fam.*) polizonte, *m.*; rimero. —*v.t.* (*fam.*) pillar.

cope (1) [koup], *n.* capa, capucho.
cope (2) [koup], *v.i.* hacer frente a, manejárselas con (*with*).
coping ['koupiŋ], *n.* albardilla.
copious ['koupiəs], *a.* copioso.
copper ['kɔpə], *n.* cobre, *m.*; (*fam.*) polizonte, *m.*, guindilla, *m.*; vellón (*para monedas*), *m.*; calderilla (*dinero suelto*); caldera (*para hervir*).
coppery ['kɔpəri], *a.* cobrizo; cobreño.
coppice ['kɔpis], **copse** [kɔps], *n.* soto.
copy ['kɔpi], *n.* copia; ejemplar, *m.*, número; (*print.*) manuscrito.—*v.t.* copiar.
copyist ['kɔpiist], *n.* copista, *m.*
copyright ['kɔpirait], *n.* propriedad literaria; — *reserved,* queda hecho el depósito que marca la ley.
coquette [kɔ'ket], *n.* coqueta.
coquettish [kɔ'ketiʃ], *a.* coqueta, coquetón.
coral ['kɔrəl], *a.* coralino.—*n.* coral, *m.*
cord [kɔ:d], *n.* cuerda, cordel, cordón, *m.*; **spinal** —, médula espinal.
cordial ['kɔ:diəl], *a.* cordial.—*n.* cordial, licor tónico, *m.*
cordite ['kɔ:dait], *n.* cordita.
cordon ['kɔ:dən], *n.* (*mil. etc.*) cordón, *m.*
corduroy ['kɔ:djurɔi], *n.* pana.
core [kɔ:], *n.* corazón, *m.*; centro; alma; (*elec.*) núcleo.
coriander [kɔri'ændə], *n.* culantro.
cork [kɔ:k], *n.* corcho; tapón, *m.*—*v.t.* tapar con corcho.
corkscrew ['kɔ:kskru:], *n.* sacacorchos, *m.*
cormorant ['kɔ:mərənt], *n.* corvejón, *m.*
corn [kɔ:n], *n.* grano; trigo; (*U.S.*) maíz, *m.*; (*anat.*) callo; (*U.S., fam.*) lo trillado y cursi. —*v.t.* acecinar.
cornea ['kɔ:niə], *n.* córnea.
corned-beef ['kɔ:nd'bi:f], *n.* carne prensada.
corner ['kɔ:nə], *n.* esquina (*exterior*); rincón (*interior*), *m.*; recodo (*de carretera*); (*com.*) monopolio.—*v.t.* arrinconar; (*com.*) acaparar.
corner-stone ['kɔ:nəstoun], *n.* piedra angular.
cornet ['kɔ:nit], *n.* corneta; cucurucho.
corn-field ['kɔ:nfi:ld], *n.* trigal; (*U.S.*) maizal, *m.*
corn-flour ['kɔ:nflauə], *n.* harina de maíz.
cornflower ['kɔ:nflauə], *n.* aciano.
cornice ['kɔ:nis], *n.* cornisa.
Cornish ['kɔ:niʃ], *a., n.* rel. a, natural de Cornualles.
Cornwall ['kɔ:nwəl], *n.* Cornualles, *m.*
corny ['kɔ:ni], *a.* calloso; (*fam.*) trillado y cursi.
coronary ['kɔrənəri], *a.* coronario.
coronation [kɔrə'neiʃən], *n.* coronación, *f.*
coroner ['kɔrənə], *n.* juez (*m.*) de guardia.
coronet ['kɔrənət], *n.* corona nobiliaria.
corporal ['kɔ:pərəl], *a.* corporal.—*n.* (*mil.*) cabo.
corporate ['kɔ:pərit], *a.* corporativo.
corporation [kɔ:pə'reiʃən], *n.* ayuntamiento; corporación, *f.*
corporeal [kɔ:'pɔ:riəl], *a.* corpóreo.
corps [kɔ:], *n.* (*mil. etc.*) cuerpo.
corpse [kɔ:ps], *n.* cadáver, *m.*
corpulent ['kɔ:pjulənt], *a.* corpulento.
corpuscle ['kɔ:pʌsl], *n.* corpúsculo.
corral [kɔ'ra:l], *n.* corral, *m.*
correct [kɔ'rekt], *a.* correcto.—*v.t.* corregir.
correction [kə'rekʃən], *n.* corrección, *f.*

corrective [kə'rektiv], *a., n.* correctivo.
correctness [kə'rektnis], *n.* corrección, *f.*
correlate ['kɔrəleit], *v.t.* correlacionar.
correspond [kɔrəs'pɔnd], *v.i.* corresponder; cartearse.
correspondence [kɔrəs'pɔndəns], *n.* correspondencia.
correspondent [kɔrəs'pɔndənt], *n.* correspondiente, corresponsal, *m.f.*
corresponding [kɔrəs'pɔndiŋ], *a.* correspondiente.
corridor ['kɔridɔ:], *n.* pasillo, corredor, *m.*
corroborate [kə'rɔbəreit], *v.t.* corroborar.
corrode [kə'roud], *v.t.* corroer.
corrosion [kə'rouʒən], *n.* corrosión, *f.*
corrosive [kə'rouziv], *a., n.* corrosivo.
corrugate ['kɔrugeit], *v.t.* arrugar; acanalar; corrugar; ***corrugated iron,*** hierro acanalado *o* ondulado.
corrupt [kə'rʌpt], *a.* corrompido.—*v.t.* corromper.
corruption [kə'rʌpʃən], *n.* corrupción, *f.*
corsage [kɔ:'sa:ʒ], *n.* corpiño.
corset ['kɔ:sit], *n.* corsé, *m.*
Corsica ['kɔ:sikə], *n.* Córcega.
Corsican ['kɔ:sikən], *a., n.* corso.
Corunna [kɔ'rʌnə], *n.* La Coruña.
corvette [kɔ:'vet], *n.* (*naut.*) corbeta.
cosmic ['kɔzmik], *a.* cósmico.
cosmopolitan [kɔzmə'pɔlitən], *a.* cosmopolita.
Cossack ['kɔsæk], *a., n.* cosaco.
cosset ['kɔsit], *v.t.* mimar.
cost [kɔst], *n.* costa.—*v.t., v.i.* costar.
Costa Rican ['kɔstə'ri:kən], *a., n.* costarriqueño, costarricense, *m.f.*
costermonger ['kɔstəmʌŋgə], **coster** ['kɔstə], *n.* (*Brit.*) vendedor ambulante (*de frutas etc.*), *m.*
costliness ['kɔstlinis], *n.* suntuosidad, *f.*
costly ['kɔstli], *a.* suntuoso; costoso.
costume ['kɔstju:m], *n.* traje, *m.*, vestido; disfraz, *m.*; — ***jewel(le)ry,*** joyas de fantasía.
costumier [kɔs'tju:miə], *n.* sastre (*m.*) de teatro.
cosy ['kouzi], *a.* cómodo, agradable.
cot [kɔt], *n.* cuna; catre, *m.*; choza.
coterie ['koutəri], *n.* pandilla.
cottage ['kɔtidʒ], *n.* choza, cabaña; — ***cheese,*** requesón, *m.*
cotter ['kɔtə], *n.* chaveta.
cotton [kɔtn], *n.* algodón, *m.*; — ***gin,*** desmotadera de algodón; — ***waste,*** desperdicios *o* hilacha de algodón; — ***wool,*** algodón en rama, guata. —*v.i.* (*fam.*) aficionarse(***to,*** a).
couch [kautʃ], *n.* canapé, sofá, *m.*; lecho.—*v.t.* expresar.
couch-grass ['ku:tʃgra:s], *n.* (*bot.*) grama.
cough [kɔf], *n.* tos, *f.*—*v.i.* toser; **to** — **up,** (*fam.*) pagar.
could [kud] [CAN].
council ['kaunsil], *n.* concilio; ayuntamiento; concejo; — **of war,** concejo de guerra.
councillor ['kaunsilə], *n.* concejal, *m.*
counsel ['kaunsəl], *n.* consejo; consejero; abogado.—*v.t.* aconsejar.
count (1) [kaunt], *n.* conde, *m.*
count (2) [kaunt], *n.* cálculo, cuenta; (*jur.*) cargo; (*sport*) cuento.—*v.t.* contar; **to** — **out,** (*sport*) declarar vencido.—*v.i.* contar; valer; **to** — **for,** valer; **to** — **on**

someone, contar con alguien; *to — on doing,* contar hacer; *to — one's chickens,* hijo no tener y nombre le poner.

countdown ['kauntdaun], *n.* cuenta hacia atrás.

countenance ['kauntinəns], *n.* semblante, *m.*; cara; aspecto.—*v.t.* apoyar; tolerar.

counter (1) ['kauntə], *a.* contrario, opuesto. —*v.t.* oponerse a; contradecir.

counter (2) ['kauntə], *n.* mostrador, *m.*; ficha.

counteract [kauntər'ækt], *v.t.* neutralizar.

counter-attraction ['kauntərətrækʃən], *n.* atracción contraria.

counterbalance [kauntə'bæləns], *v.t.* contrapesar.

counterfeit ['kauntəfi:t], *a.* contrahecho, falso.—*n.* moneda falsa; engaño.—*v.t.* contrahacer; falsificar.

counterfoil ['kauntəfɔil], *n.* talón, *m.*

countermand [kauntə'mɑ:nd], *v.t.* revocar.

counterpane ['kauntəpein], *n.* cubrecama, *m.*, colcha.

counterpart ['kauntəpɑ:t], *n.* contraparte, *f.*; copia, duplicado.

counterplot ['kauntəplɔt], *n.* contratreta.

counterpoint ['kauntəpɔint], *n.* contrapunto.

counterpoise ['kauntəpɔiz], *n.* contrapeso.

Counter-Reformation ['kauntərefə:meiʃən], *n.* Contrarreforma.

counter-revolutionary ['kauntərevəlu:ʃənəri], *a.* contrarrevolucionario.

countersign ['kauntəsain], *n.* (*mil.*) contraseña; (*com.*) refrendata.—*v.t.* (*com.*) refrendar.

countess ['kauntis], *n.* condesa.

counting-house ['kauntiŋhaus], *n.* escritorio, contaduría.

countless ['kauntlis], *a.* innumerable.

country ['kʌntri], *n.* país, *m.*, nación, *f.*; campo.

countryman ['kʌntrimən], *n.* (*pl.* **-men**) compatriota, *m. f.*; campesino.

county ['kaunti], *n.* condado, provincia; — **seat,** capital (*f.*) de condado, cabeza de partido.

coup [ku:], *n.* golpe, *m.*

coupé [ku'pei], *n.* cupé, *m.*

couple [kʌpl], *n.* par, *m.*; pareja; **married** —, matrimonio.—*v.t.* acoplar; unit; casar. —*v.i.* juntarse; casarse, copularse.

couplet ['kʌplit], *n.* dístico, versos pareados; par, *m.*

coupon ['ku:pɔn], *n.* cupón; talón, *m.*; bono.

courage ['kʌridʒ].—*n.* ánimo, valor, *m.*

courageous [kə'reidʒəs], *a.* valiente.

courier ['kuriə], *n.* estafeta, *m.*; guía, *m.*

course [kɔ:s], *n.* (*naut.*) rumbo; (*cul.*) plato; campo; curso; cauce (*m.*) de un río; hilera (*de ladrillos*); **in the — of,** durante; **of —,** por supuesto.—*v.t.* cazar.—*v.i.* correr.

court [kɔ:t], *n.* (*pol.*) corte, *f.*; (*jur.*) tribunal, *m.*; patio.—*v.t.* cortejar.

courteous ['kɔ:tjəs], *a.* cortés.

courtesan ['kɔ:tizæn], *n.* cortesana, ramera.

courtesy ['kɔ:tizi], *n.* cortesía; reverencia.

court-house ['kɔ:thaus], *n.* palacio de justicia.

courtier ['kɔ:tjə], *n.* cortesano, palaciego.

courtly ['kɔ:tli], *a.* cortés, cortesano.

court-martial ['kɔ:t'mɑ:ʃəl], *n.* (*pl.* **courts-martial**) consejo de guerra.—*v.t.* someter a consejo de guerra.

courtship ['kɔ:tʃip], *n.* cortejo; noviazgo.

courtyard ['kɔ:tjɑ:d], *n.* patio.

cousin ['kʌzin], *n.* primo.

cove (1) [kouv], *n.* (*geog.*) ensenada.

cove (2) [kouv], *n.* (*fam.*) tío.

covenant ['kʌvənənt], *n.* (*Bibl.*) alianza; pacto.

cover ['kʌvə], *n.* tapa, cubierta; velo, pretexto; cubierto (*en la mesa*); portada (*de una revista*); forro.—*v.t.* cubrir; incluir.

coverage ['kʌvəridʒ], *n.* alcance, *m.*

coverlet ['kʌvəlit], *n.* cubrecama, *m.*, colcha.

covert ['kʌvat], *a.* cubierto; escondido, secreto. —*n.* asilo, guarida.

covet ['kʌvit], *v.t.*, *v.i.* codiciar.

covetous ['kʌvitəs], *a.* codicioso.

covetousness ['kʌvitəsnis], *n.* codicia.

cow [kau], *n.* vaca.—*v.t.* intimidar.

coward [kauəd], *n.* cobarde *m.*

cowardice ['kauədis], *n.* cobardía.

cowardly ['kauədli], *a.* cobarde.

cowbell ['kaubel], *n.* cencerro.

cowboy ['kaubɔi], *n.* vaquero.

cower ['kauə], *v.i.* agacharse, acobardarse.

cow-herd ['kauhə:d], *n.* vaquero, pastor de vacas.

cow-hide ['kauhaid], *n.* piel (*f.*) de vaca, cuero.

cowl [kaul], *n.* cogulla; caperuza; caballete, *m.*

cowpox ['kaupɔks], *n.* vacuna.

cowry ['kauri], *n.* cauri, *m.*

cowslip ['kauslip], *n.* (*bot.*) primavera.

coxcomb ['kɔkskoum], *n.* cresta de gallo; mequetrefe, *m.*

coxswain ['kɔksən], *n.* (*naut.*) timonel, *m.*

coy [kɔi], *a.* tímido; coquetón.

crab [kræb], *n.* cangrejo.

crab-apple ['kræbæpl], *n.* manzana silvestre.

crabbed ['kræbid], *a.* áspero; enredoso.

crack [kræk], *a.* de primera clase.—*n.* grieta; estallido; chiste, *m.*; (*fam.*) esfuerzo.—*v.t.* agrietar; romper; fraccionar; *to — up,* alabar.—*v.i.* agrietarse; cascarse (*la voz*); desbaratarse; *to — up,* perder la salud *o* el ánimo.

crack-brained ['krækbreind], *a.* mentecato.

cracker ['krækə], *n.* (*esp. U.S.*) galleta; petardo.

crackle [krækl], *n.* crepitación, *f.*—*v.i.* crujir.

crackling ['kræklin], *n.* crepitación, *f.*; chicharrón, *m.*

cradle [kreidl], *n.* cuna.—*v.t.* acunar, mecer.

craft [krɑ:ft], *n.* oficio; arte, *m.*; treta, astucia; gremio; embarcación, *f.*; avión, *m.*

craftiness ['krɑ:ftinis], *n.* astucia.

craftsman ['krɑ:ftsmən], *n.* artífice, *m.*; artesano.

crafty ['krɑ:fti], *a.* astuto, ladino, taimado.

crag [kræg], *n.* peñasco.

cram [kræm], *v.t.* embutir, rellenar, henchir; cebar.—*v.i.* atracarse (*de comida*); aprender apresuradamente.

cramp [kræmp], *n.* (*med.*) calambre, *m.*; (*eng.*) abrazadera.—*v.t.* engrapar; apretar; *to — one's style,* cortarle las alas a uno.

cranberry ['krænbəri], *n.* arándano.

crane [krein], *n.* (*orn.*) grulla; (*eng.*) grúa.

cranium ['kreinjəm], *n.* cráneo, casco.

crank [kræŋk], *n.* manivela, manubrio, biela; (*fam.*) chiflado.—*v.t.* (*eng.*) arrancar con la manivela.

crankcase ['kræŋkkeis], *n.* (*eng.*) cárter, *m.*

crankshaft ['kræŋkʃɑ:ft], *n.* (*eng.*) cigüeñal, *m.*

cranky ['kræŋki], *a.* chiflado, excéntrico.

cranny ['kræni], *n.* grieta.
crape [kreip], *n.* crespón negro,
crash [kræʃ], *n.* estallido; desplome, *m.*;
fracaso; quiebra.—*v.t.* estrellar.—*v.i.* chocar; desplomarse; quebrar; estrellarse.
crass [kræs], *a.* tosco, basto; torpe.
crate [kreit], *n.* (caja de) embalaje, *m.*, jaula;
banasta, cuévano.—*v.t.* embalar con tablas.
crater ['kreitə], *n.* cráter, *m.*
cravat [krə'væt], *n.* corbata.
crave [kreiv], *v.t.* anhelar, ansiar; pedir,
suplicar.
craven ['kreivən], *a.* cobarde.
craving ['kreiviŋ], *n.* anhelo.
crawfish ['krɔːfiʃ], *n.* langostino; cámbaro;
cangrejo de río.
crawl [krɔːl], *n.* reptación, *f.*, gateo; (*natación*)
crawl, *m.*, arrastre, *m.*
crayfish ['kreifiʃ], [CRAWFISH].
crayon ['kreiən], *n.* clarión, *m.*; lápiz (*m.*) de
color.
craze [kreiz], *n.* manía; moda.—*v.t.* enloquecer; grietar.
craziness ['kreizinis], *n.* locura.
crazy ['kreizi], *a.* loco; desvencijado; — **bone,**
(*U.S.*) [FUNNY BONE].
creak [kriːk], *n.* chirrido, rechinamiento.—*v.i.*
chirriar, rechinar.
cream [kriːm], *n.* nata, crema.—*v.t.* desnatar.
crease [kriːs], *n.* pliegue, *m.*; arruga; doblez, *f.*,
raya (*del pantalón*).—*v.t.* plegar; arrugar.
create [kri'eit], *v.t.* crear, producir, causar.
creation [kri'eiʃən], *n.* creación, *f.*
creative [kri'eitiv], *a.* creativo, creador.
creator [kri'eitə], *n.* creador; inventor, *m.*
creature ['kriːtʃə], *n.* criatura.
credential [kri'denʃəl], *a.* credencial.—*n.pl.*
(cartas) credenciales, *f.pl.*
credibility [kredi'biliti], *n.* credibilidad,
verosimilitud, *f.*
credible ['kredibl], *a.* creíble, verosímil.
credit ['kredit], *n.* crédito; **on** —, al fiado, a
crédito.—*v.t.* creer; acreditar.
creditable ['kreditəbl], *a.* honorable.
creditor ['kreditə], *n.* acreedor.
credulity [kri'djuːliti], *n.* credulidad, *f.*
credulous ['kredjuləs], *a.* crédulo.
creed [kriːd], *n.* fe, *f.*; credo, símbolo (de la
fe).
creek [kriːk], *n.* cala, ensenada; (*U.S.*)
arroyo.
creep [kriːp], *n.* arrastramiento.—*pl.* (*fam.*)
hormigueo.—*v.i. irr.* arrastrarse, deslizarse; hormiguear.
creeper ['kriːpə], *n.* (planta) trepadora.
creepy ['kriːpi], *a.* hormigueante.
cremate [kri'meit], *v.t.* incinerar.
cremation [kri'meiʃən], *n.* cremación, incineración (*f.*) de cadáveres.
crematorium [kremə'tɔːriəm], *n.* crematorio.
crenellate ['krenəleit], *v.t.* almenar, dentar.
creole ['kriːoul], *a.*, *n.* criollo; negro criollo.
creosote ['kriəsout], *n.* creosota.—*v.t.* creo-
sotar.
crept [krept], [CREEP].
crepuscular [kri'pʌskjulə], *a.* crepuscular.
crescendo [kri'ʃendou], *n.* crescendo.
crescent ['kresənt], *a.* creciente.—*n.* creciente,
(*esp. fig.*) media luna.
cress [kres], *n.* (*bot.*) mastuerzo.
crest [krest], *n.* cresta; (*her.*) cimera, cresta.—
v.t. coronar.

crestfallen ['krestfɔːlən], *a.* abatido, cabizbajo.
Cretan ['kriːtən], *a.* cretense.
Crete [kriːt], *n.* Creta.
cretin ['kretin], *n.* cretino.
crevasse [kri'væs], *n.* grieta profunda.
crevice ['krevis], *n.* grieta.
crew [kruː], *n.* tripulación, *f.*; equipo;
cuadrilla. [CROW].
crib [krib], *n.* pesebre, *m.*; belén, *m.*; camilla
de niño; (*educ.*) chuleta; (*fam.*) plagio.—*v.t.*
enjaular; (*educ.*) usar chuletas; (*fam.*)
plagiar.
crick [krik], *n.* tortícolis, *f.*
cricket (1) ['krikit], *n.* (*ent.*) grillo.
cricket (2) ['krikit], *n.* (*sport*) cricket, *m.*; (*fig.*)
juego limpio.
crikey! ['kraiki], *interj.* (*vulg.*) ¡caray!
crime [kraim], *n.* crimen, *m.*, delito.
criminal ['kriminəl], *a.*, *n.* criminal, reo.
crimson ['krimzən], *a.*, *n.* carmesí, *m.*
cringe [krindʒ], *v.i.* arrastrarse, acobardarse.
cringing ['krindʒiŋ], *a.* vil, rastrero.
crinkle [kriŋkl], *n.* arruga, pliegue, *m.*—*v.t.*
arrugar.—*v.i.* -se.
crinoline ['krinəlin], *n.* miriñaque, *m.*
cripple [kripl], *a.*, *n.* estropeado, mutilado.
—*v.* estropear, lisiar, mutilar. [COJO; MANCO.]
crisis ['kraisis], *n.* (*pl.* **crises**) crisis, *f.*
crisp [krisp], *a.* quebradizo; tostado; (*fig.*)
incisivo; fresco.—*n.pl. or* **potato crisps,**
patatas fritas (a la inglesa).—*v.t.* hacer
quebradizo; rizar.
crisscross ['kriskrɔs], *a.* entrelazado.—*v.t.*
marcar con líneas cruzadas.
criterion [krai'tiəriən], *n.* (*pl.* **criteria**
[krai'tiəriə]), criterio.
critic ['kritik], *n.* crítico.
critical ['kritikl], *a.* crítico.
criticism ['kritisizm], *n.* crítica; reseña.
criticize ['kritisaiz], *v.t.*, *v.i.* criticar.
croak [krouk], *n.* graznido.—*v.i.* graznar.
crochet ['krouʃei], *v.t.*, *v.i.* hacer ganchillo
o crochet.
crock [krɔk], *n.* cazuela; tiesto; olla; (*fam.*)
cosa agotada *o* estropeada.—*pl.* vajilla.—*v.t.*
estropear.
crockery ['krɔkəri], *n.* vajilla.
crocodile ['krɔkədail], *n.* cocodrilo; caimán,
m.; fila; — **tears,** dolor fingido.
crocus ['kroukəs], *n.* croco.
crone [kroun], *n.* (*pej.*) vieja.
crony ['krouni], *n.* compinche, *m.*
crook [kruk], *n.* curva; gancho; cayado;
criminal, *m.f.*
crooked ['krukid], *a.* curvado; torcido;
deshonesto, criminal.
croon [kruːn], *v.t.*, *v.i.* canturrear.
crop [krɔp], *n.* cosecha, recolección, (*fig.*)
colección, *f.*; (*orn.*) buche, *m.*—*pl.* la mies.—
v.t. cosechar; recortar, rapar; pacer.
—*v.i. to* — **up,** parecer, descubrirse.
cropper ['krɔpə], *n.* caída; *to* **come a** —,
caer de bruces.
cross [krɔs], *n.* enfadado, enojado; de mal
humor; contrario, adverso; *at* — **purposes,** involuntariamente en pugna.—*n.*
cruz, *f.*; cruce, *m.*—*v.t.* cruzar, atravesar;
oponerse a, contrariar; *to* — **one's mind,**
ocurrírsele a uno; *to* — **off,** tachar; *to* —
swords, medir las armas.—*v.i.* cruzar(se);
entrecortarse; *to* — **over,** pasar al otro lado.
—*v.r.* santiguarse, persignarse.

crossbar ['krɔsbɑ:], *n.* travesaño.
crossbow ['krɔsbou], *n.* ballesta.
crossbred ['krɔsbred], *a.* híbrido; mestizo.
cross-examine [krɔsig'zæmin], *v.t.* interrogar.
cross-eyed ['krɔsaid], *a.* bizco.
crossing ['krɔsiŋ], *n.* travesía; cruce, *m.*
crossroads ['krɔsroudz], *n.* encrucijada; (*fig.*) punto crítico.
cross-section ['krɔs'sekʃən], *n.* corte transversal, *m.*
crossword ['krɔswə:d], *n.* crucigrama, *m.*
crotchet ['krɔtʃit], *n.* (*mus.*) negra.
crouch [krautʃ], *n.* posición (*f.*) de agachado.— *v.i.* agacharse, agazaparse.
crow [krou], *n.* (*orn.*) corneja; cacareo, canto del gallo; grito.—*v.i.* cacarear, cantar; (*fig.*) cantar victoria, alardear.
crowbar ['kroubɑ:], *n.* pie (*m.*) de cabra, palanca (*de hierro*).
crowd [kraud], *n.* muchedumbre, *f.*, gentío; público, espectadores, *m. pl.*; vulgo.—*v.i.* apiñarse, agolparse, apretarse.
crown [kraun], *n.* corona; (*anat.*) coronilla; copa (*de sombrero*); cinco chelines.—*v.t.* coronar; (*fig.*) premiar.
crozier ['krouziə], *n.* báculo de obispo.
crucial ['kru:ʃəl], *a.* crucial, decisivo.
crucible ['kru:sibl], *n.* crisol, *m.*
crucifix ['kru:sifiks], *n.* crucifijo, Cristo.
crucifixion [kru:si'fikʃən], *n.* crucifixión, *f.*
cruciform ['kru:sifɔ:m], *a.* cruciforme.
crucify ['kru:sifai], *v.t.* crucificar; (*fig.*) atormentar, mortificar.
crude [kru:d], *a.* crudo; tosco; no refinado; bruto.
crudity ['kru:diti], *n.* crudeza.
cruel [kru:əl], *a.* cruel.
cruelty ['kru:əlti], *n.* crueldad, *f.*
cruet [kru:it], *n.* vinagrera.
cruise [kru:z], *n.* crucero; viaje (*m.*) por mar. —*v.i.* viajar por mar; cruzar.
cruiser ['kru:zə], *n.* crucero.
crumb [krʌm], *n.* miga.
crumble [krʌmbl], *v.t.* desmigajar, desmenuzar.—*v.i.* -se; desmoronarse, derrumbarse.
crumple [krʌmpl], *v.t.* arrugar.—*v.i.* -se.
crunch [krʌntʃ], *v.t.* cascar, ronchar.
crusade [kru:'seid], *n.* cruzada.
crusader [kru:'seidə], *n.* cruzado.
crush [krʌʃ], *n.* apiñamiento, aglomeración, *f.*—*v.t.* aplastar, machacar, triturar.
crust [krʌst], *n.* corteza; mendrugo; costra; capa.
crusty ['krʌsti], *a.* de mal genio, brusco.
crutch [krʌtʃ], *n.* muleta, muletilla.
crux [krʌks], *n.* lo esencial.
cry [krai], *n.* grito; alarido; **a far — from,** muy distinto de; **in full —,** acosando de cerca.—*v.i.* gritar; llorar; pregonar; **to — for,** reclamar; pedir a voces; **to — off,** renunciar; **to — out,** gritar, exclamar.
crying ['kraiiŋ], *n.* llanto, lloro; pregoneo.
crypt [kript], *n.* cripta.
cryptic ['kriptik], *a.* secreto; con doble intención.
crystallize ['kristəlaiz], *v.t.* cristalizar.—*v.i.* -se.
cub [kʌb], *n.* cachorro.
Cuban ['kju:bən], *a., n.* cubano.
cubbyhole ['kʌbihoul], *n.* chiribitil, chiscón, *m.*

cube [kju:b], *n.* cubo.—*v.t.* (*math.*) cubicar.
cubic(al) ['kju:bik(əl)], *a.* cúbico.
cubicle ['kju:bikl], *n.* cubículo.
cubit ['kju:bit], *n.* codo.
cuckold ['kʌkəld], *n.* marido cornudo.—*v.t.* poner los cuernos a.
cuckoo ['kuku:], *n.* (*orn.*) cuclillo; cucú (*canción*), *m.*
cucumber ['kju:kʌmbə], *n.* pepino, cohombro.
cud [kʌd], *n.* **to chew the —,** rumiar.
cuddle [kʌdl], *n.* abrazo cariñoso.—*v.t.* abrazar con cariño.—*v.i.* estar abrazados.
cudgel ['kʌdʒəl], *n.* porra.—*v.t.* aporrear.
cue (1) [kju:], *n.* (*theat.*) apunte, *m.*; señal, *f.*
cue (2) [kju:], *n.* taco (*de billar*).
cuff [kʌf], *n.* puño (*de camisa*); (*U.S.*) vuelta (*de pantalón*); bofetón, *m.*—*v.t.* abofetear.
cuff-links ['kʌfliŋks], *n.pl.* gemelos, *m.pl.*
cuirass [kwir'ræs], *n.* coraza.
cuisine [kwi'zi:n], *n.* cocina, manera de guisar.
culinary ['kʌlinəri], *a.* culinario.
cull [kʌl], *v.t.* escoger, espigar.
culminate ['kʌlmineit], *v.i.* culminar.
culmination [kʌlmi'neiʃən], *n.* culminación, cumbre, *f.*
culpability [kʌlpə'biliti], *n.* culpabilidad, *f.*
culpable ['kʌlpəbl], *a.* culpable.
culprit ['kʌlprit], *n.* reo, culpable, *m.f.*
cult [kʌlt], *n.* culto; secta.
cultivable ['kʌltivəbl], *a.* cultivable.
cultivate ['kʌltiveit], *v.t.* cultivar.
cultivation [kʌlti'veiʃən], *n.* cultivo; cultura.
culture ['kʌltʃə], *n.* cultura.
culvert ['kʌlvət], *n.* alcantarilla.
cumbersome ['kʌmbəsəm], *a.* embarazoso; incómodo.
cumbrous ['kʌmbrəs], *a.* pesado; incómodo.
cumulative ['kju:mjulətiv], *a.* cumulativo.
cunning ['kʌniŋ], *a.* astuto, mañoso; diestro; (*U.S.*) mono, gracioso.—*n.* astucia; (*obs.*) arte, *m.*, sutileza.
cup [kʌp], *n.* taza; jícara; copa.—*v.t.* ahuecar (en forma de taza).
cupboard ['kʌbərd], *n.* armario, alacena aparador, *m.*
cupful ['kʌpful], *n.* taza *o* lo que contiene una taza.
Cupid ['kju:pid], *n.* (*myth.*) Cupido.
cupola ['kju:pələ], *n.* cúpola.
cupreous ['kju:priəs], *a.* cobreño, cobrizo.
cur [kə:], *n.* gozque, (*fig.*) canalla, *m.*
curate ['kjuərət], *n.* cura, *m.*, adjutor, *m.*
curator [kju:'reitə], *n.* director (de museo), conservador, *m.*
curb [kə:b], *n.* barbada (*del freno*); (*fig.*) freno. [KERB].—*v.t.* refrenar. [KERB].
curd [kə:d], *n.* cuajada; requesón, *m.*
curdle [kə:dl], *v.t.* cuajar, coagular.—*v.i.* -se.
cure [kjuə], *n.* remedio; cura.—*v.t.* curar.— *v.i.* curar; curarse.
curfew ['kə:fju], *n.* queda; toque (*m.*) de queda.
curiosity [kjuri'ɔsiti], *n.* curiosidad, *f.*
curious ['kjuəriəs], *a.* curioso.
curl [kə:l], *n.* rizo, bucle, espiral, *m.*—*v.t.* rizar.—*v.i.* -se.
curlew ['kə:lju], *n.* (*orn.*) zarapito.
curly ['kə:li], *a.* rizado, ondulado.
currant ['kʌrənt], *n.* pasa (*de Corinto*); grosella.

currency ['kʌrənsi], *n.* moneda corriente, divisa; uso corriente; acceptación, *f.*
current ['kʌrənt], *a.* corriente; presente, actual.—*n.* corriente, *f.*
currently ['kʌrəntli], *adv.* actualmente; por lo general.
curriculum [kə'rikjuləm], *n.* programa (*m.*) de estudios.
curry (1) ['kʌri], *n.* (*cul.*) cari, *m.*
curry (2) ['kʌri], *v.t.* almohazar (*caballos*); *to — favour,* insinuarse.
curry-comb ['kʌrikoum], *n.* almohaza.
curse [kə:s], *n.* maldición, *f.*—*v.t.* maldecir.—*v.i.* echar pestes, maldecir.
cursed ['kə:sid], *a.* maldito.
cursive ['kə:siv], *a.* cursivo.—*n.* cursiva.
cursory ['kə:səri], *a.* precipitado; superficial.
curt [kə:t], *a.* brusco, áspero.
curtail [kə'teil], *v.t.* abreviar, reducir.
curtailment [kə'teilmənt], *n.* reducción, *f.*
curtain [kə:tn], *n.* cortina; (*theat.*) telón, *m.*
curtsy ['kə:tsi], *n.* reverencia.—*v.i.* hacer una reverencia.
curve [kə:v], *n.* curva.—*v.i.* encorvarse.
curved [kə:vd], *a.* curvo.
cushion ['kuʃən], *n.* cojín, *m.*, almohadilla.—*v.t.* amortiguar.
cuss [kʌs], *n.* (*fam.*) tunante, *m.*; *pronunciación fam. de* CURSE; (*fig.*) higo.
custard ['kʌstəd], *n.* natillas, *f.pl.*
custodian [kʌs'toudjən], *n.* custodio.
custody ['kʌstədi], *n.* custodia; *in —,* en prisión, *f.*
custom, ['kʌstəm], *n.* costumbre, *f.*; clientela.—*pl.* aduana; derechos (*m.pl.*) de aduana.
customary ['kʌstəməri], *a.* acostumbrado.
customer ['kʌstəmə], *n.* cliente, *m.*, parroquiano.
cut [kʌt], *a.* cortado; *— up,* (*fig.*) turbado.—*n.* corte, *m.*; tajada; atajo; golpe cortante, *m.*; hechura.—*v.t. irr.* cortar, recortar; hender; tallar; (*fig.*) faltar a; negar el saludo a; *to — down,* derribar, abatir; rebajar; *to — off,* amputar; desheredar; *to — out,* omitir, suprimir; *to — up,* despedazar.
cute [kju:t], *a.* (*U.S.*) mono; (*fam.*) astuto.
cutlass ['kʌtləs], *n.* sable (*m.*) de abordaje; alfanje, *m.*
cutler ['kʌtlə], *n.* cuchillero.
cutlery ['kʌtləri], *n.* cubiertos; instrumentos cortantes, *m.pl.*
cutlet ['kʌtlit], *n.* chuleta.
cut-out, ['kʌtaut], *n.* válvula de escape; portafusible, *m.*; diseño recortado.
cutter ['kʌtə], *n.* cortador, (*naut.*) cúter, *m.*
cut-throat ['kʌtθrout], *a., n.* asesino; (*fig.*) rufián, *m.*
cutting ['kʌtiŋ], *a.* incisivo, mordaz.
cuttle-fish ['kʌtlfiʃ], *n.* jibia.
cyanide ['saiənaid], *n.* cianuro.
cyclamen ['sikləmən], *n.* (*bot.*) pamporcino, ciclamino.
cycle [saikl], *n.* ciclo; (*eng.*) tiempo; bicicleta.—*v.i.* ir en bicicleta; practicar el ciclismo.
cycling ['saikliŋ], *n.* ciclismo.
cyclist ['saiklist], *n.* ciclista, *m.f.*
cyclone ['saikloun], *n.* ciclón, *m.*
cygnet ['signit], *n.* pollo del cisne.
cylinder ['silində], *n.* cilindro; *— head,* culata.
cymbal ['simbəl], *n.* címbalo.
cynic ['sinik], *n.* cínico.

cynical ['sinikəl], *a.* cínico.
cynicism ['sinisizm], *n.* cinismo.
cypress ['saiprəs], *n.* ciprés, *m.*
Cypriot ['sipriət], *a., n.* chipriote, chipriota, *m.f.*
Cyprus ['saiprəs], *n.* Chipre, *f.*
cyst [sist], *n.* (*med.*) quiste, *m.*
czar [za:], *n.* (*hist.*) zar, *m.*
Czech [tʃek], *a., n.* checo.
Czechoslovakia [tʃekouslou'vækiə], *n.* Checoeslovaquia.

D

D, d, [di:], *n.* cuarta letra del alfabeto inglés; **D,** (*mus.*) re.
dab [dæb], *n.* golpecito; brochazo.—*v.t.* frotar suavemente, tocar; dar un brochazo a.
dabble [dæbl], *v.i.* chapotear; mangonear; especular.
dactyl ['dæktil], *n.* dáctilo.
dad [dæd], **daddy** ['dædi], *n.* (*fam.*) papá, *m.*
daffodil ['dæfədil], *n.* narciso, trompón, *m.*
daft [dɑ:ft], *a.* chiflado.
dagger ['dægə], *n.* puñal, *m.*
daily ['deili], *a.* diario.—*adv.* cada día.
dainty ['deinti], *a.* delicado.—*n.* golosina.
dairy ['dɛəri], *n.* lechería.
dairy-maid ['dɛərimeid], *n.* lechera.
dais ['deiis], *n.* estrado.
daisy ['deizi], *n.* margarita.
dale [deil], *n.* valleciço.
dally ['dæli], *v.i.* retozar; holgar; rezagarse.
dam [dæm], *n.* presa; (*zool.*) madre, *f.*—*v.t.* estancar, represar.
damage ['dæmidʒ], *n.* daño, perjuicio; avería.—*v.t.* dañar, perjudicar; averiar.
damask ['dæməsk], *n.* damasco.
dame [deim], *n.* dama.
damn [dæm], *a.* maldito.—*v.t.* condenar.
damnation [dæm'neiʃən], *n.* damnación, *f.*
damp [dæmp], *a.* húmedo.—*n.* humedad, *f.*—*v.t.* humedecer; amortiguar.
dampen ['dæmpən], *v.t.* humedecer; amortiguar.
dampness ['dæmpnis], *n.* humedad, *f.*
damsel ['dæmzəl], *n.* damisela.
damson ['dæmzən], *n.* ciruela damascena.
dance [dɑ:ns], *n.* baile, *m.*; danza.—*v.t., v.i.* bailar, danzar.
dancer ['dɑ:nsə], *n.* bailador; bailarín, *m.*
dandelion ['dændilaiən], *n.* diente (*m.*) de león.
dandle [dændl], *v.t.* mecer, mimar.
dandruff ['dændrʌf], *n.* caspa.
dandy ['dændi], *a.* (*fam.*) de órdago.—*n.* pisaverde, *m.*
Dane [dein], *n.* danés, dinamarqués, *m.*
danger ['deindʒə], *n.* peligro.
dangerous ['deindʒərəs], *a.* peligroso.
dangle [dæŋgl], *v.t.* colgar (delante).
Danish ['deiniʃ], *a.* danés, dinamarqués.
dank [dæŋk], *a.* liento.
dapper ['dæpə], *a.* apuesto, gallardo.
dapple [dæpl], *n.* caballo rodado.—*v.t.* motear.

dare

dare [dɛə], *n.* reto.—*v.t.* retar, provocar.—*v.i.* atreverse, osar.
dare-devil ['dɛədevl], *n.* atrévelotodo.
daring ['dɛəriŋ], *a.* osado, atrevido.—*n.* osadía, atrevimiento.
dark [dɑːk], *a.* o(b)scuro; moreno.—*n.* o(b)scuridad, *f.*; tinieblas, *f.pl.*; noche, *f.*; *in the* —, a oscuras; *to get* —, obscurecerse, anochecer.
darken ['dɑːkən], *v.t.* obscurecer.—*v.i.* -se.
darkness ['dɑːknis], *n.* obscuridad, *f.*
darling ['dɑːliŋ], *a.*, *n.* querido.—*interj.* cariño.
darn [dɑːn], *n.* zurcido.—*v.t.* zurcir; (*fam.*) maldecir.
dart [dɑːt], *n.* dardo; saeta; (*sport*) rechilete; arranque, *m.*—*v.i.* lanzarse, volar.
dash [dæʃ], *n.* arremetida; brío; gota, rociada; raya; gran prisa.—*v.t.* frustrar; quebrar.—*v.i.* lanzarse, correr aprisa.
dash-board ['dæʃbɔːd], *n.* tablero de instrumentos (*en un coche*).
dashing ['dæʃiŋ], *a.* gallardo, bizarro, arrojado.
dastardly ['dæstədli], *a.* vil, cobarde.
date (1) [deit], *n.* fecha, data; cita (*encuentro*); *out of* —, anticuado; caducado; *up to* —, moderno; al corriente.—*v.t.* fechar, datar; citarse con.—*v.i.* datar (*from*, de).
date (2) [deit], *n.* (*bot.*) dátil, *m.*
dative ['deitiv], *a.*, *n.* dativo.
datum ['deitəm], *n.* (*pl.* **data**) dato.
daub [dɔːb], *n.* embarradura; pintarrajo.—*v.t.* embadurnar; pintarrajear.
daughter ['dɔːtə], *n.* hija.
daughter-in-law ['dɔːtərinlɔː], *n.* (*pl.* **daughters-in-law**) nuera.
daughterly ['dɔːtəli], *a.* filial, de hija.
daunt [dɔːnt], *v.t.* acobardar, desmayar, intimidar.
dauntless ['dɔːntlis], *a.* impávido.
dauphin ['dɔːfin], *n.* delfín, *m.*
Davy Jones's locker ['deivi'dʒounziz'lɔkə], *n.* (*fam.*) el fondo del mar.
daw [dɔː], *n.* graja.
dawdle ['dɔːdl], *v.i.* haraganear.
dawn [dɔːn], *n.* alba; amanecer, *m.*—*v.i.* amanecer; *it dawned on him that* . . ., se dio cuenta de que . . .
day [dei], *n.* día, *m.*; *by* —, de día; — *in,* — *out,* día tras día; — *off,* día libre; *the* — *before,* la víspera; *to win the* —, vencer, ganar la palma.
daybreak ['deibreik], *n.* amanecer, *m.*
day-dream ['deidriːm], *n.* ensueño, castillo en el aire.
daylight ['deilait], *n.* luz (*f.*) del día; día, *m.*; *in broad* —, en pleno día.
daytime ['deitaim], *n.* día, *m.*; *in* o *during the* —, de día.
daze [deiz], *n.* aturdimiento.—*v.t.* aturdir, deslumbrar.
dazzle [dæzl], *n.* deslumbramiento.—*v.t.* deslumbrar.
deacon ['diːkən], *n.* diácono.
dead [ded], *a.* muerto; (*fam.*) rendido.—*n.* *the* — *of winter,* lo más frío del invierno; *at* — *of night,* en el silencio de la noche.—*adv.* (*fam.*) completamente.
dead-beat [ded'biːt], *a.* (*fam.*) rendido.
deaden [dedn], *v.t.* amortiguar, desvirtuar.
deadline ['dedlain], *n.* fin (*m.*) del plazo.

deadlock ['dedlɔk], *n.* callejón (*m.*) sin salida, punto muerto.
deadly ['dedli], *a.* mortal, mortífero.
deaf [def], *a.* sordo; — *and dumb,* sordomudo.
deafen [defn], *v.t.* ensordecer, aturdir.
deaf-mute ['def'mjuːt], *n.* sordomudo.
deafness ['defnis], *n.* sordera.
deal [diːl], *n.* negocio; trato; reparto; (tabla de) pino; *a good* —, mucho.—*v.t.* *irr.* tratar (*with, in,* de); repartir.—*v.i.* comerciar; tratar; intervenir; comportarse.
dealer ['diːlə], *n.* comerciante; repartidor (*naipes*), *m.*
dealings ['diːliŋz], *n.pl.* relaciones, *f.pl.*; negocios, *m.pl.*
dealt [delt], [DEAL].
dean [diːn], *n.* decano; deán, *m.*
dear [diə], *a.* caro, costoso; querido, amado; — *Sir,* Muy señor mío; — *me!* ¡Dios mío!
dearth [dəːθ], *n.* escasez, *f.*
death [deθ], *n.* muerte, *f.*; — *penalty,* pena de muerte; — *throes,* agonía (de la muerte).
deathly ['deθli], *a.* mortal; cadavérico.—*adv.* como muerto o a la muerte.
death-rate ['deθreit], *n.* mortalidad, *f.*
death-rattle ['deθrætl], *n.* estertor, *m.*
death-trap ['deθtræp], *n.* situación peligrosa.
debar [di'bɑː], *v.t.* excluir.
debase [di'beis], *v.t.* envilecer; falsificar.
debatable [di'beitəbl], *a.* discutible.
debate [di'beit], *n.* debate, *m.*—*v.t.*, *v.i.* debatir.
debauch [di'bɔːtʃ], *n.* lujuria.—*v.t.* corromper.
debauchee [dibɔː'tʃiː], *n.* disoluto, calavera, *m.*
debauchery [di'bɔːtʃəri], *n.* libertinaje, *m.*
debenture [di'bentʃə], *n.* bono, vale, *m.*
debilitate [di'biliteit], *v.t.* debilitar.
debility [di'biliti], *n.* debilidad, *f.*
debit ['debit], *n.* debe, *m.*, débito.—*v.t.* debitar, adeudar.
debonair [debə'nɛə], *a.* garboso, urbano.
debris ['debri], *n.* escombros, *m.pl.*
debt [det], *n.* deuda.
debtor ['detə], *n.* deudor, *m.*
début ['deibjuː], *n.* estreno; debut, *m.*
débutante ['debjuːtɑːt], *n.* debutante, muchacha que se pone de largo.
decade ['dekeid], *n.* decenio, década.
decadence ['dekədəns], *n.* decadencia.
decadent ['dekədənt], *a.* decadente.
decamp [di'kæmp], *v.i.* decampar.
decant [di'kænt], *v.t.* decantar.
decanter [di'kæntə], *n.* garrafa.
decapitate [di'kæpiteit], *v.t.* decapitar, degollar.
decay [di'kei], *n.* podredumbre, podre, *f.*—*v.i.* pudrir(se); decaer.
deceased [di'siːst], *a.*, *n.* difunto.
deceit [di'siːt], *n.* engaño; fraude, *m.*
deceitful [di'siːtful], *a.* engañoso, falaz.
deceive [di'siːv], *v.t.* engañar; burlar.
December [di'sembə], *n.* diciembre, *m.*
decency ['diːsənsi], *n.* decencia.
decent ['diːsənt], *a.* decente.
decentralize [diː'sentrəlaiz], *v.t.* descentralizar.
deception [di'sepʃən], *n.* decepción, *f.*, engaño.

deceptive [di'septiv], *a.* engañoso.
decide [di'said], *v.t.* decidir.—*v.i.* decidir; decidirse (*to*, **a**).
decimal ['desiməl], *a.*, *n.* decimal, *m.*
decimate ['desimeit], *v.t.* diezmar.
decipher [di'saifə], *v.t.* descifrar.
decision [di'siʒən], *n.* decisión, *f.*
decisive [di'saisiv], *a.* decisivo.
deck [dek], *n.* (*naut.*) cubierta; (*U.S.*) baraja (*naipes*).—*v.t.* ataviar.
declaim [di'kleim], *v.t.* declamar.
declaration [deklə'reiʃən], *n.* declaración, *f.*
declare [di'klɛə], *v.t.* declarar; manifestar.—*v.i.* declararse.
declension [di'klenʃən], *n.* declinación, *f.*
decline [di'klain], *n.* declinación, *f.*; baja; decaimiento.—*v.t.*, *v.i.* declinar; decaer.
declivity [di'kliviti], *n.* declive, *m.*
declutch ['di:'klʌtʃ], *v.t.*, *v.i.* desembragar.
décolleté [ˌeikɔl'tei], *a.* escotado.—*n.* escote, *m.*
decompose [di:kəm'pouz], *v.t.* descomponer.—*v.i.* -se.
decomposition [di:kɔmpə'ziʃən], *n.* descomposición, *f.*
décor ['deikɔ:], *n.* decorado.
decorate ['dekəreit], *v.t.* decorar; pintar; condecorar (*honor*).
decoration [dekə'reiʃən], *n.* decoración; condecoración, *f.*
decorative ['dekərətiv], *a.* decorativo.
decorator ['dekəreitə], *n.* pintor, decorador, *m.*
decorous ['dekərəs], *a.* decoroso.
decorum [di'kɔ:rəm], *n.* decoro.
decoy [di'kɔi], *n.* señuelo, reclamo; trampa.—*v.t.* entruchar, atraer con señuelo.
decrease ['di:kri:s], *n.* disminución, *f.* decremento.—[di'kri:s], *v.t.*, *v.i.* disminuir.—*v.i.* decrecer.
decree [di'kri:], *n.* decreto.—*v.t.* decretar.
decrepit [di'krepit], *a.* decrépito.
decry [di'krai], *v.t.* afear, desacreditar.
dedicate ['dedikeit], *v.t.* dedicar.
dedication [dedi'keiʃən], *n.* dedicación, *f.*; dedicatoria.
deduce [di'dju:s], *v.t.* deducir.
deduct [di'dʌkt], *v.t.* deducir, restar.
deduction [di'dʌkʃən], *n.* deducción, *f.*
deed [di:d], *n.* hecho; hazaña; (*jur.*) escritura.
deem [di:m], *v.t.* juzgar, creer.
deep [di:p], *a.* profundo.—*n.* piélago; abismo.
deepen [di:pn], *v.t.* profundizar.
deer [diə], *n.* ciervo.
deface [di'feis], *v.t.* desfigurar.
defamation [defə'meiʃən], *n.* difamación, *f.*
defame [di'feim], *v.t.* difamar.
default [di'fɔ:lt], *n.* falta, incumplimiento.—*v.t.*, *v.i.* faltar, no cumplir.
defeat [di'fi:t], *n.* derrota.—*v.t.* derrotar, vencer.
defeatist [di'fi:tist], *a.*, *n.* derrotista, *m.f.*
defect [di'fekt, di:'fekt], *n.* defecto.
defective [di'fektiv], *a.* defectuoso; defectivo; deficiente.
defence [di'fens], *n.* defensa. **[War Office]**
defend [di'fend], *v.t.* defender.
defendant [di'fendənt], *n.* acusado; demandado.
defensive [di'fensiv], *a.* defensivo.—*n.* defensiva.

defer [di'fɔ:], *v.t.* aplazar.
deference ['defərəns], *n.* deferencia.
deferment [di'fɔ:mənt], *n.* aplazamiento.
defiance [di'faiəns], *n.* desafío; desobediencia.
defiant [di'faiənt], *a.* desafiador; desobediente.
deficiency [di'fiʃənsi], *n.* deficiencia; insolvencia.
deficient [di'fiʃənt], *a.* deficiente.
deficit ['defisit], *n.* déficit, *m.*
defile (1) ['di:fail], *n.* desfiladero.
defile (2) [di'fail], *v.t.* profanar, manchar.
define [di'fain], *v.t.* definir.
definite ['definit], *a.* definido, concreto.
definition [defi'niʃən], *n.* definición, *f.*
definitive [di'finitiv], *a.* definitivo.
deflate [di'fleit], *v.t.* desinflar.
deflation [di'fleiʃən], *n.* desinflación, *f.*
deflect [di'flekt], *v.t.* desviar.
deflection [di'flekʃən], *n.* desviación, *f.*
deflower [di:'flauə], *v.t.* desflorar.
deform [di'fɔ:m], *v.t.* deformar.
deformed [di'fɔ:md], *a.* deforme.
deformity [di'fɔ:miti], *n.* deformidad, *f.*
defraud [di'frɔ:d], *v.t.* defraudar, estafar.
defray [di'frei], *v.t.* costear, sufragar.
defrost [di:'frost], *v.t.* deshelar.
deft [deft], *a.* diestro, mañoso.
defunct [di'fʌŋkt], *a.* difunto.
defy [di'fai], *v.t.* desafiar; resistir tercamente.
degeneracy [di'dʒenərəsi], *n.* degeneración, *f.*
degenerate [di'dʒenərit], *a.*, *n.* degenerado.—[di'dʒenəreit], *v.i.* degenerar.
degradation [degrə'deiʃən], *n.* degradación, *f.*
degrade [di'greid], *v.t.* degradar.
degrading [di'greidiŋ], *a.* degradante.
degree [di'gri:], *n.* grado; (*educ.*) título.
dehydrate [di:hai'dreit], *v.t.* deshidratar.
deify ['di:ifai], *v.t.* deificar.
deign [dein], *v.i.* dignarse (*to*).
deity ['di:iti], *n.* deidad, *f.*
deject [di'dʒekt], *v.t.* abatir, desanimar.
dejection [di'dʒekʃən], *n.* abatimiento.
delay [di'lei], *n.* retraso, tardanza.—*v.t.* retrasar.—*v.i.* tardar (en).
delectable [di'lektəbl], *a.* deleitable.
delegate ['deligit], *n.* delegado.—['deligeit], *v.t.* delegar.
delegation [deli'geiʃən], *n.* delegación, *f.*
delete [di'li:t], *v.t.* borrar, suprimir.
deleterious [deli'tiəriəs], *a.* perjudicial, nocivo.
deletion [di'li:ʃən], *n.* borradura, supresión, *f.*
deliberate [di'libərit], *a.* pensado; cauto; pausado.—[di'libəreit], *v.t.*, *v.i.* deliberar.
deliberation [dilibə'reiʃən], *n.* deliberación, *f.*
delicacy ['delikəsi], *n.* delicadeza; (*cul.*) golosina.
delicate ['delikit], *a.* delicado.
delicious [di'liʃəs], *a.* delicioso.
delight [di'lait], *n.* delicia, gozo; deleite, *m.*—*v.t.* deleitar.—*v.i.* deleitarse (*in*, con, en).
delightful [di'laitful], *a.* deleitoso, encantador.
Delilah [di'lailə], *n.* Dalila.
delimit [di'limit], *v.t.* delimitar.
delineate [di'linieit], *v.t.* delinear.
delinquency [di'liŋkwənsi], *n.* delincuencia; delito.

delinquent

delinquent [di'liŋkwənt], *a.*, *n.* delincuente, *m.f.*
delirious [di'liriəs], *a.* delirante; *to be —*, delirar.
delirium [di'liriəm], *n.* delirio.
deliver [di'livə], *v.t.* libertar; entregar; asestar; distribuir (*correo*); pronunciar (*oración*); *to be delivered of,* parir.
deliverance [di'livərəns], *n.* liberación, *f.*; rescate, *m.*
delivery [di'livəri], *n.* liberación, *f.*; rescate, *m.*; distribución, *f.*; entrega; modo de expresarse; parto.
dell [del], *n.* vallejuelo.
delta ['deltə], *n.* delta.
delude [di'l(j)u:d], *v.t.* seducir, ilusionar.
deluge ['delju:dʒ], *n.* diluvio.—*v.t.* inundar.
delusion [di'l(j)u:ʒən], *n.* alucinación; decepción, *f.*
delve [delv], *v.t.* (*obs.*) cavar; *to — into,* sondear.
demagnetize [di:'mægnitaiz], *v.t.* desimant(t)ar.
demagogue ['deməgɔg], *n.* demagogo.
demand [di'mɑ:nd], *n.* demanda.—*v.t.* exigir; demandar; *to be in —,* tener demanda.
demanding [di'mɑ:ndiŋ], *a.* exigente.
demarcate ['di:mɑ:keit], *v.t.* demarcar, deslindar.
demarcation [di:mɑ'keiʃən], *n.* demarcación, *f.*, deslinde, *m.*
demean [di'mi:n], *v.r.* rebajarse, degradarse.
demeanour [di'mi:nə], *n.* conducta; porte, *m.*
demented [di'mentid], *a.* demente.
demigod ['demigɔd], *n.* semidiós, *m.*
demilitarize [di:'militəraiz], *v.t.* desmilitarizar.
demise [di'maiz], *n.* óbito.
demobilize [di:'moubilaiz], (*fam.* **demob** [di'mɔb]), *v.t.* desmovilizar.
democracy [di'mɔkrəsi], *n.* democracia.
democrat ['deməkræt], *n.* demócrata, *m.f.*
democratic [demə'krætik], *a.* democrático.
demolish [di'mɔliʃ], *v.t.* derribar, demoler.
demolition [demə'liʃən], *n.* derribo, demolición, *f.*
demon ['di:mən], *n.* demonio.
demonstrate ['demənstreit], *v.t.* demostrar.
demonstration [demənstreiʃən], *n.* demostración, *f.*
demonstrative [di'mɔnstrətiv], *a.*, *n.* demostrativo.
demoralize [di'mɔrəlaiz], *v.t.* desmoralizar.
demote [di'mout], *v.t.* (*U.S.*) degradar.
demur [di'mə:], *n.* escrúpulo, titubeo.—*v.i.* vacilar, titubear.
demure [di'mjuə], *a.* sentado, serio; gazmoño.
den [den], *n.* guarida, cubil, *m.*
denial [di'naiəl], *n.* negación, *f.*
denigrate ['denigreit], *v.t.* denigrar.
Denis ['denis], *n.* Dionisio.
denizen ['denizn], *n.* habitante, *m.f.*
Denmark ['denmɑ:k], *n.* Dinamarca.
denote [di'nout], *v.t.* denotar.
dénouement [dei'nu:mã], *n.* desenlace, *m.*
denounce [di'nauns], *v.t.* denunciar.
dense [dens], *a.* denso, espeso.
density ['densiti], *n.* densidad, *f.*

dent [dent], *n.* abolladura.—*v.t.* abollar.—*v.i.* -se.
dental [dentl], *a.*, *n.* dental, *f.*
dentifrice ['dentifris], *n.* dentífrico, pasta de dientes.
dentist ['dentist], *n.* dentista, *m.f.*
denture ['dentʃə], *n.* dentadura.
denude [di'nju:d], *v.t.* desnudar.
deny [di'nai], *v.t.* negar.
deodorant [di:'oudərənt], *a.*, *n.* desodorante, *m.*
depart [di'pɑ:t], *v.i.* partir, salir; divergir; desviarse; fallecer.
departed [di'pɑ:tid], *a.*, *n.* difunto, pasado.
department [di'pɑ:tmənt], *n.* departamento, sección, *f.*; *— store,* almacén, *m.*
departure [di'pɑ:tʃə], *n.* salida, partida; divergencia.
depend [di'pend], *v.i.* depender (*on,* de).
dependable [di'pendəbl], *a.* digno de confianza.
dependant [di'pendənt], *n.* dependiente, *m.f.*
dependence [di'pendəns], **dependency** [di'pendənsi], *n.* dependencia.
dependent [di'pendənt], *a.* dependiente.
depict [di'pikt], *v.t.* retratar, representar.
deplete [di'pli:t], *v.t.* consumir, agotar.
deplore [di'plɔ:], *v.t.* lamentar, deplorar.
deploy [di'plɔi], *v.t.* desplegar.—*v.i.* -se.
depopulate [di:'pɔpjuleit], *v.t.* despoblar.
deport [di'pɔ:t], *v.t.* deportar.
deportment [di'pɔ:tmənt], *n.* porte, *m.*, conducta; postura.
depose [di'pouz], *v.t.* deponer.
deposit [di'pɔzit], *n.* depósito.—*v.t.* depositar.—*v.i.* -se.
depot [di'depou], *n.* depósito, almacén, *m.*; (*U.S.*) estación, *f.*
deprave [di'preiv], *v.t.* depravar.
depravity [di'præviti], *n.* depravación, *f.*
deprecate ['deprikeit], *v.t.* desaprobar.
depreciate [di'pri:ʃieit], *v.t.* depreciar; abaratar.—*v.i.* depreciarse.
depredation [depri'deiʃən], *n.* depredación, *f.*
depress [di'pres], *v.t.* abatir, desalentar; deprimir.
depressing [di'presiŋ], *a.* desalentador; deprimente.
depression [di'preʃən], *n.* depresión; (*com.*) crisis, *f.*
deprive [di'praiv], *v.t.* privar.
depth [depθ], *n.* profundidad, *f.*, fondo; *in the depths of,* sumido en.
deputation [depju'teiʃən], *n.* diputación; delegación, *f.*
depute [di'pju:t], *v.t.* diputar.
deputize ['depjutaiz], *v.t.* diputar, delegar.—*v.i.* hacer las veces (*for,* de).
deputy ['depjuti], *n.* diputado; teniente, *m.*
derail [di'reil], *v.t.* hacer descarrilar.
derange [di'reindʒ], *v.t.* desarreglar; trastornar.
derelict ['derilikt], *a.* abandonado; remiso.—*n.* derrelicto.
deride [di'raid], *v.t.* mofarse de.
derision [di'riʒən], *n.* irrisión, *f.*, mofa.
derivation [deri'veiʃən], *n.* derivación, *f.*
derive [di'raiv], *v.t.*, *v.i.* derivar.
derogatory [di'rɔgətəri], *a.* despreciativo.
derrick ['derik], *n.* grúa, cabria; torre (*f.*) de taladrar.
dervish ['də:viʃ], *n.* derviche, *m.*

descant ['deskænt], *n.* discante, *m.*
descend [di'send], *v.t., v.i.* descender, bajar; caer (*on*, sobre).
descendant [di'sendənt], *n.* descendiente, *m.f.*
descendent [di'sendənt], *a.* descendente.
descent [di'sent], *n.* descenso; descendimiento; descendencia (*linaje*).
describe [dis'kraib], *v.t.* describir.
description [dis'kripʃən], *n.* descripción, *f.*
descriptive [dis'kriptiv], *a.* descriptivo.
descry [dis'krai], *v.t.* divisar.
desecrate ['desikreit], *v.t.* profanar.
desert (1) [di'zə:t], *n.* merecimiento, mérito.
desert (2) [di'zə:t], *v.t.* desertar; abandonar.
desert (3) ['dezət], *a., n.* desierto, yermo.
deserter [di'zə:tə], *n.* desertor, *m.*
desertion [di'zə:ʃən], *n.* deserción, *f.,* abandono.
deserve [di'zə:v], *v.t.* merecer.
design [di'zain], *n.* dibujo, diseño; designio, proyecto; intención, *f.*—*v.t.* diseñar, dibujar; proyectar, idear; destinar.
designate ['dezignit], *a.* designado.— ['dezigneit], *v.t.* señalar; nombrar; designar.
designing [di'zainiŋ], *a.* insidioso, intrigante.
desirable [di'zaiərəbl], *a.* deseable.
desire [di'zaiə], *n.* deseo.—*v.t.* desear.
desirous [di'zaiərəs], *a.* deseoso.
desist [di'zist], *v.i.* desistir.
desk [desk], *n.* escritorio, mesa; pupitre, *m.*
desolate ['desəlit], *a.* desolado, desierto, lúgubre.—['desəleit], *v.t.* desolar.
desolation [desə'leiʃən], *n.* desolación, *f.;* desierto.
despair [dis'pɛə], *n.* desesperación, *f.*—*v.i.* desesperar(se) (*of*, de).
desperate ['despərit], *a.* desesperado; violento.
desperation [despə'reiʃən], *n.* desesperación, *f.*
despicable [dis'pikəbl], *a.* despreciable, vil.
despise [dis'paiz], *v.t.* despreciar.
despite [dis'pait], *prep.* a pesar de.
despoil [dis'pɔil], *v.t.* despojar.
despondent [dis'pɔndənt], *a.* desalentado.
despot ['despət], *n.* déspota, *m.f.*
despotic [des'pɔtik], *a.* despótico.
dessert [di'zə:t], *n.* postre, *m.*
destination [desti'neiʃən], *n.* destino; destinación, *f.*
destine ['destin], *v.t.* destinar.
destiny ['destini], *n.* destino, sino.
destitute ['destitju:t], *a.* desamparado; desprovisto.
destitution [desti'tju:ʃən], *n.* desamparo.
destroy [dis'trɔi], *v.t.* destruir, destrozar.
destroyer [dis'trɔiə], *n.* destructor (*also naut.*), *m.*
destruction [dis'trʌkʃən], *n.* destrucción, *f.*
destructive [dis'trʌktiv], *a.* destructivo.
desultory ['desəltəri], *a.* inconexo, veleidoso.
detach [di'tætʃ], *v.t.* separar, desprender; (*mil.*) destacar.
detached [di'tætʃt], *a.* imparcial.
detachment [di'tætʃmənt], *n.* desprendimiento; desinterés, *m.;* (*mil.*) destacamento.
detail ['di:teil], *n.* detalle, pormenor, *m.;* (*mil.*) destacamento.—[di'teil], *v.t.* detallar; (*mil.*) destacar.
detain [di'tein], *v.t.* detener.
detect [di'tekt], *v.t.* descubrir; percibir.

detection [di'tekʃən], *n.* averiguación, *f.,* descubrimiento.
detective [di'tektiv], *a.* policíaco (*cuento etc.*). —*n.* detective, *m.*
detention [di'tenʃən], *n.* detención, *f.*
deter [di'tə:], *v.t.* disuadir, refrenar.
detergent [di'tə:dʒənt], *a., n.* detergente, *m.*
deteriorate [di'tiəriəreit], *v.i.* deteriorarse.
deterioration [ditiəriə'reiʃən], *n.* deterioro.
determination [ditə:mi'neiʃən], *n.* determinación, *f.*
determine [di'tə:min], *v.t.* determinar.—*v.i.* -se.
deterrent [di'terənt], *a., n.* deterrente, *m.*
detest [di'test], *v.t.* detestar.
dethrone [di'θroun], *v.t.* destronar.
detonate ['detəneit], *v.t.* hacer detonar.—*v.i.* detonar.
detour ['di:tuə], *n.* desviación, *f.,* desvío, rodeo.
detract [di'trækt], *v.t.* detraer, detractar.
detriment ['detrimənt], *n.* perjuicio.
detrimental [detri'mentl], *a.* perjudicial.
deuce [dju:s], *n.* (*fam.*) dos; *the* — *!* ¡diablos!
deuced [dju:st], *a.* (*fam.*) diabólico.
deucedly ['dju:sidli], *adv.* (*fam.*) formidablemente, muy.
devaluation [di:vælju'eiʃən], *n.* desvalorización, *f.*
devalue [di:'vælju:], *v.t.* desvalor(iz)ar.
devastate ['devəsteit], *v.t.* devastar, asolar.
devastation [devəs'teiʃən], *n.* devastación, *f.,* ruina.
develop [di'veləp], *v.t.* desarrollar; (*phot.*) revelar; (*com.*) explotar.—*v.i.* desarrollarse, evolucionar.
development [di'veləpmənt], *n.* desarrollo; (*com.*) explotación; reconstrucción; evolución, *f.;* suceso reciente.
deviate ['di:vieit], *v.i.* divergir, desviarse.
device [di'vais], *n.* artificio, invento, aparato; ardid; emblema, *m.,* lema, *m.*
devil ['devil], *n.* diablo.—*v.t.,* (*fam.*) estorbar.
devilish ['deviliʃ], *a.* diabólico.
devilment ['devilmənt], *n.* diablura.
deviltry ['deviltri], *n.* diablura.
devious ['di:viəs], *a.* tortuoso.
devise [di'vaiz], *v.t.* idear, trazar.
devoid [di'vɔid], *a.* desprovisto, falto.
devote [di'vout], *v.t.* dedicar.
devoted [di'voutəd], *a.* devoto, dedicado.
devotee [devo'ti:], *n.* devoto, dedicado.
devotion [di'vouʃən], *n.* devoción, dedicación, *f.*—*pl.* (*eccl.*) oraciones, *f.pl.*
devour [di'vauə], *v.t.* devorar.
devout [di'vaut], *a.* devoto, piadoso.
dew [dju:], *n.* rocío.—*v.t.* rociar.
dexterity [deks'teriti], *n.* destreza.
dexterous ['dekstrəs], *a.* diestro.
diabetic [daiə'betik], *a., n.* diabético.
diabolic(al) [daiə'bɔlik(əl)], *a.* diabólico.
diadem ['daiədem], *n.* diadema, *f.*
diæresis [dai'iərisis], *n.* (*pl.* **-reses**) diéresis, *f.*
diagnose ['daiəgnouz], *v.t.* diagnosticar.
diagnosis [daiəg'nousis], *n.* (*pl.* **-noses**) diagnosis, *f.*
diagonal [dai'ægənəl], *a., n.* diagonal, *f.*
diagram ['daiəgræm], *n.* diagrama, *m.,* gráfica.

dial

dial [daiəl], *n.* esfera; cuadrante, *m.*; (*tel.*) disco.—*v.t., v.i.* (*tel.*) marcar.
dialect ['daiəlekt], *n.* dialecto.
dialogue ['daiəlɔg], *n.* diálogo.
diameter [dai'æmitə], *n.* diámetro.
diamond ['daiəmənd], *n.* diamante, brillante, *m.*
diaper ['daiəpə], *n.* lienzo adamascado; (*U.S.*) pañal, *m.*
diaphragm ['daiəfræm], *n.* diafragma, *m.*; (*tel., rad.*) membrana.
diarrhoea [daiə'riə], *n.* diarrea.
diary ['daiəri], *n.* diario, jornal, *m.*; agenda.
diatribe ['daiətraib], *n.* diatriba.
dice [dais], *n.pl.* dados (*sg.* die, *q.v.*).—*v.t.* cortar en cubitos.—*v.i.* jugar a los dados.
dickens ['dikinz], *n., interj.* (*fam.*) diantre, *m.*
dictate ['dikteit], *n.* dictado, mandato.— [dik'teit], *v.t., v.i.* dictar; mandar.
dictation [dik'teiʃən], *n.* dictado.
dictator [dik'teitə], *n.* dictador, *m.*
dictatorship [dik'teitəʃip], *n.* dictadura.
diction ['dikʃən], *n.* dicción, *f.*; lenguaje, *m.*
dictionary ['dikʃənri], *n.* diccionario.
did [did], [DO].
diddle [didl], *v.t.* (*fam.*) estafar.
didn't [didnt] [DID NOT].
die (1) [dai], *n.* (*pl.* dice, *q.v.*) dado.
die (2) [dai], *n.* (*pl.* dies) troquel, *m.*, cuño; cubito.
die (3) [dai], *v.i.* morir; apagarse; *to be dying to* o *for,* (*fam.*) morirse por.
die-hard ['daihɑ:d], *a., n.* exaltado, intransigente.
diesel-engine ['di:zlendʒin], *n.* motor diesel, *m.*
diesel-oil ['di:zlɔil], *n.* gas-oil, *m.*
diet ['daiət], *n.* régimen, *m.*; dieta.—*v.i.* estar de régimen.
differ ['difə], *v.i.* diferenciar(se), diferir.
difference ['difrəns], *n.* diferencia; disensión, *f.*; *it makes no —,* da lo mismo.
different ['difrənt], *a.* diferente, distinto.
differentiate [difə'renʃieit], *v.t.* diferenciar, distinguir.
difficult ['difikəlt], *a.* difícil, dificultoso.
difficulty ['difikəlti], *n.* dificultad, *f.*; apuro.
diffident ['difidənt], *a.* desconfiado, tímido.
diffuse [di'fju:s], *a.* difuso.—[di'fju:z], *v.t.* difundir.—*v.i.* -se.
diffusion [di'fju:ʒən], *n.* difusión, *f.*
dig [dig], *n.* codazo; (*fam.*) pulla, chafaldita.— *pl.* (*fam.*) alojamiento.—*v.t., v.i. irr.* cavar; excavar; *to — up,* desenterrar.
digest ['daidʒest], *n.* digesto, recopilación, *f.*— [di'dʒest], *v.t., v.i.* digerir.
digestion [di'dʒestʃən], *n.* digestión, *f.*
digit ['didʒit], *n.* dígito.
digital ['didʒitl], *a.* digital.
dignified ['dignifaid], *a.* grave, majestuoso.
dignitary ['dignitəri], *n.* personalidad (*f.*) de alta jerarquía, dignatario.
dignity ['digniti], *n.* dignidad, *f.*
digress [dai'gres], *v.i.* divagar.
digression [dai'greʃən], *n.* digresión, divagación, *f.*
dike [daik], *n.* dique, *m.*
dilapidated [di'læpideitid], *a.* desmantelado.
dilate [dai'leit], *v.t.* dilatar.—*v.i.* -se.
dilatory ['dilətəri], *a.* lento; dilatorio.
dilemma [di'lemə], *n.* disyuntiva; dilema, *m.*
diligence ['dilidʒəns], *n.* diligencia.

diligent ['dilidʒənt], *a.* diligente, asiduo.
dilly-dally ['dili'dæli], *v.i.* haraganear.
dilute [dai'lju:t], *v.t.* diluir.
dim [dim], *a.* débil; turbio; cegato (*vista*); indistinto; (*fig.*) boto, lerdo.—*v.t.* amortiguar.—*v.i.* nublarse.
dime [daim], *n.* (*U.S.*) moneda de diez centavos.
dimension [di'menʃən], *n.* dimensión, *f.*; tamaño.
diminish [di'miniʃ], *v.t., v.i.* disminuir.
diminutive [di'minjutiv], *a.* diminuto; (*gram.*) diminutivo.—*n.* (*gram.*) diminutivo.
dimple [dimpl], *n.* hoyuelo.
din [din], *n.* estrépito, alboroto.
dine [dain], *v.i.* cenar; comer.
ding-dong ['diŋ'dɔŋ], *n.* dindán, tintín, *m.*
dinghy ['diŋgi], *n.* dinga; bote, *m.*
dingy ['dindʒi], *a.* empañado, negruzco; oscuro.
dining room ['dainiŋrum], *n.* comedor, *m.*
dinner ['dinə], *n.* cena; comida; banquete, *m.*
dint [dint], *n.* [DENT]; *by — of,* a fuerza de.
diocese ['daiəsis], *n.* diócesis, *f.*
dip [dip], *n.* zambullida; depresión, *f.*; (*fam.*) baño.—*v.t.* bajar; sumergir; batir (*bandera*).—*v.i.* bajar; sumergirse; inclinarse hacia abajo.
diphtheria [dif'θiəriə], *n.* difteria.
diphthong ['difθɔŋ], *n.* diptongo.
diploma [di'ploumə], *n.* diploma, *m.*
diplomacy [di'plouməsi], *n.* diplomacia.
diplomat ['dipləmæt], *n.* diplomático.
diplomatic [diplə'mætik], *a.* diplomático.
dire [daiə], *a.* horrendo.
direct [di'rekt, dai'rekt], *a.* directo; recto; inmediato; franco.—*v.t.* dirigir; regir; mandar.
direction [di'rekʃən], *n.* dirección, *f.*
director [di'rektə], *n.* director; gerente, *m.*
directory [di'rektəri], *n.* directorio; (*tel.*) guía.
dirge [də:dʒ], *n.* endecha.
dirigible ['diridʒibl], *a., n.* dirigible, *m.*
dirk [də:k], *n.* daga.
dirt [də:t], *n.* barro; tierra; mugre, *f.*; porquería.
dirt-cheap ['də:t'tʃi:p], *a.* (*fam.*) barato, regalado.
dirty ['də:ti], *a.* sucio; vil; obsceno, verde.
disability [disə'biliti], *n.* incapacidad, *f.*
disable [dis'eibl], *v.t.* incapacitar, inhabilitar; mutilar.
disadvantage [disəd'vɑ:ntidʒ], *n.* desventaja.
disaffected [disə'fektid], *a.* desafecto.
disagree [disə'gri:], *v.i.* disentir; desconvenir; desavenirse; no estar de acuerdo; *to — with,* sentar mal a (*comida*).
disagreement [disə'gri:mənt], *n.* desacuerdo.
disallow [disə'lau], *v.t.* negar, desaprobar.
disappear [disə'piə], *v.i.* desaparecer.
disappearance [disə'piərəns], *n.* desaparición, *f.*
disappoint [disə'pɔint], *v.t.* decepcionar, frustrar, chasquear.
disappointment [disə'pɔintmənt], *n.* desilusión, decepción, *f.*, chasco.
disapproval [disə'pru:vl], *n.* desaprobación, *f.*
disapprove [disə'pru:v], *v.t., v.i.* desaprobar (*of*).
disarm [dis'ɑ:m], *v.t., v.i.* desarmar.

disarmament [dis'ɑ:məmənt], *n.* desarme, *m.*

disarray [disə'rei], *n.* desarreglo, desorden, *m.*—*v.t.* descomponer, desarreglar.

disassociate [disə'souʃieit], *v.t.* disociar, separar.

disaster [di'zɑ:stə], *n.* desastre, *m.*

disastrous [di'zɑ:strəs], *a.* calamitoso, desastroso.

disavow [disə'vau], *v.t.* desconocer, negar.

disband [dis'bænd], *v.t.* licenciar, disolver.—*v.i.* dispersarse.

disbelief [disbi'li:f], *n.* incredulidad, *f.*

disbelieve [disbi'li:v], *v.t., v.i.* no creer, descreer.

disburse [dis'bə:s], *v.t.* desembolsar.

disbursement [dis'bə:smənt], *n.* desembolse, *m.*

disc [disk], *n.* disco.

discard [dis'kɑ:d], *v.t.* descartar.

discern [di'sə:n], *v.t.* percibir, discernir.

discernment [di'sə:nmənt], *n.* discernimiento, perspicacia.

discharge ['distʃɑ:dʒ], *n.* descarga; descargo; liberación, *f.*; cumplimiento; licencia; despedida.—[dis'tʃɑ:dʒ], *v.t.* descargar; cumplir, desempeñar; licenciar; libertar; despedir.—*v.i.* descargar(se).

disciple [di'saipl], *n.* discípulo.

disciplinary ['disiplinəri], *a.* disciplinario.

discipline ['disiplin], *n.* disciplina.—*v.t.* disciplinar.

disclaim [dis'kleim], *v.t.* renunciar; negar.

disclaimer [dis'kleimə], *n.* renuncia, negación, *f.*

disclose [dis'klouz], *v.t.* revelar, descubrir, publicar.

disclosure [dis'klouʒə], *n.* revelación, *f.*, descubrimiento.

discolour [dis'kʌlə], *v.t.* descolorar.

discomfit [dis'kʌmfit], *v.t.* desconcertar.

discomfort [dis'kʌmfət], *n.* incomodidad, *f.*—*v.t.* incomodar.

discompose [diskəm'pouz], *v.t.* inquisitar, descomponer.

disconcert [diskən'sə:t], *v.t.* desconcertar.

disconnect [diskə'nekt], *v.t.* desacoplar, desunir; (*elec.*) desconectar.

disconnected [diskə'nektid], *a.* incoherente.

disconsolate [dis'kɔnsəlit], *a.* desconsolado.

discontent [diskən'tent], *a., n.* descontento.—*v.t.* descontentar.

discontented [diskən'tentid], *a.* descontento.

discontinue [diskən'tinju:], *v.t.* descontinuar.

discord ['diskɔ:d], *n.* discordia; discordancia.

discordant [dis'kɔ:dənt], *a.* discordante.

discount ['diskaunt], *n.* descuento.—[dis'kaunt], *v.t.* descontar.

discourage [dis'kʌridʒ], *v.t.* desanimar, desalentar; disuadir.

discourse ['diskɔ:s], *n.* discurso, plática.—[dis'kɔ:s], *v.i.* discurrir.

discourteous [dis'kə:tjəs], *a.* descortés.

discourtesy [dis'kə:tisi], *n.* descortesía.

discover [dis'kʌvə], *v.t.* descubrir.

discovery [dis'kʌvəri], *n.* descubrimiento.

discredit [dis'kredit], *n.* descrédito.—*v.t.* desacreditar; descreer.

discreditable [dis'kreditəbl], *a.* ignominioso, deslustrador.

discreet [dis'kri:t], *a.* discreto.

discrepancy [dis'krepənsi], *n.* discrepancia.

discretion [dis'kreʃən], *n.* discreción, *f.*

discriminate [dis'krimineit], *v.t.* distinguir.—*v.i.* discriminar, hacer distinciones injustas.

discrimination [diskrimi'neiʃən], *n.* discernimiento; distinción (*f.*) injusta.

discus ['diskəs], *n.* disco.

discuss [dis'kʌs], *v.t.* discutir; hablar de.

discussion [dis'kʌʃən], *n.* discusión, *f.*

disdain [dis'dein], *n.* desdén, *m.*—*v.t.* desdeñar.

disdainful [dis'deinful], *a.* desdeñoso.

disease [di'zi:z], *n.* enfermedad, *f.*

disembark [disim'bɑ:k], *v.t., v.i.* desembarcar.

disembowel [disim'bauəl], *v.t.* desentrañar.

disenchant [disin'tʃɑ:nt], *v.t.* desencantar; desengañar.

disengage [disin'geidʒ], *v.t.* desenredar; desembarazar; soltar.

disentangle [disin'tæŋgl], *v.t.* desenmarañar.

disfavour [dis'feivə], *n.* disfavor; desaire, *m.*—*v.t.* desfavorecer.

disfigure [dis'figə], *v.t.* desfigurar.

disgorge [dis'gɔ:dʒ], *v.t.* desembuchar; vomitar.

disgrace [dis'greis], *n.* deshonra, vergüenza, afrenta.—*v.t.* deshonrar.

disgraceful [dis'greisful], *a.* afrentoso, deshonroso.

disgruntle [dis'grʌntl], *v.t.* amohinar.

disguise [dis'gaiz], *n.* disfraz, *m.*—*v.t.* disfrazar.

disgust [dis'gʌst], *n.* aversión, *f.*, repugnancia.—*v.t.* repugnar, dar asco ʀ.

disgusting [dis'gʌstiŋ], *a.* repugnante, asqueroso.

dish [diʃ], *n.* plato.—*pl.* vajilla.—*v.t.* — **up**, (*fam.*) servir en un plato; ofrecer.

dish-cloth [diʃkləθ], *n.* estropajo; albero.

dishearten [dis'hɑ:tn], *v.t.* descorazonar, desalentar.

dishevel [di'ʃevəl], *v.t.* desgreñar.

dishonest [dis'ɔnist], *a.* fraudulento, ímprobo, deshonrado.

dishonesty [dis'ɔnisti], *n.* improbidad, *f.*; dolo.

dishonour [dis'ɔnə], *n.* deshonor, *m.*; deshonra.—*v.t.* deshonrar; desflorar; (*com.*) no aceptar.

disillusion [disi'lu:ʒən], *n.* desilusión, *f.*—*v.t.* desilusionar.

disinclination [disinkli'neiʃən], *n.* aversión, desinclinación, *f.*

disincline [disin'klain], *v.t.* desinclinar.

disinfect [disin'fekt], *v.t.* desinfectar.

disinfectant [disin'fektənt], *n.* antiséptico, desinfectante, *m.*

disinherit [disin'herit], *v.t.* desheredar.

disintegrate [dis'intigreit], *v.t.* disgregar, desintegrar.—*v.i.* -se.

disinter [disin'tə:], *v.t.* desenterrar.

disinterested [dis'intərəstid], *a.* desprendido, imparcial.

disjoint [dis'dʒɔint], *v.t.* descoyuntar, desarticular.

disjointed [dis'dʒɔintid], *a.* (*fig.*) inconexo.

disk [disk], *n.* disco.

dislike [dis'laik], *n.* antipatía, aversión, *f.*—*v.t.* tener aversión a, desaprobar; *I — cheese*, no me gusta el queso.

dislocate [dis'loskeit], *v.t.* dislocar.

dislodge [dis'lɔdʒ], *v.t.* desalojar.

disloyal

disloyal [dis'lɔiəl], *a.* desleal.
disloyalty [dis'lɔiəlti], *n.* deslealtad, *f.*
dismal ['dizməl], *a.* lúgubre, aciago, funesto.
dismantle [dis'mæntl], *v.t.* desmontar.
dismay [dis'mei], *n.* consternación, *f.*, espanto.—*v.t.* consternar.
dismiss [dis'mis], *v.t.* despedir; licenciar; descartar.
dismissal [dis'misəl], *n.* despedida, despido; destitución, *f.*; licencia(miento).
dismount [dis'maunt], *v.t., v.i.* desmontar.—*v.i.* apearse.
disobedience [disə'bi:djəns], *n.* desobediencia.
disobedient [disə'bi:djənt], *a.* desobediente, inobediente.
disobey [disə'bei], *v.t., v.i.* desobedecer.
disorder [dis'ɔːdə], *n.* desorden, *m.*—*v.t.* desordenar.
disorderly [dis'ɔːdəli], *a.* desordenado; escandaloso.
disorganize [dis'ɔːɡənaiz], *v.t.* desorganizar.
disown [dis'oun], *v.t.* repudiar.
disparage [dis'pæridʒ], *v.t.* deslustrar, menospreciar.
disparaging [dis'pæridʒiŋ], *a.* menospreciativo.
disparity [dis'pæriti], *n.* desigualdad, *f.*
dispassionate [dis'pæʃənit], *a.* desapasionado.
dispatch [dis'pætʃ], *n.* despacho.—*v.t.* despachar; expedir.
dispel [dis'pel], *v.t.* dispersar.
dispensary [dis'pensəri], *n.* dispensario.
dispersal [dis'pəːsəl], *n.* dispersión, *f.*
disperse [dis'pəːs], *v.t.* dispersar.—*v.i.* -se.
dispersion [dis'pəːʃən], *n.* dispersión, *f.*
dispirit [di'spirit], *v.t.* desanimar.
displace [dis'pleis], *v.t.* desplazar; dislocar; remover.
display [dis'plei], *n.* exhibición, presentación, *f.*; espectáculo.—*v.t.* exhibir; ostentar.
displease [dis'pli:z], *v.t.* desagradar, disgustar.
displeasure [dis'pleʒə], *n.* desplacer, disgusto.
disposal [dis'pouzəl], *n.* disposición; venta; distribución; destrucción, *f.*; **to have at one's —,** disponer de.
dispose [dis'pouz], *v.t.* disponer; inducir; arreglar; decidir.—*v.i.* disponer (*of,* de); deshacerse (*of,* de); arreglar, terminar (*of*).
disposition [dispə'ziʃən], *n.* disposición, *f.*; natural, *m.*, indole, *f.*
dispossess [dispə'zes], *v.t.* desposeer, desposesionar.
disproof [dis'pru:f], *n.* refutación, *f.*
disproportionate [disprə'pɔːʃənit], *a.* desproporcionado.
disprove [dis'pru:v], *v.t.* refutar, confutar.
dispute [dis'pju:t], *n.* disputa.—*v.t., v.i.* disputar.
disqualify [dis'kwɔlifai], *v.t.* inhabilitar; desclasificar; descalificar.
disquiet [dis'kwaiət], *n.* inquietud, *f.*—*v.t.* inquietar.
disregard [disri'ɡaːd], *n.* desatención, *f.*; desprecio.—*v.t.* desatender; desairar; no hacer caso de, pasar por alto.
disrepair [disri'pɛə], *n.* mal estado, estropeo.
disreputable [dis'repjutəbl], *a.* desdoroso, desacreditado.
disrepute [disri'pju:t], *n.* mala fama, descrédito; **to bring into —,** desacreditar.

disrespect [disri'spekt], *n.* desacato.—*v.t.* desacatar.
disrupt [dis'rʌpt], *v.t.* trastornar, desbaratar.
dissatisfaction [disætis'fækʃən], *n.* descontento.
dissatisfied [di'sætisfaid], *a.* malcontento, descontento.
dissatisfy [di'sætisfai], *v.t.* descontentar.
dissect [di'sekt], *v.t.* disecar.
dissection [di'sekʃən], *n.* disección, *f.*
dissemble [di'sembl], *v.t.* disimular, fingir.
disseminate [di'semineit], *v.t.* difundir, propalar.
dissension [di'senʃən], *n.* disensión, *f.*, discordia.
dissent [di'sent], *n.* disidencia; disensión, *f.*—*v.i.* disentir, disidir.
dissenter [di'sentə], *n.* disidente, *m.f.*
disservice [di'səːvis], *n.* deservicio.
dissident [di'sidənt], *a., n.* disidente, *m.f.*
dissimilar [di'similə], *a.* desemejante, desigual.
dissimulate [di'simjuleit], *v.t.* disimular.
dissipate ['disipeit], *v.t.* disipar.
dissociate [di'souʃieit], *v.t.* disociar.
dissolute ['disəluːt], *a.* disoluto.
dissolution [disə'luːʃən], *n.* disolución, *f.*
dissolve [di'zɔlv], *v.t., v.i.* disolver.
dissuade [di'sweid], *v.t.* disuadir.
distaff ['distaːf], *n.* rueca; (*fig.*) las mujeres.
distance ['distəns], *n.* distancia; **in the —,** a lo lejos.
distant ['distənt], *a.* distante, lejano; frío, esquivo.
distaste [dis'teist], *n.* aversión, *f.*, disgusto.
distasteful [dis'teistful], *a.* desabrido, disgustoso.
distemper [dis'tempə], *n.* temple (*pintura*), *m.*; (*vet.*) moquillo; enfermedad, *f.*—*v.t.* destemplar; pintar al temple.
distend [dis'tend], *v.t.* hinchar.—*v.i.* -se.
distil [dis'til], *v.t.* destilar.
distillation [disti'leiʃən], *n.* destilación, *f.*
distillery [dis'tiləri], *n.* destilería, destilatorio.
distinct [dis'tiŋkt], *a.* distinto; claro, cierto.
distinction [dis'tiŋkʃən], *n.* distinción, *f.*; (*educ.*) sobresaliente, *m.*
distinctive [dis'tiŋktiv], *a.* distintivo.
distinguish [dis'tiŋgwiʃ], *v.t.* distinguir.
distort [dis'tɔːt], *v.t.* torcer.
distortion [dis'tɔːʃən], *n.* torcimiento.
distract [dis'trækt], *v.t.* distraer; enloquecer.
distraction [dis'trækʃən], *n.* distracción, *f.*; locura; frenesí, *m.*
distraught [dis'trɔːt], *a.* aturdido, atolondrado.
distress [dis'tres], *n.* pena, angustia; apuro, aprieto.—*v.t.* angustiar, penar; apurar.
distressing [dis'tresiŋ], *a.* penoso, congojoso.
distribute [dis'tribjuːt], *v.t.* distribuir, repartir.
distribution [distri'bjuːʃən], *n.* distribución, *f.*
district ['distrikt], *n.* región, *f.*, comarca; (*pol.*) distrito.
distrust [dis'trʌst], *n.* desconfianza.—*v.t.* desconfiar de.
disturb [dis'təːb], *v.t.* perturbar; molestar; desordenar.
disturbance [dis'təːbəns], *n.* disturbio; desorden, *m.*; molestia.

disuse [dis'ju:s], *n.* desuso.—[dis'ju:z], *v.t.* desusar.

ditch [ditʃ], *n.* zanja; foso.—*v.t.* zanjar; (*fam.*) echar.—*v.i.* (*aer.*) caer en el mar.

dither ['diðə], *n.* tambaleo.—*v.i.* tambalear.

ditto ['ditou], *a.*, *n.*, *adv.* idem.

ditty ['diti], *n.* cantilena, cancioncilla.

diurnal [dai'ə:nl], *a.* diurno.

divan [di'væn, 'daivæn], *n.* diván, *m.*

dive [daiv], *n.* zambullida, buceo; (*fam.*, *U.S.*) timba; guarida.—*v.i.* *irr.* tirarse, zambullirse; (*nav.*) bucear; (*aer.*) picar; meterse a prisa.

dive-bomb ['daivbɔm], *v.i.* (*aer.*) bombardear en picado.

diver ['daivə], *n.* zambullidor, *m.*; (*nav.*) buzo; (*orn.*) somorgujo.

diverge [dai'və:dʒ], *v.i.* divergir.

divergence [dai'və:dʒəns], **divergency** [dai'və:dʒənsi], *n.* divergencia.

divergent [dai'və:dʒənt], *a.* divergente.

divers ['daivəz], *a.pl.* diversos, varios.

diverse [dai'və:s], *a.* diverso, diferente.

diversion [dai'və:ʃən], *n.* diversión, *f.*, desvío.

diversity [dai'və:siti], *n.* diversidad, *f.*

divert [dai'və:t], *v.t.* desviar, apartar; divertir.

diverting [dai'və:tiŋ], *a.* divertido.

divest [dai'vest], *v.t.* despojar, desposeer.

divide [di'vaid], *v.t.* dividir.—*v.i.* -se.

dividend ['dividend], *n.* dividendo.

divine [di'vain], *a.* divino.—*n.* clérigo, predicador, *m.*—*v.t.*, *v.i.* adivinar, pronosticar.

diving ['daiviŋ], *n.* buceo; — *suit,* escafandra.

divinity [di'viniti], *n.* divinidad, *f.*; (*educ.*) teología.

division [di'viʒən], *n.* división, *f.*

divorce [di'vɔ:s], *n.* divorcio.—*v.t.* divorciarse de; divorciar (*dar un divorcio*).—*v.i.* divorciarse.

divulge [di'vʌldʒ], *v.t.* revelar, publicar, divulgar.

dizzy ['dizi], *a.* vertiginoso; ligero, desvanecido; perplejo.

do [du:], *n.(fam.)* función, *f.*—*v.t.* *irr.* hacer; bastar a; (*fam.*) estafar; (*fam.*) matar; (*fam.*) recorrer.—*v.i.* *irr.* servir, bastar; obrar; hacer; salir; hallarse; **to — away with,** destruir, acabar con; **to — up,** liar; abrochar; **to — without,** pasarse sin; **to be done for,** (*fam.*) estar hecho polvo; estar arruinado; **to have to — with,** tener que ver con; **I could — with,** me iría bien. . . .

docile ['dousail], *a.* dócil, manso, sumiso.

dock (1) [dɔk], *n.* (*naut.*) dique, *m.*; dársena; muelle, *m.*; (*jur.*) banquillo.—*v.t.* (*naut.*) poner en dique.—*v.i.* atracar en el muelle.

dock (2) [dɔk], *n.* (*bot.*) bardana.

dock (3) [dɔk], *v.t.* cercenar.

docker ['dɔkə], *n.* estibador, *m.*

docket ['dɔkit], *n.* tótulo; minuta.

dockyard ['dɔkja:d], *n.* astillero; arsenal, *m.*

doctor ['dɔktə], *n.* doctor, *m.*; (*med.*) médico.—*v.t.* (*fam.*) componer; adulterar.

doctrine ['dɔktrin], *n.* doctrina.

document ['dɔkjumənt], *n.* documento.—['dɔkjument], *v.t.* documentar.

documentary [dɔkju'mentəri], *a.* documental.

dodder ['dɔdə], *v.i.* chochear.

doddering ['dɔdəriŋ], *a.* chocho.

dodge [dɔdʒ], *n.* regate, *m.*; (*fam.*) esquinazo.—*v.t.* esquivar, evadir.—*v.i.* trampear; meterse.

dodo ['doudou], *n.* (*orn.*) dodo.

doe [dou], *n.* gama, cierva; (*zool.*) hembra.

does [dʌz], [DO].

doff [dɔf], *v.t.* quitar (*el sombrero*).

dog [dɔg], *n.* perro; (*zool.*) macho; — *Latin,* latinajo; *to go to the dogs* (*fig.*), arruinarse.

dog-ear ['dɔgiə], *n.* orejón (*de una página*), *m.*

dog-fight ['dɔgfait], *n.* refriega.

dogged ['dɔgid], *a.* terco, tozudo, obstinado.

doggerel ['dɔgərəl], *n.* coplas (*f.pl.*) de ciego.

dogma ['dɔgmə], *n.* dogma, *m.*

dogmatic [dɔg'mætik], *a.* dogmático.

dog-tired ['dɔgtaiəd], *a.* (*fam.*) rendido, hecho polvo.

doings ['du:iŋz], *n.pl.* hechos, actividad, *f.*; (*fam.*) cachivache, *m.*

doldrums ['dɔldrəmz], *n.pl.* calma chicha ecuatorial; (*fig.*) murria, desánimo.

dole [doul], *n.* soccorro para los parados; cesantía, paro; limosna; (*lit.*) angustia.—*v.t.* repartir (*out*).

doll [dɔl], *n.* muñeca.—*v.r.* **to — oneself up** (*fam.*) empapirotarse.

dollar ['dɔlə], *n.* dólar, *m.*

dolphin ['dɔlfin], *n.* delfín, *m.*

dolt [doult], *n.* zamacuco, zoquete, *m.*

domain [do'mein], *n.* dominio; heredad, *f.*

dome [doum], *n.* cúpola; cimborrio.

Domesday ['du:mzdei], *n.* día (*m.*) del Juicio final.

domestic [də'mestik], *a.*, *n.* doméstico.

domesticate [də'mestikeit], *v.t.* domesticar.

domicile ['dɔmisail], *n.* domicilio.—*v.t.* domiciliar.

dominant ['dɔminənt], *a.* dominante.

dominate ['dɔmineit], *v.t.* dominar.

domination [dɔmi'neiʃən], *n.* dominación, *f.*, dominio.

domineer [dɔmi'niə], *v.t.*, *v.i.* mandonear, dominar mucho.

Dominican [də'minikən], *a.*, *n.* (*geog.*) dominicano; (*eccl.*) dominicano, dominico.

dominion [də'minjən], *n.* dominio.

domino ['dɔminou], *n.* dominó; ficha de dominó.—*n.pl.* dominó.

don [dɔn], *n.* (*educ.*) socio (de colegio); académico, universitario.

donate [dou'neit], *v.t.* donar, contribuir.

donation [dou'neiʃən], *n.* donación, *f.*, donativo.

done [dʌn], *a.* acabado; asado, cocido; (*fam.*) rendido; — *for,* (*fam.*) rendido; muerto; arruinado, [DO].

donkey ['dɔŋki], *n.* burro, asno.

donor ['dounə], *n.* donante, donador, *m.*

don't [dount], [DO NOT].

doodle [du:dl], *v.i.* borronear.

doom [du:m], *n.* sino, hado; perdición, *f.*; juicio.—*v.t.* condenar.

doomsday [DOMESDAY].

door [dɔ:], *n.* puerta; portal, *m.*; portezuela (*de vehículo*).

door-keeper ['dɔ:ki:pə], *n.* portero.

door-knocker ['dɔ:nɔkə], *n.* aldaba.

door-man ['dɔ:mən], *n.* portero.

door-mat ['dɔ:mæt], *n.* esterilla.

doorstep ['dɔ:step], *n.* escalón (*de puerta*), *m.*

doorway ['dɔ:wei], n. portal, m.
dope [doup], n. narcótico(s); (U.S. fam.) datos, m.pl.; (fam.) bobo.—v.t. narcotizar.
dormant ['dɔ:mənt], a. latente; durmiente.
dormitory ['dɔ:mitri], n. dormitorio.
dormouse ['dɔ:maus], n. (pl. -mice) lirón, m.
dose [dous], n. dósis, f.—v.t. dosificar; medicinar.
dot [dɔt], n. punto, puntito.—v.t. puntear, motear.
dotage ['doutidʒ], n. chochez, f.
dotard ['doutəd], n. chocho.
dote [dout], v.i. chochear; to — on, idolatrar.
dotty ['dɔti], a. (fam.) chiflado, gilí.
double [dʌbl], a., n. doble, m; — bed, cama de matrimonio.—v.t. doblar.—v.i. doblarse.
double-chin [dʌbl'tʃin], n. papada.
double-cross [dʌbl'krɔs], n. (fam.) traición, f.—v.t. engañar (a un cómplice).
double-dealing [dʌbl'di:liŋ], n. doblez, m., trato doble.
double-decker [dʌbl'dekə], n. autobús (de dos pisos), m.
double-edged [dʌbl'edʒd], a. de dos filos.
double-faced [dʌbl'feist], a. doble, falaz.
doubt [daut], n. duda; no —, sin duda.—v.t., v.i. dudar.
doubtful ['dautful], a. dudoso.
doubtless ['dautlis], a. indudable.—adv. sin duda.
dough [dou], n. masa; pasta; (fam., U.S.) parné, m.
doughty ['dauti], a. valeroso.
dour [duə], a. melancólico; (Scot.) austero.
douse [daus], v.t. zambullir; apagar.
dove [dʌv], n. paloma.
dovecote ['dʌvkɔt], n. palomar, m.
dovetail ['dʌvteil], n. (carp.) cola de milano.—v.t. machihembrar a cola de milano.—v.i. cuadrar perfectamente.
dowager ['dauədʒə], n. matrona; viuda (de un hidalgo).
dowdy ['daudi], a. basto, sucio, zafio.
down (1) [daun], n. (geog.) collado.
down (2) [daun], n. (orn.) plumón, flojel, m.; vello.
down (3) [daun], n. (fam.) caída, revés, m.—v.t. (fam.) derribar; tragar.—adv. abajo.—prep. abajo (follows noun); — and out, tronado, que se ha tronado; — with.... ! iabajo.... ! to get — to, aplicarse a; llegar a; to take —, poner por escrito.
downcast ['daunka:st], a. abatido.
downfall ['daunfɔ:l], n. caída, ruina.
down-hearted [daun'ha:tid], a. desalentado.
downhill [daun'hil], adv. cuesta abajo.
downpour ['daunpɔ:], n. aguacero, chaparrón, m.
downright ['daunrait], a. categórico, total, absoluto; de siete suelas (pícaro).—adv. del todo, totalmente.
downstairs ['daunstɛəz], a. de abajo.—n. planta baja.—[daun'stɛəz], adv. abajo.
downstream [daun'stri:m], adv. río abajo.
downtown ['dauntaun], a. (U.S.) céntrico.—[daun'taun], adv. al o en el centro (de la ciudad.)
downtrodden ['dauntrɔdn], a. oprimido, tiranizado.
downward ['daunwəd], a. descendente.—adv. (also -rds [-dz]) hacia abajo; en adelante.

dowry ['dauri], n. dote, m. o f.
doze [douz], n. dormidita.—v.i. dormitar.
dozen [dʌzn], n. docena.
dozy ['douzi], a. amodorrado; lelo.
drab (1) [dræb], a. parduzco, gris.
drab (2) [dræb], n. zorra, mujerzuela.
draft [dra:ft], n. (com.) libranza, giro; bosquejo, borrador, plan, m.; (mil., U.S.) quinta.—v.t. bosquejar; redactar; (mil.) destacar, (U.S.) quintar; (U.S.) [DRAUGHT].
draftee [dra:f'ti:], n. (U.S.) quinto.
drag [dræg], n. narria (carretilla); resistencia; impedimento, traba; rastra.—v.t. arrastrar; rastrear.—v.i. arrastrarse; to — out, hacer(se) muy largo.
drag-net ['drægnet], n. red barredera.
dragon ['drægən], n. dragón, m.
dragon-fly ['drægənflai], n. libélula.
dragoon [drə'gu:n], n. (mil.) dragón, m.—v.t. regimentar.
drain [drein], n. desaguadero; desagüe, m.—v.t. desaguar; desangrar; vaciar.
drake [dreik], n. pato.
dram [dræm], n. dracma; (Scot.) copita, traguito.
drama ['dra:mə], n. drama, m.
dramatic [drə'mætik], a. dramático.
dramatist ['dræmətist], n. dramaturgo.
drank [dræŋk], [DRINK].
drape [dreip], n. colgadura.—v.t. entapizar; colgar; vestir.
draper ['dreipə], n. pañero, lencero.
drapery ['dreipəri], n. paños, m.pl., ropaje, m.; (Brit.) lencería.
drastic ['dræstik], a. drástico, violento.
draught [dra:ft], n. corriente (f.) de aire, trago, pócima; tiro; — beer, cerveza del barril. — pl. juego de damas. [DRAFT].
draughtsman ['dra:ftsmən], n. dibujante, m.
draughty ['dra:fti], a. airoso, lleno de corrientes.
draw [drɔ:], n. (sport) empate, m.; tiro; sorteo; (fam.) exitazo.—v.t. irr. dibujar; tirar (arrastrar); correr, descorrer (cortina); atraer; desenvainar (espada); cobrar (dinero); sacar; to — forth, hacer salir, ocasionar; to — up, redactar; acercar; pararse.—v.i. irr. empatar.
drawback ['drɔ:bæk], n. inconveniente, m., pega.
drawbridge ['drɔ:bridʒ], n. puente levadizo.
drawer [drɔ:], n. cajón, m., gaveta.—pl. (vestido) bragas.
drawing-pin ['drɔ:iŋpin], n. chinche, m.
drawing-room ['drɔ:iŋrum], n. salón, m., sala.
drawl [drɔ:l], n. habla lenta.—v.t., v.i. hablar muy despacio.
drawn [drɔ:n], [DRAW].
dray-horse ['dreihɔ:s], n. caballo de tiro.
dread [dred], a. pavoroso.—n. pavor, m.—v.t. temer.
dreadful ['dredful], a. espantoso; (fam.) malo.
dreadnought ['drednɔ:t], n. (naut.) gran buque acorazado.
dream [dri:m], n. sueño, ensueño.—v.i. irr. soñar (of, con).
dreamy ['dri:mi], a. soñador; vago.
dreary ['driəri], a. pesado, aburrido.
dredge [dredʒ], n. draga.—v.t. dragar.
dregs [dregz], n.pl. heces, f.pl.
drench [drentʃ], v.t. empapar, calar.

dress [dres], *n.* vestido; traje, *m.*, ropa.—*v.t.* vestir; peinar (*pelo*); (*cul.*) aderezar; curtir (*cuero*); preparar, adobar; (*med.*) curar.—*v.i.* vestir(se); **to — down,** (*fam.*) calentar las orejas a; **to — up,** vestirse de gala.
dresser ['dresə], *n.* aparador, *m.*; (*U.S.*) cómoda.
dressing ['dresiŋ], *n.* (*cul.*) aliño, salsa; (*med.*) vendaje, *m.*
dressing-gown ['dresiŋgaun], *n.* bata, peinador, *m.*
dressing-table ['dresiŋteibl], *n.* coqueta.
dressmaker ['dresmeikə], *n.* costurera, modista, *f.*
dressy ['dresi], *a.* (*fam.*) vistoso, acicalado.
drew [dru:] [DRAW].
dribble [dribl], *n.* gotita, goteo.—*v.t.* (*sport*) driblar.—*v.i.* gotear, babear.
dried [draid], *a.* paso (*fruta*). [DRY].
drift [drift], *n.* corriente, *f.*; tendencia; sentido, tenor, *m*; deriva; ventisquero.—*v.t.* amontonar; llevar.—*v.i.* ir a la deriva, derivar; flotar; dejarse llevar; amontonarse.
drill [dril], *n.* taladro; (*mil.*) instrucción, *f.*; (*agr.*) surquito para sembrar; rutina; ejercicio.—*v.t.* disciplinar, entrenar; taladrar, barrenar.—*v.i.* hacer ejercicios.
drink [driŋk], *n.* bebida.—*v.t., v.i. irr.* beber; **to — in o up,** beberse.
drinking ['driŋkiŋ], *a.* potable (*agua*); para beber.—*n.* beber, *m.*; — **trough,** abrevadero.
drip [drip], *n.* gotera.—*v.t.* verter gota a gota. —*v.i.* gotear.
dripping ['dripiŋ], *n.* pringue, *m.* o *f.*; grasa.
drive [draiv], *n.* calzada, avenida; paseo; energía; conducción; impulsión, *f.*—*v.t. irr.* conducir (*coche*); empujar, forzar; clavar; mover; arrojar; **to — at,** querer decir; **to — away o off,** ahuyentar; irse (en coche); **to — back,** rechazar; **to — mad,** volver loco.—*v.i. irr.* ir en coche.
drivel [drivl], *n.* baba; cháchara.—*v.i.* babear.
driven [drivn] [DRIVE].
driver ['draivə], *n.* conductor, *m.*
drizzle [drizl], *n.* llovizna.—*v.i.* lloviznar.
droll [droul], *a.* chancero, chusco.
dromedary ['drʌmədəri], *n.* dromedario.
drone (1) [droun], *n.* (*ent., fig.*) zángano.— *v.i.* zumbar.
drone (2) [droun], *n.* zumbido (*ruido*).
drool [dru:l], *n.* baba.—*v.i.* babear.
droop [dru:p], *n.* caída, inclinación, *f.*—*v.t.* inclinar, bajar.—*v.i.* ir cayéndose; marchitarse; decaer.
drop [drɔp], *n.* caída; baja; pendiente, *f.*; gota.—*v.t.* dejar caer; abandonar; bajar; omitir; soltar.—*v.i.* caer(se); dejarse caer; cesar; **to — a line,** (*fam.*) poner una carta; **to — in,** visitar de paso; **to — off,** decaer; dormirse; **to — out,** desaparecer; darse de baja; retirarse.
dropsy ['drɔpsi], *n.* hidropesía.
dross [drɔs], *n.* escoria.
drought [draut], *n.* sequía.
drove [drouv], *n.* manada. [DRIVE].
drown [draun], *v.t.* ahogar, anegar.—*v.i.* -se.
drowse [drauz], *v.i.* adormilarse.
drowsy ['drauzi], *a.* adormecido, amodorrado.
drub [drʌb], *v.t.* tundir, derrotar.
drudge [drʌdʒ], *n.* yunque, *m.*, burro de carga.—*v.i.* afanarse.

drudgery ['drʌdʒəri], *n.* afán, *m.*, trabajo penoso.
drug [drʌg], *n.* droga; narcótico; artículo invendible; — **addict,** morfinómano; — **store,** (*U.S.*) farmacia.—*v.t.* narcotizar.
druggist ['drʌgist], *n.* (*U.S.*) farmacéutico; droguista, *m.*
drum [drʌm], *n.* tambor, *m.*; (*anat.*) tímpano; bidón, *m.*—*v.i.* tocar el tambor; teclear, tabalear.
drummer ['drʌmə], *n.* tambor; (*U.S.*) viajante, *m.*
drumstick ['drʌmstik], *n.* baqueta, palillo; (*orn.*) muslo.
drunk [drʌŋk], *a.* borracho; **to get —,** emborracharse. [DRINK].
drunkard ['drʌŋkəd], *n.* beodo, borrachín, *m.*
drunken ['drʌŋkən], *a.* embriagado, ebrio.
drunkenness ['drʌŋkənnis], *n.* embriaguez, *f.*, borrachera.
dry [drai], *a.* seco; árido; — **goods,** (*U.S.*) lencería.—*v.t.* secar.—*v.i.* secarse; **to — up,** (*fam.*) callarse.
dry-clean [drai'kli:n], *v.t.* limpiar en seco.
dry-cleaner [drai'kli:nə], *n.* tintorero.
dry-dock [drai'dɔk], *n.* dique seco.
dryness ['drainis], *n.* sequedad, *f.*
dry-rot [drai'rɔt], *n.* pudrición seca, carcoma.
dual [dju:əl], *a.* dual, binario.
dub [dʌb], *v.t.* apellidar; doblar (*película*); armar caballero.
dubious ['dju:bjəs], *a.* dudoso; equívoco.
ducat ['dʌkit], *n.* ducado.
duchess ['dʌtʃis], *n.* duquesa.
duck [dʌk], *n.* (*orn.*) pato, pata; agachada; dril, *m.*; zambullida; (*fam.*) querido.—*v.t.* evitar; agachar; chapuzar.—*v.i.* agacharse; chapuzar.
duckling ['dʌkliŋ], *n.* patito, anadeja.
duct [dʌkt], *n.* conducto, tubo.
ductile ['dʌktail], *a.* dúctil; dócil.
dud [dʌd], *n.* cosa falsa o que no funciona; —*pl.* (*U.S. colloq.*) ropa.
dude [dju:d], *n.* (*U.S.*) caballerete, *m.*
dudgeon ['dʌdʒən], *n.* ojeriza, indignación, *f.*
due [dju:], *a.* debido; esperado; pagadero; derecho, directo.—*n.* merecido; derecho.— *pl.* abono, cuota, subscripción, *f.*; impuestos, *m.pl.*—*adv.* directamente; — **to,** debido a.
duel [dju:əl], *n.* duelo.—*v.i.* batirse en duelo.
duellist ['dju:əlist], *n.* duelista, *m.*
duet [dju:'et], *n.* dúo.
duffel [dʌfl], *n.* moletón, *m.*
duffer ['dʌfə], *n.* zamacuco, zote, *m.*
dug [dʌg], [DIG].
dug-out ['dʌgaut], *n.* trinchera, cueva; canoa.
duke [dju:k], *n.* duque, *m.*
dull [dʌl], *a.* obscuro; apagado; romo, embotado; pesado, aburrido; torpe; soso.—*v.t.* embotar; deslucir; empañar; obscurecer.
dullness ['dʌlnis], *n.* pesadez, *f.*; deslustre, *m.*; obscuridad, *f.*
duly ['dju:li], *adv.* debidamente.
dumb [dʌm], *a.* mudo; (*fam.*) estúpido.
dumbfound [dʌm'faund], *v.t.* pasmar, dejar sin habla.
dumbness ['dʌmnis], *n.* mudez; (*fam.*) estupidez, *f.*
dummy ['dʌmi], *a.* falso, postizo.—*n.* maniquí, *m.*; imitación, *f.*, contrafigura; chupete (*de niño*), *m.*

dump

dump [dʌmp], *n.* basurero (*para basura echada*); (*mil.*) depósito.—*v.t.* descargar, echar; inundar el mercado con (artículos invendibles); *to be down in the dumps,* (*fam.*) tener murria.
dumpling ['dʌmpliŋ], *n.* (*cul.*) bola de pasta cocida en un guisado.
dumpy ['dʌmpi], *a.* rechoncho, rollizo.
dun (1) [dʌn], *a., n.* bruno, pardo.
dun (2) [dʌn], *v.t.* importunar (*deudores*).
dunce [dʌns], *n.* zopenco.
dunderhead ['dʌndəhed], *n.* (*fam.*) tarugo, bolonio.
dune [dju:n], *n.* duna.
dung [dʌŋ], *n.* estiércol, *m.*; excremento.
dungeon ['dʌndʒən], *n.* mazmorra, calabozo.
duodecimo [dju:ou'desimou], *a.* en dozavo.
dupe [dju:p], *n.* primo, papanatas, *m.sg.*—*v.t.* engatusar, embaucar.
duplicate ['dju:plikit], *a., n.* duplicado; *in* —, por duplicado.—['dju:plikeit], *v.t.* duplicar.
duplicator ['dju:plikeitə], *n.* multicopista, *m.*
duplicity [dju:'plisiti], *n.* doblez, duplicidad, *f.*
durability [djuərə'biliti], *n.* durabilidad, *f.*
durable ['djuərəbl], *a.* duradero, durable.
duration [djuə'reifən], *n.* duración, *f.*
duress [djuə'res], *n.* coacción; prisión, *f.*
during ['djuəriŋ], *prep.* durante.
dusk [dʌsk], *n.* anochecer, *m.*, crepúsculo.
dusky ['dʌski], *a.* obscuro; moreno; negruzco.
dust [dʌst], *n.* polvo; cenizas (*restos mortales*), *f.pl.*; (*fam.*) alboroto.—*v.t.* quitar el polvo a, despolvorear; polvorear (*derramar*).
dustbin ['dʌstbin], *n.* receptáculo para basura, cubo de basura.
duster ['dʌstə], *n.* plumero, paño, trapo.
dust-jacket ['dʌstdʒækit], *n.* (sobre)cubierta (*de un libro*).
dustman ['dʌstmən], *n.* basurero.
dusty ['dʌsti], *a.* polvoriento; grisáceo.
Dutch [dʌtʃ], *a., n.* holandés; *double* —, algarabia, griego; *go* —, (*fam.*) pagar cada uno su escote.
Dutchman ['dʌtʃmən], *n.* holandés, *m.*
duteous ['dju:tiəs], *a.* rendido, obediente.
dutiful ['dju:tiful], *a.* concienzudo; rendido, obediente.
duty ['dju:ti], *n.* deber, *m.*; tarea; derechos (*m.pl.*) de aduana; *on* —, de guardia.
dwarf [dwɔ:f], *a., n.* enano.—*v.t.* achicar; impedir el crecimiento de.
dwell [dwel], *v.i. irr.* morar; *to* — *on,* hacer hincapié en.
dwelling ['dweliŋ], *n.* morada, vivienda.
dwindle [dwindl], *v.i.* disminuirse, menguar.
dye [dai], *n.* tinte, *m.*, color.—*v.t.* teñir; *dyed-in-the-wool,* *a.* (*fig.*) intransigente.
dying ['daiiŋ], *a.* moribundo.
dyke [DIKE].
dynamic [dai'næmik], *a.* dinámico.—*n.pl.* dinamica.
dynamo ['dainəmou], *n.* dínamo, *f.* (*S.A. m.*).
dynasty ['dinəsti], *n.* dinastía.
dysentery ['disəntri], *n.* disentería.

E

E, e [i:], *n.* quinta letra del alfabeto inglés; **E,** (*mus.*) mi.

270

each [i:tʃ], *a.* cada.—*pron.* cada uno, cada cual; — *other,* el uno al otro.—*adv.* cada uno; por persona.
eager ['i:gə], *a.* ansioso, deseoso; fogoso.
eagerness ['i:gənis], *n.* ansia; anhelo, ahinco.
eagle [i:gl], *n.* águila.
ear [iə], *n.* (*anat.*) oreja; oído; (*bot.*) espiga.
ear-drum ['iədrʌm], *n.* tímpano.
earl [ə:l], *n.* conde, *m.*
early ['ə:li], *a.* temprano; primitivo; próximo.—*adv.* temprano; al principio (*in,* de); anticipadamente; — *riser,* madrugador, *m.*; *to rise* —, madrugar.
earmark ['iəmɑ:k], *n.* marca, señal, *f.*—*v.t.* marcar; destinar.
earn [ə:n], *v.t.* ganar; ganarse; merecer.
earnest ['ə:nist], *a.* serio; celoso; atento; *in* —, en serio.
earnings ['ə:niŋz], *n.pl.* ingresos, *m.pl.*, ganancias, *f.pl.*; sueldo; jornal, *m.*
earring ['iəriŋ], *n.* pendiente, arete, *m.*
earshot ['iəʃɔt], *n.* *within* —, al alcance del oído.
earth [ə:θ], *n.* tierra; *down to* —, práctico.
earthenware ['ə:θənwɛə], *n.* loza de barro.
earthly ['ə:θli], *a.* mundano, terrenal.
earthquake ['ə:θkweik], *n.* terremoto.
earthworm ['ə:θwə:m], *n.* lombriz, *f.*
earthy ['ə:θi], *a.* terroso; basto, grosero; mundano.
earwig ['iəwig], *n.* (*ent.*) tijereta.
ease [i:z], *n.* tranquilidad; holgura; facilidad, *f.*; *at* —, cómodo, a sus anchas; *to take one's* —, ponerse a sus anchas.—*v.t.* templar, suavizar, aliviar; mover lentamente.
easel ['i:zəl], *n.* caballete, *m.*
easily ['i:zili], *adv.* fácilmente; con mucho.
east [i:st], *a.* oriental, del este.—*n.* este, oriente, Levante (*de España*), *m.*—*adv.* al este.
Easter ['i:stə], *n.* Pascua florida *o* de Resurrección.
easterly ['i:stəli], *a.* oriental.
eastern ['i:stən], *a.* oriental.
easy ['i:zi], *a.* fácil; holgado; *easy-going,* de manga ancha; — *chair,* poltrona, butaca, sillón, *m.*; *to take it* —, ir despacio; descansar.
eat [i:t], *v.t., v.i. irr.* comer; *to* — *up,* comerse; devorar.
eatable ['i:təbl], *a.* comestible.
eaten [i:tn], [EAT].
eau de Cologne ['oudəkə'loun], *n.* (agua de) Colonia.
eaves [i:vz], *n.pl.* alero, tejaroz, *m.*
eavesdrop ['i:vzdrɔp], *v.i.* espiar, escuchar, fisgonear.
ebb [eb], *n.* reflujo, menguante.—*v.i.* bajar.
ebony ['ebəni], *a.* de ébano.—*n.* ébano.
eccentric [ek'sentrik], *a., n.* excéntrico.
eccentricity [eksen'trisiti], *n.* excentricidad, *f.*
ecclesiastic [ikli:zi'æstik], *n.* eclesiástico.— (*also* **ecclesiastical**) *a.* eclesiástico.
echo ['ekou], *n.* eco.—*v.t.* repetir.—*v.i.* resonar.
éclat [ei'klɑ:], *n.* esplendor; renombre, *m.*
eclectic [e'klektik], *a.* ecléctico.
eclipse [i'klips], *n.* eclipse, *m.*—*v.t.* eclipsar.
eclogue ['eklɔg], *n.* égloga.
economic(al) [i:kə'nɔmik(əl)], *a.* económico.

economics [i:kə'nɔmiks], *n.* economía política; ciencias económicas.
economist [i:'kɔnəmist], *n.* economista, *m.f.*
economize [i:'kɔnəmaiz], *v.t., v.i.* economizar.
economy [i:'kɔnəmi], *n.* economía; frugalidad, *f.*
ecstasy ['ekstəsi], *n.* éxtasis, *f.*, delirio, rapto.
ecstatic [ek'stætik], *a.* extático.
Ecuador ['ekwədɔ:], *n.* el Ecuador.
Ecuadorian [ekwə'dɔ:riən], *a.*, *n.* ecuatoriano.
eczema ['ekzimə], *n.* eczema.
eddy ['edi], *n.* remolino.—*v.t., v.i.* remolinar.
edge [edʒ], *n.* margen, *m.* o *f.*, orilla; borde (*de carretera*), *m.*; filo (*cortante*); canto; lado; ribete, *m.*; **on** —, (*fig.*) nervioso, de mal humor.—*v.t.* orlar, ribetear (*recortar*); afilar, aguzar; mover un poco.—*v.i.* meterse de lado.
edgeways ['edʒweiz], *adv.* de lado, de canto.
edging ['edʒiŋ], *n.* ribete, orla.
edible ['edibl], *a.* comestible.
edict ['i:dikt], *n.* edicto, decreto.
edifice ['edifis], *n.* edificio; fábrica.
edify ['edifai], *v.t.* edificar (*moralmente*).
Edinburgh ['edinbərə], *n.* Edimburgo.
edit ['edit], *v.t.* redactar; dirigir.
edition [i'diʃən], *n.* edición, *f.*; tirada (*número de copias*).
editor ['editə], *n.* director (*de periódico*); redactor, *m.*
editorial [edi'tɔ:riəl], *a.* editorial.—*n.* artículo de fondo.
educate ['edjukeit], *v.t.* educar.
education [edju'keiʃən], *n.* instrucción; educación, *f.*; enseñanza; pedagogía.
educational [edju'keiʃənəl], *a.* educacional; instructivo.
eel [i:l], *n.* anguila.
e'en [i:n], *adv.* (*poet.*) [EVEN].
e'er [εə], *adv.* (*poet.*) [EVER].
eerie, eery ['iəri], *a.* espectral, miedoso.
effect [i'fekt], *n.* efecto; impresión, *f.*; **in** —, efectivamente; vigente; **to the** — **that**, en el sentido de que; **to put into** —, poner en vigor.—*v.t.* efectuar.
effective [i'fektiv], *a.* eficaz; operativo.
effectual [i'fektjuəl], *a.* eficaz.
effeminate [i'feminit], *a.* afeminado.
effervescent [efə'vesənt], *a.* efervescente.
effete [i'fi:t], *a.* gastado, estéril, decadente.
efficacious [efi'keiʃəs], *a.* eficaz.
efficacy ['efikəsi], *n.* eficacia.
efficiency [i'fiʃənsi], *n.* eficacia, eficiencia.
efficient [i'fiʃənt], *a.* eficaz, eficiente.
effigy ['efidʒi], *n.* efigie, *f.*
effort ['efət], *n.* esfuerzo.
effrontery [i'frʌntəri], *n.* descaro, desfachatez, *f.*
effusive [i'fju:siv], *a.* efusivo, derramado.
egg (1) [eg], *n.* huevo; — **custard**, flan, *m.*; — **white**, claro (de huevo).
egg (2) [eg], *v.t.* **to** — **on**, hurgar, incitar.
eggshell ['egʃel], *n.* cascarón, *m.*
ego ['i:gou], *n.* yo; ego.
egoist ['egouist], *n.* egoísta, *m.f.*
egress ['i:gres], *n.* salida.
Egypt ['i:dʒipt], *n.* Egipto.
Egyptian [i'dʒipʃən], *a.*, *n.* egipcio.
eiderdown ['aidədaun], *n.* edredón, *m.*
eight [eit], *a.*, *n.* ocho.

eighteen [ei'ti:n], *a.*, *n.* dieciocho, diez y ocho.
eighteenth [ei'ti:nθ], *a.*, *n.* décimoctavo, dieciochavo; dieciocho (*en las fechas*).
eighth [eitθ], *a.* octavo.—*n.* octavo; ocho (*en las fechas*).
eightieth ['eitjəθ], *a.*, *n.* octogésimo, ochentavo.
eighty ['eiti], *a.*, *n.* ochenta, *m.*
either ['aiðə, 'i:ðə], *a.* cualquier(a), uno u otro (*de los dos*).—*adv.* tampoco.—*conj.* o; — **...or**, o **...** o.
ejaculate [i'dʒækjuleit], *v.t.* exclamar; (*anat.*) eyacular.
eject [i'dʒekt], *v.t.* expulsar, arrojar.
ejection [i'dʒekʃən], *n.* expulsión, *f.*
eke [i:k], *v.t.* **to** — **out**, economizar, escatimar.
elaborate [i'læbərit], *a.* detallado, complicado.—[i'læboreit], *v.t.* elaborar; ampliar.
elapse [i'læps], *v.i.* transcurrir, pasar.
elastic [i'læstik], *a.*, *n.* elástico.
elasticity [ilæs'tisiti], *n.* elasticidad, *f.*
elate [i'leit], *v.t.* exaltar.
elation [i'leiʃən], *n.* exaltación, *f.*
elbow ['elbou], *n.* (*anat.*) codo; recodo (*curva*); **at one's** —, a la mano.—*v.t.* dar codazos.
elbow-room ['elbouru:m], *n.* anchura, espacio, libertad, *f.*
elder (1) ['eldə], *a.*, *n.* mayor, *m.f.*
elder (2) ['eldə], *n.* (*bot.*) saúco.
elderly ['eldəli], *a.* anciano, mayor.
eldest ['eldist], *a.* el mayor, el más viejo.
elect [i'lekt], *a.* electo, elegido.—*v.t.* elegir.
election [i'lekʃən], *n.* elección, *f.*
electioneer [ilekʃə'niə], *v.i.* hacer propaganda electoral.
electioneering [ilekʃə'niəriŋ], *n.* campaña electoral.
elector [i'lektə], *n.* elector, *m.*; votante, *m.f.*
electoral [i'lektərəl], *a.* electoral.
electric(al) [i'lektrik(əl)], *a.* eléctrico.
electrician [ilek'triʃən], *n.* electricista, *m.*
electricity [ilek'trisiti], *n.* electricidad, *f.*
electrify [i'lektrifai], *v.t.* electrificar; (*fig.*) electrizar.
electrocute [i'lektrəkju:t], *v.t.* electrocutar.
electrocution [ilektrə'kju:ʃən], *n.* electrocución, *f.*
electrode [i'lektroud], *n.* electrodo.
electron [i'lektron], *n.* electrón, *m.*
electronic [ilek'tronik], *a.* electrónico.—*n.pl.* electrónica.
elegance ['eligəns], *n.* elegancia.
elegant ['eligənt], *a.* elegante.
elegy ['elidʒi], *n.* elegía.
element ['elimənt], *n.* elemento.
elementary [eli'mentəri], *a.* elemental.
elephant ['elifənt], *n.* elefante, *m.*
elevate ['eliveit], *v.t.* elevar.
elevation [eli'veiʃən], *n.* elevación, *f.*
elevator ['eliveitə], *n.* (*U.S.*) ascensor, *m.*
eleven [i'levən], *a.*, *n.* once, *m.*
eleventh [i'levənθ], *a.*, *n.* undécimo, onceno; once (*en las fechas*); **at the** — **hour**, a última hora.
elf [elf], *n.* (*pl.* **elves**) duende, *m.*, elfo.
elfin ['elfin], **elfish** ['elfiʃ], *a.* élfino, travieso.
elicit [i'lisit], *v.t.* (son)sacar.
elide [i'laid], *v.t.* elidir.
eligible ['elidʒibl], *a.* eligible; admisible; deseable.

eligibility

eligibility [elidʒi'biliti], *n.* elegibilidad, *f.*; competencia.
eliminate [e'limineit], *v.t.* eliminar.
elision [i'liʒən], *n.* elisión, *f.*
élite [ei'li:t], *n.* la flor y (la) nata.
elixir [i'liksə], *n.* elixir, *m.*
Elizabeth [i'lizəbəθ], *n.* Isabel, *f.*
elliptical [i'liptikəl], *a.* elíptico.
elm [elm], *n.* (*bot.*) olmo.
elocution [elo'kju:ʃən], *n.* elocución, *f.*
elongate [i'lɒŋgeit], *v.t.* alargar, prolongar, extender.—*v.i.* -se.
elope [i'loup], *v.i.* fugarse con el amante.
elopement [i'loupmənt], *n.* fuga.
eloquence ['eləkwəns], *n.* elocuencia.
eloquent ['eləkwənt], *a.* elocuente.
else [els], *a.* más.—*adv.* de otro modo, de otra manera.
elsewhere ['els'wɛə], *adv.* a o en otra parte.
elude [i'lu:d], *v.t.* eludir.
elusive [i'lu:siv], *a.* evasivo.
elves [elvz], *pl.* [ELF].
emaciate [i'meisieit], *v.t.* enflaquecer, extenuar.
emanate ['eməneit], *v.i.* emanar.
emancipate [i'mænsipeit], *v.t.* emancipar.
emancipation [imænsi'peiʃən], *n.* emancipación, *f.*
embalm [em'ba:m], *v.t.* embalsamar.
embankment [em'bæŋkmənt], *n.* terraplén, dique, *m.*
embargo [im'ba:gou], *n.* embargo.—*v.t.* embargar.
embark [em'ba:k], *v.t.* embarcar.—*v.i.* -se.
embarrass [em'bærəs], *v.t.* sofocar, avergonzar; comprometer.
embarrassing [em'bærəsiŋ], *a.* vergonzoso, desconcertante.
embarrassment [em'bærəsmənt], *n.* sofoco; enredo; desconcierto; embarazo.
embassy ['embəsi], *n.* embajada.
embed [im'bed], *v.t.* encajar, empotrar; clavar.
embellish [im'beliʃ], *v.t.* hermosear; adornar.
ember ['embə], *n.* ascua, ceniza.—*pl.* rescoldo.
embezzle [im'bezl], *v.t.* malversar.
embezzlement [im'bezlmənt], *n.* desfalco, malversación, *f.*
embitter [im'bitə], *v.t.* amargar, agriar.
emblem ['embləm], *n.* emblema, *m.*, divisa.
emblematic [emblə'mætik], *a.* emblemático.
embodiment [im'bodimənt], *n.* personificación, encarnación, *f.*
embody [im'bodi], *v.t.* incorporar; personificar.
embolden [im'bouldən], *v.t.* envalentonar.
emboss [im'bos], *v.t.* labrar en relieve.
embrace [im'breis], *n.* abrazo.—*v.t.* abrazar. —*v.i.* -se.
embroider [im'broidə], *v.t.* bordar.
embroil [im'broil], *v.t.* enredar, embrollar.
embryo ['embriou], *n.* embrión, *m.*
embryonic [embri'ɒnik], *a.* embrionario.
emend [i'mend], *v.t.* enmendar.
emendation [imən'deiʃən], *n.* enmienda.
emerald ['emərəld], *n.* esmeralda.
emerge [i'mə:dʒ], *v.i.* emerger; salir.
emergency [i'mə:dʒənsi], *n.* accidente, *m.*; urgencia, crisis, *f.*; emergencia.
emery ['eməri], *n.* esmeril, *m.*; — **paper**, papel (*m.*) de esmeril.

emetic [i'metik], *a.*, *n.* emético.
emigrant ['emigrənt], *a.*, *n.* emigrante, *m.f.*
emigrate ['emigreit], *v.i.* emigrar.
emigration [emi'greiʃən], *n.* emigración, *f.*
emigré ['emigrei], *n.* emigrado.
eminence ['eminəns], *n.* eminencia.
eminent ['eminənt], *a.* eminente.
emir [e'miə], *n.* emir, *m.*
emirate ['emireit], *n.* emirato.
emissary ['emisəri], *n.* emisario.
emit [i'mit], *v.t.* emitir, exhalar.
emmet ['emit], *n.* hormiga.
emolument [i'moljumənt], *n.* emolumento.
emotion [i'mouʃən], *n.* emoción, *f.*
emotional [i'mouʃənəl], *a.* emocional.
emperor ['empərə], *n.* emperador, *m.*
emphasis ['emfəsis], *n.* énfasis, *f.*
emphasize ['emfəsaiz], *v.t.* dar énfasis a, destacar, poner de relieve, acentuar.
emphatic [im'fætik], *a.* enfático.
empire ['empaiə], *n.* imperio.
empirical [im'pirikəl], *a.* empírico.
employ [im'ploi], *n.* empleo.—*v.t.* emplear.
employee [emploi'i:], *n.* empleado.
employer [im'ploiə], *n.* patrón, jefe, *m.*
employment [im'ploimənt], *n.* empleo.
emporium [em'pɔ:riəm], *n.* emporio; bazar, *m.*
empower [im'pauə], *v.t.* facultar, autorizar.
empress ['empris], *n.* emperatriz, *f.*
empty ['empti], *a.* vacío; vano.—*v.t.* vaciar. —*v.i.* -se.
empty-handed ['empti'hændid], *a.*manivacío.
empty-headed ['empti'hedid], *a.* casquivano.
emulate ['emjuleit], *v.t.*, *v.i.* emular.
emulation [emju'leiʃən], *n.* emulación, *f.*
emulsion [i'mʌlʃən], *n.* emulsión, *f.*
enable [i'neibl], *v.t.* permitir, facilitar.
enact [i'nækt], *v.t.* promulgar (*ley*); hacer el papel de; realizar.
enactment [i'næktmənt], *n.* promulgación; representación, *f.*
enamel [i'næməl], *n.* esmalte, *m.*—*v.t.* esmaltar.
enamour [i'næmə], *v.t.* enamorar.
encamp [in'kæmp], *v.t.*, *v.i.* acampar.
enchant [in'tʃa:nt], *v.t.* encantar, hechizar.
enchanting [in'tʃa:ntiŋ], *a.* encantador.
enchantment [in'tʃa:ntmənt], *n.* encant(a-miento)o, ensalmo.
encircle [in'sə:kl], *v.t.* cercar, encerrar, rodear.
enclose [in'klouz], *v.t.* incluir; encerrar; adjuntar.
enclosed [in'klouzd], *a.*, *n.* adjunto (*en una carta*).
encompass [in'kʌmpəs], *v.t.* abarcar; cercar.
encore ['ɔŋkɔ:], *n.* propina; bis, *m.*—*v.t.* pedir una repetición de; repetir.—*interj.* ¡bis!
encounter [in'kauntə], *n.* encuentro.—*v.t.* encontrar(se con), dar con.—*v.i.* encontrarse.
encourage [en'kʌridʒ], *v.t.* animar; fomentar.
encouragement [en'kʌridʒmənt], *n.* ánimo, estímulo; fomento.
encroach [in'kroutʃ], *v.i.* pasar los límites (*on*, de).
encumber [in'kʌmbə], *v.t.* impedir, embarazar.
encumbrance [in'kʌmbrəns], *n.* estorbo, impedimento, embarazo.

encyclopedia [ensaiklou'pi:djə], *n.* enciclopedia.
end [end], *n.* fin, cabo, final, *m.*; fin, *m.*, mira, objeto; cabo suelto, pieza; colilla (*de pitillo*); *in the* —, al fin y al cabo; *on* —, de canto; *to make both ends meet*, pasar con lo que uno tiene.—*v.t., v.i.* terminar, acabar; *to* — *up*, acabar.
endanger [in'deindʒə], *v.t.* poner en peligro, arriesgar.
endear [en'diə], *v.t.* hacer querer.
endearment [en'diəmənt], *n.* palabra cariñosa; caricia.
endeavour [in'devə], *n.* conato, esfuerzo, empeño.—*v.i.* esforzarse (*to*, por).
ending ['endiŋ], *n.* fin, *m.* o *f.*, terminación, *f.*; (*gram.*) desinencia; desenlace, *m.*
endive ['endiv], *n.* endibia.
endless ['endlis], *a.* sin fin, interminable.
endorse [in'dɔːs], *v.t.* endosar; aprobar.
endow [in'dau], *v.t.* dotar (*with*, de).
endowment [in'daumənt], *n.* dotación; prenda, dote, *f.*
endue [in'dju:], *v.t.* dotar; vestir.
endurance [in'djuərəns], *n.* tolerancia; resistencia; sufrimiento; duración, *f.*
endure [in'djuə], *v.t.* aguantar; sufrir, tolerar.—*v.i.* durar, perdurar.
enemy ['enəmi], *a., n.* enemigo.
energetic [enə'dʒetik], *a.* enérgico.
energy ['enədʒi], *n.* energía.
enervate ['enəveit], *v.t.* enervar.
enfeeble [en'fi:bl], *v.t.* debilitar.
enfilade [enfi'leid], *n.* enfilada.—*v.t.* enfilar.
enfold [en'fould], *v.t.* envolver.
enforce [en'fɔːs], *v.t.* imponer, poner en vigor.
enfranchise [en'fræntʃaiz], *v.t.* franquear; dar el voto a.
engage [en'geidʒ], *v.t.* ocupar; emplear; alquilar; (*mech.*) engranar con; trabar batalla con.—*v.i.* ocuparse (*in*, en).
engaged [en'geidʒd], *a.* prometido (*novios*); ocupado.
engagement [en'geidʒmənt], *n.* noviazgo; (*mil.*) combate, *m.*; compromiso, cita.
engaging [en'geidʒiŋ], *a.* insinuante, encantador.
engender [en'dʒendə], *v.t.* engendrar.
engine ['endʒin], *n.* máquina; motor, *m.*; (*rail.*) locomotora; *two-stroke* —, motor (*m.*) de dos tiempos.
engine-driver ['endʒindraivə], *n.* maquinista, *m.*
engineer [endʒi'niə], *n.* ingeniero; (*U.S. rail.*) maquinista, *m.*—*v.t.* dirigir; maquinar.
engineering [endʒi'niəriŋ], *n.* ingeniería.
enginery ['endʒinri], *n.* maquinaria.
England ['iŋglənd], *n.* Inglaterra.
English ['iŋgliʃ], *a., n.* inglés; *the English,* los ingleses.
Englishman ['iŋgliʃmən], *n.* inglés, *m.*
Englishwoman ['iŋgliʃwumən], *n.* inglesa.
engrain [en'grein], *v.t.* teñir.
engrave [en'greiv], *v.t.* grabar.
engraving [en'greiviŋ], *n.* grabado.
engross [en'grous], *v.t.* absorber.
engulf [en'gʌlf], *v.t.* abismar; inundar.
enhance [en'hɑːns], *v.t.* realzar; encarecer.
enigma [e'nigmə], *n.* enigma, *m.*
enigmatic(al) [enig'mætik(əl)], *a.* enigmático.

enjoin [en'dʒɔin], *v.t.* mandar, encargar.
enjoy [en'dʒɔi], *v.t.* gozar; gozar de.—*v.r.* divertirse.
enjoyable [en'dʒɔiəbl], *a.* agradable.
enjoyment [en'dʒɔimənt], *n.* goce, *m.*; gusto, placer.
enlarge [en'lɑːdʒ], *v.t.* agrandar; ensanchar; ampliar, (*also phot.*)—*v.i.* ampliarse, agrandarse, ensancharse; *to enlarge on,* tratar más detalladamente.
enlargement [en'lɑːdʒmənt], *n.* ampliación, *f.*; ensanchamiento.
enlighten [en'laitn], *v.t.* ilustrar, iluminar.
enlightenment [en'laitnmənt], *n.* ilustración, *f.*
enlist [en'list], *v.t.* conseguir, granjear; (*mil.*) alistar; *enlisted soldier,* soldado raso.—*v.i.* alistarse.
enliven [en'laivn], *v.t.* avivar, animar.
enmity ['enmiti], *n.* enemistad, *f.*
ennoble [in'noubl], *v.t.* ennoblecer.
ennui [ā:'nwi], *n.* tedio, aburrimiento.
enormity [i'nɔːmiti], *n.* enormidad, *f.*
enormous [i'nɔːməs], *a.* enorme.
enough [i'nʌf], *a., adv.* bastante; *to be* —, bastar.—*interj.* ¡basta!
enrage [en'reidʒ], *v.t.* enfurecer, encolerizar.
enrapture [en'ræptʃə], *v.t.* arrebatar, embelesar.
enrich [en'ritʃ], *v.t.* enriquecer.
enrol [en'roul], *v.t.* inscribir, alistar.—*v.i.* -se.
enrolment [en'roulmənt], *n.* inscripción, *f.*
ensconce [en'skɔns], *v.t.* acomodar, resguardar.
enshrine [en'ʃrain], *v.t.* guardar como reliquia.
enshroud [en'ʃraud], *v.t.* amortajar; (*fig.*) entenebrar.
ensign ['enzən, 'ensain], *n.* bandera, pabellón, *m.*; (*mil.*) alférez, *m.*
enslave [en'sleiv], *v.t.* esclavizar.
ensnare [en'snɛə], *v.t.* entrampar.
ensue [en'sju:], *v.i.* seguirse, resultar.
ensuing [en'sju:iŋ], *a.* siguiente.
ensure [en'ʃuə], *v.t.* asegurar; asegurarse de, acierorarse de.
entail [en'teil], *v.t.* ocasionar, suponer; (*jur.*) vincular.
entangle [en'tæŋgl], *v.t.* enmarañar, enredar.
enter ['entə], *v.t.* entrar en; asentar; matricular; inscribir.—*v.i.* entrar; (*theat.*) salir; *to* — *into,* participar en; celebrar; *to* — *on,* emprender.
enterprise ['entəpraiz], *n.* empresa; iniciativa; arrojo.
enterprising ['entəpraiziŋ], *a.* emprendedor, enérgico.
entertain [entə'tein], *v.t.* divertir; considerar; abrigar; recibir.—*v.i.* recibir (*visitas*); divertir.
entertainer [entə'teinə], *n.* artista, *m.f.*; cómico, músico *etc.*
entertaining [entə'teiniŋ], *a.* divertido, entretenido.
entertainment [entə'teinmənt], *n.* diversión, *f.*; espectáculo; entretenimiento.
enthral [en'θrɔːl], *v.t.* captivar, esclavizar, encantar.
enthrone [en'θroun], *v.t.* entronizar.
enthronement [en'θrounmənt], *n.* entronización, *f.*

enthusiasm

enthusiasm [en'θju:ziæzm], *n.* entusiasmo.
enthusiast [en'θju:ziæst], *n.* entusiasta, *m.f.*
enthusiastic [enθju:zi'æstik], *a.* entusiástico.
entice [en'tais], *v.t.* tentar, seducir, incitar.
enticement [en'taismənt], *n.* tentación, seducción, incitación, *f.*
enticing [en'taisiŋ], *a.* tentador.
entire [en'taiə], *a.* entero.
entirety [en'taiəriti], *n.* entereza, totalidad, *f.*
entitle [en'taitl], *v.t.* intitular; dar derecho a, autorizar.
entity ['entiti], *n.* entidad, *f.*
entomb [en'tu:m], *v.t.* sepultar.
entomology [entoˈmolədʒi], *n.* entomología.
entrails ['entreilz], *n.pl.* entrañas, *f.pl.*
entrain [en'trein], *v.t.* mandar (en tren).—*v.i.* subir al tren.
entrance (1) ['entrəns], *n.* entrada.
entrance (2) [en'tra:ns], *v.t.* hechizar, transportar, fascinar.
entreat [en'tri:t], *v.t.* implorar, suplicar.
entrench [en'trentʃ], *v.t.* atrincherar; establecer con firmeza.
entrust [en'trʌst], *v.t.* confiar (*s.o. with s.th.,* algo a alguien).
entry ['entri], *n.* entrada; artículo (*en un libro*); (*theat.*) salida.
entwine [en'twain], *v.t.* entrelazar, entretejer.
enumerate [e'nju:məreit], *v.t.* enumerar.
envelop [en'veləp], *v.t.* envolver.
envelope ['enviloup], *n.* sobre (*para una carta*), *m.*; envoltura.
envious ['enviəs], *a.* envidioso.
environs [en'vaiərənz], *n.pl.* cercanías, *f.pl.,* contornos, *m.pl.*
environment [en'vaiərənmənt], *n.* medio, ambiente, *m.*
envisage [en'vizidʒ], *v.t.* imaginarse; figurarse.
envoy ['envoi], *n.* enviado.
envy ['envi], *n.* envidia.—*v.t.* envidiar.
enwrap [en'ræp], *v.t.* envolver.
enzyme ['enzaim], *n.* enzima.
epaulet ['epəlet], *n.* charretera.
ephemeral [i'femərəl], *a.* efímero.
epic ['epik], *a.* épico.—*n.* epopeya; épica.
epicure ['epikjuə], *n.* epicúreo.
epidemic [epi'demik], *a.* epidémico.—*n.* epidemia.
epigram ['epigræm], *n.* epigrama, *m.*
epilepsy ['epilepsi], *n.* epilepsia.
epileptic [epi'leptik], *a.* epiléptico.
epilogue ['epiloɡ], *n.* epílogo.
Epiphany [i'pifəni], *n.* Epifanía, día (*m.*) de los Reyes (Magos).
episcopal [i'piskəpəl], *a.* episcopal.
episode ['episoud], *n.* episodio.
epistle [i'pisl], *n.* epístola.
epithet ['epiθet], *n.* epíteto.
epitome [i'pitəmi], *n.* epítome, *m.*
epitomize [i'pitəmaiz], *v.t.* epitomar.
epoch ['i:pɔk], *n.* época.
epoch-making ['i:pɔkmeikiŋ], *a.* trascendental.
equable ['ekwəbl], *a.* uniforme; ecuánime.
equal ['i:kwəl], *a., n.* igual.—*v.t.* igualar; igualarse a; *to be — to,* (*fig.*) poder con.
equality [i:'kwɔliti], *n.* igualdad, *f.*
equate [i'kweit], *v.t.* igualar.
equation [i'kweiʃən], *n.* ecuación, *f.*
equator [i'kweitə], *n.* ecuador, *m.*

equatorial [ekwə'tɔ:riəl], *a.* ecuatorial.
equestrian [i'kwestriən], *a.* ecuestre.—*n.* jinete, *m.*
equilibrium [i:kwi'libriəm], *n.* equilibrio.
equine ['ekwain], *a.* equino, caballar.
equinox ['i:kwinɔks], *n.* equinoccio.
equip [i'kwip], *v.t.* equipar, aparejar.
equipment [i'kwipmənt], *n.* equipo; pertrechos, *m.pl.*; material, *m.*
equitable ['ekwitəbl], *a.* equitativo.
equity ['ekwiti], *n.* equidad, *f.*
equivalence [i'kwivələns], *n.* equivalencia.
equivalent [i'kwivələnt], *a., n.* equivalente, *m.*
equivocal [i'kwivəkəl], *a.* equívoco.
era ['iərə], *n.* era, época.
eradicate [i'rædikeit], *v.t.* extirpar.
erase [i'reiz], *v.t.* borrar, tachar.
Erasmus [i'ræzməs], *n.* Erasmo.
erasure [i'reiʒə], *n.* borradura, raspadura.
ere [ɛə], (*obs.*) [BEFORE].
erect [i'rekt], *a.* vertical, derecho, erguido.—*v.t.* erigir; montar; construir.
erection [i'rekʃən], *n.* erección; construcción, *f.*
ermine ['ə:min], *n.* armiño; (*fig.*) toga.
erode [i'roud], *v.t.* corroer; erosionar.
erosion [i'rouʒən], *n.* erosión, *f.*
erotic [i'rɔtik], *a.* erótico.
err [ə:], *v.i.* errar, marrar.
errand ['erənd], *n.* recado, mandado.
errant ['erənt], *a.* errante, erróneo; andante (*caballero*).
erratic [i'rætik], *a.* excéntrico, irregular.
erratum [e'ra:təm], *n.* (*pl.* -ata) errata.
erroneous [i'rounjəs], *a.* erróneo.
error ['erə], *n.* error, *m.*, yerro.
ersatz ['eərzæts], *a.* substitutivo.
erstwhile ['ə:stwail], *a.* antiguo.
erudite ['erudait], *a., n.* erudito.
erudition [eru'diʃən], *n.* erudición, *f.*
erupt [i'rʌpt], *v.i.* erumpir, hacer erupción.
eruption [i'rʌpʃən], *n.* erupción, *f.*
escalate ['eskəleit], *v.i.* intensificarse.
escalator ['eskəleitə], *n.* escalera móvil.
escapade ['eskəpeid], *n.* escapada; travesura.
escape [is'keip], *n.* escape, *m.*; evasión, *f.*—*v.t.* escaparse a; escapar; evitar.—*v.i.* salvarse; escaparse (*from,* de).
escarpment [is'ka:pmənt], *n.* escarpa(dura).
eschew [is'tʃu:], *v.t.* esquivar, evitar.
escort ['eskɔ:t], *n.* escolta; acompañante, *m.*—[is'kɔ:t], *v.t.* escoltar.
escutcheon [is'kʌtʃən], *n.* escudo, blasón, *f.*
Eskimo ['eskimou], *a., n.* esquimal, *m.f.*
esoteric [eso'terik], *a.* esotérico.
esparto [es'pa:tou], *n.* esparto.
especially [is'peʃəli], *adv.* especialmente.
espionage ['espiəna:ʒ], *n.* espionaje, *m.*
espousal [is'pauzl], *n.* adherencia (*of,* a).
espouse [is'pauz], *v.t.* adherirse a, sostener; (*obs.*) casarse con.
espy [es'pai], *v.t.* divisar, percibir.
esquire [es'kwaiə], *n.* escudero; (*Brit.*) don (*título*).
essay ['esei], *n.* ensayo.—[e'sei], *v.t.* ensayar.
essence ['esəns], *n.* esencia.
essential [e'senʃəl], *a., n.* esencial, *m.*
establish [is'tæbliʃ], *v.t.* establecer.
establishment [is'tæbliʃmənt], *n.* establecimiento; (*fig.*) la oligarquía.
estate [es'teit], *n.* propiedad, *f.*; herencia; heredad, *f.*, finca; estado.

esteem [es'ti:m], *n.* estima.—*v.t.* estimar, apreciar.
estimate ['estimit], *n.* estimación, *f.*, cálculo; presupuesto; tasa.—['estimeit], *v.t.* estimar, calcular.
estimation [esti'meiʃən], *n.* estimación, *f.*
estrange [es'treindʒ], *v.t.* enajenar, enemistar.
estuary ['estjuəri], *n.* estuario, desembocadura.
et cetera [et'setrə] (*abbrev.* etc.), etcétera.
etch [etʃ], *v.t.* grabar al agua fuerte.
etching ['etʃiŋ], *n.* aguafuerte, *f.*
eternal [i'tə:nəl], *a.* eterno.
eternity [i'tə:niti], *n.* eternidad, *f.*
ether ['i:θə], *n.* éter, *m.*
ethereal [i'θiəriəl], *a.* etéreo.
ethics ['eθiks], *n.pl.* ética.
ethical ['eθikəl], *a.* ético.
Ethiopia [i:θi'oupjə], *n.* Etiopía.
Ethiopian [i:θi'oupjən], *a.*, *n.* etíopio.
ethyl ['eθil, 'i:θil], *n.* etilo.
ethnology [eθ'nolədʒi], *n.* etnología.
etiquette ['etiket], *n.* etiqueta.
etymology [eti'molədʒi], *n.* etimología.
Eucharist ['ju:kərist], *n.* Eucaristía.
eulogize ['ju:lədʒaiz], *v.t.* encomiar.
eulogy ['ju:lədʒi], *n.* encomio.
eunuch ['ju:nək], *n.* eunuco.
euphemism ['ju:fəmizm], *n.* eufemismo.
Europe ['juərəp], *n.* Europa.
European [juərə'pi:ən], *a.*, *n.* europeo.
euthanasia ['ju:θə'neizjə], *n.* eutanasia.
evacuate [i'vækjueit], *v.t.* evacuar.
evacuation [ivækju'eiʃən], *n.* evacuación, *f.*
evacuee [ivækju'i:], *n.* evacuado.
evade [i'veid], *v.t.* evadir, esquivar.
evaluate [i'væljueit], *v.t.* evaluar.
evangelic(al) [i:væn'dʒelik(əl)], *a.*, *n.* evangélico.
evangelist [i'vændʒəlist], *n.* evangelista, *m.f.*
evaporate [i'væpəreit], *v.t.* evaporar.—*v.i.* -se.
evasion [i'veiʒən], *n.* evasión, *f.*, evasiva.
Eve [i:v], *n.* Eva.
eve [i:v], *n.* víspera; **on the — of**, en vísperas de; (*poet.*) tardecita.
even ['i:vən], *a.* igual, llano, liso; par (*número*); constante; **to get — with**, desquitarse *or* despicarse con.—*adv.* aún, hasta; mismo. —*v.t.* allanar.
evening ['i:vniŋ], *a.* vespertino; de etiqueta (*traje*).—*n.* tarde, *f.*, anochecer, *m.*
evenness ['i:vənnis], *n.* uniformidad, igualdad, *f.*
evensong ['i:vənsɔŋ], *n.* (*eccl.*) vísperas, *f.pl.*
event [i'vent], *n.* suceso; acto; caso; (*sport*) certamen, *m.*; **at all events,** en todo caso; **in the — of,** en caso de.
eventful [i'ventful], *a.* accidentado; memorable.
eventual [i'ventjuəl], *a.* último, final; acaecedero.
eventually [i'ventjuəli], *adv.* andando el tiempo, finalmente.
ever ['evə], *adv.* siempre; alguna vez; jamás; **hardly —,** casi nunca; **for — and —,** por siempre jamás; **— so,** (*fam.*) sumamente.
evergreen ['evəgri:n], *a.* siempre verde.—*n.* (*bot.*) siempreviva.
everlasting [evə'lɑ:stiŋ], *a.* sempiterno.
evermore [evə'mɔ:], *adv.* eternamente.
every ['evri], *a.* todo, cada; todos los, *m.pl.*

everybody ['evribɔdi], *pron.* todo el mundo, todos, *m.pl.*
everyday ['evridei], *a.* corriente, ordinario, cotidiano.
everyone ['evriwʌn], *pron.* todo el mundo, todos, *m.pl.*
everything ['evriθiŋ], *pron.* todo.
everywhere ['evriweə], *adv.* en *o* por todas partes.
evict [i'vict], *v.t.* desposeer, desahuciar.
eviction [i'vikʃən], *n.* desahucio, despojo.
evidence ['evidəns], *n.* evidencia, prueba; deposición; **in —,** visible.
evident ['evidənt], *a.* evidente, patente.
evil ['i:vil], *a.* malo.—*n.* mal, *m.*
evil-doer ['i:vildu:ə], *n.* malhechor, *m.*
evil eye ['i:vil'ai], *n.* aojo.
evoke [i'vouk], *v.t.* evocar.
evolution [i:və'lu:ʃən], *n.* evolución, *f.*
evolutionary [i:və'lu:ʃənəri], *a.* evolucionario; evolutivo.
evolve [i'vɔlv], *v.t.* desarrollar.—*v.i.* evolucionar.
ewe [ju:], *n.* oveja.
ewer [ju:ə], *n.* jarro, aguamanil, *m.*
ex- [eks-], *prefix* ex, antiguo.
exacerbate [eg'zæsəbeit], *v.t.* exacerbar.
exact [eg'zækt], *a.* exacto, preciso.—*v.t.* exigir.
exacting [eg'zæktiŋ], *a.* exigente.
exactly [eg'zæktli], *adv.* exactamente; **en punto** (*de la hora*).
exactness [eg'zæktnis], *n.* exactitud, corrección, *f.*
exaggerate [eg'zædʒəreit], *v.t.*, *v.i.* exagerar.
exaggeration [egzædʒə'reiʃən], *n.* exageración, *f.*
exalt [eg'zɔ:lt], *v.t.* exaltar.
exam [eg'zæm], *n.* (*fam.*) examen, *m.*
examination [egzæmi'neiʃən], *n.* examen, *m.*; (*med.*) reconocimiento.   **[sit]**
examine [eg'zæmin], *v.t.* examinar; reconocer; registrar.
example [eg'zɑ:mpl], *n.* ejemplo.
exasperate [eg'zɑ:spəreit], *v.t.* exasperar.
exasperation [egzɑ:spə'reiʃən], *n.* exasperación, *f.*
excavate ['ekskəveit], *v.t.* excavar.
excavation [ekskə'veiʃən], *n.* excavación, *f.*
exceed [ek'si:d], *v.t.* exceder, sobrepasar.
exceedingly [ek'si:diŋli], *adv.* sumamente.
excel [ek'sel], *v.t.* sobrepujar, avantajar.—*v.i.* sobresalir.
excellence ['eksələns], *n.* excelencia.
excellency ['eksələnsi], *n.* excelencia (*título*).
excellent ['eksələnt], *a.* excelente.
except [ek'sept], *prep.* excepto, a excepción de. —*v.t.* exceptuar.
exception [ek'sepʃən], *n.* excepción, *f.*; ofensa.
exceptionable [ek'sepʃənəbl], *a.* ofensivo, recusable.
exceptional [ek'sepʃənəl], *a.* excepcional.
excerpt ['eksə:pt], *n.* trozo, selección, *f.*, cita.
excess [ek'ses], *n.* exceso, demasía.
excessive [ek'sesiv], *a.* excesivo.
exchange [eks'tʃeindʒ], *n.* cambio, canje, *m.*; (*tel.*) central, *f.*; (*com.*) bolsa.—*v.t.* canjear, cambiar.
exchequer [eks'tʃekə], *n.* fisco, tesorería; (*Brit.*) Hacienda.

excise

excise ['eksaiz], *n.* impuesto sobre consumos. —[ek'saiz], *v.t.* extirpar.
excitable [ek'saitəbl], *a.* excitable.
excite [ek'sait], *v.t.* emocionar; excitar.
excitement [ek'saitmənt], *n.* emoción, agitación; excitación, *f.*
exciting [ek'saitiŋ], *a.* emocionante; excitante.
exclaim [eks'kleim], *v.t., v.i.* exclamar.
exclamation [eksklə'meiʃən], *n.* exclamación, *f.*; — **mark,** punto de admiración (¡!).
exclude [eks'klu:d], *v.t.* excluir.
exclusion [eks'klu:ʒən], *n.* exclusión, *f.*
exclusive [eks'klu:siv], *a.* exclusivo; — **of,** sin contar.
excommunicate [ekskə'mju:nikeit], *v.t.* descomulgar.
excommunication [ekskəmju:ni'keiʃən], *n.* excommunión, descomunión, *f.*
excrement ['ekskrimənt], *n.* excremento.
excrete [eks'kri:t], *v.t.* excretar.
excruciating [eks'kru:ʃieitiŋ], *a.* atroz, agudísimo.
excursion [eks'kə:ʃən], *n.* excursión.
excusable [eks'kju:zəbl], *a.* perdonable, excusable.
excuse [eks'kju:s], *n.* disculpa, excusa.— [eks'kju:z], *v.t.* perdonar, excusar, dispensar; — **me,** dispense, Vd. perdone.
execute ['eksikju:t], *v.t.* ejecutar; ajusticiar.
execution [eksi'kju:ʃən], *n.* ejecución, *f.*
executioner [eksi'kju:ʃənə], *n.* verdugo.
executive [ig'zekjutiv], *a.* ejecutivo.—*n.* administrador, gerente, *m.*; autoridad suprema, gobierno.
exegesis [eksi'dʒi:sis], *n.* exégesis, *f.*
exemplary [ig'zempləri], *a.* ejemplar.
exemplify [ig'zemplifai], *v.t.* ejemplificar.
exempt [ig'zempt], *a.* exento.—*v.t.* eximir, exentar.
exemption [eg'zempʃən], *n.* exención, *f.*, dispensa.
exercise ['eksəsaiz], *n.* ejercicio.—*v.t.* ejercitar; ejercer.
exert [eg'zə:t], *v.t.* desplegar; ejercer.—*v.r.* esforzarse.
exertion [eg'zə:ʃən], *n.* esfuerzo.
exhale [eks'heil], *v.t.* exhalar, emitir.—*v.i.* espirar.
exhaust [eg'zo:st], *n.* escape, *m.*—*v.t.* agotar.
exhaustion [eg'zo:stʃən], *n.* agotamiento.
exhaustive [eg'zo:stiv], *a.* exhaustivo, minucioso.
exhibit [eg'zibit], *n.* artículo exhibido.—*v.t.* exhibir.
exhibition [egzi'biʃən], *n.* exposición, *f.*; *(educ.)* beca.
exhibitor [eg'zibitə], *n.* expositor, *m.*
exhilarate [eg'ziləreit], *v.t.* alegrar, emocionar.
exhilaration [egzilə'reiʃən], *n.* regocijo, excitación, *f.*
exhort [eg'zo:t], *v.t.* exhortar.
exile ['egzail], *n.* destierro; desterrado.—*v.t.* desterrar.
exist [eg'zist], *v.i.* existir.
existence [eg'zistəns], *n.* existencia.
exit ['egzit], *n.* salida; *(stage direction)* vase.
ex-officio [eksə'fiʃiou], *a., adv.* en virtud de autoridad.
exonerate [eg'zonəreit], *v.t.* exonerar; disculpar.

exorbitant [eg'zo:bitənt], *a.* excesivo, enorme.
exorcism ['ekso:sizəm], *n.* exorcismo.
exotic [eg'zotik], *a.* exótico.
expand [eks'pænd], *v.t.* extender; ensanchar. —*v.i.* -se.
expanse [eks'pæns], *n.* extensión, *f.*
expansion [eks'pænʃən], *n.* expansión, *f.*; desarrollo.
expatiate [eks'peiʃieit], *v.i.* espaciarse.
expatriate [eks'pætriət], *a., n.* expatriado.— [eks'pætrieit], *v.t.* expatriar.
expect [eks'pekt], *v.t.* esperar, suponerse, prometerse.
expectancy [eks'pektənsi], *n.* expectación, *f.* expectativa.
expectant [eks'pektənt], *a.* expectante; encinta *(mujer)*.
expectation [ekspek'teiʃən], *n.* expectación, *f.*
expedient [eks'pi:diənt], *a.* conveniente; oportuno; ventajoso.—*n.* expediente, *m.*
expedite ['ekspədait], *v.t.* despachar, gestionar, expedir.
expedition [ekspi'diʃən], *n.* expedición, *f.*
expel [eks'pel], *v.t.* expulsar.
expend [eks'pend], *v.t.* invertir, gastar, consumir.
expendable [eks'pendəbl], *a.* gastable.
expenditure [eks'penditʃə], *n.* desembolso, gasto.
expense [eks'pens], *n.* gasto; costa.—*pl.* expensas.
expensive [eks'pensiv], *a.* costoso, caro.
experience [eks'piəriəns], *n.* experiencia.— *v.t.* experimentar.
experiment [eks'perimənt], *n.* experiencia, experimento.
expert ['ekspə:t], *a., n.* perito, experto.
expertise [ekspə:'ti:z], *n.* pericia.
expiate [eks'speiit], *v.t.* expiar.
expire [eks'paiə], *v.i.* caducar; expirar.
expiry [eks'paiəri], *n.* expiración, *f.*; fin *(m.)* de plazo.
explain [eks'plein], *v.t., v.i.* explicar.
explanation [eksplə'neiʃən], *n.* explicación, *f.*
expletive ['eksplitiv], *n.* reniego; interjección, *f.*; taco.
explicit [eks'plisit], *a.* explícito.
explode [eks'ploud], *v.t.* volar, hacer saltar; refutar.—*v.i.* estallar.
exploit ['eksploit], *n.* hazaña.—[eks'ploit], *v.t.* explotar.
exploitation [eksploi'teiʃən], *n.* explotación, *f.*
exploration [eksplə'reiʃən], *n.* exploración, *f.*
explore [eks'plo:], *v.t., v.i.* explorar.
explorer [eks'plorə], *n.* explorador, *m.*
explosion [eks'plouʒən], *n.* explosión, *f.*
explosive [eks'plouziv], *a., n.* explosivo.
exponent [eks'pounənt], *n.* expositor; exponente, *m.*; adicto.
export ['ekspo:t], *n.* exportación, *f.*—[eks'po:t], *v.t.* exportar.
expose [eks'pouz], *v.t.* exponer; desenmascarar.
expostulate [eks'postjuleit], *v.i.* protestar.
exposure [eks'pouʒə], *n.* exposición, *f.*; desenmascaramiento.
expound [eks'paund], *v.t.* exponer.
express [eks'pres], *a., n.* expreso; *(rail.)* rápido.—*v.t.* expresar.—*adv.* expresamente.
expression [eks'preʃən], *n.* expresión, *f.*
expressive [eks'presiv], *a.* expresivo.

expressly [eks'presli], *adv.* expresamente; adrede.

expulsion [eks'pʌlʃən], *n.* expulsión, *f.*

expunge [eks'pʌndʒ], *v.t.* cancelar, borrar.

expurgate ['ekspə:geit], *v.t.* expurgar.

exquisite [eks'kwizit], *a.* exquisito.

ex-serviceman [eks'sə:vismən], *n.* ex combatiente, *m.*

extant [eks'tænt], *a.* existente.

extempore [eks'tempəri], *a.* improvisado.—*adv.* de improviso.

extemporize [eks'tempəraiz], *v.i.* improvisar.

extend [eks'tend], *v.t.* extender; prolongar; alargar; ofrecer.—*v.i.* extenderse.

extension [eks'tenʃən], *n.* extensión, *f.*; (*com.*) prórroga.

extensive [eks'tensiv], *a.* extensivo, extenso.

extent [eks'tent], *n.* extensión, *f.*; punto, grado; *to a certain —*, hasta cierto punto; *to a great —*, en su mayor parte.

extenuate [eks'tenjueit], *v.t.* atenuar; extenuar; *extenuating circumstances*, circunstancias atenuantes, *f.pl.*

exterior [eks'tiəriə], *a.* exterior, externo.—*n.* exterior, *m.*

exterminate [eks'tə:mineit], *v.t.* exterminar.

external [eks'tə:nl], *a.* externo.

extinct [eks'tiŋkt], *a.* extinto.

extinction [eks'tiŋkʃən], *n.* extinción, *f.*

extinguish [eks'tiŋgwiʃ], *v.t.* extinguir; apagar.

extirpate ['ekstə:peit], *v.t.* extirpar.

extol [eks'toul], *v.t.* ensalzar.

extort [eks'tɔ:t], *v.t.* arrancar, sacar por fuerza.

extortion [eks'tɔ:ʃən], *n.* extorción, *f.*

extra ['ekstrə], *a.* adicional; de repuesto; extra.—*n.* extra, *m.*

extract ['ekstrækt], *n.* extracto.—[eks'trækt] *v.t.* extraer, sacar.

extraction [eks'trækʃən], *n.* extracción, *f.*

extradition [ekstrə'diʃən], *n.* extradición, *f.*

extraneous [eks'treinjəs], *a.* externo, ajeno.

extraordinary [eks'trɔ:dnəri], *a.* extraordinario.

extravagance [eks'trævəgəns], *n.* extravagancia; prodigalidad, *f.*

extravagant [eks'trævəgənt], *a.* extravagante; despilfarrado.

extreme [eks'tri:m], *a.* extremo; extremado.—*n.* extremo, extremidad, *f.*; *in the —*, en sumo grado.

extremist [eks'tri:mist], *a.*, *n.* extremista, *m.f.*

extremity [eks'tremiti], *n.* extremidad, *f.*

extricate ['ekstrikeit], *v.t.* desenredar, librar.

extrovert ['ekstrovə:t], *a.*, *n.* extrovertido.

extrude [eks'tru:d], *v.t.* empujar.—*v.i.* resaltar.

exuberance [eg'zju:bərəns], *n.* exuberancia.

exuberant [eg'zju:bərənt], *a.* exuberante.

exude [eg'zju:d], *v.t.* exudar, rezumar.

exult [eg'zʌlt], *v.i.* exultar.

exultation [egzʌl'teiʃən], *n.* exultación, *f.*

eye [ai], *n.* ojo; *with an — to*, con la idea de; *in the eyes of*, a los ojos de.—*v.t.* ojear; *to catch one's —*, llamar la atención a; *to see — to —*, estar de acuerdo; *to make eyes*, hacer guiños; *to shut one's —s to*, hacer la vista gorda a.

eye-ball ['aibɔ:l], *n.* globo del ojo.

eyebrow ['aibrau], *n.* ceja.

eyelash ['ailæʃ], *n.* pestaña.

eye-lid ['ailid], *n.* párpado.

eyesight ['aisait], *n.* vista.

eyesore ['aisɔ:], *n.* mácula, fealdad, *f.*

eyewash ['aiwɔʃ], *n.* (*fam.*) lisonja engañosa.

eye-witness ['aiwitnis], *n.* testigo ocular.

eyrie *or* **eyry** ['aiəri *or* 'ɛəri], *n.* aguilera, nido de ave rapaz.

F

F, f [ef], *n.* sexta letra del alfabeto inglés; *F*, (*mus.*) fa.

fable [feibl], *n.* fábula.

fabric ['fæbrik], *n.* tela, tejido; fábrica.

fabricate ['fæbrikeit], *v.t.* fabricar, forjar.

fabrication [fæbri'keiʃən], *n.* fabricación, *f.*; mentira.

fabulous ['fæbjuləs], *a.* fabuloso.

façade [fə'sɑ:d], *n.* fachada.

face [feis], *n.* cara; haz (*de encima*); faz (*del mundo*), *f.*; mueca; (*print.*) caracter, *m.*; *to save —*, salvar las apariencias.—*v.t.* encararse con, enfrentar; mirar hacia; estar en frente de; alisar, acabar; *to — the music*, (*fam.*) aceptar las consecuencias.—*v.i.* carear; *to — about*, volver la cara.—*— up to*, arrostrar.

facet ['fæsit], *n.* faceta.

facetious [fə'si:ʃəs], *a.* patoso, chistoso.

facile ['fæsail], *a.* fácil; dócil.

facilitate [fə'siliteit], *v.t.* facilitar.

facility [fə'siliti], *n.* facilidad, *f.*

facing ['feisiŋ], *n.* cubierta; paramento.—*prep.* enfrente de; (de) cara a.

facsimile [fæk'simili], *n.* facsímil(e), *m.*

fact [fækt], *n.* hecho; *in —*, en realidad.

faction ['fækʃən], *n.* facción, *f.*; tumulto.

factor ['fæktə], *n.* factor, *m.*

factory ['fæktəri], *n.* fábrica.

factual ['fæktjuəl], *a.* objetivo.

faculty ['fækəlti], *n.* facultad, *f.*

fad [fæd], *n.* guilladura; novedad, *f.*, capricho.

faddy ['fædi], *a.* quisquilloso.

fade [feid], *v.t.* desteñir.—*v.i.* marchitarse; desteñirse; *to — away*, desvanecerse.

fag [fæg], *n.* lata, afán, *m.*; (*Brit. educ.*) alumno sirviente; burro de carga, yunque, *m.*; (*fam.*) pitillo.—*v.t.* afanar, fatigar.

fag-end ['fægend], *n.* colilla (*de pitillo*); desperdicio (*trozo inútil*); retal (*trozo de tela*).

faggot ['fægət], *n.* haz, *m.*; (*fam.*).

fail [feil], *n. without —*, sin falta.—*v.t.* faltar a; (*educ.*) suspender; ser suspendido en (*un examen*).—*v.i.* fracasar; (*com.*) quebrar; ser suspendido; decaer, menguar; *not to — to*, no dejar de.

failing ['feiliŋ], *a.* decadente.—*n.* falta; fracaso; debilidad, *f.*—*prep.* a falta de.

failure ['feiljə], *n.* fracaso, malogro; (*com.*) quiebra; fracasado (*persona*); suspensión (*en un examen*), *f.*

faint [feint], *a.* débil; desmayado.—*n.* desmayo.—*v.i.* desmayarse.

faint-hearted ['feint'hɑ:tid], *a.* medroso, cobarde.

fair [fɛə], *a.* justo, imparcial; legal; propicio; rubio; blanco; hermoso, bueno (*tiempo*); admisible; (*fam.*) regular; — *play,* juego limpio, proceder leal, *m.*; — *sex,* sexo bello. —*n.* verbena; feria.

fairy ['fɛəri], *a.* de hadas.—*n.* hada; — *tale o story,* cuento de hadas; (*fig.*) patraña.

faith [feiθ], *n.* fe, *f.*; (*fig.*) palabra.

faithful ['feiθful], *a.* fiel, leal; the —, los creyentes.

faithfulness ['feiθfulnis], *n.* fidelidad, *f.*

faithless ['feiθlis], *a.* infiel, desleal.

fake [feik], *a.* (*fam.*) falso, fingido.—*n.* falsificación, *f.*; impostor (*persona*), *m.*—*v.t.* falsificar.

falcon ['fɔ:lkən], *n.* halcón, *m.*

falconry ['fɔ:lkənri], *n.* cetrería.

fall [fɔ:l], *n.* caída; baja; salto de agua; (*U.S.*) otoño.—*irr. v.i.* caer(se); ponerse (*enfermo, triste, etc.*); **to — back,** replegarse; **to — back on,** recurrir a; **to — behind,** quedarse atrás; **to — for,** (*fam.*) tragar; chiflarse por; **to — out,** desavenirse; **to — through,** fracasar, salir mal.

fallacious [fə'leiʃəs], *a.* falaz; erróneo.

fallacy ['fæləsi], *n.* falsedad, *f.*, error, *m.*; falacia.

fallen ['fɔ:lən], *n.pl.* los caídos (*de guerra*), *m.pl.* [FALL].

fallible ['fælibl], *a.* falible.

fall-out ['fɔ:laut], *n.* desperdicios nucleares, *m.pl.*

fallow ['fælou], *a.* barbechado; flavo.—*n.* barbecho.

fallow-deer ['fælou'diə], *n.* gamo.

false [fɔ:ls], *a.* falso; postizo.

false-hearted ['fɔ:ls'hɑ.tid], *a.* traicionero, pérfido.

falsehood ['fɔ:lshud], *n.* falsedad, *f.*, mentira.

falsetto [fɔ:l'setou], *n.* falsete, *m.*; falsetista, *m.f.*

falsify ['fɔ:lsifai], *v.t.* falsificar.

falsity ['fɔ:lsiti], *n.* falsedad, *f.*

falter ['fɔ:ltə], *n.* titubeo.—*v.i.* titubear, vacilar; balbucear.

fame [feim], *n.* fama.

familiar [fə'miljə], *a., n.* familiar, *m.f.*; — *with,* familiarizado con; al tanto de.

familiarize [fə'miljəraiz], *v.t.* familiarizar.

family ['fæmili], *a.* familiar.—*n.* familia.

famine ['fæmin], *n.* hambre, *f.*, carestía.

famished ['fæmiʃt], *a.* hambriento.

famous ['feiməs], *a.* famoso, célebre.

fan [fæn], *n.* abanico; (*mech.*) ventilador, *m.*; (*fam.*) aficionado.—*v.t.* abanicar; avivar.

fanatic [fə'nætik], *a., n.* fanático.

fanaticism [fə'nætisizm], *n.* fanatismo.

fancied ['fænsid], *a.* imaginario; favorecido.

fancier ['fænsiə], *n.* aficionado.

fanciful ['fænsiful], *a.* antojadizo, fantástico.

fancy ['fænsi], *a.* de fantasía; fantástico; extravagante; caprichoso; — *dress,* traje (*m.*) de fantasía.—*n.* fantasía; afición, *f.*; antojo.—*v.t.* imaginar; prendarse de; *what do you —?* ¿qué le apetece?

fanfare ['fænfɛə], *n.* toque (*m.*) de trompetas; fanfarria.

fang [fæŋ], *n.* colmillo, diente, *m.*

fanlight ['fænlait], *n.* tragaluz, *m.*, abanico.

fantastic [fæn'tæstik], *a.* fantástico.

fantasy ['fæntəsi], *n.* fantasía.

far [fɑ:], *a.* lejano, remoto.—*adv.* lejos; muy; *as — as,* hasta; en cuanto que (*with subj.*); tan lejos como; *by —,* con mucho; *so —,* hasta ahora o aquí; — *off,* lejano; a lo lejos.

far-away [fɑ:rə'wei], *a.* lejano.

farce [fɑ:s], *n.* farsa.

farcical [fɑ:sikəl], *a.* ridículo.

fare [fɛə], *n.* tarifa, pasaje, *m.*; vianda, comida. —*v.i.* pasarlo, acontecer; (*poet.*) andar.

farewell [fɛə'wel], *n.* despedida.—*interj.* ¡adiós!

far-fetched ['fɑ:'fetʃt], *a.* forzado, improbable.

farm [fɑ:m], *n.* granja; (*S.A.*) estancia.—*v.t.* cultivar; arrendar.

farmer ['fɑ:mə], *n.* granjero; labrador, *m.*

farmhouse ['fɑ:mhaus], *n.* granja, cortijo, alquería.

farmyard ['fɑ:mjɑ:d], *n.* corral, *m.*

far-reaching ['fɑ:ri:tʃiŋ], *a.* de gran alcance.

farther ['fɑ:ðə], *a.* más lejano.—*adv.* más lejos.

farthest ['fɑ:ðist], *a.* más lejano.—*adv.* lo más lejos.

farthing ['fɑ:ðiŋ], *n.* cuarto de penique.

fascinate ['fæsineit], *v.t.* fascinar.

fascinating ['fæsineitiŋ], *a.* fascinador.

fascination [fæsi'neiʃən], *n.* fascinación, *f.*

fascism ['fæʃizm], *n.* fascismo.

fascist ['fæʃist], *a., n.* fascista, *m.f.*

fashion ['fæʃən], *n.* moda; estilo; manera; elegancia; *after a —,* en cierto modo.—*v.t.* forjar, formar.

fashionable ['fæʃnəbl], *a.* de moda; de buen tono, elegante.

fast (1) [fɑ:st], *a.* rápido; adelantado (*reloj*); disoluto, ligero.—*adv.* rápidamente, aprisa.

fast (2) [fɑ:st], *n.* ayuno.—*v.i.* ayunar.

fast (3) [fɑ:st], *a.* fijo, constante; *to make—,* (*naut.*) amarrar.—*adv.* firmemente; profundamente.

fasten [fɑ:sn], *v.t.* atar; cerrar; fijar; abrochar.—*v.i.* fijarse; cerrarse; *to — on,* asirse de.

fastener ['fɑ:snə], *n.* cierre, *m.*, asilla.

fastidious [fæs'tidiəs], *a.* melindroso, quisquilloso.

fasting ['fɑ:stiŋ], *n.* ayuno.

fastness ['fɑ:stnis], *n.* rapidez, *f.*; fijeza, firmeza; plaza fuerte; ligereza.

fat [fæt], *a.* gordo, grueso; pingüe; *to get —,* engordar.—*n.* grasa, sebo; *to live off the — of the land,* vivir a cuerpo del rey.

fatal [feitl], *a.* fatal; mortal.

fate [feit], *n.* hado, sino; suerte, *f.*

fated ['feitid], *a.* fatal; predestinado (a la muerte).

father ['fɑ:ðə], *n.* padre, *m.*—*v.t.* engendrar; prohijar; originar; atribuir.

father-in-law ['fɑ:ðərinlɔ:], *n.* (*pl.* **fathers-in-law**) suegro.

fatherland ['fɑ:ðəlænd], *n.* patria.

fatherly ['fɑ:ðəli], *a.* paternal.

fathom ['fæðəm], *n.* (*naut.*) · braza.—*v.t.* sondear; profundizar; (*fig.*) entender.

fatigue [fə'ti:g], *n.* fatiga; (*mil.*) faena.—*v.t.* fatigar.

fatten [fætn], *v.t.* engordar, cebar.

fatty ['fæti], *a.* graso, grasoso; (*fam.*) gordinflón.

fatuous ['fætjuəs], *a.* fatuo; ilusorio; necio.

faucet ['fɔ:sit], *n.* (*U.S.*) [TAP].

fault [fɔ:lt], *n.* culpa; defecto; falta; (*geol.*) falla; (*elec.*) avería; *at* —, culpable; *it is John's* —, Juan tiene la culpa.—*v.t.* hallar una falta.

fault-finder ['fɔ:ltfaində], *n.* criticón, *m.*

faultless ['fɔ:ltlis], *a.* perfecto; cabal; sin falta.

faulty ['fɔ:lti], *a.* defectuoso.

favour ['feivə], *n.* favor, *m.*; (*com.*) grata, atenta (*carta*); *in* — *of*, a favor de; *to be in* — *of*, estar por; ser partidario de.—*v.t.* favorecer.

favourable ['feivərəbl], *a.* favorable.

favourite ['feivrit], *a.* favorito, predilecto. —*n.* favorito.

fawn (1) [fɔ:n], *a.* color de cervato.—*n.* cervato.

fawn (2) [fɔ:n], *v.i.* adular, bailar el agua delante (*on*, a).

fear [fiə], *n.* miedo, temor, *m.*—*v.t.*, *v.i.* temer.

fearful ['fiəful], *a.* temeroso; espantoso.

fearless ['fiəlis], *a.* intrépido, audaz.

fearsome ['fiəsəm], *a.* miedoso; terrible.

feasible ['fi:zibl], *a.* factible, hacedero; dable.

feast [fi:st], *n.* festín, banquete, *m.*; (*eccl.*) fiesta; abundancia.—*v.t.* banquetear, regalar.—*v.i.* festejarse.

feat [fi:t], *n.* hazaña, proeza.

feather ['feðə], *n.* pluma; (*fig.*) humor, *m.*; clase, *f.*; *white* —, cobardía.—*v.t.* *to* — *one's nest*, hacer su agosto.

feather-brained ['feðəbreind], *a.* casquivano.

featherweight ['feðəweit], *a.* ligero como una pluma; (*sport*) peso pluma.

feature ['fi:tʃə], *n.* facción (*cara*), *f.*; rasgo, característica; parte (*f.*) principal. —*pl.* facciones, *f.pl.*—*v.t.* destacar; ofrecer; presentar.

February ['februəri], *n.* febrero.

fecundity [fə'kʌnditi], *n.* fecundidad, *f.*

fed [fed], [FEED].—*a.* — *up*, (*fam.*) harto (*with*, de).

federal ['fedərəl], *a.* federal.

federate ['fedəreit], *v.t.* federar.

federation [fedə'reiʃən], *n.* federación, *f.*

fee [fi:], *n.* honorario; derechos, *m.pl.*; (*jur.*) herencia.

feeble [fi:bl], *a.* débil; flaco; enfermizo.

feed [fi:d], *n.* alimentación, *f.*; pienso; (*fam.*) comilona.—*v.t.* *irr.* alimentar; dar de comer a.—*v.i.* *irr.* comer; alimentarse (*on*, de).

feel [fi:l], *n.* tacto; sensación, *f.*—*v.t.* *irr.* sentir; tocar, tentar, palpar; sondear; tomar (*el pulso*).—*v.i.* *irr.* sentirse; ser al tacto; estar; *to* — *for*, buscar a tientas; condolerse de; *to* — *cold, hot, hungry, thirsty*, tener frío, calor, hambre, sed; *to* — *like*, tener ganas de; *to* — *sorry*, sentirlo; compadecerse (*for*, de).

feeler ['fi:lə], *n.* (*ent.*) antena, palpo; (*zool.*) tentáculo; (*fig.*) tentativa, tanteo.

feeling ['fi:liŋ], *n.* sensación, *f.*; sentimiento; parecer, *m.*—*pl.* sensibilidad, *f.*

feet [fi:t], [FOOT].

feign [fein], *v.t.* fingir, aparentar, simular.

felicitation [filisi'teiʃən], *n.* felicitación, *f.*

felicitous [fi'lisitəs], *a.* feliz, oportuno.

felicity [fi'lisiti], *n.* felicidad, *f.*; ocurrencia oportuna.

feline ['fi:lain], *a.*, *n.* felino.

fell [fel], *v.t.* talar (*árbol*); derribar. [FALL].

fellow ['felou], *a.* Spanish uses prefix con-; — *countryman*, compatriota, *m.f.*—*n.* socio; miembro; compañero; igual, *m.*; (*fam.*) tío, sujeto.

fellow-creature ['felou'kri:tʃə], *n.* semejante, *m.f.*

fellow-feeling ['felou'fi:liŋ], *n.* compañerismo.

fellow-man ['felou'mæn], *n.* prójimo.

fellowship ['felouʃip], *n.* compañerismo; (*educ.*) pensión, *f.*, beca.

fellow-soldier ['felou'souldʒə], *n.* conmilitón, *m.*

fellow-traveller ['felou'trævələ], *n.* (*fig.*) comunistoide, *m.f.*; compañero de viaje.

felon ['felən], *n.* reo, criminal.

felony ['feləni], *n.* delito de mayor cuantía.

felt (1) [felt], *n.* fieltro.

felt (2) [felt] [FEEL].

female ['fi:meil], *a.* hembra, femenino.—*n.* hembra.

feminine ['feminin], *a.* femenino; mujeril.

fen [fen], *n.* pantano, laguna.

fence [fens], *n.* cerca, seto; traficante (*m.*) en objetos robados; *to sit on the* —, estar a ver venir; no participar, no comprometerse. —*v.t.* cercar, defender.—*v.i.* esgrimir.

fencing ['fensiŋ], *n.* esgrima; cercas, *f.pl.* materiales (*m.pl.*) para cercas.

fend [fend], *v.t.* parar, resguardar.—*v.i.* defenderse (*off*).

fender ['fendə], *n.* guardafuegos,*m. inv.*; (*U.S.*, *aut.*) guardabarros, *m. inv.*

fennel ['fenəl], *n.* hinojo.

ferment ['fə:ment], *n.* fermento, fermentación, *f.*—*v.t.*, *v.i.* [fə'ment], fermentar.

fern [fə:n], *n.*(*bot.*) helecho.

ferocious [fə'rouʃəs], *a.* feroz.

ferocity [fə'rɔsiti], *n.* ferocidad, *f.*

ferret ['ferit], *n.* (*zool.*) hurón, *m.*—*v.t.* huronear (*out*).

ferry ['feri], *n.* barco para pasar un río; trasbordador, *m.*; balsadero.—*v.t.* balsear (*río*); llevar a la otra orilla, trasbordar.

fertile ['fə:tail], *a.* fértil, fecundo.

fertility [fə:'tiliti], *n.* fertilidad, fecundidad, *f.*

fertilize ['fə:tilaiz], *v.t.* fertilizar; fecundar; abonar.

fertilizer ['fə:tilaizə], *n.* (*agr.*) abono, fertilizante, *m.*

fervent ['fə:vənt], *a.* fervoroso.

fervour ['fə:və], *n.* fervor, *m.*

fester ['festə], *v.t.* enconar.—*v.i.* enconarse; pudrir.

festival ['festivəl], *n.* fiesta; festival, *m.*

festive ['festiv], *a.* festivo.

festivity [fes'tiviti], *n.* festividad, *f.*

festoon [fes'tu:n], *n.* festón, *m.*—*v.t.* festonear.

fetch [fetʃ], *v.t.* traer, ir por; hacer venir; producir; (*fam.*) pegar (*golpe*); captar, atraer.

fetching ['fetʃiŋ], *a.* atractivo, llamativo.

fête [feit], *n.* fiesta.—*v.t.* festejar.

fetid ['fetid], *a.* fétido, hediondo.

fetish ['fetiʃ], *n.* fetiche, *m.*

fetter ['fetə], *n.* grillo, hierro.—*v.t.* engrillar.

feud [fju:d], *n.* saña vieja; enemistad (*f.*) tradicional entre dos familias.—*v.i.* luchar, oponerse con saña.

feudal ['fju:dəl], *a.* feudal.

fever ['fi:və], *n.* fiebre, *f.*, calentura.

feverish ['fi:vriʃ], *a.* febril, calenturiento.

few

few [fju:], *a.pl.*, pocos; *a* —, unos cuantos; *the* —, la minoría.

fiancé(e) [fi'ɔ:nsei], *n.* novio, novia, prometido, prometida.

fiasco [fi'æskou], *n.* fiasco.

fib [fib], *n.* trola, trápala, mentira.—*v.i.* embustear, mentir.

fibre ['faibə], *n.* fibra, hebra.

fibreglass ['faibəglɑ:s], *n.* vidrio fibroso.

fibrous ['faibrəs], *a.* fibroso.

fickle [fikl], *a.* veleidoso, inconstante.

fiction ['fikʃən], *n.* ficción, *f.*; literatura novelesca.

fictional ['fikʃənəl], *a.* ficcionario; novelesco.

fictitious [fik'tiʃəs], *a.* ficticio; fingido.

fiddle [fidl], *n.* (*fam.*) violín, *m.*; engañifa; *fit as a* —, en buena salud.—*v.t.* falsear, estafar.—*v.i.* tocar el violín; embustear; *to* — *with*, manosear, perder tiempo en; *to play second* —, estar subordinado (*to*, a).

fiddler ['fidlə] *n.* (*fam.*) violinista, *m.f.*; embustero.

fiddlesticks! ['fidlstiks], *interj.* ¡tonterías! ¡qué va!

fiddling ['fidliŋ], *a.* trivial.

fidelity [fi'deliti], *n.* fidelidad, *f.*

fidget ['fidʒit], *n.* persona inquieta.—*v.i.* inquietarse, azogarse.

field [fi:ld], *n.* campo; (*sport*) participantes, *m.pl.*

field-day ['fi:lddei], *n.* día (*m.*) de mucha actividad.

field-glasses ['fi:ldglɑ:siz], *n.pl.* gemelos, prismáticos, *m.pl.*

field-marshal ['fi:ld'mɑ:ʃəl], *n.* mariscal, *m.*

fiend [fi:nd], *n.* demonio, diablo; fiero.

fiendish ['fi:ndiʃ], *a.* diabólico.

fierce [fiəs], *a.* feroz, fiero; furioso, violento.

fiery ['faiəri], *a.* ardiente, fogoso.

fife [faif], *n.* pífano.

fifteen [fif'ti:n], *a., n.* quince, *m.*

fifteenth [fif'ti:nθ], *a., n.* décimoquinto, quinceno; quince (*en las fechas*).

fifth [fifθ], *a.* quinto.—*n.* quinto; cinco (*en las fechas*); (*mus.*) quinta.

fifth-columnist ['fifθ'kɔləmist], quintacolumnista, *m.f.*

fiftieth ['fiftiiθ], *a., n.* quincuagésimo.

fifty ['fifti], *a., n.* cincuenta, *m.*

fifty-fifty ['fifti'fifti], *a., adv.* (*fam.*) mitad y mitad, a medias.

fig [fig], *n.* higo; — *tree*, higuera; *I don't give a* — *for it*, no me importa un bledo o higo.

fight [fait], *n.* pelea, lucha; pujanza.—*v.t. irr.* combatir, pelearse con, luchar con *o* contra. —*v.t. irr.* pelear, lidiar, luchar (*for*, por); *to pick a* — *with*, meterse con; *to* — *it out*, decidirlo luchando; *to* — *shy of*, evadir.

fighter ['faitə], *n.* combatiente, luchador; (*aer.*) caza, *m.*

fighting ['faitiŋ], *n.* combate, *m.*, lucha, batalla; — *chance*, posibilidad (*f.*) de éxito pero con riesgos.

figment ['figmənt], *n.* ficción, invención, *f.*

figurative ['figjurətiv], *a.* figurativo, figurado.

figure ['figə], *n.* figura; (*anat.*) talle, *m.*, tipo, línea; precio; cifra.—*v.t.* figurar; calcular; *to* — *out*, descifrar.—*v.i.* figurar(se); *to* — *on*, contar con.

figurehead ['figəhed], *n.* figurón, *m.*

filch [filtʃ], *v.t.* sisar, birlar.

file (1) [fail], *n.* carpeta, fichero.—*v.t.* archivar; registrar.

file (2) [fail], *n.* lima (*herramienta*).—*v.t.* limar.

file (3) [fail], *n.* fila.—*v.i.* desfilar.

filibuster ['filibʌstə], *n.* filibustero.—*v.t., v.i.* (*U.S. pol.*) impedir la aprobación de una ley *etc.*

filigree ['filigri:], *n.* filigrana.

filing cabinet ['failiŋkæbinət], *n.* archivador, *m.*; fichero.

filing-card ['failiŋkɑ:d], *n.* ficha.

filings ['failiŋz], *n.pl.* limalla.

Filipino [fili'pi:nou], *a., n.* filipino.

fill [fil], *n.* terraplén, *m.*; hartazgo; *to have one's* — *of*, hartarse de.—*v.t.* llenar; tapar; *to* — *in*, rellenar, completar.—*v.i.* llenarse; bañarse (*de lágrimas*); hartarse; *to* — *in*, terciar, hacer las veces (*for*, de).

fillet ['filit], *n.* filete, *m.*

filling ['filiŋ], *n.* relleno; empastadura (*de dientes*); — *station*, (*U.S.*) [SERVICE STATION].

fillip ['filip], *n.* capirotazo; estímulo.—*v.t.* dar un capirotazo a; estimular.

filly ['fili], *n.* potra; (*fam.*) retozona.

film [film], *n.* película; capa (*polvo*).—*v.t.* rodar, filmar.

film star ['filmstɑ:], *n.* estrella del cine.

filmy ['filmi], *a.* pelicular; diáfano.

filter ['filtə], *n.* filtro.—*v.t.* filtrar.

filter-tipped ['filtə'tipt], *a.* con filtro, emboquillado.

filth [filθ], *n.* mugre, suciedad; obscenidad, *f.*

filthy ['filθi], *a.* mugriento, sucio; obsceno.

fin [fin], *n.* aleta.

final [fainl], *a.* final; último; terminante.—*n.* final, *m.* o *f.*

finale [fi'nɑ:li], *n.* final, *m.*

finance ['fainæns], *n.* finanzas, *f.pl.*, hacienda. —*v.t.* financiar.

financial [fai'nænʃəl], *a.* financiero.

financier [finæn'siə], *n.* financiero.

finch [fintʃ], *n.* (*orn.*) pinzón, *m.*

find [faind], *n.* hallazgo.—*v.t. irr.* hallar, encontrar.—*v.i. irr.* fallar, pronunciar un fallo; *to* — *out*, averiguar, descubrir.

finding ['faindiŋ], *n.* (*jur.*) fallo, resultando.

fine (1) [fain], *a.* fino; excelente; bueno (*tiempo*); delicado; (*fam.*) magnífico; — *arts*, bellas artes.

fine (2) [fain], *n.* multa (*castigo*).—*v.t.* multar.

fineness ['fainnis], *n.* fineza; finura.

finery ['fainəri], *n.* galas, *f.pl.*, atavíos, *m.pl.*

finesse [fi'nes], *n.* sutileza, tino.

finger ['fiŋgə], *n.* dedo; manecilla (*de reloj*); *to have at one's* — *tips*, saber al dedillo; *to twist round one's little* —, saber manejar completamente a (*una persona*).— *v.t.* manosear; (*mus.*) pulsar, teclear.

finger-nail ['fiŋgəneil], *n.* uña.

finger-print ['fiŋgəprint], *n.* huella digital.

finicky ['finiki], *a.* melindroso, remilgado.

finish ['finiʃ], *n.* final, remate, *m.*; acabamiento.—*v.t.* acabar, terminar; pulir; (*fam.*) matar, arruinar.—*v.i.* acabar; *to* — *off*, rematar; matar; acabar con; *to* — *with*, acabar con, romper con.

Finland ['finlənd], *n.* Finlandia.

Finn [fin], **Finnish** ['finiʃ], *a., n.* finlandés, finés, *m.*

fir [fɔ:], *n. (bot.)* abeto.

fire [faiə], *n.* fuego; incendio; **to be on —,** arder, estar ardiendo; **to catch —,** encenderse; **to miss —,** hacer fogonazo, fallar; **to set on —,** pegar fuego a; **under —,** *(mil.)* expuesto al fuego.—*v.t.* disparar *(armas)*; encender; incendiar; lanzar *(proyectil)*; cocer *(en el horno)*; hacer explotar *(cargas)*; *(fam.)* despedir, dar pasaporte a.—*v.i.* hacer fuego, disparar; encenderse.

fire-arm ['faiəra:m], *n.* arma de fuego.

fire-brigade ['faiəbrigeid], *n.* cuerpo de bomberos.

fire-engine ['faiərendʒin], *n.* bomba de incendios.

fire-escape ['faiəreskeip], *n.* escalera de incendios.

fireman ['faiəmən], *n.* bombero; *(rail.)* fogonero.

fireplace ['faiəpleis], *n.* chimenea, hogar, *m.*

fireside ['faiəsaid], *n.* hogar, *m.*

firewood ['faiəwud], *n.* leña.

fireworks ['faiəwə:ks], *n.* fuegos artificiales, *m.pl.*; *(fam.)* jarana.

firing-squad ['fairiŋskwɔd], *n.* pelotón *(m.)* de fusilamiento.

firm (1) [fɔ:m], *a.* firme.

firm (2) [fɔ:m], *n. (com.)* razón *(f.)* social, empresa, firma.

firmament ['fɔ:məmənt], *n.* firmamento.

firmness ['fɔ:mnis], *n.* firmeza.

first [fɔ:st], *a., n., adv.* primero; **— of all,** ante todo; **— at —,** al principio, en primer lugar; **— aid,** cura de urgencia, primeros auxilios; **— floor,** *(Brit.)* piso principal, piso segundo; *(U.S.)* planta baja.

firstborn ['fɔ:stbɔ:n], *a., n.* primogénito.

first-class [fɔ:st'kla:s], *a.* de primera clase.

first-hand [fɔ:st'hænd], *a., adv.* de primera mano.

first-rate [fɔ:st'reit], *a.* de primera categoría, excelente.

firth [fɔ:θ], *n.* estuario, ría.

fiscal ['fiskəl], *a., n.* fiscal, *m.*

fish [fiʃ], *n. (ichth.)* pez, *m.*; *(cul.)* pescado.—*v.t., v.i.* pescar; **to — for,** *(fig.)* buscar.

fishbone ['fiʃboun], *n.* espina, raspa.

fisherman ['fiʃəmən], *n.* pescador, *m.*

fishing ['fiʃiŋ], *a.* pesquero.—*n.* pesca; **— rod,** caña de pescar.

fishmonger ['fiʃmʌŋɡə], *n.* pescadero.

fish-pond ['fiʃpɔnd], *n.* vivero.

fishwife ['fiʃwaif], *n.* pescadera; *(fig.)* marimacho.

fishy ['fiʃi], *a.* que huele *o* sabe a pescado; *(fam.)* sospechoso, dudoso, inverosímil.

fission ['fiʃən], *n.* fisión; escisión, *f.*

fissure ['fiʃə], *n.* grieta; fisura.—*v.t.* hender.—*v.i.* henderse.

fist [fist], *n.* puño; *(print.)* manecilla.

fisticuff ['fistikʌf], *n.* puñetazo.

fit (1) [fit], *a.* apto; conveniente; sano; decente; digno.—*n.* ajuste, encaje, *m.*—*v.t.* sentar; ajustar, encajar; cuadrar con; equipar.—*v.i.* encajar; sentar.

fit (2) [fit], *n. (med.)* acceso; ataque; arranque.

fitful ['fitful], *a.* espasmódico.

fitness ['fitnis], *n.* conveniencia; aptitud; buena salud, *f.*

fitting ['fitiŋ], *a.* propio, conveniente; justo.—*n.* prueba; ajuste, *m.*—*pl.* accesorios, *m.pl.*

five [faiv], *a., n.* cinco.

five-year plan ['faivjiə'plæn], *n.* plan quinquenal, *m.*

fix [fiks], *n. (fam.)* apuro, aprieto.—*v.t.* fijar; arreglar; **to — up,** *(fam.)* componer; organizar; **to — on,** clavar en; elegir.

fixation [fik'seiʃən], *n.* fijación, *f.*

fixed [fikst], *a.* fijo.

fixture ['fikstʃə], *n.* mueble fijo, *m.*; accesorio; instalación *(f.)* fija; soporte, *m.*—*pl.* habilitaciones, guarniciones, *f.pl.*

fizz [fiz], *n.* efervescencia.—*v.i.* chisporrotear.

flabbergast ['flæbəga:st], *v.t. (fam.)* pasmar, aturdir.

flabby ['flæbi], *a.* lacio, flojo.

flag (1) [flæg], *n.* bandera. —*v.t.* hacer señales con una bandera.

flag (2) [flæg], *v.i.* flaquear, flojear, aflojar.

flag (3) [flæg], *n.* losa.—*v.t.* enlosar.

flag (4) [flæg], *n. (bot.)* lirio.

flagon ['flæɡən], *n.* jarro, frasco.

flag-pole ['flæɡpoul], *n.* asta.

flagrant ['fleiɡrənt], *a.* escandaloso, notorio.

flag-ship ['flæɡʃip], *n. (naut.)* capitana, buque *(m.)* insignia.

flail [fleil], *n.* mayal, *m.*—*v.t.* azotar, golpear.

flair [fleə], *n.* don especial, *m.*, instinto.

flak [flæk], *n.* fuego antiaéreo.

flake [fleik], *n.* copo *(de nieve)*; escama, hojuela.—*v.t.* hacer escamas.—*v.i.* deshacerse en escamas.

flamboyant [flæm'bɔiənt], *a.* flameante; ampuloso.

flame [fleim], *n.* llama.—*v.i.* llamear; inflamarse.

flamingo [flə'miŋɡou], *n.* flamenco.

flange [flændʒ], *n.* pestaña; realce, *m.*

flank [flæŋk], *n.* lado; costado; flanco.—*v.t.* flanquear.

flannel ['flænəl], *n.* franela.

flap [flæp], *n.* faldeta; hoja plegadiza; aletazo; *(fam.)* trastorno.—*v.t.* batir, sacudir, golpear.—*v.i.* aletear.

flare [fleə], *n.* llamarada; cohete *(m.)* de señales; destello.—*v.i.* destellar; **to — up,** encolerizarse; recrudecer.

flash [flæʃ], *n.* destello, relámpago; rayo; instante *(phot.)* flash, *m.*—*v.t.* hacer brillar; lanzar; transmitir rápidamente.—*v.i.* relampaguear.

flashlight ['flæʃlait], *n.* linterna eléctrica.

flashy ['flæʃi], *a.* chillón, charro, ostentoso.

flask [flɑ:sk], *n.* frasco, redoma.

flat [flæt], *a.* plano; llano; raso; liso; chato *(nariz)*; mate, flojo; insípido; terminante.—*n.* piso; llano; pantano; *(mus.)* bemol, *m.*; *(U.S.)* pneumático desinflado; pinchazo.

flatten ['flætn], *v.t.* allanar; desazonar.—*v.i.* allanarse.

flatter ['flætə], *v.t.* lisonjear; sentar bien a.—*v.r.* hacerse la ilusión *(that,* de que).

flatterer ['flætərə], *n.* lisonjero.

flattery ['flætəri], *n.* lisonja, adulación, *f.*

flaunt [flɔ:nt], *v.t.* ostentar, hacer alarde de.

flavour ['fleivə], *n.* sabor, *m.*; gustillo; *(cul.)* condimento.—*v.t.* sazonar, condimentar.

flaw [flɔ:], *n.* defecto, tacha.—*v.t.* agrietar, afear.

flawless ['flɔ:lis], *a.* sin tacha, entero.

flax [flæks], *n.* lino.

flay [flei], *v.t.* desollar; despellejar.

flea [fli:], *n.* pulga.
flea-bite ['fli:bait], *n.* picadura de pulga; nonada.
fleck [flek], *n.* punto, veta.—*v.t.* puntear, vetear.
fled [fled], [FLEE].
fledg(e)ling ['fledʒliŋ], *n.* volantón, *m.*; novato.
flee [fli:], *v.t., v.i. irr.* huir.
fleece [fli:s], *n.* vellón, *m.*; lana.—*v.t.* esquilar; (*fam.*) pelar.
fleet [fli:t], *a.* raudo, veloz.—*n.* (*aer., naut.*) flota; (*naut.*) armada.—*v.i.* volar, pasar rápidamente.
fleeting ['fli:tiŋ], *a.* fugaz; transitorio.
Fleming ['flemiŋ], *n.* flamenco.
Flemish ['flemiʃ], *a., n.* flamenco.
flesh [fleʃ], *n.* carne, *f.*; (*fig.*) familia; *in the* —, en persona; vivo; — *and blood,* carne y hueso.
flesh-pots ['fleʃpɔts], *n.pl.* (*fig.*) vida regalona.
fleshy ['fleʃi], *a.* carnoso; carnal; gordo.
flew [flu:], [FLY].
flex [fleks], *n.* (*elec.*) cordón, *m.*—*v.t.* doblar.
flexible ['fleksibl], *a.* flexible.
flick [flik], *n.* golpecito rápido.—*pl.* (*fam.*) el cine.—*v.t.* dar un golpecito a; tirar; chasquear.
flicker ['flikə], *n.* llama *o* luz (*f.*) vacilante; temblor, *m.*—*v.i.* temblar; oscilar.
flight [flait], *n.* huída, fuga; vuelo; tramo (*escalera*); *to take* —, alzar el vuelo; huir.
flighty ['flaiti], *a.* caprichoso, frívolo.
flimsy ['flimzi], *a.* débil, endeble; fútil.
flinch [flintʃ], *v.i.* encogerse, apocarse.
fling [fliŋ], *n.* tiro violento; baile escocés, *m.*—*v.t. irr.* arrojar; *to have one's* —, correrla, echar una cana al aire.
flint [flint], *n.* pedernal, *m.*
flip [flip], *n.* capirotazo.—*v.t.* dar un capirotazo a.
flippant ['flipənt], *a.* frívolo, impertinente.
flirt [flə:t], *n.* coqueta, coquetón, *m.,* flirt, *m.f.*; tirón, *m.*—*v.t.* tirar, lanzar, mover rápidamente.—*v.i.* flirtear, galantear, coquetear (*with,* con); jugar (*with,* con).
flirtatious [flə:'teiʃəs], *a.* coqueta, coquetón.
flit [flit], *v.i.* revolotear; (*fam.*) mudar de casa.
float [flout], *n.* veleta (*pesca*); boya; carro.—*v.t.* (*com.*) lanzar; emitir; (*naut.*) poner a flote.—*v.i.* flotar.
floating['floutiŋ], *a.* flotante, boyante; a flote; de tránsito.
flock (1) [flɔk], *n.* rebaño; bandada (*pájaros*).
flock (2) [flɔk], *n.* borra.—*v.i.* congregarse; venir de tropel.
floe [flou], *n.* témpano.
flog [flɔg], *v.t.* azotar; (*low*) vender.
flood [flʌd], *n.* inundación, *f.,* diluvio; (*fig.*) torrente, *m.*—*v.t.* inundar.—*v.i.* desbordar.
floor [flɔ:], *n.* suelo, piso; fondo; *to take the* —, tomar la palabra.—*v.t.* derribar.
flop [flɔp], *n.* (*fam.*) birria, fracaso; ruido sordo.—*v.i.* agitarse; caer pesadamente; (*fam.*) salir calabaza, fracasar.
floral ['flɔ:rəl], *a.* floral.
florid ['flɔrid], *a.* florido; encarnado (*cara*).
florin ['flɔrin], *n.* florín (*dos chelines*), *m.*
florist ['flɔrist], *n.* florero, florista.
flotilla [flou'tilə], *n.* flotilla.
flotsam ['flɔtsəm], *n.* pecio(s).

flounce (1) [flauns], *n.* volante (*costura*), *m.*
flounce (2) [flauns], *v.i.* saltar de enojo.
flounder (1) ['flaundə], *n.* (*ichth.*) platija.
flounder (2), *v.i.* forcejear, revolcarse.
flour [flauə], *n.* harina.
flourish ['flʌriʃ], *n.* floreo; molinete, *m.,* rúbrica; rasgo.—*v.t.* blandir, menear.—*v.i.* florecer, medrar.
flout [flaut], *v.t.* mofarse de.
flow [flou], *n.* flujo.—*v.i.* fluir; manar.
flower [flauə], *n.* flor, *f.*; (*fig.*) la flor y la nata.—*v.i.* florecer.
flower-bed ['flauəbed], *n.* macizo, cuadro.
flowering ['flauəriŋ], *a.* floreciente; florido.—*n.* florecimiento; floración, *f.*
flower-pot ['flauəpɔt], *n.* maceta, tiesto.
flowery ['flauəri], *a.* florido.
flowing ['flouiŋ], *a.* corriente; ondeante.
flown [floun], [FLY].
'flu [flu], *n.* (*fam.*) gripe, *f.*
fluctuate ['flʌktjueit], *v.i.* fluctuar.
flue [flu:], *n.* humero; tamo.
fluency ['flu:ənsi], *n.* fluidez, *f.*
fluent ['flu:ənt], *a.* flúido.
fluently ['flu:əntli], *adv.* corrientemente.
fluff [flʌf], *n.* pelusa, borra, plumón, *m.*
fluffy ['flʌfi], *a.* fofo; mullido; velloso.
fluid [flu:id], *a., n.* flúido.
fluke [flu:k], *n.* chiripa.
flung [flʌŋ], [FLING].
fluorescent [fluə'resənt], *a.* fluorescente.
flurry ['flʌri], *n.* ráfaga, racha.—*v.t.* aturrullar.
flush (1) [flʌʃ], *a.* copioso; próspero; robusto.—*n.* rubor, *m.*; bochorno; abundancia; ataque febril, *m.*; floración, *f.*—*v.t.* abochornar; animar; limpiar con un chorro de agua.—*v.i.* abochornarse.
flush (2) [flʌʃ], *a.* rasante, enrasado.—*v.t.* nivelar.
flush (3) [flʌʃ], *v.t.* (*hunt.*) levantar.—*v.i.* fluir precipitadamente.
flush (4) [flʌʃ], *n.* flux, *m.*
fluster ['flʌstə], *n.* aturdimiento.—*v.t.* aturrullar.
flute [flu:t], *n.* flauta.—*v.t.* estriar.
flutter ['flʌtə], *n.* aleteo; agitación, *f.*—*v.t.* sacudir.—*v.i.* aletear.
flux [flʌks], *n.* flujo; mudanza frecuente.
fly [flai], *n.* (*pl.* **flies**) (*ent.*) mosca; bragueta (*de pantalones*); telar, *m.*—*pl.* (*theat.*) bambalina.—*v.t. irr.* (*aer.*) dirigir; hacer volar.—*v.i. irr.* volar; *to* — *over,* trasvolar; *to* — *open,* abrirse de repente.
flying ['flaiiŋ], *a.* volante.—*n.* aviación, *f.*; *with* — *colours,* con banderas desplegadas.
fly-leaf ['flaili:f], *n.* hoja de guarda.
flyover [flaiouvə], *n.* viaducto.
foal [foul], *n.* potro.—*v.i.* parir.
foam [foum], *n.* espuma.—*v.i.* espumar.
focus ['foukəs], *n.* enfoque, *m.*; foco.—*v.t.* enfocar.
fodder ['fɔdə], *n.* forraje, *m.*
foe [fou], *n.* enemigo.
fog [fɔg], *n.* niebla.—*v.t.* empañar, velar.—*v.i.* obscurecer; velarse.
fog-horn ['fɔghɔ:n], *n.* sirena de niebla.
foggy ['fɔgi], *a.* nebuloso, brumoso.
foible ['fɔibl], *n.* lado flaco, flaqueza.
foil (1) [fɔil], *n.* hojuela; contraste.
foil (2) [fɔil], *n.* florete, *m.*—*v.t.* frustrar.

foist [fɔist], *v.t.* vender *o* hacer aceptar algo con engaño (*on*, a).
fold [fould], *n.* pliegue; redil, *m.*—*v.t.* plegar, doblar.—*v.i.* plegarse, doblarse; *to — up*, doblar; doblarse; (*fam.*) fracasar.
folder ['fouldə], *n.* carpeta.
folding ['fouldiŋ], *a.* plegadizo.
foliage ['fouliidʒ], *n.* follaje, *m.*
folio ['fouliou], *a.* en folio.—*n.* folio.
folk [fouk], *n.* gente, *f.*; pueblo.
folk-dance ['foukdɑːns], *n.* baile popular, *m.*
folklore ['fouklɔː], *n.* folklore, *m.*
folk-song ['fouksɔŋ], *n.* canción popular, *f.*
follow ['folou], *v.t.* seguir.—*v.i.* seguir(se); *to — on*, seguir; continuar; *to — up*, reforzar; seguir; *as follows*, como sigue.
follower ['folouə], *n.* secuaz, *m.f.*, seguidor, *m.*
following ['folouiŋ], *a.* siguiente.—*n.* secuaces, *m.pl.*, séquito; aficionados, *m.pl.*
folly ['foli], *n.* locura, desatino.
foment [fou'ment], *v.t.* fomentar.
fond [fɔnd], *a.* cariñoso; (*obs.*) tonto; *— of*, aficionado a; encariñado de.
fondle [fɔndl], *v.t.* acariciar.
font [fɔnt], *n.* (*eccl.*) pila.
food [fuːd], *n.* alimento.
food-stuffs ['fuːdstʌfs], *n.pl.* productos alimenticios, *m.pl.*
fool [fuːl], *a.* (*fam.*) tonto, loco.—*n.* tonto, bobo; bufón, *m.*; *fool's errand*, caza de grillos.—*v.t.* embaucar.—*v.i.* tontear; *to make a — of*, poner en ridículo; *to play the —*, hacer el tonto; *to — with*, frangollar; jugar con.
foolhardy ['fuːlhɑːdi], *a.* temerario; arriesgado.
foolish ['fuːliʃ], *a.* tonto, bobo.
fool-proof ['fuːlpruːf], *a.* a prueba de impericia; cierto, seguro.
foot [fut], *n.* (*pl.* **feet**) pie, *m.*; (*mil.*) infantería; *on —*, de *o* a pie; *to put one's — down*, (*fam.*) imponer la disciplina; *to put one's — in it*, (*fam.*) meter la pata.—*v.t.* pagar (*cuenta*).—*v.i.* (*fam.*) ir a pie.
football ['futbɔːl], *n.* futbol, balompié; balón, *m.*, pelota.
foothold ['futhould], *n.* posición segura, arraigo, pie, *m.*
footing ['futiŋ], *n.* posición segura, arraigo; *on an equal —*, en condiciones iguales; *on a war —*, en pie de guerra.
footlights ['futlaits], *n.* (*theat.*) candilejas.
footman ['futmən], *n.* lacayo.
footmark ['futmɑːk], *n.* huella.
footnote ['futnout], *n.* nota al pie de la página; (*fig.*) glosa, apéndice, *m.*
footpath ['futpɑːθ], *n.* senda, vereda.
foot-print ['futprint], *n.* huella, pisada.
footsore ['futsɔː], *a.* despeado.
footstep ['futstep], *n.* paso.
footwear ['futweə], *n.* calzado.
fop [fɔp], *n.* currutaco, pisaverde, *m.*
for [fɔː], *prep.* para; por; a; de; como; a pesar de.—*conj.* pues, puesto que; *as —*, en cuanto a; *O — ..! ¡* quién tuviera. ... !
forage ['fɔridʒ], *n.* forraje, *m.*—*v.t.*, *v.i.* forrajear.
foray ['fɔrei], *n.* correría.—*v.t.* saquear.
forbade [fɔː'beid *or* -'bæd], [FORBID].
forbear (1) [FOREBEAR].

forbear (2) [fɔː'beə], *v.t.*, *v.i. irr.* abstenerse, detenerse (de).
forbearance [fɔː'beərəns], *n.* paciencia, abstención, *f.*
forbid [fɔː'bid], *v.t. irr.* vedar, prohibir.
forbidding [fɔː'bidiŋ], *a.* adusto; repugnante.
force [fɔːs], *n.* fuerza; *in —*, en grandes números; vigente.—*v.t.* forzar.
forceful ['fɔːsful], *a.* potente, eficaz.
forceps ['fɔːseps], *n. inv.* fórceps, *m. inv.*, pinzas, *f.pl.*
forcible ['fɔːsibl], *a.* violento; eficaz.
ford [fɔːd], *n.* vado.—*v.t.* vadear.
fore [fɔː], *a.* delantero.—*n.* delantera, cabeza. —*prefix.* pre-, ante-.
forearm ['fɔːrɑːm], *n.* antebrazo.
forebear ['fɔːbeə], *n.* antepasado.
forebode [fɔː'boud], *v.t.* presagiar.
foreboding [fɔː'boudiŋ], *n.* presentimiento; presagio.
forecast ['fɔːkɑːst], *n.* pronóstico.—*v.t.*, *v.i. irr.* (*conjug. like* CAST) pronosticar; prever.
forecastle [fouksl], *n.(naut.)* castillo de proa.
forefather ['fɔːfɑːðə], *n.* antepasado.
forefinger ['fɔːfiŋgə], *n.* dedo índice.
forego [fɔː'gou], *v.t. irr.* (*conjug. like* GO) preceder.
foregoing ['fɔːgouiŋ], *a.*, *n.* precedente, anterior.
foregone ['fɔːgɔn], *a.* inevitable (*conclusión*); [FOREGO].
foreground ['fɔːgraund], *n.* primer término.
forehead ['fɔrid], *n.* frente, *f.*
foreign ['fɔrin], *a.* extranjero; ajeno; extraño; *— affairs*, asuntos exteriores; *Foreign Office*, ministerio de asuntos exteriores.
foreigner ['fɔrinə], *n.* extranjero.
forelock ['fɔːlɔk], *n.* copete, mechón, *m.*
foreman ['fɔːmən], *n.* capataz; (*jur.*) presidente, *m.*
foremost ['fɔːmoust], *a.* (más) delantero; primero, principal.—*adv.* primero.
forensic [fɔ'rensik], *a.* forense.
forerunner ['fɔːrʌnə], *n.* precursor, *m.*
foresee [fɔː'siː], *v.t. irr.* (*conjug. like* SEE) prever.
foreshadow [fɔː'ʃædou], *v.t.* presagiar.
foresight ['fɔːsait], *n.* previsión, *f.*, providencia.
forest ['fɔrist], *a.* forestal.—*n.* bosque, *m.*, selva.
forestall [fɔː'stɔːl], *v.t.* prevenir; acopiar, acaparar.
forestry ['fɔristri], *n.* silvicultura, ingeniería forestal.
foretaste ['fɔːteist], *n.* goce anticipado; muestra.
foretell [fɔː'tel], *v.t. irr.* (*conjug. like* TELL) predecir.
forethought ['fɔːθɔːt], *n.* premeditación; consideración, *f.*, prudencia.
forever [fɔr'evə], *adv.* (*U.S.*) [FOR EVER].
foreword ['fɔːwəːd], *n.* prefacio, prólogo.
forfeit ['fɔːfit], *n.* multa, pena; prenda.—*v.t.* perder el derecho a.
forgave [fɔ'geiv] [FORGIVE].
forge [fɔːdʒ], *n.* fragua; herrería.—*v.t.* fraguar, forjar; falsificar; *to — ahead*, ir avanzando.
forgery ['fɔːdʒəri], *n.* falsificación, *f.*
forget [fɔː'get], *v.t. irr.* olvidar, olvidarse de.

forgetful

forgetful [fɔː'getful], *a.* olvidadizo.
forget-me-not [fɔː'getminɔt], *n.* (*bot.*) nomeolvides, *m.sg.*
forgive [fɔː'giv], *v.t. irr.* (*conjug. like* GIVE) perdonar.
forgiveness [fɔː'givnis], *n.* perdón, *m.*
forgo [fɔː'gou], *v.t. irr.* (*conjug. like* GO) privarse de.
forgot(ten) [fɔː'gɔt(n)] [FORGET].
fork [fɔːk], *n.* (*cul.*) tenedor, *m.*; horca, horquilla; (*rail.*) ramal, *m.*; bifurcación, *f.*—*v.t.* ahorquillar.—*v.i.* bifurcarse.
forlorn [fɔː'lɔːn], *a.* desamparado, desesperado.
form [fɔːm], *n.* forma; impreso, papeleta cédula; (*educ.*) clase, *f.*, grado.—*v.t.* formar. —*v.i.* formarse.
formal ['fɔːməl], *a.* formal; solemne.
formality [fɔː'mæliti], *n.* etiqueta; formalidad, *f.*; pormenor, *m.*
formation [fɔː'meiʃən], *n.* formación, *f.*
former ['fɔːmə], *a.* anterior; antiguo; *the* —, aquél.
formidable ['fɔːmidəbl], *a.* formidable.
formula ['fɔːmjulə], *n.* fórmula.
forsake [fɔː'seik], *v.t. irr.* abandonar, dejar.
forsaken [fɔː'seikən], **forsook** [fɔː'suk] [FORSAKE].
fort [fɔːt], *n.* fortaleza, fortín, *m.*
forth [fɔːθ], *adv.* adelante; fuera; en adelante; *and so* —, y así sucesivamente.
forthcoming ['fɔːθkʌmiŋ], *a.* próximo; dispuesto.
forthwith [fɔːθ'wiθ], *adv.* sin dilación, *f.*
fortieth [fɔː'tiiθ], *a., n.* cuadragésimo; cuarentavo.
fortification [fɔːtifi'keiʃən], *n.* fortificación, *f.*
fortify ['fɔːtifai], *v.t.* fortificar; fortalecer.
fortitude ['fɔːtitjuːd], *n.* fortaleza, firmeza.
fortnight ['fɔːtnait], *n.* quincena, quince días.
fortress ['fɔːtris], *n.* fortaleza.
fortuitous [fɔː'tjuːitəs], *a.* fortuito.
fortunate ['fɔːtjunit], *a.* afortunado.
fortune ['fɔːtjuːn], *n.* fortuna.
fortune-teller ['fɔːtjuːn'telə], *n.* adivino sortílego.
forty ['fɔːti], *a., n.* cuarenta, *m.*
forum ['fɔːrəm], *n.* foro, plaza; juzgado.
forward ['fɔːwəd], *a.* delantero; precoz; adelantado; atrevido.—*n.* delantero.—*v.t.* hacer seguir (*carta*); promover.—*adv.* adelante; en adelante.
forwards ['fɔːwədz], *adv.* (hacia) adelante.
fossil ['fɔsil], *a., n.* fósil, *m.*
foster ['fɔstə], *a.* adoptivo.—*v.t.* criar; fomentar.
fought [fɔːt], [FIGHT].
foul [faul], *a.* sucio, asqueroso; obsceno; fétido; vil; atroz; obstruido; — *play*, traición, *f.*, juego sucio.—*n.* falta, juego sucio.—*v.t.* enredar; obstruir; ensuciar; *to fall — of*, enredarse con *o* en.
foul-mouthed ['faulmauðd], *a.* deslenguado.
found (1) [faund], *v.t.* fundar.
found (2) [faund], *v.t.* (*metal*) fundir.
found (3) [faund], [FIND].
foundation [faun'deiʃən], *n.* fundamento; cimiento; fundación, *f.*
foundling ['faundliŋ], *n.* expósito.
foundry ['faundri], *n.* fundición, *f.*, fundería.

fount [faunt] (*poet.*), **fountain** ['fauntin], *n.* fuente, *f.*
fountain-pen ['fauntin'pen], *n.* pluma estilográfica.
four [fɔː], *a., n.* cuatro; *on all fours*, a gatas.
fourteen [fɔː'tiːn], *a., n.* catorce, *m.*
fourteenth [fɔː'tiːnθ], *a., n.* decimo-cuarto, catorzavo; catorce (*en las fechas*).
fourth [fɔːθ], *a.* cuarto.—*n.* cuarto; cuatro (*en las fechas*); (*mus.*) cuarta.
fowl [faul], *n.* ave, *f.*; gallina, gallo.—*n.pl.* aves en general.
fox [fɔks], *n.* (*zool., fig.*) zorro.—*v.t.* confundir.
foxglove ['fɔksglʌv], *n.* (*bot.*) dedalera.
foxy ['fɔksi], *a.* zorruno; taimado.
foyer ['fɔiei], *n.* salón de entrada *o* descanso, zaguán, *m.*
fracas ['frækɑː], *n.* riña, gresca.
fraction ['frækʃən], *n.* fracción, *f.*, quebrado.
fracture ['fræktʃə], *n.* fractura, rotura.—*v.t.* fracturar.—*v.i.* -se.
fragile ['frædʒail], *a.* frágil.
fragment ['frægmənt], *n.* fragmento.
fragrance ['freigrəns], *n.* fragancia.
fragrant ['freigrənt], *a.* fragante.
frail [freil], *a.* frágil, delicado, débil.
frailty ['freilti], *n.* debilidad, *f.*
frame [freim], *n.* marco; armazón, *f.*; armadura; talle, *m.*; estado; sistema, *m.*—*v.t.* formar, fraguar; enmarcar, colocar en marco; servir de marco a; (*fam.*) incriminar (*a un inocente*).
framework ['freimwɔːk], *n.* armadura, armazón, *f.*
franc [fræŋk], *n.* franco.
France [frɑːns], *n.* Francia.
franchise ['fræntʃaiz], *n.* sufragio; franquicia.
Francis ['frɑːnsis], *n.* Francisco.
Franciscan [fræn'siskən], *a., n.* franciscano.
frank [fræŋk], *a.* franco.—*v.t.* franquear.
frankincense ['fræŋkinsens], *n.* olíbano, incienso.
frankness ['fræŋknis], *n.* franqueza.
frantic ['fræntik], *a.* frenético.
fraternal [frə'təːnl], *a.* fraternal.
fraternize ['frætənaiz], *v.i.* fraternizar.
fraud [frɔːd], *n.* fraude, *m.*, timo; (*fam.*) tramposo.
fraudulent ['frɔːdjulənt], *a.* fraudulento.
fraught [frɔːt], *a.* cargado, lleno (*with*, de).
fray (1) [frei], *n.* contienda.
fray (2) [frei], *v.t.* raer, rozar.—*v.i.* raerse; deshilacharse.
freak [friːk], *a.* monstruoso; extraordinario.— *n.* rareza, fenómeno, monstruosidad, *f.*
freakish ['friːkiʃ], *a.* raro, monstruoso.
freckle [frekl], *n.* peca.—*v.t.* motear.
freckly ['frekli], *a.* pecoso.
free [friː], *a.* libre; gratis; liberal; — *and easy*, desenvuelto; — *rein*, rienda suelta. —*adv.* gratis; libremente.—*v.t.* libertar, librar; exentar.
freebooter ['friːbuːtə], *n.* pirata, *m.*; filibustero.
freedom ['friːdəm], *n.* libertad, *f.*
free-for-all ['friːfɔːr'ɔːl], *n.* sarracina.
freehold ['friːhould], *n.* (*jur.*) feudo franco.
freelance ['friːlɑːns], *a.* independiente.—*n.* mercenario.
Freemason ['friːmeisən], *n.* francmasón, *m.*

furtive

freeze [fri:z], *n.* helada.—*v.t.* irr. helar; congelar.—*v.i.* irr. helarse.

freight [freit], *n.* carga; flete, *m.*; mercancías, *f.pl.*

French [frentʃ], *a.*, *n.* francés; — *bean*, judía verde; — *window(s)*, ventana con puerta.

Frenchman ['frentʃmən], *n.* francés, *m.*

Frenchwoman ['frentʃwumən], *n.* francesa.

frenzy ['frenzi], *n.* frenesí, *m.*

frequency ['fri:kwənsi], *n.* frecuencia.

frequent ['fri:kwənt], *a.* frecuente.—[fri'kwent], *v.t.* frecuentar.

fresh [freʃ], *a.* fresco; nuevo; dulce (*agua*); puro; novicio; (*fam.*) fresco, atrevido.

freshen [freʃn], *v.t.* refrescar.—*v.i.* -se.

freshness ['freʃnis], *n.* pureza; frescura.

fret (1) [fret], *n.* calado; (*mus.*) traste, *m.*—*v.t.* recamar; adornar con calados.

fret (2) [fret], *n.* roce, *m*; enfado.—*v.t.* rozar; raer.—*v.i.* apurarse, incomodarse; raerse.

fretful ['fretful], *a.* mohíno, descontentadizo.

fretwork ['fretwə:k], *n.* calado.

friar [fraiə], *n.* fraile, *m.*

friary ['fraiəri], *n.* convento de frailes.

friction ['frikʃən], *n.* fricción, *f.*; rozamiento.

Friday ['fraidei], *n.* viernes, *m. inv.*

fried [fraid], *a.* frito.

friend [frend], *n.* amigo.—*interj.* (*mil.*) gente (*f.*) de paz.

friendly ['frendli], *a.* amistoso, amigable; benévolo.

friendship ['frendʃip], *n.* amistad, *f.*

frieze [fri:z], *n.* (*arch.*) friso.

frigate ['frigət], *n.* fragata.

fright [frait], *n.* susto.

frighten [fraitn], *v.t.* asustar; espantar; *to be frightened*, tener miedo.

frightful ['fraitful], *a.* espantoso.

frigid ['fridʒid], *a.* frío.

frill [fril], *n.* escarola, lechuga; (*fam.*) ringorrango.—*v.t.* escarolar.

fringe [frindʒ], *n.* orla, franja; borde, *m.*—*v.t.* orlar.

frisk [frisk], *v.t.* (*fam.*) cachear.—*v.i.* retozar.

fritter ['fritə], *n.* frisuelo, buñuelo.—*v.t.* malgastar, desperdiciar (*away*).

frivolous ['frivələs], *a.* frívolo.

frock [frɔk], *n.* vestido.

frock-coat ['frɔk'kout], *n.* levita.

frog [frɔg], *n.* rana; — *in the throat*, carraspera.

frogman ['frɔgmən], *n.* hombre-rana, *m.*

frolic ['frɔlik], *n.* travesura, retozo; jaleo.—*v.i.* retozar, loquear.

from [frɔm], *prep.* de; desde; por; de parte de; según.

front [frʌnt], *a.* delantero; *in* —, delante, en frente (*of*, de); — *door*, puerta principal, puerta de la calle.—*n.* frente, *m. o f.*; fachada; principio; delantera; pechera (*de vestido*); (*mil.*) frente, *m.*; apariencia falsa.

frontier ['frʌntjə], *a.* fronterizo.—*n.* frontera.

frost [frɔst], *n.* helada, escarcha.—*v.t.* escarchar.

froth [frɔθ], *n.* espuma.—*v.i.* espum(aje)ar.

frown [fraun], *n.* ceño.—*v.i.* fruncir el entrecejo, ponerse ceñudo; *to* — *at o on*, mirar con ceño.

froze(n) [frouz(n)] [FREEZE].

frugal ['fru:gəl], *a.* frugal, sobrio.

fruit [fru:t], *n.* fruta; frutas, *f.pl.*; (*fig.*) fruto.—*v.i.* dar fruto.

fruitful ['fru:tful], *a.* fructuoso, provechoso.

fruition [fru:'iʃən], *n.* fruición, *f.*, goce, *m.*; cumplimiento.

fruitless ['fru:tlis], *a.* infructuoso, vano.

frumpish ['frʌmpiʃ], *a.* desaliñado.

frustrate ['frʌstreit], *v.t.* frustrar.

frustration [frʌs'treiʃən], *n.* frustración, *f.*; desengaño.

fry [frai], *n.* fritada; pececillo(s).—*v.t.* freír.

frying-pan ['fraiiŋpæn], *n.* sartén, *f.*

fuel ['fjuəl], *n.* combustible, *m.*; (*fig.*) pábulo.—*v.t.* proveer de combustible.

fugitive ['fju:dʒitiv], *a.*, *n.* fugitivo; prófugo.

fugue [fju:g], *n.* fuga.

fulcrum ['fʌlkrəm], *n.* (*pl.* -crums *o* -cra) fulcro.

fulfil [ful'fil], *v.t.* cumplir; llenar; colmar; realizar.

fulfilment [ful'filmənt], *n.* cumplimiento; realización, *f.*

full [ful], *a.* lleno; amplio; completo (*vehículo*); pleno; fuerte; *in* —, por completo; *to the* —, enteramente; — *well*, muy bien; — *dress*, traje (*m.*) de etiqueta; uniforme (*m.*) de gala.

full-grown ['fulgroun], *n.* maduro.

fulness ['fulnis], *n.* plenitud, *f.*, hartura.

fulsome ['fulsəm], *a.* insincero; craso; repugnante.

fumble [fʌmbl], *v.i.* titubear; obrar con desmaña; buscar con las manos.

fume [fju:m], *n.* vaho; tufo.—*v.i.* vahear; humear; (*fig.*) encolerizarse.

fumigate ['fju:migeit], *v.t.* fumigar.

fun [fʌn], *n.* broma, diversión, *f.*, chacota, burla; *for o in* —, por gusto; en broma, de burlas; *to have* —, divertirse; *to make* — *of*, burlarse de.

function ['fʌŋkʃən], *n.* función, *f.*—*v.i.* funcionar.

fund [fʌnd], *n.* fondo.

fundamental [fʌndə'mentl], *a.* fundamental.—*n.pl.* fundamentos, *m.pl.*

funeral ['fju:nərəl], *a.* funerario.—*n.* funeral(es), *m.pl.*

funereal [fju:'niəriəl], *a.* fúnebre.

fungus ['fʌŋgəs], *n.* (*pl.* fungi) hongo.

funk [fʌŋk], *n.* (*fam.*) jindama.—*v.t.*, *v.i.* perder *o* evitar por cobardía.

funnel [fʌnl], *n.* embudo; (*naut.*) chimenea.

funny ['fʌni], *a.* divertido, gracioso, cómico; (*fam.*) raro;— *bone*, hueso de la alegría; *to be* —, tener gracia; *to seem* —, hacer gracia (*to*, a).

fur [fə:], *n.* piel, *f.*; (*fig.*) sarro.

furious ['fju:riəs], *a.* furioso.

furlong ['fə:lɔŋ], *n.* estadio.

furlough ['fə:lou], *n.* (*U.S. mil.*) licencia.

furnace ['fə:nis], *n.* horno.

furnish ['fə:niʃ], *v.t.* amueblar; proporcionar.

furniture ['fə:nitʃə], *n.* muebles, *m.pl.*; mueblaje, *m.*

furrow ['farou], *n.* surco.—*v.t.* surcar.

further ['fə:ðə], *a.* adicional; más lejano.—*v.t.* fomentar, promover.—*adv.* más lejos; además.

furthermore [fə:ðə'mɔ:], *adv.* además.

furthermost ['fə:ðəmoust], **furthest** ['fə:ðist], *a.*, *adv.* más lejano.

furtive ['fə:tiv], *a.* furtivo.

285

fury

fury ['fjuːri], *n.* furia.
furze [fɔːz], *n.* aulaga; retama.
fuse [fjuːz], *n.* mecha; (*elec.*) fundible, *m.—v.t.* fundir.*—v.i.* fundirse.
fuselage ['fjuːzilɑːʒ], *n.* fuselaje, *m.*
fusilier [fjuːziˈliə], *n.* fusilero.
fusion ['fjuːʒən], *n.* fusión, *f.*
fuss [fʌs], *n.* bulla, ajetreo; alharaca, hazañería.*—v.t.* mimar; molestar.*—v.i.* zangolotear, hacer alharacas; **to make a —**, armar un alboroto; hacer fiestas (*of*, a).
fussy ['fʌsi], *a.* remilgado, melindroso; exigente; molesto.
fusty ['fʌsti], *a.* mohoso, rancio.
futile ['fjuːtil], *a.* vano, inútil; fútil, frívolo.
future ['fjuːtʃə], *a.* venidero, futuro.*—n.* provenir, *m.,* futuro.
fuzzy ['fʌzi], *a.* borroso, velloso.

G

G, g [dʒiː], *n.* séptima letra del alfabeto inglés; **G,** (*mus.*) so.
gab [gæb], *n.* **the gift of the —,** (*fam.*) labia, facundia.
gabardine ['gæbədiːn], *n.* gabardina.
gabble [gæbl], *n.* cotorreo.*—v.i.* picotear.
gable [geibl], *n.* faldón, gablete, *m.*
gad [gæd], *v.i.* pindonguear.
gadabout ['gædəbaut], *n.* corretón, cantonero.
gadfly ['gædflai], *n.* tábano.
gadget ['gædʒit], *n.* (*fam.*) adminículo, dispositivo.
gag [gæg], *n.* mordaza; (*fam., U.S.*) chiste, *m.*—*v.t.* amordazar.
gage [geidʒ], *n.* prenda. [GAUGE].
gaiety ['geiiti], *n.* alegría.
gaily ['geili], *adv.* alegremente.
gain [gein], *n.* ganancia; provecho; aumento, incremento.*—v.t.* ganar.*—v.i.* ganar, avanzar; adelantarse (*reloj*); **to — on,** alcanzar.
gainsay [gein'sei], *v.t. irr.* (*conjug. like* SAY) contradecir.
gait [geit], *n.* paso, modo de andar.
gaiter ['geitə], *n.* botina; polaina.
gala ['gɑːlə], *n.* fiesta, gala.
galaxy ['gæləksi], *n.* galaxia; grupo brillante.
gale [geil], *n.* ventarrón, *m.*
Galician [gə'liʃiən], *a., n.* gallego; galiciano.
Galilean [gæli'liːən], *a., n.* galileo.
gall (1) [gɔːl], *n.* hiel, *f.*; (*fig.*) rencor, *m.,* encono.
gall (2) [gɔːl], *n.* (*bot.*) agalla; rozadura; (*fig.*) descaro.*—v.t.* irritar; amargar.
gallant ['gælənt], *a.* galante, cortés; gallardo, valiente.*—n.* galán, *m.*
gallantry ['gæləntri], *n.* gallardía; galantería; valentía.
galleon ['gæliən], *n.* galeón, *m.*
gallery ['gæləri], *n.* galería; pasadizo; balcón, *m.*
galley ['gæli], *n.* (*print., naut.*) galera.
galley-slave ['gæli'sleiv], *n.* galeote, *m.*; esclavo.
Gallicism ['gælisizəm], *n.* galicismo.
Gallicize ['gælisaiz], *v.t.* afrancesar.

galling ['gɔːliŋ], *a.* molesto, irritante.
gallon ['gælən], *n.* galón, *m.*
gallop ['gæləp], *n.* galope, *m.—v.i.* galopar.
gallows ['gælouz], *n. pl.* horca.
galore [gə'lɔː], *adv.* en abundancia.
galvanize ['gælvənaiz], *v.t.* galvanizar.
gambit ['gæmbit], *n.* gambito; táctica.
gamble [gæmbl], *n.* juego; riesgo.*—v.t.* jugar, aventurar.*—v.i.* jugar; especular.
gambler ['gæmblə], *n.* jugador, tahur, *m.*
gambling [gæmbliŋ], *n.* juego; especulación, *f.*
gambol ['gæmbəl], *n.* cabriola.*—v.i.* cabriolar, brincar.
game [geim], *a.* [GAMMY]; listo, animoso.*—n.* juego; (*sport*) partido; caza; **big —,** caza mayor.*—pl.* deportes, *m.pl.*
game-keeper ['geimkiːpə], *n.* guardamonte, *m.*
gammon ['gæmən], *n.* jamón, *m.*
gammy ['gæmi], *a.* (*fam.*) cojo.
gamp [gæmp], *n.* (*fam.*) paraguas, *m.sg.*
gamut ['gæmət], *n.* gama.
gander ['gændə], *n.* ganso; (*fam.*) mirada, ojeada.
gang [gæŋ], *n.* pandilla; cuadrilla.*—v.i.* apandillar; acometer (**up on,** en pandilla).
gangster ['gæŋstə], *n.* pandillero, gángster, *m.*
gangway ['gæŋwei], *n.* pasarela, pasamano.
gaol [dʒeil], *n.* cárcel, *f.—v.t.* encarcelar.
gaoler ['dʒeilə], *n.* carcelero.
gap [gæp], *n.* laguna; buco, buquete, *m.*
gape [geip], *v.i.* boquear; abrirse mucho; embobarse (*at*, de).
garage [gə'rɑːʒ], *n.* garaje, *m.—v.t.* poner en el garaje.
garb [gɑːb], *n.* vestidura.
garbage ['gɑːbidʒ], *n.* (*U.S.*) basura; **— can, — man,** (*U.S.*) [DUSTBIN, DUSTMAN].
garble [gɑːbl], *v.t.* mutilar, pervertir.
garden [gɑːdn], *n.* jardín (*flores*), *m.*; huerto (*legumbres*); huerta (*área fértil*); **common or —,** ordinario, corriente.*—v.t., v.i.* cultivar.
gardener ['gɑːdnə], *n.* jardinero; hortelano.
gardening ['gɑːdniŋ], *n.* jardinería; horticultura.
gargle ['gɑːgəl], *n.* gargarismo.*—v.i.* gargarizar.
garish ['gɛəriʃ], *a.* charro, ostentoso.
garland ['gɑːlənd], *n.* guirnalda.
garlic ['gɑːlik], *n.* ajo.
garment ['gɑːmənt], *n.* prenda de vestir.
garner ['gɑːnə], *v.t.* entrojar; acopiar.
garnet ['gɑːnit], *n.* granate, *m.*
garnish ['gɑːniʃ], *v.t.* adornar.
garret ['gærit], *n.* buharda, desván, *m.*
garrison ['gærisən], *n.* guarnición, *f.—v.t.* guarnicionar.
garrulous ['gæruləs], *a.* gárrulo.
garter ['gɑːtə], *n.* liga; (*her.*) jarretera.
gas [gæs], *n.* gas, *m.*; (*U.S.*) gasolina; (*fam.*) parloteo; **— station,** (*U.S.*) [SERVICE STATION].*—v.t.* atacar o matar con gas.*—v.i.* (*fam.*) parlotear.
gas-bag ['gæsbæg], *n.* (*fam.*) churrullero.
gaseous ['geisiəs], *a.* gaseoso.
gas-fitter ['gæs'fitə], *n.* gasista, *m.*
gash [gæʃ], *n.* herida, cuchillada.*—v.t.* herir, acuchillar.
gas-holder ['gæs'houldə], *n.* gasómetro.
gas-mask ['gæsmɑːsk], *n.* careta antigás.

286

gas-meter ['gæsmi:tə], *n.* contador (*m.*) de gas.
gasolene, gasoline ['gæsəli:n], *n.* (*U.S.*) gasolina. **[petrol].**
gasometer [gæ'sɔmitə], *n.* gasómetro.
gasp [gɑ:sp], *n.* boqueada; grito sofocado; anhelo entrecortado.—*v.i.* boquear, sofocarse.
gas-stove ['gæs'stouv], *n.* cocina de gas.
gastric ['gæstrik], *a.* gástrico.
gas-works ['gæswɔ:ks], *n.* fábrica de gas.
gate [geit], *n.* puerta, portillo, entrada; cancela; (*sport*) entrada, concurrencia.
gateway ['geitwei], *n.* (*fig.*) entrada.
gather ['gæðə], *v.t.* recoger; coger; cobrar; colegir; fruncir (*costura*).—*v.i.* reunirse; acumularse.
gathering ['gæðəriŋ], *n.* reunión; acumulación, *f.*
gaudy ['gɔ:di], *a.* chillón, cursi.
gauge [geidʒ], *n.* calibrador, calibre *m.*; tamaño; norma; (*rail.*) ancho de la vía.—*v.t.* calibrar; aforar; graduar; calcular.
Gaul [gɔ:l], *n.* galo (*persona*); Galia (*país*).
gaunt [gɔ:nt], *a.* desvaído, descarnado; sombrío.
gauntlet ['gɔ:ntlit], *n.* guantelete, *m.*; **to run the —**, correr (las) baquetas.
gauze [gɔ:z], *n.* gasa; cendal, *m.*
gave [geiv] [GIVE].
gawk [gɔ:k], *n.* (*fam.*) papamoscas, *m.sg.*—*v.i.* (*fam.*) papar moscas.
gawky ['gɔ:ki], *a.* desgarbado; tonto.
gay [gei], *a.* alegre, festivo; ligero.
gaze [geiz], *n.* mirada fija.—*v.i.* mirar con fijeza (*at*).
gazelle [gə'zel], *n.* gacela.
gazette [gə'zet], *n.* gaceta.
gazetteer [gæze'tiə], *n.* gacetero; diccionario geográfico.
gear [giə], *n.* (*mech.*) engranaje, *m.*; marcha; aparejo, pertrechos, *m.pl.*; rueda dentada. *v.t.*—engranar; encajar.
gear-box ['giəbɔks], *n.* caja de engranajes, cárter, *m.*; caja de velocidades.
gear-change ['giətʃeindʒ], *n.* cambio de marchas.
gear-lever ['giə'li:və], *n.* palanca de cambio.
geese [gi:s] [GOOSE].
gelatine ['dʒeləti:n], *n.* gelatina.
gem [dʒem], *n.* alhaja, joya, gema.
gender ['dʒendə], *n.* género; sexo.
gene [dʒi:n], *n.* gen, *m.*
genealogy [dʒi:ni'ælədʒi], *n.* genealogía.
general ['dʒenərəl], *n.*, *a.* general, *m.*
generalize ['dʒenrəlaiz], *v.t.*, *v.i.* generalizar.
generate ['dʒenəreit], *a.* generar; engendrar.
generation [dʒenə'reiʃən], *n.* generación, *f.*
generator ['dʒenəreitə], *n.* generador, *m.*
generic [dʒə'nerik], *a.* genérico.
generosity [dʒenə'rɔsiti], *n.* generosidad, *f.*
generous ['dʒenərəs], *a.* generoso; amplio.
genesis ['dʒenisis], *n.* génesis, *m.*
genetic [dʒə'netik], *a.* genético.—*n.pl.* genética.
Geneva [dʒi'ni:və], *n.* Ginebra.
genial ['dʒi:njəl], *a.* afable, cordial.
genital ['dʒenitl], *a.*, *n.* genital, *m.*
genitive ['dʒenitiv], *a.*, *n.* genitivo.
genius ['dʒi:niəs], *n.* genio.
genre [ʒɑ̃:r], *n.* (*lit.*) género.

genteel [dʒen'ti:l], *a.* señoril, gentil.
gentile ['dʒentail], *a.*, *n.* gentil, pagano.
gentle [dʒentl], *a.* dulce, suave; blando, benévolo; ligero.
gentlefolk ['dʒentlfouk], *n.* gente bien nacida.
gentleman ['dʒentlmən], *n.* caballero.
gentlemanly ['dʒentlmənli], *a.* caballeroso.
gentleness ['dʒentlnis], *n.* dulzura, suavidad, *f.*
gentry ['dʒentri], *n.* gente bien nacida; (*fam.*) gente, *f.*
genuine ['dʒenjuin], *a.* genuino; sincero; auténtico.
genus ['dʒi:nəs], *n.* (*pl.* **genera** ['dʒenərə]) género.
geographer [dʒi'ɔgrəfə], *n.* geógrafo.
geographic(al) [dʒiou'græfik(əl)], *a.* geográfico.
geography [dʒi'ɔgrəfi], *n.* geografía.
geological [dʒiou'lɔdʒikəl], *a.* geológico.
geologist [dʒi'ɔlədʒist], *n.* geólogo.
geology [dʒi'ɔlədʒi], *n.* geología.
geometry [dʒi'ɔmətri], *n.* geometría.
geometric [dʒiou'metrik], *a.* geométrico.
George [dʒɔ:dʒ], *n.* Jorge, *m.*
germ [dʒə:m], *n.* germen, *m.*; **— warfare**, guerra bacteriológica.
German ['dʒə:mən], *a.*, *n.* alemán, *m.*; **— measles**, rubéola.
german ['dʒə:mən], *a.* carnal.
germane [dʒə:'mein], *a.* afín, relacionado.
Germany ['dʒə:məni], *n.* Alemania.
germinate ['dʒə:mineit], *v.i.* germinar.
gesticulate [dʒes'tikjuleit], *v.i.* accionar, hacer ademanes.
gesture ['dʒestʃə], *n.* gesto, ademán, *m.*; seña; muestra.
get [get], *v.t. irr.* obtener, lograr; ir por, traer; hacer; (*fam.*) comprender.—*v.i.* hacerse, ponerse; (*fam.*) largarse; lograr pasar (**by, over, through**); **to — about**, divulgarse; reponerse y levantarse; **to — along**, largarse; ir tirando; portarse; congeniar (**with**, con); **to — at**, llegar a; (*fam.*) meterse con; **to — away**, escapar(se); partir; **to — back**, regresar, volver; **to — better**, mejorar(se); **to — by**, (*fam.*) arreglárselas; **to — down**, bajar; **to — in**, entrar en; meter; llegar; **to — off**, bajar (de); irse, escapar; **to — on**, subir (a); progresar; congeniar (**with**, con); **to — out**, salir, lograr salir; dejar (**of**); publicar(se); sacar; **to — over**, pasar por encima de; recobrarse de; vencer; **to — to**, hacer, persuadir a; **to — up**, levantarse, montar, armar; **to have got**, tener, poseer; **to have got to**, tener que; **to — angry, dark, tired** etc., enfadarse, obscurecer, cansarse etc.
get-away ['getəwei], *n.* escapatoria; arranque, *m.*
get-together ['gettə'geðə], *n.* reunión, *f.*, tertulia.
gewgaw ['gju:gɔ:], *n.* chuchería.
geyser ['gi:zə], *n.* géiser, *m.*
ghastly ['gɑ:stli], *a.* cadavérico; horrible.
gherkin ['gə:kin], *n.* pepinillo.
ghost [goust], *n.* fantasma, *m.*; espectro.
ghost-writer ['goustraitə], *n.* colaborador anónimo.
giant ['dʒaiənt], *a.* gigantesco.—*n.* gigante, *m.*
gibberish ['dʒibəriʃ], *n.* jerigonza.
gibbet ['dʒibit], *n.* horca, patíbulo.

gibe [dʒaib], *n.* pulla, mofa.—*v.i.* mofarse (*at*, de).
giblets ['dʒiblits], *n.pl.* menudillos, *m.pl.*
giddiness ['gidinis], *n.* vértigo; veleidad, *f.*
giddy ['gidi], *a.* vertiginoso; casquivano.
gift [gift], *n.* regalo; (*fig.*) dote, *f.*; prenda.
gifted ['giftid], *a.* talentoso; dotado (*with*, de).
gigantic [dʒai'gæntik], *a.* gigantesco.
giggle [gigl], *n.* risilla tonta.—*v.i.* reírse tontamente.
gild [gild], *v.t.* dorar.
gill (1) [gil], *n.* (*ichth.*) agalla.
gill (2) [dʒil], *n.* cuarto de pinta líquida.
gilt [gilt], *a., n.* dorado.
gimlet [gimlit], *n.* barrena de mano.
gin (1) [dʒin], *n.* ginebra (*bebida*).
gin (2) [dʒin], *n.* desmotadora.
ginger ['dʒindʒə], *n.* jengibre, *m.*
gingerly ['dʒindʒəli], *a.* cauteloso.—*adv.* con cautela.
gipsy ['dʒipsi], *a., n.* gitano.
gird [gə:d], *v.t.* ceñir.
girder ['gə:də], *n.* viga de acero.
girdle [gə:dl], *n.* ceñidor; faja, corsé, *m.*—*v.t.* ceñir.
girl [gə:l], *n.* chica; niña; (*fam.*) novia; — **scout**, niña exploradora.
girth [gə:θ], *n.* cincha; circunferencia.
gist [dʒist], *n.* substancia, enjundia.
give [giv], *v.t. irr.* dar; pronunciar (*oración*); otorgar, conceder; ofrecer; ocasionar; dedicar; **to — away**, regalar; tracionar, revelar; **to — back**, devolver; **to give in**, entregar; **to — out**, divulgar; **to — up**, entregar; abandonar.—*v.i. irr.* dar de sí; **to — in**, rendirse, ceder; hundirse; **to — out**, agotarse; **to — up**, rendirse.
give-and-take ['givənd'teik], *n.* tolerancia mutua.
given [givn] [GIVE]
gizzard ['gizəd], *n.* molleja.
glacial ['gleifjəl], *a.* glacial.
glacier ['glæsiə], *n.* glaciar, *m.*, helero.
glad [glæd], *a.* alegre, gozoso, contento.
gladden [glædn], *v.t.* alegrar.
glade [gleid], *n.* claro (*en un bosque*).
gladiator ['glædieitə], *n.* gladiador, *m.*
gladly ['glædli], *adv.* con mucho gusto.
glamorous ['glæmərəs], *a.* bello, lindo.
glamour ['glæmə], *n.* belleza, encanto.
glance [gla:ns], *n.* ojeada, vistazo.—*v.i.* echar un vistazo (*at*, a); ojear (*at*); desviarse (*golpes*) de soslayo (*off*).
gland [glænd], *n.* glándula.
glare [glɛə], *n.* brillo, fulgor, resplandor, *m.*; deslumbramiento; mirada indignada.—*v.i.* relumbrar; echar miradas de indignación.
glass [gla:s], *n.* vidrio; vaso, copa (*vasija*); cristal (*ventana*), *m.*; lente, *m.* o *f.*; espejo; — **case**, vitrina.—*pl.* gafas, *f.pl.*, anteojos, *m.pl.*
glass-house ['gla:shaus], *n.* invernáculo; (*mil.*) cárcel, *f.*
glassy ['gla:si], *a.* vidrioso.
glaze [gleiz], *n.* barniz, esmalte, lustre, *m.*—*v.t.* vidriar; esmaltar.
glazier ['gleiziə], *n.* vidriero.
gleam [gli:m], *n.* destello, centelleo; rayo.—*v.i.* lucir, brillar tenuemente.
glean [gli:n], *v.t.* espigar.
glee [gli:], *n.* júbilo, gozo, alegría.

gleeful ['gli:ful], *a.* jubiloso, gozoso, alegre.
glen [glen], *n.* hocino, vallecito.
glib [glib], *a.* voluble, locuaz; engañoso.
glide [glaid], *n.* deslizamiento; (*aer.*) planeo.—*v.i.* deslizarse; (*aer.*) planear.
glider ['glaidə], *n.* (*aer.*) planeador, *m.*
glimmer ['glimə], *n.* vislumbre, *m.*; luz débil, *f.*—*v.i.* brillar tenuemente.
glimpse [glimps], *n.* vislumbre, *m.*; apariencia ligera.—*v.t.* vislumbrar.
glint [glint], *n.* destello, relumbrón, *m.*—*v.i.* brillar, reflejar.
glitter ['glitə], *n.* resplandor; oropel, *m.*—*v.i.* centellear, relucir.
gloat [glout], *v.i.* relamerse, deleitarse (*over*, en).
global ['gloubəl], *a.* global.
globe [gloub], *n.* globo.
globe-trotter ['gloubtrotə], *n.* trotamundos, *m.sg.*
globule ['globju:l], *n.* glóbulo.
gloom ['glu:m], *n.* tinieblas, *f.pl.*, lobreguez, *f.*; tristeza.
gloomy ['glu:mi], *a.* tenebroso, lóbrego; triste, tétrico.
glorify ['glɔ:rifai], *v.t.* glorificar.
glorious ['glɔ:riəs], *a.* glorioso.
glory ['glɔ:ri], *n.* gloria.—*v.i.* gloriarse (*in*, de).
gloss [glɔs], *n.* lustre, barniz, *m.*; glosa.—*v.t.* satinar, lustrar; paliar; glosar; **to — over**, encubrir, paliar.
glossary ['glɔsəri], *n.* glosario.
glossy ['glɔsi], *a.* lustroso, satinado; especioso.
glove [glʌv], *n.* guante, *m.*; **to be hand in — with**, ser uña y carne, ser compinches.
glow [glou], *n.* vivo; resplandor, *m.*, brillo; viveza.—*v.i.* relucir, brillar, arder.
glow-worm ['glouwə:m], *n.* luciérnaga.
glucose ['glu:kous], *n.* glucosa.
glue [glu:], *n.* cola.—*v.t.* encolar, pegar.
glum [glʌm], *a.* moroso, tétrico, hosco.
glut [glʌt], *n.* exceso, plétora.—*v.t.* hartar, saturar; inundar (*mercado*).
glutton [glʌtn], *n.* glotón, *m.*
gluttonous ['glʌtnəs], *a.* glotón.
gluttony ['glʌtəni], *n.* glotonería; gula (*pecado*).
glycerine ['glisəri:n], *n.* glicerina.
gnarled [nɑ:ld], *a.* nudoso, retorcido.
gnash [næʃ], *v.t., v.i.* rechinar.
gnat [næt], *n.* (*ent.*) jenjén, *m.*
gnaw [nɔ:], *v.t.* roer.
gnome [noum], *n.* trasgo, gnomo.
go [gou], *n.* empuje, *m.*, energía; ida; jugada; (*fam.*) moda; ensayo.—*v.i.* ir, irse; marchar; funcionar; pasar; andar; volverse; desaparecer; caer, sentar; decirse; **to — away**, irse, marcharse; **to — by**, seguir; pasar por; **to — in**, entrar en; **to — in for**, interesarse en; **to — into**, entrar en; investigar; **to — off**, irse, alejarse; estallar; tener lugar; **to — on**, continuar; **to — out**, salir; apagarse; **to — over**, pasar por encima de; revisar; **to — with**, hacer juego con; **to — without**, dejar; pasarse sin; privarse de.
goad [goud], *n.* aguijón, *m.*—*v.t.* aguijonear.
goal [goul], *n.* meta; (*sport*) meta, portería; tanto, gol, *m.*
goal-keeper ['goulki:pə], *n.* portero, guarda-meta, *m.*
goat [gout], *n.* cabra; **billy —**, macho cabrío.

grapefruit

gobble ['gɔbl], *n.* gluglú, *m.—v.t.* engullir.—*v.i.* gluglutear.
go-between ['goubitwi:n], *n.* medianero; alcahuete, *m.*
goblet ['gɔblit], *n.* copa.
goblin ['gɔblin], *n.* trasgo, duende, *m.*
God [gɔd], *n.* Dios; **god,** *n.* dios, *m.*
godchild ['gɔdtʃaild], *n.* ahijado.
goddess ['gɔdis], *n.* diosa.
godfather ['gɔdfɑːðə], *n.* padrino.
godless ['gɔdlis], *a.* infiel, descreído, ateo.
godmother ['gɔdmʌðə], *n.* madrina.
godsend ['gɔdsend], *n.* divina merced; buena suerte, *f.*
godson ['gɔdsʌn], *n.* ahijado.
goggle [gɔgl], *n.pl.* anteojos de camino.—*v.i.* mirar pasmado (*at*), abrir los ojos mucho.
going ['gouiŋ], *a.* en marcha; próspero.—*n.* ida; estado del camino.
goings-on ['gouiŋz'ɔn], *n.pl.* (*fam.*) andanzas, *f.pl.*; jarana.
gold [gould], *n.* oro; **Gold Coast,** Costa de Oro.
golden ['gouldən], *a.* de oro, dorado.
goldfinch ['gouldfintʃ], *n.* jilguero.
goldfish ['gouldfiʃ], *n.* carpa dorada.
goldsmith ['gouldsmiθ], *n.* orfebre, orífice, *m.*
golf [gɔlf], *n.* golf, *m.*
gondola ['gɔndələ], *n.* góndola; (*aer.*) barquilla.
gone [gɔn], *a.* ido, pasado; arruinado; muerto; (*fam.*) chiflado (*on,* por).—*p.p.* [GO].
gong [gɔn], *n.* batintín, *m.,* gongo.
good [gud], *a.* bueno; — **day,** ¡buenos días! — *morning,* ¡buenos días! — *afternoon,* — *evening,* ¡buenas tardes! — *night,* ¡buenas noches!; *as — as,* tanto como, casi; *for —,* para siempre; **Good Friday,** Viernes Santo.—*n.* bien, *m.—pl.* mercancías, *f.pl.*
good-bye [gud'bai], *interj.* ¡adiós!
good-for-nothing ['gudfənʌθiŋ], *a., n.* perdido, dejado de la mano de Dios.
good-looking [gud'lukiŋ], *a.* guapo.
good-natured [gud'neitʃəd], *a.* benévolo, afable, bonachón.
goodness ['gudnis], *n.* bondad, *f.—interj.* ¡Dios mío!
goofy ['gu:fi], *a.* (*fam.*) gilí.
goose [gu:s], *n.* (*pl.* **geese**) oca; ganso (*male & generic*).
gooseberry ['gu:zbəri], *n.* uva espina, grosella.
goose-flesh ['gu:sfleʃ], **goose-pimples** ['gu:spimplz], *n.* carne de gallina.
gore [gɔː], *n.* sangre, *f.,* crúor, *m.—v.t.* acornear, coger.
gorge [gɔːdʒ], *n.* garganta; barranco.—*v.t., v.i.* engullir, traguar; hartar(se) (*on,* de).
gorgeous ['gɔːdʒəs], *a.* brillante, espléndido, bellísimo.
gorilla [gə'rilə], *n.* gorila, *m.*
gorse [gɔːs], *n.* tojo, árgoma, aulaga.
gory ['gɔːri], *a.* ensangrentado.
gosling ['gɔzliŋ], *n.* ansarino.
gospel ['gɔspəl], *n.* evangelio; (*fig.*) verdad pura.
gossamer ['gɔsəmə], *n.* telaraña finísima; gasa.
gossip ['gɔsip], *n.* chismes, *m.pl.,* chismería; chismoso.—*v.i.* chismear.
got [gɔt], [GET].

Goth [gɔθ], *n.* godo.
Gothic ['gɔθik], *a.* gótico.
gouge [gaudʒ], *n.* gubia.—*v.t.* excavar; sacar; arrancar.
gourd [guəd], *n.* calabaza.
gourmand [gur'mã], *n.* goloso.
gourmet ['gurmei], *n.* gastrónomo.
gout [gaut], *n.* gota, podagra.
govern ['gʌvən], *v.t., v.i.* gobernar; (*gram.*) regir.
governess ['gʌvənis], *n.* institutriz, *f.,* aya.
government ['gʌvənmənt], *n.* gobierno.
governor ['gʌvənə], *n.* gobernador; (*fam.*) jefe, *m.*
gown [gaun], *n.* (*educ., jur.*) toga; vestido talar; bata.
grab [græb], *n.* gancho; arrebatina; agarro.—*v.t.* agarrar; arrebatar.
grace [greis], *n.* gracia; favor, *m.*; discreción, *f.*; talante, *m.*; *to say —,* bendecir la mesa.—*v.t.* ilustrar, favorecer, hermosear.
graceful ['greisful], *a.* gracioso, agraciado.
graceless ['greislis], *a.* desgraciado; desgarbado.
gracious ['greiʃəs], *a.* gracioso; cortés; benigno.—*interj.* ¡válgame Dios!
grade [greid], *n.* grado; clase, *f.*; cuesta; (*U.S. educ.*) clase (*f.*) de escuela — *crossing,* (*U.S. rail.*) cruce (*m.*) a nivel.—*v.t.* clasificar, graduar.
gradient ['greidiənt], *n.* pendiente, *f.*
gradual ['grædjuəl], *a.* gradual; graduado.
gradually ['grædjuəli], *adv.* poco a poco.
graduate ['grædjuit], *a., n.* graduado.— ['grædjueit], *v.t.* graduar.—*v.i.* -se.
graduation [grædju'eiʃən], *n.* graduación, *f.*
graft (1) [grɑːft], *n.* (*agr., med.*) injerto.
graft (2) [grɑːft], *n.* (*U.S.*) soborno político.
graft (3) [grɑːft], *v.t., v.i.* (*agr., med.*) injertar; (*fam.*) malversar.
Grail [greil], *n.* Grial, *m.*
grain [grein], *n.* grano, granos, *m.pl.*; cereal, *m.*; fibra, veta, trepa; *against the —,* (*fig.*) a contra pelo, cuesta arriba.—*v.t.* granular; vetear.
gram [græm], [GRAMME].
grammar ['græmə], *n.* gramática.
grammarian [grə'mɛəriən], *n.* gramático.
grammatical [grə'mætikəl], *a.* gramático.
gramme [græm], *n.* gramo.
gramophone ['græməfoun], *n.* gramófono, tocadiscos, *m.sg.*
granary ['grænəri], *n.* granero, hórreo.
grand [grænd], *a.* grandioso; principal; excelente; grande.
grandchild ['græntʃaild], *n.* nieto.
granddaughter ['grændɔːtə], *n.* nieta.
grandee [græn'di:], *n.* grande (de España), *m.*
grandeur ['grændʒə], *n.* grandeza, esplendor, *m.*
grandfather ['grændfɑːðə], *n.* abuelo.
grandiose ['grændious], *a.* grandioso; hinchado.
grandmother ['grændmʌðə], *n.* abuela.
grandson ['grændsʌn], *n.* nieto.
grand-stand ['grændstænd], *n.* tribuna.
granite ['grænit], *n.* granito.
grant [grɑːnt], *n.* concesión; subvención, *f.*—*v.t.* conceder, otorgar; *to take for granted,* dar por supuesto; no apreciar debidamente.
grape [greip], *n.* uva.
grapefruit ['greipfru:t], *n.* toronja, pomelo.

289

grape-shot ['greipʃɔt], *n.* metralla.
grape-vine ['greipvain], *n.* vid, *f.*; parra; (*fig.*, *fam.*) las vías por donde corren rumores y por donde se llega a saber cosas secretas.
graph [grɑ:f], *n.* gráfica; curva.
graphic ['græfik], *a.* gráfico.
graphite ['græfait], *n.* grafito.
grapnel ['græpnəl], *n.* garabato; anclote, *m.*
grapple ['græpəl], *v.t.* agarrar.—*v.i.* luchar (*with*, con).
grasp [grɑ:sp], *n.* asimiento; alcance, *m.*; agarro; (*fig.*) poder, entendimiento.—*v.t.* agarrar, empuñar; entender.
grasping ['grɑ:spiŋ], *a.* codicioso, avaro.
grass [grɑ:s], *n.* hierba; césped, *m.*
grasshopper ['grɑ:shɔpə], *n.* saltamontes, *m.sg.*
grate (1) [greit], *n.* reja; parrilla; hogar, *m.*
grate (2) [greit], *v.t.* rallar; rechinar.—*v.i.* rechinar.
grateful ['greitful], *a.* agradecido.
gratify ['grætifai], *v.t.* satisfacer, complacer.
grating (1) ['greitiŋ], *a.* irritante.
grating (2) ['greitiŋ], *n.* reja; rejilla.
gratis ['greitis], *a.* gratuito.—*adv.* gratis.
gratitude ['grætitju:d], *n.* gratitud, *f.*, agradecimiento.
gratuitous [grə'tju:itəs], *a.* gratuito.
gratuity [grə'tju:iti], *n.* gratificación, *f.*
grave (1) [greiv], *a.* serio, grave.
grave (2) [greiv], *n.* sepultura, sepulcro, tumba. —*v.t.* grabar; *graven image,* ídolo.
gravel ['grævil], *n.* grava, guijo.
grave-yard ['greivjɑ:d], *n.* cementerio.
gravitate ['græviteit], *v.i.* gravitar.
gravity ['græviti], *n.* gravedad; (*phys.*) gravitación, *f.*
gravy ['greivi], *n.* salsa, jugo.
gray (*U.S.*), [GREY].
graze [greiz], *n.* arañazo.—*v.t.* rozar; rasguñar.—*v.i.* pacer.
grease [gri:s], *n.* grasa.—*v.t.* engrasar.
greasy ['gri:si], *a.* grasiento.
great [greit], *a.* grande; *A. the —,* A. Magno.
great- [greit], *prefix.*— *great-grandfather,* bisabuelo; *great-great-grandfather,* tatarabuelo; *great-uncle,* tío abuelo.
greatness ['greitnis], *n.* grandeza.
Greece [gri:s], *n.* Grecia.
greed [gri:d], *n.* codicia, avaricia; gula.
greedy ['gri:di], *a.* voraz, goloso; avaro.
Greek [gri:k], *a.*, *n.* griego.
green [gri:n], *a.* verde; novato; tierno, joven. —*n.* verde, *m.*—*pl.* verduras, *f.pl.*
greenery ['gri:nəri], *n.* verdura.
greengrocer ['gri:n'grousə], *n.* verdulero.
greenhouse ['gri:nhaus], *n.* invernáculo.
greenish ['gri:niʃ], *a.* verdoso.
greet [gri:t], *v.t.* saludar; presentarse a.
greeting ['gri:tiŋ], *n.* saludo.
gregarious [grə'gɛəriəs], *a.* gregario.
gremlin ['gremlin], *n.* duende, *m.*
grenade [grə'neid], *n.* granada.
grew [gru:], [GROW].
grey [grei], *a.* gris, grisáceo; — *hairs,* canas, *f.pl.*—*n.* gris, *m.*
greyhound ['greihaund], *n.* galgo.
grid [grid], *n.* rejilla; cuadriculado.
grief [gri:f], *n.* pena, quebranto, congoja.
grievance ['gri:vəns], *n.* pesar, *m.*; agravio.
grieve [gri:v], *v.t.* apenar, afligir.—*v.i.* afligirse, penar.

grill [gril], *n.* parrilla.—*v.t.* asar en parrilla; (*fam.*) interrogar.
grille [gril], *n.* rejilla.
grim [grim], *a.* fiero, severo, ceñudo.
grimace [gri'meis], *n.* mueca; visaje, *m.*—*v.i.* hacer muecas.
grime [graim], *n.* tiznado, mugre, *f.*—*v.t.* tiznar.
grimy ['graimi], *a.* tiznado, mugriento.
grin [grin], *n.* sonrisa burlona; mueca.—*v.i.* sonreír mostrando los dientes.
grind [graind], *n.* (*fam.*) zurra.—*v.t.* *irr.* moler; afilar; agobiar.—*v.i.* *irr.* rechinar.
grindstone ['graindstoun], *n.* muela; *nose to the —,* con afán, con ahinco.
grip [grip], *n.* apretón, *m.*; agarro; (*U.S.*) saco de mano.—*v.t.* asir, apretar; (*fig.*) cautivar.
grisly ['grizli], *a.* horroroso.
grist [grist], *n.* molienda; (*fig.*) provecho.
gristle ['grisl], *n.* cartílago, ternilla.
grit [grit], *n.* arena, grava; (*fig.*) tesón, *m.*— *v.t.* apretar (*los dientes*).
grizzly ['grizli], *a.* grisáceo, cano; — *bear,* oso gris.
groan [groun], *n.* gemido.—*v.i.* gemir; crujir.
grocer ['grousə], *n.* especiero; (*S.A.*) abarrotero.
groceries ['grousəriz], *n.pl.* ultramarinos; (*S.A.*) abarrotes, *m.pl.*
groggy ['grɔgi], *a.* calamocano; inseguro.
groin [grɔin], *n.* ingle, *f.*
groom [gru:m], *n.* novio; caballerizo.—*v.t.* almohazar; asear; preparar.
groove [gru:v], *n.* surco; ranura; rodada; (*fam.*) rutina.
grope [group], *v.i.* ir a tientas; *to — for,* buscar a tientas.
gross [grous], *a.* craso; total; grueso, grosero. —*n.* gruesa (*144*).
grotesque [grou'tesk], *a.* grotesco.
grotto ['grɔtou], *n.* gruta.
ground (1) [graund], *n.* tierra; suelo; terreno; fundamento; motivo; campo.—*pl.* parque, *m.*, jardines, *m.pl.*; heces, *f.pl.*, posos, *m.pl.* —*v.t.* (*aer.*) vedar que vuele.
ground (2) [graund] [GRIND].
ground-floor ['graund'flɔ:], *n.* piso bajo, planta baja.
groundless ['graundlis], *a.* infundado.
ground-nut ['graundnʌt], *n.* cacahuete, *m.*
group [gru:p], *n.* grupo.—*v.t.* agrupar.
grouse (1) [graus], *n.* (*orn.*) lagópedo.
grouse (2) [graus], *v.i.* (*fam.*) rezongo.—*v.i.* rezongar.
grove [grouv], *n.* arboleda, soto.
grovel ['grɔvəl], *v.i.* arrastrarse; envilecerse.
grow [grou], *v.t.* *irr.* cultivar; dejarse crecer (*barba*).—*v.i.* *irr.* crecer; aumentarse; ponerse; *to — old,* envejecerse.
grower ['grouə], *n.* cultivador, agricultor, *m.*
growing ['grouiŋ], *a.* creciente.—*n.* cultivo.
growl [graul], *n.* gruñido.—*v.i.* gruñir.
grown [groun], *a.* crecido; adulto.—*p.p.* [GROW].
grown-up ['groun'ʌp], *a.*, *n.* adulto, mayor.
growth [grouθ], *n.* crecimiento; (*med.*) tumor, *m.*; aumento.
grub [grʌb], *n.* gusano, gorgojo; (*fam.*) manduca.—*v.i.* hozar; cavar; escarbar.
grubby ['grʌbi], *a.* sucio.

grudge [grʌdʒ], *n.* rencor, *m.*, ojeriza.—*v.t.* envidiar; escatimar.
grudgingly ['grʌdʒiŋli], *adv.* de mala gana.
gruel [gru:əl], *n.* avenate, *m.*, gachas, *f.pl.*
gruelling ['gru:əliŋ], *a.* afanoso, agotador.
gruesome ['gru:səm], *a.* horrendo, horripilante.
gruff [grʌf], *a.* áspero, arisco.
grumble [grʌmbl], *n.* queja.—*v.i.* quejarse, refunfuñar.
grumpy ['grʌmpi], *a.* (*fam.*) rezongón, gruñón.
grunt [grʌnt], *n.* gruñido.—*v.i.* gruñir.
guarantee [gærən'ti:], *n.* garantía.—*v.t.* garantizar.
guard [gɑ:d], *n.* guardia (*cuerpo*); guardia (*señor*), *m.*; guarda; (*fig.*) prevención, *f.*, cautela; on one's —, sobre aviso, prevenido. —*v.t.* guardar, proteger; to — against, guardarse de.
guarded ['gɑ:did], *a.* cauteloso.
guardian ['gɑ:diən], *n.* guardián; tutor, *m.*
Guatemalan [gwæti'mɑ:lən], *a.*, *n.* guatemalteco.
guerrilla [gə'rilə], *n.* guerrillero.
guess [ges], *n.* conjetura.—*v.t.* suponer; adivinar.
guest [gest], *n.* huésped, *m.f.*, convidado.
guffaw [gʌ'fɔ:], *n.* carcajada.—*v.i.* reírse a carcajadas.
guidance ['gaidəns], *n.* guía, dirección, *f.*, gobierno.
guide [gaid], *n.* guía (*cosa*); guía (*señor*), *m.* —*v.t.* guiar; guided missile, proyectil dirigido.
guild [gild], *n.* gremio.
guile [gail], *n.* maña, dolo.
guillotine ['giləti:n], *n.* guillotina.—*v.t.* guillotinar.
guilt [gilt], *n.* culpa.
guiltless ['giltlis], *a.* inocente.
guilty ['gilti], *a.* culpable; reo.
guinea ['gini], *n.* guinea.
guinea-fowl ['ginifaul], *n.* gallina de Guinea *o* pintada.
Guinean ['giniən], *a.*, *n.* guineo.
guinea-pig ['ginipig], *n.* conejillo de ʰndias, cobayo.
guise [gaiz], *n.* modo; color, *m.*, pretexto; apariencia; (*obs.*) guisa.
guitar [gi'tɑ:], *n.* guitarra.
gulch [gʌltʃ], *n.* (*U.S.*) quebrada, rambla.
gulf [gʌlf], *n.* golfo.
gull [gʌl], *n.* (*orn.*) gaviota; bobo.
gullet ['gʌlit], *n.* gaznate, *m.*
gully ['gʌli], *n.* cárcava, arroyada, barranca; badén, *m.*
gulp [gʌlp], *n.* trago.—*v.i.* tragar (*down*).
gum [gʌm], *n.* goma; (*anat.*) encía.—*v.t.* engomar.
gumption ['gʌmpʃən], *n.* (*fam.*) caletre, *m.*
gun [gʌn], *n.* fusil, *m.*; pistola; cañón, *m.*
gun-boat ['gʌnbout], *n.* cañonero.
gun-fire ['gʌnfaiə], *n.* tiroteo; fuego.
gun-man ['gʌnmən], *n.* pistolero.
gunner ['gʌnə], *n.* artillero.
gunnery ['gʌnəri], *n.* artillería.
gunpowder ['gʌnpaudə], *n.* pólvora.
gunwale ['gʌnəl], *n.* borda, regala.
gu gle [gə:gl], *n.* gorgoteo; murmullo, *m.*—*v.i.* gorgotear.
gush [gʌʃ], *n.* chorro.—*v.i.* brotar, chorrear; ser extremoso.

gushing ['gʌʃiŋ], *a.* surgente; extremoso.
gust [gʌst], *n.* ráfaga; arrebato.
gusto ['gʌstou], *n.* placer, *m.*, gusto, brío.
gusty ['gʌsti], *a.* tempestuoso, borrascoso.
gut [gʌt], *n.* tripa.—*pl.* (*fam.*) valor, *m.*, valentía.
gutter ['gʌtə], *n.* gotera, canal, *m.*; arroyo.—*v.i.* gotear.
guttural ['gʌtərəl], *a.*, *n.* gutural, *f.*
guy [gai], *n.* tirante, *m.*; (*U.S. fam.*) tío, individuo.
guzzle [guzl], *v.t.* engullir.
Guyanan [gai'ɑ:nən], **Guyanese** [gaiə'ni:z], *a.*, *n.* guayanés, *m.*
gymnasium [dʒim'neiziəm], *n.* gimnasio.
gymnastics [dʒim'nastiks], *n.pl.* gimnasia.
gypsum ['dʒipsəm], *n.* yeso.
gyrate ['dʒaiəreit], *v.i.* girar.
gypsy ['dʒipsi], *a.*, *n.* gitano.
gyroscope ['dʒaiərəskoup], *n.* giroscopio.

H

H, h [eitʃ], *n.* octava letra del alfabeto inglés.
haberdasher ['hæbədæʃə], *n.* mercero, camisero.
haberdashery ['hæbədæʃəri], *n.* mercerías, *f.pl.*
habit ['hæbit], *n.* costumbre, *f.*, hábito; traje, *m.*, hábito (*vestido*); to be in the — of, soler, acostumbrar.
habitat ['hæbitæt], **habitation** [hæbi'teiʃən] *n.* habitación, *f.*
habitual [hə'bitjuəl], *a.* habitual.
habituate [hə'bitjueit], *v.t.* habituar.
hack (1) [hæk], *n.* hachazo; tos seca.—*v.t.* machetear, mellar.
hack (2) [hæk], *n.* rocín, *m.*; escritor mercenario.
hackney ['hækni], *n.* coche de alquiler; rocín, *m.*—*v.t.* gastar, vulgarizar.
hackneyed ['hæknid], *a.* trillado.
hacksaw ['hæksɔ:], *n.* sierra para metal.
had [hæd] [HAVE].
haddock ['hædək], *n.* (*ichth.*) merluza, róbalo.
haemorrhage ['heməridʒ], *n.* hemorragia.
haft [hɑ:ft], *n.* mango, asa, puño.
hag [hæg], *n.* bruja; vejarrona.
haggard ['hægəd], *a.* macilento; zahareño.
haggle [hægl], *v.i.* regatear.
The Hague [heig], *n.* La Haya.
hail (1) [heil], *n.* granizo.—*v.i.* granizar.
hail (2) [heil], *n.* saludo; llamada.—*v.t.* saludar; vocear; llamar.—*v.i.* proceder (*from*, de).
hailstone ['heilstoun], *n.* piedra de granizo.
hair [hɛə], *n.* pelo, cabello; pelillo; to split hairs, andar en quisquillas.
hairbrush ['hɛəbrʌʃ], *n.* cepillo de cabeza.
haircut ['hɛəkʌt], *n.* corte (*m.*) de pelo.
hairdresser ['hɛədresə], *n.* peluquero.
hairpin ['hɛəpin], *n.* horquilla.
hairless ['hɛəlis], *a.* pelón, pelado.
hairy ['hɛəri], *a.* peludo, peloso; velloso.
Haiti ['heiti], *n.* Haití, *m.*

Haitian ['heiʃən], *a.*, *n.* haitiano.
hake [heik], *n.* (*ichth.*) merluza.
hale (1) [heil], *a.* sano, fuerte.
hale (2) [heil], *v.t.* arrastrar.
half [hɑːf], *a.*, *adv.* medio.—*n.* (*pl.* **halves**) mitad, *f.*; — *past*, y media (*hora*); — *and* —, a medias; mitad y mitad.
half-breed ['hɑːf'briːd], **half-caste** ['hɑːf'kɑːst], *a.*, *n.* mestizo.
half-crown ['hɑːf'kraun], *n.* (*Brit.*) dos chelines con seis peniques, media corona.
half-hearted ['hɑːf'hɑːtid], *a.* sin ánimo, flojo, frío.
half-pay ['hɑːf'pei], *n.* medio sueldo.
halfpenny ['heipni], *n.* medio penique.
half-truth ['hɑːf'truːθ], *n.* verdad (*f.*) a medias.
half-way ['hɑːf'wei], *a.*, *adv.* a mitad de; a medio camino.
half-witted ['hɑːf'witid], *a.* imbécil, necio.
half-yearly ['hɑːf'jiəli], *a.*. *adv.* semestral(mente).
hall [hɔːl], *n.* vestíbulo, recibimiento, zaguán, *m.*; sala; edificio público; casa solariega.
hallelujah [hæli'luːjə], *n.*, *interj.* aleluya.
hallmark ['hɔːlmɑːk], *n.* marca de ley; (*fig.*) sello.
hallo! [hə'lou], *interj.* ¡hola!
hallow ['hælou], *v.t.* santificar.
hallucination [həluːsi'neiʃən], *n.* alucinación, *f.*
halo ['heilou], *n.* halo; aureola.
halt [hɔːlt], *a.* (*obs.*) cojo.—*n.* parada, alto.—*v.t.* parar.—*v.i.* hacer alto; vacilar.
halter ['hɔːltə], *n.* cabestro, ronzal, *m.*
halting ['hɔːltiŋ], *a.* vacilante; imperfecto.
halve [hɑːv], *v.t.* partir en dos; demediar; reducir por la mitad.—*n.pl.* [HALF].
ham [hæm], *n.* jamón; pernil, *m.*; (*fam.*) aficionado a la radio; (*fam.*) comicastro.
hamlet ['hæmlit], *n.* aldea; caserío.
hammer ['hæmə], *n.* martillo.—*v.t.* martillar; machacar; golpear.—*v.i.* martillar; repiquetear.
hammock ['hæmək], *n.* hamaca.
hamper (1) ['hæmpə], *n.* excusabaraja; cesto, cuévano.
hamper (2) ['hæmpə], *v.t.* estorbar.
hamstring ['hæmstriŋ], *v.t. irr.* (*conjug. like* STRING) desjarretar.
hand [hænd], *n.* mano, *f.*; mano de obra; obrero; letra; ayuda; (*U.S.*) aplauso; *by* —, a mano; *in* —, entre manos; dominado; de sobra, como reserva; *on* —, a la mano; disponible; *on the other* —, por otra parte; *out of* —, rebelón, desbocado; en seguida; — *to* —, cuerpo a cuerpo; — *in glove*, uña y carne; *to lend a* —, prestar ayuda; *to shake hands*, estrechar la mano (*with*, a).—*v.t.* entregar (*over*).
hand-bag ['hændbæg], *n.* bolso de mano.
hand-book ['hændbuk], *n.* manual, *m.*; guía.
hand-cart ['hændkɑːt], *n.* carretilla de mano.
handcuff ['hændkʌf], *n.pl.* esposas, *f.pl.*—*v.t.* poner esposas a.
handful ['hændful], *n.* puñado; (*fig.*) persona *o* cosa difícil.
hand-grenade ['hændgrineid], *n.* granada (de mano).
handicap ['hændikæp], *n.* obstáculo, desventaja.—*v.t.* impedir; perjudicar.
handiwork ['hændiwɔːk], *n.* obra manual.

handkerchief ['hæŋkətʃif], *n.* pañuelo.
handle [hændl], *n.* asa; mango, asidero; tirador, *m.*—*v.t.* manejar; manosear; gobernar; comerciar en.
handshake ['hændʃeik], *n.* apretón (*m.*) de manos.
handsome ['hænsəm], *a.* hermoso, guapo; generoso.
handwriting ['hændraitiŋ], *n.* letra, escritura; puño y letra.
handy ['hændi], *a.* útil; hábil; a la mano.
hang [hæŋ], *n.* caída, modo de colgar; (*fam.*) idea general; maña; bledo.—*v.t. irr.* colgar; *to* — *out*, tender; (*jur.*) ahorcar (*regular in this sense*).—*v.i.* colgar, pender; *to* — *back*, quedar por indeciso; *to* — *about*, haraganear; *to* — *fire*, suspender el fuego; *to* — *on*, agarrarse; esperar; *to* — *out*, (*fam.*) habitar.
hangar ['hæŋə], *n.* hangar, *m.*
hanger ['hæŋə], *n.* percha, colgadero.
hanger-on ['hæŋər'ɔn], *n.* mogollón, pegote; secuaz, *m.*
hanging ['hæŋiŋ], *a.* colgante.—*n.* colgadura; (*jur.*) muerte (*f.*) en la horca.
hangman ['hæŋmən], *n.* verdugo.
hang-over ['hæŋouvə], *n.* (*fig.*, *fam.*) resaca.
hanker ['hæŋkə], *v.i.* pasar anhelo (*after*, por).
haphazard ['hæp'hæzəd], *a.* casual, fortuito; sin pies ni cabeza.—*adv.* al azar, al acaso.
hapless ['hæplis], *a.* desventurado.
happen ['hæpən], *v.i.* suceder, acontecer, pasar, ocurrir; *to* —*to do*, hacer por casualidad.
happening ['hæpəniŋ], *n.* suceso, acontecimiento.
happiness ['hæpinis], *n.* felicidad, *f.*
happy ['hæpi], *a.* feliz, contento; *to be* — *to*, tener el gusto de; alegrarse de.
happy-go-lucky ['hæpigou'lʌki], *a.* irresponsable, a la buena de Dios.
harangue [hə'ræŋ], *n.* arenga.—*v.t.* arengar.
harass ['hærəs], *v.t.* hostigar, vejar.
harbinger ['hɑːbindʒə], *n.* precursor, *m.*; presagio.
harbour ['hɑːbə], *n.* puerto.—*v.t.* albergar; abrigar.
hard [hɑːd], *a.* duro; difícil; penoso; — *and fast*, riguroso.—*adv.* fuerte; duro; con ahinco; mucho.
harden ['hɑːdən], *v.t.* endurecer.—*v.i.* -se.
hard-fought ['hɑːd'fɔːt], *a.* reñido.
hard-hearted ['hɑːd'hɑːtid], *a.* duro, empedernido.
hardly ['hɑːdli], *adv.* apenas; casi no.
hardness ['hɑːdnis], *n.* dureza.
hardship ['hɑːdʃip], *n.* fatiga, apuro; privación, *f.*
hard-up ['hɑːd'ʌp], *a.* pelón, sin blanca.
hardware ['hɑːdwɛə], *n.* quincalla; — *store*, ferretería.
hardy ['hɑːdi], *a.* robusto; (*bot.*) resistente.
hare [hɛə], *n.* (*zool.*) liebre, *f.*
hare-lipped ['hɛəlipd], *a.* labihendido.
haricot bean ['hærikou'biːn], *n.* judía blanca.
hark [hɑːk], *v.t.*, *v.i.* (*obs.*) escuchar.
harlequin ['hɑːlikwin], *n.* arlequín, *m.*
harlot ['hɑːlət], *n.* ramera.
harm [hɑːm], *n.* daño, mal, *m.*, perjuicio.—*v.t.* dañar.

harmful ['hɑ:mful], *a.* dañoso, nocivo, perjudicial.
harmless ['hɑ:mləs], *a.* inocuo, inofensivo.
harmonious [hɑ:'mounjəs], *a.* armonioso.
harmony ['hɑ:məni], *n.* armonía.
harness ['hɑ:nis], *n.* arneses, *m.pl.*, jaeces,
m.pl., arreos, *m.pl.*; guarniciones, *f.pl.*
—*v.t.* enjaezar; explotar, captar (*energía*).
harp [hɑ:p], *n.* arpa.—*v.i. to — on*, porfiar en,
machacar.
harpoon [hɑ:'pu:n], *n.* arpón, *m.*—*v.t.*
arponear.
harridan ['hæridən], *n.* bruja, regañona.
harrow ['hærou], *n.* (*agr.*) grada, rastro.—*v.t.*
gradar; (*fig.*) atormentar.
Harry ['hæri], *n.* Enrique, *m.*
harry ['hæri], *v.t.* acosar, perseguir.
harsh [hɑ:ʃ], *a.* áspero, acerbo; cruel.
hart [hɑ:t], *n.* (*zool.*, *poet.*) ciervo.
harum-scarum ['hɛərəm'skɛərəm], *n.* taram-
bana, *m.f.*—*adv.* a troche y moche.
harvest ['hɑ:vist], *n.* cosecha.—*v.t.*, *v.i.*
cosechar, recoger.
has [hæz], [HAVE].
has-been ['hæzbi:n], *n.* (*fam.*) tagarote, *m.*
hash [hæʃ], *n.* picadillo; embrollo.—*v.t.* picar;
embrollar.
hasp [hæsp], *n.* broche, *m.*, manecilla.
haste [heist], *n.* prisa; *to make —*, apresurarse.
hasten [heisn], *v.t.* apresurar, precipitar.—*v.i.*
apresurarse.
hasty ['heisti], *a.* precipitado, apresurado.
hat [hæt], *n.* sombrero.
hatch [hætʃ], *n.* nidada; portezuela, trampa;
(*naut.*) escotilla.—*v.t.* empollar; (*fig.*)
tramar.—*v.i.* salir del cascarón (*out*).
hatchet ['hætʃit], *n.* hacha, destral, *m.*; *to
bury the —*, hacer la paz o (las) paces.
hatchway ['hætʃwei], *n.* escotillón, *m.*, escotilla.
hate [heit], *n.* odio, aborrecimiento.—*v.t.*
aborrecer, odiar.
hateful ['heitful], *a.* odioso; malévolo.
hatred ['heitrid], *n.* odio.
hatter ['hætə], *n.* sombrerero.
haughty ['hɔ:ti], *a.* altivo, altanero.
haul [hɔ:l], *n.* tirón; arrastre, *m.*; redada;
trayecto.—*v.t.* arrastrar; trasportar; (*naut.*)
virar.
haulage ['hɔ:lidʒ], *n.* trasporte, *m.*, acarreo.
haunch [hɔ:ntʃ], *n.* anca, cadera; pierna.
haunt [hɔ:nt], *n.* guarida, querencia.—*v.t.*
frecuentar; vagar por; obsesionar;
haunted, que tiene fantasmas.
Havana [hə'vænə], *n.* la Habana; habano,
puro (*cigarro*).
have [hæv], *v.t. irr.* tener; traer; tomar;
sentir; (*fam.*) estafar.—*auxiliary v.* haber; *to
— made*, hacer hacer; mandar hacer; *to
— to*, tener que; haber de; *the have-
nots*, los desposeídos.
haven [heivn], *n.* asilo, abrigo; puerto.
haversack ['hævəsæk], *n.* mochila.
havoc ['hævək], *n.* estrago(s).
hawk [hɔ:k], *n.* (*orn.*) azor, *m.*—*v.t.* pregonar.
—*v.i.* cazar con azores; buhonear.
hawker ['hɔ:kə], *n.* buhonero; cetrero.
hawk-eyed ['hɔ:kaid], *a.* de ojo avisor.
hawking ['hɔ:kiŋ], *n.* cetrería.
hawser ['hɔ:zə], *n.* (*naut.*) cable, *m.*, guindaleza.

hawthorn ['hɔ:θɔ:n], *n.* (*bot.*) espino blanco.
hay [hei], *n.* heno; *— fever*, alergia del heno;
romadizo; *to make — while the sun
shines*, machacar en caliente.
hayrick ['heirik], **haystack** ['heistæk], *n.*
almiar, *m.*
haywire ['heiwaiə], *a.* (*fam.*, *esp.* *U.S.*)
desarreglado; gili.—*adv.* desbaratadamente.
hazard ['hæzəd], *n.* riesgo, peligro; azar, *m.*—
v.t. aventurar; arriesgar.
hazardous ['hæzədəs], *a.* arriesgado, peligroso.
haze [heiz], *n.* calina, niebla.
hazel ['heizəl], *n.* avellano.
hazel-nut ['heizəlnʌt], *n.* avellana.
hazy ['heizi], *a.* calinoso, anieblado; confuso,
vago.
H-bomb ['eitʃbɔm], *n.* bomba-H.
he [hi:], *a.* macho.—*pron.* él.
head [hed], *a.* principal; delantero.—*n.*
cabeza; jefe, *m.*; cabecera (*cama*); res
(*de ganado*), *f.*; (*educ.*) director, *m.*; crisis, *f.*;
on his —, a su responsabilidad; —*pl.* cara
(*de moneda*).—*v.t.* acaudillar; ser el primero
de; encabezar; conducir.—*v.i.* dirigirse
(*for*, *towards*, a, hacia); *to come to a —*,
llegar a una crisis final, madurar; *to go to
one's —*, subir a la cabeza; *to lose one's —*,
perder el equilibrio por pánico; *to — off*,
interceptar.
headache ['hedeik], *n.* dolor (*m.*) de cabeza.
head-dress ['heddres], *n.* tocado.
head-first ['hed'fə:st], *adv.* de cabeza.
heading ['hediŋ], *n.* encabezamiento, título.
headland ['hedlənd], *n.* promontorio.
head-light ['hedlait], *n.* faro (*aut.*); linterna.
headline ['hedlain], *n.* cabecera, título.
headlong ['hedlɔŋ], *a.* precipitado.—*adv.* de
cabeza, de bruces.
headmaster [hed'mɑ:stə], *n.* director, *m.*
headmistress [hed'mistris], *n.* directora.
head-on ['hed'ɔn], *a.*, *adv.* de frente.
headphone ['hedfoun], *n.* auricular, *m.*
headquarters [hed'kwɔ:təz], *n.* jefatura;
(*mil.*) cuartel general, *m.*
headstrong ['hedstrɔŋ], *a.* testarudo, reacio.
headway ['hedwei], *n.* progreso, avance, *m.*
heady ['hedi], *a.* impetuoso; encabezado
(*vino*).
heal [hi:l], *v.t.* sanar, curar.—*v.i.* sanar.
health [helθ], *n.* salud; sanidad (*pública etc.*),
f.
healthy ['helθi], *a.* sano.
heap [hi:p], *n.* montón, *m.*—*v.t.* amontonar;
colmar.
hear [hiə], *v.t. irr.* oír; (*jur.*) ver; *to — about*,
oír hablar de; *to — from*, tener noticias
de, saber algo de; *to — of*, oír hablar de;
to — that, oír decir que.
heard [hə:d], [HEAR].
hearing ['hiəriŋ], *n.* oído; audición, *f.*; (*jur.*)
examen (*m.*) de testigos; *— aid*, audífono.
hearsay ['hiəsei], *n.* rumor, *m.*, fama, voz
común, *f.*; *by —*, de o por oídas.
hearse [hə:s], *n.* coche fúnebre, *m.*
heart [hɑ:t], *n.* corazón, *m.*; (*fig.*) gusto; *at
—*, en el fondo; *by —*, de memoria; *— and
soul*, con toda el alma; *to lose —*, perder
ánimo.
heartache ['hɑ:teik], *n.* congoja, cordojo,
pena.
heartbreak ['hɑ:tbreik], *n.* angustia, congoja.

hearten

hearten [hɑːtn], *v.t.* alentar.
heartfelt [ˈhɑːtfelt], *a.* sincero, cordial.
hearth [hɑːθ], *n.* hogar, *m.*
heartless [ˈhɑːtlis], *a.* desalmado; apocado.
heart-to-heart [ˈhɑːttuˈhɑːt], *a.* franco, íntimo.
hearty [ˈhɑːti], *a.* cordial; robusto; alegre; voraz.
heat [hiːt], *n.* calor, *m.*; (*sport*) carrera, corrida; (*zool.*) celo.—*v.t.* calentar; calefaccionar; acalorar.
heater [ˈhiːtə], *n.* calentador, *m.*; estufa.
heath [hiːθ], *n.* (*bot.*) brezo; brezal, *m.*
heathen [ˈhiːðən], *a., n.* pagano.
heather [ˈheðə], *n.* brezo.
heating [ˈhiːtiŋ], *n.* calefacción, *f.*
heave [hiːv], *n.* esfuerzo, alzadura; tirón, *m.*—*v.t.* alzar; lanzar con un esfuerzo; exhalar (*suspiro*).—*v.i.* ir subiendo y bajando; palpitar; vomitar; jadear; **to — to,** (*naut.*) (*irregular in this sense*) ponerse al pairo.
heaven [ˈhevən], *n.* cielo; paraíso.
heavenly [ˈhevənli], *a.* celestial; (*astr.*) celeste.
heavy [ˈhevi], *a.* pesado; grueso; denso; fuerte; difícil; abundante; grave; triste; cansado.—*adv.* pesadamente.
heavy-weight [ˈheviweit], *a.* de gran peso; de gran importancia.—*n.* (*sport*) peso fuerte.
Hebrew [ˈhiːbruː], *a., n.* hebreo.
heckle [hekl], *v.t.* importunar, interrumpir (*a un orador*).
hectic [ˈhektik], *a.* agitado, febril; (*med.*) hético.
hedge [hedʒ], *n.* seto vivo.—*v.t.* cercar; rodear; encerrar.—*v.i.* no comprometerse; esconderse; evitar una respuesta.
hedgehog [ˈhedʒhɔg], *n.* erizo.
heed [hiːd], *n.* atención, *f.*—*v.t.* hacer caso de.
heedless [ˈhiːdlis], *a.* desatento; incauto.
heel [hiːl], *n.* talón; calcañar; tacón, *m.*; **head over heels,** patas arriba; **to take to one's heels,** poner pies en polvorosa.
hefty [ˈhefti], *a.* (*fam.*) morrocotudo.
heifer [ˈhefə], *n.* vaquilla, novilla.
height [hait], *n.* altura; lo alto; colmo.
heighten [haitn], *v.t.* realzar.
heinous [ˈheinəs], *a.* nefando.
heir [ɛə], *n.* heredero.
heiress [ˈɛəris], *n.* heredera.
heirloom [ˈɛəluːm], *n.* herencia, reliquia.
held [held], [HOLD].
helicopter [ˈhelikɔptə], *n.* helicóptero.
hell [hel], *n.* infierno.
hellish [ˈheliʃ], *a.* infernal.
hello! [heˈlou], *interj.* ¡hola! ; (*tel.*) ¡diga!
helm [helm], *n.* caña del timón, timón, *m.*
helmet [ˈhelmit], *n.* casco, yelmo.
helmsman [ˈhelmzmən], *n.* timonel, *m.*
help [help], *n.* ayuda, socorro; remedio; ayudante, *m.f.*; obrero.—*v.t.* ayudar, socorrer; adelantar; servir; remediar; *it can't be helped,* no hay más remedio; **— yourself,** sírvase; *they can't — doing it,* no pueden menos de hacerlo.
helper [ˈhelpə], *n.* ayudante, *m.f.*
helpful [ˈhelpful], *a.* útil; provechoso.
helpless [ˈhelplis], *a.* desvalido; desmañado; irremediable.
helter-skelter [ˈheltəˈskeltə], *adv.* a trochemoche, al tuntún.
hem [hem], *n.* dobladillo, bastilla.—*interj.*

¡eh!—*v.t.* bastillar; *to — in,* cercar y encerrar.
hemisphere [ˈhemisfiə], *n.* hemisferio.
hemlock [ˈhemlɔk], *n.* cicuta.
hemorrhage [ˈheməridʒ], *n.* hemorragia.
hemp [hemp], *n.* cáñamo.
hen [hen], *n.* gallina; (*orn.*) hembra.
hence [hens], *adv.* de(sde) aquí; por lo tanto; *two years —,* de aquí a dos años.
henceforth [hensˈfɔːθ], **henceforward** [hensˈfɔːwəd], *adv.* de aquí en adelante.
henchman [ˈhentʃmən], *n.* secuaz, muñidor, compinche, *m.*
hen-coop [ˈhenkuːp], *n.* gallinero.
henpeck [ˈhenpek], *v.t.* dominar (*a un marido*); *henpecked husband,* bragazas, *m. inv.*
Henry [ˈhenri], *n.* Enrique, *m.*
her [həː], *pron.* la; ella.—*poss. a.* su, de ella.
herald [ˈherəld], *n.* heraldo; precursor, *m.*—*v.t.* anunciar.
heraldry [ˈherəldri], *n.* blasonería, heráldica.
herb [həːb], *n.* hierba (aromática); hortaliza.
herbalist [ˈhəːbəlist], *n.* herbolario, simplista, *m.*
herculean [həːkjuˈliːən], *a.* hercúleo.
herd [həːd], *n.* hato, manada, ganado; chusma, vulgo.—*v.t.* reunir, juntar.—*v.i.* juntarse, formar manada.
herdsman [ˈhəːdzmən], *n.* manadero, vaquero.
here [hiə], *adv.* aquí; acá; **— and there,** acá y acullá; **— is (are),** he aquí... por aquí.
hereabouts [hiərəˈbauts], *adv.* por aquí.
hereafter [hiərˈɑːftə], *n.* la vida de más allá.—*adv.* de aquí en adelante.
hereby [ˈhiəbai], *adv.* por esto medio; (*jur.*) por la presente, por éstas.
hereditary [hiˈreditəri], *a.* hereditario; heredero.
heredity [hiˈrediti], *n.* herencia.
herein [ˈhiəˈrin], *adv.* aquí dentro; adjunto.
hereon [ˈhiəˈrɔn], *adv.* en o sobre esto.
heresy [ˈherəsi], *n.* herejía.
heretic [ˈherətik], *a.* herético.—*n.* hereje, *m.f.*
heretical [həˈretikəl], *a.* herético.
hereupon [ˈhiərəˈpɔn], *adv.* en esto, a esto.
heritage [ˈheritidʒ], *n.* herencia.
hermetic [həːˈmetik], *a.* hermético.
hermit [ˈhəːmit], *n.* ermitaño.
hermitage [ˈhəːmitidʒ], *n.* ermita.
hero [ˈhiərou], *n.* héroe, *m.*
heroic [hiˈrouik], *a.* heroico.—*n.pl.* temeridad, *f.*; extravagancia.
heroin [ˈherouin], *n.* (*med.*) heroína.
heroine [ˈherouin], *n.* heroína.
heroism [ˈherouizm], *n.* heroísmo.
heron [ˈherən], *n.* garza.
herring [ˈheriŋ], *n.* arenque, *m.*; **red —,** (*fig.*) distracción, *f.*
hers [həːz], *poss. pron.* suyo, de ella; el suyo etc.
herself [həːˈself], *pron. r.* sí misma; se; ella misma.
hesitant [ˈhezitənt], *a.* vacilante, indeciso.
hesitate [ˈheziteit], *v.i.* vacilar (*to,* en).
hesitation [heziˈteiʃən], *n.* hesitación, vacilación, *f.*
heterodox [ˈhetərodɔks], *a.* heterodoxo.
heterodoxy [ˈhetərodɔksi], *n.* heterodoxia.
hew [hjuː], *v.t. irr.* desbastar, hachear, dolar.
hewn [hjuːn], [HEW].

heyday ['heidei], *n.* apogeo, época de grandeza.
hiatus [hai'eitəs], *n.* laguna; (*gram.*) hiato.
hibernate ['haibəneit], *v.i.* invernar; hibernar.
hibernation [haibə'neiʃən], *n.* invernación, *f.*
hiccough, hiccup ['hikʌp], *n.* hipo.—*v.i.* hipar.
hick [hik], *a.*, *n.* (*U.S.*) palurdo.
hid, hidden [hid, hidn], [HIDE (2)].
hide (1) [haid], *n.* cuero, pellejo, piel, *f.*; (*fam. fig.*) badana.
hide (2) [haid], *n.* escondite, *m.*, escondrijo.—*v.t. irr.* esconder, ocultar.—*v.i. irr. -se.*
hide-and-seek ['haidən'siːk], *n.* escondite, *m.*
hidebound ['haidbaund], *a.* fanático, reaccionario.
hideous ['hidiəs], *a.* horrendo, monstruoso.
hide-out ['haidaut], *n.* escondrijo.
hiding ['haidiŋ], *n.* ocultación, *f.*; retiro, escondrijo; (*fam.*) zurra; — *place,* escondrijo.
hierarchy ['haiərɑːki], *n.* jerarquía.
hieroglyph [haiəro'glif], *n.* jeroglífico.
hieroglyphic [haiəro'glifik], *a.*, *n.* jeroglífico.
high [hai], *a.* alto; arrogante; fuerte; sublime; subido; crecido; mayor (*misa*); — *and dry,* en seco; — *and low,* por todas partes;— *and mighty,* altanero.—*adv.* altamente, alto; arriba; *it is — time to . . .,* ya es hora de . . .
high-born ['haibɔːn], *a.* linajudo.
highbrow ['haibrau], *a.*, *n.* erudito, culto.
high-flown ['haiflaun], *a.* retumbante, ampuloso.
high-handed ['haihændid], *a.* despótico.
highland ['hailənd], *a.* serrano, montañés.— *n.* sierra, meseta, montaña.
highlight ['hailait], *n.* punto más notable.— *v.t.* destacar.
highly ['haili], *adv.* altamente; sumamente; con aprecio; *to think — of,* tener gran concepto de.
highness ['hainis], *n.* altura; alteza (*título*).
high-spirited ['hai'spiritid], *a.* animoso, fogoso.
high-water ['hai'wɔːtə], *n.* pleamar, *f.*, marea alta.
highway ['haiwei], *n.* camino real; carretera.
highwayman ['haiweimən], *n.* salteador, *m.*, bandolero.
hike [haik], *n.* caminata.—*v.i.* caminar por el campo.
hilarious [hi'lɛəriəs], *a.* regocijado, bullicioso.
hilarity [hi'læriti], *n.* regocijo, hilaridad, *f.*
hill [hil], *n.* colina, cuesta, cerro, collado.
hillock ['hilək], *n.* cerrejón, *m.*, montecillo.
hillside ['hilsaid], *n.* ladera.
hilly ['hili], *a.* montuoso.
hilt [hilt], *n.* puño; *up to the —,* totalmente.
him [him], *pron. le,* lo; él.
himself [him'self], *pron.* sí mismo; él mismo; se.
hind (1) [haind], *a.* trasero.
hind (2) [haind], *n.* (*zool.*) cierva.
hinder ['hində], *v.t.* estorbar, dificultar.
hindmost ['haindmoust], *a.* postrero.
hindrance ['hindrəns], *n.* obstáculo, estorbo.
hinge [hindʒ], *n.* bisagra; gozne, *m.*; charnela; (*also fig.*) quicio.—*v.t.* engoznar, enquiciar.—*v.i.* depender (**on,** de).

hint [hint], *n.* indirecta; indicación, *f.*; consejo.—*v.t.* insinuar, indicar.—*v.i.* aludir (**at,** a); pescar (**at**).
hinterland ['hintəlænd], *n.* interior, *m.*
hip (1) [hip], *n.* cadera (*de persona*).
hip (2) [hip], *n.* (*bot.*) agavanzo.
hip-bone ['hipboun], *n.* cía.
hippopotamus [hipə'potəməs], *n.* hipopótamo.
hire [haiə], *n.* alquiler, *m.*, sueldo.—*v.t.* alquilar; (*U.S.*) ajornalar.
hireling ['haiəliŋ], *n.* alquilón, *m.*, alquiladizo.
his [hiz], *poss. pron.* su; de él; suyo; el suyo.
Hispanic [his'pænik], *a.* hispánico.
Hispanist ['hispənist], *n.* hispanista, *m.f.*
hiss [his], *n.* silbido, siseo.—*v.t.*, *v.i.* silbar, sisear.
historian [his'tɔːriən], *n.* historiador, *m.*
historic(al) [his'tɔrik(əl)], *a.* histórico.
history ['histəri], *n.* historia.
histrionic [histri'ɔnik], *a.* histriónico, teatral.
hit [hit], *n.* golpe, *m.*; tiro; acierto; (*fam.*) éxito.—*v.t. irr.* golpear, pegar; dar; acertar; dar en; dar con.—*v.i. irr.* tocar, chocar; *to — on,* dar con, encontrar.
hitch [hitʃ], *n.* parada, dificultad, *f.*, avería; tirón, *m.*; nudo.—*v.t.* acoplar, atar, amarrar; tirar; (*fam.*) casar.
hitch-hike ['hitʃhaik], *v.i.* hacer autostop.
hitch-hiking ['hitʃhaikiŋ], *n.* autostop, *m.*
hither ['hiðə], *adv.* (hacia) acá; — *and thither,* acá y allá.
hitherto [hiðə'tuː], *adv.* hasta ahora.
hive [haiv], *n.* colmena; (*fig.*) enjambre, *m.*
hoard [hɔːd], *n.* repuesto, cúmulo, tesoro oculto.—*v.t.* amontonar, atesorar, acaparar.
hoarding ['hɔːdiŋ], *n.* amontonamiento; tablado de avisos; cerca provisional.
hoarfrost ['hɔːfrost], *n.* escarcha.
hoarse [hɔːs], *a.* ronco, enronquecido.
hoary ['hɔːri], *a.* cano, canoso.
hoax [houks], *n.* pajarota(da), burla.—*v.t.* mistificar, burlar.
hobble [hɔbl], *n.* traba; cojera.—*v.t.* maniatar.—*v.i.* cojear.
hobby ['hɔbi], *n.* pasatiempo; comidilla; afición, *f.*
hobby-horse ['hɔbihɔːs], *n.* caballito (*juguete*); (*fig.*) manía, tema predilecto.
hobnail ['hɔbneil], *n.* tachuela.
hobnob ['hɔbnɔb], *v.i.* codearse (**with,** con).
hobo ['houbou], *n.* (*U.S.*) vagabundo.
hock (1) [hɔk], *n.* vino del Rin.
hock (2) [hɔk], *n.* corva, jarrete, *m.*—*v.t.* (*fam.*) empeñar.
hocus-pocus ['houkəs'poukəs], *n.* birlibirloque, *m.*, engaño.
hodge-podge ['hɔdʒpɔdʒ], *n.* baturrillo.
hod [hɔd], *n.* esparavel, *m.*; cubo (*para carbón*).
hoe [hou], *n.* azadón, *m.*—*v.t.* sachar.
hog [hɔg], *n.* cerdo.—*v.t.* (*fam.*) tomar demasiado.
hoist [hɔist], *n.* cabria, grúa.—*v.t.* izar; alzar.
hold [hould], *n.* agarro; dominio; mango; (*naut.*) bodega.—*v.t. irr.* tener; sujetar; agarrar, coger; contener; sostener; celebrar; considerar.—*v.i.* valer; quedar firme; pegarse; *to — forth,* perorar; *to — one's own,* defenderse; *to — out,* ofrecer; defenderse; durar; *how many does*

holder

this car —? cuántos caben en este coche?
holder ['houldə], *n.* tenedor, posesor, *m.*; boquilla (*de pitillo*); titular (*de un documento*), *m.f.*; *letterholder*, portacartas, *m.sg.*
holding ['houldiŋ], *n.* tenencia, posesión, *f.*
hole [houl], *n.* agujero; hoyo; (*fam.*) casucha; (*fam.*) aprieto.—*v.t.* agujerear; cavar; taladrar; *to — up*, esconderse.
holiday ['hɔlidei], *n.* fiesta; vacación, *f.*; *on —*, de vacaciones; de veraneo; *— maker*, veraneante, *m.f.*
holiness ['houlinis], *n.* santidad, *f.*
Holland ['hɔlənd], *n.* Holanda.
hollow ['hɔlou], *a.* hueco, ahuecado; insincero.—*n.* hueco, cavidad, *f.*—*v.t.* ahuecar.
holly ['hɔli], *n.* (*bot.*) acebo.
holy ['houli], *n.* santo, sagrado.
homage ['hɔmidʒ], *n.* homenaje, *m.*
home [houm], *a.* doméstico, casero; natal, nacional.—*n.* casa, hogar, *m.*; asilo, hospicio; patria; *at —*, en casa; recepción (*fiesta*), *f.*—*v.i.* dirigirse, guiarse (*on, hacia*).—*adv.* a casa; en casa; (*fig.*) en el blanco.
homely ['houmli], *a.* casero, llano, acogedor; (*U.S.*) feo.
home-made ['houm'meid], *a.* de fabricación casera, casero.
homesick ['houmsik], *a.* nostálgico.
homesickness [houm'siknis], *n.* morriña de la tierra, añoranza.
homestead ['houmsted], *n.* finca solariega; (*U.S.*) granja.
homeward(s) ['houmwəd(z)], *adv.* hacia casa.
home-work ['houmwə:k], *n.* (*educ.*) deber, *m.*
homicide ['hɔmisaid], *n.* homicida (*persona*), *m.f.*; homicidio (*crimen*).
homing missile ['houmiŋ'misail], *n.* proyectil autodirigido.
homogeneous [hɔmɔ'dʒi:njəs], *a.* homogéneo.
Honduran [hɔn'dju:rən], *a.*, *n.* hondureño.
Honduras [hɔn'dju:rəs], *n.* Honduras, *f.sg.*
honest ['ɔnist], *a.* honrado, recto, probo; sincero; fiel.
honesty ['ɔnisti], *n.* honradez, rectitud; sinceridad, *f.*
honey ['hʌni], *n.* miel, *f.*
honeycomb ['hʌnikoum], *n.* panal, *m.*—*v.t.* perforar, apanalar.
honeyed ['hʌnid], *a.* meloso; enmelado.
honeymoon ['hʌnimu:n], *n.* luna de miel.
honeysuckle ['hʌnisʌkl], *n.* madreselva.
honorary ['ɔnərəri], *a.* honorario.
honour ['ɔnə], *n.* honor, *m.*; honra.—*v.t.* honrar; aceptar.
honourable ['ɔnərəbl], *a.* honroso; honorable.
hood [hud], *n.* capucha, capriote, *m.*, caperuza; cubierta (*de coche*).—*v.t.* encapirotar.
hoodlum ['hu:dləm], *n.* (*U.S. fam.*) maleante, *m.*
hoodwink ['hudwiŋk], *v.t.* emprimar, engañar.
hoof [hu:f], *n.* (*pl.* hooves) casco, pezuña.
hook [huk], *n.* gancho; anzuelo (*para pescar*); corchete, *m.*; *by — or by crook*, a buenas o a malas, a todo trance.—*v.t.* enganchar; coger, pescar.—*v.i.* doblarse.
hooked [hukt], *a.* ganchudo; aguileña (*nariz*).
hooky ['huki], *n.* (*U.S.*) *to play —*, hacer novillos.

hooligan ['hu:ligən], *n.* gamberro.
hoop [hu:p], *n.* aro; collar, *m.*—*v.t.* enarcar.
hooray! [hu'rei], *interj.* ¡viva! ¡bravo!
hoot [hu:t], *n.* ululato; grito.—*v.t.* sisear; sonar.—*v.i.* ulular; reír a carcajadas.
hooves [hu:vz]. [HOOF].
hop (1) [hɔp], *n.* brinco, saltito.—*v.i.* brincar; andar a saltitos; (*fam.*) viajar.
hop (2) [hɔp], *n.* (*bot.*) lúpulo, hombrecillo.
hope [houp], *n.* esperanza.—*v.t.*, *v.i.* esperar.
hopeful ['houpful], *a.* esperanzado; alentador; prometedor.
hopeless ['houplis], *a.* desesperado; desesperanzado.
horde [hɔ:d], *n.* horda.
horizon [hə'raizn], *n.* horizonte, *m.*
horizontal [hɔri'zɔntl], *a.*, *n.* horizontal, *f.*
hormone ['hɔ:moun], *n.* hormona, *f.*, hormón, *m.*
horn [hɔ:n], *n.* cuerno; (*mus.*) trompa; (*aut.*) bocina.
hornet ['hɔ:nit], *n.* avispón, *m.*
horny ['hɔ:ni], *a.* córneo; calloso.
horoscope ['hɔrəskoup], *n.* horóscopo.
horrible ['hɔribl], *a.* horrible.
horrid ['hɔrid], *a.* horroroso; malísimo.
horrify ['hɔrifai], *v.t.* horripilar, horrorizar.
horror ['hɔrə], *n.* horror, *m.*
hors d'oeuvres ['ɔ:'də:vrə], *n.pl.* entremeses, *m.pl.*
horse [hɔ:s], *n.* caballo; (*mil.*) caballería; (*carp. etc.*) caballete, burro; potro; *dark —*, persona misteriosa o desconocida; *to ride the high —*, ser envanecido y mandón.
horseback ['hɔ:sbæk], *a.*, *adv. on —*, a caballo.
horse-chestnut ['hɔ:s'tʃesnʌt], *n.* castaño de Indias (*árbol*); castaña de Indias (*fruta*).
horse-dealer ['hɔ:s'di:lə], *n.* chalán, caballista, *m.*
horse-laugh ['hɔ:slɑ:f], *n.* carcajada.
horseman ['hɔ:smən], *n.* jinete, *m.*
horseplay ['hɔ:splei], *n.* payasada.
horsepower ['hɔ:spauə], *n.* caballo de vapor *o* de fuerza.
horseshoe ['hɔ:sʃu:], *n.* herradura.
horsewhip ['hɔ:shwip], *n.* látigo.—*v.t.* azotar, zurriagar.
horsewoman ['hɔ:swumən], *n.* amazona.
hors(e)y ['hɔ:si], *a.* caballuno; caballar.
horticulture ['hɔ:tikʌltʃə], *n.* horticultura.
hose [houz], *n.* manga, manguera (*para el agua*); calzas, *f.pl.*, calceta (*ropa*).
hosiery ['houzjəri], *n.* medias; calcetería.
hospitable ['hɔspitəbl], *a.* hospitalario.
hospital ['hɔspitl], *n.* hospital, *m.*, clínica.
hospitality [hɔspi'tæliti], *n.* hospitalidad, *f.*
host (1) [houst], *n.* huésped, *m.*; mesonero; anfitrión, *m.*
host (2) [houst], *n.* hueste (*multitud*), *f.*
hostage ['hɔstidʒ], *n.* rehén, *m.*
hostel ['hɔstəl], *n.* parador, *m.*; residencia.
hostess ['houstis], *n.* huéspeda; patrona; (*aer.*) azafata.
hostile ['hɔstail], *a.* hostil, enemigo.
hostility [hɔs'tiliti], *n.* hostilidad, *f.*
hot [hɔt], *a.* caliente; cálido (*clima*); caluroso (*tiempo*); ardiente, apasionado; (*cul.*) picante; (*fam.*) insoportable; *to be —*, hacer calor (*tiempo*), tener calor (*persona*); *— air*, palabrería; *— water*, (*fam.*) apuro, aprieto.

hurt

hotbed ['hɔtbed], *n.* (*agr.*) almajara; (*fig.*) sementera.
hotel [(h)ou'tel], *n.* hotel, *m.*
hotelier [(h)ou'teliə], *n.* hotelero.
hothead ['hɔthed], *n.* alborotador, *m.*, temerario.
hotheaded ['hɔthedid], *a.* temerario.
hothouse ['hɔthaus], *n.* invernáculo.
hound [haund], *n.* podenco, sabueso.—*pl.* jauría.
hour [auə], *n.* hora.
houri ['huəri], *n.* hurí, *f.*
hourly ['auəli], *a.*, *adv.* (a) cada hora; por horas.
house [haus], *n.* casa; (*pol.*) cámara; (*fig.*) público, entrada; — *arrest*, arresto domiciliario; — *coat*, bata; *House of Commons*, Cámara de los Comunes.— [hauz], *v.t.* dar casa a, alojar; (*mech.*) encajar.
house-breaking ['hausbreikiŋ], *n.* escalo.
household ['haushould], *a.* casero, familiar.—*n.* casa, familia.
housekeeper ['hauski:pə], *n.* ama de llaves; mujer (*f.*) de casa.
housekeeping ['hauski:piŋ], *n.* gobierno doméstico.
housemaid ['hausmeid], *n.* criada.
house-warming ['hauswɔ:miŋ], *n.* estreno (de una casa).
housewife ['hauswaif], *n.* madre de familia, mujer casera.
house-work ['hausweːk], *n.* quehaceres domésticos, limpieza.
housing ['hauziŋ], *n.* vivienda; casas; (*mech.*) caja, encaje, *m.*
hove [houv], [HEAVE].
hovel ['hɔʌəl], *n.* casucha, choza mala.
hover ['hɔvə], *v.i.* cernerse; rondar; colgar.
hovercraft ['hɔvəkrɑːft], *n.* aereodeslizador, *m.*
how [hau], *adv.*, *conj.* como, de qué modo; cuán, cuanto; — *many*, cuantos; — *much*, cuanto.—*interj.* ¡cómo! ¡qué!—*interrog.* ¿cómo? ¿cuánto? — *far is it to X?* ¿cuánto hay de aquí a X?
however [hau'evə], *adv.* sin embargo; como quiera; — *big it is*, por grande que sea.
howitzer ['hauitsə], *n.* obús, *m.*
howl [haul], *n.* aullido, alarido.—*v.i.* aullar, chillar; soltar carcajadas.
howler ['haulə], *n.* (*fam.*) patochada, gazapo.
hoyden ['hɔidn], *n.* tunantuela.
hub [hʌb], *n.* (*mech.*) cubo; (*fig.*) eje, *m.*
hubbub ['hʌbʌb], *n.* alboroto, bulla.
huckster ['hʌkstə], *n.* (*U.S.*) buhonero.
huddle ['hʌdl], *n.* tropel, *m.*; (*fam.*) conchabanza.—*v.i.* acurrucarse; arracimarse.
hue (1) [hjuː], *n.* matiz, tinte, *m.*
hue (2) [hjuː], *n.* — *and cry*, vocería, alarma.
huff [hʌf], *n.* enfado súbito.—*v.t.* enojar; soplar (*juego de damas*).
hug [hʌg], *n.* apretón, abrazo fuerte, *m.*—*v.t.* abrazar, apretar; navegar muy cerca de.
huge [hjuːdʒ], *a.* enorme, inmenso.
hulk [hʌlk], *n.* casco; carraca; masa.
hulking ['hʌlkiŋ], *a.* grueso, pesado, enorme.
hull [hʌl], *n.* casco; armazón, *f.*
hullabaloo [hʌləbə'luː], *n.* baraúnda, bulla.
hum [hʌm], *n.* zumbido; tarareo.—*v.t.* canturrear, tararear.—*v.i.* canturrear; zumbar.
human ['hjuːmən], *a.*, *n.* humano.
humane [hjuː'mein], *a.* humanitario.

humanist ['hjuːmənist], *n.* humanista, *m.f.*
humanitarian [hjuːmæni'tɛəriən], *a.*, *n.* humanitario.
humanity [hjuː'mæniti], *n.* humanidad, *f.*
humble [hʌmbl], *a.* humilde.—*v.t.* humillar; *to eat — pie*, desdecirse, someterse.
humbleness ['hʌmblnəs], *a.* humildad, *f.*
humbug ['hʌmbʌg], *n.* bambolla; patraña; farsante (*persona*), *m.f.*
humdrum ['hʌmdrʌm], *a.* monótono, pesado, rutinario.
humid ['hjuːmid], *a.* húmedo.
humidity [hjuː'miditi], *n.* humedad, *f.*
humiliate [hjuː'milieit], *v.t.* humillar, degradar.
humiliation [hjuːmili'eifən], *n.* humillación, *f.*
humility [hjuː'militi], *n.* humildad, *f.*
humming-bird ['hʌmiŋbəːd], *n.* (*orn.*) colibrí, picaflor, *m.*
humorist ['hjuːmərist], *n.* humorista, *m.f.*
humorous ['hjuːmərəs], *a.* humorístico, chistoso.
humour ['hjuːmə], *n.* humor, *m.*—*v.t.* seguir el humor de, acomodarse a.
hump [hʌmp], *n.* joroba, corcova.—*v.t.* encorvar.
humpback ['hʌmpbæk], *n.* joroba; jorobado (*persona*).
Hun [hʌn], *n.* huno; (*pej.*) alemán, *m.*
hunch [hʌntʃ], *n.* joroba; (*fam.*) corazonada. —*v.t.* encorvar.
hunchback ['hʌntʃbæk], *n.* joroba; jorobado (*persona*).
hunchbacked ['hʌntʃbækt], *a.* jorobado.
hundred ['hʌndrəd], *a.* cien; ciento.—*n.* ciento; centenar.
hundredth ['hʌndrədθ], *a.*, *n.* centésimo.
hundredweight ['hʌndrədweit], *n.* quintal (50.8 *kgs.*), *m.*
hung [hʌŋ], [HANG].
Hungarian [hʌŋ'gɛəriən], *a.*, *n.* húngaro.
Hungary ['hʌŋgəri], *n.* Hungría.
hunger ['hʌŋgə], *n.* hambre, *f.*—*v.i.* hambrear; anhelar (*for*).
hungry ['hʌŋgri], *a.* hambiento (*for*, de); *to be —*, tener hambre.
hunt [hʌnt], *n.* caza; cacería; busca.—*v.t.* cazar; buscar.—*v.i.* cazar, buscar (*for*).
hunter ['hʌntə], *n.* cazador, *m.*; perro *o* caballo de caza.
hunting ['hʌntiŋ], *a.* de caza; cazador.—*n.* caza; cacería, montería.
huntsman ['hʌntsmən], *n.* cazador, *m.*; montero.
hurdle [həːdl], *n.* zarzo; (*also sport*) valla; (*fig.*) obstáculo.—*v.t.* saltar, vencer; cercar con vallas.
hurdy-gurdy ['həːdiˈgəːdi], *n.* (*mus.*) organillo, zanfonía.
hurl [həːl], *v.t.* lanzar, arrojar.
hurly-burly ['həːliˈbəːli], *n.* trulla, alboroto.
hurrah! [huˈrɑː], **hurray!** [huˈrei], *interj.* ¡viva!
hurricane ['hʌrikən], *n.* huracán, *m.*
hurry ['hʌri], *n.* prisa.—*v.t.* dar prisa a, apresurar; hacer con prisa.—*v.i.* or **hurry up**, darse prisa, apresurarse.
hurt [həːt], *n.* daño; herida; dolor; mal, *m.*—*v.t. irr.* dañar; doler; lastimar; herir.—*v.i. irr.* doler, hacer daño.

297

hurtful

hurtful ['hə:tful], *a.* dañoso; malicioso.
hurtle [hə:tl], *v.t.* arrojar.—*v.i.* arrojarse; chocar.
husband ['hʌzbənd], *n.* marido, esposo.—*v.t.* dirigir; economizar; cultivar.
husbandry ['hʌzbəndri], *n.* labranza, granjería; buen gobierno, economía.
hush [hʌʃ], *n.* silencio, quietud, *f.*—*v.t.* callar. —*v.i.* callar(se); *to — up*, echar tierra a (*escándalo etc.*).—*interj.* ¡chitón! ¡chito!
hush-hush ['hʌʃ'hʌʃ], *a.* muy secreto.
husk [hʌsk], *n.* cáscara, vaina, hollejo.—*v.t.* pelar, mondar.
husky ['hʌski], *a.* ronco, rauco (*voz*); (*fam.*) fortachón.—*n.* (*zool.*) perro esquimal.
hussy ['hʌsi, 'hʌzi], *n.* tunanta, descarada.
hustle [hʌsl], *n.* prisa; bulla.—*v.t.* empujar; dar prisa a.—*v.i.* darse prisa; patullar.
hut [hʌt], *n.* cabaña, choza, cobertizo.
hutch [hʌtʃ], *n.* conejera; arca; cabaña.
hyacinth ['haiəsinθ], *n.* jacinto.
hybrid ['haibrid], *a.*, *n.* híbrido.
hydrant ['haidrənt], *n.* boca de riego.
hydraulic [hai'drɔ:lik], *a.* hidráulico.
hydrochloric [haidro'klɔrik], *a.* clorhídrico.
hydroelectric [haidroi'lektrik], *a.* hidroeléctrico.
hydrogen ['haidrədʒən], *n.* hidrógeno; — *bomb*, bomba de hidrógeno.
hyena [hai'i:na], *n.* hiena.
hygiene ['haidʒi:n], *n.* higiene, *f.*
hygienic [hai'dʒi:nik], *a.* higiénico.
hymn [him], *n.* himno.
hyper- ['haipə], *prefix.* hiper-, excesivamente.
hyperbole [hai'pə:bəli], *n.* hipérbole, *f.*
hyphen ['haifən], *n.* guión, *m.*
hyphenate ['haifəneit], *v.t.* escribir con guión, insertar un guión.
hypnosis [hip'nousis], *n.* hipnosis, *f.*
hypnotic [hip'nɔtik], *a.*, *n.* hipnótico.
hypnotism ['hipnətizm], *n.* hipnotismo.
hypnotize ['hipnətaiz], *v.t.* hipnotizar.
hypochondriac [haipo'kɔndriæk], *a.*, *n.* hipocondríaco.
hypocrisy [hi'pɔkrisi], *n.* hipocresía.
hypocrite ['hipəkrit], *n.* hipócrita, *m.f.*
hypocritical [hipə'critikəl], *a.* hipocrítico.
hypodermic [haipo'də:mik], *a.* hipodérmico.—*n.* (jeringa) hipodérmica.
hypothesis [hai'pɔθisis], *n.* hipótesis, *f.*
hypothetical [haipo'θetikəl], *a.* hipotético.
hysteria [his'tiəri], *n.* histeria, histerismo.
hysteric(al) [his'terik(əl)], *a.* histérico.
hysterics [his'teriks], *n.pl.* histerismo, paroxismo histérico.

I

I, (1) **i** [ai], *n.* novena letra del alfabeto inglés.
I (2) [ai], *pron.* yo.
Iberian [ai'biəriən], *a.* ibérico.—*n.* íbero.
ibex ['aibeks], *n.* íbice, *m.*, cabra montés.
ice [ais], *n.* hielo; helado; (*cul.*) garapiña.—*v.t.* helar; poner hielo en; garapiñar.—*v.i.* helarse.

iceberg ['aisbə:g], *n.* iceberg, *m.*, témpano de hielo.
icebox ['aisbɔks], *n.* (*U.S.*) nevera.
ice-cream ['ais'kri:m], *n.* helado.
Iceland ['aislənd], *n.* Islandia.
Icelander ['aislændə], *n.* islandés (*persona*), *m.*
Icelandic [ais'lændik], *a.* islandés.—*n.* islandés (*idioma*), *m.*
icicle ['aisikl], *n.* carámbano, canelón, *m.*
icing ['aisiŋ], *n.* garapiña, costra de azúcar; (*aer.*) helamiento.
iconoclast [ai'kɔnoklæst, ai'kɔnoklɑ:st], *n.* iconoclasta, *m.f.*
icy ['aisi], *a.* helado, frío.
I'd [aid] [I WOULD, I SHOULD, I HAD].
idea [ai'diə], *n.* idea.
ideal [ai'diəl], *a.*, *n.* ideal, *m.*
idealist [ai'diəlist], *n.* idealista, *m.f.*
idealistic [aidiə'listik], *a.* idealista.
idealize [ai'diəlaiz], *v.t.* idealizar.
identical [ai'dentikəl], *a.* idéntico.
identify [ai'dentifai], *v.t.* identificar.
identity [ai'dentiti], *n.* identidad, *f.*
ideology [aidi'ɔlədʒi], *n.* ideología.
idiocy ['idiəsi], *n.* idiotez, necedad, *f.*
idiom ['idjəm], *n.* modismo, idiotismo; lenguaje, *m.*; estilo.
idiot ['idiət], *n.* idiota, *m.f.*
idiotic [idi'ɔtik], *a.* idiota.
idle [aidl], *a.* ocioso; perezoso; vano (*inútil*) —*v.t. to — away*, malgastar (*tiempo*).—*v.i.* holgazanear; marchar despacio.
idleness ['aidlnis], *n.* ociosidad; pereza; paro.
idler ['aidlə], *n.* holgazán, haragán, *m.*
idol [aidl], *n.* ídolo.
idolater [ai'dɔlətə], *n.* idólatra, *m.*
idolatress [ai'dɔlətris], *n.* idólatra, *f.*
idolatry [ai'dɔlətri], *n.* idolatría.
idolize ['aidəlaiz], *v.t.* idolatrar.
idyll ['idil], *n.* idilio.
if [if], *conj.* si; — *so*, si es así.—*n.* (*fam.*) pero, duda.
igloo ['iglu:], *n.* iglú, *m.*
ignite [ig'nait], *v.t.* encender.—*v.i.* -se.
ignition [ig'niʃən], *n.* encendido, ignición, *f.*
ignoble [ig'noubl], *a.* innoble; infame.
ignominious [ignə'miniəs], *a.* ignominioso.
ignominy ['ignəmini], *n.* ignominia.
ignoramus [ignə'reiməs], *n.* ignorante, *m.f.*
ignorance ['ignərəns], *n.* ignorancia.
ignorant ['ignərənt], *a.* ignorante; indocto; *to be — of*, ignorar, desconocer.
ignore [ig'nɔ:], *v.t.* no hacer caso de, desconocer, desairar; rechazar.
I'll [ail] [I WILL, I SHALL].
ill [il], *a.* enfermo, malo.—*n.* mal, *m.*; *to take —*, tomar a mal.—*adv.* mal; poco.
ill- [il], *prefix.* mal-, des-.
illegal [i'li:gəl], *a.* ilegal.
illegitimacy [ili'dʒitiməsi], *n.* ilegitimidad, *f.*
illegitimate [ili'dʒitimit], *a.* ilegítimo.
ill-fated [il'feitid], *a.* malogrado.
ill-gotten [il'gɔtən], *a.* mal adquirido.
illicit [i'lisit], *a.* ilícito.
illiteracy [i'litərəsi], *n.* analfabetismo; incultura.
illiterate [i'litərit], *a.* analfabeto; iliterato.
ill-mannered [il'mænəd], *a.* malcriado, mal educado, descortés.
illness ['ilnis], *n.* enfermedad, *f.*
illogical [i'lɔdʒikəl], *a.* ilógico.

illogicality [iləd3i'kæliti], *n.* falta de lógica.
ill-tempered [il'tempəd], *a.* desabrido, de mal genio.
ill-timed [il'taimd], *a.* inoportuno.
illuminate [i'lju:mineit], *v.t.* iluminar; alumbrar.
illumination [ilju:mi'neiʃən], *n.* iluminación, *f.*; alumbrado.
illumine [i'lju:min], *v.t.* iluminar, alumbrar.
ill-use [il'ju:z], *v.t.* maltratar.
illusion [i'lju:ʒən], *n.* ilusión, *f.*
illustrate ['iləstreit], *v.t.* ilustrar.
illustration [iləs'treiʃən], *n.* ilustración, *f.*; grabado, lámina.
illustrious [i'lʌstriəs], *a.* ilustre, preclaro.
I'm [aim] [I AM].
image ['imid3], *n.* imagen, *f.*; (*gram.*) metáfora.
imaginary [i'mæd3inəri], *a.* imaginario.
imagination [imæd3i'neiʃən], *n.* imaginación, *f.*
imagine [i'mæd3in], *v.t.*, *v.i.* imaginar(se).
imbecile ['imbisi:l], *a.*, *n.* imbécil, *m.f.*
imbed [im'bed], *v.t.* enclavar, encajar.
imbibe [im'baib], *v.t.* beber, embeber(se en *o* de), empapar(se de).
imbroglio [im'brouliou], *n.* embrollo, enredo.
imbue [im'bju:], *v.t.* imbuir (*with*, de, en).
imitate ['imiteit], *v.t.* imitar, remedar.
imitation [imi'teiʃən], *n.* imitación, *f.*
imitator ['imiteitə], *n.* imitador, *m.*
immaculate [i'mækjulit], *a.* inmaculado.
immaterial [imə'tiəriəl], *a.* sin importancia; inmaterial.
immature [imə'tjuə], *a.* inmaturo, verde.
immaturity [imə'tjuəriti], *n.* inmadurez, *f.*
immediate [i'mi:djət], *a.* inmediato.
immediately [i'mi:djətli], *adv.* en seguida, inmediatamente.
immense [i'mens], *a.* inmenso, vasto.
immigrant ['imigrənt], *a.*, *n.* inmigrante, *m.f.*
immigration [imi'greiʃən], *n.* inmigración, *f.*
imminent ['iminənt], *a.* inminente.
immobilize [i'moubilaiz], *v.t.* inmovilizar.
immoderate [i'mɔdərit], *a.* inmoderado.
immodest [i'mɔdist], *a.* inmodesto, impúdico.
immodesty [i'mɔdisti], *n.* inmodestia, impudicia.
immoral [i'mɔrəl], *a.* inmoral.
immorality [imə'ræliti], *n.* inmoralidad, *f.*
immortal [i'mɔ:təl], *a.* inmortal.
immortality [imɔ:'tæliti], *n.* inmortalidad, *f.*
immortalize [i'mɔ:təlaiz], *v.t.* inmortalizar.
immune [i'mju:n], *a.* inmune (*to*, contra).
immunize [i'mjunaiz], *v.t.* inmunizar.
imp [imp], *n.* diablillo, duende, *m.*
impact ['impækt], *n.* choque, *m.*, impacto.
impair [im'pɛə], *v.t.* empeorar, perjudicar.
impale [im'peil], *v.t.* empalar, atravesar.
impart [im'pɑ:t], *v.t.* comunicar; hacer saber.
impartial [im'pɑ:ʃəl], *a.* imparcial.
impassable [im'pɑ:səbl], *a.* intransitable.
impasse [im'pɑ:s], *n.* callejón (*m.*) sin salida.
impassive [im'pæsiv], *a.* impasible.
impatience [im'peiʃəns], *n.* impaciencia.
impatient [im'peiʃənt], *a.* impaciente.
impeach [im'pi:tʃ], *v.t.* acusar, encausar, denunciar.

impeccable [im'pekəbl], *a.* impecable.
impede [im'pi:d], *v.t.* dificultar, impedir.
impediment [im'pedimənt], *n.* impedimento.
impel [im'pel], *v.t.* impeler, impulsar.
impend [im'pend], *v.i.* amenazar; pender; ser inminente.
impenitent [im'penitənt], *a.*, *n.* impenitente.
imperative [im'peritiv], *a.* imperativo, imperioso.—*n.* (*gram.*) imperativo.
imperfect [im'pə:fikt], *a.*, *n.* imperfecto.
imperfection [impə'fekʃən], *n.* imperfección, *f.*; defecto.
imperforate [im'pə:fərit], *a.* sin dentar (*sello*).
imperial [im'piəriəl], *a.* imperial.
imperialism [im'piəriəlizm], *n.* imperialismo.
impersonal [im'pə:sənəl], *a.* impersonal.
impersonate [im'pə:səneit], *v.t.* imitar, fingir ser; personificar.
impertinent [im'pə:tinənt], *a.* impertinente.
impervious [im'pə:vjəs], *a.* impermeable; impersuasible.
impetuous [im'petjuəs], *a.* impetuoso.
impetus ['impitəs], *n.* ímpetu, *m.*
impinge [im'pind3], *v.i.* tocar, incidir (**on**, en).
impious ['impiəs], *a.* impío.
implacable [im'plækəbl], *a.* implacable.
implant [im'plɑ:nt], *v.t.* (in)plantar.
implement [im'plimənt], *n.* herramienta, utensilio.—['impliment], *v.t.* poner en ejecución.
implicate ['implikeit], *v.t.* implicar, enredar.
implication [impli'keiʃən], *n.* insinuación; implicación, *f.*
implicit [im'plisit], *a.* implícito; absoluto.
implied [im'plaid], *a.* implícito (**by**, en).
implore [im'plɔ:], *v.t.* suplicar, implorar.
imply [im'plai], *v.t.* implicar, suponer; insinuar, dar a entender.
impolite [impə'lait], *a.* descortés.
import ['impɔ:t], *n.* importación, *f.*; importancia; tenor, *m.*, sentido.—[im'pɔ:t], *v.t.* importar.
importance [im'pɔ:təns], *n.* importancia.
important [im'pɔ:tənt], *a.* importante.
importune [im'pɔ:tju:n], *v.t.* importunar.
impose [im'pouz], *v.t.* imponer; abusar (**on**, de).
imposing [im'pouziŋ], *a.* imponente.
imposition [impə'ziʃən], *n.* imposición, *f.*; abuso; (*educ.*) tarea extraordinaria.
impossibility [impɔsi'biliti], *n.* imposibilidad, *f.*
impossible [im'pɔsibl], *a.* imposible.
impostor [im'pɔstə], *n.* impostor, *m.*
impotence ['impətəns], *n.* impotencia.
impotent ['impətənt], *a.* impotente.
impoverish [im'pɔvəriʃ], *v.t.* empobrecer.
impracticable [im'præktikəbl], *a.* impracticable, infactible.
impractical [im'præktikəl], *a.* irrealizable; poco práctico.
impregnable [im'pregnəbl], *a.* inexpugnable.
impregnate [im'pregneit], *v.t.* impregnar.
impresario [impre'sa:riou], *n.* empresario.
impress [im'pres], *v.t.* imprimir; impresionar; inculcar.
impression [im'preʃən], *n.* impresión, *f.*
impressive [im'presiv], *a.* impresionante.

imprint

imprint ['imprint], *n.* pie (*m.*) de imprenta; marca.—[im'print], *v.t.* estampar, imprimir, grabar.

imprison [im'prizən], *v.t.* encarcelar.

imprisonment [im'prizənmənt], *n.* encarcelamiento.

improbable [im'prɔbəbl], *a.* improbable.

impromptu [im'promptju:], *a.* impremeditado, de improviso.—*n.* improvisación, *f.* —*adv.* improvisando.

improper [im'prɔpə], *a.* indecoroso; impropio.

impropriety [imprə'praiəti], *n.* indecencia; impropiedad, *f.*

improve [im'pru:v], *v.t.* mejorar; perfeccionar (*on*).—*v.i.* mejorar(se); perfeccionarse.

improvement [im'pru:vmənt], *n.* mejoramiento; mejoría; mejora.

improvise ['imprəvaiz], *v.t., v.i.* improvisar.

imprudent [im'pru:dənt], *a.* imprudente.

impudence ['impjudəns], *n.* impudencia, desfachatez, *f.*

impudent ['impjudənt], *a.* impudente, desfachatado.

impugn [im'pju:n], *v.t.* impugnar, poner en tela de juicio.

impulse ['impʌls], *n.* impulso.

impulsive [im'pʌlsiv], *a.* impulsivo.

impunity [im'pju:niti], *n.* impunidad, *f.*

impure [im'pjuə], *a.* impuro.

impurity [im'pjuəriti], *n.* impureza; impuridad, *f.*

impute [im'pju:t], *v.t.* imputar.

in [in], *prep.* en; dentro de; de; con.—*adv.* en casa; dentro.

in- [in-], *prefix.* in-, des-.

inability [inə'biliti], *n.* inhabilidad; incapacidad, *f.*

inaccessible [inæk'sesibl], *a.* inasequible; inaccesible.

inaccuracy [in'ækjurisi], *n.* incorrección, inexactitud, *f.*

inaccurate [in'ækjurit], *a.* incorrecto, inexacto.

inactive [in'æktiv], *a.* inactivo.

inadequate [in'ædikwit], *a.* inadecuado, insuficiente.

inadvertent [inəd'və:tənt], *a.* inadvertido.

inadvisable [inəd'vaizəbl], *a.* no aconsejable, imprudente.

inane [in'ein], *a.* vano, inane, sandio.

inanimate [in'ænimit], *a.* inanimado.

inapplicable [in'æplikəbl], *a.* inaplicable.

inappropriate [inə'prouppriit], *a.* poco apropriado, inadecuado.

inarticulate [ina:'tikjulit], *a.* inarticulado; incapaz de expresarse.

inasmuch as [inəz'mʌtʃəz], *conj.* visto que; en cuanto.

inattentive [inə'tentiv], *a.* desatento.

inaudible [in'ɔ:dibl], *a.* inaudible.

inaugurate [in'ɔ:gjureit], *v.t.* inaugurar.

inauspicious [inɔ:'spiʃəs], *a.* desfavorable, poco propicio.

inborn ['inbɔ:n], *a.* innato.

inbreed ['in'bri:d], *v.t. irr.* (*conjug. like* BREED) engendrar dentro de la misma estirpe; dotar de . . . al nacer.

Inca ['iŋkə], *a.* incaico.—*n.* inca, *m.f.*

incantation [inkæn'teiʃən], *n.* conjuro.

incapable [in'keipəbl], *a.* incapaz.

incapacitate [inkə'pæsiteit], *v.t.* incapacitar.

incarcerate [in'ka:səreit], *v.t.* encarcelar, aprisionar.

incarnate [in'ka:nit], *a.* encarnado.—['inka:neit], *v.t.* encarnar.

incarnation [inka:'neiʃən], *n.* encarnación, *f.*

incautious [in'kɔ:ʃəs], *a.* incauto, descuidado.

incendiary [in'sendjəri], *a., n.* incendiario.

incense (1) ['insens], *n.* incienso.—*v.t.* incensar.

incense (2) [in'sens], *v.t.* encolerizar, exasperar.

incentive [in'sentiv], *a.* incentivo.—*n.* incentivo, aliciente, *m.*

inception [in'sepʃən], *n.* comienzo, estreno.

incessant [in'sesənt], *a.* incesante, sin cesar.

incest ['insest], *n.* incesto.

inch [intʃ], *n.* pulgada; *within an — of*, a dos dedos de.—*v.t., v.i.* mover(se) poco a poco.

incident ['insidənt], *a., n.* incidente, *m.*

incidental [insi'dentl], *a.* incidental.

incinerate [in'sinəreit], *v.t.* incinerar.

incipient [in'sipiənt], *a.* incipiente.

incision [in'siʒən], *n.* incisión, *f.*

incite [in'sait], *v.t.* incitar, instigar.

inclement [in'klemənt], *a.* inclemente.

inclination [inkli'neiʃən], *n.* inclinación, *f.*

incline ['inklain], *n.* declive, *m.*—[in'klain], *v.t.* inclinar.—*v.i.* inclinarse (**to, a**).

include [in'klu:d], *v.t.* incluir.

inclusive [in'klu:siv], *a.* inclusivo.

incognito [in'kɔgnitou], *a.* incógnito.—*adv.* de incógnito.

incoherent [inkou'hiərənt], *a.* incoherente.

income ['inkəm], *n.* renta, ingresos, *m.pl.* rédito.

income-tax ['inkəmtæks], *n.* impuesto de utilidades, impuesto sobre renta.

incommode [inkə'moud], *v.t.* incomodar.

incompatible [inkəm'pætibl], *a.* incompatible.

incompetence [in'kɔmpitəns], *n.* incompetencia.

incompetent [in'kɔmpitənt], *a.* incompetente.

incomplete [inkəm'pli:t], *a.* incompleto.

incomprehensible [inkɔmpri'hensibl], *a.* incomprensible.

inconceivable [inkən'si:vəbl], *a.* inconcebible.

inconclusive [inkən'klu:siv], *a.* inconcluyente, indeciso.

incongruity [inkɔn'gru:iti], *n.* incongruencia.

incongruous [in'kɔŋgruəs], *a.* incongruo.

inconsequent [in'kɔnsikwənt], *a.* inconsecuente.

inconsequential [inkɔnsi'kwenʃəl], *a.* inconsecuente; sin importancia.

inconsiderable [inkən'sidərəbl], *a.* insignificante.

inconsiderate [inkən'sidərit], *a.* desconsiderado.

inconsistent [inkən'sistənt], *a.* inconsistente, inconsecuente.

inconstant [in'kɔnstənt], *a.* inconstante.

incontinent [in'kɔntinənt], *a.* incontinente.

inconvenience [inkən'vi:niəns], *n.* incomodidad, *f.*; inconveniente, *m.*, molestia.—*v.t.* incomodar.

inconvenient [inkən'vi:niənt], *a.* inconveniente, incómodo, molesto.

incorporate [in'kɔ:pəreit], *v.t.* incorporar; formar una sociedad anónima.
incorrect [inkə'rekt], *a.* incorrecto.
incorrigible [in'kɔridʒibl], *a.* incorregible.
increase ['inkri:s], *n.* aumento; ganancia; progenie, *f.*—[in'kri:s], *v.t., v.i.* aumentar.
increasingly [in'kri:siŋli], *adv.* cada vez más, con creces.
incredible [in'kredibl], *a.* increíble.
incredulous [in'kredjuləs], *a.* incrédulo.
increment ['inkrimənt], *n.* incremento, aumento.
incriminate [in'krimineit], *v.t.* acriminar, incriminar.
incubate ['inkjubeit], *v.t., v.i.* incubar.
incubator ['inkjubeitə], *n.* incubadora.
inculcate ['inkʌlkeit], *v.t.* inculcar.
incumbent [in'kʌmbənt], *a.* incumbente.—*n.* (*eccl.*) beneficiado; *to be — on*, incumbir a.
incur [in'kə:], *v.t.* contraer, incurrir en; causarse.
incurable [in'kjuərəbl], *a.* incurable.
incursion [in'kə:ʃən], *n.* incursión, *f.*, correría.
indebted [in'detid], *a.* adeudado; obligado.
indecency [in'di:sənsi], *n.* indecencia.
indecent [in'di:sənt], *a.* indecente.
indecision [indi'siʒən], *n.* indecisión, *f.*
indecisive [indi'saisiv], *a.* indeciso.
indecorous [indi'kɔ:rəs], *a.* indecoroso.
indeed [in'di:d], *adv.* de veras, por cierto.
indefinite [in'definit], *a.* indefinido.
indelible [in'delibl], *a.* indeleble.
indemnify [in'demnifai], *v.t.* indemnizar.
indemnity [in'demniti], *n.* indemnización, indemnidad, *f.*
indent [in'dent], *v.t.* mellar; (*print.*) sangrar.
indenture [in'dentʃə], *n.* contrato (de aprendizaje).
independence [indi'pendəns], *n.* independencia.
independent [indi'pendənt], *a.* independiente.
indescribable [indis'kraibəbl], *a.* indescriptible.
index ['indeks], *n.* (*pl.* **-dexes, -dices**) índice, *m.*
India ['indjə], *n.* la India.
Indian ['indjən], *a., n.* indio; *India ink*, tinta china.
india-rubber ['indjərʌbə], *n.* goma.
indicate ['indikeit], *v.t.* indicar.
indication [indi'keiʃən], *n.* indicación, *f.*
indicative [in'dikətiv], *a., n.* indicativo.
indicator ['indikeitə], *n.* indicador, *m.*
indict [in'dait], *v.t.* (*jur.*) acusar, procesar.
indictment [in'daitmənt], *n.* (auto de) acusación, *f.*
indifference [in'difrəns], *n.* indiferencia.
indifferent [in'difrənt], *a.* indiferente; pasadero, regular.
indigenous [in'didʒinəs], *a.* indígena, natural.
indigent ['indidʒənt], *a.* indigente.
indigestion [indi'dʒestʃən], *n.* indigestión, *f.*
indignant [in'dignənt], *a.* indignado.
indignation [indig'neiʃən], *n.* indignación, *f.*
indignity [in'digniti], *n.* indignidad, *f.*
indigo ['indigou], *n.* índigo; añil, *m.*
indirect [indi'rekt], *a.* indirecto.
indiscreet [indis'kri:t], *a.* indiscreto.
indiscretion [indis'kreʃən], *n.* indiscreción, *f.*

indiscriminate [indis'kriminit], *a.* promiscuo; indistinto.
indispensable [indis'pensəbl], *a.* indispensable, imprescindible.
indisposed [indis'pouzd], *a.* indispuesto, maldispuesto.
indisposition [indispə'ziʃən], *n.* indisposición, *f.*
indisputable [indis'pju:təbl], *a.* indisputable, irrebatible.
indistinct [indis'tiŋkt], *a.* indistinto, confuso.
indistinguishable [indis'tiŋgwiʃəbl], *a.* indistinguible.
individual [indi'vidjuəl], *a.* individual.—*n.* individuo.
Indo-China [indou'tʃainə], *n.* la Indochina.
indoctrinate [in'dɔktrineit], *v.t.* adoctrinar, catequizar.
Indo-European [indoujuərə'piən], *a., n.* indoeuropeo.
indolence ['indələns], *n.* indolencia.
indomitable [in'dɔmitəbl], *a.* indómito, indomable.
Indonesian [ində'ni:zjən], *a., n.* indonesio.
indoor ['indɔ:], *a.* de puertas adentro; interior.
indoors [in'dɔ:z], *adv.* en casa, dentro.
indorse [in'dɔ:s], *v.t.* endosar; respaldar.
induce [in'dju:s], *v.t.* inducir; ocasionar.
inducement [in'dju:smənt], *n.* aliciente, *m.*, incentivo.
indulge [in'dʌldʒ], *v.t.* gratificar; mimar.—*v.i.* entregarse (*in*, a), gozar.
indulgence [in'dʌldʒəns], *n.* (*eccl.*) indulgencia; mimo; abandono.
indulgent [in'dʌldʒənt], *a.* indulgente.
industrial [in'dʌstriəl], *a.* industrial.
industrialist [in'dʌstriəlist], *n.* industrial, *m.*
industrialize [in'dʌstriəlaiz], *v.t.* industrializar.
industrious [in'dʌstriəs], *a.* industrioso, aplicado.
industry ['indəstri], *n.* industria.
inebriate [i'ni:brieit], *v.t.* embriagar.
inedible [i'nedibl], *a.* no comestible.
ineffable [i'nefəbl], *a.* inefable.
ineffective [ini'fektiv], *a.* ineficaz.
ineffectual [ini'fektjuəl], *a.* ineficaz.
inefficiency [ini'fiʃənsi], *n.* ineficacia.
inefficient [ini'fiʃənt], *a.* ineficaz; ineficiente.
inept [i'nept], *a.* inepto.
inequality [ini'kwɔliti], *n.* desigualdad, *f.*
inert [i'nə:t], *a.* inerte.
inertia [i'nə:ʃə], *n.* inercia; desidia.
inescapable [inis'keipəbl], *a.* ineludible.
inevitable [i'nevitəbl], *a.* inevitable.
inexact [inig'zækt], *a.* inexacto.
inexhaustible [inig'zɔ:stibl], *a.* inagotable.
inexpedient [iniks'pi:djənt], *a.* impropio, inoportuno, imprudente.
inexpensive [iniks'pensiv], *a.* barato.
inexperienced [iniks'piəriənst], *a.* inexperto.
inexpert [ineks'pə:t], *a.* imperito.
inexplicable [i'neksplikəbl], *a.* inexplicable.
infallible [in'fælibl], *a.* infalible.
infamous ['infəməs], *a.* infame.
infamy ['infəmi], *n.* infamia.
infancy ['infənsi], *n.* infancia.
infant ['infənt], *a.* infantil.—*n.* niño; infante, *m.*; (*educ.*) párvulo; (*jur.*) menor, *m.f.*
infantile ['infəntail], *a.* infantil; aniñado.
infantry ['infəntri], *n.* infantería.

infatuate

infatuate [inˈfætjueit], *v.t.* amartelar, apasionar; engreír.
infatuation [infætjuˈeiʃən], *n.* encaprichamiento, apasionamiento.
infect [inˈfekt], *v.t.* inficionar, infectar, contagiar.
infection [inˈfekʃən], *n.* infección. *f.*
infectious [inˈfekʃəs], *a.* contagioso, infeccioso.
infer [inˈfəː], *v.t.* inferir; (*fam.*) dar a entender.
inferior [inˈfiəriə], *a.*, *n.* inferior, *m.*
inferiority [infiəriˈoriti], *n.* inferioridad, *f.*
infernal [inˈfəːnəl], *a.* infernal.
inferno [inˈfəːnou], *n.* infierno.
infertile [inˈfəːtail], *a.* estéril, infecundo.
infest [inˈfest], *v.t.* infestar; apestar; plagar.
infidel [ˈinfidəl], *a.*, *n.* infiel, *m.f.*
infidelity [infiˈdeliti], *n.* infidelidad, deslealtad, *f.*
infiltrate [ˈinfiltreit], *v.t.* infiltrar; infiltrarse en.
infinite [ˈinfinit], *a.*, *n.* infinito.
infinitive [inˈfinitiv], *a.*, *n.* infinitivo.
infinity [inˈfiniti], *n.* infinidad, *f.*; (*math.*) infinito.
infirm [inˈfəːm], *a.* enfermizo, doliente; débil; inestable.
infirmary [inˈfəːməri], *n.* enfermería; hospital, *m.*
infirmity [inˈfəːmiti], *n.* dolencia, achaque, *m.*; inestabilidad, *f.*
inflame [inˈfleim], *v.t.* inflamar, encender.—*v.i.* inflamarse.
inflammable [inˈflæməbl], *a.* inflamable.
inflammation [infləˈmeiʃən], *n.* inflamación, *f.*
inflate [inˈfleit], *v.t.* inflar, hinchar.—*v.i.* inflarse.
inflation [inˈfleiʃən], *n.* inflación, *f.*; (*fig.*) hinchazón, *f.*
inflect [inˈflekt], *v.t.* dar (las) inflexión(es) a.
inflection, inflexion [inˈflekʃən], *n.* inflexión.
inflict [inˈflikt], *v.t.* infligir (*on*, a).
influence [ˈinfluəns], *n.* influencia, influjo.—*v.t.* influenciar, influir sobre *o* en.
influenza [influˈenzə], *n.* gripe, *f.*
influx [ˈinflʌks], *n.* afluencia.
inform [inˈfɔːm], *v.t.* informar.
informal [inˈfɔːməl], *a.* familiar; (*pej.*) informal (*impolite*).
informality [infɔːˈmæliti], *n.* sencillez, *f.*, falta de ceremonia; informalidad, *f.*
informant [inˈfɔːmənt], *n.* informante, *m.f.*, informador, *m.*
information [infəˈmeiʃən], *n.* informes, *m.pl.*, información, *f.*
informer [inˈfɔːmə], *n.* delator, soplón, *m.*
infraction [inˈfrækʃən], *n.* infracción, *f.*
infrequent [inˈfriːkwənt], *a.* infrecuente.
infringe [inˈfrindʒ], *v.t.* violar, infringir.
infuriate [inˈfjuərieit], *v.t.* enfurecer.
infuse [inˈfjuːz], *v.t.* infundir.
ingenious [inˈdʒiːniəs], *a.* ingenioso, genial.
ingenuity [indʒiˈnjuːiti], *n.* ingeniosidad, *f.*
ingenuous [inˈdʒenjuəs], *a.* ingenuo.
inglorious [inˈglɔːriəs], *a.* obscuro; deshonroso.
ingot [ˈiŋgət], *n.* lingote, *m.*
ingrained [inˈgreind], *a.* muy pegado *o* arraigado.

ingratiate [inˈgreiʃieit], *v.r.* insinuarse (*with*, con).
ingratitude [inˈgrætitjuːd], *n.* ingratitud, *f.* desagradecimiento.
ingredient [inˈgriːdiənt], *n.* ingrediente, *m.*
inhabit [inˈhæbit], *v.t.* habitar.
inhabitant [inˈhæbitənt], *n.* habitante, *m.f.*
inhale [inˈheil], *v.t.*, *v.i.* aspirar.
inherent [inˈhiərənt], *a.* inherente; innato.
inherit [inˈherit], *v.t.* heredar.
inheritance [inˈheritəns], *n.* herencia.
inhibit [inˈhibit], *v.t.* inhibir.
inhibition [inhiˈbiʃən], *n.* inhibición, *f.*
inhospitable [inhɔsˈpitəbl], *a.* inhospitalario, inhospedable.
inhuman [inˈhjuːmən], *a.* inhumano, desalmado.
inimitable [iˈnimitəbl], *a.* inimitable.
iniquitous [iˈnikwitəs], *a.* inicuo, malvado.
iniquity [iˈnikwiti], *n.* iniquidad, *f.*
initial [iˈniʃəl], *a.*, *n.* inicial, *f.*—*v.t.* rubricar; marcar.
initiate [iˈniʃieit], *n.* iniciado.—*v.t.* iniciar.
initiative [iˈniʃiətiv], *n.* iniciativa.
inject [inˈdʒekt], *v.t.* inyectar.
injection [inˈdʒekʃən], *n.* inyección, *f.*
injunction [inˈdʒʌŋkʃən], *n.* mandato; entredicho.
injure [ˈindʒə], *v.t.* dañar; herir; injuriar.
injurious [inˈdʒuəriəs], *a.* dañoso; injurioso.
injury [ˈindʒəri], *n.* lesión, *f.*, herida; daño.
injustice [inˈdʒʌstis], *n.* injusticia.
ink [iŋk], *n.* tinta.—*v.t.* entintar.
inkling [ˈiŋkliŋ], *n.* noción, *f.*, sospecha.
inkwell [ˈiŋkwel], *n.* tintero.
inky [ˈiŋki], *a.* negro; manchado de tinta.
inlaid [ˈinleid], *a.* embutido.
inland [ˈinlənd] *a.* interior.—[ˈinˈlænd], *adv.* tierra adentro.
inlet [ˈinlet], *n.* abra, ensenada, cala.
inmate [ˈinmeit], *n.* residente, *m.f.*; asilado; preso.
inmost [ˈinmoust], *a.* el más íntimo *o* recóndito.
inn [in], *n.* posada, mesón, *m.*, fonda.
innate [iˈneit], *a.* innato, ingénito.
inner [ˈinə], *a.* interior; — *tube*, cámara de aire.
innermost [INMOST].
innings [ˈiniŋz], *n.sg.* (*sport*) turno; (*fig.*) turno, goce, *m.*
innkeeper [ˈinkiːpə], *n.* posadero, mesonero.
innocence [ˈinəsəns], *n.* inocencia.
innocent [ˈinəsənt], *a.* inocente.
innovate [ˈinoveit], *v.t.* innovar.
innovation [inoˈveiʃən], *n.* innovación, *f.*
innuendo [injuˈendou], *n.* indirecta, insinuación, *f.*
innumerable [iˈnjuːmərəbl], *a.* innumerable.
inoculate [iˈnɔkjuleit], *v.t.* inocular.
inoffensive [inəˈfensiv], *a.* inofensivo.
inopportune [iˈnɔpətjuːn], *a.* inoportuno; intempestivo.
inordinate [iˈnɔːdinit], *a.* excesivo, desordenado.
inorganic [inɔːˈgænik], *a.* inorgánico.
input [ˈinput], *n.* gasto; energía invertida; lo que se invierte.
inquest [ˈiŋkwest], *n.* indagación judicial, *f.*
inquire [inˈkwaiə], *v.i.* preguntar (*about, after*, por; *of*, a); investigar (*into*).

inquiry [in'kwaiəri], *n.* pesquisa, investigación, *f.*; pregunta.
inquisition [inkwi'ziʃən], *n.* inquisición, *f.*
inquisitive [in'kwizitiv], *a.* curioso, preguntón.
inquisitor [in'kwizitə], *n.* inquisidor, *m.*
inroad ['inroud], *n.* incursión, *f.*; desgaste, *m.*
insane [in'sein], *a.* loco, demente, insano.
insanity [in'sæniti], *n.* locura, insania, demencia.
insatiable [in'seiʃəbl], *a.* insaciable.
inscribe [in'skraib], *v.t.* inscribir; grabar.
inscription [in'skripʃən], *n.* inscripción, *f.*
inscrutable [in'skru:təbl], *a.* inescrutable, insondable.
insect ['insekt], *n.* insecto.
insecticide [in'sektisaid], *n.* insecticida, *m.*
insecure [insi'kjuə], *a.* inseguro; precario.
insecurity [insi'kjuəriti], *n.* inseguridad, *f.*
insensible [in'sensibl], *a.* insensible; inconsciente.
inseparable [in'sepərəbl], *a.* inseparable.
insert [in'sə:t], *v.t.* insertar.
inside ['insaid], *a.*, *n.* interior, *m.*; — *information*, informes secretos; — *out*, al revés. — [in'saidz], *n.pl.* *(fam.)* entrañas, *f.pl.*—[in'said], *adv.* dentro, hacia dentro.—*prep.* dentro de.
insight ['insait], *n.* perspicacia, penetración, *f.*
insignia [in'signiə], *n.pl.* insignias, *f.pl.*
insignificant [insig'nifikənt], *a.* insignificante.
insincere [insin'siə], *a.* insincero.
insinuate [in'sinjueit], *v.t.* insinuar.
insipid [in'sipid], *a.* insípido, soso.
insipidity [insi'piditi], *n.* insipidez, *f.*
insist [in'sist], *v.i.* insistir (*on*, en).
insistence [in'sistəns], *n.* insistencia.
insistent [in'sistənt], *a.* insistente.
insolence ['insələns], *n.* descaro, insolencia.
insolent ['insələnt], *a.* descarado, insolente.
insoluble [in'sɔljubl], *a.* in(di)soluble.
insolvent [in'sɔlvənt], *a.* insolvente.
insomnia [in'sɔmniə], *a.* insomnio.
inspect [in'spekt], *v.t.* inspeccionar.
inspection [in'spekʃən], *n.* inspección, *f.*
inspector [in'spektə], *n.* inspector, *m.*
inspiration [inspi'reiʃən], *n.* inspiración, *f.*
inspire [in'spaiə], *v.t.* inspirar; *to be inspired by,* inspirarse en.
inspiring [ins'paiəriŋ], *a.* inspirador, inspirante.
instability [instə'biliti], *n.* inestabilidad, *f.*
install [in'stɔ:l], *v.t.* instalar.
installation [instə'leiʃən], *n.* instalación *f.*
instalment [in'stɔ:lmənt], *n.* entrega; plazo (*pago*). [**plazo**].
instance ['instəns], *n.* ejemplo, caso; instancia; *for* —, por ejemplo.
instant ['instənt], *a.* inmediato; corriente.—*n.* instante; mes corriente, *m.*
instantaneous [instən'teinjəs], *a.* instantáneo.
instantly ['instəntli], *a.* al instante.
instead [in'sted], *adv.* en su lugar.—*prep.* en lugar, en vez (*of*, de).
instep ['instep], *n.* empeine, *m.*
instigate ['instigeit], *v.t.* instigar.
instil [in'stil], *v.t.* instilar.
instinct ['instiŋkt], *n.* instinto.
instinctive [in'stiŋktiv], *a.* instintivo.

institute ['institju:t], *n.* instituto.—*v.t.* instituir.
institution [insti'tju:ʃən], *n.* institución, *f.*; uso establecido.
instruct [in'strʌkt], *v.t.* instruir; mandar.
instruction [in'strʌkʃən], *n.* instrucción; indicación, *f.*
instructive [in'strʌktiv], *a.* instructivo.
instructor [in'strʌktə], *n.* instructor, *m.*
instrument ['instrumənt], *n.* instrumento.
instrumental [instru'mentl], *a.* instrumental.
insubordinate [insə'bɔ:dinit], *a.* insubordinado.
insubordination [insəbɔ:di'neiʃən], *n.* insubordinación, *f.*
insufferable [in'sʌfərəbl], *a.* insufrible, inaguantable.
insufficient [insə'fiʃənt], *a.* insuficiente.
insular ['insjulə], *a.* insular; estrecho de miras.
insulate ['insjuleit], *v.t.* aislar.
insulation [insju'leiʃən], *n.* aislamiento.
insulator ['insjuleitə], *n.* aislador, *m.*
insult ['insʌlt] *n.* insulto.—[in'sʌlt], *v.t.* insultar.
insulting [in'sʌltiŋ], *a.* insultante.
insuperable [in'sju:pərəbl], *a.* insuperable.
insurance [in'ʃuərəns, in'ʃɔ:rəns], *n.* seguro.
insure [in'ʃuə, in'ʃɔ:], *v.t.* asegurar.
insurgent [in'sə:dʒənt], *a.*, *n.* insurrecto, insurgente.
insurrection [insə'rekʃən], *n.* insurrección, *f.*
intact [in'tækt], *a.* intacto, íntegro, incólume.
intake ['inteik], *n.* admisión; entrada.
intangible [in'tændʒibl], *a.* intangible.
integer ['intidʒə], *n.* *(math.)* entero.
integral ['intigrəl], *a.* íntegro; integral; solidario.
integrate ['intigreit], *v.t.* integrar.
integration [inti'greiʃən], *n.* integración, *f.*
integrity [in'tegriti], *n.* integridad, *f.*; entereza.
intellect ['intilekt], *n.* intelecto.
intellectual [inti'lektjuəl], *a.*, *n.* intelectual.
intelligence [in'telidʒəns], *n.* inteligencia; información, *f.*
intelligent [in'telidʒənt], *a.* inteligente.
intelligible [in'telidʒibl], *a.* inteligible.
intemperance [in'tempərəns], *n.* intemperancia; exceso.
intemperate [in'tempərit], *a.* intemperante; inclemente.
intend [in'tend], *v.t.* proponerse, pensar.
intended [in'tendid], *n.* *(fam.)* prometido, prometida.
intense [in'tens], *a.* intenso.
intensify [in'tensifai], *v.t.* intensificar.—*v.i.* -se.
intensity [in'tensiti], *n.* intensidad, *f.*
intensive [in'tensiv], *a.* intensivo.
intent [in'tent], *a.* atentísimo; resuelto (*on*, a); *to be* — *on,* pensar sólo en.—*n.* intento; intención, *f.*; sentido; *to all intents and purposes,* prácticamente; virtualmente.
intention [in'tenʃən], *n.* intención, *f.*; fin, *m.*
intentional [in'tenʃənəl], *a.* intencional, intencionado.
inter [in'tə:], *v.t.* enterrar.
inter ['intə], *prefix.* entre-.

intercede [intə'si:d], v.i. interceder.
intercept [intə'sept], v.t. interceptar, atajar.
interchange [intə'tʃeindʒ], n. intercambio.—v.t. intercambiar.—v.i. -se.
intercommunicate [intəkə'mju:nikeit], v.i. comunicarse.
intercourse [intəkɔ:s], n. trato, intercambio; comercio; coito.
interdict ['intədikt], n. interdicto, entredicho.
interest ['intərəst], n. interés, m.—v.t. interesar.
interesting ['intərəstiŋ], a. interesante.
interfere [intə'fiə], v.i. meterse (in, en); estorbar (with).
interference [intə'fiərəns], n. intrusión, f.; estorbo; (rad.) interferencia.
interim ['intərim], a. interino; in the —, ínterin, entre tanto.
interleave [intə'li:v], v.t. interfoliar.
interlock [intə'lɔk], v.t. trabar, engargantar.—v.i. -se.
interloper ['intəloupə], n. intruso.
interlude ['intəlju:d], n. intermedio, intervalo.
intermediary [intə'mi:djəri], a., n. intermediario.
intermediate [intə'mi:djət], a. intermedi(ari)o.
interment [in'tə:mənt], n. entierro.
interminable [in'tə:minəbl], a. interminable.
intermingle [intə'miŋgl], v.t. entreverar, entremezclar.—v.i. -se.
intermittent [intə'mitənt], a. intermitente.
intern [in'tə:n], v.t. internar, encerrar.
internal [in'tə:nəl], a. interno, interior.
international [intə'næʃənəl], a. internacional.
internment [in'tə:nmənt], n. internación, f.
interpolate [in'tə:pəleit], v.t. interpolar.
interpret [in'tə:prit], v.t. interpretar.
interpretation [intə:pri'teiʃən], n. interpretación, f.
interpreter [in'tə:pritə], n. intérprete, m.
interrogate [in'terəgeit], v.t. interrogar.
interrogation [interə'geiʃən], n. interrogación, f.; — mark, punto de interrogación.
interrogative [intə'rɔgətiv], a., n. interrogativo.
interrogator [in'terəgeitə], n. interrogante, m.f.
interrupt [intə'rʌpt], v.t. interrumpir.
interruption [intə'rʌpʃən], n. interrupción, f.
interval ['intəvəl], n. intervalo; intermedio, descanso.
intervene [intə'vi:n], v.i. intervenir; mediar; ocurrir.
intervention [intə'venʃən], n. intervención, f.
interview ['intəvju], n. entrevista.—v.t. entrevistar.
interweave [intə'wi:v], v.t. irr. (conjug. like WEAVE) entretejer.
intestate [in'testeit], a. (ab)intestado.
intestine [in'testin], n. intestino.
intimacy ['intiməsi], n. intimidad, f.
intimate (1) ['intimit], a. íntimo.
intimate (2) ['intimeit], v.t. intimar; indicar.
intimidate [in'timideit], v.t. intimidar.
into ['intu], prep. en, hacia el interior de.
intolerable [in'tɔlərəbl], a. intolerable.

intolerance [in'tɔlərəns], n. intolerancia.
intolerant [in'tɔlərənt], a. intolerante.
intonation [intə'neiʃən], n. entonación, f.
intone [in'toun], v.t. entonar; salmodiar.
intoxicate [in'tɔksikeit], v.t. embriagar.
intoxicating [in'tɔksikeitiŋ], a. embriagante.
intransigent [in'trænsidʒənt], a. intransigente.
intransitive [in'trɑ:nsitiv], a. intransitivo.
intrepid [in'trepid], a. intrépido.
intricacy ['intrikəsi], n. intrincación, f.
intricate ['intrikit], a. intrincado.
intrigue ['intri:g], n. intriga.—[in'tri:g], v.t. fascinar.—v.i. intrigar.
intriguer [in'tri:gə], n. intrigante, m.f.
intriguing [in'tri:giŋ], a. intrigante; fascinador.
intrinsic [in'trinsik], a. intrínseco.
introduce [intrə'dju:s], v.t. introducir; presentar (gente).
introduction [intrə'dʌkʃən], n. introducción; presentación, f.
introductory [intrə'dʌktəri], a. introductivo; proemial.
intrude [in'tru:d], v.i. estorbar, entremeterse.
intruder [in'tru:də], n. intruso, entremetido.
intrusion [in'tru:ʒən], n. intrusión, f.
intrust [in'trʌst], v.t. confiar.
intuition [intju:'iʃən], n. intuición, f.
intuitive [in'tju:itiv], a. intuitivo.
inundate ['inʌndeit], v.t. inundar.
inure [i'njuə], v.t. avezar, endurecer.
invade [in'veid], v.t. invadir.
invader [in'veidə], n. invasor, m.
invading [in'veidiŋ], a. invasor.
invalid (1) [in'vælid], a. inválido, nulo.
invalid (2) ['invəlid], a., n. inválido, enfermo.
invalidate [in'vælideit], v.t. invalidar.
invaluable [in'væljuəbl], a. inestimable, precioso.
invariable [in'vɛəriəbl], a. invariable.
invasion [in'veiʒən], n. invasión, f.
invective [in'vektiv], n. invectiva.
inveigh [in'vei], v.i. prorrumpir en invectivas.
inveigle [in'vi:gl, in'veigl], v.t. seducir, engatusar.
invent [in'vent], v.t. inventar.
invention [in'venʃən], n. invención, f., hallazgo; invento.
inventor [in'ventə], n. inventor, m.
inventory ['invəntəri], n. inventario, catálogo.
inversion [in'və:ʃən], n. inversión, f.
invert [in'və:t], v.t. invertir, transponer.
invertebrate [in'və:tibreit], a., n. invertebrado.
invest [in'vest], v.t. invertir (dinero); (mil.) sitiar; investir (honor).
investigate [in'vestigeit], v.t. investigar.
investigation [investi'geiʃən], n. investigación, f.
investment [in'vestmənt], n. inversión, f.; (mil.) cerco.
investor [in'vestə], n. inversionista, m.f.
inveterate [in'vetərit], a. inveterado, habitual.
invidious [in'vidjəs], a. detestable, odioso; injusto.
invigorate [in'vigəreit], v.t. vigorizar.
invincible [in'vinsibl], a. invencible.
inviolate [in'vaiəlit], a. inviolado.
invisible [in'vizibl], a. invisible.

invitation [invi'teiʃən], *n.* invitación, *f.*, convite, *m.*
invite [in'vait], *v.t.* invitar, convidar.
inviting [in'vaitiŋ], *a.* seductor, halagante, provocativo.
invoice ['invɔis], *n.* factura.—*v.t.* facturar.
invoke [in'vouk], *v.t.* invocar.
involuntary [in'vɔləntri], *a.* involuntario.
involve [in'vɔlv], *v.t.* implicar; envolver; enredar.
invulnerable [in'vʌlnərəbl], *a.* invulnerable.
inward ['inwəd], *a.* interior.
inwards ['inədz], *n.pl.* (*fam.*) tripas, entrañas, *f.pl.*—['inwədz], *adv.* hacia dentro.
iodine ['aiədi:n], *n.* yodo.
iota [ai'outə], *n.* iota; (*fig.*) jota, tilde, *f.*
Iran [i'rɑ:n], *n.* Irán, *m.*
Iranian [i'reinjən], *a.*, *n.* iranés, *m.*, iranio.
Iraq [i'rɑ:k], *n.* Irak, *m.*
Iraqi [i'rɑ:ki], *a.*, *n.* iraquiano, iraqués, *m.*
irascible [i'ræsibl], *a.* irascible, colérico.
irate [ai'reit], *a.* airado.
ire [aiə], *n.* (*poet.*) ira.
Ireland ['aiələnd], *n.* Irlanda.
iris ['aiəris], *n.* (*anat.*) iris, *m.*; (*bot.*) lirio.
Irish ['aiəriʃ], *a.* irlandés.—*n.* irlandés (*idioma*), *m.*
Irishman ['aiəriʃmən], *n.* irlandés, *m.*
irksome ['ə:ksəm], *a.* cargante, molesto.
iron [aiən], *n.* hierro; plancha (*para vestidos*); *iron curtain*, telón (*m.*) de acero.—*v.t.* planchar; *to iron out*, allanar (*problemas*).
ironclad ['aiənklæd], *a.*, *n.* acorazado.
ironic(al) [aiə'rɔnik(əl)], *a.* irónico.
ironmonger ['aiənmʌŋgə], *n.* ferretero, quincallero.
ironmongery ['aiənmʌŋgəri], *n.* ferretería, quincalla.
irony ['aiərəni], *n.* ironía.
irrational [i'ræʃənəl], *a.* irracional.
irregular [i'regjulə], *a.* irregular.
irregularity [iregju'læriti], *n.* irregularidad, *f.*
irrelevance [i'reləvəns], *n.* inaplicabilidad, *f.*
irrelevant [i'reləvənt], *a.* inaplicable, fuera de propósito.
irreligion [iri'lidʒən], *n.* irreligión, *f.*
irreligious [iri'lidʒəs], *a.* irreligioso.
irreparable [i'repərəbl], *a.* irreparable.
irrepressible [iri'presibl], *a.* incontenible.
irresistible [iri'zistibl], *a.* irresistible.
irresolute [i'rezəlju:t], *a.* irresoluto.
irrespective [iris'pektiv], *a.* independiente; aparte, sin hacer caso (*of*, de).
irresponsible [iris'pɔnsibl], *a.* irresponsable.
irreverence [i'revərəns], *n.* irreverencia.
irreverent [i'revərənt], *a.* irreverente.
irrevocable [i'revəkəbl], *a.* irrevocable.
irrigate ['irigeit], *v.t.* regar, irrigar.
irrigation [iri'geiʃən], *n.* riego, irrigación, *f.*
irritable ['iritəbl], *a.* irritable, enfadadizo.
irritate ['iriteit], *v.t.* irritar.
is [iz], [BE].
Islam [iz'lɑ:m], *n.* el Islam.
Islamic [iz'læmik], *a.* islámico.
island ['ailənd], *n.* isla.
islander ['ailəndə], *n.* isleño.
isle [ail], *n.* (*poet.*) isla.
isn't [iznt], [IS NOT].
isolate ['aisəleit], *v.t.* aislar.
isolation [aisə'leiʃən], *n.* aislamiento.
Israel ['izreil], *n.* Israel, *m.*
Israeli [iz'reili], *a.*, *n.* israelí, *m.f.*

Israelite ['izriəlait], *n.* (*Bibl.*) israelita, *m.f.*
issue ['iʃju:], *n.* tirada; emisión, *f.*; número (*de una revista*); resultado; asunto discutido; progenie, *f.*; *at* —, en disputa.—*v.t.* emitir; publicar.—*v.i.* salir; provenir; *to join* —, disputar.
isthmus ['isməs], *n.* istmo.
it [it], *pron.* ello; lo, la; le.
Italian [i'tæljən], *a.*, *n.* italiano.
italic [i'tælik], *a.* itálico, bastardillo.—*n.pl.* bastardilla, cursiva.
italicize [i'tælisaiz], *v.t.* subrayar.
Italy ['itəli], *n.* Italia.
itch [itʃ], *n.* picazón, comezón, *f.*; prurito.—*v.i.* comer, picar; sentir prurito (*to*, de).
itchy ['itʃi], *a.* hormigoso.
item ['aitəm], *n.* ítem, *m.*, párrafo, artículo; detalle, *m.*
itemize ['aitəmaiz], *v.t.* detallar.
itinerant [ai'tinərənt], *a.* ambulante viandante.
itinerary [ai'tinərəri], *n.* itinerario.
its [its], *poss. a.* su; suyo.
itself [it'self], *pron.* sí (mismo); se.
ivory ['aivəri], *n.* marfil, *m*; *Ivory Coast,* Costa de Marfil.
ivy ['aivi], *n.* hiedra.

J

J, j [dʒei], *n.* décima letra del alfabeto inglés.
jab [dʒæb], *n.* hurgonazo, pinchazo; codazo.—*v.t.* pinchar; dar un codazo a.
jabber ['dʒæbə], *n.* chapurreo.—*v.t.*, *v.i.* chapurrear.
jack [dʒæk], *n.* (*mech.*) gato, cric, *m.*; (*zool.*) macho; (*fam.*) mozo; marinero; sota (*naipes*); burro; sacabotas, *m.sg.*
jackal ['dʒækɔ:l], *n.* chacal, *m.*
jackass ['dʒækæs], *n.* burro; (*orn.*) martín, *m.*
jack-boot ['dʒækbu:t], *n.* bota alta.
jack-in-office ['dʒækin'ɔfis], *n.* oficial engreído.
jack-in-the-box ['dʒækinðə'bɔks], *n.* caja de sorpresa.
jack-knife ['dʒæknaif], *n.* navaja (sevillana *o* de Albacete).
jack-of-all-trades ['dʒækəvɔ:l'treidz], *n.* dije, factótum, *m.*
Jack Tar ['dʒæk'tɑ:], *n.* lobo de mar.
jade (1) [dʒeid], *a.* verde.—*n.* (*min.*) jade, *m.*
jade (2) [dʒeid], *n.* picarona, mujerzuela; rocín, *m.*—*v.t.* cansar.
jaded ['dʒeidid], *a.* cansado, ahito.
jagged ['dʒægid], *a.* mellado, aserrado.
jaguar ['dʒægjuə], *n.* jaguar, *m.*
jail [dʒeil], *n.* cárcel, *f.*—*v.t.* encarcelar.
jailer ['dʒeilə], *n.* carcelero.
jalopy [dʒə'lɔpi], *n.* (*fam.*) coche ruinoso.
jam [dʒæm], *n.* conserva, mermelada; agolpamiento, apiñadura; (*fam.*) aprieto.—*v.t.* apiñar; estrechar; atorar; (*rad.*) perturbar.—*v.i.* apiñarse; trabarse; atascarse.

Jamaican

Jamaican [dʒə'meikən], *a.*, *n.* jamaicano.
James [dʒeimz], *n.* Jaime, Diego, Santiago.
jamming ['dʒæmiŋ], *n.* (*rad.*) perturbación, *f.*
Jane [dʒein], *n.* Juana.
jangle ['dʒæŋgl], *n.* cencerreo; riña.—*v.t.* hacer cencerrear.—*v.i.* cencerrear; reñir.
janitor ['dʒænitə], *n.* (*U.S.*) portero, conserje, *m.*
January ['dʒænjuəri], *n.* enero.
Japan [dʒə'pæn], *n.* Japón, *m.*; **japan,** *n.* laca.
Japanese [dʒæpə'niːz], *a.*, *n.* japonés.
jar (1) [dʒɑː], *n.* vaso, tarro, orza, jarro.
jar (2) [dʒɑː], *n.* sacudida.—*v.t.* sacudir; bazucar; irritar.—*v.i.* sacudirse; chirriar.
jargon ['dʒɑːgən], *n.* jerga.
jasmine ['dʒæzmin], *n.* jazmín, *m.*
jasper ['dʒæspə], *n.* jaspe, *m.*
jaundice ['dʒɔːndis], *n.* (*med.*) ictericia; (*fig.*) envidia.—*v.t.* amargar.
jaunt [dʒɔːnt], *n.* (*fam.*) caminata, excursión, *f.*
jaunty ['dʒɔːnti], *a.* airoso, garboso.
javelin ['dʒævəlin], *n.* jabalina.
jaw [dʒɔː], *n.* quijada; (*fam.*) cháchara.—*pl.* (*fig.*) garras, *f.pl.*
jay [dʒei], *n.* (*orn.*) arrendajo.
jaywalker ['dʒeiwɔːkə], *n.* peatón imprudente, *m.*
jazz [dʒæz], *n.* jazz, *m.*
jealous ['dʒeləs], *a.* celoso.
jealousy ['dʒeləsi], *n.* celos, *m.pl.*
jeep [dʒiːp], *n.* coche (*m.*) militar pequeño.
jeer [dʒiə], *n.* mofa, befa.—*v.i.* mofarse (*at,* de).
jelly ['dʒeli], *n.* jalea, gelatina.
jelly-fish ['dʒelifiʃ], *n.* medusa, aguamar, *m.*
Jemmy ['dʒemi], *n.* palanqueta.
jeopardize ['dʒepədaiz], *v.t.* arriesgar, poner en peligro.
jeopardy ['dʒepədi], *n.* riesgo, peligro.
jerk (1) [dʒɔːk], *n.* tirón, arranque; tic, *m.*; (*pej.*) tío.—*v.t.* sacudir.—*v.i.* moverse a tirones; sacudir(se).
jerk (2) [dʒɔːk], *v.t.* tasajear (*carne*).
jerry-built ['dʒeribilt], *a.* mal construido.
Jerusalem [dʒə'ruːsələm], *n.* Jerusalén, *f.*
jest [dʒest], *n.* chanza, broma.—*v.i.* chancear.
jester ['dʒestə], *n.* bufón, *m.*; bromista, *m.f.*
Jesuit ['dʒezjuit], *a.*, *n.* jesuita, *m.*
Jesus ['dʒiːzəs], *n.* Jesús;—*Christ,* Jesucristo.
jet (1) [dʒet], *n.* chorro; surtidor; mechero.
jet (2) [dʒet], *n.* (*min.*) azabache, *m.*
jet-aeroplane ['dʒet'ɛərəplein], *n.* avion (*m.*) de chorro *o* de reacción.
jet-engine ['dʒet'endʒin], *n.* motor (*m.*) a chorro.
jetsam ['dʒetsəm], *n.* echazón, *f.*, pecio.
jettison ['dʒetisən], *v.t.* echar a la mar; desechar.
jetty ['dʒeti], *n.* malecón, muelle, *m.*
Jew [dʒuː], *n.* judío.
jewel [dʒuːəl], *n.* joya, alhaja.
jeweller ['dʒuːələ], *n.* joyero.
jewel(le)ry ['dʒuːəlri], *n.* joyas, *f.pl.*; joyería.
Jewess [dʒuː'es], *n.* judía.
Jewish ['dʒuːiʃ], *a.* judío.
Jewry ['dʒuəri], *n.* judería.
jib (1) [dʒib], *n.* aguilín, pescante (*de una grúa*); (*naut.*) foque, *m.*—*v.i.* virar.
jib (2) [dʒib], *v.i.* negarse, resistirse (*at,* a).
jibe [dʒaib], *n.* befa, pulla.—*v.i.* mofarse (*at,* de).
jiffy ['dʒifi], *n.* (*fam.*) santiamén, *m.*

jig [dʒig], *n.* giga (*baile*); (*mech.*) gálibo; criba.
jigger ['dʒigə], *n.* criba; criba de vaivén; (*naut.*) palo de mesana.
jig-saw ['dʒigsɔː], *n.* sierra de vaivén; rompecabezas (*juguete*), *m.inv.*
jilt [dʒilt], *v.t.* plantar, dejar colgado, dar calabazas a.
Jim(my) ['dʒim(i)], *n.* Jaimito.
jimmy ['dʒimi], (*U.S.*) [JEMMY].
jingle [dʒingl], *n.* cascabeleo; rima pueril, aleluya.—*v.t.* hacer sonar.—*v.i.* cascabelear.
jingoism ['dʒiŋgouizm], *n.* jingoísmo.
jinx [dʒinks], *n.* cenizo, gafe, *m.*
jitters ['dʒitəz], *n.pl.* (*fam.*) jindama, miedo.
Joan [dʒoun], *n.* Juana; — *of Arc,* Juana de Arco.
job [dʒɔb], *n.* tarea; empleo, oficio; destajo; agiotaje, *m.*; negocio; (*print.*) remiendo; — *lot,* lote, *m.*, saldo; *odd* —, tarea pequeña.
jobber ['dʒɔbə], *n.* corredor; agiotista, *m.*
jockey ['dʒɔki], *n.* jockey, *m.*—*v.t.* maniobrar.
jocular ['dʒɔkjulə], *a.* jocoso.
jocund ['dʒɔkənd], *a.* jocundo, jovial.
Joe [dʒou], *n.* Pepe, *m.*
jog [dʒɔg], *n.* empujoncito; trote, *m.*; — *trot,* trote de perro.—*v.t.* empujar; refrescar (*la memoria*).—*v.i.* seguir adelante, irse defendiendo.
John [dʒɔn], *n.* Juan, *m.*; — *Bull,* el inglés típico, Inglaterra.
join [dʒɔin], *n.* juntura.—*v.t.* juntar, unir, ensamblar; ingresar en; asociarse a; librar (*batalla*); unirse con.—*v.i.* juntarse.
joiner ['dʒɔinə], *n.* ebanista, *m.*; carpintero.
joinery ['dʒɔinəri], *n.* ebanistería.
joint [dʒɔint], *a.* común, mutuo; unido, solidario.—*prefix.* co-.—*n.* juntura, unión; (*anat.*) coyuntura, articulación, *f.*; (*U.S.; fam.*) sitio de reunión; tabernucho; (*cul.*) pedazo, tajada (*de carne*); *to put out of* —, descoyuntar.—*v.t.* articular; juntar; ensamblar.
joint-stock company ['dʒɔint'stɔk'kʌmpəni], *n.* sociedad anónima.
joist [dʒɔist], *n.* viga, vigueta.
joke [dʒouk], *n.* chiste, *m.*, broma; *joking aside,* sin broma, en serio.—*v.i.* chancear; hablar en broma.
joker ['dʒoukə], *n.* bromista, *m.f.*; comodín (*naipes*), *m.*
jolly ['dʒɔli], *a.* festivo, jovial, alegre; (*fam.*) agradable; *Jolly Roger,* bandera negra de los piratas.—*adv.* (*fam.*) muy.
jolt [dʒoult], *n.* sacudión, *m.*; salto.—*v.t.* sacudir.—*v.i.* traquear.
Jonah ['dʒounə], *n.* Jonás, *m.*; (*fam.*) gafe, *m.*, cenizo.
Jordan [dʒɔːdn], *n.* Jordán (*río*), *m.*; Jordania (*país*).
Jordanian [dʒɔː'deinjən], *a.*, *n.* jordano.
Joseph ['dʒouzif], *n.* José, *m.*
jostle ['dʒɔsl], *v.t.* codear, empujar.
jot [dʒɔt], *n.* jota, tilde, *f.*—*v.t.* apuntar (*down*).
journal [dʒɔːnl], *n.* diario; revista.
journal-bearing ['dʒɔːnl'bɛəriŋ], *n.* cojinete, *m.*, chumacera.
journalism ['dʒɔːnəlizm], *n.* periodismo.
journalist ['dʒɔːnəlist], *n.* periodista, *m.f.*
journey ['dʒɔːni], *n.* viaje, *m.*—*v.i.* viajar.
joust [dʒaust], *n.* torneo, justa.—*v.i.* justar.

jovial ['dʒouvjəl], *a.* jovial, alegre.
jowl [dʒaul], *n.* carrillo; quijada.
joy [dʒɔi], *n.* alegría, gozo.
joyful ['dʒɔiful], *a.* alegre, gozoso.
joy-ride ['dʒɔiraid], *n.* paseo de placer en coche.
joy-stick ['dʒɔistik], *n.* (*aer.*) palanca de mando.
jubilant ['dʒu:bilənt], *a.* jubiloso.
jubilation [dʒu:bi'leiʃən], *n.* júbilo.
jubilee ['dʒu:bili:], *n.* jubileo; bodas (*f.pl.*) de oro.
judge [dʒʌdʒ], *n.* juez, *m.* (*of,* en).—*v.t., v.i.* juzgar (*by,* por).
judg(e)ment ['dʒʌdʒmənt], *n.* juicio; discreción, *f.*; sentencia.
judicial [dʒu'diʃəl], *a.* judicial.
judiciary [dʒu'diʃiəri], *n.* judicatura.
judicious [dʒu'diʃəs], *a.* juicioso, cuerdo.
jug [dʒʌg], *n.* jarra, jarro; (*fam.*) cárcel, *f.,* banasto.
juggle [dʒʌgl], *v.t.* escamotear; **to — with,** falsear.—*v.i.* hacer juegos malabares.
juggler ['dʒʌglə], *n.* malabarista, *m.f.*
jugular ['dʒʌgjulə], *a.* yugular.
juice [dʒu:s], *n.* zumo, jugo; (*fam.*) electricidad, *f.*; gasolina.
juicy ['dʒu:si], *a.* jugoso; (*fam.*) picante.
July [dʒu'lai], *n.* julio.
jumble [dʒʌmbl], *n.* enredo, revoltijo. —*v.t.* emburujar, revolver.
jumble-sale ['dʒʌmblseil], *n.* venta de trastos.
jumbo ['dʒʌmbou], *n.* (*fam.*) elefante, *m.*
jump [dʒʌmp], *n.* salto.—*v.t., v.i.* saltar; **to — at,** aceptar, coger en seguida; **to — to,** darse prisa; deducir sin reflexión.
jumper (1) ['dʒʌmpə], *n.* saltador, *m.*
jumper (2) ['dʒʌmpə], *n.* jersey, *m.*
jumpy ['dʒʌmpi], *a.* asustadizo.
junction ['dʒʌŋkʃən], *n.* juntura; empalme (*ferrocarril*), *m.*
juncture ['dʒʌŋktʃə], *n.* juntura; ocasión, *f.*; coyuntura.
June [dʒu:n], *n.* junio.
jungle [dʒʌŋgl], *n.* jungla, selva.
junior ['dʒu:njə], *a.* menor, más joven; juvenil; hijo (*nombre*).—*n.* menor, *m.f.*
junk (1) [dʒʌŋk], *n.* trastos, chatarra.
junk (2) [dʒʌŋk], *n.* (*naut.*) junco.
junketing ['dʒʌŋkitiŋ], *n.* festín, *m.*
jurisdiction [dʒuəriz'dikʃən], *n.* jurisdicción, *f.*
jurist ['dʒuərist], *n.* jurista, *m.f.*
juror ['dʒuərə], *n.* jurado.
jury ['dʒuəri], *n.* jurado.
jury-box ['dʒuəribɔks], *n.* tribuna del jurado.
jury-mast ['dʒuərima:st], *n.* (*naut.*) bandola.
just [dʒʌst], *a.* justo.—*adv.* justamente; apenas, casi; hace muy poco; sólo; (*fam.*) muy; **to have —,** acabar de; **— now,** hace poco; ahora mismo.
justice ['dʒʌstis], *n.* justicia; juez, *m.*
justify ['dʒʌstifai], *v.t.* justificar.
jut [dʒʌt], *n.* saledizo.—*v.i.* proyectarse (*out*).
jute [dʒu:t], *n.* yute, *m.*
juvenile ['dʒu:vinail], *a.* juvenil.—*n.* joven, menor, *m.f.*
juxtapose [dʒʌkstə'pouz], *v.t.* yuxtaponer.

K

K, k [kei], *n.* undécima letra del alfabeto inglés.
kaf(f)ir ['kæfiə], *a., n.* (*pej.*) cafre, *m.f.*
kale [keil], *n.* col, *f.*
kaleidoscope [kə'laidəskoup], *n.* cal(e)idoscopio.
kangaroo [kæŋgə'ru:], *n.* canguro.
keel [ki:l], *n.* quilla.
keen [ki:n], *a.* agudo; afilado; ansioso, entusiasmado; aficionado (*on,* a).
keep [ki:p], *n.* mantenimiento; (*fort.*) torre, *f.*; **for keeps,** (*fam.*) para siempre.—*v.t. irr.* guardar, quedarse con; criar (*un ganado*); cumplir (*una promesa*); mantener; detener; celebrar.—*v.i. irr.* quedar; mantenerse; no dañarse; **to — away,** tener alejado; mantenerse alejado; no acercarse; **to — back,** retener; no acercarse; **to — down,** sujetar; **to — on,** no quitarse; seguir, continuar; **to — quiet,** estarse callado.
keeper ['ki:pə], *n.* encargado; guardia, *m.f.,* custodio.
keeping ['ki:piŋ], *n.* custodia; celebración, *f.*; **in — with,** de acuerdo con; **in safe —,** en buenas manos.
keg [keg], *n.* cuñete, *m.,* barrilito.
ken [ken], *n.* alcance mental, *m.*
kennel [kenl], *n.* perrera.
kept [kept] [KEEP].
kerb [kə:b], *n.* bordillo de acera, adoquín, *m.* [CURB].
kernel [kə:nl], *n.* almendra; (*fig.*) meollo.
kestrel ['kestrəl], *n.* (*orn.*) cernícalo.
kettle [ketl], *n.* caldero; tetera.
kettledrum ['ketldrʌm], *n.* timbal, *m.*
key [ki:], *a.* clave.—*n.* llave, *f.*; tecla (*de piano*); (*fig.*) clave, *f.*; (*mus.*) tono.
key-hole ['ki:houl], *n.* ojo de la llave.
key-note ['ki:nout], *n.* nota tónica; (*fig.*) idea básica.
keystone ['ki:stoun], *n.* piedra clave.
khaki ['ka:ki], *a., n.* caqui, *m.*
kick [kik], *n.* coz, *f.,* puntapié, *m.*; culatazo (*de un fusil*); (*fam.*) gusto vivo.—*v.t., v.i.* cocear, dar puntapiés (a); patalear.
kid [kid], *n.* cabrito; (*fam.*) nene, *m.,* niño. —*v.t.* (*fam.*) embromar.
kid-gloves ['kid'glʌvz], *n.pl.* guantes (*m.pl.*) de cabritilla; (*fig.*) blandura, delicadeza.
kidnap ['kidnæp], *v.t.* secuestrar, raptar.
kidnapping ['kidnæpiŋ], *n.* secuestro, rapto.
kidney ['kidni], *n.* riñón, *m.*
kidney-bean ['kidni'bi:n], *n.* judía pinta *o* verde.
kill [kil], *n.* muerte, *f.,* matanza.—*v.t.* matar.
killer ['kilə], *n.* matador, *m.,* asesino.
killing ['kiliŋ], *a.* (*fam.*) agobiante; (*hum.*) ridículo.—*n.* matanza; asesinato.
kill-joy ['kildʒɔi], *n.* aguafiestas, *m.sg.*
kiln [kiln], *n.* horno; ladrillera.
kilo ['ki:lou], *n.* kilo, kilogramo.
kilogram(me) ['kiləgræm], *n.* kilogramo.
kilometre ['kiloumi:tə], *n.* kilómetro.
kilt [kilt], *n.* falda escocesa.
kin [kin], *n.* deudos; **next of —,** parientes próximos.

307

kind

kind [kaind], *a.* bondadoso; afectuoso (*recuerdos*).—*n.* clase, *f.*, género, especie, *f.*; **in** —, de la misma moneda; en mercancías (*en vez de dinero*); — **of**, (*fam.*) algo.
kindergarten ['kindəgɑ:tn], *n.* jardín (*m.*) de la infancia.
kind-hearted [kaind'hɑ:tid], *a.* bondadoso.
kindle [kindl], *v.t.* encender.—*v.i.* -se.
kindly ['kaindli], *a.* benigno.—*adv.* bondadosamente; *not to take* — *to*, aceptar de mala gana.
kindness ['kaindnis], *n.* bondad, *f.*
kindred ['kindrid], *a.* semejante; allegado.— *n.* parentela, parientes, *m.pl.*
king [kiŋ], *n.* rey, *m.*
kingdom ['kiŋdəm], *n.* reino.
kingfisher ['kiŋfiʃə], *n.* martín pescador, *m.*
kingly ['kiŋli], *a.* regio, real.
king-pin ['kiŋpin], *n.* pivote central, *m.*; bolo central.
kink [kiŋk], *n.* enroscadura; arruga; (*fam.*) capricho, manía.
kinsfolk ['kinzfouk], *n.* parientes, deudos, *m.pl.*
kinsman ['kinzmən], *n.* deudo, pariente, *m.*
kiosk ['ki:ɔsk], *n.* quiosco.
kipper ['kipə], *n.* arenque (*m.*) ahumado.
kirk [kə:k], *n.* (*Scot.*) iglesia.
kiss [kis], *n.* beso.—*v.t.*, *v.i.* besar(se).
kit [kit], *n.* avíos, *m.pl.*, equipo, pertrechos, *m.pl.*
kitchen ['kitʃin], *n.* cocina; — *garden*, huerto.
kite [kait], *n.* cometa; (*orn.*) milano.
kith and kin ['kiθənd'kin], *n.* parientes y amigos.
kitten [kitn], *n.* gatito.
kitty (1) ['kiti], *n.* (*fam.*) minino (*gatito*).
kitty (2) ['kiti], *n.* puesta (*polla*).
knack [næk], *n.* tranquillo, truco.
knapsack ['næpsæk], *n.* mochila, barjuleta.
knave [neiv], *n.* bribón, *m.*; sota (*naipes*); (*obs.*) villano; mozo.
knavery ['neivəri], *n.* bellaquería.
knead [ni:d], *v.t.* amasar.
knee [ni:], *n.* rodilla; (*fig.*) codo; *on his knees*, de rodillas.
knee-cap ['ni:kæp], *n.* rótula.
knee-deep ['ni:'di:p], *a.* metido hasta las rodillas.
knee-high ['ni:'hai], *a.* hasta las rodillas (de alto).
kneel [ni:l], *v.i. irr.* arrodillarse.
knell [nel], *n.* doble, *m.*, toque (*m.*) de difuntos; mal agüero.
knelt [nelt] [KNEEL].
knew [nju:] [KNOW].
knickers ['nikəz], *n.* bragas, *f.pl.*, cucos, *m.pl.*
knick-knack ['niknæk], *n.* chuchería, bujería.
knife [naif], *n.* (*pl.* **knives**) cuchillo.—*v.t.* acuchillar; apuñalar.
knight [nait], *n.* caballero; — *errant*, caballero andante.—*v.t.* armar caballero.
knighthood ['naithud], *n.* caballería.
knit [nit], *v.t. irr.* hacer de punto; unir; fruncir (*la frente*).—*v.i. irr.* hacer punto; hacer calceta; unirse, trabarse.
knitting ['nitiŋ], *n.* labor (*m.*) de punto.
knives [naivz] [KNIFE].
knob [nɔb], *n.* botón, *m.*; protuberancia.
knock [nɔk], *n.* golpe, *m.*; llamada, alda-

bonazo (*a la puerta*).—*v.t.* golpear; *to* — *about*, estar *o* ir por ahí; *to* — *down*, derribar; atropellar (*coche*); *to* — *out*, sacar a golpes; dejar sin sentido (con un puñetazo).—*v.i.* llamar (*a la puerta*); pistonear (*motor*).
knocker ['nɔkə], *n.* aldaba (*de la puerta*).
knock-kneed ['nɔkni:d], *a.* zambo, patizambo.
knock-out ['nɔkaut], *a.* decisivo; final.—*n.* fuera (*m.*) de combate, knock-out, *m.*
knoll [noul], *n.* otero, loma.
knot [nɔt], *n.* nudo; lazo.—*v.t.* anudar.—*v.i.* -se.
knotty ['nɔti], *a.* nudoso; (*fig.*) espinoso.
know [nou], *v.t., v.i. irr.* saber (*un hecho*); conocer (*por los sentidos*); *in the* —, (*fam.*) enterado; *to* — *best*, saber lo que más conviene; *to* — *how to*, saber; *to* — *what's what*, saber cuántas son cinco.
know-all ['nouɔ:l], *n.* (*fam.*) sabelotodo.
know-how ['nouhau], *n.* (*fam.*) conocimiento técnico; tranquillo.
knowingly ['nouiŋli], *adv.* a sabiendas.
knowledge ['nɔlidʒ], *n.* conocimiento(s); erudición, *f.*; ciencia; *to my* —, que yo sepa.
known [noun] [KNOW].
knuckle [nʌkl], *n.* nudillo, artejo; codillo, jarrete (*carne*), *m.*—*v.i. to* — *down*, ponerse (*to it*, al trabajo); someterse; *to* — *under*, someterse.
Koran [kɔ'rɑ:n], *n.* Alcorán, Corán, *m.*
Korea [kɔ'riə], *n.* Corea.
Korean [kɔ'riən], *a., n.* coreano.
Kuwait [ku'weit], *n.* Estado del Kuwait.

L

L, l [el], *n.* duodécima letra del alfabeto inglés.
lab [læb], *n.* (*fam.*) [LABORATORY].
label [leibl], *n.* etiqueta, rótula, letrero; rotuelo (*de un libro*); (*fam.*) nombre, *m.*—*v.t.* rotular; apodar.
laboratory ['læbrətəri], *n.* laboratorio.
laborious [lə'bɔ:riəs], *a.* laborioso, penoso.
labour ['leibə], *n.* trabajo; obreros, *m.pl.*, mano (*f.*) de obra; (*med.*) parto; *Labour Party*, (*pol.*) partido laborista.—*v.t.* macear, machacar; trillar.—*v.i.* trabajar, forcejar; padecer, sufrir (*under*).
laboured ['leibəd], *a.* penoso; forzado.
labourer ['leibərə], *n.* peón, *m.*, bracero, jornalero.
laburnum [lə'bə:nəm], *n.* (*bot.*) codeso, laburno.
labyrinth ['læbirinθ], *n.* laberinto.
lace [leis], *n.* encaje; cordón (*de un zapato*), *m.*—*v.t.* atar (*un zapato*); añadir licor a.
lacerate ['læsəreit], *v.t.* lacerar.
lack [læk], *n.* falta, carencia, escasez, *f.*—*v.t.* carecer de; necesitar.—*v.i.* faltar.
lackadaisical ['lækə'deizikəl], *a.* cachazudo.
lackey ['læki], *n.* lacayo.
lacking ['lækiŋ], *a.* falto, carente (*in*, de).
laconic [lə'kɔnik], *a.* lacónico.

laudable

lacquer ['lækə], *n.* laca, barniz, *m.—v.t.* laquear.
lad [læd], *n.* chaval, *m.*
ladder ['lædə], *n.* escalera (de mano); carrera (*en una media*).
laden [leidn], *a.* cargado.
ladle [leidl], *n.* cucharón, *m.*
lady ['leidi], *n.* dama, señora.
lady-in-waiting ['leidiin'weitiŋ], *n.* dama de servicio.
lady-killer ['leidikilə], *n.* (*fam.*) tenorio.
ladyship ['leidiʃip], *n.* señoría (*título*).
lag (1) [læg], *n.* retraso.—*v.i.* rezagarse.
lag (2) [læg], *v.t.* proteger con fieltro (*tubos*).
lag (3) [læg], *n.* (*fam.*) preso.
laggard ['lægəd], *a., n.* rezagado.
lagoon [lə'guːn], *n.* laguna.
laid [leid], *a., p.p.* [LAY]; — up, fuera de servicio; enfermo.
lain [lein], [LIE].
lair [lɛə], *n.* cubil, *m.*, guarida.
laird [lɛəd], *n.* (*Scot.*) señor hacendado.
laity ['leiiti], *n.* los legos.
lake [leik], *n.* lago; laca (*color*).
lamb [læm], *n.* cordero.
lame [leim], *a.* cojo; flojo.—*v.t.* encojar.
lameness ['leimnis], *n.* cojera; defecto; flojedad, *f.*
lament [læ'ment], *n.* lamento.—*v.t., v.i.* lamentar(se).
lamentable ['læməntəbl], *a.* lamentable.
lamentation [læmən'teiʃən], *n.* lamentación, *f.*
lamina ['læminə], *n.* lámina.
lamp [læmp], *n.* lámpara; farol, *m.*
lampoon [læm'puːn], *n.* pasquín, *m.—v.t.* pasquinar.
lamp-post ['læmppoust], *n.* pie o poste (*m.*) de farol.
lance [lɑːns], *n.* lanza; (*med.*) lanceta; — corporal, (*mil.*) cabo menor.—*v.t.* abrir con lanceta.
lancer ['lɑːnsə], *n.* lancero.
lancet ['lɑːnsit], *n.* lanceta.
land [lænd], *n.* tierra; terreno.—*v.t.* desembarcar; poner en tierra; sacar a la tierra.—*v.i.* desembarcar; (*aer.*) aterrizar; ir a parar.
landed ['lændid], *a.* hacendado.
landing ['lændiŋ], *n.* desembarco; desembarcadero (*sitio*); (*aer.*) aterrizaje, *m.*; descanso (*de la escalera*).
landlady ['lændleidi], *n.* mesonera; patrona.
landlord ['lændlɔːd], *n.* mesonero; patrón, *m.*
land-lubber ['lændlʌbə], *n.* marinero de agua dulce.
landmark ['lændmɑːk], *n.* mojón, *m.*; marca; punto culminante o de referencia.
land-owner ['lændounə], *n.* terrateniente, *m.f.*
landscape ['lændskeip], *n.* paisaje, *m.*
landslide ['lændslaid], *n.* derrumbe, *m.*, argayo, desprendimiento de tierra; (*pol.*) victoria aplastante.
lane [lein], *n.* senda, vereda, callejuela; (*aer., naut.*) ruta, derrotero.
language ['læŋgwidʒ], *n.* lenguaje (*estilo*), *m.*; lengua, idioma, *m.*
languid ['læŋgwid], *a.* lánguido, flojo.
languish ['læŋgwiʃ], *v.i.* languidecer, penar.
languor ['læŋgə], *n.* languidez, *f.*
lank [læŋk], *a.* flaco; lacio; descarnado.
lanky ['læŋki], *a.* (*fam.*) larguirucho.

lantern ['læntən], *n.* linterna.
Laos [laus], *n.* Laos, *m.*
Laotian ['lauʃən], *a., n.* laocio, laosiano.
lap (1) [læp], *n.* regazo; (*sport*) etapa; doblez, *f.*, traslapo.—*v.t.* traslapar.—*v.i.* -se.
lap (2) [læp], *n.* chapaleteo (*de agua*).—*v.t.* lamer; beber a lengüetadas.—*v.i.* lamer.
lap-dog ['læpdɔg], *n.* perrillo faldero.
lapel [lə'pel], *n.* solapa.
Lapland ['læplænd], *n.* Laponia.
Lapp [læp], *n.* lapón (*persona*), *m.*
Lappish ['læpiʃ], *a.* lapón.—*n.* lapón (*idioma*), *m.*
lapse [læps], *n.* lapso; yerro; transcurso (*periodo*); caducidad, *f.—v.i.* recaer; caducar.
lapwing ['læpwiŋ], *n.* (*orn.*) avefría.
larceny ['lɑːsəni], *n.* hurto, latrocinio.
larch [lɑːtʃ], *n.* (*bot.*) alerce, *m.*
lard [lɑːd], *n.* manteca (de cerdo).—*v.t.* (*cul.*) mechar; (*fig.*) entreverar.
larder ['lɑːdə], *n.* despensa.
large [lɑːdʒ], *a.* grande, grueso; at —, en general; en libertad.
largess ['lɑːdʒes], *n.* largueza.
lariat ['læriət], *n.* lazo.
lark (1) [lɑːk], *n.* (*orn.*) alondra.
lark (2) [lɑːk], *n.* (*fam.*) calaverada, parranda.—*v.i.* bromear.
larynx ['læriŋks], *n.* laringe, *f.*
lascivious [lə'siviəs], *a.* lascivo.
lash [læʃ], *n.* látigo; latigazo; (*anat.*) pestaña.—*v.t.* azotar; atar.
lashing ['læʃiŋ], *n.* azotamiento; atadura, ligadura.—*pl.* gran cantidad, *f.*
lass [læs], *n.* chavala.
lasso [læ'suː], *n.* lazo.—*v.t.* lazar.
last (1) [lɑːst], *a.* último; postr(im)ero; pasado; — night, anoche; — straw, colmo, acabóse, *m.*; — week, la semana pasada. —*n.* el último.—*adv.* la última vez; por último; at —, por fin.
last (2) [lɑːst], *n.* horma (*para los zapatos*).—*v.i.* durar, continuar, seguir; conservarse.
lasting ['lɑːstiŋ], *a.* duradero.
latch [lætʃ], *n.* cerrojo, picaporte, *m.—v.t.* cerrar con picaporte.
latchkey ['lætʃkiː], *n.* llavín, *m.*
late [leit], *a.* tardío; reciente; avanzado (*hora*); difunto, lamentado; — lamented, fallecido.—*adv.* tarde; to be —, ser tarde; llevar un retraso; of —, recientemente.
late-comer ['leitkʌmə], *n.* rezagado.
lately ['leitli], *adv.* estos días, últimamente.
latent ['leitənt], *a.* latente.
lateral ['lætərəl], *a.* lateral.
latex ['leiteks], *n.* látex, *m.*
lath [lɑːθ], *n.* listón, *m.*
lathe [leið], *n.* torno.
lather ['lɑːðə], *n.* espuma de jabón.
Latin ['lætin], *a., n.* latino; latín (*idioma*), *m.*; — America, la América Latina, Hispanoamérica.
latitude ['lætitjuːd], *n.* latitud, *f.*
latrine [lə'triːn], *n.* letrina.
latter ['lætə], *a.* posterior, moderno; the —, éste.
lattice ['lætis], *n.* celosía, enrejado.—*v.t.* enrejar.
laud [lɔːd], *n.* loa.—*v.t.* loar.
laudable ['lɔːdəbl], *a.* laudable, loable.

309

laugh

laugh [lɑːf], *n.* risa.—*v.i.* reír(se); *to — at,* reírse de; *to — off,* tomar a risa.
laughable [ˈlɑːfəbl], *a.* risible.
laughing [ˈlɑːfiŋ], *a.* risueño.—*n.* risa.
laughingly [ˈlɑːfiŋli], *adv.* entre risas; risiblemente.
laughing-stock [ˈlɑːfiŋstɔk], *n.* hazmerreír, *m.*
laughter [ˈlɑːftə], *n.* risa.
launch [lɔːntʃ], *n.* lancha.—*v.t.* lanzar; botar (*un navío*).—*v.i.* lanzarse.
lauching-pad [ˈlɔːntʃiŋpæd], *n.* plataforma de lanzamiento.
launder [ˈlɔːndə], *v.t.* lavar y planchar.
laundress [ˈlɔːndris], *n.* lavandera.
laundry [ˈlɔːndri], *n.* lavadero; ropa lavada.
laureate [ˈlɔːrieit], *a.,* *n.* laureado.
laurel [ˈlɔrəl], *n.* laurel, lauro, *m.*
lava [ˈlɑːvə], *n.* lava.
lavatory [ˈlævətəri], *n.* lavabo, retrete, *m.*
lavender [ˈlævində], *n.* espliego, alhucema.
lavish [ˈlæviʃ], *a.* pródigo.—*v.t.* prodigar, desparramar.
law [lɔː], *n.* ley, *f.*; derecho (*asignatura*); — *and order,* paz pública.
law-abiding [ˈlɔːəbaidiŋ], *a.* pacífico, formal, probo.
law-breaker [ˈlɔːbreikə], *n.* transgresor, *m.,* criminal, *m.f.*
law-court [ˈlɔːkɔːt], *n.* tribunal (*m.*) de justica.
lawful [ˈlɔːful], *a.* legal, lícito, legítimo.
law-giver [ˈlɔːgivə], *n.* legislador, *m.*
lawless [ˈlɔːlis], *a.* desaforado.
lawn [lɔːn], *n.* césped, *m.*
lawn-mower [ˈlɔːnmouə], *n.* segadora de césped.
law-suit [ˈlɔːsjuːt], *n.* pleito.
lawyer [ˈlɔːjə], *n.* abogado.
lax [læks], *a.* laxo, vago; negligente.
laxative [ˈlæksətiv], *a.* laxativo.—*n.* laxante, *m.*
laxity [ˈlæksiti], *n.* laxitud, flojedad, *f.*; descuido, dejadez, *f.*
lay (1) [lei], *a.* seglar, lego, profano.
lay (2) [lei], *n.* caída, orientación, *f.*; balada.—*v.t. irr.* poner, colocar; echar, tender; matar (*polvo etc.*); poner (*huevos, la mesa*); calmar; conjurar (*aparecido*); achacar; trazar (*proyectos*); *to — aside,* poner a un lado; *to — down,* declarar, sentar; rendir (*armas*); dar (*vida*); *to — waste,* asolar, devastar.—*v.i. irr.* poner (*gallinas*); apostar; *to — oneself open to,* exponerse a.
layer [leiə], *n.* capa, cama, lecho; estrato.
layette [leiˈet], *n.* canastilla.
layman [ˈleimən], *n.* lego; (*fig.*) profano.
lay-out [ˈleiaut], *n.* disposición, *f.*; plan, *m.*
laze [leiz], *v.i.* holgazanear.
laziness [ˈleizinis], *n.* pereza.
lazy [ˈleizi], *a.* perezoso.
lazy-bones [ˈleizibounz], *n.* (*fam.*) gandul, *m.* vago.
lea [liː], *n.* (*poet.*) prado.
lead (1) [led], *n.* plomo.
lead (2) [liːd], *n.* delantera; primacía; dirección, *f.*; (*theat.*) papel principal, *m.*; (*elec.*) conductor, *m.*—*v.t. irr.* conducir; acaudillar; dirigir; llevar.—*v.i. irr.* ser el primero; conducir; mandar; *to — up to,* resultar en, conducir a.
leaden [ledn], *a.* plomizo; muy pesado; de plomo.

leader [ˈliːdə], *n.* caudillo; líder; director, *m.*; artículo de fondo (*en un periódico*).
leadership [ˈliːdəʃip], *n.* jefatura, mando; dotes (*m.pl.*) de mando.
leading [ˈliːdiŋ], *a.* principal; eminente; director; — *lady,* dama; — *man,* primer galán, *m.*
leaf [liːf], *n.* (*pl.* **leaves**) hoja.—*v.i.* echar hojas; *to — through,* hojear.
leaflet [ˈliːflit], *n.* hojuela; hoja volante.
leafy [ˈliːfi], *a.* frondoso.
league [liːg], *n.* liga.
leak [liːk], *n.* gotera; escape, *m.*; (*naut.*) vía de agua.—*v.i.* hacer agua; escaparse, salirse; *to — out,* trascender.
leaky [ˈliːki], *a.* llovedizo; que hace agua.
lean [liːn], *a.* magro; flaco; pobre.—*n.* molla, carne mollar, *f.*—*v.t. irr.* apoyar, arrimar.—*v.i. irr.* apoyarse, arrimarse; inclinarse; *to — out,* asomarse (*of,* a).
leaning [ˈliːniŋ], *a.* inclinado.—*n.* propensión, *f.,* tendencia.
lean-to [ˈliːntuː], *a.,* *n.* colgadizo.
leap [liːp], *n.* salto; — *year,* año bisiesto.—*v.t., v.i. irr.* saltar.
learn [ləːn], *v.t., v.i. irr.* aprender; *to — of,* saber.
learned [ˈləːnid], *a.* docto, erudito.
learner [ˈləːnə], *n.* principiante, aprendiz, *m.*
learning [ˈləːniŋ], *n.* erudición, *f.,* ciencia.
lease [liːs], *n.* arriendo.—*v.t.* arrendar.
leasehold [ˈliːshould], *n.* censo.
leash [liːʃ], *n.* traílla.
least [liːst], *a.* el menor, el más pequeño.—*adv.* menos; lo menos; *at —,* al menos, por lo menos.
leather [ˈleðə], *n.* cuero.
leathery [ˈleðəri], *a.* correoso.
leave [liːv], *n.* permiso; (*mil.*) licencia.—*v.t. irr.* dejar; (*jur.*) legar; salir de.—*v.i. irr.* salir; irse; *to — alone,* dejar en paz; *to — out,* omitir; *to take one's — of,* despedirse de.
leaven [levn], *n.* levadura.—*v.t.* leudar.
leaves [liːvz] [LEAF].
leave-taking [ˈliːvteikiŋ], *n.* despedida.
leavings [ˈliːviŋz], *n.pl.* sobras, *f.pl.*; desechos, *m.pl.*
Lebanese [lebəˈniːz], *a.,* *n.* libanés.
Lebanon [ˈlebənən], *n.* el Líbano.
lecher [ˈletʃə], *n.* lujurioso.
lecherous [ˈletʃərəs], *a.* lujurioso.
lechery [ˈletʃəri], *n.* lujuria.
lectern [ˈlektən], *n.* atril, facistol, *m.*
lecture [ˈlektʃə], *n.* conferencia; — *theatre,* aula, anfiteatro.—*v.t.* sermonear.—*v.i.* dar conferencias.
lecturer [ˈlektʃərə], *n.* conferenciante, *m.f.,* profesor universitario.
led [led], [LEAD].
ledge [ledʒ], *n.* anaquel, *m.*; tonga; repisa.
ledger [ˈledʒə], *n.* libro mayor.
lee [liː], *n.* (*naut.*) sotavento, socaire, *m.*
leech [liːtʃ], *n.* sanguijuela; (*obs.*) médico.
leek [liːk], *n.* puerro.
leer [liə], *n.* mirada lasciva, mirada de reojo.—*v.i.* mirar con lascivia, mirar de reojo (*at*).
lees [liːz], *n.pl.* heces, *f.pl.*
leeward [ˈluːəd], *a.* de sotavento.
leeway [ˈliːwei], *n.* (*naut.*) deriva; tardanza; libertad, *f.*
left [left], *a.* izquierdo.—*n.* izquierda.

left-handed ['left'hændid], *a.* zurdo.
left-overs ['leftouvəz], *n.pl.* sobras.
left-wing ['left'wiŋ], *a.* izquierdista.
leg [leg], *n.* pierna; pata; etapa; *to pull some-one's* —, tomar el pelo a; *on one's last legs*, a la muerte, de capa caída.
legacy ['legəsi], *n.* legado.
legal ['li:gəl], *a.* legal.
legate ['legit], *n.* legado.
legation [li'geiʃən], *n.* legación, *f.*
legend ['ledʒənd], *n.* leyenda.
legendary ['ledʒəndri], *a.* legendario.
legible ['ledʒibl], *a.* legible.
legion ['li:dʒən], *n.* legión, *f.*
legislate ['ledʒisleit], *v.t., v.i.* legislar.
legislation [ledʒis'leiʃən], *n.* legislación, *f.*
legitimate [li'dʒitimit], *a.* legítimo.
leg-up ['legʌp], *n. (fam.)* ayuda.
leisure ['leʒə], *n.* ocio, ratos libres, *m.pl.*
leisurely ['leʒəli], *a.* pausado.
lemon ['lemən], *n.* limón, *m.*
lemonade [lemə'neid], *n.* limonada.
lend [lend], *v.t. irr.* prestar.
length [leŋθ], *n.* largura, largo; *at* —, por fin; *to go to any length(s)*, hacer todo lo posible.
lengthen ['leŋθən], *v.t.* alargar.
lengthy ['leŋθi], *a.* prolongado, largo.
lenient ['li:njənt], *a.* clemente.
lens [lenz], *n.* lente, *m.* o *f.*
Lent [lent], *n.* Cuaresma.
lent [lent] [LEND].
lentil ['lentil], *n.* lenteja.
leopard ['lepəd], *n.* leopardo.
leper ['lepə], *n.* leproso.
leprosy ['leprəsi], *n.* lepra.
lese-majesty [li:z'mædʒisti], *n.* lesa majestad, *f.*
less [les], *a.* menor.—*adv.* menos; — *and* —, cada vez menos.
lessen [lesn], *v.t.* minorar, disminuir.—*v.i.* disminuirse; amainar *(viento)*.
lesson [lesn], *n.* lección; clase, *f.*; *to be a* — *to*, escarmentar.
lest [lest], *conj.* para que no, de miedo que.
let (1) [let], *v.t. irr.* dejar; alquilar; *to* — *by*, dejar pasar; *to* — *down*, bajar; desilusionar, dejar colgado; *to* — *go*, soltar; *to* — *know*, hacer saber, avisar; *to* — *off*, disparar; perdonar; — *him come*, que venga; — *us say*, digamos.
let (2) [let], *n. without* —, sin estorbo.
lethal ['li:θəl], *a.* letal.
lethargic [lə'θɑ:dʒik], *a.* letárgico.
let's [lets] [LET US].
letter ['letə], *n.* carta *(correo)*; letra *(del alfabeto)*.—*pl.* letras *(literatura)*.
letter-box ['letəbɔks], *n.* buzón, *m.*
lettuce ['letis], *n.* lechuga.
Levant [lə'vænt], *n.* Levante, *m.*
level ['levəl], *a.* nivelado, llano, raso; cuerdo; *to do one's* — *best*, hacer su posible.—*n.* nivel, *m.*; llano.—*v.t.* allanar, anivelar; apuntar.
level-crossing ['levəl'krɔsiŋ], *n.* paso a nivel.
level-headed ['levəl'hedid], *a.* sensato.
lever ['li:və], *n.* palanca.
leveret ['levərit], *n.* lebratillo.
leviathan [lə'vaiəθən], *n.* leviatán, *m.*
levity ['leviti], *n.* ligereza, veleidad, *f.*
levy ['levi], *n. (mil.)* leva; exacción, recaudación, *f.*—*v.t. (mil.)* reclutar; recaudar.
lewd [lju:d], *a.* salaz, lascivo.

lexical ['leksikəl], *a.* léxico.
lexicon ['leksikən], *n.* léxico.
liability [laiə'biliti], *n.* responsibilidad, *f.*; desventaja.
liable ['laiəbl], *a.* responsable; sujeto, expuesto; propenso.
liaison [li'eizən], *n.* coordinación, *f.*, enlace, *m.*; amorío.
liar [laiə], *n.* mentiroso.
libel ['laibəl], *n.* calumnia.—*v.t.* calumniar.
liberal ['libərəl], *a., n.* liberal, *m.f.*
liberate ['libəreit], *v.t.* liber(t)ar.
liberation [libə'reiʃən], *n.* liberación, *f.*
liberator ['libəreitə], *n.* liber(t)ador, *m.*
Liberian [lai'biəriən], *a., n.* liberiano.
libertine ['libəti:n], *a., n.* libertino.
liberty ['libəti], *n.* libertad, *f.*
librarian [lai'breəriən], *n.* bibliotecario.
library ['laibrəri], *n.* biblioteca.
Libya ['libjə], *n.* la Libia.
Libyan ['libjən], *a., n.* libio.
lice [lais] [LOUSE].
licence ['laisəns], *n. (U.S. license)* licencia; permiso; libertinaje, *m.*; *driving* —, permiso de conducir; — *number*, (número de) matrícula.—*v.t.* licenciar; autorizar.
licentious [lai'senʃəs], *a.* licencioso.
lichen ['laikən, 'litʃin], *n.* liquen, *m.*
licit ['lisit], *a.* lícito.
lick [lik], *n.* lamedura.—*v.t.* lamer; *(fam.)* tundear; vencer.
licorice ['likəris], *n.* regaliz, *m.*
lid [lid], *n.* tapa, tapadera, cobertera.
lie (1) [lai], *n.* mentira.—*v.t., v.i.* mentir; *to give the* — *to*, desmentir.
lie (2) [lai], *n.* situación, *f.*—*v.i. irr.* yacer; echarse; hallarse; *to* — *down*, acostarse.
liege [li:dʒ], *a.* feudal.—*n.* vasallo; señor, *m.*
lieu [lju:], *n. in* — *of*, en vez de.
lieutenant [lu:'tenənt], *n.* lugarteniente; *(mil.)* teniente, *m.*
life [laif], *a.* vital; vitalicio; perpetuo.—*n. (pl.* **lives)** vida; vivacidad, *f.*; — *insurance*, seguro de vida.
life-boat ['laifbout], *n.* lancha salvavidas.
lifeless ['laiflis], *a.* muerto; exánime; flojo.
lifelike ['laiflaik], *a.* vivo, natural.
lifelong ['laiflɔŋ], *a.* de toda la vida.
lifetime ['laiftaim], *n.* curso de la vida, vida.
lift [lift], *n.* alzamiento; *(Brit.)* ascensor, *m.*; *(fam.)* invitación *(f.)* para subir a un coche.—*v.t.* levantar, elevar, alzar; reanimar; *(fam.)* sisar, hurtar.
light [lait], *a.* ligero; leve; claro *(color)*; rubio.—*n.* luz; lumbre, *f.*, fuego.—*pl.* bofes, *m.pl.*—*v.t. irr.* encender; alumbrar, iluminar *(up)*.
lighten [laitn], *v.t.* aligerar; alegrar.—*v.i.* relampaguear.
lighter (1) ['laitə], *n.* mechero.
lighter (2) ['laitə], *n. (naut.)* barcaza, gabarra.
light-fingered [lait'fiŋgəd], *a.* largo de uñas.
light-headed [lait'hedid], *a.* casquivano; mareado.
light-hearted [lait'hɑ:tid], *a.* alegre, festivo.
lighthouse ['laithaus], *n.* faro.
lighting ['laitiŋ], *n.* alumbrado; encendido.
lightning ['laitniŋ], *n.* relámpago, relampagueo, rayo.
light-ship ['laitʃip], *n.* buque faro.

like

like (1) [laik], *a.* semejante; probable.—*n.* semejante, *m.*—*prep.* como, igual que; *to look* —, parecerse a.

like (2) [laik], *n.* gusto.—*v.t.* gustar de; *I — this*, esto me gusta; *when you* —, cuando Vd. quiera.

likelihood ['laiklihud], *n.* probabilidad. *f.*

likely ['laikli], *a.* probable.

liken ['laikən], *v.t.* comparar, asemejar.

likewise ['laikwaiz], *adv.* también, igualmente.

liking ['laikiŋ], *n.* gusto, afición, *f.*

lilac ['lailək], *n.* lila.

lilt [lilt], *n.* ritmo, paso alegre.

lily ['lili], *n.* azucena, lirio.

limb [lim], *n.* miembro; brazo; rama (*árbol*).

limbo ['limbou], *n.* limbo.

lime (1) [laim], *n.* cal, *f.*

lime (2) [laim], *n.* lima (*fruta*).

lime (3) [laim], *n.* (*bot.*) tilo.

lime-kiln ['laimkiln], *n.* calera.

lime-light ['laimlait], *n.* (*theat.*) luz (*f.*) del proyector; (*fig.*) luz (*f.*) de la publicidad.

limerick ['limərik], *n.* copla jocosa.

limestone ['laimstoun], *n.* piedra caliza.

limit ['limit], *n.* límite, *m.*; (*fam.*) colmo.—*v.t.* limitar.

limitation [limi'teiʃən], *n.* limitación, *f.*

limited ['limitid], *a.* limitado; *— company*, sociedad anónima.

limp [limp], *a.* flojo, blando.—*n.* cojera.—*v.i.* cojear.

limpet ['limpit], *n.* lapa, lápade, *f.*

limpid ['limpid], *a.* cristalino.

linden ['lindən], *n.* (*bot.*) tilo.

line [lain], *n.* línea; renglón, *m.*; cuerda; raya; (*rail.*) vía; descendencia; (*com.*) ramo; especialidad, *f.*; *in — with*, de acuerdo con; *hard lines*, (*fam.*) lástima, mala suerte.— *v.t.* poner en fila o línea; forrar.—*v.i. to — up*, hacer cola.

lineage ['liniidʒ], *n.* linaje, *m.*

lineal ['liniəl], **linear** ['liniə], *a.* lineal.

linen ['linin], *n.* lino, lienzo.

liner ['lainə], *n.* transatlántico.

linger ['liŋgə], *v.i.* tardar, demorarse.

lingerie ['lɛ̃ʒriː], *n.* ropa blanca de mujer.

lingo ['liŋgou], *n.* (*fam.*) jerga.

linguist ['liŋgwist], *n.* lingüista, *m.f.*

linguistic [liŋ'gwistik], *a.* lingüístico.

lining ['lainiŋ], *n.* forro; rayado.

link (1) [liŋk], *n.* eslabón, *m.*—*v.t.* eslabonar, juntar.

link (2) [liŋk], *n.* (*pl.*) campo de golf.

linnet ['linit], *n.* pardillo.

linoleum [lin'ouljəm], *n.* linóleo.

linseed ['linsiːd], *n.* linaza.

lint [lint], *n.* hilas.

lion ['laiən], *n.* león, *m.*; *lion's share*, parte (*f.*) del león.

lioness ['laiənis], *n.* leona.

lip [lip], *n.* labio; (*low*) descaro.

lip-service ['lipsə:vis], *n.* jarabe (*m.*) de pico.

lipstick ['lipstik], *n.* barra o lápiz (*m.*) de labios.

liquefy ['likwifai], *v.t.* liquidar.—*v.i.* -se.

liqueur [li'kjuə], *n.* licor, *m.*

liquid ['likwid], *a., n.* líquido.

liquidate ['likwideit], *v.t.* liquidar.

liquor ['likə], *n.* licor, *m.*; (*U.S.*) bebidas alcohólicas, *f.pl.*

liquorice [LICORICE].

Lisbon ['lizbən], *n.* Lisboa.

lisp [lisp], *n.* ceceo.—*v.i.* cecear.

list (1) [list], *n.* lista.—*v.t.* hacer una lista de.

list (2) [list], *n.* (*naut.*) ladeo, escora.—*v.i.* (*naut.*) ir a la banda, escorar.

listen [lisn], *v.i.* escuchar (*to*).

listener ['lisnə], *n.* oyente, *m.*, *f.*

listless ['listlis], *a.* apático, indiferente.

lit [lit] [LIGHT].

litany ['litəni], *n.* letanía.

literal ['litərəl], *a.* literal.

literary ['litərəri], *a.* literario.

literate ['litərit], *a.* que sabe leer y escribir; literato.

literature ['litərətʃə], *n.* literatura.

lithe [laið], *a.* ágil, cimbreño.

lithograph ['liθogrɑːf *or* -græf], *n.* litografía.

litigant ['litigənt], *n.* litigante, *m.f.*

litigate ['litigeit], *v.i.* litigar.

litigation [liti'geiʃən], *n.* litigación, *f.*

litmus ['litməs], *n.* (*chem.*) tornasol, *m.*

litre ['liːtə], *n.* litro.

litter ['litə], *n.* basura, desechos; litera camilla; paja; ventregada, camada.—*v.t.* esparcir, echar basura en; desordenar.

little [litl], *a.* pequeño; poco; *— finger*, dedo meñique.—*adv.* poco; *a* —, un poco (de); algún tanto; *— by* —, poco a poco; *to think — of*, tener en poco.

liturgical [li'tə:dʒikl], *a.* litúrgico.

liturgy ['litədʒi], *n.* liturgia.

live (1) [liv], *v.t.* llevar (*una vida*); vivir; *to — down*, borrar (el recuerdo de).—*v.i.* vivir; *to — up to*, cumplir, honrar.

live (2) [laiv], *a.* vivo; cargado (*elec.*, *munición*); ardiente: natural.

livelihood ['laivlihud], *n.* vida, subsistencia.

lively ['laivli], *a.* vivo, vivaz, brioso.

liver ['livə], *n.* (*anat.*) hígado.

livery ['livəri], *n.* librea; de alquiler.

lives [laivz] [LIFE].

livestock ['laivstɔk], *n.* ganado.

livid ['livid], *a.* lívido; (*fam.*) negro.

living ['liviŋ], *a.* vivo, viviente.—*n.* vida; modo de ganar la vida; (*eccl.*) beneficio.

living-room ['liviŋrum], *n.* sala de estar.

lizard ['lizəd], *n.* lagarto, lagartija.

load [loud], *n.* carga.—*pl.* (*fam.*) una barbaridad de.—*v.t.* cargar.

loadstone [LODESTONE].

loaf [louf], *n.* (*pl.* **loaves**) pan, *m.*; hogaza.—*v.i.* gandulear.

loafer ['loufə], *n.* haragán, gandul, *m.*

loam [loum], *n.* marga.

loan [loun], *n.* préstamo; empréstito.—*v.t.* prestar.

loath [louθ], *a.* poco dispuesto.

loathe [louð], *v.t.* detestar, abominar.

loathing [Houðiŋ], *n.* detestación, *f.*, asco.

loathsome ['louðsəm], *a.* asqueroso, nauseabundo.

loaves [louvz] [LOAF].

lobby ['lɔbi], *n.* vestíbulo; (*pol.*) cabilderos, *m.pl.*—*v.t.* cabildear.

lobe [loub], *n.* lóbulo.

lobster ['lɔbstə], *n.* langosta.

local ['loukəl], *a.* local.

localize ['loukəlaiz], *v.t.* localizar.

locate [lou'keit], *v.t.* situar; localizar.

loch [lɔk, lɔx], *n.* (*Scot.*) ría; lago.

lock [lɔk], *n.* cerradura; esclusa (*de canal*); bucle (*pelo*), *m.*; (*mech.*) cámara (*aire*); **under — and key**, debajo de llave; —, **stock and barrel**, todo; del todo.—*v.t.* cerrar con llave; trabar; **to — up,** (*fam.*) encarcelar. —*v.i.* cerrarse; trabarse.

lock-jaw ['lɔkdʒɔ:], *n.* trismo, tétano.

lock-out ['lɔkaut], *n.* (*com., pol.*) cierre, *m.*; paro forzoso.

locksmith ['lɔksmiθ], *n.* cerrajero.

lock-up ['lɔkʌp], *n.* (*fam.*) calabozo.

locomotive [louka'moutiv], *n.* locomotora.

locust ['loukəst], *n.* (*ent.*) langosta.

lode [loud], *n.* (*min.*) venero, veta.

lodestone ['loudstoun], *n.* piedra imán.

lodge [lɔdʒ], *n.* casita; pabellón, *m.*; portería; logia.—*v.t.* alojar; hospedar; fijar, plantar; presentar (*una queja*).—*v.i.* alojarse.

lodger ['lɔdʒə], *n.* huésped, *m.*, inquilino.

lodging ['lɔdʒiŋ], *n.* alojamiento.—*pl.* pensión, *f.*, cuartos alquilados, *m.pl.*

loft [lɔft], *n.* desván; pajar, *m.*

lofty ['lɔfti], *a.* encumbrado; excelso; altivo.

log [lɔg], *n.* tronco, leño; (*naut., aer.*) diario de navegación *o* de vuelo; (*fam.*) logaritmo.

logarithm ['lɔgəriðəm], *n.* logaritmo.

log-book ['lɔgbuk], *n.* (*naut.*) cuaderno de bitácora; (*aer.*) diario de vuelo.

loggerheads ['lɔgəhedz], *n.pl.* **to be at —,** estar reñidos, venir a las manos.

logic ['lɔdʒik], *n.* lógica.

logical ['lɔdʒikəl], *a.* lógico.

logwood ['lɔgwud], *n.* campeche, *m.*

loin [lɔin], *n.* (*anat.*) ijada; lomo.

loiter ['lɔitə], *v.i.* haraganear, tardar.

loiterer ['lɔitərə], *n.* vago, haragán, *m.*

loll [lɔl], *v.i.* colgar, repantigarse.

lollipop ['lɔlipɔp], *n.* paleta, dulce (*m.*) en palito.

London ['lʌndən], *n.* Londres, *m.*

Londoner ['lʌndənə], *n.* londinense, *m.f.*

lone [loun], *a.* solo, solitario.

loneliness ['lounlinis], *n.* soledad, *f.*

lonely ['lounli], *a.* (*U.S.* **lonesome**) solo, solitario, triste.

long [lɔŋ], *a.* largo.—*adv.* mucho tiempo, mucho; **as — as,** mientras que; con tal que; **how —,** cuánto tiempo; **— ago,** hace mucho tiempo; **so —!** (*fam.*) ¡hasta luego! **— v.i.** morirse, anhelar (**for,** por); ansiar; **to be — in,** tardar en.

long-distance ['lɔŋ'distəns], *a., adv.* (*tel.*) interurbano. **[trunk-call]**

longhand ['lɔŋhænd], *n.* escritura ordinaria.

longing ['lɔŋiŋ], *n.* anhelo, ansia.

longitude ['lɔndʒitju:d], *n.* longitud, *f.*

long-lived ['lɔŋlivd], *a.* de larga vida, duradero.

longshoreman ['lɔŋʃɔːmən], *n.* estibador, *m.*

long-standing ['lɔŋstændiŋ], *a.* que existe desde hace mucho tiempo.

long-winded [lɔŋ'windid], *a.* palabrero, interminable.

look [luk], *n.* mirada; aspecto, aire, *m.*—*v.i.* parecer; **to — after,** cuidar; **to — at,** mirar; **to — for,** buscar; **to — into,** investigar; **to — like,** parecerse a; **to — on,** juzgar, tener (**as,** por); **to — out,** tener cuidado; **to — out for,** aguardar; guardarse de; **to — up,** buscar; (*fam.*) mejorar; (*fam.*) visitar; **to — (out) on(to),** dar a.

looker-on [lukə'rɔn], *n.* (*pl.* **lookers-on**) espectador, mirón, *m.*

looking-glass ['lukiŋglɑ:s], *n.* espejo.

look-out ['lukaut], *n.* atalaya (*sitio*), *f.*; atalaya (*hombre*), *m.*; **on the — for,** a la mira de.

loom (1) [lu:m], *n.* telar, *m.*

loom (2) [lu:m], *v.i.* asomar; amenazar.

loony ['lu:ni], *a.* (*fam.*) chiflado.

loop [lu:p], *n.* lazo; recodo vuelta; recoveco; presilla; (*aer.*) rizo.—*v.t.* enlazar; doblar; atar.—*v.i.* formar lazo(s); recodar; **to — the —,** rizar el rizo.

loophole ['lu:phoul], *n.* abertura; (*mil.*) aspillera; (*fig.*) escapatoria.

loose [lu:s], *a.* suelto; flojo; disoluto; vago; **to set —,** libertar; soltar; **to come —,** desprenderse.—*v.t.* soltar; desatar.

loosen [lu:sn], *v.t.* aflojar; desatar.

loot [lu:t], *n.* botín, *m.*—*v.t.* saquear, pillar.

lop [lɔp], *v.t.* desmochar, podar (*off*).

lope [loup], *n.* zancada, paso largo.

lop-sided [lɔp'saidid], *a.* al sesgo, desequilibrado.

loquacious [lou'kweiʃəs], *a.* locuaz.

lord [lɔ:d], *n.* señor; (*Brit.*) lord; **Our Lord,** Nuestro Señor; **House of Lords,** Cámara de los Lores; **Lord Chamberlain,** Camarero Mayor; **Lord's Prayer,** padrenuestro.—*v.i.* **to — it over,** señorear altivamente.

lore [lɔ:], *n.* saber popular, *m.*

lorry ['lɔri], *n.* (*Brit.*) camión, *m.*

lose [lu:z], *v.t., v.i. irr.* perder.

loss [lɔs], *n.* pérdida; **at a —,** perplejo.

lost [lɔst] [LOSE].

lot [lɔt], *n.* mucho, gran cantidad; suerte, *f.*, sino; partija, lote, *m.*, solar (*sitio para construir casas etc.*), *m.*; **to draw lots,** echar suertes.

loth [LOATH].

lotion ['louʃən], *n.* loción, *f.*

lottery ['lɔtəri], *n.* lotería.

lotus ['loutəs], *n.* loto.

loud [laud], *a.* alto, fuerte, ruidoso; (*fam.*) vistoso, chillón; cursi.

loud-speaker [laud'spi:kə], *n.* (*rad. etc.*) altavoz, *m.*

lounge [laundʒ], *n.* salón, *m.*; gandulería.—*v.i.* recostarse, repantigarse; haraganear.

louse [laus], *n.* (*pl.* **lice**) piojo.

lousy ['lauzi], *a.* piojoso; (*fam.*) malísimo, sucio; (*fam.*) colmado (*de dinero*).

love [lʌv], *n.* amor, *m.*; cariño; (*sport*) cero; **in —,** enamorado (**with,** de).—*v.t.* querer, amar; (*fam.*) gustar de.

love affair ['lʌvə'fɛə], *n.* amores, *m.pl.*; (*pej.*) amorío.

lovely ['lʌvli], *a.* hermoso; precioso.

lover ['lʌvə], *n.* amante; querido.

loving ['lʌviŋ], *a.* cariñoso.

low (1) [lou], *a.* bajo; desanimado; ruin.— *adv.* bajo; **Low Countries,** Países Bajos; **— water** *o* **tide,** marea baja, bajamar, *f.*; **— gear,** primera marcha.—*adv.* bajo; **to lie —,** tenerse escondido.

low (2) [lou], *v.i.* mugir (*vacas*).

low-brow ['loubrau], *a.* (*fam.*) poco culto.

lower [louə], *v.t., v.i.* bajar.—*compar. of* LOW.

lowly ['louli], *a.* humilde.

loyal ['lɔiəl], *a.* leal, fiel.

loyalty ['lɔiəlti], *n.* lealtad, *f.*

lozenge ['lɔzindʒ], *n.* pastilla; (*geom., her.*) losange, *m.*

lubricant

lubricant ['lu:brikənt], *a., n.* lubricante, *m.*
lubricate ['lu:brikeit], *v.t.* lubricar.
lucid ['lju:sid], *a.* luciente; lúcido.
luck [lʌk], *n.* suerte, *f.*
lucky ['lʌki], *a.* afortunado, dichoso; *to be —,* tener (buena) suerte.
lucrative ['lu:krətiv], *a.* lucrativo.
lucre ['lu:kə], *n.* lucro, el vil metal.
ludicrous ['lu:dikrəs], *a.* absurdo, ridículo.
luggage ['lʌgidʒ], *n.* equipaje, *m.*
lugubrious [lu'gju:briəs], *a.* lóbrego, funesto.
lukewarm ['lu:kwɔ:m], *a.* tibio.
lull [lʌl], *n.* momento de calma, tregua.—*v.t.* calmar, adormecer.—*v.i.* calmarse; amainar.
lullaby ['lʌləbai], *n.* canción (*f.*) de cuna, nana.
lumbago [lʌm'beigou], *n.* lumbago.
lumber ['lʌmbə], *n.* maderaje, *m.*, madera; trastos, *m.pl.*
lumbering ['lʌmbəriŋ], *a.* pesado, torpe, desmañado.
lumberjack ['lʌmbədʒæk], *n.* hachero, leñador, *m.*
lumber-room ['lʌmbərum], *n.* leonera, trastera.
lumber-yard ['lʌmbəyɑ:d], *n.* madería.
luminous ['lju:minəs], *a.* luminoso.
lump [lʌmp], *n.* pedazo; bulto; borujo; chichón, *m.*; — *sugar*, azúcar (*m.*) en terrón; — *sum*, pago *o* suma total.—*v.t.* aterronar; juntar; (*fam.*) aguantar.—*v.i.* aterronarse.
lumpy ['lʌmpi], *a.* borujoso, aterronado.
lunacy ['lu:nəsi], *n.* locura, demencia.
lunatic ['lu:nətik], *a., n.* loco; — *asylum,* manicomio.
lunch [lʌntʃ], *n.* almuerzo.—*v.i.* almorzar.
luncheon ['lʌntʃən], *n.* almuerzo de ceremonia.
lung [lʌŋ], *n.* pulmón, *m.*
lunge [lʌndʒ], *n.* estocada; arremetida.—*v.i.* dar una estocada (*at*, a); arremetir.
lupin(e) ['lu:pin], *n.* lupino, altramuz, *m.*
lurch [lə:tʃ], *n.* sacudida; guiñada, bandazo; *to leave in the —,* dejar en las astas del toro.—*v.i.* dar una sacudida; tambalearse; (*naut.*) guiñar, dar un bandazo.
lure [ljuə], *n.* señuelo, añagaza.—*v.t.* atraer con señuelo; seducir, entruchar.
lurid ['ljuərid], *a.* ominoso, espeluznante.
lurk [lə:k], *v.i.* acechar.
luscious ['lʌʃəs], *a.* exquisito, rico.
lush [lʌʃ], *a.* lozano.
lust [lʌst], *n.* lujuria; codicia; deseo vehemente.—*v.i.* codiciar (*after*); lujuriar.
lustful ['lʌstful], *a.* lujurioso.
lustre ['lʌstə], *n.* lustre, *m.*, brillo.
lusty ['lʌsti], *a.* recio, robusto, forzudo.
lute [lju:t], *n.* laúd, *m.*
Luther ['lu:θə], *n.* Lutero.
Lutheran ['lu:θərən], *a., n.* luterano.
Luxemb(o)urg ['lʌksəmbə:g], *n.* Luxemburgo.
Luxemburger ['lʌksəm'bə:gə], *n.* luxemburgués.
Luxemburgian ['lʌksəm'bə:gjən], *a.* luxemburgués.
luxuriant [lʌg'zjuəriənt], *a.* lujuriante.
luxuriate [lʌg'zjuərieit], *v.i.* crecer con lozanía; lozanear; abundar.
luxurious [lʌg'zjuəriəs], *a.* lujoso.
luxury ['lʌkʃəri], *n.* lujo.

lying (1) ['laiiŋ], *a.* mentiroso.—*n.* **mentiras,** *f.pl.*
lying (2) ['laiiŋ] [LIE (2)].
lynch [lintʃ], *v.t.* linchar.
lynx [liŋks], *n.* lince, *m.*
lyre [laiə], *n.* lira.
lyric ['lirik], *a.* lírico.—*n.* lírica; letra (*de una canción*).
lyrical ['lirikəl], *a.* lírico.

M

M, m [em], *n.* letra decimotercera del alfabeto inglés.
ma'am [ma:m] [MADAM].
macabre [mə'ka:br], *a.* macabro.
macaroni [mækə'rouni], *n.* macarrones, *m.pl.*
mace (1) [meis], *n.* maza (*ceremonial*).
mace (2) [meis], *n.* macia (*especia*).
Machiavelli [mækiə'veli], *n.* Maquiavelo.
Machiavellian [mækiə'veliən], *a.* maquiavélico.—*n.* maquiavelista, *m.f.*
machination [mæki'neiʃən], *n.* maquinación, *f.*
machine [mə'ʃi:n], *n.* máquina.—*v.t.* hacer a máquina.
machinery [mə'ʃi:nəri], *n.* maquinaria.
machine-gun [mə'ʃi:ngʌn], *n.* ametralladora.
mackerel ['mækərəl], *n.* (*pl.* **mackerel**) caballa.
mackintosh ['mækintɔʃ], *n.* impermeable, *m.*, gabardina.
mad [mæd], *a.* loco; enojado; *to go —,* volverse loco.
madam ['mædəm], *n.* señora; (*fam.*) descarada.
madcap ['mædkæp], *n.* botarate, *m.*
madden [mædn], *v.t.* enloquecer; enojar.
made [meid], *a.* hecho; próspero. [MAKE].
made-up [meid'ʌp], *a.* falso, ficticio; hecho; compuesto; pintado.
madhouse ['mædhaus], *n.* manicomio.
madman ['mædmən], *n.* loco.
madness ['mædnis], *n.* locura.
magazine [mægə'zi:n], *n.* revista; recámara (*de un fusil*); almacén; polvorín, *m.*; (*naut.*) santabárbara.
maggot ['mægət], *n.* cresa.
magic ['mædʒik], *a.* mágico.—*n.* magia; brujería.
magician [mə'dʒiʃən], *n.* mágico; brujo.
magistrate ['mædʒistreit], *n.* magistrado, juez, *m.*
magnanimous [mæg'næniməs], *a.* magnánimo.
magnate ['mægneit], *n.* magnate, *m.*
magnesium [mæg'ni:zjəm], *n.* magnesio.
magnet ['mægnit], *n.* imán, *m.*
magnetic [mæg'netik], *a.* magnético.
magnetism ['mægnitizm], *n.* magnetismo.
magnetize ['mægnitaiz], *v.t.* magnetizar.
magnificence [mæg'nifisəns], *n.* magnificencia.
magnificent [mæg'nifisənt], *a.* magnífico.

314

magnify ['mægnifai], *v.t.* magnificar.
magnifying glass ['mægnifaiiŋ'glɑːs], *n.* lupa.
magnitude ['mægnitjuːd], *n.* magnitud, *f.*
magpie ['mægpai], *n.* (*orn.*) urraca, picaza.
mahogany [mə'hogəni], *n.* caoba.
Mahomet, *n.* [mə'homit] [MOHAMMED].
maid [meid], *n.* criada; doncella; virgen, *f.*
maiden [meidn], *a.* primero, de estreno; virginal.—*n.* doncella.
mail (1) [meil], *n.* correo; cartas, *f.pl.* — **box,** buzón, *m.*; — **man,** cartero. —*v.t.* echar al correo, mandar por correo.
mail (2) [meil], *n.* malla.
mail-bag ['meilbæg], *n.* valija.
mail-train ['meiltrein], *n.* tren correo.
maim [meim], *v.t.* mutilar.
main [mein], *a.* principal; mayor (*calle*); maestro.—*n.* robustez, *f.*; (*poet.*) océano; cañería maestra; cable maestro; **in the —,** principalmente.
mainland ['meinlænd], *n.* continente, *m.,* tierra firme.
maintain [mein'tein], *v.t.* mantener.
maintenance ['meintinəns], *n.* mantenimiento; conservación, *f.*
maize [meiz], *n.* maíz, *m.*
majestic [mə'dʒestik], *a.* majestuoso.
majesty ['mædʒisti], *n.* majestad, *f.*
major ['meidʒə], *a.* principal; mayor.—*n.* mayor (*m.f.*) de edad; (*mil.*) comandante, mayor, *m.*; — **general,** general (*m.*) de división.
Majorca [mə'dʒɔːkə], *n.* Mallorca.
Majorcan [mə'dʒɔːkən], *a., n.* mallorquín, *m.*
majordomo ['meidʒə'doumou], *n.* mayordomo.
majority [mə'dʒɔriti], *n.* mayoría.
make [meik], *n.* marca, fabricación, *f.*; hechura.—*v.t. irr.* hacer; producir; fabricar; ganar (*dinero*); pronunciar (*una oración*); forzar, obligar; calcular; **to — after,** correr en pos de; **to — as if to,** hacer como que, fingir; **to — away with,** llevarse; matar; **to — fast,** amarrar; **to — good,** reparar; indemnizar; tener éxito; **to — off,** escaparse; **to — out,** descifrar; explicar; **to — up,** inventar; recompensar (*for*); formar; reconciliar(se); pintarse; maquillar(se); **to — up one's mind,** decidirse; **to — sense,** tener sentido; **to — way,** abrir paso.
make-believe ['meikbili:v], *a.* fingido.—*n.* artificio, simulación, *f.*
Maker ['meikə], *n.* Creador, *m.*; **maker,** *n.* fabricante, *m.*
makeshift ['meikʃift], *a.* provisional.—*n.* suplente; expediente, *m.*
make-up ['meikʌp], *n.* cosméticos, *m.pl.*; composición, *f.*; (*theat.*) maquillaje, *m.*
makeweight ['meikweit], *n.* contrapeso; suplente, *m.*
making ['meikiŋ], *n.* fabricación, *f.*; hechura; éxito.
mal- [mæl], *prefix.* mal-, des-.
maladjusted [mælə'dʒʌstid], *a.* inadaptado, mal adaptado.
malady ['mælədi], *n.* dolencia, enfermedad, *f.*
malaria [mə'lɛəriə], *n.* paludismo.
Malaysian [mə'leiʒən], *a., n.* malaysia.
malcontent ['mælkəntent], *a., n.* malcontento.
male [meil], *a., n.* macho (*animales*); varón (*personas*), *m.*

malediction [mæli'dikʃən], *n.* maldición, *f.*
malefactor ['mælifæktə], *n.* malhechor, maleante, *m.*
malevolence [mə'levələns], *n.* malevolencia.
malevolent [mə'levələnt], *a.* malévolo.
malformed [mæl'fɔːmd], *a.* deformado.
malice ['mælis], *n.* malicia; rencor, *m.*
malicious [mə'liʃəs], *a.* malicioso.
malign [mə'lain], *a.* maligno.—*v.t.* calumniar.
malignant [mə'lignənt], *a.* maligno.
malinger [mə'liŋgə], *v.i.* fingirse enfermo.
malingerer [mə'liŋgərə], *n.* enfermo fingido.
mallard ['mæləd], *n.* (*orn.*) pato silvestre, lavanco.
malleable ['mæliəbl], *a.* maleable.
mallet ['mælit], *n.* mazo.
mallow ['mælou], *n.* (*bot.*) malva.
malmsey ['mɑːmzi], *n.* malvasía.
malnutrition [mælnju(:)'triʃən], *n.* desnutrición, *f.*
malpractice [mæl'præktis], *n.* abuso, procedimientos ilegales, *m.pl.*
malt [mɔːlt], *n.* malta.
Maltese [mɔːl'tiːz], *a., n.* maltés, *m.*
maltreat [mæl'triːt], *v.t.* maltratar.
maltreatment [mæl'triːtmənt], *n.* **maltrato.**
mammal ['mæməl], *a., n.* mamífero.
mammoth ['mæməθ], *a.* gigantesco.—*n.* mamut, *m.*
man [mæn], *n.* (*pl.* **men**) hombre; varón, *m.*; criado; pieza (*ajedrez etc.*); **no —,** nadie; **to a —,** todos; unánimemente; **— and boy,** desde la mocedad.—*v.t.* guarnecer, (*naut.*) tripular.
manacle ['mænəkl], *n.* manilla, esposas, *f.pl.*—*v.t.* maniatar, poner esposas a.
manage ['mænidʒ], *v.t. n.* manejar; (*com.*) dirigir.—*v.i.* arreglárselas; conseguir (*to*).
management ['mænidʒmənt], *n.* manejo; gerencia, dirección, *f.*
manager ['mænidʒə], *n.* gerente, director, *m.*; apoderado; empresario; ahorrador, *m.*
manageress [mænidʒə'res], *n.* directora.
mandarin ['mændərin], *n.* mandarín, *m.*; mandarina (*fruta*).
mandate ['mændeit], *n.* mandato.
mandolin ['mændəlin], *n.* mandolina.
mane [mein], *n.* crin (*de caballo*), *f.*; melena (*de león*).
man-eater ['mæniːtə], *n.* caníbal, *m.f.*, antropófago.
maneuver [mən'uːvə], (*U.S.*) [MANOEUVRE].
manfully ['mænfuli], *adv.* valientemente.
manganese [mæŋgə'niːz], *n.* manganeso.
mange [meindʒ], *n.* sarna.
manger ['meindʒə], *n.* pesebre, *m.*
mangle [mæŋgl], *n.* calandria; exprimidor, *m.*—*v.t.* pasar por el exprimidor; mutilar, despedazar.
mangy ['meindʒi], *a.* sarnoso.
manhole ['mænhoul], *n.* pozo de registro, buzón, *m.*
manhood ['mænhud], *n.* virilidad, *f.*; los hombres; edad viril, *f.*
mania ['meinjə], *n.* manía.
maniac ['meiniæk], *a., n.* maniático.
manicure ['mænikjuə], *n.* manicura.
manifest ['mænifest], *a., n.* manifiesto.—*v.t.* manifestar.
manifesto [mæni'festou], *n.* manifiesto.
manifold ['mænifould], *a.* múltiple.

manikin ['mænikin], *n.* maniquí, *m.*
manipulate [mə'nipjuleit], *v.t.* manipular.
mankind [mæn'kaind], *n.* humanidad, *f.*, el género humano; los hombres.
manliness ['mænlinis], *n.* virilidad, *f.*
manly ['mænli], *a.* viril; varonil.
manna ['mænə], *n.* maná, *m.*
mannequin ['mænikin], *n.* modelo, *f.*
manner ['mænə], *n.* manera.—*pl.* costumbres, *f.pl.*, modales, *m.pl.*
mannered ['mænəd], *a.* amanerado; educado.
mannerism ['mænərizm], *n.* hábito; amaneramiento.
mannerly ['mænəli], *a.* cortés, urbano.
mannish ['mæniʃ], *a.* hombruno.
manoeuvre [mə'nu:və], *n.* maniobra.—*v.t.* hacer maniobrar.—*v.i.* maniobrar.
man-of-war ['mænəv'wɔ:], *n.* (*pl.* **men-of-war**) buque (*m.*) de guerra.
manor ['mænə], *n.* casa señorial, finca solariega; feudo.
mansion ['mænʃən], *n.* palacio, casa señorial.
manslaughter ['mænslɔ:tə], *n.* homicidio accidental *o* no premeditado.
mantel [mæntl], *n.* manto.
mantelpiece ['mæntlpi:s], *n.* repisa de chimenea.
mantilla [mæn'tilə], *n.* mantilla.
mantle [mæntl], *n.* manto, capa; manguito (*gas*).—*v.t.* tapar, cubrir.
manual ['mænjuəl], *a.*, *n.* manual, *m.*
manufacture [mænju'fæktʃə], *n.* fabricación, *f.*—*v.t.* fabricar, manufacturar.
manufacturer [mænju'fæktʃərə], *n.* fabricante, *m.*
manure [mə'njuə], *n.* estiércol, *m.*—*v.t.* abonar, estercolar.
manuscript ['mænjuskript], *a.*, *n.* manuscrito.
many ['meni], *a.*, *pron.* muchos; gran número (de); *a good* o *great* —, muchísimos; *how* —, cuántos; *so* —, tantos; *too* —, demasiados; de sobra.
many-coloured ['meni'kʌləd], *a.* multicolor.
many-sided ['meni'saidid], *a.* multilátero, versátil, polifacético.
map [mæp], *n.* mapa, *m.*, plan, *m.*—*v.t.* planear, trazar el mapa de (*out*).
maple [meipl], *n.* arce, *m.*
mar [ma:], *v.t.* echar a perder, desfigurar.
maraud [mə'rɔ:d], *v.t.* merodear por.
marauder [mə'rɔ:də], *n.* merodeador, *m.*
marauding [mə'rɔ:diŋ], *a.* merodeante.—*n.* merodeo.
marble [ma:bl], *n.* mármol, *m.*; bolita, canica (*juguete*).—*v.t.* marmolizar.
March [ma:tʃ], *n.* marzo.
march (1) [ma:tʃ], *n.* marcha.—*v.t.* hacer marchar.—*v.i.* marchar.
march (2) [ma:tʃ], *n.* marca (*frontera*).
marchioness ['ma:ʃənis], *n.* marquesa.
march-past ['ma:tʃ'pa:st], *n.* desfile, *m.*
mare [mɛə], *n.* yegua; *mare's nest,* parto de los montes.
Margaret ['ma:gərit], *n.* Margarita.
margarine ['ma:dʒəri:n, 'ma:gəri:n], *n.* margarina.
margin ['ma:dʒin], *n.* margen (*de un papel*), *m.* o *f.*; reserva.
marginal ['ma:dʒinəl], *a.* marginal.
marigold ['mærigould], *n.* (*bot.*) maravilla; clavelón, *m.*

marijuana [mæri'hwa:nə], *n.* mariguana.
marine [mə'ri:n], *a.* marítimo, marino.—*n.* marina; soldado de la marina.
mariner ['mærinə], *n.* marinero.
marital ['mæritəl], *a.* marital.
maritime ['mæritaim], *a.* marítimo.
mark [ma:k], *n.* marca, señal, *f.*; indicio; traza, vestigio; nota, calificación (*en un examen*), *f.*; blanco (*tiro*); signo; rango; marco (*moneda*).—*v.t.* marcar; notar; señalar; anotar.
market ['ma:kit], *n.* mercado.—*v.t.* vender; comerciar en.
market-garden ['ma:kit'ga:dn], *n.* huerta, granja.
marksman ['ma:ksmən], *n.* tirador, *m.*, buen tiro.
marksmanship ['ma:ksmənʃip], *n.* buena puntería.
marmalade ['ma:məleid], *n.* mermelada.
maroon (1) [mə'ru:n], *a.*, *n.* marrón, *m.*
maroon (2) [mə'ru:n], *v.t.* abandonar, aislar.
marquee [ma:'ki:], *n.* tienda grande.
marquess, marquis ['ma:kwis], *n.* marqués, *m.*
marriage ['mæridʒ], *n.* matrimonio; casamiento; (*fig.*) maridaje, *m.*
marriageable ['mæridʒəbl], *a.* casadero.
marriage-licence ['mæridʒ'laisəns], *n.* dispensa de amonestación.
married ['mærid], *a.* casado; conyugal.
marrow ['mærou], *n.* médula, meollo; (*bot.*) calabaza.
marry ['mæri], *v.t.* casar; casarse con; (*fig.*) maridar.—*v.i.* casarse.
Mars [ma:z], *n.* Marte, *m.*
Marseilles [ma:'seilz], *n.* Marsella.
marsh [ma:ʃ], *n.* pantano; marisma.
marshal ['ma:ʃəl], *n.* mariscal, *m.*—*v.t.* ordenar, regimentar.
marshy ['ma:ʃi], *a.* pantanoso, palustre.
mart [ma:t], *n.* mercado, emporio.
marten ['ma:tin], *n.* marta, garduña.
martial ['ma:ʃəl], *a.* marcial, bélico. [COURT-MARTIAL].
martin ['ma:tin], *n.* (*orn.*) avión, *m.*
martyr ['ma:tə], *n.* mártir, *m.f.*—*v.t.* martirizar.
martyrdom ['ma:tədəm], *n.* martirio.
marvel ['ma:vəl], *n.* maravilla.—*v.i.* maravillarse (*at*, de).
marvellous ['ma:viləs], *a.* maravilloso.
Marxism ['ma:ksizm], *n.* marxismo.
Marxist ['ma:ksist], *a.*, *n.* marxista, *m.f.*
Mary ['mɛəri], *n.* María.
marzipan ['ma:zipæn], *n.* mazapán, *m.*
mascot ['mæskət], *n.* mascota.
masculine ['mæskjulin], *a.* masculino.
mash [mæʃ], *n.* masa; amasijo.—*v.t.* magullar, majar, aplastar.
mask [ma:sk], *n.* máscara.—*v.t.* enmascarar.
mason [meisn], *n.* albañil; (franco)masón, *m.*
masonic [mə'sɔnik], *a.* masónico.
masonry ['meisnri], *n.* albañilería; mampostería, ladrillos, piedras *etc.*; masonería.
masquerade [mæskə'reid], *n.* mascarada; farsa.—*v.i.* enmascararse; hacer una farsa; hacerse pasar (*as*, por).
mass (1) [mæs], *n.* masa; multitud. *f.*; bulto.—*v.t.* amasar; juntar en masa.—*v.i.* juntarse en masa.
mass (2) [mæs, ma:s], *n.* (*eccl.*) misa.

massacre ['mæsəkə], *n.* matanza, carnicería. —*v.t.* degollar, destrozar.
massage ['mæsɑ:dʒ], *n.* masaje, *m.*— [mə'sɑ:dʒ], *v.t.* masar, sobar.
masseur [mæ'sə:], *n.* masajista, *m.*
masseuse [mæ'sə:z], *n.* masajista.
massive ['mæsiv], *a.* macizo, enorme.
mass-meeting ['mæs'mi:tiŋ], *n.* mitin popular, *m.*
mass-production ['mæsprə'dʌkʃən], *n.* fabricación (*f.*) en serie.
mast [mɑ:st], *n.* (*naut.*) mástil, *m.*, palo; (*rad.*) torre, *f.*
master ['mɑ:stə], *a.* maestro.—*n.* maestro; patrón; dueño; (*educ.*) profesor, *m.*; perito; amo.—*v.t.* dominar.
masterful ['mɑ:stəful], *a.* imperioso; perito.
masterly ['mɑ:stəli], *a.* magistral.
masterpiece ['mɑ:stəpi:s], *n.* obra maestra.
mastery ['mɑ:stəri], *n.* dominio; maestría.
masthead ['mɑ:sthed], *n.* tope, *m.*
masticate ['mæstikeit], *v.t.* masticar.
mastiff ['mæstif], *n.* mastín, *m.*, alano.
mat (I) [mæt], *n.* estera; greña.—*v.t.* esterar; enredar.—*v.i.* enredarse.
mat (2) [mæt], *a.* mate.
match (I) [mætʃ], *n.* igual; pareja; boda; (*sport*) partido.—*v.t.* hacer juego con; igualar.
match (2) [mætʃ], *n.* cerilla, fósforo.
match-box ['mætʃbɔks], *n.* cajetilla.
match-maker ['mætʃmeikə], *n.* casamentero (*entre novios*).
mate (I) [meit], *n.* compañero; (*naut.*) contramaestre, *m.*; (*fam.*) camarada, amigo.— *v.i.* acoplarse.
mate (2) [meit], *n.* (*chess*) mate, *m.*—*v.t.* (*chess*) dar mate a.
material [mə'tiəriəl], *a.* material; importante. —*n.* material, *m.*; materia; tela, género.
materialism [mə'tiəriəlizm], *n.* materialismo.
materialist [mə'tiəriəlist], *n.* materialista, *m.f.*
materialistic [mətiəriə'listik], *a.* materialista.
materialize [mə'tiəriəlaiz], *v.t.* realizar; dar cuerpo a.—*v.i.* realizarse; tomar cuerpo.
maternal [mə'tə:nəl], *a.* materno; maternal.
maternity [mə'tə:niti], *n.* maternidad, *f.*
mathematical [mæθə'mætikəl], *a.* matemático.
mathematician [mæθəmə'tiʃən], *n.* matemático.
mathematics [mæθə'mætiks], *n.* matemáticas, *f.pl.*
matinée ['mætinei], *n.* función (*f.*) de tarde.
matins ['mætinz], *n.pl.* maitines, *m.pl.*
matriculate [mə'trikjuleit], *v.t.* matricular.— *v.i.* -se.
matriculation [mətrikju'leiʃən], *n.* matrícula.
matrimonial [mætri'mounjəl], *a.* matrimonial, conyugal.
matrimony ['mætriməni], *n.* matrimonio.
matrix ['mætriks], *n.* (*pl.* **matrices**) matriz, *f.*
matron ['meitrən], *n.* matrona.
matter ['mætə], *n.* materia; asunto; motivo; importancia; (*med.*) pus, *m.*; **as a — of fact,** en realidad; **a — of,** cosa de; **no —,**

no importa.—*v.i.* importar; supurar; **to be the — with,** pasar a.
matter-of-fact ['mætərəv'fækt], *a.* prosaico.
Matthew ['mæθju:], *n.* Mateo.
mattress ['mætris], *n.* colchón, *m.*
mature [mə'tjuə], *a.* maduro; (*com.*) pagadero.—*v.t.*, *v.i.* madurar; (*com.*) vencer.
maturity [mə'tjuəriti], *n.* madurez, *f.*; (*com.*) vencimiento.
maudlin ['mɔ:dlin], *a.* sensiblero; calamocano.
maul [mɔ:l], *v.t.* sobar; maltratar; destrozar.
Maundy Thursday ['mɔ:ndi'θə:zdei], *n.* jueves santo.
mausoleum [mɔ:sə'liəm], *n.* mausoleo.
mauve [mouv], *a.* color (*m.*) de malva.—*n.* malva.
mawkish ['mɔ:kiʃ], *a.* sensiblero, ñoño.
maxim ['mæksim], *n.* máxima.
maximum ['mæksiməm], *a.* máximo.—*n.* máximum, *m.*
May [mei], *n.* mayo.
may [mei], *v. aux. irr.* poder; tener permiso; *it — be,* puede ser.
maybe ['meibi], *adv.* acaso, tal vez.
mayor [mɛə], *n.* alcalde, *m.*
mayoress ['mɛərəs], *n.* alcaldesa.
maze [meiz], *n.* laberinto.
me [mi:], *pron.* me; mí; *with —,* conmigo.
meadow ['medou], *n.* prado, pradera.
meagre ['mi:gə], *a.* escaso; flaco.
meal (I) [mi:l], *n.* comida.
meal (2) [mi:l], *n.* harina.
mealy-mouthed ['mi:li'mauðd], *a.* meloso, mojigato.
mean (I) [mi:n], *a.* tacaño; ruin; malintencionado.
mean (2) [mi:n], *a.* medio, mediano (*ordinario*).—*n.* medio, promedio.—*pl.* medios; manera; recursos, dinero; *by all means,* no faltaba más; *by no means,* de ninguna manera; *by some means,* de alguna manera.
mean (3) [mi:n], *v.t. irr.* querer decir, significar.—*v.i. irr.* proponerse, pensar.
meander [mi'ændə], *n.* meandro.—*v.i.* serpentear.
meaning ['mi:niŋ], *n.* significado, sentido.
meaningful ['mi:ninful], *a.* significativo.
meaningless ['mi:niŋlis], *a.* sin sentido.
meanness ['mi:nnis], *n.* mezquindad, *f.*, tacañería; ruindad, *f.*
meant [ment] [MEAN].
meantime ['mi:ntaim], *n.* interín, *m.*; *in the —,* entretanto.
meanwhile ['mi:n'hwail], *adv.* entretanto.
measles [mi:zlz], *n.* sarampión, *m.*
measure ['meʒə], *n.* medida; (*mus.*) compás, *m.*; medio, gestión, *f.*; (*jur.*) proyecto de ley.—*v.t.*, *v.i.* medir.
measured ['meʒəd], *a.* deliberado; mesurado; rítmico.
measurement ['meʒəmənt], *n.* medida; mensuración, *f.*
meat [mi:t], *n.* carne, *f.*; *cold —,* fiambre, *m.*; *minced —,* picadillo.
meaty ['mi:ti], *a.* carnoso; (*fig.*) jugoso, substancial.
Mecca ['mekə], *n.* la Meca.
mechanic [mə'kænik], *n.* mecánico.—*pl.* mecánica.
mechanical [mə'kænikəl], *a.* mecánico; maquinal.

mechanism

mechanism ['mekǝnizm], *n.* mecanismo.
mechanize ['mekǝnaiz], *v.t.* mecanizar.
medal [medl], *n.* medalla.
medallion [mǝ'dæljǝn], *n.* medallón, *m.*
meddle [medl], *v.i.* entremeterse.
meddler ['medlǝ], *n.* entremetido, intruso.
meddlesome ['medlsǝm], *a.* entremetido.
meddling ['medliŋ], *a.* entremetido.—*n.* oficiosidad, *f.*
mediaeval [MEDIEVAL].
mediate ['mi:dieit], *v.t.*, *v.i.* mediar.
medical ['medikǝl], *a.* médico, de medicina.
medicament ['medikǝmǝnt], *n.* medicamento.
medicinal [me'disinl], *a.* medicinal.
medicine [medsn], *n.* medicina.
medicine-man ['medsnmæn], *n.* curandero.
medieval [medi'i:vǝl], *a.* medieval.
mediocre ['mi:dioukǝ], *a.* mediocre, mediano.
mediocrity [mi:di'ɔkriti], *n.* mediocridad, *f.*
meditate ['mediteit], *v.i.* meditar.
meditation [medi'teiʃǝn], *n.* meditación, *f.*
Mediterranean [meditǝ'reinjǝn], *a.*, *n.* Mediterráneo.
medium ['mi:djǝm], *a.* mediano.—*n.* (*pl.* -ums *o* -a) medio.
medley ['medli], *n.* mescolanza, fárrago.
meek [mi:k], *a.* manso, dócil.
meet [mi:t], *n.* (*sport*) concurso.—*v.t.* *irr.* encontrar; encontrarse con; recibir; honrar; cumplir.—*v.i.* *irr.* encontrarse (*with*, con).
meeting ['mi:tiŋ], *n.* reunión, *f.*; (*pol.*) mitin, *m.*; encuentro.
megacycle ['megǝsaikl], *n.* megaciclo.
megalomaniac [megǝlou'meiniæk], *a.*, *n.* megalómano.
megaphone ['megǝfoun], *n.* portavoz, *m.*, megáfono.
melancholia [melǝn'kouljǝ], *n.* melancolía.
melancholic [melǝn'kɔlik], *a.*, *m.* melancólico.
melancholy ['melǝnkɔli], *a.* melancólico.—*n.* melancolía.
melee ['melei], *n.* refriega.
mellow ['melou], *a.* suave, meloso; maduro.—*v.t.* suavizar.—*v.i.* suavizarse.
melodious [mi'loudjǝs], *a.* melodioso.
melodrama ['melǝdra:mǝ], *n.* melodrama, *m.*
melodramatic [melǝudrǝ'mætik], *a.* melodramático.
melody ['melǝdi], *n.* melodía.
melon ['melǝn], *n.* melón, *m.*
melt [melt], *v.t.* fundir, derretir.—*v.i.* fundirse, derretirse; deshacerse.
melting pot ['meltiŋpɔt], *n.* crisol, *m.*
member ['membǝ], *n.* miembro; socio; vocal (*de un comité*), *m.*
membership ['membǝʃip], *n.* personal, *m.*, socios, *m.pl.*; el ser miembro o socio.
membrane ['membrein], *n.* membrana.
memo ['memou], *n.* (*fam.*) apunte, *m.*
memoir ['memwa:], *n.* memoria.
memorandum [memǝ'rændǝm], *n.* (*pl.* -da) memorándum, *m.*
memorial [mǝ'mɔ:rjǝl], *a.* conmemorativo.—*n.* monumento.
memorize ['memǝraiz], *v.t.* aprender de memoria.
memory ['memǝri], *n.* memoria; recuerdo.
men [men] [MAN].
menace ['menis], *n.* amenaza.—*v.t.*, *v.i.* amenazar.

menagerie [mi'nædʒǝri], *n.* colección (*f.*) de fieras, zoo, *m.*
mend [mend], *n.* remiendo.—*v.t.* remendar, componer, reparar.
mendicant ['mendikǝnt], *a.*, *n.* mendicante, *m.*
menfolk ['menfouk], *n.pl.* hombres, *m.pl.*
menial ['mi:njǝl], *a.* servil.—*n.* lacayo.
mental ['mentǝl], *a.* mental.
mentality [men'tæliti], *n.* mentalidad, *f.*
menthol ['menθɔl], *n.* mentol, *m.*
mention ['menʃǝn], *n.* mención, *f.*—*v.t.* mencionar.
menu ['menju:], *n.* menú, *m.*, minuta.
mercantile ['mǝ:kǝntail], *a.* mercantil.
mercenary ['mǝ:sinri], *a.*, *n.* mercenario.
merchandise ['mǝ:tʃǝndaiz], *n.* mercancías, *f.pl.*, mercadería.
merchant ['mǝ:tʃǝnt], *a.* mercante.—*n.* mercader, comerciante, *m.*
merciful ['mǝ:siful], *a.* clemente, misericordioso.
merciless ['mǝ:silis], *a.* desapiadado, desalmado.
mercury ['mǝ:kjuri], *n.* mercurio.
mercy ['mǝ:si], *n.* misericordia, clemencia; gracia; *at the — of*, a la merced de.
mere (1) [miǝ], *a.* mero, solo.
mere (2) [miǝ], *n.* (*poet.*) lago.
meretricious [meri'triʃǝs], *a.* de oropel, charro.
merge [mǝ:dʒ], *v.t.* combinar, fusionar.—*v.i.* fusionarse; convertirse (*into*, en).
merger ['mǝ:dʒǝ], *n.* (*com.*) fusión (*f.*) de empresas.
meridian [mǝ'ridiǝn], *a.*, *n.* meridiano.
meringue [mǝ'ræŋ], *n.* merengue, *m.*
merit ['merit], *n.* mérito, merecimiento.—*v.t.*, *v.i.* merecer.
meritorious [meri'tɔ:rjǝs], *a.* meritorio.
mermaid ['mǝ:meid], *n.* sirena.
merriment ['merimǝnt], *n.* regocijo, alegría.
merry ['meri], *a.* alegre.
merry-go-round ['merigouraund], *n.* tiovivo.
merry-maker ['merimeikǝ], *n.* parrandista, *m.f.*, juerguista, *m.f.*
mesh [meʃ], *n.* malla, red, *f.*
mesmerize ['mezmǝraiz], *v.t.* hipnotizar.
mess (1) [mes], *n.* desorden, *m.*, enredo; bazofia.—*v.t.* ensuciar; desordenar.—*v.i.* — *about*, perder el tiempo.
mess (2) [mes], *n.* (*mil. etc.*) rancho.—*v.i.* hacer rancho.
message ['mesidʒ], *n.* mensaje, *m.*, recado.
messenger ['mesindʒǝ], *n.* mensajero.
Messiah [mǝ'saiǝ], *n.* Mesías, *m.sg.*
messy ['mesi], *a.* sucio; desordenado.
mestizo [mes'ti:zou], *a.*, *n.* mestizo.
metal [metl], *a.* metálico.—*n.* metal, *m.*; grava (*de caminos*).
metallic [mǝ'tælik], *a.* metálico.
metaphor ['metǝfǝ], *n.* metáfora.
metaphorical [metǝ'fɔrikǝl], *a.* metafórico.
metaphysical [metǝ'fizikǝl], *a.* metafísico.
metaphysics [metǝ'fiziks], *n.* metafísica.
meteor ['mi:tjǝ:], *n.* estrella fugaz, bólido; meteoro (*tiempo*).
meteorite ['mi:tjǝrait], *n.* meteorito.
meteorology [mi:tjǝ'rɔlǝdʒi], *n.* meteorología.

minimize

meter ['mi:tə], *n.* contador, *m.*; (*U.S.*) metro. —*v.t.* medir.
methane ['meθein], *n.* metano.
method ['meθəd], *n.* método.
methodic(al) [mə'θɔdik(əl)], *a.* metódico.
methyl ['meθil], *n.* metilo.
meticulous [mə'tikjuləs], *a.* meticuloso, minucioso.
métier ['meitiei], *n.* oficio, aptitud, *f.*
metre ['mi:tə], *n.* metro.
metric ['metrik], *a.* métrico.
metronome ['metrənoum], *n.* metrónomo.
metropolis [mi'trɔpəlis], *n.* metrópoli, *f.*
metropolitan [metrə'pɔlitən], *a., n.* metropolitano.
mettle [metl], *n.* brío, vigor, *m.*; *to be on one's* —, estar dispuesto a hacer lo mejor posible; *to put on one's* —, estimular.
mew (1) [mju:], *n.* maullido.—*v.i.* maullar, miar (*gatos*).
mew (2) [mju:], *n.* (*orn.*) gaviota.
mews [mju:z], *n.pl.* caballeriza; callejuela (*en Londres*).
Mexican ['meksikən], *a., n.* mejicano.
Mexico ['meksikou], *n.* Méjico.
miaow [mi'au], *n.* miau, *m.*, maullido.—*v.i.* maullar.
Michael ['maikəl], *n.* Miguel, *m.*
microbe ['maikroub], *n.* microbio.
microfilm ['maikroufilm], *n.* microfilm, *m.*
microphone ['maikrəfoun], *n.* micrófono.
microscope ['maikrəskoup], *n.* microscopio.
microscopic [maikrə'skɔpik], *a.* microscópico.
mid [mid], *a.* medio; *in mid-air*, en el aire; *in mid-winter* o *mid-summer*, en pleno invierno o verano.
midday ['mid'dei], *n.* mediodía, *m.*
middle [midl], *a.* medio, central; — *finger*, dedo del corazón; *Middle Ages*, Edad Media; *Middle East*, Oriente Medio.—*n.* centro, medio, mitad, *f.*; mediados (*m.pl.*) del mes; promedio.
middle-aged ['midl'eidʒd], *a.* de mediana edad.
middle-class ['midl'klɑ:s], *a.* de la clase media.
middleman ['midlmæn], *n.* (*com.*) corredor, *m.*, intermediario.
middling ['midliŋ], *a.* regular, mediano.
midge [midʒ], *n.* mosquito.
midget ['midʒit], *a., n.* enano.
midland ['midlənd], *a.* del centro, del interior.—*n. pl. the Midlands*, región (*f.*) central de Inglaterra.
midnight ['midnait], *n.* medianoche, *f.*
midriff ['midrif], *n.* diafragma, *m.*
midshipman ['midʃipmən], *n.* guardia marina, *m.*
midst [midst], *n.* centro.—*prep.* (*poet.*) entre; *in the* — *of*, en medio de.
midway ['mid'wei], *adv.* a (la) mitad del camino.
midwife ['midwaif], *n.* (*pl.* midwives) partera, comadrona.
mien [mi:n], *n.* semblante, *m.*
might [mait], *n.* poderío, poder, *m.*, fuerza. [MAY].
mighty ['maiti], *a.* poderoso; (*fam.*) muy.
migraine ['mi:grein], *n.* jaqueca.
migrant ['maigrənt], *a.* migratorio.
migrate [mai'greit], *v.i.* emigrar.

migration [mai'greiʃən], *n.* migración, *f.*
Mike [maik], *n.* Miguelito.
mike [maik], *n.* (*fam.*) micrófono.
milch [miltʃ], *a.f.* (*obs.*) lechera (*vaca*).
mild [maild], *a.* suave, templado, ligero.
mildew ['mildju:], *n.* mildeu, *m.*, moho.
mile [mail], *n.* milla.
mileage ['mailidʒ], *n.* kilometraje, *m.*
milestone ['mailstoun], *n.* piedra miliar; (*fig.*) hito.
milieu ['mi:ljə:], *n.* ambiente, *m.*
militant ['militənt], *a.* militante.
militarism ['militərizm], *n.* militarismo.
military ['militəri], *a.* militar.—*n.* milicia, militares, *m.pl.*
militate ['militeit], *v.i.* militar.
militia [mi'liʃə], *n.* milicia.
milk [milk], *n.* leche, *f.*—*v.t.* ordeñar.
milkmaid ['milkmeid], *n.* lechera.
milkman ['milkmən], *n.* lechero.
milksop ['milksɔp], *n.* marica, *m.*
milky ['milki], *a.* lechoso; *Milky Way*, Vía Láctea.
mill [mil], *n.* molino; fábrica; *to go through the* —, pasarlo mal.—*v.t.* moler; fabricar; acordonar (*monedas*).—*v.i.* hormiguear.
millennium [mi'lenjəm], *n.* milenio, milenario.
miller ['milə], *n.* molinero; fabricante, *m.*
millet ['milit], *n.* mijo.
millibar ['miliba:], *n.* milibar, *m.*
milligram(me) ['miligræm], *n.* miligramo.
millimetre ['milimi:tə], *n.* milímetro.
milliner ['milinə], *n.* sombrerero.
million ['miljən], *n.* millón, *m.*
millionaire [miljə'nɛə], *n.* millonario.
millionth ['miljənθ], *a., n.* millonésimo.
mill-pond ['milpɔnd], *n.* alberca, represa.
mill-race ['milreis], *n.* caz, *m.*
millstone ['milstoun], *n.* muela de molino.
mime [maim], *n.* mimo.—*v.t.* remedar.
mimic ['mimik], *a.* mímico.—*n.* mimo, remedador, *m.*—*v.t.* remedar.
mimicry ['mimikri], *n.* mímica, remedo.
minaret ['minəret], *n.* alminar, *m.*
mince [mins], *n.* picadillo.—*v.t.* picar, desmenuzar; (*fig.*) medir (*palabras*).
mincemeat ['minsmi:t], *n.* carne picada, cuajado.
mincing ['minsiŋ], *a.* remilgado.
mind [maind], *n.* mente, *f.*; juicio; ánimo; parecer, *m.*; intención, *f.*, deseo; *to bear in* —, tener presente o en cuenta; *to change one's* —, cambiar de opinión; *to make up one's* —, decidirse.—*v.t.* cuidar; tener en cuenta; *to* — *one's own business*, no meterse en lo que no le toca a uno.—*v.i.* molestar a; *do you* —? ¿le molesta? *never* —, no se preocupe.
mindful ['maindful], *a.* atento (*of*, a).
mine (1) [main], *poss. pron.* mío, el mío.
mine (2) [main], *n.* mina.—*v.t.* minar.
miner ['mainə], *n.* minero; (*mil.*) minador, *m.*
mineral ['minərəl], *a., n.* mineral, *m.*; (*Brit.*) gaseosa.
mine-sweeper ['mainswi:pə], *n.* dragaminas, *m. inv.*
mingle [miŋgl], *v.t.* mezclar.—*v.i.* -se.
miniature ['minətʃə], *a.* en miniatura.—*n.* miniatura.
minimal ['miniməl], *a.* mínimo.
minimize ['minimaiz], *v.t.* reducir al mínimo.

319

minimum

minimum ['minimǝm], *a.*, *n.* mínimo.
mining ['mainiŋ], *n.* minería; (*mil.*) minado.
minion ['minjǝn], *n.* paniaguado.
minister ['ministǝ], *n.* ministro.—*v.t.*, *v.i.* ministrar.
ministerial [mini'stiǝriǝl], *a.* ministerial.
ministry ['ministri], *n.* ministerio.
mink [miŋk], *n.* visón, *m.*
minnow ['minou], *n.* pececillo, foxino.
minor ['mainǝ], *a.*, *n.* menor, *m.f.*
minority [mai'nɔriti], *n.* minoría.
minster ['minstǝ], *n.* basílica, catedral, *f.*
minstrel ['minstrǝl], *n.* juglar, *m.*
mint (1) [mint], *n.* sin usar.—*n.* casa de moneda.—*v.t.* acuñar.
mint (2) [mint], *n.* (*bot.*) menta, yerbabuena.
minus ['mainǝs], *a.*, *n.*, *prep.* menos.
minute (1) [mai'nju:t], *a.* diminuto.
minute (2) ['minit], *n.* minuto.—*pl.* actas.
minute-hand ['minit'hænd], *n.* minutero.
minuteness [mai'nju:tnis], *n.* menudencia.
minutiae [mai'nju:ʃii], *n.pl.* minucias, *f. pl.*
minx [miŋks], *n.* (*zool.*) marta; descarada.
miracle ['mirikl], *n.* milagro.
miraculous [mi'rækjulǝs], *a.* milagroso.
mirage [mi'rɑ:ʒ], *n.* espejismo.
mire [maiǝ], *n.* fango, lodo.
mirror ['mirǝ], *n.* espejo.—*v.t.* reflejar.
mirth [mǝ:θ], *n.* regocijo, júbilo.
miry ['maiǝri], *a.* fangoso, cenagoso.
mis- [mis], *prefix.* des-, mal-.
misadventure [misǝd'ventʃǝ], *n.* infortunio, contratiempo.
misanthrope ['misǝnθroup], *n.* misántropo.
misapprehension [misæpri'henʃǝn], *n.* equivocación, *f.*
misbegotten [misbi'gɔtn], *a.* bastardo.
misbehave [misbi'heiv], *v.i.* portarse mal.
misbehaviour [misbi'heiviǝ], *n.* mala conducta; desmán, *m.*
miscarriage [mis'kæridʒ], *n.* aborto, malogro.
miscarry [mis'kæri], *v.i.* malparir, abortar; salir mal.
miscellaneous [misǝ'leiniǝs], *a.* misceláneo.
miscellany [mi'selǝni], *n.* miscelánea.
mischief ['mistʃi:f], *n.* daño; diablura, travesura; **to make —**, sembrar cizaña.
mischievous ['mistʃivǝs], *a.* travieso; dañoso, malicioso.
misconception [miskǝn'sepʃǝn], *n.* concepto erróneo.
misconduct [mis'kɔndʌkt], *n.* mala conducta, mal porte, *m.*
misconstrue [miskǝn'stru:], *v.t.* interpretar mal.
miscreant ['miskriǝnt], *a.*, *n.* malvado, maleante, *m.*
misdeed [mis'di:d], *n.* malhecho.
misdemeanour [misdi'mi:nǝ], *n.* delito, fechoría.
misdirect [misdi'rekt], *v.t.* dirigir mal.
miser ['maizǝ], *n.* avaro.
miserable ['mizǝrǝbl], *a.* desgraciado, miserable.
miserly ['maizǝli], *a.* avariento, tacaño.
misery ['mizǝri], *n.* miseria; pena, dolor, *m.*
misfire [mis'faiǝ], *v.i.* fallar.
misfit ['misfit], *n.* lo que no cae bien; persona desequilibrada.
misfortune [mis'fɔ:tʃǝn], *n.* desventura.

misgiving [mis'giviŋ], *n.* recelo, duda, desconfianza.
misguided [mis'gaidid], *a.* equivocado, descarriado.
mishap [mis'hæp], *n.* percance, *m.*, contratiempo.
misinform [misin'fɔ:m], *v.t.* informar mal.
misinterpret [misin'tǝ:prit], *v.t.* interpretar mal.
mislay [mis'lei], *v.t. irr.* (*conjug. like* LAY) extraviar, traspapelar.
mislead [mis'li:d], *v.t. irr.* (*conjug. like* LEAD) despistar, engañar.
misleading [mis'li:diŋ], *a.* engañoso.
misnomer [mis'noumǝ], *n.* nombre inapropiado.
misogyny [mi'sɔdʒini], *n.* misoginia.
misplace [mis'pleis], *v.t.* colocar mal; prestar (*fe*) a quien no la merece.
misprint ['misprint], *n.* errata (de imprenta).
misrepresent [misrepri'zent], *v.t.* falsificar, pervertir.
misrule [mis'ru:l], *n.* desgobierno.
Miss [mis], *n.* Señorita.
miss [mis], *n.* falta; fracaso, malogro; tiro errado.—*v.t.* echar de menos (*gente, cosas*); perder (*el tren*); no hallar; omitir; errar (*el blanco*); pasar por alto.—*v.i.* errar el blanco; malograr; **to just —**, por poco no coger.
missal ['misǝl], *n.* misal, *m.*
missel thrush ['misǝl θrʌʃ], *n.* charla, zorzal, *m.*
misshapen [mis'ʃeipǝn], *a.* deforme.
missile ['misail], *n.* proyectil, *m.*; **guided —**, proyectil teleguiado.
missing ['misiŋ], *a.* desaparecido; **to be —**, faltar.
mission ['miʃǝn], *n.* misión, *f.*; acometido.
missionary ['miʃǝnri], *a.*, *n.* misionario, misionero.
misspell [mis'spel], *v.t. irr.* (*conjug. like* SPELL) deletrear mal.
misspelling [mis'speliŋ], *n.* falta ortográfica.
mist [mist], *n.* neblina; (*U.S.*) llovizna.
mistake [mis'teik], *n.* error, *m.*; malentendido; falta.—*v.t. irr.* (*conjug. like* TAKE) comprender mal; tomar (*for*, por).
mistaken [mis'teikǝn], *a.* equivocado, errado, erróneo; **to be —**, equivocarse, engañarse.
Mister ['mistǝ], *n.* (el) señor, *m.*
mistletoe ['misǝltou], *n.* (*bot.*) muérdago.
mistook [mis'tuk] [MISTAKE].
Mistress, Mrs. ['misiz], *n.* (la) señora, Sra. (de); **mistress** [mistris], *n.* señora; (*educ.*) maestra, profesora, *n.*; (*pej.*) querida.
mistrust [mis'trʌst], *n.* desconfianza.—*v.t.*, *v.i.* desconfiar (de).
misty ['misti], *a.* nebuloso.
misunderstand [misʌndǝ'stænd], *v.t. irr.* (*conjug. like* STAND) entender mal.
misunderstanding [misʌndǝ'stændiŋ], *n.* malentendido.
misuse [mis'ju:s], *n.* mal uso.—[mis'ju:z], *v.t.* usar mal de; emplear mal.
mite (1) [mait], *n.* pizca; blanca (*moneda*).
mite (2) [mait], *n.* (*zool.*) ácaro; chiquitín, *m.*
mitigate ['mitigeit], *v.t.* atenuar, mitigar.
mitre ['maitǝ], *n.* (*eccl.*) mitra; (*carp.*) inglete, *m.*
mitt, mitten [mit, mitn], *n.* mitón, *m.*, manopla.

320

mix [miks], *n.* mezcla.—*v.t.* mezclar.—*v.i.* mezclarse; *to* —*up*, confundir.
mixed [mikst], *a.* mezclado; mixto (*matrimonio, sexos etc.*); *to get* — *up in*, enredarse en.
mixer ['miksə], *n.* mezclador, *m.*; *to be a good mixer*, (*fam.*) tener don de gentes.
mixture ['mikstʃə], *n.* mezcla, mixtura.
mix-up ['miksʌp], *n.* (*fam.*) lío, enredo.
mizzen ['mizən], *n.* (*naut.*) mesana.
moan [moun], *n.* gemido.—*v.i.* gemir.
moat [mout], *n.* foso.
mob [mɔb], *n.* populacho, gentuza, gentío.—*v.t.* festejar, atropellar.
mobile ['moubail], *a.* móvil.
mobilize ['moubilaiz], *v.t.* movilizar.
mock [mɔk], *a.* simulado, fingido.—*n.* mofa, burla.—*v.t., v.i.* mofarse, burlarse (*de*).
mockery ['mɔkəri], *n.* mofa, escarnio; irrisión, *f.*; remedo.
mock-up ['mɔkʌp], *n.* maqueta, modelo.
mode [moud], *n.* modo; moda.
model ['mɔdəl], *a.* modelo, *inv.*—*n.* modelo; modelo (*moda*), *f.*—*v.t., v.i.* modelar.
moderate ['mɔdərit], *a.* moderado.— ['mɔdəreit], *v.t.* moderar.
moderation [mɔdə'reiʃən], *n.* moderación, *f.*
modern [mɔdn], *a.* moderno.
modernistic [mɔdə'nistik], *a.* modernista.
modernize ['mɔdənaiz], *v.t.* modernizar.—*v.i.* -se.
modest ['mɔdist], *a.* humilde; modesto; moderado.
modesty ['mɔdisti], *n.* humildad, *f.*, recato; modestia.
modicum ['mɔdikəm], *n.* pitanza.
modification [mɔdifi'keiʃən], *n.* modificación, *f.*
modify ['mɔdifai], *v.t.* modificar.
modulate ['mɔdjuleit], *v.t.* modular.
Mohammed [mou'hæmid], *n.* Mahoma, *m.*
Mohammedan [mou'hæmidən], *a., n.* mohametano.
moist [mɔist], *a.* húmedo.
moisten [mɔisn], *v.t.* humedecer, mojar.—*v.i.* -se.
moisture ['mɔistʃə], *n.* humedad, *f.*
molar ['moulə], *a.* molar.—*n.* molar, *m.*, muela.
molasses [mɔ'læsiz], *n.* melaza.
mold (*U.S.*) [MOULD].
mole (1) [moul], *n.* (*zool.*) topo.
mole (2) [moul], *n.* (*anat.*) lunar, *m.*
mole (3) [moul], *n.* (*naut.*) malecón, *m.*
molecular [mɔ'lekjulə], *a.* molecular.
molecule ['mɔlikjuːl], *n.* molécula.
molest [mɔ'lest], *v.t.* incomodar; vejar.
mollify ['mɔlifai], *v.t.* mitigar, suavizar; apaciguar.
mollusk ['mɔlʌsk], *n.* molusco;(*cul.*)marisco.
molt (*U.S.*) [MOULT].
molten ['moultən], *a.* fundido, derretido.
moment ['moumənt], *n.* momento; (*fig.*) importancia.
momentary ['mouməntəri], *a.* momentáneo.
momentous [mou'mentəs], *a.* trascendental.
momentum [mou'mentəm], *n.* ímpetu, *m.*
monarch ['mɔnək], *n.* monarca, *m.*
monarchist ['mɔnəkist], *a., n.* monarquista, *m.f.*, monárquico.
monarchy ['mɔnəki], *n.* monarquía.

monastery ['mɔnəstri], *n.* monasterio, convento.
monastic [mə'næstik], *a.* monástico.
Monday ['mʌndei], *n.* lunes, *m.sg.*
monetary ['mʌnitəri], *a.* monetario.
money ['mʌni], *n.* dinero.
money-bag ['mʌnibæg], *n.* talega, bolso.
money-bags ['mʌnibægz], *n.* (*fam.*) ricacho.
money-box ['mʌnibɔks], *n.* hucha.
money-lender ['mʌnilendə], *n.* prestamista, *m.f.*
monger ['mʌngə], *n.* traficante, tratante, *m.*
Mongol ['mɔngəl], *a., n.* mongol, *m.f.*
Mongolia [mɔn'gouljə], *n.* la Mogolia.
Mongolian [mɔn'gouljən], *a., n.* mogol, *m.*
mongrel ['mʌngrəl], *a., n.* mestizo.
monitor ['mɔnitə], *n.* monitor, *m.*—*v.t.* controlar.
monk [mʌnk], *n.* monje, *m.*
monkey ['mʌnki], *n.* mono.—*v.i.* tontear, hacer monadas.
monocle ['mɔnəkl], *n.* monóculo.
monogamy [mɔ'nɔgəmi], *n.* monogamia.
monogram ['mɔnəgræm], *n.* monograma, *m.*
monologue ['mɔnəlɔg], *n.* monólogo.
monopolize [mə'nɔpəlaiz], *v.t.* monopolizar, acaparrar.
monopoly [mə'nɔpəli], *n.* monopolio.
monorail ['mɔnoureil], *n.* monorriel, *m.*
monosyllable ['mɔnəsiləbl], *n.* monosílabo.
monotheism ['mɔnouθiːizm], *n.* monoteísmo.
monotonous [mə'nɔtənəs], *a.* monótono.
monotony [mə'nɔtəni], *n.* monotonía.
monsignor [mɔn'siːnjɔː], *n.* monseñor *m.*
monsoon [mɔn'suːn], *n.* monzón, *m.*
monster ['mɔnstə], *n.* monstruo.
monstrance ['mɔnstrəns], *n.* (*eccl.*) custodia.
monstrosity [mɔns'trɔsiti], *n.* monstruosidad, *f.*
monstrous ['mɔnstrəs], *a.* monstruoso.
month [mʌnθ], *n.* mes, *m.sg.*
monthly ['mʌnθli], *a.* mensual.—*adv.* mensualmente.
monument ['mɔnjumənt], *n.* monumento.
monumental [mɔnju'mentl], *a.* monumental.
moo [muː], *n.* mugido.—*v.i.* mugir.
mood [muːd], *n.* genio, humor, talante, *m.*; mal humor, *m.*
moody ['muːdi], *a.* irritable, tosco; caviloso; caprichoso.
moon [muːn], *n.* luna.
moonbeam ['muːnbiːm], *n.* rayo lunar.
moonlight ['muːnlait], *n.* luna, luz (*f.*) de la luna.
moonshine ['muːnʃain], *n.* sueños dorados, *m.pl.*, ilusión, *f.*
moonstruck ['muːnstrʌk], *a.* aturdido; lunático.
Moor [muə], *n.* moro.
moor (1) [muə], *n.* páramo, brezal, *m.*
moor (2) [muə], *v.t.* amarrar.
Moorish ['muəriʃ], *a.* moro.
moorland ['muələænd], *n.* brezal, *m.*, páramo.
moose [muːs], *n.* alce, *m.*, mosa.
moot [muːt], *a.* batallona (*cuestión*).—*n.* junta.
mop [mɔp], *n.* estropajo, aljofifa; mueca; mechón, *m.*
mope [moup], *v.i.* estar abatido.

moral

moral ['mɔrəl], a. moral.—n. moraleja.—pl. moral, f.

morale [mɔ'ra:l], n. moral, f.

morality [mə'ræliti], n. moralidad, f.

moralize ['mɔrəlaiz], v.t., v.i. moralizar.

moratorium [mɔrə'tɔ:riəm], n. moratoria.

morbid ['mɔ:bid], a. morboso, malsano.

more [mɔ:], a., n., adv. más; no —, no ya; no más; the — ... the —, cuanto más ... tanto más.

moreover [mɔ:'rouvə], adv. además, por otra parte.

morgue [mɔ:g], n. depósito de cadáveres.

moribund ['mɔribʌnd], a. moribundo.

morn [mɔ:n], n. (poet.) mañana.

morning ['mɔ:niŋ], n. mañana; early —, madrugada.

Moroccan [mə'rɔkən], a., n. marroquí, m.f.

Morocco [mə'rɔkou], n. Marruecos, m.sg.

morose [mə'rous], a. bronco, lóbrego.

morphia ['mɔ:fjə], morphine ['mɔ:fi:n], n. morfina.

morphology [mɔ:'fɔlədʒi], n. morfología.

morrow ['mɔrou], n. (obs.) mañana, el día siguiente.

morsel ['mɔ:səl], n. bocado; manjar.

mortal ['mɔ:təl], a., n. mortal, m.f.

mortality [mɔ:'tæliti], n. mortalidad; mortandad, f.

mortar ['mɔ:tə], n. mortero; (arch.) argamasa.

mortgage ['mɔ:gidʒ], n. hipoteca.—v.t. hipotecar.

mortician [mɔ:'tiʃən], n. (U.S.) director (m.) de pompas fúnebres.

mortify ['mɔ:tifai], v.t. mortificar; (fig.) humillar.

mortise ['mɔ:tis], n. mortaja, muesca; — and tenon joint, ensambladura de caja y espiga.

mortuary ['mɔ:tjuəri], n. depósito de cadáveres.

Mosaic [mou'zeiik], a. mosaico.

mosaic [mou'zeik], a., n. mosaico.

Moscow ['mɔskou], n. Moscú, f.

Moses ['mouziz], n. Moisés, m.sg.

Moslem ['mɔzləm], [MUSLIM].

mosque [mɔsk], n. mezquita.

mosquito [mɔs'ki:tou], n. mosquito.

moss [mɔs], n. musgo.

mossy ['mɔsi], a. musgoso.

most [moust], a. más; la mayoría de.—n. lo más; la mayoría.—adv. más; lo más; to make the — of, sacar el mayor partido de.

mostly ['moustli], adv. principalmente, en su mayor parte.

mote [mout], n. mota.

moth [mɔθ], n. (ent.) mariposa nocturna; polilla (en tela).

moth-eaten ['mɔθi:tn], a. apolillado.

mother ['mʌðə], n. madre, f.; — tongue, lengua materna.—v.t. servir de madre a; mimar.

motherhood ['mʌðəhud], n. maternidad, f.

mother-in-law ['mʌðərinlɔ:], n. (pl. mothers-in-law) suegra.

motherly ['mʌðəli], a. maternal.

motif [mou'ti:f], n. motivo, tema, m.

motion ['mouʃən], n. movimiento; señal, f.; moción (en un debate), f.; in —, en marcha; — picture, (U.S. cine.) película; to carry a motion, adoptar una moción.—v.t. señalar, indicar.

motionless ['mouʃənlis], a. inmoble, inmóvil.

motivate ['moutiveit], v.t. motivar.

motivation [mouti'veiʃən], n. motivación, f.

motive ['moutiv], a., n. motivo.

motley ['mɔtli], a. abigarrado.—n. mezcla, abigarrada.

motor ['moutə], a. de motor.—n. motor, m.—v.i. pasear en coche, recorrer en coche.

motor-bike ['moutəbaik], n. (fam.) moto, f.

motor-boat ['moutəbout], n. canoa automóvil; gasolinera.

motor-car ['moutəka:], n. coche, m., automóvil, m.

motor-cycle ['moutəsaikl], n. motocicleta.

motor-cyclist ['moutəsaiklist], n. motociclista, m.f.

motoring ['moutəriŋ], n. automovilismo.

motorist ['moutərist], n. automovilista, m.f.

motorize ['moutəraiz], v.t. motorizar.

motorway ['moutəwei], n. autopista.

mottle ['mɔtl], n. veta, mancha.—v.t. motear, jaspear.

motto ['mɔtou], n. lema, m.

mould (1) [mould], n. (bot.) moho.—v.t. enmohecer.—v.i. enmohecerse.

mould (2) [mould], n. molde, m.; índole, f.—v.t. moldear, amoldar.

moulder ['mouldə], v.i. enmohecerse, desmoronarse.

moulding ['mouldiŋ], n. moldura; formación, f.

mouldy ['mouldi], a. mohoso, enmohecido.

moult [moult], n. muda.—v.t., v.i. mudar (la pluma).

mound [maund], n. montón, m., terrero; terraplén, m.; dique, m.

mount [maunt], n. monte, m.; montura, cabalgadura; montaje, m.—v.t., v.i. montar.

mountain ['mauntin], a. montañoso, montañés.—n. montaña; to make a — out of a molehill, hacer de una pulga un elefante.

mountain-climbing ['mauntin'klaimiŋ], n. alpinismo.

mountaineer [maunti'niə], n. montañés; alpinista, m.f.

mountainous ['mauntinəs], a. montañoso.

mountain-range ['mauntin'reindʒ], n. cordillera; sierra.

mountebank ['mauntibæŋk], n. saltimbanqui, m.

mounting ['mauntiŋ], n. montaje; engaste, m.

mourn [mɔ:n], v.t. llorar, lamentar.—v.i. lamentarse; estar de luto.

mourner ['mɔ:nə], n. enlutado; afligido; paid —, plañidera.

mourning ['mɔ:niŋ], n. luto; in —, de luto.

mouse [maus], n. (pl. mice) ratón, m.

mouse-hole ['maushoul], n. ratonera.

mouse-trap ['maustræp], n. ratonera, trampa.

moustache [məs'ta:ʃ], n. bigote, m.

mouth [mauθ], n. boca; orificio; desembocadura (de un río); down in the —, cariacontecido; to make one's — water, hacerse agua la boca.—[mauð], v.t. articular, pronunciar; meter en la boca.

mouth-organ ['mauθɔ:gən], n. armónica (de boca).

mouth-piece ['mauθpi:s], *n.* boquilla; (*fig.*) portavoz, *m.*
movable ['mu:vəbl], *a.* móvil, movible.—*n.pl.* bienes muebles, *m.pl.*
move [mu:v], *n.* movimiento; paso; jugada, turno; *it's your* —, le toca a Vd.—*v.t.* mover; trasladar; conmover (*emoción*).—*v.i.* moverse; mudar de casa; avanzar; *to* — *in,* tomar posesión (de); entrar en acción; *to* — *away,* apartar(se).
movement ['mu:vmənt], *n.* movimiento.
movie ['mu:vi], *n.* (*U.S. fam.*) película.—*pl.* cine, *m.*
moving ['mu:vin], *a.* motor, motriz; conmovedor, emocionante.—*n.* traslado; cambio; mudanza.
mow [mou], *v.t.* (*p.p. also* **mown**) segar.
mower [mouə], *n.* segador, *m.*; segadora (*máquina*).
much [mʌtʃ], *a., n., adv.* mucho; *as* —, tanto; *how* —, cuánto; *too* —, demasiado; *so* —, tanto; — *of a muchness,* (*fam.*) otro que tal, casi lo mismo.
muck [mʌk], *n.* estiércol, *m.*; (*fig.*) porquería.—*v.t.* (*fam.*) ensuciar, estropear (*up*).
muck-raker ['mʌkreikə], *n.* buscavidas, *m.f. inv.*
mucky ['mʌki], *a.* (*fam.*) puerco, sucio.
mud [mʌd], *n.* barro, lodo, fango; *to sling at,* llenar de fango.
muddle [mʌdl], *n.* lío, enredo, embrollo.—*v.t.* confundir, embrollar; aturdir.—*v.i. to* — *along,* ir a la buena de Dios, obrar confusamente.
muddy ['mʌdi], *a.* barroso, fangoso; turbio.—*v.t.* enturbiar.
mudguard ['mʌdgɑ:d], *n.* guardabarros, *m.sg.*
muezzin [mu'ezin], *n.* almuédano.
muff (1) [mʌf], *n.* manguito.
muff (2) [mʌf], *n.* (*fam.*) chapucería.—*v.t.* (*fam.*) chapucear, frangollar.
muffin ['mʌfin], *n.* mollete, *m.*, bollo.
muffle [mʌfl], *n.* mufla; funda.—*v.t.* amortiguar; embozar.
muffler ['mʌflə], *n.* bufanda; (*U.S. mech.*) silenciador, *m.*
mufti ['mʌfti], *n.* traje paisano; muftí, *m.*
mug [mʌg], *n.* cubilete, pichel, *m.*; (*low*) jeta; (*low*) tío, fulano.
muggy ['mʌgi], *a.* sofocante, bochornoso.
mulatto [mju'lætou], *a., n.* mulato.
mulberry ['mʌlbəri], *n.* (*bot.*) morera (*árbol*); mora (*fruta*).
mule [mju:l], *n.* mulo, mula.
multilateral [mʌlti'lætərəl], *a.* multilátero.
multiple ['mʌltipl], *a.* múltiple.—*n.* múltiplo.
multiplication [mʌltipli'keiʃən], *n.* multiplicación, *f.*
multiply ['mʌltiplai], *v.t.* multiplicar.—*v.i.* -se.
multitude ['mʌltitju:d], *n.* multitud, *f.*
mum [mʌm], *a.* (*fam.*) callado.—*n.* (*fam.*) mamá, *f.*
mumble [mʌmbl], *n.* mascullada.—*v.t., v.i.* mascullar, farfullar.
mumbo-jumbo ['mʌmbou'dʒʌmbou], *n.* fetiche, *m.*; música celestial.
mummy (1) ['mʌmi], *n.* momia.
mummy (2) ['mʌmi], *n.* (*fam.*) mamá, *f.*
mumps [mʌmps], *n.* parótidas, *f.pl.,* lamparones, *m.pl.*

munch [mʌntʃ], *v.t., v.i.* masticar, ronchar.
mundane ['mʌndein], *a.* mundano.
municipal [mju'nisipəl], *a.* municipal.
municipality [mju:nisi'pæliti], *n.* municipio.
munificent [mju'nifisənt], *a.* munífico.
munitions [mju'niʃənz], *n.pl.* municiones, *f.pl.*
mural ['mjuərəl], *a.* mural.—*n.* pintura mural.
murder ['mə:də], *n.* asesinato, homicidio.—*v.t.* asesinar; (*fig.*) destripar.
murderer ['mə:dərə], *n.* asesino.
murderess ['mə:dəris], *n.* asesina.
murderous ['mə:dərəs], *a.* asesino.
murk [mə:k], *n.* tinieblas *f.pl.*; cerrazón, *f.*
murky ['mə:ki], *a.* lóbrego, tenebroso; borrascoso.
murmur ['mə:mə], *n.* murmullo.—*v.t., v.i.* murmurar.
muscle [mʌsl], *n.* músculo.
muscular ['mʌskjulə], *a.* muscular; musculoso.
muse [mju:z], *n.* musa.—*v.i.* meditar.
museum [mju'zi:əm], *n.* museo.
mushroom ['mʌʃrum], *n.* champiñón, *m.*, seta.—*v.i.* aparecer de la noche a la mañana.
mushy ['mʌʃi], *a.* (*fam.*) pulposo; sensiblero.
music ['mju:zik], *n.* música.
musical ['mju:zikəl], *a.* músico, musical.
musician [mju'ziʃən], *n.* músico.
musk [mʌsk], *n.* almizcle, *m.*
musket ['mʌskit], *n.* mosquete, *m.*
musketeer [mʌski'tiə], *n.* mosquetero.
Muslim ['mʌzlim], *a., n.* musulmán, *m.*
muslin ['mʌzlin], *n.* muselina.
mussel [mʌsl], *n.* mejillón, *m.*, almeja.
must [mʌst], *n.* moho; zumo, mosto.—*v. aux. irr.* (*existe solamente en el tiempo presente*) deber, tener que; deber de.
mustard ['mʌstəd], *n.* mostaza.
muster ['mʌstə], *n.* asamblea, reunión, *f.*; revista, alarde, *f.*, lista; *to pass* —, ser aceptable.—*v.t.* reunir, juntar; cobrar (*ánimo*).
musty ['mʌsti], *a.* mohoso, rancio.
mutant ['mju:tənt], *a., n.* mutante, *m.*
mutation [mju'teiʃən], *n.* mutación, *f.*
mute [mju:t], *a., n.* mudo.—*v.t.* poner sordina a.
mutilate ['mju:tileit], *v.t.* mutilar.
mutineer [mju:ti'niə], *n.* amotinado, sedicioso.
mutiny ['mju:tini], *n.* motín, *m.*, sublevación, *f.*—*v.i.* amotinarse.
mutter ['mʌtə], *v.t., v.i.* murmurar, refunfuñar.
mutton [mʌtn], *n.* carnero (*carne*).
mutual ['mju:tjuəl], *a.* mutuo.
muzzle [mʌzl], *n.* bozal, *m.*, mordaza; boca (*de un fusil*).—*v.t.* amordazar, embozar.
my [mai], *poss. pron.* mi.
myopic [mai'opik], *a.* miope.
myrrh [mə:], *n.* mirra.
myrtle [mə:tl], *n.* mirto, arrayán, *m.*
myself [mai'self], *pron.* yo mismo; me, a mí mismo.
mysterious [mis'tiəriəs], *a.* misterioso.
mystery ['mistəri], *n.* misterio.
mystic ['mistik], *a., n.* místico.
mysticism ['mistisizm], *n.* misticismo.
mystify ['mistifai], *v.t.* dejar perplejo, mistificar.

myth [miθ], *n*. mito, leyenda.
mythical ['miθikəl], *a*. mítico.
mythology [mi'θɔlədʒi], *n*. mitología.

N

N, n [en], *n*. décimocuarta letra del alfabeto inglés.
nab [næb], *v.t.* (*fam.*) agarrar.
nadir ['neidiə], *n*. nadir, *m*.
nag (1) [næg], *n*. jaca.
nag (2) [næg], *n*. (*fam.*) regañona.—*v.t.*, *v.i.* regañar, jeringar.
nail [neil], *n*. clavo; (*anat.*) uña.—*v.t.* clavar.
naive [nai'i:v], *a*. ingenuo, cándido.
naiveté [nai'i:vtei], *n*. ingenuidad, candidez, *f*.
naked ['neikid], *a*. desnudo; **with the — eye,** a simple vista.
name [neim], *n*. nombre, *m*.; **by —,** de nombre; **to call names,** poner motes (a); **what is your —?** ¿cómo se llama Vd.? —*v.t.* nombrar; bautizar; apodar.
nameless ['neimlis], *a*. sin nombre; desconocido.
namely ['neimli], *adv.* a saber.
name-plate ['neimpleit], *n*. placa.
namesake ['neimseik], *n*. tocayo.
nanny ['næni], *n*. (*fam.*) niñera.
nanny-goat ['nænigout], *n*. cabra.
nap (1) [næp], *n*. duermevela, *m.*, siestecita.—*v.i.* echar una siestecita; **to catch napping,** coger desprevenido.
nap (2) [næp], *n*. lanilla (*de tela*).
nape [neip], *n*. nuca.
naphtha ['næfθə], *n*. nafta.
napkin ['næpkin], *n*. servilleta; pañal (*para un niño*), *m*.
Naples [neiplz], *n*. Nápoles, *f*.
Napoleon [nə'pouljən], *n*. Napoleón, *m*.
Napoleonic [nəpouli'ɔnik], *a*. napoleónico.
narcissus [nɑː'sisəs], *n*. narciso.
narcotic [nɑː'kɔtik], *a.*, *n*. narcótico.
narrate [næ'reit], *v.t.* narrar, relatar.
narration [næ'reiʃən], *n*. narración, *f*.
narrative ['nærətiv], *a*. narrativo.—*n*. narrativa.
narrow ['nærou], *a*. estrecho, angosto; intolerante.—*n.pl.* angostura.—*v.t.* enangostar, estrechar.—*v.i.* -se.
narrow-minded ['nærou'maindid], *a*. intolerante, mojigato.
narrowness ['nærounis], *n*. estrechez, *f*.
nasal ['neizəl], *a*. nasal.
nastiness ['nɑːstinis], *n*. suciedad, *f.*; horror, *m.*; ruindad, *f*.
nasty ['nɑːsti], *a*. sucio, puerco; indecente; intratable; odioso.
natal ['neitəl], *a*. natal.
nation ['neiʃən], *n*. nación, *f*.
national ['næʃənəl], *a.*, *n*. nacional, *m.f.*
nationalist ['næʃnəlist], *a.*, *n*. nacionalista, *m.f.*
nationality [næʃə'næliti], *n*. nacionalidad, *f*.
nationalize ['næʃnəlaiz], *v.t.* nacionalizar.

native ['neitiv], *a*. nativo, indígena.—*n*. natural, indígena, *m.f.*
nativity [nə'tiviti], *n*. nacimiento, natividad, *f*.
natty ['næti], *a*. garboso, majo, elegante.
natural ['nætʃurəl], *a*. natural.
naturalize ['nætʃurəlaiz], *v.t.* naturalizar.
nature ['neitʃə], *n*. naturaleza.
naught [nɔːt], *n*. nada, cero; **to come to —,** frustrarse.
naughty ['nɔːti], *a*. travieso, desobediente; pícaro.
nausea ['nɔːsiə], *n*. náusea.
nauseate ['nɔːsieit], *v.t.* dar asco (a).
nauseating ['nɔːsieitiŋ], *a*. asqueroso, nauseabundo.
nautical ['nɔːtikəl], *a*. náutico; **— mile,** milla marina.
naval ['neivəl], *a*. naval.
Navarre [nə'vɑː], *n*. Navarra.
Navarrese [nævə'riːz], *a.*, *n*. navarro.
nave [neiv], *n*. (*arch.*) nave, *f*.
navel ['neivəl], *n*. (*anat.*) ombligo.
navigable ['nævigəbl], *a*. navegable; marinero (*barco*).
navigate ['nævigeit], *v.t.*, *v.i.* navegar.
navigation [nævi'geiʃən], *n*. navegación, *f*.
navvy ['nævi], *n*. bracero, peón, *m*.
navy ['neivi], *n*. marina.
navy-blue ['neivi'bluː], *a.*, *n*. azul marino.
nay [nei], *adv.* (*obs.*, *dial.*) no.
Nazi ['nɑːtsi], *a.*, *n*. nazi, nacista, *m.f.*
Nazi(i)sm ['nɑːts(iː)izm], *n*. nazismo.
neap-tide ['niːp'taid], *n*. marea muerta, bajamar, *f*.
near [niə], *a*. cercano; próximo; **— at hand,** a mano.—*adv.* cerca.—*prep.* cerca de.—*v.t.* acercarse a.
nearby ['niəbai], *a*. cercano, vecino.—[niə'bai], *adv.* cerca.
nearly ['niəli], *adv.* casi; por poco.
near-sighted ['niə'saitid], *a*. miope.
neat [niːt], *a*. aseado; esmerado; sin mezcla.
'neath [niːθ], *prep.* (*poet.*) so, bajo.
neatness ['niːtnis], *n*. aseo; pulidez, *f.*, primor, *m*.
nebula ['nebjulə], *n*. nebulosa.
nebulous ['nebjuləs], *a*. nebuloso.
necessary ['nesisəri], *a*. necesario.—*n*. lo necesario.
necessitate [nə'sesiteit], *v.t.* necesitar, requerir.
necessity [nə'sesiti], *n*. necesidad, *f*.
neck [nek], *n*. cuello; golete (*de una botella*), *m.*; (*geog.*) península; **— and —,** parejos; **— or nothing,** todo o nada.
neckerchief ['nekətʃiːf], *n*. pañuelo de cuello.
necklace ['neklis], *n*. collar, *m*.
necropolis [ne'krɔpəlis], *n*. necrópolis, *f*.
nectar ['nektə], *n*. néctar, *m*.
née [nei], *a.f.* nacida; **Anne Smith — Brown,** Anne Brown de Smith.
need [niːd], *n*. necesidad, *f.*; **in —,** necesitado.—*v.t.* necesitar, hacer falta a; **if need(s) be,** si fuera necesario.
needful ['niːdful], *a*. necesario.
needle [niːdl], *n*. aguja.
needless ['niːdlis], *a*. innecesario.
needlework ['niːdlwəːk], *n*. labor, *f.*, costura.
needs [niːdz] *adv.* necesariamente, forzosamente.
needy ['niːdi], *a*. necesitado, menesteroso.

ne'er [nɛə], *adv.* (*poet.*) nunca.
ne'er-do-well ['nɛədu:wel], *n.* dejado de la mano de Dios.
negation [ni'geiʃən], *n.* negación, *f.*, negativa.
negative ['negətiv], *a.* negativo.—*n.* (*gram.*) negación, *f.*; (*phot.*) negativo; negativa (*repulsa*).
neglect [ni'glekt], *n.* descuido, negligencia.—*v.t.* abandonar, descuidar, desatender.—*v.i.* dejar, olvidarse (*to*, de).
neglectful [ni'glektful], *a.* negligente.
negligence ['neglidʒəns], *n.* negligencia.
negligent ['neglidʒənt], *a.* negligente.
negligible ['neglidʒəbl], *a.* sin importancia, insignificante.
negotiable [ni'gouʃəbl], *a.* negociable; transitable.
negotiate [ni'gouʃieit], *v.t.* negociar; salvar, transitar.—*v.i.* negociar.
negotiation [nigouʃi'eiʃən], *n.* negociación, *f.*
Negress ['ni:gris], *n.* (*pej.*) negra.
Negro ['ni:grou], *a.*, *n.* negro.
neigh [nei], *n.* relincho.—*v.i.* relinchar.
neighbour ['neibə], *n.* vecino; (*fig.*) prójimo.
neighbourhood ['neibəhud], *n.* vecindad, *f.*
neighbouring ['neibəriŋ], *a.* vecino.
neighbourly ['neibəli], *a.* buen vecino, amigable.
neither ['naiðə, 'ni:ðə], *a.* ninguno (de los dos).—*adv.* tampoco.—*conj.* — ... *nor*, ni ... ni.
neon ['ni:ɔn], *n.* neón, *m.*
Nepal [ni'pɔ:l], *n.* el Nepal.
Nepalese [nepə'li:z], *a.*, *n. inv.* nepalés, *m.*
nephew ['nefju:], *n.* sobrino.
nepotism ['nepətizm], *n.* nepotismo.
Nero ['niərou], *n.* Nerón, *m.*
nerve [nə:v], *n.* nervio; (*fam.*) descaro; **to get on one's nerves**, irritar, fastidiar, exasperar.
nerve-racking ['nə:vrækiŋ], *a.* exasperante, agobiante.
nervous ['nə:vəs], *a.* nervioso; tímido; — **breakdown**, crisis nerviosa.
nest [nest], *n.* nido.—*v.i.* anidar; buscar nidos.
nest-egg ['nesteg], *n.* hucha, peculio.
nestle [nesl], *v.t.* arrimar, abrigar.—*v.i.* arrimarse, abrigarse.
net (1) [net], *n.* red, *f.*—*v.t.* coger (en red); ganar.
net (2) [net], *a.* neto.
nether ['neðə], *a.* inferior.
Netherlands ['neðələndz], **The**, *n.pl.* los Países Bajos.
netting ['netiŋ], *n.* malla, red, *f.*, redes, *f.pl.*
nettle [netl], *n.* ortiga.—*v.t.* picar, irritar.
network ['netwə:k], *n.* red, *f.*
neurotic [njuə'rotik], *a.*, *n.* neurótico.
neuter ['nju:tə], *a.*, *n.* neutro.
neutral ['nju:trəl], *a.* neutral; neutro.
neutrality [nju:'træliti], *n.* neutralidad, *f.*
never ['nevə], *adv.* nunca, (no) jamás.
nevertheless [nevəðə'les], *adv.* no obstante, a pesar de eso.
new [nju:], *a.* nuevo; **New World**, Nuevo Mundo; **New York**, Nueva York; **New Zealand**, Nueva Zelandia; **New Zealander**, neocelandés, *m.*
new-comer ['nju:kʌmə], *n.* recién venido.
new-fangled [nju:'fæŋgld], *a.* inventado por novedad, nuevo.

newly ['nju:li], *adv.* nuevamente; (*before p.p.*) recién.
newly-wed ['nju:li'wed], *a.*, *n.* recién casado.
newness ['nju:nis], *n.* novedad, *f.*; inexperiencia.
news [nju:z], *n.sg.* noticias; **piece of —**, noticia; **—reel**, (*cine.*) actualidades, *f.pl.*
newscast ['nju:zka:st], *n.* (*U.S.*) noticiario.
newspaper ['nju:zpeipə], *n.* periódico; — **reporter** o — **man**, periodista, *m.*
newt [nju:t], *n.* tritón, *m.*
next [nekst], *a.* próximo; que viene; — **day**, el día siguiente; — **door**, la casa de al lado.—*adv.* luego, después; la próxima vez; **what —?** y luego ¿ qué ?—*prep.* junto (*to*, a), al lado (*to*, de); casi (*to*).
nib [nib], *n.* punta (*de pluma*).
nibble [nibl], *v.t.* mordiscar, picar.
Nicaraguan [nikə'rægjuən], *a.*, *n.* nicaragüense, *m.f.*, nicaragüeño.
nice [nais], *a.* fino; preciso; (*fam.*) simpático, agradable, amable; decente.
nicely ['naisli], *adv.* con exactitud; finamente; amablemente.
nicety ['naisəti], *n.* sutileza; precisión, *f.*
niche [nitʃ], *n.* nicho.
Nick [nik], *n.* **Old Nick**, patillas, *m.sg.*, el Diablo.
nick [nik], *n.* muesca, mella; **in the — of time**, a pelo, al momento preciso.—*v.t.* hacer muescas en, cortar; (*low*) robar.
nickel ['nikəl], *n.* níquel, *m.*
nick-nack ['niknæk], *n.* fruslería, friolera.
nickname ['nikneim], *n.* apodo.—*v.t.* motejar, apodar.
nicotine ['nikəti:n], *n.* nicotina.
niece [ni:s], *n.* sobrina.
nifty ['nifti], *a.* (*fam.*) guapo, de órdago.
Niger ['naidʒə], *n.* República del Níger; Níger (*río*), *m.*
niggardly ['nigədli], *a.*, *adv.*, tacaño.
nigger ['nigə], *n.* (*pej.*) negro.
nigh [nai], *adv.*, *prep.* (*poet.*) [NEAR].
night [nait], *n.* noche, *f.*; **at o by —**, de noche; **first —**, (*theat.*, *cine.*) estreno.
night-dress ['naitdres], *n.* camisón, *m.* camisa de dormir.
nightfall ['naitfɔ:l], *n.* anochecer, *m.*
nightingale ['naitiŋgeil], *n.* ruiseñor, *m.*
nightly ['naitli], *a.* nocturno.—*adv.* cada noche.
nightmare ['naitmɛə], *n.* pesadilla.
night-watchman [nait'wotʃmən], *n.* sereno; vigilante, *m.*
nihilist ['naiilist], *a.*, *n.* nihilista, *m.f.*
nil [nil], *n.* cero; nada.
the Nile [nail], *n.* el Nilo.
nimble [nimbl], *a.* ágil, listo.
nincompoop ['ninkəmpu:p], *n.* badulaque, *m.*, majadero.
nine [nain], *a.*, *n.* nueve, *m.*
ninepins ['nainpinz], *n.* juego de bolos.
nineteen [nain'ti:n], *a.*, *n.* diecinueve, diez y nueve, *m.*
nineteenth [nain'ti:nθ], *a.*, *n.* décimonono, diecinueveavo; diecinueve (*en las fechas*).
ninetieth ['naintiəθ], *a.*, *n.* nonagésimo, noventavo.
ninety ['nainti], *a.*, *n.* noventa, *m.*
ninth [nainθ], *a.*, *n.* noveno, nono.
nip [nip], *n.* mordisco; pellizco; quemadura; traguito.—*v.t.* mordiscar; pellizcar; cortar.

nipper ['nipə], *n.* (*fam.*) chaval, *m.—pl.* tenazas, pinzas.
nipple [nipl], *n.* pezón, *m.*; tetilla.
nit [nit], *n.* liendre, *f.*
nitrate ['naitreit], *n.* nitrato.
nitre ['naitə], *n.* nitro.
nitric ['naitrik], *a.* nítrico.
nitrogen ['naitrədʒən], *n.* nitrógeno.
nitwit ['nitwit], *n.* (*fam.*) bobatel, *m.*
no [nou], *a.* ninguno; — *good*, inútil, sin valor; *to be — use* (*for anything*), no servir para nada.—*adv.* no.
Noah [nouə], *n.* Noé, *m.*
nobility [nou'biliti], *n.* nobleza.
noble [noubl], *a.*, *n.* noble, *m.f.*
nobleman ['noublmən], *n.* noble, *m.*
nobody ['noubədi], *pron.* nadie.—*n.* persona insignificante.
nocturnal [nɔk'tə:nəl], *a.* nocturno.
nod [nɔd], *n.* seña afirmativa hecha con la cabeza; cabezada.—*v.t.* inclinar (la cabeza). —*v.i.* cabecear; inclinar la cabeza.
node [noud], *n.* nudo.
noise [nɔiz], *n.* ruido. *to — abroad,— v.t.* divulgar.
noiseless ['nɔizlis], *a.* silencioso.
noisy ['nɔizi], *a.* ruidoso.
nomad ['noumæd], *n.* nómada, *m.f.*
nomadic [nou'mædik], *a.* nómada.
nominal ['nɔminəl], *a.* nominal.
nominate ['nɔmineit], *v.t.* nombrar, nominar.
nominative ['nɔminətiv], *a.*, *n.* nominativo.
nominee [nɔmi'ni:], *n.* propuesto, candidato nombrado.
non- [nɔn], *prefix.* des-, no, falta de ...
nonage ['nɔnidʒ], *n.* minoría, infancia.
nonagenarian [nɔnədʒi'neəriən], *a.*, *n.* noventón, *m.*, nonagenario.
nonchalant ['nɔnʃələnt], *a.* descuidado, indiferente.
non-commissioned officer ['nɔnkəmiʃənd 'ɔfisə], *n.* suboficial, *m.*, cabo, sargento.
non-committal [nɔnkə'mitl], *a.* evasivo.
nonconformist [nɔnkən'fɔ:mist], *a.*, *n.* disidente, *m.f.*
nondescript ['nɔndiskript], *a.* indefinible, indeterminable.
none [nʌn], *pron.* ninguno; nada; nadie; — *the less*, a pesar de eso, sin embargo.
nonentity [nɔ'nentiti], *n.* nada, ficción, *f.*; persona insignificante, nulidad, *f.*
nones [nounz], *n.pl.* (*eccl.*) nona.
nonplus ['nɔn'plʌs], *v.t.* confundir, dejar perplejo.
non-profitmaking [nɔn'prɔfitmeikiŋ], *a.* no comercial.
nonsense ['nɔnsəns], *n.* tontería, disparate, *m.*; estupidez, *f.*
nonsensical [nɔn'sensikəl], *a.* disparatado, desatinado.
non-stop ['nɔn'stɔp], *a.*, *adv.* sin parar.
noodle (1) [nu:dl], *n.* tallarín, *m.*, fideo.
noodle (2) [nu:dl], *n.* (*fam.*) simplón, *m.*
nook [nuk], *n.* rincón, *m.*, ángulo.
noon [nu:n], *n.* mediodía, *m.*
noose [nu:s], *n.* lazo, corredizo; trampa; dogal (*para ahorcar a un criminal*), *m.*
nor [nɔ:], *conj.* ni. [NEITHER].
norm [nɔ:m], *n.* norma.
normal ['nɔ:məl], *a.* normal.—*n.* estado normal.

normalcy ['nɔ:məlsi] (*U.S.*), **normality** [nɔ:'mæliti], *n.* normalidad, *f.*
Norman ['nɔ:mən], *a.*, *n.* normando.
Norse [nɔ:s], *a.*, *n.* nórdico, noruego (*idioma*).
north [nɔ:θ], *a.* septentrional.—*n.* norte, *m.*; *North America*, Norteamérica.
northeast [nɔ:θ'i:st], *a.*, *n.* nordeste, *m.*
northerly ['nɔ:ðəli], *a.* que viene del norte, boreal.
northern ['nɔ:ðən], *a.* septentrional, norteño; del norte; *Northern Lights*, aurora boreal.
northerner ['nɔ:ðənə], *n.* norteño.
northwest [nɔ:θ'west], *a.*, *n.* noroeste, *m.*
Norway ['nɔ:wei], *n.* Noruega.
Norwegian [nɔ:'wi:dʒən], *a.*, *n.* noruego.
nose [nouz], *n.* nariz, *f.*; hocico (*de animales*); olfato; *to blow one's —*, sonarse las narices; *to talk through one's —*, ganguear; *to turn up one's — at,* menospreciar, desdeñar.
nose-dive ['nouzdaiv], *n.* descenso en picado.
nosegay ['nouzgei], *n.* ramillete, *m.*
nostalgia [nɔs'tældʒə], *n.* nostalgia, añoranza.
nostalgic [nɔs'tældʒik], *a.* nostálgico.
nostril ['nɔstril], *n.* nariz, *f.*, ventana de la nariz.
nostrum ['nɔstrəm], *n.* panacea.
nosy ['nouzi], *a.* (*fam.*) curioso, entremetido.
not [nɔt], *adv.* no.
notable ['noutəbl], *a.* notable.
notary ['noutəri], *n.* notario.
notch [nɔtʃ], *n.* mella, muesca.—*v.t.* mellar.
note [nout], *n.* nota; billete (*dinero*), *m.*; apunte, *m.*; *of —*, notable.—*v.t.* notar; apuntar.
note-book ['noutbuk], *n.* cuaderno.
noted ['noutid], *a.* conocido, eminente.
noteworthy ['noutwə:ði], *a.* digno de atención, notable.
nothing ['nʌθiŋ], *n.*, *pron.* nada; cero; *for —*, gratis; *to be good for —*, no servir para nada; *to have — to do with*, no tener que ver con; *to make — of*, no comprender; *to think — of*, tener en poco.
nothingness ['nʌθiŋnis], *n.* nada, *f.*
notice ['noutis], *n.* aviso; letrero; anuncio, cartel, *m.*; despedida; atención, reseña; notificación, *f.*; *at short —*, a corto plazo.—*v.t.* observar, notar, fijarse en.
noticeable ['noutisəbl], *a.* perceptible.
notice-board ['noutisbɔ:d], *n.* tablón (*m.*) o tablero de avisos.
notify ['noutifai], *v.t.* avisar, notificar.
notion ['nouʃən], *n.* noción, *f.—pl.* (*U.S.*) [HABERDASHERY.]
notoriety [noutə'raiəti], *n.* notoriedad, *f.*
notorious [nou'tɔ:riəs], *a.* notorio; de mala fama.
notwithstanding [nɔtwiθ'stændiŋ], *prep.* a pesar de.—*adv.* no obstante.
nougat ['nu:gɑ:], *n.* turrón, *m.*
nought [nɔ:t], *n.* nada; cero. [NAUGHT.]
noun [naun], *n.* sustantivo, nombre, *m.*
nourish ['nʌriʃ], *v.t.* alimentar, nutrir; (*fig.*) abrigar.
nourishing ['nʌriʃiŋ], *a.* nutritivo.
nourishment ['nʌriʃmənt], *n.* nutrimento.
novel ['nɔvəl], *a.* nuevo, insólito.—*n.* novela.
novelist ['nɔvəlist], *n.* novelista, *m.f.*
novelty ['nɔvəlti], *n.* novedad, innovación, *f.*
November [nou'vembə], *n.* noviembre, *m.*
novice ['nɔvis], *a.*, *n.* novicio.

now [nau], *adv.* ahora, ya; — *and then*, de vez en cuando; — ... —, ora ... ora, ya ... ya; *just* —, hace poco.
nowadays ['nauədeiz], *adv.* hoy día.
nowhere ['nouwɛə], *adv.* en ninguna parte.
noxious ['nɔkʃəs], *a.* nocivo, dañoso.
nozzle [nɔzl], *n.* boquerel, *m.*, boquilla.
nuance ['nu:ɑ:ns], *n.* matiz, *m.*
nuclear ['nju:kliə], *a.* nuclear.
nucleus ['nju:kliəs], *n.* núcleo.
nude [nju:d], *a.* desnudo; *in the* —, desnudo, en cueros.
nudge [nʌdʒ], *n.* codacito.—*v.t.* dar un codacito a.
nudist ['nju:dist], *n.* nudista, *m.f.*
nugget ['nʌgit], *n.* pepita (*de oro etc.*).
nuisance ['nju:səns], *n.* molestia, incomodidad, fastidio; *what a* — *!* ¡qué lata!
null [nʌl], *a.* nulo.
nullify ['nʌlifai], *v.t.* anular.
nullity ['nʌliti], *n.* nulidad, *f.*
numb [nʌm], *a.* entumecido.—*v.t.* entumecer.
number ['nʌmbə], *n.* número; *to look after* — *one*, barrer hacia dentro; — *one*, (*fam.*) mingas.—*v.t.* numerar; *to be numbered among*, considerarse uno de.
numeral ['nju:mərəl], *a.* numeral.—*n.* número.
numerical [nju:'merikəl], *a.* numérico.
numerous ['nju:mərəs], *a.* numeroso.
numskull ['nʌmskʌl], *n.* bobo, zote, bodoque, *m.*
nun [nʌn], *n.* religiosa, monja.
nuncio ['nʌnsiou], *n.* nuncio.
nunnery ['nʌnəri], *n.* convento de monjas.
nuptial ['nʌpʃəl], *a.* nupcial.—*n.pl.* nupcias, *f.pl.*
nurse [nə:s], *n.* enfermera; niñera.—*v.t.* criar, alimentar; cuidar; amamantar; fomentar.
nursemaid ['nə:smeid], *n.* niñera.
nursery ['nə:səri], *n.* cuarto de los niños; (*agr.*) semillero, plantel, *m.*; — *rhyme*, copla infantil.
nursing ['nə:siŋ], *n.* oficio de enfermera; amamantamiento.
nursing-home ['nə:siŋhoum], *n.* clínica de reposo; clínica de maternidad.
nurture ['nə:tʃə], *v.t.* educar; criar; (*fig.*) cebar (*pasión*).
nut [nʌt], *n.* nuez, *f.*; tuerca (*de tornillo*); (*fam.*) calamorra, cabeza; (*fam.*) estrafalario, loco.
nutcrackers ['nʌtkrækəz], *n.pl.* cascanueces, *m. inv.*
nutmeg ['nʌtmeg], *n.* nuez moscada.
nutriment ['nju:trimənt], *n.* nutrimento.
nutrition [nju:'triʃən], *n.* nutrición, *f.*
nutritious [nju:'triʃəs], *a.* nutritivo.
nutshell ['nʌtʃel], *n.* cáscara de nuez; *in a* —, (*fig.*) en una palabra.
nuzzle [nʌzl], *v.t.* hozar.—*v.i.* arrimarse.
nymph [nimf], *n.* ninfa.

O

O (1), **o** [ou], *n.* decimoquinta letra del alfabeto inglés.

O (2) **oh** [ou], *interj.* O; — *if only it were*, ¡Ojalá que fuera!
o' [ə] [OF].
oaf [ouf], *n.* tonto, zoquete, *m.*
oak [ouk], *n.* roble, *m.*; — *apple*, agalla.
oar [ɔ:], *n.* remo; remero; *oarlock*, chumacera.
oarsman ['ɔ:zmən], *n.* remero.
oasis [ou'eisis], *n.* (*pl.* **oases**) oasis, *m.*
oath [ouθ], *n.* juramento; blasfemia, (*fam.*) taco.
oatmeal ['outmi:l], *n.* harina de avena; gachas, *f.pl.*
oats [outs], *n.pl.* avena.
obedience [ə'bi:djəns], *n.* obediencia.
obedient [ə'bi:djənt], *a.* obediente.
obeisance [ə'beisəns], *n.* reverencia; homenaje, *m.*
obelisk ['ɔbilisk], *n.* obelisco.
obese [ou'bi:s], *a.* obeso, gordo.
obey [ou'bei], *v.t.*, *v.i.* obedecer.
obituary [ə'bitjuəri], *a.* necrológico.—*n.* necrología, obituario.
object ['ɔbdʒikt], *n.* objeto.—[əb'dʒekt], *v.t. v.i.* objetar.
objection [əb'dʒekʃən], *n.* objeción, *f.*; inconveniente, *m.*
objectionable [əb'dʒekʃənəbl], *a.* inadmisible; desagradable.
objective [ɔb'dʒektiv], *a.*, *n.* objetivo.
objectivity [ɔbdʒek'tiviti], *n.* objetividad, *f.*
objector [əb'dʒektə], *n.* objetante, *m.f.*
obligation [ɔbli'geiʃən], *n.* obligación, *f.*; precepto.
obligatory [ə'bligətri], *a.* obligatorio.
oblige [ə'blaidʒ], *v.t.* obligar, constreñir; complacer, favorecer; *to be obliged for*, estar agradecido por; *to be obliged to*, estar obligado a.
obliging [ə'blaidʒiŋ], *a.* servicial.
oblique [ə'bli:k], *a.* oblicuo; sesgado; indirecto.
obliterate [ə'blitəreit], *v.t.* borrar, destruir.
obliteration [əblitə'reiʃən], *n.* borradura, destrucción, *f.*
oblivion [ə'bliviən], *n.* olvido.
oblivious [ə'bliviəs], *a.* absorto; olvidadizo.
oblong ['ɔblɔŋ], *a.* oblongo, apaisado.—*n.* cuadrilongo.
obnoxious [ɔb'nɔkʃəs], *a.* odioso, detestable.
oboe ['oubou], *n.* oboe, *m.*
obscene [ɔb'si:n], *a.* obsceno.
obscenity [ɔb'seniti], *n.* obscenidad, *f.*
obscure [ɔb'skjuə], *a.* oscuro.—*v.t.* oscurecer.
obscurity [ɔb'skjuəriti], *n.* oscuridad, *f.*
obsequies ['ɔbsikwiz], *n.pl.* exequias, *f.pl.*
obsequious [əb'si:kwiəs], *a.* servil, zalamero.
observatory [əb'zə:rvətri], *n.* observatorio.
observe [əb'zə:v], *v.t.* observar; guardar.
obsess [əb'ses], *v.t.* obsesionar.
obsession [əb'seʃən], *n.* obsesión, *f.*
obsidian [ɔb'sidiən], *n.* (*min.*) obsidiana.
obsolescent [ɔbsou'lesənt], *a.* algo anticuado.
obsolete ['ɔbsəli:t], *a.* anticuado, desusado.
obstacle ['ɔbstikəl], *n.* obstáculo.
obstetrician [ɔbste'triʃən], *n.* obstétrico, médico partero.
obstinacy ['ɔbstinəsi], *n.* testarudez, obstinación, *f.*; porfía.
obstinate ['ɔbstinit], *a.* obstinado, testarudo; porfiado.
obstreperous [ɔb'strepərəs], *a.* turbulento, desmandado.
obstruct [əb'strʌkt], *v.t.* obstruir, estorbar.

obstruction [əb'strʌkʃən], *n.* obstrucción, *f.*; obstáculo, estorbo.
obtain [əb'tein], *v.t.* obtener.—*v.i.* prevalecer.
obtrude [əb'truːd], *v.t.* imponer.—*v.i.* entrometerse.
obtrusion [əb'truːʒən], *n.* imposición, *f.*
obtuse [əb'tjuːs], *a.* obtuso; torpe.
obtuseness [əb'tjuːsnis], *n.* terquedad, *f.*; falta de inteligencia, torpeza.
obverse ['ɔbvəːs], *n.* anverso.
obviate ['ɔbvieit], *v.t.* evitar, apartar, obviar.
obvious ['ɔbviəs], *a.* evidente, manifiesto, obvio.
occasion [ə'keiʒən], *n.* ocasión, *f.*—*v.t.* ocasionar.
occasional [ə'keiʒənəl], *a.* poco frecuente; de circunstancia.
occasionally [ə'keiʒnəli], *adv.* de vez en cuando.
occident ['ɔksidənt], *n.* occidente, *m.*
occidental [ɔksi'dentl], *a.*, *n.* occidental, *m.f.*
occiput ['ɔksipʌt], *n.* occipucio, colodrillo.
occult [ə'kʌlt], *a.* oculto; mágico.
occupancy ['ɔkjupənsi], *n.* tenencia, ocupación, *f.*
occupant ['ɔkjupənt], *n.* inquilino; ocupante, *m.f.*
occupation [ɔkju'peiʃən], *n.* ocupación, *f.*; inquilinato; profesión, *f.*
occupational [ɔkju'peiʃənəl], *a.* profesional.
occupier ['ɔkjupaiə], *n.* inquilino.
occupy ['ɔkjupai], *v.t.* ocupar; habitar.
occur [ə'kəː], *v.i.* acontecer, suceder; encontrarse; ocurrir, venir a la mente.
occurrence [ə'kʌrəns], *n.* acontecimiento, suceso; ocurrencia.
ocean ['ouʃən], *n.* océano; *oceans of,* (*fam.*) la mar de.
Oceania [ouʃi'einjə], *n.* (*geog.*) Oceanía.
ocelot ['ousələt], *n.* (*zool.*) ocelote, *m.*
ochre ['oukə], *n.* ocre, *m.*
o'clock [ə'klɔk] [CLOCK].
octagon ['ɔktəgən], *n.* octágono.
octagonal [ɔk'tægənəl], *a.* octágono.
octane ['ɔktein], *n.* octano.
octave ['ɔktiv], *n.* (*mus.*, *eccl.*) octava.
October [ɔk'toubə], *n.* octubre, *m.*
octopus ['ɔktəpəs], *n.* pulpo.
octosyllabic [ɔktousi'læbik], *a.* octosílabo.
ocular ['ɔkjulə], *a.* ocular, visual.
odd [ɔd], *a.* impar (*número*); extraño, raro; sobrante; *three hundred* —, trescientos y pico.
odds [ɔdz], *n.pl.* ventaja, puntos de ventaja; *it makes no* —, lo mismo da; *to be at* —, estar de punta; — *and ends,* cabos sueltos, trocitos.
ode [oud], *n.* oda.
odious ['oudjəs], *a.* detestable.
odium ['oudjəm], *n.* odio, oprobio.
odorous ['oudərəs], *a.* fragrante, oloroso.
odour ['oudə], *n.* olor, perfume, *m.*
odourless ['oudəlis], *a.* inodoro.
Odysseus [o'disjuːs], *n.* (*myth.*) Odiseo.
Odyssey ['ɔdisi], *n.* (*myth.*) Odisea.
Œdipus ['iːdipəs], *n.* (*myth.*) Edipo.
of [ɔv, əv], *prep.* de.
off [ɔf], *a.* malo; errado; libre; podrido; (*elec.*) cortado.—*adv.* lejos; — *and on,* por intervalos.—*prep.* de, desde, fuera de.
offal ['ɔfəl], *n.* menudillos, desperdicios, *m.pl.*

offence [ə'fens], *n.* ofensa, agravio; crimen, *m.*
offend [ə'fend], *v.t.*, *v.i.* ofender; transgresar.
offender [ə'fendə], *n.* delincuente, *m.f.*; ofensor, *m.*
offensive [ə'fensiv], *a.* ofensivo, desagradable. —*n.* ofensiva, ataque, *m.*
offer ['ɔfə], *n.* oferta.—*v.t.* ofrecer; proponer. —*v.i.* ofrecerse.
offering ['ɔfəriŋ], *n.* ofrenda; sacrificio.
off-hand ['ɔf'hænd], *a.* descomedido, informal; improvisado.
office ['ɔfis], *n.* oficina; oficio, cargo; despacho; (*U.S. med.*) consultorio.
officer ['ɔfisə], *n.* oficial, *m.*; funcionario; agente (*m.*) de policía.
official [ə'fiʃəl], *a.* oficial.—*n.* funcionario; encargado.
officialdom [ə'fiʃəldəm], *n.* burocracia.
officially [ə'fiʃəli], *adv.* oficialmente, de oficio.
officiate [ə'fiʃieit], *v.i.* oficiar (*as,* de).
officious [ə'fiʃəs], *a.* entremetido, oficioso.
offing ['ɔfiŋ], *n.* (*naut.*) largo; *in the* —, inminente.
off-peak ['ɔf'piːk], *a.* de las horas de menos carga; — *heater,* termos (*m.sg.*) de acumulación.
offprint ['ɔfprint], *n.* separata.
offset ['ɔfset], *v.t.* compensar, equivaler.
offshoot ['ɔfʃuːt], *n.* vástago; retoño.
offside [ɔf'said], *a.*, *adv.* fuera de juego.
offspring ['ɔfspriŋ], *n.* vástago, descendiente, *m.*; descendencia.
often [ɔfn], *adv.* a menudo, muchas veces; *how* — ? ¿cuántas veces ?
ogive ['oudʒaiv], *n.* (*arch.*) ojiva.
ogle [ougl], *v.t.* guiñar, ojear.
ogre ['ougə], *n.* ogro, monstruo.
oh [O].
ohm [oum], *n.* (*elec.*) ohmio.
oho! [ou'hou], *interj.* ¡ajá!
oil [ɔil], *n.* aceite, *m.*; petróleo; (*art.*) óleo; — *pipe-line,* oleoducto.—*v.t.* engrasar, aceitar.
oil-can ['ɔilkæn], *n.* aceitera.
oilcloth ['ɔilklɔθ], *n.* hule, *m.*, encerado.
oilskin ['ɔilskin], *n.* hule, *m.*
oil-stove ['ɔilstouv], *n.* estufa de aceite *o* petróleo.
oil-tanker ['ɔiltæŋkə], *n.* (buque) petrolero.
oily ['ɔili], *a.* aceitoso, grasiento; (*fig.*) zalamero.
ointment ['ɔintmənt], *n.* ungüento, pomada.
O.K. [ou'kei], *a.*, *interj.* (*fam.*) muy bien, está bien.
old [ould], *a.* viejo; antiguo; añejo; *how* — *are you?* ¿cuántos años tiene Vd. ? *of* —, antiguamente, antaño; — *fogey,* vejarrón, vejete.
olden ['ouldən], *a.* (*poet.*) antiguo.
old-fashioned [ould'faʃənd], *a.* chapado a lo antiguo.
oldish ['ouldiʃ], *a.* algo viejo.
old maid [ould'meid], *n.* solterona.
Old Testament [ould 'testəmənt], *n.* Antiguo Testamento.
old-world ['ouldwəːld], *a.* antañón, de antaño; del Mundo Antiguo.
oleander [ouli'ændə], *n.* adelfa, baladre, *m.*
olfactory [ɔl'fæktəri], *a.* olfactorio.
oligarch ['ɔligɑːk], *n.* oligarca, *m.*

oligarchy ['ɔligɑːki], *n.* oligarquía.
olive ['ɔliv], *a.* aceitunado.—*n.* (*bot.*) olivo, aceituno (*árbol*); aceituna (*fruta*); oliva (*color*); — **oil,** aceite de oliva.
Olympian [ɔ'limpiən],**Olympic** [ɔ'limpik], *a.* olímpico.—*n.pl.* **the Olympics,** los Olímpicos (*Juegos olímpicos*).
Olympus [ɔ'limpəs], (*myth., geog.*) Olimpo.
omelette ['ɔmlit], *n.* tortilla (de huevos).
omen ['oumen], *n.* agüero, presagio.
ominous ['ɔminəs], *a.* ominoso, de mal agüero.
omission [o'miʃen], *n.* omisión, *f.*
omit [o'mit], *v.t.* omitir, excluir.
omnibus ['ɔmnibʌs], *a.* general.—*n.* autobús, *m.*
omnipotence [ɔm'nipotəns], *n.* omnipotencia.
omnipotent [ɔm'nipotənt], *a.* omnipotente.
omniscient [ɔm'nisiənt], *a.* omnisciente, omniscio.
on [ɔn], *prep.* sobre, en, encima de; respecto a; — **account of,** a causa de; — **arriving,** al llegar; — **board,** a bordo (de); — **condition that,** con tal que; — **the right,** a la derecha.—*adv.* **the light is** —, la luz está encendida; **he has his hat** —, lleva el sombrero puesto; — **and off,** de vez en cuando; **and so** —, y así sucesivamente; — **and** —, continuamente, sin parar.
once [wʌns], *adv.* una vez; **at** —, en seguida; — **upon a time there was . . .,** érase una vez . . .—*conj.* una vez que.
one [wʌn], *a.* uno; cierto; **it's all** —, lo mismo da.—*pron.* uno; **any** —, cualquiera; **every** —, cada uno; — **by** —, uno a uno; **no** —, nadie; **some** —, [SOMEONE]; **that's the** —, ése es.
one-eyed ['wʌnaid], *a.* tuerto.
one-handed ['wʌn'hændid], *a.* manco.
one-horse ['wʌnhɔːs], *a.* (*fam.*) de poca monta.
oneness ['wʌnnis], *n.* unidad, *f.*
onerous ['ɔnərəs], *a.* oneroso.
oneself [wʌn'self], *pron.* si, sí mismo; uno mismo.
one-sided ['wʌn'saidid], *a.* parcial.
one-way ['wʌn'wei], *a.* de dirección única.
onion ['ʌnjən], *n.* cebolla.
on-looker ['ɔnlukə], *n.* testigo, espectador.
only ['ounli], *a.* único, solo.—*adv.* sólo, solamente.—*conj.* sólo que; **if** — . . . ¡ojalá . . . !
only-begotten ['ounlibi'gotn], *a.* unigénito.
onomatopœia [ɔnəmætə'piːə], *n.* onomatopeya.
onrush ['ɔnrʌʃ], *n.* embestida.
onset ['ɔnset], *n.* primer ataque, *m.,* acceso.
onslaught ['ɔnslɔːt], *n.* ataque violento, *m.*
onto ['ɔntuː], *prep.* en, sobre, encima de; a.
onus ['ounəs], *n.* carga.
onward ['ɔnwəd], *a.* avanzado.—*adv.* (also **onwards** ['ɔnwədz]) (en) adelante.
onyx ['ɔniks], *n.* ónice, *m.*
ooze [uːz], *n.* cieno, limo; rezumo.—*v.t.* manar, sudar, rezumar.—*v.i.* rezumar(se), manar.
opal ['oupəl], *n.* ópalo.
opaque [ou'peik], *a.* opaco, oscuro.
ope [oup], *v.t., v.i.* (*poet.*) [OPEN].
open ['oupən], *a.* abierto; — **sea,** alta mar; — **secret,** secreto a voces.—*n.* **in the** —, al aire libre.—*v.t.* abrir.—*v.i.* abrirse; **to** — **on,** dar a.

opening ['oupəniŋ], *n.* abertura; (*theat.*) estreno; inauguración, *f.*
open-minded [oupən'maindid], *a.* receptivo, imparcial.
opera ['ɔprə], *n.* ópera.
operate ['ɔpəreit], *v.t.* actuar; dirigir.—*v.i.* funcionar; operar; ser vigente; **to** — **on,** (*med.*) operar.
operatic [ɔpə'rætik], *a.* operístico, de ópera.
operating-theatre ['ɔpəreitiŋθiətə], *n.* quirófano.
operation [ɔpə'reiʃən], *n.* operación, *f.*; funcionamiento; (*med.*) intervención quirúrgica.
operative ['ɔpərətiv], *a.* operativo; vigente.—*n.* operario.
operator ['ɔpəreitə], *n.* telefonista, *m.f.*
ophthalmic [ɔf'θælmik], *a.* oftálmico.
opiate ['oupieit], *n.* opiata, narcótico.
opine [ou'pain], *v.t., v.i.* (*obs.*) opinar.
opinion [ou'pinjən], *n.* opinión, *f.*, parecer, *m.*
opinionated [ou'pinjəneitid], *a.* dogmático, presuntuoso.
opium ['oupiəm], *n.* opio.
opossum [ou'pɔsəm], *n.* (*zool.*) zarigüeya.
opponent [ɔ'pounənt], *n.* adversario; contrincante, *m.f.*
opportune ['ɔpətjuːn], *a.* oportuno.
opportunist [ɔpə'tjuːnist], *a., n.* oportunista, *m.f.*
opportunity [ɔpə'tjuːniti], *n.* ocasión; oportunidad, *f.*
oppose [ɔ'pouz], *v.t.* oponer(se a).
opposing [ɔ'pouziŋ], *a.* opuesto; contrario.
opposition [ɔpə'ziʃən], *n.* oposición, *f.*
oppress [ɔ'pres], *v.t.* oprimir, gravar.
oppression [ɔ'preʃən], *n.* opresión, *f.*
oppressive [ɔ'presiv], *a.* opresivo.
oppressor [ɔ'presə], *n.* opresor, *m.*
opt [ɔpt], *v.i.* optar (**for,** a, por).
optician [ɔp'tiʃən], *n.* óptico; oculista, *m.f.*
optics ['ɔptiks], *n.* óptica.
optimism ['ɔptimizm], *n.* optimismo.
optimist ['ɔptimist], *n.* optimista, *m.f.*
optimistic [ɔpti'mistik], *a.* optimista.
optimum ['ɔptiməm], *a.* óptimo.—*n.* grado óptimo.
option ['ɔpʃən], *n.* opción, *f.*
optional ['ɔpʃənəl], *a.* facultativo, optativo.
opulence ['ɔpjuləns], *n.* opulencia.
opulent ['ɔpjulənt], *a.* opulento.
opus ['oupəs] (*pl.* **opera** ['ɔprə]), *n.* (*mus., lit.*) opus, *m.*
or [ɔː], *conj.* o; o sea.
oracle ['ɔrəkl], *n.* oráculo.
oral ['ɔːrəl], *a.* oral.
orange ['ɔrindʒ], *a.* anaranjado.—*n.* naranja (*fruta*), naranjo (*árbol*).
oration [ɔ'reiʃən], *n.* discurso, oración, *f.*
orator ['ɔrətə], *n.* orador, *m.*
oratory ['ɔrətri], *n.* oratoria; (*eccl.*) oratorio.
orb [ɔːb], *n.* orbe, *m.*
orbit ['ɔːbit], *n.* órbita.—*v.t., v.i.* orbitar.
orchard ['ɔːtʃəd], *n.* huerto, vergel, *m.*
orchestra ['ɔːkistrə], *n.* orquesta. [stall (1)]
orchid ['ɔːkid], *n.* orquídea.
ordain [ɔː'dein], *v.t.* ordenar (*eccl.* **as** (priest etc.), de).
ordeal [ɔː'diəl], *n.* (*hist.*) ordalías, *f.pl.*; aprieto.

329

order

order ['ɔːdə], *n.* orden, *m.*; (*eccl.*, *mil.*) orden, *f.*; (*com.*) pedido; *in — to*, para; *in — that*, para que; *out of —*, desarreglado; no funciona.—*v.t.* mandar, ordenar; (*com.*) pedir; encargar.
orderly ['ɔːdəli], *a.* ordenado, en orden.—*n.* (*mil.*) ordenanza, *m.*; (*med.*) practicante, *m.f.*
ordinal ['ɔːdinəl], *a.* ordinal.
ordinance ['ɔːdinəns], *n.* ordenanza.
ordinary ['ɔːdinəri], *a.* ordinario, regular.
ordination [ɔːdi'neiʃən], *n.* ordenación, *f.*
ordnance ['ɔːdnəns], *n.* municiones, *f.pl.*
ore [ɔː], *n.* mena.
organ ['ɔːgən], *n.* órgano.
organic [ɔː'gænik], *a.* orgánico.
organism ['ɔːgənizm], *n.* organismo.
organization [ɔːgənai'zeiʃən], *n.* organización, *f.*
organize ['ɔːgənaiz], *v.t.* organizar.—*v.i.* -se.
orgy ['ɔːdʒi], *n.* orgia.
Orient ['ɔːriənt], *n.* oriente, *m.*— ['ɔːrient], *v.t.* orientar.
oriental [ɔːri'entəl], *a.*, *n.* oriental, *m.f.*
orientate ['ɔːrienteit], *v.t.* orientar.—*v.i.* -se.
orientation [ɔːrien'teiʃən], *n.* orientación, *f.*
orifice ['ɔrifis], *n.* orificio.
origin ['ɔridʒin], *n.* origen, *m.*
original [ɔ'ridʒinəl], *a.* original.
originality [ɔridʒi'næliti], *n.* originalidad, *f.*
originate [ɔ'ridʒineit], *v.t.* originar.—*v.i.* -se.
originator [ɔ'ridʒineitə], *n.* inventor, *m.*
ornament ['ɔːnəmənt], *n.* adorno, ornamento.—*v.t.* ornamentar.
ornamental [ɔːnə'mentl], *a.* ornamental.
ornate [ɔː'neit], *a.* florido, ornado.
ornithology [ɔːni'θɔlədʒi], *n.* ornitología.
orphan ['ɔːfən], *a.*, *n.* huérfano.—*v.t.* dejar huérfano a.
orphanage ['ɔːfənidʒ], *n.* orfanato.
orthodox ['ɔːθodɔks], *a.* ortodoxo.
orthodoxy ['ɔːθodɔksi], *n.* ortodoxia.
orthography [ɔː'θɔgrəfi], *n.* ortografía.
orthopaedic [ɔː'θouˈpiːdik], *a.* ortopédico.
oscillate ['ɔsileit], *v.i.* oscilar.
oscillation [ɔsi'leiʃən], *n.* oscilación, *f.*
osier ['ouziə], *n.* (*bot.*) mimbrera, sauce, *m.*
ostensible [ɔs'tensibl], *a.* ostensible, supuesto.
ostentation [ɔsten'teiʃən], *n.* ostentación, *f.*, pompa.
ostentatious [ɔsten'teiʃəs], *a.* ostentoso; vanaglorioso.
ostler ['ɔslə], *n.* establero, mozo de cuadra.
ostracize ['ɔstrəsaiz], *v.t.* desterrar; negar el trato social a.
ostrich ['ɔstritʃ], *n.* avestruz, *m.*
other ['ʌðə], *a.* otro; *every — day*, un día sí y otro no.—*adv.* — *than*, además de, aparte de.
otherwise ['ʌðəwaiz], *adv.* de otro modo, si no.
otter ['ɔtə], *n.* nutria.
Ottoman ['ɔtoumən], *a.*, *n.* otomano; **otto-man**, *n.* sofá, *m.*, otomana.
ouch! [autʃ], *interj.* ¡aj! ¡ay!
ought [ɔːt], *n.* (*obs.*) algo; nada [AUGHT].—*v. irr.* *you — to*, Vd. debiera *or* debería.
ounce [auns], *n.* onza.
our [auə], *a.* nuestro.
ours [auəz], *pron.* el nuestro.
ourselves [auə'selvz], *pron.* *pl.* nosotros mismos.
oust [aust], *v.t.* desalojar, expulsar.

out [aut], *adv.* fuera; — *of*, de; fuera de; sin; — *to*, con intención de; *it is —*, se acaba de publicar; se sabe ya.—*prefix.* sobre-.
out-and-out ['autənd'aut], *adv.* de siete suelas.
outbid [aut'bid], *v.t.* *irr.* (*conjug. like* BID) mejorar, sobrepujar.
outbreak ['autbreik], *n.* estallido, arranque, *m.*
outburst ['autbəːst], *n.* arranque *m.*
outcast ['autcɑːst], *n.* paria, *m.f.*
outclass [aut'clɑːs], *v.t.* aventajar.
outcome ['autkʌm], *n.* resultado.
outcry ['autcrai], *n.* vocería, alboroto.
outdate [aut'deit], *v.t.* anticuar.
outdid [aut'did] [OUTDO].
outdistance [aut'distəns], *v.t.* rezagar, dejar atrás.
outdo [aut'duː], *v.t.* *irr.* (*conjug. like* DO) exceder, sobrepujar.
outdoor [aut'dɔː], *a.* al aire libre.
outer ['autə], *a.* exterior.
outermost ['autəmoust], *a.* extremo, más exterior.
outface [aut'feis], *v.t.* desafiar, arrostrar.
outfall ['autfɔːl], *n.* desembocadero.
outfit ['autfit], *n.* equipo; juego (*colección*); traje (*vestido*), *m.*; cuerpo, grupo.—*v.t.* equipar.
outflank [aut'flæŋk], *v.t.* flanquear.
outgoing ['autgouiŋ], *a.* saliente.—*n.* salida.—*pl.* gastos, *m.pl.*
outgrow [aut'grou], *v.t.* crecer más que; ser ya grande para; dejar (*vestidos de niños, etc.*).
outhouse ['authaus], *n.* accesoria, tejadillo.
outing ['autiŋ], *n.* excursión, *f.*, caminata.
outlandish [aut'lændiʃ], *a.* estrambótico, estrafalario.
outlast [aut'lɑːst], *v.t.* sobrevivir a, durar más que.
outlaw ['autlɔː], *n.* forajido, proscrito.—*v.t.* proscribir.
outlay ['autlei], *n.* desembolso inicial.
outlet ['autlet], *n.* salida; desaguadero.
outline ['autlain], *n.* contorno; esbozo.—*v.t.* esbozar.
outlive [aut'liv], *v.t.* sobrevivir a.
outlook ['autluk], *n.* perspectiva.
outlying ['autlaiiŋ], *a.* remoto, de las cercanías.
outmoded [aut'moudid], *a.* fuera de moda.
outnumber [aut'nʌmbə], *v.t.* exceder en número.
out-of-date [autəv'deit], *a.* anticuado.
out-of-doors [autəv'dɔːz], *adv.* al aire libre.
outpace [aut'peis], *v.t.* dejar atrás.
out-patient ['autpeiʃənt], *n.* enfermo no hospitalizado.
outpost ['autpoust], *n.* avanzada.
outpour [aut'pɔː], *n.* chorreo, derrame, *m.*
output ['autput], *n.* rendimiento, producción, *f.*
outrage ['autreidʒ], *n.* atrocidad, *f.*, atropello.—*v.t.* violar; violentar; enojar mucho.
outrageous [aut'reidʒəs], *a.* atroz.
outrank [aut'ræŋk], *v.t.* aventajar, exceder en grado.
outright ['autrait], *a.* cabal, rotundo.—[aut'rait], *adv.* sin reserva; al instante; de una vez.

outrun [aut'rʌn], *v.t.* dejar atrás corriendo; pasar el límite de.

outsell [aut'sel], *v.t.* vender más que.

outset ['autset], *n.* principio, comienzo.

outshine [aut'ʃain], *v.t.* eclipsar, brillar más que.

outside [aut'said], *n.* exterior, *m.*; *at the* —, a más tirar.—*adv.* fuera.—['autsaid], *a.* exterior, externo.—*prep.* fuera de.

outsider [aut'saidə], *n.* forastero; intruso; (*sport*) caballo desconocido en una carrera, caballo no favorito.

outsize ['autsaiz], *a.* de tamaño extraordinario.

outskirts ['autskə:ts], *n.pl.* afueras, cercanías, *f.pl.*, arrabales, *m.pl.*

outspoken [aut'spoukən], *a.* franco, boquifresco.

outstanding [aut'stændiŋ], *a.* sobresaliente; destacado; (*com.*) pendiente.

outstretch [aut'stretʃ], *v.t.* extender, alargar.

outstrip [aut'strip], *v.t.* sobrepujar, vencer, adelantarse a.

outward ['autwəd], *a.* exterior, externo.—*adv.* (also **outwards** ['autwədz]) hacia fuera.

outwardly ['autwədli], *adv.* fuera, de fuera; al parecer.

outweigh [aut'wei], *v.t.* preponderar.

outwit [aut'wit], *v.t.* burlar(se de), ser más listo que.

outworn [aut'wɔːn], *a.* gastado.

oval ['ouvəl], *a.* oval(ado).—*n.* óvalo.

ovary ['ouvəri], *n.* ovario.

ovation [ou'veiʃən], *n.* ovación, *f.*

oven ['ʌvən], *n.* horno, hornillo.

over ['ouvə], *adv.* (por) encima; al otro lado; demasiado; (*U.S.*) de nuevo, otra vez; patas arriba; durante; allá; *all* —, por todas partes; *it is all* —, se acabó ya; — *and again*, repetidas veces; *please turn* — (*P.T.O.*), a la vuelta.—*prep.* sobre; (por) encima de; a través de; más de; — *and above*, además de.—*prefix.* sobre-, demasiado (*e.g.* —*active*, demasiado activo.)

overall ['ouvərɔːl], *a.* general, cabal, total.—*n.* delantal, mandil, *m.*—*n.pl.* zafones, *m.pl.*, mono.

overawe [ouver'ɔː], *v.t.* intimidar.

overbalance [ouvə'bæləns], *v.t.* hacer perder el equilibrio; volcar, derribar.—*v.i.* caerse, perder el equilibrio.

overbearing [ouvə'bɛəriŋ], *a.* imperioso, altanero.

overboard ['ouvəbɔːd], *a.* al agua.

overcast [ouvə'kaːst], *a.* anublado.

overcharge [ouvə'tʃaːdʒ], *v.t.* hacer pagar demasiado; (*mech. etc.*) sobrecargar.

overcloud [ouvə'klaud], *v.t.* anublar.

overcoat ['ouvəkout], *n.* abrigo, sobretodo, gabán, *m.*

overcome [ouvə'kʌm], *v.t. irr.* (*conjug. like* COME) superar, domar.

overcrowded [ouvə'kraudid], *a.* atestado.

overdo [ouvə'duː], *v.t. irr.* (*conjug. like* DO) exagerar; hacer demasiado.

overdose ['ouvədous], *n.* dosis excesiva.

overdraft ['ouvədraːft], *n.* sobregiro, giro en descubierto.

overdraw [ouvə'drɔː], *v.i.* exceder el crédito.

overdrive ['ouvədraiv], *n.* sobremarcha (*coche*).

overdue [ouvə'djuː], *a.* atrasado; vencido y no pagado.

overeat [ouvə'iːt], *v.i.* comer demasiado.

overflow ['ouvəflou], *n.* reboso; diluvio; rebosadero.—[ouvə'flou], *v.i.* desbordarse, rebosar.

overflowing [ouvə'flouiŋ], *a.* abundante, desbordante.

overgrown [ouvə'groun], *a.* entapizado; demasiado grande.

overhang ['ouvəhæŋ], *n.* alero (*techo*); proyección, *f.*—[ouvə'hæŋ], *v.t. irr.* (*conjug. like* HANG) colgar sobre; amenazar.

overhaul ['ouvəhɔːl], *n.* recorrido, reparación, *f.*—[ouvə'hɔːl], *v.t.* componer, repasar, registrar.

overhead ['ouvəhed], *a.* de arriba; elevado.— *n.* (*usually pl.*) gastos generales.—[ouvə'hed], *adv.* arriba, en lo alto; (por) encima.

overhear [ouvə'hiːə], *v.t. irr.* (*conjug. like* HEAR) oír por casualidad.

overjoyed [ouvə'dʒɔid], *a.* encantadísimo.

overland ['ouvəlænd], *a., adv.* por tierra, por vía terrestre.

overlap ['ouvəlæp], *n.* solapo, solapadura.— [ouvə'læp], *v.t.* solapar.—*v.i.* solaparse; coincidir.

overlook [ouvə'luk], *v.t.* pasar por alto; traspapelar; dar a, dar vista.

overlord ['ouvəlɔːd], *n.* jefe supremo.

overnight [ouvə'nait], *adv.* durante la noche; toda la noche.

overpass ['ouvəpaːs], *n.* (*U.S.*) [FLYOVER].

overpopulation [ouvəpɔpju'leiʃən], *n.* exceso de población.

overpower [ouvə'pauə], *v.t.* supeditar, subyugar; colmar, abrumar.

overrate [ouvə'reit], *v.t.* apreciar con exceso.

overreach [ouvə'riːtʃ], *v* '. exceder.

override [ouvə'raid], *v.t. irr.* (*conjug. like* RIDE) rechazar; fatigar.

overrule [ouvə'ruːl], *v.t.* rechazar; anular; desechar.

overrun [ouvə'rʌn], *v.t. irr.* (*conjug. like* RUN) invadir; plagar, infestar; exceder.

overseas [ouvə'siːz], *a.* de ultramar.—*adv.* en ultramar.

overseer ['ouvəsiːə], *n.* capataz, *m.*

overshadow [ouvə'ʃædou], *v.t.* sombrear; (*fig.*) eclipsar.

overshoot [ouvə'ʃuːt], *v.t.* pasar la raya.

oversight ['ouvəsait], *n.* descuido, inadvertencia.

overstate [ouvə'steit], *v.t.* exagerar.

overstatement [ouvə'steitmənt], *n.* exageración, *f.*

overstep [ouvə'step], *v.t.* traspasar.

overstrung [ouvə'strʌŋ], *a.* demasiado excitable.

overt ['ouvət], *a.* manifiesto, patente.

overtake [ouvə'teik], *v.t. irr.* (*conjug. like* TAKE) alcanzar y pasar, adelantarse a; sorprender.

overtax [ouvə'tæks], *v.t.* agobiar.

overthrow ['ouvəθrou], *n.* derrocamiento, derribo.—[ouvə'θrou], *v.t. irr.* (*conjug. like* THROW) derrocar, derribar.

overtime ['ouvətaim], *n.* horas extraordinarias, *f.pl.*

overture ['ouvətjuə], *n.* obertura.

overturn [ouvə'təːn], *v.t.* volcar, trastornar.

overvalue [ouvə'væljuː], *v.t.* apreciar demasiado.

overweening

overweening [ouvə'wi:niŋ], *a.* engreído, presuntuoso.
overweight [ouvə'weit], *a.* gordo con exceso.
overwhelm [ouvə'hwelm], *v.t.* abrumar; engolfar; colmar.
overwhelming [ouvə'hwelmiŋ], *a.* abrumador; irresistible.
overwrought [ouvə'rɔːt], *a.* sobreexcitado, agotado por un exceso de trabajo *o* de pena.
Ovid ['ɔvid], *n.* Ovidio.
owe [ou], *v.t.* deber.—*v.i.* tener deudas.
owing ['ouiŋ], *a.* debido; — *to,* a causa de.
owl [aul], *n.* lechuza, buho, mochuelo.
own [oun], *a.* propio.—*v.t.* poseer, tener; reconocer, confesar; *to — up,* (*fam.*) confesar.
owner ['ounə], *n.* propietario, dueño.
ownerless ['ounəlis], *a.* sin dueño; mostrenco.
ownership ['ounəʃip], *n.* propiedad, posesión, *f.*
ox [ɔks], *n.* (*pl.* **oxen** ['ɔksən]) buey, *m.*
oxide ['ɔksaid], *n.* óxido.
oxidize ['ɔksidaiz], *v.t.* oxidar.
oxygen ['ɔksidʒən], *n.* oxígeno.
oyez! ['oujez], *interj.* ¡oíd!
oyster ['ɔistə], *n.* ostra.
ozone ['ouzoun], *n.* ozono.

P

P, p [pi:], *n.* décimosexta letra del alfabeto inglés; *to mind one's p's and q's,* ir con cuidado, tener cuidado.
pace [peis], *n.* paso; marcha, andadura; velocidad, *f.*; *to keep — with,* ir al mismo paso que; mantenerse al corriente de.—*v.t.* recorrer; marcar el paso para; *to — out,* medir a pasos.—*v.i.* pasear(se); ambular; *to — up and down,* dar vueltas.
pacific [pə'sifik], *a.* pacífico; sosegado; *the Pacific (Ocean),* el Océano Pacífico.
pacification [pæsifi'keiʃən], *n.* pacificación, *f.*
pacifier ['pæsifaiə], *n.* chupete (*de niño*), *m.*
pacifism ['pæsifizm], *n.* pacifismo.
pacifist ['pæsifist], *a.*, *n.* pacifista, *m.f.*
pacify ['pæsifai], *v.t.* pacificar; tranquilizar; conciliar.
pack [pæk], *n.* fardo; lío; carga; paquete, *m.*; manada; jauría; — *of cards,* baraja de naipes; — *of lies,* sarta de mentiras; — *of thieves,* cuadrilla de malhechores. —*v.t.* embalar; empaquetar; apretar; atestar; llenar.—*v.i.* hacer la maleta; *to — up,* (*fam.*) liar el hato; *to send packing,* (*fam.*) dar calabazas a, mandar a la porra.
package ['pækidʒ], *n.* paquete, *m.*; fardo.— *v.t.* empaquetar.
packer ['pækə], *n.* embalador, *m.*
packet ['pækit], *n.* paquete, *m.*; cajetilla; (*mar.*) paquebote, *m.*; *to make one's —,* (*fam.*) hacer su pacotilla; *to cost a —,* (*fam.*) costar un dineral.
pack-horse ['pæk'hɔːs], *n.* caballo de carga.
packing ['pækiŋ], *n.* embalaje, *m.*; *to do one's —,* hacer la maleta.
packing-case ['pækiŋkeis], *n.* caja de

embalaje.
pack-saddle ['pæksædl], *n.* albarda.
pact [pækt], *n.* pacto; *to make a —,* pactar.
pad [pæd], *n.* almohadilla, cojinete, *m.*; (*sport*) espinillera.—*v.t.* almohadillar; rellenar, forrar; meter paja en.
padding ['pædiŋ], *n.* borra, algodón, *m.*; almohadilla; (*fig.*) paja.
paddle [pædl], *n.* canalete, *m.*, zagual, *m.*; paleta.—*v.t.* remar.—*v.i.* chapotear.
paddle-steamer ['pædlsti:mə], *n.* vapor (*m.*) de paletas.
paddock ['pædək], *n.* prado; parque, *m.*; picadero.
padlock ['pædlɔk], *n.* candado.—*v.t.* cerrar con candado.
padre ['pɑːdri], *n.* cura castrense, páter, *m.*
pagan ['peigən], *a.*, *n.* pagano.
paganism ['peigənizm], *n.* paganismo.
page (1) [peidʒ], *n.* paje, *m.*, escudero (*muchacho*).—*v.t.* hacer llamar por el paje.
page (2) [peidʒ], *n.* página, hoja (*de un libro*). —*v.t.* paginar.
pageant ['pædʒənt], *n.* espectáculo, procesión *f.*; pompa.
pageantry ['pædʒəntri], *n.* pompa, aparato; ostentación, *f.*
paid [peid], *pret.,p.p.* [PAY].
paid-up share ['peidʌp'ʃɛə], *n.* acción liberada.
pail [peil], *n.* cubo, pozal, *m.*
pain [pein], *n.* dolor, *m.*; sufrimiento; tormento; *labour pains,* dolores (*m.pl.*) de parto; *on — of death,* so pena de muerte; *to take pains,* tomarse trabajo, esforzarse; *to be in —,* sufrir.—*v.t.* doler; afligir; atormentar.
pained [peind], *a.* dolorido; afligido.
painful ['peinful], *a.* doloroso; angustioso; molesto; arduo.
painless ['peinlis], *a.* sin dolor.
painstaking ['peinzteikiŋ], *a.* cuidadoso; diligente; concienzudo.
paint [peint], *n.* pintura.—*v.t.*, *v.i.* pintar; *to — the town red,* andar de parranda, (*fam.*) correrla.
paint-box ['peintbɔks], *n.* caja de pinturas.
paint-brush ['peintbrʌʃ], *n.* pincel, *m.*; brocha.
painter ['peintə], *n.* pintor, *m.*; (*naut.*) boza.
painting ['peintiŋ], *n.* pintura; cuadro.
pair [pɛə], *n.* par, *m.*; pareja.—*v.t.* parear; emparejar; aparear; casar.—*v.i.* parearse; aparearse; casarse; *to — off,* formar pareja.
pajamas [pə'dʒɑːməz], *n.pl.* pijama, *m.*
Pakistan [pɑːkis'tɑːn], *n.* el Paquistán.
Pakistani [pɑːkis'tɑːni], *a.*, *n.* pakistano, pakistaní, *m.f.*
pal [pæl], *n.* (*fam.*) amigo, compañero.
palace ['pælis], *n.* palacio.
palatable ['pælətəbl], *a.* sabroso, apetitoso; aceptable.
palate ['pælit], *n.* paladar, *m.*
palatial [pə'leiʃəl], *a.* palaciego; suntuoso.
pale (1) [peil], *a.* pálido; descolorido; claro (*color*); tenue (*luz*); *to grow —,* palidecer.
pale (2) [peil], *n.* estaca; límite, *m.*
paleness ['peilnis], *n.* palidez, *f.*
palette ['pælit], *n.* paleta.
palette-knife ['pælitnaif], *n.* espátula.
paling ['peiliŋ], *n.* palizada, estacada.
palisade [pæli'seid], *n.* palizada, estacada.

332

parakeet

pall (1) [pɔ:l], *n.* palio; manto; paño mortuorio.
pall (2) [pɔ:l], *v.i.* perder el sabor.
pall-bearer ['pɔ:lbɛərən], *n.* doliente, *m.*
palliate ['pælieit], *v.t.* paliar, mitigar; excusar, disculpar.
palliative ['pæljətiv], *a., n.* paliativo.
pallid ['pælid], *a.* pálido, descolorido.
pallor ['pælə], *n.* palidez, *f.*
palm [pɑ:m], *n.* palma; — *tree,* palmera; *Palm Sunday,* Domingo de Ramos.—*v.t.* enpalmar; *to — off,* defraudar con; (*fam.*) dar gato por liebre.
palmist ['pɑ:mist], *n.* quiromántica, *m.f.*
palmistry ['pɑ:mistri], *n.* quiromancia.
palm-oil ['pɑ:mɔil], *n.* aceite (*m.*) de palma.
palmy ['pɑ:mi], *a.* palmar; floreciente; próspero.
palpable ['pælpəbl], *a.* palpable.
palpitate ['pælpiteit], *v.i.* palpitar.
palpitating ['pælpiteitiŋ], *a.* palpitante.
palpitation [pælpi'teiʃən], *n.* palpitación, *f.*
palsied ['pɔ:lzid], *a.* paralizado, paralítico.
palsy ['pɔ:lzi], *n.* parálisis, *f.*—*v.t.* paralizar.
paltriness ['pɔ:ltrinis], *n.* mezquindad, *f.*
paltry ['pɔ:ltri], *a.* mezquino; despreciable.
pamper ['pæmpə], *v.t.* mimar.
pamphlet ['pæmflit], *n.* folleto.
pamphleteer [pæmfli'tiə], *n.* folletista, *m.f.*
pan [pæn], *n.* cazuela; cacerola; cazoleta (*de fusil*); *flash in the* —, fuego de paja.—*v.t.* separar (el oro en una gamella).
panacea [pænə'siə], *n.* panacea.
panache [pə'næʃ], *n.* penacho.
Panama [pænə'mɑ:], *n.* Panamá, *m.*; *Panama hat,* sombrero de jipijapa.
Panamanian [pænə'meinjən], *a., n.* panameño.
pancake ['pænkeik], *n.* hojuela, fruta de sartén; — *landing,* (*aer.*) aterrizaje brusco; *Pancake* (*Tues*)*day,* martes (*m.*) de Carnaval.
panda ['pændə], *n.* panda, *m. f.*
pandemonium [pændi'mounjəm], *n.* pandemonio; estrépito.
pander ['pændə], *n.* alcahuete, *m.*—*v.i.* alcahuetear; *to — to,* mimar; prestarse a.
pane [pein], *n.* (hoja de) vidrio; cristal, *m.*; cuadro.
panegyric [pæni'dʒirik], *a., n.* panegírico.
panel [pænl], *n.* entrepaño; artesón, *m.*; tabla; registro; jurado; — *doctor,* médico de seguros.—*v.t.* labrar a entrepaños; (*arch.*) artesonar.
panelled ['pænəld], *a.* entrepañado; artesonado.
panelling ['pænəliŋ], *n.* entrepaños, *m.pl.*; artesonado.
pang [pæŋ], *n.* punzada, dolor agudo; remordimiento, congoja.
panic ['pænik], *n.* pánico; espanto, terror, *m.* —*v.i.* espantarse.
panic-stricken ['pænikstrikən], *a.* aterrorizado, despavorido.
pannier ['pæniə], *n.* alforja.
panoply ['pænəpli], *n.* panoplia.
panorama [pænə'rɑ:mə], *n.* panorama, *m.*
panoramic [pænə'ræmik], *a.* panorámico.
pansy ['pænzi], *n.* pensamiento, trinitaria; (*fam.*) maricón, *m.*

pant [pænt], *n.* jadeo; palpitación, *f.*—*v.i.* jadear; palpitar; hipar (*perro*).
pantechnicon [pæn'teknikən], *n.* carro de mudanzas.
pantheism ['pænθiizm], *n.* panteísmo.
pantheon ['pænθiən], *n.* panteón, *m.*
panther ['pænθə], *n.* pantera.
panties ['pæntiz], *n.pl.* pantalones (*de mujer*), *m.pl.*; bragas, *f.pl.*
panting ['pæntiŋ], *a.* jadeante.—*n.* jadeo; resuello; palpitación, *f.*
pantomime ['pæntəmaim], *n.* pantomima; revista; mímica; *in* —, por gestos *o* señas.
pantry ['pæntri], *n.* despensa.
pants [pænts], *n.pl.* (*fam.*) calzoncillos; pantalones, *m.pl.*
panzer division ['pænzədi'viʒən], *n.* división (*f.*) motorizada.
pap [pæp], *n.* teta; pezón, *m.*; papilla.
papacy ['peipəsi], *n.* papado, pontificado.
papal ['peipəl], *a.* papal, pontificio; — *bull,* bula pontificia; — *see,* sede apostólica.
paper ['peipə], *a.* de papel.—*n.* papel, *m.*; hoja de papel; documento; disertación, *f.*; conferencia; periódico; examen escrito; — *bag,* saco de papel.—*pl.* credenciales, *m.pl.*—*v.t.* empapelar.
paper-chase ['peipəʃeis], *n.* rally-paper, *m.*
paper-clip ['peipəklip], *n.* clip, *m.*
paper-hanger ['peipəhæŋə], *n.* empapelador, *m.*
paper-hanging ['peipəhæniŋ], *n.* empapelado.
papering ['peipəriŋ], *n.* empapelado.
paper-knife ['peipənaif], *n.* cortapapeles, *m. inv.*
paper-mill ['peipəmil], *n.* fábrica de papel.
paper-money ['peipə'mʌni], *n.* papel moneda, *m.*
paper-weight ['peipəweit], *n.* pisapapeles, *m. inv.*
papier-mâché ['pæpjei'mɑ:ʃei], *n.* cartón piedra, *m.*
papist ['peipist], *a., n.* papista, *m.f.*
papoose [pə'pu:s], *n.* niño indio.
papyrus [pə'paiərəs], *n.* papiro.
par [pɑ:], *n.* par, *f.*; *above* —, a premio; *at* —, a la par; *below* —, a descuento; *to be on a — with,* estar al nivel de, ser igual a.
parable ['pærəbl], *n.* parábola.
parachute ['pærəʃu:t], *n.* paracaídas, *m.sg.*; — *troops,* cuerpo de paracaidistas.—*v.i.* lanzarse en paracaídas.
parachutist ['pærəʃu:tist], *n.* paracaidista, *m.f.*
parade [pə'reid], *n.* procesión, *f.*; desfile, *m.*, revista; paseo; alarde, *m.*, pompa; — *ground,* campo de instrucción; plaza de armas.—*v.t.* hacer alarde de; pasar revista a. —*v.i.* desfilar; pasearse.
paradise ['pærədais], *n.* paraíso; (*fig.*) jauja; *bird of* —, ave (*f.*) del paraíso.
paradox ['pærədɔks], *n.* paradoja.
paradoxical [pærə'dɔksikəl], *a.* paradójico.
paraffin ['pærəfin], *n.* parafina, kerosina.
paragon ['pærəgən], *n.* dechado.
paragraph ['pærəgrɑ:f], *n.* párrafo; suelto; *new* —, punto y aparte.
Paraguay ['pærəgwai], *n.* el Paraguay.
Paraguayan [pærə'gwaiən], *a., n.* paraguayo.
parakeet ['pærəki:t], *n.* perico.

333

parallel

parallel ['pærəlel], *a.* paralelo; igual; semejante, análogo; — **bars,** paralelas.—*n.* paralelo, línea paralela; semejanza; cotejo; (*mil.*) paralela; *without* —, sin ejemplo.— *v.t.* poner en paralelo; cotejar, comparar.

parallelism ['pærəlelizm], *n.* paralelismo.

parallelogram [pærə'leləgræm], *n.* paralelogramo.

paralyse ['pærəlaiz], *v.t.* paralizar.

paralysis [pə'rælisis], *n.* parálisis; (*fig.*) paralización, *f.*

paralytic [pærə'litik], *a., n.* paralítico.

paramount ['pærəmaunt], *a.* supremo, sumo.

paramour ['pærəmuə], *n.* amante, *m.;* querida.

paranoia [pærə'nɔiə], *n.* paranoia.

parapet ['pærəpit], *n.* parapeto.

paraphernalia [pærəfə'neiljə], *n.* (*jur.*) bienes parafernales, *m.pl.;* atavíos, *m.pl.;* pertrechos, *m.pl.*

paraphrase ['pærəfreiz], *n.* paráfrasis, *f.*—*v.t.* parafrasear.

parasite ['pærəsait], *n.* parásito.

parasitic [pærə'sitik], *a.* parásito; (*med.*) parasítico.

parasol [pærə'sɔl], *n.* quitasol, *m.;* sombrilla.

paratroops ['pærətru:ps], *n.pl.* paracaidistas, *m.pl.*

parcel [pɑ:sl], *n.* paquete, *m.,* bulto; parcela (*de tierra*).—*v.t.* empaquetar, envolver; *to* — *out,* repartir.

parch [pɑ:tʃ], *v.t.* secar; abrasar.—*v.i.* secarse.

parched [pɑ:tʃt], *a.* sediento, seco; — *with thirst,* muerto de sed.

parchedness ['pɑ:tʃidnis], *n.* aridez, sequedad, *f.*

parchment ['pɑ:tʃmənt], *n.* pergamino; parche (*de un tambor*), *m.*

pardon [pɑ:dn], *n.* perdón, *m.;* absolución, *f.;* amnistía; *to beg* —, pedir perdón, disculparse; — *?¿* cómo *?*—*v.t.* perdonar; absolver; amnistiar.

pardonable ['pɑ:dnəbl], *a.* perdonable, disculpable, excusable.

pardoner ['pɑ:dnə], *n.* vendedor (*m.*) de indulgencias; perdonador, *m.*

pare [pɛə], *v.t.* cortar; pelar; reducir.

parent ['pɛərənt], *n.* padre, *m.;* madre, *f.;* antepasado.—*pl.* padres, *m.pl.*

parentage ['pɛərəntidʒ], *n.* parentela; linaje, *m.;* familia, alcurnia; extracción, *f.,* origen, *m.*

parental [pə'rentəl], *a.* paternal; maternal.

parenthesis [pə'renθisis], *n.* (*pl.* **-theses**) paréntesis, *m.*

parenthetical [pærən'θetikəl], *a.* entre paréntesis.

parenthood ['pɛərənthud], *n.* paternidad; maternidad, *f.*

paring ['pɛəriŋ], *n.* raedura, peladura; corteza, cortadura; desecho, desperdicio.

paring-knife ['pɛəriŋnaif], *n.* trinchete, *m.*

Paris ['pæris], *n.* París, *m.*

parish ['pæriʃ], *a.* parroquial.—*n.* parroquia; — *church,* parroquia; — *clerk,* sacristán, *m.;* — *priest,* cura, *m.*

parishioner [pə'riʃənə], *n.* parroquiano; feligrés, *m.*

Parisian [pə'rizjən], *a., n.* parisiense, *m.f.*

parity ['pæriti], *n.* paridad, *f.*

park [pɑ:k], *n.* parque, *m.;* jardín (público),

m.; car —, parque de automóviles. —*v.t.* estacionar; aparcar.—*v.i.* estacionarse, aparcarse.

parking ['pɑ:kiŋ], *n.* estacionamiento; — *lights,* luces (*f.pl.*) de estacionamiento; — *place,* parque (*m.*) de estacionamiento; *no* —, ¡prohibido estacionarse!

park-keeper ['pɑ:kki:pə], *n.* guardián, *m.*

parlance ['pɑ:ləns], *n.* lenguaje, *m.*

parley ['pɑ:li], *n.* (*mil.*) parlamento.—*v.i.* parlamentar.

parliament ['pɑ:ləmənt], *n.* parlamento; cortes, *f.pl.*

parliamentary [pɑ:lə'mentəri], *a.* parlamentario; — *immunity,* inviolabilidad (*f.*) parlamentaria.

parlour ['pɑ:lə], *n.* sala de recibo; locutorio; — *games,* juegos, (*m.pl.*) de prendas.

Parnassus [pɑ:'næsəs], *n.* Parnaso.

parochial [pə'roukiəl], *a.* parroquial, parroquiano; (*fig.*) provincial.

parodist ['pærədist], *n.* parodista, *m.f.*

parody ['pærədi], *n.* parodia.—*v.t.* parodiar.

parole [pə'roul], *n.* promesa de honor.—*v.t.* poner en libertad bajo palabra.

paroxysm ['pærəksizm], *n.* paroxismo; acceso.

parricide ['pærisaid], *n.* parricidio (*crimen*); parricida (*persona*), *m.f.*

parrot ['pærət], *n.* papagayo, loro.

parry ['pæri], *n.* parada; quite, *m.*—*v.t., v.i.* parar; evitar.

parse [pɑ:z], *v.t.* analizar.

parsimonious [pɑ:si'mounjəs], *a.* parsimonioso.

parsimony ['pɑ:siməni], *n.* parsimonia.

parsing ['pɑ:ziŋ], *n.* análisis, *m.* o *f.*

parsley ['pɑ:sli], *n.* perejil, *m.*

parsnip ['pɑ:snip], *n.* chirivía.

parson [pɑ:sn], *n.* clérigo; cura anglicano, *m.*

parsonage ['pɑ:sənidʒ], *n.* rectoría.

part [pɑ:t], *n.* parte, *f.;* porción, *f.;* trozo; pieza; región, *f.;* lugar, *m.;* papel (*de un actor*), *m.;* (*mus.*) voz, *f.;*—*pl.* prendas, dotes, partes, *f.pl., for my* —, por mi parte; *foreign parts,* el extranjero *in* —, en parte; *in parts,* por entregas; *spare* —, pieza de recambio; — *owner,* conpropietario; *to take* — *in,* tomar parte en; *to take in good* —, tomar a bien; *to play a* —, desempeñar un papel; *to take a person's* —, ser partidario de alguien.—*v.t.* distribuir, repartir; abrir; *to* — *one's hair,* hacerse la raya.—*v.i.* partir, despedirse; *to* — *from,* despedirse de; separarse de; *to* — *with,* deshacerse de.

partake [pɑ:'teik], *v.t.irr.* (*conjug. like* TAKE) participar de; tomar parte en.—*v.i.* tomar algo; *to* — *of,* comer de; beber de.

partial ['pɑ:ʃəl], *a.* parcial; aficionado.

partiality [pɑ:ʃi'æliti], *n.* parcialidad, *f.;* preferencia.

participant [pɑ:'tisipənt], *n.* participante, *m.f.*

participate [pɑ:'tisipeit], *v.i.* participar (de); tomar parte (en).

participation [pɑ:tisi'peiʃən], *n.* participación, *f.*

participle ['pɑ:tisipl], *n.* participio.

particle ['pɑ:tikl], *n.* partícula; átomo, pizca.

particular [pə'tikjulə], *a.* particular; especial; individual; exacto; escrupuloso; *in* —, en particular; *to be* — *about,* ser exigente en cuanto a.—*n.* particular, pormenor, *m.*; circunstancia.—*pl.* detalles, *m.pl.*

particularize [pə'tikjulɔraiz], *v.t.* particularizar; especificar.

parting ['pɑ:tiŋ], *n.* despedida; separación, *f.*; raya; bifurcación, *f.*; *the* — *of the ways,* el punto decisivo.

partisan [pɑ:ti'zæn], *a.* partidario.—*n.* partidario; guerrillero.

partition [pɑ:'tiʃən], *n.* partición; división; pared, *f.*, tabique, *m.*—*v.t.* partir, dividir.

partly ['pɑ:tli], *adv.* en parte.

partner ['pɑ:tnə], *n.* socio, asociado; compañero; pareja; consorte, *m.f.*

partnership ['pɑ:tnəʃip], *n.* asociación; sociedad, *f.*, compañía; *to take into* —, tomar como socio; *to go into* —, asociarse.

partook [pɑ:'tuk] [PARTAKE].

partridge ['pɑ:tridʒ], *n.* perdiz, *f.*

party ['pɑ:ti], *n.* partido; grupo; reunión; (*jur.*) parte, *f.*; interesado; *to be a* — *to,* ser cómplice en.

parvenu ['pɑ:vənju:], *a.*, *n.* advenedizo.

pass [pɑ:s], *n.* paso; desfiladero; salvoconducto; permiso, licencia; crisis, *f.*; (*sport*) pase, *m.*; estocada (*esgrima*); aprobación (*examen*), *f.*; *free* —, billete (*m.*) de favor. —*v.t.* pasar; alargar; aventajar; tolerar; aprobar (*un examen*); evacuar; *to* — *sentence,* pronunciar sentencia; (*fam.*) *to* — *the buck,* echar la carga.—*v.i.* pasar; cesar, desaparecer; *to* — *away,* fallecer, morir; *to* — *by,* pasar cerca de; (*fig.*) pasar por; *to* — *for,* pasar por; *to* — *on,* seguir andando; fallecer; *to* — *out,* salir; (*fig.*) desmayarse; *to* — *over,* atravesar; excusar; pasar por; *to* — *through,* atravesar; traspasar; (*fig.*) experimentar; *to bring to* —, ocasionar; *to come to* —, suceder. [overtake]

passable ['pɑ:səbl], *a.* transitable; tolerable; regular.

passage ['pæsidʒ], *n.* pasaje, *m.*; travesía; viaje, *m.*; tránsito; entrada; pasillo; callejón, *m.*

pass-book ['pɑ:sbuk], *n.* libreta de banco.

passenger ['pæsindʒə], *n.* pasajero, viajero; peatón, *m.*

pass-key ['pɑ:ski:], *n.* llave maestra, *f.*

passer-by ['pɑ:sə'bai], *n.* (*pl.* **passers-by**) transeúnte, paseante, *m.f.*

passing ['pɑ:siŋ], *a.* pasajero, fugaz, momentáneo; *in* —, de paso.—*n.* paso, pasada; muerte, *f.*, fallecimiento; aprobación, *f.*—*adv.* (*poet.*) sumamente.

passion ['pæʃən], *n.* pasión, *f.*; ira; ardor, *m.*; *Passion Sunday,* Domingo de Pasión; *to fly into a* —, montar en cólera.

passionate ['pæʃənit], *a.* apasionado; irascible; ardiente; impetuoso.

passion-flower ['pæʃənflauə], *n.* pasionaria, *f.*

passive ['pæsiv], *a.* pasivo.—*n.* voz pasiva.

Passover ['pɑ:souvə], *n.* pascua.

passport ['pɑ:spɔ:t], *n.* pasaporte, *m.*

password ['pɑ:swɔ:d], *n.* contraseña.

past [pɑ:st], *a.* pasado; terminado; antiguo; — *president,* ex presidente, *m.*—*n.* pasado; historia; pretérito; (*fam.*) *to have a* —,

tener malos antecedentes.—*adv.* más allá.— *prep.* después de; más allá de; sin; fuera de; incapaz de; — *caring,* no le importa ya; *it is ten* — *six,* son las seis y diez.

paste [peist], *a.* imitado.—*n.* pasta; engrudo. —*v.t.* pegar; engrudar.

pasteboard ['peistbɔ:d], *a.* de cartón.—*n.* cartón, *m.*

pastel ['pæstəl], *n.* (*art.*) pastel, *m.*

pasteurization [pɑ:stərai'zeiʃən], *n.* pasteurización, *f.*

pasteurize ['pɑ:stəraiz], *v.t.* pasteurizar.

pastille ['pæsti:l], *n.* pastilla.

pastime ['pɑ:staim], *n.* pasatiempo.

past-master ['pɑ:st'mɑ:stə], *n.* maestro consumado.

pastor ['pɑ:stə], *n.* pastor, *m.*

pastoral ['pɑ:stərəl], *a.* pastoril.—*a.*, *n.* (*eccl.*) pastoral, *f.*

pastry ['peistri], *n.* pasta; pastel, *m.*; pastelería.

pastry-cook ['peistrikuk], *n.* pastelero.

pasture ['pɑ:stʃə], *n.* pasto; prado, pradera.— *v.t.* pastar, apacentar.—*v.i.* pastar, pacer.

pasty ['peisti], *a.* pálido; pastoso.—*n.* ['pæsti], empanada.

pat (1) [pæt], *n.* golpecito; caricia; (*fig.*) — *on the back,* elogio.—*adv.* a propósito; fácilmente.—*v.t.* dar golpecitos; acariciar.

pat (2) [pæt], *n.* — *of butter,* pedacito de mantequilla.

patch [pætʃ], *n.* remiendo; parche, *m.*; pedazo; lunar postizo; mancha; (*fam.*) *not to be a* — *on,* no llegar a los zancajos de.—*v.t.* remendar; (*fam.*) chafallar; (*fig.*) *to* — *up,* hacer las paces.

patchy ['pætʃi], *a.* cubierto de parches; (*fig.*) desigual.

paten ['pætən], *n.* (*eccl.*) patena.

patent ['pætənt], *a.* patente; evidente; — *leather,* charol, *m.*; — *medicine,* específico farmacéutico.—*n.* patente, *f.*; — *of nobility,* carta de hidalguía; — *applied for,* patente solicitada.—*v.t.* obtener una patente; conceder una patente.

paternal [pə'tə:nl], *a.* paterno, paternal.

paternity [pə'tə:niti], *n.* paternidad, *f.*

path [pɑ:θ], *n.* senda, sendero; camino; trayectoia.

pathetic [pə'θetik], *a.* patético.

pathological [pæθə'lɔdʒikəl], *a.* patológico.

pathologist [pə'θɔlədʒist], *n.* patólogo.

pathology [pə'θɔlədʒi], *n.* patología.

pathos ['peiθɔs], *n.* lo patético.

pathway ['pɑ:θwei], *n.* senda, sendero.

patience ['peiʃəns], *n.* paciencia; *to play* —, hacer solitarios (*naipes*); *to lose* —, perder la paciencia, impacientarse.

patient ['peiʃənt], *a.* paciente.—*n.* paciente, *m.f.*; enfermo.

patois ['pætwɑ:], *n.* dialecto.

patriarch ['peitriɑ:k], *n.* patriarca, *m.*

patriarchal [peitri'ɑ:kəl], *a.* patriarcal.

patrician [pə'triʃən], *a.*, *n.* patricio.

patrimony ['pætriməni], *n.* patrimonio.

patriot ['pætriət], *n.* patriota, *m.f.*

patriotic [pætri'ɔtik], *a.* patriótico.

patriotism ['pætriətizm], *n.* patriotismo.

patrol [pə'troul], *n.* patrulla; ronda.—*v.t.*, *v.i.* patrullar; rondar.

patron ['peitrən], *n.* mecenas, *m.sg.*; protector, *m.*; patrono; cliente, *m.f.*; — *saint,* santo patrón, santa patrona.
patronage ['pætrənidʒ], *n.* patronato; patrocinio; clientela; superioridad, *f.*
patroness ['peitrənes], *n.* protectora; patrona.
patronize ['pætrənaiz], *v.t.* patrocinar; proteger; ser parroquiano de; tratar con arrogancia.
patronizing ['pætrənaizin], *a.* que patrocina; altivo.
patter ['pætə], *n.* ruido; golpecitos, *m.pl.*; parladuría.—*v.i.* patear; hacer ruido.
pattern ['pætən], *n.* modelo; muestra; patrón, *m.*; norma.
paunch [pɔːntʃ], *n.* panza, barriga.
pauper ['pɔːpə], *n.* pobre, *m.f.*
pause [pɔːz], *n.* pausa; cesación, *f.*—*v.i.* pausar; detenerse.
pave [peiv], *v.t.* empedrar, enlosar; (*fig.*) *to — the way for,* facilitar el camino para.
pavement ['peivmənt], *n.* pavimento; pavimentado; acera.
pavilion [pə'viljən], *n.* pabellón, *m.*; tienda; quiosco.
paving ['peivin], *n.* empedrado, pavimento.
paving-stone ['peivinstoun], *n.* losa, adoquín, *m.*
paw [pɔː], *n.* pata; garra.—*v.t.* arañar; manosear.—*v.i.* piafar.
pawn (1) [pɔːn], *n.* empeño; (*fig.*) prenda; *in* —, empeñado; — *ticket,* papeleta de empeño.—*v.t.* empeñar; dar en prenda.
pawn (2) [pɔːn], *n.* peón (*ajedrez*), *m.*
pawnbroker ['pɔːnbroukə], *n.* prestamista, *m.f.*
pawnshop ['pɔːnʃɔp], *n.* casa de préstamos, monte (*m.*) de piedad.
pay [pei], *n.* paga; salario; sueldo; jornal, *m.*, recompensa; (*mil.*) soldada.—*v.t.* (*pret., p.p.* **paid**) pagar; recompensar; satisfacer; gastar; presentar; *to — attention,* prestar atención; *to — back,* devolver; (*fig.*) pagar en la misma moneda; *to — by instalments,* pagar a plazos; *to — in full,* saldar; *to — a call,* hacer una visita; *to — off,* pagar y despedir; redimir; *to — out,* largar, arriar (*cordel*).—*v.i.* pagar; ser provechoso; sufrir un castigo; *to — through the nose,* costar un ojo de la cara; *to — for it,* (*fig.*) pagarlas.
payable ['peiəbl], *a.* pagadero.
pay-day ['peidei], *n.* día (*m.*) de pago.
payee [pei'iː], *n.* (*com.*) portador, *m.*
payer [peiə], *n.* pagador, *m.*
paymaster ['peimɑːstə], *n.* pagador, *m.*; (*mil.*) habilitado.
Paymaster-General ['peimɑːstə'dʒenərəl], *n.* ordenador (*m.*) de pagos.
payment ['peimənt], *n.* pago, paga; (*fig.*) recompensa; premio; *cash* —, pago en especie; *on — of,* mediante el pago de; — *in advance,* pago adelantado.
pay-roll ['peiroul], *n.* nómina.
pea [piː], *n.* guisante, *m.*
peace [piːs], *n.* paz; quietud; tranquilidad, *f.*; sosiego; *to hold one's* —, callarse; *to make* —, hacer las paces.
peaceable ['piːsəbl], *a.* pacífico; apacible.
peaceful ['piːsful], *a.* tranquilo; pacífico.
peace-loving ['piːslʌvin], *a.* pacífico.

peace-maker ['piːsmeikə], *n.* conciliador, *m.*
peace-offering ['piːsɔfərin], *n.* sacrificio propiciatorio.
peach [piːtʃ], *n.* melocotón, *m.*
peacock ['piːkɔk], *n.* pavón, *m.*, pavo real.
peahen ['piːhen], *n.* pava real.
peak [piːk], *n.* pico; cumbre, *f.*; punta; visera; (*fig.*) apogeo, auge, *m.*; — *hours,* horas de mayor tráfico.
peaked [piːkt], *a.* puntiagudo; con visera; (*fam.*) enfermizo.
peal [piːl], *n.* repique (*de campanas*), *m.*; estruendo; sonido; — *of laughter,* carcajada.—*v.t.* tañer.—*v.i.* repicar; sonar.
peanut ['piːnʌt], *n.* cacahuete, *m.*
pear [pɛə], *n.* pera; — *tree,* peral, *m.*
pearl [pəːl], *n.* perla.
pearl-barley ['pəːl'bɑːli], *n.* cebada perlada.
pearl-grey ['pəːl'grei], *a.* gris de perla.
pearly ['pəːli], *a.* perlino.
peasant ['pezənt], *n.* campesino.
peasantry ['pezəntri], *n.* campesinos, *m.pl.*
pea-shooter ['piːʃuːtə], *n.* cerbatana.
peat [piːt], *n.* turba.
peat-bog ['piːtbɔg], *n.* turbera.
peaty ['piːti], *a.* turboso.
pebble [pebl], *n.* guijarro, guija.
pebbly ['pebli], *a.* guijarroso, guijoso.
peccadillo [pekə'dilou], *n.* pecadillo.
peck [pek], *n.* picotazo; besito.—*v.t.* picotear; rozar con los labios.
peculiar [pi'kjuːljə], *a.* peculiar, particular; característico; extraño.
peculiarity [pikjuːli'æriti], *n.* peculiaridad, particularidad, *f.*
pecuniary [pi'kjuːnjəri], *a.* pecuniario.
pedagogic [pedə'gɔdʒik], *a.* pedagógico.
pedagogue ['pedəgɔg], *n.* pedagogo.
pedagogy ['pedəgɔdʒi], *n.* pedagogía.
pedal [pedl], *n.* pedal, *m.*—*v.i.* pedalear.
pedant ['pedənt], *n.* pedante, *m.f.*
pedantic [pə'dæntik], *a.* pedante.
pedantry ['pedəntri], *n.* pedantería.
peddle [pedl], *v.t.* revender.—*v.i.* ser buhonero.
peddling ['pedlin], *n.* buhonería.
pedestal ['pedistl], *n.* pedestal, *n.*
pedestrian [pə'destriən], *a.* pedestre; (*fig.*) trillado, prosaico.—*n.* peatón, *m.*; — *crossing,* cruce (*m.*) de peatones.
pedigree ['pedigriː], *a.* de raza, de casta.—*n.* genealogía; raza.
pediment ['pedimənt], *n.* (*arch.*) frontón, *m.*
pedlar ['pedlə], *n.* buhonero.
peel [piːl], *n.* corteza, hollejo, piel, *f.*—*v.t.* pelar.—*v.i.* pelarse; desconcharse (*pintura*).
peeling ['piːlin], *n.* peladura; desconchadura.
peep (1) [piːp], *n.* ojeada; vista.—*v.i.* atisbar; mostrarse.
peep (2) [piːp], *n.* pío.—*v.i.* piar.
peep-hole ['piːphoul], *n.* mirilla.
peep-show ['piːpʃou], *n.* óptica.
peer (1) [piə], *n.* par, *m.*; igual; noble, *m.f.*
peer (2) [piə], *v.i.* escudriñar.
peerage ['piəridʒ], *n.* dignidad (*f.*) de par; aristocracia.
peeress ['piəres], *n.* paresa.
peerless ['piəlis], *a.* sin par, incomparable.
peevish ['piːviʃ], *a.* enojadizo; displicente.
peevishness ['piːviʃnis], *n.* mal humor, *m.* displicencia.

peg [peg], *n.* clavija; estaca; colgadero; pinza; *to take down a* —, bajar los humos a.— *v.t.* enclavijar, clavar.—*v.i. to — away,* batirse el cobre.

pejorative [ˈpiːdʒərətiv, pəˈdʒɔrətiv], *a.* peyorativo.

pelican [ˈpelikən], *n.* pelicano.

pellet [ˈpelit], *n.* pelotilla; píldora; bolita.

pell-mell [ˈpelˈmel], *adv.* a trochemoche; atropelladamente.

pelt (1) [pelt], *n.* piel, *f.*; pellejo.

pelt (2) [pelt], *n.* golpe, *m.*—*v.t.* arrojar, apedrear, azotar.—*v.i.* llover.

pelvis [ˈpelvis], *n.* pelvis, *f.*

pen (1) [pen], *n.* pluma.—*v.t.* escribir.

pen (2) [pen], *n.* corral, *m.*; pollera.—*v.t.* acorralar, encerrar.

penal [ˈpiːnəl], *a.* penal; — *servitude,* trabajos forzados, *m.pl.*

penalize [ˈpiːnəlaiz], *v.t.* penar, castigar.

penalty [ˈpenəlti], *n.* pena, castigo; multa; (*sport*) penalty, *m.*

penance [ˈpenəns], *n.* penitencia.

pence [pens] [PENNY].

pencil [ˈpensil], *n.* lápiz, *m.*—*v.t.* escribir, dibujar, marcar con lápiz.

pendant [ˈpendənt], *n.* pendiente; gallardete, *m.*

pending [ˈpendiŋ], *a.* pendiente.—*prep.* hasta, en espera de.

pendulum [ˈpendjuləm], *n.* péndulo, péndola.

penetrability [penitrəˈbiliti], *n.* penetrabilidad, *f.*

penetrable [ˈpenitrəbl], *a.* penetrable.

penetrate [ˈpenitreit], *v.t.*, *v.i.* penetrar.

penetrating [ˈpenitreitiŋ], *a.* penetrante.

penetration [peniˈtreiʃən], *n.* penetración, *f.*

penguin [ˈpeŋgwin], *n.* pingüino.

penicillin [peniˈsilin], *n.* penicilina.

peninsula [piˈninsjulə], *n.* península.

peninsular [piˈninsjulə], *a.* peninsular.

penis [ˈpiːnis], *n.* pene, *m.*

penitence [ˈpenitəns], *n.* penitencia.

penitent [ˈpenitənt], *a.*, *n.* penitente, *m.f.*

penitential [peniˈtenʃəl], *a.* penitencial.

penitentiary [peniˈtenʃəri], *a.* penitenciario. —*n.* casa de corrección; presidio.

penknife [ˈpennaif], *n.* cortaplumas *m.sg.*

penmanship [ˈpenmənʃip], *n.* caligrafía.

pen-name [ˈpenneim], *n.* seudónimo.

penniless [ˈpenilis], *a.* sin dinero, sin blanca; indigente.

penny [ˈpeni], *n.* (*pl.* **pennies** *o* **pence**) penique, *m.*; (*fam.*) dinero.

pennyworth [ˈpeniwəːθ], *n.* valor (*m.*) de un penique.

pension [ˈpenʃən], *n.* pensión, *f.*; beca; retiro;—*v.t.* pensionar; *to — off,* jubilar.

pensioner [ˈpenʃənə], *n.* pensionista, *m.f.*; inválido.

pensive [ˈpensiv], *a.* pensativo, meditabundo; cabizbajo.

pentagon [ˈpentəgən], *n.* pentágono.

pentameter [penˈtæmitə], *n.* pentámetro.

Pentecost [ˈpentikəst], *n.* Pentecostés, *m.*

pent-up [ˈpentʌp], *a.* encerrado; enjaulado; (*fig.*) reprimido.

penultimate [penˈʌltimit], *a.* penúltimo.

penurious [piˈnjuəriəs], *a.* indigente, muy pobre; escaso; tacaño.

penury [ˈpenjuri], *n.* penuria.

peony [ˈpiəni], *n.* peonía.

people [ˈpiːpl], *n.* pueblo; nación, *f.*; gente, *f.*; personas, *f.pl.*; vulgo; súbditos, *m.pl.*; familia; *common* —, gentuza; — *say,* se dice.—*v.t.* poblar.

pepper [ˈpepə], *n.* pimienta; pimiento.—*v.t.* sazonar con pimienta; acribillar; salpimentar.

peppermint [ˈpepəmint], *n.* menta; pastilla de menta.

peppery [ˈpepəri], *a.* picante; (*fig.*) irascible.

per [pəː], *prep.* por; — *annum,* al año; — *cent,* por ciento; — *hour,* por hora.

perambulate [pəˈræmbjuleit], *v.t.*, *v.i.* recorrer.

perambulator [pəˈræmbjuleitə], *n.* coche (*m.*) de niño.

perceive [pəˈsiːv], *v.t.* percibir; darse cuenta de, comprender; discernir.

percentage [pəˈsentidʒ], *n.* porcentaje, *m.*

perceptible [pəˈseptibl], *a.* perceptible; sensible.

perception [pəˈsepʃən], *n.* percepción; sensibilidad, *f.*

perceptive [pəˈseptiv], *a.* perceptivo.

perch (1) [pəːtʃ], *n.* (*ichth.*) perca.

perch (2) [pəːtʃ], *n.* percha; pértica.—*v.t.* posar.—*v.i.* posarse.

percolate [ˈpəːkəleit], *v.t.* colar, filtrar.—*v.i.* colarse, filtrarse.

percolator [ˈpəːkəleitə], *n.* filtro, colador, *m.*

percussion [pəˈkʌʃən], *n.* percusión, *f.*; choque, *m.*

perdition [pəˈdiʃən], *n.* perdición, *f.*; ruina.

peremptory [ˈperəmptəri], *a.* perentorio; imperioso.

perennial [pəˈrenjəl], *a.* perenne, perpetuo. —*n.* planta vivaz.

perfect [ˈpəːfikt], *a.* perfecto; acabado.— [pəˈfekt], *v.t.* perfeccionar.

perfectible [pəˈfektəbl], *a.* perfectible.

perfection [pəˈfekʃən], *n.* perfección, *f.*; *to* —, a la perfección.

perfectionist [pəˈfekʃənist], *n.* perfeccionista, *m.f.*

perfidious [pəˈfidjəs], *a.* pérfido.

perfidy [ˈpəːfidi], *n.* perfidia.

perforate [ˈpəːfəreit], *v.t.* perforar, agujerear.

perforation [pəːfəˈreiʃən], *n.* perforación, *f.*; agujero.

perform [pəˈfɔːm], *v.t.* ejecutar; desempeñar; representar.—*v.i.* representar, desempeñar un papel; tocar; cantar; hacer trucos.

performance [pəˈfɔːməns], *n.* ejecución, realización, *f.*; desempeño; representación, *f.*; *first* —, estreno.

performer [pəˈfɔːmə], *n.* ejecutante, *m.f.*; actor, *m.*; actriz, *f.*; artista, *m.f.*

perfume [ˈpəːfjuːm], *n.* perfume, *m.*; aroma, fragancia.—[pəːˈfjuːm], *v.t.* perfumar; aromatizar, embalsamar.

perfumer [pəːˈfjuːmə], *n.* perfumista, *m.f.*

perfunctoriness [pəˈfʌŋktərinis], *n.* descuido; superficialidad, *f.*

perfunctory [pəˈfʌŋktəri], *a.* perfunctorio; superficial; negligente.

perhaps [pəˈhæps], *adv.* quizá, quizás, tal vez.

peril [ˈperil], *n.* peligro; riesgo.

perilous [ˈperiləs], *a.* peligroso, arriesgado.

perimeter [pəˈrimitə], *n.* perímetro.

337

period [ˈpiəriəd], *n.* período; edad, *f.*, tiempo; época; término, plazo; (*U.S.*) punto final; (*med.*) menstruación, *f.*, regla; — *costume*, vestido de época.

periodic [piəriˈɔdik], *a.* periódico.

periodical [piəriˈɔdikəl], *a.* periódico.—*n.* revista.

peripheral [pəˈrifərəl], *a.* periférico.

periphery [pəˈrifəri], *n.* periferia.

periphrastic [periˈfræstik], *a.* perifrástico.

periscope [ˈperiskoup], *n.* periscopio.

perish [ˈperiʃ], *v.i.* perecer; marchitarse; acabar, fenecer.

perishable [ˈperiʃəbl], *a.* perecedero.

perjure [ˈpəːdʒə], *v.t.* perjurar; *to — oneself*, perjurarse.

perjurer [ˈpəːdʒərə], *n.* perjuro, perjurador, *m.*

perjury [ˈpəːdʒəri], *n.* perjurio; *to commit* —, jurar en falso.

perk [pəːk], *v.i.* levantar la cabeza; *to — up*, (*fam.*) reponerse; cobrar ánimo.

perky [ˈpəːki], *a.* desenvuelto, gallardo; alegre.

permanence [ˈpəːmənəns], *n.* permanencia; estabilidad, *f.*

permanent [ˈpəːmənənt], *a.* permanente; estable; fijo; — *wave*, ondulación permanente, *f.*

permeate [ˈpəːmieit], *v.t.* impregnar; infiltrar.

permissible [pəˈmisəbl], *a.* permisible, admisible.

permission [pəˈmiʃən], *n.* permiso, licencia.

permissive [pəˈmisiv], *a.* permisivo, tolerado.

permit [ˈpəːmit], *n.* permiso; licencia; pase, *m.*—[pəˈmit], *v.t.* permitir; tolerar.

permutation [pəːmjuːˈteiʃən], *n.* permutación, *f.*

pernicious [pəˈniʃəs], *a.* pernicioso.

peroration [perəˈreiʃən], *n.* peroración, *f.*

peroxide [pəˈrɔksaid], *n.* peróxido.

perpendicular [pəːpənˈdikjulə], *a.*, *n.* perpendicular, *f.*

perpetrate [ˈpəːpitreit], *v.t.* perpetrar, cometer.

perpetration [pəːpiˈtreiʃən], *n.* perpetración, comisión, *f.*

perpetrator [ˈpəːpitreitə], *n.* perpetrador; autor, *m.*

perpetual [pəˈpetjuəl], *a.* perpetuo; continuo, incesante; eterno.

perpetuate [pəˈpetjueit], *v.t.* perpetuar, eternizar; inmortalizar.

perpetuity [pəːpiˈtjuiti], *n.* perpetuidad, *f.*; *in* —, para siempre.

perplex [pəˈpleks], *v.t.* confundir, aturdir, embrollar.

perplexed [pəˈplekst], *a.* perplejo, confuso.

perplexing [pəˈpleksiŋ], *a.* inquietante; confuso, intricado.

perplexity [pəˈpleksiti], *n.* perplejidad, confusión, *f.*

persecute [ˈpəːsikjuːt], *v.t.* perseguir; molestar.

persecution [pəːsiˈkjuːʃən], *n.* persecución, *f.*

persecutor [ˈpəːsikjuːtə], *n.* perseguidor, *m.*

perseverance [pəːsiˈviərəns], *n.* perseverancia.

persevere [pəːsiˈviə], *v.i.* perseverar.

persevering [pəːsiˈviəriŋ], *a.* perseverante.

Persia [ˈpəːʃə], *n.* Persia.

Persian [ˈpəːʃən], *a.* persa.—*n.* persa, *m.f.*

persist [pəˈsist], *v.i.* persistir; empeñarse; permanecer.

persistence [pəˈsistəns], *n.* persistencia.

persistent [pəˈsistənt], *a.* persistente.

person [ˈpəːsn], *n.* persona; *in* —, en persona.

personable [ˈpəːsnəbl], *a.* bien parecido.

personage [ˈpəːsənidʒ], *n.* personaje, *m.*

personal [ˈpəːsnəl], *a.* personal; particular; íntimo; en persona.

personality [pəːsəˈnæliti], *n.* personalidad, *f.*

personification [pəːsɔnifiˈkeiʃən], *n.* personificación, *f.*

personify [pəːˈsɔnifai], *v.t.* personificar.

personnel [pəːsəˈnel], *n.* personal, *m.*

perspective [pəˈspektiv], *n.* perspectiva.

perspicacious [pəːspiˈkeiʃəs], *a.* perspicaz.

perspicacity [pəːspiˈkæsiti], *n.* perspicacia.

perspicuity [pəːspiˈkjuiti], *n.* perspicuidad, *f.*

perspiration [pəːspəˈreiʃən], *n.* transpiración, *f.*, sudor, *m.*

perspire [pəˈspaiə], *v.i.* transpirar, sudar.

persuade [pəˈsweid], *v.t.* persuadir; inducir, mover.

persuader [pəˈsweidə], *n.* persuasor, *m.*

persuasion [pəˈsweiʒən], *n.* persuasión; opinión, *f.*; secta.

persuasive [pəˈsweiziv], *a.* persuasivo.

persuasiveness [pəˈsweizivnis], *n.* persuasiva.

pert [pəːt], *a.* listo; desenvuelto, fresco.

pertain [pəˈtein], *v.i.* pertenecer; tocar; referirse.

pertinacious [pəːtiˈneiʃəs], *a.* pertinaz.

pertinacity [pəːtiˈnæsiti], *n.* pertinacia, tenacidad, *f.*

pertinence [ˈpəːtinəns], *n.* pertinencia.

pertinent [ˈpəːtinənt], *a.* pertinente, atinado.

pertness [ˈpəːtnis], *n.* viveza; desenvoltura, frescura.

perturb [pəˈtəːb], *v.t.* perturbar, inquietar, agitar.

perturbation [pəːtəˈbeiʃən], *n.* perturbación, *f.*

Peru [pəˈruː], *n.* el Perú.

perusal [pəˈruːzəl], *n.* lectura; escudriño.

peruse [pəˈruːz], *v.t.* leer con cuidado; escudriñar.

Peruvian [pəˈruːvjən], *a.*, *n.* peruano.

pervade [pəːˈveid], *v.t.* penetrar; llenar; difundirse por.

pervasive [pəːˈveiziv], *a.* penetrante.

perverse [pəˈvəːs], *a.* perverso, depravado; obstinado; petulante.

perverseness [pəˈvəːsnis], *n.* perversidad, obstinación, *f.*

perversion [pəˈvəːʃən], *n.* perversión, *f.*

pervert [ˈpəːvəːt], *n.* pervertido; renegado.—[pəˈvəːt], *v.t.* pervertir, corromper; falsificar.

pervious [ˈpəːvjəs], *a.* penetrable; permeable.

pessary [ˈpesəri], *n.* pesario.

pessimism [ˈpesimizm], *n.* pesimismo.

pessimist [ˈpesimist], *n.* pesimista, *m.f.*

pessimistic [pesiˈmistik], *a.* pesimista.

pest [pest], *n.* insecto nocivo; peste, *f.*; (*fig.*) plaga; mosca.

pester [ˈpestə], *v.t.* molestar, importunar.

pestilence [ˈpestiləns], *n.* pestilencia, peste, *f.*

pestilential [pestiˈlenʃəl], *a.* pestífero, pestilente.

pestle [pesl], *n.* pistadero, mano (*f.*) de mortero.

pet (1) [pet], *n.* animal doméstico; favorito; niño mimado; (*fam.*) querido, querida.—*v.t.* mimar; acariciar.
pet (2) [pet], *n.* despecho, mal humor, *m.*
petal [petl], *n.* pétalo.
peter ['pi:tə], *v.i.* **to — out,** agotarse; desaparecer.
petition [pi'tiʃən], *n.* petición, *f.*; memorial, *m.*; súplica; instancia.—*v.t.* pedir; suplicar; dirigir un memorial.
petitioner [pi'tiʃənə], *n.* peticionario.
petrify ['petrifai], *v.t.* petrificar.—*v.i.* petrificarse.
petrol ['petrəl], *n.* gasolina; **— pump,** surtidor (*m.*) de gasolina; **— station,** puesto de gasolina.
petroleum [pi'trouljəm], *n.* petróleo.
petticoat ['petikout], *n.* enagua.
pettifogger ['petifɔgə], *n.* picapleitos, *m.sg.*; sofista, *m.f.*
pettiness ['petinis], *n.* pequeñez; mezquindad, *f.*; insignificancia.
petty ['peti], *a.* pequeño; mezquino; insignificante; **— cash,** gastos menores; **— larceny,** hurto menor; **— officer,** suboficial, *m.*; **— thief,** ratero.
petulance ['petjuləns], *n.* displicencia, mal humor, *m.*
petulant ['petjulənt], *a.* displicente, mal humorado.
pew [pju:], *n.* banco de iglesia.
pewter ['pju:tə], *a.* de peltre.—*n.* peltre, *m.*
phalanx ['fælæŋks], *n.* falange, *f.*
phallic ['fælik], *a.* fálico.
phantasmagoria [fæntæzmə'gɔ:rjə], *n.* fantasmagoría.
phantom ['fæntəm], *n.* fantasma, *m.*, espectro, sombra.
pharisaic [færi'seiik], *a.* farisaico.
pharisee ['færisi:], *n.* fariseo.
pharmaceutical [fɑ:mə'sju:tikəl], *a.* farmacéutico.
pharmacist ['fɑ:məsist], *n.* farmacéutico.
pharmacy ['fɑ:məsi], *n.* farmacia.
phase [feiz], *n.* fase, *f.*; aspecto.
pheasant ['fezənt], *n.* faisán, *m.*
phenomenal [fi'nɔminəl], *a.* fenomenal.
phenomenon [fi'nɔminən], *n.* (*pl.* **phenomena** [fi'nɔminə]) fenómeno.
phial ['faiəl], *n.* redoma.
philander [fi'lændə], *v.i.* galantear.
philanderer [fi'lændərə], *n.* tenorio, galanteador, *m.*
philandering [fi'lændəriŋ], *n.* galanteo.
philanthropic [filən'θrɔpik], *a.* filantrópico.
philanthropist [fi'lænθrəpist], *n.* filántropo.
philanthropy [fi'lænθrəpi], *n.* filantropía.
philatelic [filə'telik], *a.* filatélico.
philatelist [fi'lætəlist], *n.* filatelista, *m.f.*
philately [fi'lætəli], *n.* filatelia.
philharmonic [filhɑ:'mɔnik], *a.* filarmónico.
Philippine ['filipi:n], *a.* filipino.—*n.pl.* **Filipinas** (*islas*).
Philistine ['filistain], *a.*, *n.* filisteo.
philologist [fi'lɔlədʒist], *n.* filólogo.
philology [fi'lɔlədʒi], *n.* filología.
philosopher [fi'lɔsəfə], *n.* filósofo; **philosopher's stone,** piedra filosofal.
philosophical [filə'sɔfikəl], *a.* filosófico.
philosophize [fi'lɔsəfaiz], *v.i.* filosofar.
philosophy [fi'lɔsəfi], *n.* filosofía.
philtre ['filtə], *n.* filtro.

phlebitis [fli'baitis], *n.* flebitis, *f.*
phlegm [flem], *n.* flema.
phlegmatic [fleg'mætik], *a.* flemático.
Phoenician [fi'ni:ʃən], *a.*, *n.* fenicio.
phoenix ['fi:niks], *n.* fénix, *f.*
phonetic [fə'netik], *a.* fonético.—*n.pl.* fonética.
phoney ['founi], *a.* falso; espurio.
phonograph ['founəgrɑ:f], *n.* fonógrafo.
phonology [fə'nɔlədʒi], *n.* fonología.
phosphate ['fɔsfeit], *n.* fosfato.
phosphorescent [fɔsfə'resənt], *a.* fosforescente.
phosphorus ['fɔsfərəs], *n.* fósforo.
photogenic [foutə'dʒenik], *a.* fotogénico.
photograph ['foutəgrɑ:f], *n.* fotografía, foto, *f.*—*v.t.* fotografiar.
photographer [fə'tɔgrəfə], *n.* fotógrafo.
photographic [foutə'græfik], *a.* fotográfico.
photography [fə'tɔgrəfi], *n.* fotografía.
photogravure [foutəgrə'vjuə], *n.* fotograbado.
photostat ['foutoustæt], *n.* fotostato.
phrase [freiz], *n.* frase, *f.*—*v.t.* frasear, expresar, redactar.
phrase-book ['freizbuk], *n.* libro de frases.
phraseology [freizi'ɔlədʒi], *n.* fraseología.
phrenetic [fri'netik], *a.* frenético.
physical ['fizikəl], *a.* físico.
physician [fi'ziʃən], *n.* médico.
physicist ['fizisist], *n.* físico.
physics ['fiziks], *n.* física.
physiognomy [fizi'ɔnəmi], *n.* fisonomía.
physiological [fiziə'lɔdʒikəl], *a.* fisiológico.
physiologist [fizi'ɔlədʒist], *n.* fisiólogo.
physiology [fizi'ɔlədʒi], *n.* fisiología.
physiotherapy [fiziə'θerəpi], *n.* fisioterapia.
physique [fi'zi:k], *n.* físico, presencia.
pianist ['pi:ənist], *n.* pianista, *m.f.*
piano ['pjænou], *n.* piano; **grand —,** piano de cola; **baby grand (—),** piano de media cola; **upright —,** piano vertical; **— stool,** taburete (*m.*) de piano; **— tuner,** afinador (*m.*) de pianos; **to play the —,** tocar el piano.
piccolo ['pikəlou], *n.* flautín, *m.*
pick (1) [pik], *n.* escogimiento; lo mejor.—*v.t.* escoger, elegir; picar; limpiar, mondar; abrir con ganzúa; **to — a bone,** roer un hueso; (*fig.*) ajustar cuentas; **to — and choose,** vacilar; **to — a quarrel,** buscar camorra; **to — someone's pocket,** limpiar la faltriquera a; **to — off,** arrancar; fusilar; **to — out,** escoger; distinguir, reconocer; **to — up,** recoger, coger; levantar; adquirir; trabar amistad con; aprender; interceptar.—*v.i.* comer poco; escoger; **to — up,** recobrar la salud, reponerse.
pick (2) [pik], *n.* pico.
pick-axe ['pikæks], *n.* zapapico.
picket ['pikit], *n.* estaca; piquete, *m.*—*v.t.* cercar con estacas; poner piquetes.
picking ['pikiŋ], *n.* recolección, *f.*; escogimiento; robo.—*pl.* desperdicios, *m.pl.*; ganancias, *f.pl.*
pickle [pikl], *n.* escabeche, *m.*; encurtido; (*fam.*) apuro.—*v.t.* escabechar, encurtir.
picklock ['piklɔk], *n.* ganzúa.
pick-me-up ['pikmi:ʌp], *n.* tónico; **trinquis,** *m.*
pickpocket ['pikpɔkit], *n.* ratero.

339

picnic

picnic ['piknik], *n.* partida de campo, picnic, *m.*—*v.i.* hacer un picnic.
pictorial [pik'tɔ:riəl], *a.* pictórico, gráfico.
picture ['piktʃə], *n.* cuadro; retrato; ilustración, *f.*; imagen, *f.*; grabado; fotografía; película; — *book*, libro de estampas; — *frame*, marco; *to go to the pictures*, ir al cine.
picturesque [piktʃə'resk], *a.* pintoresco.
pie [pai], *n.* pastel, *m.*, empanada; *to put a finger in the* —, meter cuchara; *to eat humble* —, bajar las orejas.
piece [pi:s], *n.* pedazo; trozo; porción, *f.*; pieza; — *of paper*, papelito, hoja de papel; — *of ground*, parcela de tierra; — *of furniture*, mueble, *m.*; — *of news*, noticia; *to come to pieces*, deshacerse; *to cut to pieces*, destrozar; *to go to pieces*, hacerse pedazos; *to pull to pieces*, despedazar; *to take to pieces*, desmontar.—*v.t.* unir; remendar.
piecemeal ['pi:smi:l], *adv.* en pedazos; por partes.
piece-work ['pi:swə:k], *n.* trabajo a destajo.
pied [paid], *a.* pío; abigarrado.
pier [piə], *n.* embarcadero; malecón, *m.*; pila.
pierce [piəs], *v.t.* penetrar; agujerear; traspasar.—*v.i.* penetrar.
piercing ['piəsiŋ], *a.* penetrante; cortante.
piety ['paiəti], *n.* piedad, devoción, *f.*
piffle [pifl], *n.* disparates, *m.pl.*, patrañas, *f.pl.*
pig [pig], *n.* puerco, cerdo; lingote, *m.*; *guinea* —, conejillo de Indias; *to buy a* — *in a poke*, comprar a ciegas.—*v.i. to* — *it*, (*fam.*) vivir como cochinos.
pigeon (I) ['pidʒin], *n.* pichón, *m.*, paloma; *carrier* —, paloma mensajera.
pigeon (2) ['pidʒin], *n. that's his* —, (*fam.*) con su pan se lo coma.
pigeon-hole ['pidʒinhoul], *n.* casilla.—*v.t.* encasillar.
pigeon-toed ['pidʒin'toud], *a.* patituerto.
pigheaded ['pig'hedid], *a.* cabezudo, terco.
pig-iron ['pigaiən], *n.* lingote (*m.*) de fundición.
piglet ['piglit], *n.* cerdito.
pigment ['pigmənt], *n.* pigmento.—*v.t.* pigmentar.
pigmy ['pigmi], *n.* pigmeo.
pigskin ['pigskin], *n.* piel (*f.*) de cerdo.
pigsty ['pigstai], *n.* pocilga.
pigtail ['pigteil], *n.* coleta, trenza.
pike (I) [paik], *n.* sollo; pica, chuzo.
pike (2) [paik], *n.* (*ichth.*) lucio.
pikestaff ['paiksta:f], *n.* asta de pica; *as plain as a* —, a bola vista.
pile (I) [pail], *n.* pila, montón, *m.*; pira; mole, *f.*, edificio grande; *atomic* —, pila atómica; *to make one's* —, (*fig.*) hacer su pacotilla. —*v.t.* apilar, amontonar.—*v.i. to* — *up*, amontonarse.
pile (2) [pail], *n.* pilote, *m.*, estaca.—*v.t.* clavar estacas.
pile (3) [pail], *n.* pelo.
piles [pailz], *n.pl.* (*med.*) hemorroides, *f.pl.*
pilfer ['pilfə], *v.t.* hurtar, ratear, sisar.
pilfering ['pilfəriŋ], *n.* ratería, sisa.
pilgrim ['pilgrim], *n.* peregrino, romero.
pilgrimage ['pilgrimidʒ], *n.* peregrinación, *f.*, romería.
pill [pil], *n.* píldora.

pillage ['pilidʒ], *n.* saqueo.—*v.t.* saquear, pillar.
pillager ['pilidʒə], *n.* saqueador, *m.*
pillar ['pilə], *n.* pilar, *m.*, columna; (*fig.*) sostén, *m.*; *from* — *to post*, de Ceca en Meca; —*of strength*, (*fam.*) roca.
pillar-box ['piləbɔks], *n.* buzón, *m.*
pillion ['piljən], *n.* grupa; grupera; *to ride* —, ir a la grupa.
pillory ['piləri], *n.* picota.—*v.t.* empicotar.
pillow ['pilou], *n.* almohada.—*v.t.* apoyar.
pillow-case ['piloukeis], *n.* funda de almohada.
pilot ['pailət], *n.* piloto.—*v.t.* pilotar, pilotear; guiar.
pilotage ['pailətidʒ], *n.* pilotaje; (*naut.*) practicaje, *m.*
pimp [pimp], *n.* alcahuete, *m.*—*v.i.* alcahuetear.
pimpernel ['pimpənel], *n.* pimpinela.
pimple [pimpl], *n.* grano.
pin [pin], *n.* alfiler, *m.*; clavija; clavo; prendedor, *m.*; *pins and needles*, agujetas, *f.pl.*, aguijones, *m.pl.*—*v.t.* prender con alfileres; enclavijar; sujetar.
pinafore ['pinəfɔ:], *n.* delantal, *m.*
pince-nez ['pɛ̃snei], *n.* quevedos, *m.pl.*
pincers ['pinsəz], *n.pl.* tenazas; pinzas, *f.pl.*
pinch [pintʃ], *n.* pellizco; pulgarada; polvo; apuro; dolor, *m.*; *at a* —, en caso de apuro. —*v.t.* pellizcar; apretar; hurtar, birlar; coger, prender.—*v.i.* pellizcar; apretar; economizar.
pincushion ['pinkuʃən], *n.* acerico.
pine (I) [pain], *n.* pino; madera de pino.
pine (2) [pain], *v.i.* languidecer, consumirse; *to* — *for*, suspirar por; *to* — *away*, languidecer, morirse de pena.
pineapple ['painæpl], *n.* piña; ananás, *m.sg.*
pine-cone ['painkoun], *n.* piña.
pine-needle ['painni:dl], *n.* pinocha.
ping-pong ['piŋpɔŋ], *n.* 'ping-pong', *m.*, tenis (*m.*) de mesa.
pin-head ['pinhed], *n.* cabeza de alfiler.
pinion ['pinjən], *n.* piñón, *m.*; ala; alón, *m.*; —*v.t.* atar las alas; maniatar; trincar.
pink (I) [piŋk], *a.* rosado.—*n.* clavel, *m.*; color (*m.*) de rosa; casaquín (*m.* de caza); modelo; *in the* —, en sana salud.
pink (2) [piŋk], *v.i.* picar.
pinking ['piŋkiŋ], *n.* picadura.
pin-money ['pinmʌni], *n.* alfileres, *m.pl.*
pinnace ['pinis], *n.* pinaza.
pinnacle ['pinəkl], *n.* pináculo; cumbre, *f.*
pin-point ['pinpɔint], *n.* punta de alfiler.
pint [paint], *n.* pinta.
pioneer [paiə'niə], *n.* explorador; iniciador; (*mil.*) zapador, *m.*—*v.t.* explorar; introducir.
pious [paiəs], *a.* piadoso, pío, devoto.
pip [pip], *n.* pepita; moquillo; punto.
pipe [paip], *n.* pipa; cañón, *m.*, tubo; trino; (*mus.*) caramillo; (*naut.*) silbo; *waste* —, tubo de relleno, desaguadero; *water* —, cañería; — *clay*, blanquizal, *m.*—*v.t.* silbar; conducir con cañerías.—*v.i.* tocar la gaita; silbar; trinar.
pipe-cleaner ['paipkli:nə], *n.* limpiapipas, *m.sg.*
pipe-line ['paiplain], *n.* cañería; oleoducto.
piper ['paipə], *n.* flautista, *m.f.*; gaitero.
piping ['paipiŋ], *n.* cañería; cordoncillo; trino; — *hot*, hirviente.

piquancy ['pi:kənsi], *n.* picante, *m.*
piquant ['pi:kənt], *a.* picante.
pique [pi:k], *n.* pique, *m.*—*v.t.* picar, irritar; **to — oneself on,** jactarse de; **to be piqued,** estar enojado.
piracy ['paiərəsi], *n.* piratería.
pirate ['paiərit], *n.* pirata, *m.*; (*fig.*) plagiario.—*v.t.* falsificar; plagiar.—*v.i.* piratear; plagiar.
pirouette [piru'et], *n.* pirueta.—*v.i.* hacer piruetas.
pistil ['pistil], *n.* pistilo.
pistol [pistl], *n.* pistola; **— shot,** pistoletazo.
piston ['pistən], *n.* émbolo, pistón, *m.*; (*mus.*) llave, *f.*; **— ring,** aro del pistón; **— rod,** biela; **— stroke,** carrera del émbolo.
pit [pit], *n.* hoyo; foso; (*theat.*) platea; precipicio; boca (*del estómago*).—*v.t.* marcar con hoyos; competir.
pitch (1) [pitʃ], *n.* pez, *f.*, alquitrán, *m.*
pitch (2) [pitʃ], *n.* tiro, alcance, *m.*; pendiente, *f.*; (*mus.*) tono; (*sport*) cancha; (*fig.*) grado; (*naut.*) cabezada; **— and toss,** cara o cruz.—*v.t.* colocar; arrojar, tirar; *pitched battle,* batalla campal.—*v.i.* caer; (*naut.*) cabecear.
pitcher (1) ['pitʃə], *n.* cántaro, jarro.
pitcher (2) ['pitʃə], *n.* (*sport*) lanzador (*m.*) de pelota.
pitchfork ['pitʃfɔ:k], *n.* horquilla.
pitching ['pitʃiŋ], *n.* cabeceo.
piteous ['pitiəs], *a.* lastimero; compasivo.
pitfall ['pitfɔ:l], *n.* trampa; (*fig.*) peligro latente.
pith [piθ], *n.* meollo; médula; (*fig.*) médula; fuerza; quinta esencia.
pithy ['piθi], *a.* meduloso; (*fig.*) enérgico; expresivo.
pitiable ['pitjəbl], *a.* lastimoso, digno de compasión; despreciable.
pitiful ['pitiful], *a.* compasivo; lastimero; miserable.
pitiless ['pitilis], *a.* despiadado.
pitilessness ['pitilisnis], *n.* inhumanidad, *f.*
pittance ['pitəns], *n.* pitanza; zatico.
pitted ['pitid], *a.* picado.
pity ['piti], *n.* piedad, compasión, *f.*; *what a —,* qué lástima; *to take — on,* tener lástima de; *to move to —,* enternecer.—*v.t.* compadecer, tener lástima de.
pivot ['pivət], *n.* pivote, *m.*; (*fig.*) eje, *m.*, punto de partida.—*v.i.* girar sobre un eje.
pixy ['piksi], *n.* duende, *m.*
placard ['plæka:d], *n.* cartel, *m.*
placate [plə'keit], *v.t.* apaciguar, aplacar.
place [pleis], *n.* lugar, *m.*; sitio; puesto; plaza; residencia; punto; posición, *f.*; asiento; *in the first —,* en primer lugar; *in — of,* en lugar de; *out of —,* fuera de lugar; mal a propósito; *to take —,* ocurrir, verificarse; *to give —,* ceder el paso.—*v.t.* poner; colocar; fijar.
placid ['plæsid], *a.* plácido, apacible; sosegado.
placing ['pleisiŋ], *n.* posición; colocación, *f.*
plagiarism ['pleidʒiərizm], *n.* plagio.
plagiarist ['pleidʒiərist], *n.* plagiario.
plagiarize ['pleidʒiəraiz], *v.t.*, *v.i.* plagiar.
plague [pleig], *n.* plaga, peste, *f.*—*v.t.* plagar; (*fig.*) atormentar, importunar.
plaice [pleis], *n.* platija.
plain [plein], *a.* raso, igual, llano; sencillo; claro, evidente; sincero, natural; puro; feo;

— chant, canto llano *o* gregoriano; **— truth,** pura verdad.—*n.* llano, llanura; (*geom.*) plano.
plain-spoken ['plein'spoukən], *a.* franco.
plaintiff ['pleintif], *n.* demandante, *m.f.*
plaintive ['pleintiv], *a.* quejumbroso, lamentoso.
plait [plæt], *n.* trenza.—*v.t.* trenzar; tejer.
plan [plæn], *n.* plan, *m.*, proyecto; plano.—*v.t.* proyectar, planear; trazar.
plane (1) [plein], *n.* (*geom.*) plano; (*carp.*) cepillo; (*fam.*) avión, *m.*—*v.t.* acepillar, alisar.
plane (2) [plein], *n.* (*bot.*) plátano.
planet ['plænit], *n.* planeta, *m.*
planetary ['plænitəri], *a.* planetario.
plank [plæŋk], *n.* tabla.
planking ['plæŋkiŋ], *n.* entablado, tablazón, *m.*
planner ['plænə], *n.* proyectista, *m.f.*, planificador, *m.*
planning ['plæniŋ], *a.* planificación, *f.*
plant [pla:nt], *n.* planta; instalación, *f.*—*v.t.* plantar; colocar, establecer; inculcar.
plantain ['plæntin], *n.* llantén, *m.*
plantation [plæn'teiʃən], *n.* plantación, *f.*
planter ['pla:ntə], *n.* plantador, *m.*; colono.
planting ['pla:ntiŋ], *n.* plantación; introducción, *f.*
plant-pot ['pla:ntpɔt], *n.* florero, tiesto.
plaque [pla:k], *n.* placa; medalla.
plaster ['pla:stə], *n.* yeso; argamasa; (*med.*) emplasto; **— of Paris,** escayola.—*v.t.* enyesar; poner emplastos; (*fig.*) embadurnar.
plasterer ['pla:stərə], *n.* yesero.
plastering ['pla:stəriŋ], *n.* acción (*f.*) de enyesar; enyesado.
plastic ['plæstik], *a.* plástico.—*n.* plástico.—*pl.* materias plásticas, *f.pl.*
plasticine ['plæstisi:n], *n.* plasticina.
plasticity [plæs'tisiti], *n.* plasticidad, *f.*
plate [pleit], *n.* plato; plancha; lámina; vajilla; placa; electrotipo; dentadura postiza.—*v.t.* planchear; platear; niquelar; blindar.
plateau ['plætou], *n.* meseta, altiplanicie, *f.*
plate-glass ['pleit'gla:s], *n.* vidrio plano.
platform ['plætfɔ:m], *n.* plataforma; (*rail.*) andén, *m.*
platinum ['plætinəm], *n.* platino.
platitude ['plætitju:d], *n.* perogrullada; trivialidad, *f.*
platonic [plə'tɔnik], *a.* platónico.
Platonism ['pleitənizm], *n.* platonismo.
platoon [plə'tu:n], *n.* sección, *f.*
plausibility [plɔ:zə'biliti], *n.* plausibilidad, *f.*
plausible ['plɔ:zibl], *a.* plausible.
play [plei], *n.* juego; recreo; diversión, *f.*; movimiento; (*theat.*) comedia, drama, *m.*; pieza; (*mech.*) holgura; **— on words,** retruécano; *to bring into —,* poner en movimiento.—*v.t.* (*mus.*) tocar; tañer; (*theat.*) desempeñar el papel de, representar; manipular, mover; *to — the fool,* hacer el tonto; *to — at,* jugar a; *to — off,* contraponer; *to — second fiddle,* hacer un papel secundario.—*v.i.* jugar; (*mus.*) tocar, tañer; representar; divertirse, recrearse; juguetear; (*mech.*) moverse; *to — fair,* jugar limpio; *to — false,* engañar.
playbill ['pleibil], *n.* cartel, *m.*

player

player [pleiə], *n.* jugador, *m.*; (*mus.*) músico, tocador, *m.*; (*theat.*) actor, *m.*, actriz, *f.*
playfellow [ˈpleifelou], *n.* compañero de juego.
playful [ˈpleiful], *a.* travieso, juguetón.
playgoer [ˈpleigouə], *n.* aficionado al teatro.
playground [ˈpleigraund], *n.* patio de recreo.
playing [ˈpleiiŋ], *n.* juego.
playing-cards [ˈpleiiŋkɑːdz], *n.pl.* naipes, *m.pl.*
playing-field [ˈpleiiŋfiːld], *n.* campo de deportes.
plaything [ˈpleiθiŋ], *n.* juguete, *m.*
playtime [ˈpleitaim], *n.* hora de recreo.
playwright [ˈpleirait], *n.* dramaturgo.
plea [pliː], *n.* excusa, pretexto; súplica; (*jur.*) declaración; acción, *f.*
plead [pliːd], *v.t.* defender; alegar.—*v.i.* (*jur.*) abogar, pleitear; declarar; interceder; suplicar.
pleasant [ˈplezənt], *a.* agradable; ameno; simpático.
pleasantness [ˈplezəntnis], *n.* agrado; placer, *m.*; amabilidad, *f.*
pleasantry [ˈplezəntri], *n.* chanza.
please [pliːz], *v.t.* gustar, agradar, contentar.—*v.i.* gustar, agradar; tener a bien, placer; — *God!* ¡plega a Dios! — *go in,* tenga la bondad de entrar, haga el favor de entrar; *to be hard to* —, ser muy exigente.—*interj.* por favor.
pleased [pliːzd], *a.* contento, satisfecho; encantado.
pleasing [ˈpliːziŋ], *a.* agradable, grato; placentero.
pleasurable [ˈpleʒərəbl], *a.* divertido; agradable.
pleasure [ˈpleʒə], *n.* gusto, placer, *m.*; satisfacción, *f.*; deseo; *to take — in,* disfrutar de; complacerse en; *at* —, a voluntad.
pleasure-boat [ˈpleʒəbout], *n.* bote (*m.*) de recreo.
pleasure-trip [ˈpleʒətrip], *n.* excursión, *f.*
pleat [pliːt], *n.* pliegue, *m.*—*v.t.* plegar.
plebeian [pliˈbiːən], *a.* plebeyo.
plectrum [ˈplektrəm], *n.* plectro.
pledge [pledʒ], *n.* prenda; empeño; brindis, *m.*—*v.t.* empeñar; brindar por; prometer; *to — one's word,* dar su palabra.
plenitude [ˈplenitjuːd], *n.* plenitud, *f.*
plentiful [ˈplentiful], *a.* abundante, copioso.
plenty [ˈplenti], *n.* abundancia; de sobra.
plethora [ˈpleθərə], *n.* plétora.
pleurisy [ˈpluːrisi], *n.* pleuresía.
pliable [ˈplaiəbl], *a.* flexible; dócil.
pliant [ˈplaiənt], *a.* flexible; dócil.
pliers [ˈplaiəz], *n.pl.* alicates, *m.pl.*
plight [plait], *n.* apuro.—*v.t.* **empeñar;** prometer en matrimonio.
plinth [plinθ], *n.* plinto.
plod [plɔd], *v.i.* andar despacio y con dificultad; (*fig.*) trabajar con perseverancia.
plot [plɔt], *n.* parcela; trama, conjuración, *f.*; proyecto; argumento.—*v.t.* trazar; urdir.—*v.i.* conspirar.
plotter [ˈplɔtə], *n.* conspirador, *m.*, conjurado.
plotting [ˈplɔtiŋ], *n.* conspiración; delineación, *f.*
plough [plau], *n.* arado.—*v.t.*, *v.i.* arar; surcar (*las ondas*).
ploughman [ˈplaumən], *n.* arador, *m.*
ploughshare [ˈplauʃeə], *n.* reja de arado.

plover [ˈplʌvə], *n.* avefría.
plow (*U.S.*) [PLOUGH].
pluck [plʌk], *n.* tirón, *m.*; asadura; (*fam.*) valor, *m.*—*v.t.* coger; desplumar; (*mus.*) puntear; *to — up courage,* sacar ánimos.
plucky [ˈplʌki], *a.* (*fam.*) valiente, animoso.
plug [plʌg], *n.* tapón, *m.*; (*elec.*) enchufe, *m.*; nudillo; rollo (*de tabaco*).—*v.t.* tapar, atarugar; rellenar; *to — in,* enchufar.
plum [plʌm], *n.* ciruela; (*fig.*) golosina; — *tree,* ciruelo.
plumage [ˈpluːmidʒ], *n.* plumaje, *m.*
plumb [plʌm], *a.* perpendículo; recto.—*adv.* a plomo.—*v.t.* aplomar; (*naut.*) sondar.
plumber [ˈplʌmə], *n.* fontanero.
plumbing [ˈplʌmiŋ], *n.* fontanería; cañerías, *f.pl.*
plumb-line [ˈplʌmlain], *n.* plomada.
plum-cake [ˈplʌmkeik], *n.* pastel (*m.*) de fruta.
plume [pluːm], *n.* pluma; penacho.—*v.t.* desplumar; adornar con plumas.
plummet [ˈplʌmit], *n.* plomada; (*naut.*) sonda.
plump [plʌmp], *a.* rollizo, gordiflón.—*v.t.* dejar caer; hinchar; *to — for,* (*fig.*) votar por, favorecer.—*v.i.* hincharse; caer a plomo.
plumpness [ˈplʌmpnis], *n.* gordura.
plunder [ˈplʌndə], *n.* pillaje, botín, *m.*—*v.t.* saquear; pillar.
plunge [plʌndʒ], *n.* sumersión, *f.*; (*fig.*) paso.—*v.t.* chapuzar; sumergir; hundir.—*v.i.* sumergirse; precipitarse; encabritarse (*caballo, buque, etc.*); jugarse el todo.
plunger [ˈplʌndʒə], *n.* émbolo.
pluperfect [pluːˈpəːfikt], *a.*, *n.* pluscuamperfecto.
plural [ˈpluərəl], *a.*, *n.* plural, *m.*
plurality [pluəˈræliti], *n.* pluralidad, *f.*
plus [plʌs], *a.*, *adv.* más; (*math.*, *elec.*) positivo; — *fours,* pantalones (*m.pl.*) de golf.
plush [plʌʃ], *n.* felpa.
plutocracy [pluːˈtɔkrəsi], *n.* plutocracia.
plutocrat [ˈpluːtəkræt], *n.* plutócrata, *m.f.*
ply [plai], *n.* doblez; inclinación, *f.*; *three* —, tres hojas.—*v.t.* aplicar; emplear; ejercer; *to — with,* servir con; importunar con.—*v.i.* ir y venir; hacer el servicio.
pneumatic [njuːˈmætik], *a.* neumático.
pneumonia [njuːˈmouniə], *n.* pulmonía.
poach (1) [poutʃ], *v.t.* escalfar (*huevos*).
poach (2) [poutʃ], *v.t.* cazar o pescar en terreno vedado; (*fig.*) invadir; hurtar.—*v.i.* cazar o pescar en terreno vedado; meterse en los negocios de otros.
poacher [ˈpoutʃə], *n.* cazador ilegal, *m.*
poaching [ˈpoutʃiŋ], *n.* caza ilegal.
pock [pɔk], *n.* pústula.
pocket [ˈpɔkit], *n.* bolsillo; (*min.*) depósito; (*fig.*) bolsa; tronera (*billar*); *in* —, con ganancia; *out of* —, con pérdida.—*v.t.* meter en el bolsillo; tomar; *to — one's pride,* tragarse el orgullo.
pocket-book [ˈpɔkitbuk], *n.* cartera.
pocket-handkerchief [ˈpɔkitˈhæŋkətʃif], *n.* pañuelo de bolsillo.
pocket-knife [ˈpɔkitnaif], *n.* cortaplumas, *m.sg.*
pocket-money [ˈpɔkitmʌni], *n.* alfileres, *m.pl.*

pock-marked ['pɔkmɑːkd], *a.* picado de viruelas.
pod [pɔd], *n.* vaina.
poem ['pouim], *n.* poema, *m.*, poesía.
poet ['pouit], *n.* poeta, *m.*
poetaster [poui'tæstə], *n.* poetastro.
poetess ['pouitis], *n.* poetisa.
poetic [pou'etik], *a.* poético.
poetics [pou'etiks], *n.sg.* poética.
poetry ['pouitri], *n.* poesía.
pogrom ['pɔgrəm], *n.* pogrom, *m.*
poignancy ['pɔinjənsi], *n.* patetismo; acerbidad, *f.*; fuerza.
poignant ['pɔinjənt], *a.* conmovedor; patético; agudo.
point [pɔint], *n.* punto; punta; (*geog.*) cabo; (*rail.*) aguja; agudeza; cuestión, *f.*; detalle; fin, *m.*; peculiaridad, *f.*; (*com.*) entero; *to be on the — of,* estar a punto de; *to come to the —,* venir al caso; *to score a —,* ganar un tanto; *in — of,* tocante a; *on all points,* de todos lados; *in —,* a propósito; *in — of fact,* en efecto; *— of view,* punto de vista; *— of order,* cuestión (*f.*) de orden.—*v.t.* afilar, puntuar; rejuntar; *to — out,* señalar; *to — a moral,* inculcar una moral.—*v.i.* señalar; mostrar la caza; *to — at,* señalar con el dedo; *to — to,* indicar.
point-blank ['pɔint'blæŋk], *a., adv.* de punto en blanco.
pointed ['pɔintid], *a.* afilado, puntiagudo; (*arch.*) ojival; (*fig.*) directo; intencionado.
pointer ['pɔintə], *n.* puntero; perro perdiguero; aguja; (*fig.*) índice, *m.*
pointing ['pɔintiŋ], *n.* puntería; relleno de juntas.
pointless ['pɔintlis], *a.* sin punta; fútil.
poise [pɔiz], *n.* equilibrio; aplomo; porte, *m.*— *v.t.* balancear; pesar.—*v.i.* estar suspendido.
poison [pɔizn], *n.* veneno.—*v.t.* envenenar.
poisoner ['pɔizne], *n.* envenenador.
poisonous ['pɔiznəs], *a.* venenoso.
poke [pouk], *n.* empujón, *m.*—*v.t., v.i.* hurgar; atizar (*fuego*); empujar; *to — one's nose in,* meterse en todo; *to — fun at,* burlarse de.
poker (1) ['poukə], *n.* hurgón; atizador, *m.*
poker (2) ['poukə], *n.* poker, *m.*
poky ['pouki], *a.* pequeño; miserable.
Poland ['poulənd], *n.* Polonia.
polar ['poulə], *a.* polar; *— bear,* oso blanco.
polarize ['pouləraiz], *v.t.* polarizar.
Pole [poul], *n.* polaco.
pole [poul], *n.* (*geog., geom.*) polo; (*sport*) pértiga; palo; mástil.
poleaxe ['poulæks], *n.* hachuela de mano.—*v.t.* aturdir.
polecat ['poulkæt], *n.* mofeta.
polemic [pə'lemik], *n.* polémica.
police [pə'liːs], *n.* policía; *— constable,* agente (*m.*) de policía; *— force,* policía; *— station,* comisaría.—*v.t.* mantener el orden público en; administrar.
policeman [pə'liːsmən], *n.* policía, *m.*
policewoman [pə'liːswumən], *n.* agente femenino de policía.
policy ['pɔlisi], *n.* política; sistema, *m.*; curso de acción; póliza de seguro.
poliomyelitis [pouliomaiə'laitis], *n.* poliomielitis, *f.*
Polish ['pouliʃ], *a.* polaco, polonés.
polish ['pɔliʃ], *n.* pulimento; cera; barniz, *m.*; tersura; (*fig.*) urbanidad, *f.*—*v.t.* pulir; dar

brillo; (*fig.*) civilizar; *to — off,* (*fam.*) terminar; acabar con; engullir.
polished ['pɔliʃt], *a.* pulido; culto; cortés.
polisher ['pɔliʃə], *n.* pulidor, *m.*; *French —,* barnizador, *m.*
polite [pə'lait], *a.* cortés, bien educado.
politeness [pə'laitnis], *n.* cortesía.
politic ['pɔlitik], *a.* político.
political [pə'litikəl], *a.* político.
politician [pɔli'tiʃən], *n.* político.
politics ['pɔlitiks], *n.pl.* política; ciencias políticas, *f.pl.*
polka ['pɔlkə], *n.* polca.
polka-dotted ['pɔlkə'dɔtid], *a.* de *o* con lunares.
poll [poul], *n.* lista electoral; escrutinio; cabeza; votación, *f.*; colegio electoral.—*v.t.* descabezar; podar; descornar; escrutar; dar voto; recoger (*votos*).
pollen ['pɔlin], *n.* polen, *m.*
polling ['pouliŋ], *n.* votación, *f.*
pollute [pə'luːt], *v.t.* ensuciar; contaminar; profanar.
pollution [pə'luːʃən], *n.* contaminación; profanación; corrupción, *f.*
polygamous [pə'ligəməs], *a.* polígamo.
polygamy [pə'ligəmi], *n.* poligamia.
polyglot ['pɔliglɔt], *a.,* *n.* poligloto.
polygon ['pɔligən], *n.* polígono.
Polynesian [pɔli'niːzjən], *a.,* *n.* polinesio.
polysyllabic ['pɔlisi'læbik], *a.* polisílabo.
polytechnic [pɔli'teknik], *a.* politécnico.
polytheism ['pɔliθiːizm], *n.* politeísmo.
pomade [pə'meid], *n.* pomada.
pomegranate ['pɔmigrænit], *n.* granada.
pommel ['pʌml], *n.* pomo.—*v.t.* aporrear.
pomp [pɔmp], *n.* pompa, fausto.
pompom ['pɔmpɔm], *n.* pompón, *m.*
pomposity [pɔm'pɔsiti], *n.* pomposidad, *f.*
pompous ['pɔmpəs], *a.* pomposo.
pond [pɔnd], *n.* estanque, *m.*, charca.
ponder ['pɔndə], *v.t.* ponderar, pesar, estudiar.—*v.i.* meditar.
ponderous ['pɔndərəs], *a.* abultado; pesado.
pontiff ['pɔntif], *n.* pontífice, *m.*
pontifical [pɔn'tifikəl], *a.* pontificio.
pontificate [pɔn'tifikit], *n.* pontificado.— [pɔn'tifikeit], *v.t.* pontificar.
pontoon [pɔn'tuːn], *n.* pontón, *m.*
pony ['pouni], *n.* jaca.
poodle [puːdl], *n.* perro de lanas.
pooh-pooh [puːˈpuː], *v.t.* tratar con desprecio.
pool [puːl], *n.* estanque, *m.*; charco; rebalsa; polla (*en el juego*); conjunto; *football pool(s),* quiniela(s).—*v.t.* combinar.
poop [puːp], *n.* popa.
poor [puə], *a.* pobre; infeliz; malo; *the —,* los pobres.
poor-box ['puəbɔks], *n.* cepillo de pobres.
poor-house ['puəhaus], *n.* casa de caridad.
pop [pɔp], *n.* detonación, *f.*; taponazo; (*fam.*) gaseosa.—*v.t.* meter de repente; disparar; hacer saltar.—*v.i.* saltar; dar un chasquido; *to — in,* (*fam.*) visitar; entrar de repente; *to — off,* (*fam.*) marcharse; estirar la pata; *to — out,* (*fam.*) salir.— *interj.* ¡pum!
pop (2) [pɔp], *n.* (*fam.*) música yeyé.
Pope [poup], *n.* papa, *m.*
popery ['poupəri], *n.* papismo.
poplar ['pɔplə], *n.* álamo.
poplin ['pɔplin], *n.* popelina.

poppy ['pɔpi], *n.* amapola, adormidera.
populace ['pɔpjuləs], *n.* pueblo; populacho.
popular ['pɔpjulə], *a.* popular.
popularity [pɔpju'læriti], *n.* popularidad, *f.*
popularize ['pɔpjuləraiz], *v.t.* popularizar, vulgarizar.
populate ['pɔpjuleit], *v.t.* poblar.
population [pɔpju'leiʃən], *n.* población, *f.*
populous ['pɔpjuləs], *a.* populoso.
porcelain ['pɔːslin], *n.* porcelana.
porch [pɔːtʃ], *n.* pórtico; vestíbulo.
porcupine ['pɔːkjupain], *n.* puerco espín.
pore (1) [pɔː], *n.* poro.
pore (2) [pɔː], *v.i.* **to — over,** leer con mucha atención.
pork [pɔːk], *n.* carne (*f.*) de cerdo.
pornographic [pɔːnə'græfik], *a.* pornográfico.
pornography [pɔː'nɔgrəfi], *n.* pornografía.
porous ['pɔːrəs], *a.* poroso.
porpoise ['pɔːpəs], *n.* marsopa.
porridge ['pɔridʒ], *n.* puches, *m.* o *f.* *pl.*
port (1) [pɔːt], *n.* puerto; porta.
port (2) [pɔːt], *n.* vino de Oporto.
port (3) [pɔːt], *n.* (*naut.*) babor (*costado izquierdo*), *m.*
portable ['pɔːtəbl], *a.* portátil.
portal [pɔːtl], *n.* portal, *m.*
portcullis [pɔː'tkʌlis], *n.* rastrillo.
portend [pɔː'tend], *v.t.* presagiar.
portent ['pɔːtent], *n.* augurio, presagio.
portentous [pɔː'tentəs], *a.* portentoso, ominoso.
porter ['pɔːtə], *n.* portero, mozo; conserje, *m.*; cerveza negra.
portfolio [pɔː't'fouljou], *n.* cartera; carpeta; (*pol.*) ministerio.
porthole ['pɔːthoul], *n.* porta.
portion ['pɔːʃən], *n.* porción, parte, *f.*; dote, *m.* o *f.*
portly ['pɔːtli], *a.* corpulento.
portmanteau [pɔː't'mæntou], *n.* maleta.
portrait ['pɔːtreit], *n.* retrato.
portraiture ['pɔːtritʃə], *n.* retrato; pintura.
portray [pɔː'trei], *v.t.* retratar; describir.
portrayal [pɔː'treiəl], *n.* representación, *f.*; pintura.
Portugal ['pɔːtjugəl], *n.* Portugal, *m.*
Portuguese [pɔːtju'giːz], *a.,* *n.* portugués, *m.*
pose [pouz], *n.* actitud, postura; afectación, *f.*—*v.t.* plantear; colocar.—*v.i.* colocarse; adoptar posturas; **to — as,** dárselas de, hacerse pasar por.
poser ['pouzə], *n.* problema, *m.*; pregunta difícil.
position [pə'ziʃən], *n.* posición; situación; condición; actitud, *f.*; puesto; **in a — to,** en estado de.
positive ['pɔzətiv], *a.* positivo; categórico.—*n.* (*phot.*) (prueba) positiva; (*elec.*) positivo.
possess [pə'zes], *v.t.* poseer, tener; gozar de; dominar.
possession [pə'zeʃən], *n.* posesión, *f.*; **to take — of,** apoderarse de; entrar en.
possessive [pə'zesiv], *a.* posesivo.
possessor [pə'zesə], *n.* poseedor, *m.*
possibility [pɔsi'biliti], *n.* posibilidad, *f.*
possible ['pɔsibl], *a.* posible; **as soon as —,** cuanto antes.
post (1) [poust], *n.* correo; poste, *m.*; puesto; **by return of —,** a vuelta de correo;

— **office,** casa de correos.—*v.t.* echar al correo; fijar; colocar; tener al corriente.
post (2) [poust], *prefix.* después de; — **mortem,** autopsia; — **war,** (de la) postguerra.
postage ['poustidʒ], *n.* porte, *m.,* franqueo; — **stamp,** sello.
postal ['poustəl], *a.* postal; — **order,** giro postal.
postcard ['poustkaːd], *n.* tarjeta postal.
poster ['poustə], *n.* cartel, *m.*
posterior [pɔs'tiəriə], *a.* posterior.—*n.* trasero.
posterity [pɔs'teriti], *n.* posteridad, *f.*
postern ['poustəːn], *n.* posterna.
post-haste ['poust'heist], *a.* apresurado; **a** toda prisa.
posthumous ['pɔstjuməs], *a.* póstumo.
postman ['poustmən], *n.* (*pl.* **-men**) cartero.
postmark ['poustmaːk], *n.* matasellos, *m. inv.*
postmaster ['poustmaːstə], *n.* administrador (*m.*) de correos.
post-paid ['poust'peid], *a.* franco.
postpone [pous'poun], *v.t.* aplazar.
postponement [pous'pounmənt], *n.* aplazamiento.
postscript ['pous(t)skript], *n.* posdata.
postulate ['pɔstjuleit], *n.* postulado.—*v.t.* postular.
posture ['pɔstʃə], *n.* postura, actitud; situación, *f.*
posy ['pouzi], *n.* ramillete, *m.*
pot [pɔt], *n.* olla, marmita; orinal, *m.*—*v.t.* preservar; plantar en tiestos.
potage [pɔ'taːʒ], *n.* potaje, *m.*
potash ['pɔtæʃ], *n.* potasa.
potassium [pə'tæsjəm], *n.* potasio.
potato [pə'teitou], *n.* patata; **sweet —,** batata.
pot-belly ['pɔt'beli], *n.* panza; **pot-bellied,** panzudo.
pot-boiler ['pɔtbɔilə], *n.* obra hecha de prisa para ganarse la vida.
potency ['poutənsi], *n.* potencia, fuerza.
potent ['poutənt], *a.* potente, fuerte.
potentate ['poutənteit], *n.* potentado.
potential [pə'tenʃəl], *a.* potencial; virtual.
potentiality [pətenʃi'æliti], *n.* potencialidad, *f.*
pothole ['pɔthoul], *n.* bache, *m.*
pothook ['pɔthuk], *n.* garabato; palote, *m.*
potion ['pouʃən], *n.* poción, *f.*
pot-luck ['pɔt'lʌk], *n.* fortuna del puchero.
potman ['pɔtmən], *n.* mozo de taberna.
pot-pourri ['poupu'riː], *n.* (*mus.*) popurrí, *m.*; (*fig.*) baturillo.
pot-shot ['pɔt'ʃɔt], *n.* tiro al azar.
potter (1) ['pɔtə], *n.* alfarero.
potter (2) ['pɔtə], *v.i.* andar de vagar.
pottery ['pɔtəri], *n.* alfarería.
pouch [pautʃ], *n.* bolsa; tabaquera, petaca.
poultice ['poultis], *n.* emplasto.—*v.t.* bizmar.
poultry ['poultri], *n.* volatería.
poultry-farming ['poultri'faːming], *n.* avicultura.
pounce [pauns], *n.* calada.—*v.i.* calarse.
pound (1) [paund], *n.* libra.
pound (2) [paund], *n.* corral (*m.*) de concejo.
pound (3) [paund], *v.t.* golpear.
pour [pɔː], *v.t.* verter; vaciar; derramar.—*v.i.* fluir; **to — with rain,** diluviar, llover a cántaros.
pouring ['pɔːring], *a.* torrencial.
pout [paut], *n.* pucherito.—*v.i.* hacer pucheritos.

pouting ['pautiŋ], *n.* pucheritos, *m.pl.*
poverty ['povəti], *n.* pobreza.
powder ['paudə], *n.* polvo; pólvora.—*v.t.*
pulverizar; polvorear.—*v.i.* pulverizarse;
ponerse polvos.
powdery ['paudəri], *a.* polvoriento.
power [pauə], *n.* poder, *m.*; fuerza; facultad,
f.; potencia; — *of attorney*, (*jur.*) procuración, *f.*; *the Great Powers*, las grandes
potencias; *the powers that be*, los que
mandan.
powerful ['pauəful], *a.* poderoso, potente;
fuerte; eficaz.
powerless ['pauəlis], *a.* impotente; ineficaz.
power-station ['pauəsteiʃən], *n.* terma,
central (*f.*) de energía eléctrica.
pox [poks], *n.* viruelas,*f.pl.*; sífilis,*f.*
practicable ['præktikəbl], *a.* practicable,
factible.
practical ['præktikəl], *a.* práctico; — *joke*,
broma.
practice ['præktis], *n.* práctica; costumbre,*f.*;
experiencia; profesión, *f.*; clientela; ejercicio; *to put into* —, poner en obra;*out of*
—, desentrenado.
practise ['præktis], *v.t.* practicar; ejercer;
entrenarse en.—*v.i.* practicar; estudiar.
practised ['præktist], *a.* experimentado.
practitioner [præk'tiʃənə], *n.* practicante, *m.*;
médico.
pragmatic [præg'mætik], *a.* pragmático,
práctico.
prairie ['prɛəri], *n.* pradera; pampa.
praise [preiz], *n.* elogio; alabanza.—*v.t.*
elogiar, alabar.
praiseworthy ['preizwɔːði], *a.* digno de
alabanza, loable.
pram [præm], *n.* (*fam.*) [PERAMBULATOR].
prance [prɑːns], *n.* cabriola.—*v.i.* cabriolar,
encabritarse.
prank [præŋk], *n.* travesura.
prate [preit], *v.i.* chacharear.
prattle [prætl], *n.* cháchara.—*v.t.* balbucear.
—*v.i.* chacharear.
prawn [prɔːn], *n.* gamba.
pray [prei], *v.t., v.i.* rezar; suplicar; implorar.
prayer [prɛə], *n.* oración, *f.*; plegaria;
súplica; — *book*, devocionario.
praying ['preiiŋ], *n.* rezo; suplicación, *f.*
preach [priːtʃ], *v.t., v.i.* predicar.
preacher ['priːtʃə], *n.* predicador, *m.*
preaching ['priːtʃiŋ], *n.* predicación, *f.*
preamble [priː'æmbl], *n.* preámbulo.
prearrange [priːə'reindʒ], *v.t.* arreglar de
antemano, predisponer.
prebendary ['prebəndəri], *n.* prebendado.
precarious [pri'kɛərjəs], *a.* precario; incierto,
inseguro.
precariousness [pri'kɛərjəsnis], *n.* estado
precario, condición (*f.*) incierta; incertidumbre, inseguridad, *f.*
precaution [pri'kɔːʃən], *n.* precaución, *f.*
precautionary [pri'kɔːʃənəri], *a.* preventivo.
precede [pri'siːd], *v.t.* preceder, anteceder;
exceder en importancia.—*v.i.* tener la
primacía ir delante.
precedence [pri'siːdəns], *n.* prioridad; superioridad, *f.*; precedencia.
precedent ['presidənt], *n.* precedente, *m.*
preceding [pri'siːdiŋ], *a.* precedente.
precept ['priːsept], *n.* precepto.
preceptor [pri'septə], *n.* preceptor, *m.*

precinct ['priːsiŋkt], *n.* recinto; barrio.—*pl.*
recinto.
precious ['preʃəs], *a.* precioso; de gran valor;
querido.—*adv.* (*fam.*) — *little*, muy poco.
precipice ['presipis], *n.* precipicio.
precipitant [pri'sipitənt], *a.* precipitado.
precipitate [pri'sipiteit], *v.t.* precipitar.—*v.i.*
precipitarse.
precipitation [prisipi'teiʃən], *n.* precipitación, *f.*; (*chem.*) precipitado.
precipitous [pri'sipitəs], *a.* precipitoso,
escarpado.
precise [pri'sais], *a.* preciso; exacto; justo;
escrupuloso; puntual; (*fam.*) pedante,
ceremonioso.
precision [pri'siʒən], *n.* precisión, *f.*; exactitud;
escrupulosidad, *f.*
preclude [pri'kluːd], *v.t.* impedir; excluir.
precocious [pri'kouʃəs], *a.* precoz.
preconceive [priːkən'siːv], *v.t.* preconcebir.
preconception [priːkən'sepʃən], *n.* opinión
(*f.*) preconcebida; prejuicio.
precursor [pri'kɔːsə], *n.* precursor, *m.*
predatory ['predətəri], *a.* rapaz; voraz.
predecessor ['priːdisesə], *n.* predecesor, *m.*;
antepasado.
predestination [priːdesti'neiʃən], *n.* predestinación, *f.*
predestine [priː'destin], *v.t.* predestinar.
predetermine [priːdi'tɔːmin], *v.t.* predeterminar.
predicament [pri'dikəmənt], *n.* apuro;
(*phil.*) predicamento.
predicate ['predikit], *n.* predicado.—
['predikeit], *v.t.* afirmar.
predict [pri'dikt], *v.t.*—predecir, pronosticar.
prediction [pri'dikʃən], *n.* predicción, *f.*;
pronóstico.
predilection [priːdi'lekʃən], *n.* predilección,*f.*
predispose [priːdis'pouz], *v.t.* predisponer.
predisposition [priːdispə'ziʃən], *n.* predisposición, *f.*
predominance [pri'dominəns], *n.* predominio.
predominant [pri'dominənt], *a.* predominante.
predominate [pri'domineit], *v.i.* predominar.
pre-eminence [priː'eminəns], *n.* preeminencia; primacía.
pre-eminent [priː'eminənt], *a.* preeminente;
extraordinario.
preen [priːn], *v.i.* limpiar las plumas; *to —
oneself*, jactarse.
preface ['prefis], *n.* prólogo; (*eccl.*) prefacio.
—*v.t.* poner un prólogo.
prefatory ['prefətəri], *a.* preliminar.
prefect ['priːfekt], *n.* prefecto.
prefecture ['priːfektjuə], *n.* prefectura.
prefer [pri'fɔː], *v.t.* preferir; ascender; presentar.
preferable ['prefərəbl], *a.* preferible.
preference ['prefərəns], *n.* preferencia.
preferential [prefə'renʃəl], *a.* preferente.
preferment [pri'fɔːmənt], *n.* promoción, *f.*;
ascenso; puesto eminente.
prefix ['priːfiks], *n.* prefijo.—*v.t.* prefijar.
pregnancy ['pregnənsi], *n.* embarazo, preñez
f.
pregnant ['pregnənt], *a.* embarazada, preñada, encinta; (*fig.*) fértil.
prehensile [pri'hensail], *a.* prensil.
prehistoric [priːhis'torik], *a.* prehistórico.

prejudge [pri:'dʒʌdʒ], *v.t.* prejuzgar.
prejudice ['predʒudis], *n.* prejuicio; (*jur.*) perjuicio.—*v.t.* perjudicar; influir.
prejudicial [predʒju'diʃəl], *a.* perjudicial.
prelate ['prelit], *n.* prelado.
preliminary [pri'liminəri], *a.*, *n.* preliminar, *m.*
prelude ['prelju:d], *n.* preludio; presagio.—*v.t.*, *v.i.* preludiar.
premature [premə'tjuə], *a.* prematuro.
premeditate [pri:'mediteit], *v.t.* premeditar.
premeditation [pri:medi'teiʃən], *n.* premeditación, *f.*
premier ['premiə], *a.* primero, principal.—*n.* primer ministro; presidente (*m.*) del consejo.
première ['premiɛə], *n.* estreno.
premise ['premis], *n.* premisa.—*pl.* recinto; local, *m.*; tierras, *f.pl.*
premium ['pri:mjəm], *n.* premio; (*com.*) prima; *at a —*, a prima; (*fig.*) en gran demanda.
premonition [pri:mə'niʃən], *n.* presentimiento.
preoccupation [pri:ɔkju'peiʃən], *n.* preocupación, *f.*
preoccupied [pri:'ɔkjupaid], *a.* preocupado; absorto.
preoccupy [pri:'ɔkjupai], *v.t.* preocupar.
preordain [pri:ɔ:'dein], *v.t.* preordenar; predestinar.
prepaid [pri:'peid], *a.* porte pagado. [PREPAY].
preparation [prepə'reiʃən], *n.* preparación; disposición, *f.*; (*med.*) preparado.
preparatory [pri'pærətəri], *a.* preparatorio; preliminar.
prepare [pri'pɛə], *v.t.* preparar; equipar; aderezar.—*v.i.* prepararse.
preparedness [pri'pɛədnis], *n.* estado de preparación.
prepay [pri:'pei], *v.t.* (*conjug. like* PAY) pagar por adelantado.
preponderance [pri'pɔndərəns], *n.* preponderancia.
preposition [prepə'ziʃən], *n.* preposición, *f.*
prepossessing [pri:pə'zesiŋ], *a.* atractivo.
preposterous [pri'pɔstərəs], *a.* absurdo, ridículo.
prerequisite [pri:'rekwizit], *a.*, *n.* requisito.
prerogative [pri'rɔgətiv], *n.* prerrogativa.
presage ['presidʒ], *n.* presagio.—[pri'seidʒ], *v.t.* presagiar.
presbyterian [prezbi'tiəriən], *a.*, *n.* presbiteriano.
presbytery ['prezbitəri], *n.* presbiterio.
prescient ['pri:ʃiənt], *a.* presciente.
prescribe [pris'kraib], *v.t.*, *v.i.* prescribir; (*med.*) recetar; (*jur.*) dar leyes.
prescription [pris'kripʃən], *n.* prescripción, *f.*; (*med.*) receta.
presence ['prezəns], *n.* presencia; aparición, *f.*; — *of mind*, presencia de ánimo.
present (1) ['prezənt], *a.* presente; actual; *to be — at*, asistir a.—*n.* presente, *m.*; actualidad, *f.*
present (2) [pri'zent], *v.t.* presentar; regalar, dar; manifestar.—['prezənt], *n.* regalo, presente, *m.*
presentable [pri'zentəbl], *a.* presentable.
presentation [prezən'teiʃən], *n.* presentación, *f.*; — *copy*, ejemplar (*m.*) de regalo.
present-day ['prezənt'dei], *a.* actual.

presentiment [pri'zentimənt], *n.* presentimiento.
presently ['prezəntli], *adv.* luego, dentro de poco; (*U.S.*) al presente.
preservation [prezə'veiʃən], *n.* preservación; conservación, *f.*
preservative [pri'zə:vətiv], *a.*, *n.* preservativo.
preserve [pri'zə:v], *n.* conserva; compota; coto.—*v.t.* preservar; conservar; proteger; garantizar.
preside [pri'zaid], *v.i.* presidir; *to — over*, presidir.
presidency ['prezidənsi], *n.* presidencia.
president ['prezidənt], *n.* presidente, *m.*; presidenta.
presidential [prezi'denʃəl], *a.* presidencial.
presiding [pri'zaidiŋ], *a.* que preside; tutelar.
press (1) [pres], *n.* urgencia; apretón, *m.*; armario; muchedumbre, *f.*; imprenta; prensa; *in the —*, en prensa; *— agent*, agente (*m.*) de publicidad; *— box*, tribuna de la prensa.—*v.t.* apretar; prensar; exprimir; abrumar; oprimir; obligar; apremiar; acosar; planchar; insistir.—*v.i. to — on*, avanzar; apretar el paso; *to — for*, exigir.
press (2) [pres], *n.* leva forzada.—*v.t.* hacer levas.
press-gang ['pres'gæŋ], *n.* ronda de matrícula.
pressing ['presiŋ], *a.* urgente, importuno, apremiante.—*n.* presión, *f.*; prensadura; expresión (*f.*) (de zumo); planchado.
press-stud ['presstʌd], *n.* botón automático.
pressman ['presmən], *n.* tirador, *m.*; periodista, *m.f.*
pressure ['preʃə], *n.* presión; opresión, *f.*; peso; apremio; impulso; apretón, *m.*
pressure-cooker ['preʃə'kukə], *n.* olla exprés, autoclave, *f.*
pressure-gauge ['preʃə'geidʒ], *n.* manómetro.
prestige [pres'ti:ʒ], *n.* prestigio.
presumable [pri'zju:məbl], *a.* presumible.
presume [pri'zju:m], *v.t.* presumir; suponer.—*v.i.* presumir; jactarse; abusar.
presumption [pri'zʌmpʃən], *n.* suposición, presunción, *f.*; insolencia.
presumptive [pri'zʌmptiv], *a.* presunto; presuntivo.
presumptuous [pri'zʌmptjuəs], *a.* presuntuoso, presumido.
presuppose [pri:sə'pouz], *v.t.* presuponer.
pretence [pri'tens], *n.* pretexto; afectación, *f.*; fingimiento; pretensión, *f.*; *false pretences*, apariencias fingidas, *f.pl.*; *under — of*, so pretexto de.
pretend [pri'tend], *v.t.* fingir.—*v.i.* fingir; pretender.
pretender [pri'tendə], *n.* pretendiente, *m.*; hipócrita, *m.f.*
pretension [pri'tenʃən], *n.* pretensión, *f.*; simulación, *f.*
pretentious [pri'tenʃəs], *a.* presumido; hinchado.
pretentiousness [pri'tenʃəsnis], *n.* hinchazón, *m.*
preterite ['pretərit], *n.* pretérito.
pretext ['pri:tekst], *n.* pretexto.
prettiness ['pritinis], *n.* lo bonito; gracia.

pretty ['priti], *a.* bonito; guapo, lindo; mono.—*adv.* bastante; muy; casi.

prevail [pri'veil], *v.i.* prevalecer, predominar; vencer; *to — upon,* persuadir.

prevailing [pri'veiliŋ], *a.* predominante; general; común.

prevalence ['prevələns], *n.* predominio.

prevalent ['prevələnt], *a.* prevaleciente; predominante; general; común.

prevaricate [pri'værikeit], *v.i.* tergiversar.

prevarication [priværi'keiʃən], *n.* tergiversación, *f.*

prevent [pri'vent], *v.t.* prevenir, impedir; evitar.

preventable [pri'ventəbl], *a.* evitable.

prevention [pri'venʃən], *n.* prevención, *f.*; estorbo.

preventive [pri'ventiv], *a.* preventivo.—*n.* preservativo.

preview ['pri:vju:], *n.* representación privada; vista de antemano.

previous ['pri:vjəs], *a.* previo, anterior.

prey [prei], *n.* presa; víctima; *bird of —,* ave (*f.*) de rapiña.—*v.i.* *to — on,* devorar; hacer presa; oprimir.

price [prais], *n.* precio; valor, *m.*; premio; — *list,* tarifa; *at any —,* cueste lo que cueste; *not at any —,* por nada del mundo.—*v.t.* evaluar; fijar el precio de.

priceless ['praislis], *a.* sin precio; (*fam.*) divertidísimo.

prick [prik], *n.* aguijón, *m.*; picadura; alfilerazo; pinchazo; remordimiento.—*v.t.* picar; punzar; atormentar; avivar.

prickle [prikl], *n.* espina; escozor, *m.*

prickly ['prikli], *a.* espinoso; — *pear,* higo chumbo.

pride [praid], *n.* soberbia; orgullo; aparato, pompa; *to take — in,* estar orgulloso de.— *v.r.* *to — oneself on,* jactarse de.

priest [pri:st], *n.* sacerdote; cura, *m.*

priestess ['pri:stis], *n.* sacerdotisa.

priesthood ['pri:sthud], *n.* sacerdocio.

priestly ['pri:stli], *a.* sacerdotal.

prig [prig], *n.* fatuo.

priggish ['prigiʃ], *a.* fatuo.

prim [prim], *a.* etiquetero, almidonado.

primacy ['praiməsi], *n.* primacía.

primary ['praiməri], *a.* primario.

primate ['praimit], *n.* (*eccl.*) primado.

prime [praim], *a.* primero; de primera clase; excelente; principal.—*n.* aurora; principio; (*fig.*) flor, *f.*, nata; (*eccl.*) prima; (*math.*) número primo.—*v.t.* cebar (*las armas*); preparar.

primer ['praimə], *n.* abecedario; libro escolar; cebador, *m.*

primeval [prai'mi:vəl], *a.* primitivo.

priming ['praimiŋ], *n.* cebo (*de armas*); preparación; imprimación; instrucción, *f.*

primitive ['primitiv], *a.* primitivo; anticuado.

primness ['primnis], *n.* gravedad afectada; escrupulosidad, *f.*

primogeniture [praimou'dʒenitʃə], *n.* primogenitura.

primordial [prai'mɔ:djəl], *a.* primordial.

primrose ['primrouz], *a.* de color amarillo claro.—*n.* primavera.

prince [prins], *n.* príncipe, *m.*

princely ['prinsli], *a.* principesco; magnífico.

princess [prin'ses], *n.* princesa.

principal ['prinsəpəl], *a.* principal.—*n.*

principal; director; rector; (*jur.*) causante, *m.*

principality [prinsi'pæliti], *n.* principado.

principle ['prinsəpl], *n.* principio.

print [print], *n.* impresión, *f.*; imprenta; grabado; prueba positiva; molde, *m.*; huella; estampado; *in —,* en letra de molde; impreso; *out of —,* agotado.—*v.t.* imprimir; estampar; tirar; publicar; (*fig.*) grabar; (*phot.*) tirar una prueba.

printed ['printid], *a.* impreso; — *fabric,* (tejido) estampado; — *matter,* impresos, *m.pl.*

printer ['printə], *n.* impresor, *m.*; tipógrafo.

printing ['printiŋ], *n.* imprenta; tipografía; impresión; estampación, *f.*; — *house,* imprenta; — *press,* prensa tipográfica.

prior [praiə], *a.* anterior.—*n.* prior, *m.*

prioress ['praiəris], *n.* priora.

priority [prai'ɔriti], *n.* prioridad, *f.*

priory ['praiəri], *n.* priorato.

prise [praiz], *v.t.* *to — open,* abrir a la fuerza.

prism [prizm], *n.* prisma, *m.*

prison [prizn], *n.* cárcel, *f.*; prisión, *f.*; — *camp,* campamento de prisioneros.

prisoner ['priznə], *n.* prisionero; preso; *to take —,* prender.

privacy ['praivəsi, 'privəsi], *n.* soledad, *f.*, retiro; secreto.

private ['praivit], *a.* particular, personal; privado; secreto; confidencial; *in —,* confidencialmente; en secreto; — *individual,* particular, *m.f.*; — *parts,* vergüenzas, *f.pl.* —*n.* soldado raso.

privateer [praivə'tiə], *n.* corsario.

privation [prai'veiʃən], *n.* privación, *f.*; carencia.

privet ['privit], *n.* alheña.

privilege ['privilidʒ], *n.* privilegio; exención, *f.*—*v.t.* privilegiar.

privy ['privi], *a.* privado; cómplice; enterado; *Privy Council,* Consejo Privado.—*n.* retrete, *m.*

prize [praiz], *n.* premio; *first —,* premio mayor; premio gordo (*de lotería*).—*v.t.* estimar, apreciar.

prize-fight ['praiz'fait], *n.* partido de boxeo.

prize-fighter ['praiz'faitə], *n.* boxeador, *m.*

probability [prɔbə'biliti], *n.* probabilidad, *f.*

probable ['prɔbəbl], *a.* probable.

probate ['proubeit], *n.* verificación (*f.*) (*de testamentos*).

probation [prə'beiʃən], *n.* probación, *f.*; (*jur.*) libertad vigilada.

probationary [prə'beiʃnəri], *a.* de probación.

probationer [prə'beiʃnə], *n.* novicio, aprendiz, *m.*

probe [proub], *n.* tienta, sonda; (*fig.*) investigación, *f.*—*v.t.* tentar; escudriñar.

probity ['proubiti], *n.* probidad, *f.*

problem ['prɔbləm], *n.* problema, *m.*

problematic [prɔbli'mætik], *a.* problemático.

procedure [prə'si:dʒə], *n.* procedimiento.

proceed [prə'si:d], *v.i.* proceder; seguir adelante; *to — against,* armar un pleito contra.

proceeding [prə'si:diŋ], *n.* procedimiento; conducta; transacción, *f.*—*pl.* actas, *f.pl.*; proceso.

proceeds ['prousi:dz], *n.pl.* producto; ganancias, *f.pl.*

process ['prouses], *n.* proceso; procedimiento; método; curso.—*v.t.* procesar; esterilizar.

procession [prə'seʃən], *n.* (*eccl.*) procesión, *f.*; (*mil.*) desfile, *m.*; cortejo.

proclaim [prə'kleim], *v.t.* proclamar; publicar.

proclamation [proklə'meiʃən], *n.* proclamación; publicación, *f.*; edicto.

proclivity [prə'kliviti], *n.* proclividad, *f.*

procrastinate [prou'kræstineit], *v.i.* dilatar; vacilar.

procrastination [proukræsti'neiʃən], *n.* dilación; vacilación, *f.*

procreate ['proukrieit], *v.t.* procrear.

procreation [proukri'eiʃən], *n.* procreación, *f.*

proctor ['proktə], *n.* procurador; censor (de una universidad), *m.*

procure [prə'kjuə], *v.t.* conseguir, obtener; alcahuetear.

procurer [prə'kjuərə], *n.* alcahuete, *m.*

procuress ['prokjuəris], *n.* alcahueta.

prod [prod], *n.* punzada; pinchazo.—*v.t.* punzar; pinchar.

prodigal ['prodigəl], *a.*, *n.* pródigo.

prodigality [prodi'gæliti], *n.* prodigalidad, *f.*

prodigious [prə'didʒəs], *a.* prodigioso.

prodigy ['prodidʒi], *n.* prodigio.

produce ['prodju:s], *n.* producto; provisiones, *f.pl.*—[prə'dju:s], *v.t.* producir; causar; mostrar; (*geom.*) prolongar; fabricar; (*theat.*) poner en escena; (*com.*) rendir.

producer [prə'dju:sə], *n.* productor, *m.*; (*theat.*) director (*m.*) de escena.

product ['prodʌkt], *n.* producto; resultado.

production [prə'dʌkʃən], *n.* producción, *f.*; producto; (*theat.*) dirección (escénica), *f.*

productive [prə'dʌktiv], *a.* productivo.

productivity [prodʌk'tiviti], *n.* productividad, *f.*

profanation [profə'neiʃən], *n.* profanación, *f.*

profane [prə'fein], *a.* profano.—*v.t.* profanar.

profanity [prə'fæniti], *n.* profanidad, *f.*

profess [prə'fes], *v.t.* profesar; afirmar; declarar; fingir.

professed [prə'fest], *a.* declarado; profeso; fingido.

profession [prə'feʃən], *n.* profesión, declaración, *f.*

professional [prə'feʃənl], *a.*, *n.* profesional, *m.f.*

professor [prə'fesə], *n.* catedrático; profesor, *m.*

professorial [profə'sɔ:rjəl], *a.* de un catedrático; profesorial.

professorship [prə'fesəʃip], *n.* cátedra.

proffer ['profə], *v.t.* ofrecer; proponer.

proficiency [prə'fiʃənsi], *n.* habilidad, *f.*, pericia.

proficient [prə'fiʃənt], *a.* experto, perito.

profile ['proufail], *n.* perfil, *m.*; *in* —, de perfil.—*v.t.* perfilar.

profit ['profit], *n.* provecho; utilidad, *f.*; ventaja; (*com.*) ganancia.—*v.t.* aprovechar. —*v.i.* ganar; (*com.*) sacar ganancia; *to* — *by*, aprovechar.

profitable ['profitəbl], *a.* provechoso, útil; lucrativo.

profiteer [profi'tiə], *n.* estraperlista, *m.f.*—*v.i.* usurear.

profitless ['profitlis], *a.* infructuoso.

profligacy ['profligəsi], *n.* libertinaje, *m.*

profligate ['profligit], *a.*, *n.* libertino.

profound [prə'faund], *a.* profundo.

profundity [prə'fʌnditi], *n.* profundidad, *f.*

profuse [prə'fju:s], *a.* profuso; pródigo.

profusion [prə'fju:ʒən], *n.* profusión; prodigalidad, *f.*

progenitor [prou'dʒenitə], *n.* progenitor, *m.*

progeny ['prodʒini], *n.* prole, *f.*

prognosis [prog'nousis], *n.* pronóstico; prognosis, *f.*

prognosticate [prog'nostikeit], *v.t.* pronosticar.

prognostication [prognosti'keiʃən], *n.* pronosticación, *f.*

programme ['prougræm], *n.* programa, *m.*; *programmed learning*, instrucción programada.

progress ['prougres], *n.* progreso; desarrollo; curso; *to make* —, hacer progresos.— [prə'gres], *v.i.* progresar; avanzar.

progression [prə'greʃən], *n.* progresión, *f.*

progressive [prə'gresiv], *a.* progresivo.

prohibit [prə'hibit], *v.t.* prohibir; impedir.

prohibition [proui'biʃən], *n.* prohibición, *f.*; prohibicionismo (*de bebidas alcohólicas*).

prohibitive [prə'hibitiv], *a.* prohibitivo.

project ['prodʒekt], *n.* proyecto, plan, *m.*— [prə'dʒekt], *v.t.* proyectar.—*v.i.* sobresalir; destacarse.

projectile [prə'dʒektail], *a.* arrojadizo.—*n.* proyectil, *m.*

projecting [prə'dʒektiŋ], *a.* saliente; saltón (*ojos, dientes, etc.*).

projection [prə'dʒekʃən], *n.* proyección, *f.*; lanzamiento.

proletarian [prouli'tɛərjən], *a.*, *n.* proletario.

proletariat [prouli'tɛərjət], *n.* proletariado.

prolific [prə'lifik], *a.* prolífico; fecundo.

prolix ['prouliks], *a.* prolijo.

prolixity [prou'liksiti], *n.* prolijidad, *f.*

prologue ['proulog], *n.* prólogo.—*v.t.* prologar.

prolong [prə'loŋ], *v.t.* prolongar.

prolongation [proulɔŋ'geiʃən], *n.* prolongación, *f.*

promenade [promi'na:d], *n.* paseo; bulevar, *m.*—*v.i.* pasearse.

prominence ['prominəns], *n.* prominencia; protuberancia; eminencia.

prominent ['prominənt], *a.* prominente; eminente; saltón (*ojos, dientes etc.*).

promiscuous [prə'miskjuəs], *a.* promiscuo.

promiscuousness [prə'miskjuəsnis], **promiscuity** [promis'kju:iti], *n.* promiscuidad, *f.*

promise ['promis], *n.* promesa; esperanza; *to break one's* —, faltar a su palabra; *to keep one's* —, cumplir su palabra; *a man of* —, un hombre de porvenir.—*v.t.*, *v.i.* prometer.

promising ['promisiŋ], *a.* prometedor, que promete.

promissory ['promisəri], *a.* promisorio; — *note*, pagaré, *m.*

promontory ['proməntri], *n.* promontorio.

promote [prə'mout], *v.t.* promover, fomentar; ascender; (*com.*) negociar.

promoter [prə'moutə], *n.* promotor, *m.*; empresario.

promotion [prə'mouʃən], *n.* promoción, *f.*; ascenso; fomento.

348

prompt [prɔmpt], *a.* pronto; puntual; diligente; rápido; en punto (*de la hora*).
prompter [ˈprɔmptə], *n.* apuntador, *m.*
prompting [ˈprɔmptiŋ], *n.* sugestión, *f.*—*pl.* dictados, *m.pl.*
promulgate [ˈprɔmɔlgeit], *v.t.* promulgar; publicar.
promulgation [prɔmɔlˈgeiʃən], *n.* promulgación; publicación, *f.*
prone [proun], *a.* postrado; propenso.
proneness [ˈprounnis], *n.* postración; propensión, *f.*
prong [prɔŋ], *n.* horquilla; diente, *m.*; punta.
pronged [prɔŋd], *a.* dentado; provisto de púas.
pronoun [ˈprounaun], *n.* pronombre, *m.*
pronounce [prəˈnauns], *v.t.* pronunciar.
pronounced [prəˈnaunst], *a.* marcado.
pronouncement [prəˈnaunsmənt], *n.* pronunciamiento.
pronunciation [prənʌnsiˈeiʃən], *n.* pronunciación, *f.*
proof [pru:f], *a.* impenetrable.—*n.* prueba; demostración, *f.*; ensayo.—*v.t.* impermeabilizar.
prop [prɔp], *n.* apoyo, puntal, *m.*; rodrigón, *m.*; (*min.*) entibo.—*v.t.* apoyar; ahorquillar; acodalar; apuntalar.
propaganda [prɔpəˈgændə], *n.* propaganda.
propagandist [prɔpəˈgændist], *n.* propagandista, *m.f.*
propagate [ˈprɔpəgeit], *v.t.* propagar.—*v.i.* propagarse.
propagation [prɔpəˈgeiʃən], *n.* propagación, *f.*
propel [prəˈpel], *v.t.* propulsar.
propeller [prəˈpelə], *n.* propulsor, *m.*; hélice, *f.*
propensity [prəˈpensiti], *n.* propensión, *f.*, tendencia.
proper [ˈprɔpə], *a.* propio; particular; apropiado; decoroso; exacto.
property [ˈprɔpəti], *n.* propiedad, *f.*; bienes, *m.pl.*; hacienda.—*pl.* (*theat.*) accesorios, *m.pl.*
prophecy [ˈprɔfisi], *n.* profecía.
prophesy [ˈprɔfisai], *v.t., v.i.* profetizar.
prophet [ˈprɔfit], *n.* profeta, *m.*
prophetess [ˈprɔfitis], *n.* profetisa.
prophetic [prəˈfetik], *a.* profético.
propitiate [prəˈpiʃieit], *v.t.* propiciar; apaciguar.
propitiation [prəpiʃiˈeiʃən], *n.* propiciación, *f.*
propitiatory [prəˈpiʃiətəri], *a.* propiciatorio.
propitious [prəˈpiʃəs], *a.* propicio, favorable.
proportion [prəˈpɔːʃən], *n.* proporción; porción, *f.*; *in — as,* a medida que; *out of —,* desproporcionado.
proportional [prəˈpɔːʃənəl], *a.* proporcional, en proporción.
proportionate [prəˈpɔːʃnit], *a.* proporcionado.
proposal [prəˈpouzəl], *n.* proposición, *f.*; propósito; oferta; declaración, *f.*
propose [prəˈpouz], *v.t.* proponer; brindar.—*v.i.* tener la intención de; declararse.
proposer [prəˈpouzə], *n.* proponente, *m.f.*
proposition [prɔpəˈziʃən], *n.* proposición, *f.*; propósito, proyecto.
propound [prəˈpaund], *v.t.* proponer; presentar.
proprietary [prəˈpraiətəri], *a.* propietario.

proprietor [prəˈpraiətə], *n.* propietario, dueño.
proprietress [prəˈpraiətris], *n.* propietaria, dueña.
propriety [prəˈpraiəti], *n.* decoro; corrección, *f.*
propulsion [prəˈpʌlʃən], *n.* propulsión, *f.*
prorogue [prəˈroug], *v.t.* prorrogar; suspender.
prosaic [prouˈzeiik], *a.* prosaico.
proscribe [prouˈskraib], *v.t.* proscribir.
proscription [prouˈskripʃən], *n.* proscripción, *f.*
prose [prouz], *a.* en prosa.—*n.* prosa; — **writer,** prosista, *m.f.*
prosecute [ˈprɔsikjuːt], *v.t.* proseguir; (*jur.*) procesar.
prosecution [prɔsiˈkjuːʃən], *n.* prosecución; (*jur.*) acusación; parte actora.
prosecutor [ˈprɔsikjuːtə], *n.* demandante, actor, *m.*
proselyte [ˈprɔsilait], *n.* prosélito.
prosody [ˈprɔsədi], *n.* prosodia.
prospect [ˈprɔspekt], *n.* perspectiva; esperanza; probabilidad, *f.*; *to have good prospects,* tener porvenir.—[prəˈspekt], *v.t., v.i.* explorar.
prospective [prəˈspektiv], *a.* previsor; en perspectiva.
prospector [ˈprɔspəktə], *n.* explorador, operador, *m.*
prospectus [prəˈspektəs], *n.* prospecto, programa, *m.*
prosper [ˈprɔspə], *v.t., v.i.* prosperar.
prosperity [prɔsˈperiti], *n.* prosperidad, *f.*
prosperous [ˈprɔspərəs], *a.* próspero; adinerado.
prostitute [ˈprɔstitjuːt], *n.* prostituta, ramera.—*v.t.* prostituir.
prostitution [prɔstiˈtjuːʃən], *n.* prostitución, *f.*
prostrate [ˈprɔstreit], *a.* postrado; tendido.—[prɔsˈtreit], *v.t.* postrar; derribar; rendir.—*v.i.* postrarse.
prostration [prɔsˈtreiʃən], *n.* postración, *f.*; abatimiento.
protect [prəˈtekt], *v.t.* proteger, amparar.
protection [prəˈtekʃən], *n.* protección, *f.*, amparo; salvoconducto; (*pol.*) proteccionismo.
protective [prəˈtektiv], *a.* protector.
protector [prəˈtektə], *n.* protector, *m.*
protectorate [prəˈtektərit], *n.* protectorado, *m.*
protein [ˈproutiːn], *n.* proteína.
protest [ˈproutest], *n.* protesta.—[prəˈtest], *v.t.* protestar.—*v.i.* protestar; quejar(se).
Protestant [ˈprɔtistənt], *a., n.* protestante, *m.f.*
Protestantism [ˈprɔtistəntizm], *n.* protestantismo.
protestation [prɔtesˈteiʃən], *n.* protesta, protestación, *f.*
protocol [ˈproutəkɔl], *n.* protocolo.
protoplasm [ˈproutəplæzm], *n.* protoplasma, *m.*
prototype [ˈproutətaip], *n.* prototipo.
protract [prəˈtrækt], *v.t.* prolongar, dilatar.
protractor [prəˈtræktə], *n.* (*math.*) transportador, *m.*
protrude [prəˈtruːd], *v.t.* sacar fuera.—*v.i.* salir fuera; sobresalir.

protuberance [prə'tju:bərəns], *n.* protuberancia.

protuberant [prə'tju:bərənt], *a.* prominente.

proud [praud], *a.* orgulloso; noble; soberbio; arrogante; espléndido.

prove [pru:v], *v.t.* probar; demostrar; (*jur.*) verificar.—*v.i.* resultar.

provenance ['prɔvinəns], *n.* origen, *m.*

proverb ['prɔvə:b], *n.* refrán, *m.*, proverbio.

proverbial [prə'və:bjəl], *a.* proverbial.

provide [prə'vaid], *v.t.* proveer; proporcionar.—*v.i.* abastecer, proveer lo necesario; *provided that,* con tal que.

providence ['prɔvidəns], *n.* providencia.

provident ['prɔvidənt], *a.* próvido.

providential [prɔvi'denʃəl], *a.* providencial.

provider [prə'vaidə], *n.* proveedor, *m.*

province ['prɔvins], *n.* provincia; (*fig.*) esfera.

provincial [prə'vinʃəl], *a.* provincial.—*n.* provinciano.

provision [prə'viʒən], *n.* provisión; estipulación, *f.*—*pl.* víveres, *m.pl.*—*v.t.* aprovisionar.

provisional [prə'viʒənl], *a.* provisional.

proviso [prə'vaizou], *n.* condición, estipulación, *f.*

provocation [prɔvə'keiʃən], *n.* provocación, *f.*

provocative [prə'vɔkətiv], *a.* provocativo, provocador.

provoke [prə'vouk], *v.t.* provocar; encolerizar; inducir.

provoking [prə'voukin], *a.* provocativo.

provost ['prɔvəst], *n.* preboste; director de colegio; (*Scot.*) alcalde, *m.*

prow [prau], *n.* proa.

prowess ['prauis], *n.* proeza.

prowl [praul], *v.t., v.i.* rondar.

prowler ['praulə], *n.* rondador, *m.*

proximity [prɔk'simiti], *n.* proximidad, *f.*

proxy ['prɔksi], *n.* poder, *m.*; apoderado; delegado; *by* —, por poderes.

prude [pru:d], *n.* mojigato.

prudence ['pru:dəns], *n.* prudencia.

prudent ['pru:dənt], *a.* prudente.

prudery ['pru:dəri], *n.* mojigatería.

prudish ['pru:diʃ], *a.* mojigato.

prune (1) [pru:n], *n.* ciruela pasa.

prune (2) [pru:n], *v.t.* podar.

pruning ['pru:nin], *n.* poda.

pruning-knife ['pru:ninnaif], *n.* podadera.

prurient ['pruəriənt], *a.* lascivo, salaz.

Prussian ['prʌʃən], *a., n.* prusiano.

pry (1) [prai], *v.i.* espiar; fisgonear, entremeterse.

pry (2) [prai], *v.t.* (*mech.*) alzaprimar.

prying ['praiin], *a.* fisgón, curioso.—*n.* fisgoneo; curiosidad, *f.*

psalm [sɑ:m], *n.* salmo.

psalmist ['sɑ:mist], *n.* salmista, *m.*

psalter ['sɔ:ltə], *n.* salterio.

pseudo ['sju:dou], *a.* seudo.

pseudonym ['sju:dənim], *n.* seudónimo.

psychiatrist [sai'kaiətrist], *n.* (p)siquiatra, *m.f.*

psychiatry [sai'kaiətri], *n.* (p)siquiatría.

psychic ['saikik], *a.* (p)síquico.

psycho-analyse [saikou'ænəlaiz], *v.t.* (p)sicoanalizar.

psycho-analysis [saikouə'næləsis], *n.* (p)sicoanálisis, *m.* o *f.*

psycho-analyst [saikou'ænəlist], *n.* (p)sicoanalista, *m.f.*

psychological [saikə'lɔdʒikəl], *a.* (p)sicológico.

psychologist [sai'kɔlədʒist], *n.* (p)sicólogo.

psychology [sai'kɔlədʒi], *n.* (p)sicología.

psychopathic [saikou'pæθik], *a.* (p)sicopático.

pub [pʌb], *n.* (*fam.*) taberna.

puberty ['pju:bəti], *n.* pubertad, *f.*

pubic ['pju:bik], *a.* púbico.

public ['pʌblik], *a., n.* público; — *house,* taberna.

publican ['pʌblikən], *n.* tabernero.

publication [pʌbli'keiʃən], *n.* publicación, *f.*

publicity [pʌb'lisiti], *n.* publicidad, *f.*

public-spirited ['pʌblik'spiritid], *a.* patriótico.

publish ['pʌbliʃ], *v.t.* publicar.

publisher ['pʌbliʃə], *n.* editor, *m.*

puce [pju:s], *a.* color de pulga.

puck [pʌk], *n.* duende, *m.*; trasgo.

pucker ['pʌkə], *n.* arruga; fruncido.—*v.t.* arrugar; fruncir.

pudding ['pudin], *n.* pudín, *m.*; *black* —, morcilla.

puddle [pʌdl], *n.* charco.

puerile ['pjuərail], *a.* pueril.

puff [pʌf], *n.* soplo; resoplido; bocanada (*de humo*); borla (*para polvos*); jactancia; bollo. —*v.t., v.i.* hinchar; soplar.

puffy ['pʌfi], *a.* hinchado; jadeante.

pugilism ['pju:dʒilizm], *n.* pugilato.

pugilist ['pju:dʒilist], *n.* boxeador, *m.*

pugnacious [pʌg'neiʃəs], *a.* pugnaz.

pugnacity [pʌg'næsiti], *n.* pugnacidad, *f.*

pull [pul], *n.* tirón, *m.*; sacudida; tirador (*de puerta*), *m.*; (*fam.*) influencia; ventaja; atracción, *f.*; fuerza.—*v.t.* tirar; arrastrar; sacar; remar; chupar; *to* — *away,* arrancar; quitar con violencia; *to* — *back,* retirar hacia atrás; retener; *to* — *down,* derribar; humillar; *to* — *off,* quitarse (*vestidos*) (*fam.*) conseguir; *to* — *one's leg,* (*fam.*) tomar el pelo a uno; *to* — *out,* sacar; *to* — *to pieces,* hacer pedazos; *to* — *up,* desarraigar.—*v.i.* tirar; remar; *to* — *in* o *up,* enfrenar; parar; *to* — *round,* (*fam.*) reponerse; *to* — *through,* salir de apuros; reponerse.

pulley ['puli], *n.* polea; (*naut.*) garrucha.

pulmonary ['pʌlmənəri], *a.* pulmonar.

pulp [pʌlp], *n.* pulpa; carne (*de fruta*), *f.*; pasta (*para hacer papel*).—*v.t.* reducir a pulpa.

pulpit ['pulpit], *n.* púlpito.

pulsate [pʌl'seit], *v.i.* pulsar.

pulse [pʌls], *n.* pulso; pulsación, *f.*; latido; (*fig.*) ritmo; *to feel the* —, tomar el pulso. —*v.i.* pulsar, latir.

pulverize ['pʌlvəraiz], *v.t.* pulverizar.

pumice ['pʌmis], *n.* piedra pómez.

pump [pʌmp], *n.* bomba; escarpín; surtidor, *m.*—*v.t.* bombear; (*fig.*) sondear; *to* — *up,* inflar.

pumpkin ['pʌmpkin], *n.* calabaza, calabacera.

pun [pʌn], *n.* retruécano, juego de palabras.

Punch [pʌntʃ], *n.* Polichinela, *m.*

punch [pʌntʃ], *n.* puñetazo; punzón, *m.*; taladro; ponche (*bebida*), *m.*—*v.t.* punzar; dar puñetazos.

punctilious [pʌŋk'tiljəs], *a.* puntilloso, escrupuloso.

punctiliousness [pʌŋk'tiljəsnis], *n.* puntualidad, *f.*

punctual ['pʌŋktjuəl], *a.* puntual.

punctuality [pʌŋktju'æliti], *n.* puntualidad, *f.*

punctuate ['pʌŋktjueit], *v.t.* puntuar; (*fig.*) interponer.

punctuation [pʌŋktju'eiʃən], *n.* puntuación, *f.*

puncture ['pʌŋktʃə], *n.* pinchazo; perforación, *f.*; picada.—*v.t.* pinchar; perforar; picar.

pungency ['pʌndʒənsi], *n.* naturaleza picante; mordacidad, *f.*

pungent ['pʌndʒənt], *a.* picante; mordaz.

punish ['pʌniʃ], *v.t.* castigar.

punishable ['pʌniʃəbl], *a.* punible.

punishment ['pʌniʃmənt], *n.* castigo; pena.

punitive ['pju:nitiv], *a.* punitivo.

punt [pʌnt], *n.* batea.

punter (1) ['pʌntə], *n.* el que va en una batea.

punter (2) ['pʌntə], *n.* pelete, apostador, *m.*

puny ['pju:ni], *a.* delicado, encanijado; pequeño.

pup [pʌp], *n.* cachorro.—*v.i.* parir.

pupil (1) [pju:pl], *n.* (*anat.*) pupila, niña del ojo.

pupil (2) [pju:pl], *n.* discípulo, alumno.

puppet ['pʌpit], *n.* títere, *m.*; muñeca; (*fig.*) maniquí, *m.*

puppy ['pʌpi], *n.* perrillo; cachorro.

purchase ['pə:tʃəs], *n.* compra; adquisición, *f.*; palanca.—*v.t.* comprar; adquirir.

pure [pjuə], *a.* puro.

purgation [pə:'geiʃən], *n.* purgación, *f.*

purgative ['pə:gətiv], *a.* purgativo.—*n.* purga.

purgatory ['pə:gətəri], *n.* purgatorio.

purge [pə:dʒ], *n.* purga; purgación; depuración, *f.*—*v.t.* purgar; depurar.

purification [pjuərifi'keiʃən], *n.* purificación, *f.*

purify ['pjuərifai], *v.t.* purificar; refinar; depurar.

purist ['pjuərist], *n.* purista, *m.f.*

puritan ['pjuəritən], *a., n.* puritano.

puritanical [pjuəri'tænikəl], *a.* puritano.

purity ['pjuəriti], *n.* pureza.

purloin [pə:'loin], *v.t.* robar, hurtar.

purple [pə:pl], *a.* purpúreo.—*n.* púrpura, violeta.

purport ['pə:pət], *n.* sentido; objeto.— [pə:'pɔ:t], *v.t.* significar; indicar; pretender.

purpose ['pə:pəs], *n.* intención, *f.*; objeto; utilidad, *f.*; propósito; *to no* —, inútilmente; *to the* —, al propósito; *on* —, adrede.—*v.t., v.i.* proponerse.

purposeful ['pə:pəsful], *a.* resuelto.

purposeless ['pə:pəslis], *a.* vago; sin objeto.

purposely ['pə:pəsli], *adv.* expresamente, adrede.

purr [pə:], *n.* ronroneo.—*v.i.* ronronear.

purse [pə:s], *n.* bolsa.—*v.t.* embolsar; apretar (*los labios*).

purser ['pə:sə], *n.* contador, *m.*

pursue [pə:'sju:], *v.t.* seguir; continuar; perseguir.

pursuer [pə:'sju:ə], *n.* perseguidor, *m.*

pursuit [pə:'sju:t], *n.* perseguimiento; busca; prosecución; ocupación, *f.*

purvey [pə:'vei], *v.t.* proveer; abastecer.

purveyor [pə:'veiə], *n.* abastecedor, proveedor, *m.*

push [puʃ], *n.* empujón, *m.*; impulso; empuje;

ataque, *m.*; esfuerzo; momento crítico; *at a* —, (*fam.*) en caso de necesidad.—*v.t.* empujar; impeler; apretar; importunar; ayudar; insistir en; *to* — *away*, rechazar; *to* — *off*, desatracar; *to* — *down*, derribar. —*v.i.* empujar; dar un empujón; *to* — *back*, retroceder; *to* — *off*, (*fam.*) coger la calle; *to* — *in*, entrometerse.

pushing ['puʃiŋ], *a.* enérgico; agresivo.

pusillanimous [pju:si'læniməs], *a.* pusilánime.

put [put], *v.t. irr.* poner, meter; colocar; expresar; lanzar; presentar; hacer (*una pregunta*); *to* — *away*, apartar; repudiar; ahorrar; (*fam.*) comerse; *to* — *back*, atrasar; devolver; *to* — *by*, poner de lado; ahorrar; *to* — *down*, deponer; humillar; apuntar; *to* — *forth*, publicar; brotar; *to* — *forward*, adelantar; exponer; *to* — *in*, meter, introducir; entrar en un puerto; *to* — *in for*, solicitar; *to* — *in mind*, recordar; *to* — *into practice*, poner en uso; *to* — *in writing*, poner por escrito; *to* — *off*, dilatar; aplazar; quitarse; desilusionar; *to* — *on*, ponerse; fingir; imponer; *to* — *out*, echar fuera; brotar; dislocar; apagar; publicar; irritar; *to* — *over*, sobreponer; diferir; exponer; *to* — *an end to*, acabar con; *to* — *a stop to*, poner coto a; *to* — *to*, añadir; exponer; *to* — *to bed*, acostar; *to* — *to death*, dar la muerte; *to* — *to flight*, ahuyentar; *to* — *to the vote*, poner a votación; *to* — *together*, juntar, reunir; *to* — *up*, poner en venta; aumentar; edificar; proponer; poner (*dinero*); presentarse como candidato; alojar; *to* — *up with*, aguantar; *to* — *upon*, poner en; persuadir; oprimir.

putrefaction [pju:tri'fækʃən], *n.* putrefacción, *f.*

putrefy ['pju:trifai], *v.t.* pudrir.—*v.i.* -se.

putrid ['pju:trid], *a.* podrido, pútrido.

putty ['pʌti], *n.* masilla.—*v.t.* poner masilla.

puzzle [pʌzl], *n.* enigma, *m.*; rompecabezas, *m.sg.*; problema, *m.*; perplejidad, *f.*—*v.t.* traer perplejo; desconcertar; confundir; embrollar.—*v.i.* estar perplejo.

puzzling ['pʌzliŋ], *a.* extraño.

pygmy ['pigmi], *n.* pigmeo.

pyjamas [pə'dʒɑ:məz], *n.pl.* pijama, *m.*

pylon ['pailən], *n.* pilón; poste, *m.*

pyramid ['pirəmid], *n.* pirámide, *f.*

pyre [paiə], *n.* pira.

the Pyrenees [pirə'ni:z], *n.pl.* los Pirineos.

pyrotechnic [pairou'teknik], *a.* pirotécnico.— *n.* pirotécnica.

python ['paiθən], *n.* pitón, *m.*

Q

Q, q [kju:], *n.* decimoséptima letra del alfabeto inglés.

quack [kwæk], *n.* graznido (*del pato*); (*fam.*) matasanos, *m.sg.*—*v.i.* graznar (*un pato*), parpar.

quackery ['kwækəri], *n.* charlatanismo.
quadrangle ['kwɔdræŋgl], *n.* cuadrángulo; (*arch.*) patio; (*abbr.* **quad** [kwɔd]) patio (*de colegio*).
quadruped ['kwɔdruped], *n.* cuadrúpedo.
quadruplet ['kwɔdruplit] (*abbr.* **quad** [kwɔd]), *n.* cuatrillizo, cuadrúpleto.
quaff [kwɔf], *v.t.* beber de un trago.
quagmire ['kwæɡmaiə], *n.* cenagal, *m.*
quail (1) [kweil], *n.* (*orn.*) codorniz, *f.*
quail (2) [kweil], *v.i.* acobardarse, temblar.
quaint [kweint], *a.* curioso, pintoresco.
quake [kweik], *n.* terremoto.—*v.i.* estremecerse, temblar.
Quaker ['kweikə], *a.*, *n.* cuáquero.
qualification [kwɔlifi'keiʃən], *n.* calificación, *f.*; requisito; atenuación, *f.—pl.* competencia, capacitación, *f.*
qualified ['kwɔlifaid], *a.* competente; calificado.
qualify ['kwɔlifai], *v.t.* calificar; capacitar, habilitar.—*v.i.* capacitarse; tener derecho (*for*, a).
quality ['kwɔliti], *n.* calidad, *f.*
qualm [kwɑːm], *n.* escrúpulo; basca.
quandary ['kwɔndəri], *n.* atolladero, perplejidad, *f.*
quantity ['kwɔntiti], *n.* cantidad, *f.*
quantum ['kwɔntəm], *a.* cuántico.—*n.* cuanto, cuántum, *m.*
quarantine ['kwɔrəntiːn], *n.* cuarentena.—*v.t.* poner en cuarentena.
quarrel ['kwɔrəl], *n.* riña, disputa.—*v.i.* reñirse.
quarrelsome ['kwɔrəlsəm], *a.* pendenciero.
quarry (1) ['kwɔri], *n.* cantera.—*v.t.* explotar una cantera.
quarry (2) ['kwɔri], *n.* ralea, presa (*víctima*).
quart [kwɔːt], *n.* cuarto de galón.
quarter ['kwɔːtə], *n.* cuarto; barrio; parte; piedad, *f.*; **to give no —**, no dar cuartel.—*pl.* vivienda, alojamiento; (*mil.*) cuartel, *m.*; **at close quarters**, (de) muy cerca.—*v.t.* cuartear, descuartizar; alojar.
quarterly ['kwɔːtəli], *a.* trimestral.
quartermaster ['kwɔːtəmɑːstə], *n.* (*mil.*) comisario.
quartet [kwɔː'tet], *n.* cuarteto.
quarto ['kwɔːtou], *a.* en cuarto, 4°.
quartz [kwɔːts], *n.* cuarzo.
quash [kwɔʃ], *v.t.* anular.
quatrain ['kwɔtrein], *n.* cuarteto.
quaver ['kweivə], *n.* temblor, *m.*; (*mus.*) trémolo; corchea (*nota*).—*v.i.* temblar; (*mus.*) trinar.
quay [kiː], *n.* muelle, *m.*
queasy ['kwiːzi], *a.* bascoso; remilgado.
queen [kwiːn], *n.* reina; dama (*naipes*).—*v.i.* **to — it**, darse tono, hacerse la reina.
queenly ['kwiːnli], *a.* de reina, como reina.
queer [kwiːə], *a.* curioso, raro; (*fam.*) malucho; (*low*) maricón; **in — street**, pelado, apurado.—*v.t.* **to — the pitch**, poner chinitas.
quell [kwel], *v.t.* reprimir, sofocar; sosegar.
quench [kwentʃ], *v.t.* apagar (*fuego, sed*).
query ['kwiːəri], *n.* pregunta, duda; (*U.S.*) punto de interrogación (?).—*v.t.* dudar; poner en tela de juicio.
quest [kwest], *n.* demanda, búsqueda.
question ['kwestʃən], *n.* pregunta; cuestión (*asunto*), *f.*; **beyond —**, fuera de duda;

out of the —, imposible; **to be in —**, tratarse de; **there is no —**, no cabe duda; **— mark**, punto de interrogación.—*v.t.* interrogar; poner en duda; desconfiar de.
questionable ['kwestʃənəbl], *a.* cuestionable; dudoso; sospechoso.
questionnaire [kwestʃə'nɛə], *n.* cuestionario.
queue [kjuː], *n.* cola.—*v.i.* hacer cola.
quibble [kwibl], *n.* sutileza.—*v.i.* sutilizar.
quibbler ['kwiblə], *n.* pleitista, *m.f.*
quick [kwik], *a.* rápido; listo; vivo.—*n.* carne viva, lo vivo; **the —**, los vivos; **to cut to the —**, herir en lo vivo.—*adv.* aprisa, pronto.
quicken ['kwikən], *v.t.* avivar.—*v.i.* -se.
quicklime ['kwiklaim], *n.* cal viva.
quickly ['kwikli], *adv.* rápidamente, pronto.
quicksand ['kwiksænd], *n.* arena movediza.
quicksilver ['kwiksilvə], *n.* azogue, *m.*
quickstep ['kwikstep], *n.* pasacalle, *m.*
quid (1) [kwid], *n.* mascada de tabaco.
quid (2) [kwid], *n.* (*Brit. fam.*) libra esterlina.
quiescent [kwi'esənt], *a.* tranquilo; quiescente.
quiet ['kwaiət], *a.* callado, silencioso; quieto; **to be —**, callar.—*n.* silencio.—*v.t.* tranquilizar, acallar.
quill [kwil], *n.* cañón (*m.*) de pluma; púa.
quilt [kwilt], *n.* colcha.—*v.t.* acolchar.
quince [kwins], *n.* membrillo.
quinine [kwi'niːn], *n.* quinina.
quinquennium [kwin'kweniəm], *n.* quinquenio.
quintessence [kwin'tesəns], *n.* quintaesencia.
quintuplet ['kwintjuplit] (*abbr.* **quin** ['kwin]), *n.* quintillizo, quintúpleto.
quip [kwip], *n.* pulla, agudeza.—*v.i.* echar pullas.
quire [kwaiə], *n.* mano (*f.*) de papel.
quirk [kwəːk], *n.* rareza, capricho.
quit [kwit], *v.t.* irr. (*U.S.*) abandonar.—*v.i.* rendirse; marcharse; rajarse.
quite [kwait], *adv.* del todo, completamente.
quits [kwits], *adv.* (*fam.*) **to be —**, estar desquitado(s), quedar en paz.
quitter ['kwitə], *n.* (*U.S.*) dejado, remolón, *m.*
quiver ['kwivə], *n.* aljaba, carcaj; tremor, *m.* —*v.i.* temblar.
Quixote ['kwiksət], *n.* Quijote, *m.*
quixotic [kwik'sɔtik], *a.* quijotesco.
quiz [kwiz], *n.* (*pl.* **quizzes**) examen, *m.*; interrogatorio.—*v.t.* (*fam.*) interrogar.
quizzical ['kwizikəl], *a.* curioso, raro; guaso.
quoit [k(w)ɔit], *n.* tejo, herrón, *m.*
quorum ['kwɔːrəm], *n.* quórum, *m. inv.*
quota ['kwoutə], *n.* cuota, cupo.
quotation [kwou'teiʃən], *n.* cita; (*com.*) cotización, *f.*; **— marks**, comillas, *f.pl.*
quote [kwout], *n.* cita.—*pl.* (*U.S.*) comillas, *f.pl.*—*v.t.* citar; (*com.*) cotizar.
quotient ['kwouʃənt], *n.* cociente, *m.*

R

R, r [ɑː], *n.* decimoctava letra del alfabeto inglés; **the three Rs**, las primeras letras.

rabbi ['ræbai], *n.* rabino.
rabbit ['ræbit], *n.* conejo; *(fig.)* novicio.
rabble [ræbl], *n.* gentuza, populacho.
rapid ['ræbid], *a.* rabioso.
rabies ['reibi:z], *n.* rabia.
race (1) [reis], *n. (sport)* carrera; corriente *(f.)* de agua.—*v.t.* competir en una carrera con; acelerar demasiado.—*v.i.* correr en una carrera; ir de prisa; acelerarse demasiado.
race (2) [reis], *n.* raza; *human* —, género humano.
race-track ['reistræk], *n.* hipódromo.
racial ['reiʃəl], *a.* racial.
racing ['reisiŋ], *n.* carreras *(de caballos), f.pl.*
rack (1) [ræk], *n.* estante, *m.*; percha; *(rail.)* red,*f.*; tormento; caballete,*m.*—*v.t.* torturar; *to — one's brains,* devanarse los sesos.
rack (2) [ræk], *n. — and ruin,* ruina total.
racket ['rækit], *n. (fam.)* jaleo *(ruido); (fam.)* estafa.
racketeer [ræki'tiə], *n.* trapacista, *m.*
racquet ['rækit], *n.* raqueta *(para tenis).*
racy ['reisi], *a.* picante, chispeante.
radar ['reidɑ:], *n.* radar, *m.*
radiant ['reidjənt], *a.* radiante, brillante.
radiate ['reidieit], *v.t.* radiar.—*v.i.* irradiar.
radiation [reidi'eiʃən], *n.* radiación,*f.*
radiator ['reidieitə], *n.* radiador, *m.*
radical ['rædikəl], *a., n.* radical, *m.f.*
radio ['reidjou], *n.* radio, *f.* [WIRELESS].
radioactive [reidjou'æktiv], *a.* radiactivo.
radioactivity [reidjouæk'tiviti], *n.* radiactividad, *f.*
radish ['rædiʃ], *n.* rábano.
radium ['reidjəm], *n.* radio.
radius ['reidjəs], *n.* radio.
raffle [ræfl], *n.* sorteo, rifa, tómbola.—*v.t.* rifar.
raft [rɑ:ft], *n.* balsa.
rafter ['rɑ:ftə], *n.* viga, cabrio.
rag [ræg], *n.* trapo, harapo; *(fam.)* jolgorio, fisga.—*v.t. (fam.)* tomar el pelo a.
ragamuffin ['rægəmʌfin], *n.* pelagatos, *m.sg.*
rage [reidʒ], *n.* rabia, furia; *(fam.)* furor, *m.,* boga.—*v.i.* encolerizarse, rabiar; bramar.
ragged ['rægid], *a.* harapiento; áspero; desigual.
raging ['reidʒiŋ], *a.* violento; bramador.
raid [reid], *n.* correría; ataque, *m.*—*v.t.* invadir, atacar.
rail (1) [reil], *a.* ferroviario.—*n.* carril, riel, *m.*; barra; barandilla; *by* —, por ferrocarril; *to go off the rails,* descarrilarse.—*v.t.* cercar.
rail (2) [reil], *v.i.* injuriar *(at),* mofarse *(at, de).*
railing ['reiliŋ], *n.* barandilla, antepecho.
raillery ['reiləri], *n.* escarnio, burla.
railroad ['reilroud], *n. (U.S.)* ferrocarril, *m.*
railway ['reilwei], *a.* ferroviario.—*n.* ferrocarril, *m.*
railway-carriage ['reilwei'kæridʒ], *n.* vagón, coche, *m.*
railwayman ['reilweimən], *n.* ferroviario.
raiment ['reimənt], *n.* indumento.
rain [rein], *n.* lluvia.—*v.t., v.i.* llover; *— or shine,* llueva o no.
rainbow ['reinbou], *n.* arco iris.
raincoat ['reinkout], *n.* impermeable, *m.,* gabardina.
rainfall ['reinfɔ:l], *n.* lluvia, precipitación,*f.*
rainstorm ['reinstɔ:m],*n.* aguacero, chubasco.

rainy ['reini], *a.* lluvioso; — *day,* *(fig.)* necesidad futura.
raise [reiz], *n. (U.S.)* subida, aumento.—*v.t.* alzar, levantar; subir; reunir *(dinero);* criar *(animales etc.);* cultivar; armar *(un lío);* suscitar *(observaciones).*
raiser ['reizə], *n.* cultivador, *m.*; ganadero.
raisin ['reizin], *n.* pasa, uva pasa.
raja(h) ['rɑ:dʒə], *n.* rajá, *m.*
rake (1) [reik], *n.* rastrillo.—*v.t.* rastrillar; atizar *(fuego);* escudriñar; *(mil.)* barrer.
rake (2) [reik], *n. (fig.)* libertino.
rakish ['reikiʃ], *a.* airoso, elegante; libertino.
rally ['ræli], *n.* reunión, *f.*; concurso.—*v.t.* reunir; recobrar.—*v.i.* reunirse; recobrar las fuerzas.
ram [ræm], *n.* carnero; *(mil.)* ariete, *m.*—*v.t.* chocar con; atacar con espolón.
ramble [ræmbl], *n.* paseo, excursión, *f.*—*v.i.* pasearse; vagar, serpentear; divagar.
rambling ['ræmbliŋ], *a.* errante; incoherente; enorme.—*n.* divagación, *f.*
ramp [ræmp], *n.* rampa.
rampant ['ræmpənt], *a.* desenfrenado; *(her.)* rampante.
rampart ['ræmpɑ:t], *n.* baluarte, *m.,* muralla.
ramshackle ['ræmʃækl], *a.* desvencijado.
ran [ræn] [RUN].
ranch [rɑ:ntʃ], *n.* hacienda, ganadería, rancho.
rancid ['rænsid], *a.* rancio.
rancour ['ræŋkə], *n.* rencor, *m.,* encono.
random ['rændəm], *a.* casual, al azar; *at* —, al azar, a troche y moche.
rang [ræŋ] [RING].
range [reindʒ], *n.* serie, *f.*; alcance, *m.*; terrenos *(m.pl.)* de pasto; hornillo; duración, *f.*—*v.t.* colocar, poner en fila, ordenar.—*v.i.* extenderse; variar; vagar.
ranger ['reindʒə], *n.* guardia, *m.*; guardabosque, *m.*
rank (1) [ræŋk], *a.* notorio; violento; lozano.
rank (2) [ræŋk], *n.* rango; grado; *(mil.)* fila *(línea).*—*pl. (mil.)* soldados rasos, *m.pl.*—*v.t.* colocar; ordenar.—*v.i.* ocupar un puesto.
rankle [ræŋkl], *v.t.* irritar, inflamar.—*v.i.* enconarse.
ransack ['rænsæk], *v.t.* saquear, rebuscar.
ransom ['rænsəm], *n.* rescate, *m.*—*v.t.* rescatar.
rant [rænt], *v.i.* desvariar, delirar.
rap [ræp], *n.* golpe seco; *(fig.)* bledo.—*v.t., v.i.* dar un golpecito seco (a), tocar.
rapacious [rə'peiʃəs], *a.* rapaz.
rape [reip], *n.* estupro.—*v.t.* violar.
rapid ['ræpid], *a.* rápido.—*n.pl.* rabión, *m.*
rapidity [rə'piditi], *n.* rapidez,*f.*
rapier ['reipiə], *n.* espadín, estoque, *m.*
rapt [ræpt], *a.* arrebatado, absorto.
rapture ['ræptʃə], *n.* éxtasis, *m.*
rare [rɛə], *a.* raro; sobresaliente, poco común; *(cul.)* medio asado.
rarefy ['rɛərifai], *v.t.* rarificar.
rarity ['rɛəriti], *n.* rareza.
rascal ['rɑ:skəl], *n.* bribón, tunante, *m.*
rase [reiz] [RAZE].
rash (1) [ræʃ], *a.* temerario, arrojado.
rash (2) [ræʃ], *n.* erupción, *f.,* brote, *m.*
rasher (1) ['ræʃə], *n.* torrezno, lonja.
rasher (2) ['ræʃə], *compar.* [RASH] (1).
rashness ['ræʃnis], *n.* temeridad, *f.*
rasp [rɑ:sp], *n.* escofina, raspa; sonido estridente.—*v.t.* raspar.

raspberry ['rɑ:zbəri], *n.* frambuesa (*fruta*); frambueso (*planta*).
rasping ['rɑ:spiŋ], *a.* áspero, ronco.
rat [ræt], *n.* (*zool.*) rata; (*pej.*) canalla, *m.f.*; **to smell a —,** (*fam.*) tener sus malicias.— *v.i.* **to — on,** delatar, soplar.
ratable [RATEABLE].
ratchet ['rætʃit], *n.* trinquete, *m.*
rate (1) [reit], *n.* razón, *f.*; (*com.*) tasa, tipo; velocidad, *f.*; modo; calidad, *f.*; **at any —,** de todos modos; **at the — of,** a razón de.— *pl.* (*Brit.*) impuestos locales sobre propiedad inmueble.—*v.t.* estimar, valuar.—*v.i.* ser considerado.
rate (2) [reit], *v.t.* regañar.
rateable ['reitəbl], *a.* sujeto a contribución.
ratepayer ['reitpeiə], *n.* contribuyente, *m.f.*
rather ['rɑ:ðə], *adv.* algo, bastante; más bien; **I had** o **would —,** preferiría.
ratification [rætifi'keiʃən], *n.* ratificación, *f.*
ratify ['rætifai], *v.t.* ratificar.
rating ['reitiŋ], *n.* valuación, capacidad, *f.*; (*Brit.*) marinero.
ratio ['reiʃiou], *n.* razón, *f.*
ration ['ræʃən], *n.* ración, *f.*—*v.t.* racionar.
rational [ræʃənəl], *a.* racional.
rationalize ['ræʃənəlaiz], *v.t.* hacer racional, racionalizar.
rationing ['ræʃəniŋ], *n.* racionamiento.
rattle [rætl], *n.* carraca; sonajero; traqueteo; **death —,** estertor, *m.*, agonia.—*v.t.*, *v.i.* traquetear; (*fam.*) meter miedo.
rattle-snake ['rætlsneik], *n.* crótalo, serpiente (*f.*) de cascabel.
raucous ['rɔ:kəs], *a.* ronco.
ravage ['rævidʒ], *n.* estrago.—*v.t.* estragar.
rave [reiv], *v.i.* delirar; **to — about,** estar loco por.
ravel ['rævəl], *v.t.* deshilar, desenredar; (*obs.*) enredar.
raven ['reivən], *a.* negro, lustroso.—*n.* cuervo.
ravenous ['rævinəs], *a.* voraz, hambriento.
ravine [ræ'vi:n], *n.* hondonada, barranco.
ravish ['ræviʃ], *v.t.* violar; arrebatar.
ravishing ['ræviʃiŋ], *a.* encantador.
raw [rɔ:], *a.* crudo; verde; bisoño, novato; **— deal,** (*fam.*) mala pasada; **— materials,** materias primas.
ray (1) [rei], *n.* rayo.
ray (2) [rei], *n.* (*ichth.*) raya.
rayon ['reijon], *n.* rayón, *m.*
raze [reiz], *v.t.* arrasar.
razor ['reizə], *n.* navaja; **safety —,** maquinilla de afeitar; **— blade,** hoj(it)a de afeitar, cuchilla.
re (1) [rei, ri:], *prep.* (*jur., com.*) concerniente a.
re (2) [ri:], *prefix.* re-; de nuevo, otra vez, volver a.
reach [ri:tʃ], *n.* alcance, *m.*; extensión, *f.*— *v.t.* alcanzar, llegar a; alargar.—*v.i.* extenderse; alcanzar; **to — for,** intentar, alcanzar; alargar la mano para coger.
react [ri:'ækt], *v.i.* reaccionar.
reaction [ri:'ækʃən], *n.* reacción, *f.*
reactionary [ri:'ækʃənəri], *a., n.* reaccionario.
reactor [ri:'æktə], *n.* reactor, *m.*
read [ri:d], *v.t. irr.* leer; recitar; **to — out,** leer en voz alta; **to — through,** repasar. —*v.i. irr.* leer; rezar.—[red], *p.p. and past of* [READ].
readable ['ri:dəbl], *a.* leíble; legible.

reader ['ri:də], *n.* lector, *m.*; (*educ., Brit.*) catedrático auxiliar, catedrático asociado.
readily ['redili], *adv.* de buena gana; pronto; facilmente.
readiness ['redinis], *n.* preparación; expedición; disponibilidad, *f.*; agudeza.
reading ['ri:diŋ], *n.* lectura.
reading-room ['ri:diŋ'rum], *n.* sala de lectura.
ready ['redi], *a.* listo, preparado; dispuesto; contante (*dinero*).
re-afforestation [ri:əfɔris'teiʃən], *n.* repoblación (*f.*) de montes.
reagent [ri:'eidʒənt], *n.* reactivo.
real ['ri:əl], *a.* real; auténtico, verdadero; (*jur., U.S.*) inmueble; **— estate,** (*U.S.*) bienes raíces, *m.pl.*
realism ['ri:əlizm], *n.* realismo.
realist ['ri:əlist], *n.* realista, *m.f.*
realistic [ri:ə'listik], *a.* realista.
reality [ri'æliti], *n.* realidad, *f.*
realization [riəlai'zeiʃən], *n.* realización; comprensión, *f.*
realize ['riəlaiz], *v.t.* darse cuenta de; (*com. etc.*) realizar.
realm [relm], *n.* reino.
ream [ri:m], *n.* resma.
reap [ri:p], *v.t.* cosechar, segar.
rear (1) [riə], *a.* posterior; trasero; último.— *n.* parte posterior, *f.*; zaga; fondo; cola.
rear (2) [riə], *v.t.* levantar, elevar.—*v.i.* empinarse, encabritarse (*caballo*).
rear-admiral ['riə'ædmirəl], *n.* contraalmirante, *m.*
rearguard ['riəgɑ:d], *n.* retaguardia.
rearm [ri:'ɑ:m], *v.t.* rearmar.—*v.i.* -se.
rearmanent [ri:'ɑ:məmənt], *n.* rearme, *m.*
rearmost ['riəmoust], *a.* postrero, último.
reason ['ri:zən], *n.* razón, *f.*; **by — of,** a causa de; **there is no — to,** no hay para qué; **within —,** dentro de lo razonable; **to stand to —,** ser razonable.—*v.t., v.i.* razonar.
reasonable ['ri:zənəbl], *a.* razonable.
reasoning ['ri:zəniŋ], *n.* razonamiento.
reassurance [ri:ə'ʃɔ:rəns], *n.* certeza restablecida.
reassure [ri:ə'ʃɔ:], *v.t.* asegurar, tranquilizar.
reassuring [ri:ə'ʃɔ:riŋ], *a.* tranquilizador.
rebate ['ri:beit], *n.* descuento, rebaja.—*v.t.* rebajar.
rebel ['rebəl], *a., n.* rebelde, *m.f.*—[ri'bel], *v.i.* rebelarse.
rebellion [ri'beljən], *n.* rebelión, *f.*
rebellious [ri'beljəs], *a.* rebelde, revoltoso.
rebirth [ri:'bə:θ], *n.* renacimiento.
rebound ['ri:baund], *n.* rebote, *m.*—[ri'baund], *v.i.* rebotar.
rebuff [ri'bʌf], *v.t.* desairar.—*n.* repulsa.
rebuild [ri:'bild], *v.t. irr.* (*conjug. like* BUILD) reconstruir.
rebuke [ri'bju:k], *v.t.* censurar, reprender.
rebut [ri'bʌt], *v.t.* refutar.
rebuttal [ri'bʌtəl], *n.* refutación, *f.*
recall [ri'kɔ:l], *v.t.* recordar; llamar, hacer volver.
recant [ri'kænt], *v.i.* retractarse.
recapitulate [ri:kə'pitjuleit], *v.t., v.i.* recapitular.
recapture [ri:'kæptʃə], *n.* recobro.—*v.t.* recobrar; represar.
recast [ri:'kɑ:st], *v.t.* refundir.

recede [ri'si:d], *v.i.* retirarse, retroceder.
receipt [ri'si:t], *n.* recibo.—*pl.* entradas, *f. pl.*
receive [ri'si:v], *v.t.* recibir; (*jur.*) receptar.
receiver [ri:'si:və], *n.* receptor, *m.*; (*jur.*) síndico; receptador (*de objetos robados*), *m.*
recent ['ri:sənt], *a.* reciente; próximo (*historia*).
recently ['ri:səntli], *adv.* recientemente; (*before p.p.*) recién.
receptacle [ri'septəkl], *n.* receptáculo, recipiente, *m.*
reception [ri'sepʃən], *n.* recepción, *f.*; acogida.
recess [ri'ses], *n.* descanso, vacaciones, *f.pl.*; nicho.
recipe ['resipi], *n.* receta.
recipient [ri'sipjənt], *n.* recibidor, *m.*
reciprocal [ri'siprəkəl], *a.* recíproco.
reciprocate [ri'siprəkeit], *v.t.* reciprocar.
recital [ri'saitl], *n.* recital, *m.*
recitation [resi'teiʃən], *n.* recitación, *f.*
recite [ri'sait], *v.t.* recitar.
reckless ['reklis], *a.* precipitado, temerario.
reckon ['rekən], *v.t.* calcular; **to — on,** contar con; **to — up,** adicionar.
reckoning ['rekəniŋ], *n.* cálculo; ajuste (*m.*) de cuentas; juicio final.
reclaim [ri'kleim], *v.t.* reclamar.
reclamation [reklə'meiʃən], *n.* reclamación, *f.*
recline [ri'klain], *v.t.* reclinar.—*v.i.* -se.
recluse [ri'klu:s], *n.* hermitaño; persona retirada.
recognition [rekəg'niʃən], *n.* reconocimiento.
recognize ['rekəgnaiz], *v.t.* reconocer.
recoil [ri'kɔil], *n.* reculada, retroceso.—*v.i.* recular.
recollect [rekə'lekt], *v.t.* recordar.
recollection [rekə'lekʃən], *n.* recuerdo.
recommend [rekə'mend], *v.t.* recomendar.
recommendation [rekəmen'deiʃən], *n.* recomendación, *f.*
recompense ['rekəmpens], *n.* recompensa.—*v.t.* recompensar.
reconcile ['rekənsail], *v.t.* reconciliar.—*v.r.* resignarse; **to become reconciled,** reconciliarse.
reconciliation [rekənsili'eiʃən], *n.* reconciliación, *f.*
reconnaissance [ri'kɔnisəns], *n.* reconocimiento.
reconnoitre [rekə'nɔitə], *v.t., v.i.* reconocer.
reconquer [ri:'kɔŋkə], *v.t.* reconquistar.
reconsider [ri:kən'sidə], *v.t.* reconsiderar.
reconstruct [ri:kən'strʌkt], *v.t.* reconstruir.
record ['rekɔ:d], *n.* historia personal, antecedentes, *m.pl.*; (*mus.*) disco; registro; (*sport*) record, *m.*, marca.—*pl.* anales, *m.pl.*; archivo.—[ri'kɔ:d], *v.t.* registrar, anotar; grabar (*sonidos*).
recorder [ri'kɔ:də], *n.* juez municipal, *m.*; (*mus.*) caramillo.
recount [ri'kaunt], *v.t.* recontar; narrar (*un cuento*).
recoup [ri'ku:p], *v.t.* recobrar, desquitar.—*v.i.* recobrarse.
recourse [ri'kɔ:s], *n.* recurso; **to have — to,** recurrir a.
recover [ri'kʌvə], *v.t.* recobrar, recuperar.—*v.i.* reponerse; resarcirse.
recovery [ri'kʌvəri], *n.* recobro, recuperación, *f.*
recreation [rekri'eiʃən], *n.* recreo.

recriminate [ri'krimineit], *v.t., v.i.* recriminar.
recrimination [rikrimi'neiʃən], *n.* recriminación, reconvención, *f.*
recruit [ri'kru:t], *n.* recluta, *m.*, quinto.—*v.t.* reclutar.
recruiting [ri'kru:tiŋ], *n.* reclutamiento.
rectangle ['rektæŋgl], *n.* rectángulo.
rectangular [rek'tæŋgjulə], *a.* rectangular.
rectify ['rektifai], *v.t.* rectificar.
rectitude ['rektitju:d], *n.* rectitud, probidad, *f.*
rector ['rektə], *n.* rector, *m.*; cura anglicano.
recumbent [ri'kʌmbənt], *a.* reclinado.
recuperate [ri'k(j)u:pəreit], *v.t.* recobrar, recuperar.—*v.i.* recuperarse.
recur [ri'kə:], *v.i.* repetirse.
recurrent [ri'kʌrənt], *a.* periódico; recurrente.
red [red], *a.* rojo, colorado; (*pol.*) rojo; tinto (*vino*); **— letter day,** día señalado; **— tape,** (*fam.*) burocratismo; papeleo.—*n.* rojo; (*pol.*) rojo.
red-cap ['redkæp], *n.* (*fam.*) policía militar, *m.*; (*U.S.*) [PORTER].
redcoat ['redkout], *n.* (*fam., hist.*) soldado inglés.
redden [redn], *v.t.* enrojecer.—*v.i.* enrojecerse; ponerse colorado.
reddish ['rediʃ], *a.* rojizo.
redeem [ri'di:m], *v.t.* redimir, rescatar; (*com.*) cumplir; amortizar.
redeemer [ri'di:mə], *n.* redentor, *m.*
redemption [ri'dempʃən], *n.* redención, *f.*
redhead ['redhed], *n.* pelirrojo.
red-hot ['red'hot], *a.* calentado al rojo, cadente.
redness ['rednis], *n.* rojez, *f.*
redolent ['redələnt], *a.* fragante; reminiscente.
redouble [ri'dʌbl], *v.t.* redoblar.
redoubt [ri'daut], *n.* reducto.
redound [ri'daund], *v.i.* redundar (*to,* en).
redress [ri'dres], *n.* reparación; compensación, *f.*; remedio.—*v.t.* reparar; remediar.
redskin ['redskin], *n.* piel roja, *m.*
reduce [ri'dju:s], *v.t.* reducir; reducirse; **to be reduced to,** verse obligado a.
reduction [ri'dʌkʃən], *n.* reducción, *f.*; (*com.*) descuento.
redundancy [ri'dʌndənsi], *n.* redundancia; sobra.
redundant [ri'dʌndənt], *a.* redundante, de sobra.
re-echo [ri:'ekou], *v.t.* repetir como eco, retumbar.
reed [ri:d], *n.* (*bot.*) cañavera, carrizo; (*mus.*) lengüeta.
reef [ri:f], *n.* arrecife, *m.*
reefer ['ri:fə], *n.* (*fam.*) pitillo de mariguana.
reek [ri:k], *n.* tufo, vaho.—*v.i.* vahear; oler (*of,* a).
reel [ri:l], *n.* carrete, *m.*; devanadera.—*v.i.* **to — off,** soltar con facilidad, decir sin dificultad alguna una serie de.
reel (2) [ri:l], *v.i.* tambalear.
reel (3) [ri:l], *n.* baile escocés, *m.*
re-enter [ri:'entə], *v.t.* volver a entrar (**en**).
re-entry [ri:'entri], *n.* nueva entrada.
refectory [ri'fektəri], *n.* refectorio.
refer [ri'fə:], *v.t.* referir.—*v.i.* referirse, aludir (*to,* a).
referee [refə'ri:], *n.* árbitro; garante, *m.*

reference

reference ['refərəns], *n.* referencia; alusión, *f.*; consulta.
referendum [refə'rendəm], *n.* referéndum, *m.*, plebiscito.
refill ['ri:fil], *n.* relleno, recambio.
refine [ri'fain], *v.t.* refinar.
refined [ri'faind], *a.* refinado; fino; pulido.
refinement [ri'fainmənt], *n.* refinamiento; sutileza; elegancia.
refinery [ri'fainəri], *n.* refinería.
refit ['ri:fit], *n.* reparación, *f.*, recorrido.— [ri:'fit], *v.t.* reparar, componer.
reflect [ri'flekt], *v.t.* reflejar.—*v.i.* reflexionar.
reflection [ri'flekʃən], *n.* reflejo; reflexión, *f.*; reproche, *m.*
reflective [ri'flektiv], *a.* reflexivo.
reflector [ri'flektə], *n.* reflector, *m.*
reflex ['ri:fleks], *n.* reflejo.
reflexive [ri'fleksiv], *a.* reflexivo.
refloat [ri:'flout], *v.t.* poner a flote de nuevo, desvarar.
reforestation [ri:foris'teiʃən], *n.* (U.S.) [RE-AFFORESTATION].
reform [ri'fo:m], *n.* reforma.—*v.t.* reformar. —*v.i.* -se.
Reformation [refɔ:'meiʃən], *n.* (hist.) Reforma.
reformatory [ri'fɔ:mətəri], *n.* casa de corrección.
refraction [ri'frækʃən], *n.* refracción, *f.*
refresh [ri'freʃ], *v.t.* refrescar.
refreshing [ri'freʃiŋ], *a.* refrescante.
refreshment [ri'freʃmənt], *n.* refresco.
refrigeration [rifridʒə'reiʃən], *n.* refrigeración, *f.*
refrigerator [ri'fridʒəreitə], *n.* nevera, frigorífico.
refuge ['refju:dʒ], *n.* refugio; asilo; *to take —,* refugiarse.
refugee [refju:'dʒi:], *n.* refugiado.
refusal [ri'fju:zəl], *n.* negación, *f.*, negativa.
refuse (1) ['refju:s], *n.* basura, desechos, *m. pl.*
refuse (2) [ri'fju:z], *v.t.* rechazar; *to — to,* negarse a.
refute [ri'fju:t], *v.t.* refutar.
regain [ri'gein], *v.t.* recobrar.
regal ['ri:gəl], *a.* real, regio.
regale [ri'geil], *v.t.* regalar, agasajar.
regalia [ri'geiliə], *n.pl.* regalías; insignias reales, *f.pl.*
regard [ri'gɑ:d], *n.* mirada; miramiento, consideración, *f.*; respecto, concepto, motivo; *out of — for,* por respeto a; *to pay — to,* tener miramientos por; *with — to,* respecto a; *without — for,* sin hacer caso de.—*pl.* recuerdos, saludos.—*v.t.* considerar; tocar a; *as regards,* en cuanto a.
regarding [ri'gɑ:diŋ], *prep.* tocante a.
regardless [ri'gɑ:dlis], *a.* desatento.—*adv.* cueste lo que cueste; *— of,* sin reparar en.
regatta [ri'gætə], *n.* regata.
regency ['ri:dʒənsi], *n.* regencia.
regenerate [ri'dʒenərit], *a.* regenerado.— [ri:'dʒenəreit], *v.t.* regenerar.
regent ['ri:dʒənt], *n.* regente, *m.*
regicide ['redʒisaid], *n.* regicida (persona), *m.f.*, regicidio (crimen).
regime [rei'ʒi:m], *n.* régimen, *m.*
regiment ['redʒimənt], *n.* regimiento.— ['redʒiment], *v.t.* regimentar.
region ['ri:dʒən], *n.* región, *f.*

regional ['ri:dʒənəl], *a.* regional.
register ['redʒistə], *n.* registro; matrícula; lista; contador, *m* ←*v.t.* registrar, inscribir, matricular.—*v.i.* inscribirse, registrarse.
registrar [redʒis'trɑ:], *n.* registrador, *m.*, archivero.
registry ['redʒistri], *n.* archivo, registro.
regress [ri'gres], *v.i.* retroceder.
regression [ri'greʃən], *n.* regresión, *f.*
regret [ri'gret], *n.* pesadumbre, *f.*, pesar, *m.* —*pl.* excusas, *f.pl.*—*v.t.* sentir; arrepentirse de.
regrettable [ri'gretəbl], *a.* lamentable.
regular ['regjulə], *a.*, *n.* regular, *m.f.*
regularity [regju'læriti], *a.*, *n.* regularidad, *f.*
regularize ['regjuləraiz], *v.t.* regularizar.
regulate ['regjuleit], *v.t.* regular.
regulation [regju'leiʃən], *n.* ordenanza, regla, reglamento; regulación, *f.*
regurgitate [ri'gə:dʒiteit], *v.t.* expeler, vomitar.—*v.i.* regurgitar.
rehabilitate [ri:hæ'biliteit], *v.t.* rehabilitar.
rehash ['ri:hæʃ], *n.* refundición, *f.*, refrito.— [ri:'hæʃ], *v.t.* rehacer, refundir.
rehearsal [ri'hə:səl], *n.* ensayo.
rehearse [ri'hə:s], *v.t.* ensayar.
reign [rein], *n.* reinado.—*v.i.* reinar.
reimburse [ri:im'bə:s], *v.t.* reembolsar.
rein [rein], *n.* rienda; *free —,* rienda suelta. —*v.t.* gobernar, refrenar.
reindeer ['reindiə], *n.* reno.
reinforce [ri:in'fɔ:s], *v.t.* reforzar; *reinforced concrete,* hormigón armado.
reinforcement [ri:in'fɔ:smənt], *n.* refuerzo.
reinstate [ri:in'steit], *v.t.* reinstalar.
reiterate [ri:'itəreit], *v.t.* reiterar.
reject [ri'dʒekt], *v.t.* rechazar.
rejection [ri'dʒekʃən], *n.* rechazamiento.
rejoice [ri'dʒois], *v.i.* regocijarse; celebrar (at).
rejoicing [ri'dʒoisiŋ], *n.* regocijo.
rejoin [ri'dʒoin], *v.t.* reunirse con.—*v.i.* contestar (hablar).
rejoinder [ri'dʒoində], *n.* réplica, contrarréplica.
rejuvenate [ri'dʒu:vəneit], *v.t.* rejuvenecer.
relaid [ri:'leid] [RELAY (2)].
relapse [ri'læps], *n.* recaída, reincidiva.—*v.i.* recaer, reincidir.
relate [ri'leit], *v.t.* referir, narrar; relacionar. —*v.i.* relacionarse con, tocar a (to).
related [ri'leitid], *a.* emparentado.
relation [ri'leiʃən], *n.* pariente, *m.f.*; parentesco; relación, *f.*; *in — to,* respecto a.
relationship [ri'leiʃənʃip], *n.* relación, *f.*; parentesco; afinidad, *f.*
relative ['relətiv], *a.* relativo.—*n.* pariente, *m.f.*
relativity [relə'tiviti], *n.* relatividad, *f.*
relax [ri'læks], *v.t.* relajar; aliviar.—*v.i.* calmarse, descansar.
relaxation [rilæk'seiʃən], *n.* relajación, *f.*; descanso, recreo.
relay (1) ['ri:lei], *n.* relevo; (elec.) relé, *m.*— [ri:'lei], *v.t.* relevar; retransmitir; llevar.
relay (2) [ri:'lei], *v.t.* recolocar.
relay-race ['ri:lei'reis], *n.* carrera de relevos.
release [ri'li:s], *n.* liberación; producción; cesión, *f.*; escape, *m.*—*v.t.* libertar; publicar; soltar; aliviar.
relegate ['reləgeit], *v.t.* relegar.
relent [ri'lent], *v.i.* aplacarse, desenojarse.

relentless [ri'lentlis], *a.* implacable; emperdernido.
relevant ['reləvənt], *a.* pertinente.
reliable [ri'laiəbl], *a.* fidedigno; seguro.
relic ['relik], *n.* reliquia.
relief [ri'li:f], *n.* alivio; relieve, *m.*; (*mil.*) relevo; socorro.
relieve [ri'li:v], *v.t.* relevar; aliviar; socorrer.
religion [ri'lidʒən], *n.* religión, *f.*
religious [ri'lidʒəs], *a.*, *n.* religioso.
relinquish [ri'liŋkwiʃ], *v.t.* abandonar, ceder.
relish ['reliʃ], *n.* saborcillo; condimento; goce, *m.—v.t.* paladear, saborear; gozar de.
reluctance [ri'lʌktəns], *n.* aversión, *f.*, desgana.
reluctant [ri'lʌktənt], *a.* renuente, mal dispuesto.
rely [ri'lai], *v.i.* confiar (**on**, en), contar (**on**, con).
remain [ri'mein], *v.i.* quedar, quedarse; *it remains to be done*, queda por hacer.
remainder [ri'meində], *n.* residuo, restante, *m.*, resto.
remains [ri'meinz], *n.pl.* restos, *m.pl.*
remand [ri'mɑ:nd], *v.t.* reencarcelar; — *home*, casa de corrección.
remark [ri'mɑ:k], *n.* observación, *f.—v.t.*, *v.i.* observar, notar; *to — on*, comentar.
remarkable [ri'mɑ:kəbl], *a.* notable, singular.
remedy ['remidi], *n.* remedio.—*v.t.* remediar.
remember [ri'membə], *v.t.* recordar, acordarse de.
remembrance [ri'membrəns], *n.* memoria, recuerdo solemne.
remind [ri'maind], *v.t.* recordar (*of*).
reminder [ri'maində], *n.* recordatorio.
reminisce [remi'nis], *v.i.* entregarse a los recuerdos.
reminiscent [remi'nisənt], *a.* evocador (*of*, de).
remiss [ri'mis], *a.* negligente.
remission [ri'miʃən], *n.* remisión, *f.*
remit [ri'mit], *v.t.* remitir; trasladar.
remittance [ri'mitəns], *n.* giro, remesa.
remnant ['remnənt], *n.* residuo; retazo, **retal**, *m.*; resto.
remorse [ri'mɔ:s], *n.* remordimiento.
remorseless [ri'mɔ:slis], *a.* implacable.
remote [ri'mout], *a.* remoto; — *control*, telecontrol, *m.*, mando a distancia.
removal [ri'mu:vəl], *n.* traslado; eliminación, *f.*
remove [ri'mu:v], *n.* grado; traslado.—*v.t.* quitar, sacar; trasladar.
remunerate [ri'mju:nəreit], *v.t.* remunerar.
Renaissance [rə'neisəns], *n.* Renacimiento.
renascence [ri'næsəns], *n.* renacimiento.
rend [rend], *v.t. irr.* desgarrar; hender.
render ['rendə], *v.t.* rendir; dar, prestar; hacer, poner; verter; interpretar; *to — down*, derretir.
rendezvous ['rɔ:ndeivu:], *n.* (*pl.* **rendezvous** ['rɔ:ndeivu:z]) cita, lugar (*m.*) de cita.
renegade ['renigeid], *a.*, *n.* renegado, apóstata, *m.f.*
renew [ri'nju:], *v.t.* renovar.—*v.i.* renovarse.
renewal [ri'nju:əl], *n.* renovación, *f.*; prórroga.
renounce [ri'nauns], *v.t.* renunciar.
renovate ['renouveit], *v.t.* renovar.
renown [ri'naun], *n.* renombre, *m.*
renowned [ri'naund], *a.* renombrado.

rent (I) [rent], *n.* alquiler, *m.* renta.—*v.t.* alquilar.
rent (2) [rent], *n.* desgarro, raja.
rental ['rentəl], *n.* arriendo.
renunciation [rinʌnsi'eiʃən], *n.* renunciación, *f.*
repair [ri'pɛə], *n.* remiendo, reparación, *f.*; *in good —*, en buen estado.—*v.t.* reparar, remendar; remontar (*zapatos*).—*v.i.* dirigirse.
reparation [repə'reiʃən], *n.* reparación, *f.*
repartee [repɑ:'ti:], *n.* réplica, respuesta aguda.
repast [ri'pɑ:st], *n.* yantar, *f.*
repatriate [ri:'pætrieit], *v.t.* repatriar.
repay [ri'pei], *v.t.* (*conjug. like* PAY) recompensar, reembolsar.
repeal [ri'pi:l], *v.t.* revocar.
repeat [ri'pi:t], *n.* repetición, *f.—v.t.*, *v.i.* repetir.
repel [ri'pel], *v.t.* repugnar; rechazar.
repellent [ri'pelənt], *a.* repulsivo, repelente.
repent [ri'pent], *v.i.* arrepentirse (de).
repentance [ri'pentəns], *n.* arrepentimiento.
repentant [ri'pentənt], *a.*, *n.* arrepentido.
repercussion [ri:pə'kʌʃən], *n.* repercusión, *f.*
repertoire ['repətwɑ:], *n.* repertorio.
repetition [repi'tiʃən], *n.* repetición, *f.*
rephrase [ri:'freiz], *v.t.* reformular.
replace [ri'pleis], *v.t.* reemplazar; reponer.
replacement [ri'pleismənt], *n.* reemplazo; reposición, *f.*; (*mech. etc.*) repuesto, pieza de repuesto.
replenish [ri'pleniʃ], *v.t.* rellenar, resarcir.
replete [ri'pli:t], *a.* repleto.
replica ['replikə], *n.* réplica, duplicado.
reply [ri'plai], *n.* respuesta, contestación, *f.—v.i.* responder, contestar.
report [ri'pɔ:t], *n.* informe, reportaje, *m.*; voz, *f.*; estallido.—*v.t.* relatar, dar parte de; denunciar.—*v.i.* presentarse.
reporter [ri'pɔ:tə], *n.* reportero.
repose [ri'pouz], *n.* reposo.—*v.i.* reposar.
reprehend [repri'hend], *v.t.* reprender, censurar.
reprehensible [repri'hensibl], *a.* reprensible, censurable.
represent [repri'zent], *v.t.* representar.
representative [repri'zentətiv], *a.* representativo.—*n.* representante, *m.f.*
repress [ri'pres], *v.t.* reprimir.
repression [ri'preʃən], *n.* represión, *f.*
reprieve [ri'pri:v], *n.* suspensión (*f.*) de castigo.—*v.t.* suspender el castigo de; aliviar.
reprimand ['reprimɑ:nd], *n.* reprimenda, reprensión, *f.—v.t.* reprender, censurar.
reprint ['ri:print], *n.* tirada aparte; reimpresión, *f.*—[ri:'print], *v.t.* reimprimir.
reprisal [ri'praizəl], *n.* represalia.
reproach [ri'proutʃ], *n.* reproche, *m.—v.t.* reprochar.
reprobate ['reproubeit], *a.*, *n.* réprobo.
reproduce [ri:prə'dju:s], *v.t.* reproducir.—*v.i.* -se.
reproduction [ri:prə'dʌkʃən], *n.* reproducción, *f.*
reproof [ri'pru:f], *n.* reprobación, *f.*, reproche, *m.*
reprove [ri'pru:v], *v.t.* reprobar, censurar.
reptile ['reptail], *a.*, *n.* reptil, *m.*

republic

republic [ri'pʌblik], *n.* república.
republican [ri'pʌblikən], *a., n.* republicano.
repudiate [ri'pju:dieit], *v.t.* repudiar.
repugnance [ri'pʌgnəns], *n.* repugnancia.
repugnant [ri'pʌgnənt], *a.* repugnante.
repulse [ri'pʌls], *n.* repulsa.—*v.t.* repulsar, repeler.
repulsion [ri'pʌlʃən], *n.* repulsión, aversión, *f.*
repulsive [ri'pʌlsiv], *a.* repulsivo, repelente.
reputable ['repjutəbl], *a.* respetable, fidedigno.
reputation [repju:'teiʃən], *n.* reputación, *f.*, nombre, *m.*
repute [ri'pju:t], *n.* reputación, *f.*—*v.t.* reputar; **to be reputed to be,** tener fama de.
reputedly [ri'pju:tidli], *adv.* según dicen.
request [ri'kwest], *n.* petición, solicitud, *f.*; **on —,** a pedido.—*v.t.* rogar, suplicar, pedir.
requiem ['rekwiem], *n.* réquiem, *m.*
require [ri'kwaiə], *v.t.* necesitar; exigir.
requirement [ri'kwaiəmənt], *n.* requisito, necesidad, *f.*
requisite ['rekwizit], *a.* necesario, debido.— *n.* requisito.
requisition [rekwi'ziʃən], *n.* requisición, *f.*— *v.t.* requisar.
requite [ri'kwait], *v.t.* corresponder a.
reredos ['riərədɒs], *n.* (*eccl.*) retablo.
rescind [ri'sind], *v.t.* rescindir, abrogar.
rescue ['reskju:], *n.* rescate, *m.*; salvamento, liberación, *f.*; socorro.—*v.t.* salvar, rescatar, libertar.
research [ri'sə:tʃ], *n.* investigación, *f.*—*v.i.* investigar.
resemblance [ri'zembləns], *n.* semejanza, parecido.
resemble [ri'zembl], *v.t.* parecerse a.
resent [ri'zent], *v.t.* resentirse de.
resentful [ri'zentful], *a.* resentido.
resentment [ri'zentmənt], *n.* resentimiento.
reservation [rezə'veiʃən], *n.* reservación, *f.*; reserva; salvedad, *f.*
reserve [ri'zə:v], *n.* reserva.—*v.t.* reservar.
reservist [ri'zə:vist], *a., n.* reservista, *m.f.*
reservoir ['rezəvwa:], *n.* embalse, *m.*, depósito; pantano; (*fig.*) mina.
reshape [ri:'ʃeip], *v.t.* reformar.
reside [ri'zaid], *v.i.* residir, morar.
residence ['rezidəns], *n.* residencia.
resident ['rezidənt], *a., n.* residente, *m.f.*
residential [rezi'denʃəl], *a.* residencial.
residual [ri'zidjuəl], *a.* residual.
residue ['rezidju:], *n.* residuo, resto.
resign [ri'zain], *v.t.* resignar.—*v.i.* dimitir; resignarse.
resignation [rezig'neiʃən], *n.* dimisión; resignación, *f.*
resilient [ri'ziljənt], *a.* elástico, resaltante; vivo, activo.
resin ['rezin], *n.* resina.
resist [ri'zist], *v.t.* resistir a.—*v.i.* resistirse.
resistance [ri'zistəns], *n.* resistencia.
resistant [ri'zistənt], *a.* resistente.
resolute ['rezəlju:t], *a.* resuelto.
resolution [rezə'lju:ʃən], *n.* resolución, *f.*
resolve [ri'zɔlv], *n.* resolución, determinación, *f.*—*v.t.* resolver.—*v.i.* resolverse (*into,* a).
resonant ['rezənənt], *a.* resonante.
resort [ri'zɔ:t], *n.* recurso; estación, *f.*, lugar

(*m.*) de veraneo; concurso.—*v.i.* recurrir (*to,* a).
resound [ri'zaund], *v.t.* hacer resonar.—*v.i.* resonar.
resource [ri'sɔ:s], *n.* recurso.
resourceful [ri'sɔ:sful], *a.* ingenioso, avisado.
respect [ri'spekt], *n.* respeto, estimación, *f.*; respecto; **in — of, with — to,** respecto a.—*pl.* saludos, *m.pl.*—*v.t.* respetar, acatar.
respectability [rispektə'biliti], *n.* respectabilidad, *f.*
respectable [ris'pektəbl], *a.* respetable.
respectful [ris'pektful], *a.* respetuoso.
respecting [ris'pektiŋ], *prep.* (con) respecto a.
respective [ris'pektiv], *a.* respectivo; sendo.
respiration [respi'reiʃən], *n.* respiración, *f.*
respite ['respait, 'respit], *n.* tregua, respiro; plazo.
resplendent [ris'plendənt], *a.* resplandeciente.
respond [ris'pɔnd], *v.i.* responder.
response [ris'pɔns], *n.* respuesta.
responsibility [rispɔnsi'biliti], *n.* responsabilidad, *f.*
responsible [ris'pɔnsibl], *a.* responsable.
responsive [ris'pɔnsiv], *a.* sensible, responsivo.
rest (1) [rest], *n.* descanso; reposo; estribo; pausa; **at —,** en reposo; en paz.—*v.t.* descansar, apoyar, colocar.—*v.i.* descansar; **to — with,** tocar a, correr a cuenta de.
rest (2) [rest], *n.* resto; **the —,** lo demás; los demás.—*v.i.* verse, hallarse, estar; **to — assured,** estar seguro.
restaurant ['restərənt, 'restrã], *n.* restaurante, restóran, *m.*
restful ['restful], *a.* tranquilo, sosegado.
restitution [resti'tju:ʃən], *n.* restitución, *f.*
restive ['restiv], *a.* inquieto.
restless ['restlis], *a.* inquieto, impaciente; insomne.
restlessness ['restlisnis], *n.* desasosiego; insomnio.
restoration [restɔ:'reiʃən], *n.* restauración, *f.*
restore [ri'stɔ:], *v.t.* restaurar; restituir.
restrain [ri'strein], *v.t.* refrenar; encerrar.
restraint [ri'streint], *n.* mesura, comedimiento; freno; restricción, *f.*
restrict [ri'strikt], *v.t.* restringir.
restriction [ri'strikʃən], *n.* restricción, *f.*
restrictive [ri'striktiv], *a.* restrictivo.
result [ri'zʌlt], *n.* resultado; resulta.—*v.i.* resultar; **to — in,** acabar por, terminar en.
resultant [ri'zʌltənt], *a., n.* resultante, *m.*
resume [ri'zju:m], *v.t.* reasumir; reanudar; volver a ocupar (*un asiento*).—*v.i.* seguir, recomenzar.
résumé ['rezju:mei], *n.* resumen, *m.*, sumario.
resumption [ri'zʌmpʃən], *n.* reasunción, *f.*
resurgence [ri'sə:dʒəns], *n.* resurgimiento.
resurrect [rezə'rekt], *v.t., v.i.* resucitar.
resurrection [rezə'rekʃən], *n.* resurrección, *f.*
resuscitate [ri'sʌsiteit], *v.t.* resucitar.
retail ['ri:teil], *a., adv.* al por menor.—*n.* venta al por menor, reventa.—[ri'teil], *v.t.* vender al por menor; repetir, contar.
retailer ['ri:teilə], *n.* tendero, vendedor al por menor, *m.*
retain [ri'tein], *v.t.* retener; contratar.
retainer [ri'teinə], *n.* partidario, criado; honorario (*pago*).
retaliate [ri'tælieit], *v.i.* desquitarse, vengarse.

retaliation [ri'tæli'eiʃən], *n.* desquite, *m.*, represalias, *f.pl.*
retard [ri'tɑːd], *v.t.* atrasar.
retch [retʃ], *v.i.* arquear, tener bascas.
retention [ri'tenʃən], *n.* retención, *f.*
retentive [ri'tentiv], *a.* retentivo.
reticence ['retisəns], *n.* reticencia, reserva.
reticent ['retisənt], *a.* reservado.
retina ['retinə], *n.* retina.
retinue ['retinjuː], *n.* séquito, comitiva.
retire [ri'taiə], *v.t.* retirar; jubilar.—*v.i.* retirarse; jubilarse; acostarse.
retirement [ri'taiəmənt], *n.* jubilación, *f.*; retiro; — *pension*, pensión vitalicia.
retiring [ri'taiəriŋ], *a.* tímido, retraído; dimitente.
retort [ri'tɔːt], *n.* réplica; retorta.—*v.i.* replicar.
retouch [riː'tʌtʃ], *v.t.* retocar.
retrace [ri'treis], *v.t.* desandar; repasar.
retract [ri'trækt], *v.t.* retractar.—*v.i.* -se.
retraction [ri'trækʃən], *n.* retracción, *f.*
retreat [ri'triːt], *n.* retiro (*lugar*); retirada (*hecho*).—*v.i.* retirarse.
retribution [retri'bjuːʃən], *n.* retribución, *f.*, castigo.
retrieve [ri'triːv], *v.t.* cobrar; resarcirse de.
retriever [ri'triːvə], *n.* perro cobrador, sabueso.
retrograde ['retrougreid], *a.* retrógrado.
retrospective [retrou'spektiv], *a.* retrospectivo.
retroussé [ri'truːsei], *a.* respingado.
return [ri'tɔːn], *n.* vuelta; devolución, *f.*; correspondencia; (*pol.*) resultado; (*com.*) rédito; — *ticket*, billete (*m.*) de ida y vuelta; *in* —, en cambio; en recompensa; *many happy returns*, feliz cumpleaños, felicidades.—*v.t.* devolver; rendir; dar; elegir; corresponder a (*un favor*).—*v.t.* volver; regresar. [**post** (1)]
reunion [riː'juːnjən], *n.* reunión, *f.*
reunite [riːjuː'nait], *v.t.* reunir; reconciliar.—*v.i.* -se.
reveal [ri'viːl], *v.t.* revelar.
reveille [ri'væli], *n.* (*mil.*) diana.
revel ['revəl], *n.* jerga, francachela.—*v.i.* ir de parranda; gozarse (*in*, de).
revelation [revə'leiʃən], *n.* revelación, *f.*; (*Bib.*) Apocalipsis, *m.*
reveller ['revələ], *n.* juerguista, *m.f.*
revelry ['revəlri], *n.* jarana, juerga.
revenge [ri'vendʒ], *n.* venganza.—*v.t.* vengar, vengarse de.—*v.i.* vengarse.
revengeful [ri'vendʒful], *a.* vengativo.
revenue ['revənjuː], *n.* rentas públicas, *f.pl* (*com.*) rédito; ingresos, *m.pl.*; aduana.
reverberate [ri'vəːbəreit], *v.t.* reflejar.—*v.i.* resonar, retumbar.
reverberation [rivəːbə'reiʃən], *n.* retumbo; reverberación, *f.*
revere [ri'viə], *v.t.* reverenciar, venerar.
reverence ['revərəns], *n.* reverencia.
reverend ['revərənd], *a., n.* reverendo.
reverent ['revərənt], *a.* reverente.
reverie ['revəriː], *n.* ensueño.
reversal [ri'vəːsəl], *n.* reversión, *f.*, cambio; revocación, *f.*
reverse [ri'vəːs], *a.* contrario.—*n.* revés, *m.*; reverso; contratiempo.—*v.t.* invertir; revocar; *to — the charges*, (*tel.*) cobrar al

número llamado.—*v.i.* invertirse; ir hacia atrás.
reversible [ri'vəːsibl], *a.* reversible; ɩ dos caras.
reversion [ri'vəːʃən], *n.* reversión, *f.*
revert [ri'vəːt], *v.i.* recudir; (*jur.*) revertir; saltar atrás.
review [ri'vjuː], *n.* revista; (*lit.*) reseña.—*v.t.* repasar; (*lit.*) reseñar; (*mil.*) revistar, pasar en revista.
revile [ri'vail], *v.t.* ultrajar, injuriar.
revise [ri'vaiz], *v.t.* revisar; repasar; corregir.
revision [ri'viʒən], *n.* revisión, *f.*; repaso; corrección, *f.*
revival [ri'vaivəl], *n.* renacimiento; restauración; (*rel.*) despertamiento; (*theat.*) reestreno.
revive [ri'vaiv], *v.t.* resucitar; restaurar; reanimar; (*theat.*) reestrenar.—*v.i.* resuscitar; reanimarse; volver en si.
revoke [ri'vouk], *v.t.* revocar.
revolt [ri'voult], *n.* sublevación, rebelión, *f.*—*v.t.* dar asco a, repugnar.—*v.i.* rebelarse; sentir repulsión.
revolting [ri'voultiŋ], *a.* repugnante.
revolution [revə'luːʃən], *n.* revolución, *f.*
revolutionary [revə'luːʃənəri], *a., n.* revolucionario.
revolutionize [revə'luːʃənaiz], *v.t.* revolucionar.
revolve [ri'vɔlv], *v.t.* hacer girar; ponderar.—*v.i.* girar.
revolver [ri'vɔlvə], *n.* revólver, *m.*
revolving [ri'vɔlviŋ], *a.* giratorio.
revue [ri'vjuː], *n.* (*theat.*) revista.
revulsion [ri'vʌlʃən], *n.* revulsión; reacción, *f.*
reward [ri'wɔːd], *n.* premio, recompensa; retribución, *f.*—*v.t.* recompensar, premiar.
rewarding [ri'wɔːdiŋ], *a.* provechoso; satisfaciente.
reword [riː'wəːd], *v.t.* expresar *o* formular de otra manera.
rhapsody ['ræpsədi], *n.* rapsodia.
rhetoric ['retərik], *n.* retórica.
rhetorical [ri'tɔrikəl], *a.* retórico.
rheum [ruːm], *n.* reuma.
rheumatic [ru'mætik], *a.* reumático.—*n.pl.* (*fam.*) reumatismo.
rheumatism ['ruːmətizm], *n.* reumatismo.
Rhine [rain], *n.* Rin, *m.*
rhinocerous [rai'nɔsərəs] (*fam. rhino* ['rainou]), *n.* rinoceronte, *m.*
rhizome ['raizoum], *n.* rizoma, *m.*
Rhodesia [rou'diːzjə], *n.* la Rodesia.
rhododendron [roudə'dendrən], *n.* rododendro.
Rhône [roun], *n.* Ródano, *m.*
rhubarb ['ruːbɑːb], *n.* ruibarbo.
rhyme [raim], *n.* rima; *without* — *or reason*, sin ton ni son.—*v.t., v.i.* rimar.
rhymester ['raimstə], *n.* poetastro, rimador, *m.*
rhythm ['riðm], *n.* ritmo.
rhythmic ['riðmik], *a.* rítmico.
rib [rib], *n.* costilla; varilla (*de un abanico, etc.*); nervadura.—*v.t.* (*fam.*) tomar el pelo a.
ribald ['ribəld], *a.* grosero, escabroso.
ribaldry ['ribəldri], *n.* grosería, escabrosidad, *f.*
riband ['ribənd], *n.* cinta; listón, *m.*
ribbing ['ribiŋ], *n.* costillaje, *m.*; nervadura; burlas, *f.pl.*
ribbon ['ribən], *n.* cinta.

rice

rice [rais], *n.* arroz, *m.*; — *pudding*, arroz con leche.
rich [ritʃ], *a.* rico; *(fig.)* rico; *(fam.)* divertido y ridículo.—*n.pl.* —*es* ['ritʃiz], riquezas, *f. pl.*
Richard ['ritʃəd], *n.* Ricardo.
rick [rik], *n.* almiar, *m.*
rickets ['rikits], *n. pl.* raquitis, *f.*, raquitismo.
rickety ['rikiti], *a.* raquítico; *(fig.)* desvencijado.
rickshaw ['rikʃɔ:], *n.* riksha, *m.*
ricochet ['rikəʃei], *n.* rebote, *m.—v.i.* rebotar.
rid [rid], *v.t.* desembarazar, librar; *to get — of,* quitar de en medio, deshacerse de.
riddance ['ridəns], *n.* *good* —! ¡adiós, gracias! ¡de buena me he librado!
ridden [ridn], [RIDE].
riddle (1) [ridl], *n.* enigma, *m.*, acertijo.
riddle (2) [ridl], *n.* garbillo, criba.—*v.t.* cribar *(tamizar)*; acribillar *(con agujeros, balas).*
ride [raid], *n.* paseo.—*v.t.* montar; surcar *(el mar)*; tiranizar.—*v.i.* cabalgar, montar; pasear; flotar.
rider ['raidə], *n.* caballero, jinete, *m.*; pasajero; añadidura.
ridge [ridʒ], *n.* espinazo, lomo; caballete, *m.*
ridicule ['ridikju:l], *n.* ridículo, irrisión, *f.—v.t.* poner en ridículo, ridiculizar.
ridiculous [ri'dikjuləs], *a.* ridículo.
riding ['raidiŋ], *a.* de montar.—*n.* equitación, *f.*
rife [raif], *a.* abundante, corriente; lleno *(with,* de).
riff-raff ['rifræf], *n.* bahorrina, gentuza.
rifle (1) [raifl], *n.* rifle, fusil, *m.—v.t.* rayar *(fusil).*
rifle (2) [raifl], *v.t.* pillar.
rifleman ['raiflmən], *n.* fusilero.
rift [rift], *n.* raja, hendedura; desavenencia.
rig (1) [rig], *n.* aparejo, jarcias, *f.pl.*; *(fam.)* traje, *m.—v.t.* enjarciar; aparejar; *(fam.)* emperifollar.
rig (2) [rig], *v.t. (fam.)* manipular, falsificar.
rigging (1) ['rigin], *n.* aparejos, *m.pl.*, jarcias, *f.pl.*
rigging (2) ['rigin], *n.* manipulación, *f.*, forcejeos, *m.pl.*
right [rait], *a.* correcto; derecho; *to be* —, tener razón; — *angle,* ángulo recto; *in his — mind,* en sus cabales.—*n.* derecho; título; derecha *(lado)*; *by* —, en derecho.—*v.t.* rectificar; enderezar.—*adv.* correctamente; en buen estado; mismo; bien; *all* —, muy bien; — *away,* en seguida; — *or wrong,* a tuertas o a derechas; *to put* —, enderezar, corregir; encaminar, orientar.
righteous ['raitʃəs], *a.* justo, virtuoso.
righteousness ['raitʃəsnis], *n.* virtud, *f.*, justicia.
rightful ['raitful], *a.* legítimo, justo.
rigid ['ridʒid], *a.* rígido, tieso; riguroso, rigoroso.
rigidity [ri'dʒiditi], *n.* rigidez, *f.*
rigor mortis ['rigə'mɔ:tis], *n.* rigor *(m.)* de la muerte.
rigorous ['rigərəs], *a.* riguroso, rigoroso.
rigour ['rigə], *n.* rigor, *m.*
rile [rail], *v.t. (fam.)* picar, exasperar.
rim [rim], *n.* canto, borde, *m.*; llanta *(de una rueda).—v.t.* cercar.
rime (1) [raim], *n.* escarcha.
rime (2) [raim], [RHYME].

rind [raind], *n.* corteza.
ring (1) [riŋ], *n.* sortija, anillo; círculo; plaza, ruedo; corro *(gente).—v.t.* cercar, rodear; anillar.
ring (2) [riŋ], *n. (tel.)* llamada; repique, *m.*, campaneo.—*v.t. irr.* sonar; tocar; *(tel.)* llamar.—*v.i. irr.* sonar; resonar, zumbar; *to — up,* llamar por teléfono.
ringleader ['riŋli:də], *n.* cabecilla, *m.*
rink [riŋk], *n.* pista de patinar.
rinse [rins], *n.* enjuague, *m.—v.t.* enjuagar.
riot ['raiət], *n.* tumulto, alboroto, motín, *m.*; orgía; *to run* —, desenfrenarse.—*v.i.* amotinarse, alborotarse.
riotous ['raiətəs], *a.* alborotado, amotinado.
rip [rip], *n.* rasgón, *m.*, rasgadura; *(fam.)* gamberro, pícaro.—*v.t.* descoser; rasgar; arrancar.—*v.i.* rasgarse; correr.
ripe [raip], *a.* maduro.
ripen ['raipən], *v.t., v.i.* madurar.
ripeness ['raipnis], *n.* madurez, *f.*
riposte [ri'post], *n.* réplica aguda.
ripping ['ripin], *a. (fam.)* de órdago.
ripple [ripl], *n.* rizo, oleadita.—*v.i.* rizarse.
rise [raiz], *n.* subida; cuesta; aumento; salida; origen, *m.*; *to give — to,* ocasionar, motivar.—*v.i. irr.* levantarse; subir; salir; surgir; nacer, brotar.
risen [rizn] [RISE].
rising ['raizin], *a.* saliente *(sol)*; ascendiente; que sube.—*n.* sublevación, *f.*
risk [risk], *n.* riesgo.—*v.t.* arriesgar; arriesgarse a.
risky ['riski], *a.* arriesgado.
risqué ['riskei], *a.* escabroso, picante.
rissole ['risoul], *n.* risol, *m.*
rite [rait], *n.* rito.
ritual ['ritjuəl], *a., n.* ritual, *m.*
ritualist ['ritjuəlist], *a., n.* ritualista, *m.f.*
rival ['raivəl], *a., n.* rival, *m.f.—v.t.* rivalizar con.
rivalry ['raivəlri], *n.* rivalidad, *f.*
river ['rivə], *a.* fluvial.—*n.* río; — *bed,* cauce, *m.*
riverside ['rivəsaid], *n.* ribera.
rivet ['rivit], *n.* remache, *m.—v.t.* remachar; clavar *(los ojos en).*
rivulet ['rivjulit], *n.* riachuelo, arroyo.
roach (1) [routʃ], *n. (ichth.)* leucisco.
roach (2) [routʃ], *n. (ent.)* cucaracha.
road [roud], *n.* camino; carretera; *(naut.)* rada; — *map,* mapa itinerario.
road-block ['roudblɔk], *n.* barricada.
roadside ['roudsaid], *n.* borde, *m.*
roam [roum], *v.t.* vagar por.—*v.i.* vagar, vagabundear.
roan [roun], *a., n.* roano.
roar [rɔ:], *n.* bramido, rugido.—*v.i.* rugir, bramar; estallar.
roast [roust], *a., n.* asado.—*v.t.* asar; tostar.—*v.i.* -se.
roastbeef ['roust'bi:f], *n.* rosbif, *m.*
rob [rob], *v.t.* robar.
robber ['robə], *n.* ladrón, *m.*
robbery ['robəri], *n.* robo.
robe [roub], *n.* túnica; traje talar, *m.—v.t.* vestir, ataviar.—*v.i.* vestirse, ataviarse de ceremonia.
robin ['robin], *n. (orn.)* petirrojo.
robot ['roubɔt], *n.* robot, *m.*
robust [rou'bʌst], *a.* robusto; fornido, membrudo.

rock (1) [rɔk], *n.* roca; peñón, *m.*; (*fam.*) **on the rocks**, pelado; sobre hielo (*bebida*).
rock (2) [rɔk], *v.t.* mecer; sacudir.—*v.i.* bambolear; mecerse.
rocker ['rɔkə], *n.* mecedora; balancín, *m.*
rocket ['rɔkit], *n.* cohete, *m.*—*v.i.* subir hasta las nubes.
rocking-chair ['rɔkintʃɛə], *n.* mecedora.
rocky ['rɔki], *a.* rocoso, roqueño; poco firme; **Rockies** o **Rocky Mountains,** Montañas Rocosas, *f.pl.*
rococo [rə'koukou], *a., n.* rococó, *m.*
rod [rɔd], *n.* varilla; caña de pescar; pértica; jalón, *m.*; vástago; (*fam., U.S.*) pistola; **to rule with a — of iron,** governar con mano de hierro; **to spare the —,** no castigar (*a un niño travieso*).
rode [roud], [RIDE].
rodent ['roudənt], *a., n.* roedor, *m.*
rodeo ['roudiou, rou'deiou], *n.* rodeo, circo.
roe (1) [rou], *n.* (*ichth.*) hueva.
roe (2) [rou], *n.* (*zool.*) corzo.
rogation [rou'geiʃən], *n.* rogación, *f.*, rogativa.
rogue [roug], *n.* bribón, *m.*, bellaco.
roguery ['rougəri], *n.* picardía, bellaquería; travesura.
role [roul], *n.* papel, *m.*
roll [roul], *n.* rollo; registro, rol, *m.*; panecillo; balanceo; retumbo del trueno; oleaje, *m.*; **to call the —,** pasar lista.—*v.t.* hacer rodar; arrollar; liar (*cigarrillo*); mover; vibrar; redoblar (*tambor*).—*v.i.* rodar; balancearse; dar vueltas; retumbar; **to — up,** arrollar; (*fam.*) llegar; **to — up one's sleeves,** arremangarse; **to — in money,** nadar en dinero.
roller ['roulə], *n.* rodador, *m.*; ruedecilla; ola grande; **— bearing,** cojinete (*m.*) de rodillos; **— skate,** patín (*m.*) de ruedas; **— towel,** toalla sin fin.
rollicking ['rɔlikiŋ], *a.* turbulento, retozón.
rolling-pin ['rouliŋpin], *n.* rodillo, hataca.
rolling-stock ['rouliŋstɔk], *n.* (*rail.*) material móvil, *m.*
rolling stone ['rouliŋ'stoun], *n.* (*fig.*) persona veleidosa.
roly-poly ['rouli'pouli], *a.* rechoncho.—*n.* pudín (*m.*) en forma de rollo.
Roman ['roumən], *a., n.* romano; **— nose,** nariz aguileña; **roman,** *n.* (*print.*) redondo.
Romance [rou'mæns], *a.* románico.—*n.* romance, *m.*
romance [rou'mæns], *n.* romance, *m.*; romanticismo; amor, *m.*; ficción, *f.*—*v.i.* fingir fábulas.
Romanesque [roumə'nesk], *a.* románico.
Romania [rou'meiniə] [RUMANIA].
Romanian [rou'meiniən] [RUMANIAN].
romantic [rou'mæntik], *a., n.* romántico.
romanticism [rou'mæntisizm], *n.* romanticismo.
romp [rɔmp], *n.* retozo, juego animado.—*v.i.* retozar, triscar, juguetear.
rompers ['rɔmpəz], *n.pl.* traje (*m.*) de juego; **in —,** en pañales.
rood [ru:d], *n.* crucifijo; la Cruz.
roof [ru:f], *n.* tejado, techo; paladar (*boca*), *m.*
roofing ['ru:fiŋ], *n.* material (*m.*) para techos.
rook [ruk], *n.* grajo, cuervo merendero; roque (*ajedrez*), *m.*—*v.t.* (*fam.*) estafar.
rookery ['rukəri], *n.* colonia de grajos.

rookie ['ru:ki], *n.* (*U.S. fam.*) bisoño.
room [ru:m], *n.* cuarto, habitación, *f.*; sitio, espacio; oportunidad, *f.*; **there is — for,** cabe(n).
rooming house ['ru:miŋhaus], *n.* (*U.S.*) casa de cuartos alquilados.
roomy ['ru:mi], *a.* holgado, espacioso.
roost [ru:st], *n.* percha; gallinero; **to rule the —,** mandar, tener vara alta.—*v.i.* posar.
rooster ['ru:stə], *n.* gallo.
root [ru:t], *n.* raíz, *f.*; (*fig.*) origen, *m.*; **to take —,** arraigar, echar raíces.—*v.i.* desarraigar (*up o out*); hocicar; echar raíces.
rope [roup], *n.* cuerda, soga; **to know the ropes,** saber cuántas son cinco.—*v.i.* atar; coger con lazo.—*v.i.* **to — in,** (*fam.*) implicar; (*U.S.*) embaucar.
ropy ['roupi], *a.* pegajosa, fibroso; viscoso.
rosary ['rouzəri], *n.* (*eccl.*) rosario; jardín (*m.*) de rosales.
rose (1) [rouz], *a.* rosado; **to see everything through rose-coloured spectacles,** verlo todo color de rosa.—*n.* rosa; rosal (*mata*), *m.*; roseta (*de una manguera*); **under the —,** bajo cuerda.
rose (2) [rouz], [RISE].
rosebush ['rouzbuʃ], *n.* rosal, *m.*
rosemary ['rouzməri], *n.* romero.
rosette [rou'zet], *n.* rosa.
rosewood ['rouzwud], *n.* palisandro.
rosin ['rɔzin], *n.* resina.
roster ['rɔstə], *n.* lista de turnos; horario.
rostrum ['rɔstrəm], *n.* tribuna.
rosy ['rouzi], *a.* rosado, color (*m.*) de rosa; (*fam.*) feliz, alegre.
rot [rɔt], *n.* podre, podredumbre, *f.*; (*fam.*) tontería, disparate, *m.*—*v.t.* pudrir.—*v.i.* pudrirse.
rotary ['routəri], *a.* rotativo.
rotate [rou'teit], *v.t.* hacer girar.—*v.i.* girar; alternar.
rotation [rou'teiʃən], *n.* rotación; **in —,** por turnos.
rote [rout], *n.* rutina maquinal; **by —,** de memoria.
rotten [rɔtn], *a.* podrido; corrompido; (*fam.*) ruin.
rotter ['rɔtə], *n.* (*fam.*) calavera, *m.*, sinvergüenza, *m.*
rouble [ru:bl], *n.* rublo.
roué ['ru:ei], *n.* libertino.
rouge [ru:ʒ], *n.* arrebol, colorete, *m.*
rough [rʌf], *a.* áspero; tosco; borrascoso; aproximado; turbulento; bruto; **— diamond,** (*fig.*) persona inculta pero de buen fondo; **— draft,** borrador, *m.*—*v.t.* hacer áspero; bosquejar; **to — it,** vivir sin comodidades.
rough-and-ready ['rʌfənd'redi], *a.* tosco pero eficaz.
roughen [rʌfn], *v.t.* poner tosco or áspero.—*v.i.* ponerse áspero.
roughness ['rʌfnis], *n.* aspereza, rudeza, tosquedad, *f.*; borrasca; rigor, *m.*; agitación, *f.*
roughshod ['rʌfʃɔd], *adv.* **to ride — over,** imponerse con arrogancia a.
roulette [ru:'let], *n.* ruleta.
Roumania [RUMANIA].
Roumanian [RUMANIAN].

round [raund], *a.* redondo; rotundo.—*n.* círculo; ronda; giro; tiro, bala; recorrido.— *v.t.* arredondar, redondear; volver.—*v.i.* redondearse; volverse; **to — off**, redondear; rematar; **to — up**, encerrar, recoger.—*adv.* alrededor; por ahí; por todas partes; **to go —**, rodear, pasar dando un rodeo; ser bastante; dar vueltas; **to come —**, rodear; venir por; volver en sí; **to stand —**, rodear; circundar.—*prep.* al rededor de; **a la vuelta de** (*una esquina*). [**return**]

roundabout [′raundəbaut], *a.* indirecto.—*n.* tío vivo; glorieta, redondel (*de carreteras*), *m.*

roundhand [′raundhænd], *n.* letra redonda.

round-shouldered [′raund′fouldəd], *a.* cargado de espaldas.

round-up [′raundʌp], *n.* encierro, rodeo.

rouse [rauz], *v.t.* despertar; animar; levantar.

rousing [′rauziŋ], *a.* emocionante, conmovedor.

rout [raut], *n.* derrota, fuga.—*v.t.* derrotar.

route [ru:t], *n.* ruta.

routine [ru:′ti:n], *a.* rutinario.—*n.* rutina.

rove [rouv], *v.t.* vagar por; torcer.—*v.i.* vagar.

rover [′rouvə], *n.* vagabundo; pirata, *m.*; buque (*m.*) de piratas.

row (1) [rou], *n.* fila; hilera; remadura; paseo en barca.—*v.t.*, *v.i.* remar.

row (2) [rau], *n.* pendencia, camorra; alboroto.—*v.i.* armar camorra, reñirse.

rowdy [′raudi], *a.*, *n.* pendenciero, gamberro.

rowing [′rouiŋ], *n.* remo.

rowlock [′rʌlək], *n.* chumacera.

royal [′rɔiəl], *a.* real.

royalism [′rɔiəlizm], *n.* realismo.

royalty [′rɔiəlti], *n.* realeza; familia real. —*pl.* derechos de autor.

rub [rʌb], *n.* roce, *m.*; (*fig.*) pega.—*v.t.* frotar; fregar; (*fig.*) molestar.—*v.i.* frotar; **to — out**, borrar.

rubber [′rʌbə], *n.* goma, caucho; goma de borrar; **— band**, liga de goma.

rubberneck [′rʌbənek], *n.* (*U.S. fam.*) turista boquiabierto.

rubber-stamp [′rʌbə′stæmp], *n.* estampillo. —*v.t.* firmar por rutina.

rubbery [′rʌbəri], *a.* elástico.

rubbish [′rʌbiʃ], *n.* basura; necedad, *f.*

rubble [rʌbl], *n.* ripios, escombros, *m.pl.*

rubicund [′ru:bikʌnd], *a.* rubicundo.

rubric [′ru:brik], *n.* rúbrica.

ruby [′ru:bi], *n.* rubí, *m.*

rucksack [′ruksæk], *n.* mochila, barjuleta.

rudder [′rʌdə], *n.* timón, gobernalle, *m.*

ruddy [′rʌdi], *a.* rojizo; rubicundo; coloradote.

rude [ru:d], *a.* tosco; descortés, informal; insolente.

rudeness [′ru:dnis], *n.* descortesía, insolencia; rudeza.

rudiment [′ru:dimənt], *n.* rudimento.

rudimentary [ru:di′mentəri], *a.* rudimentario.

rue [ru:], *v.t.* sentir, arrepentirse de.

rueful [′ru:ful], *a.* lastimoso, lamentable.

ruff [rʌf], *n.* lechuguilla (*collar*), golilla; collarín; (*orn.*) combatiente, *m.*

ruffian [′rʌfiən], *n.* tunante, bergante, bribón, *m.*

ruffle [rʌfl], *v.t.* arrugar; rizar; desaliñar; vejar.

rug [rʌg], *n.* alfombra, tapete, *m.*; manta.

rugged [′rʌgid], *a.* recio; escabroso.

ruin [′ru:in], *n.* ruina.—*v.t.* arruinar.

ruination [ru:i′neiʃən], *n.* ruina, perdición, *f.*

ruinous [′ru:inəs], *a.* ruinoso.

rule [ru:l], *n.* regla; autoridad, gobierno; **as a —**, generalmente, por regla general; **to be the —**, ser de regla; **to make it a — to**, imponerse la regla de.—*v.t.* gobernar, mandar; regir; determinar, disponer; **to — out**, excluir, no admitir; **to — over**, gobernar.—*v.i.* regir, señorear; prevalecer, ser vigente.

ruler [′ru:lə], *n.* gobernante, *m.*; regla.

ruling [′ru:liŋ], *n.* rayado; (*jur. etc.*) fallo.

rum (1) [rʌm], *a.* (*fam.*) raro, sospechoso.

rum (2) [rʌm], *n.* ron, *m.*

Rumania [ru:′meiniə], *n.* Romania.

Rumanian [ru:′meiniən], *a.*, *n.* rumano.

rumba [′rʌmbə], *n.* rumba.

rumble (1) [rʌmbl], *n.* retumbo, rumor bajo. —*v.i.* retumbar, rugir.

rumble (2) [rʌmbl], *v.t.* (*fam.*) cazar, descubrir.

ruminant [′ru:minənt], *a.*, *n.* rumiante, *m.f.*

ruminate [′ru:mineit], *v.t.*, *v.i.* rumiar; ponderar.

rummage [′rʌmidʒ], *n.* trastos viejos, *m.pl.*— *v.t.*, *v.i.* escudriñar, buscar desordenadamente.

rumour [′ru:mə], *n.* rumor, chisme, *m.* —*v.t.* **it is rumoured that**, corre la voz de que.

rump [rʌmp], *n.* nalga, anca; resto.

rumple [rʌmpl], *v.t.* arrugar, desaliñar.

rumpus [′rʌmpəs], *n.* batahola.

run [rʌn], *n.* corrida, curso, carrera; viajecito; serie; duración, *f.*; tanto (*de cricket*); **in the long —**, a la larga; **on the —**, en fuga; escapado.—*v.t. irr.* dirigir; pasar; correr; presentar.—*v.i. irr.* correr; manar; viajar; correrse; funcionar; ser candidato; **to — across**, tropezar con; cruzar corriendo; **to — after**, perseguir; **to — away**, fugarse, escaparse; **to — down**, gotear; agotarse; cazar y matar; atropellar; desprestigiar; **to — in**, entrar corriendo; (*fam.*) detener; **to — dry**, secarse; **to — foul of**, incurrir el enojo de; **to — off**, salvarse, huir; **to — out**, salir corriendo; agotarse; expirar, caducar; **to — out of**, no tener más; **to — over**, repasar; atropellar; rebosar. [**ladder**]

runaway [′rʌnəwei], *a.*, *n.* fugitivo, tránsfuga, *m.f.*

rung (1) [rʌŋ], *n.* escalón, *m.*

rung (2) [rʌŋ] [RING].

runner [′rʌnə], *n.* corredor; contrabandista, *m.*; (*bot.*) sarmiento.

runner-bean [′rʌnə′bi:n], *n.* judía verde.

runner-up [′rʌnər′ʌp], *n.* subcampeón, *m.*

running [′rʌniŋ], *a.* corriente; corredizo; seguido; en marcha; **— in**, en rodaje.—*n.* carrera, corrida; marcha; dirección, *f.*; **in the —**, con esperanzas todavía; **— costs**, gastos corrientes.

running-board [′rʌniŋbɔ:d], *n.* estribo.

runt [rʌnt], *n.* redrojo.

runway [′rʌnwei], *n.* pista de aterrizaje.

rupee [ru:′pi:], *n.* rupia.

rupture [′rʌptʃə], *n.* ruptura; hernia.—*v.t.* romper; causar una hernia.—*v.i.* romperse.

rural [′ruərəl], *a.* rural.

ruse [ruːz], *n.* ardid, *f.*, artimaña.
rush (1) [rʌʃ], *n.* acometida; tropel, *m.*; prisa; demanda extraordinaria; (*U.S.*) lucha estudiantil; — *hour*, hora de tráfico intenso. —*v.t.* llevar con gran prisa; hacer con gran prisa; atacar con prisa, sorprender.—*v.i.* ir de prisa; hacer con prisa.
rush (2) [rʌʃ], *n.* (*bot.*) junco.
rusk [rʌsk], *n.* galleta, rosca.
russet ['rʌsit], *a.* rojizo, bermejizo.
Russia ['rʌʃə], *n.* Rusia.
Russian ['rʌʃən], *a.*, *n.* ruso.
rust [rʌst], *n.* orín, herrín, *m.*, moho; (*bot.*) tizón, *m.*, roña.—*v.t.* enmohecer, aherrumbrar.—*v.i.* -se, oxidarse.
rustic ['rʌstik], *a.*, *n.* rústico; campesino.
rusticate ['rʌstikeit], *v.t.* desterrar al campo; (*educ.*) expulsar temporalmente.—*v.i.* rusticar.
rustle [rʌsl], *n.* crujido, susurro.—*v.t.* hacer crujir; robar ganado.—*v.i.* crujir, susurrar; (*U.S.*) patear, pernear; *to — up*, (*fam.*) improvisar.
rustler ['rʌslə], *n.* ladrón (*m.*) de ganado.
rusty ['rʌsti], *a.* herrumbroso, mohoso, oxidado; (*fig.*) casi olvidado por falta de práctica.
rut (1) [rʌt], *n.* bache, *m.*, rodada, surco.— *v.t.* hacer rodadas en.
rut (2) [rʌt], *n.* (*zool.*) celo.—*v.i.* bramar; estar en celo.
ruthless ['ruːθlis], *a.* desalmado, despiadado.
rye [rai], *n.* centeno; (*U.S.*) whisky (*m.*) de centeno.

S

S, s [es], *n.* décimonona letra del alfabeto inglés.
Sabbath ['sæbəθ], *n.* sábado (*judío*); domingo (*cristiano*).
sable [seibl], *a.* sable; negro.—*n.* marta.
sabotage ['sæbətɑːʒ], *n.* sabotaje, *m.*—*v.t.* sabotear.
saboteur [sæbə'təː], *n.* saboteador, *m.*
sabre ['seibə], *n.* sable, *m.*
saccharine ['sækərin], *n.* sacarina.
sack (1) [sæk], *n.* saco; *to give the —*, despedir; *to get the —*, ser despedido.—*v.t.* meter en un saco; despedir.
sack (2) [sæk], *n.* (*mil.*) saqueo.—*v.t.* saquear.
sack (3) [sæk], *n.* (*obs.*) vino.
sackcloth ['sækkloθ], *n.* harpillera; (*eccl.*) cilicio.
sacrament ['sækrəmənt], *n.* sacramento.
sacramental [sækrə'mentl], *a.* sacramental.
sacred ['seikrid], *a.* sagrado; consagrado.
sacrifice ['sækrifais], *n.* sacrificio.—*v.t.*, *v.i.* sacrificar.
sacrificial [sækri'fiʃəl], *a.* del sacrificio.
sacrilege ['sækrilidʒ], *n.* sacrilegio.
sacrilegious [sækri'lidʒəs], *a.* sacrílego.
sacristan ['sækristən], *n.* sacristán, *m.*
sacristy ['sækristi], *n.* sacristía.

sad [sæd], *a.* triste; pensativo; funesto; (*fig.*) travieso.
sadden [sædn], *v.t.* entristecer.
saddle [sædl], *n.* silla de montar; (*mec.*) silla. —*v.t.* ensillar; cargar.
saddle-bag ['sædlbæg], *n.* alforja.
sadism ['sædizm, 'seidizm], *n.* sadismo.
sadist ['sædist, 'seidist], *n.* sadista, *m.f.*
sadistic [sæ'distik], *a.* sadista.
sadness ['sædnis], *n.* tristeza.
safe [seif], *a.* seguro; incólume, salvo; intacto; cierto; digno de confianza; — *and sound*, sano y salvo.—*n.* caja fuerte o de caudales; alacena.
safe-conduct ['seif'kɔndʌkt], *n.* salvoconducto.
safeguard ['seifgɑːd], *n.* protección; precaución, *f.*—*v.t.* proteger.
safety ['seifti], *n.* seguridad; — *belt*, salvavidas, *m.inv.*; — *catch*, fiador, *m.*; — *pin*, imperdible, *m.*
safety-valve ['seiftivælv], *n.* válvula de seguridad.
saffron ['sæfrən], *a.* azafranado.—*n.* azafrán, *m.*
sag [sæg], *v.i.* ceder, doblegarse; flaquear.
saga ['sɑːgə], *n.* saga; epopeya.
sagacious [sə'geiʃəs], *a.* sagaz; sutil.
sagacity [sə'gæsiti], *n.* sagacidad, *f.*
sage (1) [seidʒ], *a.* sabio; sagaz.—*n.* sabio.
sage (2) [seidʒ], *n.* (*bot.*) salvia.
said [sed], *a.* dicho; citado. [SAY].
sail [seil], *n.* vela; paseo en barco; aspa (*de molino*); *under full —*, a toda vela; *to set —*, hacerse a la vela; zarpar.—*v.t.* gobernar (*un barco*); navegar por.—*v.i.* navegar; zarpar; flotar.
sailcloth ['seilklɔθ], *n.* lona.
sailing ['seilin], *n.* navegación, *f.*; *plain —*, (*fig.*) progreso fácil.
sailing-boat ['seilinbout], *n.* barco de vela.
sailor ['seilə], *n.* marinero; (*mil.*) marino.
saint [seint], *a.* San, *m.*; Santo (*before male names beginning with Do- or To-*)-; Santa; *St. Bernard*, perro de San Bernardo.—*n.* santo; santa; (*fig.*) ángel, *m.*
saintliness ['seintlinis], *n.* santidad, *f.*
sake [seik], *n.* causa; amor, *m.*; *for the — of*, por amor de; *for your —*, por Vd.; por su propio bien.
salacious [sə'leiʃəs], *a.* salaz.
salad ['sæləd], *n.* ensalada.
salad-bowl ['sælədboul], *n.* ensaladera.
salad-dressing ['sæləd'dresin], *n.* mayonesa.
salaried ['sælərid], *a.* asalariado.
salary ['sæləri], *n.* salario, sueldo.
sale [seil], *n.* venta; subasta; demanda; *for —*, *on —*, de o en venta.
salesman ['seilzmən], *n.* dependiente (*de tienda*); viajante, *m.*
saleswoman ['seilzwumən], *n.* dependienta (*de tienda*).
salient ['seiljənt], *a.* saliente; conspicuo.—*n.* saliente, *m.*
saliva [sə'laivə], *n.* saliva.
sallow ['sælou], *a.* cetrino.
sallowness ['sælounis], *n.* amarillez, *f.*
sally ['sæli], *n.* salida.—*v.i.* hacer una salida.
salmon ['sæmən], *a.* (*also* **salmon-pink**) de color (*m.*) de salmón.—*n.* salmón, *m.*
saloon [sə'luːn], *n.* sala; salón, *m.*; cámara (*de un vapor*); (*U.S.*) taberna.

363

salt

salt [sɔ:lt], *a.* salado; salobre.—*n.* sal, *f.*; sabor, *m.*; *old* —, lobo de mar; — *cellar*, salero; *he is not worth his* —, no vale el pan que come; *to take with a pinch of* —, creer con cierta reserva.—*v.t.* salar; salpimentar.

saltpetre [sɔ:lt'pi:tə], *n.* salitre, *m.*

salty ['sɔ:lti], *a.* salado; salobre.

salubrious [sə'lju:briəs], *a.* salubre, saludable.

salutary ['sæljutəri], *a.* saludable.

salutation [sælju'teiʃən], *n.* salutación, *f.*, saludo.

salute [sə'lju:t], *n.* saludo; salva.—*v.t., v.i.* saludar.

Salvador(i)an [sælvə'dɔ:r(i)ən], *a., n.* salvadoreño.

salvage ['sælvidʒ], *n.* salvamento.—*v.t.* salvar.

salvation [sæl'veiʃən], *n.* salvación, *f.*

salve [sɑ:v, sælv], *n.* pomada; remedio.—*v.t.* curar; remediar; tranquilizar; salvar.

salver ['sælvə], *n.* bandeja.

Samaritan [sə'mæritn], *a., n.* samaritano.

same [seim], *a.* mismo; idéntico; igual; *much the — as,* casi como; *it is all the — to me,* me es igual, me da lo mismo; *all the* —, sin embargo.

sameness ['seimnis], *n.* identidad, *f.*; parecido.

sample [sɑ:mpl], *n.* muestra.—*v.t.* probar.

sanatorium [sænə'tɔ:riəm], *n.* sanatorio.

sanctify ['sæŋktifai], *v.t.* santificar.

sanctimonious [sæŋkti'mounjəs], *a.* beato, mojigato.

sanction ['sæŋkʃən], *n.* sanción, *f.*—*v.t.* sancionar, autorizar.

sanctity ['sæŋktiti], *n.* santidad; inviolabilidad, *f.*

sanctuary ['sæŋktjuəri], *n.* santuario; asilo; *to take* —, acogerse a sagrado.

sand [sænd], *n.* arena; — *dune,* duna.—*pl.* playa.

sandal [sændl], *n.* sandalia; alpargata.

sandalwood ['sændlwud], *n.* sándalo.

sand-paper ['sændpeipə], *n.* papel (*m.*) de lija.

sand-pit ['sændpit], *n.* arenal, *m.*

sandstone ['sændstoun], *n.* arenisca.

sandwich ['sændwidʒ], *n.* sandwich, *m.,* bocadillo.—*v.t.* insertar.

sandy ['sændi], *a.* arenoso; rufo (*de pelo*).

sane [sein], *a.* cuerdo; prudente.

sang [sæŋ] [SING].

sanguinary ['sæŋgwinəri], *a.* sanguinario.

sanguine ['sæŋgwin], *a.* confiado, optimista; sanguíneo.

sanitary ['sænitəri], *a.* sanitario.

sanitation [sæni'teiʃən], *n.* higiene, *f.*; sanidad pública, *f.*; instalación sanitaria, *f.*

sanity ['sæniti], *n.* cordura; sentido común; prudencia.

Santa Claus ['sæntə'klɔ:z], *n.* Papá Noel, *m.*; los Reyes Magos.

sap (1) [sæp], *n.* savia; (*fam.*) necio.

sap (2) [sæp], *v.t.* zapar; (*fig.*) agotar, debilitar.

sapling ['sæpliŋ], *n.* árbol joven, *m.*

sapper ['sæpə], *n.* zapador, *m.*

sapphire ['sæfaiə], *n.* zafiro.—*a.* de color (*m.*) de zafiro.

sarcasm ['sɑ:kæzm], *n.* sarcasmo.

sarcastic [sɑ:'kæstik], *a.* sarcástico.

sardine [sɑ:'di:n], *n.* sardina.

sardonic [sɑ:'dɔnik], *a.* sardónico.

sash (1) [sæʃ], *n.* faja; cinturón, *m.*

sash (2) [sæʃ], *n.* marco (*de ventana*); — *window,* ventana de guillotina.

sat [sæt] [SIT].

Satan ['seitən], *n.* Satanás, *m.*

satanic [sə'tænik], *a.* satánico.

satchel ['sætʃəl], *n.* cartapacio; cartera.

sate [seit], *v.t.* hartar, saciar.

satellite ['sætəlait], *a., n.* satélite, *m.*

satiate ['seiʃieit], *v.t.* hartar, saciar; satisfacer.

satiety [sə'taiəti], *n.* hartura, saciedad, *f.*

satin ['sætin], *n.* raso.

satiny ['sætini], *a.* arrasado.

satire ['sætaiə], *n.* sátira.

satirical [sə'tirikəl], *a.* satírico.

satirist ['sætirist], *n.* escritor (*m.*) satírico.

satirize ['sætiraiz], *v.t.* satirizar.

satisfaction [sætis'fækʃən], *n.* satisfacción, *f.*; contento; recompensa; pago (*de una deuda*).

satisfactory [sætis'fæktəri], *a.* satisfactorio; expiatorio.

satisfy ['sætisfai], *v.t.* satisfacer; convencer; pagar; apagar (*la sed*).

saturate ['sætʃəreit], *v.t.* saturar; (*fig.*) imbuir.

saturation [sætʃə'reiʃən], *n.* saturación, *f.*

Saturday ['sætədei], *n.* sábado.

satyr ['sætə], *n.* sátiro.

sauce [sɔ:s], *n.* salsa; compota; (*fam.*) insolencia.

sauce-boat ['sɔ:sbout], *n.* salsera.

saucepan ['sɔ:spən], *n.* cacerola.

saucer ['sɔ:sə], *n.* platillo; *flying* —, platillo volante.

saucy ['sɔ:si], *a.* respondón, impudente.

Saudi Arabia ['saudiə'reibjə], *n.* la Arabia Saudita.

saunter ['sɔ:ntə], *n.* paseo, vuelta.—*v.i.* vagar, pasearse.

sausage ['sɔsidʒ], *n.* salchicha; chorizo.

savage ['sævidʒ], *a.* salvaje; feroz; cruel.—*n.* salvaje, *m.f.*

savagery ['sævidʒri], *n.* salvajismo; ferocidad; crueldad, *f.*

save [seiv], *v.t.* salvar; ahorrar (*dinero*); conservar; evitar.—*v.i.* ahorrar.—*prep.* salvo, excepto.—*conj.* sino, a menos que.

saving ['seiviŋ], *a.* económico, frugal; calificativo.—*n.* ahorro; salvedad, *f.*—*pl.* ahorros; *savings bank,* caja de ahorros. —*prep.* salvo, excepto.

saviour ['seivjə], *n.* salvador, *m.*

savour ['seivə], *n.* sabor, *m.*, gusto, dejo.— *v.t.* saborear; sazonar.—*v.i.* saber, oler (*of,* a).

savoury ['seivəri], *a.* sabroso, apetitoso; agradable.—*n.* entremés salado.

saw (1) [sɔ:], *n.* (*carp.*) sierra.—*v.t.* aserrar. —*v.i.* usar una sierra.

saw (2) [sɔ:], *n.* refrán, *m.*

saw (3) [sɔ:] [SEE].

sawdust ['sɔ:dʌst], *n.* serrín, *m.*

sawmill ['sɔ:mil], *n.* molino de aserrar, aserradero.

Saxon ['sæksən], *a., n.* sajón.

saxophone ['sæksəfoun], *n.* saxófono.

say [sei], *n. to have a — in the matter,* entrar en el asunto.—*v.t. irr.* decir; recitar; *no sooner said than done,* dicho y hecho. —*v.i.* decir; *you don't —!* ¿de veras? *that is to* —, es decir.

saying ['seiiŋ], *n.* dicho; refrán, *m.*, proverbio; *as the — is o goes*, como se dice.

scab [skæb], *n.* costra; escabro; (*fam.*) esquirol, *m.*

scabbard ['skæbəd], *n.* vaina.

scabby ['skæbi], *a.* costroso; roñoso; (*fig.*) despreciable.

scaffold ['skæfəld], *n.* andamio; cadalso.

scaffolding ['skæfəldiŋ], *n.* andamiaje, *m.*

scald [skɔːld], *n.* escaldadura.—*v.t.* escaldar.

scale (1) [skeil], *n.* platillo de balanza; (*math.*, *mus.*) escala; *on a large —*, en gran escala; *on a small —*, en pequeña escala; *to —*, a escala.—*pl.* balanza.—*v.t.* escalar; *to — down*, reducir.

scale (2) [skeil], *n.* (*zool.*) escama; laminita. —*v.t.* escamar.

scallop ['skɔləp], *n.* venera; (*sew.*) festón, *m.*

scalp [skælp], *n.* pericráneo; cuero cabelludo. —*v.t.* quitar la cabellera.

scalpel ['skælpəl], *n.* escalpelo.

scaly ['skeili], *a.* escamoso; incrustado.

scamp [skæmp], *n.* bribón, *m.*

scamper ['skæmpə], *v.i.* escaparse, escabullirse.

scan [skæn], *v.t.* escudriñar; escandir (*versos*).

scandal ['skændl], *n.* escándalo; difamación, *f.*

scandalize ['skændəlaiz], *v.t.* escandalizar.

scandalous ['skændələs], *a.* escandaloso; vergonzoso; calumnioso.

Scandinavia [skændi'neivjə], *n.* Escandinavia.

Scandinavian [skændi'neivjən], *a.*, *n.* escandinavo.

scansion ['skænʃən], *n.* escansión, *f.*

scant [skænt], **scanty** ['skænti], *a.* escaso; insuficiente.

scapegoat ['skeipgout], *n.* cabeza de turco, víctima propiciatoria.

scar [skaː], *n.* cicatriz, *f.*—*v.t.* marcar con una cicatriz.

scarce [skɛəs], *a.* escaso; raro; *to make oneself —*, largarse.

scarcely ['skɛəsli], *adv.* apenas; no bien; con dificultad.

scarcity ['skɛəsiti], *n.* escasez, *f.*; rareza; carestía.

scare [skɛə], *n.* susto; alarma.—*v.t.* asustar; intimidar; *to — away*, ahuyentar.

scarecrow ['skɛəkrou], *n.* espantajo.

scarf [skaːf], *n.* bufanda; pañuelo.

scarlet ['skaːlit], *a.* de color escarlata.—*n.* escarlata; *— fever*, escarlatina.

scathing ['skeiðiŋ], *a.* mordaz, cáustico.

scatter ['skætə], *v.t.* esparcir; derramar; dispersar.—*v.i.* dispersarse; disiparse.

scatter-brained ['skætəbreind], *a.* atolondrado.

scattered ['skætəd], *a.* disperso.

scavenge ['skævindʒ], *v.t.* recoger la basura.

scavenger ['skævindʒə], *n.* basurero; animal (*m.*) que se alimenta de carroña.

scenario [si'naːriou], *n.* escenario; guión, *m.*

scene [siːn], *n.* escena; vista; lugar, *m.*; escándalo; *behind the scenes*, entre bastidores; *to come on the —*, entrar en escena.

scene-painter ['siːnpeintə], *n.* escenógrafo.

scenery ['siːnəri], *n.* decorado; paisaje, *m.*

scene-shifter ['siːnʃiftə], *n.* tramoyista, *m.f.*

scenic ['siːnik], *a.* escénico; pintoresco.

scent [sent], *n.* olor, *m.*; fragancia; perfume,

m.; pista; *to throw off the —*, despistar.—*v.t.* husmear; perfumar; sospechar.

sceptic ['skeptik], *n.* escéptico.

sceptical ['skeptikəl], *a.* escéptico.

scepticism ['skeptisizm], *n.* escepticismo.

sceptre ['septə], *n.* cetro.

schedule ['skedjuːl], *n.* lista; horario; programa, *m.*—*v.t.* inventariar; *to be scheduled to o for*, haber de, deber.

scheme [skiːm], *n.* plan, *m.*, proyecto; diagrama, *m.*; esquema, *m.*; ardid, *m.*; *colour —*, combinación (*f.*) de colores.—*v.i.* formar planes; intrigar.

schemer ['skiːmə], *n.* proyectista, *m.f.*; intrigante, *m.f.*

schism [sizm], *n.* cisma, *m.* o *f.*

scholar ['skɔlə], *n.* alumno; estudiante, *m.f.*; erudito; becario.

scholarly ['skɔləli], *a.* de estudiante; erudito.

scholarship ['skɔləʃip], *n.* erudición, *f.*; beca.

scholastic [skə'læstik], *a.* escolástico; pedantesco.

school [skuːl], *n.* escuela; colegio (*particular*); instituto (*del estado*); facultad, *f.*; departamento (*de universidad*); (*ichth.*) banco; *boarding —*, colegio de internos; *— book*, libro de clase; *in —*, en clase.—*v.t.* instruir, enseñar; disciplinar.

schoolboy ['skuːlbɔi], *n.* alumno.

schooling ['skuːliŋ], *n.* enseñanza, educación; formación, *f.*

schoolmaster ['skuːlmaːstə], *n.* maestro de escuela; profesor, *m.*

schoolmistress ['skuːlmistris], *n.* maestra; profesora.

schooner ['skuːnə], *n.* goleta; vaso, copa.

science ['saiəns], *n.* ciencia.

scientific [saiən'tifik], *a.* científico; sistemático.

scientist ['saiəntist], *n.* hombre (*m.*) de ciencia, científico.

scintillate ['sintileit], *v.i.* chispear, centellear.

scissors ['sizəz], *n.pl.* tijeras, *f.pl.*

scoff [skɔf], *n.* mofa, burla.—*v.i.* mofarse, burlarse (*at*, de).

scoffer ['skɔfə], *n.* mofador, *m.*

scold [skould], *v.t.* reñir, reprender.

scolding ['skouldiŋ], *n.* regaño, reprensión, *f.*

scoop [skuːp], *n.* pala de mano; cucharón (*m.*) de draga; ganancia; reportaje sensacional, *m.*—*v.t.* sacar con pala o cuchara; vaciar; ganar; *to — out*, excavar.

scooter ['skuːtə], *n.* patinete (*de niño*); scúter, *m.*

scope [skoup], *n.* alcance, *m.*; esfera de acción; plan, *m.*

scorch [skɔːtʃ], *v.t.* chamuscar; tostar; abrasar, agostar (*el sol*).

scorching ['skɔːtʃiŋ], *a.* ardiente, abrasador; (*fig.*) mordaz.

score [skɔː], *n.* muesca; (*sport*) tanteo; señal, *f.*; motivo; raya; veintena (*20*); (*mus.*) partitura; *to pay off old scores*, saldar cuentas viejas.—*v.t.* rayar, marcar; tachar; apuntar; (*mus.*) orquestar; (*sport*) ganar (*puntos*); marcar (*un gol*).—*v.i.* llevar ventaja (*over*, a).

scorn [skɔːn], *n.* desdén, *m.*, desprecio.—*v.t.* despreciar, desdeñar; burlarse de.

scornful ['skɔːnful], *a.* desdeñoso.

scorpion ['skɔːpjən], *n.* escorpión, *m.*

Scot [skɔt], *n.* escocés, *m.*

Scotch [skɔtʃ], *n.* whisky escocés, *m.*
Scotland ['skɔtlənd], *n.* Escocia.
Scots [skɔts], *a.* escocés.
Scotsman ['skɔtsmən] [SCOT].
Scotswoman ['skɔtswumən], *n.* escocesa.
Scottish ['skɔtiʃ] [SCOTS].
scoundrel ['skaundrəl], *n.* canalla, *m.*
scour [skauə], *v.t., v.i.* fregar; limpiar; recorrer.
scourge [skɔ:dʒ], *n.* azote, *m.*; (*fig.*) plaga.— *v.t.* azotar; castigar.
scout [skaut], *n.* (*mil.*) explorador, *m.*—*v.i.* explorar, reconocer.
scowl [skaul], *n.* ceño.—*v.i.* ponerse ceñudo; *to — at,* mirar con ceño.
scowling ['skaulin], *a.* ceñudo.—*n.* ceño.
scraggy ['skrægi], *a.* descarnado, flaco.
scramble [skræmbl], *n.* trepa; contienda.— *v.t.* revolver (*huevos*).—*v.i.* trepar; andar a la rebatiña; **scrambled eggs,** huevos revueltos, *m.pl.*
scrap [skræp], *n.* pedacito; fragmento; riña, camorra.—*pl.* desperdicios; sobras.—*v.t.* echar a la basura.—*v.i.* reñise.
scrap-book ['skræpbuk], *n.* album (*m.*) de recortes.
scrape [skreip], *n.* acción *o* efecto *o* ruido de raspar; lío; dificultad, *f.*—*v.t.* raspar, rascar; restregar (*los pies*); *to — together,* amontonar poco a poco.—*v.i. to — through,* aprobar por milagro.
scratch [skrætʃ], *n.* arañazo, rasguño; borradura; línea de partida.—*v.t.* rascar; hacer un rasguño; arañar; cavar; retirar de una carrera.—*v.i.* arañar; retirarse.
scrawl [skrɔ:l], *n.* garabato.—*v.t.* garabatear.
scrawny ['skrɔ:ni], *a.* esquelético.
scream [skri:m], *n.* chillido.—*v.t., v.i.* chillar, gritar.
screech [skri:tʃ], *n.* chillido.—*v.t., v.i.* chillar.
screen [skri:n], *n.* biombo; mampara; (*eccl.*) cáncel, *m.*; pantalla (*de cine*); (*mil.*) cortina; abrigo.—*v.t.* abrigar; esconder; proteger; cribar; proyectar (*una película*).
screw [skru:], *n.* tornillo; rosca; (*aer., naut.*) hélice, *f.*; tacaño; (*fam.*) carcelero.—*v.t.* atornillar; oprimir; torcer; apretar.—*v.i.* dar vueltas; *to — down,* fijar con tornillo; *to — in,* atornillar; *to — up,* cerrar con tornillo; *to — up one's courage,* tomar coraje.
screwdriver ['skru:draivə], *n.* destornillador, *m.*
scribble [skribl], *n.* garrapatos, *m.pl.*—*v.t.* escribir de prisa.—*v.i.* garrapatear.
script [skript], *n.* escritura; letra cursiva; (*print.*) plumilla; texto; manuscrito; guión, *m.*
scriptural ['skriptʃərəl], *a.* bíblico.
Scripture ['skriptʃə], *n.* Sagrada Escritura.
scroll [skroul], *n.* rollo; voluta; rúbrica.
scrub [skrʌb], *n.* fregado; matorral, *m.*—*v.t.* fregar; restregar.
scrubbing ['skrʌbin], *n.* fregado.
scrubbing-brush ['skrʌbinbrʌʃ], *n.* cepillo de fregar.
scruff [skrʌf], *n.* nuca.
scruffy ['skrʌfi], *a.* (*fam.*) desaliñado, ruin.
scrum [skrʌm], *n.* mêlée, *f.*
scruple [skru:pl], *n.* escrúpulo.—*v.i.* tener escrúpulos.

scrupulous ['skru:pjuləs], *a.* escrupuloso; temoroso; exacto.
scrupulousness ['skru:pjuləsnis], *n.* escrupulosidad; meticulosidad, *f.*
scrutineer [skru:ti'niə], *n.* escrutador, *m.*
scrutinize ['skru:tinaiz], *v.t.* escudriñar; escrutar.
scrutiny ['skru:tini], *n.* escrutinio.
scuffle [skʌfl], *n.* pelea, sarracina.—*v.i.* pelear, forcejear.
scull [skʌl], *n.* remo.—*v.t.* remar.
scullery ['skʌləri], *n.* fregadero, trascocina.
sculptor ['skʌlptə], *n.* escultor, *m.*
sculptress ['skʌlptris], *n.* escultora.
sculptural ['skʌlptʃərəl], *a.* escultural.
sculpture ['skʌlptʃə], *n.* escultura.—*v.t.* esculpir.
scum [skʌm], *n.* espuma; hez, *f.*; (*fig.*) canalla.
scurf [skə:f], *n.* caspa.
scurrility [skʌ'riliti], *n.* grosería.
scurrilous ['skʌriləs], *a.* grosero.
scurry ['skʌri], *n.* fuga precipitada; remolino.—*v.i.* escabullirse.
scurvy ['skə:vi], *a.* vil, ruin.—*n.* escorbuto.
scuttle (1) [skʌtl], *n.* escotillón, *m.*—*v.t.* (*naut.*) echar a pique.—*v.i.* apretar a correr, escabullirse.
scuttle (2) [skʌtl], *n.* fuga precipitada.
scuttle (3) [skʌtl], *n.* cubo.
scythe [saið], *n.* guadaña.—*v.t.* guadañar.
sea [si:], *n.* mar, *m.* o *f.*; (*fig.*) abundancia; — *level,* nivel (*m.*) del mar; — *water,* agua salada; *at —,* en el mar; (*fig.*) perplejo; *high —,* alta mar; *to put to —,* hacerse a la vela, zarpar.
seafarer ['si:feərə], *n.* marinero.
seafaring ['si:feərin], *a.* marino.—*n.* vida del marinero.
sea-green ['si:'gri:n], *a.* verdemar.
seagull ['si:gʌl], *n.* gaviota.
sea-horse ['si:hɔ:s], *n.* caballo marino.
seal (1) [si:l], *n.* sello; timbre, *m.*—*v.t.* sellar; estampar; cerrar (*cartas*); confirmar; *to — up,* cerrar.
seal (2) [si:l], *n.* (*zool.*) foca.
sealing-wax ['si:linwæks], *n.* lacre, *m.*
sealskin ['si:lskin], *n.* piel (*f.*) de foca.
seam [si:m], *n.* costura; (*med.*) sutura; arruga; cicatriz, *f.*; (*geol., min.*) filón, *m.*, veta, capa.
seaman ['si:mən], *n.* marinero.
seamanship ['si:mənʃip], *n.* náutica, marinería.
seamstress ['si:mstris], *n.* costurera.
séance ['seiɑ:ns], *n.* sesión (*f.*) de espiritistas.
seaplane ['si:plein], *n.* hidroavión, *m.*
seaport ['si:pɔ:t], *n.* puerto de mar.
sear [siə], *v.t.* chamuscar; cauterizar.
search [sə:tʃ], *n.* registro; busca; examen, *m.*—*v.t.* registrar; investigar.—*v.i.* buscar (*for*).
searching ['sə:tʃin], *a.* penetrante, escrutador.
searchlight ['sə:tʃlait], *n.* reflector, *m.*
search-warrant ['sə:tʃwɔrənt], *n.* auto de registro.
sea-shore ['si:'ʃɔ:], *n.* playa.
seasick ['si:sik], *a.* mareado; *to be —,* marearse.
seasickness ['si:siknis], *n.* mareo.

season [si:zn], *n.* estación (*del año*); sazón, *f.*; tiempo; temporada; — *ticket,* billete (*m.*) de abono; *in* —, en sazón; del tiempo; *out of* —, fuera de estación; *closed*—, veda.—*v.t.* sazonar; acostumbrar; templar; imbuir.—*v.i.* madurarse.

seasonable ['si:znəbl], *a.* oportuno, tempestivo; de estación.

seasoning ['si:zniŋ], *n.* condimento; salsa; madurez; aclimatación, *f.*

seat [si:t], *n.* asiento; banco; silla; fondillos (*de los pantalones*), *m.pl.*; sitio, puesto; mansión; (*theat.*) localidad, *f.*; (*pol.*) escaño; *to hold a — in Parliament,* ser diputado a Cortes.—*v.t.* sentar; tener asientos para.

sea-wall ['si:wɔ:l], *n.* dique, *m.*

seaweed ['si:wi:d], *n.* alga marina.

seaworthy ['si:wə:ði], *a.* en buen estado.

secede [si'si:d], *v.i.* separarse.

secession [si'seʃən] *n.* secesión, *f.*

secessionist [si'seʃənist], *n.* separatista, *m.f.*, secesionista, *m.f.*

secluded [si'klu:did], *a.* apartado, solitario.

seclusion [si'klu:ʒən], *n.* reclusión, *f.*; apartamiento; soledad, *f.*

second ['sekənd], *a.* segundo; inferior; igual, otro; — *class* o *rate,* de segunda clase; — *lieutenant,* alférez, *m.*; — *sight,* doble vista; — *to none,* inferior a nadie; *on* — *thoughts,* después de pensarlo bien; — *fiddle,* papel secundario; — *nature,* otra naturaleza; *to come off — best,* llevar lo peor.—*n.* segundo; dos (*en las fechas*), *m.*; padrino; (*mus.*) segunda; momento.—*pl.* mercancías (*f.pl.*) de calidad inferior.—*v.t.* apoyar; secundar; ayudar.

secondary ['sekəndri], *a.* secundario; subordinado; accesorio.

second-hand ['sekənd'hænd], *a., adv.* de segunda mano.

secondly ['sekəndli], *adv.* en segundo lugar.

secrecy ['si:krəsi], *n.* secreto, reserva; misterio.

secret ['si:krit], *a., n.* secreto; — *service,* servicio de espionaje.

secretarial [sekrə'teəriəl], *a.* de secretario.

secretariat [sekrə'teəriət], *n.* secretaría.

secretary ['sekrətəri], *n.* secretario; secretaria; (*pol.*) ministro.

secrete [si'kri:t], *v.t.* esconder, ocultar; (*med.*) secretar.

secretion [si'kri:ʃən], *n.* escondimiento; (*anat.*) secreción, *f.*

secretive [si'kri:tiv], *a.* callado, reservado.

sect [sekt], *n.* secta.

sectarian [sek'teəriən], *a., n.* sectario.

section ['sekʃən], *n.* sección; porción; subdivisión, *f.*; (*mil.*) pelotón, *m.*

sectional ['sekʃənəl], *a.* seccionario; hecho de secciones.

sector ['sektə], *n.* sector, *m.*

secular ['sekjulə], *a.* seglar, profano.

secularize ['sekjuləraiz], *v.t.* secularizar.

secure [si'kjuə], *a.* seguro; cierto; firme.—*v.t.* asegurar; adquirir.

security [si'kjuəriti], *n.* seguridad, *f.*; fiador, *m.*; *to stand — for,* salir fiador por.—*pl.* (*com.*) valores, *m.pl.*, títulos, *m.pl.*

sedate [si'deit], *a.* formal, serio; sosegado.

sedative ['sedətiv], *a., n.* sedativo.

sedentary ['sedəntəri], *a.* sedentario.

sediment ['sedimənt], *n.* sedimento.

sedimentary [sedi'mentəri], *a.* sedimentario.

sedition [si'diʃən], *n.* sedición, *f.*

seditious [si'diʃəs], *a.* sedicioso.

seduce [si'dju:s], *v.t.* seducir.

seducer [si'dju:sə], *n.* seductor, *m.*

seduction [si'dʌkʃən], *n.* seducción, *f.*

seductive [si'dʌktiv], *a.* seductivo; persuasivo.

sedulous ['sedjuləs], *a.* asiduo.

see (1) [si:], *n.* sede, *f.*; *Holy See,* Santa Sede.

see (2) [si:], *v.t., v.i. irr.* ver; mirar; comprender; visitar; recibir visitas; acompañar; *to* — *about,* hacerse cargo de; *to* — *into,* examinar a fondo; *to* — *the point,* caer en la cuenta; *let's* —, vamos a ver; *to* — *the sights,* visitar los monumentos; — *you tomorrow,* hasta mañana.

seed [si:d], *n.* semilla, simiente, *f.*; pepita (*de fruta*); (*fig.*) germen, *m.*; progenie, *f.*; *to run to* —, granar.—*v.t.* sembrar; despepitar.—*v.i.* granar.

seedy ['si:di], *a.* granado; (*fam.*) andrajoso; indispuesto.

seeing ['si:iŋ], *n.* vista; visión, *f.*; — *is believing,* ver y creer.—*conj.* — *that,* visto que.

seek [si:k], *v.t. irr.* buscar; procurar; pretender, solicitar; pedir; *to* — *after* o *for,* buscar; *to* — *out,* buscar por todos lados.

seem [si:m], *v.i.* parecer.

seeming ['si:miŋ], *a.* aparente.

seemingly ['si:miŋli], *adv.* al parecer.

seemliness ['si:mlinis], *n.* decoro.

seemly ['si:mli], *a.* decente, decoroso.

seen [si:n] [SEE].

seep [si:p], *v.i.* rezumarse.

seer [siə], *n.* profeta, *m.*; vidente; veedor, *m.*

seesaw ['si:sɔ:], *n.* columpio (*de niños*); vaivén, *m.*—*v.i.* balancear; columpiarse.

seethe [si:ð], *v.i.* hervir; (*fig.*) bullir.

segment ['segmənt], *n.* segmento.

segregate ['segrigeit], *v.t.* segregar.—*v.i.* -se.

segregation [segri'geiʃən], *n.* segregación, *f.*

seize [si:z], *v.t.* asir, coger; (*jur.*) secuestrar; prender; apoderarse de; (*fig.*) comprender; *to* — *up,* (*mech.*) atascarse.

seizure [si'ʒə], *n.* asimiento; captura; (*med.*) ataque, *m.*; (*jur.*) secuestro.

seldom ['seldəm], *adv.* rara vez.

select [si'lekt], *a.* selecto, escogido; exclusivo. —*v.t.* escoger.

selection [si'lekʃən], *n.* selección, *f.*; *to make a* —, escoger.

selective [si'lektiv], *a.* selectivo.

self [self], *a.* mismo; propio.—*n.* (*pl.* **selves**) personalidad, *f.*; el yo.—*pron.* se, sí mismo.

self-acting ['self'æktiŋ], *a.* automático.

self-centred ['self'sentəd], *a.* egocéntrico.

self-confidence ['self'kɔnfidəns], *n.* confianza en sí mismo.

self-conscious ['self'kɔnʃəs], *a.* apocado.

self-consciousness ['self'kɔnʃəsnis], *n.* timidez, *f.*

self-contained ['selfkən'teind], *a.* reservado; completo; independiente.

self-control ['selfkən'troul], *n.* dominio de sí mismo.

self-defence ['selfdi'fens], *n.* defensa propia.

self-denial ['selfdi'naiəl], *n.* abnegación, *f.*

self-esteem ['selfes'ti:m], *n.* amor propio.

self-evident ['self'evidənt], *a.* patente.

self-government

self-government ['self'gʌvənmənt], *n.* autonomía.
self-importance ['selfim'pɔːtəns], *n.* altivez, *f.*, orgullo.
self-interest ['self'intərəst], *n.* propio interés.
selfish ['selfiʃ], *a.* interesado, egoísta.
selfishness ['selfiʃnis], *n.* egoísmo.
selfless ['selflis], *a.* desinteresado.
self-love ['self'lʌv], *n.* amor propio.
self-made ['self'meid], *a.* levantado por sus propios esfuerzos.
self-portrait ['self'pɔːtreit], *n.* autorretrato.
self-preservation ['selfprezə'veiʃən], *n.* defensa de sí mismo.
self-reliant ['selfri'laiənt], *a.* confiado en sí mismo.
self-respect ['selfri'spekt], *n.* respecto de sí mismo; dignidad, *f.*
self-sacrifice ['self'sækrifais], *n.* abnegación, *f.*
self-satisfied ['self'sætisfaid], *a.* satisfecho de sí mismo.
self-starter ['self'stɑːtə], *n.* arranque automático.
self-styled ['self'staild], *a.* que se llama a sí mismo.
self-sufficient ['selfsə'fiʃənt], *a.* que basta a sí mismo.
self-supporting ['selfsə'pɔːtiŋ], *a.* independiente.
sell [sel], *v.t., v.i. irr.* vender; *to — for cash,* vender al contado; *to — off,* saldar; *to — on credit,* vender al fiado.
seller ['selə], *n.* vendedor, *m.*
selves [selvz] [SELF].
semaphore ['seməfɔː], *n.* semáforo.
semblance ['sembləns], *n.* apariencia; máscara.
semen ['siːmen], *n.* semen, *m.*
semi- ['semi], *prefix.* semi; medio.
semicircle ['semisəːkl], *n.* semicírculo.
semicircular [semi'səːkjulə], *a.* semicircular.
semicolon ['semikoulən], *n.* punto y coma.
seminar ['seminɑː], *n.* seminario.
seminary ['seminəri], *n.* seminario; colegio.
semiquaver ['semikweivə], *n.* semicorchea.
Semitic [si'mitik], *a.* semítico.
semitone ['semitoun], *n.* semitono.
senate ['senit], *n.* senado.
senator ['senətə], *n.* senador, *m.*
send [send], *v.t. irr.* enviar, mandar; remitir; arrojar; conceder; infligir; volver (*loco, etc.*); *to — away,* despedir; *to — back,* devolver, mandar volver; *to — down,* hacer bajar; (*fam.*) suspender; *to — for,* enviar a buscar; *to — in,* hacer entrar; introducir; *to — off,* expedir; despedir; *to — out,* hacer salir; enviar; emitir; *to — up,* hacer subir; lanzar; (*fam.*) parodiar; (*fam.*) enviar a la cárcel; *to — word,* mandar aviso.
sender ['sendə], *n.* remitente, *m.f.*
send-off ['send'ɔf], *n.* despedida.
senile ['siːnail], *a.* senil.
senility [si'niliti], *n.* senilidad, *f.*
senior ['siːnjə], *a.* mayor, de mayor edad; superior en grado; más antiguo; padre.
seniority [siːni'ɔriti], *n.* ancianidad, *f.*; precedencia.
sensation [sen'seiʃən], *n.* sensación, *f.*
sensational [sen'seiʃənl], *a.* sensacional.
sense [sens], *n.* sentido; juicio; *to be out of one's senses,* haber perdido el juicio;

common —, sentido común; *to come to one's senses,* volver en sí; recobrar el sentido común.
senseless ['senslis], *a.* sin sentido; disparatado, absurdo.
sensibility [sensi'biliti], *n.* sensibilidad, *f.*
sensible ['sensibl], *a.* cuerdo, sensato; sensible; consciente (de); perceptible.
sensitive ['sensitiv], *a.* sensitivo; sensible; impresionable; delicado.
sensitivity [sensi'tiviti], *n.* sensibilidad, *f.*; delicadeza.
sensitize ['sensitaiz], *v.t.* sensibilizar.
sensory ['sensəri], *a.* sensorio.
sensual ['sensjuəl], *a.* sensual; voluptuoso.
sensualism ['sensjuəlizm], *n.* sensualismo.
sensualist ['sensjuəlist], *n.* sensualista, *m.f.*
sensuality [sensju'æliti], *n.* sensualidad, *f.*
sensuous ['sensjuəs], *a.* sensorio.
sensuousness ['sensjuəsnis], *n.* sensualidad, *f.*
sent [sent] [SEND].
sentence ['sentəns], *n.* (*gram.*) frase, oración, *f.*; (*jur.*) sentencia; máxima.—*v.t.* sentenciar, condenar.
sententious [sen'tenʃəs], *a.* sentencioso.
sentient ['senʃənt], *a.* sensible.
sentiment ['sentimənt], *n.* sentimiento; opinión, *f.*
sentimental [senti'mentl], *a.* sentimental; tierno.
sentimentality [sentimen'tæliti], *n.* sentimentalismo; sensiblería.
sentinel ['sentinl], **sentry** ['sentri], *n.* centinela, *m.f.*
sentry-box ['sentriboks], *n.* garita de centinela.
separable ['sepərəbl], *a.* separable.
separate ['sepərit], *a.* separado, distinto; segregado.—['sepəreit], *v.t.* separar, dividir.—*v.i.* separarse.
separation [sepə'reiʃən], *n.* separación, *f.*
separatist ['sepərətist], *a., n.* separatista, *m.f.*
sepia ['siːpjə], *n.* sepia.
September [səp'tembə], *n.* se(p)tiembre, *m.*
septic ['septik], *a.* séptico.
sepulchral [si'pʌlkrəl], *a.* sepulcral.
sepulchre ['sepəlkə], *n.* sepulcro.
sequel ['siːkwəl], *n.* resultado; consecuencia; continuación, *f.*
sequence ['siːkwəns], *n.* serie; sucesión, *f.*; consecuencia.
sequestered [si'kwestəd], *a.* aislado, remoto.
sequin ['siːkwin], *n.* lentejuela.
seraph ['serəf], *n.* serafín, *m.*
seraphic [sə'ræfik], *a.* seráfico.
serenade [seri'neid], *n.* serenata.—*v.t.* dar una serenata.
serene [si'riːn], *a.* sereno.
serenity [si'reniti], *n.* serenidad, *f.*
serf [səːf], *n.* siervo.
serfdom ['səːfdəm], *n.* servidumbre, *f.*
serge [səːdʒ], *n.* estameña.
sergeant ['sɑːdʒənt], *n.* sargento.
sergeant-major ['sɑːdʒənt'meidʒə], *n.* sargento instructor.
serial ['siəriəl], *a.* de o en serie; por entregas.—*n.* novela por entregas; drama por episodios.
series ['siəriːz], *n.* serie, *f.*
serious ['siəriəs], *a.* serio; grave; sincero; importante.

seriously ['siəriəsli], *adv.* **to take —,** tomar en serio.
seriousness ['siəriəsnis], *n.* seriedad; gravedad, *f.*
sermon ['sə:mən], *n.* sermón, *m.*
sermonize ['sə:mənaiz], *v.t., v.i.* predicar, sermonear.
serpent ['sə:pənt], *n.* serpiente, *f.*; (*mus.*) serpentón, *m.*
serrated [se'reitid], *a.* dentellado; serrado.
serried ['serid], *a.* apretado, apiñado.
serum ['siərəm], *n.* suero.
servant ['sə:vənt], *n.* criado; criada; servidor, *m.*; empleado.
serve [sə:v], *v.t.* servir; ser útil a; manejar; (*jur.*) entregar (*una citación etc.*); cumplir (*una condena*); tratar.—*v.i.* servir (*as,* de); bastar; **to — for,** servir para; **to — time,** cumplir una condena; **to — one's time,** terminar el aprendizaje; **to — one's turn,** bastar; **it serves you right,** lo tienes merecido.
server ['sə:və], *n.* servidor, *m.*; (*eccl.*) acólito; bandeja.
service ['sə:vis], *n.* servicio; servicio de mesa; (*eccl.*) oficio; (*sport*) saque, *m.*; **at your —,** a la disposición de Vd.; **out of —,** desacomodado, 'no funciona'; **to be of — to,** ser útil a; **coffee —,** juego de café; **diplomatic —,** cuerpo diplomático; **on active —,** en acto de servicio; en el campo de batalla.
serviceable ['sə:visəbl], *a.* servible, útil; duradero; servicial.
service-station ['sə:vissteiʃən], *n.* (estación) gasolinera.
servile ['sə:vail], *a.* servil; adulador.
servility [sə:'viliti], *n.* servilismo.
serving ['sə:viŋ], *a.* sirviente.
serving-maid ['sə:viŋmeid], *n.* criada.
servitude ['sə:vitju:d], *n.* servidumbre, esclavitud, *f.*; **penal —,** trabajos forzados.
session ['seʃən], *n.* sesión, *f.*; junta; curso académico; **petty sessions,** tribunal (*m.*) de primera instancia.
set [set], *a.* obstinado, terco; establecido, prescrito; ajustado; inmóvil, fijo; engastado; forzado.—*n.* aparato (*de radio*); (*theat.*) decoración, *f.*; juego; clase, colección, *f.*; grupo; posición, *f.*; movimiento; tendencia; porte, *m.*; triscamiento (*de una sierra*); juego (*de herramientas etc.*); inclinación, *f.*; partido (*de tenis*).—*v.t. irr.* fijar; poner; plantar; establecer, instalar; preparar; (*print.*) componer; engastar, montar (*joyas*); (*mus.*) poner en música; (*med.*) reducir; encasar (*un hueso roto*); (*naut.*) desplegar (*velas*); tender (*lazos*); regular (*un reloj*).—*v.i.* ponerse (*el sol*); cuajarse (*un líquido*); fluir (*una corriente*); **to — about doing something,** ponerse a hacer una cosa; **to — upon each other,** venir a las manos; **to — against,** oponer; **to be — against,** detestar; **to — aside,** poner a un lado; abrogar; **to — at,** estimar en; **to — at rest,** poner en reposo; **to — back,** hacer retroceder; **to — before,** presentar; **to — down,** imputar; poner por tierra; poner por escrito; **to — fire to,** pegar fuego a; **to — forth,** exponer; avanzar; ponerse en camino; **to — free,** poner en libertad; **to — in motion,** poner en movimiento; **to — off,** adornar; poner en

relieve; salir; **to — one's heart on,** tener ilusión por; **to — one's teeth on edge,** dar dentera; **to — out,** ponerse en camino; hacer ver; **to — to rights,** rectificar; **to — on,** atacar; **to — to work,** poner(se) a trabajar; **to — up,** exaltar; fundar; establecerse; montar; **to — upon,** asaltar.
setback ['setbæk], *n.* revés, *m.*, contrariedad, *f.*
settee [se'ti:], *n.* canapé, sofá, *m.*
setting ['setiŋ], *n.* fondo; puesta (*del sol*); engaste (*de joyas*); (*naut.*) dirección, *f.*; fraguado (*del cemento*); (*theat.*) decorado; (*mus.*) arreglo; marco; aliño (*de huesos*).
settle [setl], *v.t.* colocar; establecer; sosegar; poblar, colonizar; poner fin a; clarificar; resolver; afirmar, asegurar; saldar; satisfacer; arreglar; **to — accounts,** ajustar cuentas; **to — on,** escoger; señalar (*una pensión etc.*).—*v.i.* establecerse; calmarse; hacer sedimento; decidirse; clarificarse; **to — down,** establecerse; calmarse; asentarse; ponerse (*to,* a).
settled [setld], *a.* fijo; establecido; determinado; poblado; sereno.
settlement ['setlmənt], *n.* establecimiento; colonia; colonización, *f.*; ajuste, *m.*; solución, *f.*; (*com.*) saldo, liquidación, *f.*; (*jur.*) dote, *m.*; traspaso.
settler ['setlə], *n.* colono.
seven [sevn], *a., n.* siete, *m.*
seventeen [sevn'ti:n], *a., n.* diecisiete, diez y siete, *m.*
seventeenth [sevn'ti:nθ], *a., n.* décimoséptimo; diez y siete (*en las fechas*), *m.*
seventh [sevnθ], *a., n.* séptimo.—*n.* séptima parte; siete (*en las fechas*), *m.*; (*mus.*) séptima.
seventieth ['sevntiəθ], *a., n.* septuagésimo.
seventy ['sevnti], *a., n.* setenta, *m.*
sever ['sevə], *v.t.* separar; romper.
several ['sevərəl], *a.* varios; distinto respectivo.
severance ['sevərəns], *n.* separación, *f.*
severe [si'viə], *a.* severo; riguroso; duro; austero; fuerte; grave.
severity [si'veriti], *n.* severidad; gravedad, *f.*; inclemencia (*del tiempo*).
sew [sou], *v.t., v.i. irr.* coser.
sewage ['sju:idʒ], *n.* aguas (*f.pl.*) de albañal; alcantarillado.
sewer [sjuə], *n.* albañal, *m.*, alcantarilla, cloaca.
sewing ['souiŋ], *n.* costura.
sewing-machine ['souiŋmə'ʃi:n], *n.* máquina de coser.
sex [seks], *n.* sexo; **the fair —,** el bello sexo.
sexless ['sekslis], *a.* neutro; frío.
sexton ['sekstən], *n.* sacristán, *m.*; sepulturero.
sexual ['seksjuəl], *a.* sexual.
sexuality [seksju'æliti], *n.* sexualidad, *f.*
shabby ['ʃæbi], *a.* raído; andrajoso; pobre; ruin; mezquino.
shack [ʃæk], *n.* choza.
shackle [ʃækl], *n.* grillo, esposa; traba.—*v.t.* encadenar, poner esposas; estorbar.
shade [ʃeid], *n.* sombra; matiz, *m.*; pantalla (*de lámpara*); visera; espectro; toldo.—*v.t.* sombrear; esfumar; amparar.
shading ['ʃeidiŋ], *n.* (*art*) degradación, *f.*, sombreado.

shadow

shadow ['ʃædou], *n.* sombra; (*art*) toque (*m.*) de obscuro.—*v.t.* obscurecer, sombrear; seguir de cerca.

shadowy ['ʃædoui], *a.* umbroso; vago.

shady ['ʃeidi], *a.* sombreado; sombrío; (*fig.*) sospechoso.

shaft [ʃɑ:ft], *n.* flecha; asta, mango (*de un arma etc.*); (*mech.*) eje, *m.*; vara (*de un carro*); pozo (*de mina, de ascensor*); rayo (*de luz*).

shaggy ['ʃægi], *a.* velludo, peludo; lanudo.

shake [ʃeik], *n.* meneo; sacudida; apretón (*m.*) de manos; temblor; (*fam.*) periquete, *m.* —*v.t. irr.* sacudir; menear; agitar; hacer temblar; desalentar; debilitar; estrechar (*la mano*); *to — one's head,* mover la cabeza; *to — off,* librarse de; sacudir; despistar; *to — up,* sacudir, remover.—*v.i.* estremecerse; trepidar; dar un apretón de manos.

shaking ['ʃeikiŋ], *a.* tembloroso.—*n.* sacudimiento; meneo; temblor, *m.*

shaky ['ʃeiki], *a.* trémulo; poco firme; dudoso.

shall [ʃæl], *v.i. aux. irr.* tener que; (*when it simply indicates the future, the future tense is used in Spanish*).

shallow ['ʃælou], *a.* somero, poco profundo; (*fig.*) superficial.—*n.* bajío.

sham [ʃæm], *a.* fingido; falso.—*n.* impostura, farsa.—*v.t., v.i.* simular, fingir.

shamble ['ʃæmbl], *n.* paso pesado y lento.— *pl.* matadero; (*fig.*) carnicería.—*v.i.* andar arrastrando los pies.

shambling ['ʃæmbliŋ], *a.* pesado, lento.

shame [ʃeim], *n.* vergüenza; ignominia; afrenta; lástima; *to put to —,* avergonzar.—*v.t.* avergonzar; afrentar.

shamefaced ['ʃeim'feist], *a.* tímido, vergonzoso; avergonzado.

shameful ['ʃeimful], *a.* vergonzoso, escandaloso; indecente.

shameless ['ʃeimlis], *a.* desvergonzado; indecente.

shamelessness ['ʃeimlisnis], *n.* desvergüenza; impudicia.

shampoo [ʃæm'pu:], *n.* champú, *m.*—*v.t.* dar un champú a.

shamrock ['ʃæmrɔk], *n.* trébol blanco.

shank [ʃæŋk], *n.* zanca; (*mech.*) asta.

shape [ʃeip], *n.* forma; bulto; talle; molde; fantasma, *m.*; *to put into —,* dar forma a. —*v.t.* formar, dar forma; ordenar; modificar; concebir; tallar.

shapeless ['ʃeiplis], *a.* informe; disforme.

shapelessness ['ʃeiplisnis], *n.* informidad; deformidad, *f.*

shapely ['ʃeipli], *a.* simétrico; bien formado.

share (1) [ʃɛə], *n.* parte, porción, *f.*; cuota; (*com.*) acción, *f.*; interés, *m.*—*v.t.* dividir; compartir; tomar parte en; distribuir; *to — out,* repartir.—*v.i.* participar; tomar parte (en).

share (2) [ʃɛə], *n.* reja (*del arado*).

shareholder ['ʃɛəhouldə], *n.* accionista, *m.f.*

shark [ʃɑ:k], *m.* tiburón; (*fam.*) caimán, *m.*

sharp [ʃɑ:p], *a.* agudo; astuto; vivo; cortante; repentino; afilado; penetrante; áspero; picante; mordaz; fino (*de oído*); severo; violento; listo; bien definido; (*mus.*) sostenido.—*adv.* en punto; puntualmente.— *n.* (*mus.*) sostenido.

sharp-edged ['ʃɑ:p'edʒd], *a.* aguzado.

sharpen ['ʃɑ:pən], *v.t.* afilar; aguzar; amolar.

sharpener ['ʃɑ:pənə], *n.* amolador, afilador, *m.*; *pencil —,* cortalápiz, *m.*; *knife —,* chaira.

sharper ['ʃɑ:pə], *n.* fullero; timador, *m.*

sharp-eyed ['ʃɑ:p'aid], *a.* de vista penetrante.

sharp-featured ['ʃɑ:p'fi:tʃəd], *a.* cariagüileño.

sharpness ['ʃɑ:pnis], *n.* agudeza; aspereza.

sharp-witted ['ʃɑ:p'witid], *a.* perspicaz.

shatter ['ʃætə], *v.t.* hacer pedazos; romper; frustrar (*esperanzas*).—*v.i.* hacerse pedazos; romperse.

shave [ʃeiv], *n.* afeitada; *to have a close —,* (*fig.*) escapar por un pelo.—*v.t.* afeitar; acepillar; rozar.—*v.i.* afeitarse.

shaving ['ʃeiviŋ], *n.* afeitada; acepilladura.

shaving-brush ['ʃeiviŋbrʌʃ], *n.* brocha de afeitar.

shaving-soap ['ʃeiviŋsoup], *n.* jabón (*m.*) de afeitar.

shawl [ʃɔ:l], *n.* chal, *m.*

she [ʃi:], *pron.* ella; la; hembra.

sheaf [ʃi:f], *n.* (*pl.* **sheaves**) gavilla; haz (*de flechas*), *m.*; lío, paquete (*de papeles*), *m.*

shear [ʃiə], *v.t. irr.* tonsurar; esquilar (*ovejas*); cortar; tundir (*tela*).

shears [ʃiəz], *n.* tijeras grandes, *f.pl.*; (*mech.*) cizallas, *f.pl.*

sheath [ʃi:θ], *n.* vaina.

sheathe [ʃi:ð], *v.t.* envainar; (*naut.*) aforrar.

sheaves [ʃi:vz] [SHEAF].

she-cat ['ʃi:kæt], *n.* gata.

she-devil ['ʃi:devil], *n.* diabla.

shed (1) [ʃed], *n.* cabaña; cobertizo.

shed (2) [ʃed], *v.t. irr.* quitarse *or* desprenderse de; mudar, derramar.

sheen [ʃi:n], *n.* brillo, lustre, *m.*

sheep [ʃi:p], *n.* (*pl.* **sheep**) oveja; carnero; *black —,* (*fig.*) garbanzo negro; *to make sheep's eyes at,* lanzar miradas de carnero degollado.

sheep-dip ['ʃi:pdip], *n.* desinfectante (*m.*) para ganado.

sheep-dog ['ʃi:pdɔg], *n.* perro de pastor.

sheepfold ['ʃi:pfould], *n.* majada.

sheepish ['ʃi:piʃ], *a.* vergonzoso, tímido.

sheep-shearing ['ʃi:p'ʃiəriŋ], *n.* esquileo.

sheer (1) [ʃiə], *a.* puro; transparente; acantilado.—*adv.* de un golpe; a pico.

sheer (2) [ʃiə], *v.t., v.i.* desviar.

sheet [ʃi:t], *n.* hoja, plancha; sábana; mortaja; extensión (*de agua*), *f.*; (*naut.*) escota; — *anchor,* ancla de la esperanza.

sheikh [ʃeik], *n.* jeque, *m.*

shekel ['ʃekl], *n.* siclo; (*fam.*) cuarto.

shelf [ʃelf], *n.* (*pl.* **shelves**) anaquel, estante, *m.*; banco de arena; *to be left on the —,* (*fig.*) quedarse para tía.

shell [ʃel], *n.* casco; cáscara; concha; coraza; caparazón, *m.*; cubierta; (*mil.*) granada; *tortoise —,* carey, *m.*—*v.t.* desvainar; descascarar; (*mil.*) bombardear.

shellfish ['ʃelfiʃ], *n.* marisco.

shelling ['ʃeliŋ], *n.* bombardeo.

shelter ['ʃeltə], *n.* amparo, abrigo; asilo; refugio.—*v.t.* abrigar; amparar; ocultar.— *v.i.* refugiarse, abrigarse.

sheltered ['ʃeltəd], *a.* abrigado; retirado.

shelve (1) [ʃelv], *v.t.* poner sobre un estante; proveer de estantes; (*fig.*) aplazar indefinidamente.

shelve (2) [ʃelv], *v.i.* inclinarse.

shelves [ʃelvz] [SHELF].
shelving [ˈʃelviŋ], *a.* inclinado, en declive.—*n.* estantería; declive, *m.*
shepherd [ˈʃepəd], *n.* pastor, *m.*—*v.t.* guiar.
shepherdess [ˈʃepədis], *n.* pastora.
sherry [ˈʃeri], *n.* vino de Jerez.
shield [ʃiːld], *n.* escudo; (*fig.*) amparo, defensa.—*v.t.* amparar.
shield-bearer [ˈʃiːldbeərə], *n.* escudero.
shift [ʃift], *n.* cambio; expediente, *m.*; artificio; camisa; tanda, turno (*de obreros*).—*v.t.* trasladar; mover; quitar.—*v.i.* moverse; cambiar(se); variar.
shiftless [ˈʃiftlis], *a.* incapaz; perezoso.
shifty [ˈʃifti], *a.* astuto; falso; furtivo.
shilling [ˈʃiliŋ], *n.* chelín, *m.*
shimmer [ˈʃimə], *n.* luz trémula; resplandor, *m.*—*v.i.* rielar.
shin [ʃin], *n.* espinilla.—*v.t. to — up*, trepar.
shine [ʃain], *n.* brillo.—*v.t. irr.* pulir; dar lustre a (*los zapatos*).—*v.i.* relucir, resplandecer, brillar; distinguirse.
shining [ˈʃainiŋ], *a.* brillante, radiante, resplandeciente.
shiny [ˈʃaini], *a.* brillante, lustroso.
ship [ʃip], *n.* buque, *m.*, barco.—*v.t.* embarcar; (*com.*) expedir; armar (*remos etc.*).
shipbuilder [ˈʃipbildə], *n.* constructor (*m.*) de buques.
shipbuilding [ˈʃipbildiŋ], *n.* construcción naval, *f.*
shipment [ˈʃipmənt], *n.* embarque, *m.*; remesa.
shipper [ˈʃipə], *n.* remitente; importador; exportador, *m.*
shipping [ˈʃipiŋ], *n.* barcos, buques, *m.pl.*; (*com.*) embarque, *m.*
shipshape [ˈʃipʃeip], *a.* en buen orden; bien arreglado.
shipwreck [ˈʃiprek], *n.* naufragio.—*v.t.* hacer naufragar; *to be shipwrecked*, naufragar.
shipyard [ˈʃipjaːd], *n.* astillero.
shire [ʃaiə], *n.* condado.
shirk [ʃəːk], *v.t.* evitar, esquivar; faltar a.
shirt [ʃəːt], *n.* camisa; *in one's shirt-sleeves*, en mangas de camisa.
shirt-front [ˈʃəːtfrʌnt], *n.* pechera.
shiver [ˈʃivə], *n.* estremecimiento, escalofrío; fragmento.—*v.t.* romper, hacer pedazos.—*v.i.* tiritar, temblar.
shivery [ˈʃivəri], *a.* tembloroso; friolero.
shoal [ʃoul], *n.* banco (*de arena, de peces*); muchedumbre, *f.*
shock [ʃɔk], *n.* choque, *m.*; susto; (*med.*) postración nerviosa, *f.*; (*elec.*) sacudida.—*v.t.* sacudir; chocar; escandalizar.
shocking [ˈʃɔkiŋ] *a.* espantoso; ofensivo; escandaloso.
shod [ʃɔd] [SHOE].
shoddy [ˈʃɔdi], *a.* de pacotilla; espurio.—*n.* lana regenerada.
shoe [ʃuː], *n.* zapato; herradura (*de caballo*); (*mech.*) zapata; *to be in someone's shoes*, estar en el pellejo de uno.—*v.t. irr.* herrar.
shoe-horn [ˈʃuːhɔːn], *n.* calzador, *m.*
shoe-lace [ˈʃuːleis], *n.* lazo.
shoemaker [ˈʃuːmeikə], *n.* zapatero.
shoe-shop [ˈʃuːʃɔp], *n.* zapatería.
shone [ʃɔn] [SHINE].
shook [ʃuk] [SHAKE].
shoot [ʃuːt], *n.* retoño; partida de caza.—*v.t. irr.* disparar, tirar; lanzar; vaciar; fusilar;

pegar un tiro (*a*); empujar; hacer (*una película*).—*v.i.* tirar, disparar; brotar; lanzarse; latir (*un dolor*); caer (*una estrella*); *to — off*, tirar; llevarse; *to — up*, espigarse (*plantas, niños etc.*); subir rápidamente.
shooting [ˈʃuːtiŋ], *n.* caza con escopeta; tiro; tiroteo.—*a. — star*, estrella fugaz.
shooting-range [ˈʃuːtiŋreindʒ], *n.* campo de tiro.
shooting-stick [ˈʃuːtiŋstik], *n.* bastón asiento.
shop [ʃɔp], *n.* tienda; *to talk —*, hablar de negocios.—*v.i.* (*also to go shopping*) ir de compras.
shopkeeper [ˈʃɔpkiːpə], *n.* tendero.
shoplifter [ˈʃɔpliftə], *n.* ladrón (*m.*) de tiendas.
shopping [ˈʃɔpiŋ], *n.* compras *f.pl.*; *—centre*, barrio de tiendas.
shop-window [ˈʃɔpˈwindou], *n.* escaparate, *m.*
shore (1) [ʃɔː], *n.* costa; playa; orilla (*de un río*).
shore (2) [ʃɔː], *v.t. to — (up)*, apuntalar.
shorn [ʃɔːn] [SHEAR].
short [ʃɔːt], *a.* corto; bajo; breve; escaso; insuficiente; brusco; (*com.*) alcanzado; *in —*, en suma; *to fall — of*, no llegar a; ser inferior a; *to be — of*, carecer de; *— of*, fuera de, menos; *to cut —*, interrumpir bruscamente; *to run —*, faltar; *— cut*, atajo.—*n.pl.* calzones cortos, *m.pl.*—*adv.* brevemente; bruscamente.
shortage [ˈʃɔːtidʒ], *n.* falta; carestía.
short-circuit [ˈʃɔːtˈsəːkit], *n.* corto circuito.
shortcoming [ˈʃɔːtˈkamiŋ], *n.* defecto.
shorten [ˈʃɔːtn], *v.t.* acortar.—*v.i.* acortarse.
shorthand [ˈʃɔːthænd], *n.* taquigrafía, estenografía.
short-handed [ˈʃɔːtˈhændid], *a.* falto de mano de obra.
shortly [ˈʃɔːtli], *adv.* pronto; brevemente; bruscamente.
shortness [ˈʃɔːtnis], *n.* cortedad, *f.*
short-sighted [ˈʃɔːtˈsaitid], *a.* miope; (*fig.*) poco perspicaz.
short-sightedness [ˈʃɔːtˈsaitidnis], *n.* miopía; (*fig.*) falta de perspicacia.
shot (2) [ʃɔt], *a.* tornasolado.—*n.* perdigón, *m.*; bala; tiro; tirador, *m.*; tirada; (*min.*) barreno; (*fam.*) ensayo. [SHOOT].
shotgun [ˈʃɔtgan], *n.* escopeta.
should [ʃud] [SHALL].
shoulder [ˈʃouldə], *n.* hombro; espalda.—*v.t.* echarse a la espalda; (*fig.*) cargar con; codear; *— arms!* ¡armas al hombro!
shoulder-blade [ˈʃouldəbleid], *n.* omoplato.
shoulder-strap [ˈʃouldəstræp], *n.* tirante, *m.*
shout [ʃaut], *n.* grito.—*v.t., v.i.* gritar.
shouting [ˈʃautiŋ], *n.* gritos, *m.pl.* aclamación, *f.*
shove [ʃʌv], *n.* empujón, *m.*—*v.t., v.i.* empujar.
shovel [ʃʌvl], *n.* pala.—*v.t.* traspalar.
show [ʃou], *n.* exposición, *f.*; espectáculo; función, *f.*; pompa, aparato; seña; apariencia; negocio; *to make a — of*, hacer gala de.—*v.t. irr.* indicar; mostrar; hacer ver; demostrar; descubrir, exponer; explicar; conducir; *to — off*, exhibir; lucir (*vestidos*); *to — out*, acompañar a la puerta; *to — up*, hacer subir; exponer (*un fraude*).—*v.i.* parecer; mostrarse; *to — off*, pavonearse; *to — up*, presentarse.
show-case [ˈʃoukeis] *n.* vitrina.

shower [ʃauə], *n.* chubasco; (*fig.*) lluvia; abundancia; — *bath,* ducha; *to take a* —, ducharse.—*v.t.* derramar.—*v.i.* llover.
showery [ˈʃauəri], *a.* lluvioso.
showiness [ˈʃouinis], *n.* ostentación, *f.*
shown [ʃoun] [SHOW].
showy [ˈʃoui], *a.* vistoso, ostentoso.
shrank [ʃræŋk] [SHRINK].
shred [ʃred], *n.* harapo; fragmento; pizca.—*v.t.* desmenuzar.
shrew [ʃru:], *n.* (*zool.*) musaraña; (*fig.*) fiera.
shrewd [ʃru:d], *a.* sagaz, perspicaz; sutil.
shrewdness [ˈʃru:dnis], *n.* sagacidad, *f.*, perspicacia; sutileza.
shriek [ʃri:k], *n.* chillido, grito agudo.—*v.i.* chillar; gritar.
shrill [ʃril], *a.* agudo, estridente.
shrimp [ʃrimp], *n.* camarón, *m.*; quisquilla; (*fam.*) hombrecillo.
shrine [ʃrain], *n.* relicario; sepulcro de santo; capilla.
shrink [ʃriŋk], *v.t.* irr. encoger; reducir.—*v.i.* encogerse; contraerse; disminuir; (*fig.*) temblar; retirarse; *to — from,* huir de.
shrinkage [ˈʃriŋkidʒ], *n.* encogimiento; contracción; reducción, *f.*
shrinking [ˈʃriŋkiŋ], *a.* tímido.
shrivel [ˈʃrivəl], *v.t.* arrugar; marchitar.—*v.i.* arrugarse; marchitarse; avellanarse.
shroud [ʃraud], *n.* mortaja.—*pl.* (*naut.*) obenques, *m.pl.*—*v.t.* amortajar; velar.
Shrove Tuesday [ʃrouvˈtju:zd(e)i], *n.* martes (*m.*) de carnaval.
shrub [ʃrʌb], *n.* arbusto.
shrubbery [ˈʃrʌbəri], *n.* arbustos, *m.pl.*
shrug [ʃrʌg], *n.* encogimiento de hombros.—*v.i.* encogerse de hombros.
shrunk [ʃrʌŋk], **shrunken** [ˈʃrʌŋkən] [SHRINK].
shudder [ˈʃʌdə], *n.* estremecimiento; vibración, *f.*—*v.i.* estremecerse; vibrar.
shuffle [ˈʃʌfl], *n.* barajadura; embuste, *m.*—*v.t.* mezclar (*papeles*); barajar (*naipes*); arrastrar (*los pies*); *to — off,* esquivar; largarse arrastrando los pies.
shun [ʃʌn], *v.t.* rehuir, evitar, esquivar; apartarse de.
shunt [ʃʌnt], *v.t.* apartar; (*rail.*) desviar.
shunting [ˈʃʌntiŋ], *n.* (*rail.*) maniobras, *f.pl.*
shut [ʃʌt], *v.t.* irr. cerrar.—*v.i.* cerrarse; juntarse; *to — down,* cerrar; parar (*fábrica*); *to — in,* encerrar; rodear; *to — off,* cortar; *to — out,* excluir; *to — up,* cerrar; encerrar; (*fam.*) hacer callar; callarse.
shutter [ˈʃʌtə], *n.* postigo; persiana; contraventana; (*phot.*) obturador, *m.*
shuttle [ˈʃʌtl], *n.* lanzadera.
shuttle-cock [ˈʃʌtlkɔk], *n.* volante, *m.*
shy (1) [ʃai], *a.* tímido.—*n.* respingo.—*v.i.* respingar; asustarse.
shy (2) [ʃai], *n.* lanzamiento; prueba.—*v.t.* lanzar.
shyness [ˈʃainis], *n.* timidez, *f.*
Siamese [saiəˈmi:z], *a.*, *n.* siamés.
Sicilian [siˈsiljən], *a.*, *n.* siciliano.
Sicily [ˈsisili], *n.* Sicilia.
sick [sik], *a.* nauseado, mareado; enfermo; *to be — of,* estar harto de; *to be —,* estar enfermo; vomitar.
sick-bed [ˈsikbed], *n.* lecho de enfermo.
sicken [sikn], *v.t.* marear; dar asco a; hartar.—*v.i.* enfermar(se), caer enfermo; marearse.

sickening [ˈsikniŋ], *a.* nauseabundo; repugnante; fastidioso.
sickle [sikl], *n.* hoz, *f.*
sickly [ˈsikli], *a.* enfermizo; nauseabundo; — *sweet,* empalagoso.
sickness [ˈsiknis], *n.* enfermedad, *f.*; náusea.
side [said], *n.* lado; margen, *m.*, orilla; falda (*de colina*); partido; (*sport*) equipo; costado; ijada (*de animal*); *to be on the — of,* estar por; *on all sides,* por todas partes; *wrong — out,* al revés.—*v.i.* *to — with,* declararse por.
sideboard [ˈsaidbɔ:d], *n.* aparador, *m.*
side-car [ˈsaidkɑ:], *n.* sidecar, *m.*
side-glance [ˈsaidglɑ:ns], *n.* mirada de soslayo.
side-light [ˈsaidlait], *n.* luz lateral, *f.*
sidelong [ˈsaidlɔŋ], *a.* lateral, oblicuo.—*adv.* de lado; de soslayo.
side-show [ˈsaidʃou], *n.* función secundaria.
side-street [ˈsaidstri:t], *n.* callejuela.
side-track [ˈsaidtræk], *n.* apartadero; desvío.
sideways [ˈsaidweiz], *adv.* de lado; oblicuamente; de soslayo.
side-whiskers [ˈsaidhwiskəz], *n.pl.* patillas, *f.pl.*
siding [ˈsaidiŋ], *n.* apartadero.
sidle [saidl], *v.i.* ir de lado; *to — up to,* acercarse furtivamente a.
siege [si:dʒ], *n.* sitio, asedio; *to lay —,* poner, sitio.
sieve [siv], *n.* tamiz, *m.*, cedazo.—*v.t.* tamizar; cerner.
sift [sift], *v.t.* cerner; escudriñar; separar.
sigh [sai], *n.* suspiro.—*v.i.* suspirar; *to — for,* anhelar.
sight [sait], *n.* vista; visión, *f.*; aspecto; espectáculo; mira (*de fusil*); *to come into* —, asomarse; *in* —, a la vista; *out of* —, perdido de vista; *to catch — of,* vislumbrar; *to lose — of,* perder de vista; *to know by* —, conocer de vista.—*v.t.* avistar; ver; apuntar.
sightseeing [ˈsaitsi:iŋ], *n.* visita de los monumentos.
sightseer [ˈsaitsi:ə], *n.* turista, *m.f.*
sign [sain], *n.* señal, *f.*; signo (*del zodíaco*); marca; síntoma, *m.*; seña; muestra; huella.—*v.t.* firmar; (*eccl.*) persignar; señalar.
signal [ˈsignəl], *a.* insigne, notable.—*n.* señal, *f.*—*v.t.*, *v.i.* hacer señas, señalar.
signal-box [ˈsignəlbɔks], *n.* garita de señales.
signatory [ˈsignətəri], *n.* signatario.
signature [ˈsignitʃə], *n.* firma.
signboard [ˈsainbɔ:d], *n.* muestra, letrero.
significance [sigˈnifikəns], *n.* significación, *f.*; importancia.
significant [sigˈnifikənt], *a.* significativo.
signify [ˈsignifai], *v.t.* significar; expresar; importar.
signpost [ˈsainpoust], *n.* indicador (*m.*) de dirección.
silence [ˈsailəns], *n.* silencio.—*interj.* ¡silencio! —*v.t.* imponer silencio a; mandar callar; silenciar.
silencer [ˈsailənsə], *n.* silenciador, *m.*
silent [ˈsailənt], *a.* silencioso; *to remain —,* guardar silencio. [**sleeping**]
silhouette [siluˈet], *n.* silueta.—*v.t.* destacar.
silk [silk], *n.* seda; *shot —,* seda tornasolada.
silkworm [ˈsilkwə:m], *n.* gusano de seda.
silky [ˈsilki], *a.* sedoso; (*fig.*) suave.

sill [sil], *n.* umbral (*de puerta*), *m.*; antepecho, repisa (*de ventana*).
silliness ['silinis], *n.* simpleza; tontería.
silly ['sili], *a.* tonto, imbécil; disparatado.
silt [silt], *n.* aluvión, *m.*
silver ['silvǝ], *a.* de plata; argentino; — *birch*, abedul, *m.*; — *paper*, papel (*m.*) de estaño; — *plate*, vajilla de plata; — *wedding*, bodas (*f.pl.*) de plata.—*n.* plata; monedas (*f.pl.*) de plata (*dinero*); vajilla de plata.—*v.t.* platear; azogar; blanquear.
silversmith ['silvǝsmiθ], *n.* platero.
silvery ['silvǝri], *a.* plateado; argentino.
similar ['similǝ], *a.* semejante, parecido.
similarity [simi'læriti], *n.* semejanza.
simile ['simili], *n.* símil, *m.*
simmer ['simǝ], *v.i.* hervir a fuego lento; *to — down*, (*fig.*) moderarse poco a poco.
simper ['simpǝ], *v.i.* sonreírse afectadamente.
simple [simpl], *a.* sencillo; simple; ingenuo; mero; necio.
simple-minded ['simpl'maindid], *a.* ingenuo.
simpleton ['simpltǝn], *n.* papanatas, *m.sg.*
simplicity [sim'plisiti], *n.* sencillez; simplicidad, *f.*
simplification [simplifi'keiʃǝn], *n.* simplificación, *f.*
simplify ['simplifai], *v.t.* simplificar.
simulate ['simjuleit], *v.t.* simular, fingir.
simulation [simju'leiʃǝn], *n.* simulación, *f.*, fingimiento.
simultaneous [simǝl'teinjǝs], *a.* simultáneo.
sin [sin], *n.* pecado.—*v.i.* pecar.
since [sins], *adv.* desde; desde entonces; *long —*, hace mucho.—*conj.* ya que, puesto que; desde que.—*prep.* desde.
sincere [sin'siǝ], *a.* sincero.
sincerity [sin'seriti], *n.* sinceridad, *f.*
sinew ['sinju:], *n.* tendón, *m.*; (*fig.*) fuerza.
sinewy ['sinju:i], *a.* fibroso; fuerte.
sinful ['sinful], *a.* pecador (*persona*); pecaminoso (*hecho*).
sinfulness ['sinfulnis], *n.* pecado; perversidad, *f.*
sing [siŋ], *v.t. irr.* cantar; elogiar.—*v.i.* cantar; zumbar (*los oídos*).
singe [sindʒ], *v.t.* chamuscar.
singer ['siŋǝ], *n.* cantante, *m.f.*; cantor, *m.*
singing ['siŋiŋ] *a.* cantante.—*n.* canto; zumbido (*de los oídos*).
single [siŋgl], *a.* único; sencillo; solo; individual; soltero (*no casado*); — *file*, fila india; — *combat*, combate singular, *m.*; — *ticket*, billete sencillo, *m.*—*v.t. to — out*, escoger.
single-breasted ['siŋgl'brestid], *a.* recto.
single-handed ['siŋgl'hændid], *a.* solo, sin ayuda.
single-minded ['siŋgl'maindid], *a.* sin doblez; de una sola idea.
singlet ['siŋglit], *n.* camiseta.
singly ['siŋgli], *adv.* a solas; separadamente, uno a uno.
singular ['siŋgjulǝ], *a., n.* singular, *m.*
singularity [siŋgju'læriti], *n.* singularidad, *f.*
sinister ['sinistǝ], *a.* siniestro.
sink [siŋk], *n.* fregadero, pila; sumidero; (*fig.*) sentina.—*v.t. irr.* hundir, sumergir, echar a pique; excavar; bajar, disminuir; hacer caer; invertir; ocultar; grabar.—*v.i.* hundirse, sumergirse, grabarse (*en la memoria*); caer;

penetrar; bajar, disminuir; irse a pique; debilitarse; *to — to one's knees*, caer de rodillas.
sinner ['sinǝ], *n.* pecador, *m.*
sinuous ['sinjuǝs], *a.* sinuoso, tortuoso.
sinus ['sainǝs], *n.* seno.
sip [sip], *n.* sorbo.—*v.t.* sorber, beber a sorbos; saborear.
siphon ['saifǝn], *n.* sifón, *m.*—*v.t.* sacar con sifón.
sir [sǝ:], *n.* señor, *m.*; caballero.
sirloin ['sǝ:lɔin], *n.* solomillo.
sister ['sistǝ], *n.* hermana; (*eccl.*) sor, *f.*
sister-in-law ['sistǝrinlɔ:], *n.* (*pl.* **sisters-in-law**) cuñada.
sisterly ['sistǝli], *a.* de hermana.
sit [sit], *v.t. to — an examination*, examinarse.—*v.i., v.i.* sentarse; posarse; empollar; celebrar sesión; formar parte (*on*, de); sentar; montar (*a caballo*); servir de modelo; *to — by*, sentarse al lado de; *to — down*, sentarse; *to — up*, incorporarse; velar.
site [sait], *n.* sitio; solar, *m.*
sitting ['sitiŋ], *n.* asentada; empolladura; nidada (*de pajarillos*); sesión, *f.*
sitting-room ['sitiŋrum], *n.* sala de estar.
situated ['sitjueitid], *a.* situado.
situation [sitju'eiʃǝn], *n.* situación, *f.*; empleo.
six [siks], *a., n.* seis, *m.*; *at sixes and sevens*, en estado de desorden.
sixpence ['sikspǝns], *n.* (moneda de) seis peniques, *m.pl.*
sixteen [siks'ti:n], *a., n.* diez y seis, dieciséis, *m.*
sixteenth [siks'ti:nθ], *a., n.* décimosexto; dieciseisavo; diez y seis (*en las fechas*), *m.*
sixth [siksθ], *a.* sexto.—*n.* sexta parte, *f.*; **seis** (*en las fechas*), *m.*; (*mus.*) sexta.
sixtieth ['sikstiǝθ], *a.* sexagésimo; sesenta.— *n.* sexagésima parte, *f.*
sixty ['siksti], *a., n.* sesenta, *m.*
sizable ['saizǝbl], *a.* bastante grande.
size (1) [saiz], *n.* tamaño; medida; talle *m.*; dimensión, *f.*; diámetro; corpulencia; número (*de zapatos etc.*); cola.—*v.t.* medir; clasificar según el tamaño; encolar; *to — up*, tomar las medidas a; considerar.
size (2) [saiz], *n.* cola.—*v.t.* encolar.
sizzle [sizl], *n.* chisporroteo.—*v.i.* chisporrotear.
skate (1) [skeit], *n.* patín, *m.*
skate (2) [skeit], *n.* (*ichth.*) raya.
skater ['skeitǝ], *n.* patinador, *m.*
skating ['skeitiŋ], *n.* patinaje, *m.*
skating-rink ['skeitiŋriŋk], *n.* pista de patinar.
skein [skein], *n.* madeja.
skeleton ['skelitn], *n.* esqueleto; armadura; esbozo; — *key*, llave maestra.
sketch [sketʃ], *n.* esbozo; croquis, *m.*; (*theat.*) entremés, *m.*—*v.t.* esbozar; dibujar.
sketchy ['sketʃi], *a.* bosquejado; incompleto.
skewer ['skju:ǝ], *n.* broqueta.—*v.t.* espetar.
ski [ski:], *n.* esquí, *m.*—*v.i.* esquiar.
skid [skid], *n.* (*aut.*) patinazo.—*v.i.* patinar.
skidding ['skidiŋ], *n.* patinaje, *m.*
ski-ing ['ski:iŋ], *n.* el esquiar.
skilful ['skilful], *a.* hábil.
skill [skil], *n.* habilidad, *f.*
skilled [skild], *a.* hábil, diestro.
skim [skim], *v.t.* desnatar (*la leche*); espumar; rozar; leer superficialmente.

skimp [skimp], *v.t.* escatimar; frangollar.—*v.i.* ser tacaño.
skin [skin], *n.* piel, *f.*; cutis, *m.*; cáscara, pellejo *(de fruta)*; odre *(para vino)*, *m.*; *soaked to the* —, calado hasta los huesos. —*v.t.* despellejar; pelar; *(fam.)* desollar.
skin-deep ['skin'di:p], *a.* superficial.
skinflint ['skinflint], *n.* avaro.
skinny ['skini], *a.* flaco, descarnado.
skip [skip], *n.* brinco.—*v.t.* pasar por alto; omitir.—*v.i.* brincar; saltar a la comba; escaparse.
skipping ['skipiŋ], *n.* acción *(f.)* de saltar; comba.
skipping-rope ['skipiŋroup], *n.* comba.
skirmish ['skə:miʃ], *n.* escaramuza.—*v.i.* escaramuzar.
skirt [skə:t], *n.* falda; faldón *(de chaqueta)*, *m.*; margen, *m.*; *(fam.)* chica.—*v.t.* ladear.
skirting ['skə:tiŋ], *n.* zócalo.
skit [skit], *n.* parodia.
skittle [skitl], *n.* bolo.—*pl.* juego de bolos.
skull [skʌl], *n.* cráneo; calavera.
skull-cap ['skʌlkæp], *n.* casquete, *m.*
skunk [skʌŋk], *n.* mofeta.
sky [skai], *n.* cielo.
sky-blue ['skai'blu:], *a., n.* azul celeste, *m.*
sky-high [skai'hai], *a.* hasta las nubes.
skylark ['skailɑ:k], *n.* alondra.
skylight ['skailait], *n.* claraboya.
sky-line ['skailain], *n.* horizonte, *m.*
sky-scraper ['skaiskreipə], *n.* rascacielos, *m.sg.*
slab [slæb], *n.* plancha; losa.
slack [slæk], *a.* flojo; débil; negligente; perezoso; lento; *(com.)* encalmado.
slacken ['slækən], *v.t., v.i.* aflojar; relajar; amainar *(el viento)*; reducir.
slacker ['slækə], *n.* gandul, *m.*
slackness ['slæknis], *n.* flojedad, *f.*; descuido; pereza; desanimación, *f.*
slacks [slæks], *n.pl.* pantalones, *m.pl.*
slag [slæg], *n.* escoria.
slag-heap ['slæghi:p], *n.* escorial, *m.*
slain [slein] [SLAY].
slake [sleik], *v.t.* apagar *(la sed)*; satisfacer.
slam (1) [slæm], *n.* portazo.—*v.t.* cerrar de golpe.—*v.i.* cerrarse de golpe.
slam (2) [slæm], *n.* capote *(naipes)*, *m.*
slander ['slɑ:ndə], *n.* calumnia.—*v.t.* calumniar.
slanderer ['slɑ:ndərə], *n.* calumniador, *m.*
slanderous ['slɑ:ndərəs], *a.* calumnioso.
slang [slæŋ], *n.* argot, *m.*, jerga.
slant [slɑ:nt], *n.* inclinación; oblicuidad, *f.*; *on the* —, inclinado; oblicuo.—*v.t.* inclinar.—*v.i.* inclinarse.
slanting ['slɑ:ntiŋ], *a.* oblicuo; inclinado.
slap [slæp], *n.* bofetada.—*v.t.* pegar; golpear.
slapdash ['slæpdæʃ], *a.* descuidado; chapucero.
slash [slæʃ], *n.* cuchillada; latigazo; corte, *m.* —*v.t.* acuchillar; azotar; cortar.
slate [sleit], *n.* pizarra; — *quarry*, pizarral, *m.*—*v.t.* empizarrar; *(fam.)* censurar.
slate-coloured ['sleitkʌləd], *a.* apizarrado.
slaughter ['slɔ:tə], *n.* matanza; carnicería.— *v.t.* matar.
slaughter-house ['slɔ:təhaus], *n.* matadero.
Slav [slɑ:v], *a., n.* eslavo.
slave [sleiv], *n.* esclavo.—*v.i.* trabajar como esclavo.

slave-driver ['sleivdraivə], *n.* capataz *(m.)* de esclavos.
slaver (1) ['sleivə], *n.* negrero.
slaver (2) ['slævə], *n.* baba.—*v.i.* babosear.
slavery ['sleivəri], *n.* esclavitud, *f.*
slave-trade ['sleiv'treid], *n.* trata de esclavos; *white* —, trata de blancas.
slavish ['sleiviʃ], *a.* servil.
Slavonic [slə'vɔnik], *a.* eslavo.
slay [slei], *v.t. irr.* matar.
slayer ['sleiə], *n.* matador, *m.*
sledge [sledʒ], *n.* trineo.
sledge-hammer ['sledʒhæmə], *n.* acotillo.
sleek [sli:k], *a.* liso, lustroso; pulcro; obsequioso.—*v.t.* alisar.
sleekness ['sli:knis], *n.* lisura; gordura.
sleep [sli:p], *n.* sueño; *to put to* —, adormecer; *to go to* —, dormirse.—*v.i. irr.* dormir; *to* — *on*, consultar con la almohada; seguir durmiendo; *to* — *like a top*, dormir como un lirón; *to* — *it off*, dormirla.
sleeper ['sli:pə], *n.* durmiente, *m.f.*; *(rail.)* traviesa; coche-cama, *m.*
sleepiness ['sli:pinis], *n.* somnolencia; letargo.
sleeping ['sli:piŋ], *a.* durmiente; *(com.)* — *partner*, socio comanditario.
sleeping-car ['sli:piŋkɑ:], *n.* coche-cama, *m.*
sleepless ['sli:plis], *a.* insomne; *a* — *night*, una noche blanca.
sleep-walker ['sli:pwɔ:kə], *n.* somnámbulo.
sleep-walking ['sli:pwɔ:kiŋ], *n.* somnambulismo.
sleepy ['sli:pi], *a.* soñoliento; letárgico; *to be* —, tener sueño.
sleet [sli:t], *n.* aguanieve, *f.*—*v.i.* caer aguanieve.
sleeve [sli:v], *n.* manga; *(mech.)* manguito.
sleeveless ['sli:vlis], *a.* sin manga.
sleigh [slei], *n.* trineo.
sleight [slait], *n.* — *of hand*, juego de manos, prestidigitación, *f.*
slender ['slendə], *a.* delgado, tenue, esbelto; escaso; pequeño; — *hope*, esperanza remota; — *means*, renta corta.
slenderness ['slendənis], *n.* delgadez, esbeltez; pequeñez; escasez, *f.*
slept [slept] [SLEEP].
slew [slu:] [SLAY].
slice [slais], *n.* rebanada *(de pan)*; lonja, tajada; pala *(para pescado)*.—*v.t.* cortar en lonjas, *etc.*; tajar; cortar.
slicer ['slaisə], *n.* rebanador, *m.*
slick [slik], *a. (fam.)* mañoso.
slide [slaid], *n. (photo.)* diapositiva; resbalón, *m.*; portaobjetos *(para el microscopio)*, *m.sg.*; encaje *(de un bastidor)*, *m.*; desprendimiento *(de rocas)*; *(mus.)* ligado; *(mech.)* guía; pasador *(para el pelo)*, *m.* — *v.i. irr.* resbalar, deslizarse; pecar; *to* — *over*, pasar por alto; *to let things* —, dejar rodar la bola.
slide-rule ['slaidru:l], *n.* regla de cálculo.
sliding ['slaidiŋ], *a.* corredizo; resbaladizo.— *n.* deslizamiento.
sliding-door ['slaidiŋ'dɔ:], *n.* puerta corrediza.
sliding-scale ['slaidiŋ'skeil], *n.* escala graduada.
slight [slait], *a.* ligero; escaso; pequeño; débil; insignificante.—*n.* desaire, *m.*, desprecio.— *v.t.* despreciar, desairar.
slighting ['slaitiŋ], *a.* despreciativo.

slim [slim], *a.* delgado; tenue; escaso.—*v.i.* adelgazarse.

slime [slaim], *n.* cieno; baba.

slimming ['slimiŋ], *n.* adelgazamiento.

slimy ['slaimi], *a.* viscoso, limoso; (*fig.*) servil.

sling [sliŋ], *n.* honda; (*med.*) cabestrillo.—*v.t.* tirar; suspender.

slink [sliŋk], *v.i. irr.* escabullirse.

slip [slip], *n.* resbalón; tropezón; desliz, *m.*; equivocación, *f.*; tira (*de papel*); combinación (*de mujer*),*f.*; funda (*de almohada*); (*bot.*) vástago; escapada; *to give someone the—,* escaparse de alguien.—*v.t.* deslizar; soltar; dislocar (*un hueso*).—*v.i.* deslizarse, resbalar; salirse (*de su sitio*); escurrirse; equivocarse; cometer un desliz; correr; *to — away,* escabullirse; *to — into,* introducirse en; vestirse; *to — off,* quitarse; *to let the opportunity —,* perder la ocasión.

slipper ['slipə], *n.* pantuflo; zapatilla.

slippery ['slipəri], *a.* resbaladizo; escurridizo; poco firme; sin escrúpulos.

slipshod ['slipʃɔd], *a.* descuidado, chapucero.

slit [slit], *n.* resquicio; cortadura.—*v.t. irr.* hender; cortar; *to — the throat,* degollar.

sliver ['slivə], *n.* astilla.

slobber ['slɔbə], *n.* baba.—*v.i.* babosear.

sloe [slou], *n.* endrina (*fruta*); endrino (*árbol*).

slogan ['slougən], *n.* grito de combate; mote, slogan, *m.*

slop [slɔp], *n.* charco.—*pl.* agua sucia.—*v.t.* derramar.—*v.i.* derramarse.

slope [sloup], *n.* inclinación, *f.*; falda (*de colina*). — *v.i.* inclinarse, estar en declive.

sloping ['sloupiŋ], *a.* inclinado, en declive.

sloppy ['slɔpi], *a.* aguoso; lodoso; chapucero.

slot [slɔt], *n.* muesca; ranura.

slot-machine ['slɔtməʃi:n], *n.* tragaperras, *m. inv.*

slouch [slautʃ], *n.* inclinación (*f.*) del cuerpo.—*v.i.* ir cabizbajo.

slovenly ['slʌvnli], *a.* desaseado; sucio; descuidado.

slow [slou], *a.* lento; tardo; torpe; pesado; *the clock is five minutes —,* el reloj lleva cinco minutos de atraso.—*v.t., v.i. to — down,* ir más despacio; retrasar.

slowcoach ['sloukoutʃ], *n.* perezoso.

slowly ['slouli], *adv.* despacio.

slow-motion ['slou'mouʃən], *n.* velocidad reducida, *f.*

slowness ['slounis], *n.* lentitud, *f.*; tardanza; torpeza.

slow-witted ['slou'witid], *a.* torpe.

sludge [slʌdʒ], *n.* cieno, lodo.

slug [slʌg], *n.* (*zool.*) babosa; bala (*munición*).—*v.t.* (*fam.*) aporrear, golpear).

sluggish ['slʌgiʃ], *a.* perezoso; lento; flojo.

sluice [slu:s], *n.* esclusa; canal, *m.* —*v.t. to — down,* lavar; regar.

sluice-gate ['slu:sgeit], *n.* compuerta.

slum [slʌm]. *n.* barrio pobre, suburbio.

slumber ['slʌmbə], *n.* sueño.—*v.i.* dormitar.

slump [slʌmp], *n.* baja.—*v.i.* caerse; bajar.

slung [slʌŋ] [SLING].

slunk [slʌŋk] [SLINK].

slur [slə:], *n.* estigma, *m.*; (*mus.*) ligado.—*v.t.* comerse palabras; ligar; manchar; *to — over,* pasar por encima de.

slush [slʌʃ], *n.* aguanieve, *f.*; cieno; (*fig.*) ñoñería.

slushy ['slʌʃi], *a.* fangoso; (*fig.*) ñoño.

slut [slʌt], *n.* pazpuerca; ramera.

sly [slai], *a.* astuto, taimado; disimulado; *on the —,* a hurtadillas.

slyness ['slainis], *n.* astucia; disimulo.

smack (1) [smæk], *n.* sabor, *m.*; dejo.—*v.i.* saber (of, a).

smack (2) [smæk], *n.* beso sonado y fuerte; bofetada, cachete, *m.*; chasquido (*de látigo*).—*v.t.* dar una bofetada o un cachete.

smack (3) [smæk], *n.* lancha de pescar.

small [smɔ:l], *a.* pequeño; menudo; corto; bajo (*de estatura*); mezquino; poco; de poca importancia; — *change,* (dinero) suelto; — *fry,* pececillos, *m.pl.*; gente menuda o de poca importancia; — *hours,* altas horas de la noche; — *print,* carácter (*m.*) de letra menuda; — *talk,* trivialidades,*f.pl.*

smallish ['smɔ:liʃ], *a.* bastante pequeño.

smallness ['smɔ:lnis], *n.* pequeñez, *f.*; insignificancia.

smallpox ['smɔ:lpɔks], *n.* viruelas, *f.pl.*

smart [smɑ:t], *a.* vivo; listo; elegante.—*n.* escozor, dolor, *m.*—*v.i.* picar, escocer; dolerse.

smarten [smɑ:tn], *v.t.* embellecer.

smartness ['smɑ:tnis], *n.* viveza; habilidad, *f.*; elegancia.

smash [smæʃ], *n.* rotura; fracaso; ruina, quiebra; accidente, *m.*; — *and grab raid,* robo violento.—*v.t.* romper; quebrar; aplastar, destrozar.—*v.i.* romperse; quebrarse; hacer bancarrota; *to — up,* quebrar.

smattering ['smætəriŋ], *n.* tintura; conocimiento superficial.

smear [smiə], *n.* mancha; calumnia.—*v.t.* untar; manchar, ensuciar; (*fig.*) calumniar.

smell [smel], *n.* olfato; olor, *m.*—*v.t. irr.* oler; (*fig.*) percibir; *to — a rat,* (*fig.*) oler el poste.—*v.i.* oler (*of,* a); oler mal.

smelling ['smeliŋ], *a. foul —,* hediondo; *sweet —,* oloroso.—*n.* acción (*f.*) de oler.

smelling-salts ['smeliŋsɔlts], *n.pl.* sales inglesas,*f.pl.*

smelt (1) [smelt], *v.t.* fundir.

smelt (2) [smelt] [SMELL].

smelting ['smeltiŋ]. *n.* fundición, *f.*

smile [smail], *n.* sonrisa.—*v.i.* sonreír(se); (*fig.*) ser propicio.

smiling ['smailiŋ], *a.* risueño, sonriente.

smirk [smə:k], *n.* sonrisa afectada.—*v.i.* sonreír afectadamente.

smite [smait], *v.t. irr.* herir; golpear; castigar; encantar; doler.

smith [smiθ], *n.* herrero.

smithereens [smiðə'ri:nz], *n.pl.* añicos, *m.pl.*

smithy ['smiði], *n.* fragua.

smitten ['smitn] [SMITE].

smock [smɔk], *n.* blusa.

smoke [smouk], *n.* humo.—*v.t.* fumar; ahumar; ennegrecer.—*v.i.* humear; fumar.

smokeless ['smouklis], *a.* sin humo.

smoker ['smoukə], *n.* fumador, *m.*; (*rail.*) coche (*m.*) para fumadores.

smoke-screen ['smoukskri:n], *n.* cortina de humo.

smoke-signal ['smouksignəl], *n.* ahumada.

smoking ['smoukiŋ], *a.* humeante.—*n.* el fumar, *m.*; *no —,* se prohibe fumar.

smoking-jacket ['smoukiŋdʒækit], *n.* batín, *m.*

smoky ['smouki], *a.* humeante; ahumado.

smooth

smooth [smu:ð], *a.* liso; suave; manso (*del agua*); uniforme; igual; lisonjero; afable.— *v.t.* allanar; alisar; igualar; acepillar; calmar; *to — over,* exculpar.
smoothness ['smu:ðnis], *n.* lisura; igualdad; suavidad; afabilidad, *f.*
smooth-tongued ['smu:ð'tʌŋd], *a.* lisonjero, obsequioso.
smote [smout] [SMITE].
smother ['smʌðə], *v.t.* ahogar, sofocar; suprimir; apagar.
smoulder ['smouldə], *v.i.* arder sin llama; (*fig.*) arder; estar latente.
smouldering ['smouldəriŋ], *a.* que arde lentamente; latente.
smudge [smʌdʒ], *n.* mancha.—*v.t.* tiznar; manchar.
smug [smʌg], *a.* presumido; farisaico.
smuggle [smʌgl], *v.t.* pasar de contrabando. —*v.i.* contrabandear.
smuggler ['smʌglə], *n.* contrabandista, *m.f.*
smuggling ['smʌgliŋ], *n.* contrabando.
smugness ['smʌgnis], *n.* satisfacción (*f.*) de sí mismo.
smut [smʌt], *n.* mancha (*de hollín*); (*fig.*) indecencia.
smutty ['smʌti], *a.* tiznado; (*fig.*) verde.
snack [snæk], *n.* tentempié, *m.*, merienda.
snag [snæg], *n.* pega, tropiezo; nudo.
snail [sneil], *n.* caracol, *m.*; *snail's pace,* paso de tortuga.
snake [sneik], *n.* culebra, serpiente, *f.*
snap [snæp], *a.* repentino, inesperado.—*n.* chasquido; castañeteo (*con los dedos*); mordedura; cierre (*de resorte*); vigor, *m.*; período corto (*de frío*); (*photo.*) instantánea. —*v.t.* morder; chasquear; romper; cerrar de golpe; castañetear (*los dedos*); sacar una instantánea.—*v.i.* chasquear; partirse; romperse; hablar bruscamente; *to — at,* tratar de morder; *to — off,* romper(se); *to — up,* coger.
snappy ['snæpi], *a.* irritable; vigoroso.
snare [snɛə], *n.* lazo, trampa; red, *f.*—*v.t.* enredar.
snarl [snɑ:l], *n.* regaño, gruñido.—*v.i.* regañar, gruñir.
snatch [snætʃ], *n.* agarro; ratito; fragmento. —*v.t.* agarrar; disfrutar.
sneak [sni:k], *n.* mandilón, *m.*, chivato.—*v.i.* colarse (en).
sneaking ['sni:kiŋ], *a.* vil; furtivo; secreto.
sneer [sniə], *n.* sonrisa de desprecio; mofa.— *v.i.* mirar *o* hablar con desprecio; *to — at,* mofarse de.
sneeze [sni:z], *n.* estornudo.—*v.i.* estornudar.
sniff [snif], *v.t.* olfatear.—*v.i.* resollar.
snigger ['snigə], *n.* risa disimulada.—*v.i.* reírse disimuladamente.
snip [snip], *n.* tijeretada; recorte (*de paño*), *m.* —*v.t.* tijeretear.
sniper ['snaipə], *n.* paco, tirador apostado, *m.*
snivel [snivl], *v.i.* moquear; lloriquear.
snivelling ['snivliŋ], *a.* mocoso; llorón.
snob [snɔb], *n.* esnob, *m.f.*
snobbish ['snɔbiʃ], *a.* esnob.
snoop [snu:p], *v.i.* espiar, curiosear.
snooze [snu:z], *n.* siesta.—*v.i.* dormitar.
snore [snɔ:], *n.* ronquido.—*v.i.* roncar.
snoring ['snɔ:riŋ], *n.* ronquido.
snort [snɔ:t], *n.* bufido, resoplido.—*v.i.* bufar, resoplar.

snout [snaut], *n.* hocico.
snow [snou], *n.* nieve, *f.*—*v.i.* nevar; *to — up,* aprisionar con nieve.
snowball ['snoubɔ:l], *n.* bola de nieve.
snow-bound ['snoubaund], *a.* aprisionado por la nieve.
snow-capped ['snoukæpt], *a.* coronado de nieve.
snowdrift ['snoudrift], *n.* acumulación (*f.*) de nieve.
snowdrop ['snoudrɔp], *n.* campanilla de invierno.
snowfall ['snoufɔ:l], *n.* nevada.
snowflake ['snoufleik], *n.* copo de nieve.
snowman ['snoumæn], *n.* figura de nieve.
snow-plough ['snouplau], *n.* quitanieves, *m.inv.*
snow-shoe ['snouʃu:], *n.* raqueta de nieve.
snowstorm ['snoustɔ:m], *n.* ventisca.
snow-white ['snou'hwait], *a.* blanco como la nieve.
snowy ['snoui], *a.* nevoso.
snub [snʌb], *n.* repulsa; desaire, *m.*; nariz chata.—*v.t.* desairar; repulsar; tratar con desdén.
snub-nosed ['snʌb'nouzd], *a.* chato.
snuff [snʌf], *n.* moco (*de candela*); rapé, *m.* —*v.t.* oler; despabilar (*una candela*).
snuff-box ['snʌfbɔks], *n.* tabaquera.
snug [snʌg], *a.* cómodo; caliente; escondido.
snuggle [snʌgl], *v.i.* acomodarse; *to — up to,* arrimarse a.
so [sou], *adv.* así; de este modo; tan; tanto; de igual modo; también; por tanto; aproximadamente; — *as to,* para; a fin de que; — *on and — forth,* etcétera; — *that,* de modo que, para que; — *much,* tanto; — *be it,* así sea; — *far,* hasta aquí; — *to speak,* por decirlo así.
soak [souk], *n.* remojo; (*fam.*) borrachín, *m.*— *v.t.* remojar; *to — up,* empapar.—*v.i.* estar en remojo.
so-and-so ['souənd'sou], *n.* fulano (de tal).
soap [soup], *n.* jabón, *m.*—*v.t.* jabonar.
soap-dish ['soupdiʃ], *n.* jabonera.
soap-suds ['soupsʌdz], *n.pl.* jabonaduras, *f.pl.*
soapy ['soupi], *a.* jabonoso.
soar [sɔ:], *v.i.* remontarse, encumbrarse.
sob [sɔb], *n.* sollozo.—*v.i.* sollozar.
sober ['soubə], *a.* sobrio; sereno; modesto; obscuro; *to — up,* desemborrachar; calmar. —*v.i.* *to — up,* volverse sobrio.
sober-minded ['soubəmaindid], *a.* grave.
sobriety [sou'braiəti], *n.* sobriedad; moderación; seriedad, *f.*
so-called ['sou'kɔ:ld], *a.* llamado, supuesto.
soccer ['sɔkə], *n.* fútbol, *m.*
sociable ['souʃəbl], *a.* sociable.
social ['souʃəl], *a.* social; sociable.—*n.* velada.
socialism ['souʃəlizm], *n.* socialismo.
socialist ['souʃəlist], *a.*, *n.* socialista, *m.f.*
society [sə'saiəti], *n.* sociedad, *f.*; mundo elegante; compañía.
sociological [sousiə'lɔdʒikəl], *a.* sociólogo.
sociologist [sousi'ɔlədʒist], *n.* sociólogo.
sociology [sousi'ɔlədʒi], *n.* sociología.
sock (1) [sɔk], *n.* calcetín, *m.*
sock (2) [sɔk], *n.* (*fam.*) puñetazo.—*v.t.* (*fam.*) pegar.

socket ['sɔkit], *n.* hueco; *(mech.)* cubo, caja; cuenca *(del ojo);* fosa *(de un hueso);* *(elec.)* enchufe, *m.*; alvéolo *(de un diente).*

sod [sɔd], *n.* césped, *m.*

soda ['soudə], *n.* sosa, soda.

soda-water ['soudə'wɔːtə], *n.* (agua de) seltz *o* sifón, *m.*

sodden [sɔdn], *a.* saturado.

sodomy ['sɔdəmi], *n.* sodomía.

sofa ['soufə], *n.* sofá, *m.*

soft [sɔft], *a.* suave; blando; dulce; tonto; — *drinks,* bebidas no alcohólicas.

soften [sɔfn], *v.t.* ablandar; enternecer; suavizar.—*v.i.* ablandarse; enternecerse.

softening ['sɔfniŋ], *n.* ablandamiento; enternecimiento.

softness ['sɔftnis], *n.* blandura; suavidad, *f.*; dulzura; debilidad *(f.)* de carácter.

soggy ['sɔgi], *a.* empapado, saturado.

soil [sɔil], *n.* tierra.—*v.t.* ensuciar.

soiled [sɔild], *a.* sucio.

soirée ['swaːrei], *n.* velada.

sojourn ['sɔdʒɔːn], *n.* residencia.—*v.i.* residir.

solace ['sɔləs], *n.* solaz, *m.*, consuelo.—*v.t.* solazar; consolar.

solar ['soulə], *a.* solar.

sold [sould], [SELL].

solder ['sɔldə], *n.* soldadura.—*v.t.* soldar.

soldering ['sɔldəriŋ], *n.* soldadura.

soldering-iron ['sɔldəriŋ'aiən], *n.* soldador, *m.*

soldier ['souldʒə], *n.* soldado; militar, *m.*

sole (1) [soul], *a.* único, solo; exclusivo.

sole (2) [soul], *n.* (anat.) planta; suela *(del zapato).*—*v.t.* solar *(zapatos).*

sole (3) [soul], *n.* (ichth.) lenguado.

solemn ['sɔləm], *a.* solemne, grave.

solemnity [sɔ'lemniti], *n.* solemnidad, *f.*

solemnize ['sɔləmnaiz], *v.t.* solemnizar.

solicit [sɔ'lisit], *v.t.* solicitar; rogar, implorar.

solicitor [sɔ'lisitə], *n.* abogado.

solicitous [sɔ'lisitəs], *a.* solícito; deseoso; inquieto.

solicitude [sɔ'lisitjuːd], *n.* solicitud, *f.*; cuidado; preocupación, *f.*

solid ['sɔlid], *a.* sólido; macizo; serio; unánime.—*n.* sólido.

solidarity [sɔli'dæriti], *n.* solidaridad, *f.*

solidify [sɔ'lidifai], *v.t.* solidificar.—*v.i.* solidificarse.

solidity [sɔ'liditi], *n.* solidez; unanimidad, *f.*

soliloquy [sɔ'liləkwi], *n.* soliloquio.

solitaire [sɔli'tɛə], *n.* solitario.

solitary ['sɔlitəri], *a.* solitario; solo, único; *in — confinement,* incomunicado.

solitude ['sɔlitjuːd], *n.* soledad, *f.*

solo ['soulou], *n.* solo.—*a.* — *flight,* vuelo a solas.

soloist ['soulouist], *n.* solista, *m.f.*

soluble ['sɔljubl], *a.* soluble.

solution [sɔ'luːʃən], *n.* solución, *f.*

solve [sɔlv], *v.t.* resolver.

solvency ['sɔlvənsi], *n.* solvencia.

solvent ['sɔlvənt], *a.* disolvente; *(com.)* solvente.—*n.* disolvente, *m.*

sombre ['sɔmbə], *a.* sombrío.

some [sʌm], *a.* un poco de, algo de; alguno; algunos, unos.—*pron.* algo; algunos; algunas.

someone ['sʌmwʌn], **somebody** ['sʌmbədi], *pron.* alguien, *m.f.*; — *else,* otro, otra persona; *to be —,* ser un personaje.

somehow ['sʌmhau], *adv.* de alguna manera.

somersault ['sʌməsɔːlt], *n.* salto mortal.—*v.i.* dar un salto mortal.

something ['sʌmθiŋ], *pron.* alguna cosa, algo; — *else,* otra cosa; *to have — to do,* tener que hacer.—*adv.* algún tanto.

sometime ['sʌmtaim], *adv.* algún día; en algún tiempo; — *last week,* durante la semana pasada; — *or other,* tarde o temprano; — *soon,* dentro de poco.

sometimes ['sʌmtaimz], *adv.* algunas veces, a veces.

somewhat ['sʌmwɔt], *adv.* algo, algún tanto.

somewhere ['sʌmwɛə], *adv.* en alguna parte; — *else,* en otra parte.

somnolence ['sɔmnələns], *n.* somnolencia.

somnolent ['sɔmnələnt], *a.* soñoliento; soporífero.

son [sʌn], *n.* hijo.

sonata [sɔ'nɑːtə], *n.* sonata.

song [sɔŋ], *n.* canción, *f.*; canto; poesía; *(fig.)* bagatela; *Song of Songs,* el Cantar de los Cantares; *drinking —,* canción báquica; *to sell for a —,* vender por un pedazo de pan.

song-bird ['sɔŋbəːd], *n.* ave cantora.

song-book ['sɔŋbuk], *n.* cancionero.

songster ['sɔŋstə], *n.* cantor, *m.*; ave cantora.

son-in-law ['sʌninlɔː], *n.* *(pl.* **sons-in-law)** yerno.

sonnet ['sɔnit], *n.* soneto.

sonorous ['sɔnərəs], *a.* sonoro.

soon [suːn], *adv.* pronto; dentro de poco; *as — as,* luego que; *as — as possible,* cuanto antes; — *after,* poco después.

sooner ['suːnə], *adv., compar. of* SOON; más pronto; antes; *I would — die,* antes la muerte; *the — the better,* cuanto antes mejor; — *or later,* tarde o temprano; *no — said than done,* dicho y hecho; *no — had he come than . . .,* apenas había venido cuando . . .; *I would — go,* preferiría ir.

soot [sut], *n.* hollín, *m.*

soothe [suːð], *v.t.* calmar; aliviar.

soothing ['suːðiŋ], *a.* calmante; consolador.

soothsayer ['suːθseiə], *n.* adivino.

sooty ['suti], *a.* cubierto de hollín; negro; obscurecido.

sop [sɔp], *n.* sopa; soborno.

sophisticated [sɔ'fistikeitid], *a.* mundano; culto; elegante.

sophistication [səfisti'keiʃən], *n.* mundanería; cultura.

sophistry ['sɔfistri], *n.* sofistería.

soporific [sɔpə'rifik], *a.* soporífero.

sopping ['sɔpiŋ], *a.* calado, empapado.

soppy ['sɔpi], *a.* empapado; lluvioso.

soprano [sɔ'prɑːnou], *n.* soprano, tiple, *m.f.*

sorcerer ['sɔːsərə], *n.* mago, brujo.

sorceress ['sɔːsəris], *n.* bruja.

sorcery ['sɔːsəri], *n.* hechicería, sortilegio.

sordid ['sɔːdid], *a.* sórdido; bajo.

sordidness ['sɔːdidnis], *n.* sordidez, *f.*; bajeza.

sore [sɔː], *a.* doloroso; violento; extremo; enojado; — *throat,* mal *(m.)* de garganta.—*n.* llaga; úlcera.

soreness ['sɔːnis], *n.* dolor, *m.*; *(fig.)* amargura.

sorrow ['sɔrou], *n.* pesar, *m.*, pesadumbre, *f.*, tristeza; duelo.

sorrowful ['sɔrəful]. *a.* afligido; triste.
sorrowing ['sɔrouiŋ], *a.* afligido.—*n.* aflicción, *f.*
sorry ['sɔri], *a.* arrepentido; afligido; despreciable; *I am* —, lo siento.
sort [sɔːt], *n.* clase, especie, *f.*; *all sorts of people,* toda clase de gente; *nothing of the* —, nada de eso; *out of sorts,* indispuesto; *a good* —, (*fam.*) buen tipo.—*v.t.* separar; clasificar; *to* — *out,* escoger y arreglar.
so-so ['sousou], *a.* regular.
sot [sɔt], *n.* zaque, *m.*
sought [sɔːt] [SEEK].
soul [soul], *n.* alma; espíritu, *m.*; ánima; ser; corazón, *m.*; *All Souls' Day,* Día de los Difuntos; — *in purgatory,* alma en pena.
soulful ['soulful], *a.* conmovedor; espiritual.
soulfulness ['soulfulnis], *n.* sensibilidad; espiritualidad, *f.*
soulless ['soullis], *a.* sin alma; despreciable.
sound (I) [saund], *a.* sano; entero; (*com.*) solvente; seguro; profundo; sólido; válido.—*adv.* bien.
sound (2) [saund], *n.* estrecho (*de mar*).
sound (3) [saund], *n.* sonido; son; ruido; sonda.—*v.t.* tocar; sonar; anunciar, publicar, celebrar.—*v.i.* sonar, hacer ruido; resonar.
sound (4) [saund], *v.t.* (*med.*) sondar, tentar; (*naut.*) sondear.
sound-barrier ['saund'bæriə], *n.* barrera del sonido.
sounding ['saundiŋ], *a.* sonoro.—*n.* sondeo. —*pl.* sondas, *f.pl.*
soundness ['saundnis], *n.* salud, *f.*; fuerza, validez, solidez, *f.*
sound-proof ['saundpruːf], *a.* aislado de todo sonido.
sound-track ['saundtræk], *n.* guía sonora.
sound-wave ['saundweiv], *n.* onda sonora.
soup [suːp], *n.* sopa; *clear* —, consommé, *m.*; *thick* —, puré, *m.*; *in the* —, (*fam.*) en apuros.
soup-plate ['suːp'pleit], *n.* plato sopero.
soup-tureen ['suːptjuˈriːn], *n.* sopera.
sour [sauə], *a.* agrio, ácido; áspero; — *grapes!* ¡están verdes!—*v.t.* agriar.
source [sɔːs], *n.* fuente, *f.*; nacimiento (*de un río*); foco; *to have from a good* —, saber de buena tinta.
sourness ['sauənis], *n.* acidez, *f.*, agrura; aspereza.
south [sauθ], *a.* meridional, del sur; *South American,* sudamericano; *South African,* sudafricano.—*n.* mediodía, sur, *m.*
south-east ['sauθ'iːst], *n.* sudeste, *m.*
south-easterly ['sauθ'iːstəli], *a.* hacia el sudeste; del sudeste.
south-eastern ['sauθ'iːstən], *a.* del sudeste.
southerly ['sʌðəli], *a.* meridional; hacia el sur.
southern [sʌðən], *a.* del sur, meridional.
southward ['sauθwəd], *a.* del sur.—*adv.* hacia el sur.
south-west ['sauθ'west], *n.* sudoeste, *m.*
south-westerly ['sauθ'westəli], *a.* hacia el sudoeste; del sudoeste.
south-western ['sauθ'westən], *a.* del sudoeste.
souvenir ['suːvəniə], *n.* recuerdo.
sovereign ['sɔvrin], *a.*, *n.* soberano.
Soviet ['souvjet], *a.* soviético.—*n.* soviet, *m.*
sow (I) [sau], *n.* puerca, cerda; jabalina.
sow (2) [sou], *v.t.*, *v.i. irr.* sembrar; esparcir;

to — *one's wild oats,* (*fig.*) correr sus mocedades.
sower [souə], *n.* sembrador, *m.*
sowing ['souiŋ], *n.* siembra; sembradura.
sown [soun] [SOW (2)].
spa [spaː], *n.* balneario.
space [speis], *n.* espacio; intervalo; período. —*v.t.* espaciar.
spacious ['speiʃəs], *a.* espacioso; amplio.
spaciousness ['speiʃəsnis], *n.* espaciosidad; amplitud, *f.*
spaceman ['speismæn], *n.* astronauta, *m.*; hombre (*m.*) del espacio.
space-ship ['speisʃip], *n.* astronave, *f.*
space-suit ['speissjuːt], *n.* escafandra espacial.
spade [speid], *n.* pala; espada (*naipes*); *to call a* — *a* —, llamar al pan pan y al vino vino.
Spain [spein], *n.* España.
span [spæn], *n.* palmo; espacio; vano (*de puente*); envergadura (*de alas*).—*v.t.* medir a palmos; cruzar; extenderse sobre.
spangle [spæŋgl], *n.* lentejuela.—*v.t.* adornar con lentejuelas; sembrar.
Spaniard ['spænjəd], *n.* español, *m.*
spaniel ['spænjəl], *n.* perro de aguas.
Spanish ['spæniʃ], *a.*, *n.* español, *m.*
Spanish-American ['spæniʃəˈmerikən], *a.*, *n.* hispanoamericano.
spank [spæŋk], *n.* nalgada.—*v.t.* zurrar.
spanking ['spæŋkiŋ], *a.* veloz.—*n.* zurra.
spanner ['spænə], *n.* llave (inglesa), *f.*
spar (I) [spaː], *n.* (*min.*) espato.
spar (2) [spaː], *n.* (*naut.*) percha.
spar (3) [spaː], *n.* boxeo; riña.—*v.i.* boxear.
spare [speə], *a.* disponible, de sobra; de repuesto; escaso; enjuto; — *part,* pieza de repuesto; — *time,* tiempo desocupado; — *wheel,* rueda de recambio.—*v.t.* ahorrar; escatimar; pasarse sin; evitar; perdonar; hacer gracia de; dedicar (*el tiempo*); *to have to* —, tener de sobra.
sparing ['speəriŋ], *a.* escaso; frugal.
spark [spaːk], *n.* chispa; (*fam.*) pisaverde, *m.* —*v.t. to* — *off,* instigar.—*v.i.* chispear.
spark(ing) plug ['spaːkiŋplʌg], *n.* bujía (de encendido).
sparkle [spaːkl], *n.* centelleo; brillo.—*v.i.* centellear; brillar; ser espumoso (*de ciertos vinos*).
sparkling ['spaːkliŋ], *a.* centelleante; brillante; espumante (*vino*).
sparrow ['spærou], *n.* gorrión, *m.*
sparrow-hawk ['spærouhɔːk], *n.* gavilán, *m.*
sparse [spaːs], *a.* esparcido, claro.
Spartan ['spaːtən], *a.*, *n.* espartano.
spasm [spæzm], *n.* espasmo; ataque, *m.*
spasmodic [spæzˈmɔdik], *a.* espasmódico.
spastic ['spæstik], *a.* (*med.*) espasmódico.
spat (I) [spæt], *n.* polaina (*para los pies*).
spat (2) [spæt] [SPIT].
spate [speit], *n.* crecida; (*fig.*) torrente, *m.*
spatial ['speiʃəl], *a.* espacial.
spatter ['spætə], *n.* salpicadura; rociada.— *v.t.* salpicar; regar; manchar.—*v.i.* rociar.
spawn [spɔːn], *n.* freza; producto.—*v.t.*, *v.i.* desovar; engendrar.
speak [spiːk], *v.t.*, *v.i. irr.* hablar; decir; pronunciar; *to* — *for itself,* (*fig.*) hablar por sí; — *one's mind,* decir lo que se piensa; *to* — *out,* hablar claro; *to* — *up,* elevar la voz, hablar más alto; *to* — *up for,* hablar por; *so to* —, por decirlo así.

Speaker ['spi:kə], *n. (Brit.)* Presidente *(m.)* de la Cámara de los Comunes.
speaker ['spi:kə], *n.* el que habla; orador, *m.*
speaking ['spi:kiŋ], *a.* hablante; para hablar. —*n.* habla, discurso; — *trumpet,* portavoz, *m.*; — *tube,* tubo acústico; *they are not on* — *terms,* no se hablan.
spear [spiə], *n.* lanza; venablo; arpón *(de pesca), m.—v.t.* alancear; arponear.
spear-head ['spiəhed], *n.* punta de lanza.
special ['speʃəl], *a.* especial; extraordinario; particular.
specialist ['speʃəlist], *n.* especialista, *m.f.*
speciality [speʃi'æliti], *n.* especialidad; peculiaridad, *f.*
specialize ['speʃəlaiz], *v.t.* especializar.—*v.i.* -se.
species ['spi:ʃi:z], *n. (pl.* species) especie, *f.*
specific [spi'sifik], *a., n.* específico; — *gravity,* peso específico.
specification [spesifi'keiʃən], *n.* especificación, *f.*
specify ['spesifai], *v.t.* especificar.
specimen ['spesimin], *n.* espécimen, *m.*; ejemplo.
specious ['spi:ʃəs], *a.* especioso.
speck [spek], **speckle** [spekl], *n.* manchita; punto, átomo.—*v.t.* manchar.
spectacle ['spektəkl], *n.* espectáculo; exposición, *f.*; escena.—*pl.* gafas, *f.pl.*
spectacular [spek'tækjulə], *a.* espectacular.
spectator [spek'teitə], *n.* espectador, *m.*
spectral ['spektrəl], *a.* espectral.
spectre ['spektə], *n.* espectro, fantasma, *m.*
spectrum ['spektrəm], *n.* espectro.
speculate ['spekjuleit], *v.i.* especular.
speculation [spekju'leiʃən], *n.* especulación, *f.*
speculative ['spekjulətiv], *a.* especulativo.
speculator ['spekjuleitə], *n.* especulador, *m.*
sped [sped] [SPEED].
speech [spi:tʃ], *n.* palabra; lenguaje, *m.*; habla, discurso; idioma, *m.*
speechless ['spi:tʃlis], *a.* mudo; sin habla; desconcertado.
speed [spi:d], *n.* rapidez; velocidad, *f.*; presteza; prisa; *at full* —, a toda velocidad; *with all* —, a toda prisa.—*v.t. irr.* ayudar; despedir; acelerar; hacer salir bien. —*v.i. irr.* correr; darse prisa; marchar con velocidad excesiva.
speed-boat ['spi:dbout], *n.* lancha de carrera.
speedily ['spi:dili], *adv.* aprisa; prontamente.
speediness ['spi:dinis], *n.* celeridad, rapidez, *f.*; prisa.
speed-limit ['spi:dlimit], *n.* velocidad máxima.
speed-way ['spi:dwei], *n.* pista de ceniza.
speedy ['spi:di], *a.* rápido; pronto.
spell (1) [spel], *n.* hechizo, encanto.—*v.t. irr.* deletrear; significar; *how do you* —...? ¿cómo se escribe...?
spell (2) [spel], *n.* turno; rato; temporada.
spellbound ['spelbaund], *a.* fascinado, encantado.
spelling ['speliŋ], *n.* deletreo, ortografía.
spelt [spelt] [SPELL].
spend [spend], *v.t. irr.* gastar; consumir; agotar; pasar *(tiempo).—v.i. irr.* hacer gastos.
spendthrift ['spendθrift], *n.* pródigo, manirroto.
spent [spent] [SPEND].

sperm [spə:m], *n.* esperma.
sperm-whale ['spə:m'hweil], *n.* cachalote, *m.*
sphere [sfiə], *n.* esfera; — *of influence,* zona de influencia.
spherical ['sferikəl], *a.* esférico.
sphinx [sfiŋks], *n.* esfinge, *f.*
spice [spais], *n.* especia; *(fig.)* sabor, *m.*; dejo.—*v.t.* especiar.
spick-and-span ['spikənd'spæn], *a.* más limpio que una patena; flamante *(nuevo).*
spicy ['spaisi], *a.* especiado; aromático; *(fig.)* picante.
spider ['spaidə], *n.* araña; *spider's web,* telaraña.
spidery ['spaidəri], *a.* parecido a una araña.
spigot ['spigət], *n.* espiche, *m.*
spike [spaik], *n.* clavo; *(bot.)* espiga; espliego. —*v.t.* clavar *(un cañón).*
spill (1) [spil], *n.* vuelco.—*v.t. irr.* derramar; volcar; *to* — *the beans,* soltar el gato.
spill (2) [spil], *n.* astilla.
spin [spin], *n.* vuelta; paseo.—*v.t. irr.* hilar; hacer girar; *to* — *out,* prolongar; *to* — *a yarn,* contar un cuento.—*v.i. irr.* hilar; girar; dar vueltas *(vértigo).*
spinach ['spinidʒ], *n.* espinaca(s).
spinal [spainl], *a.* espinal; — *column,* columna vertebral.
spindle [spindl], *n.* huso; *(mech.)* eje, *m.*
spine [spain], *n. (anat.)* espinazo; *(bot.)* espina; *(zool.)* púa.
spinner ['spinə], *n.* hilandero.
spinney ['spini], *n.* arboleda.
spinning ['spiniŋ], *n.* hilado.
spinning-top ['spiniŋtɔp], *n.* trompo.
spinning-wheel ['spiniŋhwi:l], *n.* torno de hilar.
spinster ['spinstə], *n.* soltera.
spiny ['spaini], *a.* espinoso.
spiral [spaiərəl], *a., n.* espiral, *f.*; — *staircase,* escalera en caracol.
spire (1) [spaiə], *n.* aguja *(de iglesia).*
spire (2) [spaiə], *n.* espira.
spirit ['spirit], *n.* espíritu, *m.*; alma; ánimo; energía; agudeza; espectro; temperamento; ingenio; alcohol, *m.—pl.* licores, *m.pl.*; *low spirits,* abatimiento; *high spirits,* alegría; *to keep up one's spirits,* mantener el valor.
spirited ['spiritid], *a.* fogoso; animoso.
spirit-level ['spiritlevəl], *n.* nivel *(m.)* de aire.
spiritual ['spiritjuəl], *a.* espiritual.
spiritualism ['spiritjuəlizm], *n.* espiritismo.
spit (1) [spit], *n.* asador, espetón *(para cocer), m.—v.t.* espetar.
spit (2) [spit], *n.* saliva.—*v.t., v.i. irr.* escupir *(out).*
spit (3) [spit], *n.* lengua de tierra.
spite [spait], *n.* rencor, *m.,* ojeriza, malevolencia; *in* — *of,* a pesar de.—*v.t.* dar pesar a.
spiteful ['spaitful], *a.* rencoroso, malévolo.
spitefulness ['spaitfulnis], *n.* malevolencia, *f.*
spittle [spitl], *n.* saliva.
spittoon [spi'tu:n], *n.* escupidera.
splash [splæʃ], *n.* chapoteo; *(fam.)* sensación, *f.—v.t.* salpicar; *(fam.)* tratar sensacionalmente.—*v.i.* chapotear.
splay-footed ['spleifutid], *a.* zancajoso.
spleen [spli:n], *n. (anat.)* bazo; rencor, *m.*; esplín, *m.*
splendid ['splendid], *a.* espléndido, magnífico, glorioso.

splendour ['splendə], *n.* resplandor, *m.*; esplendor, *m.*; magnificencia.
splice [splais], *n.* empalme, *m.—v.t.* empalmar; juntar; (*fam.*) casar
splint [splint], *n.* tablilla.
splinter ['splintə], *n.* astilla.—*v.t.* astillar. —*v.i.* romperse en astillas.
split [split], *n.* hendidura, grieta; división, *f.*, cisma.—*v.t. irr.* hender; dividir; (*fig.*) desunir.—*v.i. irr.* henderse; dividirse; partirse; **to — on,** (*fam.*) denunciar.
splutter ['splʌtə], *n.* chisporroteo; balbuceo; —*v.t.*, *v.i.* chisporrotear; balbucir.
spoil [spoil], *n.* botín, *m.—v.t. irr.* estropear; corromper; mimar; saquear.—*v.i.* estropearse.
spoilt [spoilt] [SPOIL].
spoke (1) [spouk], *n.* rayo; peldaño.
spoke (2) [spouk], **spoken** ['spoukən] [SPEAK].
spokesman ['spouksmən], *n.* portavoz, *m.*
sponge [spʌndʒ], *n.* esponja; — **cake,** bizcocho; **to throw up the —,** (*fig.*) darse por vencido.—*v.t.* limpiar con esponja.—*v.i.* (*fig.*) vivir de gorra.
sponger ['spʌndʒə], *n.* gorrista, *m.f.*
spongy ['spʌndʒi], *a.* esponjoso.
sponsor ['sponsə], *n.* fiador, *m.*; padrino; madrina.
spontaneity [spontə'ni:iti], *n.* espontaneidad, *f.*
spontaneous [spon'teinjəs], *a.* espontáneo.
spool [spu:l], *n.* canilla, carrete, *m.*
spoon [spu:n], *n.* cuchara.—*v.t.* sacar con cuchara.
spoonful ['spu:nful], *n.* cucharada.
sporadic [spə'rædik], *a.* esporádico.
spore [spɔ:], *n.* espora.
sport [spɔ:t], *n.* deporte, *m.*; pasatiempo; broma; objeto de broma; **to make — of,** burlarse de.—*pl.* concurso de atletismo.—*v.t.* lucir, ostentar.—*v.i.* divertirse, jugar.
sporting ['spɔ:tiŋ], *a.* deportivo; de buena disposición; — **chance,** posibilidad (*f.*) de éxito.
sportive ['spɔ:tiv], *a.* juguetón.
sportsman ['spɔ:tsmən], **sportswoman** ['spɔ:tswumən], *n.* deportista, *m.f.*
spot [spot], *n.* sitio, lugar, *m.*; mancilla; mancha; gota (*de lluvia*); grano; poco; **on the —,** en al acto.—*v.t.* motear, manchar; observar.
spotless ['spotlis], *a.* limpio, sin mancha, inmaculado.
spotlight ['spotlait], *n.* proyector, *m.*; luz (*f.*) del proyector.—*v.t.* señalar.
spotted ['spotid], *a.* manchado; con manchas; con lunares (*diseño*).
spotty ['spoti], *a.* lleno de manchas.
spouse [spauz], *n.* esposo; esposa.
spout [spaut], *n.* tubo, cañería; canalón, *m.*; cuello (*de vasija*); pico (*de tetera etc.*); chorro.—*v.t.* arrojar; echar; recitar.—*v.i.* brotar, chorrear; (*fam.*) hablar.
sprain [sprein], *n.* torcedura.—*v.t.* torcer.
sprang [spræŋ] [SPRING].
sprat [spræt], *n.* sardineta.
sprawl [sprɔ:l], *v.i.* extenderse; recostarse (en).
spray [sprei], *n.* rocío (*de agua*); espuma (*del mar*); pulverizador, *m.*; ramita.—*v.t.* rociar, pulverizar.
spread [spred], *n.* extensión; propagación, *f.*; colcha (*de cama*); (*fam.*) banquete, *m.—*

v.t. irr. tender, extender; desplegar; difundir; divulgar; diseminar; poner.—*v.i. irr.* extenderse; desplegarse; propagarse; difundirse.
spree [spri:], *n.* parranda; **to go on a —,** ir de parranda.
sprig [sprig], *n.* ramita; espiga.
sprightly ['spraitli], *a.* alegre, despierto.
spring [spriŋ], *a.* primaveral.—*n.* primavera; muelle, resorte, *m.*; brinco, salto; elasticidad, *f.*; manantial, *m.*, fuente, *f.—v.t. irr.* soltar; dar de golpe; **to — a leak,** hacer agua.—*v.i. irr.* brincar, saltar; brotar; originarse; **to — back,** saltar hacia atrás; **to — up,** brotar; surgir.
springtime ['spriŋtaim], *n.* primavera.
springy ['spriŋi], *a.* elástico.
sprinkle ['spriŋkl], *v.t.* rociar; salpicar.
sprinkling ['spriŋkliŋ], *n.* rociadura; pequeño número, poco.
sprint [sprint], *n.* sprint, *m.—v.i.* sprintar.
sprout [spraut], *n.* retoño.—*pl.* bretones, coles (*f.pl.*) de Bruselas.—*v.i.* germinar; retoñar.
sprung [sprʌŋ] [SPRING].
spun [spʌn] [SPIN].
spur [spə:], *n.* espuela; espolón (*de gallo*), *m.*; (*fig.*) estímulo; **on the — of the moment,** de sopetón.—*v.t.* espolear; poner(se) espuelas; (*fig.*) estimular.
spurious ['spjuəriəs], *a.* espurio; falso.
spurn [spə:n], *v.t.* despreciar; rechazar.
spurt [spə:t], *n.* chorro; esfuerzo repentino.—*v.t.* hacer chorrear; lanzar.—*v.i.* chorrear; brotar; hacer un esfuerzo supremo.
spy [spai], *n.* espía, *m.f.*;—*v.t.* divisar; observar; **to — out,** explorar.—*v.i.* ser espía.
spy-glass ['spaiglɑ:s], *n.* catalejo.
spying ['spaiiŋ], *n.* espionaje, *m.*
squabble [skwobl], *n.* riña, disputa.—*v.i.* reñir, disputar.
squad [skwod], *n.* escuadra; pelotón, *m.*
squadron ['skwodrən], *n.* (*aer.*) escuadrilla; (*naut.*) escuadra; (*mil.*) escuadrón, *m.*
squadron-leader ['skwodrən'li:də], *n.* comandante, *m.*
squalid ['skwolid], *a.* escuálido; mezquino.
squall [skwo:l], *n.* chillido; ráfaga; (*fig.*) tempestad, *f.—v.i.* chillar.
squally ['skwo:li], *a.* tempestuoso; violento.
squalor ['skwolə], *n.* escualidez, *f.*
squander ['skwondə], *v.t.* malgastar; desperdiciar; derrochar.
square [skwεə], *a.* cuadrado; justo; honrado; categórico; (*fam.*) fuera de moda; — **deal,** trato honrado; — **root,** raíz cuadrada. —*n.* (*geom.*) cuadrado; casilla, escaque (*de ajedrez*), *m.*; plaza; (*mil.*) cuadro. — *v.t.* cuadrar; escuadrar; ajustar; nivelar; **to — the account,** saldar la cuenta.—*v.i.* cuadrar; conformarse, ajustarse.
squareness ['skwεənis], *n.* cuadratura; honradez, *f.*
squash [skwoʃ], *n.* aplastamiento; apiñamiento (*gentío*); calabaza; pulpa (*de fruta*). —*v.t.* aplastar.—*v.i.* -se.
squashy ['skwoʃi], *a.* blando.
squat [skwot], *a.* rechoncho.—*v.i.* agacharse, agazaparse; ocupar sin derecho.
squatter ['skwotə], *n.* intruso, colono usurpador.
squawk [skwo:k], *n.* graznido.—*v.i.* graznar.

squeak [skwiːk], *n.* chillido; chirrido; *to have a narrow* —, escapar por milagro.—*v.i.* chillar; chirriar; crujir.
squeal [skwiːl], *n.* chillido, grito agudo.—*v.i.* ' chillar; (*fam.*) cantar.
squeamish ['skwiːmiʃ], *a.* delicado; remilgado; asqueado.
squeeze [skwiːz], *n.* estrujón; apretón, *m.*; *tight* —, (*fig.*) aprieto.—*v.t.* estrujar; apretar; sacar; arrancar; *to* — *in,* hacer sitio para.—*v.i. to* — *through,* pasar por fuerza; *to* — *in,* entrar con dificultad.
squelch [skwelt ʃ], *v.t.* despachurrar.—*v.i.* chapotear.
squib [skwib], *n.* buscapiés, *m.inv.*, petardo; pasquinada (*sátira*).
squid [skwid], *n.* calamar, *m.*
squint [skwint], *n.* estrabismo; mirada furtiva; (*fam.*) vistazo.—*v.i.* bizcar.
squint-eyed ['skwintaid], *a.* bizco.
squire [skwaiə], *n.* escudero; hacendado.
squirm [skwəːm], *n.* retorcimiento.—*v.i.* retorcerse.
squirrel ['skwirəl], *n.* ardilla.
squirt [skwəːt], *n.* chorro; jeringa; (*fam.*) majadero.—*v.t.* lanzar.—*v.i.* chorrear.
stab [stæb], *n.* puñalada; (*fig.*) punzada.—*v.t.* apuñalar.
stability [stə'biliti], *n.* estabilidad, *f.*; firmeza.
stable (1) [steibl], *a.* estable; firme.
stable (2) [steibl], *n.* cuadra; establo (*para vacas*).—*v.t.* poner en la cuadra.
stack [stæk], *n.* niara (*de heno*); montón; pabellón (*de fusiles*); cañón (*de chimenea*), *m.*; (*fam.*) abundancia.—*v.t.* hacinar; amontonar.
stadium ['steidjəm], *n.* estadio.
staff [staːf], *n.* báculo; palo; bordón (*de peregrino*), *m.*; vara; asta (*de bandera*); personal, *m.*; (*mil.*) estado mayor; (*mus.*) pentagrama, *m.*
stag [stæg], *n.* ciervo.
stage [steidʒ], *n.* tablas, *f.pl.*; escena; andamio, etapa; estado; — *hand,* tramoyista, *m.*; — *manager,* director (*m.*) de escena; *by easy stages,* poco a poco; a pequeñas etapas; *to go on the* —, hacerse actor; *to put on the* —, poner en escena.—*v.t.* poner en escena; organizar.
stage-coach ['steidʒkoutʃ], *n.* diligencia.
stage-fright ['steidʒfrait], *n.* miedo al público.
stagger ['stægə], *n.* tambaleo.—*v.t.* desconcertar; escalonar (*horas etc.*).—*v.i.* tambalear.
staggering ['stægəriŋ], *a.* tambaleante; (*fig.*) asombroso.
stagnant ['stægnənt], *a.* estancado; paralizado.
stagnate [stæg'neit], *v.i.* estancarse.
stagnation [stæg'neiʃən], *n.* estancación; paralización, *f.*
stag-party ['stægpaːti], *n.* reunión (*f.*) de hombres solos.
staid [steid], *a.* serio, formal.
stain [stein], *n.* mancha; descoloración, *f.*; tinte, *m.*—*v.t.* manchar; teñir; descolorar; *stained glass,* vidrio de color.
stainless ['steinlis], *a.* sin mancha; inmaculado; inoxidable (*acero*).
stair [stɛə], *n.* escalón, *m.*, peldaño.—*pl.* escalera.
staircase ['stɛəkeis], *n.* escalera.

stake [steik], *n.* estaca; (*agr.*) rodrigón; (*com.*) interés, *m.*; apuesta (*en los juegos*).—*v.t.* estacar; apostar; *to* — *a claim,* hacer una reclamación.
stalactite ['stæləktait], *n.* estalactita.
stalagmite ['stæləgmait], *n.* estalagmita.
stale [steil], *a.* viejo; pasado; cansado.
stalemate ['steilmeit], *n.* tablas, *f.pl.* (*ajedrez*); empate, *m.*
staleness ['steilnis], *n.* rancidez; vejez, *f.*
stalk (1) [stɔːk], *n.* (*bot.*) tallo; pie (*de copa*), *m.*
stalk (2) [stɔːk], *n.* paso majestuoso.—*v.t.* cazar al acecho.—*v.i.* andar con paso majestuoso.
stall (1) [stɔːl], *n.* puesto (*de establo*); (*theat.*) butaca; sitial (*de coro*), *m.*; barraca.
stall (2) [stɔːl], *v.t.* cortar (*máquina*).—*v.i.* pararse; dilatar; poner obstáculos.
stallion ['stæljən], *n.* garañón, *m.*
stalwart ['stɔːlwət], *a.*, *n.* fornido; leal, *m.*
stamina ['stæminə], *n.* vigor, *m.*
stammer ['stæmə], *n.* tartamudeo; balbuceo.—*v.i.* tartamudear; balbucir.
stamp [stæmp], *n.* sello; timbre, *m.*, marca; estampilla; cuño; mano de mortero; (*fig.*) temple, *m.*, clase, *f.*; patada.—*v.t.* estampar; imprimir; sellar; timbrar; fijar el sello; acuñar; patear; apisonar; estigmatizar.—*v.i.* patear.
stampede [stæm'piːd], *n.* estampida; pánico.—*v.t.* ahuyentar; dispersar en pánico.—*v.i.* salir de estampía; huir con pavor.
stanch [staːntʃ], *v.t.* restañar.
stand [stænd], *n.* posición, *f.*; tribuna; sostén, *m.*; puesto; (*mus.*) atril, *m.*; parada (*de taxis*); resistencia; *to make a* — *against,* oponerse a.—*v.t. irr.* poner de pie; poner; tolerar; resistir; convidar.—*v.i. irr.* estar; ser; estar de pie; ponerse en pie; sostenerse; parar(se); quedar(se); estancarse; presentarse como candidato; durar; estar vigente; *to* — *against,* oponerse a; *to* — *aloof,* mantenerse separado; *to* — *aside,* dejar pasar; mantenerse separado; *to* — *back,* recular; *to* — *by,* sostener; ser espectador; atenerse a; estar listo; *to* — *for,* representar; significar; presentarse como candidato para; tolerar; *to* — *in for,* sustituir; *to* — *in need of,* necesitar; *to* — *in the way of,* cerrar el paso a; impedir; *to* — *on end,* erizarse (*el pelo*); *to* — *out,* resistir; destacarse; *to* — *up,* ponerse en pie; *to* — *up for,* defender; volver por.
standard ['stændəd], *a.* normal; clásico; — *work,* obra clásica.—*n.* marco; norma; nivel, *m.*; ley (*del oro*), *f.*; (*mech.*) poste; pie; estandarte, *m.*, bandera; *gold* —, patrón (*m.*) de oro.
standardize ['stændədaiz], *v.t.* hacer uniforme; controlar.
standing ['stændiŋ], *a.* derecho, de pie; constante; permanente, fijo; vigente; — *army,* ejército permanente.—*n.* posición; reputación; duración; antigüedad, *f.*; — *room,* sitio para estar de pie (*en un teatro etc.*)
stand-offish [stænd'ɔfiʃ], *a.* altanero.
standpoint ['stændpoint], *n.* punto de vista.
standstill ['stændstil], *n.* parada; pausa completa.
stank [stæŋk] [STINK].
stanza ['stænzə], *n.* estrofa.

staple

staple (1) [steipl], *a.* corriente; principal.—*n.* producto principal (*de un país*); fibra; materia prima.

staple (2) [steipl], *n.* grapa, picolete, *m.*

star [sta:], *n.* estrella; asterisco; *Stars and Stripes*, las barras y las estrellas.—*v.t.* estrellar; (*theat.*) presentar como estrella; señalar con asterisco.—*v.i.* ser estrella.

starch [sta:tʃ], *n.* almidón, *m.*—*v.t.* almidonar.

starchy ['sta:tʃi], *a.* almidonado; (*med.*) feculoso; (*fig.*) tieso.

stare [steə], *n.* mirada fija.—*v.i.* abrir grandes ojos; mirar fijamente; *to — in the face,* saltar a la vista.

starfish ['sta:fiʃ], *n.* estrella de mar.

staring ['steəriŋ], *a.* que mira fijamente; llamativo.

stark [sta:k], *a.* rígido; árido; completo; — *naked,* en cueros.

starlight ['sta:lait], *n.* luz (*f.*) de las estrellas.

starling ['sta:liŋ], *n.* estornino.

starlit ['sta:lit], **starry** ['sta:ri], *a.* estrellado.

star-spangled ['sta:spæŋgld], *a.* sembrado de estrellas.

start [sta:t], *n.* sobresalto; comienzo, principio; salida, partida; arranque, *m.*; ventaja.—*v.t.* empezar; poner en marcha; espantar (*caza*); dar la señal de partida; provocar; iniciar; abrir.—*v.i.* asustarse; dar un salto; ponerse en marcha; salir (*un tren*); arrancar (*un coche*); comenzar; combarse (*madera*); *to — back,* saltar hacia atrás; emprender el viaje de regreso; *to — out,* salir; *to — up,* ponerse en marcha.

starter ['sta:tə], *n.* iniciador; (*sport*) stárter; (*aut.*) arranque, *m.*

startle [sta:tl], *v.t.* asustar; alarmar.

starvation [sta:'veiʃən], *n.* hambre; inanición, *f.*

starve [sta:v], *v.t.* matar de hambre.—*v.i.* morir de hambre.

state [steit], *a.* de estado, estatal; público; de gala.—*n.* estado; dignidad, *f.*; pompa; *in* —, con gran pompa; *in a* —, (*fam.*) agitado.—*v.t.* exponer; decir; proponer (*un problema*). **[Foreign Office]**

statecraft ['steitkra:ft], *n.* arte (*m.*) de gobernar.

stately ['steitli], *a.* imponente, majestuoso.

statement ['steitmənt], *n.* declaración; exposición, *f.*; resumen, *m.*; (*com.*) estado de cuenta.

statesman ['steitsmən], *n.* estadista, *m.*

statesmanlike ['steitsmənlaik], *a.* propio de un estadista.

statesmanship ['steitsmənʃip], *n.* arte (*m.*) de gobernar.

static ['stætik], *a.* estático.—*n.* perturbación atmosférica o eléctrica.

statics ['stætiks], *n.* estática.

station ['steiʃən], *n.* puesto; condición social; (*rail.*) estación, *f.*; (*rad.*) emisora; — *master,* jefe (*m.*) de estación.—*v.t.* colocar.

stationary ['steiʃənəri], *a.* estacionario, inmóvil.

stationery ['steiʃənəri], *n.* papelería.

statistical [stə'tistikl], *a.* estadístico.

statistics [stə'tistiks], *n. pl.* estadística.

statue ['stætju:], *n.* estatua.

statuesque [stætju'esk], *a.* escultural.

statuette [stætju'et], *n.* figurilla.

stature ['stætʃə], *n.* estatura.

status ['steitəs], *n.* estado; posición; reputación, *f.*

statute ['stætju:t], *n.* estatuto, ley, *f.*

statutory ['stætjutəri], *a.* establecido; estatuario.

staunch [stɔ:ntʃ], *a.* firme; leal; constante.

stave [steiv], *n.* duela; (*mus.*) pentagrama, *m.*—*v.t. irr. to — in,* abrir boquete en; quebrar; *to — off,* diferir; evitar; apartar.

stay (1) [stei], *n.* estancia; residencia; suspensión, *f.*; parada; freno.—*v.t.* detener; posponer.—*v.i.* permanecer, quedar(se); detenerse; hospedarse; *to — in,* quedarse en casa; *to — on,* permanecer; *to — up,* no acostarse.

stay (2) [stei], *n.* puntal; sostén; (*naut.*) estay, *m.*—*pl.* corsé, *m.*

stead [sted], *n.* lugar, *m.*; *to stand in good* —, ser útil.

steadfast ['stedfa:st], *a.* constante; firme; leal.

steady ['stedi], *a.* firme; fijo; seguro; formal; constante; uniforme.—*v.t.* hacer firme; estabilizar; calmar.

steak [steik], *n.* filete; biftec, *m.*

steal [sti:l], *v.t., v.i. irr.* robar, hurtar; *to — away,* escabullirse; *to — in,* entrar furtivamente.

stealth [stelθ], *n.* astucia; cautela; *by —,* a hurtadillas.

stealthy ['stelθi], *a.* furtivo; cauteloso.

steam [sti:m], *n.* vapor, *m.*—*v.t.* saturar; cocer al baño María; empañar (*ventanas*).—*v.i.* echar vapor.

steamboat ['sti:mbout], *n.* [STEAMSHIP].

steam-engine ['sti:mendʒin], *n.* máquina de vapor.

steamer ['sti:mə], *n.* [STEAMSHIP].

steam-hammer ['sti:m'hæmə], *n.* maza de fragua.

steam-roller ['sti:mroulə], *n.* apisonadora.

steamship ['sti:mʃip], *n.* vapor, *m.*

steel [sti:l], *a.* de acero.—*n.* acero; afilón, *m.*; *cold —,* arma blanca; *stainless —,* acero inoxidable.—*v.t.* acerar; endurecer.

steep (1) [sti:p], *a.* escarpado; acantilado; empinado (*de escaleras*); exorbitante (*de precios*).—*n.* despeñadero.

steep (2) [sti:p], *n.* remojo.—*v.t.* empapar; remojar.

steeple [sti:pl], *n.* aguja.

steeplechase ['sti:pltʃeis], *n.* carrera de obstáculos.

steeplejack ['sti:pldʒæk], *n.* reparador (*m.*) de campanarios.

steepness ['sti:pnis], *n.* carácter escarpado.

steer (1) [stiə], *v.t.* gobernar; conducir.—*v.i.* navegar; timonear; conducirse; *to — clear of,* evitar.

steer (2) [stiə], *n.* novillo.

steering ['stiəriŋ], *n.* gobierno; (mecanismo de) dirección, *f.*

steering-wheel ['stiəriŋhwi:l], *n.* volante, *m.*

stem (1) [stem], *n.* (*bot.*) tallo; tronco; pie (*de copa*), *m.*; (*gram.*) raíz, *f.*; tubo (*de pipa*); *from — to stern,* de proa a popa.

stem (2) [stem], *v.t.* ir contra; resistir; contener; estancar.

stench [stentʃ], *n.* hedor, *m.*; tufo.

stencil [stensl], *n.* patrón (*m.*) para estarcir; estarcido; cliché (*duplicador*), *m.*—*v.t.* estarcir.

stenographer [ste'nɔgrəfə], *n.* estenógrafo.
step [step], *n.* paso; escalón, *m.*; grado; huella; (*mus.*) intervalo; — **ladder**, escalera de tijera; *in* —, a compás; *to* **keep in** —, llevar el paso; *watch your* —! ¡tenga cuidado! *to retrace one's steps*, volver sobre sus pasos; *to take steps*, tomar medidas.—*v.i. irr.* dar un paso; pisar; caminar; *to* — *aside*, desviarse; *to* — *back*, retroceder; *to* — *down*, bajar; *to* — *in*, entrar; *to* — *on*, pisar; *to* — *out*, salir; apearse; dar pasos grandes; *to* — *over*, atravesar; *to* — *up*, subir; aumentar.
stepbrother ['stepbrʌðə], *n.* hermanastro.
stepdaughter ['stepdɔ:tə], *n.* hijastra.
stepfather ['stepfɑ:ðə], *n.* padrastro.
stepmother ['stepmʌðə], *n.* madrastra.
stepsister ['stepsistə], *n.* hermanastra.
stepson ['stepsʌn], *n.* hijastro.
stereophonic [stiəriə'fɔnik], *a.* estereofónico.
stereoscopic [stiəriəs'kɔpik], *a.* estereoscópico.
stereotype ['stiəriətaip], *n.* estereotipia.—*v.t.* estereotipar.
sterile ['sterail], *a.* estéril; árido.
sterility [ste'riliti], *n.* esterilidad; aridez, *f.*
sterilization [sterilai'zeiʃən], *n.* esterilización, *f.*
sterilize ['sterilaiz], *v.t.* esterilizar.
sterilizer ['sterilaizə], *n.* esterilizador, *m.*
sterling ['stə:liŋ], *a.* esterlina; (*fig.*) genuino.
stern (1) [stə:n], *a.* austero; rígido; áspero.
stern (2) [stə:n], *n.* (*naut.*) de popa.—*n.* popa.
sternness ['stə:nnis], *n.* austeridad, severidad, *f.*
stethoscope ['steθəskoup], *n.* estetoscopio.
stevedore ['sti:vədɔ:], *n.* estibador, *m.*
stew [stju:], *n.* estofado; (*fig.*) agitación, *f.*—*v.t.* estofar; hervir; cocer (*fruta*).
steward ['stju:ədl], *n.* administrador, *m.*; mayordomo; despensero; camarero (*en los vapores*).
stewpan ['stju:pæn], **stewpot** ['stju:pɔt], *n.* cazuela, olla.
stick (1) [stik], *n.* palo; estaca; leña; vara; bastón, *m.*; (*mus.*) batuta; barra; tallo; (*fig.*) *in a cleft* —, entre la espada y la pared.
stick (2) [stik], *v.t. irr.* hundir; clavar; meter; fijar; picar; pegar; tolerar; *to* — *out*, sacar.—*v.i. irr.* estar clavado; clavarse; pegarse; quedar; detenerse; atascarse; encallarse; perseverar; *to* — *at*, persistir en; detenerse ante; tener escrúpulos sobre; *to* — *at nothing*, no tener escrúpulos; *to* — *by*, sostener; *to* — *close*, mantenerse juntos; *to* — *out*, sobresalir; proyectar; *to* — *to*, pegarse a; mantener; perseverar en; *to* — *up for*, defender.
stickiness ['stikinis], *n.* viscosidad, *f.*
sticking-plaster ['stikiŋplɑ:stə], *n.* esparadrapo.
stickler ['stiklə], *n.* rigorista, *m.f.*
sticky ['stiki], *a.* pegajoso, viscoso; (*fig.*) difícil.
stiff [stif], *a.* tieso; duro; inflexible; espeso; almidonado; severo, difícil; frío; alto (*precio*); fuerte (*brisa*); — *neck*, torticolis, *m.*
stiffen [stifn], *v.t.* atiesar; endurecer; reforzar; espesar; aterir (*de frío*).—*v.i.* atiesarse; endurecerse; robustecerse; obstinarse; enderezarse; aterirse; refrescar (*el viento*).

stiffener ['stifnə], *n.* contrafuerte, *m.*
stiffness ['stifnis], *n.* tiesura; rigidez; severidad; obstinación; dificultad, *f.*
stifle [staifl], *v.t.* ahogar; apagar; suprimir.—*v.i.* ahogarse.
stigma ['stigmə], *n.* estigma, *m.*
stigmatize ['stigmətaiz], *v.t.* estigmatizar.
still (1) [stil], *a.* inmóvil; quedo, tranquilo; no espumoso (*vino*); — *life*, naturaleza muerta; *to keep* —, no moverse.—*adv.* todavía, aún; no obstante; siempre.—*n.* silencio; (*cine.*) retrato de propaganda.—*v.t.* hacer callar; calmar; detener.
still (2) [stil], *n.* alambique, *m.*
still-born ['stilbɔ:n], *a.* nacido muerto.
stillness ['stilnis], *n.* silencio; quietud, tranquilidad, *f.*
stilt [stilt], *n.* zanco.
stilted ['stiltid], *a.* hinchado, pomposo.
stimulant ['stimjulənt], *a., n.* estimulante, *m.*
stimulate ['stimjuleit], *v.t.* estimular, excitar.
stimulating ['stimjuleitiŋ], *a.* estimulante; inspirador.
stimulation [stimju'leiʃən], *n.* estímulo; excitación, *f.*
stimulus ['stimjuləs], *n.* estímulo; incentivo.
sting [stiŋ], *n.* aguijón (*de insecto*), *m.*; mordedura (*de culebra*); estímulo; (*bot.*) púa.—*v.t., v.i. irr.* picar; morder, estimular; atormentar.
stinginess ['stindʒinis], *n.* tacañería.
stingy ['stindʒi], *a.* tacaño; pequeño.
stink [stiŋk], *n.* hedor, *m.*—*v.i. irr.* heder, apestar.
stinking ['stiŋkiŋ], *a.* hediondo.
stint [stint], *n.* tarea; límite, *m.*—*v.t.* limitar; escatimar.
stipend ['staipend], *n.* estipendio, salario.
stipendiary [stai'pendjəri], *a., n.* estipendiario.
stipulate ['stipjuleit], *v.t.* estipular.
stipulation [stipju'leiʃən], *n.* estipulación; condición, *f.*
stir [stə:], *n.* movimiento; conmoción, *f.*; bullicio.—*v.t.* agitar; mover; revolver; conmover; inspirar; atizar; *to* — *up*, despertar, fomentar.—*v.i.* moverse; levantarse (*de la cama*).
stirring ['stə:riŋ], *a.* conmovedor, emocionante.—*n.* movimiento; el revolver.
stirrup ['stirəp], *n.* estribo.
stitch [stitʃ], *n.* puntada; punto; punzada (*dolor*).—*v.t., v.i.* coser; (*med.*) suturar; *to* — *up*, remendar; suturar.
stoat [stout], *n.* armiño.
stock [stɔk], *a.* corriente; del repertorio; — *phrase*, frase hecha.—*n.* tronco; injerto; estirpe (*de familia*), *f.*; (*com.*) valores, *m.pl.*; capital, *m.*; surtido (*de mercancías*); caldo; provisión, *f.*; reserva; ganado; (*bot.*) alhelí, *m.*; culata (*de fusil*); alzacuello; *to take* —, hacer inventario; *Stock Exchange*, Bolsa.—*pl.* cepo.—*v.t.* abastecer; proveer.
stockade [stɔ'keid], *n.* estacada, empalizada.—*v.t.* empalizar.
stockbroker ['stɔkbroukə], *n.* corredor (*m.*) de valores, bolsista, *m.*
stockholder ['stɔkhouldə], *n.* accionista, *m.f.*
stocking ['stɔkiŋ], *n.* media.
stocktaking ['stɔkteikiŋ], *n.* inventario.
stocky ['stɔki], *a.* rechoncho.
stoic ['stouik], *a., n.* estoico.

stoicism ['stouisizm], *n.* estoicismo.
stoke [stouk], *v.t.* alimentar; echar carbón.
stoke-hold ['stoukhould], **stoke-room** ['stoukrum], *n.* cuarto de calderas.
stoker ['stoukə], *n.* fogonero.
stole (1) [stoul], *n.* estola.
stole (2) [stoul], **stolen** ['stoulən] [STEAL].
stolid [stolid], *a.* estólido; impasible.
stolidity [stɔ'liditi], *n.* estolidez; impasibilidad, *f.*
stomach ['stʌmək], *n.* estómago; vientre, *m.*; (*fig.*) apetito; valor, *m.*—*v.t.* digerir; (*fig.*) aguantar.
stone [stoun], *a.* de piedra.—*n.* piedra; hueso, pepita (*de fruta*); **to leave no — unturned,** (*fig.*) hacer todo lo posible.—*v.t.* apedrear; deshuesar (*la fruta*); revestir de piedras.
stone-cold ['stoun'kould], *a.* frío como la piedra.
stone-deaf ['stoun'def], *a.* completamente sordo.
stone-quarry ['stounkwori], *n.* pedrera.
stony ['stouni], *a.* pedregoso; (*fig.*) empedernido, duro, insensible.
stood [stud] [STAND].
stool [stu:l], *n.* taburete, *m.*
stool-pigeon ['stu:lpidʒən], *n.* soplón, *m.*
stoop [stu:p], *n.* inclinación, *f.*; cargazón (*f.*) de espaldas.—*v.i.* inclinarse; ser cargado de espaldas; rebajarse, humillarse.
stooping ['stu:piŋ], *a.* inclinado; cargado (*de espaldas*).—*n.* inclinación, *f.*
stop [stɔp], *n.* parada; cesación; detención; interrupción; suspensión, *f.*; (*mus.*) registro; **full —,** punto; **to make a —,** detenerse; **to put a — to,** poner coto a. —*v.t.* detener, parar; cortar; reprimir; suspender; poner fin a; obstruir; tapar; restañar; cesar (de); evitar; **to — up,** tapar.—*v.i.* parar(se), detenerse; cesar; quedarse; terminar; **to — at nothing,** no tener escrúpulos.
stop-cock ['stɔpkɔk], *n.* llave (*f.*) de agua.
stop-gap ['stɔpgæp], *n.* tapagujeres, *m.sg.*
stoppage ['stɔpidʒ], *n.* cesación; interrupción; obstrucción, *f.*; parada.
stopper ['stɔpə], *n.* tapón, *m.*
stop-press ['stɔp'pres], *n.* noticias (*f.pl.*) de última hora.
stop-watch ['stɔpwɔtʃ] *n.* cronógrafo.
storage ['stɔːridʒ], *n.* almacenaje, *m.*; **— battery,** (*U.S.*) [ACCUMULATOR].
store [stɔː], *n.* abundancia; provisión, *f.*; depósito, almacén, *m.*; tienda; **to set — by,** estimar en mucho.—*pl.* pertrechos, *m.pl.*; provisiones, *f.pl.*—*v.t.* proveer; acumular; tener en reserva; almacenar.
storeroom ['stɔːrum], *n.* despensa.
storey ['stɔːri] [STOREY (2)].
stork [stɔːk], *n.* cigüeña.
storm [stɔːm], *n.* tempestad, *f.*, tormenta; tumulto, *m.* (*mil.*) asalto; **to take by —,** tomar por asalto; **— in a teacup,** tempestad (*f.*) en un vaso de agua.—*v.t.* asaltar.—*v.i.* bramar de cólera.
stormy ['stɔːmi], *a.* tempestuoso; turbulento.
story (1) ['stɔːri], *n.* historia; cuento; anécdota; argumento.
story (2), **storey** ['stɔːri], *n.* piso; **a four-story house,** casa de cuatro pisos.
stout (1) [staut], *a.* fornido; corpulento; fuerte; firme; resuelto; intrépido.

stout (2) [staut], *n.* cerveza negra.
stoutness ['stautnis], *n.* corpulencia; solidez, *f.*; fuerza; valor, *m.*
stove (1) [stouv], *n.* horno, estufa.
stove (2) [stouv] [STAVE].
stow [stou], *v.t.* colocar; esconder; (*naut.*) estibar.—*v.i.* **to — away,** embarcarse clandestinamente.
stowaway ['stouəwei], *n.* polizón, *m.*
straddle [strædl], *v.t., v.i.* montar a horcajadas.
strafe [strɑːf], *v.t.* bombardear intensamente.
straggle [strægl], *v.i.* rezagarse; dispersarse; extenderse.
straggler ['stræglə], *n.* rezagado.
straggling ['strægliŋ], *a.* rezagado; disperso; desordenado.
straight [streit], *a.* derecho; recto, directo; lacio (*pelo*); ordenado; justo; honrado; franco; **— face,** cara seria.—*adv.* derecho; en línea directa; directamente; **— away,** en seguida.
straighten [streitn], *v.t.* poner derecho; enderezar; poner en orden, arreglar; **to — out,** poner en orden.—*v.i.* **to — up,** erguirse.
straightforward [streit'fɔːwəd], *a.* honrado; sincero; sencillo; directo.
strain (1) [strein], *n.* tensión; tirantez, *f.*; esfuerzo; torcedura; estilo; exceso; (*mus.*) melodía.—*v.t.* estirar; forzar; esforzar; torcer (*un músculo*); forzar (*la vista*); aguzar (*el oído*); obligar demasiado; abusar de; filtrar; colar.
strain (2) [strein], *n.* raza; (*biol.*) cepa; vena; disposición heredada.
strainer ['streinə], *n.* coladero.
strait [streit], *n.* estrecho; apuro.
straiten [streitn], *v.t.* estrechar; limitar.
strait-jacket ['streitdʒækit], *n.* camisa de fuerza.
strait-laced [streit'leist], *a.* (*fig.*) mojigato.
strand (1) [strænd], *n.* playa; ribera.—*v.t., v.i.* encallar; **to be stranded,** quedarse abandonado; (*fig.*) quedarse colgado.
strand (2) [strænd], *n.* hebra; hilo, sarta; cabo, ramal.
strange [streindʒ], *a.* extraño, singular; extraordinario; desconocido.
strangeness ['streindʒnis], *n.* rareza; novedad, *f.*
stranger ['streindʒə], *n.* desconocido; forastero; extranjero.
strangle [stræŋgl], *v.t.* estrangular; ahogar.
strangler ['stræŋglə], *n.* estrangulador, *m.*
strangulation [stræŋgju'leiʃən], *n.* estrangulación, *f.*
strap [stræp], *n.* correa.—*v.t.* atar con correas.
strapping ['stræpiŋ], *a.* robusto.
stratagem ['strætədʒəm], *n.* estratagema, ardid, *m.*
strategic [strə'ti:dʒik], *a.* estratégico.
strategist ['strætidʒist], *n.* estratego.
strategy ['strætidʒi], *n.* estrategia.
stratosphere ['strætəsfiə], *n.* estratosfera.
stratum ['strɑːtəm], *n.* estrato.
straw [strɔː], *n.* paja; **to be the last —,** ser el colmo.
strawberry ['strɔːbəri], *n.* fresa.
straw-coloured ['strɔːkʌləd], *a.* pajizo.
stray [strei], *a.* perdido, descarriado.—*n.* animal perdido.—*v.i.* descarriarse, perder el camino; errar.

streak [stri:k], *n.* raya; rayo (*de luz*); vena; — *of lightning*, relámpago.—*v.t.* rayar.
streaky ['stri:ki], *a.* rayado.
stream [stri:m], *n.* corriente, *f.*; arroyo; torrente, *m.*; chorro.—*v.i.* correr, manar, brotar, fluir; chorrear.
streamer ['stri:mə], *n.* gallardete, *m.*
street [stri:t], *n.* calle, *f.*; *the man in the* —, el hombre medio; el ciudadano típico.
street-walker ['stri:twɔ:kə], *n.* prostituta.
strength [streŋθ], *n.* fuerza; validez; intensidad, *f.*
strengthen ['streŋθən], *v.t.* fortificar; reforzar; confirmar.—*v.i.* fortificarse; reforzarse.
strenuous ['strenjuəs], *a.* enérgico; arduo.
stress [stres], *n.* importancia; tensión, compulsión, *f.*; acento; (*mech.*) esfuerzo; *to lay great* — *on*, insistir en; dar mucha importancia a.—*v.t.* insistir en; dar énfasis a; acentuar.
stretch [stretʃ], *n.* tensión, *f.*; estirón, *m.*; esfuerzo; extensión, *f.*—*v.t.* extender; alargar; estirar; dilatar; ensanchar; exagerar; *to* — *a point*, hacer una concesión.—*v.i.* extenderse; dar de sí; estirarse; desperezarse; *to* — *out*, extenderse.
stretcher ['stretʃə], *n.* camilla.
stretcher-bearer ['stretʃəbeərə], *n.* camillero.
strew [stru:], *v.t. irr.* esparcir, derramar.
strewn [stru:n] [STREW].
stricken ['strikən], *a.* herido; afligido.
strict [strikt], *a.* estricto; exacto; severo.
strictly ['striktli], *adv. strictly speaking*, en rigor.
strictness ['striktnis], *n.* rigor, *m.*; severidad, *f.*
stride [straid], *n.* paso largo, tranco.—*v.t. irr.* cruzar a grandes trancos; montar a horcajadas.—*v.i.* andar a pasos largos.
strident ['straidənt], *a.* estridente; (*fig.*) chillón.
strife [straif], *n.* disputa, lucha; rivalidad, *f.*
strike [straik], *n.* golpe, *m.*; huelga; (*min.*) descubrimiento de un filón.—*v.t. irr.* golpear; pegar; herir; tocar, chocar contra; encender (*un fósforo*); acuñar (*moneda*); cerrar (*un trato*); dar (*la hora*); parecer; dar una impresión; ocurrírsele a uno (*una idea*); descubrir, encontrar; adoptar (*una postura*); arriar (*una bandera*); hacer (*un balance*); nivelar; desmontar (*una tienda*); *to* — *against*, chocar contra; *to* — *down*, derribar; acometer; *to* — *off*, borrar; *to* — *out*, borrar, tachar; *to* — *up*, trabar (*amistad*); *it strikes me*, me parece; *how does it* — *you?* ¿qué te parece?—*v.i. irr.* golpear; (*naut.*) encallar; declararse en huelga; sonar; arraigar; dar la hora; estallar; *to* — *back*, dar golpe por golpe; *to* — *home*, dar en el vivo; *to* — *out*, asesar un puñetazo; arrojarse; *to* — *up*, empezar a tocar.
striker ['straikə], *n.* huelguista, *m.f.*
striking ['straikiŋ], *a.* sorprendente, notable; impres.onante; fuerte.
string [striŋ], *n.* bramante, *m.*; ristra (*de cebollas*); cinta; cuerda (*de un arco*); hilera; (*mus.*) cuerda; (*fig.*) sarta, serie, *f.*; — *beans*, judías verdes; *to pull strings*, (*fig.*) manejar los hilos.—*v.t. irr.* (*mus.*) encordar; ensartar; quitar las fibras; *to* — *out*, extender en fila; *to* — *up*, ahorcar.

stringed [striŋd], *a.* encordado; — *instrument*, instrumento de cuerda.
stringency ['strindʒənsi], *n.* aprieto; estrechez, severidad, *f.*
stringent ['strindʒənt], *a.* estricto, severo.
stringy ['striŋi], *a.* fibroso; correoso.
strip [strip], *n.* tira; listón (*de madera*), *m.* —*v.t.* desnudar; despojar; robar; descortezar.—*v.i.* desnudarse.
stripe [straip], *n.* raya, lista; azote; (*mil.*) galón, *m.*—*v.t.* rayar.
strive [straiv], *v.i. irr.* esforzarse; contender; pugnar.
strode [stroud] [STRIDE].
stroke [strouk], *n.* golpe, *m.*; (*mech.*) golpe del émbolo; plumada; pincelada; campanada (*de un reloj*); tacada (*en el billar*); (*med.*) ataque, *m.*; caricia con la mano; *not a* —, absolutamente nada; — *of genius*, rasgo ingenioso; — *of luck*, golpe de fortuna. —*v.t.* acariciar.
stroll [stroul], *n.* paseo.—*v.i.* pasearse, vagar.
stroller ['stroulə], *n.* paseante, *m.f.*
strong [strɔŋ], *a.* fuerte, vigoroso, robusto; poderoso; concentrado; firme; enérgico; resuelto; vivo; pronunciado; *ten thousand* —, de diez mil hombres.
strong-box ['strɔŋbɔks], *n.* caja de caudales.
stronghold ['strɔŋhould], *n.* fortaleza; (*fig.*) refugio.
strong-minded ['strɔŋ'maindid], *a.* resuelto; de firmes creencias.
strove [strouv] [STRIVE].
struck [strʌk] [STRIKE].
structural ['strʌktʃərəl], *a.* estructural.
structure ['strʌktʃə], *n.* construcción, *f.*; edificio; estructura.
struggle ['strʌgl], *n.* lucha, disputa, conflicto. —*v.i.* luchar; esforzarse; contender.
strum [strʌm], *v.t.* rasgar (*la guitarra etc.*).
strung [strʌŋ] [STRING].
strut (1) [strʌt], *n.* pavonada.—*v.i.* pavonearse.
strut (2) [strʌt], *n.* (*carp.*) jabalcón, *m.*
stub [stʌb], *n.* cabo; talón (*de cheque*), *m.*; colilla (*de pitillo*); fragmento.—*v.t.* apagar (*out*).
stubble [stʌbl], *n.* rastrojo; barba.
stubborn ['stʌbən], *a.* terco; inquebrantable; persistente.
stubbornness ['stʌbənnis], *n.* obstinación, terquedad, *f.*
stuck [stʌk] [STICK].
stud (1) [stʌd], *n.* tachón, *m.*; botón (*m.*) de camisa.—*v.t.* tachonar; (*fig.*) adornar.
stud (2) [stʌd], *n.* caballeriza.
student ['stju:dənt], *a.* estudiantil.—*n.* estudiante, *m.f.*
studio ['stju:diou], *n.* estudio.
studious ['stju:djəs], *a.* estudioso, aplicado; solícito.
study ['stʌdi], *n.* estudio; gabinete, *m.*; meditación, *f.*—*v.t., v.i.* estudiar.
stuff [stʌf], *n.* materia; esencia; cachivaches, *m.pl.*; tela, estofa.—*v.t.* henchir; llenar; rellenar; apretar.
stuffing ['stʌfiŋ], *n.* rehenchimiento; relleno.
stuffy ['stʌfi], *a.* mal ventilado; (*fig.*) hinchado.
stultify ['stʌltifai], *v.t.* embrutecer; invalidar.
stumble [stʌmbl], *n.* traspié, tropezón, *m.*— *v.i.* tropezar; *to* — *across*, hallar casualmente, tropezar con.

stumbling-block

stumbling-block ['stʌmbliŋblɔk], *n.* tropiezo; impedimento.
stump [stʌmp], *n.* tocón (*de árbol*), *m.*; troncho (*de col*); muñón (*de brazo etc.*); raigón (*de muela*); poste, *m.—v.t.* dejar perplejo.
stun [stʌn], *v.t.* aturdir con un golpe; pasmar; atolondrar.
stung [stʌŋ] [STING].
stunk [stʌŋk] [STINK].
stunning ['stʌniŋ], *a.* aturdidor; (*fam.*) estupendo.
stunt (1) [stʌnt], *n.* reclamo llamativo; ejercicio de proeza.
stunt (2) [stʌnt], *v.t.* impedir el crecimiento de.
stupefy ['stju:pifai], *v.t.* causar estupor; atontar; pasmar.
stupendous [stju:'pendəs], *a.* estupendo.
stupid ['stju:pid], *a.* estúpido; estupefacto.
stupidity [stju:'piditi], *n.* estupidez, *f.*; tontería.
stupor ['stju:pə], *n.* estupor, *m.*
sturdiness ['stə:dinis], *n.* robustez; tenacidad, *f.*
sturdy ['stə:di], *a.* robusto; tenaz.
sturgeon ['stə:dʒən], *n.* esturión, *m.*
stutter ['stʌtə], *n.* tartamudeo.—*v.i.* tartamudear.
stuttering ['stʌtəriŋ], *a.* tartamudo.—*n.* tartamudeo.
sty (1) [stai], *n.* pocilga.
sty (2), **stye** [stai], *n.* (*med.*) orzuelo.
style [stail], *n.* estilo; manera de obrar; moda; modelo; tratamiento; tono; clase, *f.—v.t.* nombrar.
stylish ['staili ʃ], *a.* elegante; a la moda.
stylize ['stailaiz], *v.t.* estilizar.
suave [swɑ:v], *a.* urbano, tratable.
suavity ['swɑ:viti], *n.* urbanidad, *f.*
subaltern ['sʌbəltən], *n.* subalterno.
subcommittee ['sʌbkəmiti], *n.* subcomisión, *f.*
subconscious [sʌb'kɔnʃəs], *a.* subconsciente. —*n.* subconsciencia.
subdivide [sʌbdi'vaid], *v.t.* subdividir.
subdivision ['sʌbdiviʒən], *n.* subdivisión, *f.*
subdue [səb'dju:], *v.t.* sojuzgar, reprimir; dominar; amansar; suavizar.
sub-editor ['sʌbeditə], *n.* subdirector, *m.*
subject ['sʌbdʒikt], *a.* sujeto; sometido.— *n.* (*pol.*) súbdito; tema, *m.*, asunto; (*educ.*) asignatura.—[səb'dʒekt], *v.t.* sujetar, someter, subyugar.
subjection [səb'dʒekʃən], *n.* sujeción, *f.*, sometimiento.
subjective [səb'dʒektiv], *a.* subjetivo.
subjugate ['sʌbdʒugeit], *v.t.* subyugar, someter.
subjugation [sʌbdʒu'geiʃən], *n.* subyugación, *f.*
subjunctive [səb'dʒʌŋktiv], *a.*, *n.* subjuntivo.
sublimate ['sʌblimeit], *v.t.* sublimar.
sublimation [sʌbli'meiʃən], *n.* sublimación, *f.*
sublime [sə'blaim], *a.* sublime; supremo; *the —,* lo sublime.
sublimity [sə'blimiti], *n.* sublimidad, *f.*
submarine ['sʌbməri:n], *a.*, *n.* submarino.
submerge [səb'mə:dʒ], *v.t.* sumergir; ahogar. —*v.i.* sumergirse.
submersion [səb'mə:ʃən], *n.* sumersión, *f.*
submission [səb'miʃən], *n.* sumisión; rendición, *f.*
submissive [səb'misiv], *a.* sumiso.

submit [səb'mit], *v.t.* someter; presentar.— *v.i.* someterse; rendirse.
subnormal [sʌb'nɔ:məl], *a.* subnormal.
subordinate [sə'bɔ:dinit], *a.*, *n.* subordinado. —[sə'bɔ:dineit], *v.t.* subordinar.
subscribe [səb'skraib], *v.t.*, *v.i.* subscribir; abonarse.
subscriber [səb'skraibə], *n.* subscriptor, *m.*; abonado.
subscription [səb'skripʃən], *n.* subscripción, *f.*; cuota; abono.
subsequent ['sʌbsikwənt], *a.* subsiguiente.
subservient [səb'sə:vjənt], *a.* útil; servil; subordinado.
subside [səb'said], *v.i.* calmarse; callarse; cesar; bajar (*el agua*); hundirse; disminuir.
subsidence [səb'saidəns], *n.* hundimiento; desplome, *m.*; bajada; poso; (*fig.*) apaciguamiento.
subsidiary [səb'sidjəri], *a.* subsidiario.
subsidize ['sʌbsidaiz],*v.t.* subvencionar.
subsidy ['sʌbsidi], *n.* subvención, *f.*
subsist [səb'sist], *v.i.* subsistir.
subsistence [səb'sistəns], *n.* subsistencia, *f.*
subsoil ['sʌbsɔil], *n.* subsuelo.
substance ['sʌbstəns], *n.* substancia.
substantial [səb'stænʃəl], *a.* substancial, sólido; verdadero.
substantiate [səb'stænʃieit], *v.t.* verificar; justificar; substanciar.
substantive ['sʌbstəntiv], *a.*, *n.* substantivo.
substitute ['sʌbstitju:t], *n.* substituto.—*v.t.* substituir.
substitution [sʌbsti'tju:ʃən],*n.*substitución,*f.*
substratum [sʌb'strɑ:təm], *n.* (*pl.* **substrata**) substrato.
subterfuge ['sʌbtəfju:dʒ], *n.* subterfugio; evasión, *f.*
subterranean [sʌbtə'reinjən], *a.* subterráneo.
subtle [sʌtl], *a.* sutil; penetrante; hábil; astuto.
subtlety ['sʌtlti], *n.* sutileza; agudeza; astucia.
subtract [səb'trækt], *v.t.* substraer, restar.
subtraction [səb'trækʃən], *n.* substracción, *f.*, resta.
suburb ['sʌbə:b], *n.* suburbio.—*pl.* afueras, *f.pl.*
suburban [sə'bə:bən], *a.* suburbano.
subversion [səb'və:ʃən], *n.* subversión, *f.*
subversive [səb'və:siv], *a.* subversivo.
subvert [səb'və:t], *v.t.* subvertir.
subway ['sʌbwei], *n.* pasaje subterráneo, *m.*; (*U.S.*) metro.
succeed [sək'si:d], *v.t.* suceder (a); seguir (a). —*v.i.* tener éxito; ser el sucesor; *to — in,* lograr, conseguir.
succeeding [sək'si:diŋ], *a.* subsiguiente, futuro.
success [sək'ses], *n.* éxito.
successful [sək'sesful], *a.* próspero, afortunado; *to be —,* tener éxito.
succession [sək'seʃən], *n.* sucesión, *f.*; *in —,* sucesivamente.
successor [sək'sesə], *n.* sucesor, *m.*; heredero.
succinct [sək'siŋkt], *a.* sucinto, conciso.
succour ['sʌkə], *n.* socorro, auxilio.—*v.t.* socorrer.
succulent ['sʌkjulənt], *a.* suculento.
succumb [sə'kʌm], *v.i.* sucumbir; rendirse.
such [sʌtʃ], *a.* tal; semejante, parecido.—*adv.* tan.—*pron.* tal; el (la, lo, los, las) que.

superannuated

suchlike ['sʌtʃlaik], *a.* semejante, tal; de esta clase.
suck [sʌk], *n.* succión, *f.*; chupada; **to give —**, (*obs.*) amamantar.—*v.t.* chupar; mamar.
sucker ['sʌkə], *n.* lechón, chupador, *m.*; (*bot.*) retoño; (*zool.*) ventosa; (*fam.*) primo.
sucking-pig ['sʌkiŋpig], *n.* lechoncito, cochinillo.
suckle [sʌkl], *v.t.* amamantar.
suction ['sʌkʃən], *n.* succión, *f.*
suction-pump ['sʌkʃən'pʌmp], *n.* bomba aspirante.
Sudan [su'dɑːn], *n.* el Sudán.
Sudanese [sudə'niːz], *a.*, *n.* sudanés, *m.*
sudden [sʌdn], *a.* imprevisto, impensado; súbito; precipitado; **all of a —**, de repente.
suddenly ['sʌdnli], *adv.* de repente, súbitamente.
suddenness ['sʌdnnis], *n.* calidad repentina, brusquedad, *f.*
suds [sʌdz], *n.pl.* jabonaduras, *f.pl.*, espuma.
sue [sjuː], *v.t.* demandar, pedir en juicio; **to — for**, pedir; **to — for damages**, demandar por daños y perjuicios.
suede [sweid], *a.* de ante.—*n.* ante, *m.*
suet ['s(j)uːit], *n.* sebo.
suffer ['sʌfə], *v.t.* sufrir, padecer; tolerar, aguantar; permitir.—*v.i.* sufrir.
sufferance ['sʌfərəns], *n.* tolerancia.
sufferer ['sʌfərə], *n.* sufridor, *m.*; enfermo; víctima.
suffering ['sʌfəriŋ], *a.* doliente, sufriente.—*n.* sufrimiento, dolor, *m.*
suffice [sə'fais], *v.t.* satisfacer.—*v.i.* bastar.
sufficiency [sə'fiʃənsi], *n.* suficiencia.
sufficient [sə'fiʃənt], *a.* suficiente, bastante.
suffix ['sʌfiks], *n.* sufijo.
suffocate ['sʌfəkeit], *v.t.* sofocar, ahogar; apagar.—*v.i.* sofocarse, ahogarse.
suffocation [sʌfə'keiʃən], *n.* sofocación, *f.*, ahogo.
suffrage ['sʌfridʒ], *n.* sufragio.
suffuse [sə'fjuːz], *v.t.* bañar, cubrir; extender.
sugar ['ʃugə], *n.* azúcar, *m.*—*v.t.* azucarar; **to — the pill**, (*fig.*) dorar la píldora.
sugar-beet ['ʃugəbiːt], *n.* remolacha.
sugar-bowl ['ʃugəboul], *n.* azucarero.
sugar-cane ['ʃugəkein], *n.* caña de azucar.
sugar-coated ['ʃugəkoutid], *a.* confitado.
sugar-tongs ['ʃugətɔŋz], *n.pl.* tenacillas, *f.pl.*
sugary ['ʃugəri], *a.* azucarado; (*fig.*) meloso.
suggest [sə'dʒest], *v.t.* sugerir; insinuar; indicar; aconsejar; evocar.—*v.r.* ocurrirse (*una idea*).
suggestion [sə'dʒestʃən], *n.* sugestión; insinuación, *f.*
suggestive [sə'dʒestiv], *a.* sugestivo; picante.
suicidal [sjui'saidl], *a.* suicida.
suicide ['sjuisaid], *n.* suicidio (*hecho*); suicida (*persona*), *m.f.*; **to commit —**, suicidarse.
suit [sjuːt], *n.* petición, *f.*; cortejo; pleito; traje, *m.*; palo (*naipes*); serie, *f.*; **to follow —**, jugar el mismo palo; (*fig.*) seguir el ejemplo.—*v.t.* convenir; ir bien, sentar; agradar.
suitability [sjuːtə'biliti], *n.* conveniencia; aptitud, *f.*
suitable ['sjuːtəbl], *a.* apropiado, apto, a propósito, conveniente.
suitcase ['sjuːtkeis], *n.* maleta.

suite [swiːt], *n.* juego (*de muebles etc.*); serie, *f.*; séquito.
suitor ['sjuːtə], *n.* pretendiente, *m.*; (*jur.*) demandante, *m.f.*
sulk [sʌlk], *n.* mohina.—*v.i.* ponerse mohino.
sulky ['sʌlki], *a.* mohino, malhumorado.
sullen ['sʌlən], *a.* hosco, taciturno; sombrío.
sullenness ['sʌlənnis], *n.* hosquedad, taciturnidad, *f.*, mal humor, *m.*
sully ['sʌli], *v.t.* manchar, empañar; desdorar.
sulphur ['sʌlfə], *n.* azufre, *m.*
sulphurous ['sʌlfərəs], *a.* sulfuroso.
sultan ['sʌltən], *n.* sultán, *m.*
sultana [sʌl'tɑːnə], *n.* sultana.
sultry ['sʌltri], *a.* bochornoso, sofocante.
sum [sʌm], *n.* (*math.*) suma; problema, *m.*; total, *m.*; (*com.*) cantidad, *f.*; resumen, *m.*—*v.t.* sumar; **to — up**, recapitular; resumir.
summarize ['sʌməraiz], *v.t.* resumir, compendiar.
summary ['sʌməri], *a.* sumario; somero.—*n.* sumario, resumen, *m.*
summer ['sʌmə], *a.* estival, de verano.—*n.* verano, estío.
summer-house ['sʌməhaus], *n.* cenador, *m.*
summit ['sʌmit], *n.* cima, cumbre, *f.*
summon ['sʌmən], *v.t.* citar; mandar; llamar; invocar; **to — up**, animar.
summons ['sʌmənz], *n.* citación, *f.*; requerimiento.
sumptuous ['sʌmptjuəs], *a.* suntuoso, magnifico.
sumptuousness ['sʌmptjuəsnis], *n.* suntuosidad, *f.*, magnificencia.
sun [sʌn], *n.* sol, *m.*—*v.r.* tomar el sol.
sun-bathing ['sʌnbeiðiŋ], *n.* baño de sol.
sunbeam ['sʌnbiːm], *n.* rayo de sol.
sun-blind ['sʌnblaind], *n.* toldo para el sol.
sunburn ['sʌnbəːn], *n.* quemadura del sol; bronceado.
sunburnt ['sʌnbəːnt], *a.* moreno, tostado por el sol, bronceado.
Sunday ['sʌnd(e)i], *a.* dominical.—*n.* domingo.
sunder ['sʌndə], *v.t.* separar, hender.
sun-dial ['sʌndaiəl], *n.* reloj (*m.*) de sol.
sundown ['sʌndaun], *n.* puesta del sol.
sundry ['sʌndri], *a.* varios.—*n.pl.* **sundries**, artículos diversos, *m.*
sunflower ['sʌnflauə], *n.* girasol, *m.*
sung [sʌŋ] [SING].
sun-glasses ['sʌnglɑːsiz], *n.pl.* gafas (*f.pl.*) de sol.
sunk [sʌŋk] [SINK].
sunken ['sʌŋkən], *a.* hundido.
sunlight ['sʌnlait], *n.* luz (*f.*) del sol.
sunny ['sʌni], *a.* expuesto al sol, asoleado; (*fig.*) risueño; alegre; **to be —**, hacer sol.
sunrise ['sʌnraiz], *n.* salida del sol; **from — to sunset**, de sol a sol.
sunset ['sʌnset], *n.* puesta del sol.
sunshade ['sʌnʃeid], *n.* quitasol, *m.*
sunshine ['sʌnʃain], *n.* luz (*f.*) del sol; **in the —**, al sol.
sunstroke ['sʌnstrouk], *n.* insolación, *f.*
sup [sʌp], *n.* sorbo.—*v.t.* sorber, beber.—*v.i.* (*obs.*) cenar.
superabundance [sjuːpərə'bandəns], *n.* superabundancia.
superabundant [sjuːpərə'bandənt], *a.* superabundante.
superannuated [sjuːpər'ænjueitid], *a.* jubilado; anticuado.

387

superb

superb [sju'pə:b], *a.* soberbio; espléndido.
supercilious [sju:pə'siljəs], *a.* desdeñoso, altivo.
superficial [sju:pə'fiʃəl], *a.* superficial.
superficiality [sju:pəfiʃi'æliti], *n.* superficialidad, *f.*
superfluity [sju:pə'flu:iti], *n.* superfluidad, *f.*, sobra.
superfluous [sju:'pə:fluəs], *a.* superfluo.
superhuman [sju:pə'hju:mən], *a.* sobrehumano.
superimpose [sju:pərim'pouz], *v.t.* sobreponer.
superintend [sju:prin'tend], *v.t.* dirigir, vigilar, superentender.
superintendent [sju:prin'tendənt]. *n.* superintendente, *m.f.*
superior [sju'piərjə], *a.* superior; altivo.—*n.* superior, *m.*; *Mother Superior,* superiora.
superiority [sjupiəri'oriti], *n.* superioridad, *f.*
superlative [sju'pə:lətiv], *a.*, *n.* superlativo.
superman ['sju:pəmæn], *n.* superhombre, *m.*
supernatural [sju:pə'nætʃrəl], *a.* sobrenatural.
supersede [sju:pə'si:d], *v.t.* reemplazar, suplantar.
superstition [sju:pə'stiʃən], *n.* superstición, *f.*
superstitious [sju:pə'stiʃəs], *a.* supersticioso.
supervene [sju:pə'vi:n], *v.i.* sobrevenir.
supervise ['sju:pəvaiz], *v.t.* superentender, vigilar, dirigir.
supervision [sju:pə'viʒən], *n.* superintendencia, dirección, *f.*, vigilancia.
supervisor ['sju:pəvaizə], *n.* superintendente, *m.f.*
supper ['sʌpə], *n.* cena; *to have —,* cenar.
supplant [sə'plɑ:nt], *v.t.* suplantar.
supple [sʌpl], *a.* flexible; ágil; dócil; servil, lisonjero.
supplement ['sʌplimənt], *n.* suplemento; apéndice, *m.*—[sʌpli'ment], *v.t.* suplementar, complementar.
supplementary [sʌpli'mentəri], *a.* suplementario, adicional.
suppliant ['sʌpljənt], *a.*, *n.* suplicante, *m.f.*
supplicate ['sʌplikeit], *v.t.* suplicar.
supplication [sʌpli'keiʃən], *n.* súplica, suplicación, *f.*
supplier [sə'plaiə], *n.* suministrador, proveedor, *m.*
supply [sə'plai], *n.* suministro, provisión, *f.*; cantidad suficiente, *f.*; substituto; (*com.*) oferta; *— and demand,* oferta y demanda. —*pl.* **supplies,** pertrechos, *m.pl.*; provisiones, *f.pl.*—*v.t.* proveer; suministrar; proporcionar; suplir, reemplazar.
support [sə'po:t], *n.* sostén, *m.*; apoyo; *in — of,* en favor de.—*v.t.* sostener, apoyar; mantener; aguantar; defender; vindicar; *to — oneself,* ganarse la vida.
supporter [sə'po:tə], *n.* defensor, *m.*; partidario.
suppose [sə'pouz], *v.t.* suponer; figurarse; creer.
supposition [sʌpə'ziʃən], *n.* suposición, hipótesis, *f.*
suppress [sə'pres], *v.t.* suprimir; reprimir; ocultar; contener.
suppression [sə'preʃən], *n.* supresión; represión, *f.*
supremacy [sju'preməsi], *n.* supremacía.

supreme [sju'pri:m], *a.* supremo; sumo.
surcharge ['sə:tʃɑ:dʒ], *n.* sobrecarga.
sure [ʃuə], *a.* seguro, cierto; *to be —,* seguramente; estar seguro; *to make — of,* asegurarse de.—*adv.* (*fam.*) seguramente, ciertamente.
sure-footed i'ʃuə'futid], *a.* de pie firme.
sureness ['ʃuənis], *n.* seguridad, *f.*, certeza.
surety ['ʃuəti], *n.* garante, *m.f.*; garantía.
surf [sə:f], *n.* rompiente, *m.*, resaca.
surface ['sə:fis], *a.* superficial.—*n.* superficie, *f.*—*v.t.* allanar.—*v.i.* salir a la superficie.
surfeit ['sə:fit], *n.* ahito; (*fig.*) empalago.—*v.t.* saciar.
surf-riding ['sə:fraidiŋ], *n.* patinaje (*m.*) sobre las olas.
surge [sə:dʒ], *n.* oleada.—*v.i.* agitarse, bullir; embravecerse (*el mar*); romper (*las olas*).
surgeon ['sə:dʒən], *n.* cirujano.
surgery ['sə:dʒəri], *n.* cirugía.
surgical ['sə:dʒikəl], *a.* quirúrgico.
surliness ['sə:linis], *n.* acedía, mal genio; taciturnidad, *f.*
surloin [SIRLOIN].
surly ['sə:li], *a.* agrio, malhumorado; taciturno.
surmise ['sə:maiz], *n.* conjetura, suposición, *f.*—[sə:'maiz], *v.t.* conjeturar; suponer.
surmount [sə:'maunt], *v.t.* vencer, superar; coronar.
surname ['sə:neim], *n.* apellido.—*v.t.* nombrar, llamar.
surpass [sə:'pɑ:s], *v.t.* superar; exceder.
surpassing [sə:'pɑ:siŋ], *a.* incomparable.
surplice ['sə:plis], *n.* sobrepelliz, *f.*
surplus ['sə:pləs], *a.* sobrante.—*n.* sobras, *f.pl.*, sobrante, *m.*, exceso; (*com.*) superávit, *m.*
surprise [sə praiz], *n.* sorpresa, asombro.—*v.t.* sorprender, asombrar; coger de improviso.
surprising [sə'praiziŋ], *a.* sorprendente.
surrealism [sə'riəlizm], *n.* surrealismo.
surrender [sə'rendə], *n.* rendición, *f.*, entrega; sumisión, *f.*; (*jur.*) cesión, *f.*—*v.t.* rendir, entregar; ceder; renunciar a.—*v.i.* entregarse, rendirse.
surreptitious [sʌrəp'tiʃəs], *a.* subrepticio.
surround [sə'raund], *n.* borde, *m.*—*v.t.* rodear, cercar; sitiar.
surrounding [sə'raundiŋ], *a.* vecino; alrededor, *inv.*—*n.pl.* alrededores, *m.pl.*, cercanías, *f.pl.*; ambiente, *m.*
survey ['sə:vei], *n.* apeo; vista; inspección, *f.*, examen, *m.*—[sə:'vei], *v.t.* apear (*tierras*); inspeccionar (*casas*); mirar; examinar.
surveying [sə'veiiŋ], *n.* agrimensura.
surveyor [sə:'veiə], *n.* agrimensor; inspector, *m.*
survival [sə'vaivəl], *n.* supervivencia; reliquia.
survive [sə'vaiv], *v.t.*, *v.i.* sobrevivir; subsistir.
survivor [sə'vaivə], *n.* sobreviviente, *m.f.*
susceptibility [səsepti'biliti], *n.* susceptibilidad; propensión, *f.*
susceptible [sə'septibl], *a.* susceptible; sensible; impresionable; enamoradizo.
suspect ['sʌspekt], *a.*, *n.* sospechoso.—[səs'pekt], *v.t.* sospechar; conjeturar; dudar.—*v.i.* tener sospechas.
suspend [səs'pend], *v.t.* suspender.

suspenders [səs'pendəz], *n.pl.* ligas, *f.pl.*; (*U.S.*) tirantes (*m.pl.*) del pantalón.
suspense [səs'pens], *n.* incertidumbre, *f.*
suspension [səs'penʃən], *n.* suspensión, *f.*
suspension-bridge [səs'penʃənbridʒ], *n.* puente colgante, *m.*
suspicion [səs'piʃən], *n.* sospecha; conjetura; pizca, dejo.
suspicious [səs'piʃəs], *a.* sospechoso; suspicaz.
sustain [səs'tein], *v.t.* sostener, sustentar, mantener; apoyar; confirmar; (*mus.*) prolongar; **to — a loss,** sufrir una pérdida.
sustenance ['sʌstinəns], *n.* mantenimiento; sustento, alimentos, *m.pl.*
swab [swɔb], *n.* fregajo; (*med.*) torunda; (*naut.*) lampazo.—*v.t.* fregar; (*naut.*) lampacear.
swagger ['swægə], *n.* fanfarria; pavoneo.—*v.i.* fanfarrear; pavonearse.
swaggering ['swægəriŋ], *a.* fanfarrón, majo.
swallow (1) ['swɔlou], *n.* trago.—*v.t.* tragar, engullir; retractar.
swallow (2) ['swɔlou], *n.* (*orn.*) golondrina.
swam [swæm] [SWIM].
swamp [swɔmp], *n.* pantano.—*v.t.* sumergir, echar a pique; mojar; (*fig.*) hundir.
swampy ['swɔmpi], *a.* pantanoso.
swan [swɔn], *n.* cisne, *m.*
swank [swæŋk], *n.* farolero; farolería.—*v.i.* fanfarrear; darse tono.
swap [swɔp], *n.* cambio, trueque, *m.*—*v.t.* cambiar, trocar.
swarm [swɔ:m], *n.* enjambre, *m.*; caterva, multitud, *f.*—*v.i.* enjambrar; pulular, hormiguear; abundar.
swarthy ['swɔ:ði], *a.* moreno.
swashbuckler ['swɔʃbʌklə], *n.* matasiete, *m.*
swat [swɔt], *v.t.* matar (*moscas*).
swathe [sweið], *v.t.* fajar, envolver; vendar.
sway [swei], *n.* ascendiente, *m.*, influencia; poder, *m.*, imperio; vaivén, *m.*, balanceo, oscilación, *f.*; bamboleo; **to hold —,** gobernar.—*v.t.* inclinar; influir; cimbrar; dominar, gobernar; mecer, oscilar.—*v.i.* inclinarse; oscilar; bambolearse, tambalearse.
swear [sweə], *v.t. irr.* jurar; declarar bajo juramento; **to — in,** hacer prestar juramento a.—*v.i. irr.* jurar; blasfemar; hacer votos; **to — by,** (*fam.*) poner confianza implícita en; **to — to,** atestiguar.
sweat [swet], *n.* sudor, *m.*; (*fig.*) trabajo duro.—*v.t.* hacer sudar.—*v.i.* sudar.
sweating ['swetiŋ], *n.* transpiración; explotación, *f.*
sweaty ['sweti], *a.* sudoroso.
Swede [swi:d], *n.* sueco.
swede [swi:d], *n.* (*bot.*) nabo sueco.
Sweden ['swi:dn], *n.* Suecia.
Swedish ['swi:diʃ], *a., n.* sueco.
sweep [swi:p], *n.* barredura; extensión, *f.*; alcance, *m.*; curva; envergadura (*de alas*); gesto.—*v.t. irr.* barrer; deshollinar; pasar por; arrebatar; examinar (*con la mirada*); **to — along,** arrastrar; **to — aside,** apartar con un gesto desdeñoso; **to — away,** barrer; llevar; **to — up,** barrer; **to be swept off one's feet,** ser arrebatado.—*v.i. irr.* barrer; pasar rápidamente por; marchar majestuosamente; extenderse; **to — along,** pasar majestuosamente; **to — on,** seguir su marcha.

sweeper ['swi:pə], *n.* barrendero.
sweeping ['swi:piŋ], *a.* comprehensivo; demasiado amplio *o* general; **— changes,** cambios radicales.
sweepstake ['swi:psteik], *n.* lotería.
sweet [swi:t], *a.* dulce; oloroso; melodioso; encantador; amable; bonito.—*n.* dulzura; dulce, bombón, *m.*; persona querida.
sweet-corn ['swi:tkɔ:n], *n.* mazorca.
sweeten ['swi:tn], *v.t.* endulzar, azucarar.
sweetheart ['swi:thɑ:t], *n.* enamorada, novia; enamorado, novio.
sweetness ['swi:tnis], *n.* dulzura; bondad, *f.*; fragancia.
sweet-pea ['swi:t'pi:], *n.* guisante (*m.*) de olor.
sweet-smelling ['swi:t'smeliŋ], *a.* fragante.
sweet-toothed ['swi:t'tu:θd], *a.* goloso.
sweet-william ['swi:t'wiljəm], *n.* clavel barbado.
swell [swel], *n.* oleada, oleaje, *m.*; hinchazón, *f.*; ondulación (*del terreno*), *f.*; (*mus.*) crescendo; aumento; (*fam.*) petimetre, *m.*—*v.t. irr.* hinchar; aumentar; envanecer.—*v.i. irr.* hincharse; entumecerse (*el mar*); crecer; envanecerse.
swelling ['sweliŋ], *n.* hinchazón, *f.*; (*med.*) tumefacción, *f.*
swelter ['sweltə], *v.i.* abrasarse; sudar la gota gorda.
swept [swept] [SWEEP].
swerve [swə:v], *n.* desviación, *f.*—*v.i.* torcerse; desviarse.
swift [swift], *a.* veloz, rápido; pronto; repentino.—*n.* (*orn.*) vencejo.
swiftness ['swiftnis], *n.* velocidad, rapidez; prontitud, *f.*
swim [swim], *n.* nadada, baño; **to be in the —,** estar al corriente.—*v.t. irr.* pasar a nado; hacer flotar; mojar.—*v.i. irr.* nadar; flotar; resbalar; inundarse; abundar; **my head swims,** se me va la cabeza.
swimmer ['swimə], *n.* nadador, *m.*
swimming ['swimiŋ], *n.* natación, *f.*; (*med.*) vértigo.
swimming-costume ['swimiŋ'kɔstju:m], *n.* traje (*m.*) de baño.
swimming-pool ['swimiŋpu:l], *n.* piscina.
swindle ['swindl], *n.* estafa, timo.—*v.t.* estafar, timar.
swindler ['swindlə], *n.* estafador, *m.*
swine [swain], *n.* (*inv.*) puerco, cerdo; (*fig.*) cochino.
swing [swiŋ], *n.* oscilación, *f.*, balanceo; vaivén, *m.*; ritmo; columpio; alcance, *m.*; **in full —,** en plena operación.—*v.t. irr.* columpiar; mecer; hacer oscilar; blandir.—*v.i. irr.* oscilar; columpiarse; balancearse; dar vueltas; (*naut.*) bornear; (*fam.*) ser ahorcado.
swinging ['swiŋiŋ], *a.* oscilante; rítmico.—*n.* oscilación, *f.*; balanceo; vaivén, *m.*
swish [swiʃ], *n.* silbo; crujido; susurro.—*v.t.* blandir; agitar, menear; azotar.—*v.i.* silbar; susurrar; crujir.
Swiss [swis], *a., n.* suizo.
switch [switʃ], *n.* varilla; látigo; cabellera postiza; (*rail.*) apartadero, aguja; (*elec.*) conmutador, interruptor, *m.*—*v.t.* azotar; (*elec.*) interrumpir; trasladar; **to — off,** (*elec.*) desconectar, cortar; **to — on,** (*elec.*) conectar, encender.

switchboard ['switʃbɔːd], *n.* cuadro de distribución.
Switzerland ['switsələnd], *n.* Suiza.
swivel [swivl], *n.* alacrán, torniquete, *m.—v.i.* girar sobre un eje.
swollen ['swoulən] [SWELL].
swoon [swuːn], *n.* desmayo.—*v.i.* desmayarse.
swoop [swuːp], *n.* calada.—*v.i.* abatirse, abalanzarse.
sword [sɔːd], *n.* espada; **to put to the —,** pasar a cuchillo.
sword-belt ['sɔːdbelt], *n.* talabarte, *m.*
sword-fish ['sɔːdfiʃ], *n.* pez espada, *m.*
sword-play ['sɔːdplei], *n.* esgrima.
swordsman ['sɔːdzmən], *n.* espadachín, *m.*
swore [swɔː], **[sworn]** [swɔːn] [SWEAR].
swum [swʌm] [SWIM].
swung [swʌŋ] [SWING].
sycamore ['sikəmɔː], *n.* sicómoro.
sycophant ['sikəfənt], *n.* adulador, *m.*
sycophantic [sikə'fæntik], *a.* adulatorio.
syllabic [si'læbik], *a.* silábico.
syllable ['siləbl], *n.* sílaba.
syllabus ['siləbəs], *n.* programa, *m.*
syllogism ['silədʒizm], *n.* silogismo.
symbol ['simbəl], *n.* símbolo.
symbolic [sim'bɔlik], *a.* simbólico.
symbolism ['simbəlizm], *n.* simbolismo.
symbolist ['simbəlist], *n.* simbolista, *m.f.*
symbolize ['simbəlaiz], *v.t.* simbolizar.
symmetrical [si'metrikəl], *a.* simétrico.
symmetry ['simitri], *n.* simetría.
sympathetic [simpə'θetik], *a.* compasivo; simpático.
sympathize ['simpəθaiz], *v.i.* simpatizar; compadecerse.
sympathizer ['simpəθaizə], *n.* partidario.
sympathy ['simpəθi], *n.* compasión, *f.*; simpatía.
symphonic [sim'fɔnik], *a.* sinfónico.
symphony ['simfəni], *n.* sinfonía.
symptom ['simptəm], *n.* síntoma, *m.*; indicio.
symptomatic [simptə'mætik], *a.* sintomático.
synagogue ['sinəgɔg], *n.* sinagoga.
synchronize ['siŋkrənaiz], *v.t.* sincronizar. —*v.i.* sincronizarse; coincidir.
syncopation [siŋkə'peiʃən], *n.* síncopa.
syndicate ['sindikit], *n.* sindicato.—['sindikeit], *v.t.* sindicar.
synonym ['sinənim], *n.* sinónimo.
synonymous [si'nɔniməs], *a.* sinónimo.
synopsis [si'nɔpsis], *n.* sinopsis, *f.*
syntactic [sin'tæktik], *a.* sintáctico.
syntax ['sintæks], *n.* sintaxis, *f.*
synthesis ['sinθisis], *n.* síntesis, *f.*
synthesize ['sinθisaiz], *v.t.* sintetizar.
synthetic [sin'θetik], *a.* sintético.
syphillis ['sifilis], *n.* sifilis, *f.*
syphon [SIPHON].
Syrian ['siriən], *a., n.* sirio.
syringe ['sirindʒ], *n.* jeringa.—*v.t.* jeringar.
syrup ['sirəp], *n.* jarabe; almíbar, *m.*
system ['sistim], *n.* sistema, *m.*; método.
systematic [sisti'mætik], *a.* sistemático, metódico.
systematize ['sistimətaiz], *v.t.* sistematizar; metodizar.

T

T, t [tiː], *n.* vigésima letra del alfabeto inglés; ***T-square,*** regla T.
tab [tæb], *n.* oreja; etiqueta; **to keep tabs on,** saber localizar.
tabernacle ['tæbənækl], *n.* tabernáculo.
table [teibl], *n.* mesa; tabla; lista; índice, *m.*; **to lay the —,** poner la mesa; **to turn the tables,** volverse la tortilla.—*v.t.* entablar *(una petición)*; enumerar; *(U.S.)* aplazar.
table-cloth ['teiblklɔθ], *n.* mantel, *m.*
tableau ['tæblou], *n. (pl.* **tableaux)** cuadro.
table-lamp ['teibllæmp], *n.* quinqué, *m.*
table-land ['teibllænd], *n.* meseta.
table-linen ['teibllinin], *n.* mantelería.
tablespoon ['teiblspuːn], *n.* cuchara grande.
tablet ['tæblit], *n.* placa; losa; *(med.)* pastilla.
table-talk ['teiblɔːk], *n.* conversación *(f.)* de sobremesa.
taboo [tə'buː], *n.* tabú, *m.*
tabulate ['tæbjuleit], *v.t.* tabular, catalogar.
tacit ['tæsit], *a.* tácito.
taciturn ['tæsitəːn], *a.* taciturno.
tack [tæk], *n.* tachuela, puntilla; hilván, *m. (costura)*; *(naut.)* bordada; *(fig.)* cambio de política.—*v.t.* clavar con tachuelas; hilvanar *(costura)*; *(fig.)* añadir.—*v.i. (naut.)* virar; *(fig.)* cambiar de política.
tackle [tækl], *n.* aparejo; avíos *m.pl.*; *(naut.)* poleame, *m.* —*v.t.* agarrar, asir; **atacar;** *(fig.)* abordar.
tact [tækt], *n.* discreción, *f.*
tactful ['tæktful], *a.* discreto.
tactical ['tæktikəl], *a.* táctico.
tactics ['tæktiks], *n.pl.* táctica.
tactile ['tæktail], *a.* tangible; táctil.
tactless ['tæktlis], *a.* indiscreto.
tadpole ['tædpoul], *n.* renacuajo.
taffeta ['tæfitə], *n.* tafetán, *m.*
tag (1) [tæg], *n.* herrete, *m.*; ctiqueta; refrán, *m.*
tag (2) [tæg], *n.* **to play —,** jugar al marro.
tail [teil], *n.* cola, rabo; fin, *m.—pl.* cruz *(de una moneda),* *f.*, frac *(vestido),* *m.*; **to turn —,** volver la espalda.—*v.t.* seguir, pisar los talones a.—*v.i.* **to — off,** disminuir.
tail-coat ['teilkout], *n.* frac, *m.*
tail-end ['teil'end], *n.* extremo.
tail-light ['teil'lait], *n.* farol trasero.
tailor ['teilə], *n.* sastre, *m.*; **tailor's shop,** sastrería.—*v.t.* adaptar; entallar.
tailoress ['teilərəs], *n.* sastra, modista.
tail-piece ['teil'piːs], *n.* apéndice, *m.*
taint [teint], *n.* mancha; corrupción, contaminación, *f.—v.t.* corromper; contaminar.
take [teik], *v.t. irr.* tomar; coger; traer; llevar; aceptar; quitar; conducir; suponer; *(math.)* restar; sacar *(una fotografía)*; dar *(un paseo)*; **to — aback,** desconcertar; **to — away,** quitar; *(math.)* restar; **to — back,** *(fig.)* retractar; **to — down,** bajar; escribir al dictado; humillar; **to — for granted,** dar por sentado; **to — in,** comprender; admitir; dar asilo; encoger; *(fig.)* engañar; **to — off,** quitar; cortar; *(fam.)* imitar; arrancar; **to — on,** encargarse de; **to — on trust,** tomar a crédito; **to — out,** sacar con; sacar; llevar afuera; extraer; **to — over,** encargarse de; **to — to pieces,** desarmar; **to — up,** subir;

empezar; ocupar (*un sitio*); adoptar; acortar (*un vestido*); **to be taken with** o **to take a fancy to,** aficionarse a; **to — care of,** cuidar; —*v.i.* lograr, tener éxito; prender; arraigarse. **to — after,** parecerse a; **to — off,** (*aer.*) despegar; **to — to,** empezar a; aplicarse a; aficionarse a; **to — up with,** trabar amistad con; **to — care,** tener cuidado; **to — the chair,** presidir; **to — fright,** cobrar miedo; **to — to one's heels,** huir; **to — leave of,** despedirse de; **to — no notice,** no hacer caso; **to — pains,** darse molestia; esmerarse; **to — pity on,** compadecerse de; **to — place,** verificarse, suceder; **to — shelter,** refugiarse.—*n.* toma; (*photo.*) tomada.

take-off ['teikɔf], *n.* caricatura; (*aer.*) despegue, *m.*

taken ['teikən] [TAKE].

taking ['teikiŋ], *a.* encantador, atractivo; contagioso.—*n.* toma; secuestro.—*pl.* ingresos, *m.pl.*

talcum powder ['tælkəm'paudə], *n.* polvo de talco.

tale [teil], *n.* cuento; **old wives' —,** patraña, cuento de viejas; **to tell tales,** contar historias; chismear.

tale-bearer ['teilbɛərə], *n.* chismoso.

talent ['tælənt], *n.* talento, ingenio.

talented ['tæləntid], *a.* talentoso.

talisman ['tælizmən], *n.* talismán, *m.*

talk [tɔːk], *n.* conversación, *f.*; charla; rumor, *m.*—*v.t., v.i.* hablar; **to — into,** persuadir; **to — out of,** disuadir; **to — over,** discutir; persuadir.

talkative ['tɔːkətiv], *a.* hablador, locuaz.

tall [tɔːl], *a.* alto; (*fig.*) exagerado.

tallow ['tælou], *n.* sebo.

tally ['tæli], *n.* tarja; cuenta; **to keep —,** llevar la cuenta.—*v.t.* llevar la cuenta.—*v.i.* concordar.

talon ['tælən], *n.* garra, uña.

tambourine [tæmbə'riːn], *n.* pandereta.

tame [teim], *a.* manso; sumiso; soso.—*v.t.* domar; reprimir.

tameness ['teimnis], *n.* mansedumbre; sumisión, *f.*

tamer ['teimə], *n.* domador, *m.*

tamper ['tæmpə], *v.i.* meterse (en); estropear; falsificar (*with*).

tan [tæn], *a.* de color de canela.—*n.* bronceado. —*v.t.* curtir; poner moreno; tostar; (*fam.*) zurrar.—*v.i.* ponerse moreno, broncearse.

tandem ['tændəm], *n.* tándem, *m.*

tang [tæŋ], *n.* sabor, *m.*; dejo picante; retintín, *m.*

tangent ['tændʒənt], *a.*, *n.* tangente, *f.*

tangerine [tændʒə'riːn], *n.* tangerina.

tangible ['tændʒibl], *a.* tangible.

tangle [tæŋgl], *n.* enredo, maraña.—*v.t.* enredar.—*v.i.* enredarse, enmarañarse.

tank [tæŋk], *n.* tanque, *m.*; cisterna; (*mil.*) tanque, *m.*, carro (de combate).

tankard ['tæŋkəd], *n.* pichel, *m.*

tanker ['tæŋkə], *n.* petrolero.

tanned [tænd], *a.* bronceado, moreno; curtido.

tanner ['tænə], *n.* curtidor, *m.*, noquero.

tantalize ['tæntəlaiz], *v.t.* atormentar, provocar.

tantamount ['tæntəmaunt], *a.* **to be — to,** equivaler a.

tantrum ['tæntrəm], *n.* perra, pataleta, berrinche, *m.*

tap (1) [tæp], *n.* palmadita.—*v.t.* dar una palmadita a.

tap (2) [tæp], *n.* grifo (*de agua*); **on —,** en tonel; (*fig.*) a la mano.—*v.t.* decentar; horadar; sangrar; (*elec.*) derivar; escuchar (*conversaciones telefónicas*).

tape [teip], *n.* cinta.

tape-measure ['teipmeʒə], *n.* cinta métrica.

taper ['teipə], *n.* bujía; (*eccl.*) cirio.—*v.t.* afilar.—*v.i.* rematar en punta.

tape-recorder ['teiprikɔːdə], *n.* magnetófono.

tape-recording ['teiprikɔːdiŋ], *n.* grabación (*f.*) en cinta.

tapestry ['tæpəstri], *n.* tapiz, *m.*

tapeworm ['teipwəːm], *n.* tenia, lombriz solitaria.

tapioca [tæpi'oukə], *n.* tapioca.

tar [taː], *n.* alquitrán, *m.*—*v.t.* alquitranar, embrear; **to — and feather,** embrear y emplumar.

tardiness ['taːdinis], *n.* lentitud, *f.*, tardanza.

tardy ['taːdi], *a.* tardío; lento.

tare (1) [tɛə], *n.* (*bot.*) yero; (*Bibl.*) cizaña.

tare (2) [tɛə], *n.* (*com.*) tara.

target ['taːgit], *n.* blanco; **— practice,** tiro al blanco.

tariff ['tærif], *n.* tarifa.

tarmac ['taːmæk], *n.* (*aer.*) pista.

tarnish ['taːniʃ], *n.* deslustre, *m.*—*v.t.* deslustrar.—*v.i.* deslustrarse.

tarpaulin [taːˈpɔːlin], *n.* alquitranado, encerado.

tarry ['tæri], *v.i.* tardar; detenerse.

tart (1) [taːt], *a.* ácido, agrio.

tart (2) [taːt], *n.* tarta, pastelillo; (*low*) mujerzuela.

tartan ['taːtən], *n.* tartán, *m.*

Tartar ['taːtə], *a.*, *n.* tártaro.

tartar ['taːtə], *n.* tártaro; **cream of —,** crémor tártaro, *m.*

task [taːsk], *n.* tarea; empresa; **to take to —,** reprender, llamar a capítulo.

tassel ['tæsəl], *n.* borla.

taste [teist], *n.* gusto; sabor, *m.*; un poco; muestra; prueba; buen gusto; afición, *f.*; **to have a — for,** tener afición a; **in bad (good) —,** de mal (buen) gusto.—*v.t.* gustar; probar.—*v.i.* saber (of, a).

tasteful ['teistful], *a.* de buen gusto.

tasteless ['teistlis], *a.* insípido; de mal gusto.

tasty ['teisti], *a.* sabroso, apetitoso.

tatter ['tætə], *n.* andrajo.

tattered ['tætəd], *a.* andrajoso.

tatting ['tætiŋ], *n.* frivolité, *f.*

tattoo (1) [tæ'tuː], *n.* tatuaje, *m.*—*v.t.* tatuar.

tattoo (2) [tæ'tuː], *n.* (*mil.*) retreta.

tattooing (1) [tæ'tuːiŋ], *n.* tatuaje, *m.*

tattooing (2) [tæ'tuːiŋ], *n.* tamboreo.

taught [tɔːt], [TEACH].

taunt [tɔːnt], *n.* escarnio, mofa.—*v.t.* provocar; **to — with,** echar en cara.

taut [tɔːt], *a.* tieso.

tautness ['tɔːtnis], *n.* tensión, *f.*

tautology [tɔːˈtɔlədʒi], *n.* tautología.

tavern ['tævən], *n.* taberna, mesón, *m.*

tawdry ['tɔːdri], *a.* charro, chillón, cursi.

tawny ['tɔːni], *a.* leonado.

tax

tax [tæks], *n.* impuesto; — *collector*, recaudador (*m.*) de contribuciones.—*v.t.* imponer contribuciones; (*jur.*) tasar; cargar; *to — with*, acusar de.

taxable ['tæksəbl], *a.* sujeto a impuestos.

taxation [tæk'seiʃən], *n.* imposición (*f.*) de contribuciones *o* impuestos.

tax-free ['tæks'fri:], *a.* libre de impuestos.

taxi ['tæksi], *n.* taxi, *m.*—*v.i.* ir en taxi; (*aer.*) correr por tierra.

taxidermist ['tæksidə:mist], *n.* taxidermista, *m.f.*

taxidermy ['tæksidə:mi], *n.* taxidermia.

taxi-driver ['tæksidraivə], *n.* taxista, *m.*

taximeter ['tæksimi:tə], *n.* taxímetro.

taxi-stand ['tæksi'stænd], *n.* parada de taxis.

tax-payer ['tækspeiə], *n.* contribuyente, *m.f.*

tea [ti:], *n.* té, *m.*; merienda; — *-caddy*, bote (*m.*) para té; — *rose*, rosa de té.

teach [ti:tʃ], *v.t. irr.* enseñar.—*v.i.* ser profesor.

teacher ['ti:tʃə], *n.* maestro, profesor, *m.*; maestra, profesora.

tea-chest ['ti:tʃest], *n.* caja para té.

teaching ['ti:tʃiŋ], *a.* docente.—*n.* enseñanza; doctrina.

tea-cosy ['ti:kouzi], *n.* cubretetera, *m.*

teacup ['ti:kʌp], *n.* taza para té.

teak [ti:k], *n.* teca.

team [ti:m], *n.* yunta, pareja (*bueyes*); equipo.—*v.t.* enganchar.—*v.i. to — up* (*with*), asociarse (con).

teamwork ['ti:mwə:k], *n.* cooperación, *f.*

teapot ['ti:pɔt], *n.* tetera.

tear (1) [teə], *n.* rasgón, *m.*—*v.t. irr.* romper; rasgar; despedazar; arañar; *to — away*, arrancar; *to — down*, derribar; *to — up*, desarraigar; hacer pedazos.—*v.i.* rasgarse; romper; correr precipitadamente; *to — away*, irse corriendo; *to — down*, bajar corriendo; *to — oneself away*, arrancarse; *to — up*, subir corriendo.

tear (2) [tiə], *n.* lágrima; gota; *to shed tears*, llorar.

tearful ['tiəful], *a.* lloroso.

tearfully ['tiəfuli], *adv.* entre lágrimas.

tear-gas ['tiəgæs], *n.* gas lacrimógeno.

tease [ti:z], *n.* fastidio; (*fam.*) guasa; (*fam.*) guasón, *m.*—*v.t.* fastidiar; embromar; tomar el pelo (a); cardar (*lana*).

tea-set ['ti:set], *n.* juego de té.

teaspoon ['ti:spu:n], *n.* cucharita.

teat [ti:t], *n.* pezón, *m.*; teta.

tea-time ['ti:taim], *n.* hora del té.

technical ['teknikəl], *a.* técnico.

technicality [tekni'kæliti], *n.* cosa técnica; tecnicismo; detalle técnico.

technician [tek'niʃən], *n.* técnico.

technique [tek'ni:k], *n.* técnica.

technological [teknə'lɔdʒikəl], *a.* tecnológico.

technologist [tek'nɔlədʒist], *n.* tecnólogo.

technology [tek'nɔlədʒi], *n.* tecnología.

tedious ['ti:djəs], *a.* tedioso, aburrido.

tedium ['ti:djəm], *n.* tedio.

teem [ti:m], *v.i.* rebosar; pulular; diluviar.

teeming ['ti:miŋ], *a.* prolífico, fecundo; torrencial.

teenager ['ti:neidʒə], *n.* adolescente, *m.f.*

teeter ['ti:tə], *v.i.* balancearse.

teeth [ti:θ] [TOOTH].

teethe [ti:ð], *v.i.* echar los dientes.

teething ['ti:ðiŋ], *n.* dentición, *f.*

teething-ring ['ti:ðiŋriŋ], *n.* chupador, *m.*

teetotal [ti:'toutl], *a.* abstemio.

teetotaller [ti:'toutlə], *n.* abstemio.

telegram ['teligræm], *n.* telegrama, *m.*

telegraph ['teligrɑ:f, -græf], *n.* telégrafo; — *pole*, poste telegráfico.—*v.t.*, *v.i.* telegrafiar.

telegraphy [ti'legrəfi], *n.* telegrafía.

telepathy [ti'lepəθi], *n.* telepatía.

telephone ['telifoun], *n.* teléfono; — *directory*, guía telefónica; — *exchange*, central telefónica, *f.*; — *number*, número de teléfono; — *operator*, telefonista, *m.f.*; *to be on the —*, estar comunicando; tener teléfono.—*v.t.*, *v.i.* telefonear, llamar por teléfono.

telephone-booth ['telifounbu:θ], *n.* cabina telefónica.

telephonic [teli'fɔnik], *a.* telefónico.

telephonist [ti'lefənist], *n.* telefonista, *m.f.*

telescope ['teliscoup], *n.* telescopio.—*v.t.* enchufar.—*v.i.* enchufarse.

telescopic [telis'kɔpik], *a.* telescópico.

televise ['telivaiz], *v.t.* transmitir por televisión.

television ['teliviʒən], *n.* televisión, *f.*

tell [tel], *v.t. irr.* contar; decir; expresar; manifestar; comunicar; revelar; marcar (*la hora*); *to — off*, regañar.—*v.i. irr.* decir; producir efecto.

teller ['telə], *n.* narrador; escrutador; pagador, *m.*

telling ['teliŋ], *a.* eficaz, notable.

tell-tale ['telteil], *a.* revelador.—*n.* soplón, *m.*

temerity [ti'meriti], *n.* temeridad, *f.*

temper ['tempə], *n.* temple; carácter, *m.*; mal genio; *bad —*, mal humor, *m.*; *good —*, buen humor; *to lose one's —*, enojarse.—*v.t.* templar; moderar.

temperament ['tempərəmənt], *n.* temperamento.

temperamental [tempərə'mentl], *a.* caprichoso; natural.

temperance ['tempərəns], *n.* templanza, moderación, *f.*; abstinencia.

temperate ['tempərit], *a.* moderado; templado.

temperature ['tempritʃə], *n.* temperatura; (*med.*) fiebre, *f.*

tempered ['tempəd], *a.* templado; *hot —*, irascible.

tempest ['tempist], *n.* tempestad, *f.*

tempestuous [tem'pestjuəs], *a.* tempestuoso.

temple (1) [templ], *n.* templo.

temple (2) [templ], *n.* (*anat.*) sien, *f.*

temporal ['tempərəl], *a.* temporal.

temporary ['tempərəri], *a.* provisional, interino.

temporize ['tempəraiz], *v.i.* contemporizar.

tempt [tempt], *v.t.* tentar; atraer.

temptation [temp'teiʃən], *n.* tentación, *f.*

tempter ['temptə], *n.* tentador, *m.*

tempting ['temptiŋ], *a.* tentador, atrayente.

temptress ['temptris], *n.* tentadora.

ten [ten], *a.*, *n.* diez, *m.*

tenable ['tenəbl], *a.* defendible, sostenible.

tenacious [ti'neiʃəs], *a.* tenaz; adhesivo; porfiado.

tenacity [ti'næsiti], *n.* tenacidad, *f.*; porfía.

tenancy ['tenənsi], *n.* tenencia; inquilinato.

tenant ['tenənt], *n.* arrendatario, inquilino; morador, *m.*

tench [tentʃ], *n.* (*ichth.*) tenca.
tend [tend], *v.t.* guardar; cuidar; vigilar.—*v.i.* tender, propender.
tendency ['tendənsi], *n.* tendencia, propensión, *f.*
tendentious [ten'denʃəs], *a.* tendencioso.
tender (1) ['tendə], *a.* tierno; compasivo; blando; escrupuloso.
tender (2) ['tendə], *n.* (*com.*) oferta, propuesta; *legal* —, curso legal.—*v.t.* ofrecer; presentar.
tender (3) ['tendə], *n.* (*naut.*) falúa; (*rail.*) ténder, *m.*
tenderness ['tendənis], *n.* ternura; escrupulosidad, *f.*
tendon ['tendən], *n.* (*anat.*) tendón, *m.*
tendril ['tendril], *n.* zarcillo.
tenement ['tenimənt], *n.* vivienda; casa de vecindad.
tenet ['tenit], *n.* dogma, *m.*, principio.
tenfold ['tenfould], *a.* décuplo.—*adv.* diez veces.
tennis ['tenis], *n.* tenis, *m.*; — *ball*, pelota de tenis; — *court*, pista de tenis.
tenor ['tenə], *n.* curso; tenor, *m.*, contenido; (*mus.*) tenor, *m.*
tense (1) [tens], *a.* tieso; tirante; tenso.
tense (2) [tens], *n.* (*gram.*) tiempo.
tension ['tenʃən], *n.* tensión, (*pol.*) tirantez, *f.*
tent [tent], *n.* tienda; — *pole*, mástil (*m.*) de tienda.
tentacle ['tentəkl], *n.* tentáculo.
tentative ['tentətiv], *a.* tentativo.
tenterhooks ['tentəhuks], *n.pl.* on —, en ascuas.
tenth [tenθ], *a.* décimo.—*n.* décimo, décima parte; diez (*en las fechas*), *m.*
tenuous ['tenjuəs], *a.* tenue; delgado; sutil.
tenure ['tenjuə], *n.* tenencia; duración, *f.*
tepid ['tepid], *a.* tibio.
tercentenary [tə:sen'ti:nəri], *n.* tercer centenario.
term [tə:m], *n.* plazo, período; trimestre (*de escuela*); límite, *m.*; término.—*pl.* condiciones, *f.pl.*; tarifa; *to be on good terms with*, estar en buenas relaciones con; *to come to terms*, llegar a un arreglo.—*v.t.* llamar.
terminal ['tə:minl], *a.* terminal.—*n.* término; (*elec.*) borne, *m.*
terminate ['tə:mineit], *v.t.*, *v.i.* terminar.
termination [tə:mi'neiʃən], *n.* terminación, *f.*
terminology [tə:mi'nɔlədʒi], *n.* terminología.
terminus ['tə:minəs], *n.* estación terminal, *f.*
termite ['tə:mait], *n.* termita, *m.*
terrace ['teris], *n.* terraza.—*v.t.* terraplenar.
terra-cotta ['terə'kɔtə], *n.* terracota.
terrain [te'rein], *n.* terreno.
terrestrial [ti'restriəl], *a.* terrestre.
terrible ['teribl], *a.* terrible.
terrific [tə'rifik], *a.* espantoso; (*fam.*) estupendo.
terrify ['terifai], *v.t.* espantar, aterrar.
territorial [teri'tɔ:riəl], *a.* territorial.
territory ['teritəri], *n.* territorio; región, *f.*
terror ['terə], *n.* terror, *m.*, espanto; (*fam.*) fiera.
terrorism ['terərizm], *n.* terrorismo.
terrorist ['terərist], *n.* terrorista, *m.*
terrorize ['terəraiz], *v.t.* aterrorizar.
terse [tə:s], *a.* conciso, sucinto; brusco.
terseness['tə:snis],*n.*concisión;brusquedad,*f.*

test [test], *n.* prueba; examen, *m.*; criterio; análisis, *m.*; ensayo; *to put to the* —, poner a prueba; *to stand the* —, soportar la prueba; — *match*, partido internacional de cricket *o* rugby; — *pilot*, piloto de pruebas; — *tube*, tubo de ensayo.—*v.t.* probar, poner a prueba; ensayar.
testament ['testəmənt], *n.* testamento; *New Testament*, Nuevo Testamento; *Old Testament*, Antiguo Testamento.
testicle ['testikl], *n.* testículo.
testify ['testifai], *v.t.*, *v.i.* declarar; (*jur.*) testificar.
testimonial [testi'mounjəl], *n.* recomendación, *f.*; certificado.
testimony ['testiməni], *n.* testimonio.
testiness ['testinis], *n.* mal humor, *m.*
testy ['testi], *a.* enojadizo, irascible.
tetanus ['tetənəs], *n.* tétano.
tether ['teðə], *n.* traba, maniota; *to be at the end of one's* —, quedar sin recursos; acabarse la paciencia.—*v.t.* trabar, atar.
Teuton ['tju:tən], *n.* teutón, *m.*
Teutonic [tju:'tɔnik], *a.* teutónico.
text [tekst], *n.* texto; tema, *m.*
text-book ['tekstbuk], *n.* libro de texto, manual, *m.*
textile ['tekstail], *a.* textil.—*n.* textil, *m.*; tejido.
textual ['tekstjuəl], *a.* textual.
texture ['tekstʃə], *n.* textura.
Thai [tai], *a.*, *n.* tailandés, *m.*
Thailand ['tailænd], *n.* Tailandia.
Thames [temz], *n.* Támesis, *m.*; *to set the — on fire*, inventar la pólvora.
than [ðæn], *conj.* que; de; del (de la, de los, de las) que; de lo que.
thank [θæŋk], *v.t.* dar las gracias a; — *God*, gracias a Dios; — *you*, gracias; *to* — *for*, agradecer.
thankful ['θæŋkful], *a.* agradecido.
thankless ['θæŋklis], *a.* ingrato.
thanks [θæŋks], *n.pl.* gracias; — *to*, gracias a.
thanksgiving ['θæŋksgiviŋ], *n.* acción (*f.*) de gracias.
that [ðæt], *a.* (*pl.* those) ese, *m.*; esa; aquel, *m.*; aquella.—*pron.* ése, *m.*; ésa; eso; aquél, *m.*; aquélla; aquello; (*replacing noun*) el; la; lo.—*rel. pron.* que; quien; el cual; la cual; lo cual; el que; la que; lo que.—*conj.* que; para que; para.
thatch [θætʃ], *n.* barda.—*v.t.* bardar.
thaw [θɔ:], *n.* deshielo.—*v.t.* deshelar; derretir; (*fig.*) ablandar.—*v.i.* deshelarse; derretirse; (*fig.*) ablandarse.
the [ðə *before vowel* ði:], *art.* el; la; lo; los; las.—*adv.* (*before a comparative*) cuanto ... tanto (más).
theatre ['θiətə], *n.* teatro; quirófano (*hospital*); — *attendant*, acomodador, *m.*
theatrical [θi'ætrikəl], *a.* teatral.—*n.pl.* funciones teatrales, *f.pl.*; *amateur theatrical*, función (*f.*) de aficionados.
thee [ði:], *pron.* (*obs.*, *eccl.*) te; ti.
theft [θeft], *n.* robo, hurto.
their [ðɛə], *a.* su; sus; suyo; suya; suyos; suyas; de ellos, de ellas.
theirs [ðɛəz], *pron.* el suyo; la suya; los suyos; las suyas; de ellos, de ellas.
theism ['θiːizm], *n.* teísmo.
theist ['θiːist], *n.* teísta, *m.f.*
them [ðem], *pron.* ellos; ellas; los; las; les.

theme [θi:m], *n.* tema, *m.*; tesis, *f.*
themselves [ðəm'selvz], *pron. pl.* ellos mismos; ellas mismas; sí mismos; se.
then [ðen], *adv.* entonces; luego, después; *now and* —, de vez en cuando; *now* —, ahora bien; *and what* — *?* ¿y qué más? *there and* —, en el acto.—*conj.* pues; por consiguiente.
thence [ðens], *adv.* desde allí; por eso; por consiguiente.
thenceforth ['ðens'fɔ:θ], *adv.* de allí en adelante.
theocracy [θi'ɔkrəsi], *n.* teocracia.
theodolite [θi'ɔdəlait], *n.* teodolito.
theologian [θiə'loudʒən], *n.* teólogo.
theological [θiə'lɔdʒikəl], *a.* teológico.
theology [θi'ɔlədʒi], *n.* teología.
theorem ['θiərəm], *n.* teorema, *m.*
theoretical [θiə'retikəl], *a.* teórico.
theorist ['θiərist], *n.* teórico.
theorize ['θiəraiz], *v.i.* teorizar.
theory ['θiəri], *n.* teoría.
theosophy [θi'ɔsəfi], *n.* teosofía.
therapeutic [θerə'pju:tik], *a.* terapéutico.
therapy ['θerəpi], *n.* terapia.
there [ðeə], *adv.* ahí, allí, allá; *all* —, (*fam.*) en sus cabales; *down* —, allí abajo; *up* —, allí arriba; *who's* — *?* ¿quién llama? — *is* o *are,* hay; — *they are,* helos ahí.—*interj.* ¡vaya! ¡toma! ¡ya ves! —, — *!* ¡vamos!
thereabouts [ðeərə'bauts], *adv.* por ahí; cerca de; aproximadamente.
thereafter [ðeər'ɑ:ftə], *adv.* después de eso.
thereby [ðeə'bai], *adv.* de ese modo; por allí cerca.
therefore ['ðeəfɔ:], *adv.* por eso, por lo tanto.
therein [ðeər'in], *adv.* allí dentro; en esto, en eso.
thereof [ðeər'ɔv], *adv.* de esto, de eso.
thereupon [ðeərə'pɔn], *adv.* encima; por consiguiente; luego, en eso.
therm [θə:m], *n.* unidad térmica.
thermal ['θə:məl], *a.* termal.
thermodynamics [θe:moudai'næmiks], *n.pl.* termodinámica.
thermometer [θə'mɔmitə], *n.* termómetro.
thermonuclear [θə:mou'nju:kljə], *a.* termonuclear.
thermos flask ['θə:məs'flɑ:sk], *n.* termos, *m. inv.*
thermostat ['θə:məstæt], *n.* termostato.
these [ði:z], *a.pl.* [THIS] estos, estas.—*pron. pl.* éstos; éstas.
thesis ['θi:sis], *n.* tesis, *f.*
Thespian ['θespjən], *a.* dramático.
they [ðei], *pron. pl.* ellos; ellas.
thick [θik], *a.* espeso; grueso; denso; turbio; apretado; numeroso; lleno; indistinto; estúpido; (*fam.*) íntimo; *that's a bit* — *!* ¡eso es un poco demasiado! —*n.* espesor, *m.*; lo más denso; *the* — *of the fight,* lo más reñido del combate; *to go through* — *and thin,* atropellar por todo; *in the* — *of,* en el centro de, en medio de.—*adv.* densamente; continuamente.
thicken ['θikən], *v.t.* espesar; aumentar.—*v.i.* espesarse; aumentar; complicarse.
thickening ['θikəniŋ], *n.* hinchamiento; (*cul.*) espesante, *m.*
thicket ['θikit], *n.* maleza, matorral, *m.*
thick-headed ['θik'hedid], *a.* torpe, estúpido.
thick-lipped ['θik'lipt], *a.* bezudo.

thickness ['θiknis], *n.* espesor, *m.*; densidad, *f.*; consistencia; pronunciación indistinta.
thickset ['θik'set], *a.* doblado; rechoncho.
thick-skinned ['θik'skind], *a.* paquidermo; (*fig.*) insensible.
thief [θi:f], *n.* ladrón, *m.*
thigh [θai], *n.* muslo.
thigh-bone ['θaiboun], *n.* fémur, *m.*
thimble [θimbl], *n.* dedal, *m.*
thin [θin], *a.* delgado; flaco; tenue; ligero; escaso; aguado; insubstancial; *to grow* —, enflaquecer.
thine [ðain], *pron.* (*obs., eccl.*) el tuyo; la tuya; los tuyos; las tuyas.—*a.* tu; tus; tuyo; tuya; tuyos; tuyas.
thin-faced ['θin'feist], *a.* de cara delgada.
thing [θiŋ], *n.* cosa; *poor* — *!* ¡pobre! *no such* —, nada de eso; *the* —, lo que está de moda; *to be just the* —, venir al pelo.
think [θiŋk], *v.t., v.i. irr.* pensar; creer; imaginar; considerar; *to* — *of,* pensar en; acordarse de; pensar de; *as you* — *fit,* como Vd. quiera; *to* — *highly of,* tener buen concepto de; *to* — *proper,* creer conveniente; *what do you* — *of this?* ¿qué le parece? *to* — *out,* resolver; proyectar; *to* — *over,* pensar.
thinker ['θiŋkə], *n.* pensador, *m.*
thinking ['θiŋkiŋ], *a.* pensador; inteligente.— *n.* pensamiento, reflexión, *f.*; juicio; *to my way of* —, a mi parecer.
thin-lipped ['θin'lipt], *a.* de labios apretados.
thinness ['θinnis], *n.* delgadez; flaqueza; tenuidad; escasez, *f.*; pequeño número; poca consistencia.
thin-skinned ['θin'skind], *a.* sensible.
third [θə:d], *a.* tercero; — *party,* tercera persona.—*n.* tercio, tercera parte; tres (*en las fechas*), *m.*; (*mus.*) tercera.
thirst [θə:st], *n.* sed, *f.*; (*fig.*) ansia.—*v.i.* tener sed (*for,* de).
thirsty ['θə:sti], *a.* sediento; *to be* —, tener sed.
thirteen ['θə:'ti:n], *a., n.* trece, *m.*
thirteenth ['θə:'ti:nθ], *a.* decimotercio.—*n.* décimotercio; trece (*en las fechas*), *m.*
thirtieth ['θə:tiiθ], *a.* trigésimo.—*n.* trigésimo; treinta (*en las fechas*).
thirty ['θə:ti], *a., n.* treinta, *m.*
this [ðis], *a.* (*pl.* **these**) este; esta.—*pron.* éste; ésta; esto.
thistle [θisl], *n.* cardo.
thistle-down ['θisldaun], *n.* papo de cardo.
thither ['ðiðə], *adv.* allá, hacia allá; a ese fin.
Thomas ['tɔməs], *n.* Tomás, *m.*
thong [θɔŋ], *n.* correa.
thorax ['θɔ:ræks], *n.* (*pl.* **thoraces** [-æsi:z]) (*anat.*) tórax, *m. inv.*
thorn [θɔ:n], *n.* espina; espino.
thorny ['θɔ:ni], *a.* espinoso.
thorough ['θʌrə], *a.* completo; perfecto; concienzudo.
thoroughbred ['θʌrəbred], *a.* de casta.
thoroughfare ['θʌrəfeə], *n.* vía pública.
thoroughgoing ['θʌrəgouiŋ], *a.* completo; concienzudo.
thoroughness ['θʌrənis], *n.* esmero, minuciosidad, *f.*
those [ðouz], *a.pl.* [THAT] esos; esas; aquellos; aquellas.—*pron. pl.* ésos; esas; aquéllos; aquéllas; los; — *who,* los que; las que; quienes; — *which* o — *that,* los que; las que.

tick

thou [ðau], *pron.* (*obs., eccl.*) tú.
though [ðou], *conj.* aunque; sin embargo; a pesar de que; *as* —, como si.
thought [θɔːt], *n.* pensamiento; reflexión, *f.*; concepto; propósito; cuidado; (*fam.*) migaja; *on second thoughts*, después de pensarlo bien.
thoughtful ['θɔːtful], *a.* pensativo; previsor; atento.
thoughtfulness ['θɔːtfulnis], *n.* reflexión; previsión; atención, *f.*
thoughtless ['θɔːtlis], *a.* descuidado; irreflexivo; inconsiderado; necio.
thoughtlessness ['θɔːtlisnis], *n.* descuido; irreflexión; inconsideración; necedad, *f.*
thousand ['θauzənd], *a.* mil.—*n.* mil; millar, *m.*
thousandth ['θauzəndθ], *a., n.* milésimo.
thrash [θræʃ], *v.t.* azotar; trillar; (*fam.*) derrotar; *to* — *out*, ventilar.
thrashing ['θræʃiŋ], *n.* paliza; trilla; — *floor*, era.
thrashing-machine ['θræʃiŋməʃiːn], *n.* trilladora.
thread [θred], *n.* hilo; hebra; filete, *m.*; (*fig.*) hilo.—*v.t.* enhebrar; ensartar; colarse a través de.
threadbare ['θredbɛə], *a.* raído; muy usado; (*fig.*) usado.
threat [θret], *n.* amenaza.
threaten [θretn], *v.t., v.i.* amenazar (*to*, con).
threatening ['θretniŋ], *a.* amenazador.
three [θriː], *a., n.* tres, *m.*
three-cornered ['θriː'kɔːnəd], *a.* triangular; — *hat*, sombrero de tres picos; tricornio.
threefold ['θriːfould], *a.* triple.
threepence ['θrepəns], *n.* tres peniques, *m.pl.*
three-ply ['θriː'plai], *a.* triple; de tres hilos *o* capas (*lana*).
threescore ['θriː'skɔː], *a., n.* sesenta, *m.*
thresh [θreʃ] [THRASH].
threshold ['θreʃould], *n.* umbral, *m.*; (*fig.*) principio.
threw [θruː] [THROW].
thrice [θrais], *adv.* tres veces.
thrift [θrift], *n.* ahorro; frugalidad, *f.*
thriftless ['θriftlis], *a.* manirroto.
thrifty ['θrifti], *a.* económico, frugal.
thrill [θril], *n.* estremecimiento; emoción, *f.*—*v.t.* emocionar.—*v.i.* estremecerse, emocionarse.
thriller ['θrilə], *n.* novela policíaca.
thrilling ['θriliŋ], *a.* emocionante; penetrante.
thrive [θraiv], *v.i. irr.* prosperar; crecer; desarrollarse con ímpetu.
thriving ['θraiviŋ], *a.* próspero; floreciente; vigoroso.
throat [θrout], *n.* garganta; *to clear the* —, aclarar la voz.
throaty ['θrouti], *a.* ronco.
throb [θrɔb], *n.* latido, pulsación, *f.*—*v.i.* latir, palpitar.
throbbing ['θrɔbiŋ], *a.* palpitante.—*n.* latido, pulsación, *f.*
throe [θrou], *n.* dolor, *m.*, agonía; *throes of childbirth*, dolores (*m.pl.*) de parto.
thrombosis [θrɔm'bousis], *n.* trombosis, *f.*
throne [θroun], *n.* trono; (*fig.*) corona.
throng [θrɔŋ], *n.* muchedumbre, multitud, *f.*

—*v.t.* apretar; llenar de bote en bote.—*v.i.* apinarse.
throttle [θrɔtl], *n.* regulador, *m.*; estrangulador, *m.*—*v.t.* estrangular; (*fig.*) ahogar.
through [θruː], *prep.* por; a través de; por medio de; entre; por causa de; gracias a.—*adv.* a través; enteramente, completamente; desde el principio hasta el fin; de un lado a otro; *to carry* —, llevar a cabo; *to fall* —, (*fig.*) fracasar; *to be wet* —, mojarse hasta los huesos.—*a.* — *train*, tren directo.
throughout [θruː'aut], *adv.* en todas partes; de un extremo a otro.—*prep.* por todo.
throw [θrou], *n.* tiro; echada; lance, *m.*—*v.t. irr.* echar, lanzar, arrojar; derribar; desmontar; *to* — *aside*, desechar; *to* — *away*, tirar; desechar; *to* — *back*, devolver; *to* — *down*, echar al suelo; derribar; *to* — *in*, echar dentro; insertar; *to* — *off*, quitarse; despojarse de; *to* — *open*, abrir de par en par; *to* — *out*, echar fuera; emitir; rechazar; expeler; *to* — *up*, echar al aire; levantar; renunciar a; (*fam.*) vomitar, arrojar.
throw-back ['θroubæk], *n.* atavismo.
thrown [θroun] [THROW].
thrush [θrʌʃ], *n.* (*orn.*) tordo.
thrust [θrʌst], *n.* golpe; ataque; empujón, *m.*; estocada; (*mech.*) empuje, *m.*, presión, *f.*—*v.t. irr.* introducir; meter; empujar; tirar; *to* — *upon*, imponer.—*v.i. irr.* acometer; meterse, introducirse; tirar una estocada; empujar.
thud [θʌd], *n.* ruido sordo.
thug [θʌg], *n.* rufián, criminal, *m.*
thumb [θʌm], *n.* pulgar, *m.*; *under the* — *of*, (*fig.*) en el poder de.—*v.t.* hojear (*through*); emporcar con los dedos.
thumb-stall ['θʌmstɔːl], *n.* dedil, *m.*
thumb-tack ['θʌmtæk], *n.* (*U.S.*) [DRAWING PIN].
thump [θʌmp], *n.* golpe, *m.*, puñetazo.—*v.t., v.i.* golpear; aporrear.
thunder ['θʌndə], *n.* trueno; estruendo.—*v.t., v.i.* tronar; retumbar; (*fig.*) fulminar.
thunderbolt ['θʌndəboult], *n.* rayo.
thunderclap ['θʌndəklæp], *n.* trueno.
thundering ['θʌndəriŋ], *a.* de trueno; (*fam.*) terrible; muy grande.—*n.* trueno.
thunderstorm ['θʌndəstɔːm], *n.* tormenta, tronada.
thunderstruck ['θʌndəstrʌk], *a.* estupefacto.
Thursday ['θɔːzd(e)i], *n.* jueves, *m.*
thus [ðʌs], *adv.* así; de este modo; — *far*, hasta aquí; hasta ahora.
thwart [θwɔːt], *v.t.* frustrar.
thy [ðai], *a.* (*obs., eccl.*) tu; tus; tuyo; tuya; tuyos; tuyas.
thyme [taim], *n.* tomillo.
thyroid ['θairɔid], *a.* tiroideo; — *gland*, tiroides, *m.sg.*
thyself [ðai'self], *pron.* (*obs., eccl.*) tú mismo; ti mismo.
tiara [ti'ɑːrə], *n.* tiara.
tic [tik], *n.* tic nervioso.
tick (1) [tik], *n.* (*zool.*) ácaro.
tick (2) [tik], *n.* tictac, *m.*; contramarca.—*v.t.* marcar contra.—*v.i.* hacer tictac.
tick (3) [tik], *n.* funda de colchón.
tick (4) [tik], *n.* (*fam.*) crédito.

395

ticket ['tikit], *n.* billete, *m.*; entrada; papeleta; etiqueta; (*U.S. pol.*) candidatura; *to buy a* —, sacar un billete; — *collector,* revisor, *m.*; — *office,* taquilla.—*v.t.* marcar.
ticket-window ['tikit'windou], *n.* taquilla.
tickle [tikl], *n.* cosquillas, *f.pl.*—*v.t.* hacer cosquillas a; divertir; halagar.—*v.i.* hacer cosquillas.
tickling ['tiklin], *n.* cosquillas, *f.pl.*
ticklish ['tikliʃ], *a.* cosquilloso; espinoso; *to be* —, tener cosquillas.
tidal [taidl], *a.* de marea; — *wave,* mareajada.
tide [taid], *n.* marea; estación, *f.*, tiempo; corriente, *f.*; *high* —, marea alta, pleamar, *f.*; *low* —, marea baja, bajamar, *f.*; *to go with the* —, seguir la corriente.—*v.t. to* — *over,* ayudar; superar.
tidiness ['taidinis], *n.* aseo; buen orden, *m.*
tidy ['taidi], *a.* aseado; ordenado; (*fam.*) considerable.—*v.t.* asear, poner en orden; limpiar.
tie [tai], *n.* lazo, atadura; nudo; corbata; (*sport*) empate, *m.*; partido; (*fig.*) obligación, *f.*; — *pin,* alfiler (*m.*) de corbata.—*v.t.* atar; ligar; sujetar; limitar; anudar; *to* — *up,* atar; envolver; (*naut.*) amarrar.—*v.i.* atarse; (*sport*) empatar.
tier [tiə], *n.* fila.
tiger ['taigə], *n.* tigre, *m.*
tight [tait], *a.* apretado; tieso; estrecho; ajustado; bien cerrado; hermético; escaso; (*fam.*) borracho; (*fam.*) tacaño; — *corner,* (*fig.*) aprieto; *to be tight-fisted,* ser como un puño.—*adv.* fuertemente, estrechamente, bien; *to hold* —, tener bien.
tighten [taitn], *v.t.* apretar, estrechar.
tight-rope ['taitroup], *n.* cuerda de volatinero; — *walker,* volatinero, equilibrista, *m.f.*
tights [taits], *n.pl.* mallas, *f.pl.*, leotardos, *m.pl.*
tigress ['taigris], *n.* tigresa.
tile [tail], *n.* teja; baldosa; azulejo.—*v.t.* tejar, embaldosar.
till (1) [til], *n.* cajón (*m.*) de mostrador.
till (2) [til], *v.t.* cultivar.
till (3) [til], *prep.* hasta.—*conj.* hasta que.
tiller (1) ['tilə], *n.* labrador, *m.*
tiller (2) ['tilə], *n.* (*naut.*) caña del timón.
tilt [tilt], *n.* inclinación, *f.*; ladeo; justa.—*v.t.* inclinar; ladear.—*v.i.* inclinarse; ladearse; justar.
timber ['timbə], *n.* madera de construcción; viga; árboles, *m.pl.*
timbered ['timbəd], *a.* enmaderado; arbolado.
timbre [tɛ̃:mbr], *n.* timbre, *m.*
time [taim], *n.* tiempo; época, edad; estación, *f.*; hora; vez, *f.*; plazo; ocasión, *f.*; (*mus.*) compás, *m.*; (*mil.*) paso; *at a* — o *at the same* —, a la vez, al mismo tiempo; no obstante; *at times,* a veces; *at any* —, a cualquier hora; *behind the times,* pasado de moda; *in* —, a tiempo; con el tiempo; *at no* —, nunca; *in the day-* —, de día; *in the night-* —, de noche; *every* —, cada vez; *in our times,* en nuestros días; *from* — *to* —, de vez en cuando; *from this* — *forward,* desde hoy en adelante; *out of* —, (*mus.*) fuera de compás; *for the* — *being,* por ahora; *to arrange a* —, fijar un día; *to mark* —, (*mil., fig.*) marcar

el paso; *to have a good* —, pasarlo bien; *to take* —, tardar; necesitar tiempo; *to be on* —, llegar en punto; *what* — *is it?* ¿qué hora es?—*v.t.* calcular el tiempo de; hacer con oportunidad; calcular.
time-exposure ['taimikspouʒə], *n.* exposición, *f.*
time-honoured ['taimɔnəd], *a.* venerable.
timeless ['taimlis], *a.* eterno.
timely ['taimli], *a.* oportuno.
time-piece ['taimpi:s], *n.* reloj, *m.*
time-table ['taimteibl], *n.* horario; itinerario.
timid ['timid], *a.* tímido.
timidity [ti'miditi], *n.* timidez, *f.*
timorous ['timərəs], *a.* timorato.
tin [tin], *n.* estaño; lata; hojalata; — *can,* lata.—*v.t.* estañar; envasar en lata; cubrir con hojalata.
tinder ['tində], *n.* yesca.
tinder-box ['tindəbɔks], *n.* yescas, *f.pl.*
tinfoil ['tinfɔil], *n.* papel (*m.*) de estaño.
tinge [tindʒ], *n.* matiz, tinte, *m.*; (*fig.*) dejo.—*v.t.* matizar.
tingle [tingl], *n.* picazón, *f.*; hormigueo.—*v.i.* picar; estremecerse.
tinker ['tinkə], *n.* calderero.—*v.t., v.i.* remendar; *to* — *with,* chafallar.
tinkle [tinkl], *n.* retintín, *m.*; cencerreo.—*v.i.* tintinar.
tinned [tind], *a.* en lata, en conserva.
tin-opener ['tinoupnə], *n.* abrelatas, *m. inv.*
tin-plate ['tinpleit], *n.* hojalata.
tinsel ['tinsəl], *n.* oropel, *m.*
tint [tint], *n.* matiz; color; tinte, *m.*—*v.t.* matizar; colorar; teñir.
tiny ['taini], *a.* muy pequeño, minúsculo.
tip [tip], *n.* punta; cabo; extremidad, *f.*; inclinación, *f.*; propina; aviso oportuno; golpecito.—*v.t.* inclinar; voltear; dar una propina a; poner regatón.—*v.i.* inclinarse; dar propina; *to* — *over,* volcarse.
tipple [tipl], *n.* bebida.—*v.i.* empinar el codo.
tipsy ['tipsi], *a.* achispado.
tiptoe ['tiptou], *n.* punta del pie; *on* —, de puntillas.
tiptop ['tip'tɔp], *a.* espléndido.
tirade [tai'reid], *n.* diatriba.
tire [taiə], *n.* (*U.S.*) [TYRE]—*v.t.* cansar; aburrir; *to* — *out,* agotar.—*v.i.* cansarse; aburrirse.
tired ['taiəd], *a.* cansado.
tiredness ['taiədnis], *n.* cansancio.
tireless ['taiəlis], *a.* incansable.
tiresome ['taiəsəm], *a.* molesto; aburrido.
tissue ['tisju:], *n.* tejido; tisú, *m.*; (*fig.*) sarta; — *-paper,* papel (*m.*) de seda.
tit (1) [tit], *n.* (*orn.*) paro.
tit (2) [tit], *n.* only in — *for tat,* tal para cual.
titbit ['titbit], *n.* golosina.
tithe [taið], *n.* diezmo.—*v.t.* diezmar.
titillate ['titileit], *v.t.* titilar.
titivate ['titiveit], *v.i.* emperifollarse; ataviarse.
title [taitl], *n.* título; derecho; documento.
titled [taitld], *a.* titulado.
title-page ['taitlpeidʒ], *n.* portada.
title-role ['taitlroul], *n.* papel principal, *m.*
titter ['titə], *n.* risita sofocada.—*v.i.* reír entre dientes.
titular ['titjulə], *a.* titular; nominal.

to [tu:], *prep.* a; hacia; por; para; de; en; hasta; con; que; (*hora*) menos; — *his face*, en cara; *from town — town*, de pueblo en pueblo.—*adv.* — *and fro*, de un lado a otro, de aquí para acullá; *to come —*, volver en sí.

toad [toud], *n.* sapo.

toadstool ['toudstu:l], *n.* hongo.

toady ['toudi], *n.* lameculos (*fam.*), *m.f. inv.*—*v.t.* adular (*to*).

toast [toust], *n.* pan tostado; brindis, *m.*—*v.t.* tostar; brindar.

tobacco [tə'bækou], *n.* tabaco; — *pouch*, tabaquera; — *plantation*, tabacal, *m.*

tobacconist [tə'bækənist], *n.* tabaquero, tabacalero; *tobacconist's*, estanco, tabaquería.

toboggan [tə'bəgən], *n.* tobogán, *m.*

today [tə'dei], *n.* el día de hoy.—*adv.* hoy; hoy día; actualmente.

toddle [tɔdl], *v.i.* hacer pinitos.

toe [tou], *n.* dedo del pie; pie, *m.*; punta; *big* —, dedo gordo del pie; *from top to —*, de pies a cabeza.—*v.t.* *to — the line*, conformarse.

toffee ['tɔfi], *n.* caramelo.

together [tə'geðə], *a.* junto.—*adv.* juntamente; junto; al mismo tiempo; de seguida; — *with*, con; junto con; a la vez que.

toil (1) [tɔil], *n.* trabajo penoso.—*v.i.* afanarse; *to —* (*up a hill*), subir (*una cuesta*) con pena.

toil (2) [tɔil], *n.* (*usually pl.*) lazos, *m.pl.*; redes, *f.pl.*

toilet ['tɔilit], *n.* tocado; atavío; retrete, *m.*; — *paper*, papel higiénico, *m.*

token ['toukən], *n.* signo; muestra; recuerdo; *as a — of*, en señal de.

told [tould] [TELL].

tolerable ['tɔlərəbl], *a.* tolerable; regular.

tolerance ['tɔlərəns], *n.* tolerancia; indulgencia.

tolerant ['tɔlərənt], *a.* tolerante; indulgente.

tolerate ['tɔləreit], *v.t.* tolerar; permitir.

toleration [tɔlə'reiʃən], *n.* tolerancia.

toll (1) [toul], *n.* peaje, *m.*; derecho de molienda.

toll (2) [toul], *n.* tañido (*de campanas*).—*v.t., v.i.* tañer.

toll-gate ['toul'geit], *n.* barrera de peaje.

Tom [tɔm], *dimin.* Tomás.

tomato [tə'ma:tou], *n.* tomate, *m.*; — *plant*, tomatera.

tomb [tu:m], *n.* tumba.

tombstone ['tu:mstoun], *n.* piedra sepulcral.

tom-cat ['tɔmkæt], *n.* gato macho.

tome [toum], *n.* tomo.

tomfoolery [tɔm'fu:ləri], *n.* tontería.

tomorrow [tə'mɔrou], *adv., n.* mañana; *the day after —*, pasado mañana.

ton [tʌn], *n.* tonelada; *tons of*, (*fam.*) un montón de.

tone [toun], *n.* tono; acento; sonido; matiz, *m.*—*v.t.* entonar; *to — down*, amortiguar; suavizar; *to — in with*, armonizarse con; *to — up*, robustecer.

tongs [tɔnz], *n.pl.* tenazas, *f.pl.*

tongue [tʌn], *n.* lengua; clavo (*de hebilla*); badajo (*de campana*); oreja (*de zapato*); *to hold one's —*, callarse.

tongue-tied ['tʌntaid], *a.* mudo; (*fig.*) turbado.

tongue-twister ['tʌntwistə], *n.* trabalenguas, *m. inv.*

tonic ['tɔnik], *a.* tónico.—*n.* (*med.*) tónico; (*mus.*) tónica.

tonight [tə'nait], *adv.* esta noche.

tonnage ['tʌnidʒ], *n.* tonelaje, *m.*

tonsil ['tɔnsil], *n.* amígdala.

tonsillitis [tɔnsi'laitis], *n.* tonsilitis, amigdalitis, *f.*

too [tu:], *adv.* demasiado; también, además.

took [tuk] [TAKE].

tool [tu:l], *n.* herramienta; instrumento; utensilio; (*fig.*) agente, *m.f.*—*v.t.* labrar con herramienta.

tooth [tu:θ], *n.* (*pl.* teeth) diente, *m.*; muela; púa (*de peine*); (*fig.*) paladar, *m.*; *to cut one's teeth*, echar los dientes; *to gnash one's teeth*, rechinarse los dientes; *to have a sweet —*, ser goloso; *to pick one's teeth*, limpiarse o curarse los dientes; *in the teeth of*, contra; *false teeth*, dentadura postiza; *set of teeth*, dentadura.

toothache ['tu:θeik], *n.* dolor (*m.*) de muelas.

toothbrush ['tu:θbrʌʃ], *n.* cepillo para dientes.

toothless ['tu:θlis], *a.* desdentado; sin púas.

tooth-paste ['tu:θpeist], *n.* pasta de dientes.

toothpick ['tu:θpik], *n.* palillo, mondadientes, *m. inv.*

top (1) [tɔp], *a.* de encima; superior; principal; primero.—*n.* cima, cumbre, *f.*; copa (*de árbol*); ápice, *m.*; coronilla (*de cabeza*); superficie, *f.*; cabeza (*de página*); coronamiento; capota (*de vehículo*); *from — to bottom*, de arriba abajo; *from — to toe*, de pies a cabeza.

top (2) [tɔp], *n.* peonza; *to sleep like a —*, dormir como un tronco.

topaz ['toupæz], *n.* topacio.

top-coat ['tɔpkout], *n.* sobretodo.

top-dog ['tɔp'dɔg], *n.* (*fam.*) gallito.

toper ['toupə], *n.* borrachín, *m.*

top-hat ['tɔp'hæt], *n.* sombrero de copa.

topic ['tɔpik], *n.* tema, *m.*, asunto.

topical ['tɔpikəl], *a.* tópico; actual.

topmost ['tɔpmoust], *a.* más alto.

topography [tə'pɔgrəfi], *n.* topografía.

topple [tɔpl], *v.t.* derribar, hacer caer.—*v.i.* venirse abajo; tambalearse.

topsyturvy ['tɔpsi'tə:vi], *a.* trastornado.—*adv.* en desorden, patas arriba.

torch [tɔ:tʃ], *n.* antorcha, tea; *electric —*, linterna, lamparilla.

torch-bearer ['tɔ:ʃbeərə], *n.* hachero.

torchlight ['tɔ:tʃlait], *n.* luz (*f.*) de antorcha.

tore [tɔ:] [TEAR].

torment ['tɔ:ment], *n.* tormento, tortura; angustia.—[tɔ:'ment], *v.t.* atormentar, torturar.

torn [tɔ:n] [TEAR].

tornado [tɔ:'neidou], *n.* tornado.

torpedo [tɔ:'pi:dou], *n.* torpedo.—*v.t.* torpedear.

torpedo-boat [tɔ:'pi:dəbout], *n.* torpedero.

torpedo-tube [tɔ:'pi:dəutju:b], *n.* tubo lanzatorpedos.

torpid ['tɔ:pid], *a.* torpe; entorpecido.

torpor ['tɔ:pə], *n.* letargo, torpor, *m.*, entorpecimiento.

torrent ['tɔrənt], *n.* torrente, *m.*

torrential [tə'renʃəl], *a.* torrencial.

torrid ['tɔrid], *a.* tórrido.

tort [tɔ:t], *n.* (*jur.*) tuerto.

tortoise ['tɔ:təs], *n.* tortuga.
tortoise-shell ['tɔ:təʃel], *n.* carey, *m.*
tortuous ['tɔ:tjuəs], *a.* tortuoso.
torture ['tɔ:tʃə], *n.* tortura, tormento.—*v.t.* torturar; martirizar.
torturer ['tɔ:tʃərə], *n.* atormentador, *m.*
toss [tɔs], *n.* sacudimiento; movimiento (*de cabeza*); cogida (*de toro*).—*v.t.* lanzar, echar; coger, acornear; mover (*la cabeza*); **to — aside,** echar a un lado; **to — in a blanket,** mantear; **to — up,** echar al aire; jugar a cara o cruz.—*v.i.* (*naut.*) cabecear.
tot (1) [tɔt], *n.* nene, *m.*; nena; copita.
tot (2) [tɔt], *v.t.* **to — up,** sumar.
total [toutl], *a.* total; entero, completo.—*n.* total, *m.*, suma.—*v.t.* sumar.—*v.i.* ascender a.
totality [tou'tæliti], *n.* totalidad, *f.*
totem ['toutəm], *n.* totem, *m.*
totter ['tɔtə], *v.i.* bambolearse; estar para caerse.
tottering ['tɔtəriŋ], *a.* vacilante; tambaleante.
touch [tʌtʃ], *n.* tacto; contacto; toque, *m.*; ataque ligero; (*fam.*) sablazo; **in — with,** en contacto con.—*v.t.* tocar, tentar; alcanzar; conmover; importar; (*fam.*) dar un sablazo a; **to — off,** descargar; **to — up,** retocar; **to — upon,** tratar ligeramente de.—*v.i.* tocarse; **to — down,** aterrizar.
touching ['tʌtʃiŋ], *a.* conmovedor, patético.—*prep.* tocante a.
touch-line ['tʌtʃlain], *n.* (*sport*) línea de toque.
touchstone ['tʌtʃstoun], *n.* piedra de toque.
touchy ['tʌtʃi], *a.* susceptible.
tough [tʌf], *a.* duro; resistente; fuerte; (*fam.*) difícil.
toughen [tʌfn], *v.t.* endurecer.—*v.i.* -se.
toughness ['tʌfnis], *n.* dureza; fuerza; dificultad, *f.*
tour [tuə], *n.* viaje, *m.*, excursión, *f.*; **on —,** (*theat.*) de gira.—*v.t., v.i.* viajar (por).
tourist ['tuərist], *n.* turista, *m.f.*
touristic [tuə'ristik], *a.* turístico.
tournament ['tuənəmənt], *n.* torneo, *m.*
tousle [tauzl], *v.t.* despeinar.
tout [taut], *n.* buhonero; revendedor (*de billetes*), *m.*—*v.i.* **to — for,** pescar, solicitar.
tow [tou], *n.* remolque, *m.*; **in —,** a remolque.—*v.t.* remolcar.
towards [tə'wɔ:dz], *prep.* hacia; cerca de; para con; tocante a.
towel ['tauəl], *n.* toalla.
tower ['tauə], *n.* torre, *f.*—*v.i.* elevarse; (*fig.*) destacarse.
towering ['tauəriŋ], *a.* elevado; dominante; (*fig.*) violento.
town [taun], *n.* ciudad, *f.*; pueblo, población, *f.*; **— council,** concejo municipal; **— hall,** ayuntamiento.
town-planning ['taun'plæniŋ], *n.* urbanismo.
townsman ['taunzmən], *n.* ciudadano.
toxic ['tɔksik], *a.* tóxico.
toxin ['tɔksin], *n.* toxina.
toy [tɔi], *n.* juguete, *m.*—*v.i.* jugar.
toyshop ['tɔiʃɔp], *n.* juguetería.
trace [treis], *n.* huella; vestigio; tirante, *m.*; (*fig.*) dejo.—*v.t.* trazar; calcar; localizar; descubrir; **to — back,** hacer remontar.
tracing ['treisiŋ], *n.* calco; **— paper,** papel (*m.*) para calcar.
track [træk], *n.* huella; pista; (*rail.*) vía; senda; ruta; **beaten —,** senda trillada;

to keep — of, no perder de vista.—*v.t.* seguir la pista de; rastrear.
tract [trækt], *n.* tracto; región, *f.*; folleto; (*anat.*) vía.
tractable ['træktəbl], *a.* dócil.
traction ['trækʃən], *n.* tracción, *f.*
traction-engine ['trækʃən'endʒin], *n.* máquina de tracción.
tractor ['træktə], *n.* tractor, *m.*
trade [treid], *n.* comercio; tráfico; profesión, *f.*; **free —,** libre cambio; cambio; **— mark,** marca de fábrica; **— union,** sindicato; **— unionist,** sindicalista, *m.f.*; **— winds,** vientos alisios.—*v.t.* cambiar.—*v.i.* comerciar, traficar; **to — on,** explotar.
trader ['treidə], *n.* comerciante, traficante, *m.f.*; mercader, *m.*
tradesman ['treidzmən], *n.* tendero; artesano; **tradesman's entrance,** puerta de servicio.
trading ['treidiŋ], *a.* comerciante, mercantil.—*n.* comercio.
tradition [trə'diʃən], *n.* tradición, *f.*
traditional [trə'diʃənl], *a.* tradicional.
traduce [trə'dju:s], *v.t.* denigrar.
traffic ['træfik], *n.* tráfico; circulación, *f.*; **— island,** salvavidas, *m.inv.*; **— jam,** atasco de la circulación; **— light,** semáforo; **— circle,** círculo de tráfico.—*v.i.* traficar.
tragedian [trə'dʒi:djən], *n.* trágico.
tragedy ['trædʒidi], *n.* tragedia.
tragic ['trædʒik], *a.* trágico.
tragi-comedy ['trædʒi'kɔmidi], *n.* tragicomedia.
trail [treil], *n.* pista, huella, rastro; sendero; cola.—*v.t.* arrastrar; rastrear.—*v.i.* arrastrar.
trailer ['treilə], *n.* cazador; (*aut.*) remolque, *m.*; (*cine.*) anuncio de película; (*bot.*) tallo rastrero.
train [trein], *n.* tren, *m.*; séquito; cola (*de traje*); serie, *f.*—*v.t.* amaestrar; enseñar; (*sport*) preparar; entrenar; apuntar (*un cañón*).—*v.i.* educarse; entrenarse.
trainer ['treinə], *n.* amaestrador; instructor; (*sport*) preparador, entrenador, *m.*
training ['treiniŋ], *n.* instrucción, *f.*; (*sport*) entrenamiento; **— college,** escuela normal.
trait [trei(t)], *n.* rasgo, característica.
traitor ['treitə], *n.* traidor, *m.*
trajectory [trə'dʒektəri], *n.* trayectoria.
tram [træm], *n.* tranvía, *m.*
trammel ['træməl], *n.* traba; estorbo.—*v.t.* trabar.
tramp [træmp], *n.* vagabundo; caminata; ruido de pisadas; **— steamer,** vapor volandero.—*v.t.* vagar por.—*v.i.* ir a pie; vagabundear; patear.
trample [træmpl], *n.* pisoteo.—*v.t.* pisotear; **to — on,** (*fig.*) atropellar, maltratar.
trance [trɑ:ns], *n.* rapto, arrobamiento; (*med.*) catalepsia.
tranquil ['træŋkwil], *a.* tranquilo.
tranquillizer ['træŋkwilaizə], *n.* (*med.*) tranquilizador, *m.*
tranquillity [træŋ'kwiliti], *n.* tranquilidad, *f.*
transact [træn'zækt], *v.t.* despachar; llevar a cabo.
transaction [træn'zækʃən], *n.* negocio; transacción, *f.*—*pl.* actas, *f.pl.*
transatlantic ['trænzət'læntik], *a.* transatlántico.

transcend [træn'send], *v.t.* superar, trascender.

transcendence [træn'sendəns], *n.* trascendencia; superioridad, *f.*

transcendent [træn'sendənt], *a.* trascendental; superior.

transcribe [træns'kraib], *v.t.* transcribir.

transcript ['trænskript], *n.* traslado.

transcription [træns'kripʃən], *n.* transcripción, *f.*

transept ['trænsept], *n.* crucero.

transfer ['trænsfə:], *n.* transferencia; traslado; (*jur.*) cesión, *f.*; calcomanía.—[træns'fə:], *v.t.* trasladar, transferir; ceder.

transferable [træns'fə:rəbl], *a.* transferible.

transfiguration [trænsfigju'reiʃən], *n.* transfiguración, *f.*

transfigure [træns'figə], *v.t.* transfigurar.

transfix [træns'fiks], *v.t.* traspasar.

transform [træns'fɔ:m], *v.t.* transformar.

transformation [trænsfə'meiʃən], *n.* transformación, *f.*

transformer [træns'fɔ:mə], *n.* transformador, *m.*

transfusion [træns'fju:ʒən], *n.* transfusión, *f.*

transgress [træns'gres], *v.t.* traspasar; violar. —*v.i.* pecar.

transgression [træns'greʃən], *n.* transgresión, *f.*, pecado.

transgressor [træns'gresə], *n.* transgresor, pecador, *m.*

transient ['trænzjənt], *a.* transitorio.

transit ['trænsit], *n.* tránsito; *in* —, de tránsito.

transition [træn'siʃən], *n.* transición, *f.*

transitional [træn'siʃənl], *a.* de transición.

transitive ['trænsitiv], *a.* transitivo.

transitory ['trænsitəri], *a.* transitorio.

translatable [træns'leitəbl], *a.* traducible.

translate [træns'leit], *v.t.* traducir; (*eccl.*) trasladar.

translation [træns'leiʃən], *n.* traducción; versión, *f.*; (*eccl.*) traslado.

translator [træns'leitə], *n.* traductor, *m.*

translucent [trænz'lu:sənt], *a.* translúcido.

transmigration [trænzmai'greiʃən], *n.* transmigración, *f.*

transmission [trænz'miʃən], *n.* transmisión, *f.*

transmit [trænz'mit], *v.t.* transmitir; remitir.

transmitter [trænz'mitə], *n.* transmisor, emisor, *m.*

transmute [trænz'mju:t], *v.t.* transmutar.

transparency [træns'pærənsi], *n.* transparencia; transparente, *m.*

transparent [træns'pærənt], *a.* transparente.

transpire [træns'paiə], *v.i.* transpirar; (*fam.*) acontecer.

transplant [træns'plɑ:nt], *v.t.* trasplantar.

transport ['trænspɔ:t], *n.* transporte, *m.*; arrobamiento.—[træns'pɔ:t], *v.t.* transportar; deportar; arrebatar.

transportable [træns'pɔ:təbl], *a.* transportable.

transportation [trænspɔ:'teiʃən], *n.* transporte, *m.*; deportación, *f.*

transpose [træns'pouz], *v.t.* transponer; (*mus.*) trasportar.

transposition [trænspə'ziʃən], *n.* transposición, *f.*

transubstantiation [trænsʌbstænʃi'eiʃən], *n.* transubstanciación, *f.*

trap [træp], *n.* trampa; pequeño coche; (*mech.*) sifón, *m.*; (*low*) boca; *to fall into a* —, caer en la trampa.—*v.t.* coger con trampa; (*fig.*) tender un lazo a.—*v.i.* armar lazos. [TRAPS].

trapdoor ['træpdɔ:], *n.* escotillón, *m.*, trampa.

trapeze [trə'pi:z], *n.* trapecio.

trapper ['træpə], *n.* cazador (*con trampas*), *m.*

trappings ['træpiŋz], *n.pl.* jaeces, *m.pl.*; arreos, *m.pl.*

traps [træps], *n.pl.* (*fam.*) trastos, *m.pl.*

trash [træʃ], *n.* cachivaches, *m.pl.*; (*U.S.*, *fam.*) basura; gentuza; disparates, *m.pl.*

trashy ['træʃi], *a.* sin valor, despreciable.

traumatic [trɔ:'mætik], *a.* traumático.

travail ['træveil], *n.* dolores (*m.pl.*) de parto; afán, *m.*—*v.i.* estar de parto; afanarse.

travel [trævl], *n.* el viajar, viajes, *m.pl.*—*v.t.* recorrer.—*v.i.* viajar; andar.

traveller ['trævlə], *n.* viajero; (*com.*) viajante, *m.f.*; *traveller's cheque*, cheque (*m.*) de viajero.

travelling ['trævliŋ], *a.* de viaje; viajero.—*n.* viajes, *m.pl.*

traverse ['trævə:s], *a.* transversal.—*adv.* al través.—*n.* travesaño; (*jur.*) denegación, *f.*; (*mil.*) través, *m.*—*v.t.* atravesar, cruzar; (*jur.*) negar.

travesty ['trævisti], *n.* parodia.—*v.t.* parodiar.

trawl [trɔ:l], *n.* jábega.—*v.t.*, *v.i.* pescar a la rastra.

trawler ['trɔ:lə], *n.* barco pesquero de rastreo.

tray [trei], *n.* bandeja; cajón, *m.*

treacherous ['tretʃərəs], *a.* traidor, pérfido.

treachery ['tretʃəri], *n.* traición, *f.*, perfidia.

treacle [tri:kl], *n.* melado; melaza.

tread [tred], *n.* paso, pisada; huella (*de escalón*); llanta (*de neumático*).—*v.t.* *irr.* pisar; pisotear; hollar.—*v.i. irr.* pisar (*on*); *to* — *under foot*, pisotear.

treadle [tredl], *n.* pedal, *m.*

treadmill ['tredmil], *n.* molino de rueda de escalones; (*fig.*) tráfago.

treason [tri:zn], *n.* traición, *f.*

treasonable ['tri:znəbl], *a.* traidor.

treasure ['treʒə], *n.* tesoro; — *trove*, tesoro hallado.—*v.t.* atesorar.

treasurer ['treʒərə], *n.* tesorero.

Treasury ['treʒəri], *the*, *n.* Ministerio de Hacienda.

treasury ['treʒəri], *n.* tesorería.

treat [tri:t], *n.* regalo; placer, *m.*, gusto; festín, *m.*—*v.t.* tratar; convidar; obsequiar. —*v.i.* convidar; *to* — *of*, tratar de; *to* — *with*, negociar con.

treatise ['tri:tiz], *n.* tratado.

treatment ['tri:tmənt], *n.* tratamiento; conducta.

treaty ['tri:ti], *n.* tratado, pacto.

treble [trebl], *a.* triple; (*mus.*) atiplado.—*n.* (*mus.*) tiple, *m.*; — *clef*, clave (*f.*) de sol.— *v.t.* triplicar.—*v.i.* triplicarse.

tree [tri:], *n.* árbol, *m.*; horma (*de zapatos*); arzón (*de silla*), *m.*; *fruit* —, frutal, *m.*; *to bark up the wrong* —, (*fig.*) errar el tiro.

trek [trek], *n.* viaje, *m.*—*v.i.* viajar, caminar.

trellis ['trelis], *n.* enrejado; espaldera.

tremble [trembl], *n.* temblor, *m.*—*v.i.* temblar.

trembling ['trembliŋ], *a.* tembloroso; trémulo.

tremendous [tri'mendəs], *a.* tremendo.

tremor ['tremǝ], *n.* temblor, *m.*; estremecimiento.
tremulous ['tremjulǝs], *a.* tembloroso, trémulo.
trench [trentʃ], *n.* foso, zanja; (*mil.*) trinchera.—*v.t.* atrincherar.—*v.i.* hacer fosos.
trenchant ['trentʃǝnt], *a.* penetrante.
trencher ['trentʃǝ], *n.* trinchero.
trend [trend], *n.* rumbo, curso; tendencia.
trepidation [trepi'deiʃǝn], *n.* trepidación, *f.*
trespass ['trespǝs], *n.* pecado; violación, *f.*—*v.i.* pecar; entrar en propiedad sin derecho; infringir.
trespasser ['trespǝsǝ], *n.* pecador, *m.*; intruso.
tress [tres], *n.* trenza, rizo.
trestle [tresl], *n.* caballete, *m.*
trial ['traiǝl], *n.* prueba; tentativa; desgracia; (*jur.*) proceso, vista de una causa; **on —,** a prueba; (*jur.*) en juicio; **to stand —,** ser procesado; **— run,** marcha de ensayo.
triangle ['traiæŋgl], *n.* triángulo.
triangular [trai'æŋgjulǝ], *a.* triangular.
tribal [traibl], *a.* de la tribu, tribal.
tribe [traib], *n.* tribu, *f.*
tribesman ['traibzmǝn], *n.* miembro de una tribu.
tribulation [tribju'leiʃǝn], *n.* tribulación, *f.*
tribunal [trai'bju:nl], *n.* tribunal, *m.*
tributary ['tribjutǝri], *a.*, *n.* tributario.
tribute ['tribju:t], *n.* tributo; contribución, *f.*
trick [trik], *n.* engaño; maña; truco; ardid, *m.*; baza (*naipes*); **dirty —,** perrada; **to play a — on,** burlar.—*v.t.* engañar; adornar.—*v.i.* trampear.
trickery ['trikǝri], *n.* engaño; adornos, *m.pl.*
trickle [trikl], *n.* chorrito.—*v.i.* gotear.
tricky ['triki], *a.* tramposo; (*fam.*) espinoso.
tricycle ['traisikl], *n.* triciclo.
trident ['traidǝnt], *n.* tridente, *m.*
tried [traid], *a.* probado, leal.
triennial [trai'enjǝl], *a.* trienal.
trifle [traifl], *n.* bagatela, fruslería, poca cosa; (*cul.*) dulce (*m.*) de crema; (*fig.*) un poquito.—*v.i.* juguetear; **to — with,** jugar con.
trifling ['traifliŋ], *a.* frívolo.
trigger ['trigǝ], *n.* gatillo.
trigonometry [trigǝ'nɔmitri], *n.* trigonometría.
trilby ['trilbi], *n.* sombrero flexible.
trill [tril], *n.* trino; vibración, *f.*—*v.i.* trinar.
trillion ['triljǝn], *n.* trillón; (*U.S.*) billón, *m.*
trilogy ['trilǝdʒi], *n.* trilogía.
trim [trim], *a.* ajustado; en buen estado; elegante.—*n.* atavío; orden, *m.*, estado.—*v.t.* arreglar; ajustar; decorar; despabilar (*una lámpara*); recortar; (*carp.*) acepillar; (*naut.*) orientar.
trimming ['trimiŋ], *n.* guarnición, *f.*; ajuste, *m.*; (*naut.*) orientación, *f.*—*pl.* accesorios, *m.pl.*
trimness ['trimnis], *n.* aseo; esbeltez, *f.*
trinity ['triniti], *n.* trinidad, *f.*
trinket ['triŋkit], *n.* dije, *m.*
trio ['tri:ou], *n.* trío.
trip [trip], *n.* zancadilla; traspié, *m.*; excursión, *f.*, viaje, *m.*—*v.t.* hacer caer; dar una zancadilla a; (*fig.*) coger en falta (*up*).—*v.i.* tropezar; ir con paso ligero; (*fig.*) equivocarse.
tripartite [trai'pɑ:tait], *a.* tripartito.

tripe [traip], *n.* callos, *m.pl.*; (*fam.*) disparate, *m.*
triphthong ['trifθɔŋ], *n.* triptongo.
triple [tripl], *a.* triple.—*v.t.* triplicar.—*v.i.* triplicarse.
triplet ['triplit], *n.* trillizo; (*mus.*) tresillo; (*poet.*) terceto.
triplicate ['triplikit], *a.* triplicado.—['triplikeit], *v.t.* triplicar.
tripod ['traipɔd], *n.* trípode, *m.*
tripper ['tripǝ], *n.* excursionista, *m.f.*
trite [trait], *a.* trillado.
triumph ['traiǝmf], *n.* triunfo.—*v.i.* triunfar.
triumphal [trai'ʌmfǝl], *a.* triunfal.
triumphant [trai'ʌmfǝnt], *a.* triunfante.
trivial ['triviǝl], *a.* trivial; frívolo.
triviality [trivi'æliti], *n.* trivialidad; frivolidad, *f.*
trod [trɔd], **trodden** [trɔdn] [TREAD].
troglodyte ['trɔglǝdait], *n.* troglodita, *m.f.*
Trojan ['troudʒǝn], *a.*, *n.* troyano.
trolley ['trɔli], *n.* trole, *m.*; carro. **[tram]**
trolley-bus ['trɔlibʌs], *n.* trolebús, *m.*
trollop ['trɔlǝp], *n.* ramera; cochina.
trombone [trɔm'boun], *n.* trombón, *m.*
troop [tru:p], *n.* tropa; tropel, *m.*; compañía; escuadrón, *m.*—*pl.* tropas, *f.pl.*—*v.i.* ir en tropel; apinarse; **to — off,** retirarse en tropel.
trooper ['tru:pǝ], *n.* soldado de caballería.
trophy ['troufi], *n.* trofeo.
tropic ['trɔpik], *a.*, *n.* trópico.
tropical ['trɔpikǝl], *a.* tropical.
trot [trɔt], *n.* trote, *m.*—*v.t.* hacer trotar; **to — out,** (*fig.*) salir con.—*v.i.* trotar.
troth [trouθ], *n.* fe, *f.*; palabra de honor; **to plight one's —,** desposarse.
trouble [trʌbl], *n.* pena; molestia; dificultad, *f.*; estorbo; inquietud, *f.*; **to be in —,** hallarse en un apuro; (*fam.*) estar preñada; **to cause —,** armar un lío; **to be worth the —,** valer la pena.—*v.t.* molestar; turbar; incomodar; importunar; pedir, rogar.—*v.i.* darse molestia; incomodarse; apurarse.
troubled [trʌbld], *a.* turbado; preocupado.
troublesome ['trʌblsǝm], *a.* molesto; fastidioso; importuno; difícil.
trough [trɔf], *n.* artesa; gamella; tragadero (*del mar*).
trounce [trauns], *v.t.* zurrar.
troupe [tru:p], *n.* compañía.
trousers ['trauzǝz], *n.pl.* pantalones, *m.pl.*
trousseau ['tru:sou], *n.* ajuar, *m.*
trout [traut], *n.* trucha.
trowel ['trauǝl], *n.* paleta; desplantador, *m.*
Troy [trɔi], *n.* Troya.
truancy ['tru:ǝnsi], *n.* tuna.
truant ['tru:ǝnt], *a.* tunante.—*n.* novillero; **to play —,** hacer novillos.
truce [tru:s], *n.* tregua.
truck (I) [trʌk], *n.* carro; camión, *m.*; autocamión, *m.* **[van** (2)]
truck (2) [trʌk], *n.* cambio; relaciones, *f.pl.*; (*U.S.*) hortalizas, *f.pl.*
truculence ['trʌkjulǝns], *n.* agresividad, *f.*; truculencia.
truculent ['trʌkjulǝnt], *a.* agresivo; truculento.
trudge [trʌdʒ], *v.i.* ir a pie; andar con pena.
true [tru:], *a.* verdadero; leal; sincero; **a plomo.**
truffle [trʌfl], *n.* trufa.

truism ['tru:izm], *n.* perogrullada.
trump (1) [trʌmp], *n.* triunfo (*naipes*); (*fam.*) joya.—*v.t.* cortar con el triunfo.—*v.i.* jugar triunfo.
trump (2) [trʌmp], *v.t.* **to — up**, inventar.
trump (3) [trʌmp], *n.* son de trompeta; **the last —**, el día del Juicio Final.
trumpet ['trʌmpit], *n.* trompeta; **to blow one's own —**, alzar el gallo.—*v.t.*, *v.i.* trompetear; (*fig.*) divulgar.
trumpeter ['trʌmpitə], *n.* trompetero, trompeta *m.*
truncate [trʌŋ'keit], *v.t.* truncar.
truncation [trʌŋ'keiʃən], *n.* truncamiento.
truncheon ['trʌntʃən], *n.* porra.
trundle [trʌndl], *v.t.*, *v.i.* rodar.
trunk [trʌŋk], *n.* tronco; trompa (*de elefante*); baúl, *m.*—*pl.* taparrabo; bañador, *m.*; calzoncillos, *m.pl.* **[boot(1)]**
trunk-call ['trʌŋk'kɔ:l], *n.* conferencia interurbana.
trunk-road ['trʌŋkroud], *n.* carretera principal.
truss [trʌs], *n.* haz, armazón, *m.*; (*med.*) braguero.
trust [trʌst], *n.* confianza; crédito; esperanza; (*jur.*) fideicomiso; (*com.*) trust, *m.*; **to hold in —**, guardar en depósito; **on —**, al fiado.—*v.t.* tener confianza en; creer en.—*v.i.* esperar; confiar (**in**, en).
trustee [trʌs'ti:], *n.* guardián, *m.*; (*jur.*) depositario.
trustworthy ['trʌstwə:ði], *a.* fidedigno.
trusty ['trʌsti], *a.* leal; seguro; firme.
truth [tru:θ], *n.* verdad, *f.*; **the plain —**, la pura verdad.
truthful ['tru:θful], *a.* veraz; verdadero.
try [trai], *n.* prueba; tentativa; (*sport*) tiro.—*v.t.*, *v.i.* intentar, procurar, tratar de; probar; emprender; verificar; exasperar, fatigar; (*jur.*) ver, procesar; **to — hard**, esforzarse (**to**, a, por); **to — on**, probar; **to — out**, poner a prueba; ensayar.
trying ['traiiŋ], *a.* difícil; molesto; fatigoso.
tryst [trist], *n.* cita; lugar (*m.*) de cita.
tsetse ['tsetsi], *n.* tsetsé, *f.*
tub [tʌb], *n.* cuba; artesón, *m.*
tuba ['tju:bə], *n.* tuba.
tube [tju:b], *n.* tubo; (*rail.*) metro; (*radio etc.*) tubo; **inner —**, cámara de aire.
tuber ['tju:bə], *n.* (*bot.*) tubérculo.
tubercular [tju:'bə:kjulə], *a.* tuberculoso.
tuberculosis [tju:'bə:kju'lousis], *n.* tuberculosis, *f.*
tubing ['tju:biŋ], *n.* tubería.
tub-thumper ['tʌbθʌmpə], *n.* (*fam.*) gerundio.
tubular ['tju:bjulə], *a.* tubular.
tuck [tʌk], *n.* pliegue, *m.*; alforza; (*fam.*) dulces, *m.pl.*—*v.t.* alforzar; **to — in**, arropar.—*v.i.* **to — into**, (*fam.*) comerse.
Tuesday ['tju:zd(e)i], *n.* martes, *m.*
tuft [tʌft], *n.* manojo; moño; penacho; copete, *m.*
tug [tʌg], *n.* tirón; (*naut.*) remolcador, *m.*; **— of war**, lucha de la cuerda.—*v.t.*, *v.i.* tirar (de) (**at**, de).
tuition [tju:'iʃən], *n.* instrucción, *f.*
tulip ['tju:lip], *n.* tulipán, *m.*
tulle [tju:l], *n.* tul, *m.*
tumble [tʌmbl], *n.* caída; voltereta.—*v.t.* derribar; desarreglar.—*v.i.* caer; voltear; **to**

— down, venirse abajo; **to — to it**, (*fam.*) caer en la cuenta.
tumble-down ['tʌmbldaun], *a.* desvencijado, destartalado.
tumbler ['tʌmblə], *n.* volatinero; vaso.
tummy ['tʌmi], *n.* (*fam.*) barriguita, tripita.
tumour ['tju:mə], *n.* tumor, *m.*
tumult ['tju:mʌlt], *n.* alboroto; tumulto.
tumultuous [[tju:'mʌltjuəs], *a.* tumultuoso.
tun [tʌn], *n.* cuba, tonel, *m.*
tuna ['tju:nə], *n.* atún, *m.*
tune [tju:n], *n.* aire, *m.*, armonía; melodía; **in —**, afinado; (*fig.*) de acuerdo; **out of —**, desafinado; **to the — of**, (*fam.*) hasta la suma de.—*v.t.* afinar; sintonizar (*radio etc.*); ajustar (*motores*).—*v.i.* templar (**up**); sintonizar (**in**) (**to**, con).
tuneless ['tju:nlis], *a.* discorde.
tuner ['tju:nə], *n.* afinador; (*rad.*) sintonizador, *m.*
tunic ['tju:nik], *n.* túnica.
tuning ['tju:niŋ], *n.* afinación; sintonización, *f.*
tuning-fork ['tju:niŋfɔ:k], *n.* diapasón, *m.*
Tunisia [tju:'niziə], *n.* Túnez, *f.*
Tunisian [tju:'niziən], *a.*, *n.* tunecino.
tunnel [tʌnl], *n.* túnel, *m.*—*v.t.*, *v.i.* construir un túnel; minar.
turban ['tə:bən], *n.* turbante, *m.*
turbine ['tə:bain], *n.* turbina.
turbojet ['tə:boudʒet], *n.* turborreactor, *m.*
turbot ['tə:bət], *n.* (*ichth.*) rodaballo.
turbulent ['tə:bjulənt], *a.* turbulento.
tureen [tju:'ri:n], *n.* sopera.
turf [tə:f], *n.* césped, *m.*; turba; carreras (*f.pl.*) de caballos.
turgid ['tə:dʒid], *a.* turgente; (*fig.*) hinchado.
Turk [tə:k], *n.* turco.
Turkey ['tə:ki], *n.* Turquía.
turkey ['tə:ki], *n.* pavo; pava.
Turkish ['tə:kiʃ], *a.*, *n.* turco.
turmoil ['tə:mɔil], *n.* tumulto, alboroto.
turn [tə:n], *n.* giro, vuelta; paseo; vez, *f.*; dirección, *f.*; inclinación, *f.*; oportunidad, *f.*; procedimiento; servicio; provecho; **good —**, favor, *m.*; **bad —**, mala pasada; **at every —**, a cada instante; **to do a good —**, prestar un servicio; **to take a —**, dar una vuelta; **to take turns**, turnar, alternar.—*v.t.* hacer girar, dar vueltas a; invertir; dar nueva dirección a; adaptar; convertir; volver; traducir; torcer; dar asco; infatuar; perturbar; tornear; redondear (*una frase*); **to — against**, hacerse enemigo de; **to — aside**, desviar; **to — away**, despedir, rechazar; **to — back**, volver atrás; **to — one's back on**, volver la espalda a; **to — down**, doblar, plegar; rechazar; **to — from**, desviar de; **to — in**, volver adentro; (*fig.*) entregar; **to — into**, cambiar en; **to — off**, cerrar; **to — on**, abrir; encender; **to — out**, arrojar; apagar; volver del revés; **to — over**, recorrer; invertir; volcar; entregar; **to — round**, volver; **to — the stomach**, dar asco; **to — to good account**, poner a provecho; **to — up**, volver arriba; revolver; **to — upon**, revolver sobre; **to — upside down**, trastornar.—*v.i.* volver; volverse; girar; ponerse; agriarse (*la leche*); infatuarse; perturbarse; resultar; tornearse; (*naut.*) virar; **to — about**, volverse; **to — aside**, desviarse; **to — away**, volverse; **to — back**,

retroceder; *to — in,* volverse adentro; doblarse; (*fam.*) ir a la cama; *to — into,* entrar en; convertirse en; *to — off,* desviarse; torcer; *to — out,* resultar; suceder; salir; *to — over,* revolverse; *to — round,* volverse; *to — to,* ponerse a; dirigirse a; *to — up,* volver arriba; (*fam.*) llegar; acontecer; *to — upon,* volver sobre; depender de.

turncoat ['tə:nkout], *n.* renegado.

turning ['tə:niŋ], *n.* vuelta.

turning-point ['tə:niŋpoint], *n.* punto decisivo.

turnip ['tə:nip], *n.* nabo.

turnout ['tə:naut], *n.* vestidos, *m.pl.*; entrada *o* salida de personas; (*com.*) producto neto.

turnover ['tə:nouvə], *n.* pastel, *m.*; (*com.*) ventas, *f.pl.*

turnstile ['tə:nstail], *n.* torniquete, *m.*

turntable ['tə:nteibl], *n.* plato (giratorio).

turpentine ['tə:pəntain], *n.* trementina.

turpitude ['tə:pitju:d], *n.* infamia, torpeza.

turquoise ['tə:kwoiz], *n.* turquesa.

turret ['tʌrət], *n.* torrecilla.

turtle [tə:tl], *n.* tortuga de mar; *to turn —,* voltear patas arriba; volcar(se).

turtle-dove ['tə:tldʌv], *n.* tórtola.

tusk [tʌsk], *n.* colmillo.

tussle [tʌsl], *n.* riña.—*v.i.* luchar.

tutelar ['tju:tilə], *a.* tutelar.

tutor ['tju:tə], *n.* preceptor, *m.*; ayo.—*v.t.* enseñar.—*v.i.* dar clases.

tutorial [tju:'tɔ:riəl], *n.* seminario.

tutoring ['tju:təriŋ], *n.* instrucción, *f.*

twain [twein], *n.* (*poet.*) dos, *m.f.pl.*

twaddle [twɔdl], *n.* disparates, *m.pl.*

twang [twæŋ], *n.* sonido vibrante; gangueo; punteado de una cuerda; acento.—*v.i.* ganguear.—*v.t.* rasguear.

'twas [twɔz] [IT WAS].

tweed [twi:d], *n.* cheviot, *m.*

tweezers ['twi:zəz], *n.pl.* tenacillas, pinzas, *f.pl.*

twelfth [twelfθ], *a.* duodécimo; *Twelfth Night,* día (*m.*) de los Reyes.—*n.* duodécimo, duodécima parte; doce (*en las fechas*), *m.*

twelve [twelv], *a., n.* doce, *m.*

twentieth ['twentiiθ], *a.* vigésimo.—*n.* veintavo; vigésima parte; veinte (*en las fechas*), *m.*

twenty ['twenti], *a., n.* veinte, *m.*

twice [twais], *adv.* dos veces.

twiddle [twidl], *v.t.* jugar con.

twig [twig], *n.* ramita.

twilight ['twailait], *a.* crepuscular.—*n.* crepúsculo.

twill [twil], *n.* tela asargada.

twin [twin], *a., n.* mellizo, gemelo.

twine [twain], *n.* cordel, *m.*—*v.t.* enroscar; ceñir.—*v.i.* entrelazarse.

twin-engined ['twin'endʒind], *a.* bimotor.

twinge [twindʒ], *n.* punzada; (*fig.*) remordimiento.

twinkle [twiŋkl], *n.* centelleo; pestañeo.—*v.i.* centellear; brillar.

twinkling ['twiŋkliŋ], *n.* brillo; centelleo; (*fig.*) instante, *m.*; *in the — of an eye,* en un abrir y cerrar de ojos; en un santiamén.

twirl [twə:l], *n.* vuelta, rotación, *f.*; pirueta.—*v.t.* hacer girar; dar vueltas a.—*v.i.* girar; dar vueltas.

twist [twist], *n.* torzal, *m.*; mecha; sacudida; peculiaridad, *f.*; recodo; torsión, *f.*; trenza; rollo (*de tabaco*).—*v.t.* torcer; enroscar; trenzar; falsificar.—*v.i.* torcerse; serpentear; retorcerse.

twister ['twistə], *n.* torcedor; tromba marina, tornado.

twisting ['twistiŋ], *a.* sinuoso.

twitch [twitʃ], *n.* tirón, *m.*; contracción nerviosa, *f.*—*v.t.* arrancar.—*v.i.* crisparse; moverse.

twitter ['twitə], *n.* piada, gorjeo.—*v.i.* piar, gorjear.

two [tu:], *a., n.* dos, *m.*; *to put — and — together,* caer en la cuenta.

two-faced ['tu:'feist], *a.* de dos caras; (*fig.*) de dos haces.

twofold ['tu:fould], *a.* doble.—*adv.* doblemente.

two-headed ['tu:'hedid], *a.* de dos cabezas.

two-legged ['tu:'legid], *a.* bípedo.

twopence ['tʌpəns], *n.* dos peniques, *m.pl.*

twopenny ['tʌpni], *a.* de dos peniques; (*fig.*) de tres al cuarto.

two-ply ['tu:'plai], *a.* de dos hilos *o* capas.

two-seater ['tu:'si:tə], *a.* de dos asientos.

two-step ['tu:step], *n.* paso doble.

two-way ['tu:wei], *a.* de dos direcciones.

type [taip], *n.* tipo; letra de imprenta.—*v.t., v.i.* escribir a máquina.

type-case ['taipkeis], *n.* caja de imprenta.

type-setter ['taipsetə], *n.* cajista, *m.f.*

typewriter ['taipraitə], *n.* máquina de escribir.

typewriting ['taipraitiŋ], *n.* mecanografía.

typewritten ['taipritn], *a.* escrito a máquina.

typhoid ['taifoid], *n.* fiebre tifoidea.

typhoon [tai'fu:n], *n.* tifón, *m.*

typhus ['taifəs], *n.* tifus, *m.*

typical ['tipikəl], *a.* típico.

typify ['tipifai], *v.t.* simbolizar.

typist ['taipist], *n.* mecanógrafo.

typography [tai'pɔgrəfi], *n.* tipografía.

tyrannical [ti'rænikəl], *a.* tiránico.

tyrannize ['tirənaiz], *v.t., v.i.* tiranizar.

tyrannous ['tirənəs], *a.* tiránico.

tyranny ['tirəni], *n.* tiranía.

tyrant ['taiərənt], *n.* tirano.

tyre [taiə], *n.* neumático; llanta (*de carro*).

U

U, u [ju:], *n.* vigésima primera letra del alfabeto inglés.

ubiquitous [ju:'bikwitəs], *a.* ubicuo.

udder ['ʌdə], *n.* ubre, *f.*

ugliness ['ʌglinis], *n.* fealdad, *f.*

ugly ['ʌgli], *a.* feo; repugnante.

Ukraine [ju:'krein], *n.* Ucrania.

Ukrainian [ju:'kreiniən], *a., n.* ucranio.

ulcer ['ʌlsə], *n.* úlcera.

ulcerate ['ʌlsəreit], *v.t.* ulcerar.—*v.i.* ulcerarse.

ulterior [ʌl'tiəriə], *a.* ulterior; *— motive,* intención oculta.

ultimate ['ʌltimit], *a.* último; esencial, fundamental.

ultimatum [ˌʌlti'meitəm], *n.* ultimátum, *m.*
ultra ['ʌltrə], *a.* extremo, exagerado.—*prefix.* ultra-.
ultraviolet [ˌʌltrə'vaiəlit], *a.* ultravioleta.
umbrage ['ʌmbridʒ], *n.* (*poet.*) sombraje, *m.*; resentimiento; **to take** —, picarse (*at*, de).
umbrella [ʌm'brelə], *n.* paraguas, *m.sg.*; — **stand**, paragüero.
umpire ['ʌmpaiə], *n.* (*sport*) árbitro; arbitrador, *m.*—*v.t.*, *v.i.* arbitrar.
un- [ʌn], *prefix, variously translated in Spanish by* in–, des–, no, sin, poco.
unabridged [ʌnə'bridʒd], *a.* no abreviado; íntegro.
unacceptable [ʌnək'septəbl], *a.* inaceptable.
unaccompanied [ʌnə'kʌmpənid], *a.* no acompañado, solo.
unaccomplished [ʌnə'kʌmpliʃt], *a.* inacabado, imperfecto, incompleto.
unaccountable [ʌnə'kauntəbl], *a.* inexplicable; irresponsable.
unaccustomed [ʌnə'kʌstəmd], *a.* desacostumbrado.
unacquainted [ʌnə'kweintid], *a.* desconocido; **to be** — **with**, no conocer; ignorar.
unadulterated [ʌnə'dʌltəreitid], *a.* sin mezcla, natural; puro.
unadventurous [ʌnəd'vəntʃərəs], *a.* nada aventurero; tímido.
unadvisable [ʌnəd'vaizəbl], *a.* poco conveniente; imprudente.
unaffected [ʌnə'fektid], *a.* sin afectación, natural, franco; no afectado.
unalterable [ʌn'ɔːltərəbl], *a.* inalterable; invariable.
unanimity [juːnə'nimiti], *n.* unanimidad, *f.*
unanimous [juː'næniməs], *a.* unánime.
unanswerable [ʌn'ɑːnsərəbl], *a.* incontestable, incontrovertible.
unapproachable [ʌnə'proutʃəbl], *a.* inaccesible.
unarmed [ʌn'ɑːmd], *a.* desarmado; indefenso.
unashamed [ʌnə'ʃeimd], *a.* sin vergüenza.
unassuming [ʌnə'sjuːmiŋ], *a.* sin pretensiones, modesto.
unattainable [ʌnə'teinəbl], *a.* inasequible.
unattractive [ʌnə'træktiv], *a.* poco atractivo, antipático.
unavailing [ʌnə'veiliŋ], *a.* infructuoso, inútil, vano.
unavoidable [ʌnə'vɔidəbl], *a.* inevitable.
unaware [ʌnə'weə], *a.* ignorante; inconsciente.
unawares [ʌnə'weəz], *adv.* **to take** —, coger desprevenido.
unbearable [ʌn'beərəbl], *a.* intolerable, insoportable.
unbecoming [ʌnbi'kʌmiŋ], *a.* impropio, inconveniente; indecoroso; que sienta mal.
unbeliever [ʌnbi'liːvə], *n.* incrédulo; descreído.
unbias(s)ed [ʌn'baiəst], *a.* imparcial.
unbidden [ʌn'bidn], *a.* no convidado; espontáneo.
unborn [ʌn'bɔːn], *a.* no nacido todavía.
unbosom [ʌn'buzəm], *v.t.* confesar; **to** — **oneself**, abrir su pecho.
unbound [ʌn'baund], *a.* sin encuadernar.
unbounded [ʌn'baundid], *a.* ilimitado, infinito.
unbreakable [ʌn'breikəbl], *a.* inquebrantable.
unbridled [ʌn'braidld], *a.* desenfrenado.

unbroken [ʌn'broukən], *a.* intacto, entero; indomado; no interrumpido, ininterrumpido.
unbuckle [ʌn'bʌkl], *v.t.* deshebillar.
unburden [ʌn'bəːdn], *v.t.* descargar; aliviar; (*fig.*) **to** — **oneself**, desahogarse.
unbutton [ʌn'bʌtn], *v.t.* desabotonar, desabrochar.
uncanny [ʌn'kæni], *a.* misterioso; pavoroso.
unceasing [ʌn'siːsiŋ], *a.* incesante, sin cesar.
uncertain [ʌn'səːtn], *a.* incierto, dudoso; indeciso, irresoluto.
uncertainty [ʌn'səːtnti], *n.* incertidumbre; irresolución, *f.*
unchain [ʌn'tʃein], *v.t.* desencadenar.
unchangeable [ʌn'tʃeindʒəbl], *a.* invariable, inmutable.
unchaste [ʌn'tʃeist], *a.* impúdico, incasto.
unchecked [ʌn'tʃekt], *a.* desenfrenado; no verificado.
unclaimed [ʌn'kleimd], *a.* no reclamado.
uncle [ʌŋkl], *n.* tío; (*fam.*) prestamista, *m.*
unclean [ʌn'kliːn], *a.* sucio, impuro; inmundo.
unclothe [ʌn'klouð], *v.t.* desnudar.
uncoil [ʌn'kɔil], *v.t.* desarrollar.—*v.i.* desovillarse.
uncomfortable [ʌn'kʌmfətəbl], *a.* incómodo; molesto, desagradable; preocupado.
uncommon [ʌn'kɔmən], *a.* poco común, raro, extraño; infrecuente; extraordinario.
uncompromising [ʌn'kɔmprəmaiziŋ], *a.* inflexible.
unconcerned [ʌnkən'səːnd], *a.* indiferente, frío; despreocupado.
unconditional [ʌnkən'diʃənl], *a.* incondicional, absoluto.
unconquerable [ʌn'kɔŋkərəbl], *a.* invencible.
unconscious [ʌn'kɔnʃəs], *a.* inconsciente; sin sentido; espontáneo; inconsciente.
unconstitutional [ʌnkɔnsti'tjuːʃənl], *a.* anticonstitucional.
uncontrollable [ʌnkən'trouləbl], *a.* irrefrenable, ingobernable.
unconventional [ʌnkən'venʃənl], *a.* poco convencional; excéntrico; original.
uncork [ʌn'kɔːk], *v.t.* destapar.
uncouple [ʌn'kʌpl], *v.t.* desconectar; soltar.
uncouth [ʌn'kuːθ], *a.* tosco, grosero.
uncover [ʌn'kʌvə], *v.t.* descubrir; desabrigar; destapar.
unction ['ʌŋkʃən], *n.* unción, *f.*; ungüento; (*fig.*) hipocresía; fervor, *m.*
unctuous ['ʌŋktjuəs], *a.* untuoso, zalamero.
uncurl [ʌn'kəːl], *v.t.* desrizar.—*v.i.* desrizarse; destorcerse.
undamaged [ʌn'dæmidʒd], *a.* indemne.
undated [ʌn'deitid], *a.* sin fecha.
undaunted [ʌn'dɔːntid], *a.* intrépido; denodado.
undecided [ʌndi'saidid], *a.* indeciso; irresoluto.
undefended [ʌndi'fendid], *a.* indefenso.
undefined [ʌndi'faind], *a.* indefinido.
undeniable [ʌndi'naiəbl], *a.* incontestable, innegable.
under ['ʌndə], *a.* bajo; inferior; subordinado.—*adv.* abajo; debajo; menos; **to keep** —, subyugar.—*prep.* bajo, debajo de; inferior a; menos de; al mando de; — **age**, menor de edad; — **arms**, bajo las armas; — **consideration**, en consideración; — **cover**, al

abrigo; — *pain of*, so pena de; — *steam*, al vapor; — *way*, en marcha.
underarm ['ʌndərɑːm], *n.* sobaco, axila.
undercarriage ['ʌndəkærɪdʒ], *n.* (*aer.*) tren (*m.*) de aterrizaje.
underclothes ['ʌndəklouðz], *n.pl.* ropa interior.
undercurrent ['ʌndəkʌrənt], *n.* corriente (*f.*) submarina; (*fig.*) tendencia oculta.
undercut ['ʌndəkʌt], *n.* filete, *m.*—[ʌndə'kʌt], *v.t.* socavar; baratear.
under-developed ['ʌndədi'veləpt], *a.* subdesarrollado; (*phot.*) no revelado bastante.
underdog ['ʌndədɒg], *n.* víctima; débil, *m.*
underdone [ʌndə'dʌn], *a.* medio asado.
underestimate [ʌndər'estimeit], *v.t.* desestimar.
underfoot [ʌndə'fut], *adv.* debajo de los pies.
undergo [ʌndə'gou], *v.t. irr.* (*conjug. like* GO) padecer, sufrir; pasar por.
undergraduate [ʌndə'grædjuit], *n.* estudiante (*m.*) no licenciado.
underground ['ʌndəgraund], *a.* subterráneo. —*n.* metro.—[ʌndə'graund], *adv.* bajo tierra.
undergrowth ['ʌndəgrouθ], *n.* maleza.
underhand [ʌndə'hænd], *a.* clandestino, solapado.—*adv.* a escondidas, bajo mano.
underlie [ʌndə'lai], *v.t. irr.* (*conjug. like* LIE) estar debajo de; ser la razón fundamental de.
underline [ʌndə'lain], *v.t.* subrayar.
underling [ʌndə'lɪŋ], *n.* subordinado, paniaguado.
underlying [ʌndə'laɪɪŋ], *a.* fundamental.
undermine [ʌndə'main], *v.t.* socavar; minar.
underneath [ʌndə'niːθ], *adv.* debajo.— ['ʌndəniːθ], *prep.* bajo, debajo de.
underpaid [ʌndə'peid], *a.* mal pagado.
underprivileged [ʌndə'privilidʒd], *a.* menesteroso.
underrate [ʌndə'reit], *v.t.* desestimar, menospreciar.
underside ['ʌndəsaid], *n.* revés, envés, *m.*
undersigned [ʌndə'saind], *a., n.* infrascrito, abajo firmado.
understand [ʌndə'stænd], *v.t. irr.* (*conjug. like* STAND) comprender; saber; conocer; tener entendido; sobrentender.—*v.i.* comprender; tener entendido.
understandable [ʌndə'stændəbl], *a.* comprensible.
understanding [ʌndə'stændɪŋ], *n.* entendimiento; comprensión, *f.*; acuerdo.
understatement ['ʌndəsteitmənt], *n.* moderación (*f.*) excesiva.
understudy ['ʌndəstʌdi], *n.* (*theat.*) sobresaliente, *m.f.*—*v.t.* sustituir.
undertake [ʌndə'teik], *v.t. irr.* (*conjug. like* TAKE) encargarse de, emprender.
undertaker ['ʌndəteikə], *n.* director (*m.*) de pompas fúnebres.
undertaking ['ʌndəteikɪŋ], *n.* empresa funeraria, [ʌndə'teikɪŋ], empresa; (*jur.*) garantía.
undertone ['ʌndətoun], *n.* voz baja, tonillo; (*art*) color apagado.
undervalue [ʌndə'vælju:], *v.t.* menospreciar.
underwear ['ʌndəweə], *n.* ropa interior.
underworld ['ʌndəwə:ld], *n.* infierno; heces (*f.pl.*) de la sociedad, hampa.
underwrite ['ʌndərait], *v.t. irr.* (*conjug. like* WRITE) (*com.*) asegurar, reasegurar.

underwriter ['ʌndəraitə], *.ı.* asegurador, reasegurador, *m.*
undeserved [ʌndi'zə:vd], *a.* inmerecido.
undesirable [ʌndi'zaiərəbl], *a.* no deseable; pernicioso, indeseable.
undigested [ʌndi'dʒestid], *a.* indigesto.
undignified [ʌn'dignifaid], *a.* sin dignidad.
undiminished [ʌndi'miniʃt], *a.* no disminuido; continuo; íntegro.
undisciplined [ʌn'disiplind], *a.* indisciplinado.
undisclosed [ʌndis'klouzd], *a.* no revelado.
undivided [ʌndi'vaidid], *a.* indiviso, íntegro, completo.
undo [ʌn'duː], *v.t.* (*conjug. like* DO) deshacer; desatar; anular; (*fig.*) arruinar.
undoing [ʌn'duːɪŋ], *n.* anulación, *f.*; ruina.
undoubted [ʌn'dautid], *a.* indudable, evidente.
undress [ʌn'dres], *v.t.* desnudar, desvestir.— *v.i.* desnudarse.
undressed [ʌn'drest], *a.* desnudo; no preparado; (*com.*) en bruto.
undue [ʌn'djuː], *a.* excesivo, indebido; injusto.
undying [ʌn'daiiŋ], *a.* inmortal, imperecedero.
unearth [ʌn'ə:θ], *v.t.* desenterrar; (*fig.*) sacar a luz.
unearthly [ʌn'ə:θli], *a.* sobrenatural; misterioso; espantoso.
uneasiness [ʌn'iːzinis], *n.* inquietud, *f.*; malestar, *m.*; incomodidad, *f.*
uneasy [ʌn'iːzi], *a.* inquieto; incómodo; turbado.
uneatable [ʌn'iːtəbl], *a.* incomible.
unemployed [ʌnim'plɔid], *a.* sin trabajo, desocupado.—*n.* desocupado, cesante, *m.*
unemployment [ʌnim'plɔiment], *n.* paro (forzoso), cesantía.
unending [ʌn'endɪŋ], *a.* sin fin, perpetuo.
unequal [ʌn'iːkwəl], *a.* desigual; — *to the task of*, incapaz de.
unequalled [ʌn'iːkwəld], *a.* sin igual, sin par.
unequivocal [ʌni'kwivəkəl], *a.* inequívoco.
unerring [ʌn'ə:rɪŋ], *a.* infalible.
uneven [ʌn'iːvən], *a.* desigual; impar; escabroso.
uneventful [ʌni'ventful], *a.* sin incidentes; tranquilo.
unexampled [ʌnig'zɑːmpld], *a.* sin igual, único.
unexpected [ʌniks'pektid], *a.* imprevisto, inesperado; repentino.
unexpressed [ʌniks'prest], *a.* tácito, sobrentendido; no expresado.
unfading [ʌn'feidɪŋ], *a.* inmarcesible; inmortal.
unfailing [ʌn'feilɪŋ], *a.* inagotable; infalible, seguro.
unfair [ʌn'feə], *a.* injusto; desleal; parcial.
unfaithful [ʌn'feiθful], *a.* infiel; desleal; inexacto.
unfaithfulness [ʌn'feiθfulnis], *n.* infidelidad; deslealtad; inexactitud, *f.*
unfaltering [ʌn'fɔ:ltərɪŋ], *a.* firme.
unfamiliar [ʌnfə'miljə], *a.* poco familiar; desconocido.
unfashionable [ʌn'fæʃnəbl], *a.* fuera de moda.
unfasten [ʌn'fɑːsən], *v.t.* desatar; desabrochar; soltar.

unfathomable [ʌn'fæðəməbl], *a.* insondable, impenetrable.

unfavourable [ʌn'feivərəbl], *a.* desfavorable, adverso.

unfinished [ʌn'finiʃt], *a.* incompleto, inacabado.

unfit [ʌn'fit], *a.* inepto; impropio, inconveniente; indigno; enfermo.

unflagging [ʌn'flægiŋ], *a.* infatigable; persistente.

unflinching [ʌn'flintʃiŋ], *a.* determinado, resuelto.

unfold [ʌn'fould], *v.t.* desplegar; desenvolver.—*v.i.* descubrirse; desarrollarse; abrirse.

unforeseen [ʌnfɔ:'si:n], *a.* imprevisto.

unforgettable [ʌnfə'getəbl], *a.* inolvidable.

unforgivable [ʌnfə'givəbl], *a.* inexcusable.

unfortunate [ʌn'fɔ:tʃənit], *a.*, *n.* desdichado, desgraciado, infeliz, *m.f.*

unfriendly [ʌn'frendli], *a.* hostil; perjudicial; insociable.

unfrock [ʌn'frɔk], *v.t.* exclaustrar.

unfurl [ʌn'fɔ:l], *v.t.* desplegar.

unfurnished [ʌn'fɔ:niʃt], *a.* desamueblado; desprovisto.

ungainly [ʌn'geinli], *a.* desgarbado.

ungentlemanly [ʌn'dʒentlmənli], *a.* de mal tono; indigno de un caballero.

ungodliness [ʌn'gɔdlinis], *n.* impiedad, *f.*

ungodly [ʌn'gɔdli], *a.* impío, irreligioso.

ungracious [ʌn'greiʃəs], *a.* desagradable, ofensivo.

ungrammatical [ʌngrə'mætikəl], *a.* antigramatical, incorrecto.

ungrateful [ʌn'greitful], *a.* ingrato; desagradable.

unguarded [ʌn'gɑ:did], *a.* indefenso; indiscreto; desprevenido.

unhappiness [ʌn'hæpinis], *n.* desgracia, infelicidad, *f.*

unhappy [ʌn'hæpi], *a.* desgraciado, infeliz; malhadado; inoportuno.

unharmed [ʌn'hɑ:md], *a.* ileso; indemne.

unhealthy [ʌn'helθi], *a.* enfermizo; malsano.

unheard [ʌn'hɔ:d], *a.* sin ser oído; desconocido.

unheard of [ʌn'hɔ:dɔv], *a.* inaudito, sin ejemplo.

unhesitating [ʌn'heziteitiŋ], *a.* resuelto; pronto.

unhesitatingly [ʌn'heziteitiŋli], *adv.* sin vacilar, sin reservas.

unhinge [ʌn'hindʒ], *v.t.* desgoznar; (*fig.*) trastornar.

unholy [ʌn'houli], *a.* impío.

unhook [ʌn'huk], *v.t.* descolgar; desenganchar.

unhoped [ʌn'houpt], *a.* — **for**, inesperado.

unhurt [ʌn'hɔ:t], *a.* ileso, incólume, sano y salvo; indemne.

unicorn ['ju:nikɔ:n], *n.* unicornio.

unification [ju:nifi'keiʃən], *n.* unificación, *f.*

uniform ['ju:nifɔ:m], *a.* uniforme; invariable.—*n.* uniforme, *m.*

uniformity [ju:ni'fɔ:miti], *n.* uniformidad, *f.*

unify ['ju:nifai], *v.t.* unificar.

unimaginable [ʌni'mædʒinəbl], *a.* inimaginable.

unimpaired [ʌnim'pɛəd], *a.* no deteriorado; intacto.

unimpeachable [ʌnim'pi:tʃəbl], *a.* irreprensible, intachable.

unimportant [ʌnim'pɔ:tənt], *a.* insignificante, sin importancia.

uninformed [ʌnin'fɔ:md], *a.* ignorante.

uninhabited [ʌnin'hæbitid], *a.* inhabitado, desierto.

uninjured [ʌn'indʒəd], *a.* ileso.

uninspired [ʌnin'spaiəd], *a.* sin inspiración; pedestre.

unintelligible [ʌnin'telidʒibl], *a.* ininteligible.

unintentional [ʌnin'tenʃənl], *a.* involuntario.

uninterested [ʌn'intərestid], *a.* no interesado.

union ['ju:njən], *n.* unión, *f.*; *Union of Soviet Socialist Republics,* Unión (*f.*) de Repúblicas Socialistas Soviéticas.

unique [ju:'ni:k], *a.* único, sin igual.

unison ['ju:nizn], *n.* unisonancia; *in —,* al unísono.

unit ['ju:nit], *n.* unidad, *f.*

Unitarian [ju:ni'teəriən], *a.*, *n.* unitario.

unite [ju:'nait], *v.t.* unir; incorporar; juntar.—*v.i.* unirse; incorporarse; juntarse.

united [ju:'naitid], *a.* unido; *United Arab Republic,* República Árabe Unida; *United Kingdom,* Reino Unido; *United Nations,* Naciones Unidas; *United States,* los Estados Unidos.

unity ['ju:niti], *n.* unidad, *f.*

universal [ju:ni'vɔ:səl], *a.* universal; general; *— joint,* cardán, *m.*

universality [ju:nivə:'sæliti], *n.* universalidad; generalidad, *f.*

universe ['ju:nivə:s], *n.* universo.

university [ju:ni'vɔ:siti], *n.* universidad, *f.*

unjust [ʌn'dʒʌst], *a.* injusto.

unjustifiable [ʌn'dʒʌstifaiəbl], *a.* injustificable.

unkempt [ʌn'kempt], *a.* despeinado; desaseado.

unkind [ʌn'kaind], *a.* poco amable; duro; desfavorable.

unknowingly [ʌn'nouiŋli], *adv.* sin saberlo; involuntariamente.

unknown [ʌn'noun], *a.* desconocido, ignoto.—*n.* (*math.*) incógnita.

unlace [ʌn'leis], *v.t.* desenlazar; desatar.

unladylike [ʌn'leidilaik], *a.* impropio de una señora; de mal tono.

unlawful [ʌn'lɔ:ful], *a.* ilegal.

unless [ʌn'les], *conj.* a menos que, a no ser que; excepto.

unlicensed [ʌn'laisənst], *a.* sin licencia; no autorizado.

unlike [ʌn'laik], *a.* disímil; diferente.—*prep.* a diferencia de, no como.

unlikely [ʌn'laikli], *a.* inverosímil, improbable.

unlimited [ʌn'limitid], *a.* ilimitado, inmenso.

unload [ʌn'loud], *v.t.* descargar; aligerar; deshacerse de.

unlock [ʌn'lɔk], *v.t.* abrir; (*fig.*) descubrir.

unlooked-for [ʌn'luktfɔ:], *a.* inopinado.

unloose [ʌn'lu:s], *v.t.* soltar; desatar.

unlucky [ʌn'lʌki], *a.* desgraciado, infeliz; funesto.

unmanageable [ʌn'mænidʒəbl], *a.* ingobernable, indomable.

unmanly [ʌn'mænli], *a.* afeminado.

unmannerly [ʌn'mænəli], *a.* mal educado.

unmarried [ʌn'mærid], *a.* soltero; célibe.

unmask [ʌn'mɑ:sk], *v.t.* desenmascarar; quitar el velo a, descubrir.
unmindful [ʌn'maindful], *a.* desatento; negligente.
unmistakable [ʌnmis'teikəbl], *a.* inequívoco, evidente.
unmoved [ʌn'mu:vd], *a.* fijo; firme; impasible.
unnatural [ʌn'nætʃərəl], *a.* innatural; desnaturalizado; artificial.
unnecessary [ʌn'nesisəri], *a.* innecesario, superfluo.
unnerve [ʌn'nə:v], *v.t.* acobardar.
unnoticed [ʌn'noutist], *a.* inadvertido, inobservado.
unobserved [ʌnəb'zə:vd], *a.* desapercibido.
unobtainable [ʌnəb'teinəbl], *a.* inasequible.
unobtrusive [ʌnəb'tru:siv], *a.* discreto.
unoccupied [ʌn'ɔkjupaid], *a.* desocupado; libre.
unofficial [ʌnə'fiʃəl], *a.* no oficial.
unorthodox [ʌn'ɔ:θədɔks], *a.* heterodoxo.
unpack [ʌn'pæk], *v.t.* desempaquetar; vaciar. —*v.i.* desempaquetar; deshacer las maletas.
unpalatable [ʌn'pælətəbl], *a.* desagradable.
unparalleled [ʌn'pærəleld], *a.* sin paralelo, sin igual.
unpardonable [ʌn'pɑ:dnəbl], *a.* imperdonable.
unpatriotic [ʌnpætri'ɔtik], *a.* antipatriótico.
unperturbed [ʌnpə'tə:bd], *a.* impasible.
unpleasant [ʌn'pleznt], *a.* desagradable.
unpopular [ʌn'pɔpjulə], *a.* impopular.
unpopularity [ʌnpɔpju'læriti], *n.* impopularidad, *f.*
unpractical [ʌn'præktikəl], *a.* impráctico.
unpractised [ʌn'præktist], *a.* inexperto.
unprecedented [ʌn'presidəntid], *a.* sin precedente.
unprejudiced [ʌn'predʒudist], *a.* imparcial.
unprepared [ʌnpri'pɛəd], *a.* sin preparación, desprevenido.
unpretentious [ʌnpri'tenʃəs], *a.* sin pretensiones, modesto.
unprincipled [ʌn'prinsipld], *a.* sin conciencia, inmoral.
unprofitable [ʌn'prɔfitəbl], *a.* improductivo; inútil.
unprotected [ʌnprə'tektid], *a.* sin protección.
unprovoked [ʌnprə'voukt], *a.* no provocado, sin motivo.
unpublished [ʌn'pʌbliʃt], *a.* inédito.
unpunished [ʌn'pʌniʃt], *a.* impune.
unqualified [ʌn'kwɔlifaid], *a.* incapaz; sin título; absoluto.
unquestionable [ʌn'kwestʃənəbl], *a.* indudable, indiscutible.
unravel [ʌn'rævəl], *v.t.* deshilar; (*fig.*) desembrollar.
unreadable [ʌn'ri:dəbl], *a.* ilegible.
unreal [ʌn'ri:əl], *a.* irreal; ilusorio; falso.
unreasonable [ʌn'ri:znəbl], *a.* irrazonable; extravagante; exorbitante.
unrelated [ʌnri'leitid], *a.* no relacionado; sin parentesco.
unreliable [ʌnri'laiəbl], *a.* indigno de confianza; informal; incierto.
unremitting [ʌnri'mitiŋ], *a.* incesante; incansable.
unrepentant [ʌnri'pentənt], *a.* impenitente.
unrequited [ʌnri'kwaitid], *a.* no correspondido.

unreserved [ʌnri'zə:vd], *a.* no reservado; franco.
unrest [ʌn'rest], *n.* inquietud, *f.*, desasosiego.
unrestrained [ʌnris'treind], *a.* desenfrenado.
unrestricted [ʌnris'triktid], *a.* sin restricción.
unrewarded [ʌnri'wɔ:did], *a.* no recompensado.
unrighteous [ʌn'raitʃəs], *a.* injusto, malo.
unrighteousness [ʌn'raitʃəsnis], *n.* injusticia, maldad, *f.*
unrivalled [ʌn'raivəld], *a.* sin igual.
unroll [ʌn'roul], *v.t.* desarrollar.—*v.i.* desarrollarse.
unruffled [ʌn'rʌfld], *a.* sereno; no arrugado, liso.
unruly [ʌn'ru:li], *a.* indomable, ingobernable.
unsaddle [ʌn'sædl], *v.t.* desensillar.
unsafe [ʌn'seif], *a.* inseguro; peligroso.
unsatisfactory [ʌnsætis'fæktəri], *a.* poco satisfactorio.
unsatisfied [ʌn'sætisfaid], *a.* descontento; no satisfecho; no convencido.
unsavoury [ʌn'seivəri], *a.* insípido; desagradable; (*fig.*) sucio, indeseable.
unscathed [ʌn'skeiðd], *a.* ileso.
unscrew [ʌn'skru:], *v.t.* destornillar.—*v.i.* destornillarse.
unscrupulous [ʌn'skru:pjuləs], *a.* poco escrupuloso.
unseasonable [ʌn'si:znəbl], *a.* fuera de sazón, intempestivo; inoportuno.
unseat [ʌn'si:t], *v.t.* derribar; (*pol.*) echar abajo.
unseemly [ʌn'si:mli], *a.* indecente; indecoroso; impropio.
unseen [ʌn'si:n], *a.* inapercibido; invisible; oculto.
unselfish [ʌn'selfiʃ], *a.* desinteresado; generoso.
unselfishness [ʌn'selfiʃnis], *n.* desinterés, *m.*; generosidad, *f.*
unserviceable [ʌn'sə:visəbl], *a.* inservible, inútil.
unsettle [ʌn'setl], *v.t.* desarreglar; agitar.
unsettled [ʌn'setld], *a.* inconstante; agitado; indeterminado; (*com.*) pendiente.
unshakable [ʌn'ʃeikəbl], *a.* firme; imperturbable.
unshaken [ʌn'ʃeikən], *a.* firme.
unsheathe [ʌn'ʃi:ð], *v.t.* desenvainar.
unshrinkable [ʌn'ʃriŋkəbl], *a.* que no se encoge.
unshrinking [ʌn'ʃriŋkiŋ], *a.* intrépido.
unsightly [ʌn'saitli], *a.* feo.
unskilled [ʌn'skild], *a.* inhábil, inexperto.
unsociable [ʌn'souʃəbl], *a.* insociable, huraño.
unsophisticated [ʌnsə'fistikeitid], *a.* cándido; inexperto.
unsound [ʌn'saund], *a.* podrido; defectuoso; erróneo; enfermo; heterodoxo; *of — mind,* insano.
unsparing [ʌn'spɛəriŋ], *a.* generoso; implacable.
unspeakable [ʌn'spi:kəbl], *a.* indecible; execrable.
unspoilt [ʌn'spɔilt], *a.* intacto; no despojado; ileso; no mimado.
unstable [ʌn'steibl], *a.* inestable; inconstante.
unsteady [ʌn'stedi], *a.* inestable; inconstante; inseguro.

unstudied [ʌn'stʌdid], *a.* no estudiado; natural.
unsuccessful [ʌnsək'sesful], *a.* sin éxito; infructuoso.
unsuitable [ʌn'sju:təbl], *a.* impropio, inconveniente; incongruo.
unsupported [ʌnsə'pɔ:tid], *a.* sin apoyo.
unsurmountable [ʌnsə'mauntəbl], *a.* insuperable.
unsurpassed [ʌnsə'pɑ:st], *a.* sin igual.
unsuspecting [ʌnsəs'pektiŋ], *a.* confiado.
unswerving [ʌn'swə:viŋ], *a.* constante; directo.
unsymmetrical [ʌnsi'metrikl], *a.* asimétrico.
unsympathetic [ʌnsimpə'θetik], *a.* incompasivo; antipático.
unsystematic [ʌnsistə'mætik], *a.* sin sistema.
untainted [ʌn'teintid], *a.* puro, no corrompido.
untamed [ʌn'teimd], *a.* indomado.
untenable [ʌn'tenəbl], *a.* insostenible.
unthinkable [ʌn'θiŋkəbl], *a.* inconcebible.
unthinking [ʌn'θiŋkiŋ], *a.* desatento, inconsiderado; indiscreto.
untidy [ʌn'taidi], *a.* desarreglado; desaseado.
untie [ʌn'tai], *v.t.* desatar, desligar.
until [ʌn'til], *prep.* hasta.—*conj.* hasta que.
untimely [ʌn'taimli], *a.* inoportuno, intempestivo; prematuro.
untiring [ʌn'taiəriŋ], *a.* infatigable.
unto [ʌntu], *prep.* (*obs.*) hacia, a.
untold [ʌn'tould], *a.* no dicho; no narrado; incalculable; **to leave —,** no decir; dejar en el tintero.
untouched [ʌn'tʌtʃt], *a.* intacto.
untrained [ʌn'treind], *a.* inexperto; indisciplinado.
untranslatable [ʌntræns'leitəbl], *a.* intraducible.
untried [ʌn'traid], *a.* no experimentado.
untrodden [ʌn'trɔdn], *a.* no frecuentado; virgen.
untroubled [ʌn'trʌbld], *a.* tranquilo, calmo.
untrue [ʌn'tru:], *a.* falso; engañoso; infiel.
untrustworthy [ʌn'trʌstwə:ði], *a.* indigno de confianza.
untruth [ʌn'tru:θ], *n.* mentira.
untruthful [ʌn'tru:θful], *a.* mentiroso.
unusual [ʌn'ju:ʒuəl], *a.* poco común, inusitado, desacostumbrado.
unutterable [ʌn'ʌtərəbl], *a.* indecible.
unvarying [ʌn'vɛəriiŋ], *a.* invariable, uniforme.
unveil [ʌn'veil], *v.t.* quitar el velo; descubrir.
unversed [ʌn'və:st], *a.* inexperto.
unwarranted [ʌn'wɔrəntid], *a.* injustificable; (*com.*) no garantizado.
unwary [ʌn'wɛəri], *a.* incauto, imprudente.
unwavering [ʌn'weivəriŋ], *a.* resuelto, firme.
unwelcome [ʌn'welkəm], *a.* mal acogido; inoportuno; molesto.
unwell [ʌn'wel], *a.* indispuesto.
unwholesome [ʌn'houlsəm], *a.* insalubre, malsano.
unwilling [ʌn'wiliŋ], *a.* desinclinado, no dispuesto.
unwind [ʌn'waind], *v.t. irr.* (*conjug. like* WIND) desenvolver, desarrollar.—*v.i.* desenvolverse, desarrollarse.
unwise [ʌn'waiz], *a.* imprudente, indiscreto.
unwittingly [ʌn'witiŋli], *adv.* inconscientemente.

unwomanly [ʌn'wumənli], *a.* impropio de una mujer.
unwonted [ʌn'wountid], *a.* inusitado, insólito.
unworthiness [ʌn'wə:ðinis], *n.* indignidad, *f.*
unworthy [ʌn'wə:ði], *a.* indigno.
unwrap [ʌn'ræp], *v.t.* desenvolver.
unwritten [ʌn'ritn], *a.* no escrito.
unyielding [ʌn'ji:ldiŋ], *a.* firme, inflexible.
up [ʌp], *a.* ascendente; **the — train.** el tren ascendente.—*n.pl.* **ups and downs,** vicisitudes, *f.pl.*—*adv.* arriba; hacia arriba; levantado; de pie; (*fam.*) acabado; (*fam.*) enterado; **— and down,** arriba y abajo, por todas partes; **— there,** allá arriba, **to go —, to take —,** subir; **to speak —,** hablar alto; **it's not — to much,** (*fam.*) no vale gran cosa; **it's — to you,** a ti te toca; **to be well — in,** estar al corriente de; **time's —,** es la hora; **what's —?** ¿qué pasa? **hard —,** pobre; **to be — in arms,** sublevarse.—*prep.* en lo alto de; hacia arriba de; a lo largo de; en el interior de; **to catch —,** alcanzar; **— to date,** hasta la fecha; al corriente; de última moda; **— to now,** hasta ahora.
upbraid [ʌp'breid], *v.t.* reprender.
upbringing ['ʌpbriŋiŋ], *n.* crianza.
upheaval [ʌp'hi:vəl], *n.* trastorno.
uphill ['ʌphil], *a.* ascendente; penoso.—[ʌp'hil], *adv.* cuesta arriba.
uphold [ʌp'hould], *v.t. irr.* (*conjug. like* HOLD) apoyar, sostener; defender.
upholster [ʌp'houlstə], *v.t.* tapizar.
upholsterer [ʌp'houlstərə], *n.* tapicero.
upholstery [ʌp'houlstəri], *n.* tapicería.
upkeep ['ʌpki:p], *n.* manutención; conservación, *f.*
uplift ['ʌplift], *n.* elevación, *f.*; (*fam.*) fervor, *m.*—[ʌp'lift], *v.t.* elevar.
upon [ʌ'pɔn], *prep.* [ON].
upper ['ʌpə], *a. compar. of* UP; superior, más alto; **— hand,** (*fig.*) ventaja; **— deck,** (*naut.*) cubierta alta.
upper-cut ['ʌpəkʌt], *n.* golpe (*m.*) de abajo arriba.
uppermost ['ʌpəmoust], *a.* más alto; predominante.
upright ['ʌprait], *a.* derecho; vertical; recto.—*n.* soporte, montante, *m.*
uprightness ['ʌpraitnis], *n.* rectitud, *f.*
uprising [ʌp'raiziŋ], *n.* insurrección, *f.*
uproar ['ʌprɔ:], *n.* alboroto, conmoción, *f.,* estrépito.
uproarious [ʌp'rɔ:riəs], *a.* tumultuoso, estrepitoso.
uproot [ʌp'ru:t], *v.t.* desarraigar; (*fig.*) extirpar.
upset ['ʌpset], *n.* trastorno; vuelco.—[ʌp'set], *v.t. irr.* (*conjug. like* SET) trastornar; desarreglar; contrariar; derribar; volcar; perturbar.—*v.i.* volcarse.
upsetting [ʌp'setiŋ], *a.* perturbante; inquietante.
upshot ['ʌpʃɔt], *n.* resultado.
upside down ['ʌpsaid'daun], *adv.* de arriba abajo, al revés; en desorden, patas arriba.
upstairs [ʌp'stɛəz], *adv.* arriba.
upstanding [ʌp'stændiŋ], *a.* recto, honrado.
upstart ['ʌpstɑ:t], *a., n.* advenedizo.
upstream ['ʌpstri:m], *adv.* agua arriba.
upward(s) ['ʌpwəd(z)], *adv.* hacia arriba.
uranium [juə'reinjəm], *n.* uranio.

407

urban

urban ['ɔːbən], *a.* urbano.
urbane [ɔːˈbein], *a.* urbano, fino.
urchin ['ɔːtʃin], *n.* pilluelo.
urge [ɔːdʒ], *n.* impulso; deseo.—*v.t.* empujar; estimular; pedir con ahinco, recomendar con urgencia.
urgency ['ɔːdʒənsi], *n.* urgencia.
urgent ['ɔːdʒənt], *a.* urgente.
urinate ['juərineit], *v.i.* orinar.
urine ['juərin], *n.* orina.
urn [ɔːn], *n.* urna.
Uruguay [uru'gwai], *n.* el Uruguay.
Uruguayan [uru'gwaiən], *a.,* *n.* uruguayo.
us [ʌs], *pron.* nos; nosotros.
usable ['juːzəbl], *a.* servible.
usage ['juːzidʒ], *n.* uso, costumbre, *f.*; tratamiento.
use [juːs], *n.* uso, empleo; costumbre; necesidad, *f.*; provecho; utilidad, *f.*; *of no* —, inútil; *to make* — *of,* aprovechar; utilizar; *to have no* — *for,* no necesitar; tener en poco; *what is the* — *of it?* ¿ para qué sirve ?—[juːz], *v.t.* usar, emplear, utilizar; acostumbrar; manejar; gastar; tratar; *to* — *up,* agotar; *to be used to, to* — *to,* acostumbrar, soler.
useful ['juːsful], *a.* útil; provechoso.
useless ['juːslis], *a.* inútil; vano.
usher ['ʌʃə], *n.* ujier, (*theat.*) acomodador, *m.*—*v.t.* introducir; anunciar (*in*).
usherette [ʌʃəˈret], *n.* (*theat.*) acomodadora.
usual ['juːʒuəl], *a.* usual, acostumbrado; general; *as* —, como siempre, como de costumbre.
usurer ['juːʒurə], *n.* usurero.
usurious [juːˈʒjuəriəs], *a.* usurario.
usurp [juːˈzɔːp], *v.t.* usurpar; arrogarse.
usurper [juːˈzɔːpə], *n.* usurpador, *m.*
usury ['juːʒuri], *n.* usura.
utensil [juːˈtensl], *n.* utensilio; herramienta.
utilitarian [juːtiliˈtɛəriən], *a.,* *n.* utilitario.
utility [juːˈtiliti], *n.* utilidad, *f.*; ventaja.
utilize ['juːtilaiz], *v.t.* utilizar, servirse de; explotar.
utmost ['ʌtmoust], *a.* extremo; más lejano; mayor.—*n.* todo lo posible.
Utopian [juːˈtoupjən], *a.* utópico.
utter (1) ['ʌtə], *a.* completo; extremo.
utter (2) ['ʌtə], *v.t.* decir, pronunciar; dar.
utterance ['ʌtərəns], *n.* expresión; pronunciación, *f.*
uxorious [ʌkˈsɔːriəs], *a.* uxorio, gurrumino.

V

V, v [viː], *n.* vigésima segunda letra del alfabeto inglés.
vacancy ['veikənsi], *n.* vacío; vacancia; vacuidad, *f.*; laguna.
vacant ['veikənt], *a.* vacío; libre; vacante; distraído.
vacate [vəˈkeit], *v.t.* dejar vacante; (*jur.*) rescindir.
vacation [vəˈkeiʃən], *n.* vacación, *f.*, vacaciones, *f.pl.*

vaccinate ['væksineit], *v.t.* vacunar.
vaccination [væksiˈneiʃən], *n.* vacunación, *f.*
vaccine ['væksiːn], *n.* vacuna.
vacillate ['væsileit], *v.i.* vacilar.
vacillating ['væsileitiŋ], *a.* vacilante.
vacillation [væsiˈleiʃən], *n.* vacilación, *f.*
vacuity [væˈkjuːiti], *n.* vacuidad, *f.*
vacuous ['vækjuəs], *a.* vacío; fatuo.
vacuum ['vækjuəm], *n.* vacío; — *cleaner,* aspiradora (*de polvo*); — *flask,* termos, *m.sg.*; — *pump,* bomba neumática.
vacuum-brake ['vækjuəmbreik], *n.* freno al vacío.
vagabond ['vægəbɔnd], *a.,* *n.* vagabundo.
vagary [vəˈgɛəri], *n.* capricho; divagación, *f.*
vagina [vəˈdʒainə], *n.* vagina.
vagrancy ['veigrənsi], *n.* vagancia.
vagrant ['veigrənt], *a.,* *n.* vagabundo.
vague [veig], *a.* vago.
vagueness ['veignis], *n.* vaguedad, *f.*
vain [vein], *a.* vano; vanidoso; *in* —, en vano, en balde.
vainglorious [veinˈglɔːriəs], *a.* vanaglorioso.
vainglory [veinˈglɔːri], *n.* vanagloria.
vale [veil], *n.* valle, *m.*
valediction [væliˈdikʃən], *n.* despedida; vale, *m.*
valedictory [væliˈdiktəri], *a.* de despedida.
Valencian [vəˈlensjən], *a.,* *n.* valenciano.
valet ['vælit, 'vælei], *n.* criado; sirviente, *m.*
valiant ['væljənt], *a.* valiente, animoso.
valid ['vælid], *a.* válido, valedero; vigente.
validate ['vælideit], *v.t.* validar.
validity [vəˈliditi], *n.* validez, *f.*
valise [vəˈliːz], *n.* maleta, saco de viaje.
valley ['væli], *n.* valle, *m.*
valorous ['vælərəs], *a.* valiente, valeroso.
valour ['vælə], *n.* valor, *m.*, valentía.
valuable ['væljuəbl], *a.* valioso; estimable.—*n.pl.* objetos (*m.pl.*) de valor.
valuation [væljuˈeiʃən], *n.* valuación, tasación; estimación, *f.*
value ['væljuː], *n.* valor, *m.*—*v.t.* valorar, tasar; tener en mucho.
valueless ['væljulis], *a.* sin valor.
valuer ['væljuə], *n.* tasador, *m.*
valve [vælv], *n.* (*mech.*) válvula; (*biol.*) valva.
vamp (1) [væmp], *n.* pala (*de zapato*); remiendo; (*mus.*) acompañamiento improvisado.—*v.t.* poner palas; remendar; (*mus.*) improvisar un acompañamiento.
vamp (2) [væmp], *n.* (*fam.*) sirena, ninfa.—*v.t.* (*fam.*) engatusar.
vampire ['væmpaiə], *n.* vampiro.
van (1) [væn], *n.* vanguardia.
van (2) [væn], *n.* camioneta, furgoneta; *delivery* —, camión (*m.*) de reparto; *removal* —, carro de mudanzas; *mail* —, camión postal; *guard's* —, furgón, *m.*
vandal ['vændəl], *n.* vándalo.
vandalism ['vændəlizm], *n.* vandalismo.
vane [vein], *n.* veleta; aspa; paleta.
vanguard ['vængɑːd], *n.* vanguardia.
vanilla [vəˈnilə], *n.* vainilla.
vanish ['væniʃ], *v.i.* desaparecer; desvanecerse.
vanishing ['væniʃiŋ], *a.*—*cream,* crema (para el cutis).—*n.* desaparición, *f.*; — *point,* punto de fuga.
vanity ['væniti], *n.* vanidad, *f.*
vanquish ['vænkwiʃ], *v.t.* vencer, derrotar.

vantage ['vɑ:ntidʒ], n. ventaja; — *point*, posición ventajosa.
vapid ['væpid], a. insípido, insulso.
vapidity [væ'piditi], n. insipidez, insulsez, f.
vaporization [veipərai'zeiʃən], n. vaporización, f.
vaporize ['veipəraiz], v.t. vaporizar.—v.i. vaporizarse.
vapour ['veipə], n. vapor, m., humo, vaho.
variability [vɛəriə'biliti], n. variabilidad, f.
variable ['vɛəriəbl], a., n. variable, f.
variance ['vɛəriəns], n. variación, f.; desacuerdo; *at* —, en desacuerdo.
variant ['vɛəriənt], a., n. variante, f.
variation [vɛəri'eiʃən], n. variación, f.
varicose ['værikous], a. varicoso; — *vein*, várice, f.
varied ['vɛərid], a. variado.
variegate ['vɛərigeit], v.t. abigarrar, matizar.
variegated ['vɛərigeitid], a. abigarrado; jaspeado.
variegation [vɛəri'geiʃən], n. abigarramiento.
variety [və'raiəti], n. variedad, diversidad, f.
various ['vɛəriəs], a. vario.
varlet ['vɑ:lit], n. (obs.) lacayo; bribón, m.
varnish ['vɑ:niʃ], n. barniz, m.; *nail* —, esmalte (m.) de uñas.—v.t. barnizar; (fig.) disimular.
varnishing ['vɑ:niʃiŋ], n. barnizado; vidriado.
varsity ['vɑ:siti], n. (fam.) universidad, f.
vary ['vɛəri], v.t., v.i. variar.
varying ['vɛəriiŋ], a. variante, diverso.
vase [vɑ:z], n. jarrón, m.; urna.
vassal ['væsəl], a., n. vasallo.
vast [vɑ:st], a. vasto; inmenso.
vastness ['vɑ:stnis], n. inmensidad, f.
vat [væt], n. cuba, tina; *wine* —, lagar, m.
Vatican ['vætikən], a., n. Vaticano.
vaudeville ['voudəvil], n. teatro de variedades.
vault (1) [vɔ:lt], n. bodega (de vino); (arch.) bóveda.—v.t. abovedar.
vault (2) [vɔ:lt], n. salto.—v.t. saltar.—v.i. (sport) saltar con pértiga.
vaunt [vɔ:nt], n. jactancia.—v.t. alardear, hacer gala de.—v.i. jactarse.
veal [vi:l], n. ternera.
veer [viə], v.t., v.i. virar.
vegetable ['vedʒitəbl], a. vegetal.—n. legumbre, f.; *green vegetables*, hortalizas, f.pl.; — *garden*, huerto.
vegetarian [vedʒi'tɛəriən], a., n. vegetariano.
vegetate ['vedʒiteit], v.i. vegetar.
vegetation [vedʒi'teiʃən], n. vegetación, f.
vehemence ['vi:iməns], n. vehemencia; intensidad, f.
vehement ['vi:imənt], a. vehemente; apasionado.
vehicle ['vi:ikl], n. vehículo.
veil [veil], n. velo.—v.t. velar.
vein [vein], n. vena; (geol.) veta; (carp.) hebra; (fig.) rasgo; humor, m.
vellum ['veləm], n. vitela.
velocity [vi'lɔsiti], n. velocidad, rapidez, f.
velvet ['velvit], a. aterciopelado; de terciopelo; (fig.) dulce.—n. terciopelo.
venal ['vi:nəl], a. venal.
venality [vi:'næliti], n. venalidad, f.
vend [vend], v.t. vender.
vendor ['vendə], n. vendedor, m.
veneer [vi'niə], n. chapa; (fig.) apariencia.—v.t. chapear; (fig.) disimular.
veneering [vi'niəriŋ], n. chapeado.

venerable ['venərəbl], a. venerable.
venerate ['venəreit], v.t. venerar.
veneration [venə'reiʃən], n. veneración, f.
venereal [vi'niəriəl], a. venéreo; — *disease*, mal (m.) venéreo.
Venetian [vi'ni:ʃən], a., n. veneciano; — *blind*, persiana.
Venezuelan [vene'zweilən], a., n. venezolano.
vengeance ['vendʒəns], n. venganza.
vengeful ['vendʒful], a. vengativo.
venial ['vi:njəl], a. venial.
veniality [vi:ni'æliti], n. venialidad, f.
venison [venzn], n. venado.
venom ['venəm], n. veneno.
venomous ['venəməs], a. venenoso; malicioso.
vent [vent], n. abertura; respiradero; (fig.) desahogo; expresión, f.—v.t. ventilar; desahogar; dejar escapar; *to* — *one's feelings*, desahogarse.
ventilate ['ventileit], v.t. ventilar; (fig.) discutir.
ventilation [venti'leiʃən], n. ventilación, f.
ventilator ['ventileitə], n. ventilador, m.
ventriloquism [ven'trilәkwizm], n. ventriloquia.
ventriloquist [ven'trilәkwist], n. ventrílocuo.
venture ['ventʃə], n. ventura; riesgo; aventura; especulación, f.—v.t. aventurar, arriesgar; *to* — *an opinion*, expresar una opinión.—v.i. aventurarse, arriesgarse, correr riesgo; *to* — *abroad*, atreverse a salir; *nothing ventured, nothing gained*, quien no se aventura, no ha ventura.
venturesome ['ventʃəsəm], a. aventurero, atrevido; peligroso.
Venus ['vi:nəs], n. Venus, f.
veracious [və'reiʃəs], a. veraz, verídico.
veracity [ve'ræsiti], n. veracidad, f.
verandah [və'rændə], n. veranda.
verb [və:b], n. verbo.
verbal ['və:bəl], a. verbal.
verbatim [və:'beitim], a., adv. palabra por palabra.
verbose [və:'bous], a. verboso, prolijo.
verbosity [və:'bɔsiti], n. verbosidad, f.
verdant ['və:dənt], a. verde, floreciente.
verdict ['və:dikt], n. (jur.) veredicto, fallo.
verdure ['və:djə], n. verdura.
verge [və:dʒ], n. vara; borde, margen, m.; *on the* — *of*, al borde de; (fig.) a punto de.
verger ['və:dʒə], n. sacristán, m.; macero.
verification [verifi'keiʃən], n. verificación, f.
verily ['verili], adv. (obs.) en verdad.
verify ['verifai], v.t. verificar, averiguar.
verisimilitude [verisi'militju:d], n. verosimilitud, f.
veritable ['veritəbl], a. verdadero.
vermilion [və'miljən], a. bermejo.—n. bermellón, m.
vermin ['və:min], n. sabandijas, f.pl.
verminous ['və:minəs], a. verminoso.
vermouth ['və:məθ], n. vermut, m.
vernacular [və'nækjulə], a., n. vernáculo.
vernal [və:nl], a. vernal, primaveral.
versatile ['və:sətail], a. versátil; de muchos talentos; adaptable.
versatility [və:sə'tiliti], n. adaptabilidad, f.; muchos talentos, m.pl.
verse [və:s], n. verso; estrofa; versículo.
versed [və:st], a. versado.
versification [və:sifi'keiʃən], n. versificación, f.

versifier

versifier ['vəːsifaiə], *n.* versificador, *m.*
versify ['vəːsifai], *v.t., v.i.* versificar.
version ['vəːʃən], *n.* versión; traducción, *f.*
versus ['vəːsəs], *prep.* contra.
vertebra ['vəːtibrə], *n.* (*pl.* **-brae** [-bri])
vértebra.
vertebrate ['vəːtibrit], *a.*, *n.* vertebrado.
vertex ['vəːteks], *n.* (*pl.* **-tices** [-tisiːz])
(*geom., anat.*) vértice, *f.*; (*fig.*) cenit, *m.*
vertical ['vəːtikəl], *a.* vertical.
verve [vəːv], *n.* brío.
very ['veri], *a.* mismo; verdadero; perfecto.—
adv. muy; mucho.
vespers ['vespəz], *n. pl.* (*eccl.*) vísperas, *f.pl.*
vessel [vesl], *n.* vasija, recipiente, *m.*; barco;
(*anat.*) vaso.
vest [vest], *n.* camiseta; (*U.S.*) chaleco.—*v.t.*
(*poet.*) vestir; revestir; ceder; **vested
interests**, intereses (*m.pl.*) creados.
vestibule ['vestibjuːl], *n.* vestíbulo; zaguán,
m.
vestige ['vestidʒ], *n.* vestigio.
vestment ['vestmənt], *n.* hábito.—*pl.* (*eccl.*)
vestimentas, *f.pl.*
vestry ['vestri], *n.* sacristía; vestuario.
vet [vet]. *n.* (*fam.*) veterinario.—*v.t.* (*fam.
Brit.*) escudriñar.
veteran ['vetərən], *a.*, *n.* veterano.
veterinary ['vetərinəri], *a.* veterinario;
— **science,** veterinaria; — **surgeon,**
veterinario.
veto ['viːtou], *n.* veto.—*v.t.* poner el veto;
vedar.
vex [veks], *v.t.* irritar; enfadar.
vexation [vek'seiʃən], *n.* irritación, *f.*;
enfado.
vexatious [vek'seiʃəs], *a.* irritante; enfadoso.
vexing ['veksiŋ], *a.* irritante; enfadoso.
V.H.F. [viːeitʃ'ef], (*abbrev.*) **very high frequency,** ondas (*f.pl.*) ultracortas.
via ['vaiə], *prep.* por, vía.
viability [vaiə'biliti], *n.* viabilidad, *f.*
viable ['vaiəbl], *a.* viable.
viaduct ['vaiədʌkt], *n.* viaducto.
vial ['vaiəl], *n.* frasco, ampolleta.
viaticum [vai'ætikəm], *n.* viático.
vibrant ['vaibrənt], *a.* vibrante.
vibrate [vai'breit], *v.t., v.i.* vibrar.
vibration [vai'breiʃən], *n.* vibración, *f.*
vicar ['vikə], *n.* cura anglicano; vicario.
vicarage ['vikəridʒ], *n.* vicaría.
vicarious [vai'kɛəriəs], *a.* vicario; experimentado *o* padecido por otro.
vice (1) [vais], *n.* vicio; defecto.
vice (2) [vais], *n.* tornillo de banco.
vice (3) [vais], *prefix.* vice.
vice-admiral ['vais'ædmərəl], *n.* vice-
almirante, *m.*
vice-president ['vais'prezidənt], *n.* vice-
presidente, *m.*
viceroy ['vaisroi], *n.* virrey, *m.*
viceroyalty [vais'roiəlti], *n.* virreinato.
vice versa ['vaisi'vəːsə], *adv.* viceversa.
vicinity [vi'siniti], *n.* vecindad; proximidad, *f.*
vicious ['viʃəs], *a.* vicioso.
viciousness ['viʃəsnis], *n.* viciosidad; depravación, *f.*
vicissitude [vi'sisitjuːd], *n.* vicisitud, *f.*
victim ['viktim], *n.* víctima.
victimization [viktimai'zeiʃən], *n.* tiraniza-
ción, *f.*

victimize ['viktimaiz], *v.t.* hacer víctima;
sacrificar; tiranizar.
victor ['viktə], *n.* víctor, vencedor, *m.*
Victorian [vik'toːriən], *a.*, *n.* victoriano.
victorious [vik'toːriəs], *a.* victorioso, vencedor.
victory ['viktəri], *n.* victoria.
victuals ['vitəlz], *n.pl.* vituallas, *f.pl.*, víveres,
m.pl.
videlicet [VIZ.].
vie [vai], *v.i.* competir, rivalizar.
Vienna [vi'enə], *n.* Viena.
Viennese [viə'niːz], *a.*, *n.* vienés, *m.*
Vietnamese [vjetnæ'miːz], *a.*, *n.* vietnamés,
vietnamita, *m.*
view [vjuː], *n.* vista; panorama, *m.*; inspección,
f.; parecer, *m.*, opinión, *f.*; apariencia;
intención, *f.*; **with a — to,** con motivo
de; **in — of,** en vista de; **in the — of,** en
la opinión de—*v.t.* examinar; inspeccionar;
mirar; considerar.
viewer ['vjuːə], *n.* espectador; inspector, *m.*;
televidente, *m.f.*
view-finder ['vjuːfaində], *n.* enfocador, *m.*
vigil ['vidʒil], *n.* vigilia; vela; **to keep —
over,** vigilar; velar.
vigilance ['vidʒiləns], *n.* vigilancia.
vigilant ['vidʒilənt], *a.* vigilante; despierto.
vignette [vi'njet], *n.* viñeta.
vigorous ['vigərəs], *a.* vigoroso, enérgico.
vigour ['vigə], *n.* vigor, *m.*
Viking ['vaikiŋ], *a.*, *n.* vikingo.
vile [vail], *a.* vil; infame.
vileness ['vailnis], *n.* vileza; bajeza; infamia.
vilification [vilifi'keiʃən], *n.* difamación, *f.*,
vilipendio.
vilify ['vilifai], *v.t.* difamar, vilipendiar.
villa ['vilə], *n.* villa, casa de campo.
village ['vilidʒ], *n.* aldea, pueblecito.
villager ['vilidʒə], *n.* aldeano, lugareño.
villain ['vilən], *n.* malvado.
villainous ['vilənəs], *a.* infame; malvado.
villainy ['viləni], *n.* infamia; maldad, *f.*
villein ['vilən], *n.* (*hist.*) villano.
vim [vim], *n.* (*fam.*) energía.
vindicate ['vindikeit], *v.t.* vindicar.
vindication [vindi'keiʃən], *n.* vindicación, *f.*
vindictive [vin'diktiv], *a.* vengativo; rencoroso.
vindictiveness [vin'diktivnis], *n.* deseo de
venganza; rencor, *m.*
vine [vain], *n.* vid, *f.*, parra; enredadera.
vinegar ['vinigə], *n.* vinagre, *m.*
vinegary ['vinigəri], *a.* vinagroso.
vineyard ['vinjəd], *n.* viña, viñedo.
vinous ['vainəs], *a.* vinoso.
vintage ['vintidʒ], *a.* añejo; antiguo, **veterano.**
—*n.* vendimia.
vintner ['vintnə], *n.* vinatero.
viola (1) [vi'oulə], *n.* (*mus.*) viola.
viola (2) ['vaiolə], *n.* (*bot.*) viola.
violate ['vaiəleit], *v.t.* violar.
violation [vaiə'leiʃən], *n.* violación.
violence ['vaiələns], *n.* violencia.
violent ['vaiələnt], *a.* violento.
violet ['vaiəlit], *a.* violado.—*n.* (*bot.*) **violeta.**
violin [vaiə'lin], *n.* violín, *m.*
violinist [vaiə'linist], *n.* violinista, *m.f.*
violoncello [vaiələn'tʃelou], *n.* violoncelo.
viper ['vaipə], *n.* víbora.
viperish ['vaipəriʃ], *a.* viperino.
Virgil ['vəːdʒil], *n.* Virgilio.

vulgarism

Virgilian [vəˈdʒiljən], *a.* virgiliano.
virgin [ˈvəːdʒin], *a.*, *n.* virgen, *f.*
virginal [ˈvəːdʒinl], *a.* virginal.—*n.pl.* (*mus.*) espineta.
virginity [vəːˈdʒiniti], *n.* virginidad, *f.*
virile [ˈvirail], *a.* viril, varonil.
virility [viˈriliti], *n.* virilidad, *f.*
virtual [ˈvəːtjuəl], *a.* virtual.
virtue [ˈvəːtjuː], *n.* virtud, *f.*; excelencia; **by — of,** en virtud de.
virtuosity [vəːtjuˈɔsiti], *n.* virtuosidad, *f.*
virtuoso [vəːtjuˈouzou], *n.* virtuoso.
virtuous [ˈvəːtjuəs], *a.* virtuoso.
virulence [ˈviruləns], *n.* virulencia.
virulent [ˈvirulənt], *a.* virulento.
virus [ˈvairəs], *n.* virus, *m.*
visa [ˈviːzə], *n.* visado.
visage [ˈvizidʒ], *n.* semblante, *m.*
viscount [ˈvaikaunt], *n.* vizconde, *m.*
viscountess [ˈvaikauntis], *n.* vizcondesa.
viscous [ˈviskəs], *a.* viscoso.
visibility [viziˈbiliti], *n.* visibilidad, *f.*
visible [ˈvizibl], *a.* visible.
Visigoth [ˈvizigɔθ], *a.*, *n.* visigodo.
vision [ˈviʒən], *n.* visión, *f.*
visionary [ˈviʒənəri], *a.*, *n.* visionario.
visit [ˈvizit], *n.* visita.—*v.t.* visitar, hacer una visita a.—*v.i.* **to go visiting,** ir de visita.
visitation [viziˈteiʃən], *n.* visitación, *f.*
visiting [ˈvizitiŋ], *a.* de visita.—*n.* **— card,** tarjeta de visita.
visitor [ˈvizitə], *n.* visita; visitador, *m.*
visor [ˈvaizə], *n.* visera (*de casco*).
vista [ˈvistə], *n.* vista, perspectiva.
visual [ˈviʒjuəl], *a.* visual.
visualize [ˈviʒjuəlaiz], *v.t.* imaginar.
vital [vaitl], *a.* vital; escencial.—*n.pl.* partes vitales, *f.pl.*; (*fig.*) entrañas, *f.pl.*
vitality [vaiˈtæliti], *n.* vitalidad, *f.*
vitalize [ˈvaitəlaiz], *v.t.* vivificar, vitalizar.
vitamin [ˈvitəmin], *n.* vitamina.
vitiate [ˈviʃieit], *v.t.* viciar; infectar; invalidar.
vitreous [ˈvitriəs], *a.* vítreo, vidrioso.
vitriol [ˈvitriəl], *n.* vitriolo.
vitriolic [vitriˈɔlik], *a.* vitriólico.
vituperate [viˈtjuːpəreit], *v.t.* vituperar.
vituperation [vitjuːpəˈreiʃən], *n.* vituperio.
vivacious [viˈveiʃəs], *a.* animado, vivaracho.
vivacity [viˈvæsiti], *n.* vivacidad, *f.*, viveza.
viva voce [ˈvaivəˈvousi], *a.* oral.—*n.* examen (*m.*) oral.—*adv.* de viva voz.
vivid [ˈvivid], *a.* brillante; intenso; vivaz; gráfico.
vividness [ˈvividnis], *n.* brillantez; intensidad; vivacidad, *f.*
vivify [ˈvivifai], *v.t.* vivificar.
vivisection [viviˈsekʃən], *n.* vivisección, *f.*
vixen [ˈviksən], *n.* zorra; (*fig.*) arpía.
viz. [viz], *adv.* (*abbrev. of* **videlicet** [viˈdeliset]) a saber.
vizier [viˈziə], *n.* visir, *m.*
vocabulary [vouˈkæbjuləri], *n.* vocabulario.
vocal [ˈvoukəl], *a.*, *n.* vocal, *f.*
vocalist [ˈvoukəlist], *n.* cantante, *m.f.*
vocalization [voukəlaiˈzeiʃən], *n.* vocalización, *f.*
vocalize [ˈvoukəlaiz], *v.t.* vocalizar.
vocation [vouˈkeiʃən], *n.* vocación, *f.*
vocational [vouˈkeiʃənəl], *a.* profesional; práctico.
vocative [ˈvokətiv], *a.* *n.* (*gram.*) vocativo.
vociferate [voˈsifəreit], *v.t.*, *v.i.* vociferar.

vociferation [vosifəˈreiʃən], *n.* vociferación, *f.*
vociferous [voˈsifərəs], *a.* vocinglero, clamoroso.
vodka [ˈvodkə], *n.* vodca, *m.*
vogue [voug], *n.* boga, moda; **in —,** en boga, de moda.
voice [vois], *n.* voz, *f.*; **in a loud —,** en voz alta; **in a low —,** en voz baja.—*v.t.* proclamar; expresar; sonorizar.
void [void], *a.* vacío; (*jur.*) nulo, inválido.—*n.* vacío.—*v.t.* invalidar, anular.
volatile [ˈvɔlətail], *a.* volátil; voluble.
volatilize [vɔˈlætilaiz], *v.t.* volatilizar.—*v.i.* volatilizarse.
volcanic [vɔlˈkænik], *a.* volcánico.
volcano [vɔlˈkeinou], *n.* volcán, *m.*
vole [voul], *n.* ratón (*m.*) campestre; campañol, *m.*
volition [voˈliʃən], *n.* volición; voluntad, *f.*
volley [ˈvɔli], *n.* descarga, andanada; salva; (*sport*) voleo.
volt [voult], *n.* (*elec.*) voltio.
voltage [ˈvoultidʒ], *n.* voltaje, *m.*
volubility [vɔljuˈbiliti], *n.* volubilidad, locuacidad, *f.*
voluble [ˈvɔljubl], *a.* gárrulo, locuaz.
volume [ˈvɔljuːm], *n.* tomo; volumen, *m.*
voluminous [vəˈljuːminəs], *a.* voluminoso.
voluntary [ˈvɔləntəri], *a.* voluntario.
volunteer [vɔlənˈtiə], *a.*, *n.* (*mil.*) voluntario.—*v.t.* ofrecer; expresar.—*v.i.* ofrecerse; (*mil.*) alistarse.
voluptuary [vəˈlʌptjuəri], *a.*, *n.* voluptuoso.
voluptuous [vəˈlʌptjuəs], *a.* voluptuoso.
voluptuousness [vəˈlʌptjuəsnis], *n.* voluptuosidad, *f.*
vomit [ˈvomit], *n.* vómito.—*v.t.*, *v.i.* vomitar.
vomiting [ˈvomitiŋ], *n.* vómito.
voodoo [ˈvuːduː], *n.* vodú, *m.*
voracious [voˈreiʃəs], *a.* voraz.
voracity [voˈræsiti], *n.* voracidad, *f.*
vortex [ˈvoːteks], *n.* vórtice, *m.*
votary [ˈvoutəri], *n.* devoto; partidario.
vote [vout], *n.* voto; votación, *f.*; **— of confidence,** voto de confianza; **— of thanks,** voto de gracias; **to put to the —,** poner a votación.—*v.t.*, *v.i.* votar.
voter [ˈvoutə], *n.* votante, *m.f.*; elector, *m.*
voting [ˈvoutiŋ], *n.* votación, *f.*; **— paper,** papeleta de votación.
votive [ˈvoutiv], *a.* votivo; **— offering,** exvoto.
vouch [vautʃ], *v.i.* afirmar; garantizar; responder (*for,* de, por).
voucher [ˈvautʃə], *n.* fiador, comprobante, *m.*; abono; recibo.
vouchsafe [vautʃˈseif], *v.t.* otorgar, conceder.
vow [vau], *n.* voto; promesa solemne; **to take a —,** hacer un voto.—*v.t.* votar, jurar, hacer voto de.
vowel [ˈvauəl], *n.* vocal, *f.*
voyage [ˈvoiidʒ], *n.* viaje, *m.*, travesía.—*v.i.* viajar por mar.
voyager [ˈvoiədʒə], *n.* viajero (por mar).
Vulcan [ˈvʌlkən], *n.* Vulcano.
vulcanize [ˈvʌlkənaiz], *v.t.* vulcanizar.
vulgar [ˈvʌlgə], *a.* vulgar; grosero, de mal gusto; **— fraction,** fracción común, *f.*
vulgarism [ˈvʌlgərizm], *n.* vulgarismo; vulgaridad, *f.*

vulgarity [vʌl'gæriti], *n.* vulgaridad, *f.*; grosería.
vulgarize ['vʌlgəraiz], *v.t.* vulgarizar.
Vulgate ['vʌlgit], *n.* Vulgata.
vulnerability [vʌlnərə'biliti], *n.* vulnerabilidad, *f.*
vulnerable ['vʌlnərəbl], *a.* vulnerable.
vulture ['vʌltʃə], *n.* buitre, *m.*

W

W, w ['dʌblju:], *n.* vigésima tercera letra del alfabeto inglés.
wad [wɔd], *n.* taco; fajo; atado.
wadding ['wɔdiŋ], *n.* borra; relleno; algodón, *m.*
waddle ['wɔdl], *n.* anadeo.—*v.i.* anadear.
wade [weid], *v.t.*, *v.i.* vadear; andar en el agua; **to — in,** (*fig.*) meterse en; (*fig.*) **to — through,** leer con dificultad.
wader ['weidə], *n.* ave zancuda.—*pl.* botas (*f.pl.*) de vadear.
wafer ['weifə], *n.* (*eccl.*) hostia; oblea; barquillo.
waffle [wɔfl], *n.* fruta de sartén; (*fig.*) palabrería.
waft [wɔft], *n.* ráfaga.—*v.t.* llevar por el aire; hacer flotar.
wag (1) [wæg], *n.* coleada; meneo.—*v.t.* menear.—*v.i.* menearse.
wag (2) [wæg], *n.* bromista, *m.f.*
wage [weidʒ], *n.* jornal, *m.*, salario, sueldo. —*v.t.* hacer; emprender; **to — war,** hacer guerra.
wage-earner ['weidʒə:nə], *n.* jornalero, asalariado.
wager ['weidʒə], *n.* apuesta; **to lay a —,** hacer una apuesta.—*v.t.*, *v.i.* apostar.
waggish ['wægiʃ], *a.* zumbón, guaso.
waggishness ['wægiʃnis], *n.* guasa.
waggle [wægl], *n.* meneo.—*v.t.* menear.—*v.i.* menearse.
waggon ['wægən], *n.* carro; (*rail.*) vagón, *m.*; **on the —,** (*fam.*) sin beber nada alcohólico.
waggoner ['wægənə], *n.* carretero.
wagtail ['wægteil], *n.* aguzanieves, *f.sg.*
waif [weif], *n.* expósito; animal abandonado.
wail [weil], *n.* gemido, lamento.—*v.t.* lamentar.—*v.i.* lamentarse, gemir.
wainscot ['weinskət], *n.* friso de madera.
waist [weist], *n.* cintura; corpiño; (*naut.*) combés, *m.*
waist-band ['weistbænd], *n.* pretina.
waistcoat ['weiskəut], *n.* chaleco.
waist-deep ['weist'di:p], *a.* hasta la cintura.
waist-line ['weistlain], *n.* cintura.
wait [weit], *n.* espera; pausa; tardanza; **to lie in —,** acechar (*for*).—*v.t.*, *v.i.* esperar, aguardar; servir; **to — for,** esperar a; **to keep waiting,** hacer esperar; **to — at table,** servir a la mesa.
waiter ['weitə], *n.* camarero, mozo.
waiting ['weitiŋ], *a.* que espera; de servicio. —*n.* espera; **— room,** sala de espera; antesala.

waitress ['weitris], *n.* camarera, criada.
waive [weiv], *v.t.* renunciar, abandonar.
wake (1) [weik], *n.* vigilia; velatorio.—*v.t.* irr. despertar.—*v.i.* irr. despertar(se).
wake (2) [weik], *n.* (*naut.*) estela; **in the — of,** en la estela de, después de.
wakeful ['weikful], *a.* despierto; vigilante.
waken ['weikən], *v.t.*, *v.i.* despertar.
Wales [weilz], *n.* País de Gales, *m.*
walk [wɔ:k], *n.* paseo; modo de andar; avenida; paso; profesión, *f.*, carrera; **to go for a —,** dar un paseo.—*v.t.* hacer andar; sacar a paseo; recorrer; llevar al paseo; **to — the streets,** callejear.—*v.i.* andar, ir a pie, caminar; pasear(se), dar un paseo; **to — away,** marcharse; **to — back,** volver a pie; **to — down,** bajar a pie; **to — in,** entrar; **to — out,** salir; salir en huelga; **to — up,** subir a pie; **to — up and down,** ir y venir.
walking ['wɔ:kiŋ], *n.* andar, pasear, *m.*; paseo; **— pace,** paso de andadura; **— tour,** excursión (*f.*) a pie.
walking-stick ['wɔ:kiŋstik], *n.* bastón, *m.*
walk-out ['wɔ:kaut], *n.* huelga.
walk-over ['wɔ:kouvə], *n.* triunfo fácil.
wall [wɔ:l], *n.* muro; pared, *f.*; muralla; **garden —,** tapia; **partition —,** tabique, *m.*; **— socket,** (*elec.*) enchufe, *m.*; **walls have ears,** las paredes oyen.—*v.t.* cercar con un muro; amurallar; **to — in,** murar; **to — up,** tapiar.
wallet ['wɔlit], *n.* cartera; bolsa de cuero.
wallflower ['wɔ:lflauə], *n.* alhelí, *m.*
wallop ['wɔləp], *n.* (*fam.*) golpe, *m.*, zurra; —*v.t.* (*fam.*) zurrar.
wallow ['wɔlou], *n.* revuelco.—*v.i.* revolcarse; (*fig.*) nadar.
wallpaper ['wɔ:lpeipə], *n.* papel pintado.
walnut ['wɔ:lnʌt], *n.* nogal (*árbol*), *m.*; nuez (*fruta*), *f.*
walrus ['wɔ:lrəs], *n.* morsa.
waltz [wɔ:l(t)s], *n.* vals, *m.*—*v.i.* valsar.
wan [wɔn], *a.* pálido, descolorido, macilento.
wand [wɔnd], *n.* vara; varita.
wander ['wɔndə], *v.i.* vagar, errar; extraviarse.
wanderer ['wɔndərə], *n.* vagabundo, vagamundo.
wandering ['wɔndəriŋ], *a.* errante; nómada; delirante.—*n.* vagar, errar, *m.*; divagación, *f.*; delirio.
wane [wein], *n.* diminución, decadencia; menguante, *f.*—*v.i.* disminuir; decaer; menguar.
want [wɔnt], *n.* necesidad, falta; escasez, *f.*; deseo; **for — of,** por falta de.—*v.t.* carecer de; necesitar; desear; pasarse sin; **you are wanted,** preguntan por Vd.—*v.i.* hacer falta; estar necesitado.
wanting ['wɔntiŋ], *a.* deficiente; ausente; escaso; **to be —,** faltar.—*prep.* sin.
wanton ['wɔntən], *a.* disoluto, lascivo, travieso.—*n.* libertino; prostituta.
war [wɔ:], *n.* guerra; **cold —,** guerra fría o tonta; **— cry,** alarido de guerra; **— dance,** danza guerrera; **— memorial,** monumento a los caídos; **War Minister,** Ministro de la Guerra; **War Office,** Ministerio de la Guerra; **to declare —,** declarar la guerra; **to be at —,** estar en guerra.—*v.i.* guerrear, hacer la guerra.
warble ['wɔ:bl], *n.* gorjeo; trino.—*v.t.*, *v.i.* gorjear; trinar.

ward [wɔ:d], *n.* pupilo; pupilaje, *m.*; distrito electoral; crujía, sala de hospital; guarda (*llave*).—*v.t.* proteger; parar; *to — off,* desviar, evitar.

warden [wɔ:dn], *n.* guardián, *m.*; alcaide, *m.*; director, *m.*

warder ['wɔ:də], *n.* guardián, *m.*; carcelero.

wardrobe ['wɔ:droub], *n.* guardarropa, *m.*; ropa; (*theat.*) vestuario.

ware [wɛə], *n.* mercadería; loza. — *pl.* mercancías, *f.pl.*

warehouse ['wɛəhaus], *n.* almacén, *m.*

warehouseman ['wɛəhausmən], *n.* almacenero.

warfare ['wɔ:fɛə], *n.* guerra.

wariness ['wɛərinis], *n.* prudencia, cautela.

warlike ['wɔ:laik], *a.* guerrero, belicoso.

warm [wɔ:m], *a.* caliente; caluroso; tibio; ardiente; furioso; (*fam.*) fresco; *to be —,* tener calor; hacer calor; estar caliente. —*v.t.* calentar; (*fig.*) entusiasmar.—*v.i.* calentarse; (*fig.*) entusiasmarse.

warm-blooded ['wɔ:m'blʌdid], *a.* de sangre caliente; apasionado.

warm-hearted ['wɔ:m'hɑ:tid], *a.* generoso, bondadoso.

warming-pan ['wɔ:miŋpæn], *n.* calentador, *m.*

warmth [wɔ:mθ], *n.* calor, *m.*; ardor, *m.*; cordialidad, *f.*

warn [wɔ:n], *v.t.* advertir; amonestar; avisar.

warning ['wɔ:niŋ], *n.* advertencia; amonestación, *f.*; aviso.

warp [wɔ:p], *n.* urdimbre, *f.*; torcimiento.— *v.t.* torcer; pervertir.—*v.i.* torcerse; desviarse.

warped [wɔ:pt], *a.* combo; desequilibrado.

warrant ['wɔrənt], *n.* autorización, *f.*; garantía; decreto; (*com.*) orden (*f.*) de pago; razón, *f.*—*v.t.* autorizar; garantir; asegurar; justificar.

warrantable ['wɔrəntəbl], *a.* justificable.

warrantor ['wɔrəntɔ:], *n.* garante, *m.f.*

warranty ['wɔrənti], *n.* garantía; autorización, *f.*

warren ['wɔrən], *n.* conejera; vivar, *m.*, madriguera.

warrior ['wɔriə], *n.* guerrero; soldado.

wart [wɔ:t], *n.* verruga.

wary ['wɛəri], *a.* cauto, cauteloso (*of,* con).

was [wɔz] [BE].

wash [wɔʃ], *n.* lavado; ropa lavada; ropa sucia; ablución; loción, *f.*; (*naut.*) estela; (*art*) aguada.—*v.t.* lavar; bañar; (*art*) dar una capa de color a; *to — away,* quitar lavando; (*fam.*) anular.—*v.i.* lavarse; lavar ropa; *to — up,* fregar la vajilla.

wash-basin ['wɔʃbeisn], *n.* lavabo.

washer ['wɔʃə], *n.* lavador, *m.*; lavadora (*máquina*); (*mech.*) arandela.

washerwoman ['wɔʃəwumən], *n.* lavandera.

washing ['wɔʃiŋ], *n.* lavado; colada; ropa sucia.

washing-machine ['wɔʃiŋməʃi:n], *n.* lavadora.

washing-up ['wɔʃiŋ'ʌp], *n.* fregado de vajilla.

wash-leather ['wɔʃleðə], *n.* gamuza.

wash-out ['wɔʃaut], *n.* (*fam.*) fracaso.

wash-tub ['wɔʃtʌb], *n.* cuba de lavar.

wasp [wɔsp], *n.* avispa.

waspish ['wɔspiʃ], *a.* enojadizo, enconoso; mordaz.

wastage ['weistidʒ], *n.* pérdida, desgaste, *m.*

waste [weist], *a.* desierto; inútil; devastado; superfluo; — *land,* yermo; — *paper,* papel (*m.*) de desecho.—*n.* desperdicio; despilfarro; desierto; desechos, *m.pl.*; pérdida; inmensidad, devastación, *f.*—*v.t.* gastar; desperdiciar; malgastar; devastar; *to — time,* perder el tiempo.—*v.i.* gastarse, consumirse; *to — away,* demacrarse.

watch-chain ['wɔtʃtʃein], *n.* cadena de reloj.

watch-dog ['wɔtʃdɔg], *n.* perro guardián.

wasteful ['weistful], *a.* pródigo, manirroto; ruinoso.

wastefulness ['weistfulnis], *n.* prodigalidad, *f.*, gasto inútil; pérdida.

waste-paper basket ['weist'peipəbɑ:skit], *n.* cesto para papeles.

watch [wɔtʃ], *n.* vigilancia; vela; guardia; centinela; sereno; ronda; reloj, *m.*; *to be on the —,* estar de acecho, estar de guardia. —*v.t.* mirar; acechar; *to — over,* vigilar.— *v.i.* velar; hacer guardia.

watchful ['wɔtʃful], *a.* vigilante; atento.

watchfulness ['wɔtʃfulnis], *n.* vigilancia; desvelo.

watch-glass ['wɔtʃglɑ:s], *n.* cristal (*m.*) de reloj.

watch-maker ['wɔtʃmeikə], *n.* relojero.

watchman ['wɔtʃmən], *n.* vigilante, *m.*, sereno; guardián, *m.*

water ['wɔ:tə], *n.* agua; *fresh —,* agua dulce; *high —,* marea alta; *holy —,* agua bendita; *low —,* marea baja; *running —,* agua corriente; *salt —,* agua salada; *— level,* nivel (*m.*) de agua; — *main,* cañería maestra;— *man,* barquero;— *supply,* traída de aguas; — *tank,* aljibe, *m.*; — *tap,* grifo; — *wheel,* rueda hidráulica; — *wings,* nadaderas, *f.pl.*; *to make —,* orinar.—*v.t.* regar; dar de beber; aguar.—*v.i.* tomar agua; hacerse agua; *his mouth is watering,* se le hace agua la boca; *his eyes are watering,* le lloran los ojos.

water-bottle ['wɔ:təbɔtl], *n.* cantimplora.

water-carrier ['wɔ:təkæriə], *n.* aguador, *m.*

water-cart ['wɔ:təkɑ:t], *n.* carro de regar.

water-closet ['wɔ:təklɔzit], *n.* (*abbrev.* **W.C.**) retrete, *m.*

water-colour ['wɔ:təkʌlə], *n.* acuarela.

watercress ['wɔ:təkres], *n.* berro, berros, *m.pl.*

watered ['wɔ:təd], *a.* regado; — *silk,* seda tornasolada.

waterfall ['wɔ:təfɔ:l], *n.* cascada.

watering ['wɔ:təriŋ], *n.* irrigación, *f.*, riego; lagrimeo (*de los ojos*); — *can,* regadera; — *place,* balneario.

water-lily ['wɔ:təlili], *n.* nenúfar, *m.*

waterlogged ['wɔ:təlɔgd], *a.* anegado en agua.

watermark ['wɔ:təmɑ:k], *n.* filigrana (*en el papel*); nivel (*m.*) de las aguas.

water-melon ['wɔ:təmelən], *n.* sandía.

water-mill ['wɔ:təmil], *n.* aceña.

water-polo ['wɔ:təpoulou], *n.* polo acuático.

water-power ['wɔ:təpauə], *n.* fuerza hidráulica.

waterproof ['wɔ:təpru:f], *a.*, *n.* impermeable, *m.*—*v.t.* hacer impermeable.

waterspout ['wɔ:təspaut], *n.* tromba marina, manga; canalón, *m.*

watertight ['wɔːtətait], *a.* impermeable; (*fig.*) irrefutable.
waterworks ['wɔːtəwəːks], *n.pl.* obras hidráulicas, *f.pl.*; establecimiento de abastecimiento de agua; (*fam.*) lloro.
watery ['wɔːtəri], *a.* acuoso; húmedo; lloroso; insípido.
watt [wɔt], *n.* (*elec.*) vatio.
wattage ['wɔtidʒ], *n.* vatiaje, *m.*
wattle [wɔtl], *n.* zarzo; barba.
wave [weiv], *n.* ola; onda; ondulación, *f.*; movimiento de la mano; **sound** —, onda sonora; **short** —, onda corta; **long** —, onda larga.—*v.t.* ondear; ondular; blandir, agitar. —*v.i.* ondear; ondular; hacer señales; flotar.
wave-band ['weivbænd], *n.* banda de frecuencias.
wave-length ['weivleŋθ], *n.* longitud (*f.*) de onda.
waver ['weivə], *v.i.* oscilar; vacilar.
wavering ['weivəriŋ], *a.* irresoluto, vacilante. —*n.* irresolución, vacilación, *f.*
wavy ['weivi], *a.* ondulado; sinuoso.
wax [wæks], *n.* cera; — **paper**, papel (*m.*) encerado; — **taper**, blandón, *m.*—*v.t.* encerar.—*v.i.* crecer; ponerse.
waxen ['wæksən], *a.* de cera; color de cera.
waxwork ['wækswɔːk], *n.* figura de cera.
way [wei], *n.* camino, senda; vía; dirección, *f.*, rumbo; viaje, *m.*; método, modo; manera; costumbre, *f.*; — **in**, entrada; — **out**, salida; **by** — **of**, pasando por; a manera de; **that** —, por ahí; **this** —, por aquí; **which** —? ¿por dónde? **by the** —, a propósito; **right of** —, derecho de paso; **to be in the** —, estorbar; **on the** — **to**, con rumbo a; **out of the** —, fuera del camino; (*fig.*) extraordinario; **to get out of the** —, quitarse de en medio; **to get under** —, (*naut.*) hacerse a la vela; **to go out of one's** — **to**, hacer todo lo posible para; **to give** —, ceder; romper; **to get one's own** —, salir con la suya; **to lead the** —, ir delante; **to lose the** —, extraviarse; **a long** — **off**, a lo lejos; **a short** — **off**, no muy lejos.
wayfarer ['weifɛərə], *n.* viandante, *m.f.*
waylay [wei'lei], *v.t.* asechar.
wayside ['weisaid], *n.* borde (*m.*) del camino.
wayward ['weiwəd], *a.* travieso; díscolo; caprichoso.
waywardness ['weiwədnis], *n.* travesura; desobediencia.
we [wiː], *pron.* nosotros, *m.pl.*; nosotras, *f.pl.*
weak [wiːk], *a.* débil; flojo; delicado; inseguro; poco convincente; — **spot**, lado débil; punto débil.
weaken ['wiːkən], *v.t.* debilitar; disminuir.— *v.i.* debilitarse.
weakling ['wiːkliŋ], *a., n.* canijo; cobarde; alfeñique, *m.*
weakly ['wiːkli], *a.* débil; enfermizo.—*adv.* débilmente.
weakness ['wiːknis], *n.* debilidad; flojedad; imperfección, *f.*
wealth [welθ], *n.* riqueza; abundancia.
wealthy ['welθi], *a.* rico, adinerado.
wean [wiːn], *v.t.* destetar; separar.
weaning ['wiːniŋ], *n.* destete, *m.*
weapon ['wepən], *n.* arma.
wear [wɛə], *n.* uso; gasto; deterioro; moda; **for summer** —, para verano; — **and tear**, uso, depreciación, *f.*—*v.t. irr.* (*conjug. like*

TEAR) llevar, llevar puesto; vestir; mostrar; gastar; deteriorar; usar; agotar; enfadar; **to** — **away**, usar; **to** — **off**, borrar.—*v.i. irr.* usarse; gastarse; perdurar; conservarse; pasar; **to** — **away**, usarse; **to** — **off**, borrarse, quitarse; **to** — **on**, pasar lentamente; **to** — **out**, usarse.
weariness ['wiərinis], *n.* cansancio.
wearing ['wɛəriŋ], *a.* cansado.—*n.* uso; desgaste, *m.*; deterioro.
wearisome ['wiərisəm], *a.* cansado; aburrido; pesado.
weary ['wiəri], *a.* cansado, fatigado; aburrido. —*v.t.* cansar; aburrir.—*v.i.* cansarse; aburrirse.
weasel [wiːzl], *n.* comadreja.
weather ['weðə], *n.* tiempo; **what is the** — **like?** ¿qué tiempo hace? **the** — **is bad,** hace mal tiempo; **under the** —, destemplado; — **chart**, carta metereológica; — **forecast**, pronóstico del tiempo.—*v.t.* curtir; aguantar; vencer; **to** — **the storm,** resistir a la tempestad.—*v.i.* curtirse a la intemperie.
weather-beaten ['weðəbiːtn], *a.* curtido por la intemperie.
weathercock ['weðəkɔk], *n.* veleta.
weave [wiːv], *n.* tejido; textura.—*v.t.*, *v.i. irr.* tejer.
weaver ['wiːvə], *n.* tejedor, *m.*
weaving ['wiːviŋ], *n.* tejeduría; tejido.
web [web], *n.* tejido, tela; red, *f.*; lazo; (*zool.*) membrana interdigital.
web-footed ['web'futid], *a.* palmípedo.
wed [wed], *v.t.* casarse con; casar; (*fig.*) encadenar.—*v.i.* casarse.
wedding ['wediŋ], *n.* boda, casamiento; enlace, *m.*; — **cake**, pan (*m.*) de boda; — **day**, día (*m.*) de bodas; — **dress**, traje (*m.*) de boda; — **ring**, alianza, anillo de la boda.
wedge [wedʒ], *n.* cuña; calza.—*v.t.* acuñar; calzar; sujetar.
wedlock ['wedlɔk], *n.* matrimonio.
Wednesday ['wenzd(e)i], *n.* miércoles, *m.*
weed [wiːd], *n.* hierba mala; (*fam.*) tabaco; (*fam.*) madeja.—*pl.* ropa de luto.—*v.t.* escardar; (*fig.*) extirpar (**out**).
weeding ['wiːdiŋ], *n.* escarda.
weedy ['wiːdi], *a.* (*fig.*) raquítico.
week [wiːk], *n.* semana; **once a** —, una vez por semana.
weekday ['wiːkdei], *n.* día (*m.*) de entresemana.
weekend ['wiːkend], *n.* fin (*m.*) de semana.
weekly ['wiːkli], *a.* semanal.—*n.* revista semanal, semanario.
weep [wiːp], *v.t.*, *v.i. irr.* llorar.
weeping ['wiːpiŋ], *a.* lloroso; — **willow,** sauce llorón, *m.*—*n.* lloro, lágrimas, *f.pl.*
weevil ['wiːvil], *n.* gorgojo.
weft [weft], *n.* trama.
weigh [wei], *v.t.* pesar; oprimir; comparar; **to** — **anchor,** levantar el ancla; **to** — **down,** sobrecargar; (*fig.*) oprimir (**on**).— *v.i.* pesar; ser de importancia.
weighing ['weiiŋ], *n.* peso; pesada; ponderación, *f.*
weighing-machine ['weiiŋməʃiːn], *n.* báscula, máquina de pesar.
weight [weit], *n.* peso; pesadez, *f.*; pesa; cargo; **by** —, al peso; **gross** —, peso bruto; **net** —, peso neto; **to lose** —, adelgazar; **to put on** —, engordar; **to throw one's** —

wherewith

about, *(fam.)* darse importancia.—*v.t.* cargar; aumentar el peso de.
weightless ['weitlis], *a.* ingrávido.
weightlessness ['weitlisnis], *n.* ingravidez, *f.*
weighty ['weiti], *a.* de peso, pesado; *(fig.)* grave; importante.
weir [wiə], *n.* vertedero, presa de aforo.
weird [wiəd], *a.* extraño; fantástico.
welcome ['welkəm], *a.* bienvenido; grato, agradable; *you are — to it,* está a su disposición.—*n.* bienvenida; buena acogida.—*v.t.* dar la bienvenida a; saludar; acoger.—*interj.* ¡bien venido! [nada]
welcoming ['welkəmiŋ], *a.* acogedor.
weld [weld], *v.t.* soldar; *(fig.)* unir.
welder ['weldə], *n.* soldador, *m.*
welding ['weldiŋ], *n.* soldadura; unión, *f.*
welfare ['welfɛə], *n.* bienestar, *m.*; prosperidad; salud, *f.*; — *work,* servicio social.
well (1) [wel], *a.* bien; sano.—*adv.* bien; muy; *as — as,* tan bien como; *as —,* también.—*interj.* ¡bien! ¡bueno! ¡pues! — *done!* ¡bravo!
well (2) [wel], *n.* pozo; *stair —,* caja de escalera; *(naut.)* vivar, *m.*
well-aimed ['wel'eimd], *a.* certero.
well-behaved ['welbi'heivd], *a.* bien educado.
well-being ['wel'bi:iŋ], *n.* bienestar, *m.*
well-born ['wel'bɔ:n], *a.* de buena familia.
well-bred ['wel'bred], *a.* bien educado; de pura raza.
well-disposed ['weldis'pouzd], *a.* bien dispuesto.
well-educated ['wel'edjukeitid], *a.* instruido.
well-favoured ['wel'feivəd], *a.* de buen parecer.
well-founded ['wel'faundid], *a.* bien fundado.
wellingtons ['weliŋtənz], *n.pl.* botas *(f.pl.)* de goma.
well-known ['wel'noun], *a.* (bien) conocido.
well-meaning ['wel'mi:niŋ], *a.* bien intencionado.
well-read ['wel'red], *a.* erudito.
well-spent ['wel'spent], *a.* bien empleado.
well-spoken ['wel'spoukən], *a.* bien hablado; bien dicho.
well-stocked ['wel'stɔkt], *a.* bien provisto.
well-timed ['wel'taimd], *a.* oportuno.
well-to-do ['weltə'du:], *a.* acomodado.
well-wisher ['welwiʃə], *n.* bienqueriente, *m.f.*
well-worn ['wel'wɔ:n], *a.* usado; trillado.
Welsh [welʃ], *a.* galés, de Gales.—*n. the —,* los galeses.
Welshman ['welʃmən], *n.* galés, *m.*
welt [welt], *n.* ribete, *m.*; vira *(de zapato).*
welter ['weltə], *n.* tumulto; — *weight,* peso welter.
wench [wentʃ], *n. (obs.)* muchacha; *(fam.)* tía.
wend [wend], *v.t.* encaminar, dirigir; *to — one's way,* seguir su camino.
went [went] [GO].
wept [wept] [WEEP].
were [wə:] [BE].
west [west], *a.* occidental, del oeste; *West Indies,* las Antillas.—*n.* oeste, occidente, poniente, *m.*—*adv.* al oeste.
westerly ['westəli], *a.* occidental; del oeste; hacia el oeste.
western ['westən], *a.* occidental; del oeste.—*n.* novela *o* película del oeste.
westernized ['westənaizd], *a.* occidentalizado.

westward ['westwəd], *a.* occidental.—*adv.* hacia el oeste.
wet [wet], *a.* mojado; húmedo; lluvioso; *(fam.)* necio; — *paint,* recién pintado; *to get —,* mojarse; *to be —,* estar mojado; llover; — *through,* colado, mojado hasta los huesos.—*v.t.* mojar; *to — one's whistle, (fam.)* mojar el gaznate.
wetness ['wetnis], *n.* humedad, *f.*; lluvia.
whack [wæk], *n.* golpe, *m.*; tentativa; *(fam.)* porción, *f.*—*v.t.* golpear, pegar.
whale [weil], *n.* ballena; *sperm —,* cachalote, *m.*
whalebone ['weilboun], *n.* barba de ballena.
whaler ['weilə], *n.* ballenero; buque ballenero.
wharf [wɔ:f], *n.* muelle, *m.*, embarcadero, descargadero.
what [wɔt], *pron.* qué; que; cuál; cual; el cual, *etc.,* el que, *etc.;* cuanto; cuánto; — *else?* ¿y qué más? *to know what's —,* saber cuántas son cinco; *what's-his-name,* fulano de tal; *what's up?* ¿qué pasa? — *with one thing and another,* entre una cosa y otra.
whatever [wɔt'evə], *a.* todo ... que; cualquier; cual.—*pron.* cuanto; todo lo que; cualquier cosa que; — *happens,* venga lo que venga; — *you say,* diga lo que diga.
wheat [wi:t], *n.* trigo.
wheaten ['wi:tn], *a.* de trigo.
wheat-field ['wi:tfi:ld], *n.* trigal, *m.*
wheat-sheaf ['wi:tʃi:f], *n.* gavilla de trigo.
wheedle [wi:dl], *v.t.* halagar; engatusar.
wheedling ['wi:dliŋ], *a.* zalamero.—*n.* lagotería; halagos, *m.pl.*
wheel [wi:l], *n.* rueda; *potter's —,* rueda de alfarero; *front —,* rueda delantera; *rear —,* rueda trasera.—*v.t.* hacer rodar; poner ruedas en.—*v.i.* girar; dar vueltas.
wheelbarrow ['wi:lbærou], *n.* carretilla.
wheel-chair ['wi:ltʃɛə], *n.* silla de ruedas.
wheeze [wi:z], *n. (fam.)* truco.—*v.i.* jadear, respirar con dificultad.
wheezing ['wi:ziŋ], *a.* asmático.
whelk [welk], *n.* caracol *(m.)* de mar, buccino.
whelp [welp], *n.* cachorro.—*v.i.* parir.
when [wen], *adv.* cuando; cuándo; en cuanto; en que; que; y entonces.
whence [wens], *adv.* de dónde; de donde; de que; por lo que.
whenever [wen'evə], *adv.* cuandoquiera que; siempre que; cada vez que.
where [wɛə], *adv.* donde; dónde; adonde; adónde; en donde; en dónde; de donde; de dónde.
whereabouts ['wɛərəbauts], *n.* paradero.— [wɛərə'bauts], *adv.* dónde; donde.
whereas [wɛər'æz], *conj.* mientras (que); visto que, ya que.
whereby [wɛə'bai], *adv.* por (o con) el que; por qué; cómo.
wherefore [wɛə'fɔ:], *adv.* por lo cual; por qué.—*n.* porqué, *m.*
wherein [wɛər'in], *adv.* en donde; en dónde; en que; en qué.
whereof [wɛər'ɔv], *adv.* de que; cuyo.
whereon [wɛər'ɔn], *adv.* en que, sobre que.
whereupon [wɛərə'pɔn], *adv.* sobre lo cual, con lo cual.
wherever [wɛər'evə], *adv.* dondequiera (que); adondequiera (que); dónde.
wherewith [wɛə'wið], *adv.* con que; con qué.

wherewithal ['wɛəwiðɔːl], *n.* dinero necesario, cumquibus, *m.*

whet [wet], *v.t.* afilar, aguzar; (*fig.*) estimular.

whether ['weðə], *conj.* si; que; — ... *or* ..., sea (que) ... sea (que) ...

whetstone ['wetstoun], *n.* (piedra) aguzadera, piedra de afilar.

whey [wei], *n.* suero de la leche.

which [witʃ], *pron.* que; qué; cuál; cuáles; el cual, *etc.*, el que, *etc.*; quien; — *way?* ¿ por dónde ?

whichever [witʃ'evə], *pron.* cualquiera; cualesquiera; el que, *etc.*; quienquiera; quienesquiera.

whiff [wif], *n.* soplo; fragancia.

while [wail], *n.* rato; momento; tiempo; *a little* — *ago,* hace poco tiempo; *to be worth* —, valer la pena.—*conj.* mientras (que), al mismo tiempo que; si bien.—*v.t. to* — *away,* matar, entretener (*el tiempo*).

whim [wim], *n.* capricho, antojo.

whimper ['wimpə], *n.* quejido, sollozo.—*v.i.* lloriquear, gemir.

whimsical ['wimzikəl], *a* caprichoso, antojadizo; fantástico.

whine [wain], *n.* gimoteo.—*v.i.* gimotear.

whinny ['wini], *n.* relincho.—*v.i.* relinchar.

whip [wip], *n.* azote, *m.*; látigo; *to have the* — *hand,* (*fig.*) tener la sartén por el mango.—*v.t.* azotar; (*cul.*) batir; vencer; sacar; quitar; *to* — *up,* (*fig.*) excitar.

whippet ['wipit], *n.* perro lebrero.

whipping ['wipiŋ], *n.* azotamiento; — *top,* peonza.

whirl [wəːl], *n.* vuelta, rotación, *f.,* giro; (*fig.*) torbellino.—*v.t.* hacer girar.—*v.i.* girar; dar vueltas.

whirligig ['wəːligig], *n.* perinola; tíovivo.

whirlpool ['wəːlpuːl], *n.* remolino.

whirlwind ['wəːlwind], *n.* torbellino.

whirr [wəː], *n.* zumbido.—*v.i.* zumbar; girar.

whisk [wisk], *n.* cepillo; batidor, *m.*; movimiento rápido.—*v.t.* cepillar, batir; mover rápidamente; *to* — *away,* arrebatar.—*v.i.* pasar rápidamente.

whisker ['wiskə], *n.* patilla.—*pl.* bigotes, *m.pl.*; barba.

whisky ['wiski], *n.* whisky, *m.*

whisper ['wispə], *n.* cuchicheo, susurro; *in a* —, en voz baja.—*v.t., v.i.* susurrar, cuchichear; hablar al oído; murmurar.

whispering ['wispəriŋ], *n.* cuchicheo, susurro; murmullo.

whist [wist], *n.* whist, *m.*

whistle [wisl], *n.* silbo, silbido; pito; (*fam.*) gaznate, *m.*—*v.t., v.i.* silbar; *to* — *for,* llamar silbando; (*fam.*) esperar en vano.

whistling ['wisliŋ], *n.* silbido.

whit [wit], *n.* pizca; *not a* —, ni pizca.

white [wait], *a.,* *n.* blanco; clara (*de huevo*); *to go* —, ponerse pálido; *the* — *of the eye,* lo blanco del ojo; — *lie,* mentirilla; — *wine,* vino blanco.

whiten [waitn], *v.t.* blanquear.—*v.i.* -se.

whiteness ['waitnis], *n.* blancura; palidez, *f.*

whitewash ['waitwɔʃ], *n.* jalbegue, *m.*; (*fig.*) disimulación, *f.*—*v.t.* enjalbegar; (*fig.*) encubrir.

whither ['wiðə], *adv.* adonde; adónde.

whitish ['waitiʃ], *a.* blanquecino.

Whit Sunday ['wit'sʌnd(e)i], *n.* domingo de Pentecostés.

Whitsuntide ['witsəntaid], *n.* Pentecostés, *m.*

whittle [witl], *v.t.* tallar; cercenar; afilar; (*fig.*) reducir.

whizz [wiz], *n.* silbido, zumbido.—*v.i.* silbar, zumbar.

who [huː], *pron.* quién; quiénes; quien; quienes; que; el que, *etc.*

whoever [huː'evə], *pron.* quienquiera (que), cualquiera (que).

whole [houl], *a.* todo; entero; sano.—*n.* todo; totalidad, *f.*; conjunto; *on the* —, en general.

wholeness ['houlnis], *n.* totalidad; integridad, *f.*

wholesale ['houlseil], *a.* al por mayor; (*fig.*) general.—*n.* venta al por mayor.

wholesome ['houlsəm], *a.* saludable; sano.

wholly ['houli], *adv.* completamente, enteramente; del todo.

whom [huːm], *pron.* que; el que, *etc.*, el cual, *etc.*; quien; quienes; quién; quiénes.

whoop [huːp], *n.* alarido; (*med.*) estertor, *m.*—*v.i.* dar gritos; (*med.*) toser.

whooping ['huːpiŋ], *n.* alarido.

whooping-cough ['huːpiŋkɔf], *n.* tos ferina.

whore [hɔː], *n.* puta, ramera.

whose [huːz], *pron.* cuyo; del que, *etc.*, del cual, *etc.*; de quién; de quiénes.

why [wai], *n.* porqué, *m.*—*adv.* por qué; por el cual, *etc.*—*interj.* ¡cómo! ¡toma! ¡qué!

wick [wik], *n.* mecha.

wicked ['wikid], *a.* malo; perverso, malvado; malicioso.

wickedness ['wikidnis], *n.* maldad; perversidad, *f.*; pecado.

wicker ['wikə], *n.* mimbre, *m.*

wicket ['wikit], *n.* postigo; (*sport*) meta.

wide [waid], *a.* ancho; extenso; apartado; liberal; de ancho; *six feet* —, seis pies de ancho.—*adv.* lejos; completamente; *far and* —, por todas partes; — *awake,* bien despierto; — *open,* abierto de par en par.

wide-eyed ['waid'aid], *a.* con los ojos muy abiertos; asombrado; (*fig.*) inocente.

widen [waidn], *v.t.* ensanchar; extender.—*v.i.* ensancharse; extenderse.

widening ['waidniŋ], *n.* ensanche, *m.*; extensión, *f.*

widespread ['waidspred], *a.* difuso; esparcido; general.

widow ['widou], *n.* viuda.—*v.t.* enviudar, dejar viuda.

widowed ['widoud], *a.* viudo.

widower ['widouə], *n.* viudo.

widowhood ['widouhud], *n.* viudez, *f.*

width [widθ], *n.* anchura; ancho; amplitud, *f.*

wield [wiːld], *v.t.* manejar, empuñar; ejercer.

wife [waif], *n.* (*pl.* wives) mujer, *f.,* esposa; señora; *old wives' tale,* cuento de viejas, patraña.

wig [wig], *n.* peluca; cabellera.

wild [waild], *a.* salvaje; silvestre; desierto; desordenado; violento; inconstante; borrascoso; loco; extravagante; *to run* —, volver al estado primitivo; desancadenarse; *to sow one's* — *oats,* correr sus mocedades; — *beast,* fiera; *wild-cat strike,* huelga irracional; — *goose chase,* caza de grillos.—*n.pl.* desierto, yermo; región remota.

wilderness ['wildənis], *n.* desierto, yermo.

wildfire ['waildfaiə], *n.* fuego fatuo; *to spread like* —, extenderse como el fuego.

wile [wail], *n.* ardid, *m.*, engaño.
wilful ['wilful], *a.* obstinado; voluntarioso; premeditado.
wilfulness ['wilfulnis], *n.* obstinación; intención, *f.*
wiliness ['wailinis], *n.* astucia.
will [wil], *n.* albedrío; voluntad, *f.*; deseo; discreción, *f.*; testamento; *at* —, a voluntad; *to do with a* —, hacer con entusiasmo.—*v.t.* querer; mandar; legar; sugestionar.— *v. aux. irr.* querer; — *you open the window?* ¿quiere Vd. abrir la ventana? (*When it simply indicates the future, the future tense is used in Spanish*); — *you come tomorrow?* ¿ Vd. vendrá mañana ?
willing ['wiliŋ], *a.* dispuesto; servicial; deseoso; *God* —, si Dios quiere.
willingly ['wiliŋli], *adv.* de buena gana.
willingness ['wiliŋnis], *n.* buena voluntad, *f.*; consentimiento.
will-o'-the-wisp ['wiləðə'wisp], *n.* fuego fatuo.
willow ['wilou], *n.* sauce, *m.*
willowy ['wiloui], *a.* (*fig.*) cimbreño, esbelto.
will-power ['wilpauə], *n.* fuerza de voluntad.
willy-nilly ['wili'nili], *adv.* de buen o mal grado, que quiera o no.
wilt [wilt], *v.t.* marchitar; ajar.—*v.i.* marchitarse; (*fig.*) amansarse.
wily ['waili], *a.* astuto.
wimple [wimpl], *n.* toca, impla.
win [win], *n.* triunfo.—*v.t. irr.* ganar; vencer; persuadir.—*v.i. irr.* ganar; triunfar; prevalecer.
wince [wins], *n.* respingo.—*v.i.* recular; respingar.
winch [wintʃ], *n.* cabria; manubrio.
wind (1) [wind], *n.* viento; aliento; flatulencia; *to get* — *of*, husmear; *following* —, viento en popa.—*v.t.* dejar sin aliento.
wind (2) [waind], *v.t. irr.* dar cuerda a (*un reloj*); torcer; devanar, ovillar; *to* — *off*, devanar; *to* — *round*, envolver, ceñir; *to* — *up*, dar cuerda a; (*fig.*) atar cabos; (*com.*) liquidar.—*v.i. irr.* serpentear; arrollarse.
winded ['windid], *a.* jadeante.
windfall ['windfɔ:l], *n.* fruta caída del árbol; ganancia inesperada.
winding ['waindiŋ], *a.* sinuoso; tortuoso; serpentino; en espiral; — *sheet*, sudario; — *staircase*, escalera de caracol.—*n.* vuelta; tortuosidad, *f.*; (*elec.*) devanado.
winding-up ['waindiŋʌp], *n.* conclusión; (*com.*) liquidación, *f.*
windmill ['windmil], *n.* molino (de viento).
window ['windou], *n.* ventana; ventanilla; vidriera; — *frame*, marco de ventana; — *pane*, cristal, *m.*; — *sill*, antepecho o repisa de ventana; *to look out of the* —, mirar por la ventana.
window-dresser ['windoudresə], *n.* decorador (*m.*) de escaparates.
windpipe ['windpaip], *n.* tráquea.
windshield ['windʃi:ld], *n.* parabrisas, *m.inv.*; — *wiper*, limpiaparabrisas, *m.inv.*
windward ['windwəd], *a.* de barlovento.—*n.* barlovento.
windy ['windi], *a.* ventoso; (*fig.*) pomposo; cobarde; *it is* —, hace viento *o* aire.
wine [wain], *n.* vino.
wine-cellar ['wainselə], *n.* bodega.
wine-glass ['wainglɑ:s], *n.* copa.
wine-grower ['waingrouə], *n.* viticultor *m.*

wine-press ['wainpres], *n.* lagar, *m.*
wineskin ['wainskin], *n.* odre, *m.*
wine-taster ['wainteistə], *n.* catavinos (*copa*), *m.sg.*; catador (*m.*) de vinos (*persona*).
wing [wiŋ], *n.* ala; (*theat.*) bastidor, *m.*; *on the* —, al vuelo; *under one's* —, (*fig.*) bajo su protección; *in the wings*, (*theat.*) entre bastidores.—*v.t.* proveer de alas; herir en el ala; herir en el brazo.—*v.i.* volar.
winged [wiŋd], *a.* alado; (*fig.*) rápido; elevado.
wing-span ['wiŋspæn], *n.* envergadura, *f.*
wing-tip ['wiŋtip], *n.* punta de ala.
wink [wiŋk], *n.* guiño; pestañeo; un abrir y cerrar de ojos; *not to sleep a* —, no pegar los ojos; *to take forty winks*, descabezar un *o* el sueño.—*v.i.* guiñar; pestañear; (*fig.*) centellear; *to* — *at*, guiñar el ojo a; (*fig.*) hacer la vista gorda a.
winner ['winə], *n.* ganador; vencedor, *m.*
winning ['winiŋ], *a.* vencedor; que gana.— *n.* ganancia; triunfo.—*pl.* ganancias, *f.pl.*
winnow ['winou], *v.t.* aventar.
winter ['wintə], *a.* de invierno; — *sports*, deportes (*m.pl.*) de nieve.—*n.* invierno.—*v.t.* hacer invernar.—*v.i.* invernar.
wintry ['wintri], *a.* de invierno; (*fig.*) glacial.
wipe [waip], *n.* limpión, *m.*—*v.t.* enjugar; limpiar; *to* — *off*, borrar; *to* — *out*, (*fig.*) extirpar; cancelar.
wire [waiə], *n.* alambre; (*fam.*) telegrama, *m.*; — *netting*, red (*f.*) de alambre.—*v.t.* atar con alambre; proveer de alambre; (*fam.*) telegrafiar; (*elec.*) alambrar.
wireless ['waiəlis], *a.* radiotelegráfico.—*n.* radio, *f.*; radiotelegrafía; *portable* —, radio portátil; — *licence*, permiso de radiorreceptor; — *set*, aparato de radio.
wire-pulling ['waiəpuliŋ], *n.* (*fam.*) intriga secreta.
wiring ['waiəriŋ], *n.* alambrado.
wiry ['waiəri], *a.* (*fig.*) nervudo.
wisdom ['wizdəm], *n.* sabiduría.
wise [waiz], *a.* sabio; sagaz; *The Three Wise Men*, los Reyes Magos; — *guy*, (*fam.*) sabelotodo.—*n.* guisa, modo.
wish [wiʃ], *n.* deseo, anhelo.—*v.t.* desear; querer; anhelar; *to* — *good luck*, desear mucha suerte (a); *to* — *good morning*, dar los buenos días; *to* — *good-bye*, despedirse (de); *I* — *I knew!* ¡ojalá (que) supiese!
wishful ['wiʃful], *a.* deseoso; — *thinking*, sueños dorados.
wishy-washy ['wiʃiwɔʃi], *a.* insípido, flojo.
wisp [wisp], *n.* mechón, *m.*; trocito.
wistful ['wistful], *a.* triste; pensativo; ansioso.
wit [wit], *n.* ingenio; sal, *f.*; gracia; hombre (*m.*) *o* mujer (*f.*) de ingenio; *to* —, a saber. — *pl.* juicio; *to be at one's wits' end*, no saber qué hacer; *to be out of one's wits*, perder el juicio; *to live by one's wits*, vivir de gorra.
witch [witʃ], *n.* bruja.
witchcraft ['witʃkrɑ:ft], *n.* brujería.
witch-doctor ['witʃdɔktə], *n.* hechizador, *m.*; curandero.
with [wið], *prep.* con; entre; contra; de para con; — *all speed*, a toda prisa; — *that*, con esto; *away* — *you!* ¡anda!
withal [wið'ɔ:l], *adv.* con todo; además.

withdraw [wið'drɔ:], *v.t. irr (conjug. like* DRAW) retirar; quitar; retractar.—*v.i. irr.* retirarse; apartarse.

withdrawal [wið'drɔ:əl], *n.* retirada; retiro.

withdrawn [wið'drɔ:n], *a.* ensimismado.

wither ['wiðə], *v.t.* marchitar; (*fig.*) avergonzar.—*v.i.* marchitarse.

withered ['wiðəd], *a.* marchito; seco.

withering ['wiðəriŋ], *a.* que marchita; cáustico.

withers ['wiðəz], *n.pl.* cruz (*de caballo*), *f.*

withhold [wið'hould], *v.t. irr.* (*conjug. like* HOLD) retener; negar; ocultar.

within [wið'in], *adv.* dentro, adentro; en casa; (*fig.*) en el corazón.—*prep.* dentro de; — *an ace of,* por poco; — *an inch of,* (*fig.*) a dos dedos de; — *hearing,* al alcance de la voz; — *reach of,* al alcance de.

without [wið'aut], *adv.* fuera, afuera; por fuera; hacia fuera; exteriormente.—*prep.* sin; fuera de; a menos de.

withstand [wið'stænd], *v.t. irr.* (*conjug. like* STAND) oponerse a, resistir; soportar.

witless ['witlis], *a.* necio, tonto.

witness ['witnis], *n.* testigo; espectador, *m.*; testimonio; *in — whereof,* en testimonio de lo cual; *to bear —,* dar testimonio; — *for the defence,* testigo de descargo; — *for the prosecution,* testigo de cargo.—*v.t.* ser testigo de, presenciar; mostrar; (*jur.*) atestiguar.—*v.i.* dar testimonio.

witness-box ['witnisbɔks], *n.* puesto de los testigos.

witted ['witid], *a. quick —,* vivo de ingenio; *slow —,* lerdo.

witticism ['witisizm], *n.* agudeza, chiste, *m.*

witty ['witi], *a.* gracioso, salado.

wives [waivz] [WIFE].

wizard ['wizəd], *n.* brujo, hechicero, mago.

wizardry ['wizədri], *n.* brujería.

wizened ['wizənd], *a.* acartonado; marchito.

wobble [wɔbl], *v.i.* tambalearse.

woe [wou], *n.* dolor, *m.*; aflicción, *f.*; — *is me!* ¡ay de mí!

woeful ['wouful], *a.* desconsolado; funesto.

wolf [wulf], *n.* (*pl.* **wolves** [wulvz]) lobo; (*fam.*) tenorio; *to keep the — from the door,* cerrar la puerta al hambre.

woman ['wumən], *n.* (*pl.* **women**) mujer, *f.*; hembra.

woman-hater ['wumənheitə], *n.* misógino.

womanhood ['wumənhud], *n.* feminidad, *f.*; sexo femenino.

womanish ['wuməniʃ], *a.* afeminado; mujeril.

womanizer ['wumənaizə], *n.* (*fam.*) mujeriego.

womankind ['wumənkaind], *n.* sexo femenino, la mujer.

womanly ['wumənli], *a.* mujeril.

womb [wu:m], *n.* matriz, *f.*, útero, *m.*; (*fig.*) seno.

women ['wimin] [WOMAN].

won [wʌn] [WIN].

wonder ['wʌndə], *n.* admiración, *f.*; maravilla; prodigio.—*v.i.* admirarse, asombrarse (*at,* de); preguntarse.

wonderful ['wʌndəful], *a.* maravilloso.

wondering ['wʌndəriŋ], *a.* admirado; perplejo.

wonderland ['wʌndəlænd], *n.* país (*m.*) de las maravillas.

wondrous ['wʌndrəs], *a.* maravilloso.

wont [wount], *n.* costumbre, *f.*; *to be — to,* soler.

won't [wount] [WILL NOT].

woo [wu:], *v.t.* cortejar; (*fig.*) solicitar.

wood [wud], *n.* bosque, *m.*; madera; leña.

wood-carving ['wudkɑ:viŋ], *n.* talla *o* tallado de madera.

wooded ['wudid], *a.* arbolado, enselvado.

wooden [wudn], *a.* de madera; (*fig.*) torpe; — *leg,* pata de palo; — *smile,* sonrisa mecánica.

woodland ['wudlənd], *n.* bosques, *m.pl.*

woodpecker ['wudpekə], *n.* picamaderos, *m.inv.*, pájaro carpintero.

woodshed ['wudʃed], *n.* leñera.

woodwind ['wudwind], *n.* (*mus.*) madera.

woodwork ['wudwə:k], *n.* maderaje, *m.*; carpintería.

woodworm ['wudwə:m], *n.* carcoma.

wooer ['wu:ə], *n.* galanteador, pretendiente, *m.*

wooing ['wu:iŋ], *n.* galanteo.

wool [wul], *n.* lana; *to pull the — over someone's eyes,* (*fig.*) embaucar (a uno).

wool-bearing ['wulbɛəriŋ], *a.* lanar.

wool-gathering ['wulgæðəriŋ], *a.* (*fig.*) distraído.

woollen ['wulən], *a.* de lana.—*n.* tela de lana.

woolly ['wuli], *a.* lanudo, lanoso; de lana; crespo; (*fig.*) flojo, impreciso.

woolsack ['wulsæk], *n.* fardo de lana; asiento del Presidente de la Cámara de los Lores.

word [wə:d], *n.* palabra; vocablo; orden, *f.*; recado; *the Word,* (*Bible*) el Verbo; *by — of mouth,* verbalmente; *to bring —,* traer la noticia; *to keep one's —,* cumplir su palabra; *to give one's —,* dar su palabra; *to take someone's — for it,* creer (a uno); *to have a — with,* hablar con; *to have words with,* tener palabras con; *in other words,* en otros términos.—*v.t.* expresar; redactar.

wordiness ['wə:dinis], *n.* verbosidad, *f.*

wording ['wə:diŋ], *n.* fraseología; estilo; términos, *m.pl.*; redacción, *f.*

wordy ['wə:di], *a.* verboso.

wore [wɔ:] [WEAR].

work [wə:k], *n.* trabajo; obra.—*pl.* obras, fábrica; mecanismo; — *of art,* obra de arte; *to set to —,* hacer trabajar; dar empleo a; *out of —,* desocupado.—*v.t.* trabajar; explotar; producir; tallar; manejar; hacer funcionar; cultivar; efectuar; (*naut.*) maniobrar; *to — in,* hacer penetrar; *to — off,* librarse de; *to — on,* influir en; obrar sobre; mover a compasión.—*v.i.* trabajar; funcionar; tener éxito; ser eficaz; moverse; *to — at,* ocuparse de; *to — in,* penetrar en, insinuarse en; *to — out,* resultar; *not working,* no funciona.

workable ['wə:kəbl], *a.* laborable; explotable; practicable.

workaday ['wə:kədei], *a.* ordinario, prosaico.

work-box ['wə:kbɔks], *n.* caja de labor.

workday ['wə:kdei], *n.* día (*m.*) laborable.

worker ['wə:kə], *n.* trabajador, *m.*; obrero.

workhouse ['wə:khaus], *n.* asilo (de pobres).

working ['wə:kiŋ], *a.* trabajador, que trabaja; de trabajo; obrero; — *class,* clase obrera; — *clothes,* ropa de trabajo.—*n.* trabajo; fermentación, *f.*; funcionamiento; explotación, *f.*; maniobra.

workman ['wə:kmən], *n.* obrero.

workmanlike [´wɔːkmənlaik], *a.* hábil; esmerado.
workmanship [´wɔːkmənʃip], *n.* habilidad, *f.*
workroom [´wɔːkruːm], *n.* manufactura.
workshop [´wɔːkʃɔp], *n.* taller, *m.*
world [wɔːld], *n.* mundo; — *power,* potencia mundial.
worldliness [´wɔːldlinis], *n.* mundanería.
worldly [´wɔːldli], *a.* mundano; humano; profano; *to be worldly-wise,* tener mucho mundo.
world-wide [´wɔːldˈwaid], *a.* mundial.
worm [wɔːm], *n.* gusano; lombriz, *f.*; (*mech.*) tornillo sinfín.—*v.t.* to — *out,* sonsacar.—*v.i.* arrastrarse; insinuarse; *to* — *one's way into,* insinuarse en.
worm-eaten [´wɔːmiːtən], *a.* carcomido.
wormwood [´wɔːmwud], *n.* ajenjo.
worn [wɔːn], **worn-out** [´wɔːnaut], *a.* usado; raído; fatigado; gastado. [WEAR].
worrier [´wʌriə], *n.* aprensivo; pesimista, *m.f.*
worry [´wʌri], *n.* preocupación, *f.*; cuidado.— *v.t.* preocupar; molestar; importunar; desgarrar.—*v.i.* preocuparse; estar preocupado.
worse [wɔːs], *a.* (*compar. of* BAD) peor; inferior; *so much the* —, tanto peor; — *than ever,* peor que nunca; — *and* —, de mal en peor; *to get* —, empeorarse, ponerse peor.—*adv.* (*compar. of* BADLY) peor.— *n.* lo peor.
worsen [´wɔːsən], *v.t.* hacer peor; exasperar; agravar.—*v.i.* hacerse peor; exasperarse; agravarse.
worship [´wɔːʃip], *n.* adoración; veneración, *f.*; culto.—*v.t.* adorar, venerar, reverenciar. —*v.i.* adorar; dar culto.
worshipful [´wɔːʃipful], *a.* venerable.
worshipper [´wɔːʃipə], *n.* adorador; fiel, *m.*
worst [wɔːst], *a.* (*superl. of* BAD) el peor, *etc.*; pésimo.—*adv.* (*superl. of* BADLY) el peor, *etc.* —*n.* el peor, *etc.*; lo peor; *the* — *of it is,* lo peor es; *if the* — *comes to the* —, en el peor caso; *to get the* — *of it,* sacar el peor partido.—*v.t.* derrotar, vencer.
worsted [´wustid], *a.* de estambre.—*n.* estambre, *m.*
worth [wɔːθ], *a.* digno; que vale; que merece; del precio de; *to be* —, valer; ser digno de; *to be* — *while,* valer la pena.—*n.* valor, *m.*; precio; mérito.
worthiness [´wɔːðinis], *n.* valor, *m.*, mérito.
worthless [´wɔːθlis], *a.* sin valor; inútil; despreciable.
worthlessness [´wɔːθlisnis], *n.* falta de valor; inutilidad, *f.*; vileza.
worthy [´wɔːði], *a.* digno; benemérito.—*n.* hombre ilustre, *m.*; benemérita.
would [wud], [WILL]; — *that he were here!* ¡ojalá (que) estuviese aquí! — *to God!* ¡plegue a Dios!
would-be [´wudbiː], *a.* supuesto; pretendiente; frustrado.
wouldn't [wudnt] [WOULD NOT].
wound (1) [wuːnd], *n.* herida, llaga.—*v.t.* herir; lastimar; *to — to the quick,* herir en lo vivo.
wound (2) [waund] [WIND].
wounding [´wuːndiŋ], *a.* lastimador; ofensivo.
wove(n) [wouv(n)] [WEAVE].
wraith [reiθ], *n.* fantasma, *m.*

wrangle [ræŋgl], *n.* altercado; riña.—*v.i.* disputar, altercar; reñir; regatear.
wrap [ræp], *n.* bata; envoltorio.—*v.t.* envolver; embozar; ocultar; cubrir; *to be wrapped up in,* estar envuelto en; (*fig.*) estar absorto en.
wrapper [´ræpə], *n.* envoltura; embalaje, *m.*; cubierta; faja; bata.
wrapping [´ræpiŋ], *n.* envoltura; cubierta; — *paper,* papel (*m.*) de envolver.
wrath [rɔθ], *n.* furor, *m.*, ira.
wrathful [´rɔθful], *a.* enojado, furioso, airado.
wreak [riːk], *v.t.* ejecutar; descargar; *to — vengeance,* tomar venganza.
wreath [riːθ], *n.* guirnalda; corona; trenza.
wreathe [riːð], *v.t.* enguirnaldar; trenzar; entrelazar; ceñir.
wreck [rek], *n.* naufragio; barco naufragado; destrucción, *f.*; (*fig.*) ruina.—*v.t.* hacer naufragar; destruir; (*fig.*) arruinar.—*v.i.* naufragar.
wreckage [´rekidʒ], *n.* naufragio; restos, *m.pl.*
wren [ren], *n.* buscareta.
wrench [rentʃ], *n.* torcedura; tirón, arranque, *m.*; llave, *f.*—*v.t.* torcer, dislocar; arrancar.
wrest [rest], *v.t.* arrancar, arrebatar.
wrestle [resl], *v.i.* luchar.
wrestler [´reslə], *n.* luchador, *m.*
wrestling [´resliŋ], *n.* lucha.
wretch [retʃ], *n.* desgraciado, infeliz, *m.f.*
wretched [´retʃid], *a.* desgraciado; miserable; ruin; mezquino; despreciable.
wretchedness [´retʃidnis], *n.* miseria; ruindad *f.*; vileza.
wriggle [rigl], *v.i.* culebrear; retorcerse; *to — out,* escaparse; (*fig.*) extricarse.
wring [riŋ], *v.t. irr.* torcer; exprimir; *to — one's hands,* torcerse las manos; *to — the neck of,* torcer el pescuezo a.
wringer [´riŋə], *n.* torcedor; exprimidor, *m.*
wrinkle [´riŋkl], *n.* arruga; pliegue, *m.*; (*fam.*) maña.—*v.t.* arrugar.—*v.i.* arrugarse.
wrinkly [´riŋkli], *a.* arrugado.
wrist [rist], *n.* muñeca.
wrist-watch [´ristwɔtʃ], *n.* reloj (*m.*) de pulsera.
writ [rit], *n.* escritura; (*jur.*) mandamiento; orden, *f.*; *Holy Writ,* la Sagrada Escritura.
write [rait], *v.t., v.i. irr.* escribir; *to — back,* contestar a una carta; *to — down,* apuntar; *to — out,* copiar; *to — up,* redactar.
writer [´raitə], *n.* escritor; autor, *m.*
writhe [raið], *v.i.* torcerse, retorcerse.
writing [´raitiŋ], *n.* escritura; escrito; letra; *in* —, por escrito; — *paper,* papel (*m.*) de escribir; — *desk,* escritorio; — *pad,* taco de papel.
written [ritn] [WRITE].
wrong [rɔŋ], *a.* malo; injusto; erróneo; equivocado; falso; inoportuno; — *side out,* al revés; *to be* —, equivocarse; no tener razón; — *number,* número errado.—*n.* mal, *m.*; injusticia; agravio; culpa; error, *m.*; *to be in the* —, no tener razón; tener la culpa; *to do* —, hacer o obrar mal.—*adv.* mal; injustamente; equivocadamente; sin razón; al revés; *to get it* —, calcular mal; comprender mal.—*v.t.* ofender; hacer daño; agraviar; perjudicar.
wrong-doer [´rɔŋduːə], *n.* malhechor, *m.*
wrong-doing [´rɔŋduːiŋ], *n.* maleficencia.

wrongful

wrongful ['rɔŋful], *a.* injusto; falso.
wrong-headed ['rɔŋ'hedid], *a.* terco.
wrote [rout] [WRITE].
wrought [rɔːt], *a.* forjado; trabajado; excitado (*up*).
wrung [rʌŋ] [WRING].
wry [rai], *a.* torcido; irónico; — *face*, mueca.

X

X, x [eks], *n.* vigésima cuarta letra del alfabeto inglés; *X-rays*, rayos X.—*v.t.* *to X-ray*, radiografiar.
xenophobe ['zenəfoub], *n.* xenófobo.
xenophobia [zenə'foubjə], *n.* xenofobia.
Xmas ['krismɔs], *n.* (*abbrev. of* **Christmas**) (*fam.*) Navidad, *f.*
xylophone ['zailəfoun], *n.* xilófono; marimba.

Y

Y, y [wai], *n.* vigésima quinta letra del alfabeto inglés.
yacht [jɔt], *n.* yate, *m.*; — *club,* club marítimo.
yachting ['jɔtiŋ], *n.* deporte (*m.*) de vela, yachting, *m.*
yachtsman ['jɔtsmən], *n.* yachtsman, *m.*
yak [jæk], *n.* yak, *m.*
Yank [jæŋk], **Yankee** ['jæŋki], *a.,* *n.* (*fam.*) yanqui, *m.f.*
yank [jæŋk], *n.* tirón, *m.*—*v.t.* dar un tirón a.
yap [jæp], *n.* ladrido.—*v.i.* ladrar; (*fam.*) parlotear.
yard [jɑːd], *n.* yarda; corral, *m.,* patio.
yard-arm ['jɑːdɑːm], *n.* penol (de la verga), *m.*
yard-stick ['jɑːdstik], *n.* yarda de medir, criterio.
yarn [jɑːn], *n.* hilo, hilaza; (*fam.*) historia, cuento; *to spin a* —, contar una historia.
yawl [jɔːl], *n.* yola, bote, *m.*
yawn [jɔːn], *n.* bostezo.—*v.i.* bostezar; abrirse.
yawning ['jɔːniŋ], *a.* abierto.—*n.* bostezo(s).
yea [jei] [YES].
year [jiə], *n.* año; *last* —, el año pasado; *leap* —, año bisiesto; *next* —, el año que viene, el año próximo; *New Year,* Año Nuevo; *by the* —, al año; — *after* —, año tras año; *to be . . . years old*, tener . . . años; *to be getting on in years*, envejecer, irse haciendo viejo.
year-book ['jiəbuk], *n.* anuario.
yearly ['jiəli], *a.* anual.—*adv.* anualmente, cada año, una vez al año.
yearn [jəːn], *v.i.* anhelar, suspirar.

yearning ['jəːniŋ], *a.* anhelante.—*n.* anhelo.
yeast [jiːst], *n.* levadura.
yell [jel], *n.* alarido, chillido; grito.—*v.i.* chillar; gritar.
yelling ['jeliŋ], *n.* chillido(s); gritería.
yellow ['jelou], *a.* amarillo; (*fam.*) cobarde.—*n.* amarillo.
yellowish ['jelouiʃ], *a.* amarillento.
yelp [jelp], *n.* gañido.—*v.i.* gañir.
yen [jen], *n.* (*fam.*) anhelo, gana.
yes [jes], *adv.* sí; —*?* ¿de verdad? ¿qué quiere? ¿qué hay?; *to say* —, decir que sí; dar el sí.
yes-man ['jesmæn], *n.* sacristán (*m.*) de amén.
yesterday ['jestəd(e)i], *n.,* *adv.* ayer, *m.*; *the day before* —, anteayer.
yet [jet], *adv.* aún, todavía; *as* —, hasta ahora; *not* —, todavía no.—*conj.* pero, sin embargo, no obstante, con todo.
yew [juː], *n.* tejo.
yield [jiːld], *n.* producto; (*com.*) rédito; cosecha.—*v.t.* ceder; entregar; producir.—*v.i.* ceder; rendirse.
yielding ['jiːldiŋ], *a.* flexible; dócil; complaciente.—*n.* rendición, *f.,* consentimiento.
yoke [jouk], *n.* yugo; canesú (*de un vestido*), *m.*; *to throw off the* —, sacudir el yugo.—*v.t.* uncir, acoplar.
yokel ['joukəl], *n.* rústico, patán, *m.*
yolk [jouk], *n.* yema.
yonder ['jɔndə], *a.* aquel.—*adv.* allí, allá.
you [juː], *pron.* tú, vosotros, usted, ustedes; te, os, le, la, les, las; ti; sí.
young [jʌŋ], *a.* joven; nuevo; — *people,* jóvenes, *m.pl.*; *the night is* —, la noche está poco avanzada.—*n.* cría, hijuelos, *m.pl.*; *with* —, preñada (*de animales*).
younger ['jʌŋgə], *a.* más joven; menor.
youngster ['jʌŋstə], *n.* jovencito, chiquillo.
your [jɔː], *a.* tu, tus, vuestro, *etc.*; su, sus.
yours [jɔːz], *pron.* el tuyo, la tuya, *etc.*; el vuestro, la vuestra, *etc.*; el suyo, la suya, *etc.*; *yours faithfully,* queda de Vd. su atentísimo seguro servidor (*usually abbrev. to* su att. s. s.); *yours sincerely,* queda de Vd. su afectuoso (*usually abbrev. to* aff.).
yourself [jɔː'self], *pron.* tú mismo; vosotros mismos; Vd. mismo; Vds. mismos; te, os, se; ti, vosotros, usted, sí.
youth [juːθ], *n.* juventud, *f.*; joven, *m.,* chico, *m.*; jóvenes, *m.pl.*
youthful ['juːθful], *a.* joven; vigoroso.
Yugoslav ['juːgouslɑːv], *a.,* *n.* yugoeslavo.
Yugoslavia [juːgou'slɑːvjə], *n.* Yugoeslavia.
Yule [juːl], *n.* (*obs.*) Navidad, *f.*
Yule-log ['juːl'lɔg], *n.* nochebueno.
Yule-tide ['juːltaid], *n.* Navidades, *f.pl.*

Z

Z, z [zed, (*U.S.*) ziː], *n.* vigésima sexta letra del alfabeto inglés.
zany ['zeini], *a.* disparatado.—*n.* bufón, *m.*
zeal [ziːl], *n.* celo, entusiasmo.

zealot ['zelət], *n.* fanático.
zealous ['zeləs], *a.* entusiasta, apasionado.
zebra ['zi:brə, 'zebrə], *n.* cebra; — *crossing*, (tipo de) cruce (*m.*) de peatones.
zenith ['zeniθ], *n.* cenit, *m.*; apogeo.
zeppelin ['zepəlin], *n.* zepelín, *m.*
zero ['ziərou], *n.* cero; — *hour*, hora de ataque.
zest [zest], *n.* gusto, entusiasmo, deleite, *m.*
zigzag ['zigzæg], *v.t.*, *v.i.* zigzaguear.
zinc [ziŋk], *n.* cinc, *m.*; — *oxide*, óxido de cinc.
Zion ['zaiən], *n.* Sión; Jerusalén, *m.*
Zionist ['zaiənist], *n.* sionista, *m.f.*

zip [zip], *n.*(*fam.*)energía.—*v.i.* silbar; zumbar.
zipper ['zipə], *n.* (cierre) cremallera.
zircon ['zə:kən], *n.* circón, *m.*
zither ['ziðə], *n.* cítara.
zodiac ['zoudiæk], *n.* zodíaco.
zone [zoun], *n.* zona; *temperate* —, **zona** templada; *frigid* —, zona glacial.
zoo [zu:], *n.* zoo, *m.*, jardín zoológico.
zoological [zouə'lɔdʒikəl], *a.* zoológico.
zoologist [zou'ɔlədʒist], *n.* zoólogo.
zoology [zou'ɔlədʒi], *n.* zoología.
zoom [zu:m], *n.* zumbido.—*v.i.* **zumbar;** (*aer.*) empinarse.
Zulu ['zu:lu:], *a.*, *n.* zulú, *m.*

Spanish Verbs

Present Indicative	Participles	Imperative	Preterite

ORTHOGRAPHIC CHANGING VERBS

Group A. abarcar: c changes to qu before e.

abarco	abarcando		abarqué
abarcas	abarcado	abarca	abarcaste
abarca			abarcó
abarcamos			abarcamos
abarcáis		abarcad	abarcasteis
abarcan			abarcaron

Group B. ahogar: g changes to gu before e.

ahogo	ahogando		ahogué
ahogas	ahogado	ahoga	ahogaste
ahoga			ahogó
ahogamos			ahogamos
ahogáis		ahogad	ahogasteis
ahogan			ahogaron

Group C. cazar: z changes to c before e.

cazo	cazando		cacé
cazas	cazado	caza	cazaste
caza			cazó
cazamos			cazamos
cazáis		cazad	cazasteis
cazan			cazaron

Group D. vencer and esparcir: c changes to z before o and a.

venzo	venciendo		vencí
vences	vencido	vence	venciste
vence			venció
vencemos			vencimos
vencéis		venced	vencisteis
vencen			vencieron
esparzo	esparciendo		esparcí
esparces	esparcido	esparce	esparciste
esparce			esparció
esparcimos			esparcimos
esparcís		esparcid	esparcisteis
esparcen			esparcieron

Group E. coger and afligir: g changes to j before o and a.

cojo	cogiendo		cogí
coges	cogido	coge	cogiste
coge			cogió
cogemos			cogimos
cogéis		coged	cogisteis
cogen			cogieron
aflijo	afligiendo		afligí
afliges	afligido	aflige	afligiste
aflige			afligió
afligimos			afligimos
afligís		afligid	afligisteis
afligen			afligieron

Group F. delinquir: qu changes to c before o and a.

delinco	delinquiendo		delinquí
delinques	delinquido	delinque	delinquiste
delinque			delinquió
delinquimos			delinquimos
delinquís		delinquid	delinquisteis
delinquen			delinquieron

Present Subjunctive	Imperfect Subjunctive		Future Subjunctive

abarque	abarcara	abarcase	abarcare
abarques	abarcaras	abarcases	abarcares
abarque	abarcara	abarcase	abarcare
abarquemos	abarcáramos	abarcásemos	abarcáremos
abarquéis	abarcarais	abarcaseis	abarcareis
abarquen	abarcaran	abarcasen	abarcaren

ahogue	ahogara	ahogase	ahogare
ahogues	ahogaras	ahogases	ahogares
ahogue	ahogara	ahogase	ahogare
ahoguemos	ahogáramos	ahogásemos	ahogáremos
ahoguéis	ahogarais	ahogaseis	ahogareis
ahoguen	ahogaran	ahogasen	ahogaren

cace	cazara	cazase	cazare
caces	cazaras	cazases	cazares
cace	cazara	cazase	cazare
cacemos	cazáramos	cazásemos	cazáremos
cacéis	cazarais	cazaseis	cazareis
cacen	cazaran	cazasen	cazaren

venza	venciera	venciese	venciere
venzas	vencieras	vencieses	vencieres
venza	venciera	venciese	venciere
venzamos	venciéramos	venciésemos	venciéremos
venzáis	vencierais	vencieseis	venciereis
venzan	vencieran	venciesen	vencieren

esparza	esparciera	esparciese	esparciere
esparzas	esparcieras	esparcieses	esparcieres
esparza	esparciera	esparciese	esparciere
esparzamos	esparciéramos	esparciésemos	esparciéremos
esparzáis	esparcierais	esparcieseis	esparciereis
esparzan	esparcieran	esparciesen	esparcieren

coja	cogiera	cogiese	cogiere
cojas	cogieras	cogieses	cogieres
coja	cogiera	cogiese	cogiere
cojamos	cogiéramos	cogiésemos	cogiéremos
cojáis	cogierais	cogieseis	cogiereis
cojan	cogieran	cogiesen	cogieren

aflija	afligiera	afligiese	afligiere
aflijas	afligieras	afligieses	afligieres
aflija	afligiera	afligiese	afligiere
aflijamos	afligiéramos	afligiésemos	afligiéremos
aflijáis	afligierais	afligieseis	afligiereis
aflijan	afligieran	afligiesen	afligieren

delinca	delinquiera	delinquiese	delinquiere
delincas	delinquieras	delinquieses	delinquieres
delinca	delinquiera	delinquiese	delinquiere
delincamos	delinquiéramos	delinquiésemos	delinquiéremos
delincáis	delinquierais	delinquieseis	delinquiereis
delincan	delinquieran	delinquiesen	delinquieren

Spanish Verbs

Present Indicative	Participles	Imperative	Preterite

Group G. distinguir: **gu** changes to **g** before **o** and **a**.

distingo	distinguiendo		distinguí
distingues	distinguido	distingue	distinguiste
distingue			distinguió
distinguimos			distinguimos
distinguís		distinguid	distinguisteis
distinguen			distinguieron

Group H. fraguar: **gu** changes to **gü** before **e**.

fraguo	fraguando		fragüé
fraguas	fraguado	fragua	fraguaste
fragua			fraguó
fraguamos			fraguamos
fraguáis		fraguad	fraguasteis
fraguan			fraguaron

Group I. argüir: **üi** changes to **uy** before a vowel.

arguyo	arguyendo		argüí
arguyes	argüido	arguye	argüiste
arguye			arguyó
argüimos			argüimos
argüís		argüid	argüisteis
arguyen			arguyeron

Group J. bullir: **i** is elided before a vowel.

bullo	bullendo		bullí
bulles	bullido	bulle	bulliste
bulle			bulló
bullimos			bullimos
bullís		bullid	bullisteis
bullen			bulleron

Group K. tañer and ceñir: **i** is elided before a vowel; **e** in the stem sometimes changes to **i**.

taño	tañendo		tañí
tañes	tañido	tañe	tañiste
tañe			tañó
tañemos			tañimos
tañéis		tañed	tañisteis
tañen			tañeron

ciño	ciñendo		ceñí
ciñes	ceñido	ciñe	ceñiste
ciñe			ciñó
ceñimos			ceñimos
ceñís		ceñid	ceñisteis
ciñen			ciñeron

Group L. variar: **i** takes an accent when the stress falls on it.

varío	variando		varié
varías	variado	varía	variaste
varía			varió
variamos			variamos
variáis		variad	variasteis
varían			variaron

Group M. atenuar: **u** takes an accent when the stress falls on it.

atenúo	atenuando		atenué
atenúas	atenuado	atenúa	atenuaste
atenúa			atenuó
atenuamos			atenuamos
atenuáis		atenuad	atenuasteis
atenúan			atenuaron

Present Subjunctive	Imperfect Subjunctive		Future Subjunctive
distinga	distinguiera	distinguiese	distinguiere
distingas	distinguieras	distinguieses	distinguieres
distinga	distinguiera	distinguiese	distinguiere
distingamos	distinguiéramos	distinguiésemos	distinguiéremos
distingáis	distinguierais	distinguieseis	distinguiereis
distingan	distinguieran	distinguiesen	distinguieren
fragüe	fraguara	fraguase	fraguare
fragües	fraguaras	fraguases	fraguares
fragüe	fraguara	fraguase	fraguare
fragüemos	fraguáramos	fraguásemos	fraguáremos
fragüéis	fraguarais	fraguaseis	fraguareis
fragüen	fraguaran	fraguasen	fraguaren
arguya	arguyera	arguyese	arguyere
arguyas	arguyeras	arguyeses	arguyeres
arguya	arguyera	arguyese	arguyere
arguyamos	arguyéramos	arguyésemos	arguyéremos
arguyáis	arguyerais	arguyeseis	arguyereis
arguyan	arguyeran	arguyesen	arguyeren
bulla	bullera	bullese	bullere
bullas	bulleras	bulleses	bulleres
bulla	bullera	bullese	bullere
bullamos	bulléramos	bullésemos	bulléremos
bulláis	bullerais	bulleseis	bullereis
bullan	bulleran	bullesen	bulleren
taña	tañera	tañese	tañere
tañas	tañeras	tañeses	tañeres
taña	tañera	tañese	tañere
tañamos	tañéramos	tañésemos	tañéremos
tañáis	tañerais	tañeseis	tañereis
tañan	tañeran	tañesen	tañeren
ciña	ciñera	ciñese	ciñere
ciñas	ciñeras	ciñeses	ciñeres
ciña	ciñera	ciñese	ciñere
ciñamos	ciñéramos	ciñésemos	ciñéremos
ciñáis	ciñerais	ciñeseis	ciñereis
ciñan	ciñeran	ciñesen	ciñeren
varíe	variara	variase	variare
varíes	variaras	variases	variares
varíe	variara	variase	variare
variemos	variáramos	variásemos	variáremos
variéis	variarais	variaseis	variareis
varíen	variaran	variasen	variaren
atenúe	atenuara	atenuase	atenuare
atenúes	atenuaras	atenuases	atenuares
atenúe	atenuara	atenuase	atenuare
atenuemos	atenuáramos	atenuásemos	atenuáremos
atenuéis	atenuarais	atenuaseis	atenuareis
atenúen	atenuaran	atenuasen	atenuaren

Spanish Verbs

Present Indicative	Participles	Imperative	Preterite

Group **N**. creer: **i** changes to **y** before a vowel; before a consonant it takes an accent.

Present Indicative	Participles	Imperative	Preterite
creo	creyendo		creí
crees	creído	cree	creíste
cree			creyó
creemos			creímos
creéis		creed	creísteis
creen			creyeron

Group **O**. huir: **i** changes to **y** before a vowel.

Present Indicative	Participles	Imperative	Preterite
huyo	huyendo		huí[1]
huyes	huído	huye	huiste
huye			huyó
huimos			huimos
huís[1]		huid	huisteis
huyen			huyeron

Group **P**. aullar (all verbs, of any conjugation, having the diphthongs **au** or **eu** in the stem): **u** takes an accent when the stress falls on it.

Present Indicative	Participles	Imperative	Preterite
aúllo	aullando		aullé
aúllas	aullado	aúlla	aullaste
aúlla			aulló
aullamos			aullamos
aulláis		aullad	aullasteis
aúllan			aullaron

Group **Q**. garantir: defective, occurring only in those forms where the **i** is present in the verb ending, viz. the entire imperfect, preterite, future, conditional, both imperfect subjunctives, the future subjunctive and the forms of the present indicative and imperative given below.

Present Indicative	Participles	Imperative	Preterite
	garantiendo		garantí
	garantido		garantiste
			garantió
garantimos			garantimos
garantís		garantid	garantisteis
			garantieron

IRREGULAR VERBS

Present Indicative	Participles	Imperative	Future Indicative	Preterite

Group **1**. cerrar: **e** changes to **ie** when the stress falls on it.

Present Indicative	Participles	Imperative	Future Indicative	Preterite
cierro	cerrando		cerraré	cerré
cierras	cerrado	cierra	cerrarás	cerraste
cierra			cerrará	cerró
cerramos			cerraremos	cerramos
cerráis		cerrad	cerraréis	cerrasteis
cierran			cerrarán	cerraron

Group **2**. perder: **e** changes to **ie** when the stress falls on it.

Present Indicative	Participles	Imperative	Future Indicative	Preterite
pierdo	perdiendo		perderé	perdí
pierdes	perdido	pierde	perderás	perdiste
pierde			perderá	perdió
perdemos			perderemos	perdimos
perdéis		perded	perderéis	perdisteis
pierden			perderán	perdieron

Group **3**. cernir: **e** changes to **ie** when the stress falls on it.

Present Indicative	Participles	Imperative	Future Indicative	Preterite
cierno	cerniendo		cerniré	cerní
ciernes	cernido	cierne	cernirás	cerniste
cierne			cernirá	cernió
cernimos			cerniremos	cernimos
cernís		cernid	cerniréis	cernisteis
ciernen			cernirán	cernieron

[1] The accents on these two forms may be omitted in **huir** but not in any other verb.

Present Subjunctive	Imperfect Subjunctive		Future Subjunctive
crea	creyera	creyese	creyere
creas	creyeras	creyeses	creyeres
crea	creyera	creyese	creyere
creamos	creyéramos	creyésemos	creyéremos
creáis	creyerais	creyeseis	creyereis
crean	creyeran	creyesen	creyeren
huya	huyera	huyese	huyere
huyas	huyeras	huyeses	huyeres
huya	huyera	huyese	huyere
huyamos	huyéramos	huyésemos	huyéremos
huyáis	huyerais	huyeseis	huyereis
huyan	huyeran	huyesen	huyeren
aúlle	aullara	aullase	aullare
aúlles	aullaras	aullases	aullares
aúlle	aullara	aullase	aullare
aullemos	aulláramos	aullásemos	aulláremos
aulléis	aullarais	aullaseis	aullareis
aúllen	aullaran	aullasen	aullaren
	garantiera	garantiese	garantiere
	garantieras	garantieses	garantieres
	garantiera	garantiese	garantiere
	garantiéramos	garantiésemos	garantiéremos
	garantierais	garantieseis	garantiereis
	garantieran	garantiesen	garantieren
cierre	cerrara	cerrase	cerrare
cierres	cerraras	cerrases	cerrares
cierre	cerrara	cerrase	cerrare
cerremos	cerráramos	cerrásemos	cerráremos
cerréis	cerrarais	cerraseis	cerrareis
cierren	cerraran	cerrasen	cerraren
pierda	perdiera	perdiese	perdiere
pierdas	perdieras	perdieses	perdieres
pierda	perdiera	perdiese	perdiere
perdamos	perdiéramos	perdiésemos	perdiéremos
perdáis	perdierais	perdieseis	perdiereis
pierdan	perdieran	perdiesen	perdieren
cierna	cerniera	cerniese	cerniere
ciernas	cernieras	cernieses	cernieres
cierna	cerniera	cerniese	cerniere
cernamos	cerniéramos	cerniésemos	cerniéremos
cernáis	cernierais	cernieseis	cerniereis
ciernan	cernieran	cerniesen	cernieren

Spanish Verbs

Present Indicative	Participles	Imperative	Future Indicative	Preterite

Group 4. rodar: **o** changes to **ue** when the stress falls on it.

ruedo	rodando		rodaré	rodé
ruedas	rodado	**rue**da	rodarás	rodaste
rueda			rodará	rodó
rodamos			rodaremos	rodamos
rodáis		rodad	rodaréis	rodasteis
ruedan			rodarán	rodaron

Group 5. mover: **o** changes to **ue** when the stress falls on it.

muevo	moviendo		moveré	moví
mueves	movido	**mueve**	moverás	moviste
mueve			moverá	movió
movemos			moveremos	movimos
movéis		**moved**	moveréis	movisteis
mueven			moverán	movieron

Group 6. advertir: **e** (or in some cases **i**) changes to **ie** when the stress falls on it; **e** changes to **i** in some forms.

advierto	advirtiendo		advertiré	advertí
adviertes	advertido	**advierte**	advertirás	advertiste
advierte			advertirá	advirtió
advertimos			advertiremos	advertimos
advertís		**advertid**	advertiréis	advertisteis
advierten			advertirán	advirtieron

Group 7. dormir: **o** changes to **ue** when the stress falls on it; **o** changes to **u** in some forms.

duermo	durmiendo		dormiré	dormí
duermes	dormido	**duerme**	dormirás	dormiste
duerme			dormirá	durmió
dormimos			dormiremos	dormimos
dormís		**dormid**	dormiréis	dormisteis
duermen			dormirán	durmieron

Group 8. pedir: **e** changes to **i** when the stress falls on it and in some other cases.

pido	**pi**diendo		pediré	pedí
pides	pedido	**pi**de	pedirás	pediste
pide			pedirá	**pi**dió
pedimos			pediremos	pedimos
pedís		**pedid**	pediréis	pedisteis
piden			pedirán	**pi**dieron

Group 9. padecer: **c** changes to **zc** before **o** and **a**.

pade**zc**o	padeciendo		padeceré	padecí
padeces	padecido	**padece**	padecerás	padeciste
padece			padecerá	padeció
padecemos			padeceremos	padecimos
padecéis		**padeced**	padeceréis	padecisteis
padecen			padecerán	padecieron

Group 10. agorar: **o** changes to **üe** when the stress falls on it.

agüero	agorando		agoraré	agoré
agüeras	agorado	**agüera**	agorarás	agoraste
agüera			agorará	agoró
agoramos			agoraremos	agoramos
agoráis		**agorad**	agoraréis	agorasteis
agüeran			agorarán	agoraron

Group 11. andar:

ando	andando		andaré	and**uve**
andas	andado	**anda**	andarás	and**uviste**
anda			andará	and**uvo**
andamos			andaremos	and**uvimos**
andáis		**andad**	andaréis	and**uvisteis**
andan			andarán	and**uvieron**

Present Subjunctive	Imperfect Subjunctive		Future Subjunctive
ruede	rodara	rodase	rodare
ruedes	rodaras	rodases	rodares
ruede	rodara	rodase	rodare
rodemos	rodáramos	rodásemos	rodáremos
rodéis	rodarais	rodaseis	rodareis
rueden	rodaran	rodasen	rodaren
mueva	moviera	moviese	moviere
muevas	movieras	movieses	movieres
mueva	moviera	moviese	moviere
movamos	moviéramos	moviésemos	moviéremos
mováis	movierais	movieseis	moviereis
muevan	movieran	moviesen	movieren
advierta	advirtiera	advirtiese	advirtiere
adviertas	advirtieras	advirtieses	advirtieres
advierta	advirtiera	advirtiese	advirtiere
advirtamos	advirtiéramos	advirtiésemos	advirtiéremos
advirtáis	advirtierais	advirtieseis	advirtiereis
adviertan	advirtieran	advirtiesen	advirtieren
duerma	durmiera	durmiese	durmiere
duermas	durmieras	durmieses	durmieres
duerma	durmiera	durmiese	durmiere
durmamos	durmiéramos	durmiésemos	durmiéremos
durmáis	durmierais	durmieseis	durmiereis
duerman	durmieran	durmiesen	durmieren
pida	pidiera	pidiese	pidiere
pidas	pidieras	pidieses	pidieres
pida	pidiera	pidiese	pidiere
pidamos	pidiéramos	pidiésemos	pidiéremos
pidáis	pidierais	pidieseis	pidiereis
pidan	pidieran	pidiesen	pidieren
padezca	padeciera	padeciese	padeciere
padezcas	padecieras	padecieses	padecieres
padezca	padeciera	padeciese	padeciere
padezcamos	padeciéramos	padeciésemos	padeciéremos
padezcáis	padecierais	padecieseis	padeciereis
padezcan	padecieran	padeciesen	padecieren
agüere	agorara	agorase	agorare
agüeres	agoraras	agorases	agorares
agüere	agorara	agorase	agorare
agoremos	agoráramos	agorásemos	agoráremos
agoréis	agorarais	agoraseis	agorareis
agüeren	agoraran	agorasen	agoraren
ande	anduviera	anduviese	anduviere
andes	anduvieras	anduvieses	anduvieres
ande	anduviera	anduviese	anduviere
andemos	anduviéramos	anduviésemos	anduviéremos
andéis	anduvierais	anduvieseis	anduviereis
anden	anduvieran	anduviesen	anduvieren

Spanish Verbs

Present Indicative	Participles	Imperative	Future Indicative	Preterite
Group 12. asir:				
asgo	asiendo		asiré	así
ases	asido	ase	asirás	asiste
ase			asirá	asió
asimos			asiremos	asimos
asís		asid	asiréis	asisteis
asen			asirán	asieron
Group 13. caber:				
quepo	cabiendo		**cabré**	**cupe**
cabes	cabido	cabe	**cabrás**	**cupiste**
cabe			**cabrá**	**cupo**
cabemos			**cabremos**	**cupimos**
cabéis		cabed	**cabréis**	**cupisteis**
caben			**cabrán**	**cupieron**
Group 14. caer:				
caigo	cayendo		caeré	caí
caes	caído	cae	caerás	caíste
cae			caerá	cayó
caemos			caeremos	caímos
caéis		caed	caeréis	caísteis
caen			caerán	cayeron
Group 15. deducir:				
deduzco	deduciendo		deduciré	**deduje**
deduces	deducido	deduce	deducirás	**dedujiste**
deduce			deducirá	**dedujo**
deducimos			deduciremos	**dedujimos**
deducís		deducid	deduciréis	**dedujisteis**
deducen			deducirán	**dedujeron**
Group 16. dar:				
doy	dando		daré	**di**[1]
das	dado	da	darás	**diste**
da			dará	**dio**[1]
damos			daremos	**dimos**
dais		dad	daréis	**disteis**
dan			darán	**dieron**
Group 17. decir:				
digo	**diciendo**		**diré**	dije
dices	**dicho**	**di**	**dirás**	dijiste
dice			**dirá**	dijo
decimos			**diremos**	dijimos
decís		decid	**diréis**	dijisteis
dicen			**dirán**	dijeron
Group 18. estar:				
estoy	estando		estaré	**estuve**
estás	estado	**está**	estarás	**estuviste**
está			estará	**estuvo**
estamos			estaremos	**estuvimos**
estáis		estad	estaréis	**estuvisteis**
están			estarán	**estuvieron**
Group 19. haber:				
he	habiendo		**habré**	**hube**
has	habido	**hé**	**habrás**	**hubiste**
ha			**habrá**	**hubo**
hemos			**habremos**	**hubimos**
habéis		habed	**habréis**	**hubisteis**
han			**habrán**	**hubieron**

[1] In compounds **-dí, -dió.**

Present Subjunctive	Imperfect Subjunctive		Future Subjunctive
asga	asiera	asiese	asiere
asgas	asieras	asieses	asieres
asga	asiera	asiese	asiere
asgamos	asiéramos	asiésemos	asiéremos
asgáis	asierais	asieseis	asiereis
asgan	asieran	asiesen	asieren
quepa	cupiera	cupiese	cupiere
quepas	cupieras	cupieses	cupieres
quepa	cupiera	cupiese	cupiere
quepamos	cupiéramos	cupiésemos	cupiéremos
quepáis	cupierais	cupieseis	cupiereis
quepan	cupieran	cupiesen	cupieren
caiga	cayera	cayese	cayere
caigas	cayeras	cayeses	cayeres
caiga	cayera	cayese	cayere
caigamos	cayéramos	cayésemos	cayéremos
caigáis	cayerais	cayeseis	cayereis
caigan	cayeran	cayesen	cayeren
deduzca	dedujera	dedujese	dedujere
deduzcas	dedujeras	dedujeses	dedujeres
deduzca	dedujera	dedujese	dedujere
deduzcamos	dedujéramos	dedujésemos	dedujéremos
deduzcáis	dedujerais	dedujeseis	dedujereis
deduzcan	dedujeran	dedujesen	dedujeren
dé[1]	diera	diese	diere
des	dieras	dieses	dieres
dé[1]	diera	diese	diere
demos	diéramos	diésemos	diéremos
deis[2]	dierais	dieseis	diereis
den	dieran	diesen	dieren
diga	dijera	dijese	dijere
digas	dijeras	dijeses	dijeres
diga	dijera	dijese	dijere
digamos	dijéramos	dijésemos	dijéremos
digáis	dijerais	dijeseis	dijereis
digan	dijeran	dijesen	dijeren
esté	estuviera	estuviese	estuviere
estés	estuvieras	estuvieses	estuvieres
esté	estuviera	estuviese	estuviere
estemos	estuviéramos	estuviésemos	estuviéremos
estéis	estuvierais	estuvieseis	estuviereis
estén	estuvieran	estuviesen	estuvieren
haya	hubiera	hubiese	hubiere
hayas	hubieras	hubieses	hubieres
haya	hubiera	hubiese	hubiere
hayamos	hubiéramos	hubiésemos	hubiéremos
hayáis	hubierais	hubieseis	hubiereis
hayan	hubieran	hubiesen	hubieren

[1] In compounds -de, -déis.

Spanish Verbs

Present Indicative	Participles	Imperative	Future Indicative	Preterite
Group 20. hacer:				
hago	haciendo		**haré**	**hice**
haces	**hecho**	**haz**	**harás**	**hiciste**
hace			**hará**	**hizo**
hacemos			**haremos**	**hicimos**
hacéis		haced	**haréis**	**hicisteis**
hacen			**harán**	**hicieron**
Group 21. ir[1]:				
voy	**yendo**		iré	**fui**
vas	ido	**vé**	irás	**fuiste**
va			irá	**fue**
vamos			iremos	**fuimos**
vais		id	iréis	**fuisteis**
van			irán	**fueron**
Group 22. oír:				
oigo	**oyendo**		oiré	**oí**
oyes	**oído**	**oye**	oirás	**oíste**
oye			oirá	**oyó**
oímos			oiremos	**oímos**
oís		**oíd**	oiréis	**oísteis**
oyen			oirán	**oyeron**
Group 23. placer:				
plazco or plazgo	placiendo		placeré	plací
places	placido	place	placerás	placiste
place			placerá	plació or **plugo**
placemos			placeremos	placimos
placéis		placed	placeréis	placisteis
placen			placerán	placieron
Group 24. poder:				
puedo	**pudiendo**		**podré**	**pude**
puedes	podido		**podrás**	**pudiste**
puede			**podrá**	**pudo**
podemos			**podremos**	**pudimos**
podéis			**podréis**	**pudisteis**
pueden			**podrán**	**pudieron**
Group 25. poner:				
pongo	poniendo		**pondré**	**puse**
pones	**puesto**	**pon**[2]	**pondrás**	**pusiste**
pone			**pondrá**	**puso**
ponemos			**pondremos**	**pusimos**
ponéis		poned	**pondréis**	**pusisteis**
ponen			**pondrán**	**pusieron**
Group 26. querer:				
quiero	queriendo		**querré**	**quise**
quieres	querido	**quiere**	**querrás**	**quisiste**
quiere			**querrá**	**quiso**
queremos			**querremos**	**quisimos**
queréis		quered	**querréis**	**quisisteis**
quieren			**querrán**	**quisieron**

Group 27. raer: Identical with caer (14) but has the following alternative forms:
raigo or **rayo**

[1] Imperfect: **iba, -as, -a, íbamos, ibais, iban.**
[2] In compounds **-pón.**

Present Subjunctive	Imperfect Subjunctive		Future Subjunctive
haga	hiciera	hiciese	hiciere
hagas	hicieras	hicieses	hicieres
haga	hiciera	hiciese	hiciere
hagamos	hiciéramos	hiciésemos	hiciéremos
hagáis	hicierais	hicieseis	hiciereis
hagan	hicieran	hiciesen	hicieren
vaya	fuera	fuese	fuere
vayas	fueras	fueses	fueres
vaya	fuera	fuese	fuere
vayamos[1]	fuéramos	fuésemos	fuéremos
vayáis	fuerais	fueseis	fuereis
vayan	fueran	fuesen	fueren
oiga	oyera	oyese	oyere
oigas	oyeras	oyeses	oyeres
oiga	oyera	oyese	oyere
oigamos	oyéramos	oyésemos	oyéremos
oigáis	oyerais	oyeseis	oyereis
oigan	oyeran	oyesen	oyeren
plazca or plazga	placiera	placiese	placiere
plazcas	placieras	placieses	placieres
plazca	placiera or pluguiera	placiese or pluguiese	placiere or pluguiere
plazcamos	placiéramos	placiésemos	placiéremos
plazcáis	placierais	placieseis	placiereis
plazcan	placieran	placiesen	placieren
pueda	pudiera	pudiese	pudiere
puedas	pudieras	pudieses	pudieres
pueda	pudiera	pudiese	pudiere
podamos	pudiéramos	pudiésemos	pudiéremos
podáis	pudierais	pudieseis	pudiereis
puedan	pudieran	pudiesen	pudieren
ponga	pusiera	pusiese	pusiere
pongas	pusieras	pusieses	pusieres
ponga	pusiera	pusiese	pusiere
pongamos	pusiéramos	pusiésemos	pusiéremos
pongáis	pusierais	pusieseis	pusiereis
pongan	pusieran	pusiesen	pusieren
quiera	quisiera	quisiese	quisiere
quieras	quisieras	quisieses	quisieres
quiera	quisiera	quisiese	quisiere
queramos	quisiéramos	quisiésemos	quisiéremos
queráis	quisierais	quisieseis	quisiereis
quieran	quisieran	quisiesen	quisieren

raiga or raya

---

[1] Jussive vamos.

Spanish Verbs

Present Indicative	Participles	Imperative	Future Indicative	Preterite
Group 28. reír:				
río	**riendo**		reiré	**reí**
ríes	reído	**ríe**	reirás	**reíste**
ríe			reirá	**rio**
reímos			reiremos	**reímos**
reís		**reíd**	reiréis	**reísteis**
ríen			reirán	**rieron**
Group 29. roer:				
roo, **roigo** or **royo**	royendo		roeré	roí
roes	roído	roe	roerás	roíste
roe			roerá	royó
roemos			roeremos	roímos
roéis		roed	roeréis	roísteis
roen			roerán	royeron
Group 30. saber:				
sé	sabiendo		**sabré**	**supe**
sabes	sabido	sabe	**sabrás**	**supiste**
sabe			**sabrá**	**supo**
sabemos			**sabremos**	**supimos**
sabéis		sabed	**sabréis**	**supisteis**
saben			**sabrán**	**supieron**
Group 31. salir:				
salgo	saliendo		**saldré**	salí
sales	salido	**sal**	**saldrás**	saliste
sale			**saldrá**	salió
salimos			**saldremos**	salimos
salis		salid	**saldréis**	salisteis
salen			**saldrán**	salieron
Group 32. ser[1]:				
soy	siendo		seré	**fui**
eres	sido	**sé**	serás	**fuiste**
es			será	**fue**
somos			seremos	**fuimos**
sois		**sed**	seréis	**fuisteis**
son			serán	**fueron**
Group 33. tener:				
tengo	teniendo		**tendré**	**tuve**
tienes	tenido	**ten**[2]	**tendrás**	**tuviste**
tiene			**tendrá**	**tuvo**
tenemos			**tendremos**	**tuvimos**
tenéis		tened	**tendréis**	**tuvisteis**
tienen			**tendrán**	**tuvieron**
Group 34. traer:				
traigo	trayendo		traeré	**traje**
traes	traído	trae	traerás	**trajiste**
trae			traerá	**trajo**
traemos			traeremos	**trajimos**
traéis		traed	traeréis	**trajisteis**
traen			traerán	**trajeron**
Group 35. valer:				
valgo	valiendo		**valdré**	valí
vales	valido	**val** or vale	**valdrás**	valiste
vale			**valdrá**	valió
valemos			**valdremos**	valimos
valéis		valed	**valdréis**	valisteis
valen			**valdrán**	valieron

[1] Imperfect: **era, -as, -a, éramos, erais, eran.**
[2] In compounds **-tén.**

Present Subjunctive	Imperfect Subjunctive		Future Subjunctive
ría	riera	riese	riere
rías	rieras	rieses	rieres
ría	riera	riese	riere
riamos	riéramos	riésemos	riéremos
riáis	rierais	rieseis	riereis
rían	rieran	riesen	rieren
roa, roiga *or* roya	royera	royese	royere
roas	royeras	royeses	royeres
roa	royera	royese	royere
roamos	royéramos	royésemos	royéremos
roáis	royerais	royeseis	royereis
roan	royeran	royesen	royeren
sepa	supiera	supiese	supiere
sepas	supieras	supieses	supieres
sepa	supiera	supiese	supiere
sepamos	supiéramos	supiésemos	supiéremos
sepáis	supierais	supieseis	supiereis
sepan	supieran	supiesen	supieren
salga	saliera	saliese	saliere
salgas	salieras	salieses	salieres
salga	saliera	saliese	saliere
salgamos	saliéramos	saliésemos	saliéremos
salgáis	salierais	salieseis	saliereis
salgan	salieran	saliesen	salieren
sea	fuera	fuese	fuere
seas	fueras	fueses	fueres
sea	fuera	fuese	fuere
seamos	fuéramos	fuésemos	fuéremos
seáis	fuerais	fueseis	fuereis
sean	fueran	fuesen	fueren
tenga	tuviera	tuviese	tuviere
tengas	tuvieras	tuvieses	tuvieres
tenga	tuviera	tuviese	tuviere
tengamos	tuviéramos	tuviésemos	tuviéremos
tengáis	tuvierais	tuvieseis	tuviereis
tengan	tuvieran	tuviesen	tuvieren
traiga	trajera	trajese	trajere
traigas	trajeras	trajeses	trajeres
traiga	trajera	trajese	trajere
traigamos	trajéramos	trajésemos	trajéremos
traigáis	trajerais	trajeseis	trajereis
traigan	trajeran	trajesen	trajeren
valga	valiera	valiese	valiere
valgas	valieras	valieses	valieres
valga	valiera	valiese	valiere
valgamos	valiéramos	valiésemos	valiéremos
valgáis	valierais	valieseis	valiereis
valgan	valieran	valiesen	valieren

Spanish Verbs

Present Indicative	Participles	Imperative	Future Indicative	Preterite
Group **36.** venir:				
vengo	**viniendo**		vendré	**vine**
vienes	venido	**ven**[1]	vendrás	**viniste**
viene			vendrá	vino
venimos			vendremos	vinimos
venís		venid	vendréis	vinisteis
vienen			vendrán	vinieron
Group **37.** ver[2]:				
veo	viendo		veré	**vi**
ves	**visto**	**ve**	verás	viste
ve			verá	vio
vemos			veremos	vimos
veis		ved	veréis	visteis
ven			verán	vieron

[1] In compounds -**vén.**
[2] Imperfect: **veía, -as, -a, -amos, -ais, -an.**

Present Subjunctive	Imperfect Subjunctive		Future Subjunctive
venga	viniera	viniese	viniere
vengas	vinieras	vinieses	vinieres
venga	viniera	viniese	viniere
vengamos	viniéramos	viniésemos	viniéremos
vengáis	vinierais	vinieseis	viniereis
vengan	vinieran	viniesen	vinieren
vea	viera	viese	viere
veas	vieras	vieses	vieres
vea	viera	viese	viere
veamos	viéramos	viésemos	viéremos
veáis	vierais	vieseis	viereis
vean	vieran	viesen	vieren

Verbos ingleses

Presente	Pronunciación	Pretérito	Participio Pasado	Español

VERBOS IRREGULARES INGLESES

be

I am (I'm)	[ai æm, aim]	was	been	ser, estar
you are (you're)	[ju: a:; jɔ:, juə]	were		
he is (he's)	[hi: iz, hi:z]	was		
she is (she's)	[ʃi: iz, ʃi:z]	was		
it is (it's)	[it iz, its]	was		
we are (we're)	[wi: a:, wiə]	were		
you are *véase arriba*		were		
they are (they're)	[ðei a:, ðɛə]	were		

have

I have (I've)	[ai hæv, aiv]	had	had	haber, tener
you have (you've)	[ju: hæv, ju:v]	had		
he has (he's)	[hi: hæz, hi:z]	had		
she has (she's)	[ʃi: hæz, ʃi:z]	had		
we have (we've)	[wi: hæv, wi:v]	had		
they have (they've)	[ðei hæv, ðeiv]	had		

Infinitivo	Pretérito	Participio Pasado	Español
abide	**abode**	**abode**	morar
awake	**awoke**	**awoken, awakened**	despertar
bear	**bore**	**borne**	llevar; parir
beat	**beat**	**beaten**	batir
begin	**began**	**begun**	empezar
bend	**bent**	**bent**	inclinar(se)
bereave	bereaved (**bereft**)	bereaved (**bereft**)	despojar
beseech	**besought**	**besought**	impetrar
bid	**bade, bid**	**bidden, bid**	mandar
bind	**bound**	**bound**	ligar
bite	**bit**	**bitten**	morder
bleed	**bled**	**bled**	sangrar
blow	**blew**	**blown**	soplar
break	**broke**	**broken**	quebrar
breed	**bred**	**bred**	criar
bring	**brought**	**brought**	traer
build	**built**	**built**	edificar
burn	**burned, burnt**	**burned, burnt**	quemar(se)
burst	**burst**	**burst**	reventar(se)

Infinitivo	Pretérito	Participio Pasado	Español
buy	**bought**	**bought**	comprar
cast	**cast**	**cast**	arrojar
catch	**caught**	**caught**	coger
chide	**chid**	**chid, chidden**	regañar
choose	**chose**	**chosen**	escoger
cleave	cleaved, **cleft, clove**	cleaved, **cleft, cloven**[1]	hender
cling	**clung**	**clung**	adherirse
clothe	clothed (*obs.* **clad**)	**clad,** clothed	vestir
come	**came**	**come**	venir
cost	**cost**	**cost**	costar
creep	**crept**	**crept**	arrastrarse
crow	crowed, **crew**	crowed	cacarear
cut	**cut**	**cut**	cortar
dare	dared (*obs.* **durst**)	dared	osar
deal	**dealt**	**dealt**	repartir
dig	**dug**	**dug**	cavar
do	**did**	**done**	hacer
draw	**drew**	**drawn**	tirar; dibujar
dream	dreamed, **dreamt**	dreamed, **dreamt**	soñar
drink	**drank**	**drunk**	beber
drive	**drove**	**driven**	conducir
dwell	**dwelt**	**dwelt**	morar
eat	**ate**	**eaten**	comer
fall	**fell**	**fallen**	caer
feed	**fed**	**fed**	(dar de) comer
feel	**felt**	**felt**	sentir
fight	**fought**	**fought**	combatir
find	**found**	**found**	encontrar
flee	**fled**	**fled**	huir
fling	**flung**	**flung**	arrojar

[1] *Cloven* hoof.

Verbos ingleses

Infinitivo	Pretérito	Participio Pasado	Español
fly	flew	flown	volar
forbear	forbore	forborne	abstenerse
forbid	forbad(e)	forbidden	vedar
forget	forgot	forgotten	olvidar
forsake	forsook	forsaken	abandonar
freeze	froze	frozen	helar(se)
get	got	got (*U.S.* got, gotten)	obtener
gird	girded, girt	girded, girt	ceñir
give	gave	given	dar
go	went	gone	ir
grind	ground	ground	moler
grow	grew	grown	cultivar; crecer
hang[1]	hung	hung	colgar
hear	heard	heard	oír
heave	heaved, hove	heaved, hove	alzar
hew	hewed	hewed, hewn	debastar
hide	hid	hidden	esconder
hit	hit	hit	golpear
hold	held	held	tener
hurt	hurt	hurt	dañar
keep	kept	kept	guardar
kneel	knelt	knelt	arrodillarse
knit	knit, knitted	knitted	hacer punto
know	knew	known	saber
lay	laid	laid	poner
lead	led	led	conducir
lean	leant, leaned	leant, leaned	apoyar(se)
leap	leaped, leapt	leaped, leapt	saltar
learn	learned, learnt	learned, learnt	aprender
leave	left	left	dejar

[1] *Colgar.* Es regular en el sentido de *ahorcar.*

Infinitivo	Pretérito	Participio Pasado	Español
lend	lent	lent	prestar
let	let	let	dejar
lie[1]	lay	lain	yacer
light	lit, lighted	lit, lighted	iluminar
lose	lost	lost	perder
make	made	made	hacer
mean	meant	meant	querer decir
meet	met	met	encontrar(se)
melt	melted	melted	fundir
mow	mowed	mown, mowed	segar
pay	paid	paid	pagar
put	put	put	poner
quit	quit, quitted	quit, quitted	abandonar
read	read	read	leer
rend	rent	rent	desgarrar
rid	rid	rid	dezembarazar
ride	rode	ridden	montar
ring[2]	rang	rung	sonar
rise	rose	risen	levantarse
run	ran	run	correr
saw	sawed	sawn, sawed	aserrar
say	said	said	decir
see	saw	seen	ver
seek	sought	sought	buscar
sell	sold	sold	vender
send	sent	sent	enviar
set	set	set	fijar
sew	sewed	sewn, sewed	coser
shake	shook	shaken	sacudir
shear	sheared	shorn, sheared	tonsurar

[1] *Estar acostado.* En el sentido de *mentir* es regular.
[2] *Resonar.* En el sentido de *circundar* es regular.

Verbos ingleses

Infinitivo	Pretérito	Participio Pasado	Español
shed	**shed**	**shed**	quitar(se de)
shine	**shone**	**shone**	relucir
shoe	**shod**	**shod**	herrar
shoot	**shot**	**shot**	disparar
show	showed	**shown**	indicar
shrink	**shrank**	**shrunk**	encoger(se)
shut	**shut**	**shut**	cerrar (se)
sing	**sang**	**sung**	cantar
sink	**sank**	**sunk, sunken**[1]	hundir(se)
sit	**sat**	**sat**	sentarse
slay	**slew**	**slain**	matar
sleep	**slept**	**slept**	dormir
slide	**slid**	**slid**	resbalar
sling	**slung**	**slung**	tirar
slink	**slunk**	**slunk**	escabullirse
slit	**slit**	**slit**	cortar
smell	**smelt**, smelled	**smelt**	oler
smite	**smote**	**smitten**	herir
sow	sowed	**sown**, sowed	sembrar
speak	**spoke**	**spoken**	hablar
speed	**sped**	**sped**	correr
spell	**spelt**, spelled	**spelt**, spelled	deletrear
spend	**spent**	**spent**	gastar
spill	spilled, **spilt**	spilled, **spilt**	derramar
spin	**spun, span**	**spun**	hilar
spit	**spat**	**spat**	escupir
split	**split**	**split**	hender
spoil	**spoilt**, spoiled	**spoilt**, spoiled	estropear(se)
spread	**spread**	**spread**	tender
spring	**sprang**	**sprung**	brincar

[1] *Sunken* cheeks.

442

Infinitivo	Pretérito	Participio Pasado	Español
stand	**stood**	**stood**	estar (de pie)
steal	**stole**	**stolen**	robar
stick	**stuck**	**stuck**	fijar(se)
sting	**stung**	**stung**	picar
stink	**stank, stunk**	**stunk**	heder
strew	strewed	**strewn,** strewed	esparcir
stride	**strode**	**stridden**	andar a pasos largos
strike	**struck**	**struck**	golpear
string	**strung**	**strung**	ensartar
strive	**strove**	**striven**	esforzarse
swear	**swore**	**sworn**	jurar
sweep	**swept**	**swept**	barrer
swell	swelled	**swollen,** swelled	hinchar(se)
swim	**swam**	**swum**	nadar
swing	**swung**	**swung**	oscilar
take	**took**	**taken**	tomar
teach	**taught**	**taught**	enseñar
tear	**tore**	**torn**	romper
tell	**told**	**told**	contar
think	**thought**	**thought**	pensar
thrive	**throve,** thrived	thrived, **thriven**	prosperar
throw	**threw**	**thrown**	echar
thrust	**thrust**	**thrust**	empujar
tread	**trod**	**trodden**	pisar
wake	**woke**	waked, (*Brit.* **woken**)	despertar(se)
wear	**wore**	**worn**	llevar
weave	**wove**	**woven**	tejer
weep	**wept**	**wept**	llorar
wet	wetted, **wet**	wetted, **wet**	mojar
win	**won**	**won**	ganar

Verbos ingleses

Infinitivo	Pretérito	Participio Pasado	Español
wind	**wound**	**wound**	devanar
work	worked (*obs.* **wrought**)	worked (*obs.* **wrought**)	trabajar
wring	**wrung**	**wrung**	torcer
write	**wrote**	**written**	escribir

VERBOS DEFECTIVOS

Presente	Pretérito	Participio Pasado	Español
can	**could**	—	poder
may	**might**	—	tener permiso; poder
must	—	—	deber
shall	**should**	—	ir a (*futuro*)
will	**would**	—	querer; ir a (*futuro*)